MASTERPIECES

of

WORLD PHILOSOPHY

in Summary Form

Edited by
FRANK N. MAGILL

Associate Editor
IAN P. McGREAL

HARPER & ROW, PUBLISHERS

New York, Evanston, and London

B-T

PRINTED IN THE UNITED STATES OF AMERICA

ACKNOWLEDGMENTS

The articles describing the following works were prepared in whole or in part by reference to the editions indicated. The editors and staff gratefully acknowledge the use of these editions.

Euthyphro by Plato. Translated by F. J. Church. Published by Liberal Arts Press.

Republic by Plato. Translated by W. H. D. Rouse. Published by New American Library.

Organon by Aristotle. Published by Oxford University Press.

Physics by Aristotle. Translated by Hardie and Geye. Published by Clarendon Press.

On the Soul by Aristotle. Translated by J. A. Smith. Published by Random House, Inc.

Ethica Nicomachea by Aristotle. Translated by W. D. Ross. Published by Random House, Inc.

Politics by Aristotle. Translated by W. D. Ross. Published by Oxford University Press.

Rhetoric by Aristotle. Translated by W. Rhys Roberts. Published by Random House, Inc.

Poetics by Aristotle. Translated by S. H. Butcher. Published by Dover Publications, Inc.

Principal Doctrines and *Letter to Menoeceus* by Epicurus. Translated by C. Bailey. Published by Random House, Inc.

City of God by Saint Augustine. Translated by M. Dods, G. Wilson, and J. J. Smith. Published by Random House, Inc.

On the Division of Nature by Johannes Scotus Erigena. Published by Charles Scribner's Sons.

The Glosses on Porphyry by Peter Abelard. Published by Charles Scribner's Sons.

On the Reduction of the Arts to Theology by Saint Bonaventura. Translated by Sr. Emma Thérèse Healy. Published by Saint Bonaventure University.

Summa Theologica by Thomas Aquinas. Published by Benziger Brothers.

A Tract Concerning the First Principle by John Duns Scotus. Translated by Evan Roche. Published by Franciscan Institute.

William of Ockham: Selections. From *Ockham, Philosophical Writings,* translated by Philotheus Boehner, published by Thomas Nelson and Sons; *Ockham, Studies and Selections,* translated by Stephen C. Tornay, published by Open Court Publishing Company; *Selections from Medieval Philosophers,* published by Charles Scribner's Sons.

Utopia by Sir Thomas More. Published by Appleton-Century-Crofts, Inc.

The Prince by Niccolò Machiavelli. Published by Appleton-Century-Crofts, Inc.

Dialogues Concerning Cause, Principle, and One by Giordano Bruno. Translated by Sidney Greenberg. Published by King's Crown Press.

De Corpore by Thomas Hobbes. Published by Charles Scribner's Sons.

Dialogues on Metaphysics and on Religion by Nicolas de Malebranche. Translated by Morris Ginsberg. Published by The Macmillan Company.

ACKNOWLEDGMENTS

A Treatise Concerning the Principles of Human Knowledge by George Berkeley. Published by Liberal Arts Press.

The New Science by Giovanni Battista Vico. Translated by Bergin & Fisch. Published by Cornell University Press.

Man a Machine by Julien Offray de La Mettrie. Published by Open Court Publishing Company.

Freedom of the Will by Jonathan Edwards. Published by Yale University Press.

The Social Contract by Jean Jacques Rousseau. Translated by Willmoore Kendall. Published by Henry Regnery Company.

Critique of Judgment by Immanuel Kant. Translated by J. H. Bernard. Published by Hafner Publishing Company.

Philosophy of History by Georg Wilhelm Friedrich Hegel. Translated by J. Sibree. Published by Dover Publications, Inc.

Either/Or by Søren Kierkegaard. Translated by David Swenson and Lillian Swenson. Published by Princeton University Press.

Philosophical Fragments by Søren Kierkegaard. Translated by David Swenson. Published by Princeton University Press.

Concluding Unscientific Postscript by Søren Kierkegaard. Translated by David Swenson and Walter Lowrie. Published by Princeton University Press.

Essay on Liberty by John Stuart Mill. Published by Appleton-Century-Crofts, Inc.

Philosophy of the Unconscious by Eduard von Hartmann. Translated by William C. Coupland. Published by Harcourt, Brace and World, Inc.

Ethical Studies by Francis Herbert Bradley. Published by Clarendon Press.

Thus Spake Zarathustra by Friedrich Wilhelm Nietzsche. Translated by Walter Kaufmann. Published by The Viking Press.

Beyond Good and Evil by Friedrich Wilhelm Nietzsche. Published by Henry Regnery Company.

Time and Free Will by Henri Bergson. Published by George Allen and Unwin.

The World and the Individual by Josiah Royce. Published by The Macmillan Company.

Aesthetic by Benedetto Croce. Translated by Douglas Ainslie. Published by Macmillan and Company, Ltd.

An Introduction to Metaphysics by Henri Bergson. Published by G. P. Putnam's Sons.

The Life of Reason by George Santayana. Published by Charles Scribner's Sons.

Creative Evolution by Henri Bergson. Translated by Arthur Mitchell. Published by Random House, Inc.

The Nature of Truth by Harold Henry Joachim. Published by Clarendon Press.

Pragmatism by William James. Published by Longmans, Green, and Company.

The Meaning of Truth by William James. Published by Longmans, Green, and Company.

The Principle of Individuality and Value by Bernard Bosanquet. Published by Macmillan and Company, Ltd.

Ideas: General Introduction to Pure Phenomenology by Edmund Husserl. Translated by W. R. Boyce Gibson. Published by The Macmillan Company.

Our Knowledge of the External World by Bertrand Russell. Published by Open Court Publishing Company.

Three Lectures on Aesthetic by Bernard Bosanquet. Published by Macmillan and Company, Ltd.

ACKNOWLEDGMENTS

The Idea of the Holy by Rudolf Otto. Translated by J. W. Harvey. Published by Oxford University Press.

Introduction to Mathematical Philosophy by Bertrand Russell. Published by The Macmillan Company.

Space, Time, and Deity by Samuel Alexander. Published by The Humanities Press, Inc.

Tractatus Logico-Philosophicus by Ludwig Wittgenstein. Published by The Humanities Press, Inc.

Human Nature and Conduct by John Dewey. Published by Random House, Inc.

Philosophical Studies by George Edward Moore. Published by Harcourt, Brace and World, Inc.

The Philosophy of Symbolic Forms by Ernst Cassirer. Translated by Ralph Manheim. Published by Yale University Press.

I and Thou by Martin Buber. Translated by Ronald Gregor Smith. Published by T. & T. Clark.

The Mind and Its Place in Nature by Charles Dunbar Broad. Published by The Humanities Press, Inc.

Ethics by Nicolai Hartmann. Translated by Stanton Coit. Published by The Macmillan Company.

General Theory of Value by Ralph Barton Perry. Published by Harvard University Press.

The Logic of Modern Physics by Percy Williams Bridgman. Published by The Macmillan Company.

Being and Time by Martin Heidegger. Published by Max Niemeyer Verlag.

Realms of Being by George Santayana. Published by Charles Scribner's Sons.

Ethics by Frank Chapman Sharp. Published by Appleton-Century-Crofts, Inc.

The Quest for Certainty by John Dewey. Published by G. P. Putnam's Sons.

Mind and the World Order by Clarence Irving Lewis. Published by Charles Scribner's Sons.

Process and Reality by Alfred North Whitehead. Published by The Humanities Press, Inc.

The Right and the Good by William David Ross. Published by Oxford University Press.

Problems of Ethics by Moritz Schlick. Published by Prentice-Hall, Inc.

The Destiny of Man by Nicolas Berdyaev. Translated by Natalie Duddington. Published by Geoffrey Bles.

The Spirit of Mediaeval Philosophy by Étienne Henry Gilson. Translated by A. H. C. Downes. Published by Charles Scribner's Sons.

Collected Papers by Charles Sanders Peirce. Published by George Braziller.

The Two Sources of Morality and Religion by Henri Bergson. Published by Holt, Rinehart and Winston, Inc.

Degrees of Knowledge by Jacques Maritain. Published by Charles Scribner's Sons.

Perception by Henry Habberley Price. Published by Methuen and Company, Ltd.

An Idealist View of Life by Sarvepalli Radhakrishnan. Published by The Macmillan Company.

The Philosophy of Physical Realism by Roy Wood Sellars. Published by The Macmillan Company.

Art as Experience by John Dewey. Published by G. P. Putnam's Sons.

ACKNOWLEDGMENTS

Mind, Self and Society by George H. Mead. Published by The University of Chicago Press.

Philosophy and Logical Syntax by Rudolf Carnap. Published by Kegan Paul, Trench, Trubner and Company, Ltd.

Reason and Existenz by Karl Jaspers. Translated by William Earle. Published by Routledge & Kegan Paul.

Language, Truth and Logic by Alfred Jules Ayer. Published by Victor Gollancz.

Personal Realism by James Bissett Pratt. Published by The Macmillan Company.

Nature and Mind by Frederick James E. Woodbridge. Published by Columbia University Press.

The Knowledge of God and the Service of God by Karl Barth. Translated by J. L. M. Haire and Ian Henderson. Published by Hodder and Stoughton.

Logic, The Theory of Inquiry by John Dewey. Published by Holt, Rinehart, and Winston, Inc.

The Nature of Thought by Brand Blanshard. Published by George Allen and Unwin, Ltd.

An Essay on Metaphysics by Robin George Collingwood. Published by Clarendon Press.

An Inquiry into Meaning and Truth by Bertrand Russell. Published by George Allen and Unwin, Ltd.

Revelation and Reason by Heinrich Emil Brunner. Translated by Olive Wyon. Published by The Westminster Press.

Experience and Substance by De Witt Henry Parker. Published by University of Michigan Press.

The Nature and Destiny of Man by Reinhold Niebuhr. Published by Charles Scribner's Sons.

Introduction to Semantics by Rudolf Carnap. Published by Harvard University Press.

Being and Nothingness by Jean-Paul Sartre. Published by Librairie Gallimard.

Ethics and Language by Charles Leslie Stevenson. Published by Yale University Press.

An Analysis of Knowledge and Valuation by Clarence Irving Lewis. Published by Open Court Publishing Company.

Signs, Language and Behavior by Charles W. Morris. Published by Prentice-Hall, Inc.

The Concept of Mind by Gilbert Ryle. Published by Barnes and Noble, Inc.

Zen Buddhism by Daisetz T. Suzuki. Published by Doubleday and Company.

The Mystery of Being by Gabriel Marcel. Published by Henry Regnery Company.

The Rebel by Albert Camus. Published by Alfred A. Knopf, Inc.

Nature, Mind, and Death by Curt John Ducasse. Published by Open Court Publishing Company.

Systematic Theology (Volume One) by Paul Tillich. Published by The University of Chicago Press.

The Courage to Be by Paul Tillich. Published by Yale University Press.

Philosophy and Psycho-Analysis by John Wisdom. Published by Philosophical Library, Inc.

Philosophical Investigations by Ludwig Wittgenstein. Published by The Macmillan Company.

ALPHABETICAL LIST OF TITLES

ALPHABETICAL LIST OF TITLES

ALPHABETICAL LIST OF TITLES

ALPHABETICAL LIST OF TITLES

ALPHABETICAL LIST OF TITLES

ALPHABETICAL LIST OF TITLES

PREFACE

IN THIS day—the age of man's burst into space—ideas form the moving force that propels us toward our destiny. Nowhere have ideas been so profoundly evolved and so impressively expounded as in the important classics of original thought that have sprung from the minds of the world's great philosophers. In today's complex society a broadening of the base of understanding of those truths by which men ought to live is more important than ever before, for in our great heritage of ideas may be found the key to better understanding of mankind—and ourselves.

MASTERPIECES OF WORLD PHILOSOPHY IN SUMMARY FORM comprises 200 essay-reviews of philosophical works beginning with fragments from the teachings of Anaximander and tracing the course of man's most searching thoughts down to the present day. With the assistance of a score of philosophical scholars, active teachers in leading colleges and universities, we have provided an opportunity for those who are interested to find out precisely what each of these 200 philosophical classics has had to say to the mind of man.

Philosophy is not a simple subject and in this book the editors and staff do not treat it as such. Even though we have been dealing with many of the most difficult books ever written, terms such as "watered down," "popularized version," and other implications that here is a superficial approach to philosophy have had no place in our thinking. Instead, the purpose has been to distill the great thoughts advanced in these classics into compact summaries for use as an authoritative reference or as a way for the general reader to understand and appreciate the central ideas propounded in the original books.

As seekers after truth, perhaps philosophers have given closer attention to the works of their predecessors and contemporaries than any other group. A new book of serious standing on the subject of philosophy is quickly dissected by experts, critics who are relentless in their pursuit of error and who stand ready to demolish forthwith any false idea advanced. So, painstakingly, has the thread of truth been kept intact—tested, altered, its flaws mended as it passed from one hand to the next down through the centuries.

PREFACE

Logically, then, the arrangement of the articles in MASTERPIECES OF WORLD PHILOSOPHY IN SUMMARY FORM is chronological rather than alphabetical so that the emergence and impingement of ideas will be evident. The chronology is by date of publication which is not in every case the year in which the work was written, but this system preserves the sequence of influence on the orderly development of philosophic thought.

For convenience in locating an article out of time sequence, an alphabetical list of titles appears in the front section of this book and an author index appears at the end. Also appearing in the front section is the Glossary of Common Philosophical Terms. This glossary contains more than 250 definitions and is designed to assist the nonphilosopher in interpreting special meanings and connotations with which he may not be familiar. It is not surprising that the nonphilosopher may find a glossary useful; in dealing with ideas, philosophers must sometimes use language in new ways in order to express themselves.

All the material in MASTERPIECES OF WORLD PHILOSOPHY IN SUMMARY FORM was newly written expressly for this book. Despite the difficult subject matter involved we have tried to interpret the material in a way that will convey the basic ideas that the original books express—to highlight what the greatest thinkers in the history of thought said in their most important books. Staff members have endeavored to point out evidences of influences that shaped an author's thinking and his work, for such interpretations are often necessary for a full appreciation of the book in question.

MASTERPIECES OF WORLD PHILOSOPHY IN SUMMARY FORM includes a number of articles covering books dealing with Oriental philosophy. A special acknowledgment is due Professor Willem B. Roos for his article on S'aṅkara's CREST JEWEL OF WISDOM. Regular staff members—with their graduate schools and present affiliations—are listed in the front section of this book. Formal acknowledgments to the publishers of the majority of the editions used in the preparation of these 200 articles also appear in the front section.

I wish to thank Associate Editor Ian P. McGreal and each Staff Member for the invaluable assistance rendered in the preparation of MASTERPIECES OF WORLD PHILOSOPHY IN SUMMARY FORM. I am sure that all staff members share my hope that these articles will enable one to go directly to the heart of each of these 200 important writings, there to find the abiding truths that penetrating thinkers down through the centuries have laboriously wrested from the mystery of human existence.

FRANK N. MAGILL

PROJECT STAFF MEMBERS

	GRADUATE SCHOOL	PRESENT AFFILIATION
A. Cornelius Benjamin, Ph.D.	University of Michigan	University of Missouri
John Collinson, Ph.D.	The Johns Hopkins University	Wayne State University
Whitaker T. Deininger, Ph.D.	Columbia University	San Jose State College
Marvin Easterling, Ph.D.	University of Illinois	Chico State College
Jean Faurot, Ph.D.	University of Toronto	Sacramento State College
John Goldthwait, Ph.D.	Northwestern University	University of California (Davis)
W. Paul Jones, Ph.D.	Yale University	Princeton University
Kai-yu Hsu, Ph.D.	Stanford University	San Francisco State College
Robert E. Larsen, Ph.D.	University of Minnesota	San Jose State College
John Linnell, Ph.D.	University of Minnesota	Sacramento State College
Wallace Matson, Ph.D.	University of California	University of California (Berkeley)
Ian P. McGreal, Ph.D.	Brown University	Sacramento State College
Leonard Miller, Ph.D.	Cornell University	University of Washington
Bernard Peach, Ph.D.	Harvard University	Duke University

PROJECT STAFF MEMBERS

Richard H. Popkin, Ph.D.   Columbia University   Harvey Mudd College

Calvin O. Schrag, Ph.D.   Harvard University   Purdue University

Roy Wood Sellars, Ph.D.   University of Michigan   University of Michigan (Emeritus)

Erling Skorpen, Ph.D.   Yale University   Yale University

Frederick Sontag, Ph.D.   Yale University   Pomona College

Theodore Waldman, Ph.D.   University of California   State University of Iowa

GLOSSARY OF COMMON PHILOSOPHICAL TERMS

ABSOLUTE: The unconditioned, totally independent, perfect, and all-inclusive. God, as entirely unconditioned.

ABSOLUTE IDEALISM: The doctrine that reality is entirely spiritual or mental and that every aspect of reality has its being and its character only as an aspect of the whole.

ABSTRACTION: The process of forming an idea of a characteristic common to, or possibly common to, a number of objects. Also, the idea which is formed.

ACCIDENT: A characteristic which is not one of the defining characteristics of the object to which it belongs.

ACQUAINTANCE, KNOWLEDGE BY: See *knowledge by acquaintance.*

AESTHETIC ATTITUDE: The contemplation of an object for the sake of the experience of contemplating it.

AESTHETICS: The philosophy of art, beauty, and criticism.

AGENT: In ethics, the person who acts.

AGNOSTIC: One who believes agnosticism. Or, one who neither believes nor disbelieves in the existence of God.

AGNOSTICISM: The theory that it is not possible to know whether God exists.

ALTRUISM: The theory that one ought to act for the good of all concerned.

AMBIGUITY: An expression having more than one meaning.

AMORAL: Neither moral nor immoral.

AMPHIBOLY: Any argument depending for its force on a grammatical ambiguity.

ANALOGY, ARGUMENT FROM: An argument based on similarities.

ANALYSIS: The process of examining an object to discover its parts or aspects.

ANALYTIC STATEMENT: A statement which is true because of the meanings of its terms; a statement whose contradictory is an inconsistency; a statement which must be true and cannot be false. Opposite of *synthetic statement.*

ANIMISM: The belief that nature is full of spirits.

ANTECEDENT: That which is before. In logic, the conditional (if) clause in a conditional (if . . . then . . .) statement.

ANTHROPOMORPHISM: The attribution of human characteristics to God or to inanimate objects.

ANTINOMY: A contradiction between two conclusions drawn from equally credible premises.

APOLOGY: A defense by the use of intellectual argument.

A POSTERIORI STATEMENT: A factual statement; an empirical statement,

xvii

one to be confirmed or disproved by reference to evidence acquired through experience. Opposite of *a priori* statement.

A PRIORI: That which precedes and conditions experience, such as a form of intuition (as in the philosophy of Immanuel Kant, 1724-1804). Or, whatever is true independently of experience. Opposite of *a posteriori*.

A PRIORI STATEMENT: A universally and necessarily true statement, a statement which is true independently of any factual state of affairs. Opposite of *a posteriori* statement.

ARCHETYPE: An original essence, an ideal pattern of which individual things are copies, a universal. See *Idea*.

ARGUMENTUM AD HOMINEM: An argument which directs critical attack against an opponent instead of against his argument.

ARGUMENTUM AD MISERICORDIAM: An argument based on an appeal to pity.

ARGUMENTUM AD POPULUM: An argument based on an appeal to the passions and prejudices of the audience.

ARGUMENTUM AD VERECUNDIAM: An argument based on an appeal to authority.

ATMAN: In Indian philosophy, the self as distinguished from, although essentially the same as, the universal reality or world-soul, Brahma.

ATOMIC PROPOSITION: A simple proposition or statement, one which cannot be analyzed into propositions or statements. Or, the statement of a basic, atomic fact. The opposite of *molecular proposition*.

ATTRIBUTE: A property or characteristic necessary to a thing of a certain sort, an essential property. Or, any property or characteristic.

AWARENESS, ACT OF: The act of apprehending the content of consciousness; direct knowing; knowledge *of* as distinguished from knowledge *about* something; intuitive recognition; knowledge by acquaintance.

AXIOLOGY: The philosophical study of value.

AXIOM: A statement assumed to be true as the basis of a proof.

BEGGING THE QUESTION: The fallacy of assuming the conclusion of an argument by using the conclusion as a premise.

BEHAVIORISM: A method in psychology which limits empirical investigation of the mind to the study of human behavior.

BRAHMA: Also *Brahman*. The universal reality or world-soul; the supreme, all-pervasive essence and ground of the universe. See *atman*.

BUDDHISM: The philosophy or religion based on the teachings of Gautama Siddhartha (c. 563-c. 483 B.C.). The Four Noble Truths teach that life is suffering, that desire is the cause of suffering, that suffering can be eliminated, and that the way to rid oneself of suffering is by following the eight-fold path to nirvana. The eight-fold path involves right understanding, right resolve, right speech, right conduct, right living, right effort, right intuition, and right concentration.

CALVINISM: The theology based on the teachings of John Calvin (1509-1564). The doctrines include belief in the total depravity of man, predestination, irresistibility of grace, and the absolute sovereignty of God.

CARTESIANISM: The philosophy of René Descartes (1596-1650). Descartes used a method of systematic doubt by which he arrived at the idea which served as the foundation of his philosophy: "Cogito, ergo sum," "I think, therefore I exist."

CATEGORICAL IMPERATIVE: In the philosophy of Kant, the unconditional moral law for all rational beings; the purely formal principle of moral action: "Act only according to a maxim by which you can at the same time will that it shall become a universal law." See also *practical imperative.*

CATEGORY: A fundamental class; a basic conception; one of the primary ideas to which all other ideas can be reduced.

CATHARSIS: In Aristotle's *Poetics,* the purgation or elimination of the emotions of pity and fear by the dramatic resolution in tragedy.

CAUSE: In Aristotelian philosophy four kinds of cause are distinguished: *material* cause, that out of which something is made; *formal* cause, the plan or idea by reference to which something is made; *final* cause, the purpose for which something is made; and *efficient* cause, the act or event which produces the result.

CHÜN-TZU: In Chinese philosophy, the ideal man, the benevolent man, one who practices *jen.*

CLASS: A collection which results if a number of entities possess a common property. An empty class is a potential collection, a class which has no members.

COGITO, ERGO SUM: See *Cartesianism.*

COGNITION: Any kind of knowledge process. Or, the product of the knowledge process.

COHERENCE THEORY OF TRUTH: The theory that truth is a property not of individual statements or propositions but of the totality of ideas or of the absolutely inclusive idea.

CONCEPT: Any idea. Or, any universal which can be the object of thought.

CONCEPTUALISM: The theory that general terms have meaning because universals exist as concepts in the mind. See also *nominalism, moderate realism,* and *Platonic realism.*

CONDITIONAL STATEMENT: Any statement of the form "If . . . then . . ."

CONNOTATION: The properties common to whatever is designated by a particular term. Or, the defining properties of a term. Or, the ideas and images associated with the use of a particular term.

CONSEQUENT: That which is after. In logic, the closing clause of a conditional statement.

CONSISTENCY: The logical relation which holds between propositions which are not contradictory. Or, the relation between entities which may be parts of a whole.

CONTENT OF CONSCIOUSNESS: Whatever is directly apprehended in experience, as distinguished from awareness, the act of experiencing content; the datum of experience.

CONTINGENCY: A state of affairs which need not occur; a state of affairs which may or may not occur.

CONTRADICTION: The logical relation which holds between two statements or propositions which cannot both be true and cannot both be false in that the truth of either involves the falsity of the other.

CONTRARIES: The logical relation which holds between two statements or propositions if they cannot both be true but may both be false.

GLOSSARY OF COMMON PHILOSOPHICAL TERMS

CORRESPONDENCE THEORY OF TRUTH: The theory that a statement or proposition is true if it corresponds to a matter of fact; to correspond to a fact, a statement must somehow designate the fact.

COSMOGONY: A theory concerning the creation of the universe.

COSMOLOGICAL ARGUMENT: An argument which purports to prove the existence of God by maintaining that there must have been a first cause which initiated the causal sequence of contingent things.

COSMOLOGY: The philosophic study of basic causes and processes in the universe; an inquiry into the structure of the universe.

CRITICAL REALISM: The theory that most existing things do not depend for their existence upon being perceived or conceived in mind; the theory that knowledge of independently existing things is possible even when the ideas by which things are known differ in existence and in character from the things known.

DATUM: The given element. Or, whatever is presented as the content of consciousness.

DEDUCTION: The mode of reasoning which involves passing from one or more propositions to other propositions logically implied by the former.

DEFINIENDUM: A word to be defined.

DEFINIENS: An expression used to define a word.

DEFINITION: The process of explaining the meaning of a term. Or, the expression used to explain the meaning of a term; the statement of the equivalence in meaning of a *definiendum* and *definiens*.

DEISM: The belief that God is unconcerned with the world he created. Or, the view that God can be understood by the use of reason and by reference to natural phenomena.

DENOTATION: The class of entities to which a term refers; whatever a term designates.

DEONTOLOGICAL ETHICS: Any theory of the right and the wrong which relates moral value not to the value of the consequences of human action but to the formal nature of the act; an ethics which regards an act as right if it conforms to moral principle.

DESCRIPTION, KNOWLEDGE BY: See *knowledge by description*.

DETERMINISM: The theory that every event has a cause and an effect and that the character of any event is entirely a function of its cause.

DHARMA: In Indian philosophy, the cosmic law, virtue, the right.

DIALECTIC: The art of rational discourse. Or, the method of philosophical inquiry by the use of questions and answers. Or, the critical treatment of paradoxes arising out of the misapplication of categories. Or, the method of constructing ideas by resolving apparent contradictories.

DICTUM DE OMNI ET NULLO: The Aristotelean principle of syllogistic logic which states that whatever can be affirmed or denied of the whole of a class may be affirmed or denied of a part.

DILEMMA: An argument composed of two conditional (if . . . then . . .) propositions and an alternative (either . . . or . . .) proposition, usually used to show that if either of the alternatives is chosen, the result is an unsatisfactory state of affairs.

DING AN SICH: The thing-in-itself, whatever exists independently of human knowledge.

DIRECT KNOWLEDGE: Awareness of feeling, thought, emotion, or any content of consciousness. See also *awareness, intuition.*

DIVISION: The process of distinguishing the species within a genus. Or, the product of such a process.

DUALISM: Any metaphysical theory which reduces the kinds of existing things to two basic substances.

EGOCENTRIC PREDICAMENT: The peculiar situation in which any knower finds himself when he attempts to discover something which is not dependent for its existence upon being known.

EGOISM, ETHICAL: The theory that one ought to act so as to secure the greatest possible good for oneself.

EGOISM, PSYCHOLOGICAL: The theory that man is so constituted that he must act to secure whatever he regards as best for himself.

ÉLAN VITAL: The life force, the basic creative principle of all living things. Or, the evolutionary principle as operative in nature.

EMANATION: The creative process in which all being is derived in a nontemporal fashion from a single source of being.

EMERGENCE: The appearance of new forms of life or matter which cannot be explained by reference to preceding forms.

EMOTIVE MEANING: The capacity of an utterance to express or to communicate feeling.

EMPATHY: The assumption of the attitude, motion, or state of mind of another as if one were the other.

EMPIRICAL STATEMENT: A statement which can be verified or shown to be false by reference to facts revealed by experience.

EMPIRICISM: The theory that all knowledge is derived from experience and that no knowledge is innate or *a priori.*

ENTELECHY: The essence or vital principle of a thing by virtue of which it is actual.

ENTHYMEME: In Aristotelian philosophy, a syllogism designed to be persuasive when used rhetorically. In modern logic, a syllogism with one of its premises or its conclusion not stated.

ENTITY: Whatever can be considered or referred to.

EPICUREANISM: The theory that happiness is the greatest good and that happiness is to be achieved by living a life of moderation in which the contemplative pleasures are preferred to the sensuous pleasures.

EPIPHENOMENALISM: The theory that mental events reflect bodily changes but have no causal influence on the body.

EPISTEMOLOGICAL DUALISM: The theory that the content of consciousness and the object known are distinct in existence even though they may be alike in essence.

EPISTEMOLOGICAL MONISM: The theory that the content of consciousness and the aspect of the object known are one in existence as well as in essence.

EPISTEMOLOGY: The philosophy of knowledge; the attempt to clarify ideas about knowledge and the methods for securing knowledge.

GLOSSARY OF COMMON PHILOSOPHICAL TERMS

ESCHATOLOGY: The theological study of such final matters as death, immortality, divine judgment, and the end of the world.

ESSENCE: The distinctive nature of a thing. Or, more broadly, any characteristic whatsoever, whether or not it is the characteristic of something.

ETERNITY: The infinite temporal duration which includes all time. Or, a state which transcends time.

ETHICAL HEDONISM: The theory that acts are right insofar as they contribute to happiness or pleasure and wrong insofar as they contribute to unhappiness or suffering.

ETHICAL RELATIVISM: The theory that the rightness and wrongness of acts are relative to, functions of, the attitudes of persons judging the acts.

ETHICS: The philosophy of morality; that part of philosophy which deals with questions concerning the nature and source of value, rightness, duty, and related matters.

EUDAEMONISM: The theory that acts are right insofar as they contribute to man's well-being or happiness. The emphasis in eudaemonism is not upon pleasure, as in hedonistic ethics, but upon the way of life most suited to man's nature.

EXCLUDED MIDDLE, PRINCIPLE OF: The principle that a proposition is either true or it is false.

EXISTENTIALISM: A philosophy which distinguishes between existence and essence and gives priority to existence; the philosophy which claims that in man existence precedes essence. The existentialist begins with the fact of an encountered existence and regards essence, or character, as contingent upon the mode of existence.

FALLACY: An unsound argument or an error in reasoning.

FATALISM: The belief that all or some events are determined by some supernatural being or power. Or, the vague belief that somehow certain events are decided upon as historical facts prior to their occurrence.

FINAL CAUSE: The end or purpose for which something was done.

FIRST MOVER: The being or power that initiated change in the universe; the first cause.

FIRST PRINCIPLE: The first cause of all contingent beings. Or, a necessary truth which serves as the foundation of a system of ideas.

FORMALISM: In ethics, the theory that moral obligation is relative to formal principles of conduct whose validity can be determined by intuitive reflection.

FREE WILL: A will, or power to decide, which is in no way causally determined. Or, an uncoerced will, a will free from the excessive influences of other persons.

GESTALT: Shape, form; the whole considered as more than the sum of its parts.

HEDONISTIC ETHICS: See *ethical hedonism*.

HEDONISTIC PARADOX: The apparent contradiction implicit in the hedonist's claim that although pleasure is the only good, pleasure should not be the sole object of desire, for if pleasure alone is sought, it will not be found.

HUMANISM: A philosophical view which emphasizes the centrality of man and rejects the supernatural.

GLOSSARY OF COMMON PHILOSOPHICAL TERMS

HYLOZOISM: The belief that all matter is living substance.

HYPOTHETICAL IMPERATIVE: Any conditional obligation of the form "If you want . . . , then you must do. . . ." See also *categorical imperative.*

HYPOTHETICAL SYLLOGISM: An argument involving a hypothetical or conditional premise (if . . . then . . .) and another premise either affirming the antecedent or denying the consequent; or an argument involving two hypothethical premises, one of which has as its antecedent the consequent of the other. (*Ex.:* If A, B; A is true; therefore, B is true. If A, B; B is false; therefore A is false. If A, B; and if B, C; therefore, if A, C.)

IDEA: In Platonic philosophy, an eternal essence, a universal archetype of things. In Berkeleian philosophy, any sense object directly known in experience.

IDEALISM: The theory that only minds (spirits) and their ideas exist.

IDENTITY, PRINCIPLE OF: The logical principle that anything is itself, that any symbol is equivalent in meaning to itself.

IDENTITY OF INDISCERNIBLES: The principle that no two things can be identical in character. In the philosophy of Gottfried Wilhelm von Leibniz (1646-1716), the principle that no two monads can have characters without a discernible difference.

IDOL: In the philosophy of Francis Bacon (1561-1626), a cause of human ignorance or error. The four classes of idols described by Bacon are the "Idols of the Tribe," inherent human habits of thought; the "Idols of the Cave," the particular weaknesses of the individual; the "Idols of the Market Place," misconceptions resulting from the misuse of language; and the "Idols of the Theater," false ideas resulting from the uncritical acceptance of authority.

IMMANENT: Being within, part of, indwelling. The opposite of *transcendent.*

IMMEDIATE VALUE: See *value, immediate.*

IMPLICATION: The logical relation which holds between one proposition and another whenever it could not be the case that the one is true and the other false.

INDETERMINISM: The theory that some events are not causally determined. Or, the theory that acts of will are not determined.

INDUCTION: The method of empirical generalization: inferring a general conclusion from a number of particular instances.

INFERENCE: The process of reasoning from one idea or set of ideas (the premises) to a conclusion. Inference is a kind of activity; implication is a logical relationship.

INFIMA SPECIES: The lowest, or ultimate, species in a system of classification.

INNATE IDEAS: Beliefs with which man is born.

INSTRUMENTAL VALUE: See *value, instrumental.*

INTERACTIONISM: The theory that body and mind causally affect each other. See also *epiphenomenalism* and *parallelism.*

INTRINSIC PROPERTY: A nonrelational property. Or, the intuitable character of an experience.

INTRINSIC VALUE: See *value, intrinsic.*

INTUITION: The faculty of knowing by mental inspection and without recourse to reason; direct knowing or awareness which is neither deductive nor inductive. Or, the product of intuitive recognition.

JEN: In Chinese philosophy, virtue, true manhood, the moral principles of true manhood.

KARMA: In Indian philosophy, deed, action. Or, the causal and moral law of the universe.

KNOWLEDGE BY ACQUAINTANCE: See *direct knowledge.*

KNOWLEDGE BY DESCRIPTION: Knowledge about a thing in terms of its properties.

LI: In Chinese philosophy, propriety, rules of conduct. Or, the rational principle, reason as law.

LOGIC: The philosophy of rational argument; the clarification of the terms of formal criticism, together with the invention or specification of forms of inference and rules for their use.

LOGICAL EMPIRICISM: The philosophy which endorses the logical analysis of language as the method of philosophy and which regards statements as meaningful only if they are either logically analytic or theoretically verifiable in experience; consequently, the philosophy which relies on logic and science and which rejects metaphysics as meaningless.

LOGICAL POSITIVISM: The earlier version of logical empiricism as developed by the Vienna Circle (Moritz Schlick, Herbert Feigl, Otto Neurath, and others) over the period 1923-1936. Chiefly distinguished from logical empiricism by its more rigid criteria of empirical meaning.

LOGICAL PRINCIPLES: The principles on which the analysis of the structure of arguments depends; namely, the principles of *identity, contradiction,* and *excluded middle.*

LOGICAL SYNTAX: See *syntax, logical.*

LOGOS: The divine reason; the creative thought or plan of the universe; the word of God.

MATERIALISM: The doctrine that everything is composed of matter; the belief that matter alone is real and that everything that exists can be understood as a form of matter. In ethics, the doctrine that material well-being and self-interest should always govern individual actions.

MATTER: In Aristotelian philosophy, pure potentiality, the unlimited, the capacity of be something.

METALANGUAGE: A language devised to describe another language.

METAPHYSICS: Speculative inquiry concerning philosophical matters which lie beyond the range of empirical inquiry. Traditionally, that part of philosophy which includes ontology, cosmology, and epistemology. Hence, in a limited sense, the study of being as such (ontology). (The term "metaphysics" was originally used by Andronicus of Rhodes (first century B.C.) as a descriptive name for that part of Aristotle's philosophy which appeared in the collection "after the *Physics.*")

MODERATE REALISM: The doctrine that universals exist in things or as concepts in mind but not as independently subsisting entities. Opposed to nominalism and to Platonic realism.

MOLECULAR PROPOSITION: A proposition which is analyzable into atomic propositions.

GLOSSARY OF COMMON PHILOSOPHICAL TERMS

MONAD: In the philosophy of Giordano Bruno (1548-1600), the individual substance, a unity of body and mind, a manifestation of divine energy. In the philosophy of Leibniz, the individual soul, active, purposive, self-contained, possessing knowledge only because of a divinely preëstablished harmony of experiences.

MONISM: In metaphysics, the theory that all reality is basically of one substance. In epistemology, the theory that the object known and the given element in experience are one in existence as well as in essence.

MYSTICISM: The belief that knowledge of reality involves the immediate awareness of God's nature and presence.

NAÏVE REALISM: The conventional opinion that the world is directly known and that it has whatever character we perceive it to have. Sometimes the term is used to refer to new realism.

NATURAL THEOLOGY: The theology, or philosophy concerning God, based on ordinary experience and not dependent on revelation.

NATURALISM: The theory that reality is understandable without reference to the supernatural.

NATURALISTIC ETHICS: Any philosophical theory concerning the right and the wrong, the obligatory, the good and the bad, which claims that value terms and moral predicates are definable empirically and that value assertions and moral judgments are empirically verifiable.

NATURALISTIC FALLACY: The fallacy defined by G. E. Moore (1873-1958) as the error of confusing some property common to good things but distinct from the property goodness with the property goodness.

NEOPLATONISM: A philosophic movement started in the beginning of the third century by Ammonius Saccas, the teacher of Plotinus (c. 204-c. 270) and Origen (c. 185-c. 254). Neoplatonism combines Platonic and Aristotelean ideas with certain conceptions from Eastern philosophy and maintains that reality is an absolute oneness, that matter is the negation of being, and that the One creates orders of being by a nontemporal process of emanation.

NEO-THOMISM: The modern philosophical movement based on the philosophy of Thomas Acquinas (c. 1225-1274).

NEUTRAL MONISM: The theory, proposed by William James (1842-1910), which claims that the elements of reality are one in kind, neither essentially mental nor essentially material, but neutral. In some contexts the neutral entities, having been related to consciousness, are described as mental; in other contexts the neutral entities, having been perceived as the aspects of physical things, are regarded as material.

NEW REALISM: The theory that physical objects exist independently of being perceived and that the knowledge of physical objects is direct in that physical objects are immediately perceived.

NIRVANA: The beatific state of union with the ultimate reality, Brahma, a state of spiritual fulfillment made possible by liberating oneself from all concern for the separated self.

NOMINALISM: The theory that general terms do not designate universal properties but are mere *flatus vocis*, vocal sounds. Opposed to Platonic realism and to moderate realism.

GLOSSARY OF COMMON PHILOSOPHICAL TERMS

NONNATURALISTIC ETHICS: Any ethics which regards value as unique and unanalyzable and which regards intuition as the only way of knowing the truth of moral claims.

NONRELATIONAL PROPERTY: A property inherent to an object and not dependent on any relation to knowing subjects; an unanalyzable quality.

NOUMENON: In the philosophy of Kant, a thing-in-itself, the unknowable reality behind phenomena.

NOUS: The second person of the Plotinian trinity; the divine mind, the intellectual principle. (Plotinus conceived of God as a trinity of the One, the ineffable creative unity; Nous, the divine mind; and the World-Soul.)

NUMINOUS: In the philosophy of Rudolf Otto (1869-1937), the unique state of mind which results from being aware of God as awesome and mysterious.

OCCASIONALISM: The theory that God causes mental phenomena to accompany physical events.

OCKHAM'S RAZOR: The scientific principle introduced by William of Ockham (c. 1280-c. 1350) to the effect that whatever explanation involves the fewest assumptions is to be preferred.

ONE: In philosophy, the One is the universe considered as the divine unity of all being.

ONTOLOGICAL ARGUMENT: In the philosophy of Saint Anselm (1033-1109), the argument that since God is the being than whom no greater can be conceived, he must exist, for it is better to exist than not to exist, and it is better to exist necessarily than to exist contingently.

ONTOLOGY: The philosophy of being as such; the study of what existence itself is, considered apart from any question as to the nature of any particular existent. The attempt to discover the fundamental categories of all being.

ORGANICISM: The cosmological theory that the universe is like an organism in that its parts are interdependent, working together for the good of the whole.

PANPSYCHISM: The doctrine that everything has a mind or soul.

PANTHEISM: The doctrine that everything is an aspect of God.

PARALLELISM: In connection with the mind-body problem, the theory that mental and physical events occur concomitantly but are not causally related. See also *epiphenomenalism* and *interactionism*.

PARSIMONY, PRINCIPLE OF: See *Ockham's razor.*

PARTICULAR: A member of a class, a thing of a kind, as distinguished from the class, the kind, the universal.

PERCEPT: A given element in perceptual experience, a sensation or sense datum.

PERSONALISM: The philosophy which regards personality as the highest good and God as the divine personality.

PHENOMENOLOGY: The philosophy of Edmund Husserl (1859-1938), which purported to be a science of the subjective, of phenomena, and of intended objects considered as intended.

PHENOMENON: An appearance, as distinguished from a thing-in-itself. See also *noumenon.*

PHILOSOPHY: Literally, the love of—and, consequently, search for—wisdom. The intellectual attempt to resolve problems having to do with the nature of matters of common experience and concern; thus, the attempt to make basic ideas clear and to justify descriptions of reality. The major fields of philosophy are aesthetics, the philosophy of art, beauty, and criticism; ethics, the philosophy of morality; logic, the philosophy of formal argument; and metaphysics, which includes epistemology, the philosophy of knowledge; ontology, the philosophy of being as such; and cosmology, the philosophy of cosmic structure.

PLATONIC REALISM: The theory that universals, or general characteristics, have a reality of their own and subsist eternally, apart from the things which embody them.

PLURALISM: Any theory which asserts that there are many ultimate substances.

POLYTHEISM: Any theory which claims that there is more than one God.

POSITIVISM: See *logical positivism*.

POTENTIALITY: An unrealized or latent capacity or power. Opposite of actuality.

PRACTICAL IMPERATIVE: In Kant's philosophy, the moral law which states, "So act as to treat humanity, whether in thine own person or in that of any other, in every case as an end withal, never as a means only." See also *categorical imperative*.

PRAGMATICS: The study of the relations of signs to those who use them; a branch of semiotic.

PRAGMATISM: As developed by Charles Sanders Peirce (1839-1914), the philosophy of meaning which holds that the idea of the sense effects of an object is the whole of the idea of the object. As a theory of truth, particularly as developed by William James, pragmatism argues that an idea is true if it works satisfactorily, leading one to anticipated experiences.

PRECISING DEFINITION: A definition which proposes a more precise meaning for a term.

PREDESTINATION: The doctrine that all events are determined by the action of God's will. Or, the doctrine that God has foreordained the eternal life of some persons.

PREËSTABLISHED HARMONY: In the philosophy of Leibniz, the theory that individual souls (monads) know reality contemporaneously with other monads, even though monads have no access to external events, because of God's causing the experiences of all monads to be harmonious with one another.

PREMISE: A proposition on which, at least in part, the conclusion of an argument is based.

PRIMA FACIE DUTIES: In the philosophy of W. D. Ross, those duties which, everything else being equal, are morally binding. Such duties are known by intuition to be duties. When *prima facie* duties conflict, further acts of intuition are needed to resolve the conflict.

PRIMARY QUALITIES: In the philosophy of John Locke (1632-1704), characteristics regarded as inseparable from physical objects and as belonging to them quite apart from any relation to other objects or to knowing minds: solidity, extension, figure, motion or rest, and number. See also *secondary qualities*.

PRIME MOVER: See *first mover*.

PRINCIPLE OF SUFFICIENT REASON: In the philosophy of Leibniz, the principle that the series of contingent events (events that need not have occurred) must be accounted for by reference to some reason or cause other than that supplied by any of the contingent events in the series.

PROPERTY: Any characteristic. Or, any essential characteristic. Or, any defining characteristic. Or, any relational characteristic.

PROPOSITION: A state of affairs meant by a declarative sentence. Or, a declarative sentence.

PROTOCOL SENTENCE: A sentence reporting a sense response. Or, a sentence ascribing a basic sense property to some physical object.

PSYCHO-PHYSICAL PARALLELISM: See *parallelism.*

QUALE: An intrinsic quality of a sense datum.

QUALITY: Any characteristic. Or, an intrinsic nonrelational characteristic of a feeling; a kind of feeling.

RADICAL EMPIRICISM: The theory, named by William James, which claims that all things and the relations between things are matters of direct experience; hence, the theory that all terms are meaningful by reference to experience.

RATIONALISM: The theory that knowledge of reality is possible through the use of reason without reference to matters of sense experience.

REALISM: In metaphysics, the doctrine that physical objects exist independently of being thought or perceived. Also, the doctrine that universals exist (subsist) apart from things. See also *critical realism, new realism, moderate realism, Platonic realism.*

REDUCTIO AD ABSURDUM: The method of proving a proposition by showing that its contradictory involves an inconsistency or of disproving a proposition by showing that the proposition involves an inconsistency.

RELATIONAL CHARACTERISTIC: A characteristic understandable only by relating the object possessing the characteristic to some person as knowing subject; a characteristic understandable only in terms of the experiences a person would have were he to be affected by the object possessing the characteristic.

RELATIONS, PRINCIPLE OF THE INTERNALITY OF: The principle that all relations are interdependent, that the nature of any one thing affects the nature of everything else in the universe.

SAMSARA: The cycle of birth, death, and rebirth from which one can escape only by achieving nirvana.

SATORI: In Zen Buddhism, the moment of enlightenment, the sudden recognition of the unity of being.

SECONDARY QUALITIES: In the philosophy of Locke, those characteristics of physical objects which do not belong to the physical objects themselves except as powers to cause sensations; the secondary qualities are the colors, sounds, tastes, and smells of things. See also *primary qualities.*

SEMANTICS: The systematic attempt to discover the meanings of linguistic expressions as used; the branch of semiotic concerned with the meanings of signs.

SEMIOTIC: The study of signs and symbols. Semiotic includes pragmatics, the study of the uses of signs; semantics, the study of the meanings of signs; and syntactics, the study of the forms of linguistic expressions.

SENSE DATUM: The given content of a sense experience; a sense image. Or, the given content of any experience.

SENSUM: Synonym for *sense datum.*

SKEPTICISM: The philosophical position of one who maintains that knowledge is not possible. Or, the view that all knowledge is merely probable, never certain.

SOLIPSISM: The belief that only oneself exists.

SOPHISM: Fallacious and deceptive reasoning. Or, a fallacious and deceptive argument.

SOPHIST: In fifth century B.C., a Greek teacher of rhetoric, the art of politics, and basic scientific knowledge. Or, one who, at the expense of moral integrity, emphasizes success in argument or politics.

STOICISM: The ethical doctrine which endorses a life of virtue, action in accordance with the rational way of the universe, and endurance in the face of unavoidable difficulties.

SUBJECTIVE IDEALISM: The doctrine that knowledge of the world is limited to the world as a complex system of sensations; the view that matter is a complex of sensations; the claim by George Berkeley (1685-1753) that *esse est percipi:* to be is to be perceived.

SUBSISTENCE: The mode of existence, involving neither temporal nor spatial location, which is peculiar to universals, Ideas, archetypes, and other abstract entities.

SUBSTANCE: That which has properties; the enduring system of properties considered as a system in abstraction from the properties.

SUBSTRATUM: That which bears properties, the substance which is characterized.

SUMMUM BONUM: The highest good; that which is intrinsically better than any other good and which is thus qualified to serve as the end of human conduct.

SYNTACTICS: The study of the forms of linguistic expression; that branch of semiotic which is concerned with the regulation of symbols.

SYNTAX, LOGICAL: Synonym for syntactics.

SYNTHETIC STATEMENT: A statement whose truth value cannot be determined by logical analysis; a statement in which the subject does not imply the predicate. Hence, a synthetic *a priori* statement would be a statement whose truth value cannot be determined by logical analysis and which is nevertheless universally and necessarily true.

TABULA RASA: In Locke's philosophy, the term, meaning "blank tablet," used to describe the mind at birth as being without innate ideas.

TAO: The way, the order, of the universe. Also, the moral way or order corresponding to the cosmic order.

TAUTOLOGY: An analytically true statement; a statement which can be shown to be true by logical analysis.

TELEOLOGICAL ARGUMENT: An argument devised to prove God's existence by maintaining that evidence of design or purpose in nature suggests the existence of a cosmic designer.

TELEOLOGY: Any theory of ends or purposes. Or, the study of events as signs of purpose.

THEOLOGY: The philosophical study of God and of problems concerned with God. Natural theology limits itself to empirical evidence: revealed theology depends on revelation.

GLOSSARY OF COMMON PHILOSOPHICAL TERMS

TRANSCENDENT: Beyond the natural world of sense experience. Opposite of *immanent*.

TRANSCENDENTAL PHILOSOPHY: Philosophy which studies either the *a priori* form of experience or experience as formed *a priori*. Or, philosophy which regards the spiritual as the essence of reality or as a mode of being which transcends the empirical and the physical.

TRANSUBSTANTIATION: The changing of one substance into another; or the substitution of one substance for another without a change of properties.

TYCHISM: In the philosophy of Charles Sanders Peirce, the doctrine that chance events occur; the doctrine that some events are uncaused.

UNIFORMITY OF NATURE: The complete regularity of events in nature.

UNIVERSAL: A characteristic in abstraction from that which is, or may be, characterized; an Idea, archetype, or form.

UNMOVED MOVER: The first cause, or mover, not itself moved; God, as the prime mover.

VALIDITY: The property of an argument in which the premises imply the conclusion.

VALUE, IMMEDIATE: The value which something has as a result of being a direct cause of pleasure or satisfaction. Thus, aesthetic value is one kind of immediate value.

VALUE, INSTRUMENTAL: The value which something has because it is a means to something intrinsically good.

VALUE, INTRINSIC: The value which something has by virtue of its intrinsic quality; the value of something which is worth while on its own account and not merely as a means.

VEDANTA: The Indian philosophy based on the *Upanishads,* the philosophic writings which made up the last of the Vedas.

VOLUNTARISM: The theory that the will is the basic reality or controlling power of the universe.

WORLD: The universe; the system of totality of whatever exists.

WORLD GROUND: That power, or basic reality, which sustains and directs the universe.

WORLD SOUL: The spirit or creative principle which makes life possible and which endows contingent things with reality and order. See *logos*.

YANG AND YIN: In Chinese philosophy, two fundamental energy principles; *yang* is masculine, active, bright, and positive, while *yin* is feminine, passive, dark, and negative. Everything that exists is presumed to exhibit the interplay of *yang* and *yin*.

YOGA: In Indian philosophy, a method of bodily and mental discipline devised to effect the union of *atman,* or the spirit of the individual, and *Brahma,* or the world-soul.

ANAXIMANDER: FRAGMENTS

Author: Anaximander of Miletus (c.611-c.546 B.C.)
Type of work: Metaphysics
First transcribed: Sixth century B.C.

PRINCIPAL IDEAS ADVANCED

The universe arose out of an infinite "Boundless"—a mass of undifferentiated material.

The basic material of the universe was none of the elements (earth, air, fire, water), but something intermediate.

The world was generated when the hot and the cold were separated from the Boundless by its eternal motion.

The earth is shaped like a drum and is surrounded by fire-filled hoops of mist with holes on their inner sides (the sun, moon, stars).

Justice is achieved in nature by a process of a return of all things to their origins.

Thales of Miletus is traditionally credited with having been the first philosopher, since he was the first to put forward a non-mythological account of the origin and nature of things. But we know no more of his views than that he claimed that all things originated from water; and it is unlikely that he worked out this thesis in detail. It remained for his "pupil and successor" Anaximander to produce the first comprehensive natural philosophy, a system of astonishing acumen and sophistication.

Anaximander conceived his problem to be that of explaining how the present constitution of the universe developed out of a primordial condition of simplicity. Apparently he did not consider the possibility that things had always been much the same. To this extent he inherited the notion of evolution from Near Eastern mythologies, which all told of how the world had been fashioned out of a pre-existing "chaos" or homogeneous matter (usually water). But in rejecting divine personal agency, and in substituting a (more or less) continuous process for separate acts of creation, Anaximander radically transformed the idea.

Anaximander postulated an undifferentiated stuff out of which the world arose; he called it "the Boundless." This was not any one of the traditional "elements," earth, air (or rather, at that date, mist), fire, and water, but "something intermediate." Since it was no more wet than dry, and no more hot than cold, it was presumably damp and tepid. In opposition to Thales, who had held the basic stuff to be water, Anaximander conceived it as thus neutral, on the ground that the elements "are in opposition to one another—air is cold, water moist,

1

fire hot—and therefore, if any one of them were infinite, the rest would have ceased to be by this time." This is the first recorded philosophical *argument,* a criticism of a predecessor's view supported by an appeal to reason rather than to revelation or to a special mode of insight.

The Boundless was supposed to be infinite in extent and "ageless and deathless," that is, infinite in time. Anaximander, it seems, called it "divine," but only because of its agelessness and deathlessness; he did not attribute to it any characteristics of personality or (as far as we know) intelligent consciousness.

The Boundless was also said to "encompass all the worlds," implying an infinite or at least indefinitely large number of individual worlds like this one. The initial step in the generation of a world occurs when as a result of its eternal motion (we are not told how) "something capable of begetting hot and cold out of the eternal is separated off." The hot and the cold (conceived as *things,* not as qualities of a substance) separate, and at the same time a motion in rotation is imparted to them. The hot, which is fire, encircles "like the bark around a tree" the cold, which contains earth, mist, and water. In due course these latter three also separate, the earth remaining at the center of the whirl, with the water in a ring around it which is in turn enclosed in a circle of mist. The fire around the mist and water heats them until pressure builds up which, combined with the centrifugal force of the whirl, results in a cosmic explosion. The mist is caused to shut up the fire in gigantic hoops, like inner-tubes, which circle around the earth. The earth is shaped like a drum, the diameter being three times as great as the depth. We live on one of the flat surfaces. Though supported by nothing, the earth remains at the center "because of its equal distance from everything." The surface of the earth, which was at first entirely submerged, is now partly dry, and it keeps getting drier through continued evaporation. "The sea is what is left of the original moisture. The fire has dried up most of it and turned the rest salt by scorching it."

Fire-filled hoops of mist, at distances of eighteen and twenty-seven earth-radii, surround the earth and revolve around it. Each of these hoops has on its inner side one hole ("like the nozzle of a bellows," or in a more modern figure, like the valve-hole of an inner tube) through which the fire shines. The hoop eighteen earth-radii out is the moon; the outermost is the sun. The diameter of the sun, that is, of the opening in the sun-hoop, is as great as that of the earth. Eclipses and the moon's phases are explained as obstructions over the holes. (We are not told what closes them.) The stars are the innermost hoops, presumably nine earth-radii out from us. Anaximander would understandably infer that they were the hoops nearest us, for otherwise the hoops of sun and moon ought to appear as black bands in the night sky; but these thin, faint star-hoops would not interfere with the greater lights of the sun and moon.

Even if Anaximander did not affirm the rotation of the earth, his model of the world contains two very important new ideas. One is that of *an earth without material support.* All earlier, and indeed many later, cosmologists thought themselves obliged to explain the earth's fixity by providing supports. Anaximander, seeing that such shifts only moved the problem back a step or two without solving it, declared boldly that the earth stays at the center "because of its equal distance from everything."

The other new idea is that of *explanation in terms of a theory involving postulated entities.* For we certainly do not *see* the hoops; we see only the "breathing-holes." Why did Anaximander postulate the hoops, instead of resting content with a "simpler" common-sense conception of fiery spheres or discs? Our ancient sources give no hint; however, only one answer seems possible. Anaximander must have reasoned this way: heavy bodies near the earth tend to move towards the center of concentration of mass, that is, toward the center of the earth. Now the earth, being a very heavy body, should likewise move toward the greatest concentration of mass, if there is one. And there *appear* to be at least two: the sun and the moon. Therefore, if the sun and moon are what they appear to be, the earth ought to move towards them (or they towards us). Since this does not happen, the earth must really be equidistant from these bodies, despite appearances. This condition could only hold if the bodies surround the earth symmetrically, that is, are hoops, of which only the "breathing-holes" are visible. The idea of mist wrapping up fire, which seems strange to us, was natural enough to Anaximander, since lightning emerging from clouds easily suggests such a notion. We know that in fact Anaximander explained lightning in some such way: "When the wind is shut up in a cloud and bursts forth violently, the tearing of the cloud makes the noise of thunder, and the rift gives the appearance of a flash."

If this conjectural restoration of Anaximander's reasoning is correct, then Anaximander grasped the essential nature of theoretical explanation: of a law or natural regularity holding universally (in this instance, "gravitation") and accounting for (or generalized from) observation (falling bodies on the earth's surface), leading to the hypothesis of unobserved entities (the hoops) in order to render other observed phenomena (the sun and moon *not* falling) consistent with the law. This is nine-tenths of "scientific method" as now understood. Had he devised (or admitted the necessity of) some test of the hoop hypothesis, he would have had the other tenth. And even if he did not reason in this way, it seems that the hoops *must* have played this role of hypothetical entities in respect to *some* general theory, for there was no traditional or mythological incentive for supposing them. In consequence, the scientific nature of Anaximander's thought is established.

The power and originality of Anaximander's thought is displayed preeminently in his biology. Myth-making, even when it assumed a development of the cosmos as a whole, always conceived of animals, including man, as having appeared on the scene from nowhere, in their latter-day forms, either as special creations of the gods, or in some unexplained manner. In sharp contrast to this sort of facile story-telling, Anaximander worked out a theory of animal evolution based on the ideas of adaptation to environment and survival of the fittest.

His starting point was the observation that "while other animals quickly find food by themselves, man alone requires a lengthy period of suckling.

3

Hence, had he been originally as he is now, he would never have survived." That is to say, a theory of the world which in general is evolutionary is incompatible with the human species having appeared all at once (as babies?), for if it had, it could never have survived in the "state of nature." It follows that animals whose young are long immature must be the products of gradual development (presumably including socialization) from some other kind of life not so ill-fitted for the world. Furthermore, the theory that in the beginning there had been no dry land suggested, if it did not require, that all life originated in the sea. Hence "living creatures arose from the moist element as it was evaporated by the sun." The transition from marine to terrestrial life occurred thus: "The first animals were produced in the moisture, each enclosed in a prickly bark. As they advanced in age, they came out upon the drier part. When the bark broke off, they survived for a short time." As for human beings in particular, they too were "like other animals, namely fish, in the beginning. . . . At first human beings arose in the inside of fishes, and after having been reared like sharks, and become capable of protecting themselves, they were finally cast ashore and took to land." The mention of sharks was not fanciful, but based on the acute observation (to be sure, quite possibly made by somebody else) that certain sharks of the eastern Mediterranean hatch their eggs inside their bodies, so that they seem akin to mammals.

Anaximander wrote a book, the Western world's first scientific treatise, of which one sentence, or part of a sentence, has been preserved: Things return to their origins "as is ordained; for they give satisfaction and reparation to one another for their injustice according to the ordering of time. . . ." It is clear from this that Anaximander's philosophy made use of the concept of "justice," pervasive of Greek thought, according to which there is an impersonal and inexorable force in nature charged with keeping things balanced: in society and in the world at large every person, state, and element has its allotted portion, and "injustice," the encroachment of anything beyond its bounds, is followed automatically and surely by restorative retribution. The notion lies at the root both of Greek moral ideas and the conception of "laws of nature"; in the fragment of Anaximander we find it evidently being developed in the direction of the latter. It would be risky to infer anything more as to Anaximander's world-view from this half sentence. In particular, it by no means shows that Anaximander viewed the universe as "inherently moral" in any sense that we would naturally give to that expression.

Even allowing for the fact that in Greek and other Near Eastern thought before the sixth century B.C. there existed a discernible tendency toward "rationalization" of traditional myths, and that the myths themselves contained the kernels of evolutionary and natural-law concepts, it is hardly an exaggeration to say that Anaximander single-handedly invented science and philosophy as we know them. Above all, he put rationalism on such a firm foundation that, among the educated, it took mythology a thousand years to overthrow it; and even then it did not perish utterly.

Any naturalistic world-view at the beginning of the sixth century would be remarkable; it is staggering to find that the very first philosophy contained such transcendently important ideas as an unsupported earth, theoretical explanation involving inferred entities, and animal evolution from marine organisms to man in accordance with a principle of adaptation—and, quite possibly, the earth's rotation and "gravitation" in addition.

It is not surprising that Anaximander's immediate successor, Anaximenes, was incapable of such daring speculation. He accordingly taught a more "common-sense" philosophy in which the earth was held up by "mist," the unobservable hoops were abolished, and the sun, moon, and stars were "like fiery leaves," floating in the air. He was, so to speak, the first positivist. The belief that the earth needed a support continued to be held in Anaximander's homeland for a century,

down to and including Anaxagoras (whose philosophy was otherwise essentially an elaboration of Anaximander's). But the Pythagoreans adopted Anaximander's astronomy, hoops and all, at first. Since, as is well known, Copernicus and Kepler were strongly influenced by Pythagorean theories, it is possible to demonstrate a continuous chain of development in this science from Miletus to Mount Palomar. Unfortunately Anaximander's equally promising beginnings in biology bore no fruit. Though Empedocles also recognized the principle of adaptation, the details of his evolutionary theory were fantastic; and after his time the authority of Aristotle in favor of fixity of species put an end to evolutionary speculation in the ancient world. The revival two thousand years later owed nothing to Anaximander.

THE ANALECTS OF CONFUCIUS
(Lun Yü)

Author: Confucius (c.551-c.479 B.C.)
Type of work: Ethics, political philosophy, epistemology
First transcribed: Late sixth or early fifth century B.C.

PRINCIPAL IDEAS ADVANCED

Jen, *the ideal relationship among human beings, is the perfect virtue of men.*
Man is basically close to jen *by his very nature, but his action should be controlled by* li, *the rules of propriety.*
The chün-tzu, *or ideal man, is one who practices* jen *in accordance with* li; *consequently, he treasures and seeks the* tao, *the right Way.*

Confucius, to whom most of the sayings in the *Analects* are ascribed, was a descendant of an influential family of the state of Lu in the present-day Eastern Chinese province of Shantung. His family name was K'ung. His own names were Ch'iu and Chung-ni. Later he was known as K'ung Fu-tzu, meaning Master K'ung, out of respect. At the time of his birth, his family was already in reduced circumstances, but he could boast of a long line of illustrious ancestors, dating all the way back to pre-Chou dynasty times. Because of Confucius' fame, his family history is perhaps the most complete and extensive genealogy in the world. Today a man named K'ung Te-ch'eng, officially recognized as the seventy-seventh generation descendant of Confucius, still lives in Formosa.

Orphaned at an early age, Confucius went to work while still in his teens. He held a number of minor posts in the government and in the employ of the nobility. His service record and his self-cultivation soon won for him wide recognition. Students gathered around him for instruction in ethics, literature, and the art of government service. He was particularly respected for his knowledge of ancient rituals. Among his followers were men of diverse interests and temperaments. As myth and legend grew around the historical Confucius through the years, the biographical details of his life make the story of the ancient sage anything but monotonous. Confucius is said to have had to put up with one student who was too stingy to let his master borrow his umbrella; consequently, Confucius was drenched in the rain at least once. Confucius, so the legend says, had constantly to restrain a second student whose hot temper involved himself and his master in frequent difficulties. Confucius is believed to have had a narrow escape from a third disciple whose reaction against his master's ceaseless moralistic admonitions amounted to a murderous intent.

Confucius divided his time among lecturing to his students, editing reading materials for his students, and trying to persuade the men in government to adopt his ideas. If he failed in the last, he certainly succeeded remarkably well in the first two tasks, as his *Analects* (the *Lun Yü*) and its lasting influence testify. Being a collection of remembered dialogues recorded by his disciples and their pupils, there is clearly a question about the accuracy of the statements in the *Analects*. In addition, the extremely terse style of these dialogues lends itself to a variety of interpretations. However, upon a careful perusal of these sayings, many key ideas of the Confucian system emerge with clarity.

Of the central cluster of ideas that are discernible in Confucian thought, the idea of *jen* is perhaps the greatest in importance. *Jen* is the foundation of Confucian ethics because *jen* stands for the ideal relationship among human beings. The etymological significance of the Chinese character *jen* yields a key to this idea: the symbols that form this character mean "two human beings," hence the suggestion of "the ideal relationship between any two human beings." *Jen* suggests gentility, magnanimity, humanity, goodness of character, and benevolence. The last sense is the one most frequently used to translate this term. In short, *jen* is the perfect virtue of human beings; it is the only road to the peace and harmony of a society. He who embraces the principle of *jen* will treat people gently and humanely; and for him everything will go well.

In answering his disciples' questions on the existence and functions of *jen*, Confucius stressed the importance not only of internalizing the principles of *jen* to make them a part of man's natural disposition, but also of putting them into daily practice. He wanted his students to practice courtesy, magnanimity, good faith, diligence, and kindness everywhere and all the time. He came close to advocating an infinite compassion when he summed up his own exposition with a succinct command: to practice *jen* is to "love mankind" universally. Most frequently Confucius emphasized that *jen* was not a lofty metaphysical abstraction beyond the comprehension of the ordinary person. On the contrary he insisted that *jen* lay close at hand for everyone to grasp. The difficulty, as he saw it, was that few people could remain firm for long. Even among his distinguished disciples he mentioned only one who succeeded in practicing *jen* with constancy.

One detects a note of earnestness that verges on religious fervor when Confucius speaks of the importance of *jen*. With unmistakable clarity he asserts that good men sacrifice their lives in order to maintain *jen* and that never would they alter *jen* in order to survive any crisis. In this light the Confucian principles of *jen* become more than relative standards of desirable social behavior; they are notions of absolute right and justice. But, Confucius explains, the seeds of these notions are not to be found outside man's basic nature. Without anywhere giving a clear statement on his view on man's nature, Confucius nevertheless reveals his assumption that men are born basically the same and that direct expressions of the original nature of man approach much closer to *jen* than any affectation could. There is only one condition that Confucius insists on: any direct expression of one's own nature would have to be restrained by *li* (the rules of propriety) in order to adhere to the principles of *jen*.

Strictly speaking, the rules of propriety, the *li*, taken literally could mean rites, etiquette, good form, or decorum, but clearly Confucius uses this term to mean much more than mere outward expressions of formality. As an expert and an authority on ancient rites, Confucius preferred to have his students look beyond the music and pomp, the "jade and silk," and other features usually accompanying the rituals. In the *Analects* he stresses the essence of *li* as the distinguishing quality of man without which man and wild animals would be the same and human society would cease to exist. He also tells his own son to study *li* because if man does not know *li* he does not know how to behave like a man.

Li, consequently, is upheld as the evidence of man's civilization. *Li* is essential to sophisticated, cultured, and orderly living, which is the central aim of the Confucian social teachings. With *li* man can tame the wild animal in him and make himself a better member of society. In more than one statement Confucius suggests the psychological use of *li* to bring calm and poise to man at critical moments. *Li* is the Confucian prescription to save society from chaos and disorder.

True to his status as a self-appointed standard-bearer of traditional culture, Confucius does not spare any effort to impress his students with the importance of rituals. He himself would not eat unless the meal was presented and the seat arranged in the proper manner; he would not walk on foot when he kept company with the dignitaries; he would not look, listen, speak, or move until he was sure his every action was in accordance with the rules of propriety (*li*). Indeed, his own sayings and other statements about him in this book show us a man of meticulous care for proper manners. One feels that Confucius purposely did so to dramatize the cultural heritage of his state of Lu, which was closely linked to the Chou dynasty. In his philosophy Confucius champions a revival of the Chou institutions which in his political vision represent a golden past. Of course, it must be remembered that Confucius holds the spirit, the appropriateness, and the sincerity behind the rites above the formalities. He instructs his students to observe simplicity, not lavish display, as the general principle of all rites, and to ascertain the genuine sentiment behind any ritual observance, rather than the mere physical presence of etiquette. The spirit of *li*, according to Confucius, obtains only when the man practicing *li* has *jen*. Here the two key Confucian ideas come together to form the basis for the cult of *chün-tzu*.

Originally *chün-tzu* meant no more than "the son of the lord." Its more extensive use acquired for it the broader meaning of "any man of good breeding." In the repeated appearance of this term in the Confucian statements, the element of "good breeding" or family origin is no longer stressed and *chün-tzu* becomes simply "good man" or "the best of men" in contradistinction with *hsiao-jen,* "small man" or "petty man." The sense of the term in the *Analects* can also be quite adequately expressed as "the superior man" in contrast to the "inferior man."

Confucius paints in *chün-tzu* a picture of the ideal man. This perfect man has a thorough understanding of *jen* and constantly practices it. He acts always according to *li*, and the rules of

propriety are so much a part of his nature that he never can violate them. His uprightness, or the expressions of his genuine nature, is perfectly blended with that proper amount of refinement, so that he is neither pedantic nor rustic. In dealing with others he is warm-mannered. He has a will of steel and his appearance is always calm because his *jen* keeps him from anxieties, his wisdom guards him against perplexities, and his courage dispels any possible fear. While the petty-minded people think of profit, he, the *chün-tzu*, is always mindful of what is right. He may not possess much technical knowledge about details but his mind is capable of grasping what is essential and significant. Above all, the *chün-tzu* treasures and seeks the *tao*.

The Confucian *tao* is vastly different from the *tao* of mystic Taoism. Confucius speaks of the *tao* of the ancient sage-kings, meaning the Way to an ideal government and society, and of the *tao* of a virtuous man, meaning the right Way of being a man. At times Confucius treats the word *tao* as another name for righteousness and sagacity. As he does with *jen,* Confucius also speaks of *tao* with occasional outbursts of pious feeling. Thus, we hear him declare, "He who hears of *tao* in the morning may die content at night." In these instances Confucius does come close to expressing a religious dedication.

On the whole Confucius' silence on the supernatural is eloquent. In the *Analects*, he does not defend, nor does he attempt to destroy, the prevailing ideas about the world of the spirits. Instead, he unequivocally instructs his disciples to keep their minds on the affairs of men and not to be bothered

8

by questions about the spirits. He informs them that they must first learn enough about life before they inquire into life hereafter, and he himself throughout his life remained too busy studying this world to deal with the other world. When his student asks him about the relationship between the rites and the spirits, Confucius' answer is that since sincerity is the essence of the rituals, one must conduct the sacrificial rites to one's ancestors "as if they were present," and to the spirits also "as if they were present." Beyond this, so says Confucius, one should not go. It is enough "to respect the spirits and stay away from them."

Small wonder that one of his disciples declares his disappointment in trying to learn Confucius' expositions on "Heaven's ways." Confucius may be suspected of dodging the question, he may also be suspected of having no formulated ideas about the spirits, but he cannot be accused of total silence on the question of Heaven. For in many passages in this book Confucius refers to Heaven, sometimes as an invincible moral force, at other times as a Supreme Being, willful and purposeful.

Heaven to Confucius is the Supreme Being that decides in favor of the moral and the right, and Confucius envisages himself as having been commissioned by the Heavenly authority to perpetuate the sage-king's Way on earth. So he declares, when his life is threatened by the people of K'uang, "If Heaven is not going to let this culture decline, what can the people of K'uang do to me?" On another occasion of distress, Confucius comforts his friends by saying, "Heaven has created this virtue in me; what can Huan T'ui do to me?" That Confucius views Heaven's will

as always in favor of the good and always beneficial is further evinced in his statement about the regularity of the seasons and the thriving of myriad creatures. This statement has been taken by many students of Confucianism as a proof of Confucius' belief in the spontaneity of a universal amoral force that is omnipotent. This view could be correct, but if one judges by the majority of Confucius' remarks concerning Heaven, the force of the foregoing statement still tends to describe Heaven as a beneficent force that works benevolently without "elaborate explanations."

Heaven's *tao* in Confucian terms is Heaven's Way or Heaven's Will. This Will is supreme and above man's interference. If Confucius' use of the term Heaven is perfectly consistent, then Heaven's Will should also be moral and in favor of the good. Here another Confucian term is introduced, the *ming*. *Ming* could mean either a command or a destiny. When it appears in connection with Heaven as "Heaven's *ming*," it usually means Heaven's command, or Heaven's Will. When it appears alone, *ming* could mean fate or destiny. What makes Confucius' position on Heaven's Will unclear is his statement that if the Way (*tao*) is to prevail, it is fate (*ming*); and if the Way is to fail, it is also fate (*ming*). If this is the same *ming* as Heaven's command, then Heaven may not always be intent on making the Great Way prevail. This idea is what is generally understood as Confucian fatalism. In other words, fate as a shadowy necessity beyond the comprehension and control of human beings also appears in Confucian thought.

Enough is said in the *Analects* to illuminate some other Confucian ideals with regard to social and political institutions. The importance of the family as the microcosm of society is clearly implied when Confucius reminds his students to practice filial piety within the family before trying to learn how to read and write well. The significance of filial piety in the Confucian system as seen in the *Analects,* however, is not as great as has been generally believed. In his book Confucius describes this virtue as important because a man respectful toward his parents is not likely to violate the law and order of society, also because to be thankful to one's parents is a good sentiment that should be encouraged. But to uphold filial piety as the supreme human virtue is not Confucius' intent in this book; rather, it is a later development in the Confucian school of thought, elaborated and reinterpreted by the Confucian commentators on these texts. Confucius himself does not preach total, blind obedience to one's parents. He sees the virtue of a son shielding his sheep-stealing father, but he also teaches the son to remonstrate, mildly but persistently, with his erring father.

As an educator, Confucius was equally earnest in teaching his students, regardless of their social status and family origins. He believed in the equal teachability of men, but he recognized the difference in intellect and talent among men. In the *Analects* he accepts those "who are born with knowledge" as the best, and those who learn after industrious study as the second type of mind. Nowhere in this book does Confucius suggest that everybody is born socially equal and is entitled to the right to rule himself. He urges the ruler to learn the right Way to govern; he urges his students to learn to be the best ministers possible in order to assist the ruler. Confucius' view on the function of the government is that government must rule by moral excellence—a view that anticipates the whole political philosophy of Mencius.

Confucius' remark about men "born with knowledge" is extremely provocative, but unfortunately the *Analects* does not yield any adequate exposition on Confucius' view of knowledge. In discussing how to study, Confucius acknowledges his own intention "to observe and commit to memory what is observed," because he confesses that he "cannot do anything without knowing about it first." When these statements are examined together, Confucius does hint at the possibility that some people are born with knowledge; hence, these people can act spontaneously without the effort of learning how to act and without being aware of their knowledge. But Confucius carefully declines the company of people of such super intellect, and he admits that the source of his knowledge is observation and intensive study. He also rules out the attainment of knowledge through meditation without the aid of books because once he "tried to think the whole day without eating and the whole night without sleeping, but nothing came of it." Furthermore, he does not separate the attainment of knowledge from action and practice.

More important than the relation between action and knowledge is the exact identification of name with actuality, according to the Confucian teachings. The times were chaotic and the social order was confused. Hence, Confucius urged the king to behave like a king and the minister to act as one of his rank should. If the name is not correctly applied, says Confucius, then language is no longer a medium of communication. Consequently, nothing can be accomplished and men will not even know where to "put their hands or feet." From a moralistic start with a practical aim, the Confucian doctrine of rectification of names developed into a serious effort to define terms. Confucius' concern with this matter reveals his underlying assumption that the name is not just a representation of a thing, but is the very essence of the thing itself. The germ of this idea can be found in pre-Confucian thought in China's high antiquity, but Confucius' effort has added significance to this idea and made it an important development in Chinese philosophy.

In spite of its brevity and limited bulk, the *Analects* remains throughout the centuries the most authentic and rewarding source for the study of Confucius the man and his thought. In addition to the key ideas of original Confucianism, the book also illumines certain aspects of life in ancient China. The fragments of dialogues between Confucius and a few political leaders show the role the intellectuals played in a society where values were undergoing dramatic change. The dialogues also reveal how totally without restraint the states vied for supremacy in a power struggle that followed the collapse of an ancient feudal order.

The fact that certain key statements in the *Analects* have been interpreted in different ways has certainly contributed to the survival of the Confucian system. There is something in this book for everyone, from the most radical to the most conservative, if he searches hard for it. Indeed, much has been read back into the Confucian teachings, and what Confucius did actually teach has been, as a result, distorted. In spite of differences of interpretation, it seems important to note that Confucius valued most highly an orderly, peaceful, and harmonious society. To this goal he channeled all his thought and teaching. His *tao* was the Way to achieve this ideal; his *te* (virtue) was his claim that he had been invested with the knowledge of the Way; his *wen* (refinement, cultural heritage) was the heritage of institutions prevailing in an imaginary golden past derived from the ancient texts. To be sure, Confucius insisted that society would not be peaceful if each individual man did not behave properly, according to his social station. This meant that for Confucius the individual was important, but only insofar as he could help to bring about peace and harmony in society. If Confucius speculated on the position of man in the universe or dealt with other metaphysical matters, there is no sufficient evidence in this book.

HERACLITUS: FRAGMENTS

Author: Heraclitus of Ephesus (c.540-c.480 B.C.)
Type of work: Metaphysics
First transcribed: Probably early fifth century B.C.

11

There is a Logos, a Rationale, by which all things are one.

Opposites are the same (in several respects).

Although opposites are unified by their interdependence, they exist in a state of constant strife.

Everything is fire in that everything is involved in an eternal process of change and exchange.

Failure to understand the Rationale is the root of all evil.

Despite the epithet "Obscure" awarded to Heraclitus by ancient tradition, many of the less than 150 sentences from his book that have come down to us are as clear as can be. For instance, the denunciation of his fellow citizens: "The Ephesians ought to hang themselves, every one who is of age, and leave the city to the boys. They who threw out Hermodorus, the worthiest man of them, saying: 'Let no one of us be the worthiest, but if there is one, let him go somewhere else, among others.' " Or his compliments to his eminent predecessors: "Learning many things does not teach one to have intelligence; else it would have taught Hesiod and Pythagoras, also Xenophanes and Hecataeus." Or his estimate of pious individuals: "They 'purify' themselves by staining themselves with different blood, as if one who stepped into mud should wash it off with mud. But one would be thought mad, if any man should see him behaving this way. And they pray to these idols, just as if one were to have a conversation with a house— knowing naught of the nature of gods and heroes." Or such remarks about human imbecility as "Dogs bark at every one they do not know" and "Donkeys would choose garbage rather than gold." Besides Hermodorus, only Bias of Priene escaped Heraclitus'

contempt, and that was because Bias had said, "Most men are bad."

Heraclitus despised other men because he had made a discovery which he thought so obvious and important that failure to appreciate it was inexcusable. This was the discovery of what he called the *logos*—a word which cannot be translated satisfactorily; it means not only "word" but almost anything else connected with words or what words stand for: account, discourse, argument, fame, reason, formula, pattern, rationale. The last of these will be adopted here as the least objectionable rendering.

Heraclitus's book began thus: "Of this Rationale, which is eternal, men turn out to be ignorant, both before they hear it and when they hear it for the first time. For although all things occur in accordance with the Rationale, they are like novices when they are tested by such words and works as I work out, distinguishing each thing according to its nature and explaining what it is. But such things as they do when they are awake escape other men, just as they forget about what they do when asleep." To judge from the wildly divergent interpretations of Heraclitus' teaching that have been offered in two-and-a-half millennia, men are as ignorant of it now as when they heard it for the first time; and

12

this verdict no doubt applies to the present account also.

"Listening not to me but to the Rationale, it is wise to agree that all things are one." This is the succinct account of the content of the Rationale, which *is* the unity of all things. What Heraclitus meant is best explained by considering first the view he rejects. Most men suppose that the world is full of a number of things, each on its own, comprising a miscellaneous aggregation. The "learning many things" practised by men like Pythagoras and Hesiod consists in classifying the ingredients of the aggregate in accordance with a "table of opposites," and of explaining how these opposites came into being. Understanding is analysis.

This approach is utterly mistaken, Heraclitus protests. Opposites are no more capable of existing on their own than (as *we* should say) the north pole of a magnet can exist without a south pole. "They do not understand how what differs agrees with itself; back turning connection, as in bow and lyre."

About a sixth of the extant fragments deal with "opposites." They show four senses in which opposites are "the same," as Heraclitus puts it with characteristic paradox. (1) Even common sense ascribes unity to what when "analyzed" proves to be full of so-called opposites. "Over those who step into the same rivers, different and again different waters flow." "The way of letters [as in a line of writing] is straight and crooked. It is one and the same." "Beginning and end are common on the circumference of a circle." (2) Polar opposition: "They would not know the name of Justice if these

things [injustices] did not exist." "Sickness makes health pleasant and good; hunger, satiety; weariness, rest." (3) There is the special kind of polar opposition that consists in the regular succession of one thing by its opposite, so that if the one perished, so would the other: "The teacher of most men is Hesiod. They understand that he knew many things—he who did not recognize day and night; for they are one." "The cold things get hot, hot gets cold, wet gets dry, parched gets damp." (4) Many oppositions are "subjective," dependent on the point of view or nature or interests of the observer, not on essential natures: "Swine rejoice in filth." "Sea is the cleanest and the dirtiest water: for fish it is drinkable and salubrious, but for men it is undrinkable and poisonous." "Doctors who cut and burn complain that they get no adequate pay for doing these things." "The way up and down is one and the same." (That is, the same road is "the road up" to valley-dwellers and "the road down" to hill-dwellers.) Heraclitus summarizes: "Things taken together are wholes and not wholes; being brought together is being parted; concord is dissonance; and out of all things, one; and out of one, all things."

Insistence on the unity (interdependence) of opposites should not be mistaken for a denial of the existence of opposition. On the contrary, the business of opposites is to oppose, and the strife of opposites is the basic fact of existence. "It is necessary to know that war is common, and justice is strife, and all things happen in accordance with strife." "War is father of all, king of all, and he shows some to be gods and some to be men; he makes some slaves and some free." "Homer deserved to be thrown out from amongst the contestants and beaten; and Archilochus likewise," their offense having been pacifism; but to pray for the cessation of warfare amounts to desiring the end of the world. Process, not substance, was Heraclitus' fundamental ontological category.

But if the world does not consist of unrelated things, neither is it a chaos of haphazard events. What happens happens according to "measures"; the pattern of the measures is the Rationale, or Justice. "The sun will not overstep measures; if he did, Furies, guardians of Justice, would find him out." "This cosmos, the same for all, no one of gods nor of men has made, but it always was and is and will be ever-living fire, being kindled in measures and being extinguished in measures." "Wisdom is one thing: to know the Rationale of how all things are steered through all."

Philosophical speculation (as distinguished from mythology) about the nature of things had existed for hardly a century when Heraclitus wrote. His predecessors had taken it for granted (perhaps by inheritance from creation myths) that the world was made of one basic stuff, which had existed in an undifferentiated condition "in the beginning." They conceived their problems to be two: to identify this basic stuff (Thales: water; Anaximander: "the Boundless"; Anaximenes: mist; Pythagoras: number-atoms) and to describe the process of differentiation that had produced the world as we know it.

Heraclitus set himself in opposition to this tradition. The world, as a measured process, is eternal, in all its com-

plexity. To be sure, it is "ever-living fire," but "fire" is chosen as symbolic of process, not as a "basic stuff" put forward as an alternative to water or mist or what-not. "All things are exchange for fire, and fire for all things, just as merchandise is exchange for gold and gold for merchandise" has often been cited against the present interpretation, but all the statement means is that the so-called elements merge into one another in the world-process, that nothing is absolutely and eternally distinct from anything else. An obscure fragment purports to describe the exchanging: "Fire's turnings: first sea; of sea one half is earth, the other half is lightning-flash. Sea is poured out, and it is measured in the same proportion as that which it had before the earth arose."

Though Heraclitus was scornful of popular belief, he thought, like Xenophanes, that religion should be reformed, not rejected utterly. His religious position is perhaps not too misleadingly described as pantheistic. "God: day-night, winter-summer, war-peace, satiety-hunger. He changes in the same way as when there is a mixing [of oil] with spices, it is called after the fragrance of each." According to this fragment, God is the organized totality of things, the unity of all apparent opposites. God, as we might expect, takes the objective view: "To god all things are fair and good and just, but men suppose some things to be just and some unjust." That Heraclitus thought his conception of God to be a purification of the popular notion is suggested by the fragment, "That which alone is wise is one. It is unwilling and willing to be called by the name of Zeus."

Heraclitus taught immortality, but

14

only in the (somewhat attentuated) sense that the soul, like everything else in the world process, is not a stuff but a process that undergoes successive phases. "There await men, when they die, such things as they do not hope for nor expect." "Immortals-mortals, mortals-immortals, living one another's death, dying one another's life." "Death to souls is to become water, to water death is to become earth, but from earth water comes into existence, and soul from water." Although "For souls it is delight to get wet," still "When a man is drunk, he is led by an immature boy, stumbling, not heeding where he steps; his soul is wet." Hence, "A dry soul is wisest and best."

"Those who speak with intelligence must take their strength from what is common to all, as a city from law, and much more strongly. For all human laws are nourished by the one divine. It has as much power as it wishes and it suffices for all and it prevails." On the basis of this fragment Heraclitus has some claim to consideration as the founder of the philosophical theory of Natural Law. The one divine law is, of course, the Rationale, which Heraclitus conceives not only as the formula of what *is* but also as the criterion of what ought to be. "The people should fight for the law just as for the city wall." His political views were decidedly undemocratic: besides the denunciation of Hermodorus' banishers, we may cite three other fragments in this connection: "One man to me is ten thousand, if he is best"; "Also it is law to be persuaded by the counsel of one"; and "Every beast is driven to the pasture with a blow." (The last of these might stand as motto to Plato's *Republic*.)

Like Socrates, Heraclitus in effect equated moral turpitude with lack of (intellectual) understanding. Failure to apprehend the Rationale, that which is "common," is the root of all evil. "Thus one ought to follow what is common. But although the Rationale is common, the many live as if they possessed private understanding." Heraclitus frequently compares "the many" to sleepers, since "For men awake there is one common cosmos, but men asleep turn away, each one, into a private world." "It is not right to act and talk like men asleep." Unfortunately it is not clear from the extant fragments just what alteration of behavior would ensue if one decided to "follow the common"—other than that one would not get drunk, nor throw out Hermodorus.

"A man's character is [determines] his destiny," Heraclitus said, and the remark applies especially to himself. Though we have no reliable biographical information about him, Heraclitus' severe, haughty, enigmatic, yet pithy and curiously attractive style tells us all we need to know of him as a man. No one in Greek history before Socrates is so sharply delineated as an individual. It was Heraclitus' style that insured the preservation of much of his book (which must have been a short one) through copious quotations by later writers. It was his style also that led inevitably to distortions and misinterpretations of his teaching.

The two statements still most commonly attached to the name of Heraclitus are "Everything flows" and "You cannot step into the same river twice." Because of these, Heraclitus is summarized in the histories of philosophy as having taught a doctrine of perpetual change, and he is set off against

15

Parmenides, who said that there is no such thing as change. But in fact, neither of these sentences is a genuine Heraclitean fragment; both are Platonic paraphrases which are, to say the least, misleading. Though Heraclitus, as a process philosopher, was committed to the view that reality is activity, the universality of change was not central in his thought by any means; what he stressed was rather the *ordered and eternal pattern* that intelligence (as contrasted with "learning of many things") could discern in the flux of existence—the flux itself being so obvious as not to deserve comment. As for rivers, it will be recalled that what Heraclitus actually said was that one *could* step into the same river as often as one pleased—but that when one did, "different and again different waters" would flow over one's feet, the point being to illustrate the relation of transitory particulars to a fixed pattern.

In later antiquity the Stoics found in Heraclitus' pantheism and natural law doctrine much that was congenial to their own philosophy. In consequence they looked upon him (rather sentimentally) as their progenitor. In the course of accommodating his doctrines to theirs, he was made out to have taught that fire is the basic stuff of the universe and that the world process moves in cycles, each of which is terminated by a general conflagration. In the last hundred years Heraclitus has been held up to glory or obloquy as a proto-Hegelian, -Fascist, -Marxist, -Nietzschean, and -Existentialist.

The actual teachings of Heraclitus (as distinguished from *ex post facto* quoting of his apothegms to decorate opinions independently arrived at) had little influence on the course of Greek philosophy. Unlike his Milesian and Pythagorean quasi-contemporaries, Heraclitus made no contribution to the development of natural science. Perhaps he should be counted the founder of philosophical ethics for having related a moral code to a *Weltanschauung;* but the evidence bearing on this matter is slight, and it does not appear that he worked out this connection in any detailed way. And although his insistence on the Rationale as the proper object of understanding is important, credit for it must be shared with the Milesians and Pythagoreans, his sneers at their superficiality notwithstanding.

But as a stylist, phrasemaker, and critic, Heraclitus is unique. This is not said by way of patronizing him. Heraclitus compared himself to the "Sibyl with raving mouth uttering things mirthless and unadorned and unperfumed." She "reaches over a thousand years with her voice." Heraclitus has surpassed her by a factor of two-and-a-half, and still, like his doctors, cuts and burns.

THE WAY OF TRUTH and THE WAY OF OPINION

Author: Parmenides of Elea (c.515-c.456 B.C.)
Type of work: Metaphysics
First transcribed: Fifth century B.C.

Reality is a solid, homogeneous sphere.

All appearances of change and motion are illusory.

Whatever exists could not have come from nothing; it must then have come from what exists—but if the existent can come only from the existent, there is no beginning to what exists: reality is eternal and indestructible.

Since the material of the universe consists of its sensible qualities, and since to change would involve the nonexistence of qualities (which are eternal and indestructible), change is impossible.

Parmenides, it seems, began his philosophical career as a Pythagorean, but when still a young man he attained the insight that reality consists of a solid homogeneous sphere, the appearances of diversity and change being altogether illusory. He set out this extraordinary doctrine in a poem in hexameter verses, consisting of a proem, a section, "The Way of Truth," expounding and defending the theory of the Sphere, and a section, "The Way of Opinion," in which he dealt with current (probably Pythagorean) scientific theories. The "Proem" and the important "The Way of Truth" have been preserved substantially intact, but only a few fragments of "The Way of Opinion" remain.

The "Proem" is an elaborate allegorical description of Parmenides' journey into heaven. In a chariot drawn by "immortal mares" he is conducted upward by the daughters of the Sun, who bring him to the "gates of the ways of Night and Day," the keys to which "severely-chastising Justice" holds. At the entreaties of the maidens, Justice opens the portals, revealing "the goddess" (Justice?) who addresses Parmenides:

"O youth, who come to our mansion in the company of immortal charioteers, welcome! It was no evil fate but right and justice that set you to travel on this way, far indeed from the path trodden by men. Meet it is that you should inquire into all things, the unshaking heart of well-rounded truth as well as the opinions of mortals in which is no true confidence at all. Yet none the less you shall learn all things, even how seeming things—all passing through each—must really be."

The goddess warns Parmenides against relying on the senses for knowledge of reality: "Keep your thought away from this way of inquiry, and by no means let much-tried custom force you this way, to ply the unseeing eye and the ringing ear and the tongue" (considered as the organ of taste not of speech). "Rather, judge by reason the much-disputed proof which I expound." The much-disputed proof is strictly *a priori*, depending altogether on the law of identity: "Well then, I shall tell you—and do you attend and listen to my word—what are the only ways of inquiry there are to think of. The first, that IT IS, and that it is impossible for it not to be, in the way of conviction, for it follows truth. The other, that IT IS NOT, and that it must needs not be,—that, I tell you, is a path that none can learn of at all. For you could not perceive what is not —that is impossible—nor even think of it; for it is the same thing that can be thought and that can be."

17

The goddess' expressions are puzzling, for it is not English (or Greek either) to say simply, "It is." We want to know what the "it" stands for; and if "it" is (say) a radish, still the expression "A radish is" makes no sense. A radish is *what*? Nevertheless, the sense of the passage is unmistakable: if there is something real (and there is), then whatever characters it has, it has just those characters, and none other. *A is A.* It is impossible to think of A's not being A, for to *say* that A is not A would be in effect to say that the thing having the character C does *not* have the character C; and this would amount to saying something and immediately retracting it, so that altogether nothing was said. It is in this sense that "it is the same thing that can be thought and that can be." The goddess did not mean, of course, that there must be mermaids in the ocean because we can think of them. She meant that reality and thought must alike be non-contradictory.

All this is perhaps innocent enough; but the goddess is going to use the principle thus laid down as a weapon to destroy belief in the reality of the world revealed by the senses. The first step is to draw the corollary "For this shall never be proved, that what-is-not is," for "it is not possible for what is nothing to be." The thought is that the word "nothing" means "that which is-not"; consequently any sentence having the word "nothing" as its subject, and "is" as its verb, must be contradictory, "not to be thought of."

Having established this, it is easy for the goddess to prove that "what-is is uncreated and indestructible." "For what birth of it will you seek out? In what way and from what source its increase? I forbid you to say or to think

that it came from what-is-not; for how what-is-not could *be* is neither speakable nor thinkable." The argument implied is a simple dilemma: If there is an origin of what-is, that origin must be either what-is or what-is-not. But it cannot be what-is-not, for if so, the contradictory sentence "What-is-not *is* the origin of what-is" would be true, which is absurd. And of course to say that the origin of what-is is what-is, while in a sense true, is so only trivially. Therefore what-is is uncreated.

The goddess advances another argument to prove the same conclusion: "And, if it came from nothing, what need could have made it arise later rather than sooner?" This is really an argument from an assumed causal principle; even if the objection be waived that "what-is-not" is unthinkable, mere nothingness or negation could not, by definition, afford any reason or cause why something, if it were to originate out of it, should suddenly appear at one time rather than another. But without such a reason, nothing could appear at *any* time; hence, if there ever were a time at which there was just nothing at all, then there never could be anything at any other time. (This argument was attractive to many subsequent philosophers, being urged by St. Thomas Aquinas and Thomas Hobbes, among others.)

A similar argument (not given) would show that annihilation is also impossible. "Thus is generation extinguished and destruction not to be heard of."

So far the conclusions reached are only such as were agreed to by all Greek philosophers both before and after Parmenides. Nothing comes from nothing, and nothing disappears into nothing. But:

18

"Nor is it divisible, since it is all alike, and there is no more of it in one place than in another, to hinder it from holding together, nor less of it, but it is completely filled with what-is. Wherefore it is wholly continuous; for what-is is in contact with what-is. It is immovable in the bonds of mighty chains, not starting, not stopping, since generation and destruction have been banished afar, driven back by true conviction. Wherefore all these things are but names which mortals have given, believing them to be true—generation and destruction, being and not being, change of place and alteration of bright color." These astounding conclusions are drawn as corollaries, without further argument. Motion was supposed to be impossible because if anything were to move, it would have to move into empty space; but since empty space would be "what-is-not," there cannot *be* any empty space. As for "alteration of bright color" or other qualitative change, this could not take place either, for if an apple, previously green, were to become red, this would entail the disappearance of the greenness into nothing, and the appearance of redness from nothing, both equally impossible because contradictory.

The last surprise the goddess has for Parmenides is this: "It abides the same, remaining in the same place, by itself; thus it stays, rooted to the spot. For mighty Necessity keeps it in the bonds of a limit which shuts it in round about. For this reason it is not right that what-is should be without an end. For it is not wanting; if it were, there would be need of everything. . . . Since, then, it has an outermost boundary, it is limited from every side, like the mass of a well-rounded sphere, extending equally from the center in every direction." This emphatic assertion of a spatial limit to what-is is perhaps the hardest of all for us to absorb, since we immediately are led to ask, in Parmenidean fashion, What is outside it? If more of what-is, then there is no limit after all; but if what is outside of what-is is what-is-not, then it cannot exist as a limit. And indeed Parmenides' follower Melissus of Samos ventured to correct the master on this point; he asserted that what-is is spatially infinite. Parmenides' thought seems to have been that infinity (being *without* end) entails incompleteness, hence could not be predicated of what-is, which is perfect; and indeed it was characteristic of Greek thought to prefer the tidy to the vast. But this at most extenuates Parmenides without acquitting him of manifest inconsistency.

"Here shall I close my trustworthy reasoning and thinking for you about the truth," says the goddess. "Henceforward learn the beliefs of mortals, giving ear to the deceptive order of my words." After this unpromising beginning there follows an account of the nature of things, more in keeping with the general tenor of early Greek thought. We learn, for instance, that Parmenides understood that the moon shines by light "borrowed" from the sun. But the fragments of this part of the poem are too few for us to reconstruct the system at all. The purpose of including it seems to have been to forestall derisive criticism of Parmenides as ignorant of the science of his day: "I am telling you everything about this plausible cosmology, so that you may not be surpassed in insight by any mortal."

To the modern student, perhaps the most puzzling thing about Parmenides is the fact that his successors (including especially Plato) had so much reverence for him and took his arguments so seriously.

Of course, no serious thinker in the fifth century B.C. could dismiss Parmenides' conclusions merely on the ground that they were incompatible with observed fact. For philosophy, which was still a new enterprise, consisted in an investigation of the world by *reason*. And if in general the senses provided the data for the inquiry, no philosopher considered himself bound to conclude that things are in all respects as they appear to be. If the senses declared things to be thus-and-so, but reason indicated that they were otherwise, it was not by any means unheard of to dismiss the observations as deceptive. In throwing out *all* observation Parmenides only carried to an extreme a pre-existing practice.

In the second place, Parmenides, the founder of formal logic, simply *deduced the logical conclusion of the assumptions agreed on by his predecessors*. These assumptions were:

1. *Monism*: the stuff (whether water, the Boundless, mist, or fire) of which all things are made is at base of one kind only.

2. *Conservation of stuff*: this stuff, as such, is eternal, being neither created nor destroyed, neither augmented nor diminished.

3. A refusal to distinguish (or rather, the non-occurrence of the idea of distinguishing) between what *we* should call the qualities of things and the things qualified. Thus heat and brightness were not thought of as properties of a fire-substance in itself inaccessible to observation; heat and brightness literally *constituted* fire. For lack of a better word we may call this assumption *"Phenomenalism."*

4. *Reality of change.*

Once these assumptions are made explicit, Parmenides' philosophy becomes in a certain way obvious. If the stuff of things is ungenerated and indestructible, and if that stuff consists of its sensible qualities, then it is out of the question for it to change. For to say that it changes is precisely to say that it has a property at one time that it lacks at another, a conclusion that contradicts assumptions two and three. Thus what-is must be at least "frozen." But furthermore there cannot be any diversity in it, if the premise of Monism is taken seriously.

Parmenides' argument against motion on the ground that motion requires empty space, and empty space would be what is not and therefore non-existent, is an obvious sophism. Oddly, though, his successors Empedocles and Anaxagoras deferred to it and denied the possibility of a vacuum. They attempted to make reason square with observation by giving up the postulate of Monism in favor of six kinds of stuff (Empedocles) or as many stuffs as there are perceived differences (Anaxagoras); and they tried to account for motion in a plenum as displacement, illustrated by a fish swimming in a jar "full" of water. Failing to see that the argument that empty space would be nothing is independent of Parmenides' main contentions, and that change is inconsistent with the postulates of Conservation and "Phenomenalism," they exposed themselves to the Parmenidean rebuttal of Melissus, who pointed out that "if there were a many, these would have to be of the same kind as I say that the

One is. For if there is earth and water, and air and iron, and gold and fire, and if one thing is living and another dead, and if things are black and white and all that men say they really are,—if that is so, and if we see and hear aright, each one of these must be such as we first decided, and they cannot be changed or altered, but each must be just as it is."

In fact, if Parmenides' conclusions are to be escaped without abandoning either Conservation or logic, it is necessary (besides clearing up the quibble about "empty" and "nothing") to do two things: first, to distinguish between a thing and its properties (to abandon "Phenomenalism"); second, to distinguish, within properties, between qualities and relations. F. H. Bradley's *Appearance and Reality* showed, as late as 1893, how if the reality of relations is denied (if relations are conceived as qualities or predicates of the things related), then a Parmenidean view of reality is inescapable. Of the ancients, Democritus, Plato, and Aristotle were the only philosophers who displayed some grasp of Parmenides' essential points and tried to come to grips with them. It is doubtful whether any of them was altogether successful.

It should not be thought, however, that Parmenides' philosophy is free of internal problems. Besides the difficulty of the "outermost boundary," the most obvious one is this: it is not sufficient to reject sense-experience (or anything else) as illusion unless one can at least show the *possibility* of explaining, consistently with one's general position, how the illusion occurs. But such a possibility seems to be ruled out in Parmenides' system. For if we assume that in reality there exists nothing but a homogeneous rigid sphere, it seems that there can not be any illusions at all, since in order for there to be an illusion there must be—*really* be—a mind that is deceived; and a mind is by its very nature something that is changing or at least implies change (it thinks now one thought, now another).

There is the further paradox that Parmenides in effect reduced one of his premises to absurdity. As a matter of strict logic, all that Parmenides proved was that the four assumptions listed above are incompatible; the argument of itself did not show that the postulate of change was the one to be rejected. Parmenides evidently chose to deny it because of his (logically independent) argument for the impossibility of void (and perhaps also on religious grounds). Now since there is no inconsistency in assuming at once Monism, Conservation, and Change (as the Atomists were to show), Parmenides' reasoning would have been invalid without the premise of "Phenomenalism." Yet this premise seems incompatible with his conclusion that what-is is not at all what we perceive. Perhaps, however, Parmenides interpreted the third premise as implying only that what-is must have (or be) *some* kind of quality capable of entering into *some* kind of consciousness—the property in question might have been just awareness itself. The fact that Melissus argued explicitly that the One could not "suffer pain" suggests that he thought it could "suffer" *something*, in other words, be somehow conscious. This lends some slight support to the conjecture that Parmenides' sphere, though undeniably a body, was also endowed with non-discursive consciousness, whatever that might be. If so, then there is warrant for thinking of Parmenides as the father of idealism.

ANAXAGORAS: FRAGMENTS

Author: Anaxagoras of Clazomenae (c.500-c.428 B.C.)
Type of work: Metaphysics
First transcribed: Fifth century B.C.

PRINCIPAL IDEAS ADVANCED

The universe is infinite and is composed of infinitely divisible matter.
Everything that exists contains portions of every other kind of thing, but particular things are recognized by their most obvious characteristics.
Mind is matter considered as conscious and knowing.
Originally the universe was homogeneous and motionless, but as a result of the whirling influence of mind the universe became differentiated and ordered.

Anaxagoras held that the universe is infinite in extent, and composed of mind and matter; but mind is a special kind of matter. There is no empty space.

Matter is not composed of primary units; it is infinitely divisible. "Nor is there a least of what is small, but there is always a smaller; for it cannot be that what exists should cease to be by being cut." If you take a piece of a certain kind of matter—a hair, say, or a steak—and begin cutting, no matter how finely you cut it the pieces will still have the characteristics of hair or flesh. "How can hair come from what is not hair, or flesh from what is not flesh?"

Nevertheless, we eat bread, and the bread (we say) becomes hair and flesh. This is not accurate, Anaxagoras says: "The Greeks follow a wrong usage in speaking of coming into existence and passing away; for nothing comes into existence or passes away, but there is mingling and separation of things that exist. So they would be right to call coming into existence mixture, and passing away separation." The "coming into existence" of the hair is really mixture, then, and the "passing away" of the bread is separation. But mixture of what, and separation of what? Any crumb of bread, however tiny, has all the properties of the whole loaf. Bread is not *made of* bits of hair and flesh. Likewise a hair is not separable into microscopic breadcrumbs. How then can hair be a "mixture" into which bread enters, while at the same time it cannot "come from what is not hair"?

The answer is that "The things that are in one world are not divided nor cut off from one another with a hatchet." While bread contains no particles of hair, it nevertheless contains hair so to speak fused or dissolved in

22

it. And in general, "all things will be in everything; nor is it possible for them to be apart, but all things have a portion of everything. . . . And in all things many things are contained, and an equal number both in the greater and in the smaller of the things that are separated."

A loaf of bread contains "portions of everything"; that is, it contains or rather *is* a complex of *all* the sensible qualities there are. And the same is true of every crumb of the loaf. (Anaxagoras was notorious for asserting that snow is black—in the sense that even the purest white stuff yet contains a portion of every "thing," including blackness.) Yet the loaf does not appear to our senses as a primordial chaos. "Each single thing is most manifestly those things of which it has most in it." It presents us with a definite, restricted set of qualities— let us say brownness, moisture, bread-smell and bread-taste. Hair as we know it is black, shiny, oily. Hair is in bread in the sense that blackness, shininess, and oiliness are all there, but relatively in such small quantities that "the weakness of our senses prevents our discerning the truth." If we were presented (*per impossibile*) with a loaf of "pure" bread, we could not distinguish it from an ordinary loaf by looking at it, smelling it, or tasting it; but it would not nourish us. Our insides, however, are able (in an unexplained manner) to separate out the traces of hair and flesh.

Anaxagoras used the word "seeds" —"seeds of all things, having all sorts of characteristics both of color and of savor," "a multitude of innumerable seeds in no way like each other"—to indicate the diversity of quality-things to be found in even the smallest bit of

matter. But the word has no atomistic implications; anything, however large or small, that has a trace of hair in it is a hair "seed." The word occurs only twice in the extant fragments, both times in a description of world-formation, and all that is signified is that the original mixture of all things has the potentialities in it for eventual separation into the most diverse kinds of objects.

Mind, like blackness or the smell of bread, is a real stuff; consequently, it has location ("it is certainly there, where everything else is") and occupies space ("it is the thinnest of all things and the purest")—sufficient evidence, to our way of thinking, to make it a kind of matter. But it must be remembered that Anaxagoras does not make a distinction between stuff and the qualities of stuff; indeed, refusal to make this distinction is the key to his philosophy. Mind has or *is* the properties that in our experience we find it to have: it is conscious and cognitive ("it has all knowledge about everything"), and powerful, that is, manifests itself as will power or *élan vital* in living things ("mind has the greatest strength; and it has power over all things, both greater and smaller, that have life"). It is unique in not entering into mixtures: "All other things partake in a portion of everything, while Mind is infinite and self-ruled, and is mixed with nothing but is alone, itself by itself." Anaxagoras argued that "if it were not by itself, but were mixed with anything else, it would partake in all things if it were mixed with any; for in everything there is a portion of everything, and the things mixed with it would hinder it, so that it would have power over nothing in the same way that it

23

has now being alone by itself." The thought seems to be that if Mind mixed, it would lose its peculiar power just as the blackness in snow or the breadness in hair does; but this is impossible, both because what is essentially active cannot become passive, and because our minds are experienced as unities. Also "it would partake in all things if it were mixed with any"; rocks and clods would be alive—an absurdity.

But while Mind is not mixed with anything, it is *present* in some living things: "In everything there is a portion of everything except Mind, and there are some things in which there is Mind also." The power of Mind is to initiate activity (motion) in these things, and also to move and "set in order all things" from outside.

"All Mind is alike, both the greater and the smaller." It is the same mind-stuff that is present in us as in animals and vegetables. Our greater intelligence is due not to possession of a superior grade of Mind, but to our having hands.

Like every other Greek philosopher, Anaxagoras held that nothing can come from nothing, nor can anything utterly vanish. The totality of world-stuff is fixed: it is "all," and "we must know that all of them are neither more nor less; for it is not possible for them to be more than all, and all are always equal." But the world of moving, changing, differentiated things that we know is not eternal. Anaxagoras postulated a primeval condition of homogeneity and motionlessness: "All things were together, infinite both in number and in smallness; for the small too was infinite. And, when all things were together, none of them were plain, because of their smallness." "But

before they were separated off, when all things were together, not even was any color plain; for the mixture of all things prevented it—of the moist and the dry, and the warm and the cold, and the light and the dark, and of much earth that was in it, and of a multitude of innumerable seeds in no way like each other." It is perhaps permissible to think of this initial condition as a gray, dim, damp, tepid, dirty vastness. Or if you prefer, a luminosity: "Air and fire prevailed over all things, being both of them infinite; for amongst all things these are the greatest both in quantity and size"; that is, a homogeneous mixture of all things would look like air and fire, because those are what there is most of.

At some point in this mass, Mind started a whirl: "And Mind had power over the whole revolution, so that it began to revolve in the beginning. And it began to revolve first from a small beginning; but the revolution now extends over a larger space, and will extend over a larger still." We *see* the whirl of the heavenly bodies still going on overhead.

The centrifugal force of the whirl caused separation out of the homogeneous mass, "as these things revolve and are separated off by the force and speed. And the speed makes the force. Their speed is not like the speed of any of the things that are now among men, but in every way many times as fast." "And when Mind began to move things, separating off took place from all that was moved, and so much as Mind set in motion was all separated. And as things were set in motion and separated, the revolution caused them to be separated much more."

The separation resulted not just in differentiation but in a natural *order*:

"And all the things that are mingled together and separated off and distinguished are all known by Mind. And Mind set in order all things that were to be . . . and that now exist, and this revolution caused the separating off, and the thin is separated from the thick, the warm from the cold, the light from the dark, and the dry from the moist. . . . The thick and the moist and the cold and the dark came together where the earth is now, while the thin and the warm and the dry and the bright went out towards the further part of the sky." However (it is not clear how), "from the earth stones are solidified by the cold, and these rush outwards more than water." They are the sun, moon, and stars, the sun and stars being heated to incandescence by their motion, while the moon, lower down and not moving so fast, shines by the reflected light of the sun.

The process described is only a local one. Anaxagoras reasoned that Mind must "set things in order" in other parts of the boundless universe, producing other worlds: "We must suppose . . . that men have been formed in them, and the other animals that have life, and that these men have inhabited cities and cultivated fields as with us; and that they have a sun and a moon and the rest as with us; and that their earth brings forth for them many things of all kinds of which they gather the best together into their dwellings, and use them. Thus much have I said with regard to separating off, to show that it will not be only with us that things are separated off, but elsewhere too."

Anaxagoras followed Anaximenes in holding that the earth is a flat disc held up by the air. The sun, he said, is "bigger than the Peloponnese"! He correctly explained winds as due to the thinning of the air by the sun. Earthquakes are caused by the air above striking on the air under the earth; the movement of the latter causes the earth, floating on it, to rock. He understood the causes of eclipses, but thought that some lunar eclipses are caused by the interposition of invisible bodies between the sun and moon. This theory was evidently intended to explain the eclipses that occur when the sun is still above the horizon.

Contrary to the theory of Empedocles, according to which perception is a process of uniting constituents of the sense organs with like things outside them, Anaxagoras held that perception is essentially an irritation by substances unlike those that compose the organs. He worked this theory out with considerable subtlety. We see light because the pupils of our eyes are dark; this explains also why we cannot see at night. We perceive warmth and cold only when in contrast our skin is colder or warmer than the object felt; when they are at the same temperature, there is no sensation. Salt, sweet, and sour tastes are known because though these qualities are in us, there is a deficiency which makes possible a contrast. It follows that all perception is subliminal pain, as is proved by the fact that any prolonged or violent sensation is felt as painful.

As to an estimate of Anaxagoras, he was aware of the Italian philosophers—the Pythagoreans, Parmenides, Empedocles, and Zeno—and in some respects adopted their views (concerning eclipses), in others made concessions to their arguments (in rejecting a vacuum), and sometimes argued against them (his doctrine of infinite divisibility seems to stem from an attempt to refute Zeno). Primarily, however, Anaxagoras was the continuator of the Milesian school. His conception of the "beginning" and of the process of world formation, for instance, was an elaboration of Anaximander's. And like the Milesians, he was a thorough rationalist: there is no trace of mysticism in his work, and if he had any emotional reaction to his vision of the nature of things, no report of it has come down to us. The Milesians still talked of "god" and "the divine" in connection with the cosmic process, albeit these terms had become mere abstract labels for stuffs and mechanisms. In Anaxagoras, on the other hand, even the words have disappeared. Nor was his Mind an object of worship; it was not a personality, and (as Socrates complained) it was not even a cosmic Designer. It was just the projection of human cognition and will ("known" in experience as initiator of motion) without any moral or religious attributes.

In one respect, Anaxagoras' explanation of things was more consistent than that of any of his predecessors: having postulated that nothing can come from nothing, and that "things are what they seem to be" (that is, the sensible qualities *are* literally the constituents of the things), he had no difficulty (as Empedocles did) in accounting for the diversity of objects of experience. But at the same time this success was a great failure; for if there are as many principles of explanation as there are things to be explained, how can one be said to "explain" anything? Everything comes from *just* what it is. But to say that visible, concentrated hair comes from obscured, diluted hair is not to satisfy the demand that impels us to ask for explanations. Granted that we do not want to be told that hair comes from nothing, we still look for *some* sense in which "hair comes from what is not hair."

Thus the philosophy of Anaxagoras, in being the logical conclusion of the assumption that "things are what they seem to be," was—like many logical conclusions—also a cul-de-sac. Like Parmenides' similar working out of the implications of monism, it closed off one way of investigation and in doing so assured that the next advance in Greek thought (made by the atomists) would consist in denying the premise on which it rested.

Anaxagoras was the first to bring philosophy to Athens. He was also the first philosopher to suffer from Athenian religious and political bigotry. Tried and convicted of "impiety" (for his statements about the sun and moon) and allegiance to a foreign power (Persia) he was (it seems) condemned to death, but escaped to Lampsacus in Ionia, where he spent the rest of his days as an honored schoolteacher.

EMPEDOCLES: FRAGMENTS

Author: Empedocles of Acragas (c.493-c.433 B.C.)
Type of work: Metaphysics
First transcribed: Fifth century B.C.

26

Earth, air, fire, and water—stirred by love and strife—compose the world.
The universe is eternal, but it is not always arranged in the same pattern.
Particular things exist in the two intermediate stages of the cycle created by the alternating domination of Love and Strife.

Besides being a philosopher, Empedocles was a democratic statesman, the founder of an important school of medicine, and a religious leader and reformer. He also claimed to be a god.

Empedocles was the first thinker to try seriously (and to some extent successfully) to reply to Parmenides. Since what Parmenides said was that all that really exists is a solid sphere, within which there is no differentiation, no change, and no motion, one might be tempted to conclude offhand that Parmenides was mad, and that anyone who paid attention to him must have been mad also. But in fact Parmenides was a great genius: the founder, indeed, of logic. What he did was show that three assumptions, taken as self-evidently true by all investigators up to and including himself, logically entailed his odd worldview. These assumptions were, first, that nothing can come from nothing, or disappear into nothing: nothing just pops up or vanishes without a trace. The second was that there is fundamentally just *one* reality, one stuff of which particular things are modifications. The third was that whatever really exists is identical with whatever properties it really has. This last assumption was so taken for granted that no one even stated it explicitly; and it is doubtful whether anyone at the time could have done so, no alternative having been conceived. *We* should distinguish between water (H_2O) and its properties

of being wet and cold; but to the early Greeks, water was simply "the cold and wet."

Once the nature of this last assumption is grasped, it becomes obvious that Parmenides was right. For if there is just one kind of stuff, then that stuff, being identical with its properties (whatever they are), cannot possibly change. For suppose it is hot—that is, *is* "the hot." Then it cannot get cold, for if it did, "the hot" would have to disappear into nothing, and "the cold" would have to come out of nothing. Previous thinkers had supposed, naturally enough, that one particular thing might get cold without violating nothing-from-nothing as long as something else got hot to compensate for it. But this was shoddy reasoning, Parmenides pointed out. If there is just *one* reality, and it *is* (equals) hot, then it is contradictory to say that it *is* also cold.

Probably because of a propensity for religious mysticism, Parmenides' conclusions were quite agreeable to *him*. The fact that they were utterly opposed to experience did not bother him. If logic tells us one thing, and the senses tell us something else, so much the worse for the senses. "Keep your thinking clear of this way of inquiry," he warned, "nor let much-experienced habit force you down this road, where the unseeing eye and the noisy ear and the tongue rule. But decide by logic the much-disputed proof that I utter." Empedocles, however, was not prepared to abandon his senses. In an "empiricist" vein he wrote: "Come now, consider with all your powers in what way each thing is clear. Hold not your sight in greater credit as compared with your hearing, nor value your resounding ear above the clear instructions of your tongue; and do not withhold confidence in any of the other parts of your body in which there is an opening for understanding, but consider everything in the way it is clear."

Nor did Empedocles abandon logic. He realized that Parmenides' conclusion was validly drawn; therefore, if it was to be rejected, at least one of the premises leading to it would have to be thrown out. Which one? Not the third, for the simple reason that Empedocles did not realize that it *was* a premise of the argument. (This fact in due time dawned on the atomists, Leucippus and Democritus; it was their distinction between thing and quality that at length made physics as we know it possible.) And certainly not the first. Parmenides had said: "Nor will forceful credibility ever allow that anything besides itself can arise from non-being. . . . Thus is generation extinguished and destruction not to be heard of." Empedocles repeated almost verbally: "Fools!—for they have no far-reaching thoughts— who deem that what before did not exist comes into being, or that aught can perish and be utterly destroyed. For it cannot be that aught can arise from what in no way exists, and it is impossible and unheard of that Being should perish." Both Parmenides and Empedocles were fighting straw men, for *no* Greek ever questioned the maxim nothing-from-nothing.

By elimination, then, there re-

mained only the second assumption to attack: that of monism. Instead of one basic stuff, Empedocles declared that there are four (or, as we shall see, six); namely, the great world-masses, earth, air, fire, and water—what Aristotle was later to call "the elements," but which Empedocles called "roots": "Hear first the four roots of all things: shining Zeus [air], life-bringing Hera [earth], Aidoneus [fire] and Nestis [water] whose teardrops are a well-spring to mortals." These roots, like Parmenides' Being, are ungenerated, indestructible, and unchanging. Particular perishing things are temporary combinations of them: "There is no nature [*phusis,* essential being] of any of all the things that perish, nor any cessation for them of baneful death. They are only a mingling and interchange of what has been mingled. 'Nature' is but a name given to these things by men."

But before he could successfully assert a theory of change as a mixing of the unchanging, Empedocles had another Parmenidean hurdle to get over. That was the notorious denial of the possibility of motion. Parmenides had argued (independently of his main doctrine) that if anything moves, there must be empty space for it to move into; but empty space, void, would be mere "nothing," "that which is-not," and since it would be logically contradictory to say that that which is-not exists, there can be no void, hence no motion. Empedocles, whether taken in by this quibble or not, at any rate agreed that there is no void: "In the All there is naught empty and naught too full." He had an empirical reason for this view: he was the first (as far as we know) to realize that where there seems to be only empty

28

space, there is really matter, namely, air. He illustrated this conclusion by means of the *klepsydra*, a Greek kitchen gadget. It was a metal tube with a perforated bottom and an open top small enough to be stopped by holding a finger on it. It was used to remove small quantities of liquid from narrow-mouthed jars too heavy to be poured conveniently. Empedocles floridly explained its working: "When a girl, playing with a *klepsydra* of shining brass, puts the orifice of the pipe upon her comely hand, and dips the *klepsydra* into the yielding mass of silvery water—the stream does not then flow into the vessel, but the bulk of the air inside, pressing upon the close-packed perforations, keeps it out till she uncovers the compressed stream; but then air escapes and an equal volume of water runs in. In the same way, when water occupies the depths of the brazen vessel and the opening and passage is stopped up by the human hand, the air outside, striving to get in, holds the water back at the gates of the gurgling neck, pressing upon its surface, till she lets go with her hand. Then, on the contrary, just in the opposite way to what happened before, the wind rushes in and an equal volume of water runs out to make room." This discovery of air, as distinguished from wind and mist, was Empedocles' principal contribution to science.

Motion could nevertheless occur without a void and without flouting logic, Empedocles maintained, as long as the obstacle in front of the moving object could be *displaced*, as the water could not move into the *klepsydra* unless an exit was provided for the air. In general, one thing could mix with another, he held, if there were tiny

pores, like the tube of the *klepsydra*, for the substance to penetrate. He thought that when we inhale, air rushes into our bodies through the pores of the skin, the blood retiring to the center of the body; when we exhale, the blood comes back to the surface, forcing the air out.

Besides "Fire and Water and Earth and the boundless height of Air" there exist "dread Strife, too, apart from these, of equal weight to each, and Love in their midst, equal in length and breadth. . . . It is she that is believed to be implanted in the frame of mortals. It is she that makes them have thoughts of love and work the works of peace. They call her by the names of Joy and Aphrodite." Love and Strife are the forces that cause motion, though Empedocles at the same time seems to regard them as kinds of matter. But they are not conscious beings: "Aphrodite" is just that whatever-it-is, which we experience in our own selves, that impels us to union. Cosmically it causes unlike to mix with unlike. Strife, the opposite force of repulsion, causes separation and, as a result, union of like with like.

The four Roots, plus Love and Strife, are all there is. "Behold the sun, everywhere bright and warm, and all the immortal things that are bathed in heat and bright radiance. Behold the rain, everywhere dark and cold; and from the earth issue forth things close-pressed and solid. When they are in strife all these are different in form and separated; but they come together in love, and are desired by one another.

"For out of these have sprung all things that were and are and shall be —trees and men and women, beasts

29

and birds and the fishes that dwell in the waters, yea, and the gods that live long lives and are exalted in honor.

"For there are these alone; but running through one another, they take different shapes—so much does mixture change them."

Empedocles believed that the universe is eternal, but it is not always arranged in the same pattern. Love and Strife alternate in dominance. There is a time when Love unites all the Roots; in this condition, the universe is a sphere, a homogeneous mixture of the Roots and Love, Strife alone being separate, outside it. Then Strife enters the sphere and begins its work of separation, which when complete leaves each of the four Roots gathered together in unmixed purity. Then Love begins a process of mingling, eventuating in the Sphere again; after which the cycle repeats.

Particular things exist in the two intermediate stages of the cycle when neither Love nor Strife has attained supremacy. There are two kinds of "evolution" of living things corresponding to these two periods. When Love is coming in and displacing Strife, "on the earth many heads spring up without necks and arms wander bare and bereft of shoulders. Eyes stray up and down in want of brows." These *disjecta membra* are united by Love, for the most part into monsters: "Many creatures with faces and breasts looking in different directions arise; some, offspring of oxen with faces of men, while others, again, arise as offspring of men with the heads of oxen, and creatures in whom the nature of women and men is mingled, furnished with sterile organs." Only the few that happen to be capable of nourishing themselves and reproducing their kind survive. This fantasy, it will be noted, contains the germ of the idea of evolution by adaptation and survival of the fittest. However, it is inferior both in form and in underlying reasoning to the older theory of Anaximander.

In the period when Strife is gaining ascendancy over Love (which is the present stage of the world), "Fire as it was separated caused the nightborn shoots of men and tearful women to arise. . . . Whole-natured forms first arose from the earth. . . . These showed as yet neither the charming form of the limbs, nor yet the voice and organ that are proper to men." That is, they were bisexual creatures, later separated further by Strife into men and women.

The poem "Purifications" begins with a curiously charming proem: "Friends, that inhabit the great town looking down on the yellow rock of Acragas, up by the citadel, busy in goodly works, harbors of honor for the stranger, men unskilled in meanness, hail. I go about among you an immortal god, no mortal now, honored among all as is meet, crowned with fillets and flowery garlands. Whenever I come to men and women, in the flourishing towns, straightway is reverence done me; they go after me in thousands asking of me what is the way to gain; some desiring oracles, while some, who for many a weary day have been pierced by the grievous pangs of all manner of sickness, beg to hear from me the word of healing. . . . But why do I harp on these things, as if it were any great matter that I should surpass mortal, perishable men?" Though in our own days it is not unusual for eminent physicians to think of themselves in much the same way,

30

there is the difference that Empedocles *literally* believed himself a god, though a fallen one: "There is an oracle of Necessity, an ancient ordinance of the gods, eternal and sealed fast by broad oaths, that whenever one of the divinities . . . has sinfully polluted his hands with blood, or followed strife and forsworn himself, he must wander thrice ten thousand seasons [10,000 years] from the abodes of the blessed, being born throughout the time in all manners of mortal forms, changing one toilsome path of life for another. For the mighty Air drives him into the Sea, and the Sea spews him forth on the dry Earth; Earth tosses him into the beams of the blazing Sun, and he flings him back to the eddies of Air. One takes him from the other, and all reject him. One of these I now am, an exile and a wanderer from the gods, for that I put my trust in raving Strife." In this time, he says, "I have been born ere now a boy and a girl, a bush and a bird and a dumb fish in the sea." The original sin, it appears, was meat-eating, for all living creatures are akin. But deliverance is in sight: "At the last, they appear among earth-dwelling men as prophets, song-writers, physicians, and princes; and thence they rise up as gods exalted in honor, sharing the hearth of the other gods and the same table, free from human woes, safe from destiny, and incapable of being hurt."

The principal problem posed by the "Purifications" is its evident inconsistency, in teaching transmigration of souls, with the "Poem on Nature," according to which there is "no cessation of baneful death" for particular things. The only possibility of reconciling the poems seems to lie in supposing that the soul which transmigrates is a piece of Love. The soul cannot be a mixture, for all mixtures are perishable; and it is not plausible to identify it with any of the Roots. Nor could it be Strife, for its sin, we remember, consisted in "putting trust in raving Strife." It might be thought that if the soul is Love, then Love is conscious, contrary to the express statement of Empedocles that "the blood round the heart is the thought of men." However, according to a very ancient tradition of the Greeks, a man has two "souls," a blood-soul which is the seat of consciousness and a breath-soul which is the vivifying principle. It does not seem impossible that Empedocles identified the latter with the Love which admittedly is in the human body; and a particular piece of Love might somehow retain its identity even through thrice ten thousand seasons. But this is hazardous speculation, for which there is no explicit warrant either in the fragments of Empedocles' poems or in the ancient commentaries.

MO TZU

Author: Mo Ti (c.470-c.391 B.C.)
Type of work: Ethics, political philosophy, logic
First transcribed: Fourth century B.C.

Universal love is the source of the good, and by rewards and punishments human beings can be encouraged to love universally.

Uniformity of value standards is achieved by establishing the way of the most virtuous and capable "Son of Heaven" as the moral standard.

Aggressive war should never be practiced since it is neither politically nor economically advantageous.

One of the most serious challengers of Confucian ideas in the fifth century B.C. was Mo Ti, whose obscure family background encouraged much speculation about his early life on the basis of his name. It is said, not entirely without justification, that his family name, ("ink" or "black") shows that he or his ancestor must have been at one time a law breaker, because branding the convict with ink was a common practice in ancient China. His personal name, Ti, could mean a menial worker in old Chinese. Hence, his name could have been originally a nickname, indicating his origin as an ex-convict slave laborer. Whatever the truth, it is difficult to overlook the difference between the obscurity of the Mo clan and the aristocratic background of Confucius' family, particularly when one notes Mo Ti's hostility toward the Confucian school of thought.

Like Confucius, Mo Ti studied the ancient texts. He even followed the Confucian commentaries on these texts until he developed a system of his own with which he vied with Confucianism for popular acceptance. Mo Ti traveled, much as Confucius did, and he talked even more persistently to the rulers. Confucius would refuse to converse with anyone who was impolite to him, but Mo Ti forgot about ceremony as long as there was an audience. Once Mo Ti heard that the ruler

of one state was about to declare war against another. In the hope of maintaining peace he rushed to the aggressive state, walking on foot for days and nights without stopping. When his feet were sore, he simply tore pieces of his garments to bandage them and continued on his journey. Upon his arrival he found that the ruler was too much determined to carry out his war-waging plans to consider changing them. After spending much time with this ruler in vain, Mo Ti turned around and went to the attacked state where he offered his service to defend it.

On his peace missions Mo Ti was not traveling alone. He gained a considerable following, numbering in the hundreds. These disciples were devoted to their master and were trained by him personally in the arts of defensive warfare as well as in philosophy. They became a tightly knit and highly effective combat unit as they trailed after their master, galloping on their bare feet, to rescue a besieged state. Apparently they did well, for their master earned an appointment to a high post in the state of Sung. And after the master's death, the disciples elected a second master to continue the leadership of the confraternity, which lasted about a hundred years.

The work named after Mo Ti, called the *Mo Tzu*, contained fifteen books divided into seventy-one chapters. Eighteen of these chapters are lost, and of the extant fifty-three chapters, only two are likely to have been written by Mo Ti himself. The others, including six chapters quite clearly written at a date much later than his time, are his discourses recorded by someone else. Mo Ti probably said and wrote much more, for his influence was so great at one time that Mencius, the standard-bearer of Confucianism, had to bemoan that "Under the sky everyone joined either the Yang Chu or the Mo Ti school of thought." But the *Mo Tzu*, as it has come down to us, is quite sufficient in revealing the main tenets of Mohism.

The philosophical system of Mo Ti has as its basis a concept of universal love. Mo Ti regarded the lack of love among men as the principal cause of all calamities, of which the worst is the aggression of the large state against the small state, the strong taking advantage of the weak, and the many imposing their will upon the few. Even among the equally situated, Mo Ti points out in the *Mo Tzu*, people indulge in mutual injury with weapons, poison, and other hateful means. Then Mo Ti asks, "Is it out of people's loving others and wanting to benefit others" that they behave this way? He objects to the Confucian doctrine that one must love one's own parents more dearly than the kin of others and one's own state more than other fatherlands. Mo Ti's concept of universal love goes beyond an ethical prescription to cure social ills; he actually regards universal love as a source of "goodness." In his argument universal love is good because it brings untold and immeasurable benefit to mankind,

and because whatever benefits mankind must be right and good. Here we already see a strong utilitarian element in his philosophy.

The Mohist universal love is not only an ideal of perfection; it is practical and easily practicable. In the first place, Mo Ti tells us, universal love has been achieved before by the sage-kings of old. Here Mo Ti makes use of the past just as the Confucians do. Second, there is nothing that cannot be done if the rulers, or the people in power, encourage it. Mo Ti believes that if the ruler offers the lure of reward and displays the threat of punishment, then the people would go after love "like fire tending upward and water downward—nothing in the world could stop them." This is another parallel between Mohism and utilitarianism, both promoting the use of pain and pleasure to induce people to practice what is desirable.

Other Mohist ethical views are quite similar to those of the Confucians. The Mohist would go a long way in agreeing with his Confucian rival on the ideal code of social conduct. The major difference between them is that the Mohist stresses self-denial far beyond what a Confucian considers proper. A good Mohist is a this-world ascetic.

In Mohism there is a religious attitude more serious than that of the Confucians. Mo Ti himself speaks of Heaven as an identifiable deity whose will is to uphold righteousness. It must be so because "if righteousness ceased to prevail, chaos would reign over the world." It is so also because any proper standard is always set by the superior for the inferior to observe, and since Heaven is the supreme authority, even above the sovereign on earth, it is

Heaven who sets the universal standard of righteousness. Those adhering to this standard are rewarded; others violating this standard are punished. Furthermore, says Mo Ti, Heaven loves all men equally until and unless some people trespass the boundary of righteousness and forsake universal love.

The Mohist acknowledges the existence of spirits and their function as guardians of morality. He divides the spirits into three general categories: the heavenly spirits which are most superior, the mountain and river spirits which are secondary, and the spirits of dead human beings, which occupy the lowest stratum in this hierarchy. To prove the power of the spirits, particularly those of the dead, Mo Ti retells many ghost stories cited in the ancient texts and concludes with the admonition that the vengeance of the spirits is "sharp and fierce," especially when wrong is done to the innocent. Mo Ti, however, disapproves of any ritual practice to placate the spirits. He teaches his followers that they will continue to enjoy the blessing of the spirits as long as the living practice universal love and avoid harming one another.

Mo Ti is emphatic in asserting the basically equal worth of all men. He insists that the sovereign ruler must honor the virtuous and the capable regardless of "their family connection, financial status, and their physical appearances." (Here is a hint that Mo Ti himself was not quite the standard of masculine beauty of his time.) He further reiterates his belief that the ruler can use punishment and reward to make all the people strive for virtue in order that everyone have an equal chance to prove his worth. The Mohist assumption is that everybody, following the ruler's instructions, has an equal chance to change his own destiny. This view is clearly opposed to the Confucian acceptance of "fate" whose designs are above man.

Mo Ti's assumption that man is not born with a predestined pattern of his development is fully explained in Chapter Three, in which he metaphorically compares the environmental influence on man to the dyeing of silk. The one factor that influences man most, in Mo Ti's view, is his associations. Man behaves according to the company he keeps; rulers in the past failed or succeeded according to the teachers and exemplars they followed.

Already one senses a critical problem in Mo Ti's system when one examines the Mohist view on man. If men are basically equal, who then should rule and who should be ruled? Mo Ti offers two explanations of this point, one logical and the other historical. In his logical argument, Mo Ti starts from the premise that Heaven is the supreme authority that delegates his power to the sovereign king on earth. As the Son of Heaven, the king rules by observing Heaven's Will. The people must obey their king because they must bow to Heaven. In his historical argument, Mo Ti offers a recount of the evolution of society.

In the very beginning, says Mo Ti, the primeval society of man was full of strife and chaos because each individual had his own standard of behavior and no two men acted according to any common standard. As man improved and society formed, there was "a selection" of the most virtuous and capable man in the world to serve as the Son of Heaven. The Son of Heaven then issued a mandate to the people, declaring that "what the superior [the king] thinks to be right, all shall think it right; what the king thinks to be wrong, all shall think it wrong." Consequently, a uniform standard was established, and strife ceased. Mo Ti goes on to urge his readers to observe this political precedence to insure a peaceful and orderly society, but he does not make it clear how he thinks the "most virtuous and capable" was selected in the past, or should be selected in the future.

Uniformity of value standards, universal love, and nonaggression form the triad upon which Mo Ti constructed his system. The first, sometimes interpreted by later scholars as "the theory of emulating the superior," amounts to simply a standardization of views of all people, if it is carried to its logical extreme. Universal love has been discussed. The third—nonaggression—constitutes Mo Ti's most significant contribution to the ideas in the Warring States period in China's history. Mo Ti talks about righteousness and universal virtue, but he does not appear as a moralist when he deals with the question of war. He argues against aggressive war on the ground that it is not economically advantageous to attack others. He sounds extremely modern when he warns the aggressors that war lays waste lands that should be kept under productive activities. Even if a victory were won, so declares Mo Ti, "the costs of the expeditions would have exhausted the country." As a result neither the victor nor the vanquished would be fit to take their places among the nations any more. His argument is made very persuasive by his practical skill in defensive warfare, which is described with technical details in at least eleven chapters in this book. Only the conditions of the time, which were too far gone in an atmosphere of a free-for-all power struggle, prevented his views from being adopted by the chiefs of the states.

Mo Ti's utilitarianism finds another expression in his approach to economic problems. He would encourage only those economic endeavors that are useful and practical, or that contribute to the wealth and populousness of the state. The sole criterion for his judgment of the success or failure of a state is its granary and population. He is vehemently critical of any conspicuous consumption, and he believes that people should be and are actually happy if no more than the essential material supplies are abundant. As to the increase in population, his view was quite valid at a time when manpower constituted the mainspring of the state's strength and when people migrated toward the relatively orderly state to rear larger families.

Mo Ti's insistence on frugality leads him to deny the usefulness of any niceties of life. He would do away with music and rites and all other features of a cultured living. He even enjoins the artisans to cease producing carts and robes the moment the most essential needs of the people have been met, and immediately to channel their energy into the production of staple foods.

Mo Ti is remembered as the first Chinese philosopher to be seriously concerned with the logical development of an argument. In the Mo Tzu he devotes many passages to a definition of the term "dialectic." According to him, dialectic is an effort to distinguish "the right from the wrong, the good from bad governments, similarity from difference, name from actuality, benefit from harm, and certainty from uncertainty." Using his own rules for the careful development of an argument, Mo Ti makes this the first example in ancient Chinese writings to present systematic expositions supported by evidence. This is the first Chinese book to introduce the "sorites formula" and the distinction between necessary and sufficient causes. In the latter connection, Mo Ti uses an illustration of the point and the line. The point, says Mo Ti, is a necessary cause but not a sufficient cause of the line. He is also the first Chinese philosopher to draw the distinction between class and species, pointing out to his students that the former includes the latter, but not vice versa. He did much to promote the Dialectician school which flourished during and after his time.

Throughout the book Mo Ti maintains a hostile attitude toward Confucian views. His antagonism reaches its peak in Chapters Thirty-eight (missing) and Thirty-nine, which are entitled "Refutation of Confucianism." He dismisses the Confucian emphasis on rituals, acceptance of destiny, and lengthy observance of funerals. He virtually calls Confucius a hypocrite. Yet, in spite of his criticism of Confucianism, Mo Ti was in agreement with Confucius on the importance of the virtuous and the learned to the welfare of the state, as well as the importance of self-cultivation and self-discipline. Like Confucius, Mo Ti believed that no king can rule successfully without the assistance of capable and moral ministers. Also, like Confucius, Mo Ti holds the *chün-tzu*, the perfect man who conducts himself above all reproach, as an exemplar for all men to emulate.

The most significant single contribution of Mo Ti to ancient Chinese thought is the consistent exposition of his materialistic view of man's nature and his persistent reference to the pain-and-pleasure approach to human problems. To be sure, his theory that man can and must be beaten into loving his fellow men is at once paradoxical and repulsive to the idealistic Confucians, but the paradox may be more apparent than real when one realizes that both Mo Ti and Confucius assume a basically equal teachability of all men. In the development of Chinese thought, it was only a short step from Mo Ti's utilitarianism, which never completely loses sight of righteousness and virtue, to the Machiavellian realism expounded by the Legalists who rose to power at the end of the Warring States period (third century B.C.). Mo Ti's materialism is not unqualified, but all the ingredients of a more thoroughgoing materialism are present in Mo Ti's system.

That Mohism as an organized body of doctrines ceased to exert appreciable influence so soon after the death of its founder must be blamed on the aridity of the mode of life advocated by the Mohists. Mo Ti himself, as far as we know, never married, and his good disciples all led a life of ascetic dedication to their confraternity. Some of them actually died for the leader of their group. In contrast, the Confucian doctrines offer a view of life that is much more reasonable and attractive to most men.

DEMOCRITUS: FRAGMENTS

Author: Democritus of Abdera (c.460-c.370 B.C.)
Type of work: Philosophy of nature
First transcribed: Probably fourth century B.C.

PRINCIPAL IDEAS ADVANCED

Since nothing can come from nothing, and change really occurs, and motion requires a void, reality must consist of atoms moving in a void.

The only inherent properties of atoms are size, shape, and solidity; color, sweetness, bitterness, and other such qualities are attributed to objects because of the sensations occurring within experiencing organisms, but such qualities have no existence in objects.

The sensations that come from experiencing various kinds of atoms vary according to the shapes of the atoms.

The best form of government is the democratic.

The wise man is one who limits his ambition according to his ability.

In all probability credit for the fundamental ideas of the atomic theory—Greek speculation's greatest achievement—should go to Leucippus of Miletus rather than to his pupil Democritus. But we know almost nothing of Leucippus.

Rational speculation about the nature of the world began not earlier than the sixth century B.C. Four or five generations later it had progressed, in Democritus, to an essentially correct account of the nature of matter. This amazing fact has led to both exaggeration and underestimation of the Greek achievement. On the one hand, some people conclude that science stood still until the revival of the atomic theory in the seventeenth century. On the other, scientists especially are prone to point out that modern atomic physics rests on evidence derived from careful quantitative experimentation of which the Greeks knew nothing; therefore, it is said, the ancient theory was merely a lucky guess—and the Greeks made all possible guesses. A brief review of

the development of early Greek physics will show that while Democritus did not have Dalton's reasons for asserting that the world consists of atoms moving in the void, he nonetheless had some very good ones. Knowing these, we shall be able to compare ancient and modern atomism less superficially and misleadingly.

The men of Miletus, especially Anaximander, who made the break with mythological world accounts in the early sixth century B.C. took over from previous creation myths two important assumptions. First, these Milesians accepted the belief that there *was* a creation, or rather a development: the world was not always as it is now, but had in the beginning been something simple and homogeneous, like the "chaos" of the myths. Differentiation, complexity, and organization have a history. Second, the Milesians accepted the theory that there exists an impersonal force making for order and "justice" in the universe at large. The Milesians were

37

the first philosophers because they dispensed altogether with the "will of the gods" as an explanatory principle, because they assumed that the natural forces that made the universe what it is were of a kind still operative. The problem, as they conceived it, was to identify the original simple world-stuff, out of which all things had come, and to describe the process which had differentiated and organized it into the present world. Not "divine" inspiration but ordinary human reason, they thought, was capable of solving the problem. And since conclusions based on reasons invite criticism and modification, unlike revelations which can be only accepted or rejected, the history of rational speculation was progressive.

In addition to the ideas of ultimate oneness, development, and "justice" inherited from religion, the earliest philosophers assumed with "common sense" that nothing can come out of nothing, or be absolutely destroyed, and that our senses reveal to us directly the constituents of the world, at least as it is now. We feel heat and cold; we taste sweetness and bitterness; we see red and green. Heat, cold, sweetness, bitterness, red, and green are therefore *parts* of the objective world; together they make it up. We should say that these are *qualities* of matter, but early Greek thought does not make this distinction; "the hot," "the cold," "the wet," "the dry," and so on, in various combinations, *are* the stuff of things. One must simply find out the unity underlying this diversity.

Thus, for example, Anaximenes, the third of the Milesian "physicists," held that the fundamental stuff is Mist. Everything is really Mist; the things that do not appear to be Mist are Mist that has been thickened or thinned.

Very thin Mist is fire; Mist somewhat thickened is water; thickened still more it is stone.

There is an inconsistency here which Parmenides (in effect) pointed out. No doubt the theory of Anaximenes squares with observation, for fire, when cooled and "thickened," becomes smoke and smoke is easy to regard, at this stage of thought, as a kind of fog or Mist. Condensed Mist is water, and water thickened still more becomes ice, a solid, a kind of stone. But is the theory compatible with logic? Fire is (identical with) "the hot and dry"; water is (identical with) "the cold and wet". How, then, can the one be transformed into the other without violating the fundamental principle that nothing can come from nothing? Where did the *cold* come from? Where has the *hot* gone? If cold and hot are thought of (so to speak) as substances, it seems that there can be no satisfactory answer to this question. Something has come out of "nothing"; something has disappeared into "nothing." Worse still, as Parmenides saw, if there is ultimately just one stuff, that stuff must be just the kind of stuff it is, so that it cannot logically be both hot and cold, both wet and dry. Therefore *change is impossible.* If things seem to change (as they do), this must be mere illusion, for logic pronounces it contradictory.

It is important to see that Parmenides was right, *given his assumptions* of monism, nothing-from-nothing, and identity of things and qualities. Parmenides had another argument (a fallacious one) to show that the kind of change called motion cannot really occur. It is this: If a thing moves, there must be room for it to move into—that is, there must be empty space. But there cannot be any empty space, for empty space would be just "nothing," "that which is not," and the assertion that there is empty space amounts to saying "That which is not, is," a statement of contradiction.

The philosophers Empedocles and Anaxagoras tried to develop systems which would meet the logical objections of Parmenides without flying in the face of common sense. They argued that motion could occur without empty space if the moving thing *displaced* what was in front of it, as a fish swims in water. For the rest, they abandoned monism. Empedocles said that there are six basic stuffs, while Anaxagoras held that there are an infinity—as many stuffs as there are sensible discriminations—and all things are made by the mixture and separation of these stuffs.

The philosophy of Anaxagoras successfully met Parmenides' criticism, but at too high a price. While it is hard to say precisely just what it is that we are asking for when we demand an explanation of something, at any rate it is clear that an explanation is not satisfactory unless in *some* sense the ideas used in the explanation are simpler, or more unified, than the thing to be explained. But if one's explanatory principles are as diverse as the things to be explained, the requirement cannot be met. "Flour is a mixture in which flour-stuff predominates, and water is a mixture in which water-stuff predominates, and the two make bread because when they are mixed and baked the bread-stuff in both of them comes to the fore." This may be true, but it is too easy, and it does not *explain* anything.

Leucippus and Democritus discovered a better way of answering Par-

menides. As to motion, Leucippus flatly declared that "nothing" *does* exist; while Democritus more appropriately dismissed Parmenides' quibble with another: " 'Hing' exists no more than 'not-hing,' " the point of the joke being that if " 'Nothing' does not exist" is a truth of *logic*, elimination of the double negative must also produce a logical truth: " 'Hing' does exist." But "hing," so far from existing, is not even a word. (Greek for "nothing" is "mē-den," of which "mē" means "not," while "den" has no meaning in isolation.)

There is, then, a void, and things that move in it. These things are *atoms* —"uncuttables." Each separate atom is like the "reality" of Parmenides, uncreated, indestructible, unchanging. The matter in an atom is homogeneous, and nothing can happen to one internally; that is, each atom is infinitely hard. Atoms differ from one another in size and shape—that is all. They do not differ in color, for instance, but not because they are all the *same* color. They do so because they have no color at all (not even black or gray). Similarly for heat, moisture, taste, and odor. Atoms have always been (and always will be) in motion— "like the motes in a sunbeam." They jostle one another, and in their jostlings, two kinds of processes occur that result in the "coming-into-being" of the large-scale aggregates with which we are familiar. One is vortex motion, the effect of which is to separate random aggregates according to likenesses, the heavier—that is, the bigger—atoms going to the center, the lighter ones to the periphery. The other process is the hooking on to each other by atoms of like configurations.

One atom can affect another only

by colliding with it; and the outcome of a collision (hooking, or change of direction or speed) is *determined* by the sizes, shapes, and velocities of the atoms involved in the collision. But the sizes and shapes are eternal, and the velocities in their turn are outcomes of previous collisions. Therefore, there is no such thing as "chance" in nature; "Nothing happens at random," Leucippus pronounced in the one sentence of his that has survived, "but everything from a rationale and by necessity." Ideally, explanation should consist in finding out the laws of motion and impact and using these to show how one atomic configuration came about from a previous one. Such a complex act is of course impossible; however, Democritus sought to apply the fundamental idea of *mechanical causation* to observable phenomena.

There is an ancient story that illustrates his method and points up its difference from traditional concepts. Considerable interest had been aroused by the extraordinary death of a prominent man. When he was strolling along a beach, an eagle had dropped a turtle on his head. *Why?* It was recalled that an oracle had said that he would die of "a bolt from Zeus." This had been thought to be a prediction of death by a stroke of lightning. But someone pointed out that the eagle was a bird sacred to Zeus; thus, the oracle was fulfilled. This explanation satisfied most Greeks, but not Democritus. *He* went to the beach and observed the habits of eagles. He found that they were fond of turtle meat. In order to get at it, an eagle would seize a turtle in his talons, fly into the air with it, and drop it on a rock to crack the shell. This observation, together with the fact that the deceased had been bald, provided an explanation that satisfied Democritus. The curious event was shown to be one item in a natural regularity or pattern. It was unnecessary to postulate the purposes of unseen beings to account for the fact. Aristotle complained, quite unjustifiably, that Democritus "reduced the explanation of nature to the statement, 'Thus it happened formerly also.'" The fact is that Democritus understood the character of scientific explanation far better than did Aristotle.

In sum, Democritus' reason for asserting that reality consists of atoms moving in the void is that this statement can be *deduced* from the premises: (1) nothing can come from nothing, (2) change really occurs, and (3) motion requires a void. That explanation must be mechanistic also follows from these assumptions if it is further allowed that all interaction is impact. Democritus' mechanism was also the culmination of the rejection of animistic and supernatural will-forces by all his philosophical predecessors.

Democritus' atomism, and still more his mechanism, agree in principle with the fundamental tenets of modern physical science. (By "in principle" it is meant to rule out as inessential, though important, such differences as that the particles of the present-day physicists are wave-packets or whatever, and fuzzy, and hookless; what is essential is the concept of matter as somehow granular, and that physical processes are analyzable into redistributions of energy among these grains.) What modern physicists have that Democritus lacked is a conception of controlled, quantitative experimentation, together with a technique of mathematical manipulation of the data. For this reason, Democritus, though he declared that he would "rather discover one causal explanation than gain the kingdom of the Persians," failed utterly to add to detailed knowledge of nature. In fact, he was much behind his own times, still believing, for instance, that the earth is a flat disc, though the Pythagoreans had long understood its sphericity. In detailed explanations, Democritus could do no better than this: "Thunder is produced by an unstable mixture forcing the cloud enclosing it to move downward. Lightning is a clashing together of clouds by which the fire-producing atoms rubbing against each other are assembled through the porous mass into one place and pass out. And the thunderbolt occurs when the motion is forced by the very pure, very fine, very uniform and 'closely-packed' fire-producing atoms, as he himself calls them." (The foregoing is an ancient paraphrase, not a quotation from Democritus.) It must be admitted that this account of lightning is no worse than any other prior to Franklin, and a considerable improvement over "Zeus is angry."

"By convention color, by convention sweet, by convention bitter; but in reality atoms and void." Thus Democritus states his theory. The atoms alone are real, and their only inherent qualities (we can use this word now, for Democritus distinguished for the first time clearly between thing and quality) are size, shape, and solidity. Then what about color, sweet, bitter, and the rest? They are "by convention." What does this mean? Democritus held that a man's soul consists of particularly fine and spherical, hence mobile, atoms. When certain "images" from the external world—the images being, of course, themselves assemblages of atoms—impinge on the soul atoms, a

sensation is produced. The sensation occurs only within the ensouled body; hence, is not "out there" because the external world is colorless, and odorless. This is a part of the meaning of "by convention," a phrase that might be rendered as "subjective." The sensations are also subjective in the sense that they lead us to suppose, falsely, that the world is colored and odorous.

"There are two forms of knowledge, one genuine, one obscure. Of the obscure sort are all these: sight, hearing, smell, taste, touch. The genuine is distinguished from this. . . . Whenever the obscure cannot sense any farther into the minute by seeing or hearing or smelling or tasting or touching, but [it is necessary to pursue the investigation] more finely, [then the genuine, which has a finer organ of knowing,] comes up." The organ of "genuine knowledge" would seem to be the "Pure Reason" that led Democritus to deduce the atomic nature of matter. But Democritus was worried, as well he might have been, about the "obscure." He portrayed the senses speaking thus to the mind: " 'Wretched mind, getting from us your confidences you cast us down? That is your own downfall.' " For the information on which even the atomic theory is based is, after all, derived ultimately from observation through the senses.

If reality consists of matter with only its "primary qualities," what kind of reality do sensation, and thought, and consciousness in general have? This problem besets all forms of materialism and is often alleged (wrongly) to be fatal to it as a world-view. Democritus spent much effort in trying to account for sensations on atomic principles. Thus, he claimed that sour fluids consist of angular and twisted atoms, while honey is made of rounded, rather large ones. This was, of course, inconsistent with his claim that tastes are subjective effects. He could have patched up the account to some extent by considering not only the atomic constitution of the food but also that of the tongue which interacts with it; but there is no evidence that he did so. Perhaps it was despair at this problem that led him to exclaim, "In reality we know nothing. For truth is in a depth."

Materialists *should* say that sensations are not *things* at all; but Democritus held that they are illusory things. This, at any rate, is the impression we get from ancient discussions of his theory of knowledge. It may be mistaken, for the accounts all come from hostile critics who may well have misunderstood or misrepresented the great Abderite.

Unlike most Greek philosophers, Democritus was a partisan of democracy. He said: "Poverty in a democracy is as much preferable to so-called prosperity in an autocracy as freedom is to slavery." By "democracy" he meant a constitutional government, directed by public-spirited, intelligent men in the interest of all citizens.

Democritus was one of the most prolific authors of antiquity, having written, we are told, more than sixty works. All have perished. The fragments that remain fill about ten pages of ordinary print, of which eight are concerned with ethics, politics, education, and child-rearing. (Democritus thought it a risky and thankless business to have children.) Many of the ethical reflections are unbearably platitudinous: "In good fortune it is easy to find a friend, in misfortune hardest of all." Others are shrewd and worldly wise: "If you cannot understand the compliments, conclude that you are being flattered." The general tenor of the maxims is advocacy of "cheerfulness," that is, of prudence, contentment with what one has, not worrying too much: "He who would be cheerful must not busy himself with many things, either by himself or in company; and whatever he busies himself with, he should not choose what is beyond his own power and nature. But he should be so on his guard that when a stroke of fortune tempts him to excess, he puts it aside, and does not grasp at what is beyond his powers. For being well-filled is better than being stuffed." There are some fragments, however, that rise quite above this pedestrian level, embodying, in fact, teachings often credited to others, and used unfairly to belabor "crude Materialism":

"Refrain from wrongdoing not from fear but from duty."

"The doer of injustice is unhappier than the sufferer."

"Goodness is not merely in refraining from being unjust, but in not even wishing to be."

"The cause of error is ignorance of the better."

APOLOGY

Author: Plato (427-347 B.C.)
Type of work: Ethics
First transcribed: Probably one of the early dialogues

42

The oracle at Delphi declared Socrates to be the wisest of all men, and Socrates suggested that if he were superior to other men in wisdom, it was only because he was aware of his own ignorance.

Defending himself against the charge of impiety and corrupting the young, Socrates argued that the pretenders to wisdom, whom he exposed by his critical questioning, must have spread rumors about him in order to discredit him.

Socrates maintained that it would have been foolish for him to corrupt the very persons with whom he associated, for everyone knows that corrupt and evil persons harm even those who have once befriended them.

If to point out the weaknesses in a state is to do the state a service, Socrates argued, then he had better be rewarded for performing the function of gadfly to the state.

After having been condemned to death, Socrates declared that death is not to be feared, for either it is annihilation, or it is a change to a better world where one might converse with noble souls.

The word "apology," as it appears in the title of this famous dialogue, means a "defense," not a request for forgiveness. In meeting the accusation that he had corrupted the youth of Athens, Socrates did not for a moment assume an apologetic air, but with courageous faith in the worth of philosophy set forth the principles by which he governed his life.

The dialogue—which is Plato's creation, and Plato was one who knew Socrates and had grown to love him both as a teacher and a man—assumes the worth of Socrates' life and the rightness of his acts, especially of those acts of criticism which aroused the enmity of Socrates' accusers. The *Apology* is one of three dialogues describing the final days of perhaps the greatest hero in the history of philosophy, one who took philosophy seriously enough to die for it. The *Apology* reports the trial and condemnation of Socrates, the *Crito* his reasons for refusing to escape from prison, and the *Phaedo* his last conversations and death. To read the dialogues in that

order is to gain some understanding of the significance of Socrates' identification of wisdom with virtue, and some conception of the nobility of his character.

As the *Apology* opens, the prosecution, for which Meletus is the spokesman, has already stated its case. Meletus was probably merely the spokesman for the chief instigator of the trial, Anytus, respected leader of the restored democracy; the third accuser, Lycon, is barely mentioned in the dialogue. Meletus speaks only a few words, the other accusers none, but Socrates repeats the charges made against him. He begins by pointing out that almost everything they have said is false, especially their warning to the court implying that Socrates is a persuasive speaker, unless they mean by that one who speaks truth. His words will be unpremeditated but spoken with confidence in the justice of his cause; it is to truth that the jury should attend, just as it is the speaker's duty to state only the truth. There are actually two sets of charges against him, Socrates says: the present ones of impiety and corruption of the young, and some ancient ones his audience heard as children and which should now be refuted.

The latter were made by accusers largely unknown, except for Aristophanes in his burlesque of Socrates in the comedy, *The Clouds* (which was written in fun rather than ill will). These accusations were that Socrates had theories about and conducted investigations into the heavens and things below the earth (that is, pursued physical sciences), and that he could make weaker arguments appear to overcome the stronger and taught others to do the same (that is, he was a sophist). Such accusations are dangerous, Socrates argues, because uncritical listeners assume that such inquirers must be atheists. But the accusations are false, for Socrates has no knowledge of physics, not from disdain but from lack of interest. Socrates asks whether anyone present ever heard him discussing these matters. As to the charge that he has taught others professionally for fees, this, too, is false. Socrates professes (ironically) to admire Sophists such as Gorgias, Prodicus, and Hippias, who are able to persuade youths to forsake their usual company—which is free—and come to them for training in social skills—for large fees. Still, people will wonder how Socrates got this reputation if the accusations are false, so he will explain.

Perhaps he does have some degree of human wisdom, though that of the sophists is undoubtedly superhuman! The tale he will tell now concerning the kind of wisdom he does have may seem exaggerated, but judgment should be reserved until the end: Chaerephon, an old friend known to all, asked the oracle at Delphi if anyone were wiser than Socrates, and the answer was "No!" Such an answer puzzled Socrates—surely the god was speaking in riddles, for he could not be lying. So Socrates set out to see whether he could disprove the oracle by finding a wiser man. He examined a politician with a great reputation for—and the conceit of—wisdom. Not only was the man not wise, but he resented Socrates' attempt to show him that he was not. Socrates came away realizing that at least he was himself wiser in awareness of his own ignorance. Others who heard the politician's examination resented the inquiry, too, but Socrates felt it a religious duty to determine the oracle's meaning. Having queried other politicians with the same effect, he went next to the poets and found that they could not even expound their own works. Not wisdom, then, but instinct or inspiration must be the source of poetry. Proceeding to the skilled craftsmen Socrates discovered here a kind of technical knowledge he did not possess, but these men prided themselves so on their special competence that they mistakenly thought themselves expert on everything else. Naturally, Socrates' exposé of the ignorance of others made him unpopular with them, even though it was really to their good.

When bystanders heard him examine pretenders to wisdom, it was assumed that he had the knowledge, lack of which he uncovered in those questioned, even though this was not true. But the real meaning of the oracle and the upshot of Socrates' search was that God alone is really wise, and human wisdom is of relatively little value. The oracle used Socrates' name merely to make a point: " 'The wisest of you men is he who has realized, like Socrates, that in respect of wisdom he is really worthless.' " (Perhaps what Socrates actually meant here is that admission of one's errors and present lack of understanding is a necessary prerequisite of learning, for neither in theory nor in practice does Socrates deny that true wisdom is one of man's highest goods.) Thus in exposing ignorance, Socrates continues, he obeys a divine command.

Socrates tells the court that young men of leisure, having heard him questioning their elders to the latter's discomfort, have tried to imitate his techniques and have aroused further hostility which has redounded to Socrates' discredit. When victims irritated at exposure are asked what Socrates has done or taught to mislead the young, however, they have no specific evidence and so "they fall back on the stock charges against any philosopher: that he teaches his pupils about things in the heavens and below the earth, and to disbelieve in gods, and to make the weaker argument defeat the stronger." It is thus because he has revealed the truth about them in plain language that the earlier calumniators have spread these rumors about Socrates, which are the underlying causes of the present attack by Meletus, Anytus and Lycon.

Before we turn to Socrates' reply to the latter, it would be well to realize, as Professor A. E. Taylor points out, that the prosecution could not afford to present its real complaint against him. The pretext of "corruption of the young" concerned his supposed influence, discouraging unquestioning loyalty to the democracy, on former associates (Alcibiades, Critias, Charmides, and others) who had opposed the state. The charge of "irreligion" was probably related to the mutilation,

in 415 B.C., of all the Athenian statues of Hermes on the night before Alcibiades led the military expedition to Sicily, for which Alcibiades was blamed, probably falsely. But these matters were excluded from the jurisdiction of the present court by the Act of Oblivion which Anytus had sponsored. According to this act, offenses occurring under the old democracy had received general amnesty. During the year of Socrates' trial, 399 B.C., Anytus defended another person against charges of "irreligion," so it is unlikely that he actually held such a grievance against Socrates. It is likely, Professor Taylor suggests, that Anytus regarded Socrates' influence as dangerous to the restored democracy and, consequently, as one which had better be removed. Hence the trumped-up charges, the use of Meletus as mouthpiece, and the prosecution's unwillingness and inability to explain or substantiate the accusations made in public.

Consequently, on trial, Socrates exercises his argumentative abilities with humor and irony to show how ridiculous the prosecution's case is. He turns specifically to the charges of Meletus, stating them as follows: " 'Socrates is guilty of corrupting the minds of the young, and of believing in deities of his own invention instead of the gods recognized by the State.' " (Professor Taylor writes that this passage means that Socrates did not worship the official gods rather than that he did not believe in them, and that he practiced unfamiliar rites.)

Socrates now takes the line that Meletus must be joking about a serious matter in which he really has no interest. Who, he queries, exercises the best influence on the young? By a series of questions he leads Meletus to say that it is the whole Athenian citizenry—except Socrates. But this is very odd; in fact, it is exactly opposite to the case of training horses, in which the many are incompetent and only a few expert trainers improve the animals.

Furthermore, since Meletus must admit that evil people harm their associates, he must also admit that Socrates would be unbelievably stupid not to know that by corrupting his young acquaintances he would only be brewing trouble for himself; now either Socrates has not been a bad influence, or if so, it must have been unintentional. If the latter, however, what Socrates deserves according to the usual procedure is that he be given private admonition rather than punishment. But far from instructing Socrates, Meletus has avoided his company until now.

How, specifically, has Socrates corrupted the young, especially in regard to teaching belief in new deities? Does he believe in gods different from those of the state or in none at all? Meletus takes the latter alternative. Socrates suggests that Meletus has deliberately and flippantly contradicted himself in order to test Socrates' logical prowess. It is charged both that Socrates believes in no gods and that he believes in new deities, that he is an atheist and yet believes in "supernatural activities" (this refers to Socrates' famous divine "sign," or inner voice). Now one cannot believe in activities without an actor, and if Socrates believes in supernatural activities, he must believe in supernatural beings. Thus, either Meletus was trying Socrates' wit or he was desperate for a genuine charge against him.

At this point Socrates acknowledges that his destruction will be caused by the general hostility aroused by his conduct, not by these flimsy accusations, but that he has no regret for his behavior. A good man must not busily calculate the chances of life and death, but must concern himself with acting rightly. It would be most inconsistent if, after loyal military service through several engagements, Socrates were to fail through fear of death an assignment given by God himself to the philosophic life. To fear death implies knowledge of what occurs afterward, another form of the pretense to know what one does not; but to disobey a superior, human or divine, is a known evil.

Were it suggested that Socrates be acquitted on condition that he desist from his philosophical questionings, he would reply that, much as he appreciates the offer, he must still pursue his duty to God, asking Athenians, " 'Are you not ashamed that you give your attention to acquiring as much money as possible, and similarly with reputation and honour, and give no attention or thought to truth and understanding and the perfection of your soul?' " Actually, Socrates conceives his divine service as the greatest benefit ever to fall on Athens, since he urges men to put the welfare of their souls above all else. If the Athenians kill him, they will inflict more harm on themselves; Socrates believes that divine law prevents injury by an evil to a good man. Of course they can banish or kill his body, but such acts do no harm to the soul, except of course to the soul of the evildoer.

Here Socrates introduces the famous "gadfly" metaphor. Comical as it sounds, he says, "God has appointed me to this city, as though it were a

46

large thoroughbred horse which because of its great size is inclined to be lazy and needs the stimulation of some stinging fly" ("gadfly," in the Jowett translation). "It seems to me that God has attached me to this city to perform the office of such a fly; and all day long I never cease to settle here, there, and everywhere, rousing, persuading, reproving every one of you. You will not easily find another like me, gentlemen, and if you take my advice you will spare my life. I suspect, however, that before long you will awake from your drowsing, and in your annoyance you will take Anytus' advice and finish me off with a single slap; and then you will go on sleeping till the end of your days, unless God in his care for you sends someone to take my place." (While such a description of his mission might be misinterpreted as conceited, careful study of its context and of other Socratic dialogues will convince the reader that it is only the frank self-appraisal of a prophet.) As Socrates adds, proof of the sincerity of what he has said and done lies in the obvious fact of his poverty; he has neglected his private affairs in order to fulfill his duty.

Should someone ask why Socrates has not addressed himself to the state at large with his advice, the answer is that he has been forbidden to do so by the divine voice to which Meletus' charge made implicit reference and which comes to him occasionally to warn against a course of action. In regard to a political career its warning was evidently provident, for otherwise Socrates would have been dead long ago—no man, he says, can conscientiously oppose a government by the masses and champion justice and live long. He would not act wrongly in

obedience to any authority, as is evidenced by the few occasions of his public office. When a member of the Council under the old democracy, he alone opposed the unconstitutional trial of ten military commanders *en bloc,* thus risking denunciation and arrest. Later, under the oligarchy, he disobeyed an unjust order to participate in the arrest of Leon of Salamis and probably would have been executed had not the government fallen.

Toward the end of his defense, Socrates repeats that he has never taught professionally nor privately, but has allowed rich and poor to exchange questions and answers with him, and, consequently, cannot be held responsible for the good or bad career of any individual. If some of those who have listened to his discourse have been corrupted by him, Socrates challenges them to bear witness now. That no one comes is ample evidence that Meletus lies. This constitutes Socrates' defense; he will not appeal, as is usual with defendants, to the sympathy of the jury by exhibiting his children and friends. To do so would be unfitting for one of Socrates' reputation. Besides, the defendant's business is to convince the jury by facts and argument rather than by sentiment, and the jury is to decide justly, not hand out verdicts as favors. Were he to ask them to perjure themselves as jurors, this in itself would convict him of guilt. Thus Socrates ends his speech and places himself in his judges' and God's hands.

When the verdict is brought in, it is "Guilty," though obtained by a small margin, about 280 to 220. Meletus proposes the death penalty (although scholars believe Socrates' accusers did not wish to kill him but only to silence

47

or banish him, since according to current practices several alternatives of escape were open). It was customary for the convicted defendant to propose an alternate penalty and for the jury to choose which one would be enacted. But Socrates will not admit guilt; what then is his desert? Since he has not cared for money, a comfortable home, high rank, or secret societies—all the things having popular appeal—and has instead devoted himself to his mission to Athens, he says it would therefore be appropriate that he be maintained at state expense as a public benefactor. Certainly he deserves this treatment more than do Olympic horse racers!

Of course Socrates does not expect this suggestion to be taken seriously in spite of its justice. What of other possibilities? He rejects that of imprisonment, which is a known evil compared to death, which is of uncertain value. As to banishment, it is clear that he would find no more welcome in other societies than he has in Athens, for his conduct and its results would be the same. Again, he cannot give up philosophy and "mind his own business," for "to let no day pass without discussing goodness and all the other subjects about which you hear me talking and examining both myself and others is really the very best thing that a man can do, and . . . life without this sort of examination is not worth living. . . ." As to a fine, it is not likely that what he could afford would be acceptable. At this point Plato, Crito, Critobulus, and Apollodorus offer to pay a fine thirty times that which Socrates suggests, which offer he transmits to the court.

But the jury decides on the death penalty instead, and Socrates makes his final remarks. He reminds that part of the jury voting for death that nature would soon have brought about what they wished, but as it is, they will incur blame for having killed a wise man, whether he is one or not. His condemnation has resulted not from paucity of argument but from his bearing: he has not been brazen or servile, nor has he catered to their pleasure. The real difficulty is not to elude death but to outrun vice; Socrates, the old man, has been caught by the former, but they have been captured by the latter; his condemnation is by the court, but they are convicted of their wickedness by Truth. Hoping to stop his mouth by death, they will find that criticism of their actions will increase—the only escape for them is to become good men.

To those voting for acquittal, he notes that in nothing he has done this day has the inner voice opposed him, whereas in the past it sometimes stopped him in the middle of a sentence. This is clear evidence that the outcome is good and that even death is no evil. Death must be either total annihilation, in which case it is an unbroken rest, or else a change to another world; and if it is true as reported that one can there converse with the great men of time past, how rewarding! To meet Homer, Hesiod, or the great heroes of the old days, especially those similarly condemned to death unjustly, would be worth dying for again and again. To talk and argue with them would be happiness beyond description, and presumably one is not killed there for asking questions.

Socrates concludes by encouraging the friendly jurors with the belief that "nothing can harm a good man either in life or after death, and his fortunes are not a matter of indifference to the gods." He has no ill will for those who condemned him, although they are guilty of intent to harm him. As a final favor Socrates asks that his hearers treat his sons as he has treated the Athenians: if they put anything before goodness, or are self-deceived about their virtues, he asks that the jurors take their "revenge by plaguing them as I plagued you. . . ."

So ends Plato's story of the legal but unjust trial of one regarded as philosophy's first martyr. The authenticity of his report has been questioned, but scholars have pointed out that many people present at the trial, including hostile critics, would have read Plato's account and detected any substantial deviation from the facts. We may therefore regard it as an essentially accurate record of the serenity, wit, courage, and steadfastness of a philosopher whose justness gave him composure in the face of those who cheated him of life.

EUTHYPHRO

Author: Plato (427-347 B.C.)
Type of work: Ethics, philosophy of religion
First transcribed: Probably one of the early dialogues

PRINCIPAL IDEAS ADVANCED

Socrates has been charged by Meletus with corrupting the youth of Athens and with inventing new gods; and he seeks to learn from Euthyphro, who is prosecuting his own father for murder, the distinction between piety and impiety.

Euthyphro suggests that piety is prosecuting the unjust, those who have committed such crimes as murder or sacrilege; impiety is failure to prosecute such persons.

But Socrates points out that this is an example, not a definition; and thus Euthyphro suggests that piety is whatever is pleasing to the gods, and impiety is whatever is displeasing to them.

But Socrates rejects Euthyphro's definition on the ground that the gods do not agree in attitude concerning the acts of men, nor is it satisfactory to say that the pious is what all the gods love, for the pertinent question concerns the nature of piety in virtue of which the gods love it.

If, as Euthyphro then claims, piety is paying careful attention to the gods, by means of prayer and worship, for the benefit of man, then piety seems to be loved by the gods even though it is of no benefit to the gods; but this runs counter to the previous claim that piety is good not simply because the gods love it.

The *Euthyphro* deals with some of the events culminating in Socrates' trial and death, portraying Socrates just before his trial. The *Euthyphro* forms a sequence with the dialogues, the *Apology* (dealing with the trial), the *Crito* (dealing with Socrates' incarceration after his conviction), and the

49

Phaedo (dealing with the execution of Socrates by the drinking of the poison hemlock).

The *Euthyphro* is one of the best examples of the Socratic method. Socrates is portrayed as seeking wisdom about the meaning of the terms "piety" and "impiety" so that he can defend himself against the charge of being impious. Euthyphro, presumably, knows what these terms mean. Socrates tries to learn from him by asking questions and by asking him to define the terms. Each answer given by Euthyphro is scrutinized by Socrates and found to be faulty. Euthyphro complains that Socrates will not let his statements "stand still." Instead, by his persistent questioning, he makes the statements "move away," until Euthyphro no longer knows what to say. He finally quits the discussion, refusing to recognize his own ignorance concerning the matter in question, and refusing to see how dangerous it is for him, or for anyone else, to act on the basis of such complete ignorance.

The discussion begins when Socrates and Euthyphro meet at the Porch of the King Archon, where cases dealing with crimes affecting the state religion are judged. Euthyphro expresses surprise at encountering Socrates in such a place. The latter explains that he is there because he has been charged with corrupting the youth of Athens, and with inventing new gods while not believing in the old, official ones. In contrast, Euthyphro has come to court to charge his own father with murder. Socrates suggests that Euthyphro must be very wise if he knows that he is right in prosecuting his own father. Such wisdom about what is right and wrong can be of great assistance to Socrates in his own case,

so he requests details from Euthyphro.

The charge that Euthyphro is bringing against his own father is based on a very strange story. A drunken laborer, who worked on the family farm, killed one of the slaves. Euthyphro's father caught the murderer, tied him up, and threw him into a ditch. The father then sent a messenger to Athens to find out what to do. While waiting for an answer, he completely neglected the bound murderer, who died from cold and hunger before the messenger returned. Euthyphro's family insisted that the father did not actually kill the laborer, and even if he had, the laborer was a murderer anyway, so he probably deserved death. Also, they maintained, Euthyphro should not get involved, because it is impious for a son to charge his own father with murder. Euthyphro, on the other hand, insisted that he was doing the right thing.

Socrates is so impressed by Euthyphro's assurance that what he is doing is right and pious, that he asks Euthyphro to instruct him so that he will be able to go to his own trial and explain to his accusers and his judges what is right and wrong. Since piety and impiety must have the same characteristics in all actions that are pious or impious, Socrates asks Euthyphro to explain the distinction between piety and impiety.

The first definition that Euthyphro offers is that piety consists of doing what he is doing; namely, prosecuting an unjust person who has committed a serious crime, even if such a person is a parent. Impiety, on the other hand, consists of not prosecuting such an individual. To justify what he is doing, Euthyphro also points out that the Greek god, Zeus, bound up his own father, Cronos, for committing the crime of devouring some of his children, and that Cronos had also punished his father for wrongdoing.

Socrates points out that Euthyphro's statement does not actually constitute a definition of "piety," but only an illustration of one pious action. Such a statement does not really help in ascertaining if other actions are pious or impious. What is needed, instead of an example, is a statement of the essential characteristic of piety that makes all pious actions pious. Such a statement would allow one to classify all actions, since it would provide a general standard by which to judge which actions are pious and which are not. (As Plato points out over and over again in his dialogues, one does not actually know a general concept like "piety," "justice," "courage," and so on, if one can only cite examples of pious, just, or courageous activity. One cannot even be sure that these are examples of what one thinks, unless one also knows the meaning of the concepts; hence, the general knowledge is crucial for identifying and comprehending the particular examples with which we are acquainted.)

Euthyphro sees that he has not given a satisfactory definition of the term "piety" by citing the example of his case against his father. So, he offers Socrates a more general statement about "piety," saying that "what is pleasing to the gods is pious, and what is not pleasing to them is impious." Socrates congratulates him for giving him the kind of answer he wanted. All that remains, he states, is to find out if this definition is the true one. The truth will be ascertained by asking questions about the definition given.

Since Euthyphro accepts all the Greek mythological tales about quarrels and disagreements among the gods, Socrates asks him whether the gods disagree about matters of fact or matters of value. The latter, says Euthyphro. Then, Socrates argues, they are disagreeing about what pleases or displeases them. The same action is pleasing to some gods and displeasing to others, and hence, according to Euthyphro's second definition of "piety," that which is pleasing to the gods, the same action can be both pious and impious.

Euthyphro insists that this contradictory conclusion does not follow because the gods all agree on certain matters, such as that if one man unjustly kills another, he is to be punished. The gods may all agree, Socrates admits, about certain universal laws regarding punishment, but a disagreement still exists among both men and gods as to which cases fall under these laws. They disagree in their evaluations of various acts, some saying the acts are just, some that they are unjust. Even if Euthyphro is sure in his own case that the gods agree that his father's action was unjust, and that Euthyphro's action is just, it is still evident that Euthyphro's second definition of "piety" is inadequate. In view of the fact that the gods disagree about some of the actions that are pleasing or displeasing to them, an action cannot be pious simply because it pleases some gods, since the same action would have to be classed as "impious" if it displeased other gods.

A third definition is presented to overcome the problem of divine disagreements. Something is pious if *all* the gods love it, and it is impious if they *all* hate it. In cases where there is disagreement among the gods, the item

51

in question is to be classed as neither pious nor impious.

Socrates immediately begins examining this new definition by raising the most serious point that is brought up in the dialogue. He asks Euthyphro whether the gods love piety because it is pious, or whether it is pious because the gods love it. The question at issue is whether the basic characteristic that determines piety is the fact that the gods love it, or whether piety has in itself some characteristic which accounts for the fact that the gods love it. (In a more general form this question was debated in the Middle Ages, when philosophers asked whether, if something is good, it is so because God wills it, or whether God wills it because it is good. Is goodness an independent value, or is it dependent upon the divine will? It was pointed out that if the latter be true, the Ten Commandments are good and right only because God decreed them; if he had decreed the exact opposite, then the opposite would be good and right, if goodness is simply whatever God wills.)

Euthyphro holds that the gods love piety because it is pious. Socrates then shows him that he has not offered a definition, but only an effect of piety in pointing out that the gods love it. Since, according to Euthyphro, piety has certain characteristics that make it what it is, and since it is because of those characteristics that the gods love it, then he still has not given an adequate definition of "piety." He still has not revealed what the essential characteristics are that make it what it is.

Then Socrates asks Euthyphro once more to tell him what Euthyphro claims to know—namely, what piety and impiety are. By this point in the discussion, Euthyphro is bewildered; he complains that whatever he says in answer to Socrates' persistent questioning just gets up and moves away. His words and his ideas do not seem able to stay fixed and permanent. Socrates then offers to help by suggesting another way of approaching the problem.

He asks Euthyphro whether whatever is pious must also be just. When Euthyphro gives an affirmative answer, Socrates inquires whether piety is the same as justice, or whether piety is only part of what constitutes justice. The latter, he is told. In turn, Socrates demands to know what part of justice piety is. If he could find out, he tells Euthyphro, then he could go to his own trial and show his accusers that they should not prosecute him for impiety, since he would then know what piety is and would act accordingly.

In answering the question, Euthyphro offers another definition of "piety" and states that righteousness and piety are that part of justice dealing with the careful attention which should be paid to the gods. The remaining portion of justice deals with the careful attention that ought to be paid to men. Socrates requests a clarification of the meaning of the phrase, "careful attention." A clarification is needed, he points out, because in most cases where careful attention is paid to some object, like a horse or a person, the object is benefited or improved by the attention. Is this also true of the gods? Are they benefited or improved by piety? No. Therefore, it must be a different kind of attention that is involved.

To make his point clear, Euthyphro says that the kind of attention he has in mind is that which slaves pay their masters. Then, Socrates points out, piety is a type of service to the gods. Every service aims at accomplishing something. A doctor's service produces health; a shipwright's service produces a ship. But what does piety, which now seems to be a service, produce? Generally speaking, Euthyphro answers, the principal result achieved through piety, by means of words and actions in prayer and sacrifice that are acceptable to the gods, is the preservation of the state and of private families. The results of impiety are the undermining and destruction of everything.

In terms of this latest answer, Socrates again asks what piety and impiety are. Euthyphro now seems to be offering the view that piety is a science of prayer and sacrifice, a science that deals with asking of the gods and giving to them. Euthyphro insists this is exactly what he means, so Socrates proceeds to explore this latest definition of piety. To ask rightly of the gods is to ask of them what we need from them, and to give rightly to the gods is to give to them what they need from us. When Euthyphro agrees to this view Socrates points out that piety is the art of carrying on business between the gods and men. But it is a strange kind of business, since one side, man's, appears to receive all of the benefits. We are obviously benefited by what the gods give us. But what do we give in return? Also, are the gods benefited by it?

Euthyphro answers that what we give in return are honor and praise, which are gifts acceptable to the gods. Then, Socrates argues, piety is acceptable to the gods, but it does not benefit them, nor is it loved by them. Euthy-phro disagrees and insists that nothing is more loved by the gods than piety. So, Socrates asserts, piety means that which is loved by gods. Euthyphro agrees wholeheartedly.

Socrates then goes on to show Euthyphro that he has simply been talking around in a circle, and it is his own fault that his words will not stay put. They had agreed earlier in the discussion that the gods love piety because it is pious, and it is not pious because the gods love it. The fact that the gods love it is an effect of its nature and not its essential characteristic. Hence, there must be something which constitutes the fundamental characteristic of piety, that makes it what it is and causes the gods to love it. Either this conclusion is wrong, or Euthyphro has yet to answer the question, "What is piety?" Then Socrates begins all over again by asking that question.

Socrates points out once more that Euthyphro must know the answer in order to pursue his case against his father. Surely, he would not risk doing the wrong thing and offending the gods. Euthyphro wearily protests that he has no more time for the discussion, and he must rush off about his business. Socrates protests that he is left without the help he needs for his trial so that he can report that he knows what piety is, and hence will not commit any impieties in the future. At this point the dialogue ends.

The *Euthyphro* is one of the several superb short early dialogues that portray Socrates exposing the ignorance of supposedly wise men. When pressed, they are shown not to know what they are talking about. They cannot define basic concepts they deal with, such as "piety," "justice," and "courage," yet they are sure that what they are doing is pious, or just, or courageous. They are unwilling to undertake the difficult task of seeking to discover the meanings and natures of these terms. Their actions, based on their ignorance, can be disastrous, as is illustrated by both Euthyphro's charges against his father and the impending trial of Socrates.

CRITO

Author: Plato (427-347 B.C.)
Type of work: Ethics
First transcribed: Probably one of the early dialogues

PRINCIPAL IDEAS ADVANCED

Although Socrates has been unjustly accused of corrupting the young and has been sentenced to death, he refuses to escape because to escape would be to break an implicit agreement with the State to abide by its laws and judgments.

He argues that the important thing is not to live, but to live honorably.

It is never right to defend oneself against injury by an act of retaliation.

To remain in a state, after having been reared and educated under its laws, is, in effect, to agree to abide by its laws.

If Socrates were to escape a punishment legally decided upon by the State, he could no longer conduct himself as a philosopher devoted to justice and the love of wisdom.

The *Crito* is a relatively short dialogue which should be read in conjunction with and between the *Apology* and the *Phaedo.* The *Apology* gives an account of Socrates' trial and condemnation; the *Phaedo* describes his last conversations and death; the *Crito* recounts a friend's urgent plea for Socrates to avail himself of the ample opportunity to escape and the latter's justification on moral grounds for remaining in prison voluntarily, although the execution will occur two days after the present one. The dialogue is probably meant to explain Socrates' personal reasons for taking this course of inaction, rather than to prescribe a universally applicable norm for the individual unjustly condemned by the State, and some writers have suggested that Plato himself would probably have chosen to escape rather than to accept the sentence. Yet profound political, social, and moral issues are raised to which there are no easy solutions; their complications are such that readers may find their own judgments falling on either side of an exceedingly fine line.

When the dialogue opens, Socrates has been in prison a month, for no death sentences could be carried out in Athens during the annual voyage of the State vessel to Delos, in commemoration of the legendary deliverance of the city from the Minotaur by Theseus. But the ship is reportedly about to return, and Crito, having arrived at the

54

prison before dawn, is waiting for Socrates to awake, in order to break the news and try to persuade him to escape while there is yet time. It is typical of Socrates that he slumbers peacefully while Crito is wakeful and desperate, and that in the ensuing discussion it is Socrates who is the more rational and objective, though it is his own life which is at stake.

Crito's reasons for urging Socrates to escape, though perhaps on a less lofty plane than the latter's rebuttal, are not specious but are rather quite practical and persuasive. It is the weight of these, plus that of the circumstances under which Socrates was condemned, which gives the dialogue its moral significance. Crito begins by pointing out that if Socrates dies, an irreplaceable friend will have been lost, and besides, Crito will gain a reputation for loving money more than his friends, since many people will think he could have saved Socrates had he only been willing to put up the necessary cash; they will not believe that Socrates stayed in prison voluntarily.

Socrates answers that men of reason will believe only the truth; why should one regard majority opinion? Crito then points out that popular opinion is not to be taken lightly, which fact is confirmed by Socrates' present circumstances. But the philosopher replies that common people, unfortunately, are of limited capacity to do evil— since otherwise they could likewise do great good; actually they can make one neither wise nor stupid. (Here again we note the Socratic identification of wisdom and virtue, and his belief that no real evil can happen to a good man even if his body is destroyed.)

Crito acquiesces in this point but continues by assuring Socrates that he need not be concerned about any consequences to his friends if he chooses to escape (which apparently would have been quite easy under the circumstances, if not actually desired or intended by those who brought Socrates to trial). They are prepared to risk a large fine, loss of property, or other punishment. There is plenty of money available to buy off informers, and Crito knows men who will take Socrates out of the country for a moderate fee. Not only Crito's money, but also that of Simmias and Cebes—foreigners who would not be so liable to punishment—is at Socrates' disposal. At his trial Socrates had rejected banishment to a foreign society, but Crito assures him of comfort and protection among friends in Thessaly.

Furthermore, he continues, Socrates will do a wrong in voluntarily neglecting to save his life; he will be inflicting on himself the penalty his enemies wished. And what of his young sons? Will he not be failing them by leaving their education unfinished and deserting them to the lot of orphans? Crito finishes his argument by expressing once more his concern for the reputation both Socrates and his friends will incur if he refuses escape, a reputation for cowardice and lack of initiative resulting from (1) Socrates' unnecessary appearance in court (it was customary for Athenians whose conviction was probable to leave the country before trial), (2) the manner in which the defense was made (Socrates had refused all compromise and had deliberately taken a position which might, and did, result in conviction), and (3) the present situation, which will suggest sheer bungling and lack of spirit. In short, the suffering of Socrates' death will be augmented by disgrace.

To all this Socrates makes a reply remarkable for its calm, detached, and rational tenor. Much as he appreciates Crito's concern, he points out that his choice to face death is not a sudden impulse; his practice has always been to follow the course reason shows to be best. The question, then, is whether the opinions he has previously adopted are still true or whether their truth has been altered by the turn of events. We must not be frightened into a change of outlook, he reassures Crito, by imprisonment, loss of goods, or execution. With characteristic but kindly irony Socrates asks Crito to consider the matter with him, for since Crito is in no danger of death he is more likely to be impartial and objective!

Is it not true, he asks, that only some opinions are tenable and not all, that those to be respected are the good ones, and that these belong to the wise? And is it not the case that the opinions of the few qualified experts, rather than those of the masses, are to be regarded, as is illustrated in the case of athletic training? If this is true in general, then it follows that in the present case Socrates and Crito should be concerned only with what the expert in right and wrong will think, not with what the majority will say. The fact that the latter have the powers of life and death in their hands is really irrelevant to the argument.

In the considerations which follow, it is clear that Socrates is not at all interested in discussing the possibility or the means of escape, but rather its rightness or wrongness. His premises are that ". . . the really important thing is not to live, but to live well. . . . And . . . to live well means the same thing as to live honourably or

rightly." Crito's concern about expense, reputation, and the upbringing of Socrates' children are those of the common people, whose attitudes and acts are unrelated to reason. Socrates says: "Our real duty . . . is to consider one question only. . . . Shall we be acting rightly in paying money and showing gratitude to these people who are going to rescue me, and in escaping . . . or shall we really be acting wrongly in doing all this? If it becomes clear that such conduct is wrong, I cannot help thinking that the question whether we are sure to die, or to suffer any other ill effect . . . if we stand our ground and take no action, ought not to weigh with us at all in comparison with the risk of doing what is wrong."

Wrongdoing, Socrates holds, is reprehensible not merely on most but on all occasions; there are no exceptions. While most people think it natural and right to return wrongs done them, Socrates disagrees: ". . . it is never right to do a wrong or return a wrong or defend one's self against injury by retaliation. . . ." If this is so, and it is agreed that one should always fulfill morally right agreements, then it follows, Socrates concludes, that it would be wrong for him to leave without an official discharge by the State, for he would be doing the State an injury by breaking an implicit agreement with it. He explains what he means by personifying the Athenian Laws and Constitution and imagining the dialogue which might occur between them and himself were he to favor escape.

They would first point out to him that such an act would subvert the Laws and the State; the latter cannot subsist if its legal decisions are to be set aside for the benefit of individuals. But suppose that Socrates should retort that the proposed escape was in reprisal for the wrong done him by the State? The answer of the Laws to this would be that not only was there no provision made for such evasion and insubordination, but Socrates is under agreement to abide by the State's judgments. He has no legitimate complaint against them, the Laws continue, but rather positive obligations to abide by them. The Laws, by sanctioning the marriage of his parents, in a sense gave him life itself; they also provided a proper education for him. He is thus their child and servant, and as such does not have rights equal to theirs, any more than a son has the right to rebel against his father. Indeed, ". . . compared with your mother and father and all the rest of your ancestors your country is something far more precious, more venerable, more sacred, and held in greater honour both among gods and among all reasonable men. . . ." Whatever it orders one must do, unless he can justly persuade it otherwise (and of course, during the trial Socrates failed to persuade the jury, though he was confident he might have done so if given more time).

Now, in spite of all the blessings vouchsafed to Athenian citizens, the Laws continue, any young man upon reaching maturity may evaluate the political order and the administration of justice, and if he disapproves, he is free to leave the State with all his possessions. If, on the other hand, he surveys the political and judicial arrangement and voluntarily stays, his act is equivalent to an agreement to abide by the State's commands—or rather its proposals, since they are not blunt dictates and the citizen has the

choice of either obeying or persuading the State to change its decision. If Socrates should run away now, he would be more blameworthy than any other Athenian: his implicit agreement to abide by the law has been more explicit than than of any other citizen because he above all has remained at home, never crossing the border except while on military duty. Although he admired Sparta and Crete because of their good governments and respect for law, he has never emigrated to those city-states. And again, during the trial when the defendant was given the customary opportunity to propose an alternative penalty, Socrates did not choose banishment. His covenant with the State was thus made freely, consciously, and under no stress in relation to time—after all, he has spent seventy years in Athens.

Furthermore, the Laws ask, what will Socrates gain by escaping? The risk of banishment or loss of property would be inflicted upon his friends. If he entered well-ordered states, he would be regarded as a lawbreaker by their citizens and would confirm the jury's opinion of him. But if he chose to go to states with little or no respect for law and order, would that kind of life be worth while? He could not continue to converse as usual about goodness in persons and governments, for it would be hypocrisy to do so. He would not want to rear his children in such an environment, and if they remained in Athens, they would be more likely to receive good care with Socrates dead than with him alive illegally and in exile. Surely his friends, if true to their profession, would care for them.

In conclusion the Laws advise Socrates, ". . . do not think more of your children or of your life or of anything else than you think of what is right; so that when you enter the next world you may have all this to plead in your defence before the authorities there." To disobey by escaping will not really better either his friends or Socrates in this world or the next. "As it is, you will leave this place, when you do, as the victim of a wrong done not by us, the Laws, but by your fellowmen." But if he retaliates and returns evil for evil, breaking his agreement and wronging himself, his friends, his country, and the Laws themselves, he will incur the wrath of the Laws both here and in the next life.

Socrates thus concludes the speeches he has put in the mouth of the Laws and asks Crito whether he has anything to say in opposition to these arguments, which seem so persuasive that Socrates professes to be scarcely able to hear any others. Since Crito offers no refutation, the matter is decided: Socrates will obey the law even though it means his death.

Few readers will leave the *Crito* without making a personal judgment on Socrates' decision and his justification for it. The difficulty of making an adequate one is complicated by several factors: Socrates' trial, as far as we know, was legal. As Professor A. E. Taylor notes in discussing the *Apology,* the real reasons for which Socrates was prosecuted concerned matters for which general amnesty had been extended by the Act of Oblivion, and so the court could not have jurisdiction over these; hence the failure of Anytus and Meletus, Socrates' accusers, to explain their charges. However, though the ostensible charges were thus specious, and though Soc-

rates showed them to be ridiculous, the jury had voted in proper order to convict him, and so the letter of the law had been fulfilled. The very fact that this case clearly showed that an innocent and supremely good man could be condemned unjustly under the law and hence that the law needed revision was cited as an excellent reason for escape, but Socrates argued that such reform should be demanded at a time other than that at which his own fate was affected in order that reform would not be motivated by mere favoritism.

But—as Socrates makes the Laws say in the present dialogue—it is not the laws but the men administering them who wronged him. Socrates argued that respect for law in general is more valuable than one man's life lost by maladministration.

This again is a delicate point. Had the miscarriage of justice occurred merely through ignorance—though of course Socrates regarded vice as a kind of ignorance—it would have been easier to accept the sacrifice. But the reader finds it difficult to avoid feeling that the court is more intent on ridding Athens of Socrates than it is on reaching a just verdict. It is true that Socrates argued that were he to evade the death penalty, people would think him insincere in his former teaching about integrity and obedience to the law—but Crito might well have turned one of his own statements against him by replying that it is only what reasonable and wise men think that really matters. Nevertheless, the example set by escape might have been harmful to men of less comprehension.

Socrates perceived the value of consistency and stability in the State and its dispensation of justice. A state does not consist merely of the persons administering and living in it at any given time; to function best a state must have a continuity transcending the irregularities of individual fortunes. Presumably this was Socrates' intent in valuing the State above parents and ancestors, though modern Western readers may feel that Socrates revered the State too much. But whether the reader agrees with Socrates' decision here, he can hardly fail to admire the philosopher's devotion to principle, nor deny that the nobility of such a death enhances life for the living.

PROTAGORAS

Author: Plato (427-347 B.C.)
Type of work: Ethics, epistemology
First transcribed: Probably one of the early dialogues

PRINCIPAL IDEAS ADVANCED

In a discussion with the sophist Protagoras, Socrates raises some doubts concerning the claim that goodness can be taught; everyone is supposed to be qualified to speak about goodness, and good men have difficulty teaching goodness to their children.

He then wonders whether the virtues—justice, wisdom, temperance, and courage—are identical; Protagoras claims that they are not, but Socrates maneuvers Protagoras into admitting that wisdom, temperance, and justice are identical since they are all opposite to folly.

When Protagoras then insists that although three of the virtues discussed are identical, courage is different because it may be a reflection of passion, Socrates persuades him that no man is courageous who faces danger in passion and ignorance; only the wise are brave: courage is wisdom.

It is ironic, Socrates points out, that having begun by arguing that virtue cannot be taught, he ends by identifying virtue with wisdom or knowledge, which can be taught.

Plato's *Protagoras* is a brilliant dialogue. Besides being a splendid piece of argumentation, the dialogue is fine dramatically. In addition, it incorporates a picture of the sophist and a glimpse of the cultured aristocrats of the Periclean Age, facts which cannot fail to interest anyone who has a desire to know more about the life of classical Greece.

The dialogue is one of four great dialogues representing high points of Plato's literary activity, the *Republic,* the *Phaedo,* the *Symposium,* and the *Protagoras.* This was the period in which Plato reached his zenith as a literary artist. In literary quality the dialogue is surpassed only by the *Symposium,* and not all readers are willing to admit that even that work surpasses it. Philosophical development and dramatic development parallel each other precisely in the dialogue, exemplifying the high level Plato achieved in the very special literary type he used to write out his philosophy. Not only is the philosophical argument presented clearly and distinctly, but also the characters in the dialogue are drawn with great finesse. One comes to know not only the Protagorean position, but also the man Protagoras. The comic relief provided by Socrates' ridiculous analysis of Simonides' poem—a satire on the kind of literary criticism which must have been current in Periclean Athens—is a fine diversion, separating the preliminary discussion between Socrates and Protagoras from the final demonstration of the unity of the virtues. Another fine touch is the description of the sophist (Protagoras) marching back and forth in Callias' house, followed by his coterie (who are careful always to execute the necessary close order drill at the turns so that the flow of wisdom need not be interrupted). Then there is the irony of Socrates in saying how moved he is by Protagoras' long speeches, even though he cannot follow them—a remark which Socrates' subsequent arguments clearly reveal is a falsehood. Finally, there is Socrates' reduction of Protagoras to impotent fury at the end of the argument, so that when Socrates asks why he will no longer answer the questions, Protagoras explodes, "Finish the argument yourself!" Such a scene could not possibly be improved on as a description of the situation all philosophers would like to find themselves in vis-à-vis their opponents. Here is philosophical drama.

As the dialogue begins, Socrates explains to a companion how Hippocrates early one morning brought him the news that Protagoras was in Athens. Hippocrates hoped to be introduced to Protagoras by Socrates so that he might become one of Protagoras' pupils. Socrates was surprised at the request, and since it was still too early to go to Protagoras, the two friends spent the time in conversation until they could make the call. The dialogue goes back in time to that conversation.

Socrates asks Hippocrates why he wants to study with Protagoras. If he were to study with a physician he would become a physician, or if with a statuary, he would become a statuary. But what is Protagoras? The answer is that he is a sophist. But what does one learn from a sophist? Does Hippocrates wish to become a sophist? Hippocrates replies that he does not wish to become a sophist, but he thinks he can learn from Protagoras how to be a good public speaker. Such a reply does not satisfy Socrates since Hippocrates will learn from Protagoras not merely how to say something, but what to say. The sophist, Socrates points out, offers "food for the soul." The trouble is that one cannot first try a sample before buying food for the soul. The best advice in such a case is that one should exercise considerable care before letting another person "tend his soul." The two friends then go to call on Protagoras.

Socrates and Hippocrates go to the home of Callias, where Protagoras is staying, and a servant grudgingly ushers them into Protagoras' presence. This occasion offers Plato an opportunity to give the reader an amusing description of the Sophist. Protagoras is pictured as pompous and as eager for the attention his fawning disciples are paying him. He is marching back

60

and forth, passing judgment on important matters, followed by a group of admirers who cluster around him in a way that suggests reporters gathering around a celebrity today.

Protagoras' pomposity contrasts noticeably with the straightforward manner of Socrates, who, when he comes up to the sophist, introduces Hippocrates and, on his behalf, asks Protagoras what Hippocrates will learn if he studies with Protagoras. Protagoras frankly acknowledges his profession as a sophist, stating that he is the first to admit openly his profession. But Socrates is not to be put off without an answer to his question, so he asks Protagoras to state specifically what he teaches his students. Protagoras then replies that his students become better each day as a result of his instruction. Socrates asks if this means that Protagoras teaches good citizenship, that is, how to be a good man in the context of the Greek city state, and Protagoras replies that Socrates has understood him correctly.

Socrates then raises some doubts about whether this kind of goodness can be taught. He remarks that the Athenians, who are not all fools, recognize that particular men should be listened to as experts on such matters as ship building or medicine, but they regard all men as equally well qualified to speak on matters of goodness. Furthermore, men who are renowned for their personal goodness (for example, Pericles) feel that they cannot offer instruction even to their own children in this subject. So it seems that at least some persons are not willing to admit that what Protagoras professes to teach really can be taught. Can Protagoras reply to this?

Protagoras replies by launching into a long speech. He recites the fable of Prometheus and Epimetheus. Epimetheus, under Prometheus' supervision, was given the job of distributing the various qualities to the animal kingdom—swiftness to animals who were sought as prey, fur to animals who lived in cold climates, and so on—but he distributed all the qualities without leaving any for men. Prometheus then stole fire and knowledge of the industrial arts from heaven to make up for men's deficiencies. But, in spite of their knowledge, men were forced to live in cities for their mutual protection. This was impossible unless men were made ethically sensitive, so Zeus commanded Hermes to distribute conscience and moral sense to men, and to distribute them equally among all men. This myth describes the situation that exists, Protagoras says. All men are ethically sensitive, and all men must learn the principles of morality. All adults, quite properly, regard themselves as responsible for the moral education of the young, but some are better teachers than others in this area of moral instruction. Protagoras happens to be better than most people as a teacher.

Socrates professes to have been impressed by the splendid speech Protagoras has made, yet, characteristically, he has "a little question," which he is sure Protagoras can easily answer. Are the virtues—justice, wisdom, temperance, and courage—identical? Protagoras answers confidently that they are not, although they have certain likenesses and they are all parts of virtue, which itself is a unity. Socrates then presses to find out whether they are homogeneous parts of an aggregate (as a pail of water is a unity consisting of many uniform drops) or are heterogeneous parts which together make a unity (as eyes, nose, and mouth are parts of a face). Protagoras replies that they are heterogeneous elements which together make a unity.

Socrates now moves to the attack. He gets Protagoras to agree to the logical principle that a thing can have only one contrary opposite. He also gets the admission from Protagoras that *folly* is the opposite of both *wisdom* and *temperance*. This forces an alternative on Protagoras: either he must admit that wisdom is identical with temperance or he must abandon the logical principle. Protagoras reluctantly admits the identity of wisdom and temperance, and he tacitly concedes that justice and holiness, too, are identical. Socrates then pushes for the final admission, that justice and temperance are identical. However, since Protagoras senses that the argument is beginning to turn against him at this point, he tries to divert the argument. He launches into a long-winded discourse about the relativity of goods: what is good food for animals is not always good food for humans; oil may be good for massaging the body, but not good if taken as food.

But Socrates will have none of this. He pleads that he has a bad memory and therefore cannot remember long answers—he can only handle short ones. He knows Protagoras can speak either at length or with brevity, but he protests that he himself cannot manage long speeches. Will not Protagoras please confine himself to short answers? Protagoras, however, recognizing that he is losing the argument, refuses to let Socrates determine the rules for the debate. The discussion almost collapses at this point; Socrates remembers that he has an appointment

elsewhere which he must keep, and he begins taking his leave.

The listeners plead with the two disputants to continue. Plato uses this occasion to give the reader a brief glimpse of the other two sophists who are present, Hippias and Prodicus, by having them offer suggestions about how the discussion may be resumed. Prodicus urges them to "argue" but not to "wrangle" so that they will win "esteem" and not merely "praise." This type of discussion will give the hearers "gratification" rather than "pleasure," the latter reaction being concerned only with the body, while gratification is "of the mind when receiving wisdom and knowledge." Prodicus' linguistic pedantry, akin to that of some modern linguistic philosophers, emerges clearly in one paragraph to delight the reader. Hippias, too, is the butt of Plato's wit. He is made to say that all those present are really "kinsmen," by nature if not by law, and should conduct themselves as such. He is an advocate of the brotherhood of man, lofty in speech but with very little thought to fill out his speech.

Socrates finally rescues the situation by suggesting that he and Protagoras reverse their roles; Protagoras will ask the questions and Socrates will answer. Later on, when Protagoras has asked all the questions he desires, Socrates will resume his customary role as questioner. Protagoras agrees, even though he does so half-heartedly, and thus the dialogue can continue.

Protagoras is not the master of cross examination that Socrates is, however, and he soon loses the initiative. Protagoras begins questioning Socrates about a poem written by Simonides, pointing out an apparent contradiction in the poem. Socrates has a good deal of fun making long speeches which present a ridiculous literary analysis of the poem (and which show, incidentally, that he need not take a back seat to Protagoras in the matter of windiness). He appeals to Prodicus, the pseudo-expert on usage, to justify out and out equivocations; he cites the Spartans, who conceal their concern for knowledge under a counterfeit cultivation of physical prowess, as the most truly philosophical of all the Greeks. Nothing is too wild for him as he dissolves the contradiction with an exegesis of the poem which is undoubtedly a satire on the excesses of silly literary criticism in the Athens of the day. His serious point is well-taken, however, for he reminds Protagoras that one ought to judge a poem in the light of its total effect, instead of rejecting it because of one relatively minor flaw.

Socrates now gets back to the main argument. He asks Protagoras again whether the virtues are identical, and this time Protagoras admits that all are alike, with one exception—courage is different from the rest. Protagoras insists that men may be courageous either because they have knowledge or because they are in a passion. But it turns out that we do not really regard the man in a passion as courageous after all—he is foolhardy. What distinguishes the brave man from the foolhardy man who does the same deed is, of course, that the brave man knows the possible consequences of what he is doing. Thus, it turns out that courage really is identical with wisdom.

Socrates does not arrive at this conclusion directly, however. After Protagoras states that men may act bravely either out of knowledge or out of passion, Socrates shifts his attention to another problem. He raises the question whether whatever is good is also pleasant. Neither he nor Protagoras accepts the hedonistic version of this doctrine, but for the sake of the argument both agree to develop its consequences. As the reader might expect, it turns out that wisdom and courage are the same. The argument is as follows: Ordinary men believe that one always acts so as to increase the ratio of pleasure over pain for himself. However, sometimes men say that they are "overcome by pleasure," and hence do not do the good that they should. But if men always seek their own pleasure, and if whatever is good is also pleasant, this can only mean that they have chosen a lesser pleasure rather than a greater pleasure (or a lesser ratio of pleasure over pain instead of a greater ratio of pleasure over pain). If we add that no one ever knowingly does evil unless he is "overcome by pleasure," then the inference is clear that when a man does not do the good he has acted out of ignorance of what the good is. He has chosen short-range pleasure instead of long-range pleasure. This choice results only from his having failed to estimate the consequences of his act properly. Proper estimation of the consequences, however, is a matter of knowledge. So the conclusion which must be drawn is that the wise man is the good man—knowledge being identical with goodness (justice).

At the end of the argument Protagoras and Socrates part on surprisingly good terms, considering how near they came to conversational disaster earlier in the dialogue. Protagoras comments favorably on Socrates' skill in argument and predicts that he will become eminent in philosophy. Socrates courteously excuses himself and leaves. But just before these closing compliments, Socrates points out the paradoxical reversal of positions that has taken place in the course of the dialogue. Protagoras had taken the position at the beginning that virtue can be taught and said that he himself had adopted the teaching of it as his profession. At the end of the dialogue, however, Protagoras had been maintaining that virtue was not knowledge, and thus, by implication, he was denying that virtue can be taught. Socrates, on the other hand, had begun by raising doubts that virtue can be taught; he ended by identifying virtue with knowledge, thus implying that it can be taught. The reversal is not so strange as it seems at first glance, however.

Protagoras had implicitly identified virtue with skill at getting along in public affairs. Such skill cannot, of course, be taught. One must acquire it by doing it, by practicing. Socrates denies only that virtue can be taught when "virtue" is defined as a skill. If, on the contrary, virtue is not a skill, but is a form of knowledge, then of course it can be taught. Socrates has not shifted his position in any fundamental sense. At the end of the dialogue he still holds to his conviction that a skill cannot be taught. What he has done is to argue that virtue is knowledge, and, once this shift to the proper definition of virtue is made, he obviously must hold that virtue can be taught.

MENO

Author: Plato (427-347 B.C.)
Type of work: Metaphysics
First transcribed: Probably one of the early dialogues

PRINCIPAL IDEAS ADVANCED

Meno asks Socrates how to acquire virtue, and Socrates questions him in order to discover the nature of virtue; but Meno either uses the term, gives examples, or offers circular definitions.

The question arises as to how anyone can inquire about that which he does not know, for it would seem that one must know what one is inquiring about.

Socrates suggests that men's souls are immortal, and that in the course of their travels between reincarnations the souls acquire knowledge of all things; acquiring knowledge in this life, then, is an act of recollection.

Virtue can be taught if virtue is knowledge, but there appear to be no teachers of virtue; virtue must be a gift of the gods.

Plato's *Meno* is one of his early productions. It does not have the high dramatic quality characteristic of some of the dialogues Plato wrote shortly following the *Meno*; for example, the *Symposium* or the *Phaedo*. Also, the

64

philosophical problem discussed in the dialogue (whether virtue can be taught) receives better handling in other dialogues; Plato's best account of this question is found in the *Protagoras*. Nevertheless, the *Meno* is a well-known and important dialogue, for it is the *locus classicus* of one of Plato's most important philosophical doctrines—the doctrine of recollection. Indeed, it is perhaps Plato's earliest account of that doctrine, and the fullest illustration of what the doctrine came to mean to him.

The dialogue opens quite abruptly with Meno asking Socrates how one acquires virtue. Socrates replies that this question cannot be settled without first reaching agreement on a prior one, namely, what the nature of virtue itself is. As usual, Socrates professes not to know what virtue is, and, furthermore, he says that he has never met anyone else who knows. Meno naïvely remarks that Gorgias knew, to which Socrates replies that he has "forgotten" what Gorgias said. Meno then agrees to act in Gorgias' behalf, and inform Socrates on what Gorgias held virtue to be. This, of course, sets up a view which Socrates can examine and refute by his usual method of question and answer.

Meno's first attempt at defining "virtue" turns out to be formally inadequate. Instead of offering a definition of "virtue," he identifies what a man's virtue is, and what a woman's virtue is, and then says that each kind of person has his own peculiar virtue. Virtue is relative to the person and the condition in which the person finds himself. (There is one note here that Plato will pick up and make explicit in the *Republic*: that a thing's "virtue" is its *function*. He does noth-

ing with this idea here, however.) Meno's proposed definition fails since it does not define the term "virtue"; instead, he offers several other definitions, definitions which are substitution instances of the formula "the virtue of X is Y." He does not recognize that all of these presuppose some common meaning for the word "virtue" itself. Socrates, by citing a number of analogous cases, finally gets Meno to see what is involved and to offer a second definition.

Meno's second proposal is that virtue is "the power of governing mankind." This second definition does not have the same inadequacy as the first, but it still will not do, for the obvious reason that not all men govern others. Virtue must be possible for everyone, but if virtue is the power of governing, then it can be achieved only by the governors and must remain beyond the reach of the governed.

At this point Meno slips into enumerating the specific virtues, a mistake made by many of the people Socrates interrogates in the Platonic dialogues. Socrates then illustrates the kind of definition he is after by giving Meno an example of a proper definition for "figure" (in the geometrical sense).

For a third time Meno makes an attempt to define "virtue," this time by saying that "virtue is the desire for honorable things and the power of attaining them." By cross-examining Meno, Socrates draws the implications of this, showing it to be a circular definition. It amounts to saying that virtue is the power of achieving good with justice. That this is circular, in a sense, follows from Meno's admission that justice is one of the virtues. What it comes to, then, is this: Meno is saying that virtue *generally* is the power of achieving good in a *specifically* virtuous manner. This will not do, for "a specifically virtuous manner" is meaningless as long as "virtue generally" remains undefined.

At this point Meno confesses his confusion, but he tries to lay the blame on Socrates; it is characteristic of Socrates, he says, to confuse those who talk with him—Socrates is like the torpedo fish who paralyzes all with whom he comes into contact. Socrates accepts the comparison provided he can add a qualification concerning a respect in which he differs from the torpedo fish. The torpedo fish itself is not paralyzed when he comes into contact with another fish; Socrates, by contrast, is just as ignorant as those he argues with. But if this is so, Meno observes, there seems to be no point in trying to learn anything at all. He raises the stock puzzle of the eristic sophists: "How can one inquire about what one does not know; and if one already knows it, why should he inquire about it?"

In reply to this puzzle, Socrates puts forth the theory of recollection. He says that he heard from "certain wise men and women who spoke of things divine" that men's souls are immortal, and undergo an endless cycle of deaths and rebirths. In the course of these endless rebirths men's souls have come to know all things, both in this world and in the other world. Knowing, therefore, is not a matter of acquiring something new but, rather, a matter of recollecting something known but afterward forgotten. Meno is fascinated by this idea, and asks if Socrates can prove it to him. Socrates does not offer a direct proof of the theory, but he does offer what is supposedly an illustration of it by getting Meno's slave boy, who has been given no training in mathematics, to construct a proof in geometry merely by answering certain questions Socrates puts to him.

The proof itself is fairly simple, but not at all obvious. The problem is to determine how long the side of a square must be if its area is to be twice the area of a given square. Socrates diagrams a square and arbitrarily sets the side equal to two units. The area of the original square is, of course, four square units. Using the diagram, Socrates next shows the boy what the diagonal is. Then he asks the boy how many units long the sides of a square twice the area of the original square will be; that is, a figure which has an area of eight square units. At first the boy says that the side of the required figure will be four units long, but under questioning, and by referring to the diagram, he sees that this answer would yield a square whose area is sixteen square units rather than eight. He then guesses that the side of the required square should be three units long, but again he recognizes that this is not the answer since it yields a figure with an area of nine square units. Finally, he sees that by constructing a square on the diagonal of the original figure he will have the required solution, a square whose area is twice the area of the original one. Socrates, without telling the boy the answer, has elicited it merely by asking questions.

Socrates points out to Meno that the boy could not have learned the solution subsequent to his birth because he has never been given any instruction in geometry, nor did Socrates himself tell the boy the solution. Therefore, the boy must have known the solution all along, and Socrates' questions served merely as an occasion for the boy's recalling what he knew but had forgotten. The point of the example is to refute the claim of the eristic sophists that nothing can be learned. In spite of the apparent self-evidence of their paradox, the fact is that ignorant persons can come to know something as a result of intellectual inquiry. It is better to engage in inquiry, even if it merely reveals that a proposed solution is inadequate, than it is to imagine that there is no value at all in intellectual inquiry.

The discussion is shortly brought back to the original topic, whether virtue can be taught. Meno wants Socrates' own view of the matter. But Socrates replies that he cannot deal directly with this question. He must, he says, first lay down a *hypothesis*, since he and Meno have not yet defined "virtue." Considerable discussion has centered around what Socrates says here about hypotheses. He gives, as an example of a hypothesis, another illustration taken from geometry. He says that a geometrician, if asked whether a certain triangle can be inscribed within a given circle, may answer that he must first lay down a hypothesis. A. E. Taylor, in *Plato, the Man and His Work*, suggests that Socrates means that some geometrical problems are not susceptible to a general solution—only when some restriction is laid down is a solution possible. We need not pause here in an effort to determine all the niceties of the proper interpretation of the passage, however. The development of the dialogue can be seen without our having to establish Plato's meaning in all its technical detail. The point is this: Socrates is willing to discuss the ques-

tion whether virtue can be taught if Meno will grant the restriction that virtue is knowledge. This must be granted as an initial assumption (hypothesis) before the discussion can proceed. Meno agrees to the restriction.

Once it is granted that virtue is knowledge, the conclusion that it can be taught follows easily; indeed, the conclusion seems trivial. But it raises another question which is not trivial; namely, who are the teachers of virtue? Meno suspects that there must be some such teachers, but Socrates again professes ignorance; he has found none. But perhaps, Socrates suggests, Anytus, who is listening to the conversation, can tell Socrates and Meno who the teachers of virtue are.

Anytus has no uncertainties; of course there are teachers of virtue, but they are not to be found among the sophists (such as, for example, Gorgias). Any Athenian gentleman is a fine teacher of virtue. (It adds to the irony of this part of the dialogue to know that this Anytus was the leader of the group of Athenian "gentlemen" who prevailed on Meletus to bring the charges which led to the conviction and execution of Socrates.) But Socrates wants to know who taught these Athenian gentlemen who teach virtue. Obviously, Anytus responds, a previous generation of Athenian gentlemen taught them. Plato does not pursue this matter; it is clear enough to any reader that this answer leads to a troublesome regress. But on other grounds Socrates is not satisfied with this general answer. He grants that there have always been good men to be found in Athens. However, if one takes time to look at the particular histories of some of these good Athenians and their sons, he finds many cases where the father has taken care to have his sons instructed in such things as horsemanship or wrestling, and the instruction has been successful. Yet in the matter of virtue, either the sons have received no instruction, or else the instruction has not achieved its purpose, for the sons have turned out to be considerably less virtuous than the fathers. Themistocles and Pericles are good examples.

Anytus' argument has been shown to be inadequate, and he recognizes the fact, but instead of pursuing the question in the proper spirit, he loses his temper and issues a pointed warning to Socrates to watch his step in criticizing the Athenian aristocracy in this way. Socrates, in good-humored fashion, returns to Meno.

It seems, Socrates points out, that the outcome of the investigation into whether virtue can be taught is finally negative, in spite of the previous restriction. For if there are no teachers of virtue, and no scholars of virtue, then the apparent conclusion is that virtue must not be capable of being taught. Perhaps, however, another possibility should be examined. Perhaps true opinion is just as good a guide for action as is knowledge. Perhaps men can become virtuous by holding true opinions. The only drawback to this theory is that true opinions are like the statues of Daedalus —they are very valuable, but unless they are tied down they walk away. True opinions must be tied down by recollection of the truth; that is, true opinion must become knowledge. Men can get along by holding true opinions which they get from great statesmen and poets, but true opinion

must be converted into knowledge in order to become completely adequate. Virtue, then, is neither taught nor is it something which men have "by nature" (as the sophists held). It is, finally, a gift from the gods. This is the explicit conclusion of the dialogue. However, Plato obviously expects the reader to amend this conclusion on his own. Plato expects the reader to recognize that knowledge and virtue are identical, and that it is really knowledge which is the gift of the gods.

For the remainder of this article the doctrine of recollection will be considered in more detail, since it is a matter about which there is some dispute among scholars.

There is no debating the fact that Plato did hold a doctrine of recollection. References to it are to be found throughout Plato's writings, and it lies at the center of his theory of knowledge. The debate concerns just what the theory of recollection amounted to for Plato. Specifically, did Plato's belief in the doctrine of recollection include a belief in the preëxistence of the soul? Scholars have given both affirmative and negative answers to this question. The interpretation suggested in what follows is this: there is not enough evidence to show conclusively that Plato did believe in the preëxistence of the soul. Regardless of how one settles this question, however, the crucial point for Plato's theory of knowledge is that he held that knowledge is in some sense innate.

The evidence cited by those who say that Plato really did believe in the preëxistence of the soul includes the following points: (1) Socrates calls the doctrine a "glorious truth" in the

Meno; (2) the Platonic view that the Ideas are separate from the things of sense, and that the soul knows the Ideas, implies that the separation of the Ideas and the preëxistence of the soul stand or fall together; (3) the first argument for the immortality of the soul which is given in the *Phaedo* assumes the truth of the doctrine of the preëxistence of the soul. Each of these claims must be countered if one is to conclude that Plato did not hold to the preëxistence of the soul.

With reference to the first claim, that Socrates calls the doctrine a "glorious truth," one may make the following observations. Plato here adopts his standard technique for introducing a myth in presenting the doctrine in the *Meno*; that is to say, he does not put the doctrine into the mouth of Socrates directly. Instead, he has Socrates say that he heard this from certain poets and wise men. This is the device Plato repeatedly uses when he wishes to state a myth which expresses an important truth but which is not to be taken literally. Indeed, the emphasis in reading the words "glorious truth" seems to fall on "glorious" rather than on "truth," suggesting that the doctrine cannot readily be expressed in literal terms.

The second assertion above, that the separation of the Ideas and the preëxistence of the soul go together, is too strong. Certainly no one can deny that Plato asserted the separation of the Ideas and that he believed the soul was the element in a man which knows the Ideas. But Plato might very well hold these views without also holding that the soul existed before its incarnation in the body.

The third claim, that the first argument for immortality in the *Phaedo* assumes the preëxistence of the soul, neglects the fact that the first two arguments of the *Phaedo* are questioned in that dialogue, and that the conclusion of the *Phaedo* is finally made to rest on the claim that the soul is *essentially* alive; at the approach of its essential opposite, death, the soul either retires or is annihilated. Furthermore, the conclusion of the *Phaedo* is that the belief in immortality is reasonable, not certain. Plato argues that the belief in immortality is consistent with other common-sense beliefs. The conclusion of the *Phaedo* rests on *agreed* premises; Plato never claims that they are incontrovertibly *true*, as anyone who takes seriously the account of Socratic method given in the *Phaedo* should immediately recognize.

If the above arguments are sound, the most plausible conclusion is that we cannot be certain Plato held that the theory of the preëxistence of the soul was a necessary part of the doctrine of recollection. But if this is the case, the question arises: why, then, does he mention the preëxistence of the soul? When we remember that preëxistence is part of the myth, and that this means that an important truth is being expressed—though not necessarily in literal language—the proper interpretation comes readily to mind. Plato means to say by his doctrine of recollection that knowledge is not learned, but is in some sense innate. Undoubtedly Plato, who wrote his philosophy before Aristotle had made logic into an independent discipline, was not so sophisticated in logical matters as were philosophers who followed him. It would be highly unreasonable, therefore, to expect him to have recognized the significance of the relation of logical implication. A modern philosopher might say of the slave boy's demonstration that he recognized, under appropriate questioning, the logical implications of the geometrical situation Socrates diagramed, and that the ability to recognize such implications is innate. Such a view, while perhaps not the most popular current view, nevertheless is not totally disreputable. On the contrary, it represents the spirit of the rationalist tradition in philosophy as it was given expression by such important thinkers as Descartes and Spinoza. Plato's myth, it seems, is his expression of the rationalists' insight, an insight which had to wait for greater logical sophistication before it could be expressed properly. Plato had the insight, but he lacked the appropriate apparatus for expressing it in terms that contemporary philosophers easily recognize.

Regardless of how one interprets the theory of recollection as it is presented in the *Meno*, there can be no disagreement that the *Meno* is an important element in the Platonic corpus. It is probably as good a place as any to begin reading Plato. The subject of the dialogue, the relation between virtue and knowledge, is central to Plato's ethical views; the use of illustrations from geometry to clarify knowing reflects Plato's underlying mathematical bias; and the theory of recollection itself is closely tied to the central Platonic doctrine, the theory of Ideas. One who reads the *Meno* will find it a first-rate introduction to the thought of one of the truly great thinkers in the history of Western civilization.

GORGIAS

Author: Plato (427-347 B.C.)
Type of work: Philosophy of rhetoric, ethics
First transcribed: Probably one of the early dialogues

PRINCIPAL IDEAS ADVANCED

Socrates and Gorgias discuss the question concerning the uses of rhetoric, and Socrates initiates the discussion by describing rhetoric as the art of persuasion.

But, Socrates argues, if the rhetorician has no knowledge of what he proclaims, it is a case of the ignorant attempting to teach the ignorant; furthermore, if he discourses on justice, he must have knowledge of justice, and if he has knowledge of justice, he is just—consequently, he could not tolerate the unjust, which would be talking without having knowledge of what one was talking about.

Since all men desire to act for the sake of some good, no man can act as he wills if he acts in ignorance of the good; if a man acts wrongly, he acts in ignorance of the evil that he does.

Consequently, punishment should aim at rehabilitation, and it is better to be punished for one's misdeeds than to escape punishment.

70

From all this, Socrates argues, it follows that rhetoric should be used to make men aware of injustice and of the cure for injustice.

Callicles argues that natural justice is the rule of the stronger, but Socrates suggests that the wise are the strong; and Callicles then argues that the wise man seeks pleasure for himself, but Socrates shows that pleasure and pain are not identical with the good and the bad.

The *Gorgias* of Plato is an interesting if somewhat rambling dialogue in which several issues typical of Socratic inquiry are discussed. Since Socrates himself was concerned with discussion as a means of arriving at the truth, he naturally examined the claims of others to have a "vocal" way to it. The sophists were the itinerant teachers of ancient Greece, teaching their pupils to debate with others any side of an issue and to win the argument. Rhetoric was their art; by persuasion, they argued, one could control the state and gain wealth. Gorgias, one of the better-known sophists, engages Socrates in discussion over the merits and meaning of rhetoric. The position he presents is not so arbitrary as some of the claims made by other sophists, but nonetheless it is subjected to a scathing analysis by Socrates. Callicles, a rather ill-mannered member of the group, also joins in the debate. The larger question with which they are concerned is "What is the purpose of rhetoric, and, more generally, any kind of discussion?" Akin to this are discussions of justice, the role of punishment, and pleasure and pain as good and evil.

Socrates is concerned in the opening of discussion with finding out exactly what rhetoric is as an art. It is concerned with persuasive discourse and aims at giving those who practice it power over others. The recipients of this art (persuasion) are those present in the law courts and assemblies of the land and the subject matter is the just and the unjust. Supposedly, in teaching an art, the sophists know their subject and inform others. At this, Socrates discusses learning and believing, which are intimately connected with teaching and studying. When one has learned, then he has knowledge; he cannot be mistaken. If one only believes, then he can be mistaken, for there is false as well as true belief. Both Socrates and Gorgias agree that one can persuade others without regard to belief or knowledge—rhetoric apparently has to do with persuading people to believe. But as we might guess, although it is not brought up here, the Socratic method of dialectical discussion, rather than rhetoric, is the persuasion which leads to knowledge.

Gorgias holds that the rhetorician has a powerful tool by which men may gain much; they may sway anyone and accomplish anything. The rhetorician should be just, however, and should not use his power for evil consequences, although having taught it to others, he is not responsible for their misuse of it. (This point is of dramatic interest since at his trial Socrates was held responsible for the activities of his pupil, Alcibiades.)

Socrates rejects the view that one can teach anything of which one is ignorant. If the rhetorician persuades only those who are ignorant (those who know need no persuading) and he, himself, does not know—hence, is ignorant—then do we not have a case of the ignorant attempting to teach the ignorant? Gorgias has stated that the rhetorician discourses on justice, injustice, good, and evil, but if he is ignorant of these, then the same paradox holds. Gorgias has also stated that the rhetorician should not make bad use of his art, but he has admitted the possibility of his doing so. Also, under Socrates' questioning he has conceded that if the rhetorician has knowledge of the just, then he is just; but if he is just, then he cannot be unjust. Practicing his art badly would be unjust. It appears to be inconsistent that the rhetorician could make bad use of his art unless we admit that he does not know his art. For it is a Socratic principle that he who knows, knows what to do and what not to do, whereas the ignorant know neither.

Socrates then questions whether it is proper to call rhetoric an art. He proceeds in the following manner. Both the body and soul may be considered under two headings: the body under gymnastic and medicine; the soul under legislative (wherein the art of politics is found) and justice. When these divisions function properly, the individual is sound in body and soul, and his highest good is approached; but there are sham divisions which bear a resemblance to the real ones but of which there is not knowledge as in the first case but only a seeming knowledge. Socrates believes that these do not work for the best interests of the individual. They are, respectively, attiring (dressing up) and cookery, sophistry and rhetoric. They are based on experience (belief or opinion) rather than on reason, and make a pretense to knowledge.

When it is objected that those who can sway others (the rhetoricians) control the state and have real power, Socrates replies in a manner typical of him by distinguishing between the way a man acts and the way he ought to act. He argues that without knowledge men cannot do as they will. We do things not for themselves but for some sake or purpose. In so doing we do what we will. For Socrates, ultimately all that we will is done for the sake of the good. (The good is a complicated concept in Plato's philosophy. Although his explanation is not meant to be complete, it means, at least, that in willing one acts so that the health and harmony of the body and soul are maintained.) Now, if to do good is to do that which one wills, then one cannot will to do evil. (This is another instance of the Socratic maxim that no man does wrong knowingly.) But it is held that the man who can kill with impunity is in an enviable position. Socrates replies to this claim by an analysis of punishment and injustice.

Socrates holds that the man who acts because he knows what he wills is the happy man, for he is master of himself. The unjust man in ignorance knows not what he will, so that seeking what he mistakenly believes is good (no man does wrong knowingly), he is wretched in his failure to be at one with himself. Punishment is not primarily retributive but aims at the rehabilitation of the unjust man to prevent him from doing that which is bad; hence, punishment aims at his eventual happiness, for the wicked when punished are less miserable than when they go unpunished. In this view, the individual who does injustice is worse or more evil than he who suffers injustice, and certainly not to be envied. When properly administered, punishment is the medicine of the soul. If rhetoric has a use, it is to allow a man to become aware of his own injustice and seek a proper cure for it; if he be not unjust, then he had no use for rhetoric.

It is here that Callicles enters the discussion. He accuses Socrates of intentionally turning the whole of life upside down and of telling those who listen to his prattling that they are doing exactly the opposite of that which they ought to do. Philosophy may be amusing when practiced by the young, who in so doing are looked upon as precocious by their elders, but in a man it is unseemly, especially for one such as Socrates, who ought to be out earning a living instead of annoying his betters. The life that Callicles asserts is the normal one is that in which the stronger rule their inferiors by force, the better rule the worse, and the noble have more than the lowly. When this state occurs, natural justice prevails. But Socrates takes Callicles quite literally (and thus paves the way for a discussion with him since to make his position precise he has to modify his initial statement) and points out that although the many are the superior or stronger, they hold that to do injustice is more disgraceful than to suffer it. Callicles modifies his point and claims that the stronger are the more excellent, not the mob; and they are also the wiser. Socrates counters that since those who practice an art are wiser with regard to it than those who do not, trained shoemakers or cobblers ought to receive more benefits than those inferior to them in these arts. In addition, Socrates points out that the wiser may also take less than those who do not know; for example,

a wise dietitian may eat less food than the ignorant man. Knowledge does not always prescribe more but what is proper, and that may be more, less, or the same depending upon what is needed. Again, we encounter the Socratic principle that wisdom is knowing what to do and what not to do.

Callicles rejects this argument and brings up yet another, although related, position. The wise man knows how to satisfy himself, to realize his wants; the happy life is to strive for the satisfaction of pleasures. Socrates counters that the intemperate man who is never satisfied is like a leaky vessel that cannot be filled because it empties at a faster rate. Such a man is the slave of his wants; he cannot be satisfied and hence cannot be happy; it is he who wants not who is happy. For Callicles, he who wants not is dead; it is the continual gratification of desires which leads to the full life. Socrates retorts that such an all-embracing statement permits one to draw odd consequences. The man with a constant itch who spends his life in scratching must then be a happy man. The point is that unless we distinguish kinds of pleasures and pains and pursue some while avoiding others, there is not much to be gained from the sort of view that Callicles offers. Furthermore, the view under examination appears to equate pleasure with good and pain with evil, whereas Socrates holds them distinct. He proceeds as follows: it will be granted that opposites cannot exist together at the same time and in the same place. Good and evil are opposites, yet it can be shown that pleasure and pain can be present in the same individual at the same time. In order to satisfy thirst, which is painful, an individual may drink water which tastes pleasant and, according to Socrates, experience pain and pleasure at the same time in the same place. If pleasure and pain were identifiable with good and evil, then the bad man would be as good or as bad as the good man, since they have about the same amount of pleasures and pains. Lastly, with regard to this idea, when a man slakes his thirst, both the pain and the pleasure go respectively, but when a man purges evil from his soul and the good is with him, the good remains.

Callicles is now willing, as Socrates suggested earlier, to differentiate between pleasures, calling some good and others bad. But then we are back to the view that it is not pleasure alone that determines how we shall act, but rather that we must know what to choose and what not to choose as pleasures before we may pursue them; knowledge is the key to our action. This fact takes Socrates back to his earlier discussion concerning true arts, flattery, and sham. Rhetoric, as discussed by its proponents, appeals only, and indiscriminately, to the pleasure of the individual and not to the good; hence it can be classified as a sham. It is the harmony and order of the soul or the body which must be aimed for, not the gratification of passions. Harmony of the soul and body is the criterion by which we must judge their fitness; when present in the body it is called "health," when in the soul, "law." From these spring the virtues of temperance and justice; he who would practice the art of rhetoric should aim at bringing harmony to the citizenry. When a person is sick, either physically or mentally, he seeks the services of a doctor. When the physician prescribes a cure, it may well be that he forbids the satisfaction of certain wants in order to improve the patient's health.

The rhetorician who aims at getting what he wants and abusing his society is much like the tyrant discussed in Plato's *Republic*. Intent on satisfying his every desire, a slave to his passions, not knowing how to control himself, he can get the best of no one, for he knows not what is best for himself. He who would lead others must first know how to lead himself. The art of rhetoric is, as we saw, no art at all. The art of ruling, on the other hand, is perhaps the most difficult and serious art of all; it calls for men who have had experience and who have demonstrated their ability, so that when entrusted with the rule of society it will be the good or benefit of the ruled which will be their primary objective. The benefit of an individual does not reside in a misdirected search for satisfaction but in that harmony of body and soul wherein lies health and law.

SYMPOSIUM

Author: Plato (427-347 B.C.)
Type of work: Metaphysics, philosophy of love
First transcribed: Probably one of the middle dialogues

During a banquet a number of speeches praising the god Love are delivered; the first speech, by Phaedrus, makes the claim that love between virtuous men and youths is of the highest type, the chief motive to a noble life.

Pausanias distinguishes between common Love, which is of the body, and heavenly Love, which is the love of virtue and philosophy.

Eryximachus the physician argues that love is the principle of harmony which reconciles the hostile elements in the body.

Aristophanes, satirizing physiological theories of love, maintains that the human body was originally round, having four arms, four feet, a head with two faces—and so forth—and that Zeus, to punish men for rebellion, split them in two; ever since that time, the halves have sought each other avidly; the desire to be reunited is love.

Agathon praises Love as the most beautiful and youngest of the gods, possessed of all the virtues.

Socrates explains how from a love of the beauty of physical objects one can pass to the apprehension of the nature of Beauty itself, the ideal, and thereby share Love's divinity.

The *Symposium* is perhaps Plato's masterpiece as a work of art, though other dialogues are of greater philosophical import. Its great range, from discussions of physical love to an almost mystical vision of eternal, absolute beauty, makes it both art and philosophy. This range of subject and level of discussion is reflected in the original Greek and in some translations by differences in the language and style of individual speakers, and the contrasts thus afforded contribute to the dramatic excellence of the work. The dramatic effect is also enhanced by the order and structure of the dialogue, which is an account by Apollodorous of a banquet described to him by Aristodemus. At the banquet a number of speeches are given, leading up to and culminating in that of Plato's beloved teacher and paragon of philosophy, Socrates.

The dramatic poet Agathon has just won the prize for his first tragedy and is celebrating at home with his guests. Because of the aftereffects of yester-

day's drinking, it is agreed that the entertainment shall consist chiefly of conversation. Eryximachus recalls Phaedrus' frequent observation that while other gods and heroes have had ample praises and honors, Love has been singularly neglected, and so he proposes that each man deliver a speech praising this god. All agree to this proposal, Socrates remarking that he claims understanding of nothing other than this subject. Readers familiar with Socrates will see in this statement a hint that the symposium on Love will remain on no ordinary level, for Socrates, above all his contemporaries, is able to transcend the sensual.

Since the topic originated with Phaedrus, Plato's friend, he is invited to speak first. Phaedrus' speech is a rather commonplace encomium setting the stage for later speeches. He describes Love as the oldest of the gods, full of power and the author of the greatest blessings. Conceiving love of the highest type as that between virtuous men and youths, Phaedrus believes that the chief motives to the noble life are the desire for honor and the fear of dishonor and shame. The love between men is above all else the source of this motive, for the lover and the beloved hate nothing more than disgrace in each other's eyes; hence, they are courageous and self-sacrificing, even to the point of death. A nation or army constituted by such lovers would be almost invincible. Thus, Love not only serves as the chief source of virtue, but also, as seen in the stories of Alcestis and Achilles, gives happiness after death.

Pausanias thinks the foregoing is indiscriminate. Love is not one but twofold; one part is noble and one part is not. There is an elder, heavenly Aphrodite, daughter of Uranus and having no mother, and also a younger, common Aphrodite, daughter of Zeus and Dione. Therefore, there are two Loves, the offspring of each. The common Love, whose mother was of both male and female parentage, desires either women or youths and is merely of the body, without regard for good or evil, the noble or the base, and being of the body in its craving, is also like the body in temporality. The heavenly Love, however, whose mother was born from the male alone, seeks the male as the more valiant and intelligent. Lovers of this sort seek out youths of promising virtue and intellect with the intent of educating and developing them. Lovers of the body have brought only disgrace on Love, and some societies disapprove of attachments between men and youths; the question of their propriety is not simple, depending on whether the attitudes and manners involved are honorable or not. Pausanias thinks that when love of youths and the practice of philosophy and virtue

coalesce, this love is noble and mutually profitable.

While modern readers may find any variety of homosexuality distasteful, a balanced perspective requires that one remember the distinction Pausanias makes between the two kinds of love, as well as the fact that since Greek women were not educated morally and intellectually, communion with them could not attain the level of that between men.

The next speech affords a transition to a higher plane when the physician Eryximachus declares his discovery from medicine that love is indeed twofold, but not just in man; this duality is a universal principle. His position, reminiscent of Heraclitus' and Empedocles' teachings, is illustrated by the fact that in the body there are hostile loves and desires both healthy and diseased; medicine is the art of satisfying the one type, eliminating or converting the other. Hostile elements in the body must be reconciled if there is to be health, just as a proper arrangement of high and low notes is needed to produce musical harmony, and an orderly combination of short and long beats to produce rhythm. Hot and cold, moist and dry must be blended by harmonious love in order to secure the well-being of men, animals, and plants; whereas if wanton love causes an excessive degree of one element, injury follows. Even divination or communion between men and the gods is concerned with enhancing the good and curing the evil love. The former originates happiness and harmony with gods and men.

Eryximachus' speech is serious and apparently intended to be scientific, but it is followed by that of the great comic dramatist Aristophanes, who

76

satirizes current physiological theories. In order to explain the power of love properly, Aristophanes first gives the background of human nature: Originally there were three sexes—male, female, and the male-female. The body was round, having four arms, four feet, two sexual organs, and one head with two faces. This race became so powerful it attacked the gods in heaven. Zeus, in order to punish men without destroying them—since after all the gods would not wish to forego the sacrifices and worship men provided—reduced their power and doubled their number by splitting them in two. The two halves, however, sought each other avidly, and when reunited would not separate long enough to tend to the usual affairs of life; hence, they began to perish. While in the original division the face had been turned around to the sectioned side, the sexual organs had not; now Zeus contrived to move them around so that when the two halves of the man-woman came together, conception and reproduction would occur, or if two halves of males or females embraced, sexual gratification would prepare them to return to their daily tasks. Consequently, sections of the double nature lust after members of the opposite sex, but halves of the other two sexes seek their own kind. Males who seek the male, therefore, are not shameless but rather desirous of the manly and best, as is evinced by the number of statesmen so inclined. The association is not merely sexual, however; it stems from a most fundamental desire for fusion into one being. Perfect satisfaction and happiness would lie in reunion with the original other halves of our nature, but failing this, next best is to find loves congenial to us. Thus Love leads us back to our own nature in this life and the next, and hence it deserves highest praise.

So ends Aristophanes' speech, in the main highly fantastic but with a germ of truth in its description of the desire for unity. Professor A. E. Taylor even suggests that it might distantly foreshadow Socrates' coming account of the soul as longing for communion with its true good.

Agathon's turn is next. As might be expected of a dramatic poet, his remarks are rhetorically brilliant rather than philosophically cogent. He argues that Love is the most beautiful of the gods because the youngest, and the youngest because swift enough to outrun old age. Love is tender and soft because he goes about and dwells in the softest places, the hearts and souls of gods and men. He is just, neither suffering nor exerting force—all men serve him of their own wills. He is temperate, because temperance rules pleasure and no pleasure is greater than that of love. That he is courageous is evident in that Ares yielded to Aphrodite. He must be wise, for he is a poet and at his touch teaches everyone to become a poet! He is the creator of all animals, inspirer of all arts, peacemaker among the gods. His is the love of beauty rather than of deformity, and as the author of love of the beautiful he has originated every heavenly and earthly good. Agathon's praise ends in a grand flourish of words which win the acclaim of all present and which Socrates uses as occasion for pretended dismay as Agathon's successor.

Actually, however, Plato exploits this florid but somewhat vacuous panegyric as a stage setting for the more substantial and more enduring lustrous speech of Socrates. He did not realize,

Socrates says, that the intent was to praise Love by giving him every good quality without regard for the facts. Socrates knows only how to speak the truth, and he will proceed only if that is what the other wishes to hear. Upon their reassurance, Socrates begins by asking questions, as is his wont, to which the answers given by Agathon lead up to the desired conclusions. By this dialectical method he shows that since love is love *of* or desire *for* something, love cannot presently possess the object of its affection. Even when one is said to desire that which he has, what is really meant is that one desires its continued or future possession. Now it was stated that love is one of the beautiful rather than of the deformed; if so, it follows that love cannot itself be beautiful. (While this reasoning is not altogether convincing, the general point that desired qualities pertain to the object rather than to the subject's desire is plausible.) And since there is a basic identity between the good and the beautiful, it follows also that love wants, rather than has, the good.

Socrates now proceeds to an account of Love allegedly taught him by a woman of wisdom, Diotima of Mantineia. Love is neither fair (handsome or beautiful) nor good, but this does not imply that he is ugly or evil. Just as there is a mean between wisdom and ignorance—right opinion, which is not wisdom because it cannot give adequate reason for its belief, and which is not ignorance, since it is true —so there is a mean between beauty and ugliness, good and evil. Furthermore, Love is not a god, for the gods are admittedly happy, beautiful, and in possession of all goods. Love is neither mortal nor immortal, but an intermediate spirit who interprets between gods and men by forwarding prayers and sacrifices to the gods and commands and answers to men. The understanding of this function of Love is spiritual wisdom, whereas knowledge of skills and arts is of a much lower order. (Presumably this remark is intended for Agathon, who instanced Love's wisdom by showing him to be the source of poetry.)

As to Love's ancestry, Diotima told this tale: On Aphrodite's birthday the gods held a feast at which Poros (Plenty), son of Metis (Discretion), became tipsy on nectar and lay down to sleep. Penia (Poverty), having come to the door to beg as usual, saw an opportunity to better herself and lay down by Poros; thus Love was conceived. Both because Aphrodite is beautiful and Love was born on her birthday, he is now her devotee. But in accordance with his mixed parentage are his character and fortune; because of his mother he is poor, rough, squalid, without a roof over his head, but like his father he is scheming, bold, aggressive, clever, strong, a great enchanter. Neither mortal nor immortal, he flourishes at one moment, perishes the next. His intermediate nature also makes him a philosopher; gods and wise men already possess wisdom, and the ignorant are self-satisfied—this is the evil of ignorance—but Love as a mean between the ignorant and the wise is a lover of wisdom, since "wisdom is a most beautiful thing, and Love is of the beautiful. . . ." Socrates' and his companions' previous error in attributing qualities such as beauty and wisdom to Love lay in confusion between love and the beloved.

"Of what use is love to man?" Socrates asked Diotima. Her reply was that this amounted to asking what man desires in loving the beautiful; it turns out that what he really desires is possession of the good, which is what we mean by "happiness." But we cannot ask again why one desires happiness, since happiness is an ultimate end. All men seek happiness rather than something like the other half of themselves; love, then, is really "of the everlasting possession of the good." A further question concerned the manner of the pursuit of love's object. All men, Diotima continued, desire to procreate the beautiful, whether in body or in soul. Love is not, therefore, of the beautiful alone but of "generation" in beauty (of what today we would call "creativity"). This is true because only through generation or reproduction can that which is mortal gain a kind of immortality. Not only men but other animals as well love and desire immortality, and since all physical things undergo constant change and succession, the only means of attaining permanence is by generating offspring to take the parents' places. (Change is here attributed even to the soul, but Socrates and Plato believe the soul, being immortal, is not subject to those laws governing the body.) This is why procreation is desired so passionately and offspring are given such anxious care, even to the point that parents sacrifice their lives if necessary. The desire for immortality accounts also for the otherwise senseless ambition which drives so many men. In fact, Diotima said, this desire motivates all things which men do, even the practice of great virtues which men hope will keep them in memory.

Thus, some procreation is not of the body; some men are "pregnant" in body only, but some are creative in soul: they write poems or paint pictures, they conceive wisdom and virtue, best of all wisdom about the organization of states and families. Such creations of statesmen, lawmakers, and artists are preferable to human children, being more beautiful and more immortal, and the friendships out of which they are born are actually closer than those which bring forth children in the flesh.

While the reader will note how far this account of love transcends the earlier ones, it is still only of what Diotima described as the "lesser mysteries of love." Yet if practiced in the right way, these point to the higher. In a passage among the most significant in Plato, because its description of the dialectical ascent to vision of absolute beauty would apply to knowledge of the other Ideas or Forms as well, Diotima's description of beauty is recalled by Socrates.

The proper procedure in the apprehension of beauty is to begin in youth to appreciate physical or external beauty of one object, letting this inspire fair thoughts; from this, one should grow into the realization that the beauties of all physical things are related, and thus transcend narrow devotion to one. The next level is the insight that beauty of mind is preferable to that of outward appearance; at this stage the lover is moved to nurture the character and intellect of promising youths. Then he is prepared to ascend to the next (each step is progressively more abstract)—that in which the beauty of institutions and laws becomes evident. The beauty of the sciences is even higher, and he who perceives this will then proceed to a vision of a unique science, that of beauty *per se*. The final reward and the goal of this laborious ascent is apprehension of the nature (which Plato in other contexts calls the Form or Idea) of beauty: "a nature which in the first place is everlasting, not growing and decaying, or waxing and waning; secondly, not fair in one point of view and foul in another, or at one time or in one relation or at one place fair, at another . . . foul, as if fair to some and foul to others, or in the likeness of . . . any . . . part of the bodily frame, or in any form of speech or knowledge, or existing in any other being, as, for example, in an animal, or in heaven, or in earth, or in any other place but beauty absolute, separate, simple, and everlasting, which without diminution and without increase, or any change, is imparted to the ever-growing and perishing beauties of all other things. He who from these ascending under the influence of true love, begins to perceive that beauty, is not far from the end. And the true order of going . . . to the things of love, is to begin from the beauties of earth and mount upwards for the sake of that other beauty, using these as steps only, and from one going on to two, and from two to all fair forms, and from fair forms to fair practices, and from fair practices to fair notions, until from fair notions he arrives at the notion of absolute beauty, and at last knows what the essence of beauty is. This . . . is that life above all others which man should live, in the contemplation of beauty absolute. . . ."

Socrates maintains that anyone living a life of communion with the ultimately real beauty—as Diotima has described it—will share Love's divinity and reality and goodness, becoming a friend of the gods and achieving immortality as far as is possible for man. There is no better aid to this end than that of Love, and this is why and how Love ought to be praised.

As Socrates thus ends his speech, a sudden change of tone is introduced by the entrance of the drunken Alcibiades, who adequately reinforces the Socratic teaching by recalling ways in which the master practices it. Willing to participate only if the others will drink, Alcibiades empties a half-gallon wine vessel and has it filled for Socrates, calling attention to the fact, however, that Socrates can drink any amount without becoming drunk. When asked to speak, Alcibiades admits that he is in no condition to vie with others in praise of Love, and he chooses to praise Socrates instead.

Socrates, he begins, looks like a satyr; indeed, he is like the busts of Silenus which open up to reveal images of gods inside them. He is like the satyr Marsyas, too, the marvelous flute player whose melodies charm all hearers, except that Socrates pipes with words even more powerful than those of Pericles. He is the only man who is able to shame Alcibiades for neglecting his own soul to attend public affairs, and only the love of popularity tears him away from Socrates' spell. In spite of the latter's rough exterior and pretension of ignorance, he is full of temperance and true beauty, despising the popular versions of beauty, wealth, honor. While still a youth, Alcibiades became enamoured of Socrates because of the master's shining virtues, and sought to become his beloved. (But this association, had it been consummated—as it was not—would have been motivated solely by Alcibiades' desire to render service to a master admired for his wisdom and goodness and ability to impart these, for Socrates was certainly unattractive physically.) But Alcibiades recounts how his advances became more and more overt with absolutely no effect on Socrates, which made the handsome youth realize fully how genuine was the philosopher's self-control. But this was only one of many occasions in which the almost superhuman virtues of Socrates were exhibited, Alcibiades continues. While at war Socrates was able to go without food and rest with incomparable stamina; he marched better barefoot on the ice than did other soldiers whose feet were shod. Once, while engrossed in a difficult problem, Socrates stood in one spot from one dawn to the next, to the amazement of fellow soldiers who slept out in the open to keep watch on his endurance. But Socrates was not just a dreamer; he rescued Alcibiades in battle and should have had the prize for valor actually awarded to the latter. Although he seems a satyr in appearance, also like the statues with gods inside are Socrates' words, ridiculous at first but when examined found to have unparalleled significance, to be "of the most divine, abounding in fair images of virtue, and of the widest comprehension, or rather extending to the whole duty of a good and honourable man."

Shortly after Alcibiades' laud of Socrates, the formal order of the banquet breaks up; some men leave, some drink themselves to sleep. When Aristodemus awoke at dawn, there was Socrates still holding forth in argument to an audience of only Agathon and Aristophanes. When they dozed off Socrates arose and departed.

So ends a dialogue remarkable for its picture of Socrates' outward appearance, moral character, and ability to take—or leave—the earthly point of departure for the realm of reason and intellect. Especially valuable for the student of Plato is its account of the dialectical approach to the vision of Forms. Careful examination of the long quoted passage will reveal also that many other essential features of the theory of Forms are suggested there—the Forms are simple, unique, immaterial, immutable, eternal, ultimately real natures which give particular objects their being. The Form of absolute Beauty here described is obviously—on both internal and external evidence—that which Plato elsewhere calls the Good. The reader might well compare the account in the *Symposium* with those in other dialogues, especially with the Myth of the Cave in the *Republic*. But the *Symposium* glows with beauties of its own. Where else can one find such philosophical discourse on love coupled with such lovely discourse on philosophy?

PHAEDO

Author: Plato (427-347 B.C.)
Type of work: Metaphysics
First transcribed: Probably one of the middle dialogues

The philosopher is always pursuing death, for the body hinders the soul's search for knowledge, and death would bring about a separation of body and soul.

The philosopher attempts to acquire knowledge of the Ideas—those eternal forms which are copied by individual things—but to gain such knowledge he must practice a kind of death, freeing the soul so that it can discover Ideas.

Surely the soul survives the death of the body, for opposites are generated out of opposites, and life is the opposite of death.

Furthermore, we have certain ideas (such as the idea of equality) which could not have been acquired in this life; hence, we must have existed, as souls, prior to being born; we recollect the Ideas we encountered before our birth.

The *Phaedo* (named after the narrator in the dialogue) is Plato's literary and philosophical monument to the death, and to the life, of his master, Socrates. An excellent way to begin the study of philosophy is with this account of the end of the first member in the great trio in Greek thought, as written by the second. It describes the philosophic way of life as Socrates and consequently Plato saw it, explaining how the philosopher, so unlike other men in many ways, differs also in being unafraid of death. Its account of the soul's immortality ranges from the fanciful myth about the various destinies of good and evil souls to what is perhaps Socrates'—and certainly Plato's—most fundamental theory, the doctrine of forms. While the *Phaedo* must be complemented by the other Platonic dialogues in order to round out the picture of Socrates as a man and as a philosopher, it suggests powerfully the influence he and Plato have jointly exercised in the history of Western thought.

The work consists of one dialogue within another; at the request of a friend, Phaedo recounts the conversation between Socrates and his companions and the final events of the day

Socrates' unjust death sentence is executed. The inner dialogue occurs chiefly between the master and two of the several followers present, Simmias and Cebes. Quite naturally the talk turns to the true philosopher's attitude toward death.

Since Socrates appears willing to die and to justify this willingness, the question is raised: is suicide legitimate? Socrates' answer is that since men belong to the gods, the occasion of our death is in their hands, not ours. But Cebes objects that if life is divinely directed, its continuance is desirable and the voluntary escape from it would be folly. Socrates explains, however, that he expects to enjoy the company of other good and wise gods and men after death.

But a stronger defense of his position is requested. Socrates surprises his listeners by asserting that the philosopher is always pursuing death, and that it would hence be most inconsistent, now that death is at hand, to shun it. Simmias laughingly agrees that most people think the philosophic life is and deserves to be a kind of death, but he desires clarification. Socrates explains that the philosopher seeks and enjoys the pleasures of the

82

body—those of food, drink, sex, and adornment—only to the extent that they are necessary to life, and beyond this despises them. The bodily senses, desires, and feelings hinder the soul's search for knowledge of true existence. Thought is clearest, then, when the influence of the body is least felt, or when there is the greatest possible separation between body and soul ("soul" in this context includes "mind"). But what is such separation, when completed, but death itself? Hence the philosopher—whose object is truth beheld with the clear eye of the soul, not with the befuddled vision of the physical organ—is constantly practicing a kind of death.

In elaborating this position Socrates introduces the famous doctrine of forms (variously described as "essences," "absolutes," and "Ideas." The last term does not have the connotation of the common English word, and hence the others are preferable). For each class of objects and qualities (or at least for many classes) there is an absolute form or essence which is the true nature and reality shared by particular members of the class. For example, there are absolute justice, beauty, goodness, greatness, health, strength. A beautiful object, say, is beautiful not in itself but by participation to some degree in the very essence of beauty. Each absolute is pure or self-identical, unique, eternal, and perfect in its kind—since ultimately it is the kind in reality and not simply by definition for the sake of classification (although it may serve the latter purpose for the reader who rejects the Platonic metaphysics). A healthy man, for instance, becomes now more, now less healthy and eventually loses health altogether in death, but health is what

it is without relation to time. Particular things, Plato explains elsewhere, are real only on a secondary level because they are changeable and perishable; they exist only by virtue of the ideal patterns they so variously but never perfectly copy.

Socrates asks now, how are such forms known? Certainly not, strictly speaking, by the senses; with the eye we see only this or that imperfectly beautiful thing, or observe persons merely more or less just, whereas beauty, justice and the other absolutes are adequately apprehended only by an arduous and purely intellectual process: ". . . he attains to the purest knowledge of them who goes to each with the mind alone, not introducing or intruding in the act of thought, sight or any other sense together with reason, but with the very light of the mind in her own clearness searches into the very truth of each." But if forms are known by mind alone, wisdom concerning true being can mature only after death, when the mind is wholly freed.

But it has not yet been established that the soul survives; Cebes expresses the common fear that upon bodily death the soul simply disperses into nothing. Socrates therefore offers a number of considerations supporting his confidence in immortality. (One translator of the dialogue suggests that Plato does not attempt a logical proof of this belief, but even in the translation phrases such as "sufficient proof" and "logical necessity" occur. It is true, however, that the arguments used vary greatly in plausibility for a modern reader.)

It is observable, Socrates holds, that all things which are "generated" or which come into and pass out of being are generated from their opposites. Particular (rather than absolute) opposites give way to each other: that which becomes weaker must have been stronger, the worse comes from the better, and so on. Thus we find all through nature both opposite states and the processes of coming into them; otherwise, if all things passed into conditions from which there was no return, the universe would become utterly static. Imagine, for example, a world in which waking was followed only by sleeping, or in which the processes of composition were never varied by those of division. Granted this point, Socrates argues that since life and death and living and dying are opposites, and it is certain that the living die, according to this universal law of nature the living must return from the dead, and therefore the dead must exist somewhere prior to return.

Cebes now suggests that the same implication follows from Socrates' familiar account of knowledge as recollection: knowledge of true being (that is, of the forms) turns out to be a recognition of what was known in a previous existence. Let us consider our comprehension of equality, for example. If we see two similar objects we may judge that they are equal or nearly so, but how do we recognize this relative equality? Such a judgment presupposes a concept of equality *per se* to serve as a standard for comparison. The concept of perfect equality cannot be derived from sensory observation because physical objects are never precisely equal. At the same time, however—and here Socrates tempers the extreme rationalism of the earlier account of knowledge of absolutes—we are reminded of absolute equality by the sight of imper-

fectly equal things; sensation is thus a necessary but not a sufficient condition of this recognition. But since we have sensation at birth, knowledge of essences must be prior to the present life; it is recollection of what we had once known and had forgotten when the soul took on a body. It is clear then that preëxistence of the soul and that of the absolutes are equally certain.

Nevertheless, say Simmias and Cebes, we still have insufficient proof that the soul continues to exist *after* physical death. But Socrates reminds them that the latter argument, plus the one concerning opposites, does prove the point, for if the soul exists before birth (that is, in a state of "death" relative to bodily existence) and the living come from the dead, even as the dead come from the living, the soul thus exists both before and after the various bodies into which it is born. But noticing that Simmias and Cebes still evince the natural human uneasiness about the soul's future, Socrates adds another and perhaps sounder argument.

It hinges on comparison of the nature of the soul as compared to that of the body, and it concludes that if they are materially different, there is no reason to assign them a common fate. In general the composite or compound is unstable, subject to change and hence to dissolution, whereas the uncompounded or simple must be indissoluble, as are the invisible, simple, self-existent, and unchanging forms. Comparison of body and soul shows that body is like all other compound and perishable physical objects, but soul resembles the absolutes in some ways and presumably will share their permanence. This dichotomy of soul and body appears in the knowing process: if the soul relies on sensation she is dragged down to earth, as it were—to the unstable and the confused; but if she relies on her own reason she approaches the pure and eternal. Communion with the immutable breeds similarity: ". . . the soul is in the very likeness of the divine, and immortal, and intellectual, and uniform, and indissoluble, and unchangeable. . . ."

This conclusion leads Socrates to descriptions of the soul's fate after death which approach and finally cross the border between philosophy and fiction, but which, like many of Plato's myths, allegorically state significant hypotheses and profound insights. The soul's future, he says, will depend on its degree of purity in the present. Those impure souls enthralled by love of sensual pleasures and by evil passions are so weighed down by the corporeal that they may be reincarnated in animals similarly miserable in nature, such as in asses or wolves. The moderately virtuous soul might be given the body of an admirable social animal such as the ant or the bee, or perhaps even another human body. But only those souls purified of all bodily taint through philosophy may enter immediately into the blissful company of the gods and escape further reincarnation.

Philosophy is thus not merely an academic discipline or a profession; in the Platonic view it is a way of life and even the soul's salvation. Socrates describes the soul as previously shackled to the body, hoodwinked by the senses, enslaved by its own desires; worst of all, it is deceived about true reality by opinions influenced by pleasure and pain—it mistakes violence of emotion for evidence of truth. Philosophy offers release from this deception and teaches the soul to rely on her own intellectual resources. Thus, "she will calm passion, and follow reason, and dwell in the contemplation of her, beholding the true and divine. . . ."

After the almost poetic heights Socrates reaches in this account, he displays the equanimity of the truly philosophical inquirer when Simmias and Cebes still have serious doubts which he encourages them to broach. Simmias' objection presupposes the Pythagorean concept of the soul as a sort of harmony or attunement of the elements of the body, obtaining when these are in proper tension or proportion. By analogy to his previous arguments, Socrates would have to argue that the harmony of a lyre—which harmony is also invisible, perfect and divine—could survive the destruction of the instrument. But the absurdity of this suggests the absurdity of the belief that the soul exists when the body is destroyed. Cebes adds that while the soul may survive several deaths and reincarnations, yet it is possible that it finally wears out as does a body that has survived several coats.

These objections seem so cogent to the audience, just now persuaded by Socrates' train of thought, that a despair of the success of any argument whatever sets in. But Socrates warns his friends of the dangers of misology; just as one may become a misanthropist by overconfidence in men, followed by disillusionment, so may one learn to distrust all argument by accepting conclusions hastily and without sufficient attention to logic, only to discover their falsity later. But instead of adopting a cynically skeptical position that no arguments are valid, no truths about reality discoverable, we should think that the difficulty is our lack of ability, which can be improved by further effort. It is fallacious to attribute the invalidity of our own thinking to reason itself, and folly thus to forfeit the very possibility of learning the truth.

Socrates then proceeds to answer Simmias' objection by showing that it is inconsistent with previous and present admissions. Harmony or attunement is not prior to the elements organized or tuned, but the soul has been shown to exist prior to the body. Simmias cannot hold, therefore, both that knowledge is recollection and that the soul is harmony. Furthermore, harmony occurs in degrees; an instrument may be more or less in tune. But we do not think that souls are more or less souls either in themselves or relative to others. Again, if the soul were a harmony, it could contain no vice, which is inharmonious, and consequently all souls would be equally good, which of course is absurd. And finally, if soul were a harmony of bodily elements, it would be dependent upon them, but as a matter of fact the soul, especially the wise one, acts as a governor of the body, and hence is sometimes out of harmony with it.

To meet Cebes' objection that the soul may eventually deteriorate and vanish, Socrates appeals once more to the doctrine of forms to elaborate a theory of causation relevant to the problem. In his youth, he remembers, he studied physicalistic and mechanistic theories of causal explanation of human life and behavior. But the detail (and presumably the mutual inconsistencies) of these frustrated and confused him. A gleam of hope appeared in the Anaxagorean view that Mind (as universal rather than human) orders and causes all things,

which philosophy Socrates thought would show that everything was ordered for the best. If one wished to discover the ultimate causes for the shape of the earth, the positions and movements of the heavenly bodies, he need only refer to the highest good which these arrangements serve. But to his disappointment Socrates found Anaxagoras falling back on the familiar physical causes.

These offer partial but inadequate explanation of his own present behavior, Socrates continues. Of course he is engaging in his present activities in prison by means of bones, muscles, and their functions, but these are not the true causes of his behavior, which are that the Athenians have condemned him to die and he has thought it right to refuse escape and accept the penalty. Mechanistic philosophers ignore the distinction between conditions and causes (or between what Aristotle was later to call efficient and final causes); "of the obligatory and containing power of the good they think nothing. . . ." But since Socrates claims that he has been unable to discover what the nature of the best is, he offers a substitute causal theory.

While his procedure of adopting it may appear too rationalistic, further qualifications reveal much affinity to later scientific thought. His method is to select the theory judged most sound and then to accept or reject particular propositions by reference to it. But the original hypothesis is not wholly arbitrary; it can be justified either by derivation from an established theory, or (to judge from Socrates' practice) by examining its consequences for any inconsistencies. With this explanation Socrates accounts for his present assumption of the theory of forms.

We recall that an implication of the theory is that participation in the forms accounts for the characteristics of objects; Socrates insists that for him this is the only intelligible *cause* assignable. Indeed, it applies to the very processes of becoming: there is "no other way in which anything comes into existence except by participation in its own proper essence. . . ." Now two chief characteristics of forms are uniqueness and simplicity: they cannot admit their opposites. Furthermore, some particulars are so constituted that it is impossible they should admit forms opposite to those especially characteristic of their own natures; for example, the number two, having the form "even," cannot remain two and admit the form "odd." Now when we realize that what renders body alive is soul and nothing else, it appears that soul has an essential relation to life and hence cannot admit its opposite, death, any more than fire can admit cold. Hence, again the soul has been proved to be immortal, this time to the satisfaction of all those present.

It follows, then, that the soul deserves the greatest care in the present life, preparatory to the next. Socrates proceeds to give an imaginative description of the details of life after death and the various regions good and evil souls will occupy. The orthodox Christian reader will find here a number of counterparts anticipating his own traditions of heaven, hell and even purgatory. Socrates adds, however, that "A man of sense ought not to say, nor will I be very confident, that the description which I have given of the soul and her mansions is exactly true. But I do say that, inasmuch as the soul is shown to be immortal, he may venture to think, not improperly or unworthily, that something of the kind is true." The chief point is again that "there is no release or salvation from evil except the attainment of the highest virtue and wisdom."

That Socrates has by his own virtue and wisdom escaped the evil of fear of death is now abundantly evident. When the discussion is finished and he has bidden his family goodbye, only Socrates among the entire assembly keeps his composure as the final preparations are made. Admonishing his friends to restrain their sorrow (which Plato has made contagious even today), Socrates quaffs the cup of poison as cheerfully as if it were wine.

Whether or not the reasoning associated with his attitude seems entirely valid, and some of it judged formally certainly is not, there is much in the Socratic teaching which is enduringly sound and recurrently fruitful. Some doctrines, such as that of the forms, may be rejected as metaphysics while renewed as logic or epistemology. But theory aside, none can gainsay the value of Socrates' visionary courage, or fail to wish it perpetual in the human race. For an adequate intimation of the master's immortality, however, one must return to its original description by his most eminent disciple.

REPUBLIC

Author: Plato (427-347 B.C.)
Type of work: Political philosophy, metaphysics, epistemology
First transcribed: Probably one of the middle dialogues

PRINCIPAL IDEAS ADVANCED

The question arises, "What is justice?" and after some unacceptable answers, Thrasymachus suggests that justice is whatever is to the interest of the stronger party (since the stronger party makes the laws and enforces them); but Socrates argues that rulers sometimes err and that, in any case, the art of government, like other arts, is directed to the interests of those to be affected, the people themselves.

Socrates claims that the just man, provided he has knowledge, can rule both himself and others, and that the concern of the just man is not for himself alone.

To clarify the idea of justice and to prove its worth, Socrates leads a discussion concerning justice in the state; he constructs the idea of an ideal state, one which exhibits justice.

Any state needs guardians (rulers), auxiliaries (soldiers), and workers; each class does its proper business without interfering with the others; analogously, the just man is one in whom the three elements of his nature—the rational, the spirited, and the appetitive—are harmonized.

The ideal republic is one in which the classes are carefully built up by controlled breeding, education, and selection; society is communized in order to eliminate quarrels about personal property.

The guardians of the state should be educated as philosophers, having been prepared by training in music and gymnastic.

The *Republic* of Plato, perhaps the greatest single treatise written on political philosophy, has influenced strongly the thought of Western man concerning questions of justice, rule, obedience, and the good life. This is true whether one agrees with Plato's answer or, if dissatisfied, seeks a different solution. The work is also undoubtedly the best introduction to Plato's philosophy in general. Not only does it contain his ideas on the state and man, but also his famous theory of forms, his theory of knowledge, and his views of the role of music and poetry in society. Nor does he condescend in this introduction, for he presents on each of the philosophical questions mentioned a penetrating analysis which demands careful study on the part of the reader. Socrates and his illustrious student Plato force one by their dialectical technique of question and answer, of definition and exception, to take an active part in the philosophical enterprise.

The work is divided into ten books, or chapters, written as a dialogue with Socrates as the main character. One cannot fail to catch the magnificence that must be present in Plato's literary and philosophical style, for all of the available translations indicate passages of great force and beauty.

88

The opening book of the *Republic* is concerned with the question, "What is justice?" Invited by Polemarchus to the home of his father Cephalus, Socrates and others (among them Glaucon, Adeimantus, and Thrasymachus) begin, in an easy fashion, the search for an answer. A general but vague definition is defended, first by Cephalus and then by his son, Polemarchus, to the effect that justice consists in restoring what one has received from another. Socrates asks if this definition would apply in a situation in which weapons borrowed from a friend were demanded by him when quite obviously he was no longer of sound mind. It is a homely example of the type that Socrates loved to give; and, as usual, when examined, it raises important considerations. Justice, among other things, involves not only property but also conditions, such as a sound mind, which cannot be merely assumed.

The next attempt is: justice is doing good to friends and harm to enemies. But knowledge is needed in order to be able to judge who our friends and enemies are. The definition is then modified: do good to the just and harm to the unjust. Socrates brings up a point in objection which is a central feature of many of his discussions of the good life. He argues that doing harm to the unjust makes them worse than they are. He holds that it can never be just to make a man worse than he is by doing harm to him.

The most serious discussion of this book and one which sets the tone for the remainder of the *Republic* occurs next. Thrasymachus, who had been sitting by listening to the argument with ill-concealed distaste, impetu-ously breaks in and takes it up. He presents a position which has since been stated many times: justice is that which is to the advantage or interest of the stronger party, the reason being that the stronger party makes the laws. Socrates begins to attack this definition: for instance, he points out that a man does not always know what his interest is or wherein it lies. When the stronger errs in his judgment, then what? Thrasymachus replies that the ruler is not a ruler when he errs. (Note that in admitting this, Thrasymachus has already moved away from his original position and toward that of Socrates that might alone does not make right, for it is might together with some kind of knowledge capable of preventing errors that makes right.) Socrates presses his advantage further. Whenever we consider an art and its practice, be it medicine, piloting a ship, or ruling, it is done so not for the sake of the art or for its practitioner but for those who are to receive its benefits, be they patients, passengers, or the ruled.

Thrasymachus angrily declares that anyone but a philosopher could see that society "honors" the man of power over the powerless. Corrupt men with impunity dissolve contracts, and pay no taxes. People may privately proclaim the virtues of justice but publicly the opposite prevails, and men are admired and respected for daring to practice that which is ordinarily frowned upon. In fact, Thrasymachus claims, the tyrant is the happiest of men. Here Socrates points out that Thrasymachus has challenged the whole conduct of living.

Socrates repeats the point that an art is practiced for the benefit of those for whom its services are intended and not for the benefit of the practitioner. Any payment received for practicing an art is independent of the aim of the art. In ruling, the benefit is for the ruled, not the ruler. No man rules willingly; he accepts the responsibility only because he fears to be ruled by a worse man. Thrasymachus replies that ideal justice is a virtue that a man of intelligence cannot afford, whereas what is called "injustice" is in reality only good prudence. Under questioning, Thrasymachus admits that the just man does not try to get the better of other just men, but rather of unjust men who are his opposites in character. "Get the better of" appears to mean "take advantage of" in the widest possible sense. Even to instruct someone is somehow to take advantage of him. In a vein much like the one taken above, Socrates argues that in every form of knowledge and ignorance (every art or its lack), the man who knows tries to benefit those who do not know, not those who know. When the ignorant are in control, not knowing the art, they do not know in what way to practice it or on whom. Hence, they try to get the better of all—be they wise or ignorant. For Socrates, knowing one's art and for whom it is intended is a sign of virtue. "Virtue" appears to mean "the proper function of anything"; what the proper function of a thing is, however, demands appropriate study and knowledge. We saw that those who are just try to get the better of only those who are unjust and of no others, whereas the unjust try to get the better of all. The latter, then, are the ignorant and the ineffectual; the former, the intelligent, and hence the wise and the good. The soul's virtue is found in proper rule of the individual. The just man with knowledge can rule both himself and others, whereas the unjust man, factitious, disrupted, and not knowing what to do and what not to do, can rule neither himself nor others.

The first book ends as Socrates reminds his disputants that they have been getting ahead of themselves; it is a bit foolish to talk about justice (a virtue) when they have not yet defined it.

In Book II, Glaucon and Adeimantus press Socrates to prove that the just life is worth living, and Glaucon illustrates his wish by means of the legend of Gyges's ring. Gyges, so the story goes, gained possession of a ring which, when turned, made its wearer invisible. With this advantage he was able to practice evil with impunity. Socrates is to consider an individual with the advantage of a Gyges and contrast him with one who in life is his opposite. It is his task to show that the life of the just man, no matter what indignities he suffers, is worth living; nay, more, that it is preferable to that of Gyges. He is to show that virtue is its own reward no matter what the consequences.

Socrates, with misgivings, takes on the task. He suggests, inasmuch as they are searching for something not easily found, justice, that they turn to a subject which will most readily exhibit it. The state is analogous to the individual, and justice, once found in the state, will apply also to its counterpart, the individual.

He begins his quest by a kind of pseudo-historical analysis of the state. Men are not self-sufficient and thus cannot supply themselves with all the necessities of life. But by pooling their resources, and by having each man do what he is best suited to do, they will provide food, shelter, and clothing for themselves. The city thus started engages in exporting and importing, sets up markets, and steadily advances from its simple beginnings. (It should be pointed out that the *states* in ancient Greece bore a strong resemblance to the *cities* of today, both in size and population, but were independent units.) From simple needs, the people pass increasingly to luxurious wants. Since the necessities of life are no longer sufficient, the people turn to warfare to accumulate booty. Armies are needed and a new professional is born: the soldier, with appropriate characteristics. The soldiers must be as watchdogs; gentle to their friends and fierce to their enemies. (Note that in discussing the characteristics of the soldiers, a spirited group that forms only a part of the state, and analogously, a spirited part of the individual, Socrates suggests a feature formerly given as a possible definition of "justice.") The soldier must know his friends—the citizenry—and his enemies, the barbarians, and be good to the one and harm the other. This may be an aspect of justice, but it is not the complete definition. The state also needs rulers, or guardians, who are to be carefully selected and trained.

Plato holds music and gymnastics to be a significant part of the guardian training. He concludes Book II and takes up much of Book III with arguments for censorship of the tales of Hesiod and Homer, especially any wherein the gods, who ought to be examples of noble, virtuous beings, are presented as deceitful, lustful, brutal, and petty. He believed that Greek society was in the decline, that moral behavior was no longer understood or practiced by the Athenians, and that, to a large measure, the degrading tales of the gods were responsible. He no doubt mistook a symptom for a cause. The moral decline of a people involves many things of which trashy literature is only a sign; the desire for such things cannot be cured by censorship; the principle involved in censorship has other consequences which are as bad as the social evils that Plato hoped to cure. He thought, as many today do, that the young imitate in their behavior the activities they perceive in the imitative arts. If they read stories in which the "heroes" are immoral, if they see plays in which the protaganists are effeminate and slavish, then they will tend to act similarly. Plato argues that the guardians may know of such people, but to act as they do will bring about bad habits. Furthermore, to imitate means to do or be more than one thing—that is, to be both that which one imitates and also one's own self—and in this society it is enough to do or be one thing and that well.

In order to convince the inhabitants of this state that men are fit for one and only one job—to be either guardians (rulers), auxiliaries (soldiers), or workers—the rulers will institute a "noble lie." This lie or myth will be to the effect that men are molded by the gods to be one of the three types noted. Plato likens these classes to gold, silver, and bronze and holds that the people are to look upon themselves as having these "metals" in their makeup from birth. There will be some "mobility" between classes if ability is discovered, but generally they will remain static.

In Book IV, Socrates holds that the city should be neither too wealthy nor too poor, neither too large nor too small, neither too populous nor too few: one in which men and women have equal opportunity and in which each does that task for which he is best suited. Such a city will be wise and brave, temperate and just. These are the cardinal virtues, and so we are well on our way toward finding in the city those virtues we had hoped to see in the individual.

In the city, wisdom is found in the rule of the guardian; in the individual, in the rule of intelligence. To function properly, we saw, is to be virtuous. This, to Plato, is the essence of wisdom, especially since acting virtuously takes knowledge. Courage is a way of preserving the values of the city through education. Knowing what to fear and what not to fear, a knowledge gained through law, characterizes courage. Temperance is a kind of order; the naturally better part of the soul controls the worst part, as in the city the naturally superior part governs the inferior. Thus, the intelligence of the few controls the passions of the many, as a man's intelligence governs his appetites through his will. Justice, lastly, is found in the truth that each one must practice the one thing for which his nature is best suited. To do one's "business" and not to meddle with others, to have and to do that which is one's own—that is justice. Although within the class of artisans there may be some mixing of tasks —the carpenter may perform some other craft—there cannot be mixing of the classes of gold, silver, or bronze.

In Book V, Plato discusses his famous "three waves" which are needed if the ideal state is to be possible. From those who show the proper aptitude the rulers are to be selected, women as well as men. This is the first wave. The second wave is that communal life must be shared by the ruling class. Marriage and children will be held in common. All within a certain age group are to be designated "parents," a younger group, "children" and "brothers and sisters," and so on. Plato argues that family loyalty is an asset which, when practiced on a public scale, will retain its value, whereas the deficits of private family life, such as the factiousness between families, will have been eliminated. "Mine" and "not mine" now will apply to the same things. The ruler will arrange communal marriages by lot; unknown to the betrothed, however, the lottery will be fraudulently arranged for reasons of eugenics. Another myth or lie is told for the state's benefit.

The third wave, and most difficult to bring about, is that philosophers must be kings, or kings, philosophers. If this can occur, then political power and intellectual wisdom will be combined so that justice may prevail. (Recall Socrates' discussion with Thrasymachus; only when knowledge and power are joined in the ruler can true advantage or benefit befall the ruled. It is now Plato's task to characterize the philosopher and define the kind of knowledge needed.)

In Books VI and VII, he presents three magnificent analogies to explain his meaning. But first his complicated theory of forms should be mentioned. Plato believed that those features which objects of a certain kind have in common, for example, the features common to varied art objects, all beautiful, are all related to a single perfect ideal, or form, which he called "the feature itself," in this case "beauty itself." This is an intellectual reality properly "seen" by the rational element of the soul, just as the many instances are perceived by sight or by means of the other senses. The good itself, the highest of all forms, is the proper object of the philosopher's quest.

In his first analogy, Plato likens the good to the sun. Just as the sun provides light so that we may see physical objects, the good provides "light" so that the soul may perceive intellectual forms.

Plato's second analogy also emphasizes the distinction between the senses and the rational element of the soul as sources of knowing. We are to imagine a line whose length has been divided into two unequal parts; furthermore, these parts are then to be divided in the same proportion as the first division. If we label the line AE, the first point of division C and the other two points of the subdivisions B and D, then the following proportions hold:

$$\frac{CE}{AC} = \frac{DE}{CD} = \frac{BC}{AB}$$

and hence $BC = CD$. Now what do these segments represent?

The first segment of the original line with its two segments Plato styles "the world of opinion," and he calls the first of its segments "conjecture" (AB) and the second "belief" (BC). As noted, we gain information of this world through our senses. We pass from creatures who let the world come to us with little or no thought (only conjecture)—a world of shadows and reflections—to persons who have beliefs as to what the shadows represent —a world of physical objects such as trees, hammers, houses.

The second segment of the original line is titled "the world of knowledge," and its sections "understanding" and "thinking" respectively; this is the world of forms mentioned in the analogy of the sun. Plato considers mathematics the mental activity most characteristic of *understanding* by the use of images. In geometry we find, among other things, an attempt to define precisely the various mathematical figures (circle, triangle, square, and so forth). Unlike the world of physical objects, which is mutable, these definitions, which state the formal properties of these objects, are unchanging. In *thinking* we find the highest form of mental activity: dialectical thought, or thinking by the use of Ideas. From contemplating the unchanging forms or Ideas of physical things, the mind progresses to the reality of perfect beauty, justice, and goodness. The process of education in the perceptual world moves from bare opinion through belief, a practical rather than a theoretical understanding of the truths of the world of things seen, to understanding and thinking, wherein the eternal truths of the world of things thought are known.

Plato's third analogy is that of the cave. We are to imagine prisoners chained in a cave in a way that all they can see is a wall in front of them. On the wall, shadows appear cast from a parapet behind them where a fire burns and where bearers carry all sorts of objects. This is, of course, analogous to the world of shadows (sense experience) represented by the segment AB of the divided line. Miraculously, a prisoner frees himself and sees the cause of the images and the light that casts them; he is in the world of belief. Noticing an opening which leads out of the cave, he crawls into the sunlight, the world of forms, and is so dazzled that he is blinded. But gradually he adjusts to the light, sees the true reality, the realm of Ideas, and is tempted to remain forever. But he is compelled by a sense of obligation to return to the cave and to instruct the chained. They disbelieve, for all they know is the world of gloom and shadows, and they would jeer him, or worse, tear him to pieces; but he persists and rededicates his life to their instruction. Thus the philosopher, having the world of forms for his contemplation, must return to be king, to rule by a sense of duty, if there is to be justice.

Plato outlines an educational program for the philosopher-king which continues from the music and gymnastics taught the guardians. For ten years he studies arithmetic, geometry, solid geometry, and astronomy. He is in the realm of understanding, and the point of his mathematical training is to prepare him for study of and grasp of ideal forms. For five years he studies dialectical thought so that the ultimate principle of reason, the form of good, shall be known to him. Then, at the age of thirty-five, he begins his period of practical application of these principles, and, after fifteen years he ascends the throne at fifty.

In Book VIII, Plato, after having brought us to a glimpse of the form of the state, discusses its decline. The decline of the state is paralleled by the decline of the individuals who make it up; the state is analogous to the individual. From the rational state we move to the spirited one (the guardians), the chief virtue of which is honor; when the spirited element is again dominated by appetites, then wealth is sought and the oligarchy born. From wealth we go to the government of the many who, overthrowing the few, proclaim the virtues of the group. Appealing to the mob, the demogogue takes over and the full decline of the ideal state and man has occurred. There is a weird similarity; from love of reason to insatiable lust, the state and the individual have degenerated. There is the rule of one in both cases, but we have gone from one who knows what to do and what not to do to one who knows nothing and whose every impulse is his master. The man of intelligence uses his reason to direct his will and thus to control his appetites, but the tyrant controls nothing. He is controlled by his appetites. A man who is slave to his appetites is master of nothing; the man who is master of nothing is the most miserable of men. He is always in pain. Thus Book IX closes, with the passage from true pleasure to pain, from the just man to the unjust. Socrates has shown Glaucon and Adeimantus what the happy life, the just life, is.

Book X contains the famous Myth of Er, which will not be discussed here, but it also touches somewhat on what Plato means by "Idea" or "form" and on the danger of art in the state. His analysis will be mentioned briefly. To each class of particulars that have something in common, Plato holds there is a form or Idea in which these particulars participate and which gives them their common quality. The quality is a reflection of the Idea; so a bed painted by an artist has as its model a physical bed which has in common with other beds the Idea of "bedness" itself. There can be but one Idea-form of beds, for if there were another, the two forms would have a third in which they would participate, and so on, *ad infinitum*. Plato's criticism of art as imitation was based on the claim that art is three steps removed from reality (since works of art are copies of the aspects of things, and things are themselves copies of the Ideas).

The *Republic* closes with an argument for the immortality of the soul. The soul's only illness is injustice; yet injustice is not fatal. By loving justice —by harmonizing reason, spirit, and appetite—man can keep his soul healthy, and the soul will prosper forever.

PHAEDRUS

Author: Plato (427-347 B.C.)
Type of work: Metaphysics, philosophy of love, philosophy of rhetoric
First transcribed: Probably one of the middle dialogues

PRINCIPAL IDEAS ADVANCED

Lysias is reported by Phaedrus as having argued that it is better to be loved by one who does not love than by one who does, for the lover is moved by passion and can do harm.

Socrates at first agrees that love is irrational and therefore harmful, but on reflection he maintains that madness is sometimes divine, and that love is a kind of divine madness.

The soul is like a winged charioteer driving a team of horses; the charioteer, if inspired by love of the ideal, is reason or intelligence in control of the good horse (will) and the bad horse (passion).

Souls which have seen the most of Being, having known the eternal forms or Ideas of all things, pass into the bodies of philosophers, or lovers of wisdom; souls which are disciplined and full of wisdom return to their heavenly home.

Good rhetoric depends on having true knowledge; the Sophists are mistaken in claiming that the appearance of knowledge is all that is necessary.

The *Phaedrus* was probably composed around 370 B.C., after the *Republic* but before the six late dialogues, the *Sophist,* the *Statesman,* the *Philebus,* the *Timaeus,* the *Critias,* and the *Laws.* One of the principal reasons for placing the *Phaedrus* after the *Republic* is the number of passages in the *Phaedrus* which would be difficult to understand except in the light of the *Republic.*

The dramatic date of the dialogue is about 410 B.C., about ten years before the trial and death of Socrates. The *Phaedrus* is a direct dialogue; that is, Plato does not use in this dialogue a narrator who retells to someone else a conversation of Socrates. The scene, a walk outside the walls of Athens to a shady spot along the banks of the river Ilissus, is an unusual setting for Socrates. There are only two characters, Socrates and Phaedrus; Phaedrus also participates in two earlier dialogues, the *Protagoras* and the *Symposium*.

There are several possible answers to the question, "What is the Phaedrus about?" Love, rhetoric, philosophy are all possible answers, since all three subjects are significantly involved in the dialogue. Love is the subject of all three of the set speeches included in the *Phaedrus*; this does not, however, necessarily make love the subject of the dialogue. Rhetoric is examined and criticized, and then proposals are made for a reformed rhetoric capable of serving philosophy. Perhaps the most significant feature of this dialogue is Plato's continuation of his effort to justify philosophy as the most worthy life of the soul against the opposing claims of the Sophists. The dialogue also presents a special method of philosophy, dialectic, which involves collection and division.

The *Phaedrus* opens with a meeting between Socrates and Phaedrus. Phaedrus has spent the morning listening to a speech of Lysias on the subject of love. Socrates accompanies Phaedrus to a shady spot along the river Ilissus where Phaedrus reads a copy of Lysias' speech.

Scholars disagree on the genuineness of this long speech attributed in the dialogue to Lysias. Whether this speech was actually written by Lysias, or whether it is a clever caricature by Plato, it illustrates the reasons for Plato's criticism of the rhetoric of the Sophists. The speech argues on the basis of self-interest the advantage of yielding to someone who does not love rather than to someone who does love. The basic reason offered for yielding to someone who does not love rather than to a genuine lover is that a lover is prevented by his passion from making careful calculations and is therefore likely to injure his beloved.

When Socrates criticizes this speech of Lysias as repetitious and inferior to what he has heard from others on the same subject, Phaedrus challenges Socrates to construct a better speech. Socrates reluctantly agrees. Since Socrates insists that successful deliberation must follow definition, he begins his speech with a definition of love as irrational desire directed toward physical beauty, analogous to gluttony, which is irrational desire directed toward food. From this definition, which is the basis for Lysias' speech but is not the definition Socrates develops in his second speech, Socrates concludes that the lover is more likely than the non-lover to harm the beloved. After this first speech, Socrates declares his remarks to be, along with Lysias' speech, foolish, irreverent, and blasphemous. Socrates then proposes to atone for his offence in treating love as evil by delivering a second speech.

Socrates begins his second speech by denying the assumption of the first two speeches that all madness is evil. He asserts that madness is divine rather than evil when it inspires prophets to foretell the future, when it heals the sick by ritual purification, and when it stimulates the poet to the frenzy of composition. Socrates then declares that he will prove love to be a fourth type of divine madness. The first step in this proof is the argument for the immortality of the soul. This argument, which rests on the nature of the soul as the self-moving principle of motion, recurs in Book X of the *Laws* but is not present in two earlier considerations of immortality in the *Phaedo* and the *Republic*.

Although the immortality of the soul is demonstrated by argument, the nature of the soul is described indirectly by one of the most famous of Plato's myths. The soul is compared to a winged charioteer driving a team of winged horses. All the horses and charioteers corresponding to the souls of the gods are good, but the pair of horses corresponding to the human soul has one good horse and one evil horse. The souls travel through the heavens, but human souls lose their wings, fall to earth, and join bodies to form living beings. The three parts of the human soul are the same as those mentioned in the *Republic:* the winged charioteer corresponds to reason, the good horse to will or spirit, and the bad horse to the passions.

No human souls are able to follow the chariots of the gods to the place where true Being dwells, where the souls of the gods see with the eye of reason such Forms or Ideas as Justice, Temperance, and Knowledge. In no human soul are the horses so completely under the control of the charioteer that the fullest vision of true Being can be achieved. However, some souls rise higher and thus come closer and see more than the others before falling back and losing their wings. The type of life assigned to a human soul at birth depends on how close the soul has come to the full vision of Being. Souls that have seen the most enter into the bodies of philosophers. Then, in descending order, souls that have seen less of Being enter into the following types of persons: a law-abiding ruler, a statesman, an athlete or physician, a prophet, a poet, a farmer, and finally the two lowest types, a Sophist and a tyrant.

After each period of a thousand years a soul enters another human form until she finally regains her wings. Between the end of one life and the beginning of the next is a period of reward or punishment as earned in the previous life. It is possible for a human soul after the first life to be born in an animal, and for a human soul which has been born in an animal to be again born in a man. But all souls born into human beings must have had some vision of Being, since only this vision of the Forms can explain how human souls can pass to universal concepts of reason from the particular impressions of the senses. For most souls it takes ten thousand years to regain wings and return to their heavenly home. A philosopher, however, who chooses the philosophic life three times regains wings in only three thousand years.

The love of beauty is called by Socrates the fourth and highest type of divine madness since one who pursues the beautiful things of this world is reminded of the vision of the Form Beauty and thus of the other proper objects of contemplation, Justice, Temperance, and the other Forms. Through love the soul begins to regain its wings. The struggle in the soul of the lover against the purely physical carnal desires is represented in the myth by the difficult struggle of the charioteer to subdue the behavior of the bad horse. The highest form of love results from the complete subjection of physical desires by both the lover and the beloved. The happiest lovers are those who achieve the philosophical life by the victory of the higher elements in their souls over the lower. Socrates concludes his second speech with a prayer to the god of Love by which he atones for the blasphemous attack on love of his earlier speeches.

Phaedrus praises this speech of Socrates and then agrees with Socrates that there is nothing bad in writing a speech but only in writing a bad speech. Socrates then proposes to examine the nature of good and bad writing. According to Socrates, the first requirement of a good speech is knowledge. Phaedrus replies with the claim of the defenders of rhetoric that what is believed to be knowledge by the audience is required rather than genuine knowledge. Socrates points out that rhetoric as the skill of persuasion depends on misrepresenting things. In order to mislead successfully, the rhetorician must himself have knowledge. Socrates then turns again to Lysias' speech which reveals Lysias' lack of knowledge and his inability to organize a speech properly. On the other hand, Socrates finds in his own two speeches an illustration of the philosophical method, dialectic. The method of dialectic, which also looms large in the *Sophist,* the *Statesman,* and the *Philebus,* involves collection and division. Collection of similars under a single form and the division of generic forms into more specific forms (the Form of Living Thing into the Form of Plant and the Form of Animal) are essential to the definition which must begin successful discussion.

Socrates reviews for Phaedrus the claims of the teachers of rhetoric and urges that allowances be made for their mistaken claims, since their ignorance of dialectic prevents them from properly defining rhetoric. As a positive example, Pericles' superiority in rhetoric is explained by his study of the philosopher Anaxagoras.

The claim of the teachers of rhetoric that knowledge of the truth is not necessary since probability or likeness to truth is enough for success is again rejected. A successful orator must have knowledge of his subject, knowledge about his audience, and the ability to use the method of dialectic. Even then, competence will be achieved only by those who practice diligently. The wise man who becomes a successful orator will not direct his skill toward his fellow men, but toward speaking what is pleasing to the gods. Speaking the truth rather than manipulating the audience is the goal of the wise man. Writing on paper is inferior to writing in the soul of the learner because a written composition can easily fall into the hands of those who are unable to understand it.

The dialogue ends appropriately with Socrates' prayer to the gods, a prayer that the inward life may not be hampered by outward possessions.

THEAETETUS

Author: Plato (427-347 B.C.)
Type of work: Epistemology
First transcribed: Probably one of the middle dialogues

Theaetetus suggests that knowledge is perception, and Socrates identifies the theory as the Protagorean view that man is the measure of all things; but since the Protagorean theory applies only to sensation, and since it is possible to see without knowing what one sees, or to know without seeing, the theory is unsatisfactory.

The Protagorean doctrine that the world of sense experience is a flux is unacceptable to Socrates because if everything were flux, knowledge would be impossible, for knowledge involves the unchanging by reference to which the changing is understood.

To understand the raw data of sense one must refer to Ideas, the forms or natures of sensible things; thus, one could not know by perception alone. [The Ideas are not specifically mentioned.]

The proposal that knowledge is true opinion does not provide a criterion for deciding definitely whether an opinion is true; nor is it satisfactory to say that knowledge is true opinion supported by reasons, for such an account is circular.

The *Theaetetus* is one of the finest of Plato's dialogues dating from his middle period. Scholars are agreed that the dialogue was written later than the *Meno* and the *Republic*, but prior to the *Statesman* and the *Laws*. Thus it is placed in the same period as the *Parmenides* and the *Sophist*. It may well have been written as a tribute to the historical Theaetetus shortly after Theaetetus' death from wounds suffered in battle. This conjecture rests on the fact that the speakers who introduce the main dialogue—but play no other role—refer to the return of the dying Theaetetus. This event serves as an occasion for them to read together a report of a conversation which took place a number of years previously between Socrates and Theaetetus. At the time, Socrates was awaiting his trial, so we are to assume that Socrates was seventy years old and that Theaetetus was a youth of about sixteen.

The dialogue proper opens with a conversation between Theodorus (Theaetetus' teacher) and Socrates in which Theodorus praises Theaetetus highly.

Socrates is impressed, and he calls the boy over to converse with him to see if Theodorus' estimate is a fair one. Socrates tells Theaetetus of his occupation as an intellectual midwife and requests Theaetetus to let him use his art to see if Theaetetus has anything to give birth to. The boy responds eagerly but respectfully, and the philosophical portion of the dialogue gets under way.

Socrates asks Theaetetus for a definition of knowledge, and Theaetetus replies that knowledge is perception. This possibility is then examined. Socrates, using his customary question and answer technique, proceeds to make the definition more precise. He begins by identifying the theory as that of Protagoras. With this identification the theory is recognized as the familiar Protagorean view that "Man is the measure of all things." What the view comes to, Socrates states, is an identification of appearance with reality: "What *seems* or *appears* to me *is* to me." The world of knowledge is in some sense private to each knower. The

99

theory is thus applied to sensation, which is interpreted as an interaction or resultant of two elements, a sense stimulus and the sensory response. The stimulus is given status as something objectively real. Nevertheless, since each knower's sense organs are private, and the knowledge he obtains is conditioned by this private character, the result is a private world of knowledge.

Socrates wishes to clarify the theory still more, however. To do so, he points out that certain puzzles can arise if the theory is not fully understood. There are three "laws" which seem to be true, yet incompatible with experience: (1) No object can become greater or smaller without having something added to or subtracted from it. (2) No object to which nothing is either added or subtracted is made greater or smaller. (3) Any object which now is, but previously was not, must have suffered becoming. Against the background of these three apparently self-evident laws it seems impossible that Socrates can now be taller than Theaetetus, but yet within a year be shorter than Theaetetus, unless Socrates himself undergoes some change in height.

The resolution of the apparent conflict between the facts (Socrates' first being taller, then shorter, than Theaetetus) and the three laws rests on recognizing that the theory of sensation Socrates has attributed to Protagoras differs from the theory of sensation which is presupposed in generating the puzzles. The three laws, when taken in conjunction with the fact of Socrates' becoming shorter than Theaetetus, produce the puzzle only when largeness and smallness are interpreted as nonrelational properties; that is to say, only when they are interpreted as absolute qualities which inhere in an object without making any reference to another object. In Plato's earlier dialogue, the *Phaedo*, there is a suggestion that size is an absolute rather than a relational property, that Socrates is short because of the presence of Shortness (the Idea) in Socrates. In such a view, the comparison of Socrates and Theaetetus would involve one in saying that initially Tallness was present in Socrates, and then, a year later (without Socrates having undergone any change), Shortness is present in Socrates. If sensation yields knowledge of the real, and Socrates becomes shorter than Theaetetus in virtue of Shortness replacing Tallness, one cannot say that Socrates really remains unchanged—yet Socrates does remain the same height. The contradiction lies in saying that Socrates changes and that Socrates does not change.

The account of sensation developed in this dialogue, however, is that the sensation of Socrates' height is the result of an interaction between the sense stimulus and the sense organ. This is a more sophisticated account which, it should be noted, is intended to deal with sense experience, not with knowledge of the Ideas. The Ideas cannot be known by sensation, so a part of the problem—*really* knowing the Tallness in Socrates—is dispelled. What can be sensed is the world of becoming, and this, for Plato and Socrates, is a world of flux, not the world which truly can be known. But the sensation—that which can be "known" on the basis of the theory under consideration—is a product of the interaction of an element from the flux with the private sense organ of an individual knower. The externally real combines with a private sense organ to give rise to sensation. The real, as Protagoras understood it, may very well be a collection of apparently contradictory qualities, but the world of "knowledge" is private since it is conditioned by the privacy of the knower's sense organs. All sense knowledge is relative to a particular knower at a particular time. Thus, there is no contradiction in saying that Socrates now is taller than Theaetetus, but later is shorter than Theaetetus. There is no stable, unchanging background to give rise to the (apparent) contradictions. The "laws" are thus revealed as resting on the conviction that there is an abiding, changeless structure to the world of sensation; once this abiding character is rejected in favor of a flux, the "laws" lose their point. The external world is a flux, the knower himself is in flux, and sensation is a product of the two. If either changes, there is a different sensation.

The theory is now fully stated, and Socrates moves on to the criticism of it. He first makes some rather trivial objections. He points out, in the first place, that the theory does not justify taking *man* as the measure of all things. With just as good reason one might take a pig or a horse as the measure, if knowledge is merely an interaction between a flux and a private sense organ. The criticism is not developed seriously; nevertheless, there is a purpose in making it. It suggests (although it does not explicitly state) a crucial element in the discussion of knowing; namely, that a judging mind is involved wherever there is a genuine case of knowing. A judging mind is precisely what a pig or horse lacks; thus, it is ridiculous to say that a pig is the measure of all

things. The other criticisms Socrates makes at this time also imply the same point, that a judging mind must be included in any theory of knowing. But the point is not elaborated at this time since it would destroy the dramatic quality of the dialogue to develop it at this point. Three additional criticisms are made here: (1) The theory, since it rejects any common world shared by two knowers, provides no justification for Protagoras' life as a teacher. Protagoras cannot justify his role as a teacher who corrects his pupils unless he is in some sense the measure of his pupils' worlds. (2) Sensations cannot be all there is to knowing since this would imply that one who cannot read would nevertheless *know* what is said on a page of writing when he merely *sees* it. Yet this clearly is not the case. (3) The theory would require one to deny that a man who closes his eyes knows what he has just seen.

Socrates next undertakes to defend Protagoras against these criticisms. He states that Protagoras would regard the criticisms as irrelevant since what should be refuted is either (a) the claim that men's sensations are private, or (b) the claim that the object causing the sensation is private. Still speaking on behalf of Protagoras, Socrates adds that the earlier criticisms missed the point and spirit of Protagoras' position. Protagoras could offer a justification of his teaching by pointing to the analogous case of a physician. The physician does not deny the reality of his patient's (distorted) world; instead, he changes the condition of the patient so that the patient's world is changed (thus losing its distortion). The wine really is bitter to a sick man, but the physician makes him well so that the same wine tastes sweet to the man when he has recovered from his illness. (In a sense, this is to say that Socrates-sick is not the same man as Socrates-well.) We can admit that the wine is both bitter and sweet without thereby destroying the right of the physician to perform his beneficial work. This justification, however, rests on restricting our concern to what is *useful* rather than on raising the question of what is *true*. Questions of *truth* concern the external object of knowledge; questions of *utility* can be restricted to the state of the knower. Protagoras, as teacher, can justify modifying the state of the knower without rejecting his claim that the object is a part of a private world in which there is no difference between what *appears* and what *is*. The earlier criticism has not touched Protagoras' real claim; namely, that what *seems* or *appears* to be true for an individual knower *is* true for that knower.

After a digression, Socrates turns to a more serious criticism of the position of Protagoras, one which takes into account the justification Socrates has offered on behalf of Protagoras. Socrates is quite willing to admit that the Protagorean position is a fair account of what occurs in immediate sensation. The world of becoming, for Plato and Socrates, is a flux, and men's sensations are private. One cannot taste the apple another man is tasting, nor does any man ever see a particular apple tree from quite the same perspective as that of his companion. And the "seeming" of the immediate data of sense is the "reality" of the immediate data of sense. But the problem of knowledge is wider than the problem of data. A theory of knowledge must account for other judgments besides those concerning the immediate data of sense, and it is

this fact that finally undercuts the Protagorean theory. Once one recognizes that there is more to the problem of knowing than merely giving an account of the direct awareness of uninterpreted sense experience, the weakness of the Protagorean position becomes obvious. Socrates raises the question of justifying judgments which have a future reference; thus, he broadens the scope of the discussion to include a problem Protagoras' theory cannot explain. A physician and his patient, for example, may disagree today about whether the patient will have a fever tomorrow. It is clear that both cannot be judging truly, and obviously the physician's prediction is more reliable than is the patient's. Both men are judging about a fact which is not at the moment a part of the immediate experience of either of them, and both cannot be right in their judgments; clearly one of them (the physician) is a better "measure" than is the other. When the consideration of knowing is thus broadened to include more than merely men's immediate experience, the Protagorean theory is seen to be inadequate.

Socrates next moves to a more critical examination of the doctrine that the world of sense experience is a flux. He examines the position of the followers of Heraclitus. Heraclitus had said that everything is in flux and that a person cannot step into the same river twice since "new waters are ever flowing." Some of his followers, however, had gone beyond this claim in saying that one cannot step into the same river even once. What these followers sensed, apparently, was that if everything is an absolute flux, then there is no point at all to mentioning "same." "Same" is a word which has meaning only in contrast with change, but if all is utter change, there is nothing which can be said to be "the same." This doctrine meshes well with the Protagorean doctrine; in fact, it is the Protagorean position stated in its most extreme form. Socrates therefore wishes to consider it.

The crucial point which the Heraclitean analysis omits is the recognition that there must be something which is exempt from the flux if there is to be any knowledge at all. If the world is nothing but a flux, in this extreme Heraclitean sense, then the knowledge is impossible. Socrates rejects both the unrelieved flux of the extreme Heracliteans and its opposite number, the unchanging unity of the followers of Parmenides. Knowledge, in the strict sense, is of elements like the Parmenidean One, but the (almost) knowledge we have of the world of becoming is of a flux which moves within limits that are unchanging and fixed after the manner of the Parmenidean unity. The world of sense experience, for Plato, is a flux—as the Heracliteans recognized—but insofar as this world of sense experience can be known, it must be viewed against an unchanging set of limits having the character of the Parmenidean One. Knowledge of the world of sense experience, then, involves both the changing and the unchanging; neither is by itself sufficient to account for our knowledge. Absolute flux is radically unknowable.

From this criticism of the extreme Heraclitean position Socrates moves on to a total rejection of the definition of knowledge which Theaetetus initially put forth; namely, that knowledge is perception. At the beginning of the examination of this theory Soc-

rates had laid down two criteria for knowledge which now serve as a basis for the rejection of Theaetetus' first proposal. Socrates at that point stated —and Theaetetus had assented—that knowledge was (1) of the real and (2) infallible. The examination of the theory that knowledge is perception has issued in the recognition that sensation may very well yield something which is infallible, but it has also revealed that it is not of the real, since the real is fixed and unchanging, not an ultimate flux. Yet Socrates goes even further in refuting Theaetetus' initial proposal. He introduces a consideration which had been hinted at earlier but was then left undeveloped; namely, that knowledge involves a mind which interprets the deliverances of sense. Before anything even remotely resembling knowledge is achieved, the raw data of sense must be interpreted. A man may taste an apple, but he cannot judge that it is sweet without evaluating the sense experience in the light of a standard which is not in itself part of the raw taste of the apple; he must know what sweetness is before he can determine that the apple tastes sweet. This standard—which is the Idea Sweetness, the reader realizes, even though Plato avoids specific mention of the Ideas in this dialogue—must be unchanging and real. It can be known, and it serves as the standard in terms of which the raw data of sense are interpreted. But the sense organs by themselves cannot know the standard. On the contrary, it is the mind which knows the standard and judges that the sense experience is of such and such a character in the light of this standard. Uninterpreted sense experience, therefore, cannot possibly be knowledge; even if it is interpreted, it still has as its object something which is less than real, and the interpretation presupposes a standard which is the genuine object of knowledge. When pursued far enough, the examination of sense experience leads to the Platonic position that knowledge must be restricted to the Ideas; we cannot have genuine knowledge of the world of becoming. Plato reserves the discussion of the Ideas in their own right for the *Sophist,* but the *Theaetetus* prepares the ground for this later direct analysis of knowing.

Theaetetus' first attempt to define knowledge has thus proved to be inadequate in the light of Socrates' examination of it. If the dialogue is to continue, Theaetetus must offer a new definition. This he does, proposing now that knowledge is true opinion. The examination of this possibility occupies Socrates and Theaetetus in the next portion of the dialogue. However, if there is any significance to the definition of knowledge as "true opinion," there must be something which is *false* opinion. It is to the elucidation of mistaken belief, or false opinion, then, that Socrates turns at this point.

Two well-known analogies occur in the account of false belief: the wax tablet analogy and the bird cage analogy. Socrates first suggests that belief may be analogous to fitting a new sense experience into an impression left in a wax tablet by a previous experience. When the new sense experience matches the impression in the wax, there is a case of true belief; but when the new experience is fitted into an impression which does not match, the result is mistaken belief.

The bird cage analogy takes into account some complications which the wax tablet analogy overlooks. The wax tablet analogy cannot account for mistaken belief about matters which do not have reference to sense experience. For example, a man might believe that 7 plus 5 equals 11, a mathematical belief which does not rest on sense experience. This situation is likened to a man who has a cage full of birds. At some time in the past he has gotten possession of the birds (learned the truths of mathematics) and put them into the cage. Later, he reaches into the cage to get possession of a particular bird. He may think he has grasped a parrot, even though in fact he has a pigeon in his hand. Analogously, a man who once learned that 7 plus 5 equals 12 may, when he tries to recall this truth, mistakenly believe that 7 plus 5 equals 11. He has in his possession, but not in his hand, the truth; thus, he describes incorrectly what he has in his hand.

These two accounts have a common feature. Both involve the interpretation of some conceptual object. It is the interpretation that brings in the difficulty, for whether one mistakenly judges that a stone is an apple (sense object) or whether one mistakenly judges that 7 plus 5 equals 11 (mathematical object), he still is making an interpretation. Yet if the interpretation yields genuine knowledge it must be infallible and of the real. A mistaken belief is clearly not infallible. If one knows, and knows that he knows, his initial judgment cannot be fallible. Neither the wax tablet analogy nor the bird cage analogy yields such certainty, however, and they therefore fail to do the job. Plato and Socrates want a psychological criterion for separating true from false beliefs. Neither the wax tablet nor the bird cage yields such a psychological criterion. Both accounts of mistaken belief are therefore inadequate, but the discussion is broken off at this point since further analysis would require Plato to introduce the Ideas, something he wishes to postpone until the *Sophist*.

Theaetetus has one final proposal to make. He suggests that the difficulty encountered in the examination of false belief may be overcome by defining knowledge as true belief accompanied by a reason or correct explanation. This will indeed do the job, but it has one crucial flaw; namely, it is a circular definition of knowledge. What the definition comes to is that knowledge is true opinion that is known to be true. An adequate definition, however, cannot use the term to be defined in the definition of the term. Theaetetus' final suggestion is inadequate, just as his earlier proposals have been.

The conclusion of the dialogue, then, is that knowledge is neither sensation nor true opinion—not even true opinion accompanied by an explanation. Theaetetus has labored, but he has not brought forth a legitimate intellectual offspring. Nevertheless, Socrates says, the discussion has been of value to Theaetetus, for he does not now think that he knows something which he does not know, and if he attempts to define knowledge again at a later time his present efforts will help him to avoid certain pitfalls.

The overt conclusion of the dialogue may be negative, but for one who reads Plato intelligently and enters into the dialogue as an attentive, though silent, participant, the positive conclusion is nevertheless obvious, even though it is not explicitly stated: Knowledge can only be of the Forms or Ideas. To give an adequate account of knowing one must introduce the Ideas. This task Plato postpones until the *Sophist*, the dialogue which naturally follows the *Theaetetus*.

One can hardly read the *Theaetetus* without feeling that here is philosophy unsurpassed. Plato's problems, for the most part, retain their vitality, and his solutions retain their interest, even after more than two thousand years. And when philosophical excellence of the very first order is given expression in literary and dramatic form of equally high quality, there is very little that can be said in criticism. Part of Plato's appeal undoubtedly results from the fact that he usually is occupied in rejecting inadequate positions, leaving his own positive doctrine to be worked out by the reader as the implicit alternative. And it is certainly true that Plato made mistakes. Yet when his mistakes are all pointed out, and an allowance is made for his indirect manner of arguing for his own doctrine, the fact remains that the Platonic position today is still in its essentials the same as that Plato himself held; the necessary corrections are minor. Platonism is a live alternative today. And the student who wishes to see the inadequacies of a simple-headed empiricism which thinks it can do without a judging mind in accounting for knowledge can do no better than to study carefully Plato's *Theaetetus*.

PARMENIDES

Author: Plato (427-347 B.C.)
Type of work: Epistemology
First transcribed: Probably one of the later dialogues

PRINCIPAL IDEAS ADVANCED

Zeno has argued that if Being is many, it must be both like and unlike, which is impossible; but Zeno forgets that, although the universals likeness and unlikeness are not identical, particular things can be alike in some respect, and unlike in some other respect.

Socrates claims that there are absolute ideas (forms) of the just, the beautiful, the good, and the true; but perhaps there are no ideas of vile materials such as mud, hair, and dirt.

Parmenides has various criticisms of the Doctrine of Ideas: If an Idea is one and yet exists in many things, it is separated from itself; and if Ideas cover things with only parts of themselves, anything partaking of smallness would be smaller than absolute smallness.

Furthermore, Parmenides argues, the Doctrine of Ideas leads to an infinite regress of Ideas; and if the Ideas are absolute, they cannot be known by us.

Parmenides then demonstrates his sophistical skill by arguing that if the one is, the one is not; and if the one is not, nothing is.

The *Parmenides* is fascinating as a penetrating criticism of the Doctrine of Ideas in its undeveloped state, as propounded by the youthful Socrates. According to the report given by Antiphon—a report of the conversation between Parmenides and Socrates, with some assistance from Zeno and Aristoteles—Socrates met Parmenides when the latter was about sixty-five years old and famous for his poem *On Nature,* in which he argued, with great ingenuity, that "All is one." It may very well be that this conversation occurred as reported, but what is more likely is that Plato, having heard that at one time young Socrates met the aging Parmenides, used this bit of historical information as a dramatic center about which to build a summary of Parmenidean criticism of his Doctrine of Ideas, taking some of the edge off the criticism by portraying Socrates as clever but immature in his thinking. Consequently, the *Parmenides* serves as evidence that Plato was never entirely satisfied with the Doctrine of Ideas, that, like all great philosophers, he kept coming back to his central thesis, subjecting it to critical scrutiny and modifying it in accordance with the discoveries of its weaknesses.

The presentation of the dialogue is somewhat complicated. Cephalus repeats an account originally given by Antiphon of the meeting between Parmenides and Socrates. The actual conversation presumably occurred several years earlier.

Socrates had gone with others to hear the writings of Zeno, who was visiting Athens with Parmenides. After hearing Zeno read from some of his writings, Socrates summed up

Zeno's thesis as stating that "if being is many, it must be both like and unlike, and . . . this is impossible. . . ." The youthful Socrates then pointed out that this was simply a roundabout way of supporting Parmenides' doctrine that All is one, for to claim that Being is *not many* and to state that it *is one* is to make one and the same claim.

Zeno agreed with Socrates, but he defended himself by saying that his argument was designed to show the inconsistency in upholding the doctrine that Being is not one, but many.

Socrates then professed not to see the extraordinariness of saying that things could be both like and unlike. It would be paradoxical, he agreed, to say in regard to the *Idea* of likeness that it could somehow partake of unlikeness; after all, the likeness that things might share could not in itself, as an absolute nature, be unlikeness. But things—as distinguished from absolute Ideas, or natures—could very well be alike in some respect or to some degree, and unlike in some other respect or degree. To say that things are one simply because it is possible to speak of them as partaking of the Idea oneness, while at the same time they might, in some other respect, partake of the Idea of the many, is only to utter a truism. The impression left by Socrates' argument was that the view held by Parmenides and Zeno might very well be trivial, nothing but a truism.

Apparently both Parmenides and Zeno were upset and impressed by Socrates' criticism, but the venerable Parmenides had no intention of allowing Socrates to escape scrutiny of his own views. He began to probe Socrates' distinction between *Ideas* in themselves (or kinds of things) and *things* of certain kinds (partaking of Ideas). He drew from Socrates the admission that Socrates believed in Ideas (such as the Idea of likeness) which can be considered as distinct from that which partakes of the Ideas. Socrates emphatically asserted that there are absolute Ideas of the just, the beautiful, the good and such matters, but he was not certain that there are Ideas of man, fire, and water—and he was certain that there are no absolute Ideas of such vile materials as hair, mud, and dirt. Nevertheless, Socrates did admit that he sometimes thought that there is an Idea of everything—that even the most vile things partake of absolute Ideas—but that he was afraid that this extreme view would turn out to be nonsensical. Parmenides replied, in a somewhat condescending manner, that Socrates' reluctance to extend his view was caused by Socrates' youth, that the time would come when he would "not despise even the meanest things. . . ."

Then, by using the language of things to talk about Ideas, Parmenides attempted to show the difficulties of claiming that many things can partake of a single absolute nature or Idea. If the whole Idea is one and exists as one in many things, then it is separated from itself (resulting in a condition, Parmenides suggested implicitly, which would not be possible). Socrates responded by saying that the Idea is like the day—"one and the same in many places at once. . . ." But Parmenides then took advantage of this spatial metaphor to argue that just as a sail spread over many men covers each with only a part of itself, so an Idea spread over many things would cover each with only a part—not the whole

—of itself. But if Ideas cover things with only parts of themselves, then things partaking of equality, for example, would in fact be partaking of less than equality (since but a part of equality); and things partaking of smallness would be partaking of part of smallness, and since a part is smaller than the whole of which it is part, the part would be smaller than the absolutely small (which is absurd). Hence, Parmenides concluded, there are difficulties in Socrates' view, whether the Idea covers things as a whole or only in part. Socrates conceded that he had no ready answer to this criticism.

Another objection was then advanced by Parmenides. If one compares greatness (the Idea) to great things, it would seem that, according to Socrates' way of thought, there must be another Idea by reference to which greatness and great things can be seen to be alike in partaking of this second greatness. But there is no end to this mode of analysis, and one begins to wonder about the method.

Further criticism by Parmenides led to the rejection of the suggestion by Socrates that the Ideas might be only thoughts (for if the Ideas are *only* thoughts, the thoughts have no objects; but if, on the other hand, the thoughts are of Ideas, there are Ideas).

Socrates then proposed that Ideas are patterns and that to say that something partakes of an Idea (or nature) means only that it fits the pattern, is like the pattern in some respect. But Parmenides then used a variant of one of his former arguments to maintain that this view would involve another infinite regress of Ideas (for the pattern would be like the copy in respect of a certain Idea, and that Idea would

be like the pattern in respect of a third Idea, *ad infinitum*).

Another difficulty involved in the claim that there are absolute Ideas, Parmenides told Socrates, is that if the Ideas are absloute and not relative to us, they cannot be known by us, since all our knowledge is relative to us.

Furthermore, he went on, God surely has absolute knowledge, but if so, he cannot know human beings by reference to the absolute Ideas which he has (for the relative cannot be understood by the absolute). Yet to know them in any other way would be to know them in an inferior fashion. Thus, in Socrates' view, God is either ignorant in part, or knows in some inferior fashion.

Having made Socrates uncomfortable with his adept criticism, Parmenides then gave the young philosopher advice concerning his profession. He suggested that Socrates follow the practice of considering the consequences of any proposed hypothesis and also the consequences of the denial of the hypothesis. Socrates asked for an example, and after some urging Parmenides agreed to illustrate the method he endorsed by considering the hypothesis that one is (that Being is one) and then that one is not (that Being is not one).

To follow the logical analysis then offered by Parmenides, who supposed that he was somehow getting at the nature of reality, it is necessary to understand what might be meant by the claim that All is one—a claim sometimes put by the alternative expressions, "One is" and "Being is one." To say that All is one may be to say that whatever *is* must be one with whatever is—at least in respect of being.

(My typewriter and pencil are one in that they both *are*—they both exist.) If we try to think of something that does not exist, then it is either something that is not part of the one that is (for example, a mermaid)—or else, if it is something like empty space, then it *is* empty space; it has being, and is one with anything else that has being. And if we then refuse to talk about anything at all except in terms of its being or not being, it is of course evident that everything that *is* is one with everything (else) that is (only we should not say "else," or even "everything," since to do so involves making a distinction in terms of something other than being).

Once this game is started, it is easy to take advantage of the multiplicity of uses of the word "is" and of the word "one" to defend the claim that "One is," or that "Being is one, not many." Parmenides was so skillful at this game that his fame persists to this day, and he was persuasive enough to impress both Socrates and Plato (partly because they themselves sometimes played similar games under the same misconception: that they were learning about reality metaphysically).

To show Socrates how philosophy should be practiced Parmenides sought the aid of young Aristoteles to give him the right answers to the questions put by Parmenides. Considering first the alternative that one is, he quickly established that if one is, it cannot be many; if it cannot be many, it can neither be a whole nor have parts (since in either case it would be many). Since only something other than the one could limit the one, if the one is, it has no beginning, middle, end; hence, it is unlimited, formless,

existing nowhere, neither resting nor moving, and never in anything. The one could not be the same as or different from itself or anything other than itself; it could neither be equal to nor unequal to itself, nor to anything other; it could be neither the same age as, nor younger than, nor older than itself nor anything other. Finally, Parmenides concluded that no mode of being could be attributed to the one; consequently, the one is not. The assumption that the one is had yielded the conclusion that the one is not.

Parmenides then explored the proposition that the one is not, but only after having decided that if the one is, it partakes of being; and if it partakes of being, it must have being in every part and be infinitely multiple, thus not one. And further considerations only enforced the conclusion that if the one partakes of any mode of being, it must be multiple and not one. But if the one is not, and if there is consideration of the hypothesis that the one is not, then the meaning of the expression "If one is not" is known. Furthermore, there is not only knowledge of the one which is not, but the one which is not must be something if it can be considered; but, on the other hand, being cannot be attributed to the one, since it is not. As that which is not, the one must be different from the others which are; and it must be like itself, which is not. Working out the implications of various interpretations of the ambiguous claim that the one is not, Parmenides finally came to the conclusion that if the one is not, nothing is, and he finished by saying: "Let this much be said; and further let us affirm what seems to be the truth, that, whether one is or is not, one and the others in relation to themselves and one another, all of them, in every way, are and are not, and appear to be and appear not to be."

It is worth one's while to attend to the logical play (undertaken in dead seriousness) in the latter part of the *Parmenides,* if only to learn what happens when a philosopher mistakes logical facts for facts about the world; and the uselessness of such analysis makes the earlier discussion, concerning the Platonic Ideas, seem all the more important by contrast. One receives the impression that Plato (and Socrates) enjoyed the game that logic makes possible, but at the same time they tended to regard sophistical skills as unimportant, even improper, when contrasted with the practice of true philosophy.

As a final example of the sort of word play that occupied Parmenides and led to his famous thesis that "All is one," a passage is now quoted—elementary in its logical development, but sparkling enough to impress his uncritical listeners, the youthful Socrates, the guileless Aristoteles: ". . . the one which is not, if it is to maintain itself, must have the being of not-being as the bond of not-being, just as being must have as a bond the not-being of not-being in order to perfect its own being; for the truest assertion of the being of being and of the not-being of not-being is when being partakes of the being of being and not of the being of not-being—that is, the perfection of being; and when not-being does not partake of the not-being of not-being but of the being of not being—that is the perfection of not-being."

"Most true," commented the guileless Aristoteles.

SOPHIST

Author: Plato (427-347 B.C.)
Type of work: Epistemology, metaphysics
First transcribed: Probably one of the later dialogues

PRINCIPAL IDEAS ADVANCED

The sophist claims that in teaching the art of rhetoric he teaches all useful knowledge.

Parmenides' claim—that the real is one being—is false, for the term "real" must refer to one Idea and the term "one" to another.

Those who claim that only the tangible is real are mistaken, for Ideas are real; and life, soul, and intelligence are also real, yet none of these is tangible.

The task of the philosopher in his search for wisdom is to seek to discover which Ideas combine and which do not.

The sophist claims that we cannot speak of what is not, but he is mistaken for to speak of what is not is simply to speak of that which exists as not having certain forms (Ideas).

The sophist is an image-maker who teaches the art of deception through the use of language; he is no true philosopher.

There is still some controversy over the question whether Plato intended to write a triology among his dialogues consisting of the *Statesman*, the *Sophist*, and the *Philosopher*. The latter dialogue was never written, but it seems likely that it was planned, since the first two are concerned with the search for definitions which will not only delimit the statesman and the sophist, but will also show wherein, if at all, they differ from the philosopher. It was thus supposed that Plato intended to write a concluding dialogue in which the philosopher would be defined and in which the search for the type of knowledge appropriate to him would be ended. In the *Sophist* Plato aims at a definition of the sophist and of the kind of activity that properly belongs to him. The dialogue *Theaetetus* is also intimately connected to this series, for in it Plato begins the quest for a proper definition of knowledge and for an answer to many of the problems that plagued him as he worked out his theory of ideas. The *Sophist* follows the *Theaetetus* and carries on the search for an answer.

In setting out to define "sophist" Plato makes use of the technique of classification by which he goes from the most general terms to the more specific in seeking to describe the nature of a sophist. He makes use of a similar approach in the *Statesman* in order to distinguish the true ruler from apparent ones. In their pursuit of the nature of the sophist, Socrates and a stranger from Elea point out many facets of his character, especially with regard to what he professes to know,

which indicate to them that although a correct definition ought to point to that, and that alone, which is essential to the nature of the sophist, they find that he professes to be master of many arts. The sophist shows as his most pronounced trait the ability to discourse persuasively; he claims that through the art of rhetoric he can give one knowledge in all fields. It is denied by the stranger that one can have knowledge in all fields, a denial in accord with Plato's view expressed throughout his works, and emphasized in *The Republic*, that one can know and do only one thing well. Therefore, the sophist, although he proclaims himself expert in many areas, must have and present only the appearance or image of a subject rather than the reality. Sophistry, if it is an art (for how can the practitioners of sham be artists?), is the art of image-making. The stranger then pursues an analysis of image-making.

Image-making has two parts or kinds. In the first place, one may copy an original; examples are the craftsman who copies a natural object and the painter who makes a likeness of someone's face. In the second place, there are those who make semblances —what appear to be likenesses, but are in some way out of proportion. The second type of image-making raises certain questions. What is meant by this world of semblances? A semblance is apparently not real, and yet it cannot be said to be unreal or nothing, for it is something. But what kind of a something? Plato is again struggling with the Parmenidean problem of the existence of a world of appearances, which is neither of the world of forms or ideas nor of the world of not-being or nothing; rather, it seems to hover somewhere in between, to be a world of change, of becoming.

The Eleatic stranger had previously proclaimed himself, or had been proclaimed, a student of Zeno and of Parmenides, and he shows his indebtedness to them in his pursuit of these questions. The concern over the world of appearances brings up related problems over the judgments made about that world. For in dealing with that which is not real (that is, that which changes), we must use negative judgments, yet these judgments apparently refer to some object. Plato is emphasizing that when we use a locution such as "is not" we seem to be denying the existence of something. But of what? There is nothing that we can be talking about since apparently it, whatever it is, is not, and hence is not anything. This sort of puzzle sets off a discussion in the *Sophist* over certain aspects of epistemology and ontology that had troubled pre-Socratic philosophers and to which Plato addressed himself. The discussion concerns the three realms of not-being (nothing), becoming, and being, and what sort of knowledge and judgment is appropriate to each.

In discussing the worlds of reality and appearance, the stranger dismisses rather quickly that of not-being or the totally unreal. Generally speaking, the totally unreal cannot be the subject of discourse because our statements cannot have *no* reference whatsoever; we cannot talk about nothing. In addition, the very attempt to do so is ambiguous and misleading. We seem to be talking about something, the totally unreal, and we use pronouns as if they referred to a thing; and yet, as noted, we are not talking about anything. There is a sense in which we contradict ourselves when we attempt to talk about nothing, since we must talk about something.

There is still a puzzle which must be solved: when we use a statement which either tells us that something is or that something is not, then of either alternative we can say that it is true or it is false. In either case we seem to be stating a sentence which conveys meaning. Hence, we cannot always be talking about the totally unreal or the meaningless when we utter negative or even false judgments. It remains to be seen if this problem can be treated successfully. The analysis given by Parmenides (who is the stranger's inspiration) that there is only that which is or is not cannot be adequate; false statements seem to refer to something "in between." Thus Plato parts company with Parmenides and holds that the realm of becoming, events in space and time which undergo change, has a status which cannot be ignored by the philosopher. Before this realm is examined, however, some attention must be given to what is meant by the "real." The Eleatic stranger begins by reviewing what some of the earlier philosophers have said about it.

The Eleatic stranger treats briefly those who had held that hot and cold are real, or that one is but the other is not, or that the real is a third thing. When he comes to Parmenides, as we might guess, he treats him in more detail. Parmenides had claimed that the real is one being. A question is raised in that Parmenides used two names, "one" and "real," to designate this entity; how can there be two names to designate one entity? (Plato apparently believed that these two names designated two separate and distinct forms or Ideas—the form of oneness, and that of realness—hence Parmenides' analysis was not about one thing, but two.) A more detailed analysis of this view is given. If the real is a whole made up of parts, then it cannot be unity or oneness itself; these imply a lack of parts, but obviously a whole made up of parts indicates a plurality of entities. In such a case, of course, we can speak quite properly of such a whole (made up of parts) as having unity, but we cannot say that there is only one being and no other. The real is not a whole, yet wholeness exists. The real, then, cannot be what is. That realness and wholeness must exist means that there is a plurality existing. Another possibility is, if wholeness does not exist, then the real will be a plurality of many parts with no totality. But if so, it cannot then be that which is, nor can it ever become that which is.

The discovery of the unsatisfactory character of Parmenides' view of reality leads to a general discussion of idealism versus materialism as philosophical positions; Plato picturesquely calls this "the battle between the Gods and Giants," between those who dwell in the heavens—the realm of Ideas—versus those who dwell on the earth—the realm of the tangible. The Giants or materialists claim that only the tangible is real, whereas the idealists or Gods point out that moral qualities can be present in some and absent in others; these are qualities which are not tangible, yet must be admitted as real. The question as to what is real leads both camps to search for a mark or sign of the real by which they may know it. The materialists suggest, and the Eleatic stranger considers it tentatively, that only that which has the power to affect or to be affected by an agent is the real. The Eleatic stranger makes out the following objection to the materialists: the materialists demand a quality which they can sense before they proclaim something real; they admit, however, that they can be aware of the presence or absence of "justice" within themselves or others; but such awareness is not of a sensible quality but of an intellectual one, and its object, justice, is an Idea.

In discussing the idealists, the Eleatic stranger first considers the view which proclaims that only that which is changeless can be an object of knowledge and truly real. But can the changeless be an object of knowledge, if to know is to act upon in some sense? For if that which is an object of knowledge is acted upon, then it is changed; but if it is changed, then it cannot be that which is changeless. Hence, either knowledge is not that which acts upon something, or, if it is, then that which is changeless and, by definition, not capable of being acted upon, cannot be known. It is here that the Eleatic stranger questions whether only that which is changeless is real. (He thus again breaks with the Parmenidean school.) He argues that life, soul, and intelligence—all of them "objects" that undergo change—belong to the domain of the real. The school of Heraclitus is next attacked —that school which had maintained that only change, flux, was real. If all is flux there can be no intelligence in real things; for if nothing were the same from moment to moment, nothing could be known. Therefore the stranger from Elea concludes that reality must consist both of that

113

which is changeless and of that which changes, if we are to have intelligence in the world.

Plato seems to wish to bridge the gap created by the Parmenideans and the followers of Heraclitus in their construction of what is real by pointing out that each group errs when it rejects that which the other regards as real. In this dialogue the matter is not pursued further. Instead, a return to a previous discussion ensues which seems much like the one just concluded, but is different. For the discussion concerns "reality" rather than the "real," and it treats reality as a form among forms. It is in this sense that Plato holds reality to be changeless, as we shall see, and hence he does not contradict what he had just affirmed:—that the real includes that which is changeless as well as that which changes. If reality included both change and changelessness, we would have three forms rather than one—but that is impossible.

The argument brings out an important point in Platonic metaphysics. Each time a combination of forms is considered, an impasse is reached when it is revealed that there is more than one form involved in the discussion. If the one is real (or exists), then oneness, unity, reality, and existence are all involved; for if reality were not present, we could not talk of the one as real.

The Eleatic stranger then considers the questions raised in the discussion, questions concerning the possibility of the combination of forms and of negative judgments. The forms considered in this discussion are movement, rest, and reality (or existence). Some forms must be compatible with others in that some kind of combination must be possible between them if they are to be said to be real. Thus, unless movement combines with reality and unless rest does also, then neither of them is real. Not all forms are compatible in this way, however, else we would run into absurdities; for instance, movement cannot combine with rest, for if it did then we could say of movement that it is at rest, and of rest that it is in movement. The task of the philosopher in his search for wisdom and truth is to investigate which forms combine and which do not; this task is to be accomplished by philosophic discourse—by dialectic. The Eleatic stranger reminds his cohorts in discussion that their task is to seek out the sophist, who dwells in the realm of seeming or perhaps of not-being, rather than the philosopher. He suggests that after their present task is finished they may come back to the philosopher and his realm (thus giving credence to the view that Plato intended to write a dialogue called the *Philosopher*). In the search for what is real the purpose is to clarify the realm that the sophist inhabits. The stranger continues this discussion by bringing up two more forms: sameness and difference. He does so because in speaking of two or more forms we are automatically involved with sameness and difference. For rest is the same with itself (partakes of sameness), different from movement. Sameness and difference must be separate forms, for if movement and rest were equivalent to sameness then they would be equivalent to each other. That is, they would both partake of sameness and thus be the same; yet although they are the same with regard to themselves respectively, they are not with regard to each other. The same holds for difference. Having pointed out that the five forms are separate and distinct, the Eleatic stranger then considers them with regard to judgments involving the locutions "is" and "is not." He points out an important feature of the verb form "is": it has at least two senses; namely, (1) "exists" and (2) "is identical to" or "is the same as." The statements considered are as follows: (1) Motion is not (Rest). Motion is (real or exists). (2) Motion is not (the Same). Motion is the same (as itself). (3) Motion is not (the Different). Motion is different (from Difference).

The Eleatic stranger then concludes that of any form we may say that it is not (any other form) and that it is (real or exists). It is here that the break with Parmenides is complete, for it can be shown that his statement, " 'That which is' cannot 'not be' " is incorrect, since "That which is" *can* "not be" (be other than) all other existents; and thus we can have as a true statement the following: " 'What is' can 'not be.' " Furthermore, we can also have as a true statement, " 'What is not' can 'be.' " That which is not everything else is still itself (exists). Parmenides has thus been refuted in saying that "that which is" can in no sense "not be" and that "that which is not" can in no sense "be."

This argument can also be applied to the sophist and he can be shown to be wrong when he states that we cannot speak of what is not; it has been shown that we can and do so speak, when, for example, we say that "is not" means "is not the same as." Can we reconcile the problem, however, when "is not" refers to "falsity"?

The Eleatic stranger presents an analysis of statements (essentially of descriptive statements) to clarify the problem of false judgments. Of every statement it may be said that it must contain at least a name (an expression applied to that which performs the action) and a verb (an expression applied to the action). Every statement must also be about something. Lastly, every statement has a certain character; that is, we say of it that it is either true or false. The examples that the stranger considers are (1) "Theaetetus sits," and (2) "Theaetetus flies." The first is true for Theaetetus is in fact sitting. The second is false for it describes the subject Theaetetus as doing what he is not doing. Thus it states that things that are not, are (exist). It appears here that Plato in his analysis has presented us with an application of the views just worked out by the Eleatic stranger regarding the five Forms and the possibilities of combination. Falsity occurs whenever the incorrect forms are used in describing the action of the subject (assuming that the correct subject is used). In this way Plato feels that he has shown that false statements are meaningful.

Plato has so far dealt with the problem of false statements, and he has shown in what sense they are about something and in what sense they are meaningful. His analysis, although incomplete, points toward a fuller discussion which, as noted, was probably to be made in the *Philosopher*. He tackled the problem, not as he felt the sophists had done, with a shallow display of verbal paradoxes, but rather by a provocative analysis and a suggested solution in terms of his theory of forms or Ideas. Descriptive statements are about something, often tangible, performed by something or someone—thus, they denote—but, to an extent, they derive meaning from the relation they express between the action described and the form(s) partaken of. With this attempt made, the Eleatic stranger returns to a final consideration of the sophist.

He concludes that as a species of image-maker the sophist belongs to those who deal in semblances. Their forte is in the construction of contradictions which, they freely admit, are intended to confuse and deceive. The mimicry they advocate is based, not on knowledge, but on opinion; since it is an art that deals in a shadow-play of words, it is not a discourse that aims at wisdom. When sophists encourage the use of their arguments to persuade the people and gain mastery over them, their profession is that of the demagogue and not of the statesman.

STATESMAN

Author: Plato (427-347 B.C.)
Type of work: Political philosophy
First transcribed: After the *Republic* but before the *Laws*

PRINCIPAL IDEAS ADVANCED

The problem confronting the Athenian Stranger and Socrates is that of defining the ideal statesman.

The statesman, or king, is a member of the class of those who direct action; he initiates directives; and he is distinguished from those who build lifeless things by the fact that his concern is with a living herd, the citizenry.

The art of statesmanship is not a function of the kind of state to be governed; a good statesman can rule no matter what the form of government.

Laws are necessary in a state, but the ruler is more important than the laws; in many cases he must judge when the laws do not apply.

The statesman is superior to other men who practice the various arts of ruling men in that he must decide which of the other arts is to be used for the benefit of the state; in that sense, statesmanship is the art of all arts.

In Plato's political works he is mainly concerned with an analysis of the nature of the individual and of the state which is an appropriate reflection of the individual. For Plato looked upon the state as analogous to the individual, and he believed that the type of individual found in the state determined the sort of state it would be. In the *Republic* he searches for justice in the state to discover the nature of justice in the person; and, after he describes the ideal state and its ruler, he traces its decline by pointing to the concomitant decline in the soul of the individual. In the *Laws* he concentrates on the second-best state, a government of laws not men, and works out the constitution applicable to it. In the *Statesman*, written most

116

likely between the *Republic* and the *Laws*, Plato attacks the problem of defining the king who would rule in the best state, distinguishing him from sham rulers.

Plato looked upon ruling as an art, and, as with other arts, it has its subject matter which only an expert can master. People who are ill turn willingly to a physician expertly trained in the art of medicine to cure them; people who are in need of transportation between lands separated by an open sea turn to a pilot expertly trained in the art of seamanship to guide them across perilous seas; yet in the most important problem they face—conducting themselves as citizens in the state which involves their very happiness—they seem content to trust their fortunes to people untrained in statesmanship, who know nothing of the art of governing. It is as if they turned to the first person they met for medical help, or trusted anyone at all to sail them across dangerous waters. Plato believed that intelligent human beings, ignorant of an art in which they had no training, when they needed help for which the art was beneficial, would willingly turn to the expert for advice. He believed that if he could spell out the art of ruling and the training necessary to be an expert in it, intelligent people would willingly turn to true statesmen to rule them.

The Athenian Stranger points out that we are to seek a definition of the statesman as a kind of expert, and, hence, a division of forms of knowledge will be necessary. For to be an expert takes knowledge, and since this is knowledge of statecraft, statecraft should be separated from that which is other than statecraft. In addition, we must also separate knowledge into that which is applied and that which is pure. The Stranger points out that the ruler's art is closer to mental than to manual labor, and thus the distinction is needed, for the former is theoretical or pure rather than practical or applied. (In our discussion we shall use "statesmanship" and "kingship," and "statesman" and "king," as interchangeable terms respectively.)

In his search for a proper definition, the Athenian Stranger makes use of the logical technique of defining his terms by proceeding from the most general to the more particular, thus specifying what the statesman is as accurately as he can. He begins by examining appropriate subdivisions of the division of theoretical knowledge; the art of counting (which has nothing to do with applied work) and that of master builder, charged with directing action. The king is found in this class, which can itself be divided into those who give initial directives (the king) and those who pass on to others commands that are given to them (the king's ministers).

As one who issues commands, the king aims at the production of something. That which is productive may itself be divided into the lifeless and the living. The king, who is a member of the directive class, may be distinguished at this juncture from the master builder, for whereas the builder produces lifeless things, the king is concerned with ordering living creatures, in flocks rather than singly. These, it must be remembered, are flocks of tame rather than wild creatures, of men rather than animals. The art that we are looking for, then, is that of shepherding mankind; it is the art of government; and the expert,

117

the man of knowledge concerning this art, is the statesman or king, who is herder to a human, tame flock. It is a peculiar herd in that its members challenge the herder, and various members claim that they themselves are the true herders of mankind. (Thus, it is not easy to get men to accept willingly the expert in governing as properly ruling over them; they do not recognize the art for what it is.) Farmers, doctors, merchants, teachers, others, all put in their claims; some point out that even the statesman is fed by them.

Plato turns to one of his famous myths to aid us in our quest. This myth relates the reversal of the movements of heaven and earth and the changes that this brought about. Before the reversal, every herd of living creatures was watched over by a heavenly daemon. The herds were all under the great god Kronos, and they lived an idyllic existence. The reversal changed all this; when Zeus took over, the daemons left the human flocks and, unattended, they were prey to wild beasts. Men were forced to learn to protect themselves; they had no crafts and were at the mercy of nature. With mastery of crafts came protection from and the control of nature; since the gods had abandoned the flocks, human herders had to take over. The Athenian Stranger points out that the mistake they were making in defining the statesman was that they confused him with the divine herder, did not define his manner of rule, and forgot that nurture was to be subsumed under the flock in discussing the herder's function. The herder is concerned with men in flocks and it is to this fact that we must turn in our search for a definition.

In "tending men" we find that some-times rule has to be enforced and that at other times it is willingly accepted. It is important that this distinction be made, for on it depends the distinction between a tyrant and a king. The true statesman has his "tending" freely accepted by herds of free bipeds. If the state is to function properly, the rulers must be accepted willingly by the subjects; in any form of government the ruled must obey the laws or face sanctions provided in the law.

In order to understand what kingly duties entail, the Athenian Stranger continues, we must first distinguish those activities which are no part of statesmanship from statesmanship. First of all are those practical activities which contribute to the basic needs of the community and without which the community could not survive. (Nevertheless, it is not the kingly art to produce these things.) Under this category we find such workers as those who preserve what has been produced; those who produce the support of things (the carpenters, for example); those who defend us from cold as well as from enemies—such men as builders and weavers; those who provide diversion for us, the poets and musicians; those who produce the basic materials to be used in other crafts, the skinners, the lumbermen, and so on; and those who provide food and nourishment for the community. We also find in the community other groups such as slaves or merchants, civil servants and priests; but the statesman is not to be confused with any members of any of these groups, for none has independent authority and none is a ruler. Nor must we confuse the statesman with those who pretend to teach one how to rule, those who boast of their ability to argue any

118

side of an issue, the sophists who walk the land. The Athenian Stranger promises to discuss them more fully later (he does so in the *Sophist*). He then proceeds to discuss various types of states to see if the statesman fits one more than another.

There are three major types, each with two subtypes. In monarchy we have rule by one, and this may be exemplified by a tyrant or a constitutional monarchy. The next type is that in which a few wield power; this may be seen in an aristocracy or, when wealth is the criterion for rule, an oligarchy. Lastly, we have the rule of many, called a "democracy." The many may control either by force or by consent. Given that these are the forms of government, can we thus discover the art of rule?

For Plato, the art of statesmanship is not a function of the type of state. If we find a statesman capable of ruling, then, whatever the constitutional form of government under which he rules, he is to be regarded as a ruler. Plato goes on to say that this is so whether there are subjects who are rich or poor, willing or unwilling, and regardless of whether there is a code of laws.

At this juncture, the young Socrates questions whether a good governor can govern without laws. (It is here that we reach the midpoint, as it were, between the *Republic* and *Statesman*, works concerned, respectively, with the best government and its ruler, and the *Laws*, a work which discusses the second-best government, a government in which the laws are prior in importance to the character of the ruler.) The Athenian Stranger answers that the art of kingship includes the art of law making, but that the political ideal is not full authority for laws but rather for a man who understands the art and has the ability to practice it. If we consider a law as an unqualified rule of human behavior, then it cannot with perfect accuracy prescribe what is right and good for each member of the community at any one time—this takes a king. We need laws, however, because the legislator cannot give every individual his due with absolute accuracy; general codes of conduct must be spelled out for the bulk of the citizenry. In any particular case, if the statesman can legislate better than the laws, he should be permitted to do so, no matter what. Here Plato includes the possibility of forcing the citizen to accept this kind of *ad hoc* ruling.

A state in which the ruler is superior to the laws is the best state; but when that is not possible, a government of laws must be adhered to. The Athenian Stranger points out how the laws grow through the experience of legislators in dealing with the affairs of men. The knowledge that is gained is that of a science. As such, it has the force of a scientific truth of the kind that Plato considers infallible. As rules of behavior, the laws must be obeyed, and no one is to act in contravention to them. The only better situation is that in which a king, having achieved the art of statesmanship, applies the knowledge that he has gained to a particular situation. The Athenian Stranger hints at the work to be done in the *Laws* when he points out that imitative constitutions must keep strictly to the laws and never transgress written enactments or established national customs, if they mean to reproduce as far as they can that one real constitution which is government by a real statesman using real statecraft. The various

119

types of government occur when the ideal constitution is copied in various ways; thus, when copied by the wealthy, we call the rule "aristocracy," when aristocrats disobey the laws, we call that rule "oligarchy." When one governs in imitation of the truly wise ruler, we call him "king," not realizing that we are contributing to confusion; for a king who imitates the true statesman rules by right opinion without knowing the grounds for the art of statesmanship. When such a one rules not by right opinion, but by his passions, then we call him "tyrant." Although men doubt that any statesman could be superior to the laws without being corrupt, such a statesman is the only one who could govern the commonwealth worthy of the name of best state.

Previously those functions in the state which were important to the very existence of the community were distinguished from kingly duties. But what of those functions which resemble statesmanship, and what of those individuals who practice them? That is, what of generals, judges, rhetoricians, and the like, all of whom function something like a ruler, and all of whom have been suggested at one time or another for the office of ruler? Each of these men, in practicing his art, uses some form of action upon men; it may be by force (military action), or by persuasion (oratory or rhetoric), or through interpretation and judgment of the law (legal decisions). The Athenian Stranger holds that the art that decides which of the above forms of action is to be practiced is superior to the particular art decided upon. It is the statesman who decides whether to use persuasion or force against a group of men, or to take no action at all. He can use oratory which is an adjunct of statesmanship but is not statesmanship itself; thus, the statesman is superior to the rhetorician. Similarly, he can decide whether the generals are to fight or whether friendly settlement is possible; thus, he is superior to the generals. The duty of the judge is to make honest judgments in accordance with the laws made by the statesman; thus, the judge is subservient to the statesman. As an art, statesmanship is concerned with which of these other arts is to be used on the right occasion in the great enterprise of statecraft. It is the art of arts as the good is the form of forms. The statesman must develop the best in the conflicting natures of his subjects—he is a royal weaver.

PHILEBUS

Author: Plato (427-347 b.c.)
Type of work: Ethics, metaphysics
First transcribed: Probably one of the later dialogues

Principal Ideas Advanced

Philebus has maintained that pleasure is the good, while Socrates contends that wisdom is better than pleasure.

To decide the issue, Socrates considers whether a life of pleasure without wisdom or knowledge would be worth while; and he decides that if pleasure is not known, or realized, it has no value.

But a life of wisdom which is in no way pleasant is also without value.

Wisdom contributes more than pleasure does to the good, for by wisdom order and harmony are achieved, and they are the essential features of the good.

In the final ordering of goods, as a result of the discussion, measure is ranked first; second is that which is ordered by measure, the symmetrical and the beautiful; third is mind or wisdom, which possesses more of beauty, symmetry, and truth than does pleasure; fourth is the class of arts, sciences, and true opinions; and fifth is the class of pure pleasures, those accompanying the practice of the pure arts and sciences.

The *Philebus* is concerned with the question as to whether pleasure or wisdom is the good. Philebus is represented as having maintained that pleasure is the good, while Socrates has contended that wisdom, right opinion, and right reasoning are better than pleasure. It is agreed at the outset of the discussion that if a third state of being turns out to be better than either pleasure or wisdom, then neither Philebus nor Socrates will be considered the victor in the argument; but if either pleasure or wisdom turns out to be more akin to the good than the other, the victor will be the one who has defended the state allied with the better and happier life. Protarchus agrees to defend Philebus' position, and the discussion begins.

Socrates begins his criticism of Philebus' view by asking Protarchus to identify the quality common to pleasures of various sorts which Philebus designates by the word "good." Protarchus objects to the question, arguing that pleasures, insofar as they are pleasures, do not differ from one another. But after Socrates points out that it would be ridiculous to say that the various sciences, since they are all sciences, do not differ from one another, Protarchus agrees to say that there are many different kinds of pleasures, just as there are many different kinds of sciences.

The dialogue here takes a fascinating, although technical, turn. Pleasures are one, but also they are many. This fact suggests the problem of the one and the many, a problem that has nothing to do with concrete things, for an individual man, for example, can easily be one man with many parts; it has, rather, to do with the question as to how man (the universal) is one, a unity, while the class of men is many, a plurality. The problem is to explain how the one (the universal) can be distributed among the many without losing its unity. Socrates explains that his favorite way of learning is to begin with one idea, a unity, and to proceed to infinity by means of finite steps. A musician, for example, understands that sound is one, but he also knows that there are many sounds, and he realizes how these various sounds can be combined. Also, Socrates adds, if inquiry begins with the infinite, then one should proceed to the unity not directly but only by means of a definite number. Thus, beginning with the infinite number of sounds possible to man, some god or "divine man," perhaps the Egyptian Thoth, selected a definite number of sounds, and finally unified them by the art of grammar. In the present discussion the problem is to determine, in the case of the unities pleasure and wisom, the definite number of species or kinds of each, before passing on to the infinity of particular pleasures and instances of wisdom. Philebus interrupts to beg Socrates either to divide pleasure and wisdom, in the manner described, or to find between them some other way of settling the issue.

Socrates suggests that perhaps neither pleasure nor wisdom is the good, and, if so, there is no need to divide either of them into species. To settle the question as to whether either of them is the good, the proper method would be to consider, first of all, a life of pleasure without wisdom, and then a life of wisdom without pleasure; for if either is the good, it is self-sufficient and does not depend on the other. Philebus and Protarchus assent to this suggestion.

Protarchus at first is convinced that he would like nothing better than a life spent in the enjoyment of the greatest pleasures. But Socrates points out that if he had neither mind, nor memory, nor knowledge, he would have neither the intelligence nor the knowledge to know or to discover that he possessed pleasure or that he had possessed pleasure in the past; furthermore, he could not anticipate pleasure. Consequently, without knowledge life would be reduced to the kind of existence an oyster has. Viewing the alternative in this way, Protarchus loses his enthusiasm for a life of pleasure.

Socrates then considers the life of wisdom without pleasure. It, too, appears unsatisfactory. It does seem to be the case that a life of both pleasure and wisdom, a third alternative, would be superior to a life of nothing but pleasure or nothing but wisdom.

The next pertinent question, then, is the question as to whether pleasure or wisdom is the element which makes the mixed life good. Socrates claims that wisdom, or mind, is the cause of the good; if he can establish his point, Philebus' claim that pleasure is the good will not take even third place. (There is the possibility, briefly mentioned by Socrates, that the divine mind is the good; by the time the argument is over, pleasure has fallen to fifth place, and, even then, only as "pure" pleasure.)

To lay the foundation of his argument in support of mind over pleasure, Socrates introduces a principle of division according to the distinction between the finite and the infinite. The finite and the infinite form two classes; the compound of them is a third class; and the cause of the compound is the fourth.

Socrates then shows that the infinite is many and that comparatives (such as the hotter and the colder) have no definite quantity, since there is no end to the possibilities of degree; the comparative, then—whatever admits of more or less—belongs in the class of the infinite. In Socrates' terms, "the infinite . . . is their unity. . . ."

Whatever has definite quantity and is measurable is, then, finite.

When the finite and infinite are combined, a third class appears: the class of the harmonious and proportionate (since the finite is the class of the measurable and is therefore able to introduce number, or order, into the infinite). Health, music, moderate temperature, the seasons, beauty, strength, and "ten thousand other things" belong to the third class.

Protarchus is reminded that the fourth class is the cause of the union of the finite and the infinite.

It is then decided that pleasure and pain belong to the class of the infinite, the unlimited. Wisdom (knowledge, mind), however, as that which orders the universe and the elements of the universe and provides human beings with souls and minds, must belong to the fourth class: the cause of the union of the finite and infinite in a state of harmony.

Socrates then explains that pain is the consequence of the dissolution of harmony in the body; the restoration of harmony is a pleasure. The pleasure of the soul is produced by expectation, a hope of pleasure. But it is possible for a person to be in a condition of rest between periods of dissolution and restoration; and it may be that such a condition, possible to those who live a life of wisdom, is "the most divine of all lives. . . ."

The pleaures of memory are mentioned, and Protarchus is reminded that not all bodily affections reach the soul, for sometimes men are not conscious; to be conscious is to achieve union of body and soul. Memory is the preservation of consciousness, and recollection is the soul's power of recovering some feeling once experienced.

Since desire is the "endeavour of every animal . . . to the reverse of his bodily state"—as when a man who is hungry (empty) desires to be full—desire must be of the soul, or mind, which apprehends the replenishment when it occurs (remembering the state of being empty). Most men are in

an intermediate state, as, for example, those who, experiencing pain, take some pleaure in remembering past pleasures.

A distinction is then made between true pleasures and false pleasures. Those persons who beguile themselves with false fancies and opinions derive pleasure from the false; consequently, their pleasures are false. Socrates also shows how the quality and quantity of pleasures can be misjudged when they are compared with different amounts of pain; pleasures compared with pains appear to be greater than they actually are: such pleasures are also false.

The greatest of bodily changes are felt as pleasure or pain, and they appear to be greater when the body is in an unhealthy state than when it is healthy. Furthermore, the pleasures of the intemperate are more intense than those enjoyed by the wise and temperate.

Socrates then carefully outlines the class of mixed feelings, combinations of pleasure and pain which are only of the body, or only of the soul, or common to both. The pleasure of scratching an itch, for example, is a mixed feeling of the body only; and there are certain kinds of anger, belonging to the soul, which are compounds of pleasure and pain.

In explaining the ridiculous as "the vicious form of a certain habit," Socrates refers to the inscription at Delphi, "Know thyself," and asserts that the ridiculous are those who do not know themselves and who are powerless in their ignorance.

Since neither false nor mixed pleasures could possibly rank very high in the scale of values, Socrates goes on to consider true and pure pleasures.

123

If he can show that even these pleasures are inferior to wisdom or mind, he will win his case.

Having previously rejected the notion that pleasure is merely the absence of pain, Socrates classifies the true pleasures as those given by beauty of color and form, by smooth and clear sounds, by sweet smells, and by knowledge when there is no hunger (pain) for knowledge. These pleasures are true and pure because they are unmixed with pain.

Since the excessive pleasures have no measure, they are infinite; the moderate pleasures are finite. A small amount of pure pleasure is truer and more valuable than a large amount of impure, or mixed, pleasure.

Socrates then refers to the philosophical opinion that pleasure is a "generation"; that is, is relative to some absolute essence which has true being. Since pleasure is not an end, or absolute, but is feeling provoked in a generative process toward an end, and is thus allied with the instrumental, it cannot be truly good. The contrary view—that pleasure is good—would lead to the denial of the value of courage, temperance, understanding, and the other virtues; and it would further entail the absurd position that a man possessing pleasure is a man possessing virtue, or excellence, since only pleasure is good.

Turning to a consideration of knowledge, Socrates first of all distinguishes between productive knowledge (aiming at products) and educational knowledge. Arithmetic, measurement, and weighing are the pure elements of the productive arts; the rest is conjecture. Socrates claims that music, medicine, husbandry, piloting, and generalship involve more of the impure element of conjecture than does the art of the builder. Even the exact art of building, considered in its pure aspect, the arithmetical, is not always pure. One must distinguish between rough-and-ready practical calculation, where things are counted, and the pure arithmetic of the person who is concerned only with number.

Of the arts, the purest is dialectic, the science of being and reality; the knowledge at which dialectic aims is the highest kind of knowledge, the knowledge of the changeless and essential. The words "mind" and "wisdom" are most truly and exactly used to refer to the contemplation of true being.

In summarizing, Socrates reminds his listeners, Philebus and Protarchus, that neither pleasure nor wisdom in isolation is a perfect good, since neither would be acceptable without the other. The good, then, is a feature of the mixed life. At first it seems as if the greatest good could be achieved by mixing true pleasures with pure knowledge, but since life without knowledge of practical matters, to supplement knowledge of the essential, would not be worth while, all kinds of knowledge were admitted into the compound of the good. But only the true pleasures are admitted, for wisdom knows the trouble that the impure can cause. Truth, too, is added. But without measure to regulate the order of the parts of the good, no good would be possible. The mixture conceived by Socrates is regarded as the ideal because of the beauty, symmetry, and truth which order it.

The rival claims of pleasure and wisdom can now be judged by consideration of the beauty, symmetry (measure), and truth of each. On all

124

three counts, wisdom wins; it surely has more of beauty, symmetry, and truth than does pleasure.

The conclusion is now possible—the final ordering of the goods. Measure is first, because without measure nothing is worth while. Second is that which has been ordered by measure, the symmetrical and the beautiful. Mind and wisdom, as that which possesses the three essentials, is third. Then come the arts and sciences and true opinions which are the mind's activities and products. In fifth posi-

tion are the pure pleasures of the soul, the pleasures accompanying the practice of the pure arts and sciences.

Although wisdom turns out to be only third in the list of goods, Socrates wins the argument, for pleasure —and only pure pleasure at that—is fifth. Furthermore, measure and the symmetrical, the first two on the list, characterize the mind and are the mind's objectives. Insofar as pleasure is allowed at all, it is only as the pure pleasure of wisdom.

TIMAEUS

Author: Plato (427-347 B.C.)
Type of work: Cosmogony, cosmology
First transcribed: Probably one of the later dialogues

PRINCIPAL IDEAS ADVANCED

Whatever is apprehended by intelligence and reason always exists and has no becoming.

The world (the universe) must have been created, for it is a sensible, and not an intelligible, thing; the world is a living creature endowed with soul and intelligence.

The soul of the world is prior in existence and excellence to the body of the world; the soul's function is to know the rational and to rule the body.

The universal nature which receives all things without changing its own nature is "that which is"; it is eternal, formless space.

The three natures which make up reality are the Ideas (the eternal forms of things), the sensible copies of Ideas (existing objects), and space.

In most of the Socratic dialogues Socrates is either the central figure or one of the central figures. For all of his assumed deference Socrates knew himself to be the superior of his contemporaries in the art of philosophical elucidation and debate, and Plato honored him by making him the consist-

ently victorious examiner of the pretenders to wisdom. But the *Timaeus* is one of the dialogues in which Socrates assumes a minor role; his personality is off to the side, glowing as usual, but only by grace of earlier dialogues in which he figures as an intellectual hero. And the *Timaeus* is not so much

125

a dialogue—although there is some conversation—as it is a solo display of Pythagorean ideas about the origin and character of the universe by Timaeus, an enthusiastic Pythagorean astronomer.

The *Timaeus* is interesting as an exhibition of the fantastic lengths to which the imagination of man can go in the attempt to understand this mysterious universe. It is a characteristically curious mixture of immature science and mature invention—and it has almost no relevance to the scientific and philosophical problems of modern man. Nevertheless, as part of the portrait of Greek thought, as a facet in the complex entity that was Plato's realm of ideas, and as the one dialogue which —thanks to a translation by Cicero— was influential in the Middle Ages, the *Timaeus* continues to hold a place in the significant literature of philosophy.

As the dialogue begins, Socrates reminds Timaeus of a conversation on the previous day concerning the various kinds of citizens required in an ideal state. The main points of the *Republic* are reviewed: The citizens will be husbandmen, or artisans, or defenders of the state. The defenders will be warriors or political leaders, "guardians" of the state. The guardians are to be passionately dedicated to their tasks and philosophical by temperament and training. Gymnastics and music will play important parts in their education. There will be no private wives or children, but all will work together and live together in a communal way. An effort will be made, by contrived lots, to mate the good with the good, the bad with the bad; and only the good children, morally and intellectually superior, are to be educated.

Socrates, having reviewed the principle points, then invites Timaeus, Critias, and Hermocrates, as persons with practical experience in the art of politics, to tell something of their adventures so that the portrait of the ideal state can begin to take on living character.

Critias begins by telling a story about ancient Athens, a tale told to him by his great-grandfather, Dropides, who heard it from Solon, the lawgiver. Solon told of hearing from a priest of Sais that Athens was a thousand years older than Sais, which had been founded eight thousand years before the time of Solon. Both Sais and Athens were founded by Athene, the goddess, so that, both in the division of classes and in laws, the two were alike. Athens became the leader of the Hellenes against the threatening forces from the great island of Atlantis, a powerful empire larger than Libya and Asia combined. Athens defeated Atlantis, but soon afterward both empires were utterly destroyed and hidden by earthquakes and floods. Critias suggests that Socrates regard the citizens of the imaginary city (as outlined in the *Republic*) as being, not imaginary, but the citizens of the actual city of ancient Athens. The justification for this would be that the ancient city and the imagined one agree in their general features.

Socrates is charmed by the idea, and it is agreed that Timaeus will give an account commencing with the generation of the world and ending with the creation of man. Critias is then to continue the account in order to complete the process of making actual the state which has so far figured in their conversation as an imaginary one.

The remainder of the dialogue is

devoted to Timaeus' account. The dialogue *Critias* continues the conversation by giving Critias his turn in the historical-philosophical account of man's origin and progress.

After invoking the gods Timaeus asks the fascinating complex question: "What is that which always is and has no becoming; and what is that which is always becoming and never is?" The answer is thoroughly Platonic (although it is also consistently Pythagorean): "That which is apprehended by intelligence and reason is always in the same state; but that which is conceived by opinion with the help of sensation and without reason, is always in a process of becoming and perishing and never really is." This answer—that idea (whatever is apprehended by intelligence) is constant, while what is sensed is inconstant and consequently unreal—is Platonic in its giving priority to idea and in its identification of reality with whatever is constant and prior.

The next important question to be settled is whether the world did or did not have a beginning. The answer by now is obvious: if whatever can be sensed is not eternal, but comes into being or is destroyed, and if the world is sensible, then it must have come into being. But whatever comes into being must have a cause. Furthermore, since the world is fair and the maker of it must have been the best of causes, the pattern to which the artificer referred in making the copy which is the world must have been the pattern of the unchangeable—the Ideas (although the word is not used here).

Timaeus continues by stating that the world must have been patterned after a perfect, intelligent animal (an Idea), for the Deity could not have been satisfied with the imperfect, the unintelligent, or the inanimate. The world, then, became a living creature "endowed with soul and intelligence by the providence of God." In order to make the world visible, God had to use fire; in order to make it tangible, he had to use earth. Then, in order to supply two means by which a union of elements could be achieved and a world of solidity created, God introduced the elements of water and air.

Since the world had to have a shape which would comprehend all others, God made the world (the living animal) in the form of a globe. The world is one, for it is a copy of the eternal form, which is one. It has no hands or feet, but revolves in a circle.

The soul of the world was made by God to be prior in existence and excellence to the body. The soul's function is to rule the body. To compose the soul God made an essence in between the indivisible and the divisible. He then mixed this intermediate essence with the indivisible (the same) and the divisible (the other), and then divided the compound into parts, each of which contained each of the three essences. The division was very complicated, but orderly. (The formula is given, but it is too complicated to reproduce here.) The material was then made into strips, and an outer and an inner circle were formed which joined to form X's. The one circle became the circle of the same and was, consequently, undivided; the other, the circle of the other, was divided into seven circles having different orbits. (Thus the seven planets are accounted for.)

The soul and the corporeal universe were joined together. Since the soul partakes of the essences of the same, the other, and the intermediate, it alone knows the characters of the sensible world and attains to perfect knowledge of the rational.

God wanted the world to be everlasting, but eternity is not possible for a corporeal being. Hence, he created time as the image of eternity. Stars were placed in the seven orbits to make time possible.

God then made a great fire, the sun, to light up the heavens so that animals (men) might learn arithmetic by observing the stars in their courses.

The created animal was then made to have four species corresponding to the four kinds of idea involved in the original: heavenly bodies (creatures of fire), birds (creatures of the air), creatures of the water, and creatures of the earth.

Knowledge of the gods comes by tradition from those who were the children of the gods. From Earth and Heaven were born Oceanus and Tethys; Phorcys, Cronos, and Rhea were the children of the latter pair; and from Cronos and Rhea were generated Zeus and Herè.

God then used a dilution of the essence of the universe soul to prepare the souls of living things. Souls that lived properly were destined to return to their native stars, but others would be forced to reside in women or brute animals. Human beings had their bodies fashioned by those gods who were the children of the father of the gods; and the bodies were made of the four elements welded together with tiny invisible pegs. Motions within the body or upon it from external motions were carried to the soul, and the motions came to be called "sensations." Only when the soul is able to free itself from the influence of bodily motions

can it begin to revolve as it should, acquiring knowledge.

The courses of the soul are contained in the head, which is a spherical body emulating the spherical body of the universe. All the other appendages of the human being are instrumental to the soul's functioning within the head. Light is a gentle fire which merges in the eye with the fire within the body, finally affecting the soul in an act of perception.

The causes of sight must be distinguished from the purpose of sight. Sight exists to make knowledge possible: by observing heavenly bodies man acquires knowledge of time, then of numbers and of philosophy. Man learns by analogy, identifying the courses of heavenly bodies with the courses of individual souls.

Having given an account of the genesis and development of the soul and of mind in terms of the soul's activity, Timaeus considers the consequences of the presence of the four elements (earth, water, air, fire) in the universe.

In addition to the changeless, eternal pattern of things and the copies of the pattern there is the "receptacle" and "nurse" of all generation. Since the elements can pass into each other— water, for example, changing into a vapor, or air—no element is primary; in fact, one should not refer to fire, or water, or any element as "that" which is; but one should say of that which is that it is of "such" a nature, for example, fire. The universal nature which receives all things without changing its own nature is alone truly designated as "that" which is; it is formless; it is eternal space. Thus, there are three kinds of natures: the uncreated, indestructible kind of being (the eternal Ideas); the sensible copies of the eternal (the objects of opinion and sense); and space, the "home of all created things." These are called, respectively, being, generation, and space.

Originally the four elements were tossed about in space, and they were neither fair nor good; but God, by the use of form and number, brought order and goodness. The elements were made up of triangles, for they are solids, and all solids are made up of planes which are, in turn, composed of triangles. Triangles are either isosceles or scalene (with unequal sides); of these, the most beautiful is that which is such that its double is an equilateral triangle. To achieve the most beauty, the isosceles, which has but a single form, and that one of the scalene forms which is such that, doubled, an equilateral triangle is formed, must have been used by God in the creation of the elements.

Timaeus retracts his earlier statement that the elements can all pass into one another. Earth can never become anything but earth. The other three, however, can pass into one another. Since earth is the most immovable of the four elements, it must be composed of cubical forms. Water is harder to move than either fire or air; hence, it must be composed of icosahedron forms ("made up of 120 triangular elements, forming twelve solid angles, each of them included in five plane equilateral triangles, having altogether twenty bases, each of which is an equilateral triangle"). Fire is made up of the smallest and most acute bodies, pyramids; while air is composed of octahedron solids. It can now be understood why earth cannot become something other than earth: its solids cannot assume the forms necessary to the other elements.

After a discussion of the kinds of fire (flaming fire, light, and glow), the kinds of water (liquid and fusile, the latter divisible into gold, adamant, and copper; and the former into such various liquids as wine, oil, honey, and the like), and the kinds of earth (rock, stones, chemicals), Timaeus considers the effects of the elements on bodies and souls. Fire is sharp and cutting in its heat because it is made up of sharp pointed solids (pyramids: tetrahedra). Other sensations are accounted for by reference to contraction, compression, expansion, and so forth, caused by the impingement of various bodies on the sensing body. Pain is the result of a sudden change which disturbs the particles of the body; pleasure is the effect of the body's return to its natural condition.

The sensations resulting from the stimulation of the sense organs are explained as affectations caused by contractions and dilations, or by moistening or drying up, or by smothering or roughening of parts caused by the entrance of the particles of exterior objects. Sounds are blows which are transmitted to the soul, and hearing is a vibration which begins in the head and ends in the liver. Colors are flames coming from things which join with the streams of light within the body. (With great care Timaeus explains how various colors are formed by the combinations of fires.)

Returning to the account of man's origin, Timaeus argues that man's immortal soul comes from God, but man has another, mortal soul given to him by the gods who fashioned his body.

Man's mortal soul is that in him which is subject to various destructive passions, among which are the love of pleasure, and rashness and fear. The immortal soul is in the head, but the mortal soul is in the breast and thorax and is so divided that the part which has courage and passion is nearer the head, so that it might be better subject to reason.

The heart was designed by the gods to be a guard in the service of reason, sending the fire of passion to all parts of the body; and the lungs were designed to enclose the heart, thus cushioning its exertions and cooling it. The liver, solid and smooth like a mirror, was intended to distort the images of things of unworthy nature, giving them the distressing color of bile, while it also suffuses the images of worthy things with its natural sweetness. The spleen was made to keep the liver clean in order that it might function properly as the seat of divination. All parts of the body, the bowels, the bones, the marrow of the bones (which unites the soul with the body), the joints and flesh, were fashioned in such a manner as to encourage man to be a creature of reason, not appetite. Fire travels through the body, giving the red color to blood and performing such necessary tasks as the digestion of food by cutting the food with the pyramidal solids which are the material of fire. Eventually, however, as the body grows older, the triangles are blunted, and digestion becomes more difficult. Disease and death are the results of the loosening or dissolving of the bonds by which the marrow holds the body and soul together. When death results the soul, "obtaining a natural release, flies away with joy."

The diseases of the mind are of two kinds: madness and ignorance. If anyone is bad, he is so involuntarily as the result of an indisposition of the body, and indisposition is simply the lack of that fair and good proportion which means health and sanity. To achieve a proper harmony of body and soul, exercise is necessary: gymnastic for the body, music and philosophy for the soul. The human being needs the food and motion which will encourage the growth and harmony of his body and soul; and the motions most worth studying and emulating are the motions of the universe as revealed in the revolutions of the heavenly bodies. In man intellect is supposed to be superior to desire, and thus he must give particular attention to the exercise of that divine part of his soul.

Cowardly men change into women in the second generation; simple, light-minded men give rise to the race of birds; and those without philosophy, who allow the breast to rule the head, become beasts. Those who become foolish are made to crawl on the ground, devoid of feet; while the senseless and ignorant become animals of the sea.

The generation of animals is the result of desire resulting from the respiration of the seed of life rising in the marrow. When the desire of man and woman is satisfied, unseen animals pass from the man to the woman, and they mature in her.

Timaeus concludes his account by summarizing in the following manner: "The world has received animals, mortal and immortal, and is fulfilled with them, and has become a visible animal containing the visible—the sensible God who is the image of the intellectual, the greatest, best, fairest, most perfect—the one only-begotten heaven."

Thus, by giving the center of the stage to a Pythagorean, Plato sketched out a conception of the origin of the universe. Perhaps he found the analysis of things in terms of triangles a reasonable, even probable, anatomy of nature; perhaps he was intrigued, but not convinced. In any case, Plato gave full allegiance to the theory of forms, or eternal essences; and he never wavered in his endorsement of the rational mode of life. Despite the bizarre character of the philosophy contained in the *Timaeus*, the Greek love of wisdom makes itself felt and gives to the whole an enduring charm.

LAWS

Author: Plato (427-347 B.C.)
Type of work: Political philosophy
First transcribed: Probably the last dialogue

PRINCIPAL IDEAS ADVANCED

Laws are initiated when communities seek to fix custom, but societies fail when ignorance triumphs over wisdom, or when intemperance defeats temperance, or when freedom is lost or becomes license.

The best form of government is a combination of democracy and monarchy, for such a state combines freedom and wisdom.

Legislation should be designed to insure freedom, harmony, and understanding; the effort should be made to imitate the good and the gods.

Where the laws are above the ruler, the state has the possibility of salvation; the best ruler is one who can enforce the laws by persuasion and command.

The laws should provide for censorship of the improper kinds of music, dancing, poetry, eulogies, and drama; they should discourage all love but the love of soul, and they should provide for the rehabilitation of criminals.

The gods must exist since the soul, that which can move itself, is essentially dependent on the divine.

Plato's three great political treatises, the *Republic*, the *Statesman*, and the *Laws*, are unmatched of their kind and, undoubtedly, are also unsurpassed in their influence upon political thought. The first two represent his attempt to argue for and describe the political body and the ruler that would be the best or ideal, and there is a serious question as to whether he believed them possible. Some hold that the *Republic* represents Plato's attempt to sketch for us the form or Idea of the state—stateness itself, as it were—along with the art of ruling itself. The latter is more fully developed in the *Statesman*. The *Laws*, probably Plato's last work, is concerned with the sketch of a state that is second best, one in which the author no longer considers the rule of a philosopher-king, either because he no

131

longer thought it possible or because it represented an unrealizable ideal. His concern, rather, is with the rule of law.

We generally take, in our Western democracies, the position that a government of laws is superior to one of men; for we fear the arbitrary rule that may occur when tyrants are in power. Men, however, must interpret the laws, for laws do not speak for themselves. Thus, in his presentation of the ideal state, Plato described the training and qualifications of a ruler who would combine wisdom and morality with experience, so that, given any problem of governing, he would arrive at the correct solution. Why should this type of rule have been considered better than the rule of laws? A law, broadly speaking, is a command issued in *general* terms by a ruler, or by those empowered to rule, for the regulation of the conduct of the members of society. When it is held that someone has broken the law, his act must be fitted under the general law, as interpreted by properly constituted authorities. A wise man, moral in character, who, through training (education) and discipline, has attained knowledge of the good and who has spent many years in the practical application of that knowledge in governmental positions is best suited to sit in judgment of particular cases and come to decisions. For Plato, proper rule by laws demanded the ideal ruler.

In the *Laws*, an Athenian Stranger, thought by some scholars to represent Plato himself, rather than Socrates, dominates the conversation. In the opening books there ensues a discussion, reminiscent of many in earlier dialogues, of the virtues, their impor-tance to the good life, and the role of education in training the citizen to rule himself and to obey his rulers. The Athenian Stranger inquires of Megillus whether he thinks that the program in Sparta to train the young to be courageous is adequate. For, although much stress is put on endurance and resistance to pain, there is little, if any, preparation for resisting improper pleasures, especially flattery. Furthermore, in their educational scheme the Spartans have confused temperance with prohibition, by banishing revelry in all forms. Conviviality may be a benefit to the state when properly managed. In fact, the notion of "proper management" is the key to the temperance, and gaining knowledge of it a major feature of a correct education.

If we look at men, we see that they are pulled from within by pleasure and pain, and the way in which they are pulled results in virtue or vice. The way in which a man is pulled can be determined through the use of his reason in directing his will to control his passionate nature, or he can become a slave to the demands of his desires. It is the role of education to prepare him for the former, so that his acts will be virtuous and not vicious. If children are observed carefully, and their instincts toward virtue are molded into suitable habits so that they learn to do that which they ought to do—by loving what ought to be loved and hating what ought to be hated—then education will be properly administered in the city. As in the *Republic*, Plato advocates as part of the program of education the correct use of music and, again, he stresses imitation of the good as the standard by which it should be judged.

132

In Book III of the *Laws*, the Athenian Stranger turns to an analysis of legislation, one which occupies him for much of the remainder of the dialogue, and he begins by considering the origin of governments. Recounting the legend of the destruction of civilization by the deluge, he describes the rise of society again on a simple, pastoral level. Men lived by custom, remembered from the "old days," and practiced the virtues which they inherited from their parents. Legislation began when the various communities discovered the differences in their customs and vied with one another for the best. By arbitration it was decided which were best, and the communities were united into city-states, from which federations were formed. Yet Sparta and two of its neighbors had broken their federation in recent times because they lacked the wisdom to remain united. Unless legislators endeavor to plant wisdom in states and banish ignorance, not only federations but the state itself will be ruined. The Stranger points out many examples of states that have come to ruin because of excesses rather than proper management.

Persia, he claims, fell because of the servitude of the people. When the most important principle of rule, that of the wise over the ignorant, is practiced as it ought, we have a rule of law over willing subjects. When there is rule by compulsion, as in Persia, then the government will fall. On the other hand, too much freedom can also lead to the destruction of a state. The Stranger refers to the fall of Athens as a case in point. Interestingly enough, in the light of his criticisms of certain poetical practices, he traces the downfall to excesses in music. He claims that at first the music was listened to in an orderly fashion and in silence, but the poets themselves introduced noisy innovations which led to noisy confusion. In addition, freedom was replaced by license, and equality proclaimed in all things, so that the view expressed by "It's all a matter of taste" replaced norms in morality as well as etiquette. The democracy which had consisted of educated persons in the role of judges degenerated to a situation in which anyone was qualified. When freedom becomes excessive, when taste takes over, then reverence is lost and authority ignored; both the rulers and the laws are disobeyed.

In discussing a state which is well governed, Plato, in the *Laws*, indicates that his position on democracy put forth in the *Republic* (it was next to tyranny as the worst of states) has been modified. It is true that there he presented a picture of mob rule in which license and no moral laws prevailed, as in the conditions described above. That conclusion was the main feature of a democracy when discussed in the *Republic*. Now he holds that when democracy is combined with monarchy (a situation that exists in our time in the United Kingdom), it is possible to join features which make for a well-governed state: friendship and wisdom with freedom. The Athenian Stranger holds that legislation should aim to accomplish three things: (1) assure the freedom of the city, (2) promote harmony—the city should be at one with itself—and (3) foster understanding. Cleinias, who is to found a colony for Crete, asks the Athenian Stranger to develop his views on legislation further so that he may profit by them.

Speaking rather generally, the Athenian Stranger claims that it is preferable for a legislator to make laws in a state ruled by a young tyrant (king) with a good memory, one who is quick at learning, courageous, noble, and temperate. Since people tend to imitate their ruler, such a one is more likely to be obeyed and the laws of his kingdom are more likely to be the best. Besides, since he is more likely to honor the laws, he should rule, for where the law is subject and has no authority, there the state is on its way to ruin. Thus Plato, in the *Laws*, subscribes to the second-best view, for he goes on to say that where the law is above the ruler, there the state has the possibility of salvation. He stresses, as he did in the *Republic*, that the gods should be imitated, and he urges that the legislators not give two rules for one point of law.

The Athenian Stranger develops this point further by advising the legislator to define clearly the terms of his laws so that there will be no ambiguity. This will be the true sense of moderation. When the laws are made, the legislator should use both persuasion and command in framing them. The persuasive part will create good will on the part of the citizens who will be required to obey them.

It is important to realize the kinds of laws Plato is talking about. The legislator is described as framing laws to fit what we ordinarily would call a constitution. (Plato is not always clear about this point but the text supports such a view.) Both Machiavelli, in his *Discourses on Livy* (1531), and Rousseau, in *The Social Contract* (1762), are indebted to Plato as they argue for a constitution written by a stranger (as does Plato), sanctioned by the gods, consented to by the people, and so on.

In the fifth book, the Athenian Stranger gives practical advice for the securing of a virtuous state. Next to the gods, a man should honor his soul and then his body. He should live moderately, avoiding excesses, both with regard to his mental and his physical activities. Those in society who are guilty of wrongdoing, if they appear curable, should be treated gently and with forgiveness. If, however, there are citizens in the state who are beyond cure, who are incurably evil, then they must be purged. Plato, again stressing the view that evil is a kind of disease of which punishment is the cure, argues for rehabilitation over vengeance; but when rehabilitation appears fruitless, then the state should put away the individual who is of no good to himself or others. Oddly enough, from Plato's viewpoint, since no man ever does wrong knowingly, an incurable person would appear to be one who no longer can learn anything.

The state that the Athenian Stranger plans would be small in size and population. The property would be divided among the citizens as fairly and justly as possible, and great effort would be made to keep the population constant. In the best state, the Stranger proclaims, property would be held in common (as in the *Republic*); but, if it must be held privately, then the owners should be taught that they owe their possessions to the state and that basically the property belongs to the whole citizenry. The city-state should be neither too wealthy nor too poor, for the excesses of both are dangerous to civic welfare. The laws should protect the city from these extremes by limiting wealth so that no one through property shall gain undue power.

In the ensuing books Plato continues to stress education, and he points out that a crucial function of it is to help transmit and enforce the customs (favorable) that have been developed in society. Laws are only a skeleton, as it were, of the rules that govern a state. Between the "spaces," custom binds and knits the country, providing a ground for proper management of oneself. Custom can bring about reverence for the law by instilling in the young a respect for it. It is well to frown upon changes in the law, to make it difficult for changes to occur, for stability in the law is reflected in a satisfied people. (Plato was so much concerned about the disquieting effect that "wrong" music can have on the populace that he advocated laws to control music, dancing, poetry, and eulogies.) Only the good is to be stressed. Censorship of plays and other literary works for the youth will also be practiced. The Athenian Stranger knows that the young will imitate the characters they watch on the stage and read about; only if these are presented with a high regard for morality can the imitation be safe. As in the *Republic*, so in the *Laws*; Plato advocates that mathematics be taught, especially arithmetic, plane and solid geometry, and astronomy.

Since men and women are to be together in their education, some precautions must be taken to prevent promiscuity. In Book VIII, the Athenian Stranger discusses love, pointing out that there are three types which become confused and which must be carefully distinguished by the laws. The three types are (1) love of body, which leads to wantonness; (2) love of soul, which enables one to search for virtues and for a kindred soul with whom to live chastely; (3) a mixture of the two. It is the second which is to be favored by the state; the others are to be forbidden. But how will it be possible to enforce a law in support of the love of soul? Just as incest is not practiced because the customs and mores are such that it is held to be the most vile of crimes, so a similar attitude can be established regarding other vile unions. By combining the fear of impiety with a love for moderation, sexual temperance will be looked upon as a victory over base pleasures, and sufficient incentive will be provided to encourage obedience to the law. In addition, hard work will get rid of excess passion.

Although the Athenian Stranger finds it hard to believe that there will be crimes in his proposed state, he recognizes the need for a criminal law. It is here that Plato once more declares punishment a form of rehabilitation, designed to cure or improve the criminal. It is interesting that Plato considers the robbing of temples as a capital offense which, if committed by one who has been educated and trained, is punishable by death. In *The Social Contract*, Rousseau again shows the influence upon him of the works of Plato by urging a similar punishment for this kind of crime. Because Plato accepts the Socratic view that no man does wrong knowingly, and that punishment should be a cure, he feels obligated to discuss the sources of crime. He finds it in three major aspects of man's make-up. The passions, as the lowest element of the soul, may drive a man to act without reason's guidance. But to act without reason's guidance is tanta-

135

mount to slavery, and a man who is slave to his passions may perform all sorts of crimes. Related to this is the fact that a man who seeks pleasures finds that by persuasion and deceit he is led to pursue them, often to his ruin. Lastly, ignorance itself is a cause of crime. Socrates had found that he was proclaimed the wisest man in Athens because he knew that he did not know anything, whereas his fellow citizens were ignorant of their ignorance and fooled themselves into thinking that they knew. It is the conceit of wisdom that leads the ignorant man astray, causing him to commit crimes. The degree of the conceit is matched by the seriousness of the crime.

The Athenian Stranger proclaims that laws are necessary for mankind because without rules to guide them, men would be no better than savage beasts. (Again, such a position had an influence upon Rousseau, who held that society would make a man of virtue out of a creature who, acting from instinct rather than reason, was little better than a savage beast.) No man is able to know what is best for all of human society. A philosopher-king is hardly possible; thus, law and order must be chosen so that good men may be led to a good life, and those who refuse to be instructed, curbed.

In the final book (Book X) of the *Laws*, the Athenian Stranger argues that as long as the gods are held in esteem crimes of impiety will not be committed frequently. To the question of what can be done with those who do not believe in the existence of the gods, the Stranger proposes to prove their existence. He does so with a proof which shows that the soul is prior to the body, and that, since the spiritual nature of the soul is the same as that of the gods, they too must exist. The proof rests upon the soul as a source of motion. Briefly, this proof may be demonstrated as follows: Some things are in motion, others are at rest. Motion itself is of several types: (1) spinning on an axis, (2) locomotion, (3) combination, (4) separation, (5) composition, (6) growth, (7) decay, (8) destruction, (9) self-motion and motion by others, and (10) change of itself and by others. Type (10) is actually the first in terms of superiority, with (9) second. The "self-moving" principle is identified with life. Not only is the soul defined, in essence, as that which can move itself, but also it is the source of motion in all things. The body is essentially inert and has no moving power of its own; rather, it has motion produced within it. As the source of motion, the soul is prior in time to that which is moved by it. The body, which is moved by the soul, must be later than it in time. Not only is the soul the author of movement in and of the body, but of all bodies, including heavenly ones (planets, for example). Soul or spirit must exist prior to and concurrent with the heavenly bodies to have put and kept them in motion. Therefore the gods, who are spirits with spiritual qualities unencumbered by bodies, must exist.

ORGANON

Author: Aristotle (384-322 B.C.)
Type of work: Logic, metaphysics
First transcribed: c.350 B.C.

PRINCIPAL IDEAS ADVANCED

Of the categories—substance, quality, quantity, relation, action, affection, place, time, position, and state—substance is the most important, for the other categories are properties of substance.

Primary substances are the subjects of properties; they are not themselves properties: for example, individual men are primary substances.

Secondary substances are the classes of which primary substances are members: for example, the class "man" is a secondary substance.

The propositional form "If all B is A, and all C is B, then all C is A" is an axiom of logic by reference to which arguments of syllogistic form can be reduced and criticized.

Scientific arguments depend upon ultimate premises established either by induction or by intuition.

The six treatises that make up Aristotle's *Organon* are the first writings on logic as an independent discipline to appear in Western civilization. The title *"Organon"* has been used to refer to the collection since at least the sixth century, but there is no evidence that Aristotle himself referred to the treatises by this name. Aristotle's word for what today is called formal logic was "analytics." Traditionally the treatises have been ordered as follows: *Categories, On Interpretation, Prior Analytics, Posterior Analytics, Topics,* and *On Sophistical Refutations.* This order is based on the contents: the *Categories* treats of terms, the *On Interpretation* treats of propositions, the *Prior Analytics* treats of syllogisms. The remaining three treat of kinds of argument; the *Posterior Analytics* treats of apodictic (necessary) syllogisms, the *Topics* treats of dialectical (debatable) syllogisms, and the *On*

Sophistical Refutations treats of unsound arguments (informal fallacies). However, Aristotle did not write the treatises in this order, and there is no evidence to support the rather common misconception that Aristotle regarded them (except for the *Prior* and *Posterior Analytics*) as successive chapters in a systematic treatise on logic. The *Categories, Topics,* and *Sophistical Refutations* are early works, *On Interpretation* was probably written some time later, and the two *Analytics* were written last. The *Categories* is perhaps as much a work on metaphysics as it is on logic; it has considerable historical significance, but its logical content is rather meager.

There is a wealth of material discussed in the six works, but it is of very uneven importance. Large portions are tedious and out of date, while other sections are first-rate philosophy and surprisingly modern. Here a very

137

brief summary of the contents of each treatise will be given, with, following that, a somewhat more detailed account of the *Categories* and the two *Analytics*.

The Greek word "kategoria," from which our word "category" is derived, ordinarily is used simply to mean "predicate." The *Categories* is concerned with the ten ultimate kinds of predicates men can use in communicating with one another. There are references to the categories throughout the Aristotelian corpus, but at various places in his writings Aristotle departs from the list given in the *Categories*. Those listed in the *Categories* are: substance, quality, quantity, relation, action, affection, place, time, position, and state. Aristotle specifies what he means by each and points out the peculiar characteristics of each one. This work has had considerable historical importance. We shall return to it shortly.

On Interpretation opens with some grammatical distinctions. Nouns, verbs, sentences, and various kinds of propositions are characterized, and the relations between various propositional forms are traced. The traditional Square of Opposition has its roots in *On Interpretation*. The four traditional A, E, I, and O forms of propositions are discussed, although the matter of the distribution of predicate terms is not raised. (A: All S is P; E: No S is P; I: Some S is P; O: Some S is not P.) It is one of the more controversial treatises since it is the source of the view (which has plagued philosophers as gifted as Leibniz) that all propositions must finally be resolved into subject-predicate propositions, a view which modern logicians reject.

The *Prior* and *Posterior Analytics* are Aristotle's mature account of the formal theory of the syllogism and of what is today called "scientific method."

The *Topics* concerns itself with the dialectical syllogism; that is, with questions which are matters of "opinion" (in the Platonic sense). The work is an early one, and probably its contents are largely commonplaces from the Academy regarding questions which can profitably be debated. Aristotle offers common-sense advice about how to attack or defend the various views an educated Greek of fourth century Athens might expect to encounter. The work is rather tedious for the modern reader. Its significance lies in the seriousness with which Aristotle treats the problems the sophists offered to settle cheaply. It is also a reminder of the often forgotten fact that philosophy, for the Greek, was a conversational business. To philosophize, for the Greek, was to *talk*, not to reflect in private. Such a conception of philosophy as this undoubtedly led Aristotle to focus attention on the syllogism as the instrument of logical argument, since the syllogism is most effective and convincing in debate.

The *Sophistical Refutations*, although an early work, has justly been held in high regard by philosophers in all periods. It is concerned with what are today called "material fallacies." The fundamental distinction Aristotle draws between fallacies resulting from language and fallacies of relevance is still a common approach to the discussion of fallacies. Many of the fallacies he identified are still included in logic books and called by the names he gave them; for example, amphiboly and accent.

Recent scholarship has shown that so-called "traditional logic," although

138

attributed to Aristotle, is actually a synthesis made in late antiquity of some Aristotelian doctrine together with elements from an independent Stoic logic. Stoic logic is now largely lost, but it did play into the rather crude misunderstanding of Aristotle that came to be known as traditional logic. Aristotle is the discoverer of the logic of propositional functions, the branch of logic in which the range of values for the variables is terms. The Stoics discovered the logic of truth functions, or the propositional calculus, the branch of logic in which the range of values for the variables is propositions. The categorical syllogism is Aristotle's discovery; *modus ponens* and hypothetical syllogism are discoveries made by the Stoics. The extent of Aristotle's influence, however, is indicated by the name "hypothetical syllogism," which has been given to a Stoic inference form which is not syllogistic at all. The barrier traditional logic raises often prevents both a proper recognition of the Stoic achievement and a sound historical approach to and appreciation of Aristotle's syllogistic.

The ten ultimate predicates Aristotle lists in the *Categories* may be separated into two divisions, substance and the remaining nine. Substance is by far the most important; it is presupposed by all the others—they are really all characteristics or properties of substances. Within the broad category of substance, Aristotle distinguishes primary and secondary substance. Philosophers have often held that Aristotle's primary substance was the substratum of later metaphysics. Aristotle himself says that it is neither "predicable of" nor "present in" a subject, and he lists as examples the individual man or the individual horse. Secondary substances are the species of which primary substances are members; "man" and "horse," for example, are illustrations of secondary substances. We might get closer to Aristotle's doctrine if we recognize that practically everything he meant by substances could be included if we talked merely about that which is symbolized by whatever word may stand as the subject of a proposition.

But it would be going beyond the doctrine of the *Categories* to charge Aristotle with a substratum view of primary substance. Actually, Aristotle seems to mean by primary substance merely the common-sense notion of a living individual thing. After all, the term "thing" is metaphysically vague and its mere occurrence in a passage is not sufficient ground for inferring that Aristotle held a substratum doctrine. Examination of the words "predicable of" and "present in" (a subject) reveals insufficient support for a substratum view. The remarks Aristotle makes immediately following the distinction between primary and secondary substance show that by "predicable of" he means the relation between a genus or species and one of its members (for example, the species *man* is "predicable of" the *substance* Socrates), while "present in" refers to the relation between a substance and one of its attributes (for example, the *attribute* rational is "present in" the *substance* Socrates).

Before dispensing with this question, however, we should note a remark which Aristotle makes shortly following the section discussed above. He states that primary substances are most properly called substances as a result of the fact that they are the "entities which underlie everything else," and that everything else is predicated of or present in them. In another place he states that primary substances are called primary because they "underlie and are the subjects of" everything else. Now although "underlies" immediately suggests "substratum," it is important to bear in mind that the substratum doctrine was not fully developed until the medieval period, long after Aristotle's death. We should beware of anachronism and avoid attributing to Aristotle a view which was not current until after his time. If nothing is attributed to him which cannot be supported by the statements he makes in the *Categories*, it is clear that he does not there hold such a view. For the words "present in" and "predicable of" do not by themselves entail a substratum view, and "underlie and are the subjects of" are words which show that Aristotle treats "underlie" as equivalent in meaning to "are subjects." It would therefore seem wiser to recognize that there is not sufficient evidence to support the view that the *Categories* sets forth a substratum view. What Aristotle had in mind when he spoke about primary substances was simply individual living things without the metaphysical and epistemological frills which decorate the substratum doctrine.

Considerable interest has developed in Aristotle's syllogistic as it is presented in the *Prior Analytics*. Viewed on its own merits, apart from the additions and revisions of "traditional logic," the doctrine of the *Prior Analytics* is seen to be surprisingly modern and innocent of many of the charges often made against it. It lacks the refinement of contemporary functional calculi, but it nevertheless is a surprisingly sophisticated formal, axiomatic

system, needing but little to make it a completely acceptable logical calculus.

A modern logical calculus includes four elements: (1) A set of terms which are undefined (within the calculus) or "primitive" and which serve as a basis for defining all other terms in the system. Examples of such primitive terms in a logical calculus are "not" and "if . . . then . . ." and the notion of a variable. (2) Formation rules which specify which expressions are to be included as well formed and which expressions are inappropriate or not well formed. For example, we all recognize implicitly that "The instructor is tardy" is a sensible English sentence, while "The stone sang a solo" is inappropriate or not well formed. The formation rules explicitly state the conditions well formed expressions must meet. (3) Certain axioms or postulates from which the theorems of the system are derived. Euclid's axiom that the shortest distance between two points is a straight line is an example—taken from geometry rather than logic, of course—of an unproved axiom. (4) A set of rules specifying how the theorems are to be derived from the axioms.

Aristotle does not call his primitive terms by that name, but he uses "not" and "and" and "if . . . then . . ." as primitives, taking it for granted that the reader can also use them, and offering no definitions for them. In the case of variables, however, he has clearly and self-consciously arrived at the modern point of view. Throughout the *Prior Analytics* he uses letters of the alphabet in stating his syllogistic forms, and only after stating them formally does he give examples of terms which can be substituted for the variables. For example, he discusses syllogistic forms of the first figure using the letters "A," "B," and "C," and then often lists terms which can be taken as values for these variables, terms such as "horse," "man," and "animal."

The *Prior Analytics* does not include any specific formation rules, since Aristotle presupposed that he and his readers were able to recognize well-formed expressions and to rule out inappropriate expressions. He did not recognize the theoretical importance of such rules. Nor did he include explicitly stated inference rules for passing from axioms to theorems. However, a great number of proofs appear in the course of the treatise, and the proof techniques which are appropriate for deriving the theorems from the axioms are given names. Thus Aristotle illustrated the rules of proof, even though he did not lay them down as a modern logician would. The axioms are the valid moods of figure one, and the theorems are the valid moods of the other figures. The proof techniques are the techniques of "reduction," and Aristotle makes it clear that all valid moods in the second and third figures can be derived from figure one either by "conversion" (later called "direct reduction" by logicians) or by *reductio per impossible* (later called "indirect reduction" by logicians).

The axiomatic character of the *Prior Analytics* is what is most often overlooked by contemporary logicians and scholars. Aristotle is usually credited with the well-known syllogism:

All men are mortal
Socrates is a man
∴ Socrates is mortal

The form known as *Barbara*—figure one, mood AAA—is also usually attributed to Aristotle. However, neither of these is to be found in Aristotle. He did write about something which resembles these traditional forms, but it was quite different theoretically. Compare the traditional form *Barbara* with Aristotle's form:

Barbara	Aristotle's form
All M is P	If all B is A, and all C
All S is M	is B, then all C is A
∴ All S is P	

Barbara is an inference rule. It justifies asserting the conclusion on the basis of the two premises. There are three propositional forms in *Barbara,* together with the special word or symbol "therefore," the sign or mark of an inference. Aristotle's form, however, has only one proposition, and no word "therefore." It is a propositional form, not a rule of inference. Aristotle's form is really an axiom, one of four which correspond to the four valid moods of the first figure in the same way that the two forms above correspond. As axioms, then, in Aristotle's axiomatic syllogistic, there are propositions corresponding to the four valid moods of figure one. As theorems, derived by reduction, there are the valid moods of figures two and three.

There is one additional point which should be made about Aristotle's axioms, however. Contemporary logicians do not try to establish the truth of their axioms; they merely assume them and deduce their consequences. Aristotle tried to justify his axioms by appealing to the *dictum de omni et nullo;* this was his definition of the first figure. Aristotle regarded the *dictum* as self-evidently true, and he said that the first figure, which it defined, was the "perfect" figure.

The *dictum* as the definition of the first figure leads to the last point to be

141

made here about the doctrine of the *Prior Analytics*. Aristotle, as is commonly known, recognized only the first three figures. He has sometimes been charged with error here, but, as he defined the figures, there are only three. The basis for his division is the width of the middle term. If the middle term is predicated of both the major and the minor, the syllogism is second figure. If the major and the minor are both predicated of the middle, the syllogism is third figure. If the middle is predicated of one extreme, while the other extreme is predicated of the middle term, the syllogism is first figure. These exhaust the possibilities, of course, and the last definition includes both the traditional first and fourth figures. In fact, Aristotle did recognize and list the valid moods of the fourth figure, even though he (somewhat uncomfortably) treated them as strange first figure moods.

We now turn briefly to the *Posterior Analytics*, Aristotle's account of scientific method. There are two features of scientific knowledge which Aristotle stresses: its factual character and its necessary character. To know something, for Aristotle, meant knowing that an event occurred, and it meant knowing the cause of the event; this is the factual character. In addition, scientific propositions "cannot" be false; they are not merely contingently true; this is the necessary character of such knowledge. For Aristotle, then, science consists of a series of propositions which are logically systematic, have factual reference, and are necessarily true.

What gives the collection of propositions logical order is, of course, the syllogism. Scientific propositions are syllogistically demonstrated conclu-

sions from true premises. But the premises must also have been demonstrated; otherwise the conclusion is merely consistent, not necessarily true. However, it is obvious that not all premises can be syllogistically demonstrated. Ultimately the regress of demonstrations must come to an end. At this point, one has reached premises which must be justified in another manner. Aristotle offers a justification for such first premises, and this justification is the most fascinating part of the *Posterior Analytics*.

Aristotle lists six characteristics of ultimate premises. Ultimate premises (1) must be *true* propositions about things which exist (matters of fact); (2) they must be *primary*, by which Aristotle means logically indemonstrable; (3) they must be *immediate*; that is, they must be self-evident; (4) they must be *better known* than the conclusions which follow from them; (5) they must be *prior* to the conclusions in a logical sense; (6) they must state the *causes* of the events referred to by the conclusions.

Aristotle mentions two methods of establishing such ultimate premises, induction and intuition. The induction he is speaking about in the *Posterior Analytics*, however, is perfect induction, and so the question ultimately turns on the account of intuition.

At the very end of the *Posterior Analytics*, Aristotle describes intuition as a process involving the following steps: (1) sense-perception, (2) retention of the sense-percept in the soul following the removal of the external stimulus, (3) memory, (4) experience as the product of repeated memories, (5) abstraction of the universal—"the one in the many"—from experience. Here we see, however, that the justification of first premises has led to the problem of the role played by the active intellect, a matter which is more fully—though not completely satisfactorily—dealt with in Aristotle's psychology, his treatise *On the Soul*.

This brief survey should make it clear that Aristotle's claim to the title "Father of Logic" is a just one. He marked out many of the problems of logic and offered solutions which in many cases retain even today their fas-cination and pertinence. Of course, he made mistakes and his system of logic is incomplete by modern standards. But he closes the *Organon* with the comment that there was nothing written on the subject before him. He then asks to be excused for his mistakes, but thanked for the light he has shed on the matter. Surely Western civilization is deeply in the debt of Aristotle for his contributions to logic.

PHYSICS

Author: Aristotle (384-322 B.C.)
Type of work: Metaphysics, philosophy of physics
First transcribed: Fourth century B.C.

PRINCIPAL IDEAS ADVANCED

To know a thing involves understanding first principles.

Matter is potentiality, form is actuality; to each form there corresponds a special matter.

There are four types of causes: the material cause (matter); the formal cause (the kind); the final cause (the purpose); and the efficient cause (that which initiates change); in addition, change and spontaneity are kinds of causes.

Nature, defined as a principle of motion and change, is a cause that operates for a purpose.

The infinite is potential, never actual.

Place is the innermost motionless boundary of what contains; time is the number of motion in respect to before and after.

There are three kinds of change: qualitative, quantitative, and local.

There must be an unmoved mover which by eternal rotary motion imparts motion to all things.

In modern times, with the growth of natural science, most of the topics treated by Aristotle in this work would be classified as metaphysics. The collection of treatises bearing that name has come to stand for any speculative question concerning first principles, and in that light the topics of the *Physics* are closer to metaphysics than to modern questions of physics. Aristotle begins by considering the number and character of the first principles of nature, and he goes on to argue against Parmenides' speculative theo-

143

ries. Nevertheless, the topics here considered do concern first principles of the physical world, and the work is still a classic in its grasp of issues fundamental to all physical inquiry.

Book I opens by stating that it is first principles which we must come to know. To know a thing means to grasp its first principles and to have carried the analysis out to the simplest elements. We proceed from things more obvious and knowable to us and move to those principles more clear and knowable by nature. Our first question is to ask whether the first principles involved are one or more than one. As a physicist, Aristotle takes it for granted that the things which exist by nature are, either all or some of them, in motion. Speculative theories to the contrary (the idea of "Being as one and motionless") he dismisses.

One of the famous questions of the *Physics* now begins to develop: whether there is an actual infinite in the category of quantity. The infinite qua infinite, Aristotle firmly believed, is unknowable; and it is primarily this epistemological difficulty which plagues Aristotle about the infinite. The principles of physical nature cannot be either one or innumerable. A finite number is sufficient, and an infinite number would be unknowable.

In dealing with coming into being and change, Aristotle uses potentiality and actuality as explanatory concepts. What desires form is matter, and matter is the origin of potentiality and form the symbol of actuality. "Matter" Aristotle defines as the primary substratum of each thing, from which it comes to be without qualification, and which persists in the result. "Nature" Aristotle defines as a source or cause

of being moved and of being at rest in that to which it belongs primarily. But no thing has in itself the source of its own production.

In Book II we begin again on the basic problems of physics. Form is more nearly nature than matter, for a thing is more properly said to be when it has attained fulfillment (fully formed) than when it exists potentially. However, we also speak of a thing's nature as being manifest in the process of growth by which its nature is attained.

Here Aristotle pauses to make his famous distinction between physics and mathematics. Physical objects contain surfaces, volumes, lines, and points (the subject matter of mathematics), but the mathematician does not treat them as the limits of a physical body. He separates them, for in thought they are separable from motion. The objects of physics are less separable than those of mathematics. Such things are neither independent of matter nor definable in terms of matter only. Of course, matter is a relative term; to each form there corresponds a special matter.

Here Aristotle changes topics again, this time to define the (now famous) four types of causes: (1) that out of which a thing comes to be, the matter, or material cause; (2) the form or the archetype, the formal cause; (3) the end, or purpose, the final cause; and (4) the primary source of change or coming to rest, the efficient cause. And, as is not generally known, Aristotle adds to these change and spontaneity, both of which must be counted as causes. This addition is often overlooked, because these latter two causes are not amenable to knowledge, and yet any complete account must include them. Chance is unstable and is thus inscrutable to man.

Nature belongs to the class of causes which act for the sake of something, and thus it is amenable to intelligence. Those things are natural which, by a continuous movement originated by an internal principle, arrive at some completion. Nature is a cause, a cause that operates for a purpose. Nature is to be defined as a "principle of motion and change." The fulfillment of what exists potentially, insofar as it exists potentially, is motion. And it is not absurd that the actualization of one thing should be in another.

In Book III Aristotle turns to the problem of the existence of an infinite, and he readily admits that many contradictions result whether we suppose it to exist or not. Is there a sensible magnitude which is infinite? This is the physicist's problem. Aristotle begins by assuming that number is a numberable quantity. Having concluded that the sensible infinite cannot exist actually, Aristotle goes on to discuss whether it might have potential existence. The infinite has turned out to be the contrary of what is said to be. The infinite is potential, never actual. Its infinity is not a permanent actuality but consists in a process of coming to be, like time and the number of time.

"Place" is the concept under consideration in Book IV. Now if place is what primarily contains each body, it would be a limit. The place of a thing would be its form. But the place of a thing is neither a part nor a state of it, but is separable from it. And place would not have been thought of if there had not been a special kind of motion; namely, that with respect to place. Aristotle concludes that

the innermost motionless boundary of what contains is place. Furthermore, places are coincident with things, for boundaries are coincident with things and also with places.

After place, Aristotle begins his famous consideration of time. Aristotle considers it evident that time is not movement nor is it independent of movement. We perceive movement and time together. Time, he concludes, is just this—the number of motion in respect to before and after. Time, then, is a kind of number. Just as motion is a perpetual succession, so also is time. Time and movement define each other. It is obvious, then, that things which always are cannot be in time, since time by its nature is the cause of decay because change removes what now is. Yet since time is the measure of motion, it is also indirectly the measure of rest. And in conclusion we ask: Will time fail? Surely not, if motion always exists. Time has being in the same way that motion does. Every change and everything that moves is in time.

In Book V Aristotle begins to move the argument from motion toward the motionless. The goal of motion, he insists, is really immovability. Only change from subject to subject is motion, and there are three kinds of change: qualitative, quantitative, and local. In respect to substance there is no motion, because substance has no contrary among things that are. Change is not a subject. There must be a substratum underlying all processes of becoming and changing.

Book VII begins by asserting that everything that exists is in motion and must be moved by something. But this series cannot go on to infinity. Therefore, the series must come to an end, and there must be a first movement and a first moved. Here is Aristotle's famous argument for the existence of an unmoved mover from the very nature of motion itself. A great deal of the force of the argument derives from the requirements of Aristotelian knowledge. Knowing and understanding imply that the intellect has reached a state of rest and has come to a standstill, and this can be so only if the mind can find a satisfactory explanation for the origin of motion. Nevertheless, time is uncreated and motion is eternal. There must always be time.

It is clear that there never was a time when there was not motion and that the time will never come when motion will not be present. And there must be three things: the moved, the movement, and the instrument of motion. But the series must stop somewhere since the kinds of motion are limited; so there will be an end to the series. Consequently, the first thing that is in motion will derive its motion either from something that is at rest or is from itself. But that which is itself independently a cause is always prior as a cause, and this argues for the source of motion in something itself at rest. That which primarily imparts motion is itself unmoved.

There must necessarily be some such thing, which, while it has the capacity of moving something else, is itself unmoved and exempt from all change—this is the crux of Aristotle's argument. Motion, then, being eternal, that which first causes movement will also be eternal. It is sufficient, he feels, to assume only one movement, the first of unmoved things; and this will be eternal and the principle of motion to everything else. The first movement

must be something that is one and eternal. And if the first principle is permanent, the universe must also be permanent, since it is continuous with the first principle. However, motion is of two kinds. Some things are moved by an eternal unmoved movement and are therefore always in motion. Other things are moved by an agent itself in motion and changing, and so they, too, change their motion.

Locomotion, Aristotle feels, is the primary motion. Yet it is possible that there should be an infinite motion that is single and continuous. This motion is rotary motion, since rectilinear motion cannot be continuous. There cannot be a continuous rectilinear motion that is eternal. On the other hand, in motion on a circular line we find singleness and continuity. Rotation is the primary locomotion. Every locomotion is either rotary or rectilinear or a compound of the two. Rotary motion can be eternal, and thus it is prior as motion.

Aristotle concludes that there always was motion and always will be motion throughout all time. The first movement of this eternal motion is unmoved, and rotary motion alone can be eternal and is primary. If the series comes to an end, a point is reached at which motion is imparted by something that is unmoved. The only continuous motion, then, is that which is caused by the unmoved mover, and such a first unmoved mover cannot have any magnitude, is indivisible, and is without parts.

Aristotle's conclusion to the *Physics* is really only an introduction to the repetition and extension of some of the arguments later to appear in the book of edited writings entitled the *Metaphysics*. Yet in this preliminary

146

book most of the crucial concepts concerning physical nature are given a basic definition. The first principles of physics have been enumerated and defined. All that lies beyond physics is metaphysics.

ON THE SOUL
(De Anima)

Author: Aristotle (384-322 B.C.)
Type of work: Metaphysics, philosophical psychology
First transcribed: c.330 B.C.

PRINCIPAL IDEAS ADVANCED

The soul is the actual development of the potentialities of life; it is the body's source of movement, the essence of the living body, and the purpose for which the body exists.

Sensation is the process of receiving into oneself, by means of the sense organs, the forms of things.

The mind is that part of the soul by which the soul knows and thinks.

This work is divided into three books, of which the first consists mainly of a review of the opinions of Aristotle's predecessors about the soul, and refutation of their errors; the second book and the first part of the third define the soul and describe and explain the nutritive and sensitive faculties; while the rest of the third treats of the intellect.

The original meaning of the word *psyche* was "breath," and in the earliest Greek literature it had come to stand for "breath-soul," being identified with vital functions in general, while a separate blood-soul was held to be the seat of consciousness. Aristotle seems to have been unaware of this view. By his time *psyche* meant "life-principle," whether simple or complex, the inner cause of vital movements of all kinds.

Aristotle begins by describing in detail the views about the soul held by his predecessors, finding them to fall into two groups: (1) those according to which the soul is one of the elements (earth, air, fire, water) or some combination of them, or a special (material) soul-substance; and (2) the doctrine that the soul is the harmony of the body. Theories of the first kind have in common the characteristic of trying to account for bodily movements by postulating a power of self-movement in the soul. They are mistaken, for the soul cannot have any motion at all. The theories require it to have a *natural* motion, and if it had, it would (by Aristotle's doctrine of motion) have a natural place toward which it moved, a condition manifestly impossible. Aristotle treats the harmony theory very literally and unsympathetically. He interprets it as meaning that the soul is the ratio of the ele-

147

ments that go to make up the body, and he points out that since, for example, the ratio of elements in bone is different from that in flesh, there would have to be as many souls in one body as there are different kinds of tissues.

It is curious that Aristotle does not discuss the immortality of the soul. As is well known, belief in personal immortality was not widely held in Greece; however, Plato and some of his Pythagorean predecessors had taught transmigration. Aristotle declares almost at the outset that he is not inclined to think that the soul can exist separated from its bodily substratum—though he makes an exception for the intellect, which he says "seems to be an independent substance implanted within the soul and to be incapable of being destroyed." To the familiar argument that mental powers are observed to decline along with bodily ones, he replies that senility is not a defect of the mind as such, but a progressive incapability of the body to use the mind aright. This exception does not constitute an endorsement of belief in *personal* immortality, for thinking is impersonal. The arguments of Plato are not even mentioned.

In Book II Aristotle defines the soul as "the first grade of actuality of a natural body having life potentially in it." It is " 'the essential whatness' of a body." It is not really possible to understand these definitions without prior acquaintance with the whole of Aristotle's physics and metaphysics; but it is hoped that the following explanation suggested by Aristotle's discussion of causes will be of some help.

There are four questions that can be raised about a couch. (1) What is it made of (what is its *material cause*)? (2) What sort of thing is it (what is its *formal cause*)? (3) How was it made (what was its *efficient cause*)? (4) What is its purpose (what is its end or *final cause*)? When all these questions are satisfactorily answered, then (and only then) we understand the couch. And so, in general, artificial objects are produced when someone takes raw materials and by moving them imposes a form on them for a certain purpose.

The process of making a couch is to be looked upon as a movement from the potential to the actual. A heap of cloth, springs, and wood is potentially a couch; the maker's activity moves these ingredients from the state of potentiality to that of being actually a couch. These terms, however, are only relative; what is potentially a couch (the matter of a couch) is at the same time actually cloth, springs, and wood.

The world consists of particular things. Those that are not artificial are natural; and the significant difference between natural and artificial things is that while the latter have their form imposed on them from outside, the former have their own internal principles of motion (in the broadest sense, including growth). Hence everything is to be understood in the way a couch is understood: as a particular thing, a *this*, consisting of a certain matter which takes on a certain form or whatness—that is, it undergoes a process of development from a condition of potentiality to a state of actuality. We understand an acorn when we know that it is a potential oak tree, that it is the sort of thing that has the internal power of developing (organizing itself and other matter) into (not just anything but specifically) an oak tree.

Articles of furniture are classified according to their shapes. The whatness of a table is distinguished from the whatness of a chair by mere outline. But even here the difference in form amounts to a difference in *function*. What makes a thing a knife is not its shape as such but its ability to cut: the form of whatness of a knife is cutting. It is in an analogous sense that Aristotle declares the soul to be the essential whatness of a living body.

A bar of unsharpened steel is potentially a knife. When it is shaped and sharpened it is actually a knife. But the word "actually" here is ambiguous. The object is actually a knife both when it is actually cutting something and also when it is resting in a scabbard, in a condition to cut. The actuality of the knife in the scabbard Aristotle calls the "first grade of actuality" to distinguish it from the second grade, manifested only when the knife *is* cutting. And so, for the first definition of soul, the soul is not an ingredient of a body or an extra organ; it *is* the organization and functioning of the body. If a body has life potentially in it, the soul is the actuality (developed potentiality) of life. It is the "first grade" of actuality because not all the vital functions are in exercise at every moment. Hence, the immortality of the soul is out of the question. Further, it is as meaningless to ask whether soul and body are one as to wonder whether a piece of wax and its shape are one or two. It is not wrong to say that the animal is its body *plus* its soul, if care is taken to realize that this is to be interpreted in the same sense as the statement that the pupil *plus* the power of sight

constitute the eye. (It appears that Aristotle's own doctrine was not so far as he thought from the harmony-of-the-body theory.)

The soul is the life-principle. But what is it to live? It may mean "thinking or perception or local movement and rest, or movement in the sense of nutrition, decay and growth." Plants have the power of nourishing and reproducing themselves, as do all living things, "in order that, as far as their nature allows, they may partake in the eternal and divine. That is the goal toward which all things strive, that for the sake of which they do whatsoever their nature renders possible." Animals have in addition the faculty of moving from place to place, and sensation that makes movement feasible; all animals have at least the primary sense of touch, and taste, which is a kind of touch. Only man is endowed with the power of thought, which "is capable of existence in isolation from all other psychic powers." But although Aristotle distinguishes thus radically between thinking and the other psychic powers of reproduction, nourishment, and sensation, it is probably a mistake to attribute to him the doctrine that man has three (separate or separable) souls.

In all senses of cause except material cause, the soul is the cause of the body. It is the body's source or origin of movement (efficient cause), the essence of the whole living body (formal cause), and the purpose for which the body exists (final cause).

The remainder of Book II treats of the faculty of sensation and of the five senses. "By a 'sense' is meant what has the power of receiving into itself the sensible forms of things without the matter," as the wax receives the imprint of the seal. ("Sensible form" seems to mean any form that can be perceived. Thus, shapes are sensible forms, souls are not.) The process of sensing is this: the sense organ consists of two or more of the four elements in a certain ratio, the combination being such as to be suitable matter for receiving a certain range of sensible forms. When I see a hippopotamus, there is no hippopotamus (natural body, matter and form) *in* my eye. What is there is the matter of the eye, which has now taken on the sensible form of the hippopotamus and is in consequence *qualitatively* identical with the hippopotamus. I cannot see sounds or hear colors because the matter of the eye is such as to be the potentiality only of colors, the ear only of sounds. The power of the sense organ to perceive, then, is the ratio of the elements in its composition.

Sight: "What is visible is color and color is what lies upon what is in its own nature visible." In order that something may be seen, there must exist (a) a colored object, (b) a transparent medium, and (c) light. They are related as follows: All transparent things—air, water, and the "uppermost shell of the physical Cosmos"—contain a certain substance which has the power of becoming transparent. It is *actually* transparent, however, only when excited to actuality by fire, or something resembling fire (such as the phosphorescence of certain fungi and decaying flesh). Light is not a body; it is the activity of the transparent medium. When the medium is actually transparent, color is able to set it in motion, thus to communicate the sensible form to the eye.

Aristotle's discussion of sound and hearing is very accurate. He knows that sound is transmitted by vibration of the air, and he knows something of the anatomy of the ear. He remarks that voice, being "sound with a meaning," indicates the presence of soul. Voice is not just air knocking against the windpipe: we must hold our breath to speak, using the confined air as an instrument.

Aristotle observes acutely that a study of touch raises the problem whether touch is or is not a single sense. For several pairs of opposites, not just one, are perceived by touch: hot and cold, dry and moist, hard and soft. We are inferior to other animals in some of the senses, notably smell, but exceed them all in touch and in its sub-sense, taste. This (we learn to our astonishment) is the explanation of man's superior intelligence and of the superiority of one man to another: "It is to differences in the organ of touch and to nothing else that the differences between man and man in respect of natural endowment are due; men whose flesh is hard are ill-endowed by nature, men whose flesh is soft, well-endowed."

Only solutions can be tasted, Aristotle argues. The organ of taste must be something dry that can be liquefied.

All sensation is *via* a medium. Democritus erred in supposing that one can see through a vacuum. We cannot see something placed directly on the eye or hear something on the eardrum. Neither can we smell something in the nostril, unless we are breathing in. (Aristotle was puzzled, however, to find that some bloodless animals, which do not breathe, nonetheless can smell. He suggests that over the intra-nasal organ of smell we have some sort of curtain, analogous to the eyelid, which is raised only when we inhale. This the bloodless animals presumably lack.) Even the sense of touch has its medium, to wit, the flesh, which is not itself the sense organ.

Book III begins with a complicated proof that there could not be a sixth sense, nor a need for one. Aristotle continues with a discussion of the relation of the sensible object to the percipient sense. They are distinct, though their activity is one and the same: for example, the hearing and the soul are "merged in one." Both must be "found in that which has the faculty of hearing; . . . actual hearing and actual sounding appear and disappear from existence at one and the same moment." But Aristotle is no Berkeleian: as *potentialities,* one of them may exist without the other. It is wrong to say that without sight there is no white or black; this description applies only to the actualities, not to the potentialities.

There follows an obscure passage in which Aristotle seems to say that after all we do need—and indeed, we have —a sixth sense, a "common sense" which discriminates between sensations in different modalities: how else could we tell that sweet is different from white? This passage serves as a transition to the consideration of thinking and imagining which occupies most of the rest of the book.

Thinking is different from perceiving (a doctrine denied by some ancient philosophers), for (1) perception does not admit of error, while thinking does, and (2) all animals perceive, but very few think. Imagining is different from both, as being in the province of the will and not productive of emotion.

Thinking is part imagination, part judgment. Imagination is "that in virtue of which an image arises for us." It is not sensing, for (1) it takes place in dreams, (2) it is not always present, as sense is, (3) imaginations are mostly false, while sensations are always true, (4) when we (in fact) see a man, we do not say that we imagine it to be a man, and (5) visions appear to us even when our eyes are shut. Nor is imagination knowledge or intelligence or opinion, for brutes imagine but do not believe.

Nevertheless, imagination is impossible without sensation: we do not imagine what we have never sensed. Imagination is "a movement resulting from an actual exercise of a power of sense."

Mind is "the part of the soul with which the soul knows and thinks." Thinking, though it is not perceiving, is sufficiently *like* perceiving to enable us to conclude that mind is capable of being affected by forms: "Mind must be related to what is thinkable, as sense is to what is sensible." It follows that mind can have no nature (no combination of *matter* and form) of its own; for unlike the senses, the matter of which restricts their potentialities each to a certain range of possible sensations, mind is not limited in its objects. Hence, mind "before it thinks is not actually any real thing. For this reason it cannot reasonably be regarded as blended with the body." It is (potentially, not actually) "the place of forms."

The mind so far described, however, is only "passive mind." In the extremely short, obscure, and important fifth chapter we learn that though passive mind "is what it is by virtue of becoming all things," there is "another which is what it is by virtue of making all things: this is a sort of

151

positive state like light, for in a sense light makes potential colors into actual colors." This kind of mind "is not at one time knowing and at another not. When mind is set free from its present conditions it appears as just what it is and nothing more: this alone is immortal and eternal (we do not, however, remember its former activity because, while mind in this sense is impassible, mind as passive is destructible), and without it nothing thinks."

The remainder of the book is in the main a sort of appendix in which topics previously treated are considered further.

The great conception of *De Anima* is that of soul as the *function* of the body. On this account it is the sole

ancient treatise that is akin in its viewpoint to modern psychology and philosophy of mind. It is tragic that Aristotle's great authority, which sufficed to canonize so many errors for so long in other departments of science and philosophy, did not prevail in psychology. Aristotle, like the tragic heroes he describes in the *Poetics*, was not blameless in the matter: his flaw was his abandonment of his own doctrine in order to sing the ode to "active mind." While the progress of many a science has consisted in throwing off Aristotelian shackles, the reverse is true in psychology, in which Aristotle's insight had to wait almost to our own day to be rediscovered.

METAPHYSICS

Author: Aristotle (384-322 B.C.)
Type of work: Metaphysics
First transcribed: Fourth century B.C.

PRINCIPAL IDEAS ADVANCED

True knowledge is the knowledge of ultimate causes.

There are four types of causes: the formal cause (a plan or type); the final cause (a purpose); the material cause (matter, that which is used); and the efficient cause (that which initiates change).

The study of being as being involves the attempt to discover first principles of explanation.

The individual thing to which properties belong is the only true substance; substances are subjects, but never predicates.

Since properties attach themselves to individuals of a certain kind, the kind may also be called "substance"; thus, the essence of a thing is, in this sense, its substance.

Matter is potentiality, the capacity to be something; matter is unlimited which is able to be limited by form; when matter is limited by form, there is actuality.

Forms, or universals, exist only in things.

The process of change cannot go on to infinity; there must be an unmoved

152

first mover which is eternal substance and actuality; such a first mover is good; it is divine thought thinking only of thought.

Avicenna reported that he had read Aristotle's *Metaphysics* forty times and still had not understood it. Such a comment is illuminating both for metaphysics as a subject matter and for Aristotle's treatise, from which the title for this inquiry has been derived. Both are difficult to understand, but the thinker who would understand this philosophic discipline would do well to start with Aristotle. Baffling as his piece of writing is, it is still the best source of metaphysics. Its structure is puzzling, since it was put together not by Aristotle but by his students from their notes. Nor did Aristotle give the treatise its immortal name. It was placed in the collection of his writings *after* the treatise on *Physics* and so earned the name of *meta*—(after the) physics.

Accidental as this title seems, it still describes the content of the treatise fairly accurately. In modern times much of the *Physics* might be classed as metaphysics (the discussion of the infinite), and some of the topics of the *Physics* are repeated in the *Metaphysics* (change and movement); but still the *Metaphysics* does go beyond the *Physics*. First principles, not the principles of natural movement alone, are the subject now. The *Metaphysics* takes up questions beyond those of physical nature as such and moves on not only to first principles but also to an Unmoved Mover. It is true that the book (the *Metaphysics*) stands somewhat alone in Aristotle's writings. According to the way in which the *Metaphysics* is either bypassed or interpreted, much of the general interpretation of Aristotle's other works will vary.

That is, this treatise rightly occupies a metaphysical (basic) position within Aristotle's vast writings.

Book *Alpha*, which begins with the famous sentence, "All men by nature desire to know," is sometimes called the first history of philosophy. In it Aristotle reviews the theories of the Pre-Socratics and of Plato, and much information we have about the Pre-Socratics actually comes from Aristotle's accounts. Aristotle works out his own theories by a critical appraisal of other doctrines, indicating the strong and the weak points of each theory and incorporating the strong points into his own view.

Aristotle first gives a brief epistemology, describing the modes for gaining knowledge and, finally, for the achievement of wisdom. Such true knowledge can only be a knowledge of causes, particularly of ultimate causes. It is this which leads Aristotle to consider previous theories and types of cause, ending in the famous doctrine of the four kinds of cause: the *formal* cause (the plan); the *final* cause (the purpose); the *material* cause (that which is used); and the *efficient* cause (that which initiates change).

Such a theory of causation is crucial to metaphysics, since what we want is knowledge of truth, and we cannot know truth without its cause. To assure us that this can be obtained, Aristotle must affirm the existence of a first principle and the impossibility of either an infinite series or infinitely various kinds of causes. If it were otherwise, knowledge could not be obtained. Thus, a great deal of the treatise is devoted to proving that the kinds of causes are definite in number and that the existence of a first principle is certain. Knowledge comes through a grasp of causes; but if the kinds of causes were infinite in number, knowledge would be impossible (the mind can handle only finite entities). The disproof of an actual infinite, the limitation of causes to four, and the establishment of the existence of a first cause of motion—all are central if metaphysics is to achieve wisdom.

Book *Beta* turns to the traditional problem of substance. How many basic kinds of entities are there and what is it that is most stable and underlies change? Are the principles which govern both perishable and imperishable things one and the same? "Being" and "unity" are two difficult concepts, and Aristotle considers whether they are themselves substances or merely properties of things. Inevitably he becomes involved in the Platonic theory of forms. Although rejecting forms as substances, Aristotle still agrees with Plato that individuals as such are never knowable and that the knowledge of any individual thing is of its universal properties.

In Book *Gamma* Aristotle begins with the famous definition of metaphysics as the science which investigates "being as being." Other branches of philosophy treat various particular kinds of things, but metaphysics considers the one starting point of all things, the first principles and highest causes. Since being falls immediately into genera, the various sciences correspond to these genera. Yet there are certain properties peculiar to being as such, and the philosopher seeks to discover the truth about these.

To complete such basic inquiry, principles which are certain must first be found, and Aristotle gives us a statement of the principle of noncontradiction here as an example. Few principles can have the certainty which such a principle has, and one cannot demand demonstration of all things. Basic axioms cannot be proved, although they can be established indirectly by intuition or by the impossibility of their opposite being true. The starting point of demonstration cannot be demonstration but something accepted as true in itself. What the metaphysician must develop is a grasp of the basic principles which lie behind all demonstration, and then he ought to demand demonstration only of matters in which such proof is possible. He must grasp the principles of being itself.

At first glance Book *Delta* seems puzzling. Sometimes called the philosopher's lexicon, it appears to be (and is) simply an extended series of definitions of crucial terms. On closer inspection, these terms prove to be the basic metaphysical vocabulary (made up of such terms as "beginning" and "cause"). Metaphysics has always proceeded by spending time on the definition of a few key words. However, instead of attempting to give a single definition for each of these thirty or so terms, what Aristotle does is to list several common or possible meanings which may be given to each term. He does point up the more important meanings and focuses on any of metaphysical significance, but, on the whole, the book is a straightforward analysis of various common meanings given to these philosophically important terms.

The four causes are listed again here (they are not always defined in the same terms). The term "necessity" is of some special interest, since Aristotle uses it in the positive sense ("cannot be otherwise"), very much as Plato uses "eternal," whereas "necessity" for Plato in the *Timaeus* is a symbol of nonrationality and chaos. Here Aristotle denies unity as an overreaching concept and makes it merely an attribute of things. Here, also, is the famous definition of "substance" as the individual thing which is the bearer of properties and is not itself a property.

Aristotle's other doctrines can be seen through these definitions, that priority means complete actuality and absence of potency, that what is complete and excellent is what has attained its end or purpose. We find that Aristotle in defining "accident" is far from being a rigid determinist. Some aspects of the world are necessary, but events without a definite cause (except that of chance) are equally present; they are accidental. Through definitions of crucial terms, Aristotle built an outline of his view of the world's basic structure.

Scholars argue that the *Metaphysics* was not composed as a continuous work; rather, it represents a collection of pieces on similar topics. This becomes evident when, after the "lexicon," the next section begins again on the concept of knowledge through comprehending the principles and causes of things. However, this time we are led into the well-known definition of physics, mathematics, and metaphysics. Physics theorizes about such beings as admit of being moved, but are not separable from matter. Mathematics deals with things which are immovable but presumably do not exist separately, only as embodied in matter.

Metaphysics (first science) deals with things which both exist separately and are immovable and eternal. Of the accidental, there can be no scientific treatment whatsoever, in these branches of science or elsewhere.

Next Aristotle returns to the crucial question of substance, which he calls "first in every sense." The essence or the universal, the genus, and the substratum (that which underlies a thing) are all called substance. In deciding which of these meanings of substance is primary, Aristotle is never completely clear. As far as knowledge is concerned, it is clear that essence is prior. However, Aristotle is clear that he does not consider Plato's forms to be self-subsistent substances; forms, or universals, exist only in things. At the other extreme, matter as pure potentiality is unknowable in itself, and it is clear that there is no definition for the individual as such.

The causes of substances are the objects of Aristotle's search, but sensible substances all have matter and are thus subject to potentiality. Essence certainly attaches to the form and to actuality, and in that sense the form of the thing has a prior claim to be called substance. Substance is the primary category and all other categories depend on it. In virtue of the concept of substance all other beings also are said to be. And it is clear that actuality is prior to potency. "Potency" is every principle of movement or rest, whereas substance or form is actuality.

Arguing that eternal things are prior in substance to perishable things, Aristotle next begins his argument for the existence of an eternal prime mover. No eternal things exist potentially (and on these grounds he excludes the existence of an actual infinite).

Nothing which is necessary can exist potentially. Yet such eternal and necessary substances must exist, for if these did not exist, nothing would exist. In things which are from the beginning, in eternal things, there is nothing bad, nothing defective, nothing perverted. And how is there to be order unless there is something eternal and independent and permanent? In pursuing the truth one must start from the things that are always in the same state and permit no change.

The process of change cannot go on to infinity. It is necessary that there should be an eternal unmovable substance. It is impossible that movement should either have come into being or cease to be. Movement also is continuous in the sense in which time is. There must, then, be a principle whose very essence is actuality. There is something which moves without being moved, being eternal substance and actuality. The object of a desire moves in this way; it moves without being moved. The final cause, then, produces motion as being loved or desired, but all other things move by being moved.

Such a first mover exists of necessity and its mode of being is good. On such a principle the heavens and the world of nature depend. This substance cannot have any magnitude, being without parts and indivisible. The nature of divine thought is that it thinks of that which is most divine and precious, and it does not change. Change would be for the worse (involving potentiality, as it must). Since it must be of its own nature that divine thought thinks, its thinking is a

thinking on thinking. The divine thought and its object of thought are one.

The *Metaphysics* contains at this point Aristotle's famous consideration of the Platonic forms and his rejection of their separate and eternal existence. Aristotle does not deny that there are universal forms; knowledge requires them. What Aristotle refuses to do is to give them an independent and prior existence outside of particulars. Aristotle then closes the *Metaphysics* with a consideration of the status of mathematical objects. This section has often been a puzzle to scholars, for Aristotle seems to attribute certain views to Plato which are not to be found as such within the extant Platonic dialogues. Here Aristotle treats Platonic forms as if they were all thought by Plato to be numbers. These and other unexpected references to unknown Platonic theories have led scholars to guess that Aristotle knew (as Plato's pupil) of later theories developed by Plato in the Academy but not reflected in the written dialogues.

Such a puzzle is only one among many generated by the *Metaphysics*. It is a book both repetitious and vague in some of its theories, as well as unsystematic in its structure. The parts do not all fit together, and yet it has never failed to attract students to its study. It remains the classical source of metaphysics, and its problems and theories continue to be debated. It is impossible to understand the book in its entirety, and it is equally impossible to dismiss it. It remains the classical training ground for learning abstract theorizing on fundamental problems.

ETHICA NICOMACHEA

Author: Aristotle (384-322 B.C.)
Type of work: Ethics
First transcribed: Date unknown; Aristotle's lectures as recorded by his son, Nicomachus

PRINCIPAL IDEAS ADVANCED

The good is that at which all things aim; the good for man is happiness, and happiness is the realization of man's essential nature.

The virtue, or excellence, of a thing is the full development of the potentialities of its essential nature; since man is essentially a rational animal, the good for man is activity of the soul in accordance with reason.

To act in accordance with reason, to be virtuous, usually involves choosing the mean between extremes of conduct; for example, the virtue courage is the mean between rashness and cowardice.

Some kinds of acts are inherently bad and no temperate action is possible in such cases: for example, adultery and murder.

The good life involves friendship with virtuous men and development of the intellectual virtues.

The highest good for man is the contemplative life.

Dante's description of Aristotle as "the master of those who know" has an appropriate ambiguity: it suggests Aristotle's mastery of his predecessors' knowledge and also his influence, paralleled only by Plato's, on his philosophical descendants. Both aspects of this mastery are prominent in the *Ethica Nicomachea*. It is to Aristotle's credit that he gives full recognition to the contributions of other philosophers, and it is to his glory that so many basic ethical ideas of later philosophers are found in this great seminal work. While scholarly explanations of the work differ, it is generally agreed that the work was not intended for publication in its present form; it is a version of Aristotle's ethics as stated by his son, Nicomachus. The *Eudemian Ethics*, a record composed by one of Aristotle's pupils, Eudemus, supplements this work.

The *Nicomachean Ethics* is part of a vast scientific and philosophical system to which a teleological view of the universe is basic: all things are to be understood in terms of their purposes, the ends toward which they tend, ends inherent in their forms and integral to their natures. Defining the end or good of man by reference to his nature, Aristotle's ethics is a kind of naturalism, but not a reductionism failing to distinguish a higher sense of "nature" from one meaning simply "whatever is or occurs." It thus suggests (though it does not fully develop) the crucial difference between the factual and the ideal. The normative element, the "oughtness," of virtue is determined by the end or good by which virtue is understood. There is thus no nonnatural, self-subsistent, or supernatural source of obligation, but this is no loss to an ethics grounded firmly in the Aristotelian psychology and metaphysics.

Aristotle's psychological approach appears when he begins his investigation of the final good by reference to what he regards as a general fact of human and animal behavior. He cites the dictum of a predecessor that the good is "that at which all things aim." But there are many aims; some goods are desired for themselves, some for the sake of others. To avoid an infinite regression of goods merely instrumental to others, we must presuppose intrinsic goods; and if one appears to be more ultimate than any other, this will be the chief good. Its criteria will be finality and self-sufficiency—it will be valued for its own sake and its achievement will leave nothing to be desired. Everyone agrees, Aristotle notes, that happiness is thus final and self-sufficient; we desire other goods for the sake of this happiness, but never this for the sake of others. But this general agreement is merely verbal; specific descriptions of happiness are so varied that a detailed inquiry is obviously needed.

Among previous theories of the good is that of Aristotle's teacher, Plato, who held that good is a self-subsistent essence, a universal Form or Idea in which all particular good things participate, and by which alone they are good. Aristotle objects, however, that if nothing but this Form is good intrinsically, the good would be both empty of content and unattainable. In the practice of arts and sciences aiming at their own particular ends, it does not seem that a knowledge of this universal good is prerequisite. Hence Aristotle turns to a search for the specifically human good.

This must be found in man's own form and function qua man. To understand the latter, we must consider briefly the Aristotelian concept of matter and form, derived but considerably altered from that of Plato. Except for pure matter and pure form, terminal limits posited by the system rather than experienced differences in reality, the matter and form of any given thing are its two aspects of potentiality and actuality, separable only in analysis. Matter is the stuff, form the structure; matter is the *thatness*, form the *whatness*, of things. Matter without form is hardly conceivable, and form without matter is empty abstraction. Form is not mere structure, however, for what a thing is or becomes when its potentialities are actualized depends not only on shape or organization but also on function. The traditional illustration here is that of the acorn, which is a potential oak tree. Relative to the tree, the acorn is matter—an unrealized possibility which will eventuate in the actuality or form, oak tree. But the tree in turn may be matter for a higher form in case, say, it is made into a piece of furniture, and obviously the acorn itself must mature into the form, "oak tree seed," before it can function as material for the future tree. Thus the end or *telos* of the acorn is integral to its nature, and its "good" is to fulfill its formal function well—to become a strong, well-shaped tree.

The end of man must likewise be found in form, which for him is soul. "Soul" here does not have the connotations given it in Christian tradition; it is not an entity but rather a level of function of living bodies. Even plants have the nutritive function or vegetative "soul"; lower animals have this plus a sensory and appetitive or desiderative soul; the human soul has a higher level, the rational. Now the *excellence* or *virtue* of each thing, according to the meaning of the Greek *areté*, lies in the efficiency of its peculiar function; therefore "human good turns out to be activity of soul in accordance with virtue, and if there are more than one virtue, in accordance with the best and most complete."

Two broad divisions in the human soul are the irrational and the rational; the former includes the vegetative, over which reason has no direct control, and the appetitive, partially amenable to rational guidance. The rational part includes the calculative and scientific functions. Corresponding to each of these are various kinds of excellence ranged under the two main types, moral and intellectual virtues.

To reach a definition of the first type, Aristotle observes that well-being is achieved through a mean between two extremes, either of which destroys it, as the athlete's fitness is maintained by the proper amount of food, neither too much nor too little. But this is not an arithmetical mean; the proper amount of food for a wrestler would be too much for a businessman. Applying this concept to attitudes, emotions, and conduct, Aristotle develops a relational ethics which is yet not relativistic in the pejorative sense: "Virtue . . . is a state of character concerned with choice, lying in a mean, i.e., the mean relative to us, this being determined by a rational principle . . . by which the man of practical wisdom would determine it. Now it is a mean between two vices, that which depends on excess and that which depends on defect. . . ."

Examples of virtues appropriate to certain activities and attitudes are as follows:

ACTIVITY OR ATTITUDE

1. Facing death
2. Experiencing pleasure/pain
3. Giving and taking money
4. Attitude toward honor/dishonor
5. Assertion
6. Giving amusement

	VICE OF EXCESS	VIRTUE (MEAN)	VICE OF DEFECT
1.	Rashness	Courage	Cowardice
2.	Self-indulgence	Temperance	Insensibility
3.	Prodigality	Liberality	Meanness
4.	Empty vanity	Proper pride	Undue humility
5.	Boastfulness	Truth telling	Mock modesty
6.	Buffoonery	Ready wit	Boorishness

Virtue lies in feeling or acting rightly in relation to time, objects, people, motives, and manner. Though the mean is variable, since some means lie nearer one or the other extreme, there *is* a mean for most situations—that middle course recognized by the practically wise or good man. Aristotle himself notes, however, that this account of virtue and vice is not exhaustive; there are some acts and passions inherently bad, such as spite or envy, adultery or murder—there are no mean (right) ways of feeling or doing these.

Neither does the theory apply in the same way to a major virtue, justice. As a particular virtue (rather than as the Platonic justice comprehending all other virtues) justice involves the sharing of external goods such as honor or money; and the mean is an intermediate amount, while both extremes are injustice. Distributive justice is a geometrical proportion between persons judged by merit and goods awarded. If A and B are persons and C and D are things, this justice can be formulated thus: $A:B::C:D$. Equality here is thus not between persons or quantities; it lies in proportional relation. Rectificatory justice involves only the righting of wrongs in which the gain of one party equals the loss of the other, and the persons themselves are treated as equal. Since Aristotle disclaims universality for the concept of virtue as a mean, the objection of some critics to the inconsistency of his account of justice seems pointless.

The virtues and vices tend to be self-perpetuating; states of character are both causes and effects of corresponding actions. But while both acts and character are voluntary, we are clearly aware of specific choices preceding acts, while development of character is gradual and not so obvious. Nevertheless, we are responsible for both; even ignorance of the right is inexcusable if due to carelessness. The very attractiveness of false goods is due to one's character, just as that which is not really wholesome may appear so to a diseased person. Herein lies the distinguishing feature of the good man: while each character has its own concept of the noble and pleasant, the good man sees "the truth in each class of things, being as it were the norm and measure of them."

Though Aristotle's ethics is not a deontological system, it clearly was intended to develop "the sort of person that the right rule prescribes." The temperate man, for example, "craves for the things he ought, as he ought, and when he ought; and this is what rational principle directs." But the virtuous man is not burdened with a restrictive, puritanical sense of obligation; instead, he enjoys the best life by realizing his highest potentialities as a human being. This is illustrated by Aristotle's description of the properly proud man: pride, a mean between vanity and humility, "seems to be a sort of crown of the virtues; for it makes them greater, and it is not found without them." The proud man thinks himself to be *and is* worthy of great things. He is courageous, honorable and honored, noble, disdainful of the petty, liberal, dignified yet unassuming, frank in expressing his loves and hatreds, a man of few but great deeds. He is independent and incapable of centering his life in another, except for friends.

Aristotle writes at length of friendship's necessity to the good life. There are three types: friendships based on utility, those maintained for pleasure alone, and those between similarly virtuous men loved because of their goodness. The last kind is highest, rarest, and most durable.

The topic of friendship raises questions of the relations between benevolence and self-love, and here Aristotle anticipates such later writers as Hume and Bishop Joseph Butler. Our estimate of "self-love," he points out, requires distinction between higher and lower senses of the term. Selfish concern for wealth or physical pleasure is of course blameworthy, but the true lover of self is he who seeks that most fitting to his highest nature—the just, temperate, and noble. If all sought for themselves the highest good, virtue, self-love would make for the greatest common welfare. True self-love thus involves beneficence and occasionally sacrifice

160

of wealth or even life itself for the sake of friends and country. Thus the good man needs friends in order to exercise virtue fully.

The good man also needs the second major type of virtue, the intellectual, for the moral involves choice, and choice is defined as "either desiderative reason or ratiocinative desire." Good choice, then, presupposes right desire and true reasoning. The rightness and truth are measured against the right rule by which Aristotle avoids subjectivism: "there is a mark to which the man who has the rule looks . . . there is a standard which determines the mean states which we say are intermediate between excess and defect. . . ." But pure, contemplative intellect does not directly motivate, its end being truth *per se*; therefore it is the practical or productive intellect which aims at the truth in harmony with right desire. *Practical wisdom* is the intellectual virtue most intimately connected with moral virtue: "it is a true and reasoned state of capacity to act with regard to the things that are good or bad for man." It is deliberation about the contingent, not the eternal, for its concern is with selecting the best means to the good life; therefore, it is a function of the productive intellect which can command and sometimes control the irrational soul, the feelings and desires. Practical wisdom is thus a virtue of the calculative level, the lower of the two rational parts of the soul. Since it must not only calculate the means but recognize the ends, "it is not possible to be good in the strict sense without practical wisdom, nor practically wise without moral virtue." Thus, intellectual virtue is not mere cleverness.

Practical wisdom presupposes *intuitive reason*, which grasps first principles, universals, and ultimate particulars or specific facts, the raw materials with which practical wisdom does its work. Intuitive reason also furnishes the first principles with which the fourth intellectual virtue, *scientific knowledge* (logical or mathematical demonstration) operates. This virtue concerns only the eternal, the logically necessary. But the highest form of wisdom involves not only knowledge of the logical implications of first principles, but also comprehension of the principles themselves. Hence Aristotle, calling *philosophic wisdom* the combination of scientific knowledge and intuitive reason, specifies that it must be directed to the highest objects and be properly completed. From this it follows that it is not directed toward the highest human good, because "man is not the best thing in the world," not as divine, for example, as the heavenly bodies. But though not directed toward the highest human good, it *is* that good. Should a critic object that philosophic wisdom, being merely contemplative, is thus useless, Aristotle reminds us that it makes man happy not as an instrument but as the actualized end, the highest human activity. Practical wisdom's command of the body is not a mark of superiority to contemplation but, rather, prepares the way for its coming, as medicine is instrumental to health.

Before one can fully appreciate Aristotle's concept of happiness it is necessary to review his treatment of pleasure, regarded by many philosophers as the *summum bonum*. As usual, Aristotle considers arguments on both sides in some detail. He concludes not only that pleasure is a good, but also that there are cogent reasons for thinking it

161

the chief good: everyone agrees that its opposite, pain, is bad. Both beasts and men aim at pleasure (and at the start Aristotle had accepted the view that "the good is that at which all things aim"); and since pleasure is a necessary accompaniment of each activity carried to its unimpeded fulfillment, happiness would seem to be the fruition in pleasure of at least some or perhaps all of our activities. This latter consideration enters into Aristotle's final formulation of happiness, but there are compelling reasons for denying that pleasure *per se* and without qualifications is the chief good. Pleasures differ in kind, just as do activities, and since there is a pleasure proper to each activity, their values are concomitant. Some pleasures complete acts that are vicious, and some hinder the fulfillment of more worth-while activities. As Plato argued, it appears that the desirability of pleasure can be augmented by addition of other goods, such as that of wisdom, but one criterion of the final good is self-sufficiency. Pleasure, then, is but an ingredient of that good, happiness.

The modern reader must be careful not to identify this happiness with euphoria. It is a state of being, not just one of feeling. It is an activity, and since virtuous activity is also desirable for its own sake, happiness is virtuous activity. As the chief good, it involves the highest virtue, which, as we have seen, is contemplative. Contemplation is capable of more continuity than other actions, it requires fewer material necessities, its pleasures are pure and lasting. No immediately practical results follow from it, so again it appears to be loved for itself alone. As the highest human activity, it seems

most like that of the gods, and indeed it belongs to the most authoritative element in us: "that which is proper to each thing is by nature best and most pleasant for each thing; for man, therefore, the life according to reason is best and pleasantest, since reason more than anything else *is* man. This life therefore is also the happiest."

While this may strike the modern reader as an overly rationalistic or perhaps academic conclusion, Aristotle tempers it by adding that such happiness requires a complete life, including the satisfaction of bodily needs. He recognizes that few men have the ability or the opportunity to lead the life of contemplation. He claims that happiness on a secondary level is the morally virtuous life, for the moral virtues, after all, directly concern our nature in its "all too human" aspects, since it is a mixture of reason and the irrational appetites. Indeed, most men are incapable of being good through reason and self-discipline alone; they need the aid of legislation. This idea provides the subject of Aristotle's next work, the *Politica*.

If Aristotle's method should appear too speculative for the leading scientists of his day, he reminds his readers that what he has said must be reviewed and tested by reference to the facts, and should it clash with them, it must be considered mere theory. But should the reader adopt this alternative, it must be with reluctance when the theory is seen as an integral part of Aristotle's whole system. To find the most distinctive human excellence in reason and yet to allow for the most tonic exercise of the senses and appetites by conceiving both as the full fruition of man's natural potentialities, and to see

162

this actualization as part of a universally purposeful process, is to share one

of philosophy's most stirring ethical
convictions.

POLITICS

Author: Aristotle (384-322 B.C.)
Type of work: Political philosophy
First transcribed: Between 336 and 322 B.C.

PRINCIPAL IDEAS ADVANCED

The morally virtuous man performs acts according to a rational mean between
extremes of excess and deficiency; so also does the state.

The good states are monarchies, aristocracies, and polities (constitutional governments); the corresponding bad states are tyrannies, oligarchies, and radical
democracies.

Polities which lean toward the democratic form of government possess the
greatest political stability and are least liable to revolutions.

The art of government involves the use of practical wisdom.

Since the best life is one which combines action with contemplation, the ideal
state aims at providing sufficient external goods to permit the pursuit of virtue
and happiness.

Descriptions of actually existing
states are combined, in Aristotle's *Politics*, with judgments about the ideal
political community. Its eight separate
books make up a work which, most
scholars insist, their author never intended as one finished product. There
is debate about the ordering of the existing books. But in spite of the work's
variety of special topics, several dominant themes and interests prevail
throughout. One theme is the characteristic Aristotelian stress on the purposive quality of political life—the
view that a state, like any other entity
in nature, has a nature understandable
in terms of a purpose. Consequently,
one cannot properly determine the nature of citizenship unless he first
knows what, in general and particular,

the state is established to accomplish.
Another, yet related, theme concerns
the way in which political life is
viewed as an important, organized
means to the ethical development of
its members. Though the state is logically prior to the individual, according
to Aristotle, its purpose centers in the
production of the maximum human
good. The *Politics* presupposes the ethical teachings found in Aristotle's famous work on ethical life. The primary question for Aristotle is not
whether men will act politically—
since it is their natures so to act—but
rather whether they will act well.

Aristotle's insistence on the natural
basis of human political activity accounts for his central concern with the
proper education of the state's citizens.

163

Learning is induced by nature, habit, and reason. Education can influence habit and reason by modifying man's natural capacities, directing them to selected ends or kinds of action. Aristotle's conception of the way in which human ethical capacities develop affects what he says about human political roles. Two broad classes of ethical facts exist—one of them moral, the other intellectual. These classes are interdependent. The moral virtues are learned. They result from habitual kinds of conduct. The morally virtuous man performs acts according to a rational mean between extremes of excess and deficiency which require prudential judgments in specific contexts demanding action. The chief aim of the moral virtues is action rather than contemplation, doing rather than theorizing. Political activity expresses the range of virtuous actions insofar as man, as a political animal, must live in associations and devote attention to the family and to the public affairs of a commonwealth.

The matter of what makes good citizenship possible is a complicated one. The reason is that good citizenship must occur in relation to some actually existing state, of which there may be different kinds. Thus, there can be "good" citizens of "bad" states. Good citizenship need not coincide with human goodness. A man who is a good citizen of a bad state will acquire a character which produces acts foreign to the character of the morally good man. Although Aristotle preferred a state which encouraged moral activity on the part of its members, he showed sufficient realism to recognize the possibility of a wide range of states and to admit that citizenship exists as a function of the end sought after by any actually existing state. Aware of the conditions needed to produce an ideal state, Aristotle nonetheless wanted also to describe and to classify existing and possible types of political units.

Aristotle's sense of the variety of political possibilities becomes clear in his criticisms of Plato's utopian scheme sketched so brilliantly in the latter's *Republic*. He disagrees with Plato's abolition of private property and his advocacy of social communism of wives and children. Aristotle insists that Plato's recommendations are wrong in terms of both their end and their means. There can be too great a unity in any existing state. Plato's political thought wrongfully sought after an impossible kind of unity in suggesting abolition of property and the private family. Such recommendations could never lead, as means, to the minimal unity any state requires. They would increase the chances of dissension in the state. Aristotle argues that differentiation of functions is a law of nature—that things actually differ. Political philosophers must accept this fact and not seek to alter the unalterable.

In the *Laws*, written later than the *Republic*, Plato softened some earlier political suggestions by abandoning his theory of social communism. Aristotle also criticizes the *Laws* on several grounds: it fails to discuss foreign relations; it makes new states too large in territory; and it fails to limit property, population, or the respective roles of ruler and subject. Just as Aristotle insists that philosophers must never seek greater certainty in ethics than the subject-matter permits, so he argues that the political philosopher must recognize that judgments must conform to an inevitable relativity in types of political systems. "Since there are many forms of government," Aristotle asserts in Book III of the *Politics*, "there must be many varieties of citizens, and especially of citizens who are subjects. . . ." Nonetheless, he agrees with Plato that the best states—however specialized the functions of their citizens—seek the common interests of all.

When he describes existing states of his own day and age, Aristotle mentions the three which he considers best: Sparta, Crete, and Carthage. During his lifetime Aristotle also directed a study of the various constitutions, showing his interest in the empirical details of political life. Yet his empirically minded studies never paralyzed his independent judgments about the values of what he studied. Thus, Aristotle pointed out that Sparta was fit only for conducting war; the Cretan state was too narrowly a rule of the rich (oligarchy) whose cities remained safe only because of their accidental geographical inaccessibility; and the Carthaginian state relied on a policy of emigration to keep down domestic insurrection. The best existing states fail to measure up to what is possible. Aristotle realized that a description of what exists politically need not suffice either as a basis for classifying possible type of states or as a means of making clear the nature of an ideal state. In various portions of his *Politics* he devotes attention to such matters.

Like Plato, Aristotle claims that there are three broad types of states, each possessing a corresponding possible perversion. The so-called "good" types are monarchy, aristocracy, and polity. The corresponding perversions (or so-called "bad" types) of these are tyranny, oligarchy, and radical democracy. By "radical democracy" Aris-

totle means a state which permits an absolutely unrestricted manhood suffrage and the right of all, without qualification, to hold office. This classificatory scheme hides a great complexity, especially of degree, since Aristotle thinks both monarchy and aristocracy allow for at least five possible forms. The classification also contains puzzles. One is that though oligarchy is listed as a possible perversion of aristocracy, Aristotle indicates that the best state (practically, though not ideally) is a polity. A polity is defined as a state which mixes rule by the rich with rule by the poor. Ideally, then, a polity requires existence of a significantly entrenched middle class, whose interests moderate the extremes and receive furtherance through the state's machinery. A polity therefore requires a constitution which expresses elements of oligarchical interests.

To achieve a balance between oligarchy and democracy is difficult. The reason is that each type of state emphasizes a different end. Oligarchy rests on the assumption that men's political rights ought not to be equal but rather based proportionately on their possession of wealth. Democracy stresses human equality—that each shall count as one in political affairs. Neither is absolutely correct. Virtue stands as the sole general aim of statecraft, meaning that any form of political organization which produces virtuous conduct is politically justifiable. Aristotle understood that polity results from a compromise. It involves a mixed constitution. Polities may come into being in several different ways, but their constitutions must find a mean which mingles some property qualifications with offices open to lot or election. Aristotle's comments about

165

the value of a polity result, in part, from his unwillingness to consider absolute kingship the best political unit. Admitting that an absolute king who rules according to the spirit of law produces an excellent model for governing, Aristotle suggests that the rule of law receives less abuse if reserved for many citizens. He objects to monarchy because, in his estimation, it evolved as a response to the problems of a primitive social order. Monarchy often becomes simply hereditary. Its additional weaknesses are that it is subject to the passions of a single man and that no king can adequately handle all the affairs of ruling.

The need of continuity and stability in a state receives ample recognition in Aristotle's *Politics*. Yet all political systems are subject to revolutions. Existing forms of government share two general aims—"an acknowledgement of justice and proportionate equality. . . ." Men fail to translate these aims of government into adequate practice, producing conditions from which revolutions spring. In one example, Aristotle shows how the democrat's emphasis on equality leads him to think that men are equal in all things, while the oligarch's insistence on human inequality spurs him to claim too much for himself. In any state in which both the equalities among men and their inequalities fail to receive proper balancing, hardened parties tend to arise which encourage revolution on behalf of a more thorough realization of their own partial interests. The citizens possessing the highest right to rebel—men who stand out for their virtuous conduct—are those who, by their nature, seem least willing to take part in rebellions.

A student of revolutions needs to understand, first, the general feeling or attitude of those who rebel; second, the specific motivation of any rebellion (its objects); and third, the immediate factors which cause the rebellion. In all revolutions, a general cause exists in the desire for equality. This leads inferiors to revolt in hopes of attaining equality. It also causes men who are genuinely capable to rebel to achieve superiority over those who are in fact not their equals. The motivation for rebellion centers around "the desire of gain and honour, or the fear of dishonour and loss; the authors of them want to divert punishment or dishonour from themselves or their friends." Other causes play important roles. These causes of revolution include contempt, fear, insolence, increase in some aspect of the state which is disproportionate, and excessive superiority. Other kinds of causes of rebellion include intrigues at elections, unjust differences in the elements in the state, lack of care, and neglect of trivial issues over a period of time.

What causes an actual revolution depends often on the type of constitution involved. For example, Aristotle claims that democracies usually enter revolutionary times because of the demagogic intemperance of the leaders. Oligarchic states must guard against revolution-producing causes of two kinds—severe oppression of the people and personal political rivalries between important oligarchs in the state. Revolutions occur in aristocratic states when too few qualify for honors, in constitutional states when the constitution itself permits lack of justice. Aristotle insists that mixed constitutions which lean toward the democratic possess, in general, the greatest stability.

The analysis of the causes of revolutions leads Aristotle to consider how constitutions may be preserved. Obedience to the spirit of existing law requires planned defense in any moderately stable state. Such obedience extends even to small matters. Like Plato, Aristotle shows suspicion of alteration when he writes that "men should guard against the beginning of change. . . ." This remark shows that despite his awareness of variety Aristotle adopted a conservative political stance. In democracies, offices should rotate frequently; and a number of institutions are required in cases where the governing class is numerous. Aristotle advocates a fairly wide personal participation in government. He wrote for a small Greek city-state, limited in territory and numbers. For this reason many of his observations about participation in governing seem irrelevant or foreign to the modern states whose extensive territories require an underpinning of bureaucratic machinery. Aristotle makes clear, however, that magistrates and others who perform public offices should never make money. Public service should exist as a self-justifying activity of the virtuous citizen.

The moral tone of much of Aristotle's treatment of politics is apparent in his recommendations about the qualifications of men who wish to hold office in the state. In each existing state an office holder must show loyalty to the contents of the constitution. He must also possess administrative abilities of a high order and express the kind of virtue that his particular state requires. In the case of democratic governments, Aristotle never makes clear

how office holding by lot or election can guarantee that able administrators will rule. He does insist that only those who are citizens can qualify for office, and from the citizen body he excludes slaves and mechanics. Aristotle shares the cultural prejudices of his own age when he confines the virtues of the governing class (the citizen body) to the well-born and the aristocratic. A reliance on common sense runs throughout the *Politics*. Aristotle realizes that, once the purposes of governing are understood in principle, any state requires the practical wisdom of a sound statesman. Individual men must apply their knowledge of principles to specific situations. At this point the art of governing passes beyond the sphere of scientific prediction and control. Indeed, Aristotle makes clear that each and every form of state is subject to change and possible revolution, including the most tyrannically controlled states. He also indicates an unusual sensitivity to the ways in which any political form—say, democracy—must adapt itself to the special geographical and cultural circumstances with which it must in practice operate.

In the final portion of the *Politics* (Books VII and VIII) Aristotle discusses the way in which to form an ideal state as well as the educational practices necessary for its maintenance, once established. The treatment of these issues depends upon Aristotle's conception of man's nature. The human "soul" (psyche) contains an element which is subservient to a rational principle of control. This is the desiring aspect of human nature which is amenable to command and persuasion. Each man also possesses a unique capacity for rational comprehension. The best life, in Aristotle's view, is that which combines action with contemplation. The happy man will enjoy external goods, goods of the body and spiritual (intellectual) goods in some appropriate proportion. Goods of the soul exist as that to which the other goods are a necessary and enjoyable means. Individuals and states need sufficient external goods to permit the pursuit of virtue and happiness. Aristotle treats such a view as axiomatic, beyond argument.

To the question of which is the more preferable, the life of a philosopher or that of a statesman, Aristotle's answer is that political activity is not degrading, though political power can never stand as the highest good. Aristotle claims that natural capacities, developed in a proper order, can lead to the realization of the philosopher's ideal of wisdom. An important aspect of Aristotle's attitude toward the functions of political philosophizing is the manner in which he relates its aims to common sense. The political philosopher acts not so much like the scientific theorist, discovering new theories, as like the practical man who rediscovers the applicability of rules evolved in the history of political communities.

When he discusses the formation of an ideal state, Aristotle considers a small state. Its population and territory must be controlled. There must be a sufficient economic base to make the state self-sufficient. Agricultural workers, mechanics (artisans) and men of commerce are excluded from the body of the citizens. Slaves possess no rights at all. Only soldiers, priests, and rulers qualify for the rights of citizenship. These groups alone own land. Each citizen, in addition, should perform the functions of soldiering, act as priest, and rule at different periods of his life's cycle. A hard distinction should hold between rulers (citizens) and subjects (non-citizens). In addition, in any ideally formed state, attention is given to the city's planning from the standpoints of utility and beauty.

Education functions to perpetuate the state. Potential citizens learn to obey in order later to know how to rule. The legislative body of the state holds responsibility for the education of the citizens. The aim again is the production of the good man. The humanistic aim of well-rounded human development of all man's capacities is emphasized. Physical fitness is encouraged to stimulate practical and contemplative efforts. The legislative body exercises a moral watchfulness over the content of the music and tales heard by the potential citizens. Legislators control the age of marriage, determine the physical requirements of parentage, decide when exposure takes place (the Greek practice of putting infants out to die), and oversee the duration of existing marriages. These educational arrangements serve, for Aristotle, as necessary ingredients in the political perpetuation of the state.

The lasting features of Aristotle's *Politics* are its emphasis on the moral justification of a state and the way in which its author accepts the inevitability of a wide range of existing states. Through the work also runs a firm defense of common sense as the touchstone of all political philosophizing. Aristotle attempted to make sense out of politics rather than to impress individuals by proffering complicated theories. There can be no blueprint guiding the statesman's prudential judgments. Aristotle's classical work has inspired men in different times and places when political events have forced them to seek sanity rather than drama in their political thought.

RHETORIC

Author: Aristotle (384-322 B.C.)
Type of work: Philosophy of rhetoric
First transcribed: Fourth century B.C.

PRINCIPAL IDEAS ADVANCED

Rhetoric is useful for enabling truth to prevail over falsity, for providing audiences with special knowledge, for facilitating examination of both sides of an issue, and for developing the capacity for persuasive argument.

Rhetoric is concerned with matters about which men are not decided and for which no science presents adequate answers.

The most effective source of persuasion is the enthymeme; enthymemes are compressed arguments designed to appeal to the beliefs and emotions of the audience.

The materials of enthymemes are probabilities and signs; rationes esscendi are reasons, referring to probable causes, for taking something to be a fact; rationes cognoscendi are reasons for believing in facts because of signs.

Speeches are of three kinds: the political, the forensic, and the ceremonial.

Aristotle's *Rhetoric* has been of the utmost influence, direct and indirect, in Western rhetoric. Cicero and Quintilian, the great Roman rhetoricians, drew heavily upon it. Present-day textbooks of public address are considerably, often basically, Aristotelian in doctrine.

While the *Rhetoric* is predominantly a handbook to a practical art, it has an interesting philosophical orientation. It is, in fact, the answer to Plato's call, in the dialogue *Phaedrus*, for a truly philosophical rhetoric to replace the shallow sophistical doctrines characterizing existing schools. Contrary to what his contemporaries appeared to believe, Aristotle affirmed that rhetoric is a subject that can be systematically studied, not a random collection of rules of thumb. It is not a special science, like medicine or physics, but an art of general scope, like dialectic, applicable to all fields of human concern. It explains by what principles some men succeed in swaying audiences, whether by natural gifts or through practice and study. Its proper constituents are the modes of persuading the intellect; the arousing of prejudice, pity, anger, and the like are nonessentials. To move a judge by emotion is as much an abuse as to warp a carpenter's rule before using it.

Aristotle finds a fourfold usefulness of rhetoric: (1) to help truth and jus-

169

tice prevail over their opposites; (2) to provide popular audiences with the special knowledge that establishes technical truths among trained audiences; (3) to employ both persuasion and strict reasoning on opposite sides of a question so as to see them clearly, and also to confute an opponent who argues unfairly; and (4) to foster a faculty—the defense of oneself through speech and reason—which belongs to man by nature. It follows that the function of rhetoric is not simply to succeed in persuading, but to attain such success as the circumstances of each case allow.

Rhetoric is the faculty of observing in any given case the available means of persuasion. The modes of persuasion involve three factors: (1) the character of the speaker (*ethos*, ethical appeal); (2) the frame of mind of the audience (*pathos*, pathetic or emotional appeal); and (3) the actual or apparent proof of the speech itself (factual statements and arguments). The good speaker must therefore thoroughly know human nature and character, the emotions, and logic. Rhetoric is a parallel to ethics and a branch of politics; since rhetoric concerns decisions regarding human action, it necessarily involves human relationships within the framework of the established order. It is likewise a parallel to dialectic, both being faculties of discovering arguments. While dialectic is used among trained thinkers, rhetoric assumes an untrained audience. The subjects of rhetoric are those regularly debated: matters which present alternative possibilities, concerning the outcome of which men's decisions can be an influence, and for which no special science gives an adequate solution. Complete proofs may occur in the sciences, deriving from what is necessary, but not in oratory, which concerns the contingent in human affairs. As dialectic has two methods of proof, induction and the syllogism, rhetoric has their counterparts, respectively, the example and the enthymeme. The enthymeme is the most effective source of persuasion.

The principles just given decide the treatise's plan. Books I and II refer to sources for enthymemes and tell how to construct them. Since enthymemes, as the most effective means of persuasion, embrace not merely the intellectual side of argument but all its aspects, this portion also analyzes the different types of speeches, motives of conduct, the chief emotions, and types of character. All these are preliminary to the specific treatment of drawing enthymemes from commonplace beliefs. Book III, which completes the work, deals with style and arrangement of speeches.

The enthymeme is a type of syllogism. To produce one requires knowledge not only of the syllogism but also of how the enthymeme and syllogism differ, and of what their proper materials are. While interpreters of Aristotle have long taught that an enthymeme is a syllogism with one premise suppressed, James H. McBurney, writing in *Speech Monographs* in 1936, has shown that Aristotle had much more in mind. The orator must be able to secure persuasion of an untrained audience in accordance with the truth but within the limitations of the circumstances. He cannot reproduce a long or complex demonstration, as the hearers would either tire or lose the thread. The essential thing about an enthymeme is not that it is made briefer than a syllogism, but that it is

170

founded upon a more suitable basis, being drawn from material accessible and meaningful to its audience.

The proper materials of enthymemes are probabilities and signs. These will not include the first principles of the sciences, which are necessary and certain and yet do not by themselves provide solutions for problems ordinarily debated, and which are not known or understood by the general audience. Rather, there is a fairly limited number of principles of common belief, applicable to human conduct, which do bear (although not conclusively) upon such problems, and these provide the probabilities and signs for enthymemes. Aristotle supplies the chief ones under the headings "topics," "commonplaces," or "lines of argument."

The probabilities and signs useful for enthymemes, McBurney affirms, are respectively *rationes essendi,* or reasons for being of a fact, and *rationes cognoscendi,* reasons for acknowledging it. Granted a given fact, an enthymeme drawn from a *ratio essendi* would account for its existence by suggesting its cause. Reasoning thus "from a probability," by a connection that is also only probable, cannot achieve certainty in the conclusion. Yet a factual statement of some probability acquires more probability, that is, becomes more persuasive, if we are shown a cause with which its occurrence is consistent. An enthymeme drawn from a *ratio cognoscendi,* or sign, attempts to establish the occurrence or existence of a fact by citing a sign of it that has occurred. Signs are either fallible or infallible. Some enthymemes from infallible signs may claim formal validity as syllogisms, and if it is also true that the sign has actu-

ally occurred, they constitute a full proof. A further form of enthymeme is the example, proceeding by induction from one or more cases to a general principle, then from that to a new particular case.

The following typify the general "topics," "commonplaces," or "lines of argument" from which enthymemes may be drawn: "One line of positive proof is based upon consideration of the opposite of the thing in question. . . . Another line is to apply to the other speaker what he has said against yourself. . . . Another line of proof is secured by defining your terms. . . . [Others are] logical division . . . induction . . . some decision already pronounced. . . . Another line of argument is this: The things people approve of openly are not those which they approve of secretly. . . . Another line is the argument that if two results are the same their antecedents are also the same. . . . Another . . . is to show why the facts are not as supposed; pointing out that there is a reason for the false impression given."

It will be seen that this list includes a few actual material propositions but is not completely composed of such. Aristotle seems to have intended that the "commonplaces" are to be employed more as ways of thinking through a subject than as truths or propositions under which given cases may be subsumed. Each special branch of learning has also its own list of "lines of argument." Further, to add a final thought of McBurney's, the lines of argument or commonplaces are distinctly not coldly factual or logical, but have strong emotional elements such as actually do reside in the popular belief of any age. Enthymemes thus are not the orator's demonstration *as opposed to* the emotional appeal; they serve also to embody the emotional appeal as well as the intellectual elements. Commonplaces became a part of traditional rhetorical systems through the Renaissance, usually with the correct understanding that they were not mere formulas to be lifted bodily from the textbook but were really the "common places," the areas in which to search, accessible to all speakers, for the materials of persuasion. Aristotle himself emphasized that in most speeches there would be more need for the special than for the general lines of argument, and further that the life of any speech was in the speaker's knowledge and inclusion of the particular facts and circumstances of the subject on which he must speak.

The hearer is either merely an observer, doing nothing but passing on the quality of the speaker, or else he is in some capacity a judge, a person who will immediately or eventually make some decision toward which the speech is aimed. Speeches are of three kinds, which differ in the type of judge to whom they are addressed, as well as in the time concerned and the ends in view. The first kind is *political*, in which the judge or audience is a deliberative body, the time concerned is future, and the end in view is establishing the expediency or harm of a proposed action. The second kind is *forensic*, in which the judge is an actual judge or jury in court, the time concerned is past, and the aim is to establish whether an event did or did not happen, and was or was not just. The third kind is the *ceremonial*, whose audience is public, whose time is the present, and whose aim is to praise or censure.

The political speaker must be informed in five general areas of deliberation: ways and means, war and peace, national defense, imports and exports, and legislation. Since men both as individuals and as a community aim at happiness and its constituents, the orator must know what they think these to be. Hence, Aristotle gives a "popular" view of happiness, upon which "pretty well everybody agrees." He likewise describes goodness and utility, since the things men call good are those they will choose in order to secure happiness, and he sketches ways to establish the relative goodness of things disputed. He records the four forms of government (democracy, oligarchy, aristocracy, monarchy) and their natures and ends; in the knowledge of their ends practices may be advocated or condemned in political speaking. With a discussion of virtue and vice he provides suitable grounds for the ceremonial speaker. He gives the forensic speaker information about the nature and number of the incentives to wrongdoing, the state of mind of the wrongdoers, and the kind and condition of persons who are wronged. Inasmuch as all voluntary acts are or seem to be either good or pleasant, Aristotle adds a discussion of pleasure, calling it a movement by which the soul is consciously brought into its normal state of being.

As to the sources of support other than facts and logic, forensic speaking especially requires that the audience be in the right frame of mind, while deliberative speaking requires that the orator's own character should appear good. To achieve the latter, the orator requires good sense, good moral character, and good will. The emotions "are all those feelings that so change men as to affect their judgement, and that are also attended by pain or pleasure." Aristotle takes a series of important emotions and examines each as to (1) what the state of mind is of him who feels it; (2) who the others are toward whom it is directed; and (3) on what grounds it is felt. He discusses the types of human character in relation to the various emotions, moral qualities, stages of life, and conditions of fortune. A good part of the *Rhetoric* thus serves as a handbook of applied psychology from which, together with particular information, the speaker can assess a given audience and hence stir the desired emotions and invest his speech with the proper apparent character; and also from which he can understand his own emotional life and build in himself a better character.

A chapter on refutation suggests meeting an argument by inventing a counter-syllogism of the same material, namely, the ordinary opinions of men, which may often be contradictory; or else by bringing certain objections against what was said. In brief, the refutations rest upon recognition of the basis of the original arguments in mere probability and general likelihood, of which Aristotle had given notice at the outset. Of course the validly constructed enthymeme from an infallible sign that actually occurred cannot be refuted. Amplification, the making of a proposition to seem important, or the opposite, is not a line of enthymematic argument, but is a matter of the material content with which an enthymeme is filled out.

In Book III Aristotle investigates the expression of facts in language. This includes both style and arrange-

ment. Delivery is the right management of the voice to express the emotions. It is not an elevated subject of inquiry: "We ought in fairness to fight our case with no help beyond the bare facts: nothing, therefore, should matter except the proof of those facts. Still . . . other things affect the result considerably, owing to the defects of our hearers."

Good style is both clear and appropriate, avoiding meanness and undue elevation. The writer must give the impression of speaking naturally, not artificially. Language is appropriate if it expresses emotion and character and corresponds in tone to its subject matter. All recommendations regarding style are relative and must be applied with good judgment and according to the circumstances rather than uniformly and mechanically. Metaphors should be used for implanting new ideas, as they are in familiar language, yet are graphic. Their construction comes only through talent or long practice, though this treatise may indicate the principles of construction.

As to organization, Aristotle writes that sophists have needlessly proliferated the number of parts of a speech, which is basically two: stating the case and proving it. But he is willing to recognize four—introduction, statement, argument, and epilogue. The introduction should show what is the aim of the speech; occasionally it also has a remedial purpose, directed to removing or exciting prejudice. The epilogue may be used to secure the good disposition of the audience toward the speaker himself, magnify or minimize the chief fact, excite the desired emotion, and refresh his hearers' memories. Aristotle's own ending to the treatise is his example of the most direct sort of epilogue by a man of good character: "I have done. You have heard me. The facts are before you. I ask for your judgement."

POETICS

Author: Aristotle (384-322 B.C.)
Type of work: Aesthetics
First transcribed: Probably between 334 and 323 B.C.

PRINCIPAL IDEAS ADVANCED

Poetry is imitation of human life in its universal aspects.

The arts differ according to the medium, manner, and objects of imitation.

Tragedy is the imitation of serious action, achieving through pity and fear a catharsis of those emotions.

The tragic hero is a man better than most who brings about his own downfall because of a flaw in his character.

The three most important moments in a tragedy are the reversal of fortune, the discovery of the critical fact which hastens the denouement, and the suffering—the final submission of the hero.

The *Poetics* was one of Aristotle's briefest works to begin with, and only half of it has been preserved. Nevertheless, it contains so many fruitful insights and canons of literary art that it has been turned to constantly by literati and philosophers ever since Aristotle's time. It has a history of varying interpretations, as well as variant manuscripts. The present review makes use chiefly of the now standard translation and commentary of S. H. Butcher.

Unlike most of Aristotle's work, this one contains little argument. Rather, it simply analyzes poetic art as it existed in Aristotle's time and as he understood it. The lasting influence of the work attests to the worth of his observations. Modern readers of course must make adjustments for the narrower scope and achievement of literature of that day, and for the specific nature, particularly in metrics, of the Greek language.

The *Poetics* as we know it treats tragedy and (very briefly) epic poetry. A second portion on comedy has been lost. All the kinds of poetry, Aristotle finds, are modes of imitation of character, emotion, and action, but they differ in respect to (1) the medium of imitation (which includes rhythm, meter or language, and harmony or tune); (2) the manner of imitation (that is, whether staged as a play, or sung, or narrated); and (3) the objects of imitation. The objects of all artistic imitations are actions, and these always have some degree of moral quality. Hence men must be portrayed as either better than in real life, or worse, or as the same. The difference between tragedy and comedy, Aristotle affirms, is that tragedy aims at representing men as better than they actually are, and comedy as worse.

Aristotle defines tragedy as "an imitation of an action that is serious, complete, and of a certain magnitude; in language embellished with each kind of artistic ornament, the several kinds being found in separate parts of the play; in the form of action, not of narrative; through pity and fear effecting the proper purgation of these emotions." The terms of this definition have undergone much interpretation. Butcher states that action (*praxis*) for Aristotle included the whole life of the mind, as well as mere motion of the body—an inner energy working outward. This is the object imitated by drama and other arts; and under this interpretation, dramatic action is much more than physical action alone. Imitation (*mimesis*) was a term used disparagingly by Plato, and perhaps popularly, to which Aristotle gave a new meaning. Since the object of poetic imitation was human life and human nature, imitation meant an expression of the universal element in human life. Aesthetically, the real and the ideal come together in this way; the ideal is the real freed from limitations of alien influences and chance, and enabled to work out its own development from beginning to end. Thus imitation became a creative process which could improve on nature.

Purgation (*katharsis*) is applied, in the definition, to pity and fear, by which the spectator is moved. Reference to the *Politics,* to the *Rhetoric,* and to contemporary medical writings shed more light on this purgation than the *Poetics* does alone. Aristotle considered pity and fear painful emotions. Pity is what one feels upon observing another in a situation in which he would fear for himself. Just as the playing of frenzied music has the effect of calming those possessed (an actual practice in Aristotle's times), the presentation of events arousing pity and fear would allay these emotions latent in the spectator, and thus bring pleasure. These are the universal elements of human nature that it is proper for tragedy in particular to imitate.

Tragedy requires six parts: rhythm, song, metrical wording—these three are the kinds of ornament that embellish the language—spectacle (the staging of the play), character of those portrayed, and their thought. What the completeness of tragedy requires, however, is that the piece have a beginning, a middle, and an end. A beginning is that which does not necessarily follow anything, but is naturally followed by something else. An end is what must follow another thing but need not be followed by anything. A middle both follows and must be followed by something else. As to magnitude, the imitation should not be so long as to give difficulty in remembering or comprehending the action; but within this limitation, the longer it may be, the finer a creative production. Further, it must be long enough to allow naturally a change from good to bad fortune, or bad to good. The action must be both single and complete, such that to add or subtract an element of plot would disorganize or disrupt, rather than enhance, the action.

In these descriptions, Aristotle recognized the dramatic principle of unity of action which, along with the unities of time and place that he suggested, were zealously observed in neoclassical times.

Plot, Aristotle says, is the very soul of tragedy. Being the arrangement of the incidents, it is what portrays the action. "For Tragedy is an imitation, not of men, but of an action and of life, and life consists in action, and its end is a mode of action, not a quality." Character determines men's qualities, and these together with their thought determine their actions. Dramatic action, therefore, does not aim at the representation of character; character is subsidiary to the action.

Aristotle approves the origin of the plots of most Greek tragedies in Greek myth. In telling the nature of tragedy, he states that a poet is unlike a historian, not writing about what has happened but rather about what may happen. Thus he acknowledges the transformation of events by the poetic imagination. Plato had barred poets, whom he considered immoral falsifiers, from the ideal republic until they could write poetry convincingly arguing for their own reinstatement. In other words, poetry should be didactic or argumentative, and have a moral purpose. Aristotle in the *Poetics* attempts to rehabilitate poetry from this low estimate. He shows here a function of poetry which Plato had entirely overlooked, for if poetry imitates what ought to happen rather than what has happened, it imitates the universal rather than the particular. Hence poetry, Aristotle concludes, is a more philosophical and a higher thing than history.

Aristotle recognizes three parts of the plot of tragedy, calling plots complex when so divided, and simple if there are no divisions. One part is reversal of the situation, or *peripeteia*, such as when an act of the hero produces the opposite from the intended effect. Another is recognition or discovery (*anagnorisis*), in which a character acquires knowledge of a fact, producing in him love or hate toward another character. These two, when simultaneous, are most effective in arousing pity or fear. The third part of the complex plot is the final suffering. It does not turn upon a surprise as do the others, but like them will be most effective as a probable or natural outcome of other events.

What of the person chiefly concerned in these actions? The tragedy must not bring a perfectly virtuous man from prosperity to adversity, nor raise a bad man from adversity to prosperity, nor yet depict a villain receiving his deserts, for none of these would both satisfy the moral sense and still inspire pity and fear. Aristotle brings us thus to the remaining possibility, a man not eminently good and just but unmarked by vice or depravity, who is brought to adversity by some error or fault (*hamartia*). Here Aristotle seems perhaps to contradict the earlier statement that tragedy shows men better than in real life, for such would seem to be "eminently good" men. Part of the difficulty lies in the translation of *hamartia*, which has variously been rendered "tragic flaw," conveying the idea of a radical character trait like excessive pride, or "error in judgment," conveying simply a mistaken interpretation of some event. At any rate Aristotle seems to intend a hero who falls short of perfection yet is better than men usually are, and whose virtue and shortcomings both are related to the events of the drama in which he is set.

Thus the best tragedy will have a complex rather than simple plot, and since it concerns the sort of character described above, it will show a change from prosperity to adversity. The fear and pity which come from the structure of the tragedy, such as when a hero intends or performs harm to a man without knowing him to be his father or his son, is superior to the fear and pity arising from the spectacle alone, as when we see the violent act performed.

Four requirements are laid upon character. First, it must be good. Any speech or action that shows moral purpose will express character, and if the purpose is good, will express good character. Second is propriety; any trait must be appropriate to the person in whom depicted. Third, the character must be true to life. Last, it must be consistent; or if inconsistent, at least consistently inconsistent. The construction of both plot and character should aim at the necessary, the probable, and the rational. If deviations occur, they must be outside the scope of the tragedy. Both the complication and the unraveling of the plot must arise out of causes within the plot itself, and a *deus ex machina* should be used only for events antecedent or subsequent to those of the plot. And while the depiction of character should be true to life, it should be yet more beautiful, like a portrait.

The two stages of the plot are the complication and the unraveling or denouement. The complication contains everything up to the turning point to good or bad fortune. The unraveling extends from the beginning point of the change to the end of the play. The dramatist should master both. With respect to existing tragedies, there are four types: (1) the complex, depending entirely on reversal of the situation and recognition; (2) the pathetic, in which the motive is passion; (3) the

ethical, where the motives are moral; and (4) the simple. If possible, the poet should attempt to combine all elements, to produce the best type, the complex. He should not attempt to take an epic structure, which has a multiplicity of plots, and make it into a tragedy. Even the chorus should be regarded as one of the actors, and the choral songs should share in the action rather than serve as mere interludes.

As to thought, little needs to be added to what has been said in the *Rhetoric*. Thought comprises every effect produced by speech, and has as subdivisions (1) proof and refutation; (2) the excitation of the feelings such as pity, anger, fear; and (3) the suggestion of degree of importance (amplification). Just as incidents should speak for themselves without verbal exposition, the speeches should effectively produce the speaker's desired effect on their own strength.

Turning to the diction of poetry, Aristotle classifies words as either current, strange, metaphorical, ornamental, newly coined, lengthened, contracted, or altered. The latter five are used by the poet for his immediate purposes of expression or meter. A word is strange if used in another country, current if in general use in one's own. Metaphor is the transference of a name from one thing to another by certain relationships which Aristotle carefully describes. It may transfer a name from a genus to a species of it, or from species to genus, or from species to species, or by analogy or proportion, the second term is to the first as the fourth term is to the third; for example, old age is to life as evening is to day, so we may speak of "the evening of life." Sometimes one

177

of the terms is lacking, with no word existing to fill its place, but such a metaphor may still provide expression. A poet says "sowing the god-created light" where some unnamed process is to light as sowing is to seed. A command of metaphor is the greatest mark of a good writer, yet it alone cannot be taught by another, and is a mark of genius. Other embellishments may be employed to secure good effect by causing style to depart from the normal idiom—only, of course, in due proportion and with propriety. The use of these devices of language can achieve greater clarity of style. The perfection of style is to be clear without being mean.

The epic, Aristotle declares, in many ways is like tragedy. It should be constructed on dramatic principles. It too should resemble a living organism in its unity, having as its object a single action with a beginning, a middle, and an end. Epic has the same four kinds as tragedy, the simple, complex, ethical, and pathetic. It has the same parts excepting song and spectacle—that is, rhythm, poetic language, character, and thought.

The epic differs from tragedy in scale and meter. It has a special capacity for enlarging the dimensions of tragedy, for the narrator can transcend the limits of the stage. He can achieve greater diversity of materials, and can narrate simultaneous events, thus adding mass and dignity. As to meter, nature herself has taught us the proper one, the heroic or iambic hexameter which is the gravest and weightiest; for experience has shown others more suitable to other compositions and leaves us with only this still in use.

The poet should obtrude into the narrative as little as possible; many have failed, not realizing that it is not in this respect that they imitate. Homer excels in this, as he does also with respect to magnitude and unity. Again, Homer has shown the way in telling false things skillfully. He recounts one event such as would be caused by another, the earlier actually being false or impossible; and thus makes us fallaciously infer that the impossible event did occur. The diction should be elaborated in the pauses of incident, not in the action, so as not to obscure character and thought.

In a chapter near the end of the *Poetics*, Aristotle lists certain criticisms such as might be applied to a poet's work, and offers replies which the poet might make. Some dozen criticisms are gathered around five general objections: things might be called either impossible, irrational, morally harmful, contradictory, or contrary to artistic correctness. To provide a basis to combat such charges, Aristotle draws to our attention the following statements.

The poet, as an imitator, can imitate one of only three objects—things as they were or are, things as they are said or thought to be, or things as they ought to be. The vehicle of his expression is language. The standard of correctness must be acknowledged to be not the same in poetry and politics, just as it is not the same with poetry and any other art. Now the faults of poetry may be either essential or accidental. If a poet poorly imitates, through want of capacity, the error is essential. But if the error is of imputing a wrong gait to a horse or a wrong treatment to a physician, this error is not essential to the poetry but accidental.

When something is challenged as impossible, it must be justified by reference to artistic requirements (a probably rendered impossibility being preferred to an improbable possibility), or to a higher reality (the ideal sometimes serving the artist better than the actual), or to received opinion (popular report sometimes receiving greater acceptance than the actuality). The irrational and the depraved are justly censured when introduced with no artistic necessity. Seeming contradictions should be examined, as in dialectic, by asking whether the same thing is meant in both cases, in the same relation, and in the same sense. Again, if a description is called factually untrue, the poet may reply that he has described things not as they are but as they ought to be; or as men say them to be, such as the tales about the gods.

Further, if the morality of a particular act or saying is challenged, we must point out that we cannot look to that alone but must consider by whom it is done or said, and to whom, when, how, and why. Aristotle here hints, but fails to say directly, that the aesthetic question of whether an immoral act should be depicted is different from the "political" question whether that act is moral.

Various objections are met by a due regard for language, as when the critic has missed metaphorical intent, or an ambiguity, or some legitimate sense of the word used, such as its usage among a foreign people.

In his last chapter, Aristotle attacks the existing opinion that the epic is a higher form of art than the tragic. His opponents have said that the more refined is the higher, and that whatever is received as best by the better sort of audience is the most refined. The art that imitates anything and everything is most unrefined, since boorish audiences are pleased only when something of their own is thrown in, and tragedy provides gesture and spectacle to appease such an audience. The epic, not needing these, must be the higher of the two.

Aristotle meets this argument, first by diverting its force. The censure attaches not to the poetic but to the histrionic art—and the deliverer of an epic may be just as guilty of excessive gesture as an actor. Further, not all gesture and spectacle, but bad acting only, should be condemned. Again, tragedy can secure its effect without being staged, by the mere reading, so that if this fault were present, it would not be an inherent but an accidental one. Furthermore, tragedy is superior, having not only all the elements of epic, but also the accessories of song and spectacle, which produce the most vivid of pleasures; and it attains its end within narrower limits than does epic, a concentrated effect being more pleasurable than one more diluted. Finally, the tragedy is superior in unity, any epic being capable of providing the material for several tragedies. Tragedy, then, fulfills its proper function better and is a higher art than epic poetry.

MENG TZU

Author: Mencius (Meng Tzu) (c.372-c.289 B.C.)
Type of work: Ethics
First transcribed: Early third century B.C.

PRINCIPAL IDEAS ADVANCED

Every human being is born good; hence, if man maintains his original nature, he will remain good.

In man's original nature there is a sense of shame, a sense of courtesy, and a sense of right and wrong.

If man relies only on his sense perceptions without subjecting them to the control of the mind, he falls into evil ways and perverts his original nature.

If a man allows the desire for personal gain to overcome his righteousness—his sense of social obligations—he also perverts his nature.

The ideal ruler is considerate of his subjects' interests, and he provides both moral leadership and adquate social welfare.

Any person who practices the principles of humanity and righteousness with sincerity radiates the spiritual influence of the universe.

The exact date and authorship of this collection of philosophical dialogues and anecdotes have remained a subject of dispute for centuries, but there is no doubt about the existence of the man, Mencius (Meng Tzu), in the fourth to third centuries B.C. Behind the legends that have gathered around this magical name, we find a man who taught students, lectured to the rulers of his time, and expounded his political and moral philosophy in much the same way as most of the Confucians did.

When very young, Mencius lost his father, and his mother worked alone at a weaving loom to bring up the young boy. Mencius' childhood education is said to have been of the ideal kind, and his mother has been held in reverence by the Chinese as an ideal mother. It is said that she was so determined to cultivate her son's moral integrity at a very early age that she took extreme caution in her own speech and behavior in front of him. Once their landlord slaughtered a hog. When the young Mencius saw it, he asked his mother why. In jest his mother answered that the landlord was preparing a feast for him. Immediately afterwards she regretted; and in order to correct her untruthful statement she sold her badly needed clothing to buy some meat with which she actually served him a good dinner. Another time she was distressed by Mencius' fondness for play when she wanted him to concentrate on studies. After some ineffective admonition, she took out a knife and cut the warp on her loom. Since she could no longer weave, the family was without food. This drastic gesture impressed the young boy so much that he never again neglected his studies.

After studying with a disciple of Confucius' grandson, Mencius emerged in his adult life as a recognized standard-bearer of Confucianism. In his expositions on Confucius' teachings, however, Mencius ventured much further in metaphysical speculations than his master ever did. From Mencius, Confucianism gained a fully developed theory on human nature and a clear orientation toward idealism.

Mencius subscribed to the basic Confucian doctrine of *jen* (benevolence), but in elaborating on this doctrine he gave it a metaphysical basis. Confucius urged man to be humane toward others so that society might be harmonious and peaceful; Mencius urged man to be kind to others because, as he says, to be kind is man's natural propensity. Man is born good, and his evil ways are perversions. Every human being has his innate goodness; hence, if he can maintain his original nature, he will remain good. In Mencius' own language, this original good human nature is the "heart of the child," or the untainted heart. If unperverted, the original child-like heart of man will lead him toward the good, just as "water naturally flows downward." If already perverted, man can attain salvation only by returning to his original state of goodness.

How is this innate goodness of man observed? Mencius suggested that we look at the sympathetic feeling that is a part of man's nature. He uses the following illustration: anybody seeing a child about to fall into a well would immediately spring to his aid. He would do this without reflecting on the advantage and disadvantage of his action; he would not think about what merit he would gain if he rescued the child, or what blame he would have to face if he refused to reach out his hand. He would leap to save the child because the peril of the child would spontaneously fill him with a sense of alarm. This example proves the existence of a sense of mercy in every man.

With similar illustrations Mencius argued that he had proved the existence of a sense of shame, a sense of courtesy, and a sense of right and wrong in man's original nature. Together with the sense of mercy, these senses constitute the four good beginnings of man's development. According to Mencius, the sense of mercy is the beginning of *jen* (humanity); the sense of shame should lead man to righteousness; the sense of courtesy, if allowed to develop, would give man decorum; and the sense of right and wrong is the foundation for wisdom. As with man's four limbs, these four senses are already inseparable parts of any man when he is born. Also as with the four limbs, these four senses would develop to their proper healthy proportions if man would cultivate them; otherwise they wither away through misuse or desuetude.

Basing his argument on his observation of the uninstructed child, Mencius asserts in his book that man has intuitive ability and knowledge. He points out that every child "knows" how to love his parents, and as he grows he "knows" how to respect his elder brothers. The former is true *jen* (humanity) and the latter is true *i* (righteousness). Therefore, says Mencius, man is born with the innate knowledge to distinguish the right from the wrong, and the innate ability to act according to the right.

The innate knowledge and ability of man, like his basic senses or feelings, are analogous to the seeds of a plant. To allow these seeds to germinate Mencius brings forth another notion: the *"ts'ai"* of man, or man's "natural

181

powers." Thus if man exhausts his natural powers, he will realize his potential of being good, and he who does evil is failing to exercise his natural powers. Although human nature is basically good, man can be led astray by his contact with the outside world. If man relies only on his sense perceptions (on seeing, hearing, taste, and so forth) without subjecting them to the control of his mind (heart) which is the office of thinking, then he falls into evil ways. Here Mencius' theory of the "mind" is something very comparable to "reason," but we shall also see how the mind of the Mencian doctrine is closely linked to his theory of a mystic ch'i. Be it noted here that Mencius in explaining his theory of innate knowledge gives his view on the origin of evil, which is a subject not treated by Confucius himself.

Mencius never speaks of jen (humanity or benevolence) without mentioning i (righteousness). He is not the first Confucian philosopher to use this term i, but the emphasis certainly is his. Although "right," "fair," and "just" are all within the commonly accepted senses of the word "i," in Mencius' usage this word most frequently stands for a concrete sense of justice and fairness. Mencius seems to stress the importance of fulfilling one's obligations toward his fellow men. These obligations are social in nature. Thus an unfilial son is not "i" because he fails to repay his parents' kindness toward him; and a servant deserting his master is not "i" because he fails to repay his master's favors. In this light Mencius' i does not suggest anything like the Western abstract concept of righteousness. However, there is at least one place where Mencius does seem to bring in an absolute righteousness. When he warns the ruler not to abuse his subjects, Mencius states that the ruler has an obligation to protect the interest of the people. Since the ruler does not directly owe any favor to the people, Mencius in this case accepts an absolute standard of righteousness even though he fails to define it.

The social basis of the Mencian concept of righteousness creates perplexing problems when social obligations come into conflict with one another. A man is a righteous son to his father and a righteous minister to his king only so long as there is no conflict of interest between his father and his king, but this condition does not always exist. There is an anecdote in this book that illustrates such difficulties. The story concerns a warrior in ancient China who encountered his own former teacher on the battlefield, on the opposite side of no-man's-land. Remembering his obligation toward his former teacher, the warrior should show his respect to his present enemy. But as a loyal soldier to his lord, the warrior should shoot his former teacher to death. Caught in such a dilemma, the warrior won immortality and historical acclaim by a curious compromise. He broke off the points of four of his arrows and shot the arrows at his former teacher. Then he promptly withdrew with a clear conscience.

In contrast to the idea of righteousness Mencius put "li," or "profit" (not to be confused with "li," or "rules of propriety"). He blamed man's departure from righteousness to seek personal gain for the disorder and unhappiness in society. Greed leads to strife as men, both in and outside the government, go

after profit and fight for personal benefit. Only if everyone strives for that
which is right and does what he ought
to do, can the community of man
prosper in peace. This is what Mencius preached to the rulers and to his
disciples alike. It should be noted,
however, that Mencius did not dismiss
the importance of material well-being,
and the book is not always clear on
how Mencius would draw the distinction between the desirable and the undesirable kind of profit.

That Mencius recognized the need
for material well-being is evident in his
political and economic ideas. His ideal
government is one with both moral
leadership and adequate social welfare. Like Confucius himself, Mencius
advocated rule by moral excellence and
humane feeling. The ruler must be
considerate of his subjects' interests. If
the ruler is benevolent, the state will
prosper because people will not only
flock toward it but will also imitate its virtuous way of living. Since
benevolent government could bring
peace and prosperity to men without
the need for any other action, Mencius'
theory amounts to rule by moral magnetism.

Mencius was aware of the larger political and economic forces which were
at work in society in addition to the
moral forces in which he had great
confidence. He realized that a state
does not exist without people, so he advised the rulers that people must come
first, the state second, and the king last.
These are his words which the Chinese have been quoting throughout the
centuries: "People are the roots of the
nation. If the roots are not firm, the
nation collapses." Indeed the king must
win the "hearts" of his subjects; other-

wise, his administration will be doomed.
And Mencius urged the ruler to give
to and to share with the people what
they desire, and not to do to them
what they would not like. Since all
human beings like the pleasures of life,
the king must work to increase the
pleasures of life and to share them with
his people. Here Mencius clearly accepts public profit and material well-
being for everybody as something good
and moral which does not violate the
principle of righteousness.

With these declarations, Mencius appears as a champion of the people
against tyrannical governments. He is
particularly remembered for his expressions in support of the people's right to
revolt. There is enough in the sayings
attributed to Confucius himself that
implies this right to rebel. Confucius
makes the observance of Heaven's Will
a necessary condition for the ruler to
keep his throne, and he blames the
king's loss of the Heavenly Mandate
for the downfall of the former dynasty.
Mencius elaborates on this view and
makes it explicit. He calls a man without *jen* (benevolence) a scoundrel, and
a man without *i* (righteousness) a
scourge, both deserving defeat, even
death, regardless of their social station.

Much as Mencius championed the
people's right to revolt against a tyrannical ruler, this Confucian sage did not
believe in self-rule. In his book he upholds a natural division of labor in society on the basis of the different aptitudes of men. There are, he says, two
types of men: those of brain and those
of brawn. The former work with their
minds and are destined to rule, while
the latter work with their hands to
feed the former and are to be ruled by
the former. Thus he affixes an unmis-

takable stamp of approval on the Confucian attitude that only the literati, who tend to monopolize education and literature, are fit to conduct the affairs of the government.

Mencius argued that between the two types of men there is a basic difference which helps to justify their separate destinies. To state it briefly, this difference lies in the spiritual fortitude of those with education. For Mencius attributes a moral strength to the true scholar who, unlike the uneducated, alone is capable of maintaining a steadfast heart even when he is threatened with financial insecurity. For the ordinary person, an insured material provision is necessary to keep him behaving properly. What the hungry stomachs of the common people would consume first, Mencius is saying here, are moral scruples. Consequently in the *Meng Tzu* Mencius urges the intelligent ruler to look after his people's livelihood first. He demands that the ruler make certain that each farmer has around his house about an acre of land planted in mulberry trees, to enable anyone over fifty to be clothed in silk. Poultry and meat animals should be bred in season so that those over seventy will never lack a meat diet. In addition, Mencius would assign at least fifteen acres of land to any family of eight mouths in order to keep them all well-fed. The establishment of schools to teach the people Confucian principles comes last because principles can take roots only in minds when stomachs are full.

The difference between Mencius and Confucius comes into sharp relief when Mencius leaves the concrete and practical issues of the day to deal with the abstract. As we have said, in the *Meng Tzu* Mencius injects metaphysics into the Confucian system. He does so by going beyond Confucius in accepting Heaven at different times as a Supreme Being with a discerning moral will, or as a fatalistic pattern, or as the authority that creates virtue and sets the standard of righteousness. Mencius starts with his theory of human nature, and asserts that it is Heaven that gives man his innate knowledge contained in his mind (or heart—the Chinese word, *hsin,* means both heart and mind). The mind, or innate knowledge, is what makes man great because by exercising his mind man can come to "know" his original nature. Here we must note the difference between Mencius' theory of untainted heart and the mystic Taoist theory of untampered heart. The latter does not talk about man's mind and its importance.

The mysticism in the system of Mencius begins when he proceeds to tell us that when man exercises his mind to the utmost he will also come to "know" Heaven. The unerring and unwavering attitude to examine oneself in search of one's good nature is called, in Mencian terms, *ch'eng,* or sincerity. A person practicing the principles of humanity and altruism with "sincerity" can succeed in returning to his original nature which is a part of Heaven. Consequently Mencius declares that "All beings are complete within man." He who has attained this state is a perfect man, or a *chün-tzu.* The *chün-tzu* radiates a spiritual influence wherever he appears. Under his influence the ordinary people become good and the state becomes orderly. This spiritual influence, in most cases, is described by Mencius as *ch'i,* or the irresistible, all-pervading force.

The basic senses of the term, *ch'i,* include "air," "all gaseous matters," and "the air that surrounds a person." Mencius uses this term largely in the last sense. He assumes that a man with such an influential air around him must first possess that degree of spiritual perfection described above. In Mencius' ecstatic description of this all-pervading force, claiming that it flows "above and below together with Heaven and Earth," and that it "fills the entire universe between Heaven and Earth," the *ch'i* acquires puzzlingly mystic proportions.

But this Mencian concept of *ch'i* need not be a puzzle if we consider the basis of his theory. According to him, man acquires this all-pervading force by practicing the principles of humanity and morality according to the dictates of Heaven, conceived as a supreme moral voice. The process of acquiring this force, then, is a constant doing of righteous deeds without stop or affectation. Man can do so only when he uses his mind to examine himself and to rediscover the righteous senses (the four basic good senses already discussed) that come with his birth. In this analysis the mystic *ch'i* of Mencius is no more than a moral force stated metaphorically.

These are the basic tenets of an idealistic philosopher who, next to the Sung Dynasty philosopher Chu Hsi (1130-1200), perhaps did the most in establishing Confucianism as the controlling orthodoxy in Chinese thought

for at least two millennia. Much, of course, has been read back into his book. Many apologists of Chinese tradition attempt to offer Mencius as the great champion of democracy in Eastern political thought. They cite Mencius' words on the importance of people but they overlook the Mencian pattern of social hierarchy. Almost every rebel in Chinese history quoted Mencius to support his revolt against the government. At the same time every ruler found comfort in this book when he contemplated punitive campaigns to suppress rebellions. Above all, Mencius has been adopted by the Chinese state-socialists as their ancient spokesman.

In the same manner the mystic element in this book has been made use of by different schools of thought. The Taoists have always wanted to include Mencius in their ranks, and they are not entirely without justification. Certain basic elements of Taoist mysticism antedated, or at least coexisted with, Confucian thought. The theory of the all-pervading force of Mencius certainly has a familiar ring to the ears of a Taoist. These problems cannot be tackled before philological studies of the text can establish the indisputable authenticity of any statements attributed to Mencius in this book and can secure other corroborating evidence to make the full implications of these statements clear.

CHUANG TZU

Author: Chuang Chou (Chuang Tzu, c.370-c.285 B.C.)
Type of work: Metaphysics, ethics
First transcribed: c.300 B.C.

185

Tao *is the universal way of things, the all-pervading principle of all that exists; the virtue or power of every individual is a manifestation of* tao.

Distinctions between men or things, between right and wrong, are seen to be false once the universal presence of tao *is recognized.*

The only way to salvation is to identify oneself with the orderly process of all being, the tao.

Death is nothing to fear, for man lives as long as his essence, the tao *lives; and the* tao *is eternal.*

The True Man retains the unspoiled simplicity of a child; he does not concern himself with political action, but allows the tao *to take its course; he abstains from intellectual analysis and the study of abstract ideas.*

The man whose name, together with that of Lao Tzu, has become synonymous with classical Taoism was probably one of the many eccentric recluses who challenged the intellectual authority of Confucius during the Warring States period in Chinese history. Disgusted with the prevailing chaos and weary of the self-styled sages' moral preachings, these men saw the only salvation in "letting things be what they are." Legend about Chuang Chou the man tells us of his refusal to serve in the capacity of prime minister, also of his mystic wanderings and cryptic speeches. The anecdotes involving him and the statements attributed to him are extremely imaginative in character; and his words often soar to dazzling metaphysical heights. Like the *Tao Te Ching*, the thirty-three chapters of the *Chuang Tzu* contain much poetry in which we find many images identifiable with the poetic tradition founded in ancient China along the Yangtze River valley, or in relatively southern parts of China.

Like the *Tao Te Ching*, this work also expounds a theory based on the mystic universal principle called *tao*. *Tao* is the beginning of all being; hence, it could be understood as Non-Being. Having no begetter, *tao* is best expressed by what is spontaneous. From these ideas we perceive the workings of *tao* as actually nonactivity, or doing nothing that is not done by itself. In short, *tao* is the all-pervading principle that exists prior to the existence of the universe, and it is to be found in everything, no matter how trivial or base. The manifestation of this first principle in each individual thing is called *te* (virtue, power). *Tao* and *te*, thus, are actually of one essence, the former being the universal essence, and the latter the share of the former deposited in every individual being.

On this mystic concept of *tao*, Chuang Tzu (as Chuang Chou is traditionally known) has constructed his view of the universe. He does so very rarely by direct logical exposition, using instead a multitude of anecdotes, imaginary dialogues, and metaphorical parables. The universe comes into existence in accordance with *tao,* and the myriad beings in the universe each partake of *tao.* In their essence, the loftiest sage and the humblest of men are the same, their distinctions being man-made, impermanent, and never absolute. The Himalayas and the threshold of a peasant's hut are actually of the same height; the greatest of birds, the roc, really has no reason for laughing at the tiniest wren when they compare their ranges of flight. Since each follows its own way as *tao* makes it, each is as important as the other. This is Chuang Tzu's theory of relativity with which he defies the existing social institutions because they draw lines. These lines, in Chuang Tzu's view, are all false, and the concern of the Confucian and the dialectician of his time with the distinction between names and reality he thought totally irrelevant and useless.

Even the notions of right and wrong do not exist for Chuang Tzu. Right is right only because of the existence of wrong; nothing is absolutely right. Furthermore, everything is simultaneously itself (when it looks at itself) and something else (when looked upon by something else); consequently, there cannot be an absolute "this" or "that." Everything is "this" and "that" at the same time.

When someone challenged Chuang Tzu to explain how he could make such an assertion and claim it to be right when his assertion was a denial of the notion of right, Chuang Tzu dismissed the question by saying that he was not concerned with settling such an argument. He did not believe that there was any argument to be settled. He was merely proposing a third course of action or a third view transcending the ordinary right-wrong dualism.

Why is there no need to settle any argument? To begin with, everything follows *tao*. Since *tao* is always right, by virtue of the fact that it always "is so," everything is always right also. If there is conflict, then the conflict itself is also right. Chuang Tzu believed that conflict arises when man departs from *tao* and tries to act contrary to Nature's

way. He asserts, without trying to prove his assertion, that everything in the universe is inclined toward order; therefore, he denies the validity of the accepted legends about how the ancient sage-kings "worked" to bring about peace and order. Chuang Tzu preferred to see the abolition of all the man-made social and political institutions because he believed that only then could Nature's way or *tao* prevail. And *tao* will always ultimately prevail; whatever man can do will not make any lasting difference.

Nature's way is constant, and its constancy is revealed in the ceaseless change that cannot be obstructed in the universe. Every being is involved in this process of change, from one species to another, one appearance to another, or one form of its existence to another form of existence. Hence, nothing is improving or degenerating, but everything is involved in this universal cyclical motion. Man is no exception. And the only way to salvation, if it is relevant to speak of salvation in this philosophical system, is for man to understand this process and to identify himself with *tao*. In doing so man would be able to attain the axis of the wheel from which he could view the perpetual disturbance in the universe with transcendental calm. He would, then, achieve tranquillity in chaos. In this very respect Chuang Tzu's system comes close to Buddhism.

Recalling that Chuang Tzu compares man to a clod, one may say that Chuang Tzu's is not a very edifying view of man, but it is consistent with his fundamental concept of *tao*. According to him, man is part of *tao*'s making. Man has a share of *tao* just as a clod of dirt does. If he preserves this share of *tao*, he will not be lost. And

187

the way to cling to *tao* is by retaining one's original unspoiled simplicity—the state of mind of a child.

Chuang Tzu arrives at this conclusion along several lines of argument: First, the commonly accepted cultivation of the mind drives man to acquire a knowledge of artificial distinctions without real meaning. Such knowledge is not true knowledge; the only true knowledge lies in the comprehension of *tao*. Second, the artificial knowledge man acquires serves no other purpose than to create confusion and strife. Man is led by his false sense of righteousness to combat what he erroneously considers wrong. Man is encouraged by his illusion about greatness to strive for what may be actually small. Third, there is nothing that is absolutely complete except *tao* itself. Man's artificial effort to construct anything or create anything is necessarily incomplete. Man cannot attain perfect construction of anything through his own effort. Hence, whatever he undertakes to complete, he leaves something undone. What is more, the moment man makes a move, he injures something, and also himself. Hence, Chuang Tzu insists on the importance of an uncarved block, and he praises the perfection of music from a lute that has no strings.

Consistent with his theory of relativity and cyclical change, Chuang Tzu shows indifference toward death and suggests that there may be great joy after death. He decries the common practice of mourning because, as he puts it, the mourner assumes knowledge of the unknown and pretends his dislike of it. The famous story in Chapter XVIII about the death of Chuang Tzu's wife is a graphic illustration of this attitude. Chuang Tzu refuses to weep; instead, he sits with his legs crossed and beats on an inverted pot to accompany his singing. In this unconventional behavior, Chuang Tzu already expresses his idea about immortality.

Strictly speaking, the question of immortality does not exist in Chuang Tzu's system. If life and death are but phases in an irresistible cycle of change, then there is no difference between the living and the dead, or between the mortal and the immortal. Mortality becomes a problem and a source of sorrow only because man cannot free himself from the artificially constructed straitjacket of his view on life and existence. In the physical sense, man must die and there is no escape. But if man can understand Nature's way and embrace *tao*, then he lives as long as *tao* lives; hence, he is immortal. Chuang Tzu defies death by saying that if (after death) his left arm became a rooster, he would simply use it to mark the time of night. Man may die indeed, but his essence as part of the universal essence lives on forever. This is the metaphysical view of immortality in the *Chuang Tzu*.

There is also a mystic explanation of immortality offered by Chuang Tzu. A man who has succeeded in preserving his original simplicity and in maintaining his share of *tao* is called in Chuang Tzu's terms, a True Man. In order to achieve this stage, man has to rid himself of his intellectual knowledge by "fasting his mind," and "contemplating on emptiness." If he succeeds in forgetting that there are "things" in the world, he will have discarded man-made distinctions in the universe and he will have come close to a union with *tao*. What he senses will be merely an emptiness and a vastness; his appearance will resemble that of the stupid.

Then he will have attained the Mysterious Power in Nature.

So far this seems to be only an exaggerated metaphorical statement of Chuang Tzu's vision of perfect self-discipline and cultivation, but the mysticism surrounding him thickens when he goes on to describe the True Man's capacities. The best of these True Men, so says Chuang Tzu, are ethereal. They sense no heat in fire and no chill in ice. They can "mount on clouds, ride on the sun and moon, and wander at ease beyond the seas." Consequently, neither life nor death can affect them. There are many parallel stories told of this kind of spirit-travel in other ancient Chinese writings. They seem to be part of the common primitive Taoist-shamanistic traditions shared by the Chinese, particularly those in the central Yangtze River valley where Chuang Tzu is said to have lived. In this book, we find Chuang Tzu attempting to give a metaphysical explanation to these legends. It seems that he stresses the importance of "preserving oneself" by following the natural bends of things; consequently, one achieves immortality because one does not wear oneself out. This theory is illustrated in his story about the perfect butcher whose carving knife remains perpetually sharp because it always goes between the bones and tissues and never meets any resistance.

While the physical liberation of a True Man, if taken literally, amounts to a mystic vision which can hardly be rationally explained, the liberation of man's mind in the taoist fashion is not difficult to comprehend. We have seen that Chuang Tzu has no use for intellectual knowledge. To him "things are what they are," and they do what Nature dictates them to do. Man should live as part of Nature together with all other things in Nature, and desist from his futile pursuit of seeing, reading, and analyzing the universe in abstraction. The moment man ceases to confuse himself with the useless puzzles which his fellow men have created, his mind will be liberated. Then and only then will he be ready to comprehend tao.

By emptying his mind of intellectual prejudices, man will be able to see the similarity of all things. Hence, he and the myriad things will be one and he will feel that the universe is within him. Whatever he does or does not do will cause no concern or anxiety. He will thus be free to move in the universe. At this stage his happiness is true and supreme, because there is nothing about him that is not in accord with Nature.

The kind of extreme happiness that Chuang Tzu speaks of is also a result of emotional liberation. Having been intellectually liberated, man no longer sees any cause for alarm, or worry, or sorrow. Following a course completely in accord with Nature, he depends on nothing and seeks nothing. He is totally free. It is this total freedom projected into time and space that Chuang Tzu describes in his stories about the True Man. Chuang Tzu's ideal freedom is threefold: an intellectual liberation from man's prejudices and man-made restrictions, an emotional liberation through a thorough understanding of the way of all lives, and finally a total liberation when man feels no restriction because he accepts every natural course of events.

Although this work does not deal with the various aspects of what has become known as magical Taoism, Chuang Tzu's theory of the True Man and his notion of *ch'i* (gaseous matter, spirit) provide it with ample inspiration. Chuang Tzu's vague formula to achieve True-Manhood mentions the physical discipline of sitting in meditation, and the mental discipline of discarding abstract ideas. He also urges man to "listen" with his *ch'i* or to react to the outside world with his spirit, while sparing his ordinary senses. These suggestions can be related to some primitive practice of breathing exercise to aid mental concentration and ward off distracting influence. It has been said that this aspect of Taoism is a bridge between Chuang Tzu's mysticism and that of Mencius. We must not overlook, however, the fundamental difference between these two philosophers. Both believed in a mystical perfection of man through the cultivation of his *ch'i,* but while Mencius saw the road to salvation through doing socially good deeds, Chuang Tzu absolutely denied the validity of altruism.

A comparison of Chuang Tzu with Lao Tzu will show their parallelism at almost every point. As we have noted, Lao Tzu and Chuang Tzu are recognized as cofounders of the Taoist school of thought, and there is rarely any mention of one without the other. There is nevertheless one important difference between them. In advocating nonactivity, Lao Tzu stresses the difference between two extremes and warns of the disaster that inevitably follows extremity. While in urging the same thing, Chuang Tzu denies any real difference between extremes. Again, Lao Tzu advises the ruler to govern by noninterference because he believes in the inevitable reversal from one extreme to the other; hence, complete lack of rule will automatically bring rule. Chuang Tzu, on the other hand, believes in noninterference as an ideal for governing because of an alleged propensity toward order in everything.

Insofar as Chuang Tzu repeatedly criticized his contemporary moralists as useless do-gooders, his anti-intellectual attitude was clearly a reaction against the overbearing Confucians and the many other voices which at the time vied with one another in offering political cure-alls and social panaceas. Most of these moralists sought to bring order to society by urging altruism and redefinition of terms; Chuang Tzu was diametrically opposed to such activities. But in opposing his contemporary thinkers, Chuang Tzu was not unconcerned with the signs of his time; he also offered a political recipe of his own which he believed could solve all the prevalent problems. It should be noted that the *Chuang Tzu* remains an extremely important source for the study of many other less well-known schools of thought in ancient China. In several cases, Chuang Tzu's comments on some of his contemporaries provide the only information available on their philosophies.

In many ways this work has exerted even greater influence on the Chinese mind than has the *Tao Te Ching*. It has been able to do so because of the numerous imaginary and metaphorical anecdotes it contains. The metaphysical poetry of the *Tao Te Ching* is fascinating, but often it is too cryptic to be grasped. The metaphors in the *Chuang Tzu,* however, have found their way into the common pool of metaphors in Chinese literature and even in the daily language where, although their original Taoist color has been diluted through use, they have had a subtle influence on the configuration of the Chinese mind. On a higher level, such notions as the purity of man's heart (mind) and the calmness of man's emotions have become the core of quietism that has found eloquent expression in the undying poems of T'ao Ch'ien (365-427) and Wang Wei (699-750). The principles of quietude, simplicity, detachment, and leisureliness which have made these poets immortal also laid the foundation for the development of Ch'an Buddhism in China and for the theory and practice of the Chinese landscape painting— the most important Chinese contribution to art.

On the level of daily life we note the ever-present balancing influence of this school of thought on the Chinese mind, providing a measure of practical wisdom. Chuang Tzu's allegorical tales on the themes of relativity and cyclical change appear in many later works in infinite variations. For instance, the story about the death of Chuang Tzu's wife appears in a famous seventeenth century collection of traditional short stories; it again appears in an opera still being staged in modern times. One of these stories is always quoted by him who tries to comfort his friend over the loss of a dear one. Another story is used, in the form of a proverb, to advise man never to take worldly affairs too seriously. A third anecdote enables a man to live through the most trying of crises when he recalls and believes in Chuang Tzu's saying that "This, too, is Nature's way."

PRINCIPAL DOCTRINES and LETTER TO MENOECEUS

Author: Epicurus (c.342-c.270 B.C.)
Type of work: Ethics
First transcribed: Third century B.C.

PRINCIPAL IDEAS ADVANCED

Pleasure is the standard by which every good and every right action is to be judged.

No pleasure is in itself bad, and all pleasures are alike in quality.

Certain natural desires are necessary, and the gratification of such desires is preferable to the gratification of unnecessary natural desires or desires attaching to artificially cultivated tastes.

The three needs of man are equanimity, bodily health and comfort, and the exigencies of life.

To achieve the good life, a life of moderate and enduring pleasure, a man must cultivate the virtues, particularly prudence, and study philosophy.

Death is nothing to fear for while we live death is not with us; and when death comes, we no longer exist.

The *Principal Doctrines* is a collection of forty of the most important articles of Epicurus' teaching, presumably extracted by a disciple from

191

the master's voluminous works. It was widely known in ancient times, and has been preserved to us by Diogenes Laertius (probably third century) in his *Lives and Opinions of Eminent Philosophers*. Together with the *Letter to Menoeceus*, also found in Diogenes' works, it constitutes our only first-hand source for the ethical teachings of Epicurus. The most important supplementary source is Lucretius' poem, *On the Nature of Things* (first century B.C.).

Epicurus' central teaching was that pleasure is the standard by which every good is to be judged. He distinguished between feelings of pleasure and judgments concerning good and right, and he maintained that the latter, insofar as they have meaning, must refer to the former. "For we recognize pleasure as the first good innate in us, and from pleasure we begin every act of choice and avoidance, and to pleasure we return again, using the feeling as the standard by which we judge every good." (*Letter to Menoeceus.*)

No pleasure, said Epicurus, is in itself bad. He maintained that pleasures are all of the same kind. Some pleasures are more intense than others, some last longer, and some satisfy a greater portion of the body; but if these differences could be set aside, one pleasure could not be distinguished from another. Unfortunately, however, the limitations of human existence compel us to distinguish between pleasures. In actuality, the pleasure cannot be chosen in isolation, and the conditions which are necessary to our enjoying some pleasures are also annexed to pains. "For this reason, we do not choose every pleasure, but sometimes pass over many pleasures, when greater discomfort accrues to us as the result of them." (*Letter to Menoeceus.*)

Thus, Epicurus turned his attention to the consideration of desires. Some desires, he said, are natural while others are illusory. By the latter he meant physical desires of the sort which neither arise from any deprivation nor admit of definite satisfaction—desires which attach to artificially cultivated tastes. Already in his day the public supposed that he and his followers pursued the pleasures of profligacy and vice. Such was far from being the case. The reason was that such artificial desires inevitably come into conflict with natural desires which are far more important. Indeed, Epicurus held that not all natural desires are to be satisfied. He distinguished between natural desires which are necessary and those which are merely natural. The necessary ones are so exacting that we are counseled to concentrate on them alone.

The strength of Epicurus' philosophy, as over against the Cyrenaic and other philosophies of pleasure, derives from its deeper understanding of the psychology of human needs. Man has three kinds of needs that will not be denied: equanimity or peace of mind, bodily health and comfort, and the exigencies of life itself. Fortunately, according to Epicurus, few things are necessary in order to sustain life and keep the body in health, and they are comparatively easy to obtain. Illness is unavoidable, but, as he pointed out, acute pain rarely lasts long, and chronic illnesses permit a predominance of pleasure over pain in the flesh. On the whole, Epicurus seems to have expended but little thought on the necessities of life and bodily health. His main concern was with peace of mind, how to avoid unpleasantness from our fellow men, how to escape the pangs of conscience, how to avoid worry about the future, including the life beyond the grave. Such considerations gave Epicurus' philosophy a predominantly somber tone, so much so that he rarely spoke of pleasure except in a negative way, as "freedom from pain in the body and from trouble in the mind." Speaking of the three necessary desires, he said, "The right understanding of these facts enables us to refer all choice and avoidance to the health of the body and the soul's freedom from disturbance, since this is the aim of the life of blessedness." (*Letter to Menoeceus.*)

Thus, while the good in life is always simple and immediate, namely, feelings of pleasure, the art of achieving a life abundant in goodness is one that requires great skill and constant application. To this end, Epicurus recommended two sorts of means: first, the cultivation of virtue; second, the study of philosophy.

Of these two, virtue is the more important. "The man who does not possess the virtuous life cannot possibly live pleasantly," he declared. Among virtues, the chief he held to be prudence, because all other virtues were, in his view, merely special kinds of prudence.

By prudence he meant what Dostoevski once called "solving the problem of existence." It consists in knowing the worth of various satisfactions, on the one hand, and their cost, on the other. Sometimes we have to choose pains in order to secure greater pleasures; for example, having a tooth extracted. Sometimes we have to forego

pleasure because of resultant pains; for example, drinking wine when it makes one ill afterward. Epicurus spoke of a scale of comparison which the prudent man must carry about in his mind, by which he judges prospective courses of action in terms of their advantages and disadvantages.

One of the best counsels of prudence, he thought, was to make oneself independent of desire and, to this end, to accustom oneself to simple food and plain surroundings. His motive was not an ascetic one—he saw no good in deprivation for its own sake. But he contended that anyone who has learned to be satisfied with the necessities of life is freed from most of the cares of the future, since changes of fortune are unlikely to reduce a man to starvation, whereas the slightest turn may deprive a man of his luxuries. Moreover, he maintained that there is an actual overplus of pleasure in the abstemious life. Bread and water produce as great pleasures to the man who needs them as the luxuries of a wealthy table do to the reveler. Moreover, plain fare is better for health of body and alertness of mind. Furthermore, the man whose taste is not spoiled by habitual indulgence is better able to appreciate fine food and drink when, at long intervals, these are set before him.

Another counsel of prudence was to retire from the world of human affairs. Epicurus, somewhat like Hobbes, regarded man as the greatest enemy of man. To secure protection from our fellows is a natural want. But how shall one go about it? Epicurus doubted the wisdom of those who undertake to find security by competing for public honor and position. In his opinion, this is not "safe." Instead, he recommended "the immunity which results from a quiet life and the retirement from the world."

It is in connection with the harm which we may expect from our fellow men that Epicurus introduced the virtue of justice. In opposition to the teaching of Plato and Aristotle, but in agreement with that of Democritus, he denied that justice has its foundation in nature. All justice, he said, originates in "a pledge of mutual advantage to restrain men from harming one another and save them from being harmed." It does not exist among primitive tribes, and what is considered just in one country may be quite different from what is considered just in another. In fact, within the same land, as circumstances change, what was once considered just may be so no longer. For the justice of a law ultimately depends on its being to the mutual advantage of both parties to the compact.

Epicurus raised the question which Glaucon raised in Plato's *Republic*, Book II, whether it is not to the advantage of a person secretly to act unjustly if he can do so without detection. The answer is that one can never be confident that he will escape detection, and that anxiety would spoil the fruits of the crime. "The just man is most free from trouble, the unjust most full of trouble."

After virtue, Epicurus considered philosophy the second most important means for securing the life of bliss. "Let no one when young," he wrote to Menoeceus, "delay to study philosophy, nor when he is old grow weary of his study." In these words Epicurus was not recommending philosophy as a solace against the sorrows of existence nor as a diversion which yields a satisfaction of its own. By philosophy Epicurus meant a kind of mental hygiene, based on a naturalistic world-view which, if its implications were understood, would free men's minds from superstitious fear and moral anxiety.

The view of nature which recommended itself to him was that of Democritus of Abdera, who denied that the world was created by the gods or that there is any ultimate purpose in life, all things having been formed by the accidental collision of atoms falling through empty space. The man who is convinced that this is the case has, according to Epicurus, two great advantages over those who hold to traditional beliefs: first, he is freed from religious scruples; second, he is freed from the fear of death.

Epicurus did not deny the existence of the gods, which he identified with the heavenly bodies. He held that they are composed of the same fine, smooth atoms which make up the souls of men and are the basis of our reason and feelings; but because the gods are eternal and blessed in their regular motions, Epicurus found no reason to suppose that they are exacting and vengeful toward men, or indeed that they pay any attention to us. The traditional view, that the gods are the source of human misfortune and of blessedness, he explained as arising from the tendency man has to view other beings as acting like himself. He denied that such a belief is founded on sensation or has any foundation in reason. Eclipses, solstices, and other celestial phenomena which the ancients were accustomed to regard with superstitious awe, he said, are capable of explanation according to natural principles. "For if we pay attention to these we shall rightly trace the causes whence arose our mental disturbance and fear, and by learning the true causes of celestial phenomena and all other occurrences that come to pass from time to time, we shall free ourselves from all which produces the utmost fear in other men." (*Letter to Herodotus*, also cited by Diogenes.)

The fear of death seemed to him as groundless as fear of the gods. Because, at death, the soul-atoms leave man's body and are dispersed through space, a man's consciousness is dissipated, the separate atoms no longer possessing the same power and sentience which they had when together in the bodily sheath. But good and evil consist in sensations and nothing else. Therefore, according to Epicurus, there is nothing terrible in death. And if a man persuades himself of this, the anticipation of death ceases to be painful. "So death, the most terrifying of ills, is nothing to us, since so long as we exist death is not with us; but when death comes, then we do not exist. It does not then concern either the living or the dead, since for the former it is not, and the latter are no more." (*Letter to Menoeceus*.) Nor does the wise man seek length of days. "Just as

with food he does not seek simply the larger share and nothing else, but rather the most pleasant, so he seeks to enjoy not the longest period of time but the most pleasant." Such is the sweetness introduced into man's life by the knowledge that death is nothing, that he no longer has any thirst for immortality.

Epicurus was moved to modify the philosophy of Democritus in one respect. The latter held to a strictly deterministic theory of causation; but Epicurus said that, though some events happen by necessity and chance, others are within our control. It was, he said, more foolish to become "a slave to the destiny of the natural philosophers" than to follow the myths about the gods. The myths leave us some hope—the determinists only despair. The part of wisdom in these matters seemed to him, very much as it did to the Stoic Epictetus, to consist in understanding the limits of man's condition and in not expecting more than is reasonable. A man who knows these things laughs at destiny. All that he asks is a companion like himself, and then he "shall live like a god among men."

KUNG-SUN LUNG TZU

Author: Kung-sun Lung (c.330-250 B.C.)
Type of work: Logic, epistemology
First transcribed: Early third century B.C.

PRINCIPAL IDEAS ADVANCED

Universals, the properties common to many individual things, must be con sidered as distinct from individuals.

195

Thus, a white horse is not a horse, for the universal "horse" cannot be specified by color.

A hard and a white stone must be two entities, for hardness is perceptible to touch, while whiteness is perceptible only to vision.

Names refer to universals; thus, to confuse names is to confuse the natures of things, and such confusion is a cause of social disorder.

Since universals are known only through particulars, which consist of universals, everything in the universe is really a universal, and yet nothing in the universe is really a universal as such.

Only particulars change.

It has been said that ancient Chinese thought was characterized by its practical orientation. The early Chinese thinkers seem to have been preoccupied with the devising of political and social formulas to meet practical and pressing problems of their time. They gave little attention to pure abstraction.

Though this description is correct, it does not tell everything about ancient Chinese thought. In their effort to deal with the concrete problems of the world of man, the early Chinese thinkers could not avoid touching upon certain metaphysical aspects of the most fundamental of these problems. In this light it is of great interest to examine the six thin chapters of a work attributed to Kung-sun Lung, and to note the author's almost exclusive absorption in metaphysics and logic.

Kung-sun Lung had one of the few bisyllabic Chinese family names—Kung-sun. A leader of the "Dialecticians" of his time, he traveled and impressed the rulers of the various states with his outstanding oratorical and argumentative skills. His opponents, in whose works we now are able to trace a vague outline of Kung-sun Lung's life, accused him of artfully using words merely to win arguments, never to convince people completely. But Kung-sun Lung's own book, or what little portion of it that has come down to us, shows

that he was not arguing for argument's sake, but was driven by a zeal to "rectify the names" in quite the same manner as was Confucius. At least one ruler valued Kung-sun Lung's views enough to give him an important government appointment, and he spent most of his life around different princes to whom he offered his advice on how to govern. His personal political fortunes waxed and waned in proportion to the confidence he could win from his patrons.

The dialecticians of ancient China are formally known as belonging to the "School of the Name" because their primary concern was an investigation into the "names of things," or into what lies behind a name. In this work bearing his name, Kung-sun Lung quite succinctly presents a good summary of the problems which he and his fellow dialecticians treated with tireless persistence. All these problems seem to center around the key question of distinction between the universal and the particular, between the abstract Idea as the essence of things and the concrete things themselves as objects of man's sense-perception.

The name Kung-sun Lung through the years has become synonymous with his "White Horse" discourse. He himself is said to have admitted that this discourse constitutes the core of his philosophy. The argument starts with Kung-sun Lung's premise that "A white horse is not a horse."

Kung-sun Lung "proves" his thesis in several ways. To begin with, "horse" can be any kind of horse because it is a universal concept of horse. This term does not exclude any color, while the description "white horse" does so as it fits only a particular kind of horse. Hence, the two names are not equal. And again, "horse" as such also excludes "all colors," or the essence of horse (horseness) has nothing to do with color. Since horseness cannot be equal to horseness plus whiteness, a white horse is not a horse.

By the same token a white horse is not "white" either. The abstract whiteness does not involve any object that is white. Whiteness has nothing to do with "making anything white." Yet the "white" of a white horse is inseparably involved in the concrete object of a white horse; therefore, whiteness plus horseness cannot be the same as whiteness alone.

The moment the reader grasps that Kung-sun Lung is merely trying to expound on the existence of "universals" as independent entities, the famous White Horse discourse presents no difficulty to understand. With the same understanding the reader will also be able to appreciate Kung-sun Lung's position in another of his celebrated discourses, the argument on "Hard and White."

A hard and white stone is actually two entities, so says Kung-sun Lung. According to him, hardness is perceptible to man's touch while whiteness is perceptible only to man's sight. As the tactile and visual senses of man are separate, there must be two entities—a white stone and a hard stone—in a hard and white stone. In this argument Kung-sun Lung made the distinction between these entities on an epistemological basis. If only that which is perceived through man's senses constitutes an entity, then the abstraction *stoneness* does not exist. Stoneness must be perceived by man either through whiteness or hardness.

Kung-sun Lung, however, always went back to his basic distinction between a concrete thing considered as an object of sense-perception and a universal concept conceived in man's mind without the aid of any sense data. When his opponents countered his argument by saying that since both hardness and whiteness can be perceived only through the existence of a stone, the three entities are actually inseparable and one, Kung-sun Lung's answer was the same as that he used in his White Horse discourse: neither whiteness nor hardness as such depends on its attachment to any concrete object in order to exist. They exist as "independent universals." (One may say that if Kung-sun Lung had wished to be thoroughly consistent, he should have insisted that a hard and white stone is actually three separate entities.)

To prove further that whiteness as a universal exists independently, Kung-sun Lung argued that if there were no independent whiteness as such, no concrete thing could be made white by being joined with something called "white." Therefore there must be a "general whiteness"—which is the term used for the essence of "whiteness" as a universal.

These discourses are but illustrations of the views on reality and existence which Kung-sun Lung sums up in his theory of name, reference, and thing.

A thing is a concrete object. It has actuality, and it holds a position in the universe. Heaven, earth, and the myriad objects are all things. This is to say that Kung-sun Lung's "thing" is but a concrete particular.

A name is commonly understood as "pointing at" a concrete particular, or at a concrete actuality. But, according to Kung-sun Lung, a name "refers" to a universal idea. Thus, the reference of a name is a universal, not a particular. The term used by Kung-sun Lung for "reference" is *chih*, which literally means "to point at" and has been translated by some as "designation." But he stresses the common confusion of a reference (universal) with a thing (particular).

Here Kung-sun Lung was trying to show that a thing commonly goes under a name, but what a name truly refers to is not that thing alone but a universal concept of that thing. Hence, he took pains to argue about the misnaming of concrete things. The last point is part of the common intellectual tradition shared by Kung-sun Lung and many other thinkers of his time, including the Confucians. All those who included this point in their philosophical systems emphasized the moral significance of "calling a thing by its correct name." Their common belief was that a confusion of names is the direct cause of social disorder; when names are confused, men no longer know what to live by.

Kung-sun Lung made it absolutely clear that concrete things exist with or without names; hence, names and their references (universals) also exist quite separate from concrete particulars. If so, how is a universal (*chih*, reference) ever perceived? Kung-sun Lung emphasized the point that universals cannot be perceived through man's senses, unless they are joined with concrete particulars. In a lengthy and rather involved argument (Chapter III), Kung-sun Lung attempted to explain that (1) every particular consists of a number of universals; (2) no universal is perceived except through its "universal-particular" (*chih-wu*) combination or through its manifestation in a particular; (3) hence, it may be said that all things in the universe are, in essence, universals; (4) and yet nothing in the universe is really a universal as such. This argument amounts to an exposition on the existence of particulars and the subsistence of universals in space and time. As an illustration, Kung-sun Lung pointed out that while an ox and a horse do not add up to either two oxen or two horses, they do make "two" things. The universal of number subsists in the two entirely different particulars—ox and horse. Man cannot perceive number as such, for what he does perceive is an ox or a horse, which is a "universal-particular." This, in brief, is Kung-sun Lung's *tour de force* known as the theory of *chih-wu*, or universal-particular, which has caused many a sleepless night among later philosophers in China.

The last illustration appears in a separate chapter devoted to a discussion on change. In regarding every particular as only a particular combination of manifested universals, Kung-sun Lung recognized the distinction of one species of things from another. Furthermore, he even hinted at his acceptance of the distinction between genus and species. Consequently, he carried the above illustration further by declaring that there is a closer comparison between ox and horse than between ox and fowl.

If the particular consists of many manifested universals, and if universals do not change, what then does change? Kung-sun Lung's explanation is that change occurs only in the particular. The universal "right" does not change, but anything that is placed to the right can be "changed" to the left. Or, the universal "right" remains constant, but its manifestation can appear in different combinations, such as "right hand," "right leg," or "right side," for example.

The admission that particulars change led Kung-sun Lung to offer a theory of change. What is offered, however, verges on an elaboration of the "five elements" school of thought in ancient China. This school, having found its sources in the photo-philosophical and sometimes superstitious ideas of China's high antiquity, maintained a system of cyclical change, mutual destruction, and begetting of the five "basic elements" (or rather, agents, forces: water, fire, wood, metal, earth) as an explanation of life and existence. These elements were further matched to social and political institutions. Thus, when Kung-sun Lung asserts that wood should not be allowed to overcome metal, lest green displace white and the subjects usurp the prerogatives of the prime minister, he is but borrowing a page from the "five elements" school to explain the need for a fixed order in society in accordance with the natural order in the universe. Any violation of this order would bring disaster, and to confuse the proper designations of this order would be an inexcusable act of "disorderly naming."

Yet, much as Kung-sun Lung was concerned with the right use of names, there is something incongruous about attaching a "five elements" argument to the discourse on change which still centers around the distinction between universals and particulars. His argument is quite complete and consistent without bringing in the semi-metaphysical system of the five elements, and the latter really has nothing to do with Kung-sun Lung's central thesis. (His argument has caused many scholars to conclude that this portion of Chapter IV may be spurious.)

The above sums up what the existing work of *Kung-sun Lung-tzu* tells us, but no reader of this work can resist going into the paradoxes and a theory about similarity and difference attributed to this ancient philosopher by other Chinese writers of about the same time. Leaving aside the unsettled problems as to whether these points are properly attributed to Kung-sun Lung, we can at least observe here that the theory on similarity and difference, as it has become known to us, well fits Kung-sun Lung's central thesis. The theory holds that all things are, in one sense, different and, in another sense, the same. Different schools of thought in ancient China have given different explications to this statement. Kung-sun Lung and his disciples, however, explained the theory with their universal-particular dualism: since everything is but a manifestation of universals, and the latter do not change, then all things are really the same. Hence, a white horse and a yellow horse are the same because both are horse; even ox and fowl are the same because both are universal-particulars. On the other hand, every particular is different from another, so no two horses are really all alike.

Kung-sun Lung owes his popular recognition to a number of paradoxical statements that have come down to us.

None of them is preserved in the *Kung-sun Lung-tzu,* but all have become favorite subjects of discussion throughout the past two millennia. "A white horse is not a horse" is itself a paradox which, as we have seen, Kung-sun Lung made into a vehicle to carry his major argument. Other well-known paradoxes are: A fowl has three legs; fire is not hot; things never come to an end; the shadow of a flying bird never moves; an orphan calf never had a mother.

All these paradoxes can be supported if one accepts Kung-sun Lung's two main arguments: the one involving the metaphysical distinction between the universal and the particular, and the other, the epistemological distinction between one sense-perception and another. All can be explained, to a large extent, by following the same pattern of argument as that of his White horse discourse. Thus, the universal "leg" and the two actual legs of a chicken make three legs. Fire and hot are two universals which are not to be equated; also, since fire is perceived through man's eyes while "hot" is learned through man's touch, they are not the same thing and the copula "is" cannot be applied. Things as containers of universals may change their appearances but never their essences; consequently, they are never exhausted. The shadow of a flying bird moves only as a particular, but the universal of shadow neither moves nor stands still because it is not in time or space. This paradox has also been explained in the fashion of Zeno with the observation that since at any infinitesimally short instant the shadow must be standing still, it never really moves. The orphan calf, as a universal, has had no mother. Furthermore, a calf does not

become orphaned until its mother dies; hence, the moment the term "orphan calf" becames meaningful the mother of the calf is already no longer there.

Throughout the years numerous attempts were made to interpret these paradoxes in various ways, and with every attempt interest in the dialecticians as sophists was revised. It must be noted that while some of the attempted explanations are transparently trivial, others do relate themselves to fundamental problems in logic and epistemology.

Much of the difficulty in understanding Kung-sun Lung stems from the fact that Chinese is an uninflected language. Particularly in archaic Chinese, one finds absolutely no way of telling "white" apart from "whiteness." What few prepositional words there are can tolerate a large variety of interpretations, and, depending on its position in the sentence, every word can function as a verb. Bearing these features in mind, the reader can readily imagine the abstruse language in which Kung-sun Lung tried to make clear his ideas about universals and particulars. The modern reader is not the only victim, for even those of Kung-sun Lung's contemporaries who disliked him objected to his arguments on the ground that they did not "convince" man's heart. These critics, however, always admitted that they could not outwit Kung-sun Lung with words. They paid full respect to Kung-sun Lung's sophistry.

The mere fact that the dialecticians made it their principle concern to argue in abstraction has won for them a permanent position among ancient Chinese thinkers. Kung-sun Lung's interest in the proper use of names is directly related to the didactic and

moralistic Confucian doctrine of rectification of names, but the moralistic
element is almost completely submerged in his metaphysical system.
This is the very reason why the orthodox Confucians belittled the contribution of the dialecticians, describing
the latter's efforts as mere plays on
words. It is not improbable that Kung-
sun Lung and his group actually expounded a fully developed system
which, because of its powerful opposi-

tion in Confucianism, failed to survive. As a result, only a few pages
of his work remain, and very little
annotation and commentary on it has
been accumulated until quite recently.
Contempt for abstract argument as
"empty words" has been a persistent
trend in Chinese intellectual tradition, and as a result of this trend the
Kung-sun Lung Tzu has failed to win
the critical attention it deserves.

HAN FEI TZU

Author: Han Fei (c.280-c.233 B.C.)
Type of work: Political philosophy
First transcribed: Latter half of third century B.C.

PRINCIPAL IDEAS ADVANCED

Nothing interests men except material profit.

*Laws are necessary in order to control men; he who obeys the law is good, and
he who disobeys the law is bad.*

*Nothing is more important than having a prosperous state with strong armies;
to make the realization of this goal possible, the ruler should use the promise
of reward and the threat of punishment as instruments for the control of selfish
citizens.*

*To make government successful and to achieve a uniformity of standards, ac-
tualities must be made to conform with names; the behavior of citizens should
match the descriptions prescribed by the law-giving rulers.*

If laws are made according to tao, the way of nature, the state can rule itself.

*The five termites of the state are the political advisers, the scholars, the mer-
chants, the artisans, and the knights-errant.*

It is quite true that all the Chinese
philosophical schools of pre-Christian
times were concerned with political
problems and that their systems were
more in the nature of political formulae than they were pure metaphysical
speculations. But even with this understanding it is still startling to read a

book like *Han Fei Tzu* in which ethics
is totally absent and morality is completely ignored. Indeed the Legalists of
ancient China (known as *fa chia* in
Chinese, or the advocates of rule by
law) were unique in their undisguised
Machiavellian attitudes toward political realities.

201

The steadily deteriorating political and social situation of the Warring States period (end of the fifth to end of the third century B.C.) must have contributed to a hardening realism in the intellectual climate of the time, but this favorable climate alone did not give rise to the Legalist school. There were many seeds sown by the different schools of philosophers prior to the Legalists. Han Fei, to whom this book is attributed, studied with a great Confucian master named Hsün Ch'ing (Hsün Tzu, c. 320-235 B.C.). From the latter Han Fei acquired one basic concept about man's nature which was to serve as the bedrock of the Legalists' rather frightening theories.

Hsün Ch'ing distinguished himself by challenging the idealistic view of Mencius on human nature. According to Hsün, human nature is like the young craboak tree. Without restraining influence the tree will of itself grow crooked. While Hsün never lost sight of a moralistic ideal in advocating the need for education, his disciple Han Fei carried this view one step further to assert that there is nothing that interests man except material profit. The hired hand works hard only because of a promised reward, says Han Fei, and even parents do not raise their children for love but for their own future security. If this is not the case, asks Han Fei, then why do people value their baby boys so much that they drown their baby girls? (Clearly this abominable practice was actually observed in Han Fei's time.)

That there were ancient sages—a common belief shared by most people in China at that time—Han Fei did not deny. However, he believed that good men are the exception rather than the rule. Furthermore, those who are good by nature are of little value to an orderly society and a prosperous state. If the ruler relies upon the few good men to run his country, Han Fei argues, it would be like the archer who counts on the few naturally straight branches with which to make his arrows. He would not have many arrows to shoot. A few good men do not make an orderly society which requires everybody to observe the interests of society. Hence, the only thing that counts is a set of laws. He who obeys the law is good. Besides this there is no need for any other standard of good and bad, or right and wrong.

Environment offers an explanation for the existence of sages in China's golden past. In high antiquity, material supplies were abundant and people few. No one needed to rob for a living. But as population grew and the land became more crowded, the struggle for existence made manifest the true nature of man, which is profit-centered and selfish. So while in the golden past, as the Confucians explain in their teachings, a moral life was possible, the same material conditions no longer obtained. Han Fei applied this theory to explain the behavior of the legendary kings who abdicated their thrones without regret. Legend says that those sage-kings worked harder than the common peasant and enjoyed less comfort, so why should they have regrets about giving up their "burdens"? But times had changed, and the throne had become a coveted position with its accompanying comfort, power, glory, and material rewards. It is small wonder, says Han Fei, that people all aspired to the position of a ruler.

In many chapters and through various analogies Han Fei attempts to prove his theory of economic determinism. He cites the relative value of water on high mountains and near the river shore to show that man's generosity with water is conditioned by the amount of supply. He tells the story of a disobedient son—incorrigible in spite of all the affection his parents shower on him and chastened only when imprisoned—to prove that there is no reliable "moral sense" in man's nature. As evidence of the ignorance of the masses, he recounts the predicaments of several ancient sages whose benevolence was met with popular resentment. Han Fei's distrust in the ability of the people to govern themselves is absolute and complete.

The only available documentary evidence shows that Han Fei wrote this book as a result of his inability to win a position of direct influence on the ruler of his state, the state of Han. If true, it is understandable why the book reveals a constant emphasis on the art of government, and a persistent belief in the value of a prosperous state with strong armies. Toward these goals Han Fei constructed his philosophy. Since he saw material gain as the only governing force of man and could find no proof anywhere of man's intelligence, he logically turned to reward and punishment to induce man to do what should be done. Punishment and reward are what Han Fei calls the ruler's "two helms," with which the sovereign can rule successfully. In order to enable the common people to know clearly what would bring pleasure and what pain, a set of specific rules is essential. These rules are laws.

Like the carpenter's compass and square, the laws must be fixed and rigid, and their enforcement constant and consistent. The ruler must not follow the Confucian advice to respect the opinions of the learned. To do so would undermine the authority of the law and cause confusion. The ruler paying much attention to the advice of the wise will not only destroy the smooth functioning of a government; his personal position may also be endangered because his subjects would strive for cunningness with which they could either deceive or even replace the ruler. There must be only one authority and one standard, and that standard rests with the ruler alone. With legal codes as their books and law-enforcement officers as their teachers, the people need nothing else to keep them well-behaved.

The punishment-reward theory of the Legalist parallels closely the views of Mo Ti, which were common knowledge in Han Fei's time. But the real inspiration of Han Fei's belief in law is to be found in the common concern over the confusion of names. Confucius urged a rectification of names to restore a proper social hierarchy and reëstablish the desirable social relationships. The Dialecticians, such as Kung-sun Lung, examine the names to dramatize certain problems in man's knowledge. Han Fei also demanded a "search for actuality through examination of its name." Han Fei wanted a uniformity of standards, and the only way to achieve it, as he saw it, depended upon an exact correspondence between names and actualities. If the meaning of a name is not clear, then its actuality must be investigated to clarify the name. If the name is unknown, then its actuality must be searched out to arrive at a proper appellation. The important and interesting aspect of this theory is that Han Fei did not urge any adjustment of names to match actualities. On the contrary, the names provide the norm, and it is the actuality that must be adjusted to match the names. Therefore, Han Fei insisted that the ruler must hold the name in his hand, and with the name his subjects must adjust their behaviors in order to conform! Then and only then could a uniformity of standards be achieved, and government be made successful. This idea concerning the use of names represents the extreme of the evolution of the theory on "rectification of names." It is, as it has worked out, not a "search for actuality through an examination of its name," but rather a "demand that actuality conform with its name."

Once the names are fixed in the form of laws controlled by the ruler, they must be enforced so strictly that no deviation from them, for better or worse, would be tolerated. Han Fei would not hesitate to punish anyone whose claims or promises were not borne out exactly by his subsequent performance. Even if a man does more and better than his promise, he still must be punished, because the harm he does by corrupting the exact correspondence between name and actuality more than offsets the excess service he may have rendered, or the excess goods he may have produced. To Han Fei a "small loyalty" (partial fulfillment of one's promise) is detrimental to the "great loyalty" (exact fulfillment of one's promise).

A philosopher named Shen Tao, who lived shortly before Han Fei, has expounded the principle of force that comes from one's position. Han Fei quotes Shen Tao in this book and gives the latter support. According to Shen Tao, a rock acquires its smashing force only when it falls from an altitude. Depending on where an object is located, it may have greater or less power. Han Fei elaborates on this theory and acknowledges that a dragon without clouds to float him would be as miserable as an earthworm. He advises the ruler to make best use of his lofty position, for it is his sole source of power. Even the ancient sage-king would have been totally disabled if his orders had not been obeyed. Hence Han Fei urges the ruler to maintain his lofty, august position by remaining aloof from his subjects, including the top-ranking ministers. The wise sovereign rules by merely showing his "awe-inspiring majesty," without which he would be a fish without water and could do nothing.

Han Fei recognized the possibility of abuse of power in the hands of undeserving rulers, but he argued for the need of a position of power in order for anyone to rule. A good chariot can travel far even when handled by a mediocre driver, and with a good driver it can perform miracles. But if the chariot is rickety, even the best of drivers cannot make it perform well. So Han Fei would gamble on the greater odds against having many bad rulers who abuse power.

The theory of the ruler's position is one of the important aspects of statecraft which Han Fei discusses in great detail in this book. By maintaining his lofty position, the ruler of a state can command obedience and insure internal order. With order comes the opportunity to build up the strength and wealth of the state for the ultimate purpose of becoming the leader (*pa*) of all the states. This was the political ideal pursued by all the rulers of the states at that time. A collapsed old feudal order left the field wide open for power struggle. Each state sought political supremacy to rule over the entire territory of China. Thus, we read in this book lengthy arguments on how to maneuver the inter-state politics in order to acquire the status of a ruling state. Han Fei examines many historical events involving the success or failure of a ruler and comments on the causes. Invariably he finds these historical cases testifying in favor of his political philosophy.

In one aspect there is a curious similarity between Legalism and Confucianism. The Confucians believe that the best king rules by moral magnetism: if the ruler's moral virtues are perfect, his subjects and neighboring states will of themselves recognize him as their leader. Han Fei believed in rule by the magic of power: if the king's majesty is awe-inspiring, his subjects will obey without further ado. When the laws are complete, the people will know what to do without the need for the ruler to make any move.

This is an extension of the Taoist idea of non-activity. Two chapters in the *Han Fei Tzu* are devoted to an explication of Lao Tzu's *Tao Te Ching*. In giving his views on the *Tao Te Ching*, Han Fei makes it clear that he subscribes to the idea of *tao* as nature's way. There is a proper way for everything, for its existence and function. "Things have their appropriateness and materials have their right use," and since the ruler who learns of *tao* knows how to put everything in its proper place and to assign it its proper function, there is nothing else left to be done. What a ruler has to do is to set up laws according to nature's way. Then the state will go on to rule by itself. The king ultimately will rule by not ruling.

Laws backed by the ruler's infinite authority and enforced through the ruler's instruments—the ministers—will free the ruler from any personal concern. Han Fei here completes his idea of a perfect rule through non-activity. For if every part of this political mechanism functions as it should, the ruler really does not have to be concerned with government. Han Fei cites a number of historical cases in which a king indulged in comfort and yet his kingdom lasted, and Han Fei attributes this result to the good laws already set up by the king. Although in this book Han Fei stresses the importance of the king's vigilance over the welfare of his state, the suggestion that the state can rule itself while the king enjoys his life must have had a great appeal to many rulers of his time.

As we have noted, the sole criterion for judgment of right and wrong or good and bad in Legalism is: Does it contribute to the prosperity of the state and to the strength of its armies? The law, therefore, also determines reward and punishment in accordance with this very principle, which is an application of Mo Ti's utilitarianism. The ruler recognizes the "merit" of his subjects in relation to their actual material contribution to the state. Against this yardstick, the Confucians are useless and meritless because their principles of human-heartedness and rules of propriety concern only the individual's life. Encouragement given to the study of literature, praise of knight-errantry, and indulgence in idle theoretical discussions are all, in Han Fei's opinion, irrelevant to the good of the state. To uphold any one of these would pose another standard in competition with the standard of utility to the state.

The "five termites of the state" are

classified by Han Fei on this very basis. These include the traveling political advisers (a trade that flourished only in such a milieu as that of the Warring States period), the scholars, the merchants, the artisans, and the knights-errant. The first two groups use their glib tongues to confuse the rulers and undermine the laws. The merchants and artisans speculate and produce goods of no real utility, but deceive the people in order to realize undeserved increment in the process. The knights-errant take laws in their own hands, in defiance of government authority. If these people are not discouraged, says Han Fei, nobody will be willing to sweat in the fields (to produce grains) and to bleed on horseback (to fight for the state). Han Fei values only the farmers and the soldiers; this is another parallelism between Mo Ti and the Legalists.

The harshness of Han Fei's realism appealed to the power-hungry rulers of the states embroiled in a bloody political struggle; it also impressed a seasoned Legalist like Han Fei himself. The authority of the ruler, in Han Fei's own theory, had to be so absolute and infinite that to approach the ruler with any kind of advice was a dangerous undertaking at best. Chapters III and XII express the frustration of the author whose speech impediment (he was a stutterer) made the eloquence of his arguments anything but apparent.

As Chapter XI makes amply clear, the Legalist's career was a precarious one. Han Fei's theories made him extremely unpopular among the other courtiers, and he constantly risked "official execution or secret assassination." Han Fei's own life bore tragic witness

to these observations. According to the biography written by the Han dynasty historian Ssu-ma Ch'ien, Han Fei's works became known to the ruler of the state of Ch'in who harbored ruthless political ambitions. The treatises caught the fancy of this aggressive ruler, and he sought Han Fei's services so desperately that a siege of the state of Han by Ch'in soldiers was ordered. The defeated ruler of Han surrendered Han Fei. But the irony of history found its agent in a man named Li Ssu, who was Han Fei's schoolmate and fellow Legalist but somewhat inferior to Han Fei in his intellectual achievement. At this juncture Li Ssu had been advising the ruler of Ch'in for some time already. Fearing that the arrival of Han Fei in the Ch'in court would spell his political death, Li Ssu slandered Han in front of the Ch'in ruler and forged an order to demand Han Fei's suicide. Han Fei, so history tells us without further explanation, duly drank poison. He never served in the court of Ch'in.

Han Fei died, but the school of political thought that went under his name lived on and found a powerful exponent in the ruler of Ch'in. Aided by the scheming Li Ssu, and having adopted a number of Legalist measures, the state of Ch'in actually became a "prosperous state with strong armies" which conquered the whole of China in 221 B.C. and established the first really unified empire known in Chinese history. Even the Taoist element in Han Fei's system seemed to have been absorbed by the Ch'in ruler, now the first Chinese emperor. He set up severe laws, burned the Confucian theoretical books, and buried "useless" scholars. Then, when he felt that his empire was being governed quite smoothly and efficiently, he turned to search for drugs of longevity and ma-terial enjoyment, trusting his country to a rule by "non-activity."

TAO TE CHING

Author: Unknown (but erroneously attributed to Lao Tzu, born c.600 B.C.)
Type of work: Metaphysics, ethics, political philosophy
First transcribed: Late third century B.C.

PRINCIPAL IDEAS ADVANCED

Tao, *the way, is the nameless beginning of things, the universal principle underlying everything, the supreme, ultimate pattern, and the principle of growth.*

If a man takes possession of the tao, the universal principle, he becomes a Sage fit for ruling the world.

By observing Nature man learns to follow Nature's way, the tao.

The man who possesses tao must hide his power and appear soft and weak, for he who shows his power is without power; and the soft overcomes the hard.

To attain tao a man must return to the state of infancy, avoid action, and preserve the breath, the life-force, by breath control.

Perhaps more than any other ancient Chinese text this work has been a center of philological dispute through the centuries. The first question is its authorship. Legend has identified a Li Erh of the seventh century B.C. as the writer, but more reliable historical records yield only a Li Erh of the fourth century B.C. who could not have done the things attributed to him by numerous hagiographical accounts, including having been born with a beard and having taught Confucius for a period. It seems that while the historical Li Erh (or another person named Tsung, of the third century B.C.) may have actually expounded some of the ideas in this work, the story is pure fiction that the legendary Li Erh (known as Lao Tan, or Lao Tzu) composed this book all by himself shortly before he vanished beyond the mountains on the back of a blue water buffalo. In fact the *Tao Te Ching* as it has come down to us contains many telltale features which point to its collective authorship; most probably it was not written by any single author, but has grown into its present shape.

An understanding about the authorship of this work is important for a proper grasp of the central ideas behind the eighty-one short but epigrammic and sometimes cryptic chapters in this work. For however poetically integrated these ideas may be around the central theme of a mystic quietism that dates as far back as the dawning of Chinese history, there are passages in this book alluding to the many different schools of thought that contended for intellectual dominance in the early Warring States period (fifth to third century B.C.). The voice (or voices, hereafter called the "Taoist") speaking behind these epigrams is arguing against the Legalists (some call them Realists), the Confucians, and the Mohists, but the voice also seems to borrow some of the arguments of its rivals. The borrowings are possibly due both to the coexistence of these arguments, as part of the common knowledge of the intellectuals at the time this book was first put together, and to the subsequent interpolations of commentaries that became hopelessly enmeshed with the original text.

A vague notion of the "*tao*" existed among the proto-philosophical ideas in ancient China long before any Taoist, or Mohist, or Confucian expounded their respective views on this concept. It stemmed, apparently, from an early effort of the Chinese mind to search into the mystery of the universe and to discover the reason, if any, behind things. To name the unnamable, the Chinese borrowed this term, *tao*, or the "Way." The ambiguous nature of this term allows it to serve several doctrines. Hence to Confucius *tao* means the sage-king's way to social harmony; to Mo Ti, *tao* means the way to ample supply of staple foods and a populous state, and to Mencius, *tao* means the way to moral (and spiritual) perfection. But to a Taoist, *tao* could mean all these and more.

Throughout this work (and particularly in Chapter XXV), *tao* is described as the nameless beginning of all things, even prior to Heaven and Earth. *Tao* is unchanging and permeates everything; hence, *tao* must be a kind of constant, universal principle that underlies all phenomena. *Tao* has always existed and has no beginning of itself; hence, it must be comparable to the First Cause. Everything in the universe patterns itself after the dictates of a higher being, such as man patterning his ways after those of Heaven. But *tao*, being supreme, follows itself. Hence, it suggests the Ultimate Pattern. *Tao* "is so of itself," without any outside force or influence. Above all, *tao* is "always so" because it is the dynamic principle of change. It dictates the rhythm of growth and decay, but since it is itself the principle of growth it remains constant.

This is a frontal attack against the Legalist. The Legalist divides phenomena into rigid categories, and he demands that the rigidity of his system be maintained at all costs because he sees no other essence of anything except its name. The Taoist points out, in Chapter I, that the named are but the manifestations of essence. They are only the crust. What lies behind them is the real essence which is the source of all mysteries of the universe. In its application, the Taoist argument thus refutes the Legalist's emphasis on rules and regulations as the essential order of things.

As the First Cause and the Ultimate Pattern, *tao* possesses infinite power without being powerful. It does not force anything to follow its way; yet everything by virtue of being itself will of itself follow *tao*, just as water will ultimately flow downward. Any interruption of this Ultimate Pattern can be only temporary. Why, then, should a ruler employ force, as the Legalist insists he must, in order to conquer and reign over the world? Violence contrived by man is against *tao*; if only the king possesses *tao*, all the world will obey him; even Heaven and Earth will bless him and come to his aid.

The Taoist speaks metaphorically of *tao*, identifying it as the secret of all secrets, but he also goes on to suggest a way of comprehending *tao*. Since *tao* is the unchanging universal principle that dwells in everything, then everything in its original state reflects *tao*. In man the original state of existence, his infancy, comes closest to this idea. If man does not tamper with his heart (mind), so that his heart remains untainted, he has the best chance of comprehending this mysterious universal principle. Unspoiled, the *tao* in a tree trunk is as great and as efficacious as the *tao* filling the universe, so long as the tree trunk remains an "uncarved block." If carved, the block of wood becomes a few ordinary articles of daily use. But if man takes possession of the universal principle within an "uncarved block," he becomes a Sage fit for ruling the world.

Like the Confucians, the Taoist also talks about the Sages. But the Taoist Sage is not one who studies the classics, disciplines himself according to the rules of propriety, and preaches constantly to the rulers to be benevolent (as is recommended in Confucius' *Lun Yü*). On the contrary, the Taoist Sage has little use for words, because the words of *tao* are "simple and flavorless." He does not occupy himself with such useless motions as seeking audience with the rulers or teaching students, activities which kept the Confucians and the Mohists busy, because "*tao* never does, and yet through it all things are done." The life of the people becomes proportionately impoverished as Confucian rit-

uals and decorum multiply; thieves and bandits redouble at the same rate as the laws are promulgated. The Taoist Sage "does nothing," and the people of themselves behave properly. The anti-intellectual attitude of the Taoist leads him to stress non-activity because only by refraining from useless motions can the state of the "uncarved block" be preserved.

Clearly Nature in its primeval stage is the best example of the "uncarved block." Consequently, unspoiled Nature is regarded by the Taoist as the best place to observe the revelation of the universal principle or *tao*. By observing Nature man learns to follow Nature's way, the way of *tao*. This acceptance of the way of Nature as inevitable and regular and normal leads to an attitude of resignation. It is not a negative attitude undertaken with a deep sigh of regret, but a joyful acceptance of what is the perfect pattern of things and events. The Taoist does not hesitate to discourage man's efforts to undo what Nature has done. He regards such efforts as useless even should man, out of his ignorance and perversion, attempt to disobey the universal principle revealed in Nature. *Tao* is like an immense boat that drifts freely and irresistibly according to its own will, the Taoist says, and thus man does well in avoiding butting his head uselessly against this huge boat, and by riding along in it. In this idea is found the seed of the Chinese concept that the strongest is he that makes use of his enemy's strength—a concept that finds its prosaic expression in the theory of Chinese boxing. Behind this concept lies the reason why the Taoist respects whatever appears to be soft, weak, and yielding.

The multiple metaphors in this work comparing the nature of *tao* to the secret, the "dark," and the "mysterious," are not merely poetic embellishment, but revelations of the strand of primitive quietism in Taoism. Among the proto-philosophical ideas of ancient China there is the notion of *yin-yang* (negative-positive, or female-male), a pair of mutually complementary forces that are at work in and behind all phenomena. The *yin* force or element is characterized as passive, receiving, and meek (at least in appearance). Yet like the idea of the female or mother, *yin* also possesses the potential of infinite creation. Hence the *yin* principle is closer to *tao*. *Tao* is compared to "a ravine that receives all things" and, therefore, has "unlimited power." In consonance with the *yin* characteristics, the man who possesses *tao* (a Sage) must hide his power, for he who shows his power is really without power. A Taoist Sage appears to be soft and weak because it is the "soft that overcomes the hard, and the weak, the strong," and because *tao* itself is unostentatious; *tao* "produces, clothes, and feeds" all beings without claiming mastery over them, yet everything submits itself to *tao*. For the same reason the Taoist praises the infant who is soft and weak and yet is most strong because in him the universal essence is not dissipated and the harmony of *yin* and *yang* is still perfect.

In this concept lies the Taoist relativity of attributes. To a Taoist nothing is absolute except *tao* itself. Without "short," there cannot be "long." Thus, a Taoist dismisses the validity of the Dialecticians' effort to distinguish the white of a white horse from the white of a white jade. In doing so he also dismisses the Confucian effort to distinguish good from bad as useless trifling. Just as "long and short" have nothing to do with the essence of things, death and life are also two manifestations of what is so of itself (natural). To treasure the good, to prefer the rich, and to cherish life are equally meaningless, equally foolish to one having arrived at *tao*.

Since there is no real difference between acting and not acting, he who does nothing accomplishes most. This concept of non-activity, coupled with the idea that he who "moves not" endures the longest, strengthens the Taoist belief in quietism.

Throughout this book there are repeated hints at a process of attaining *tao*. The Taoist urges man to retain his untainted and untampered heart, and to return to a state of infancy, desirable because of its undissipated essence. The expression for "essence" here is *ch'i*. Generally understood as "gaseous matters," *ch'i* in ancient Chinese cosmology is closely tied in with "spirit" as distinguished from "physical substance." In man, *ch'i* is identified with breath as separate from flesh and bones. The Taoist regards man's *ch'i* as part of the universal *ch'i*, or man's life-force. Hence, to avoid dissipation man must attempt to preserve his life-force, and this effort turns out to be a process of breath control. Indeed the subsequent development of magical Taoism shows many features parallel to the esoteric Indian yoga. And practitioners of Taoist magic can always cite certain passages from this work for authority. For instance, there is at least one line (in Chapter LV) which tends to support the practice of sexual hygiene as a means of achieving *tao*.

Mysticism thickens around the Tao-

210

ist when he claims that neither poisonous insects nor wild animals can harm the infant, or that by fixing one's gaze in meditation one can achieve longevity. Three aspects are involved in these claims. First, the Taoist actually believes in a certain kind of yoga practice to prolong this life on earth. Second, in the Taoist vocabulary, the word longevity may mean endurance. That which endures in man is his essence, being part of the universal essence. Man may die, but so long as he does not lose his essence, he actually endures. The manifestation of his essence may take different forms, such as a tree or a rock, but his essence remains unchanged, hence his longevity. Third, by promoting life-nurture, the Taoist stood opposed to another school of thought prevailing at that time. Led by a philosopher named Yang Chu, this school advocated total gratification of man's physical senses as the real goal of life and the road to salvation, a doctrine clearly contrary to the Taoist emphasis on quietism.

To be with *tao* is to be free, so the *Tao Te Ching* tells us. Such a man is free because he has the infinite power which enables him to do whatever he pleases while he stays within *tao*. Metaphysically this freedom should mean spiritual emancipation and salvation—a liberation of man from the bondage of his limited orbit in this earthly world. But it can readily be seen how a man with political ambitions or a magical bend of mind could make use of this theory. Thus, we read in this book the mystic references to "travels in spirit" which take a man with *tao* through space and time to ethereal realms. It has been suggested that this book must have

had a southern Chinese origin as some passages in it allude to a southern setting; that is, to the south of the Yangtze River. That region was rich in shamanistic tradition, and a book of southern songs, collected at about the same time as the *Tao Te Ching*, contains descriptions of similar "spirit travels." It seems quite certain that these supernatural feats were part of the shamanistic belief common in the Warring States period along the middle reaches of the Yangtze River. The shamans induced trances with prayers and dances as well as through concentration and yoga-like hypnotism. Later in magical Taoism there appears a True Man, a Taoist adept at having acquired the powers to perform these superhuman feats.

As we have suggested, the *Tao Te Ching*, like most Chinese classics originating during the Warring States period, was intended to serve more as a political manual than as a purely metaphysical treatise. However, the metaphysical speculations in this book are provocative enough to have inspired many developments—some occult, some seriously philosophical—in the history of Chinese thought. The cult of nature is one of them.

Nature in the *Tao Te Ching* is amoral because it is one manifestation of the universal essence. Nature does not house more *tao* than an infant or a tree trunk, yet Nature by its grandeur has a special appeal to the Taoist. The unchanging mountains, as contrasted with the changing affairs of man, symbolize for the Taoist the principle of nonactivity, and a calm lake expresses the idea of quietude. A profound appreciation of Nature, at once aesthetic and mystic, stems from this Taoist attitude and forms the basis of a cult of nature that has played an important role in Chinese poetry and art. In philosophy, the cult of nature became the native stock upon which Indian Mahayana Buddhism was grafted to bear the fruits of Chinese Ch'an (Zen) Buddhism.

Nature also has its violent moods. Its wild destructive forces must have been the inspiration behind the passage in the *Tao Te Ching* that refers to Heaven and Earth as unkind because "they treat all beings like straw dogs," or expendable sacrificial objects. But kindness has no place in *tao* which is "always so" and unchanging. The Taoist making the above remark is not criticizing Nature but rather is stating an actuality. This attitude has encouraged many people to embrace a political absolutism which they justify and defend with the claim that they have attained *tao*.

The esoteric elements in Taoism encouraged the accumulation of magical formulas and alchemy, and through the years they influenced a large area in Chinese folk religion. A city of Taoist gods has been constructed. A Taoist clerical and lay tradition and a library of Taoist scriptures have grown to impressive proportions.

The *Tao Te Ching* deserves credit as an enduring expression of basic Chinese philosophy. The belief in the existence of a universal principle, having received such eloquent and poetic expressions in this book, leads contemplative minds to search for the profound and the true in Nature and in man himself.

THE GREAT LEARNING

Author: Attributed to Tseng Tzu (disciple of Confucius, c. fifth century B.C.), or Tzu Ssu (grandson of Confucius)
Type of work: Ethics, political philosophy
Compiled: c. end of first century B.C.

PRINCIPAL IDEAS ADVANCED

The purpose of the Ta Hsüeh *is to teach man to know the great virtue, to love the people, and to pursue the highest good.*

To make the great virtue prevail and to bring peace to the world man must first cultivate himself; only then can he cultivate his family, his state, and the world.

To cultivate oneself one must rectify the heart, but that involves making thoughts sincere, and that in turn involves extending knowledge by the investigation of things.

The pursuit of knowledge is to continue until man achieves moral excellence.

The investigation of things is an intuitive comprehension of the essence of things.

There are three principles of the art of government: the ruler should cultivate

212

his own moral stature; he should make use of wise and moral men; and he must esteem what is right above what is profitable.

Among the dozen or so great books that have exercised a controlling influence on the Chinese mind since ancient times is one called the *Li Chi,* or the *Book of Rites.* The editor of this work, Tai Sheng (c. first century B.C.), gathered together a number of treatises whose authorship he did not take pains to clarify. Most of the chapters deal with the various types of rites—from the arrangement of the most important imperial shrine to the funeral of a plain citizen—and their philosophical import. A few of these chapters, however, treat some quite fundamental philosophical problems not at all connected with any ritual. The *Ta Hsüeh (Great Learning)* is one of the latter, having been removed from the *Book of Rites,* annotated, and installed as one of four most important Confucian classics by the Sung dynasty philosopher, Chu Hsi (1130-1200). These four books are, Confucius' *Analects,* the *Meng Tzu,* the *Great Learning,* and the *Doctrine of the Mean (Chung Yung).* The last named is also a chapter of the *Book of Rites.* After Chu Hsi these four books became the primers given to every schoolboy, as well as the principal texts upon which the candidates for civil service were examined. The ideas in these books as interpreted by Chu Hsi constituted a durable intellectual orthodoxy that curtailed effectively the Buddhist influence on the Chinese mind and maintained a dominance in Chinese thought until modern times.

It is not difficult to see why this short work, which up to most recent times every schoolboy learned by heart, was used as a basic guide to man's self-cultivation. Within its ten short chapters, the author outlines a complete theory on how to bring to reality the Confucian ideal of man's life. He describes the process of making "man" worthy of his name out of an existence in ignorance. He teaches man how to attain the ideal goal of being man, which is self-perfection, in order to prepare himself for the supreme task of bringing peace and order to the world.

The very opening paragraph of the book puts forth the gist of the *Great Learning*: to teach man to know the great virtue, to love the people, and to pursue the highest good as his ultimate goal. Immediately after this statement, the reader is told that pursuing the highest good to perfect himself individually is actually the first step, whence man proceeds to influence all people with his personal virtue until the principle of great virtue is understood and accepted by all. When this condition obtains, a utopian state will exist on earth.

The author explains in greater detail the process of making the great virtue prevail. Man must first cultivate himself to perfection, then put his own house in order, then bring the same harmonious order to the state, and finally extend the same influence to all corners of the world so that there will be universal peace and prosperity. For achieving this perfection, the author urges man to "rectify his heart [mind]." However, this cannot be done unless he traces this process back to its very beginning in the following order: make his thoughts sincere, extend his knowledge, and investigate

213

things. The last is, therefore, the real beginning of man's self-cultivation.

Two problems already emerge. One is a linguistic question on the order of the last two steps. The original language could mean either "to obtain knowledge is for the purpose of understanding things," or "investigating things in order to extend knowledge." Even leaving this problem aside, the second problem remains, namely, the exact meaning of the phrase, "investigation of things." The text goes no further to explain this point, and two diametrically opposed schools of thought center their arguments precisely on this phrase.

The school headed by Chu Hsi (whose annotations, as we have noted, have become orthodox) believes in a dualism of principle and matter. As each being contains its own principle, the mind of man can comprehend the universe only after he has investigated all the principles of all things. Chapter V of the *Great Learning*, according to Chu Hsi, deals with this question. But as the entire chapter is lost except for two fragmentary phrases, Chu Hsi's annotation becomes the only authoritative conjecture. Chu says that the student must start from the principles of limited things already known to him and "search exhaustively for all the principles of all things." After a lengthy period of such concentration, the student would "suddenly penetrate" the universal principle and then his knowledge would become complete. Chu Hsi's opponents tend to entertain a monistic view and regard the universal principle as indivisible. They therefore see no value in investigating the outside world, but urge man to search within his own mind for an understanding of the universal principle.

Without going into details about this debate that lasted for centuries, it seems reasonable and acceptable to arrive at an understanding of this problem on the basis of several other key ideas in the *Great Learning*. One of these ideas is the notion of "the end" of the process of pursuing knowledge.

It has been noted that the end of this process is stated in the opening paragraph as "the highest good." To know the end of this process is important because without knowing where to stop, man would go on searching for knowledge, drifting and getting confused and being led astray by his contact with and involvement in the outside world. Consequently, he would never attain the "complete knowledge." Thus we see that the pursuit of knowledge continues until the attainment of extreme moral excellence. The *Great Learning* does not urge man to keep on accumulating objective facts and data which, as the author of this work rightly hints, are endless and confusing.

Also, in the beginning paragraph we find some elaboration on the importance of "knowing where to stop." To know where to stop, it is said, precedes the fixation of the object of pursuit. Having fixed the object of pursuit, man then and only then can achieve the peace of mind (or quiescence, or calm) which is a necessary condition for deliberation. Without deliberation, no knowledge can be obtained. Thus, without knowing where to stop in the process of pursuing knowledge, there can be no possibility of man's ever acquiring knowledge.

The next key idea is the notion of

"root and branches." This is not merely a notion of a fixed order of things—for the root precedes the branches—it is a recognition of the distinction between the principal and the adjunct, or between the essence and its extension. The overriding principle upheld in the *Great Learning* is that man must distinguish the root from the branches when he approaches anything, acquiring knowledge being no exception. To know a thing is to know its essence, and he who has learned of the essence of things possesses "complete knowledge." The author of this work considers knowledge of the distinction between the essence and the outward features of things to be the central theme of the *Great Learning*. The underlying assumption is that knowledge of phenomena is not true knowledge.

A third key idea lies in the term "peace of mind" or "quiescence." We have noted that the attainment of quiescence is necessary to acquiring knowledge. This state of mind is directly linked to the theory of "rectifying the heart [mind]." The author stresses the importance of maintaining an undisturbed mind, free from anger, anxiety, sorrow, and even the feeling of fond attachment. Only after he has succeeded in ridding his mind of all prejudices which ordinary people erroneously call knowledge, can man expect to reach true knowledge or complete knowledge. A rectified mind is a mind immune to emotional influences. Such a mind comes close to the Taoist's "empty mind," whose approach to knowledge is intuitive rather than investigative.

The author demands that man "make his thought sincere" in order to rectify his mind. Sincere thought means thought of concentration. The thought of a distracted mind cannot be sincere. When applied to the practical level of understanding, the author here is advising man to keep his mind on the object when he seeks knowledge of it. Metaphysically, the author seems to assume that knowledge can be attained only by maintaining an ever-present mind, which is still an intuitive approach to knowledge.

Another application of the idea of "making one's thought sincere" is the author's injunction that an ideal man would be careful about his action and speech even, and especially, when he is alone. When alone, man must consider himself "watched by ten eyes and pointed at by ten fingers." As a moral admonition, the author urges man to behave according to one moral standard by which he could face the world as well as himself. But as an elaboration of the notion of sincerity, the author here advocates a unity of man's being. Man's mind and his behavior are one, his inner thought and outer expression cannot contradict each other because anyone "knowing" him could see his inner self which no amount of pretension can hide. The underlying assumption here is that there is a unity of reality. The moment one perceives even a fraction of what is real and essential, he has perceived the whole.

Examining the above key ideas together, we are quite assured that what the author means by "investigation of things" is, basically, an intuitive comprehension of the essence of things which lies beyond deceptive appearances. In order to arrive at such intuitive comprehensions, man must prepare his mind for the task by "emptying his mind" of all biases and by insuring undivided concentration. Having grasped the essence of things, man stops any further pursuit of knowledge because his knowledge is already complete, and because he has reached the highest good, which is also supreme moral excellence. The wise, in other words, is also the morally good. We see how the author applies the whole theory to politics and develops a theory of the exemplar.

The final goal of self-cultivation being the maintenance of a peaceful and prosperous world, the author never loses sight of the application of his principles to politics at every point. Each of the ten chapters develops one step in the process from "investigation of things" to "bringing peace to the world." The last chapter, dealing with the art of government, occupies half of the *Great Learning*.

Three principles of the art of government are discussed in this work. The first is that people of themselves will do exactly what the ruler does. People will follow their ruler as long as the latter is "sincere"; that is to say, as long as the ruler keeps his words and deeds in agreement and consistent. In the remote past some rulers were said to have been benevolent, and other kings violent, but the people followed them equally until the sovereign proved himself to be inconsistent in that he demanded his subjects to be moral while he himself exhibited no moral scruples. People always imitate their leaders. This premise is parallel to Mo Ti's teaching in the *Mo Tzu*. Therefore, if the ruler himself sets an example, he will function as the yardstick against which the conduct of his people will be meas- ured. The *Great Learning* cites a number of historical cases to prove that the taste and value-standard of a nation change along with what the royal court upholds. The Confucian doctrine of rule by moral magnetism (see the *Meng Tzu*) thus finds another exponent in the author of this work. The ruler seeking the best way to run his state is always asked to examine his own conduct and to cultivate his own moral stature.

The second principle is to be able to recognize and make use of wise and moral men. From the sovereign down to the village chief, if the head can use good men as his assistants and expel the bad elements from positions of influence, the state will be well governed. In this effort the ruler must be "sincere"; he must not seek the good and capable merely because they are useful but because he "likes them more than he can say." He must be genuinely fond of these people and hate those who cannot practice the same principle. A minister who is jealous of others as good as he is must be removed and exiled to the "land of the barbarians and never allowed to return."

The third principle is the esteem of what is right above what is materially profitable. The ideas of righteousness and profit were made the basis for the political philosophy of Mencius, and the *Great Learning* here reaffirms the same principle by instructing the ruler to value moral excellence above material gain. A moral ruler attracts people and commands their respect. When people flock around the ruler, his domain extends. As his domain extends, the wealth of the nation also grows, and the king has no need to be concerned with any insufficiency of material supplies. It is not that the *Great Learning* disregards the solvency of a state. Rather, it stresses the importance of "accumulating wealth in the right way."

Such a morally magnetic ruler is one who appears in the eyes of his people under a paternal halo. The *Great Learning* metaphorically calls him "people's parent" and advises him to "like what the people like and hate what the people hate." What is unclear about the last statement is how it can be reconciled with the exemplar theory which sees the people as "followers" and not as the ones to make decisions. If the ruler is to observe only what the people want, then how is he to function as an exemplar?

The answer seems to lie in the confusion about a basic understanding of human nature that disturbed the philosophical world of ancient China and was not clarified even within the Confucian orthodoxy. Confucius himself was silent on this point, and his sayings merely suggest faith in the teachability of man. According to Confucius, man can be and needs to be cultivated toward the good. Mencius, the second standard-bearer of Confucianism, insisted on the innate goodness of human nature, but he did not neglect the need for self-cultivation, either. Hsün Tzu, the third great Confucian philosopher whose doctrines are said to have influenced the *Great Learning* more than did the two earlier philosophers, held a diametrically opposed view. He said that man has undesirable propensities which, if uncurbed, will inevitably lead man to evil. On the question as to what the ruler should do for the people, the *Great Learning* reflects all three views in different passages. When it says that peo-

ple follow only examples above them, the book accepts Hsün Tzu's views. When it advises the ruler to love what the people love, the book takes Mencius' theory. But in most instances the book appears to stay with Confucius himself in holding that people can be taught to follow the good, so that the responsibility of the ruler is teaching by demonstration, using himself as an example. Consequently, the cycle appears to be as follows: At first people are ignorant and seek only to meet their basic needs, which are neither good nor bad. They follow the good example of a ruler and cultivate their moral senses until the atmosphere (moral customs) of the nation becomes good. When they have attained this moral discipline, they know, generally, what is good and what is bad. Hence the ruler loves what the people love and hates what the people hate.

The influence of the key ideas in this book, however underdeveloped and ill-defined they may be in the original text, can hardly be exaggerated. After Chu Hsi, the Chinese people for the past one thousand years have used these ideas in molding the nation's ideology. Self-cultivation, explained exactly in Chu Hsi's terms, was upheld by all orthodox educators up to the very end of the nineteenth century. And self-education, explained with some variation, is still a living idea among the Marxist as well as the rightist Chinese theorists today. An authoritative pamphlet written by the Chinese Communist leader Liu Shao-ch'i (elected chairman of the People's Republic of China in 1959), instructs the youth of the nation to "set their thoughts sincere" and "watch over their behavior when alone" in order to become good communists. The whole

217

"cadre" theory in the Marxist frame, urging the good and capable to set themselves up as exemplars, is so congenial with the exemplar theory in the *Great Learning* that it won the nation overnight without encountering any resistance.

DE RERUM NATURA

Author: Lucretius (Titus Lucretius Carus, c.98-55 B.C.)
Type of work: Ethics, metaphysics, philosophy of nature
First transcribed: First century B.C.

PRINCIPAL IDEAS ADVANCED

Nothing is ever generated from nothing; nature consists of atoms moving in void.

Atoms naturally move downward, but when some swerve from their course, collisions occur; free will in human beings is a similar phenomenon.

Everything in nature is different from every other thing; the number of atoms of each shape is infinite, although the shapes of atoms are not infinite in number.

Sensed qualities are produced by combinations of atoms of various shapes, sizes, and weights.

The soul is composed of atoms; hence, at death the soul dies with the body.

Lucretius' *De rerum natura* (*On the Nature of Things*), by general agreement the greatest didactic poem in any language, is an exposition of the philosophy of Epicurus (about 340-270 B.C.). No divergence of doctrine, however minute, is to be found between Lucretius and his master.

After an invocation to Venus, symbolic of the loveliness, fruitfulness, and peace of nature, Lucretius eulogizes Epicurus as the deliverer of mankind from the superstitious terrors of religion: "When human life lay foul before the eyes, crushed on the earth beneath heavy religion, who showed her face from the regions of heaven, glowering over mortals with horrible visage, first a Greek man dared to lift mortal eyes against her and to stand up to her; neither stories of gods nor thunderbolts nor heaven with menacing growl checked him, but all the more they goaded the spirited manliness of his mind, so that he longed to be first to break through the tight locks of nature's portals. Thus the lively force of his mind prevailed, and he journeyed far beyond the flaming walls of the world and traversed the whole immensity with mind and soul, whence victorious he reports to us what limit there is to the power of each thing, and by what law each has its boundary-stone set deep. And so religion in turn is cast down under foot and trampled; the victory exalts us to heaven." (This is, of course, a great exaggeration of Epicurus' place in the history of free thought.)

218

Men make themselves miserable through fear of divine caprice in this life, and of hellfire after it. Lucretius argued that the one comes from ignorance of the workings of nature, the other from the false belief in an immortal soul. The cure for both is understanding of materialist philosophy. "Thus of necessity this terror of the mind, these darknesses, not the rays of the sun nor the bright arrows of daylight will disperse, but nature's aspect and her law."

You may think, says Lucretius to Memmius (the Roman official to whom the poem is dedicated), that the materialist philosophy is unholy. Not so: "On the contrary, that very religion has very often given birth to criminal and impious deeds." For instance, the sacrifice of Iphigenia by her father. *"Tantum religio potuit suadere malorum!*—so much of evil has religion been able to put over!"

The first law of nature is: "Nothing is ever generated from nothing, by any divine force." This Lucretius takes to be amply proved by experience. If something could come from nothing, then anything could beget anything, or things would pop up out of season, or grown men and trees would appear all at once. The observed regularity of birth and growth implies fixed seeds of all things, or in other words sufficient causes of all that happens. Nor can anything disappear into nothing; if it could, then already in the infinity of time nothing would be left. "By no means then do any of the things that are seen perish utterly; since Nature refashions one thing out of another, nor permits anything to be born unless aided by the death of something else."

Nature consists of atoms ("seeds," "beginnings"—Lucretius does not use the Greek word) too small to be seen, but nonetheless real; the winds, odors, heat, and cold show that real things can be invisible, while the drying of wet clothes and the gradual wearing away of rings and stones proves that the things we can see are made of tiny particles. Since things move, there must be void space for them to move in. Visible objects contain much void, as is proved by differences in density and by the free passage through apparently solid objects of heat and sound, of water through rocks, and of food through the tissues of the body. Besides atoms and void, there is no third kind of thing; everything else that has a name is either an essential or accidental property of these two.

Atoms are absolutely solid, containing no void within them, hence internally changeless. If they were not, there would be no large-scale objects left by now, for all would have been pulverized in infinite time. Moreover, if things were infinitely divisible, then the sum of things and the least thing would be equal, both containing an equal, since infinite, number of parts —an absurd situation (says Lucretius).

After refuting (what he takes to be) the rival theories of Heraclitus, Empedocles, and Anaxagoras, Lucretius proceeds to prove that the universe is infinite in space. Suppose it were not: then if you went to the edge of it and shot an arrow, what would happen? Either the arrow would stop, because there was something beyond to stop it, or it would not, and again there would be space beyond the presumed boundary. The number of atoms in infinite space is also infinite, for since their general tendency is to fly apart, a finite number in infinite space would have so spread out by now that the average density would be near zero, which is against observation. There is no center to the world, and no antipodes. (All the ancient atomists continued to hold that the earth is a flat disc, even though schools such as the Pythagoreans and Aristotelians, less scientific in their general principles, had long known better.)

Book I concludes with a famous passage, more applicable to the progressive nature of science than to the fossilized dogmas of Epicureanism: "These things you will learn thus, led on with little trouble; for one thing will grow clear from another, nor will blind night snatch away the road and not let you perceive Nature's ultimates. Thus things will kindle lights for things."

The proem to Book II is the longest ethical passage in the poem, depicting the peaceful serenity of the Epicurean's life, contrasted with the troubled existence of the unenlightened, who in getting and spending lay waste their powers.

Atoms move either by their own weight or by blows from other atoms. Left to themselves, atoms move "downward" (what down means in an infinite, centerless universe we are not told), all at the same speed, faster than light, because the void offers no resistance. No atom, then, would ever have hit another, if it were not for the fact that "at quite an uncertain time and at uncertain places they push out a little from their course." Thus one hits another, the second a third, and so on. Lucretius also employs this "swerve," which is supposed to occur not just "in the beginning" but even now, to account for free will in human beings— in the same way, and as irrelevantly, as some philosophers now try to but-

tress free will with Heisenberg's uncertainty principle. (Both are irrelevant because whatever we mean by free will, we certainly do not mean capriciousness.)

Everything in nature is different from every other thing: each lamb knows its own mother, one blade of wheat is not exactly like the next. The atoms too differ in their shapes. Lightning, though it is fire, "consists of more subtle and smaller figures." Honey is sweet because, being made of smooth and round bodies, it caresses the tongue and palate, while the hooked atoms of wormwood tear them. (According to atomism, all the senses are varieties of touch.) The *shapes* of atoms are not infinite in number. If they were, Lucretius infers, there would have to be some that were of enormous size. However, the number of atoms of each shape is infinite. Not every kind of particle can link with every other—that would produce monstrosities.

All combustibles contain particles capable of tossing fire abroad. Anything, such as a fruit, that has color, taste, and smell, must contain at least three kinds of constituent atoms. But no atom *by itself* has color, savor, or odor; the properties of atoms are simply solidity, size, shape, and weight. Colors and the other sensed qualities are products of atomic *arrangements*. If colors were embedded in the ultimate constituents of matter, we should be unable to account for their rapid changes without violating the principle nothing-from-nothing. (This is the main point of superiority of ancient atomism to the other schools of "physics.") Lucretius has another argument: since color, as we know, is not essentially bound up with the shape of a thing, if atoms were themselves colored, we should expect all visible things to exist in all possible colors, "even black swans"!

Nor are individual atoms endowed with consciousness. For (1) sense depends on vital motions, and hence depends on birth; (2) heavy blows can produce unconsciousness, which ought not to happen if consciousness were independent of atomic arrangements; (3) pain is the result of a disturbance, but an atom cannot be (internally) disturbed; for (4) otherwise we should be led to all sorts of absurdities, such as that not only a man but his semen would be conscious.

Lucretius makes brilliant use of the atomistic principle that just as an indefinitely large number of meanings can be conveyed by rearranging the few letters of the alphabet, "so also in things themselves, when motion, order, position, and figure are changed, the things also are bound to be changed."

There are other worlds, like this one, in the infinite universe. Indeed, the vastness and complexity of the universe is itself proof that the whole is not governed by gods: it would be too much for them. Or, if you assume intellects adequate for the task, it then becomes inexplicable why there is evil and confusion in the world.

Growth and decay pertain to worlds as much as to individuals. The vital powers of this earth are wearing out. "Indeed, already the broken and effete earth has difficulty in creating little animals, though it once created all the kinds at once, and gave birth to the huge bodies of wild beasts."

Lucretius distinguishes between the mind (animus, mens) which is what thinks in us, and the soul (anima), which is the vivifying principle: "seeds of wind and hot vapor, which take care that life shall stay in the limbs." Both, of course, are made of atoms, "extremely subtle and minute." They form a unity: "Mind and soul are joined to each other and form one nature, but the chief, so to speak, that which rules the whole body, is the Reason. . . . It is situated in the middle region of the chest." Besides atoms of wind, air, and hot vapor, the mind also contains a fourth, unnamed kind of atom, "than which nothing finer or more mobile exists." This "very soul of the whole soul" has to be postulated to account for consciousness, which is the motion of this superfine substance. (Lucretius is a consistent materialist; consciousness is not for him an unexplained product of atomic motions, distinct from them, but, like color, an "accident" of atoms of a certain kind in a certain arrangement. In other words, consciousness is an atomic process.)

Souls differ in their compositions: lions have more heat, deer more wind, oxen more air. Men differ from one another likewise, their temperaments depending on the make-up of their souls. But Lucretius is quick to add: "So tiny are the traces of the natures, which Reason could not dispel from us, that nothing prevents us living a life worthy of the gods."

The soul particles are few in number compared to those of the flesh, as we know from our inability to sense very slight stimuli.

It follows from the atomic nature of the soul that it is dispersed at death; hence consciousness ceases. Lucretius deems this point so important that he reinforces it with a multitude of observations. Lucretius points out that understanding grows with the body and decays with it; that the soul is af-

221

fected by bodily diseases, besides having some of its own; that mental ills can be cured by material medications; that "dying by pieces" in paralysis, and the twitches of recently severed limbs, show that the soul is divisible and therefore destructible; that there must be *some* soul-fragments left in the body after death, to account for the generation of worms in the corpse; that if the soul is immortal, we should remember our past existences (to the ancients, the immortality of the soul implied preëxistence as much as life *post mortem*), and to reply that it loses its memory at the shock of birth "is not, I think, to stray very far from death." Animals have souls appropriate to their bodily constitutions; this is odd on the transmigration hypothesis, even if restricted to intra-species reincarnations. And it is not only incomprehensible, but ridiculous, that souls should queue up to get into a body. In general, each thing has its appointed place: that of the soul is the body. If the soul were immortal, there would be a tremendous grotesqueness in its being so intimately linked with a mortal thing (as Lucretius contends elsewhere, there could never have been any centaurs, because the disparity in growth rates between the limbs of equine and human beings render them incompatible). Immortal things are so because they cannot be assaulted (atoms), or because they offer no resistance to blows (void), or because there is no room for them to scatter; none of these applies to the soul.

Thus fears of hell are foolish. "Death, therefore, is nothing to us, nor does it concern us in the least, inasmuch as the nature of the mind is held to be mortal. And just as we felt no ill in time gone by when the Carthagin-

ians came from all quarters to the attack, when all things under the high shore of heaven shook and trembled in horror at the fearful tumult of war, and it was in doubt to which of them would fall the rule of all things human by land and sea—so, when we shall not exist, when there shall have been a parting of body and soul by whose union we are made one, you may know that by no means can anything happen to us, who will then not be, nor move our feeling; not if earth is confounded with sea and sea with sky."

The theory of vision in atomism is that objects constantly throw off "idols" or "semblances," very thin films, of which the snake's discarded skin furnishes an example. Such "idols" enter the eye and jostle the atoms of the mind, resulting in vision. The less said about this doctrine—which, as ancient critics pointed out, cannot even explain why we cannot see in the dark, or how we can get the "idol" of an elephant into our eye—the better. Though we may remark that while the Epicurean theory is patently false and ridiculous, its ancient rivals are unintelligible.

All perceptions are true, according to the Epicureans, even those in imagination and dreams—which are perceptions of finer idols that enter the body otherwise than through the eyes. It is in inferences from perception that errors arise. Epicurus consequently held that the gods really do exist, since they are perceived in dreams. They live in the peaceful spaces between the worlds, in "quiet mansions that winds do not shake, neither do clouds drench them with rainstorms nor the white fall of snow disturb them, hardened with bitter frost; ever a cloudless sky covers them, and smiles with light widely diffused." The gods are, in short, ideal Epicureans. The mistake of men is in their false inferences that these beings trouble themselves with *us*, or even know of our existence. *True* (Epicurean) religion consists in taking these blessed beings as models and making one's own life, as far as possible, like theirs.

In discoursing of perception and imagination, Lucretius takes the opportunity to state another important principle of materialist philosophy, the denial of purposive causation. One must not suppose that our organs were created *in order to* perform their appropriate functions: this is "back-to-front perverse reasoning, for nothing at all was born in the body so that we might be able to use it, but what is once born creates its own use."

This book concludes with a discussion of sex, genetics, and embryology, containing the magnificent (but misguided) denunciation of the passion of love as "madness." It is best (we are told) not to fall in love at all; but if you do, you can still be saved if only you will open your eyes to "all the blemishes of mind and body of her whom you desire."

The world was not created by the gods. Suppose they set out to create a world, where could they get the plan for it otherwise than through observation of nature? We are to understand the origin of the world this way: "So many beginnings of things, of many kinds, already from infinite time driven on by blows and by their own weights, have kept on being carried along and hitting together, all trying to unite in all ways, creating whatever conglomerations were possible among them, so that it is no wonder that they have fallen into those dispositions also and come through those passages by which the present sum of things is carried on by renewal." But even if we knew nothing of this concourse of atoms, we ought still to reject the hypothesis of divine creation, on account of the many evils in the world. Most of the earth is uninhabitable sea, mountain, and desert; what can be lived in requires laborious clearing and cultivation, the fruits whereof are uncertain. Why are there wild beasts, diseases, untimely deaths, the helplessness of human infancy?

The world is young, for discoveries—such as the Epicurean philosophy—are still being made. The heavy earth-seeds came together and squeezed out the smoother and rounder which went to make sea, stars, sun, and moon. Lucretius gives five alternative explanations of the revolutions of the heavens; one is free to take his choice, as long as gods are not introduced. The sun and moon are about the size they appear to be (whatever that may mean).

First bushes appeared on the earth's surface, then trees, then, by spontaneous generation, birds and beasts. "Wherever there was an opportune spot, wombs grew, grasping the earth with their roots." Many monsters (though no centaurs) came out of them; in the end, all perished except those few that were capable of feeding and protecting themselves and begetting offspring. (While this account contains the notion of survival of the fittest, it is hardly an improvement over the fantasies of Empedocles, and distinctly inferior to the evolutionary speculations of Anaximander, who in the sixth century B.C. had already freed himself from the prejudice of fixity of species.)

Lucretius next proceeds to a reconstruction of the history of civilization. This passage, which has nothing to do with atomist principles, is a marvel of shrewd deduction, confirmed in almost all its details by modern anthropology and archaeology. His principle of reasoning is that certain discoveries could not have been made unless others had preceded them; for example, woven textiles must have come after iron, which is necessary for making various parts of the loom. (Of course he was mistaken—but the method is promising.)

Fire came first, and made possible stable family relationships and the development of human sympathy. "Then too neighbors began to join in friendship, anxious neither to harm nor be harmed among themselves." Language arose in these primitive societies, first as mere animal cries, but developing by the assignment of conventional names. Then kings and cities, and property and gold. Then revolts against absolute rulers, leading to the rule of law. Religion, unfortunately, also arose.

Metallurgy was discovered accidentally: first that of copper, silver, and gold, later bronze and iron.

Though this account, quite unlike most ancient philosophies, shows a knowledge of technology and of the idea of progressive development, Lucretius did not consider material progress an unalloyed blessing. Life was on balance no more secure in his day than in times of savagery; then one might be eaten by a wild beast, but one did not have looting armies to contend with. Then one might have poisoned oneself through ignorance; but for Lucretius the danger was that someone else might poison you very skillfully. Lucretius the materialist wrote: "Thus the race of men labors always in vain, and uses up its time of life in idle cares, truly because it has not learned what the limit of getting is, nor at all how far true pleasure can increase. And this, little by little, has raised life up to the height and stirred up from below the great tides of war."

Book VI consists of miscellaneous Epicurean "explanations" of phenomena such as thunder, lightning, and earthquakes, the natural causes of which need to be understood lest they provide material for religion to frighten us with. The poem, left unfinished at its author's death, ends abruptly after a translation of Thucydides' description of the plague at Athens in the second year of the Peloponnesian War.

DISCOURSES and MANUAL

Author: Epictetus (c.65-c.135)
Type of work: Ethics
First transcribed: c.120

Principal Ideas Advanced

The good life is a life of inner tranquillity which comes from conforming to nature—to reason and to truth.

224

To achieve the good life a man must master his desires, perform his duties, and think correctly concerning himself and the world.

To master desire one has only to bring desire to the level of facts; only what is within a man's power should be of concern to him.

Every man has a duty to others because each man is a citizen of the world, one of its principal parts.

To discover one's duty one should be skilled in elementary logic, in the art of disputation, and in the right use of names.

So far as is known, Epictetus left no philosophical writings. The *Discourses* (or *Diatribes*) is a transcription of some of his lectures made by a pupil, Arrian. Originally there were eight books, of which only four are known to us. The *Manual* (or *Encheiridion*), a condensed selection from the *Discourses,* was also composed by Arrian. The *Manual* is a good résumé of Epictetus' main doctrines, but the *Discourses* is rewarding for the vivid picture it calls up of Epictetus as a teacher. It catches the vigor and warmth of a wise and witty man in the act of expounding his philosophy informally. He wore his technical equipment lightly as he answered questions concerning practical difficulties, pointed out dangers in contemporary customs, and delivered short homilies suggested by current events.

For Epictetus, the goal of philosophy is not so much to understand the world as to achieve the good life, which, for him, consisted in inner tranquillity. The Stoics, of whom he was a representative, had a well-developed philosophy of nature, based on the Heraclitean doctrine that Logos or Reason governs all change. They were also competent logicians. But their chief interest lay in personal ethics, in which they applied a knowledge of physics and logic. Inner serenity, they held, consists in conforming to nature, or, which is the same thing,

following reason, or, again, discovering and living by the truth. Epictetus alluded to logic from time to time, but only rarely mentioned philosophy of nature. When he spoke of philosophy, he meant "philosophy of life." In his view, the philosopher is the wise man.

Three stages in the achievement of the good life were noted by Epictetus. The first has to do with mastering one's desires, the second with performing one's duties, and the third with thinking correctly concerning one's self and the world. He complained that students are prone to neglect the first two, which are the most important, and to overvalue the third, because students are less concerned with achieving moral excellence than with gaining a reputation as disputants. As a result, the world is flooded with vain, passionate, fault-finding fellows who have so little self-mastery that a mouse can frighten them to death; yet they boast the name of philosopher.

Epictetus put the mastery of desires first because he regarded the main business of philosophy to be the achievement of a tranquil mind. In his view, all perturbations are the result of a disproportion between our wills and the external world. The natural man supposes that happiness is possible only when the external world comes up to his expectations. The philosopher knows that this condition rarely exists, that if we build on any such hope, we are doomed to endless sorrow, which in turn leads to envy and strife. Instead of trying to bring the world up to our desires we should bring our desires to the level of actuality. Happily, this is quite within the realm of possibility because our wants are in our power, as external

In effect, the philosopher tells himself that things which are not in his power are matters of indifference, and all that matters is the use he can make of them. He may be exiled—that he cannot prevent—but does any man hinder him from going with smiles? He must die—but must he die lamenting? His leg may be fettered—but not even Zeus can overpower his will.

Epictetus recognized the difference between saying these things and doing them, and he sought various means of inculcating the habits of self-mastery. A man should daily write and meditate on extreme situations, such as how to comport himself if a tyrant puts him to torture. When enjoying anything, he should form the habit of calling up contrary appearances; for example, when embracing his child, let him whisper, "Tomorrow you will die." To overcome passions, such as anger, let each one keep a day-book in which he writes down every offense. Such are the concerns in which the philosopher ought to employ most of the time he has for thinking. "Study not to die only, but also to endure torture, and exile, and scourging, and, in a word, to give up all which is not your own." Without such practice, a man will not be prepared when unexpected trials descend upon him.

Epictetus liked to speak of the "handles" which things present to us. "Everything has two handles, the one by which it may be borne, the other by which it may not." He cited the example of a man whose brother uses him unjustly: if the man thinks of the injustice, he will not bear it; if he thinks of him as a brother, he will.

This illustration affords a good transition to the second of Epictetus' main concerns—namely, duty. It was an important part of his teaching that man is not a detached entity, but part of a whole. In a passage which is quite similar to one in the writings of St. Paul (I Corinthians XII), he compares man to one of the organs of the human body: "Do you know that as a foot is no longer a foot if it is detached from the body, so you are no longer a man if you are separated from other men? For what is a man? A part of a state, of that which first consists of gods and men; then of that which is called next to it, which is a small image of the universal state." The whole duty of man is inscribed here. Man is, as Epictetus liked to say, "a citizen of the world," and not one of the subservient parts—like the lower animals—but "one of the principal parts, for you are capable of comprehending the divine administration and of considering the connection of things." The lower creatures fulfill their functions without knowing what they do. It is the prerogative of man to understand the "connection of things." And in these connections lie his duties.

"Duties," Epictetus said, "are universally measured by relations." Among the most important for the ordinary person he listed: "engaging in public business, marrying, begetting children, venerating God, taking care of parents, and generally, having desires, aversions, pursuits of things and avoidances, in the way in which we ought to do these things, and according to our nature." The Cynics, who were in some respects the predecessors of the Stoics, used to oppose nature to society and to make a great issue of obeying the former and flouting the latter. That the Stoics of Epictetus' day should see their way to including society as part of nature is noteworthy.

But Epictetus was not ready simply to follow conventional conceptions as to what our duties are. The view that man was a citizen of the cosmos before he was a citizen of Rome has important implications. One of these is that all men, in virtue of possessing reason, are "sons of Zeus." Another is that all men are brothers. To the slave-owner, he said, "Will you not bear with your own brother, who has Zeus for his progenitor, and is like a son from the same seeds and of the same descent from above? . . . Will you not remember who you are, and whom you rule, that they are kinsmen, that they are brethren by nature, that they are the offspring of Zeus?" Conversely, the fact that a man happened to wear the emperor's crown was, in itself, no reason for obeying him. One must examine the stamp on the coin, whether it be that of a Trajan—gentle, sociable, tolerant, affectionate—or that of a Nero—passionate, resentful, violent.

As we have duties toward our fellows, so, said Epictetus, we have duties toward the gods: "to have right opinions about them, to think that they exist, and that they administer the All well and justly; and you must fix yourself in this principle, to obey them, and yield to them in everything

which happens, and voluntarily to follow it as being accomplished by the wisest intelligence." Epictetus spoke of the place appointed to an individual as being like the role assigned an actor. The actor should not complain about the role—whether it is the part of a lame man or of a magistrate. "For this is your duty, to act well the part that is given to you; but to select the part belongs to another." In another figure, he spoke of God as resembling a trainer of wrestlers who matches his athletes with suitable partners in order to bring out the best in them. Difficulties, in other words, are designed to test our souls. "For what purpose? you may say. Why, that you may become an Olympic conqueror; but it is not accomplished without sweat." Again he varied the figure: "Every man's life is a kind of warfare, and it is long and diversified. You must observe the duty of a soldier and do everything at the nod of the general."

Some of these thoughts seem far removed from the ideal of inner tranquillity which Epictetus had for his ultimate goal. "Give me a man who cares how he shall do anything, not for the obtaining of a thing." Such a passage seems close to the view which urges duty for duty's sake. But Epictetus also said that faithfulness is accompanied by the consciousness of obeying God and performing the acts of a wise and good man. What higher peace is there, he asked, than to be able to say, "Bring now, O Zeus, any difficulty that thou pleasest, for I have means given to me by thee and powers for honoring myself through the things which happen"?

The third stage in the education of a philosopher, in Epictetus' program, concerns the discipline of logic and

227

disputation. Because right thinking is a prerequisite both to the rational control of appetite and to discovering one's duty to God and man, it is imperative that every man should study to avoid "deception and rashness of judgment." But how far formal logic is necessary for this purpose was, for Epictetus, an open question. Mostly, logic was useful in debating with sophists and rhetoricians—and with Epicureans. A knowledge of elementary fallacies seemed to him sufficient for most purposes.

Of the problems which arise in connection with moral judgments, three were particularly noticed by Epictetus. The first had to do with right names. If man's duty is prescribed by relations, it is important to see things as they are. "Does a man bathe quickly? Do not say that he bathes badly, but that he bathes quickly." The right name puts the thing in the right light. Like Confucius in his *Analects,* Epictetus urged his disciples to consider what is meant by "father," "son," "man," and "citizen." Right names disclose true relations.

Similarly, inferences should be studied, so that we may not conclude from a proposition more than it really says. Epictetus used as an example the inference, "I am richer than you are, therefore I am better than you." This is invalid. Nothing follows necessarily from the premise except judgments of the order, "I have more possessions than you." Epictetus explained the function of inference as establishing assent, and that of critical thinking as

teaching us to withhold assent from what is uncertain.

Finally, it was necessary to learn the art of testing whether particular things are good. According to Epictetus, all men are by nature endowed with common moral conceptions, such as the conceptions of the good and the just; but nature does not teach us to apply these in detail. A man begins to be a philosopher when he observes that people disagree about what is good or when he casts about for some rule by which he may judge between them. There is no simple rule; but there is what Epictetus called "the art of discussion," which draws out the consequences of a man's conception so that he may see whether it agrees or conflicts with what he really wants. If it is maintained that pleasure is the good, ask such questions as these: "Is the good something that we can have confidence in?" Yes. "Can we have confidence in what is insecure?" No. "Is pleasure insecure?" Yes. Here is our answer: pleasure is not the good. Epictetus supposed that his art of discussion was the same as Socrates' dialectic, and he advised his pupils to read Xenophon's *Symposium* in order to see Socrates in action and "how many quarrels he put an end to."

Socrates was one of those held to be "saints" by the later Stoics. Another was Diogenes the Cynic. These men were, in Epictetus' view, "messengers from Zeus to men about good and bad things, to show them that they have wandered and are seeking the substance of good and evil where it is not."

228

MEDITATIONS

Author: Marcus Aurelius (Marcus Aurelius Antoninus, 121-180)
Type of work: Stoic ethics
First transcribed: Latter half of the second century

PRINCIPAL IDEAS ADVANCED

Nature is one, the divine substance, God or Reason, so that virtue for man consists in being in harmony with the way of Nature.

Virtue is the highest good.

The ideal Stoic wills to control himself in those respects in which control is possible—in desiring, believing, and responding.

Man's freedom, in a world in which all events are determined, is his power to assent or dissent to the course of events.

Nothing that is according to Nature can be evil; hence, death is not evil, nor are the ordinary misfortunes of life.

Many great works of literature and philosophy give us nothing of the sense of the persons who composed them. In the process of composition the author abstracts from his experience and his thought and, under the disguise of style, creates an immortal work in which the idiosyncratic features of his own vulnerable person are lost. But now and then, as we read, we close the gap of centuries, even of style, and come mind to mind and spirit to spirit with one who, though long dead, made such a mark in history and letters that it is as though he were making that mark still—yet responding as a person of flesh and feeling to the challenges of the world. Such a figure, at once emperor and philosopher, man of history and vulnerable man, is Marcus Aurelius; and his peculiar immortality is made possible by the personal record of his thoughts, the *Meditations*.

He was a stoic. To some modern readers the term *stoic* calls up the picture of one who, in the midst of life's threatening adventures, stands unmoved by either pleasure or pain.

To be stoical is to be one who endures, one who may suffer but who refuses to be moved by suffering.

Perhaps Marcus Aurelius was, in this sense, stoical; surely he survived the treacherous debaucheries of Lucius Aurelius Verus with whom he shared his empire, the rebellious uprisings of powerful tribes, famine and flood, the deaths of his children—but for one, who became a tyrant—and the threat of Christianity. Perhaps he also had to tolerate faithlessness in his wife—but of that we have no word from him, and rumors may be false.

But he was more than a stoic. He was a Stoic, one fallen heir to a great philosophic tradition initiated by Zeno of Cyprus and expanded and continued by Chrysippus, Panaetius, Posidonius, Seneca, and Epictetus. What is central to Stoicism is not a stonelike stubbornness in a world of suffering, but a strengthening faith in the way of Nature. Nature is one, the substance of God; and God is a divine fire which periodically consumes all things. But although the divine conflagration turns

229

all things and persons to fire—thus effectively uniting all in the purest form possible—things and persons will exist in the next cycle of existence; the cycles of existence and conflagration will succeed each other forever. Virtue for man is in willing to be in harmony with the way of Nature. Pleasure and pain are irrelevant, if the only good is Nature's way and obedience to that way. Thus, the stoical attitude is the consequence of a dedication to the Stoical ideal; it is not itself the essence of that ideal.

So conceived, Stoicism can be recognized as being close in spirit to Taoism, the philosophy and religion of ancient China, in which obedience to the Tao, the *way* of the universe, is the highest virtue. Stoicism, like Taoism, involved the belief that Nature, since it is the matter of God, works only toward the good—although the Chinese did not identify the cosmic power as fire or as God.

Finally, to fix the idea of Stoicism, it is helpful to distinguish between Stoicism and Epicureanism. Although both the Stoics and the Epicureans fostered a life of moderation in which the passions would be controlled by will and reason, the Epicureans regarded pleasure as the highest good—although, contrary to common belief, they did not endorse a program of wine, women, and song but, rather, a life of moderation in which the desire for peace and contemplation would take precedence over the desire for gratification of the senses. For the Stoics, virtue itself was the highest good, although it was generally believed that a modest kind of happiness would be the virtuous man's natural reward. Although there are other important differences, one can come to understand the essential distinction between Stoicism and Epicureanism by realizing that for the Stoics virtue was the highest good, while for the Epicureans happiness was the highest good and virtue only the means.

In Stoicism, and particularly in the later philosophy as exemplified in the *Meditations,* the ethical elements received more emphasis than the metaphysical. The early philosophy was, strangely, a pantheistic materialism— since it held that God is fire, and all Nature is God—but later Stoics were not interested in developing these ideas, and insofar as fire was mentioned it was in a metaphorical, rather than a metaphysical, way.

The Stoic ethics is not complicated; it is more an expression of dedication to Nature's way and to the control of the self than it is a specific guide to the complexities of life. The wise man, the one who becomes the ideal Stoic, is one who wills to control himself in those respects in which control is possible: in desiring, believing, and responding —and he is one who (like the Epicurean) refuses to be affected, in his desires or attitudes, by matters beyond his control or unworthy of his concern.

Nevertheless, although the ethics of Stoicism is not complicated, problems develop in connection with the metaphysical ground of the ethics. If all nature tends toward the good, and if all events are causally determined— as the Stoics believed—how is it possible for man to err, and how can man be held responsible for his actions? The Stoics were unanimous in giving assent to the claim that man is morally responsible and that his responsibility involves his freedom, and they were generally united in adhering to a strict determinism. The answer which won most favor among the Stoics, and which seems to be influential in the thinking of Marcus Aurelius, is that despite the fact that, causally speaking, events could not be other than they are, in the act of assenting or dissenting man plays a critical role in the course of events; and it is in that moment of assent or dissent that man shows his freedom and acquires his responsibility. At its most positivistic, this philosophy means that to attribute moral responsibility to man is simply to attribute to him the power, in the causal situation, of assenting or dissenting.

Although there are reflections of Stoical philosophy in the *Meditations*, the work itself is not a philosophic treatise. It is a record of the reflections of a philosophically tempered ruler, a person with moral sensitivity and intellectual awareness who never gave up the practice of examining his ideas, his motives, and his actions with the intention of refining himself. He is a generous and thoughtful man in his book, an honest man with a sense of his errors—but throughout the work Marcus seems to be sustained by a strengthening spirit, the fire or *pneuma* which is the cosmic principle of the universe. Whether or not the Roman emperor who wrote it ever intended to have it read by anyone other than himself, the *Meditations* remains an intensely personal philosophic journal by one of the greatest of the Stoics.

The book begins with expressions of gratitude—to his grandfather Verus for having taught him to refrain from passion, to his father for having inspired in him manlike behavior, to his mother for teaching him to be religious and to "content myself with a spare diet," and to his great-grandfather for having encouraged him to acquire a good education. Other friends and teachers are remembered in charming fashion. Marcus shows gratitude for having been taught to be humble as a prince while at the same time maintaining a sense of his responsibilities in public matters. He thanks the gods "That I was not long brought up by the concubine of my father; that I preserved the flower of my youth. That I took not upon me to be a man before my time, but rather put it off longer than I needed."

Within a few pages of the beginning of the *Meditations* Marcus Aurelius writes that nothing is more important than understanding "the true nature of the world, whereof thou art a part," and he gives himself sober counsel: "These things thou must always have in mind: What is the nature of the universe, and what is mine in particular: This unto that what relation it hath: what kind of part, of what kind of universe it is: And that there is nobody that can hinder thee, but that thou mayest always both do and speak those things which are agreeable to that nature, whereof thou are a part."

Again, in Book VI, Marcus writes, "He that seeth the things that are now, hath seen all that either was ever, or ever shall be, for all things are of one kind; and all like one unto another. Meditate often upon the connection of all things in the world; and upon the mutual relation that they have one unto another. For all things are after a sort folded and involved one within another, and by these means all agree well together."

To "meditate often"—this was both the duty and the practice of Marcus Aurelius. Even in the midst of war, while waiting for the next day's battle,

231

he reflected on the "connection of all things" and attempted to understand the relation of himself, a part, to that Nature of which he was a part.

He concerned himself with the problem of evil and considered whether death is evil. His conclusion was that since Nature is the means by which man and God are united, whatever man finds disagreeable is no true evil. He believed both in the justice and intelligence of the creative force in the universe and regarded it as inconceivable that Nature would be so constituted as to allow both the good and the bad to happen to good and bad men "equally and promiscuously. . . ."

His advice to himself was to spend each moment as if it were the last moment in his life. If death comes, he argues, it brings man into the company of the gods—or it brings extinction— and in either case a rational man should not be disturbed. In any event, what one loses at the moment of death is nothing more than the present moment—and it does not seem proper to complain about losing a moment of one's life. Thus he writes, "The time of a man's life is as a point; the substance of it ever flowing, the sense obscure; and the whole composition of the body tending to corruption." But what of it? For one who by the use of philosophy allows his spirit to discipline him, all things that happen are accepted contentedly, and one is assured by the conviction that "nothing that is according to nature can be evil."

It may sometimes seem that the ideal Marcus constructed is beyond reach: in his regard for community, for other men, for the way of Nature in all its manifestations, he constructed a moral pattern for himself (and, by implication, for others) that few men could

hope to attain. He enjoins himself always to keep his thoughts on worthy matters, to think only of that which he would be happy to reveal were he asked to state his thoughts; and he charges himself never to act against his will, or against community, or without examination of what he proposes to do; and he vows soberly to "let thy God that is in thee to rule over thee" so that his life might be so ordered that were the trumpet to call retreat from life, he would be ready.

But this Stoic ideal is so carefully considered and presented as the product of personal meditations that it carries with it no hint of moral pride or arrogance. Indeed, if Marcus Aurelius ever supposed he was successful in meeting the ideal, there is no sign of it in his book. For the nobility of his character we have the evidence of the testimony from those who knew him—together with the spirit of the *Meditations*—a philosophic, universe-accepting, strenuous spirit forever exploring Nature for intimations of divine intention.

We are reminded of Emerson's call for self-reliance in Marcus Aurelius' determination "to stand in no need, either of other men's help or attendance, or of that rest and tranquillity, which thou must be beholding to others for." Here again is no insensitive stubbornness but a sign of a faith in the way of Nature.

Marcus argued that if reason is common to men, then reason's law is common law, and from common law can be derived the commonweal which makes the world a city and all men the fellow citizens of it. He placed great faith in reason because he regarded it as an expression of the great ordering breath of God which pervades all Nature. The concern for other human beings fills the *Meditations,* and the spirit is much like that of the Christianity which Marcus never understood.

To live according to nature, to disdain rest and tranquillity, to be ready for death, to take misfortune as nothing evil, to be persistent in one's efforts to live like a man, to be happy as one who has faith in the purposes of God and Nature, to live with the gods and to give allegiance to the god within, to honor reason and to use it as the divine in man whereby he both recognizes and participates in the community of all men, to regard happiness as the consequence of "good inclinations of the soul, good desires, good actions"—this is the genteel, impassioned Stoical philosophy which emerges from the pages of the *Meditations.* The common conception of Stoicism as a philosophy of endurance is destroyed in the face of the fact that Marcus Aurelius' Stoicism is well-balanced, sympathetic, strenuous, idealistic, demanding—a religious call to man to use his highest powers and to control his passions.

But much of the delight of the work comes not from its philosophy—although the Stoicism developed by Marcus Aurelius is in every respect admirable—but from the author's sprightly style which, while communicating the most serious of thoughts, ever reminds us of the presence of the living thinker, a lover of men, action, and nature. Such an aphorism as "That which is not good for the beehive cannot be good for the bee" creates a pleasant image, expresses a sentiment, fixes an idea, and rounds out an argument. Again, reflecting on anger, he writes, "To them that are sick of the jaundice, honey seems bitter; and to them that are bitten by a mad dog, the water terrible; and to children, a little ball seems a fine thing. And why then should I be angry?"

Sometimes you know a man by his heroes. Marcus Aurelius writes: "Alexander, Caius, Pompeius; what are these to Diogenes, Heraclitus, and Socrates? These penetrated into the true nature of things; into all causes, and all subjects: and upon these did they exercise their power and authority. But as for those, as the extent of their error was, so far did their slavery extend." With Marcus Aurelius also the philosopher takes precedence over the soldier and emperor—both in his opinion and in ours.

Throughout all of his actions and reflections Marcus Aurelius was sustained by an unconquerable faith. He wrote that neither time nor place can limit a man's efforts to be a true man; and he regarded true manhood as made possible by reflection on God's ways as shown in the course of Nature and by calm acceptance of all circumstances. Not to accept Nature, for him, was not to accept law; and not to accept law was to be a fugitive from God. Yet to live in accordance with Nature and to accept all things, to act as directed by reason, not passion—this was not a burdensome life, but a happy one: "How happy is man in this his power that hath been granted unto him: that he needs not do anything but what God shall approve, and that he may embrace contentedly, whatsoever God doth send unto him?"

For the Stoic Marcus Aurelius, the answer was clear—and the assurance of his self-reliant faith is alive in his words:

"Herein doth consist happiness of

life, for a man to know thoroughly the true nature of everything; what is the matter, and what is the form of it:

with all his heart and soul, ever to do that which is just, and to speak the truth."

OUTLINES OF PYRRHONISM

Author: Sextus Empiricus (fl. late second and early third centuries)
Type of work: Skeptical criticism
First transcribed: Early third century

PRINCIPAL IDEAS ADVANCED

Skeptical arguments are designed to cure dogmatists of the disease of supposing that knowledge is possible.

The skeptic relies upon appearances, and he avoids the error of passing judgment.

To suppose that it is possible to judge truth and falsity is to ignore the relativity of perception and judgment.

The writings of Sextus Empiricus are the only texts that have survived from the Pyrrhonian skeptical movement of ancient times. The movement takes its name from Pyrrho of Elis (c.367-275 B.C.), who doubted that there is any way by which one can attain knowledge. He urged that judgment be suspended as to whether any particular assertion is true or false. He argued that to suspend judgment leads to a state of indifference toward the world, and to a kind of inner tranquillity which enables one to live at peace in a troubled world.

The actual school of Pyrrhonian thought began much later, in the first century B.C. It developed out of the extreme skepticism that had been prevalent in the Platonic Academy under Arcesilas (c.315-c.241 B.C.) and Carneades (c.213-c.129 B.C.). The Academic skeptics developed a series of brilliant arguments to show that

nothing can be known; they recommended that one live by probabilities. The Pyrrhonists regarded the Academics as being too dogmatic, and the former maintained their doubts, even about the skeptical contention that nothing can be known. Starting with Aenesidemus (c.100-c.40 B.C.), who had been a student at the Academy, the Pyrrhonian movement developed in Alexandria, primarily among medical doctors. Aenesidemus and his successors set forth a series of arguments against various dogmatic philosophies, including the Academic skeptics. The arguments purport to show that every dogmatic attempt to gain knowledge leads to difficulties that cannot be resolved. Instead of seeking knowledge, one should suspend judgment, thus gaining peace of mind.

Sextus Empiricus was one of the last leaders of the Pyrrhonian school. Besides the fact that he was a doctor and

234

a teacher, practically nothing is known about him. His writings—probably copies of lectures—consist of compilations of the arguments that his predecessors had worked out on any and all subjects. The *Outlines of Pyrrhonism* is a summary of the Pyrrhonian position, whereas his other works, *Against the Mathematicians* and *Against the Dogmatists*, are much more detailed expositions of the arguments that the school had developed regarding each particular area in which other philosophers had claimed to have discovered true knowledge. Sextus's writings are veritable storehouses of skeptical arguments designed to confound all other philosophers. Although very repetitious, they contain both good and bad arguments.

In the last chapter of the *Outlines of Pyrrhonism*, Sextus explains the uneven character of his book in answering the question why skeptics sometimes propound arguments which lack persuasion. The skeptic, we are told, is a lover of mankind. He is seeking to cure an ailment called "self-conceit and rashness," from which the dogmatic philosophers suffer. Just as doctors employ remedies of different strengths, depending on the condition of the patient, so, too, the skeptic employs arguments of different strengths depending upon how "sick" the dogmatic philosopher is. If the therapy can succeed with a weak argument, good. If the case is severe, a strong argument is needed. Hence, the Pyrrhonist offered a variety of arguments, good and bad, weak and strong, since his avowed aim was to cure the dogmatist of the disease of supposing that he knew something.

The *Outlines of Pyrrhonism* begins by dividing philosophers into three groups: the dogmatists, such as Aristotle and Epicurus, who say that they have discovered the truth; those such as Carneades, who say it cannot be found; and the Pyrrhonian skeptics who keep seeking for it. The aim of the Pyrrhonian arguments is to cure people from holding either of the first two views. Sextus guards himself from being accused of "secret dogmatism" by saying that the statements in his book are not to be taken as positive assertions of what is true, but only as expressions of what *appear* to him to be matters of fact.

Sextus describes skepticism as the ability or mental attitude which opposes appearances, the objects of sense experience, to judgments that can be made about them, so that suspense of judgment is achieved in which we neither affirm nor deny anything. This state is followed by the state of "quietude," in which we are untroubled and tranquil. The various dogmatic schools of Hellenistic philosophy—the Stoic, the Epicurean, and the Academic—were all looking for "peace of mind," and their theories of knowledge and of the real nature of the universe were intended to lead one to mental peace. The skeptics contend that the dogmatists never achieve peace because they worry about never knowing whether their theories are true. But the skeptic who suspends judgment achieves peace of mind, since he escapes such worry.

If the skeptic suspends judgment about everything, how does he live? Sextus answers by declaring that the skeptic accepts the world of sense experience undogmatically. It seems to the skeptic that he sees certain things, has certain feelings, and so on, but he does not know whether such is really the case. He suspends judgment about

235

all that is not immediately evident to him. Then, without judging, he follows nature and custom, so that—for example—when he seems to be hungry, he eats. He has peace of mind, since he does not judge, and he is guided in his life by his experience, his feelings, and the laws and customs of his society.

To achieve this tranquillity, one must first achieve suspension of judgment. Skeptical arguments are offered by Sextus to encourage such suspension. The first of these is the famous ten tropes, or arguments, of Aenesidemus, which show why we should suspend judgment about whether sense objects really are as they appear to be. (Sextus prefaces these and all the other arguments he sets forth with the disclaimer that he is not asserting dogmatically the exact number, nature, or truth of the arguments, but only that it seems to him that they are a set of arguments.) The ten tropes all deal with difficulties in ascertaining when features of our sense experience belong to real objects existing independently of our perceptions.

First, Sextus points out, different animals experience things differently according to the nature of their sense organs. We cannot tell which animal has the correct experience. Second, even among men, the same object is experienced differently, and we have no basis for deciding which man has the correct experience. Third, the same object affects different senses in different ways. Honey is sweet to the tongue, but sticky to the finger. We cannot tell which quality really belongs to the object. Fourth, our impressions of things vary according to our state of mind or our condition. Fifth, things appear different from different positions. Sixth, we never perceive objects individually, but only together with other objects, so that we never know what they are like by themselves. Seventh, objects look different when decomposed or analyzed than they do whole. We cannot judge which is their true nature. Eighth, everything that we perceive is seen relative to its position in space and time, so we do not know what it is like out of position. Ninth, we regard things differently according to whether they occur frequently or rarely. And tenth, since different nations and cultures have different laws and customs, we cannot judge what things are really right or wrong. These ten tropes should lead us to suspend judgment since they show that our sense impressions vary and are different, and we have no means for deciding which are correct ones.

Sextus follows with five additional tropes, or reasons for suspending judgment, attributed to Agrippa, a skeptic of a century earlier. These are more general reasons for doubting dogmatic contentions. First of all, there is interminable controversy about everything, so we cannot tell who is right. Second, every judgment must be proved, if it is to be accepted as true. But the proof will require a further proof, and so on *ad infinitum*. Third, any judgment is relative to the judge, and may not be true of the thing itself. Fourth, the dogmatists must assume something in order to make judgments, but we cannot tell if these assumptions or hypotheses are true. Fifth, the only way to escape from the infinite regress of proofs of proofs, or from starting with some unwarranted hypothesis, is to employ a circular argument in which something that is to be proved is used as part of the proof itself.

Further sets of tropes are offered, including Aenesidemus's arguments against any dogmatic theory of causation. Then the first book of the *Outlines* concludes with an explanation of skeptical terminology (showing how the skeptics can say what they do without making dogmatic assertions) and with a comparison of other Greek philosophies with Pyrrhonian skepticism.

The second and third books of the *Outlines* show why the skeptic suspends judgment with regard to knowledge claims in various specific disciplines. The second book treats problems of logic and the theory of knowledge, while the third is a collection of arguments about theology, metaphysics, mathematics, physics, and ethics. The second book, and its longer exposition in *Against the Logicians*, has attracted much attention in recent years because of the similarity of some of the views expressed to those of David Hume and of the contemporary logical positivists, analysts, and ordinary language philosophers.

The second book first presents the disturbing problem of whether the skeptic can deal with the arguments of the dogmatists without admitting that he, the skeptic, knows something, namely what the opponents are talking about. After contending that he deals only with what seems to be the dogmatists' views, Sextus turns to what he regards as crucial to any theory of true knowledge, the question whether there is any criterion for judging what is true. Philosophers disagree as to whether there is such a criterion. To settle the dispute, a criterion is needed, but it is not known whether one exists.

Further, any proposed criterion of knowledge would have to be judged by another criterion to tell if it were a true one, and that criterion by still another, and so on.

If the dogmatic philosophers insist that man is the judge or criterion of true knowledge, then a problem exists: whether all men or only some are judges of truth. If all, then another criterion is needed to settle disputes among men. If only some, then a criterion is needed to tell which men are proper judges, and under what conditions. The Stoics, for example, claim that the wise man, the Sage, is the judge. But by what standards can one tell *who* is the Sage, and whether what he says is true? Other philosophers say that the criteria are the faculties of sense and reason. But under what conditions are they the criteria? By what standards shall we judge? And whose sense and reason are standards?

It is not even obvious that anything true exists. There is controversy about this matter; so, if somebody asserts that truth exists, he will not be believed unless he offers proof. But is the proof true? Further proof has to be offered. But is *that* true? Unless some criterion of truth can be established, we cannot tell. But how can we ever determine if the criterion is the true one?

Further, one can ask, what sort of truths are they—apparent ones or nonapparent ones? Since there is disagreement about everything (and Sextus appeals to the fact that there have been philosophers who disputed everything), it is not obvious that something is true. If truths are not apparent, some standard is needed for ascertaining what is true, but all of the above difficulties arise when one attempts to apply a standard of truth.

Philosophers, especially the Stoics, maintain that they can gain true knowledge by means of signs or inferences which connect what is obvious or evident with that which is not. What is nonevident, Sextus says, falls into one of three categories: the *temporarily nonevident,* as, for example, that which is on the other side of the wall I am facing; the *naturally nonevident,* those things which can never under any circumstances be perceived, such as the pores in the skin, but which can be inferred from what is evident; and finally, the *absolutely nonevident,* whatever can never be known at all, such as whether the number of stars is odd or even. There is a type of sign, called the "suggestive sign," which connects what is obvious, our immediate experience, with what is temporarily nonevident. Smoke suggests that there is a fire. The skeptic, like anyone else, accepts suggestive signs and acts by them, because this is the natural way of relating present experience to possible future experience. But suggestive signs do not provide true knowledge, only predictions or expectations about the future course of events.

Philosophers hope to gain true knowledge by means of another kind of sign, the "indicative" one. This is defined as "an antecedent judgment in a valid hyppothetical syllogism which serves to reveal the consequent." In a syllogism of the form "If A, then B; A, therefore B," A is an indicative sign if it, itself, is evident, if it reveals that B, which is naturally nonevident, is true, and if the syllogism is valid. Sextus offers many arguments against the existence of indicative signs, including the contention that one can determine if a hypothetical syllogism is valid only if one knows whether the conse-

quent is true or false. The consequent in this case is a statement about what is naturally nonevident, which can be revealed only by an indicative sign. Hence, one is always involved in circular reasoning, since it requires knowing what is naturally nonevident to tell if an indicative sign actually exists, and one can tell what is naturally nonevident only by means of indicative signs.

Demonstrative reasoning consists of using signs to reveal conclusions. Hence, similar doubts can be cast as to whether anything at all can be demonstrated or proved. Sextus offers many arguments to show that nothing can be proved, and then, to avoid establishing the negative conclusion, he offers evidence to show that something can be proved. Therefore, one has to suspend judgment on the question.

A very brief criticism is leveled against induction, pointing out that if a general conclusion is drawn from some particular instances, it may be disproved by other cases. If generalizations can properly be made only after a review of *all* particular cases, it is obviously impossible to survey all of the data, and hence, to generalize.

The second book of the *Outlines* examines the claims of various logicians and epistemologists of ancient times, especially the Stoics and Epicureans, and shows reasons for suspending judgment as to whether there is anything that is true, and as to whether there is any method for discovering truths. The third book rapidly surveys the various sciences from theology and metaphysics to mathematics, physics, and ethics, and indicates that in each of these areas the fundamental concepts are meaningless, that the basic principles are open to question, and that, as a result, one must suspend judgment about whether anything can be known in any of these areas.

Though the skeptic accepts the customs of his society, and hence its religious views, undogmatically, Sextus points out that the arguments for the existence of God and for atheism are inconclusive, and that the conceptions of God offered by various philosophers are conflicting and often inconsistent in themselves. Further, various problems, like the problem of evil, cast doubt on the claim that a good, all-knowing deity exists.

With regard to metaphysics and physics, the basic notions, like "cause," "matter," and "body," contain difficulties. We cannot even be sure that anything causes anything else, or that bodies exist. We seem to have no way of gaining indisputable knowledge in this area. And arguments like those of Zeno of Elea, of the fifth century B.C., indicate that paradoxical conclusions can be drawn about the nature of bodies, motion, and so on.

There are also paradoxes with regard to mathematics, such as the odd argument Sextus offers to show that 6 equals 15. The whole equals the sum of its parts. The parts of 6 are 5, 4, 3, 2, and 1. Therefore, 6 equals 15.

The disagreements among philosophers and mathematicians, and the various paradoxical arguments, whether valid or not, that had been developed in ancient times suffice to raise doubts as to whether anything can be known about the world, or about mathematics. Hence, we must again suspend judgment.

When Sextus turns to ethical matters, he points out that philosophers disagree about what is good and bad. There is not even adequate evidence that anything really good or bad exists. The variety of beliefs and opinions about what is good and bad in the various known cultures leads one to suspend judgment about whether there are any objective moral values in the world. (Sextus even points out that some people and some societies condone incest and cannibalism. And who can say that they are wrong?) The skeptic lives undogmatically, not judging whether things are good or bad, but living according to the dictates of nature and society. The skeptic, like others, may suffer from physical pains, but he will avoid the additional mental suffering that results from judging that pains are bad or evil.

The writings of Sextus Empiricus seem to have had little or no influence in their own time and to have been practically unknown during the Middle Ages. Their rediscovery in the Renaissance greatly influenced many modern thinkers from Michel de Montaigne, onward, for Sextus' writings proved to be a treasurehouse of argumentation on all sorts of subjects. Philosophers such as Pierre Gassendi, George Berkeley, and David Hume, among others, used arguments from Sextus in setting forth their own theories. Pierre Bayle contended that modern philosophy began when arguments of Sextus were introduced on the philosophical scene. The arguments of the skeptic continue to stimulate twentieth century minds caught between the power of faith and the faith in power.

DE PRINCIPIIS

Author: Origen (c.185-c.254)
Type of work: Theology and metaphysics
First transcribed: c.220

PRINCIPAL IDEAS ADVANCED

God is incorporeal, the light, the truth, the good; he knows, and is known, as an intellectual being.

The Trinity is eternal; although the Intellectual Principle (Nous) and the Son are eternally generated by God the Father, they are eternal with him.

The conception of the Holy Spirit is Christianity's unique contribution to religious doctrine.

Every creature within the rational structure of the univer e has its position in relation to God as a result of what it merits because of its free action.

Scripture has a threefold meaning: the obvious sense, th? essential meaning, and the spiritual meaning.

At first glance it may be hard for the modern reader to see the relevance to philosophical questions of this central systematic work of Origen. Numerous Scriptural references fill the pages, and it is obvious that Biblical documents comprise for Origen one major test for the correctness of any theological conclusion. Moreover, the theological issues Origen chooses to consider are concerned with peculiarly Christian doctrine. Yet, to the careful reader, one who can disregard the prejudice of modern forms of expression and argument, the basic philosophical importance of Origen can soon become clear.

In the first place, it seems correct to say that Origen is the first major figure in the Christian era who wrote—in Greek—with full philosophical training and with a full sympathy toward philosophical method. Augustine is sometimes given this credit, but the truth is that before him stands Origen, to whom Augustine owes much. The revived interest in medieval philosophy has ultimately brought students back

to a concern with these formative years of the church fathers. In any inquiry into the sources of later philosophy and theology, Origen must be given wide attention. Here is an example of the kind of infusion of Greek philosophical skill into theology which gave Christian thought its unusual theoretical side and has allowed it to develop such close relationships with pagan philosophical interests.

Therefore, as one might suspect, Origen's *De Principiis* (*On the Principles*) subjected him to charges of heresy. The strong philosophical interests and training demonstrated in the past by so many famous theological figures have at times tended to lead them in this direction. If a man feels a strong attraction to philosophy, this is bound to mean that doctrine cannot win at every point. But since the original Greek text of the *De Principiis* has, for the most part, been lost, these charges are difficult to establish. The elaborated Latin translation by Rufinus contains indications that Origen's work was considerably altered in its rendering, and modern scholarship tends to find Origen not so extreme on some points as has sometimes been charged. It will always be of interest to students of the history of philosophy that Plotinus and Origen had the same philosophical teacher, Ammonius Saccas, who is sometimes said to be the founder of Neoplatonism.

Origen begins by establishing the words and teachings of Christ as a central norm, and his fame as a Biblical interpreter is widespread. To develop theological issues along the lines of philosophy, some interpretive scheme had to be devised to make Biblical thought and expression amenable to philosophical treatment. Like many a sophisticated follower of religion, Origen was caught between the rough and untechnical nature of Biblical expression and the abstract nature of technical and systematic analysis. In response, Origen attempted first of all to establish what can be taken as agreed apostolic teaching, since the church of his time provided for him no single unequivocal set of agreed doctrines.

The *Contra Celsum* (*Against Celsus*) is sometimes thought to be more immediately relevant to philosophy, since Origen wrote it during the time of Philip the Arabian to refute the attack against Christianity by the Greek philosopher Celsus. Actually, it is less philosophical in the systematic sense than the *De Principiis*, since it is in the latter work that Origen develops his principal doctrines. The *Contra Celsum* is rather contrived and often shows philosophical reason at its worst, compiling lists of apparently rational arguments in order to overwhelm an opponent's point. It is true that the *De Principiis* is much more inextricably involved with the details of Christian doctrine, but this fact should bother none but the anti-metaphysical readers.

The opening chapter of the first of the four books is titled "On God." Such a starting point must spring from systematic interests, for the Bible contains little direct discussion of the Divine Nature, and none in technical form. Later philosophy agreed with Origen in beginning immediately with a discussion of the divine attributes, until the modern period began to swing the emphasis away from metaphysics. Origen then discusses the second and third persons of the Trinity and gives an account of the origin of sin or defection. After this he considers man as a rational creature and the doctrine of last things, or eschatology. He ends the book by discussing the nature and function of angels, which to contemporary readers will seem the most artificial use of rational argument. In short, what Origen provides is a vast scheme, beginning with God and including all natural creatures in an account of the beginning and end of the world.

Origen is most concerned to prove God to be incorporeal and to deny any possible physical attributes. His love for the immaterial undoubtedly reflects his Platonic training, and Origen also stresses light symbolism in referring to God, another favorite Platonic sign. Like Augustine, Origen uses "God" as a symbol and norm for truth, but he goes on to place God beyond final human comprehension. Like the "Good" of Plato, God is too bright for direct human vision. God's incorporeality, it turns out, has its primary example in the human intellect, which Origen takes to be equally incorporeal in its operation. God is not seen as a corporeal body is seen; he is known, and he knows, as an intellectual being.

When Origen turns to Christology, we see clearly that his conception of divinity in its highest sense is personal, as is not true in Neoplatonism. The personal relationship of the three members of the Trinity is immediately apparent, and Origen establishes the coeternality of the Father and Son, despite the fact that the Son is said to have been "generated." Any Platonic, and especially Neoplatonic, framework can accept eternal generation as an intelligible concept, so that Origen's philosophical background here helps to set the theological orthodoxy. And just as *Nous*, the Intelligible-World (or Principle), in Plotinus is the source of our natural order, containing the seeds and forms of all things, so the primary function of the Son, as Origen sees it, is to be the Second Person, the divine creative agent for the natural world. The world is not eternal and the three members of the Trinity are coequal and personal in nature. This view radically distinguishes Origen and Plotinus from a basic Neoplatonism, despite the many similarities.

The Son is the truth and life of all things which exist, and Origen goes on to argue that there should be a resurrection of the type which the Son in fact undergoes in order to destroy the bond of death placed on men. But the Son is the Word (*Logos*), the intelligible structure of all things, and as such is not subject to sight but can be revealed only to the understanding. The incorporeality of the Son, and God, is again an overriding concern. Origen also takes the classical position in upholding the necessity of creation. God's omnipotence demands a world to govern and so he has no choice but to create a world through the agency of the second person of the Trinity, his Word.

Origen finds the sources for his doctrine of the Son, the divine intellectual and creative agency, in pagan philosophical views. It is interesting, and somewhat startling, to see that he considers, not the doctrine of the Son, but that of the Holy Spirit to be the unique theological idea in Christianity. No pagan before, Origen believes, had conceived of the Holy Spirit; but such teaching is, he feels, in the Bible, both in the Old and the New Testaments. The Holy Bible is the divine agent, and all rational beings, Origen asserts, partake of Reason. This is not a matter of being a Christian or not. As a measure of the importance Origen gives to the Holy Spirit, he believes that a sin committed against the Son can be forgiven but that a sin against the Holy Spirit cannot.

When Origen turns to discuss what a rational nature is, his famous doctrine of the freedom of the will becomes evident. Every rational creature is capable of earning praise or censure; and thus, if men receive censure for sin, it is not because they were incapable of different action. But among rational creatures Origen lists angels and spiritual powers of wickedness along with men. Angels and the powers of wickedness are also fully free to determine their course. Angels are free to fall, and they remain angels only as a reward for contrived choice of the good.

Every creature within the rational structure has its position because of the merit, or demerit, it has earned. The situation of every creature is the result of his own work and movement. Origen is adamant about keeping the responsibility for the fall of the angels, or the sin of man, away from God. No malignant powers were formed by God in creation, although such irrational forces now exist. They have come into being and now plague the world. Through a fall they were converted into wicked beings and that fall resulted from their own choices. Such a power was formerly holy and happy, and from that state of happiness it fell from the time that iniquity was found in it.

Our world is rationally governed, and it contained only good beings at its creation; but those beings were free to choose their own actions; they included powers and angels far stronger than man. Once such divine powers fell, because their chosen iniquity was discovered, then rational man came to have superior forces—both of good and evil—at play upon him. Man is still free to determine his choices, but not in the easy way that existed before the transformation of some good powers into evil. Spotless purity exists in the essential being of none save the Father, Son, and Holy Spirit; it is an accidental quality in every created thing and thus can easily be lost. Yet it lies within ourselves, in our own human actions, to possess either happiness or holiness.

When Origen comes to discuss the end of the world and the ultimate transformation and restoration of all things, he acknowledges immediately that such questions are not subject to strict definition but must take the form of speculative discussion. The Trinity can be set forth in propositional form; but any account of the end of the world can only be conjecture, despite its obvious basis in Scripture. How things will be after such a day is known with certainty only to God.

There is no rational creature that is not capable of both good and evil.

Since not even the devil himself was incapable of good, what we become is the result of our own decisions and not of any inevitable force. But the righteousness of man is only accidental, and it is easy for him to throw it away. Yet God has so constructed the world that no rational creature is compelled by force, against the liberty of his own will, to any course other than that to which the motives of his own mind lead him.

Origen has sketched his position, one which concedes a great deal of the directive powers of each rational individual, but he ends by admitting that his view is only a possible one. Let each reader, he says, determine for himself whether any one of the views he argues can be adopted or not. Origen trusts reason a great deal, and he makes every question of theology a matter for rational discussion; but he does not believe his conclusions to be unavoidable or inevitable.

Perhaps Origen's greatest ability is shown by the way in which he treats Scripture's place in theological argument, a particularly interesting problem in view of his obvious attachment to philosophy and to rational argument on all points. The authority of Scripture as a norm must first be agreed to, Origen says, and in that sense argument is prior to the Scripture's authority. Thus, he first set down the *reasons* which lead us to regard them as divine writings. The wide conversions to Christianity, he argues, attest to the special significance of its Scriptures. Origen argues for the deity of Christ, and thus for the divine inspiration of the Scripture which prophesied Him, so that the authority of Scripture in theology really rests upon the prior acceptance of the divinity of Christ.

Scripture is not obviously authoritative for Origen, but it becomes so for those who are convinced of Jesus' divine authority, and one can be convinced through a process of reasoning.

Scripture hides the splendor of its doctrines in common and unattractive phraseology, and the inability to see through this is one of the most frequent reasons for rejecting Scriptural passages as valid points in an argument. Thus the central problem is to state the manner in which Scripture is to be read and understood, since its validity is not immediately obvious. Here Origen introduces his famous distinction of the "spiritual meaning" as opposed to the interpretation according to the "mere letter." Origen finds certain mystical economies in the Scriptures, but to see these the words must be properly interpreted. Each individual, Origen insists, ought to receive the threefold meaning of Scripture: first, the obvious sense; second, the "soul," or essential meaning of the words; and third, the hidden wisdom or mystery of God contained in a "spiritual" meaning.

There are, then, esoteric and exoteric meanings in Scripture, and one cannot easily tell which of the three meanings will best fit a passage. Some men are better interpreters of Scripture than others and can divine the esoteric meanings of certain important passages, but the exoteric meaning is easily available, even to simple folk. This being so, not all Scriptural accounts need to be factual. That is not their purpose. Interwoven in the historical accounts are reports of events which did not occur, some which could not have happened, and some which could have happened but did not. The Biblical documents are not a pure history of events but were intended to convey meaning and truth on a threefold level, according to the scheme Origen has sketched. They reveal facts about the divine intention which no mere record of events could convey.

Many Biblical accounts cannot be believed literally—for example, God walking in paradise in the evening—and when this is so, one knows that a deeper meaning must be sought beneath the literal phrase. Such being the case, the Biblical documents are, in themselves, no simple authoritative norm in theological debate, for their normative value depends upon the prior working out, and acceptance of, a rational framework for interpreting the literature. Were the Bible to be taken literally, Origen argues, it would be incredibly irrational. Yet the passages which are true in their historical meaning are much more numerous than those which are interspersed with a purely spiritual signification. The exact reader must be careful to ascertain how far the literal meaning is true, and how far it is impossible. Certainly this places the ultimate norm in the rational judgment of the individual interpreter, since there is nothing obviously literal to compel him.

Thus Origen sets Scripture into a rational framework, making it possible to use it in support of rational theological discussion. A modern reader may at first miss the philosophical importance of Origen's analysis in the De Principiis. It is more the way in which Origen treats his material than the material itself that is philosophical. Furthermore, if Origen's approach to Scriptural authority is basically rational, his philosophical interests can be seen even more clearly in his stress upon the freedom of the will. For this is not basically a religious problem but one which a philosophical instinct might regard as important to theological doctrine. Classical philosophy had not laid a great stress on the question of freedom; the contemporary importance of the problem of man's freedom stems from the movement of philosophical minds, such as Origen's, into a religious context which stresses the relation between a creating, ordaining God and all rational beings. Origen's

philosophical background makes him sense that rational independence for man depends upon establishing some form of freedom of the will as the basis of independence from God's action. Such independence also solves the theological problem of God's responsibility for sin, which the religious doctrine stresses; and the result is to give to the question of freedom of the will a place of new importance for all succeeding philosophy.

ENNEADS

Author: Plotinus (c.204-c.270)
Type of work: Metaphysics
First transcribed: c. 256

PRINCIPAL IDEAS ADVANCED

Reality is one, and the source of all being is the One, the Divine Unity.
From the One emanates the Divine Mind (Nous), the Intellectual Principle.
The Divine Mind, in turn, spends the creative force of the One in giving rise to the Divine Soul.
The One, Nous, and the Soul make up the Divine Trinity.
While lost in the contemplation of the One, the Soul desires to return to its source of being, but in turning away from the One, it creates a lower (and hence, less perfect) order of souls and material objects by forming matter according to the Ideas of the Intellectual Principle.

Only in recent years has the full importance of Plotinus been widely recognized. Previously, Neoplatonism, of which Plotinus is the greatest representative, and Platonism had not been clearly distinguished. Lacking the original writings to compare, the Middle Ages blended the two forms of thought together without a clear notion of their distinctive qualities. Historical research and the availability of

the sources themselves have produced a growing awareness of the distinctiveness of Plotinus' thought and of his unique contributions in the *Enneads.* Its intimate connection with the Platonic tradition is readily admitted by Plotinus himself, but such closeness in origin need not mean similarity, as Plato's famous student Aristotle made clear.

In a strict sense the *Enneads* are unsystematic. Neither Porphyry's ordering of the scattered writings nor scholarly reconstruction of possible temporal sequence can make the writings form any strictly logical order. Plotinus discussed with his students a few very central philosophical problems, each of which he returned to many times, and the *Enneads* represent in content but not in form the consistency of this continual development of certain central themes.

Plotinus' metaphysical interest in the problems of the one and the many is well known, but his central interest in ethics and his fully developed aesthetic theory, which is one of the first to be elaborated, are not always so widely recognized. Most important of all, however, are Plotinus' explorations into philosophical psychology. The soul is central in all Plotinian thought, and he was the first major writer to put the analysis of the soul at the center of philosophical investigation.

The soul in Plato's world held an important place, and Plato devoted considerable time to describing it (in the *Republic* and the *Phaedrus*). Yet somehow "soul" was never reconciled with "form" as a metaphysical principle. Plotinus began where Plato left off, making soul central; and the analysis of it is more direct and extended than Plato's mythical framework could allow. Despite the importance of Plato both as to the problems Plotinus treated and as to style, what many are surprised to find upon reading Plotinus is the large amount of Aristotelianism present, as well as a wide variety of other views. In some sense, Plotinus began with Platonic problems, but his scope takes in almost all previous philosophy.

Just as Plato had a strong interest in sense perception, so also Plotinus was led by the problems of sense perception to consider the soul as of first importance. Soul is intimately related to the body and clearly is combined with it. After considering most known theories of the soul, Plotinus went on to make the soul more perfect than the body in virtue of the soul's greater unity. Soul centralizes perception and is not subject to physical division as the body is.

In Plotinus' philosophy, sensation is only the beginning of knowledge. Above that stands the soul's grasp of intelligible forms. Sensation is dependent upon the soul's close association with a physical body; but, since the soul in virtue of its greater unity stands higher in the order of being than the body, its grasp of intelligible form indicates that something in turn stands above it in the ontological order. This is the Intellectual-Principle, the locus of the intelligible forms of all things and of the principle of thought itself. This principle, which is superior to the soul, is often called the Divine Mind, since it exemplifies the union of universal thought with all of the intelligible forms of thought. This is a level of unity which exceeds that possessed by the soul, just as the soul surpasses that of the physical world.

Physical body, as it looks away from soul's guidance, tends to become sheer disorganized matter; on the other hand, as the body is subject to the soul's direction, it exemplifies harmony and order to the highest degree possible for it. As the soul's attention is absorbed by physical matter, it tends to forget itself and to be overcome with sensual desires; it goes out of itself seeking a multitude of things. But when the soul considers the Intellectual-Principle above it, then it tends to be drawn away from physical concerns and to regain its original and essential integrity, absorbed in contemplation.

The Intellectual-Principle when considered in relation to soul appears as the rational structure of our world order, but in itself it is sheer intellection, involved with no motion or change and retaining no distinction except that between thought and object. All, then, has been hierarchically arranged in the Plotinian metaphysical scheme, beginning with the soul and ascending and descending according to the degree of unity. As far removed from the multiplicity of the physical world as the Intellectual-Principle is, it still embodies the necessity of at least a distinction between thought and its object, as well as the distinctions between the various intellectual forms themselves.

Since unity has operated all along the way to delineate the various structures, Plotinus found himself driven to seek Unity itself, beyond even the division between thought and its object. Such a first principle Plotinus called the One (sometimes the Good), and it stands at the pinnacle of the hierarchy as Unity itself, from which all of the lower gradations of unity are in turn derived. These three central principles, One, Intellectual-Principle, and Soul (body is not given equal status), are nowhere simply defined, but they are refined through constant reference throughout the writings.

Evil was both a moral and a metaphysical problem for Plotinus. The deficiencies which the individual finds in this world are precisely what drove him to seek an order of existence higher than this world. Contrary to much popular opinion, Plotinus did not despise this world. Rather, he regarded the world as the fullest expression of beauty above. The natural world holds all the perfection that its lower order allows, and as such it is the very embodiment and evidence of that from which it descends, its higher origin. Yet this is not necessarily a temporal origin, since Plotinus never questioned the fact that the world is eternal. It is "origin" in the sense of the dependence of the lower orders upon the higher for the power of their existence.

Metaphysically speaking, evil was difficult for Plotinus. Since all must be accounted for by means of one principle which is without defect, the problem is to show how what is essentially perfect can eventually become bad. Plotinus did this through the image of gradually diminishing light and through increasing multiplicity. What is in itself One and perfect (the Divine Unity) as it goes out from itself to create lower orders, becomes in the process increasingly multiple and less perfect, until its final outreach is sheer matter (the negative of being), its moral equivalent, evil.

But the process which leads down from the One to the creation of matter and evil also leads upward. The soul, by looking to itself and discovering its essentially higher nature through its essential difference from its body, grasps the basic distinction which can lead it away from matter toward matter's perfect and unitary source. Seeing the gradations of unity represented in the various levels, the soul may rise by intelligence to the intelligible world and then beyond it, at least momentarily, to the One beyond intellectual distinctions.

247

The description of the One itself, of course, was an even more difficult problem for Plotinus than accounting for matter and evil. No explanation of evil is ultimately possible in a world which is eternal and whose structure is necessary. But the description of the One is of necessity baffling, and both Plotinus and his interpreters have been painfully aware of this fact. The One as the first principle of all transcends all multiplicity and therefore all distinctions, whereas an intellectual grasp depends upon the presence of at least a minimum of distinction.

Thus, the One may be approached and may be grasped, but neither directly nor intellectually. Here the famous "negative method" comes to its fullest classical use. We may deny qualities inappropriately attributed to the One more easily than we can say what its characteristics are. Indirectly, from the process of denial and of paring away, we come to some grasp of the One, but this is not a discursive understanding. Such an apprehension does not induce conversation, and Plotinus said that if we are tempted to speak about the One, to give it a set of positive characteristics, then silence is more appropriate.

This difficulty leads to what is often called Plotinus' "mysticism." And if the term is used carefully, it is quite accurate as applied to the Plotinian view. Plotinus was not needlessly vague, and surely he did not belittle the powers of reason. Everything discerned is grasped through reason's light. Yet above reason's highest level stands a more ultimate realm, the source of intelligence and all below it, a realm not itself subject to the distinctions which reason requires for its operation.

Not that the One is empty (such a thought must wait for a later time); the One is the source of all below it, containing the power of all but without itself being any single thing.

The ethical aims of Plotinus were high. Having devised this hierarchical scheme of the nature of things, each level determined by the multiplicity of its distance from the One, the goal then becomes to raise the soul in its considerations to the highest possible level. To do this, however, in some sense means that the knower must himself become the very level he contemplates. The soul ceases to be like the indefinite multiplicity below and actually becomes what it finds above it. Thus the soul tends not only to become good as it turns from matter and evil; it becomes god-like. Thus, the soul recovers the "essential man."

Beauty has a part in this conversion from the lower to the higher, and Plotinus here admitted his dependence on Plato's analysis of the use of beauty in the *Phaedrus*. The apprehension of beauty draws the soul upward, reminding it of its true self and of the higher levels open to it. Beauty represents purity, and the truly happy and virtuous life is not a thing of mixture; it is an unchanging state. By its nature beauty is present where a diversity has become a unity, which is why the pleasure derived from such beauty is itself essentially an unchanging state.

The whole process is not an easy one. It requires training and discipline. We must learn to cut away and to detach ourselves from multiple concerns. Not that they are in themselves bad or that beauty is not found in the multiplicity of the natural order, but the soul has become aware of something higher and more perfect that is possible to attain. Trained properly, the soul requires no guide for the last steps. The soul that wants the vision of beauty must first make itself beautiful through discipline and order. Action and effort are preparation for achieving a level beyond act. The Good, which is Plotinus' other name for the One, is self-sufficient, and through virtuous effort we also reach a level of essential rest.

Despite the absolute determinism of the natural structure as a whole which is eternal and without alternative, Plotinus still allowed for an area of freedom in human affairs. Some causation is due to environmental factors, but some causes originate from the soul, and this is the area of self-determination. Like Spinoza after him, Plotinus defined a free act as essentially one which springs from the individual's own nature, neither reflecting outside forces nor representing accidental features. It is the soul's clear vision of its own essential nature. Here the soul is guided by the Reason Principle above it, so that fate (freedom's opposite) prevails when action is contrary to reason. Thus Plotinus stands within the tradition: freedom means self-determination guided by rational apprehension of the structure of things.

In the Intellectual Principle above the soul no spatial distinction can be found, no division, no incompleteness. It is a living intellection as one act within a unity, whereas the soul's intellection is a more multiple and temporal affair. In keeping with the classical idea of perfection, any widespread activity would represent defeat. The various ontological levels are thus characterized by a decreasing activity as well

as by an increasing unity the nearer we move toward the One. Not that all activity is missing, but it here becomes fully realized activity.

The inequality within the natural world and the inequality of the various ontological orders all are necessary. They are, in fact, the best expression possible to the One. Gradations and completeness of every possible kind from highest to lowest, from best to worst, are the fullest expression possible for the One as the first principle of all things. Its fullness requires expression, and the widest possible variety actually expresses its perfection best. In this way Plotinus justified the presence of evil in a world which is essentially of good origin. Individual objects or events may be bad, but viewed as a part of the total panorama their place can be seen to be within a necessarily good order.

Following Plato's suggestion in the *Timaeus*, Plotinus developed the view that the natural order is like an organism. As unity "fissures out," it reaches out to the farthermost extent of things and yet embraces all in one system; but with all its differentiation it is still one organized living thing. Not everything can be equal; there must be levels from the highest to the lowest, but the overall scheme is that of the natural order as a living, self-sustaining organism.

In considering love, Plotinus made it clear that, once one has discovered the basic ontological levels and gained control over himself through discipline, there is no reason why the beauties of the natural order may not be enjoyed. Viewed properly as the descendants of yet higher orders, natural beauties may be instructive and are not to be shunned. The usual picture of Plotinus as an ascetic and as rejecting the everyday world is not accurate. One must study and discipline himself for metaphysical insight; but, although the levels above the soul are to be preferred, the natural world and human life are to be enjoyed fully as representing the best possible expression of those higher principles.

"Matter" is perhaps Plotinus' most pressing problem in his effort to see the natural order as good and as being the best expression of the One. Matter seems to be opaque and surd, and the very opposite of the light which represents the One. But Plotinus argued that, although matter is responsible for much evil and distortion, it is necessary to the One's essentially good production, since it furnishes a base for the imprinting of forms. Without matter the world would be insubstantial. Thus, despite its difficult properties, matter is necessary. As necessary to the order, it is in that sense good. This is not so much to explain matter as being in itself good as it is to account for it as necessary to the whole and as being good only in that indirect sense.

In accounting for time Plotinus foreshadows Augustine's famous discussion of time in the *Confessions*. The Intellectual-Principle is not temporal, although time lies, so to speak, self-concentrated there. Soul, on the other hand, must by nature move and produce, and thus soul's activity is the essential origin for time. This is not the soul perceived as a cosmic principle produced immediately by the Intellectual-Principle; this is soul as it turns away from its origin to produce physical structures below it. In the process of producing the other orders below it, soul clothes itself with time. If soul

withdrew and turned itself entirely toward its primal unity, time would once again disappear.

Augustine's dependence upon Plotinus for his doctrine of time is one major illustration of the now recognized importance of Plotinus for all medieval philosophy and theology. Since Plato's own writings were unavailable, Plotinus was accepted as the representative of Platonism, with no distinction drawn between Platonism and Neoplatonism. Augustine's debt to Plotinus is heavy, as Augustine acknowledges. Through Plotinus the Neoplatonic strain became extremely influential, particularly since it formed such a natural background for the rapidly developing Christian doctrine. For instance, Plotinus' ontology is based on a trinitarian concept, although the doctrine developed by Christian theologians differs from it in detail.

Spinoza and Hegel are also much in Plotinus' debt, so that in this sense much modern thought is his heir. Wherever soul is stressed as a prime object of philosophical analysis, there is a strong kinship to Plotinus. Wherever reason is powerful but is ultimately to be transcended, there rational mysticism begins and owes a debt to Plotinus. Whenever men are urged to seek their authentic existence and to turn back from multiple pursuits, the philosophical psychology and the metaphysics of Plotinus are not far away.

Contrary to some popular opinion, Plato actually stressed the practical application of philosophy, together with the constant necessity to blend practical skill with philosophical insight. Plato had his moments as a visionary, but when we turn to Plotinus we find that the whole direction of thought is

250

turned this way. Plato described his realm of forms in their perfection, but Plotinus' almost lyrical praise for the purity and repose of his Intellectual-Principle is unrestrained and unqualified. Toward this vision all thought bends, and it is not modified as it is for Plato by the necessity for return to the practical world. Plotinus knew that that vision cannot be sustained, but the return to the sense world is simply a necessity; it is never a goal.

Ethically, then, Plotinus had a single direction: upward and beyond this world's structure. But it would be false to say that this unrelieved goal involves a disparagement of the natural world. Plotinus did not disdain ordinary affairs. He loved nature, but only for what it could tell him about the source of all things and for the guidance it could provide for transcending it.

This is why the apprehension of beauty is such a stirring phenomenon for a Plotinian. Such experience is a taste here of the realm beyond being which the soul seeks. And the sense of beauty is a natural guide in detecting and in separating the higher from the lower orders within nature. Such a sensitivity to hierarchy is absolutely essential, since it is by establishing orders and levels that the mind is able to orient itself and to discern realms even beyond the natural order.

Thus the lover is very close to the philosopher, and philosophy's classical definition (the love of wisdom) fits Plotinus almost perfectly. Plato's *Phaedrus* is important here. Plotinus, like his revered predecessor, found in the phenomenon of love a philosophical key. The philosopher is stirred by love and moved by beauty; both of these experiences teach him to discern the higher from the lower in nature's

sphere. Evil is not a question at this point. The natural tendency under the influence of beauty is away from evil's home (matter) and toward beauty's source, the intellectual sphere.

In a rationalistic age, we tend to think of all structures as basically the same and as subject to the same general conditions. Plato described a world of forms different from our world, but Plotinus carried this transcendental tendency much further. In the ascent which the apprehension of beauty has launched, what we soon discover is that each level has laws of its own, until we come finally to the One itself, where even the law of identity does not hold. Below this the Intellectual-Principle has been found to be free of all distinctions, whereas division and partition are the essential elements of every lower order. To learn to read Plotinus is to stretch the mind's natural habits and to learn to think and visualize in new ways. Contrast is the proper method: bodies are exclusively many; the Supreme is exclusively one.

In some genuine sense Plotinus was an evolutionist. That is, since his theory was based upon levels each of which is different in kind from the others, his primary task was to explain how the levels are related; that is, how each lower order came from a higher principle. Plotinus' theory differs from modern evolutionary theory in that this succession is not a temporal affair. The world and all its orders were, for Plotinus, eternal. But each order is derived constantly from its superior, so that if each ontological realm exhibits basically different properties, then an evolutionary theory is required to show how something generated by one level can become unlike its origin

251

in kind. This is also the modern evolutionist's problem.

In some sense this continual attempt to trace the evolutionary cycle, now upward, now downward, is the substance of much of the *Enneads*. Beginning with the soul, Plotinus tried to explain how it could generate something different and inferior to it—physical body. Then the movement of the discourse turns upward to account for the soul's generation by the Intellectual-Principle. Finally, we reach the One, the logical terminus which the delineation of the various realms below requires.

What the modern reader gains from Plotinus is a feeling for the necessary dialectical movement between qualitatively different realms. This constant passage from the One to the Intellectual-Principle and then to the soul takes place all the while a multitude of traditional ethical and epistemological questions are being discussed. Yet, underneath this constant recovering of old ground, the picture of the Plotinian world gradually emerges crystal clear. The reader begins to see how, within such a framework as Plotinus has constructed, Plotinus could hope to deal with practical questions successfully.

In a basic sense, the Plotinian view is a contemplative one, although for reasons already explained it is incorrect to infer from this any aversion to everyday life. In addition to his contemplative quality, Plotinus was surely also speculative. He did not claim to know his doctrines with finality, but he attempted an answer to all of philosophy's most fundamental and comprehensive problems. The scope is breathtaking; and, even in an age not given to the grander views, to grasp what Plotinus saw is still an exhilarating experience that gives life and energy to the philosophical quest.

CONFESSIONS

Author: Saint Augustine (Aurelius Augustinus, 354-430)
Type of work: Theology, metaphysics (religious autobiography)
First transcribed: c.397

PRINCIPAL IDEAS ADVANCED

How can an eternal God be the cause of anything evil?

God is not the cause of evil, for evil has no genuine existence; evil is the absence of the good, the corruption of possibilities, as in the human will.

Only the parts of creation, not the whole, can partake of evil, the privation of the good.

By faith the corruption of the human will is cured.

The question as to what God was doing before he created the world is a senseless question, since "before" the creation would make sense only if God had not created time; God's creative acts are not in time.

The greatest theologian of the disintegrating ancient Roman world, St. Augustine, came to Christian faith partly "from the outside" after a trying spiritual and intellectual pilgrimage. His *Confessions* recounts episodes from a restless life finally blessed by religious peace and certainty. The work opens and closes with ardent praise for God's goodness and mercy. This unique literary classic constitutes a kind of autobiography whose details achieve significance only in the focus of a deeply experienced conversion. After the conversion everything is seen from a new perspective.

The book is the first and most universally read of its special kind of literature. Examples of this type of literature in the modern world are probably best found in aspects of the novel and in straightforward autobiographies. No other Christian writing of its kind has so influenced despairing persons or suggested so wide a range of psychological insights into the human quest after religious meaning in existence. Augustine writes of guilt and forgiveness from the vantage point of one who, threatened by the apparent worthlessness of life and haunted by a terrifying realization of the nature of human egoism, overcomes anxiety through a self-authenticating faith in the Christ of the Cross. In a world of chaos and impending destruction this faith speaks out joyously and compellingly in the *Confessions*.

The psychology of human belief is such that, given any series of experiences, men can reinterpret the significance of any of the earlier items in the light of any later ones. Likewise, men can judge the significance of any later experience in terms of an earlier one. Men's judgments about what is impor-

tant in their experiences need not follow a simple chronological ordering. Augustine writes like a man who obviously judges that an item in his experience is not only centrally crucial but, in some sense, is finally so. He reports this conversion experience in Book VIII of his *Confessions*. The significance of all items of his experience is to be decided in relation to his achievement of God's "grace"; but *that* experience is final, self-authenticating and in principle beyond any possibility of doubt or reinterpretation. That experience is the standard measure of value. Consequently, Augustine's conversion to the Christian faith leads him to reconsider even selected aspects of his earlier life in its light. Among these are his childhood sins including a youthful theft of some pears; his strong sexual appetites which involved him with concubines and produced an illegitimate son; his philosophical "errors" prior to the discovery of his Christian "truth"; and his relations with a beloved Christian mother and half-pagan father.

The *Confessions* includes confidential admissions of a man who seems preoccupied with the problem of human guilt, even inordinately so. Augustine's association of Christian faith with sexual abstinence explains the extent of his guilt-feelings though, of course, it does not explain the Christian emphasis on asceticism. So difficult and austere a standard of human conduct, once applied in human practice, may well cause even earlier slight transgressions to appear momentous. Such reasoning may well enable an unsympathetic reader to understand Augustine's otherwise puzzling concern about a childish theft of pears. Given a Christian belief in the basic sinfulness

253

of human acts, even seemingly trivial actions may take on great personal significance—since formerly trivial items making up a great part of a man's personal life will be those very ones over which a convinced Christian will think he should have control. It is as if Augustine wants to say to his readers following his conversion: How sinful man really is may be learned from an examination of seemingly unimportant acts of mine, including those of my childhood.

Two major currents dominate the predominately autobiographical books of the *Confessions* (Books I through IX). One current is an apologetic account of Augustine's intellectual search after comprehension or wisdom among some of the important "schools" popular in fourth century Roman civilization. The other is a current of continuous intellectual rootlessness—a sense of "being taken in" by a philosophical position which proves only temporarily satisfying. There is a description of the reasoned effort to understand the meaning of human existence in philosophical terms which goes side by side with the experienced failure of each tentatively grasped solution. The certainty for which Augustine thirsts is not, we soon learn, to be found in philosophy alone. Faith, and only Christian faith, is able to bring certainty, but the intellectual restlessness continues even after conversion. This restlessness receives serious attention in the contents of Books X through XIII. Nonetheless, even the philosophical quest has altered. Where previously faith was to be judged by reason, now reason is to be employed in a context involving faith.

Augustine's intellectual and spiritual quest lasted from his nineteenth until his thirty-third year. At that age he ex-perienced total conversion to Christianity. He tells how, reading from Cicero, he earlier became interested in religious issues and even turned to the Scriptures without understanding; he "was not such as could enter into it, or stoop my neck to follow its steps." He turned next to the astrologers, hoping in some material mode to discover deity. In the process he became obsessed by the problem of evil.

Teacher of rhetoric, he came to Carthage and, while "for this space of nine years . . . we lived seduced and seducing, deceived and deceiving in divers lusts," sought intellectual clarification among the Manichees, a group of men who thought a kind of divine knowledge was possible. He became disillusioned by a Manichee spokesman, who proved unable to put some of Augustine's doubts to rest and was judged adversely by the seeker. From Carthage, Augustine traveled to Rome. He did this against his mother's entreaties. In Rome he was temporarily attracted to the philosophical Academics, whose chief ability was criticism and whose philosophical tenets tended toward skepticism. Still concerned about evil—which he thought of as a kind of substance—Augustine became a catechumen in the Catholic Church. Moving to Milan, where he was at last joined by his mother, and continuing to live with the concubine who bore him a son, Augustine worried about evil, became attracted to the Platonic philosophers who sensed the ultimate unity of Being, heard St. Ambrose preach, and after a trying emotional episode was converted to Christianity.

The remainder of the *Confessions* is devoted to discussions of specific religious and philosophical topics. Three problems dominate the later books.

One is the problem of evil, which had proved such a stumbling block to Augustine's acceptance of the Christian faith. Two others are time and memory, discussed in Books X and XI, respectively. Divorced from the autobiographical nature of the earlier books, Books X through XIII contain some of the most significant of Augustine's intellectual reflections. These books indicate the extensiveness of Augustine's intellectual questioning following his emotional conversion. These books also discuss the Biblical notion of the creation of the world, as well as the ways in which Scripture may be interpreted. Only Augustine's treatments of evil, time, and memory can receive consideration in the remainder of this analysis.

Because the Christian faith requires beliefs which do not always seem to meet the demands of reason, Augustine's anguished effort to understand the origin and nature of evil proved a persistent one. His first step involved denying the Manichean dualism which made God finite and evil an objective reality. If evil were real, then God as the cause of all created things would have to contain positive evil. Intellectually, a part of Augustine's development here resulted from his reading of Platonist writers. God is to be viewed as eternal rather than as infinite. Therefore, no spatial or temporal being could be God. Yet the problem of evil remained. How can an eternal God as creator of a temporal-spatial order produce anything evil? The demands of the Christian faith permitted only one solution—the denial that evil is a substance, a genuinely objective existent.

Augustine later confesses: "And I sought 'whence is evil,' and sought in an evil way; and saw not the evil in my very search." There can be no positive evil in the world, according to Augustine's final position on the matter. There is corruption, of course. This includes the corruption of man's will. Yet the perversion of the human will is a human responsibility. God cannot be seen as the cause of such perversion. Corruption is rather the absence of good, a privation and a lack rather than a positively existing thing. It is the failure of parts of the system of Creation to harmonize for which God is not causally responsible. It is doubtful that Augustine's "solution" of the problem of evil is a clearly rational one. Rather it seems to follow from the need of faith to discover a satisfactory position which will not involve denial of God's immutability. Whatever has been caused by God to exist must be good. Evil cannot therefore possess a positive existence. It must be treated as an absence of positive goodness. Because God is a creator —though not of a universe *in* time, since there could have been no time prior to the world's existence—his immutability and absolute goodness exclude the possibility that anything could be evil from God's perspective. The parts alone and not the whole of Creation can include evil even as privation. If one's faith demands the denial of genuinely existing evil, clearly, then, whatever corruption may exist results from man's will. This corruption is to be cured, for Augustine, by faith in "my inmost Physician." A position which he defends in other writings is that which argues that God's foreknowledge of events is not incompatible with human freedom; God's foreknowledge of how men will act is not the cause of such action.

Yet Augustine's mental inquiry continued long after his conversion. The philosopher in him would not completely give way to faith. One example is his discussion of the human memory. Although inconclusive, this discussion raises a number of fascinating questions about the phenomena of human mental activity. The fact of faith is that Augustine loves his God. But *what* is it which he loves? He knows this is a unique kind of love, but he desires some clear notion of the nature of its object. He does not love bodily beauty, light, melodies, harmony of time, or the earth, when he loves God. What then can he love? The earth answers when asked: "I am not he"; and heaven, moon, sun, and other created bodies reply only: "He made us." Yet Augustine is certain he loves something when he loves God— "a kind of light, melody, fragrance, meat, embracement of my inner man." Eventually, he seeks the answer within his own consciousness. "And behold, in me there present themselves to me soul, and body, one without, the other within." God made his body, which is the corporeal aspect of his manhood. But his body cannot tell him what he loves when he loves God. It must then be the soul ("mind") by which Augustine can love his God. Mental activity must be the means by which one can know the object of his love in loving God; yet God must exist "beyond" one's own mind. This concern with mental activity ("soul") leads Augustine into his puzzlement over memory.

The memory enables Augustine to recall images rather at will, including images of the different separate senses (touch, hearing, and so forth). He can also recall items from his past personal life. He can combine these images freshly as well as consider future contingent possibilities. "Great is the force of this memory, excessive great, O my God"; so great, Augustine concludes, that it appears bottomless. Though it is by memory that Augustine knows whatever he does know, yet he cannot comprehend the full extent of his self. "Therefore is the mind too strait to contain itself." But how can one get into his own mind? Whatever is known mentally as an image came originally through the senses, as Augustine knows well. Yet he now remembers images even in the dark which are not the objects originally sensed. The memory is also an active capacity which knows reasons, laws, and numbers. It is capable of cognition. His memory recalls notions of truth and falsity. It also contains emotions like desire, joy, fear, and sorrow —which are the four great perturbations of the mind. He knows what he recognizes in naming memory but only by virtue of that which he names. Puzzlingly, Augustine even remembers forgetfulness. Augustine argues that remembering God is much like rummaging in the memory for something temporarily seeming to be lacking and finally saying: "This is it." But one, remembering, can never say, "This is it," unless it is somehow a remembered thing which has been temporarily forgotten. "What then we have utterly forgotten, though lost, we cannot even seek after."

Seeking God in the memory is, for Augustine, something like seeking happiness, if indeed they are not the same. But in seeking, men are "looking" for *something*. If the mind is essential to this search, then *what* is sought after must be like something once known but now forgotten. To say that God resides in memory is to assert that God can be known through the agency of mental activity. Yet God cannot reside in a specific part of memory. It is ultimately a mystery. Loving God is like seeking happiness. The soul ("mind") is nonetheless often tempted to seek knowledge of the object of its love through the senses. But it is obvious that what the eye, ear, nose, tongue, and fingers sense are specific things—bodily things—greatly unlike God. A mind-body dualism is characteristic of Augustine's thought. Though bodily things may be aspects of God's Creation, they are not God. Mental phenomena must be the means by which men can know God. Strangely, however, men do not always love God, at least not consciously. Yet God must somehow reside in memory even when men's mental activities are not searching for him. Coming to know God suggests a discovery. Augustine's moving words express this: "Too late loved I Thee, O Thou beauty of ancient days, yet ever new! too late I loved thee!"

The nature of time also puzzles Augustine. This puzzlement arises partly from Augustine's belief that in some sense God created the world from nothing. Yet on the view that time may be infinite, having no beginning or end, a skeptic may ask what God was doing before he created the world. Augustine refuses to commit himself to the notion of a finitely created spatial-temporal world. If time is infinite, then the world is equally so; and both time and the world yet exist as created by God. God's creative act stands "outside" time. God is therefore eternal rather than infinite. This view probably stems from Plato's influence. As eternal, God contains neither spatial

nor temporal parts. God exists in an eternal "present," possessing neither pastness nor futurity.

Augustine attempts to show how this view can prove meaningful through an analysis of the psychology of human time. Men speak of things as past, present, and future. Clearly, the past and future are in some sense nonexistent. They are *not* except in relation to some present. The past is finished and done with; the future is not yet here. Time moves only relative to some present measuring unit. What and where is this present for men? The present as a unit of measurement can in itself have no parts. Yet no unit of time is in principle removed from the possibility of further subdivision. But this suggests that one spatializes time. Yet even the man who is aware of time-movement can measure such movement only in a present. This present cannot itself be measured while operating as the necessary norm of measurement. Analogous to this human present, though absolutely unique, is God's eternity, God's present. Augustine "sees" an eternal God as involving a timeless present containing no temporal subdivisions whatever. God contains all possible reality and yet has neither past nor future. This view is related to Augustine's belief that God has complete knowledge of events, including historical ones—as if all events are somehow immediately, non-temporally available to God.

Speculations like these, plus many others, occur throughout Augustine's *Confessions*. However indecisive is Augustine's handling of such items, they help to make his book the unique work it is.

THE CITY OF GOD

Author: Saint Augustine (Aurelius Augustinus, 354-430)
Type of work: Theology
First transcribed: c. 413-426

PRINCIPAL IDEAS ADVANCED

The essential nature of man is will, and no man wills the true God to be god unless he is touched by Divine Grace.

Theology is faith seeking understanding; man has faith in order that he may understand.

History has at its beginning the Creation; at its center, Christ, and, as its consummation, the judgment and transformation.

Because God had foreknowledge, he knew that man's will would be misdirected and that evil would thereby come into the world; but he also knew that through his grace good could be brought from evil.

History is divided by two cities formed by alternative loves: the earthly city by the love of self, and the heavenly city by the love of God.

It has been held that the whole of Christian thought may be seen as variations on the essential positions of two men—St. Augustine and St. Thomas Aquinas. This contention is closely related to another—that the history of philosophy is wisely seen as variations on the work of Plato and Aristotle. It is inevitable that when a religious thinker expresses the content of his faith he will use the most appropriate words, concepts, and even systems available in his culture. Consequently, St. Augustine was a Platonist, St. Thomas was an Aristotelian. Any attempt to gloss over this fundamental difference between these two leading theologians of Christendom is to pervert both.

It was St. Thomas in the thirteenth century who was most influential in establishing Aristotelian empiricism, thereby establishing a momentous division between philosophy and theology. This was quite different from the complete separation of the two to which the Protestant Reformation came in opposing the Roman Catholic synthesis. St. Thomas held that there were certain areas unique to each discipline, while other matters could be properly understood from either perspective. The Trinity and Incarnation, for example, could be known only through revelation; the nature of the empirical world was properly the jurisdiction of philosophy, almost perfectly understood by Aristotle. But God's existence, and to a certain extent his nature, could be known either through revelation or by the processes of natural reason, operating on sense perception. Thus natural theology was strongly defended as a legitimate discipline and a fitting handmaiden of the Church.

St. Augustine, however, writing eight centuries before, drew his inspiration from Plato, strongly tempered by the theology of St. Paul. For Plato, "knowledge" through the senses was inferior to intuitive knowledge, that knowledge of the essential nature of all things without which men perceive only dim shadows in a darkened cave. Coupled with this Platonic distrust of the senses was St. Augustine's preoccupation with the problem of evil and his own personal problems of morality. At first this concern had driven him to the position of Manicheanism, that philosophy holding to a metaphysical dualism of good and evil, and to the inherent evil of matter. Disillusioned by the naïveté of its spokesmen, Augustine turned to Neoplatonism, finding there a suitable explanation of evil in terms of a theistic universe, intuitively understood. "I found there," he said, "all things but one—the *Logos* made flesh."

The significance of this omission rested in Augustine's common confession with St. Paul—"I can will what is right, but I cannot do it. For I do not do the good I want, but the evil I do not want is what I do. . . . Wretched man that I am! Who will deliver me from this body of death?" Truth is not a matter simply of knowledge but of action; to anticipate the existentialists, the problem is not knowing the truth but living the truth. With this awareness came Augustine's baptism of Neoplatonism into the Christian *Weltanschauung*—the result has been called a complete break with all previous understandings of man.

Against the Greek philosophers, Augustine insisted that to know the truth is not necessarily to do the truth, for the essential nature of man is not reason but will. Man is so created that he has no option but to love, to orient his being to some object, principle, person, with an ultimate devotion. This supreme object willed by each person characterizes his total being,

giving to him his presuppositions, motivations, rationale, vitality, and goal. There is no man without such a faith, "religion," "god." One does not reason *to* such an object, but reasons *from* it. No man believes in the true God, the God of moral demand, unless he wills so to do; but no amount of persuasion can change an unwilling will. Since man is essentially self-centered, he will always will something other than the true God to be god—man will create god in his own image. Only when man is touched by Divine Grace can he will God alone as true center.

Consequently, there must be no severance of theology and philosophy—there can be no reasoning to faith, to Truth. There can only be reasoning *from* faith. Only from the rightly oriented will, the mind already turned toward the redeeming God, can man discover Truth. The keystone of Augustinianism is this—"I believe in order to understand," or even better, theology is "faith seeking understanding." The same applies to morality, for every "virtue" that makes no reference to God is a vice. This insistence, essentially discounted by Aquinas and much of the medieval period, was revived as an essential proclamation of the Protestant Reformation. Through Kierkegaard it has become an adapted tenet of existentialism.

This understanding is the foundation for Augustine's magnum opus, *The City of God*. Augustine's writing career was largely consumed in apologetics, in defending orthodox (Nicene) Christianity against its antagonists both within and without the Church. Occasioned by the sack of Rome in 410, *The City of God* arose as an answer to pagan critics who insisted that Christianity was the principal cause of the weakening of the Roman Empire. The reasons documenting this charge ranged from the religious position that avowal of the Christian God had elicited the vengeance of the true pagan gods, to the secular charge that Christian otherworldliness had undermined the internal solidarity of the Empire. With a brilliant display of concerned patience, Augustine produced one of the most detailed, comprehensive, and definitive apologies ever written. Not only are major charges answered, but Augustine deals with every conceivable attack. He answered the critics in terms of the Christian position and defended his answers in detail from the writings of the honored spokesmen of the Empire throughout its history. Augustine's second purpose with this work was to help Christians themselves who had been weakened or perplexed by persecution and by the disastrous events of history.

Yet from this apology emerged what has made this not only a work of historic interest, but also a classic. The City of God is one of the first attempts at a theology or philosophy of history. Although Greek concepts of history differed somewhat, they were essentially in agreement that history was cyclic, characterized by an endless round of recurring events. In effect, there was no telos, no final goal, toward which history moved. St. Augustine's apology developed the cosmic implications of Christian revelation, defending history as a linear pattern. The Christian God is Triune; that is, God operates in the three eternal modes of Creator-Sustainer, Redeemer, Inspirer. History as the plane of divine activity has as its beginning Creation, as its center point God's re-

demptive act in Jesus Christ, and continues in the Spirit towards the consummation, the judgment and transformation of all into a new heaven and a new earth. From the perspective of faith the pattern of history is visible and the meaning of life perceivable. Augustine's work set the basic view of much of the Middle Ages and of Western culture as such, and he, perhaps more than any other man, provided the fundamental theology of Christendom.

The situation confronting Augustine was fraught with theological difficulties. He could easily counter petty charges, pointing to the Church as a refuge during the sacking, to Christian teachings as having tempered pagan blood-thirstiness, and to pagan respect for possessions of the Christian God. Equally easy was Augustine's proof of the moral decadence of Rome, a condition and its disastrous consequences long warned against by the Roman orators. Although Augustine may have had an apology of this scope in mind at first, the work, once begun, held vast implications. Involved here were the problems of Divine Providence, the justification of evil in a theistic world, the reconciliation of unmerited suffering, and the meaning of a history interrupted by disasters. Nothing short of a cosmology, a total world-view, could do justice to the questions forcing such an apology.

The overarching problem was providence. If God does not know what evils will occur, is he God? If he does know, is God not then either impotent or evil? Augustine answers the first question in the negative—God must have foreknowledge to be God. The problem exists only if one holds that infallible foreknowledge implies necessity. For Augustine, God can know all things without undermining free will, for *the free wills themselves* are included in the order of causes which God foreknows. It is God's knowledge of a thing which gives it not only being but also its specific nature; thus, it is *the very fact* of God's knowledge of man's free will *which makes it free*—it is known as free and not as determined. Freedom does not mean uncaused but self-caused, and it is the very self which God knows even more intimately than the self does. Consequently, God's knowledge of a person is that he will sin, not that he will be forced to sin.

In this manner God's immediate responsibility for evil is met. Yet there is a larger problem, for God still permits man in his freedom to do evil. The Empire provided the framework for Augustine's answer. The Empire, at its beginning, was dedicated to truth, justice, and the good of man—it was blessed by God. But love of liberty became love of domination; desire for virtue became intoxication for pleasure; glory in well-doing became vaunted pride. Herein is portrayed the dilemma of man from the beginning. In the beginning God created all things, and continues to create, for all would relapse into nothingness if he were to withdraw his creative power. All that God created is good, yet mutable, for having been created from nothing, it is absolutely dependent on God. Everything was graduated according to being, and the opposition of contraries serves to heighten the beauty of the universe. It was with the act of creation that time began, for time means movement and change—none of these apply to God. As a result, God's foreknowledge applies to *all* of time, for

his eternal envisagement is unchangeable; although God knows what man in his freedom will do, he also knows what he will do to bring from every evil a greater eventual good. It is in knowing all time as present that the evil in each human present is redeemed. For Augustine, everything adds to God's cosmic whole; even sinners beautify the world.

Nothing, however, is evil by nature, for all natures are God-created. Evil can be nothing but privation, lack of good. Only the will, not one's nature, is the source of evil. Both the highest of the angels and Adam became inflated by pride in their God-given capacities, craving to become ends in themselves—"ye shall be as gods." Thus evil entered the world, for men made what was good into an evil by elevating it as the *supreme* good. Sex, for example, is a good, but is made evil when claimed as the center and meaning of life. It is not the thing turned to, but the turning itself, which is evil. Since man is sustained in being by his relation to the Supreme Good, any substitution of a lesser good brings with it an ontic disruption in which man's nature is injured. Although by such action man comes to approximate a nonentity, God does not revoke his nature totally, but sustains man enough for him to be aware of his self-inflicted loss.

The result is a creature frustrated in the conflict between nature and will— "O Lord, Thou hast made us for Thyself, and we are restless until we find our rest in Thee." In first not wanting to will what he could, man now wills to do what he cannot. This is evil as privation—the impotence of an essentially good nature. Since God alone truly is, that alone which is opposed to

261

God is non-being; in willing less than fullness of being, man does not create evil but gives to non-being the existential status of being. Expressed in another way, sin is living the lie of believing oneself to be self-created, self-sustained, self-dependent. Such confusion establishes the duality, the fall, of creation—death is the most obvious consequence. Evil then has no efficient cause but a deficient one—the will. And as man is insubordinate to God, the "flesh" becomes insubordinate to the will.

In a phrase, evil is misdirected love. At this point Augustine's theory of history emerges. Adam's sin so altered man's nature, transmitted to his posterity, that human will is incapable of redirecting itself from itself as center. For such men, history is simply cyclic. But God's foreknowledge includes not simply man's fall, but God's election of some through grace to a redirected love. For these, history is linear, marked at its center by Jesus Christ, moving toward consummation in eternal life. Thus there are two histories in God's cosmic plan, indicated by two cities. These God permitted in order to show the consequences of pride and to reveal what good can be brought from evil by Grace.

Augustine's primary definition is this: "a people is an assemblage of reasonable beings bound together by a common agreement as to the objects of their love. . . ." History, from beginning to end, is divided by the two "cities" formed by these alternative loves—"the earthly by the love of self, even to the contempt of God; the heavenly by the love of God, even to the contempt of self." Of the first parents, Cain belonged to the city of men Abel to the city of God. But since all are condemned by God, those in the latter are there only because of God's undeserved election.

Augustine's descriptions of these cities is all the more interesting because he refuses to overstate his case. In the first place, he refuses, for the most part, to equate the human city with historic Rome or the divine city with the visible Church—the churches are "full of those who shall be separated by the winnowing as in the threshing-floor." These are invisible cities, and their members are interspersed in these institutions, to be separated only at the end of history. In the second place, he refrains from painting the human city with totally black strokes—"the things which this city desires cannot justly be said to be evil, for it is itself, in its own kind, better than all other human good. For it desires earthly peace for the sake of enjoying earthly goods, and it makes war in order to attain to this peace." This city is characterized not by its goods but by its supreme love of them.

With meticulous care Augustine traces the history of both cities, carefully exegeting scriptural history as both literal and as allegorical of the abiding presence of the city of God. Throughout, in event, figure, and word, Augustine sees Christ's coming prophesied and prepared for. Since not even the Jews held that they alone belonged to God, Augustine maintains that it cannot be denied that other men and nations prophesied concerning Christ, and thus many of these may belong to the heavenly city.

It was Christ who, after His resurrection, opened the Scriptures to the disciples so that they could understand the eternal foundation of history and God's dual plan. But most especially, it

262

was Christ's death, resurrection, ascension, and sending of the Holy Spirit which were the instruments of God's grace to the elect. Through His Incarnation He became Mediator, partaking of humanity so that in its purification by atonement on the Cross it could be resurrected with Him in glory and through faith men could participate in His divinity. Faith begins purification not only of the will, and thus of one's nature, but also of the mind. As Augustine says, impregnated with faith, reason may advance toward the truth. Theology and philosophy belong together because will and reason are inseparable, both in impotence and in restoration.

Throughout history those of the divine city will know suffering at the hands of the human city, yet, being of the elect, they will not fall again. No evil will be permitted ultimately evil results; through suffering God bears witness to himself, and through it the believer is tempered and corrected. Such members (striving for the ideal balance of contemplation and action) obey the laws of the earthly city and are concerned with the necessities which do not undermine faith. To the end, the true Church goes forward "on pilgrimage amid the persecutions of the world and the consolations of God," its life aimed at universal love, its endurance based on the hope of future happiness. The peace of the city of God is "the perfectly ordered and harmonious enjoyment of God, and of one another in God." But in this life such peace is more the "sol-ace of misery," and righteousness consists more in forgiveness than in the perfecting of virtues. The peace of the unbeliever is earthly pleasure, but in the life to come it will be an eternal misery of the will and passions in conflict. Expressed in terms of sin, history began with man's ability to sin or not to sin; it will end for the elect with man's higher freedom, the ability not to be able to sin, for in true freedom sin no longer has delight.

With meticulous detail, often disturbing in its literalness, Augustine outlines the epochs of future history, climaxing with the "new heaven and the new earth." Such an attempt escapes the charge of speculation, Augustine believes, because it has as its point of departure scriptural revelation, interpreted from the perspective of the Christ-event. Throughout these reflections there is a tension which has its roots in Augustine's own life. On the one hand is the rejection of this world in otherworldliness, holding alone to God's unfailing omnipotence and justice, and the eternal duality of heaven and hell. On the other hand, Augustine is world-affirming, straining for a transformational vision of which God's love gives foretaste. Both have their basis expressed in one of Augustine's concluding statements, emerging not only as a statement of faith but as a yearning hope issuing from his own tempestuous life. Speaking of that which is to be, he says that "then there shall be no more of this world, no more of the surgings and restlessness of human life. . . ."

THE CONSOLATION OF PHILOSOPHY

Author: Anicius Manlius Severinus Boethius (c.480-524)
Type of work: Ethics, metaphysics
First transcribed: 523

PRINCIPAL IDEAS ADVANCED

Boethius is a political prisoner, and he complains to Philosophy, who is a fair lady, that virtue is not rewarded; he questions God's justice.

Philosophy answers that God is the source of all things, and that through study of God's nature, Boethius can rediscover his own true nature.

Man's possessions come through good fortune; anyone who realizes this and who does not become attached to his possessions can lose them with equanimity.

Since nature is always inconstant, man should seek to be master of himself and to bear changes of fortune with a calm mind.

Truth, happiness, and even divinity may be found in man himself; man should exercise his God-given freedom to raise himself in accordance with the vision of the divine nature.

This classic of prison literature bears all of the marks of great Roman philosophical writing. Formulated as a dialogue between the prisoner Boethius and Lady Philosophy, it exhibits the unique Roman quality of combining literary appeal with technical philosophy. Whereas philosophy in Greece was for the most part academic and theoretical, when transplanted to Rome it became a widely followed way of life, as in Stoicism. It is often said that philosophy in Rome was eclectic and unoriginal; what would perhaps be more accurate to say is that the original Roman element was to mold philosophy into forms which could deal effectively with serious and perennial human problems.

Like other philosophical writers of the era, Boethius took full advantage of his knowledge of Plato, Aristotle, the Stoics, and Neoplatonism. Modern philosophers often attempt to break completely with tradition; but Boethius used and blended classical sources as the means to develop his own views. His attempt was not to construct a novel metaphysics, but to apply philosophical views to the solution of pressing problems. Boethius had done philosophical writing before, but on the whole his life had been spent as a man of affairs. For reasons shrouded in political mystery, he was imprisoned and then put to death a few months after completing this work.

The work was widely known in the Middle Ages, and Boethius, in fact, was the source of several of the prominent philosophical questions of that later period. It is still debated, however, whether Boethius was himself a Christian. It seems likely that he was, although his writing contains no specific Christian doctrine. Perhaps, like the early writings of Augustine, his intellectual discussions were strictly philosophical, even though his formal religion was Christianity.

Although *The Consolation of Philosophy* has exerted enormous influence for centuries, it is largely neglected today. Religion is more independent of philosophy, and philosophy itself seems never to have been less concerned with practical affairs than it now is. Probably the *Consolation* is now more often read outside of professional philosophical circles, but whatever its current fashion, its position as a classic of applied philosophy is secure.

Boethius opens with a lament about the sudden reversal of his circumstances, a lot which has reduced him from the role of a consul to that of a prisoner in a dungeon near Milan. As he accuses fortune of being fickle, Philosophy, in the form of a fair lady, appears to him in his cell and attempts to answer his doubts about the justice of the world. She joins him in lamenting his present plight, but tells him it is time to search for healing rather than to complain. She chides him for his lack of courage in his present state, reminding him of Plato's struggle and of Socrates' valiant death. Philosophers, she tells him, have always been at variance with the ways of men and therefore have always been subject to attack. To oppose evil men is the chief aim of all philosophers, a course that cannot help leading them into trouble repeatedly. Therefore, a philosopher must learn to reconcile his life to fate, to conquer his fear of death, and to show himself unyielding to good and bad alike.

Ever since man has been able to speak, he has complained that his just life has not been properly rewarded, either by God or by man. Boethius continues this complaint, that his prison sufferings prove the injustice of the world when they are considered as the reward for the just life he has lived. Wicked men make attacks upon his virtue, and all because he is too honest ever to have engaged in deceit. Why does God allow a wicked man to prevail against innocence? With Job and a chorus of others, Boethius questions God, whose ways are unnatural to him. "If God is, whence come evil things? If he is not, whence came good?" Thus Boethius phrases the age-old question. Why should he be exiled, condemned to death without an opportunity to defend himself, because of his too great zeal for the Senate?

Furthermore, Boethius argues, Philosophy too has been dishonored in this process, for Boethius has never sought perishable riches but has instead "followed after God." Thus, in his misfortune, Philosophy's wisdom is also brought under question. In return for kindness he has received persecutions. Even his reputation has been stained. Honest men are crushed with fear; wicked men oppress good men and prosper by doing so. At this point Philosophy scolds Boethius mildly: she tells him that his mind is so beset by passions that nothing can come close enough to him to bring any healing. Philosophy then asks the basic question on which the argument will rest: Is the universe guided by a rule of reason, or are its events random and guided by chance? If it is the latter, then no explanations for misfortune can be given. If it is the former, however, then one can question the reason and hope for a reasonable reply.

First, we must ask if there is an aim and end of all things. Is there a goal to which all nature tends? Boethius and his questioner agree that all things have their source in God. Then, if the beginning can be known, why not also the end of all things? But even more important than such cosmic questions, which establish the framework for man's life, is the fact that Boethius seems to have forgotten who he is and what his role as a man can be. He can rediscover his true nature, fortunately, through one spark within him: his knowledge of the hand that guides the universe. Through his knowledge of God and his purpose within the world Boethius can perhaps recover a true knowledge of his own nature.

What needs to be considered first, Philosophy urges, is the way of Fortune. Life cannot stand still; change must be understood. Anyone who complains over lost possessions has mistakenly assumed them to be his private property, rather than the gift of Fortune. To rise to the top is not a guarantee that the next phase may not be to sink to the bottom. Fortune, not your own just deserts, may bring you alternately high and low. These are the rules of the game, and understanding them prevents unnecessary misery. If you are violently attached to your position and possessions, they do not really satisfy you but cause you to desire more. If you are not so attached, then their loss will not disturb you.

Nature constantly changes. Why, then, should man alone wish to be exempt from cyclical flow? One thing alone is certain: nothing which is brought to birth is fixed or constant. Since these are nature's ways, nothing is wretched unless you think it so. On the other hand, if you bear everything which comes with a calm mind, then you will find your lot blessed. Why seek happiness without, when it really lies within? If you are the master of yourself, then you possess all that it is important not to lose, and even fickle Fortune cannot take that from you.

Fear alone prevents a man from being happy. Self-mastery excludes fear, and only a life based on inner calmness can ignore the raging passions which always threaten to destroy. In the light of this knowledge, why would anyone embrace as his good anything outside of himself?

No fame or power appears lasting when compared with eternity. Death has no regard for high position, however great, but claims high and low alike. And even ill fortune has its blessings: it distinguishes true friends from doubtful acquaintances. The loss of riches is a gain, since it brings you your true friends, a possession greater than riches. Love rules the universe, and men can be happy if their hearts are ruled by love. Happiness is, after all, man's highest good. And friends, who are one chief source of happiness, depend upon virtue more than upon Fortune's uncontrollable ways. They may argue over means, but they agree in their highest good and happiness.

The man who would gain true power must subdue his own wild thoughts—so Philosophy consoles Boethius. Since God is our author, no man is degenerate or base except the man who leaves his creator. Since God and the highest good form a union, every happy man is, in his happiness, divine. If it is truth that one searches for, let him only turn upon himself the light of an inward gaze. It is of no use to search elsewhere; truth, happiness, and even divinity may be found within man himself. God governs the universe for the highest good. He who turns his thoughts away from the light above is in danger of losing whatever he has won for himself here below, for he will lose his sense of direction.

Next comes the age-old question: If

there exists a good ruler of the world, why do evils exist and, what is worse, seem to go unpunished? Philosophy answers: Power is never lacking to the good, while the wicked are weak. Yet all men, good and bad alike, seek to arrive at the good, although by different means. Bad men seek the same ends that good ones do, but they do it through cupidity. Such is the weakness of wicked men that it is hard to allow that they are men at all. The power of evil is no power at all, especially since nothing evil ever reaches happiness. The wicked man is oppressed by his own passions; all good men become happy by virtue of the very fact that they are good. Therefore, as honesty is itself the reward of the honest, so wickedness is itself the punishment of the wicked. The man who loses his goodness ceases to be a man and turns into a beast.

We should love good men, for it is their due, and show pity for the evil, since to be oppressed by the disease of feeble wickedness is much more worthy of pity than of persecution. Providence is a guide for all, and there is no such thing as chance. Yet all who have reason also have the freedom of desiring and of refusing, although the working of human reason cannot approach the directness of divine foreknowledge. Such foreknowledge does not bring necessity to bear upon things as they come to pass. Man sometimes rises to see all things as God might see them and sometimes sinks down and fails to grasp such connections at all. His freedom is preserved by his lack of vision.

Near the end, having raised the question of a divine vision of all things, Boethius turns to the question of whether there are universals, and it is

here that much of the famous medieval controversy takes its start. What is comprehensible to the senses and to the imagination cannot be universal, yet reason holds to be universal what is really an individual matter comprehensible to the senses. It sees from a general point of view what is comprehensible to the senses and to the imagination, yet this is not a knowledge of real universals but only a way reason has of comprehending. Nothing set in time, for instance, can at one moment grasp the whole space of its lifetime. God, of course, sees all things in his eternal present, but man does not. Seen from God's perspective, an event may seem necessary; when examined in its own nature, it seems free and unrestrained.

In this dialogue Philosophy has the last word, and that refers to the theological problem of the difference in perspective between God and man. Consolation comes in trying to raise oneself to see the events of the world as God views them. Dejection, then, is caused by a too limited, a too human perspective; Philosophy's job is to raise man's sights, to give him divine vision. Since Philosophy can accomplish this, she is man's hope of consolation. Any individual's turn of fortune is not understandable in isolation; it must be placed in the total scheme of things, and to do this is to philosophize. Philosophy does not change events or reverse fortune, but it does provide the understanding with which the events of life may not only be accepted but also enjoyed. When Fortune reverses itself, the first cry is for restoration. Philosophy teaches that man's chief need is not for change but for understanding.

In Boethius' work we have a classic

in applied philosophy. According to the usual standards, no real argument or analysis supports the points introduced. In some sense there is not a novel doctrine here; all parts may be traced to preceding classical sources. Yet this work is itself a classic. This is true because of its historical situation, in that it came to be a source for philosophical argument. The *Consolation* raises an interconnected series of important philosophical and theological problems. Its answers are not original, but they are classical and the problems themselves perennial. In this work we see an enduring example of philosophy's application to a serious human need and of the consolation which results.

THE CREST JEWEL OF WISDOM

Author: S'aṅkara (or Shankara, Samkara, Sankaracharya, c.788-c.820)
Type of work: Metaphysics
First transcribed: Unknown

PRINCIPAL IDEAS ADVANCED

In this existence, all is illusion (maya).

To achieve liberation the wise man will discriminate between the permanent and the transitory; he will be indifferent to the fruits of action; he will achieve tranquillity of mind, self-control, cessation of action by the mind, forbearance of suffering, faith, and deep concentration on Brahman; and he will yearn to be liberated from the bonds of ignorance and egoism.

Liberation from this existence can be achieved only through direct perception of the oneness of the individual self (ātman) *with the universal self* (Brahman).

The self is none of the five sheaths of the human being.

To achieve nirvana the disciple must overcome the feeling of "I," follow his guru's teachings, study the scriptures, and come to full awareness of the truth of the mystic formula: "This is Brahman; that thou art."

It would be incorrect to speak about "the philosophy of S'aṅkara" since he and other great Indian sages never claimed a philosophy of their own but were merely expounders of the great spiritual knowledge bequeathed them by a long lineage of predecessors. They differ according to the emphasis placed upon the various aspects of that knowledge, and their greatness is measured by the degree to which they mastered it. By that measure, S'aṅkara was perhaps the greatest of the historical Hindu sages, not including, however, Gautama the Buddha.

In the East the belief is common that there is a "soul-redeeming" *truth* which can make of its possessor a divine being, one liberated from the wheel of *samsāra*, that is, from obligatory rebirth. The state of liberation, nirvana, is the supreme aim, the *sum-*

mum bonum of all six Hindu schools of philosophy, as well as of the various Buddhist sects. The Western reader must, therefore, constantly keep in mind that there are three basic doctrines of Oriental philosophy:

(1) The doctrine of *rebirth*, meaning the periodic appearance of the same human egos in new physical bodies.

(2) The doctrine of *Karma*, or moral retribution, the regulatory law under which rebirth takes place.

(3) The doctrine of *spiritual evolution* by which a relative perfection is attainable, in principle, by all beings —those of the lower kingdoms of nature included.

We can realize why no Hindu sage bothers to prove or defend these three doctrines, for they are never questioned even by an opponent. This will also explain the universal belief in India of the existence among men of advanced beings who have acquired supernormal powers (*siddhis*) and who are no longer subject to the normal laws of birth and death. Having learned the hidden secrets of nature, mainly by following the Delphic injunction "Man, know theyself!" they discovered that a thorough knowledge and understanding of their own egos enabled them to become masters not only of themselves, that is, of the actions of the outer body and the inner mind, but also of external nature to an extent that the Western reader would be inclined to call miraculous. Yet it is claimed by these sages that their supernormal powers are definitely not *supernatural*, but are exerted within the framework of nature's laws, which therefore, are able to make use of, whenever the occasion calls for the exercise of their *siddhis*.

Such a sage was S'ankara. Because of the fact that many of his successors adopted the same name, S'ankara, there is a great confusion as to his dates as well as to his writings. Many of the writings of the later S'ankaras have been fathered upon their illustrious predecessor, not always to the benefit of the latter. Although some biographers place him as early as 510 B.C., most scholars are agreed that he was born much later, about the beginning of the ninth century.

S'ankara, by writing his commentary on the *Brahma Sūtras*, in which he stressed non-dualism (*a-dvaita*), became the founder of the Advaita system of the Vedanta school of Hindu philosophy.

S'ankara's writings consist of a number of important commentaries as well as original treatises of various lengths. Of his commentaries, the one on the *Brahma Sūtras* is of the greatest importance for his followers. Also important are the ones on some of the principal *Upanishads* as well as his commentary on the *Bhagavad Gītā*.

Most of S'ankara's original treatises seem to have been written for his disciples' use only. Among these is the very short one, entitled *Ten Stanzas,* consisting of precisely ten quatrains. Somewhat longer is the *Hundred Stanzas* consisting of 101 quatrains. Of his two compendiums of Advaita philosophy, the *Thousand Teachings* consists of a part in prose of 116 numbered paragraphs and a part in verse consisting of 649 couplets arranged in nineteen chapters. The other compendium is the *Crest Jewel of Wisdom* (*Vivekacūdāmaṇi*), which consists of 581 stanzas, most of which are couplets and quatrains with a few triplets interspersed.

The Vedanta viewpoint (*vedāntadarśana*) was firmly established by Bādarāyaṇa in his *Brahma Sūtras*, also called *Vedanta Sūtras*. He is claimed to be identical with Krishna Dvaipayana who is the compiler of the Vedas, to whom also the *Purāṇas* are attributed, not to speak of the *Mahābharata*. But the Vedas were compiled 3100 B.C., according to Brahman chronology and this is, perhaps, too early a date for the *Brahma Sūtras*.

The *Brahma Sūtras* starts with an inquiry into Brahman, the world soul, then continues with a refutation of erroneous views, after which the means of reaching union with Brahman are discussed. Finally the fourth and last part is dedicated to the nature of liberation from the rounds of rebirth, and discusses the kinds of liberated beings. The *sūtras* (aphorisms) are extraordinarily terse, often consisting of only one or two words, and generally without any verb. Commentators are needed to explain these riddles. But, as one would expect, commentators are wont to disagree among themselves, and so the Vedanta school split into three main systems, known as the *Advaita*, or Non-Dualistic system; the *Viśiṣṭādvaita*, or Qualified-non-Dualistic system; and the *Dvaita*, or Dualistic system.

Of these, the first system is that of S'aṅkara and his commentary; the second is that of Rāmānuja and his great commentary (*S'rībhāṣya*); the third system is that of Madhva, or Anandatīrtha, and his *Sutrabhāṣya*.

S'aṅkara teaches the unity of the self of man with Brahman, and that their apparent separation is an illusion (*māyā*). Rāmānuja, while admitting that the self of man can unite with Brahman, claims that both are real. His system is theistic and anthropomorphic, based on religious devotion rather than on rules of logic, as is that of S'aṅkara. Madhva, however, teaches that the duality of man's soul and Brahman persists, that both are real and independent of each other. His dualism is unqualified and opposes S'aṅkara's monistic views as well as the views of Rāmānuja.

There have been other commentators on the *Brahma Sūtras*. Perhaps the most recent is Baladeva (eighteenth century), whose extensive commentary, known as *Govinda Bhāṣya*, gives the Vaisnava viewpoint, since he was a follower of S'rī Chaitanya. The *Govinda Bhāṣya* is therefore theistic, like the one by Rāmānuja.

The *Crest Jewel of Wisdom* was written by S'aṅkara to assist the would-be aspirant to spiritual wisdom in his efforts to free himself from the rounds of incessant rebirths. There is a strong similarity between the teachings and methods of S'aṅkara and the Buddha. Both aimed to teach mankind how to conquer pain and suffering, how to reach the acme of manhood, and finally how to obtain the highest spiritual state possible while still living on earth. Both considered conditioned existence as *unreal* and stressed its illusory character (*māyā*). Neither of the two had any use for personal gods (*devas*), knowing themselves superior to the latter. The Buddhists and Advaita Vedantists have been called atheists by their opponents, and Buddha as well as S'aṅkara discarded rituals completely. There is no real difference between the path leading to Buddhahood and the path leading to the state of a *Jivanmukta*. All this makes it more difficult to explain the nearly complete silence of the Buddha on the subject of the Self (*ātman*) and the almost continuous reference to the *ātman* by S'aṅkara. Buddha's silence led many Buddhists as well as non-Buddhists to believe that Buddha denied the existence of the *ātman* and, therefore, of a soul, which, of course, would contradict Buddha's statements upon a number of other subjects.

S'aṅkara's writings are too metaphysical, even for the average Hindu, to be useful for any but advanced disciples in Hindu mysticism. This he frankly admits at the outset of most of his treatises, and so in the case of the *Crest Jewel of Wisdom* he directs himself to a "wise man" (*vidvān*) who strives for liberation and has renounced his desire for the enjoyment of external objects. He advises the "wise man" to apply to a true and great spiritual teacher for guidance. After some further advice of a general nature he states the qualifications necessary for success in this venture, apart from being learned and of strong intellect: (1) *Discrimination* between things permanent and transitory; (2) *indifference* to enjoyment of the fruits of one's actions in this world and in the next; (3) the six accomplishments:

S'*ama* (tranquillity), which is a state of mind devoted to its goal;

Dama (self-control), which is the fixing in their own proper sphere of both the organs of perception and of action, after reverting them from their objects;

The height of *uparati* (cessation), which is the spontaneous abstaining from action by the mind;

Titikṣā (forbearance), which is patient endurance of all suffering, without retaliation, free from anxiety and complaint;

S'*raddhā* (faith), which is reflec-

tion and meditation on the truth of the words of the Guru and of the sacred texts; and

Samādhana (deep concentration), which is the constant fixing of the discriminating mind (*buddhi*) upon the pure Brahman, and not the indulging of the mind (*citta*); and (4) *yearning to be liberated* (*mumukṣutā*), which is the desire to be liberated by knowing one's own real nature and the bonds made through ignorance, from egoism down to the body.

The necessary qualifications for the Guru, the teacher whom the well-equipped aspirant to liberation or nirvana must now seek, are even more severe. The Guru, through whom freedom from bondage is to be attained, must be spiritually wise, conversant with sacred knowledge, sincere, and not suffering from desires; he must know the nature of Brahman; he must be one who is at rest in the Eternal, like a fire that is tranquil when destitute of fuel, one who is a river of disinterested compassion, a friend of all living creatures.

Having found such a preceptor and having asked him for guidance, the disciple, when found worthy, is then instructed by his Master, who praises him for his desire to rid himself of the bonds of ignorance (*avidyā*). He is told that liberation can only be achieved through the *direct perception* of the oneness of the individual self (*ātman*) with the universal self (Brahman). Neither the Vedas, nor the scriptures (*śastras*), nor the incantation (*mantras*), nor any medicine can help him who is bitten by the snake of ignorance.

It is necessary to know how to discriminate between spirit and non-

271

spirit, between the self and not-self.

In order to show the difference between spirit and non-spirit, the Guru outlines the visible and invisible part of nature, beginning with the grossest of man's constituent vehicles.

The *gross body* is produced from the five subtle elements, whose functions are responsible for the five senses. The Guru warns of the danger of sense enjoyments and of desires pertaining to the body, and he describes the danger in no uncertain terms.

The *internal organ* consists of *manas*, the mental faculties of postulating and doubting; the intellect, having the characteristic of certainty about things; the ego-conforming power, producing the conception "I"; and the mind, having the property of concentration.

The *vital principle* manifests itself, according to its transformations, as one of the five "vital airs."

The *subtle or astral body* is the vehicle of the five faculties, the five sense organs, the five vital airs, the five elements, ignorance, desire, and action. It is also known as the vehicle of characteristics, and is active in dreams.

The *causal body* of the self is the unmanifested condition of the three universal qualities. Its state is that of dreamless sleep. The three universal qualities are purity, action, and darkness. When the purity is unalloyed there will be perception of the self.

The Guru now defines in many ways the Supreme Spirit (*Paramātman*) through the knowledge of which Isolation (*Kaivalya*) or Freedom is obtained.

A description follows of the five sheaths (*koṣa*), another way of looking at the constituents of a human being. They are the *annamaya*-sheath, sustained by physical food—that is, the gross body; the *prāṇamaya*-sheath, the vehicle of the vital forces, through which the ego performs all the actions of the gross body; the *manomaya*-sheath, consisting of the organs of sensation and *manas*, the latter mental faculty being the cause of ignorance and consequently the cause of the bondage of conditioned existence, although the same *manas* when pure becomes the cause of liberation; the *vijñānamaya*-sheath, consisting of intellect and the powers of perception, the doer of actions and the cause of the rounds of rebirth, the embodied ego which has no beginning in time and which is the guide of all actions; the *ānandamaya*-sheath, the reflection of absolute bliss, yet not free from the quality of darkness.

The Guru explains that these five sheaths are *not the Self*. The latter is self-illumined and remains after the subtraction of these sheaths. It is the witness of the three states, of the waking, dreaming, and deep sleep state.

The disciple is now given subtler teachings about the Self and the Supreme Spirit. In a number of stanzas is repeated, paraphrasing the *Chāndogya-Upanishad*, the mystic formula: ". . . this is Brahman, that thou art (*tat tvam asi*)."

The subject of the mental impressions which are the seeds in the mind through which *karma* manifests subsequently to any act is now discussed by the Guru, and the disciple is told how to exhaust them. At the same time the disciple must overcome the feeling of "I," the power of egoism, and many stanzas are dedicated to the elaboration of this subject. Other subjects are interwoven in the discussion, such as that of *nirvikalpa samādhi*, a superior type of meditation.

The stanzas become more and more abstruse while the disciple advances in spiritual matters. The characteristics of *jivanmukta*, he who is *liberated while living on earth*, are described, and also the consequences of this achievement, especially in relation to the three kinds of *karma*.

Finally comes the moment when the disciple, through the Guru's teaching, through the evidence of the revealed scriptures, and through his own efforts, realizes the full truth and becomes absorbed in the universal self. He speaks and informs his Master about his spiritual experiences.

He tells about the Absolute (*Parabrahman*) and his spiritual bliss. He is without attachment and without limbs, sexless, and indestructible. He is neither the doer nor the enjoyer, for he is without change and without action. He is now the self-illumined *ātman*. He bows down before his Guru through whose compassion and greatly esteemed favor he has achieved the goal of his existence.

The Guru, greatly pleased, explains the position of the Knower of Brahman in the remaining stanzas. At the end, the disciple salutes his Guru respectfully. Liberated from bondage, with the Guru's permission he goes away.

ON THE DIVISION OF NATURE

Author: Johannes Scotus Erigena (c.810-c.877)
Type of work: Metaphysics
First transcribed: Ninth century

PRINCIPAL IDEAS ADVANCED

God created man in such a manner that man shares the nature of other animals as well as the celestial nature.

Our minds are ignorant and unwise, but in God the mind finds its discipline; man is an intellectual idea formed eternally in the divine mind, and for man to know he must come to full consciousness and recall the eternal ideas.

The idea by which man knows himself is his substance; consequently, man may be known through intellectual causes or by effects.

Man exists in the divine mind, for man is by his essence divine idea.

Man is by nature omniscient, but he lost the knowledge of himself and of his creator when he sinned; insofar as man can know, it is by the grace of God, who allows man to become aware of essences by acts of understanding in which the idea in man's mind and in God's mind are one.

Johannes Scotus Erigena is often regarded as the first of the real medievals. Boethius and Augustine are his only substantial predecessors, and they are several centuries earlier. Erigena was familiar with Boethius, since he wrote about his life; and he introduced classical Neoplatonism into the formative years of the medieval period through his translations from pseudo-Dionysius the Areopagite. He was also familiar with the fathers of both the Latin Church and the Greek Church. Yet, more than the fact that he is the first major writer to appear in several centuries, his importance to the Middle Ages lies in his production of one of the first complete metaphysical schemes, his *On the Division of Nature*. The Middle Ages became noted for its systematic, speculative, and constructive effort, and the tone for such effort is set here in Erigena's major work.

His Platonistic tendencies are immediately evident in the use he makes in his writing of the dialogue form. Master and Disciple answer and question each other, although the form is more that of alternating brief essays than it is of Plato's more dramatic dialogue form of rapid reply. Of course, Plato also tends to adopt a more sustained form of speech in his later dialogues, and it is perhaps primarily from the Neoplatonists that Erigena learned his writing style. Another similarity to Neoplatonism (in contrast to Plato) can be seen in the cosmic perspective which Eringena adopts. Plato's metaphysics is more fragmentary; the Neoplatonists tend naturally to deal with problems in the total setting of a cosmic scheme. Such a scheme Johannes Scotus Erigena here outlines. (The analysis which follows is of Book IV, Chapters vii-ix, available in Richard McKeon's *Selections from Medieval Philosophers*.)

Why did God create man, Erigena's Disciple asks, as one of the family of animals instead of in the form of some higher celestial creature? As it is, man needs his terrestrial body and can perceive only with the aid of perceptions received from without. With angels it is not so; no such limitations bind them, and yet man is supposed to have been made in God's image. Man's sin and fall from grace cannot account for his animal nature, since even if he had not sinned he would still be an animal. It is not by sin but by nature that man is an animal. And man's position is even more strange if we consider that he may in a future life be transmuted into a celestial form of being.

To answer his Disciple's question, the Master resorts to the divine will, saying that why God willed this is beyond inquiry, since the causes of the divine will cannot be known. Why God willed it is beyond all understanding.

Yet one can say that the whole of created nature, both visible and invisible, is present in man, and this is a valuable position. What is naturally present in the celestial essences subsists essentially in man. We can say rationally, therefore, that God wished to place man in the genus of animals for the reason that he wished to create every creature in him, and for this to be possible man had to share in all of nature and not only in celestial nature. No irrationality is implied, for everything from God can be understood and anything not from God cannot be understood because it simply is not. Things exist outside the knower, and the knowledge of them is produced in man by them. The ideas of things and the things themselves are

274

of different natures. And things must be granted to be of a more excellent nature than the ideas of them.

To continue, that which understands is better than that which is understood, and, one step more, the idea of intelligible things is older than the intelligible things themselves. The human mind derives its knowledge from things, but the things themselves were originally formed from intelligible ideas (existing in God's mind). Although our human mind is born inexpert and unwise, nevertheless it is able to find in itself its God, its expertness, and its discipline. As in God, so in man there is a kind of trinity: mind, learning, art. Still only the divine mind possesses the true idea of the human mind, since the human mind cannot of itself comprehend itself. To define man truly we must say: Man is an intellectual idea formed eternally in the divine mind.

What results is a Platonic doctrine of recollection, now transferred to the divine mind. What man essentially is, all the knowledge he can possess, is eternally contained as idea in the divine mind. To know, then, is to come to full consciousness, to recall this set of ideas eternally formed. Self-consciousness means increased knowledge of the divine nature. A true knowledge of all things is implanted in human nature, although its presence is concealed until by divine light the soul is turned to God. What else is there, then, except ideas? Accordingly, the very idea by which man knows himself may be considered his substance. Yet, how could it be that we do not always and naturally see man as this divine idea? Because (as Spinoza was to say later) all things in na-

ture may be viewed in two perspectives: either as a creature in the Word of God in which all things have been made, or as an individual considered in himself without reference to his divine origin.

Man has one substance understood in two ways: in one fashion, the human substance is perceived through its creation in intellectual causes; in the other, by its generation in effects. Accordingly, one and the same thing is spoken of as double because of the double observation of it. What difficulties do we encounter in such a theory? In order to know man's essence properly, God's nature must first be understood, for here is the true focus of knowledge. And yet, Erigena holds to the traditional assertion: it is in no way granted to the human mind to know what the essence of God is, although we may know "that it is." The result is that, although man was first rendered intelligible by understanding his essence as an idea in the divine mind, the knowledge of man is, because of this, subjected to all of the traditional difficulties surrounding the knowledge of God.

God is entirely uncircumscribed and is to be understood through no thing because he is infinite. What about man? Here, too, we deny that the human mind is *anything* and affirm only that it *is*. If the human mind were circumscribable, it could not express the image of its creator wholly, which means that because the human mind is so much like the divine it also cannot be grasped directly. The same problems which surround the divine nature now surround the human mind's understanding of its own essence, since this cannot be grasped except as part of the divine mind. Amazingly enough, even infinity is transferred to the human mind: just as the divine essence is infinite, so the human determination is not limited by any certain end. It is understood only to be, but what it *is* is never understood. Infinity, once God's unique possession, man now comes to share, and he immediately becomes subject to its rational difficulties.

Aristotle rejected infinity as an attribute of divine perfection because of its inaccessibility to rational comprehension. Transcendentalists applied unlimitedness to God in spite of the difficulties for knowledge. Now Erigena, by defining man's essence as a divine idea, subjects the understanding of human nature to the same insurmountable difficulties, since God's mind must be understood before man's essence can be found. In God, however, there is no ignorance, except the divine darkness which exceeds all understanding. Since man subsists more truly in his idea than in himself, he must be understood in and through his idea, and this is located in God, who is himself not fully knowable. Yet this cannot be avoided, for when a thing is known better, then it must be judged to exist more truly. Man, then, exists more truly as an idea in the divine mind than he does in himself, which means that God's understanding (and darkness) is involved in the knowledge of the true existence of all things, man included. Geometrical figures do not exist in themselves, for instance, but only in the theoretical structure of the discipline in which they are the figures. So man does not exist in himself truly but exists in the divine plan of which he is a part. If, therefore, geometrical bodies subsist only in their rational ideas, what is there so astonishing about the fact that natural bodies should subsist in that nature (God) in which there is the idea of them? Reality is never ultimately located in the natural world; it is in the divine mind. Intelligible things are actually prior to sensible things in the mind which understands them. The thing understood, furthermore, is preceded by the understanding soul which perceives it. Finally, the divine nature is prior to the human soul, since it provides the locus for both the soul's self-understanding and its ultimate existence.

Why should it be so difficult for man to learn these facts about his nature and his understanding? If man had not sinned, the reply comes, he certainly would not have fallen into so profound an ignorance of himself. In the fall, human nature perished entirely in all men, except in the Redeemer of the world, in whom alone it remained incorruptible. He alone was joined in a unity of substance to the Word of God, in whom all the elect by grace are made sons of God and participants of the divine substance. Before sin each creature had implanted in it a full knowledge of both itself and its creator, so that if human nature had not sinned, it would assuredly be omniscient. Sin alone separates man from God, human from divine nature. First, Erigena made man infinite by linking his self-understanding with God's understanding. Now man becomes omniscient by nature, losing this quality only through the bondage of sin.

At the present time human nature still has this perfect knowledge, both of itself, its creator, and all things (present before sin), but this perfect knowl-

276

edge is held in possibility alone. In the highest man this knowledge becomes actual again. All things are known in and are created by the Word of God; thus, the created wisdom of man knew all things before they were made. In fact, everything in the human understanding proceeds from and through that very idea of the creative wisdom. All things subsist in the divine understanding causally and in the human understanding effectually. In knowledge and in dignity, but not in time and place, the creation of man precedes those things which were created with it and by it. Yet, in the end, no created intellect can know what a thing is, since the essence of everything is involved in the problem of divine ignorance.

Man's rational processes are so great, in fact, that his understanding would naturally be equal with the angels—if he had not sinned. Man and angel are by nature so alike that they reciprocally understand each other. In fact, any two human understandings can essentially become one, since they can both apprehend ideas, and our essence and our understanding are not two things but one. Man is essentially his understanding. This is incorporeal and, ultimately, is to be seen as an idea in the divine mind. Our one true and supreme essence is the understanding made specific in the contemplation of truth. Here is an antecedent to Descartes' definition of man as a "thinking substance." Here is the final identification which makes man in his real nature so much like God and thus involves the understanding of man in the difficulties of comprehending God. Man is his knowledge; he is his ideas whose locus is in the divine mind.

God created by separating light from darkness; were there no dark element, all would be angelic nature and understanding. As it is, darkness precipitated man into ignorance as a penalty for his pride, and man could neither foresee his fall nor his misery. Were it not for the unshapeliness of darkness, all creatures would cling immutably to their creator, and men would not need to struggle for understanding. As it is, man must first see God, the presence of the idea of man in the divine mind, in order to understand his own nature. But this requires overcoming the ignorance of sin and grasping the divine nature— surely a job for an angel, unless man is first restored by divine grace.

A speculative system of such scope and daring as Erigena has presented here is quite difficult for the modern mind to grasp for many reasons. Such pure speculation, for one thing, is not very prevalent today; and, for another thing, one does not expect to find speculation of such vigor arising as the first philosophy of consequence since Augustine, who wrote nearly four centuries earlier. Here Erigena easily ranges between God and man, comprehending in his theory the whole of creation with the greatest of ease. Modern caution has restrained us from such far-ranging flights of philosophical reasoning. When we think of the Middle Ages, it is not Erigena's ideas that we think of most naturally, and it is true that they were quickly considered unorthodox by his own church. Nevertheless, they exerted a powerful influence (particularly in Platonic circles) in the fruitful centuries ahead and still stand as a monument to independent and original speculative construction.

THE BOOK OF SALVATION

Author: Avicenna (ibn-Sina, 980-1037)
Type of work: Metaphysics, philosophy of mind, epistemology
First transcribed: Early eleventh century

PRINCIPAL IDEAS ADVANCED

God is the eternal, unmoved First Mover, who exists necessarily by his own nature and who eternally generates the first created being, a pure intelligence, by a creative act of thought.

The First Intelligence creates the Second Intelligence and also the first celestial sphere and its soul; the Second Intelligence produces the Third Intelligence and the second celestial sphere; the process continues to the Tenth Intelligence, the giver of forms.

Souls are vegetable, animal, and human; the human soul is characterized by the faculties of growth, reproduction, nutrition, motion, perception, and reason.

There are five external senses and five internal senses; the internal senses are common sense, representation, imagination, estimation, and recollection.

Reason has two faculties: the practical and the theoretic; the theoretic faculty may develop to the stage of actual intellect, as activated by the Tenth Intelligence; knowledge then consists of discovering the necessary relations between universals.

In the year 529 Justinian closed the Schools of Athens, but fortunately for the West, Greek learning had been transmitted to the Near East, principally through the institutions of Alexandria and the Christian communities of Syria and Persia. Later, after the advent of Islam, this learning was fostered and developed by various Islamic philosophers and eventually carried across North Africa into Spain, where it flourished in such places as Toledo and Cordova. From the eleventh to the thirteenth centuries it trickled and then flooded into Western Europe to augment the Christians' meager and unbalanced knowledge of Greek philosophy.

Avicenna was, perhaps, the most important Islamic philosopher. Besides being a prolific writer on philosophy and religion, he was a court scholar and

physician, an active politician, a civil administrator, and the writer of medical texts which were standard works in Europe through the seventeenth century. Of his approximately one hundred works the two most important are the philosophic encyclopedia, *Kitab al-Shifa* (*The Book of Healing*), the bulk of which was known to late medieval thinkers, and an abridgment of it, *Kitab al-Nadjat* (*The Book of Salvation*). The present essay is based pri marily on the section of the *Najat* dealing with his philosophy of mind, a section translated by F. Rahman and published under the title *Avicenna's Psychology* (1952).

Before we can discuss Avicenna's philosophy of mind and his epistemology it will be necessary to outline the system within which it is elaborated. Avicenna regarded himself as an Aris totelian, but his Aristotelianism, like that of both his predecessors and successors, was influenced by the pressure of religious considerations and by the fact that the Aristotle transmitted to him had become colored by Stoic and Neoplatonic elements.

The modifications in Aristotle are evident in Avicenna's notion of God, his doctrine of creation, and his cosmology. He describes God not only as an eternal, unchanging, immaterial Unmoved Mover, but also as a being whose existence is necessary because his essence is identical with his being, as the One who is indivisible, as True Perfection, as Pure Benevolence, and as a continuously active agent intellect who, by emanation, creates the cosmos and all that is in it. Since intellect and will are identical in a pure intelligence, God can create simply by thinking. When he contemplates himself he automatically generates the first created being which is, because it stems from him, a pure intelligence.

The first created intelligence, too, can create by contemplation, but since it is a finite intelligence it can contemplate and create in different ways. In contemplating God, it creates the Second Intelligence; in contemplating its own essence and in knowing that it is a contingent being characterized by potentiality, it creates the body of the first celestial sphere; and in contemplating itself and in knowing its existence as necessary in that it flows necessarily from God, it generates the soul of the first celestial sphere.

Since the celestial sphere is attached to a body, its soul is not a pure intelligence and therefore does not create, but it does seek to emulate the perfection of its creator, the First Intelligence. It does so by contemplating the Intelligence and by perfecting its own body. Since the only change simple celestial matter can undergo is a change of position, the soul perfects celestial matter by circular motion. Hence, the First Intelligence is the final cause of both the existence and motion of the first sphere. The Second Intelligence, by contemplating the First Intelligence and by contemplating itself in the twofold manner, produces the Third Intelligence and the body and soul of the second celestial sphere, that containing the stars. In a similar manner, further intelligences and spheres are produced as the creative process works down through the spheres of Saturn, Jupiter, Mars, the sun, Venus, Mercury, and the moon. The Tenth Intelligence does not produce a sphere but it does produce sublunar things by providing souls and forms and by uniting them with suitably disposed complexes of sublunar matter. These complexes of matter come about as the four Aristotelian elements combine and recombine under the influence of the celestial spheres. The Tenth Intelligence is the Agent Intellect or Giver of Forms which looms so large in Avicenna's psychology and which provides a linkage between Aristotle's active intellect and the active intellect of the Scholastics.

Avicenna agrees with Aristotle and disagrees with the theologians in claiming that this creative process is not a temporal process and that it is not creation ex nihilo (out of nothing). Creation is not a temporal event, since time is the measure of change and thus presupposes the existence of matter, and it is not a temporal process because a cause must be contemporaneous with its effect. Furthermore, creation is not ex nihilo since form can only be imprinted on matter that is already available. Consequently, God, matter, the cosmos, and creation itself are eternal. Things exist because God exists, because he contemplates himself necessarily, and because their existence flows directly or indirectly from this contemplation. Insofar as it explains why things exist, the theory of emanation suggests a nontemporal sequence of active, efficient causes grounded in the supreme efficient cause, but it also suggests a hierarchy of essences following from one another in sequence. When God contemplates his own essence he sees the network of implications that flow from it and thus, unlike Aristotle's God, knows the cosmos in detail.

Avicenna's views influenced much subsequent philosophy. Many, if not all, of the later Christian philosophers appreciated the proof of God's existence from the existence of contingent things, the notion of God as an agent, the step in the direction of a suitable creation theory, the doctrine of intelligences as a foundation for a study of angels, God's knowledge of the world, and the identity of essence and existence in God but their sharp separation in other things. They objected to the eternity of the world, the denial of creation *ex nihilo,* the piecemeal emanation of the created world, the determinism, and the doctrine of the Agent Intellect.

Avicenna's reliance on Aristotle, and in particular on the *De anima,* is evidenced from the beginning of his psychology when he classifies souls as vegetable, animal, and human. The vegetable soul is characterized by the faculties of growth, reproduction, and nutrition; the animal has, in addition, those of motion and perception; and the human being is completed by the faculty of reason. There are really two faculties of motion in the animal soul: a psychic one characterized by desire and anger which incite motion towards objects or away from them, and a physical one that actually moves the body by contracting and relaxing the muscles. There are five external senses, each operative when the form of the sensed object is impressed on the physical sense organ. For instance, when light falls on an object it transmits an image through the transparent medium and this image is impressed on the vitreous humor of the eye where it is apprehended by the psychic faculty of sight.

Avicenna's analysis of the internal sense goes considerably beyond that of Aristotle, who did not distinguish explicitly between internal and external senses, and it anticipates in considerable detail that of the Scholastics. There are five internal senses: fantasy or common sense, representation, imagination, the estimative sense, and the recollective or retentive sense. These are unique faculties, each being associated with a different part of the brain. The common sense receives images transmitted to it by the five external senses, enabling us both to know that they differ from one another and to collate the data received from them. The function of representation or sense memory is to preserve the data received by the common sense. An external sense, such as vision, abstracts the form of a particular object from its matter, but it can do so only in the presence of the object, seeing the form with all the determinations imposed upon it by that matter and seeing it as being present in matter. The form in the representative faculty is still particular but it is not seen as being present in or presented by matter. This further abstraction makes memory possible. Imagination is the faculty that enables us to separate and combine the images preserved by representation.

The estimative faculty detects the intentions of animate things and the effects of inanimate ones, thus enabling us to discover their significance for our welfare. On the first occurrence of such an insight, such as the sheep's recognition that the skulking wolf means it no good, the response is an instinctive one in which the estimative sense operates on the images of common sense or representation to abstract the intention. Later it also seems to work by association, for after sense memory has stored up past correlations of a certain sort of visual data, say, with subsequent pain, the occurrence of such a visual datum will trigger the associated image of pain in the imagination and the estimative sense will then note the evil of that object.

Avicenna and the Scholastics note that intentions are not the objects of any of the five external senses, yet they insist, without explaining how it is possible, that intentions can be grasped only by attending to the images of common sense or representation. These intentions are particulars, but since they are nonsensible, our apprehending them marks a yet higher degree of abstraction for here we are abstracting an immaterial thing from a material thing in which it exists only accidentally. Avicenna also points out that noncognitive judgment is involved here and that this is the supreme judging faculty in the animal. Furthermore, it is the function of this faculty to guide the two motive faculties. The function of the recollective or retentive faculty is to retain the judgments or insights of the estimative faculty, just as the representative retains the images of sensible things.

The apprehension of particulars occurs only through bodily organs, for a spatial thing can be present only to another spatial thing. This is so even in the case of the faculties of imagination, representation, and estimation, despite the fact that they operate in the physical absence of the object. This point may be shown thus: imagine two squares of exactly the same size, but separated from each other, and then ask yourself how it is possible for there to be two separate squares. Since the difference cannot be accounted for as a difference of form, it must be the consequence of the same form being manifested in two different places. That is, there must be two images impressed on different areas of the middle ventricle of the brain, which is the physical seat of the psychic faculty of imagination. The point is a general one: the determinate features of our imagery can be accounted for only if the form perceived by the faculty is at the same time a form manifested in matter. This line of reasoning, which does not appear in Aristotle, influenced the Scholastics and reappears quite explicitly in Descartes.

Reason is divided into practical and theoretic faculties. With the help of the theoretic faculty the practical faculty elaborates basic moral principles such as "Tyranny is wrong," "Lying is wrong"; it considers purposes, deliberates, initiates behavior, and produces in the faculty of appetite such responses as shame and laughter.

The theoretic faculty can occur in various degrees. It may be dormant; it may develop to the point where it possesses the primary principles of

281

thought, such as "The whole is greater than its part" and "Things equal to a third are equal to one another"; or it may perfect its potentiality by grasping the secondary principles as well, and thus be in a position to think without the further acquisition of any other principles. These are the various degrees of the Potential Intellect. Finally, the intellect may actually think, exercising the capacities it has perfected at the prior stage. It is then called the Actual or Acquired Intellect. As we shall see later, this last state is not attained unless the Potential Intellect is activated by the Agent Intellect, the Tenth Intelligence.

In order to achieve its end of contemplating pure forms, theoretic reason must complete the process of abstracting forms from matter, a process already initiated by the external and internal senses. That is, it must turn to the imagination, to the images of particular objects, and, through the agency of the Agent Intellect, grasp the forms appearing there free of all the materially imposed determinations they still exhibit. This process of abstraction can be by-passed only by highly gifted individuals, such as the prophets, whose intellects are illuminated directly by the Agent Intellect, the Giver of Forms. Reason recognizes that these pure forms could be manifested in many particular cases, so it regards them as universals; but it also sees that these forms need not have been manifested at all, and therefore that they are, in themselves, neither particular nor universal.

Though he departs from Aristotle in holding that a form is not restricted to its occurrence in matter, Avicenna is not quite a Platonic realist, for he does not admit that a form can exist or subsist by itself. He introduces the famous doctrine of *ante rem, in rebus,* and *post rem,* a doctrine accepted later by Aquinas and others as the solution to the problem of universals. The essences are *ante rem* insofar as they are the exemplars in the Giver of Forms, *in rebus* insofar as they are manifested in sensible objects, and *post rem* insofar as they are grasped free of material considerations by the human intellect.

Knowledge involves the discovery of necessary relations between universals, relations noted directly by intuition, which is a kind of illumination, or established indirectly by syllogistic reasoning. While his model seems to be that of a body of knowledge derived by reason alone from universals and self-evident truths, Avicenna does point out that much of our knowledge about the world, though certain, is based partly on experience. Having noted the constant conjunction between things such as man and rationality, and day and being light, and constant disjunctions such as its not being both day and night, we cannot avoid concluding that the noted constancy reveals a necessary conjunction or disjunction. Thus we are forced to acknowledge necessary truths about the world, truths such as "Man is rational," "If it is day, then it is light," and "Either it is day or it is night." But apart from this sort of assistance, and the assistance of the internal senses as providers of data, the intellect does not need the assistance of the body. It does not operate through a physical organ, for it can know itself and is not disrupted by strong stimuli, as the physical organ of sight is disrupted by a dazzling light. Furthermore, as is required by a faculty that apprehends pure forms, it is an immaterial faculty.

In defending his view that the soul is an immaterial substance, Avicenna invokes his famous "man in the void" argument. Suppose, he says, that a man is created in a void and suppose that his feet, hands, and other physical parts are separated from him in such a way that he has no sensation of them. Under these circumstances he would have no experience of an external world and no experience of his body; nevertheless, he would still be conscious of himself. Consequently, the self he is conscious of must be an immaterial thing. Furthermore, since he can think of himself without thinking that he has a body, having a body is not essential to being a self and therefore is excluded from the nature of the self. That is to say, the immaterial self exists in its own right independently of other things and is therefore a substance. If it is associated with a body, the association is accidental. The soul is an entelechy because it governs and guides the body, but it is no more the form of the body than the pilot is the form of the ship.

This soul did not exist prior to the existence of its body, for if there were a number of preëxisting souls, they would have to differ from one another; to do so is impossible since they would not differ in form nor would they be individuated by matter. If there were one preëxisting soul, it would have to be shared by all men—an absurd idea. Therefore, the individual soul is created when there is a body suitable for it. By binding itself closely to its body the soul is influenced permanently by the peculiar nature of the body and the particular events that be-

fall it. Since the soul is a simple substance it survives the death of the body, carrying over into the hereafter the individuality it has acquired.

In these various respects Avicenna departed from the Aristotelian view of the soul in order to satisfy the requirements of theology. Thus the later Jewish and Christian philosophers welcomed his guidance when they encountered Aristotle. There is also a remarkable coincidence between Avicenna's position and arguments and those of Descartes. The influence of the "man in the void" argument is particularly evident.

To complete the survey of Avicenna's psychology, one must consider the relationship between the human intellect and the Active Intellect. The human intellect does not achieve its highest status, that of apprehending universals and the relations between them, unless it is activated by the Tenth Intelligence, which is the Active Intellect or Giver of Forms. Avicenna describes the Active Intellect as radiating a power which illuminates the potentially intelligible but actually sensible forms of imagination, thereby making them intelligible and thus present to a suitably prepared mind. In this way our potential intellect becomes an actual or acquired intellect. In this process, images are important for two reasons: first, we must abstract the form from an image of the object if we are to grasp the form as the form of an object, and second, we must compare and contrast images in order to raise our intellect to a level where the divine illumination is able to enlighten it. It is to be noted that the Active Intellect, not the human intellect, abstracts the intelligible form from the image in the imagination. Our dependence on the Giver of Forms is evinced further by the fact that since we have no intellectual memory we must reëstablish contact with it every time we think. Later, Thomas Aquinas and others objected to Avicenna's Active Intellect and insisted on fragmenting it into individual active intellects occurring as faculties of individual human souls, thus making man himself responsible for the activating of his potential intellect. They also feared, though Avicenna himself did not, that as long as we all shared the same Active Intellect, personal immortality was jeopardized. Also, they introduced intellectual memory and insisted that when intellection occurs the knower and the known become one.

Since the human intellect is able to contact the Giver of Forms more easily on subsequent occasions, it is able to perfect itself, approaching the ideal of constant contemplation of the forms. By thus emulating the Giver of Forms, which contains all intelligible forms, the soul prepares itself to enjoy a higher and more worthy status when it leaves the body. Insofar as it is the emulated intelligence, the Giver of Forms is a final and formal cause as well as an agent, and insofar as it functions in these ways it brings the human soul into the sequence of efficient, formal and final causes that stems from and culminates in God.

Besides influencing later Jewish and Christian philosophers in the various ways already indicated, Avicenna had a great influence on the work of Averroës, the other great Islamic philosopher. Anyone interested in a critical but sympathetic evaluation of Avicenna, should turn to Averroës.

MONOLOGION and PROSLOGION

Author: Saint Anselm of Canterbury (1033-1109)
Type of work: Theology
First translated: Probably after 1078

PRINCIPAL IDEAS ADVANCED

Since everything good must have a cause, and since the cause is goodness, and since God is goodness, God exists.

Since whatever exists must have a cause, and since a cause depends upon the power to cause, and since God is that power, God exists.

Since degrees of value or reality depend upon reference to absolute excellence and reality, and since God is absolute excellence and reality, God exists. [From the Monologion.]

Since God is the being than whom no greater can be conceived, and since it is better to exist in fact than merely in the imagination, God must exist in fact. [*The ontological argument.*]

God is not substance but Essence (the Father) and a set of essences (the Son);

284

as Father he is the efficient cause (the creator) of all that exists; as Son he is the formal cause (the idea).

St. Anselm was an Augustinian who was unaware of Plotinus and who lived just before the great influx of Aristotle's works through the Arabian and Jewish philosophers. His fame rests to a great extent on his belief that faith is prior to reason, a belief he expresses thus in the well-known words of the *Proslogion:* "For I do not seek to understand that I may believe, but I believe in order to understand. For this I also believe—that unless I believed, I should not understand." After we have accepted on faith the revelations given through Scripture and through the Fathers, reason is able to fulfill its secondary role of clarifying meanings and providing proofs. Yet Anselm was an ambivalent figure, for despite his emphasis on the priority of faith, he felt a very strong need to support it with proofs. Indeed, he extended the scope of reason considerably farther than did the Scholastics who followed him, for they would not have thought of trying to prove doctrines like those of the Trinity and the Incarnation. His rationalism led others to characterize him as the first of the Scholastics.

This summary will concentrate on the other element that contributed to Anselm's fame, the ontological argument as developed in the *Proslogion.* But since they are relevant, the three proofs given in his earlier work, the *Monologion,* will be considered first.

According to the first argument, the goodness of things in this world must be caused and must therefore stem from one thing that is good, or from many. But if many causes have their goodness in common, it is by virtue of this goodness that they cause good things; therefore, we must assume a common source. In either case, whether the cause be one or many, we are led to a single, unitary source of goodness. Since it is the source of all goodness, this source is not good because of something else, but is itself Goodness. (Notice that this argument depends upon a realistic doctrine of essences which will allow an essence such as *goodness* to function not only as a form but also as an active First Cause.) God is Goodness itself, not merely something that possesses goodness.

The second argument follows a similar course with respect to existence. Since whatever exists must have a cause and since an infinite regress of causes is impossible, there must either be one ultimate, nonfinite cause or several causes. If there is but one cause, we have encountered God. If there are several, then either they support each other mutually or they exist independently. The former is impossible, for that which is supported cannot be the cause of that which supports it. But if there are several independent ultimate causes, each must exist through itself, and therefore they must share this common power. Now, since it is this common power that is the source of all else, there cannot be several causes, but only one. (This proof also depends upon the above mentioned doctrine of essences.) God is not something that has this supreme power; he *is* this power.

The third proof depends upon the fact that things in the world can be ranked according to their degrees of "dignity," goodness, or reality. For instance, he says, all will admit that a horse represents a higher degree of reality than a piece of wood, for the horse is animate; similarly, a man outranks a horse, for he is rational. However, the sequence of degrees of reality cannot be an infinite one, for there must be some boundary, some limiting value by which all the rest are measured, a value which is real absolutely. If there should be several things that share this degree of reality, it is nevertheless the case that they are equal because of the common excellence they share. This excellence is the absolute reality which is the source of all relative degrees of reality.

Apparently Anselm thought these proofs too complex, for he tells us in the *Proslogion* that he searched a long time for a simpler proof. The result is the well-known ontological argument. When we think of something, Anselm says, and we are really thinking of it and not just uttering the associated verbal symbol, that thing is in our understanding. Of course, we need not understand that it exists, for we may be thinking of something which we believe does not exist, as in the case of the fool who says in his heart that God does not exist, or we may be thinking of something about whose existence we are uncertain. But in any of these cases, if we are thinking of something, if we understand *it*, then *it*, and not something else, is in the understanding. This point applies to our thought of anything, including God. However, in the case of God, we are thinking about a unique thing, for we are thinking about the greatest thing conceivable, the being "than which nothing greater can be conceived." Now if a being exists in the understanding alone, it cannot be the greatest conceivable thing, for a being that exists in reality as well as in the understanding would be greater. Consequently, since God is the greatest being conceivable he must exist in reality as well as in the understanding. Or, to put it another way, if the greatest conceivable being exists in the understanding alone, then it is not the greatest conceivable being—a conclusion which is absurd.

This argument met opposition from the beginning in the person of the monk Gaunilo, who criticized Anselm in his *In Behalf of the Fool*. First, Gaunilo says that because God's nature is essentially mysterious we do not have an idea of him. We may think we do, but we have only the verbal symbol, for when we hear the word "God," what are we to think or imagine? The proof fails, then, for the term "God" does not denote any *conceivable* thing. Second, he says that if the argument were sound, we could prove the existence of other things. By way of example he invites us to think of an island which is blessed with more good features and is therefore better than any actual land with which we are acquainted; then he suggests that we must admit its existence, since if it exists in the mind alone it would not be as good as lands which we know to exist. Third, he says that an idea or concept is only a part of the understanding itself, and that the existing object, if there is one, is something else. From the fact that an idea occurs it does not follow that something quite different in status also occurs. The fact that I am thinking of a being, thinking of it as the greatest conceivable being, and therefore thinking of it as existing necessarily, does not provide the slightest evidence that there actually is such a being, for the thought of a necessarily existing being is one thing and a necessarily existing being is another.

Anselm replies to the first objection by saying that the proof does not require a complete understanding of God, but only that we understand this much: that whatever else he may be, God is such that no greater being than he can be conceived. Even the fool must admit this much before he can refuse to believe. In reply to the second objection he says that God, unlike the blessed isle, is not thought of simply as the greatest thing of a certain type, or even as the greatest thing of all, but as the being than which nothing greater can be conceived. This latter concept can refer to only one thing, and that thing quite obviously is not the blessed isle. Later proponents of the argument, such as Descartes, make the same point by asserting that existence is contained in the essence of only one thing; namely, the greatest conceivable being.

The third objection, which has ever since been a standard one, is more difficult to handle. It seems to pinpoint an obvious defect, yet Anselm and many others were not daunted by it. In his reply to Gaunilo, Anselm hardly seems aware of it, for he simply repeats again, as if the objection had not been raised, that if we understand a thing, then it exists in the understanding. Since we are likely to feel more at home with Gaunilo's theory of ideas than with Anselm's, it will be necessary to reconstruct Anselm's doctrine in order to see why the objection seemed so unimportant to him. To do so we must explore a little further the nature of the divine being whose existence is supposed to be proved by the argument.

Anselm regarded God as self-caused, but the nature of this causation is quite mysterious. God could not have functioned as his own efficient, material, or instrumental cause, for all these causes must be prior to their effect, and not even God could exist prior to himself. For a similar reason God did not create himself. Yet he does exist through himself and from himself. By way of explication, Anselm presents us with a model, that of light. Light lights another thing by falling on it, but it also lights itself, for it is lucent. Its lucidity must come from itself, though, of course, it does not fall upon itself. Now, he says, in God the relation between *essence, to be,* and *being (existing)* is like the relation between *the light, to light,* and *lucent.* The implication is that the essence of God, the being he enjoys, and the generating of this being are one and the same thing. Like his master Augustine, Anselm conceived of God as an active essence, an activity which necessarily exists, not simply because it is active, but because its activity is the activity of existing.

In other places, too, Anselm indicates quite clearly that God is not a substance having matter and form. First, he points out that if God were such a substance he would be composite, a state impossible in a being that is the unitary source of all and in a being that has no prior cause. Furthermore, God cannot be a substance possessing such qualities as justness, wisdom, truth, and goodness; for if he were, he would be just, wise, true, and good through another and not through himself. God does not *possess* justness and wisdom; he *is* justice and wisdom. That is, as was indicated in the earlier proofs, God is identical with these essences, and since in him they are one and the same essence, God is an Essence.

We are led to this same conclusion by another route, that of creation. As pure spirit, God creates the matter of the world *ex nihilo,* but he creates it according to a model he had in mind prior to the creation. That is, as Augustine had said earlier, all the essences that are manifested in the world existed in God's thought prior to the creation. Insofar as this network of essences is the model according to which the world is created, it is the formal first cause of the world (Augustine had called the divine ideas "the reasons"), and as first cause it is identical with God. Following Augustine, Anselm says that insofar as God *is* this expression of the world he has an intelligence; he is Wisdom, the Word, the Son. But the important point as far as the ontological argument is concerned is this: God is not thought of as a substance in the ordinary sense, but as an Essence (the Father) and also as a set of essences (the Son) that function respectively as efficient and formal cause of the world. Again, as in the proofs of the *Monologion,* God the Creator is thought of as an acting essence. It is to be noted that we have in God the Father the highest degree of reality an essence can enjoy—that of an eternally acting essence that exists in and through itself.

Anselm's doctrine of creation throws still further light on the ontological argument. It is to be noted that the essences that exist prior to creation are not created, for they are the eternal exemplars. As the Son, they are sustained by God insofar as he is the ground of all, but since they *are* the intellect of God, they are not the products of a mind and they do not depend for their existence on being in a mind. Thus, there are essences which do not enjoy the highest degree of reality, but which do enjoy a degree higher than that which they would if they were mind dependent. As Anselm says, prior to their manifestation in matter, they were not nothing. Since they are consubstantial with God, they are beings in their own right. Anselm leans as far in the direction of a Platonic realism as his theology will allow him.

Anselm was not clear about the manner in which we apprehend general ideas, but he insists that these ideas are the essences we have just discussed. This follows not only from his realistic doctrine of ideas, but also from his theory of truth. When we apprehend a thing truly, we apprehend its nature, but if it exists truly, then it manifests truly the essence God intended it to manifest. Hence, when we think truly we are apprehending one or more of the essences that constitute the intellect of God. (Thus, God is Truth.) This is not to say that we apprehend essences as they exist in God, for there they are exemplars, but what we apprehend does come directly or indirectly, clearly or obscurely, from God. Since the ideas in our understanding *come* into our understanding, their existence does not depend upon our understanding and is not restricted to their occurrence there. This is what Anselm means when he says that the things we understand are in our understanding.

In speaking as if we already knew that these essences constitute the mind of God, it might seem that we beg the question which is to be settled by the ontological argument, but an account of Anselm's doctrine of creation serves to illuminate the way in which he thinks of God and of essences. In both the *Proslogion* and the *Monologion,* Anselm emphasizes the proposition that essences are characters that may be shared in common by many things and that they are ontologically prior to these things. And we may assume that he would agree with Augustine, whom he follows in so many respects, that the eternity and immutability of self-evident truths and of the essences involved in them, and the fact that many minds can share the same ideas, are sufficient evidence that general ideas are not created by mutable and independent minds. At any rate, the argument presupposes that since they are not mind dependent, essences can occur elsewhere than in minds. Thus, we can conceive of an essence enjoying a higher degree of reality, such as existing in the physical world or, perhaps, existing in such a way that it is self-sustaining. That some of the essences we apprehend also enjoy a higher degree of reality cannot be denied, for they are manifested as material objects. The only question, and the interesting one, is whether any essence we can apprehend also enjoys the supreme degree of reality. It would be worth examining the various essences we apprehend to see if there is any case where this is so. Anselm says we are led to a positive answer in the case of one and only one essence, that of the "being than which none greater can be conceived," for in this case alone the essence is such that it necessarily exists.

If we are to do justice to Anselm and understand the strong appeal this argument had for him and many others, we must be clear about the fact that throughout the argument he is talking about an essence. The premises are premises about an essence and the conclusion is a statement about this very same essence. It is not, as Gaunilo insisted, a conclusion about something else. Gaunilo's objection would be valid, as it is in the example of the blessed isle, if Anselm had concluded that an essence has been manifested in matter. But since manifestation in matter is always an accident, this is not something that could be discovered by examining an essence alone. It is crucial to the argument that existence in matter should not be thought of as the highest level of existence and that the being concerned should not be thought of as a composite of form and substance. The argument can move only from essence to Pure Essence, or *Essentia*. That is, it can only reveal to us something more about essence, and this is just what it does when it shows that one of the essences we apprehend is an active self-sustaining essence.

This discussion does not show that Anselm's argument is sound, but perhaps it does show that the whole question centers around two radically different theories about ideas, essences, and objects. Historically, philosophers who have found Anselm's argument acceptable have leaned toward a Platonic or Neoplatonic realism in which the role of essences is emphasized and that of matter minimized. The proof was not accepted by the Aristotelians who dominated the philosophic world for four or five centuries after Anselm, nor by the nominalists and empiricists who have dominated so much of philosophic thought in the last three hundred years; but it is adopted in one form or another by Descartes, Liebniz, Spinoza, and Hegel, who, despite the fact that they diverge radically from one another, are each influenced, directly or indirectly, by Plato, Plotinus, or Augustine.

289

THE GLOSSES ON PORPHYRY

Author: Peter Abelard (1079-1142)
Type of work: Epistemology
First transcribed: Early twelfth century

PRINCIPAL IDEAS ADVANCED

A universal is that which is formed to be predicated of many; since things cannot be predicated of many, only words are universals.

A universal word is imposed on things because of a common likeness conceived by the person imposing the word.

The common likeness of things is a function of the nature of things considered as causes of common conceptions.

Universals signify existent things; namely, discrete individuals; but, in a sense, universals consist in the understanding alone.

Universal words are corporeal with respect to the nature of things, and they are incorporeal with respect to the manner in which they signify.

Universals signify sensible things, but since the intrinsic substance signified is naturally separated from the things signified, universals are, in that sense, insensible.

One of the most colorful and fascinating figures of the Middle Ages was Peter Abelard. Many who know little about the technicalities of medieval logic still know about the life and loves of Abelard. Some mystery and much romance surround the events of his life, and beneath this fascination the fact that Abelard was undoubtedly one of the more skilled philosophers of the era is sometimes forgotten. For one thing, much less of his work has been translated than that of others from the same period who are, consequently, now better known. Furthermore, his particular doctrines have not gained the fame which has come to others. No matter how important *The Glosses on Porphyry* may be in a medieval setting, the idea of practicing philosophy through such commentary is not a currently accepted form. Yet it is true that few more than Porphyry

were responsible for the problems which dominated the Middle Ages, so that Abelard's glosses concern crucial issues.

This work belongs to the branch of philosophy which Abelard, following Boethius, called "rational" (the other divisions being the "speculative" and the "moral"). It corresponds most nearly to what we call logic, although it comprehends a slightly wider area of problems than perhaps our formal logic does. Porphyry prepared an introduction for the *Categories* of Aristotle and upon this Abelard comments. In spite of a lack of available Aristotelian material, he was able to construct Aristotle's doctrines with judgment. Abelard's treatment of the problem of the status of universals really ended the argument in its all-absorbing attraction; from then on it was only one among a series of problems. Abelard, it is true, was condemned by his church for his doctrines, since they seemed to lead to paganism.

Definition, division, and classification are the central logical problems to be considered first. Essential definition is the main issue and consequently all of these logical problems basically involve metaphysical issues. For there is no question but that in Porphyry's mind, and Abelard's too, logical division is division according to real structures actually present in nature. How are the creatures of the natural order divided? This question concerns as much the way of things as it does the ways of logical procedure, for in the medieval mind the two are to be worked on until they become the same. The mind adjusts its classifications to the divisions it finds in nature. Logical investigation is ontological inquiry and through it the structure of the world is grasped.

The prominent controversy regarding the status of universals is raised through logical inquiry, since it has metaphysical overtones. We cannot decide about genus and species without deciding whether universals are real. We divide according to genus and species, but we cannot be content to do this as a logical convenience. We must ask: Does such division represent anything real, when it is obvious that every individual thing is singular and not universal, representative of the species but never the species itself? Abelard asks the question: Do universals apply to things or only to words, once we have been forced to a study of universals through the study of genus and species?

Abelard must first define what a universal is. Then, after quoting Aristotle and Porphyry, he refines his own definition: that is universal which is formed to be predicated of many. The question of the ontological status of universals has been raised by a logical question and formulated in logical terms. Abelard begins by supposing that things as well as words are included within this definition.

If things as well as words are called universal, how can the universal definition be applied to things also? As usual, Abelard begins to deal with this question by considering the views of those who have formulated this problem. Many, he says, solve this issue by asserting that in different things there is present a substance essentially the same in spite of the fact that the various things differ in form. Porphyry seems to assent to this solution in arguing that by participation in the species many men are one. Other philosophers are of different opinions, and Abelard begins to formulate his own solution by finding one opinion from among these which seems to him to be closest to the truth, namely, the suggestion that individual things are different from each other not only in their forms, but also in their essences. He concludes that things cannot be universals because they are not predicated of many.

In retrospect, there seems to be no question but that much early medieval interpretation of Aristotle was substantially influenced by Neoplatonic doctrines. Abelard, like many others, was working toward the empirical stress upon the unique individual, which came to be recognized as more accurate Aristotelian doctrine. In working on the problem of the status of universals, Abelard attempted to reconcile the Platonic suggestion that universals subsist independently of things with the Aristotelian view which stressed the individual as primary and the universal as a function of the status of things, existing only in things.

Some philosophers maintain that the universal is merely a collection of many individual things, but this is too weak a status to assign to universals, in Abelard's view. He saw that, although a collection of men is called a species, when the universal *man* is predicated of each individual, it is not the whole collection of men which is predicated. A universal must be something other than a collection taken as a whole.

As most medievals came to do, obviously Abelard was trying to mediate between what he considered to be two extreme views, to work out a modified position which would give sufficient status to universals without making them in some sense more real than individuals. Being theologically oriented, he could not do away with universals or make them simply a product of language, since they are present in God's understanding and important to his way of knowing. On the other hand, like all those who became interested in Aristotle in the later Middle Ages, Abelard wanted to correct what he felt had been in error in previous ideas concerning universals and to stress the primacy of individuals and their status.

Abelard, however, could not go along with those who called single individuals predicated of many things universals, on the ground that the many things agreed with the individuals in certain respects. Neither a collection taken together, then, nor an individual thing could be called a universal; consequently, Abelard believed that universals belong to words alone. There are universal words and there are particular words. If this is so, what then had to be done was to inquire carefully into the property of universal words. What is the common cause by which the universal word is imposed and what is the conception of the common likeness of things? And more important, is the word called common because of a common cause (or respect) in which the things agree, or because of a common conception, or because of both at once? These questions, Abelard found by his examination of other doctrines, form the heart of the issue concerning universals. Dealing with these questions is the only way a solution can be hoped for.

In order to deal with the issues, Abelard argued, we must first be clear about the process of understanding itself. (This is typically Aristotelian.) When we understand the relation between the mind and the objects which it seeks to understand, and how it comes to form that understanding, then we shall learn the status of the universal. In other words, the universal is to be understood primarily as a part of the process of understanding itself. And what Abelard found is that the understanding of universals differs and is to be distinguished from the understanding of particulars.

Here Abelard turned to theology and considered the question of universals as concerning the operation of God's mind. God must have universal conceptions in his mind as a necessary part of his creative function. Man, as a human artist, however, does not need such universal patterns. Universal conceptions exist in God's mind, but not in man's, and this is one meas-

292

ure of their difference. Man does have certain intrinsic forms which do not come to him through the senses, such as rationality and mortality. (Aristotle had also realized that not all knowledge could be formed from the senses and the apprehension of individuals).

What, then, is responsible for the common reference of universal words? Is it due to a common cause of imposition or to a common conception? Abelard came to the conclusion that it is due to both, but he regarded the common cause in accordance with the nature of things as having a greater force. There is, then, a source for universal conception in the things themselves from which the understanding forms its conceptions, although some universals result merely from the formation of common conceptions. The conception of universals is formed by abstraction.

Having come this far, Abelard believed that his analysis had provided the ground necessary to propose a solution to the question about universals and their status, the question which Porphyry had originally raised. Universals signify things truly existent; they are not merely empty opinions. Nevertheless, in a certain sense they exist in the understanding alone. Again, if we divide things into either corporeal or incorporeal and ask where in this division universals belong, the answer must be that they belong to both divisions. Universals in a sense signify corporeal things in that they are imposed according to the nature of things; and yet in another sense they signify incorporeal things, with respect to the manner in which they signify.

Universals are said to subsist in sensible things; that is, they signify an intrinsic substance existing in a thing which is sensible by its exterior form. However, although they signify this substance which subsists actually in the sensible thing, at the same time they demonstrate the same substance as naturally separated from the sensible thing. Some universals are sensible with respect to the nature of things, and the same universal may be non-sensible with respect to the mode of signifying. Universals refer to sensible things, but they refer to them in an incorporeal manner. They signify both sensible things and at the same time that common conception which is ascribed primarily to the divine mind.

Singular words involve no such doubt as to their meaning. As things are discrete in themselves, so they are signified by singular words discretely, and the understanding of them refers to definite things. Universals do not have this easy reference, which is what involves the understanding of them in such difficulty. There is no definite thing, as is the case with singular words, with which they agree. Nevertheless, the multitude of things themselves is the cause of the universality of the nouns which are used to refer to them, because only that which contains many is universal. Yet the thing itself does not have the universality which the thing confers upon the word.

In some sense such a solution as Abelard has proposed—a moderate realism—could be accused of not being definite. What he did was to reject extreme solutions, on the one hand, and, on the other hand, to set the limits of the question and the mode in which the question ought to be asked. Only an extreme position is likely to be clear; any solution which attempts to hold to a moderate view is always in danger of slipping over to one of the extremes and will suffer from appearing to hold both extreme positions at once.

Yet the value in Abelard's analysis is the raising of the problems, the cast given to the question, and the elucida-

tion of the difficulties involved in any solution. The subtle analysis is to some extent illuminating in its own right, and understanding it gives us an appreciation both of Abelard and of the tradition which set his problems for him.

THE INCOHERENCE OF THE INCOHERENCE

Author: Averroës (ibn-Roshd, 1126-1198)
Type of work: Theology, metaphysics
First transcribed: Twelfth century

PRINCIPAL IDEAS ADVANCED

Since any series of causes necessary through another cause must ultimately depend upon a cause necessary in itself (a first cause), God, as the first cause, exists.

God did not create the world in time, either by willing it at the moment of creation or by willing it eternally, for to act in time is to change, and God is changeless because he is perfect.

God, as first cause and unmoved mover, does not act in time, but he produces immaterial intelligences which, because of their imperfection, can change in time.

The being of existent things is inseparable from their essence.

Averroës, the last of the great Islamic philosophers, lived roughly one hundred and fifty years after Avicenna, his philosophic rival, and about three generations after Ghazali (1058-1111) the greatest of Moslem thelogians. In his controversy with these two men he concerned himself primarily with the defense and purification of Aristotle, whom he followed as closely as he could. Since he, too, accepted such spurious works as *The Theology of Aristotle,* his interpretation is still permeated by Neoplatonic elements, but

to a lesser extent than that of Avicenna. The success of his endeavor is indicated by the fact that he was known to scholastic writers as *the* Commentator and that no less a person than Thomas Aquinas had him constantly at hand as he wrote his *Summa contra Gentiles* (c.1258-1260) and his various commentaries on Aristotle.

The Incoherence of the Incoherence was written in reply to Ghazali's book, *The Incoherence of the Philosophers,* a book in which Ghazali had attacked the philosophers, and in particular Avicenna, for advocating doctrines that were incompatible with their faith. As the title of his own book suggests, Averroës came to the defense of the philosophers by attacking the incoherence of *The Incoherence*. Adopting a position similar to that of the later medieval thinkers who distinguished between revealed and natural theology, Averroës scrupulously avoided denying any tenet of his faith; nevertheless, he sided firmly with the philosophers. His interpretations of religious doctrines were so far removed from those of the theologians that even though he was studied carefully by Hebrew and Christian philosophers, he was not recognized to any great extent by his Islamic contemporaries. Averroës' book plays a very important role in the long controversy between the philosophers and the theologians, since it is concerned chiefly with the nature and existence of God, and with the relationship between God and the cosmos. Averroës does not spell out his position in detail, for he agrees on the whole with the earlier commentators on Aristotle and with the version of Aristotle he receives from them. In particular, he agrees largely with Avicenna, disagreeing on those points, and they are important points, where he thinks Avicenna departs from Aristotle. (The reader is referred to the article on Avicenna in this book.)

Averroës agrees with Aristotle that there is a First Cause, and he accepts a modified version of Avicenna's proof from contingency. Objects whose existence is contingent rather than necessary must have a cause. If the cause is itself contingent, and if its cause is contingent, and so on, there would be an infinite regress and therefore no cause at all, a conclusion which, it can readily be seen, denies the assumption that contingent objects must have a cause. Hence, any series of contingent objects must be preceded in existence by a necessary cause which is either necessary through another or necessary without a cause—necessary in itself. But if we have a series of causes each of which is necessary through another, once more we have an infinite regress and thus no cause. Hence, any series of causes necessary through another must depend upon a cause necessary in itself—a First Cause.

The nature of this First Cause and of the way in which it causes is illuminated by Averroës' discussion of creation. Averroës agrees with the philosophers against Ghazali that the world was not created in time. The philosophers had argued that if the world was created in time, it was created directly or indirectly by God, since an infinite regress of causes is impossible. If God created it in time, then he acted at a time and therefore underwent a change in time; but unquestionably, this is an impossible state of affairs since God is perfect and changeless. To Ghazali's objection that God did not act in time, but decreed from all eternity that the world should come into being at a certain time, Averroës replies that even if God had so willed from all eternity, he must also have acted at the time of creation in order to implement his decision, for every effect must have a contemporaneous cause. Consequently, the philosopher's objection cannot be avoided. It can be shown similarly that the cosmos is incorruptible; that is, that there is no time at which it will come to an end, for this too would require a change in God. Change occurs only within the world and then only when one thing is changed into another. The world itself is eternal and everlasting.

Ghazali had already attacked Avicenna on this point, asserting that the followers of Aristotle now have a problem on their hands, for they must give some account of how an eternal First Cause produces things that have a beginning in time. The problem is complicated by the fact that Averroës and Avicenna agreed with Aristotle that since the world is eternal, infinite temporal sequences do occur. For instance, there was no time when the celestial sphere began to move and no time when the first man appeared. Why not, chides Ghazali, agree with the materialists that since there is an infinite sequence of causes, a First Cause is not only superfluous but impossible?

In reply, Averroës asks us to consider the case of the infinite sequence of past positions of a celestial sphere. Like Avicenna, he says that so far as the sphere is concerned this sequence is an accidental infinite, for the motion of the sphere at any given moment does not cause the motion it has at any other moment. First, if motion did cause motion there would be an infinite regress of causes and therefore no cause at all. Second, since motion is continuous, there are in it no discrete units that have a beginning and an end and therefore no units that could stand in a causal relationship to one another. Finally, since the cause must be contemporaneous with the effect, the causal relation cannot span an interval of time, and past motion cannot influence present motion. In the case of the celestial sphere, the motion it has at any given moment follows, not from the motion it had at some previous moment, but from its desire at that mo-

ment to emulate the perfection of the associated Intelligence. Through all eternity this Intelligence has sustained it in motion from moment to moment by continuously acting as its final cause. Since this Intelligence is itself a being whose existence is necessary through another, we are led back to the First Cause, the Unmoved Mover who stands behind the world. The Mover itself does not operate in time nor does it cause time directly, but it does produce an Intelligence which, because it is immaterial, is changeless, but which, because it is imperfect, is able to produce change of position in the sphere and thus to produce change in time.

Averroës' treatment of the infinite sequence of man begetting man is somewhat different from the preceding argument, for in this case there are discrete objects which do seem to cause one another successively. But here, too, Averroës says the sequence is, in itself, an accidental infinite. To be sure, the sequence does depend upon man, but only in several secondary senses. First, as he puts it, the third man can come from the second only if the first man has perished. That is, since the amount of matter in the universe is limited, human bodies can continue to come into existence only if others perish. Second, through the phenomena of conception and growth, man is the instrument by which God produces other men. But having functioned in both cases as a material cause by providing suitable matter, man's role is complete, for no body can produce a form in another. Directly or indirectly, the First Mover is the source of the eternal form that, when individuated by matter, animates that matter. Here again Averroës describes the Mover or one of the Intelligences as operating eternally as a final cause, again and again drawing forth from complexes of matter the form that is contained in them potentially.

Averroës then considers the question raised by Ghazali as to how it is possible for the plurality in the world to arise from the Mover, who is simple. Avicenna had argued that only one thing can emanate from God, but that this thing, the First Intelligence, is able to generate more than one thing by contemplating both itself and the Mover. Averroës replies, first, that since thought and its object are identical, the Intelligence is really identical with its thought of God and with its thought of itself and, therefore, that these thoughts are identical with each other. Hence, there is no plurality of thought and no plurality of creation. Second, he says that when Avicenna insists that only one thing can come from God, he is thinking of the Supreme Intellect as if it were a finite empirical one, but this concept is a mistake. Since our intellect is limited by matter, any particular mental act can have only one object, but since God is not so limited he can think all things even though his simplicity and changelessness preclude a plurality of acts. If it be replied that to think of all things is to have many thoughts, and that since thinker and thought are identical, God must be plural, Averroës replies that when God thinks all things he does not think them discursively as we do. In our case either we entertain images, a process which unquestionably involves spatial apprehension and thus spatial plurality, or we understand concepts by genus and species, a process which again introduces plurality. In either case, since we apprehend the object of thought by abstracting it from its material context, we apprehend it imperfectly. God, who is perfect, does not apprehend the natures of things in these ways and therefore does not apprehend them as either individual or universal. In some manner which we do not understand, he comprehends that which is plural to us but does not comprehend it as numerically plural. (This is a particular application of the general principle that any property or capacity we attribute to God must be attributed only by analogy.) God, then, is the source of all plurality even though he is simple and changeless.

Averroës accepts the Avicennian cosmology in its general outlines. The First Mover produces a number of pure Intelligences which may produce others and which cause the motions of their respective spheres or, in the case of the Agent Intellect, preside over generation and corruption in the sublunar world. The Mover is the efficient cause of these Intelligences, producing them by means of a power that it emanates, and the final and formal cause insofar as it is the thing they seek to emulate. They in turn are the efficient, final, and formal causes of the motion of the spheres. Averroës agrees with Avicenna that though prime matter is not created, the existence of material things depends upon the Mover in that he is the source of the forms and also the agent, final, and formal cause of the manifestation of any form in matter.

But despite this agreement Averroës disagrees with Avicenna on a number of points. Some, such as the number of Intelligences (over forty), and the non-linear order of the Intelligences (the Mover may have produced all of the Intelligences of the principle spheres directly) are unimportant, but others are crucial. As we have already indicated, Averroës insists that the Intelligences really are simple in that they do not contemplate themselves in several essentially different ways. It follows that the spheres are not composites of soul and body even though they are animate, and that God is the source of plurality. Consequently, God does not function as Avicenna says he does. Whether by intention or not, Avicenna left the impression that God's role in the creative process was completed when he produced the First Intelligence and that the further creative acts were contributed piecemeal by the various Intelligences acting from their own natures. In locating the source of plurality in God, Averroës is insisting that direct responsibility for the whole creative process rests with God. It is true, he says, that the Intelligences are creative agents, but they are the Mover's subordinates who, out of respect for him, implement his commands throughout the cosmos. Setting aside the theological analogy, we understand a theory such as this to mean that God's essence functions as the efficient, formal, and final cause of the First Intelligence, that this intelligence is an imperfect manifestation of the essence of God, that God as thus reflected functions once more as the efficient, formal, and final cause of an Intelligence or soul inferior to the first one, and so on down through the hierarchy.

Averroës also differes from Avicenna in a respect which anticipates the contrast between Spinoza and Leibniz, for he loosens the Avicenna bonds of necessity. To be sure, in some sense God does what he does necessarily, but this is not logical necessity, for the world he contemplates and thus produces is the best of all possible worlds. Similarly,

the various intelligences respond to God, not because it would be contradictory not to, but because they respect him. There is a definite normative element permeating the system. On the general issue of the relation between God and the world Averroës does not differ from Avicenna as greatly as he frequently says he does; nevertheless, his modifications are important and they do result in a weakening of the Neoplatonic elements, a fact that was appreciated by later Aristotelians.

Another historically important feature of Averroës' philosophy is his rejection of Avicenna's sharp distinction between essence and existence. Avicenna had insisted that except in the case of God, existence is an accident that happens to an essence. For Avicenna, existence is a condition that must be satisfied by an essence before it can occur outside a mind, a property that must be added to it. Thus, the existence of a material object does not stem from its essence, but from what happened to its essence. On the other hand, Averroës insists that the very being of an existent thing is its essence, that its being depends upon the essence and not upon what happens to the essence. For him the terms "being" and "existence" are not verb terms, but substantives applied primarily to the object itself and secondarily to the essence that makes it the sort of thing it is. Since the object is a being or existent in virtue of its essence, it is impossible to separate essence and existence save in thought. The essence itself may be regarded as an existent in a secondary sense of that term, but in this case it is impossible to separate essence and existence even in thought.

This difference between the two men is reflected in their views, inasmuch as Avicenna is very much concerned with how things come into existence and Averroës shows himself to be more concerned with the manner in which things change. Thus, in their proofs of the existence of God, Avicenna moves from the contingent existence of things to a necessarily existing ground, whereas Averroës proceeds from the occurrence of motion to an unmoved mover. Again, whereas Avicenna's Giver of Forms is bringing essences into existence by impressing them upon suitably prepared matter, Averroës' Agent Intellect is coaxing out forms nascent in complexes of matter. Averroës insists correctly that Avicenna is moving away from Aristotle and that he himself is truer to their common master. Later, Thomas Aquinas and his followers follow Avicenna in making a sharp distinction between essence and existence, but they acknowledge Averroës' objection by transforming existence from a property into an act of being that is prior in principle to essence. On the other hand, Ockham and the Averroists of the fourteenth, fifteenth, sixteenth, and seventeenth centuries insist that Averroës is right and that Avicenna and Thomas are wrong.

Another historically important feature of Averroës' philosophy is his disagreement with several aspects of Avicenna's psychology. First, and not so important, he believes that Avicenna added a superfluous faculty to the animal soul when he attributed an estimative sense to animals, a sense paralleling the cogitative sense in man. The ancients were correct, he says, in maintaining that imagination can detect intentions as well as sensible forms and that it can make judgments about these intentions. More important, Averroës gives a radically different account of the theoretic intellect. He agrees with Avicenna that the individual human intellect is activated only by the Agent Intellect which is external to us and acts on all of us alike, but he disagrees about the nature of the intellect that is activated. According to Avicenna, it is the potential intellect, an immaterial intellect, that can survive the body; but according to Averroës, it is the passive intellect, a corporeal faculty, that cannot survive the body. Averroës does admit an immaterial potential intellect in addition to the corporeal passive intellect; but it is not a personal faculty, for it is simply the Agent Intellect insofar as it individuates itself when it illuminates the passive intellect in order to prepare it for the reception of intelligible forms. Averroës thinks of the immaterial soul as being individuated when it strikes a physical object. Thus, there is no personal immortality, for individuality within the immaterial intellect disappears when the corporeal passive intellect dies. From the point of view of the Christian philosophers of the twelfth and thirteenth centuries, Averroës is correct insofar as he gives the potential and agent intellects a common status, but incorrect insofar as he denies that they are personal faculties. They preferred to modify Avicenna by eliminating the Tenth Intelligence and endowing each human being with an individual agent intellect to accompany the individual potential intellect he already has.

GUIDE FOR THE PERPLEXED

Author: Maimonides (Moses ben Maimon, 1135-1204)
Type of work: Metaphysics, theology
First transcribed: 1190

PRINCIPAL IDEAS ADVANCED

Those who have become perplexed about religious matters as a result of studying philosophy can be helped by realizing that scriptural writings may often be understood in a figurative sense.

It is precisely because of the difficulty of understanding the divine that metaphor becomes useful in religious utterances.

Once the necessity for an indirect approach to religious matters is admitted, faith becomes a way of relating oneself to a Being whose mystery is understood metaphorically.

"From Moses to Moses there was none like Moses" is a famous phrase which indicates something of Maimonides' place of importance in Jewish thought. The First Moses represents the origin of the great Jewish religious tradition and the Jewish Law. The Second Moses stands for, as is now well known, an attempt to reconcile this inherited tradition with the growing Arabian and Western philosophy and culture which were being absorbed in the eleventh century.

Intellectuals of his age were perplexed by the disparity between the Law, which meant so much to them, and the philosophical sophistication they could not resist acquiring. For them Maimonides provided a *Guide*, as well as a new summary of the Law, both of which were so successful that they have now become classics in the religious tradition as well as in secular philosophy. Can Maimonides once again serve as a guide for our time, or does our situation require new prophets? Let us begin by an inquiry into the way in which Maimonides met the need of his own day.

Maimonides addressed his *Guide* to those who had studied philosophy and had acquired knowledge and who "while firm in religious matters are perplexed and bewildered on account of the ambiguous and figurative expressions employed in holy writings." We are not, then, beginning here with philosophic reason and attempting to find a religious view which will fit it. Moses' audience was from the beginning firmly committed to its religious tradition; but, now that philosophy had penetrated religion, the question was never one as to whether religion should be maintained but only how it was to handle its philosophical content. Maimonides wrote for those whose religious roots were deep and who had held to religious practice. "The object of this treatise is to enlighten a religious man who has been trained to believe in the truth of our holy Law, who conscientiously fulfills his moral and religious duties, and at the same time has been successful in his philosophical studies." This is not the description of a hollow man.

It is not difficult to see why such a

person was "lost in perplexity and anxiety," caught in tensions he could not easily resolve. His religious training was too deeply ingrained even to consider surrendering it, and yet the new sophistication made philosophy naturally attractive. It is not that such a person had for the first time become an intellectual, since as a Jew he had inherited a long and subtle intellectual tradition; but that formerly reason had worked only within the Law, while afterwards philosophy took this same reason outside the Law and offered it new and alien foundations. This was the general cause for concern, but *Guide for the Perplexed* focuses on the particular problem of trying to explain certain words in Scripture central to the religious tradition whose common interpretation sets them at odds with philosophical refinements. Reason never ceased to accept the Law, but it found it difficult to accept any teaching based on a literal interpretation of the Law.

Furthermore, the perplexity had to be met by finding a way to live with it, since to surrender either the Law or the newly found philosophy was unacceptable. Moses' attempt is never to try to remove the source of the anxiety, as might seem natural, but to try to find a way in which to adapt to it. To surrender religion would mean to break down the context which gave meaning and continuity to Jewish life, but to surrender philosophy would be no service to religion either, since it would leave religion still disturbed by the unanswered philosophical questions. To reject philosophy would not remove the objections with which philosophy perplexes religion. Since there could be no escape from perplexity, it had to be met and accepted as the

starting point and the necessary condition.

Maimonides' first step toward meeting this perplexity is the ancient one of suggesting that the offending words in Scripture may also be understood in a figurative sense. While this is the general line of Maimonides' reply, he was quick to see that it would provide only temporary relief from perplexity unless backed up by an explanation as to why it was necessary to use figurative language in the first place. This he began to do by explaining that even in Natural Science some topics are not fully explained, that most difficult problems cannot be thoroughly understood by any one of us, and that, since men differ in degree of intelligence, truth is withheld from the multitude of ordinary men, and, therefore, their objections can be ignored. The necessity for metaphor, it seems, cannot be explained until men are convinced that reason allows only a few to reach great heights, and that even here they must all accept final limitations.

If such is the case, we are forced back to metaphor as the most adequate means available for expressing what we do know. If all obscurity could be removed from the subject, then literal terms could be used without reservation. Since literal description is completely successful only where all tinges of mystery can be removed, the acceptance of metaphorical expression depends upon the existence of some sense of mystery where God is concerned. The purely philosophical mind might have difficulty accepting mystery, even in the case of God, but what must be recognized is that Maimonides wrote for a man overtly religious, for whom the sense of mystery in the divine nature did not seem at all abnormal.

Maimonides was not fooled, it is important to note, into thinking that an allegorical interpretion of religious literature is a full explanation to a philosophical mind. Instead, the intention of this method is to show the philosophical-religious mind the reasons why to ask for a complete exposition in these matters is an exorbitant demand. The difficulty of understanding a literal impossibility arises only for the intelligent, since the ill-informed do not recognize an impossibility when it appears. Yet the intelligent observer who can admit the plausibility of a secret meaning need not reject the difficult religious doctrine at once, since he can treat it allegorically, as well as literally, to see if it may be accepted in this second mode. What is important to see here is that for Maimonides the literal meaning was never to be rejected but was always to be retained along with the more subtle metaphorical treatment.

All of this can serve to relieve philosophical perplexity, but, interestingly enough, it can do so only for one made sensitive to the limitations of human reason through a religious tradition. Without the religious sensitivity no solution can be found. The religiously untrained person simply cannot see the need for metaphorical expression. It takes some acquaintance with God, which only a religious discipline is likely to provide, to convince one of how difficult a matter it is to deal with the divine.

When the mind comprehends one thing it tends to think that it can comprehend everything, but it is just this view of knowledge which must be guarded against if the metaphorical method is to be successful in dealing with man's perplexity. If there are no limitations set for the mind, everything would theoretically be open to literal interpretation. Metaphor can become meaningful when the mind finds that it cannot go everywhere directly. Metaphor is the shortest distance between two points only when the direct path is not open to the human mind.

Here is the paradox: The religious spirit, which feeds on the sense of the final mystery within the divine nature, leads to perplexity when brought into contact with philosophical optimism and its literal, one-level mode of statement. Yet the only hope for the reconciliation without surrender is that a sense of divine mystery might force us to see that a frontal attack is not possible in the case of God. Thus, allegorical interpretation provides a genuine basis of latitude which alone is generous enough to retain both the religious sense of a divine mystery never fully disclosed, together with a philosophical directness whenever possible.

Such an interpretation of mystery and literalness together, which requires metaphorical expression, opens the way for a genuine meaning for faith. "By 'faith' we do not understand merely that which is uttered with the lips, but also that which is apprehended by the soul, the conviction that the object of belief is exactly as it is apprehended." If God is not directly approachable by literal means, faith always concerns something seen only incompletely through the figure of a symbol. Such belief cannot be compelled; but if the necessity for indirect approach is admitted in the case of objects exceeding the limits of direct grasp, metaphor becomes meaningful and faith an appropriate and possible way of relating oneself to such a Being. If all things were open to direct knowledge, a relation of faith could only seem unnecessary and inappropriate.

Metaphor is not a completely successful or controllable means of communication. We can employ only inadequate language where God is concerned, and metaphor is the best method at our disposal, since it allows the mind to get around barriers by subtle and indirect means. "We therefore make the subject clearer, and show to the understanding the way of truth by saying He is one but does not possess the attribute of unity." Here we seem to contradict ordinary expression, but this may indicate only that we are dealing with no ordinary object. By negating part of the phrase in the figurative statement we cause the sensitive mind to pass on to a grasp of God's nature, which could not be given by direct statement. What we learn from this example is that "we cannot describe the Creator by any means except by negative attributes." Metaphor and negative theology, then, are natural companions.

Positive assertions about God allow the imagination to mislead us, whereas proof by negation leads us gradually to more perfect knowledge of God. The mystery involved in the divine nature turns the ordinary situation around, so that we can now be convinced that certain qualities must be negated, whereas we cannot be as sure of positive attributes as we might be in an ordinary instance. The method of negative attributes is necessary "to direct the mind to the truth which we must believe concerning God," but it could be adopted only by one who felt the presence of mystery in the divine nature and realized the inappropriateness of frontal attack.

Our only complete knowledge concerning God, it turns out, "consists in knowing that we are unable truly to comprehend Him." God alone comprehends himself, and one not made aware of these matters too quickly jumps to the conclusion that man can know nothing about God at all. The truth lies somewhere in between, and it requires the energy of religious interest to keep from slipping into either extreme. God may be approached, but only by indirection. The negative method provides the mind with positive apprehensions of the divine nature, but not such that all mystery is removed, since God remains never fully comprehended by any being other than himself.

Thus, Maimonides has provided a context in which perplexity may be stabilized, but it is not a simple solution. He speaks to men whose sense of religious tradition is basic to them, and thus he is able to call upon their religious discipline to hold a flexible position which does not go all the way in either direction. The use of metaphor allows the literal meaning of the ordinary religious language to remain, while making room for the more subtle and refined meaning of the term in philosophical usage. A willingness to grant metapor as legitimate and applicable depends upon an agreement that knowledge reaches its limits at least in the case of God, and it is almost inconceivable that one should allow this limit to be placed on knowledge philosophically unless he had experienced some feeling of the mystery present at the center of the divine nature. Recognizing the difficulty, we employ the negative method to protect us while we look directly into the light, and the knowledge we achieve will not seem contradictory so long as it is regarded as at least partly metaphor and symbol. If a man's religious sense is strong enough to feel this, he can accept metaphor and control the anxiety which philosophical sophistication has brought to him. This is the guide for the perplexed, but only for one whose perplexity stems from a strong religious tradition and its accompanying sense of the mystery encountered whenever the mind is turned toward God.

Turning to Maimonides' doctrine of non-literal or metaphorical interpretation, we have to ask with him what it is that allows such duality of meaning without simple equivocation of terms? Maimonides' answer is that this is possible only when one finds himself dealing with a kind of existence not capable of reduction to a single level, and one is not likely to grant this if he has lost all sense of mystery in the divine nature. Philosophy can be counted on to take the mystery out of the natural order, as well it should; but it cannot be asked to provide one with some feeling for the irreducible mystery in the divine nature. The cultivation of the religious life provides the datum upon which philosophy applies itself in order to develop theology; that is, the rational statement of the divine insofar as this is possible. But if theology is not to become pure philosophy, the devotional life must have provided it with some sensitivity regarding the difficulty of handling God on our own terms.

In spite of this rather clear framework and simple objective, the casual modern reader is likely to be struck by the elaborate scholarly nature of much of the *Guide*. The opening pages are entirely given over to an exegesis or analysis of the use of certain Hebrew terms, all of which are central to Jewish religious thought. Interspersed is a discussion of the limits of man's intellect as well as an appraisal of the value of studying metaphysics. Such a diversity gives a correct picture of the blend of religious thought, scholarly study of concepts, and traditional philosophy which makes up the *Guide*. Then follows a more or less standard consideration of the nature of God and of the attributes appropriate to him.

It should be realized that the scope of the *Guide* is as wide as all traditional theology and religious thought. It is by no means simply a piece of philosophical apologetic, as might be thought from its title. Maimonides correctly sees that the only adequate way to provide a guide out of any perplexity is to take up and to discuss all of the major theological issues. To do so successfully is to provide the best, most substantial guide that can be produced. After considering the traditional attributes of God (such as unity, incorporeality), the second Moses begins Part II with a discussion of twenty-six propositions employed by philosophers to prove God's existence.

Next comes the question of creation versus the eternality of the universe, and Maimonides sets forth as best he can the way in which a doctrine of creation *ex nihilo* can be justified philosophically. Prophecy and the prophets then occupy him, as one might almost guess, for the Jewish tradition demands that prophecy be made acceptable. Visions are discussed, but evil and divine providence, as always, are the two central problems in this section. A religious belief in God runs into its greatest philosophical difficulty in trying to reconcile its conception of divinity with the evils and difficulties of the world.

It is easy to see that what Maimonides has provided is actually a comprehensive *summa* of traditional religious belief and philosophical tradition. Out of this meeting a theology is born, although its material setting within the literature of Judaism makes it appear less abstract than most modern questions. The *Guide* is actually a vast compendium of philosophical and religious material, which is then given shape through Maimonides' attempt to draw answers out of this combination. The towering position of influence which he occupies within the Jewish tradition gives some measure of his success.

Philosophy and religion in certain areas treat the same questions, but they do so in quite different ways and in quite different settings. When they are kept apart, as they can be in some ages, no conflict arises. Whenever an age becomes generally sophisticated philosophically, as was true in Maimonides' time and as is also true in our own day, then perplexity is bound to come. To those who can drop neither perspective, some reconciliation of the two bodies of material must be made. Out of the attempt to reconcile philosophy and religion each age arrives at a new theological perspective, which has implications for both technical philosophy and the religious life.

ON THE REDUCTION OF THE ARTS TO THEOLOGY

Author: Saint Bonaventura (Giovanni di Fidanza, 1221-1274)
Type of work: Theology
First transcribed: c.1250

PRINCIPAL IDEAS ADVANCED

Every kind of knowledge, if understood rightly, is knowledge of God; all of the arts reduce to theology.

God created light on the first day of creation as the source of activity in all living things, the link between soul and body.

There are two sorts of light, the created and the spiritual.

The mechanical arts are illuminated by external light, the sun; other knowledge comes from the light of sense perception, the light of philosophical knowledge, and the light of Sacred Scripture.

As seen by man, the four lights whose source is God become six because of distinctions within philosophy between rational philosophy, natural philosophy, and moral philosophy; the six lights correspond to the six days of the creation.

One central problem pervades the philosophical writings of Saint Bonaventura: the reconciliation of the mystical insights of Saint Francis of Assisi with a rational understanding of reality. For his solution Bonaventura turned to the Platonic tendency in medieval philosophy as developed by Saint Augustine, Alexander of Hales, and Robert Grosseteste. Thus, his work stands outside the Aristotelian tradition of his contemporary, Saint Thomas Aquinas. *On the Reduction of the Arts to Theology* was probably written while Saint Bonaventura was teaching at the University of Paris, and it may have been a lecture. We find in it a typical medieval scheme for the classification of knowledge.

Saint Bonaventura is often referred to by the title Doctor Seraphicus. A seraph is a ministering angel to God. Not only did Saint Bonaventura show his devotion to God in the way in which he lived, but in his writing he shows his belief in the complete absorption of every aspect of reality into the infinite goodness of God. The *Reduction* is an example of this conviction. Every kind of knowledge, if understood rightly, is knowledge of God: all of the arts reduce to theology.

The *Reduction* opens with a Biblical quotation, one from the first chapter of the epistle of James, "Every good gift and every perfect gift is from above, coming down from the Father of Lights." Light is a symbol of special importance for Saint Bonaventura. In Plato's allegory of the cave, the sun is identified with the good. This symbol came to be identified with God in the writings of the Neoplatonists and of the early Church philosophers. For Saint Bonaventura it is not the sun but light that has a special place in the created universe. Light was made by God on the first day of creation, according to the account in Genesis, while the sun was not created until the fourth

day. Light is the source of activity in all created things, the source of their extension and the source of their beauty; it is the link between the soul and the body. There are two sorts of light: the *created*, which we experience as the light of the sun, and the *spiritual* light, with which God acts upon the human soul and which is perfectly reproduced in Jesus Christ, the Son. Because of its association with Christ, light and truth have the same meaning.

Saint Bonaventura distinguishes between types of knowledge by the kinds of light which are responsible for them. The mechanical arts are illuminated by external light, the sun, which reveals their structure as artifacts. They are of seven types; weaving, armor-making, agriculture, hunting, navigation, medicine, and drama. Drama includes what we would now call the fine arts. Armor-making includes all of the implements of war. Cooking is a subdivision of the art of hunting; all sorts of buying and selling are included under navigation. By extending the meaning of terms in this way the seven mechanical arts become inclusive enough to take care of the physical needs of men.

The light of sense perception is the second light. Sense perception is directed toward a material object and is of five sorts corresponding to the five senses. Saint Bonaventura argues in accord with Saint Augustine that there are five senses because there are four elements—fire, air, water, earth—and a fifth substance, aether or light. Fire is apprehended through the sense of smell, air through hearing, water through taste, earth through touch, and light through sight. Since all created things are made up of these elements, the five senses are sufficient for man to perceive the physical universe.

Man apprehends the world by means of the third light, the light of philosophical knowledge. Through it he learns the principles and causes of the things that he perceives. There are three sorts of truth, says Saint Bonaventura, the truth of speech, of things, and of morals; and to these correspond the three types of philosophy, the rational, the natural, and the moral. The truth of speech is learned through grammar, logic, and rhetoric, which apprehend, judge, and persuade. Natural philosophy is divided into physics, which considers change as a natural process; mathematics, which considers quantity abstractly; and metaphysics, which studies being as such and which leads back to God as the first principle. Moral philosophy consists of ethics, economics, and politics, which are concerned with the individual, the family, and the state.

The fourth light illuminates the mind for the understanding of redemptive truth (veritas salutaris). It is the light of Sacred Scripture and is the highest truth because it leads beyond reason and human research, coming directly from God through inspiration. Although this truth is one in the literal sense, it is understood spiritually in three ways: the allegorical, by which we learn about God and man; the moral, by which we learn how to live; and the anagogical, by which we learn how to be united with God. These three types of truth are concerned with faith, morals, and the ultimate ends of both.

Thus, says Saint Bonaventura, there are four lights when they are considered in terms of their source, who is God; but when seen by man there are six: the light of Sacred Scripture, of sense perception, of the mechanical arts, of rational philosophy, of natural philosophy, and of moral philosophy. These six illuminations are related to the six days of creation in the order listed. The knowledge of Sacred Scripture corresponds to the creation of light on the first day, and this light permeates the whole of subsequent creation. So, too, all knowledge is contained in, and ends in, knowledge of the Sacred Scripture, going back to God from whom it came. Saint Bonaventura concludes this section of the Reduction by saying, "And there the cycle ends; the number six is complete and consequently there is rest."

It is interesting that Saint Bonaventura should mention both the circle and the number six. For him the circle is the perfect figure and six the perfect number. The circle is perfect because it is a closed figure represented by one continuous line. Six is the perfect number because it is equal to the sum of its factors, 1, 2, and 3, which are the first three numbers.

In the second part of the Reduction, Saint Bonaventura considers how each kind of knowledge leads to knowledge of the Sacred Scripture. One example from each of the five kinds of knowledge will be sufficient to explain his method.

The lowest kind of knowledge is sense perception; but just as the eye enjoys seeing, so the soul delights in its union with God. Thus there is a parallel between physical and spiritual function.

The purpose of the mechanical arts is to produce artifacts. Their production is a symbol of the generation and the incarnation of God's word. The craftsman produces the object from a pattern or idea in his mind. So God

307

creates the world and man in it to know and love him, and God became flesh to lead us from sin back to himself. In this way the mechanical arts can teach divine wisdom.

Rational philosophy deals with the three aspects of speech: the person speaking, the delivery of the speech, and the effect of the speech on the hearer. In its third aspect the purpose of speech is to express, instruct, and persuade. Speech can express only if it has an inherent likeness to its object, can instruct only if it sheds light, and can persuade only if it has power. But likeness, light, and power describe the relation of the soul to God. Saint Bonaventura quotes Saint Augustine: "He alone is a true teacher who can impress a likeness, shed light, and grant power to the heart of his hearer. He who teaches within hearts has his chair in heaven."

Natural philosophy is concerned chiefly with formal causes in matter, in the soul, and in Divine Wisdom. If we consider causes according to their effects, we find that corruptible matter can become living only by the beneficial light of incorruptible bodies: the sun, the moon, and the stars. "So too the soul can perform no living works unless it receive from the sun, that is, from Christ, the aid of his gratuitous light; unless it seek protection of the moon, that is, of the Virgin Mary, Mother of Christ, and unless it imitate the example of the other saints."

Moral philosophy is concerned primarily with right. *Right* has three meanings. It is a mean between extremes; it is conformance to a rule; and it refers to what is raised upward, that is, upright. In the second sense, he lives rightly who conforms to the rule of God.

"And so it is evident," Saint Bonaventura says in conclusion, "how the manifold Wisdom of God which is clearly revealed in Sacred Scripture, lies hidden in all knowledge and in all nature."

JOURNEY OF THE MIND TO GOD

Author: Saint Bonaventura (Giovanni di Fidanza, 1221-1274)
Type of work: Theology, epistemology
First transcribed: 1259

Principal Ideas Advanced

The six stages of the soul's powers correspond to the six stages of the ascension unto God.

God is reflected in the traces in the sensible world.

Then, in considering the powers of the self, through self-love, self-knowledge, and memory, the mind comes closer to God.

Memory, intelligence, and will are recognized as reflecting God's trinitarian nature.

By disciplined contemplation we are led even closer to the divine.

In recognizing the necessity of God's being for our understanding, the mind's work is done.

The final stage is the mind's abandonment of intellectual powers in the mystical knowledge of God.

Both the size and the title of Saint Bonaventura's most famous little work (*Itinerarium Mentis ad Deum*) belie its contents. From its size, the innocent reader might take it to be a meditation on some single point; from its title one might easily come to think of it as vague and mystical. Actually the opposite of both of these common impressions is the case. The *Itinerarium* belongs in the company of the *Summa Theologica* of Thomas Aquinas, although its brevity indicates the quite different temper of its author. Bonaventura, the "Seraphic Doctor," does not use the elaborate compendium method. Yet in brief compass we see unfurled in this work a view of nature, man, and God no less comprehensive than that contained in a many-volumed work.

As to its "mystical" qualities, what must first be grasped is that this work does in fact reflect classical mysticism but that Bonaventura's presentation of this viewpoint is both detailed and highly technical. To sketch completely the structure which Bonaventura outlines would require a quite detailed study. It is rational in every detail—right up to the point at which reason finds its own end and realizes its own boundaries. Reason will be left behind and ecstatic vision will become the goal, but this does not transpire until the very peak of possible human understanding has been reached. Only when reason has done its utmost at description and explanation can a way be seen to transcend reason. In this brief work what we find is an elaborate, intricate, and technical view, rational to its core, but aimed from the beginning at finding reason's limiting point in order thereby to leave it behind.

What is perhaps hardest for the modern mind to grasp is that Bonaventura both begins and ends with God. The modern prejudice which must be overcome here is the same one which plagues Anselm's famous "ontological argument." The contemporary philosopher is addicted to the primacy of a theory of knowledge. Before any question is asked the modern reader must inquire whether, methodologically considered, the quest is justifiable and the object knowable. Bonaventura and a host of others, on the other hand, pose the ultimate question of God at the outset just as if it were answerable. Only through the technical process of attempting to construct the answer can the success or the failure of the endeavor be discovered. The process of the attempt itself is the source of our correction. The limits of the question are recognizable, not at the beginning, but only at the end of the argument.

Not unlike the Greek invocation of the muses in the face of a difficult task, Bonaventura in the Prologue calls upon God to enlighten him in his quest. His use of the term "Father of Light" for God, and his stress upon illumination place Bonaventura well within the Augustinian and Neoplatonic tradition. God is to be immediately addressed at the outset of all serious consideration, since he is cast in the role of a first principle and as such

309

is central to any knowing process.

For all of this, the work still has a devotional element woven into it as one thread of its fabric. Francis of Assisi, the founder of Bonaventura's order, is mentioned reverentially at the outset, and Bonaventura himself claims to have undergone a vision like that experienced by Francis. However, coupled with this theme must be the awareness that Bonaventura served as a highly successful administrator, in fact as Minister General of his order. This obvious organizational skill, which daily must have called for the solution of dozens of practical problems, is balanced against the visionary quality of his writing.

Six stages of ascension to God are described in this little work. Their delineation is purely technical and rational, but Bonaventura at the same time considers prayer one means of becoming enlightened about them. To modern minds so used to splitting spirituality and rationality completely apart, such duality in Bonaventura's thought is hard to grasp. To do so, however, is also to come close to understanding the special feature of the *Itinerarium*. For all natural objects have a double side: they are at once parts of a structured natural order discoverable by reason, and at the same time, when properly viewed, may come to be seen as traces of God himself. Such divine traces are uncoverable in many places, but we begin with those which are corporeal and outside of us (as contrasted to those spiritual and interior).

Man's mind has three principal aspects, one of which is animal or sensual, another of which makes it capable of introspection, and a third in virtue of which it is able to look above itself and to grasp levels of existence higher than its own natural order. And since all natural objects have a divine side, the six stages of the soul's powers correspond to the six stages of the ascension unto God. To describe the levels of ascent to God is to delineate the soul's powers; to set forth the soul's capacities is to outline the levels through which God is to be approached.

Theology itself has three modes: symbolic, literal, and mystical. The symbolic gives proper interpretation to sensible things; the literal corresponds to an intelligible level, and the mystic transcends the level of rationality. All three are properly theology. But none of these is to be undertaken without preparation, since rectitude of the will and the clarity of unimpeded vision are necessary. Then the sensible world may be taken up for consideration, and it will be transformed upon reflection into a veritable Jacob's ladder, the sense world being as it is so full of the traces of God.

We proceed by transposing natural qualities into a divine setting. Weight, number, and measure provide a basis for grasping the power, wisdom, and immense goodness of the Creator. One inquires after the origin, course, and terminus of the natural order, and then a grasp of the various levels of natural organisms can be acquired. From this one moves to consider God as a counterpart of these levels and of this order, as spiritual, incorruptible, and immutable. The natural order is a plenitude, full of every level and variety of kind. Such munificence is a source of natural illumination for the mind in its search for the proper road to God.

God is reflected in his traces in the sensible world, and he is known not only through them but also in them.

310

The reader would move too quickly if he thought Bonaventura considered the natural order only to pass beyond it so quickly. Like others before him in his tradition, in this work Bonaventura sees the natural world as being both good and beautiful, so that to an eye sensitive to such structure God can actually be seen without taking our eyes away from the world of the senses even for a moment. The five senses are like doors. Through apprehending motion we are led to the cognition of spiritual movers, as a progress from effect to cause.

Our senses lead us to apprehension, then to delight in the natural order, and finally to judgment, which operates by abstraction and renders the sensible objects intelligible. Then, following Augustine's *On Music*, Bonaventura regards number as the outstanding examplar of God to be found in the physical world. All Platonists have been fascinated with the intelligible and yet nonsensible properties of number, especially its relation to the qualities of rhythm and proportion. The invisible things of God come to be seen, being grasped in and through the changing, sensible world. Like a sign, the sensible order leads the discerning mind to the intelligible; and, seeing this, we are led to turn from an outward vision and to consider the mind itself.

Grasping how divine things may be seen as reflected in the order of nature leads us to turn inward to consider ourselves, and here divine images appear most clearly. For the natural psychical phenomena are self-love, self-knowledge, and memory. Here Bonaventura follows Augustine's classical model and finds in these a representation of the divine Trinity. Particularly in memory the soul is most like an image of God, for God lives with all objects eternally present to him, and the soul imitates this power in the grasp of its own power of memory. Nor can we understand the being of any particular object until we come to understand Being-in-itself. Memory, intelligence, and will form in us a second reflection of God's trinitarian nature, so that when the mind considers itself, it rises through itself as through a mirror to the contemplation of the divine Trinity.

Having brought the mind so close to God in structure, Bonaventura turns to inquire why not all men see God clearly in themselves. And his answer is that most men lie so buried in the world of the senses that they are unable to regard themselves as in God's image. Here, for the first time, specifically Christian doctrine enters, since Bonaventura sees in Christ a mediator who accomplishes this needed purification and illumination. Spiritual hearing and vision must be recovered.

After the conversion of the mind to a new direction comes the disciplining of the self, and here Bernard of Clairveaux' famous "steps" are outlined to bring the soul to vision through humility and the inculcation of strict habits of thought. We must learn contemplation, and this requires a strict order in the soul. The acquired habits of the rationally ordered soul yield powers capable of leading us to the divine.

Thus, we have learned to contemplate God *outside* us in his traces in the natural and sensible order, *inside* the self through the trinitarian structure of the soul's powers, and then finally *above* the mind as the contemplative powers are strengthened by discipline. We may fix on Being-itself, rejecting, as all Neoplatonism does, any

311

positive status for non-being. Here a little dialectical exercise on being and non-being convinces us that being is actually what first enters the intellect and that this is the Being of pure actuality. Thus, analysis indicates the immediate orientation of all intellection toward Being-itself and therefore toward God. Since this orientation is at the foundation of every intellective act, it only remains for the mind to become aware of just how necessary its orientation toward God is for our understanding in every instance. For intellect to operate, the being of the divine being must be ever present as a referent and standard.

Only because we are accustomed to the lesser beings of the sensible world do we fail to recognize the mind's natural orientation and nearness to God. As the eye seems to see nothing when it sees pure light, so we seem to see sensible images and lesser beings and do not recognize the highest Being. The darkness which seems to surround Being-itself, in comparison with the ease of grasping lower objects, can now be disclosed as the fullest illumination of the mind. The purest being, necessary for every grasp of impure beings, appears only by contrast to be empty of content.

At the height we reach the traditional Platonic and Neoplatonic name for God, the Good. The fecundity of the Good is given as a rational necessity for the multiplicity of a Trinity within God, as more adequately expressing the fullness of the Good than could any less multiple first principle. Yet Bonaventura is quick to add that such rational arguments do not make the Trinity comprehensible; since it is incomprehensible, it is not fully understandable.

Having arrived at the end of the sixth step, our mind's work is done (like God's work in the days of creation), and it rests. The mind, having traversed the whole of the sensible order, then the intelligible realm, has finally understood itself and disciplined itself to raise itself to consider God himself. But the end of this gigantic and rigorous activity is rest. The mind has reached the place at which it has done all it can do; nothing more is within its power and so it must rest. Rationally it has exhausted itself and has reached its limit. Reason, illumination, devotion, and discipline have brought the mind to the pinnacle of its powers and transformed it in the process of the journey, although at the end it sees that the final vision was never far away. At the outset the goal was near but not seen. It was present from the beginning (Being-itself), but our powers were not then sufficient to grasp it directly.

What remains? By looking at sensible things the mind passed beyond them and then turned to consider itself. Now it passes not only beyond sensible things, by way of a rational dialectic, but beyond even itself. In this final passage, if the rational discipline has been perfected, all intellectual operation should at this point be abandoned. All our affection should be transferred from ourselves to God. The final step is most certainly mystical, but mysticism enters only at this final point and not before. No one can know this final phase who has not experienced it; and, even to the mind undergoing the experience, it seems like moving into death and darkness to leave rational structure behind. But the soul, having set out to find God, is now at the terminus of its itinerary

312

and willingly surrenders what it could not have surrendered before (the guidance of its rational powers) and passes over into what appears to be (as contrasted with structured reason) darkness.

How shall a modern mind appraise such a scheme and its importance to the history of, and the present developments within, philosophy? The immediate concentration upon God, the mixture of philosophy with religious discipline, as well as the view of all mundane things as immediately reflecting God—all of these are nearly the opposite of the modern approach. In some basic sense modern philosophers, as well as most Protestant theologians, are fundamentally rationalists, and to them Bonaventura's ultimate mysticism seems strange. Consequently, the *Itinerarium* has an important function to fulfill as an example of a possible and different approach.

Historically its significance cannot be overestimated. In any form of the religious life, Neoplatonism has always been extremely influential, and what we must not overlook here is that Bonaventura represents a philosophical and a theological view which has for centuries been closely associated with devout practice. Since philosophy's divorce from theology in the modern period, philosophy has been largely academic. In the *Itinerarium* we have an example of how a philosophical view can be intimately associated with, and even be determinative for, a way of life.

Out of a religious desire to see God this philosophical view arises as a disciplined guide. Such desire actually causes us to seek for and to see aspects of the natural order which might otherwise have remained unnoticed. A more abstract intellect may

derive its philosophical problems internally simply from philosophical discussion. Bonaventura finds his questions through the attempt to guide the soul toward God. Neither approach to philosophy or theology excludes the other, but a secular and a rationalistic age has trouble recognizing the legitimacy of a philosophy generated from such a practical (and in this case religious) goal.

Perhaps the most interesting comparison is to remember that Bonaventura was a contemporary of Thomas Aquinas. The two considered together offer a fascinating contrast. Both represent the use which was made of philosophy in the Middle Ages. Thomas has had wide circulation in non-Catholic and even in nonreligious circles. Bonaventura is still widely read within religious orders and in theological circles which do not receive as much public notice.

Bonaventura's little work could be considered purely as a devotional classic if it were not for its elaborate technical structure and his use of "Being" as God's primary name. Nothing indicates the presence of an abstract metaphysician more than his preference for the traditional name "Being" as opposed to more personal names for God. God is discussed in his role as a metaphysical first principle and not as an object of worship. In fact, except for the trinitarian reference, little specifically Christian or Biblical doctrine is discussed. It is only by contrast to modern anti-metaphysical interests that this work seems "religious." Actually by comparison it is both technical and abstract.

In considering Being and Non-Being, Bonaventura adopts the traditional Neoplatonic role of giving Non-

Being status only as a privation of Being, not as anything independent of or opposed to it. In fact, upon analysis it appears that nothing within the natural order can be known unless Being itself has first entered the intellect. In this way God is involved in even the simplest act of cognition, as a prerequisite for any apprehension. For a particular being to be known, Being itself must be present to the intellect, a fact that may not be recognized until after the analysis of Being and Non-Being has been carried out.

Bonaventura stresses the traditional Neoplatonic attribute of God, his unity. He possesses no diversity, and it is primarily this central characteristic of unity which places God above intellection and forces reason ultimately to transcend itself. Although God is close to and visible through the natural order, in himself his nature is quite different, reflecting none of the multiplicity of nature's variety. Because of such a basic dissimilarity any man who would have the vision of God must finally leave himself behind, in so far as he is a rational creature dealing with multiple objects.

Being which is absolutely one is seen also to be the Good, but the different ontological level involved here forces the apprehending mind to pass beyond the multiple sensible world and also beyond itself as a discursive mind. It is not so much Bonaventura's view of the order of nature which dictates this as it is his view of the Divine nature. Just as Bonaventura begins with God, so any criticism of his whole scheme must start by attempting to set forth and to defend a different view of the divine nature.

In order to see the point of Bonaventura's theory of knowledge and his theory of the orders of nature, each must be seen in its relation to his view of the divine nature, coupled with his ethical and religious goal of seeing God. In order to criticize the Seraphic Doctor's theories, what we must do is to begin with a theory of the Divine nature too. As that is altered, so also are the theory of knowledge, and the view of nature and of human psychology.

SUMMA CONTRA GENTILES

Author: Saint Thomas Aquinas (c.1225-1274)
Type of work: Theology, metaphysics
First transcribed: c. 1258-1260

PRINCIPAL IDEAS ADVANCED

The wise man is one who deals with the first beginning and the last end of the universe; truth is the final end, and the divine nature must first of all be considered if one is to understand first and last things.

No truth of faith is contrary to principles known by reason.

God understands not temporally but eternally; he understands all things at *once by understanding their intelligible counterparts, but he knows individuals as well as universals.*

God's will is free, having no cause but his own wisdom; he does not of necessity love things other than himself.

In God there is active power, but no potentiality; he is essentially infinite, and his knowledge and understanding are infinite.

Since man is a rational creature, his final happiness lies in the contemplation of God; but this end cannot be achieved in this life.

The *Summa contra Gentiles* is less widely known and much less widely read than Thomas Aquinas's later, longer, and more famous *Summa Theologica* (written from 1265 until Aquinas's death). In some sense this is strange, since the *Summa contra Gentiles* is simpler in its structure, and in that sense more readable and less involved. Perhaps the *Summa Theologica* has gained its fame through its more widespread use in church dogmatics, since it is that *Summa* which contains most of the detailed argument on doctrinal issues. By comparison, the *Contra Gentiles* is more philosophical, as its author intended and as its title implies. As such it is likely to be of more interest to the non-Catholic reader. It is true that it is an earlier work, but not so much so as to make any radical difference in Thomas's ideas, and a comparison of the basic doctrines does not reveal any wide discrepancy.

It is interesting that, whereas the *Summa Theologica* begins with an apologetic approach, explaining the relation of philosophy to theology and arguing for the existence of God, the *Contra Gentiles* begins immediately with God as he is in himself. As a work directed to the non-Christian, one might have expected the reverse. Yet in style the *Contra Gentiles* is less doctrinal and does not base its argu-

ments on a prior acceptance of Scripture as authoritative, as the *Theologica* does. The *Contra Gentiles* is more directly metaphysical, defining the "wise man" as one who deals with the first beginning and the last end of the universe. Truth is conceived of as the final end of the whole universe, and the treatise begins directly with a consideration of the divine nature as that which must be delineated if we are to explain first and last things.

Thomas Aquinas agrees with classical philosophy in holding that the chief aim of man is to achieve wisdom. In his case, however, this consists specifically in a knowledge of God. Since the Bible must be accepted as authoritative in order to be convincing, it cannot be used to prove any question about God's nature. With Jews, of course, a Christian may use the Old Testament as a basis for argument, and even a heretic may recognize the New Testament as valid evidence; he simply does not agree with the orthodox interpretation. For those who are neither heretics nor Jews, all argument must be based solely on natural reason. And then the first thing to establish is what mode of proof is possible where God is concerned. Some things true of God are beyond the scope of human reason, as, for example, that God is three in one. Other things, such as the unity and existence of God, are demonstrable under the light of natural reason. Yet human reason cannot go on further to grasp God's substance directly. Under the conditions of our present natural life, the knowledge which our understanding can obtain commences with sense data.

To discover anything true about God is exceedingly difficult, and for such arduous work not many have either the time or the natural capabilities. Some men devote themselves to business affairs and never study theology seriously. Furthermore, first of all one must master philosophy, so that a study of the divine nature requires a lot of preparation. Thus, in one sense, it is a study better suited to man's old age, when some naturally disturbing influences have subsided. As difficult as theology is and as restricted and as demanding as it is, faith was provided so that not everyone need find out about God for himself. It was necessary, Thomas argues, for the real truth about divine things to be presented to men with a fixed certainty by way of faith.

Reason and faith must agree, however, and Thomas begins by asserting that it is impossible for the truth of faith to be contrary to principles known by natural reason. No opinion or belief, Thomas is sure, is sent to man from God as an item of faith which is contrary to natural knowledge. For one thing, although as human beings our knowledge begins with sense objects, these retain in themselves some trace of the imitation of God. Here is Bonaventura's doctrine of the natural world seen as a sense world but also as one containing traces within itself of its supernatural

origin as a creation of God. Thomas also affirms the use of the negative method, another traditional doctrine. We may have some sort of knowledge of the divine nature by knowing "what it is not."

The famous proofs for God's existence also appear in the *Contra Gentiles*, but they are in briefer form than in the other *Summa* and seem less fully developed. One might have expected this work, directed at pagans as it is and not dependent upon scripture for its arguments, to make more use of the "proofs." Instead, the proofs receive less stress, and Thomas moves directly into a discussion of the divine attributes. He discusses in sequence God's eternality, his freedom from potentiality, his lack of composition, and his incorporeality. All of these are rather directly stated as if they needed little expansion.

It does not take much vision to see the *Contra Gentiles* as the framework upon which the *Summa Theologica* was finally built. The arguments need expanding, and more Biblical material is included, but the structure is very much the same. In the *Contra Gentiles* very few authors are quoted, and the argument is simply advanced in a straightforward way. Later, in the *Summa Theologica*, Thomas attempted to blend a number of important views together and to reach a more detailed conclusion. In the earlier work, however, he seems satisfied to provide the outline of the important questions and the basic structure of each argument. Little of great significance is changed in the later *Summa*, but the arguments receive a great many refinements, and the reasoning is made both more subtle and

316

more complex in order to deal with the multiplicity of views presented there.

Aquinas considers God's understanding at length and describes its difference from man's. God does not understand temporally but eternally. He does not understand by knowing an object directly but by knowing its intelligible counterpart in his own understanding. God's understanding does contain a multitude of objects, but he understands all things at once and together. Propositional truth is also present in the divine understanding, and God also knows individuals, not merely universals. Nonexistent things are known by God, even though they never will become actual, and he knows individual events, contingent upon man's action, as they will happen. In order to do this God must know the motions of the human will as well as his own will, and through these he understands evil as well as good.

Aquinas agrees to the traditional self-sufficiency of God's nature: God does not of *necessity* love things other than himself. Things outside of God need him in a way in which he does not depend on them. God's will is free, subject to no external conditions, and has no cause other than his own wisdom. His goodness is the reason why he wills all things, and in that sense it is possible to assign a reason for the choice of God's will. Will, understanding, and goodness exist in God, but not passion, since that would indicate imperfection. There is love in God but not such that he suffers from it or is subject to anything else because of it. God cannot, it is true, will evil, but such a limitation is no imperfection. God hates nothing, al-though his attributes are such that it is proper to describe him as "living."

In contrast to this extended and direct discussion of God's nature, philosophy considers man and the natural order as these things are in themselves. Philosophy makes no necessary reference to God, but the Christian faith considers natural beings, not in themselves, but inasmuch as they represent the majesty of God. Furthermore, Christians focus specifically on that in man which is directly involved in his relation to God's will. The other qualities of man are not as important in the Christian's view. The philosopher takes his stand on the immediate and natural causes of things; but the Christian argues from God as first cause, indicating what things are revealed and what we can learn about the divine nature. Philosophically we begin with creatures and then may be led to a knowledge of God; faith studies creatures only in their relation to God and so studies God first and creatures after that.

Turning then directly to God, Aquinas asserts that God's power and his action are not distinct. They are not two things, and this view actually results in a stronger doctrine of necessary predestination here than Thomas was to adopt in the *Summa Theologica*. God does not create the natural world out of anything preëxistent, and therefore he does not create merely by moving material. The act of creation means bringing a thing into being without any preëxistent material, not even potentiality. Nor is creation a successive movement. Creation takes place in an instant. A thing is at once in the act of being created and is created. Such a drastic form of creation is an action proper to God alone, and he creates directly with no intermediaries. God's power extends to every possible thing, except to those which involve a contradiction.

In God there is an active power, but no potentiality. Whatever would necessarily involve potentiality, those things are impossible to God. Nor could God make one and the same thing to be and not to be, since that would involve a contradiction. He cannot make a thing which lacks any of its essential constituents. And his will cannot be changeable; he cannot cause what once was willed not to be fulfilled. On the other hand, God's knowledge or understanding is bounded by no limits in its view. This means that God is essentially infinite, although all other things are limited. The infinite reach of God's understanding means that his knowledge extends even to things that neither are, nor shall be, nor have been.

God needs nothing and depends on nothing other than himself; every other being is in his neighbor's debt on God's account. In all these matters, God is not a debtor to any creature, but a debtor to the fulfillment of his own plan. There is no absolute necessity for the being of any creature. The creature begins to exist in time exactly when God from eternity arranged that it should begin to exist. God brought into being creation and time simultaneously. Thus, questions which concern a "before creation" are improperly asked. There is no account to be given of why he produced a creature *now,* and not before, but only why the creature has not always been. Having thus been always willed, a new thing that has not always been may be produced by God without any

change in him. But if time has not always been, we may mark a nonexistence of time prior to its being.

Multiplicity and variety characterize creation, to the end that the perfect likeness of God can be found in creatures and in each according to his measure. Taken all together, they are very good, because the order of the universe is the finest and noblest creation. Of course, in created intelligences, both potentiality and actuality are present in a way in which they are not in God. The potential intellect in man does not subsist apart from matter, but is intimately dependent on the body's functions. In each man it is individual, just as his body is individual. There is no common potential intellect which is the same for all men. Despite the individuality of the human intellect and its close association with the passive intellect, particularly with the functioning of the body, the human soul does not perish with the body but is capable of independent existence. However, this does not mean that the human soul is of the same substance as God, since they differ quite markedly in basic nature. The human soul is neither an eternally existing thing nor is it transmitted by generation, but it is brought into being by a creative act of God himself.

Aquinas's description of the divine nature is metaphysical; his doctrine of the creation of the natural order can stand on its own logical ground. It fits into Christian doctrine, it is true, but Aquinas does not expect it logically to depend upon this, nor does he consciously derive his two doctrines from specifically or exclusively Christian materials.

Two objectives of the vast scheme

remain: to consider the end of man and the created world in relation to God, and to consider finally what God can be said to have revealed. Using a quotation from the Psalms, Aquinas begins his discussion of the last end of man with the assertion that God will not abandon his creation once constituted. Every creature acts to attain some end, so that the natural world in this sense seems constantly directed toward the attainment of some goal. Furthermore, the goal desired is always some good; evil is a thing aside from the attention of an agent. In fact, the very cause of evil is something which in itself is good; and even when evil appears it never cancels out completely the good upon which it is based.

Since the end of everything is always some good, the ordained end of all things is actually the source of all good: God. God is the end of all things in the sense that all rational creatures desire to be like God, to understand him. Happiness in any ultimate sense does not consist, for man, in bodily pleasures. He knows, as a rational creature, that all final happiness lies in the contemplation of God. But this happiness is not based on a general knowledge of God, or upon the knowledge of God's existence which is to be had by demonstration. Our problem is that we cannot in this life see God is he essentially is, which means that the final happiness of man cannot be attained in this life. Nor can any created substance of its own natural power arrive at a point where he can see God as he essentially is. To achieve his aim in life, a created intelligence needs an influx of divine light enabling his intellect to be lifted up to see God.

Yet even in seeing God, no created intelligence could comprehend the divine substance or see all things that can be seen in God. Nevertheless, this is not an exclusive affair; every intelligence of every grade can, by being lifted up, partake of the vision of God. Those who do see God will see him forever, and in that final happiness every desire of man will be fulfilled. Since God is the cause of the activity in all active agents, God is everywhere and in all things. The progress toward man's final goal, then, is within the scope of divine providence. The providence of God watches immediately over all individual things. This does not deny a freedom of the will, since the action of divine providence is not direct but operates by means of secondary causes. However, the motion of the human will is caused by God and subject to his providence.

From this point Thomas moves on to consider specifically the utility of prayer, the question of fate, miracles (which God alone can work), and the purposes for the giving of a divine law for human conduct. The divine government of man here on this earth is like paternal government, since man's acts are punished or rewarded by God. Of course, not all punishments or rewards are equal. There is a distinction between venial and mortal sin, the latter being material in determining final reward or punishment. Since man cannot attain happiness for himself, he needs divine assistance, or grace. The presence in us of grace causes us to love God and produces faith. Such grace is given gratuitously. Man can, it is true, easily do good from time to time, but he needs the assistance of grace in order to persevere in good action. Man may

319

be delivered from sin, but only by grace.

All these things man needs to know, if he is to understand his final goal and the possibility for achieving it. Yet the human mind cannot of itself arrive at the direct vision of the divine substance. God cannot, Thomas has established, abandon his creation; therefore revelation is necessary in order to show man the way. God himself is prevented by his nature from descending to man, but here we reach over into the heart of Christian doctrine. For the Son of God, as a co-equal member of the Trinity, is at the same time God and capable of descending to man to make the necessary revelation to man's knowledge of his final end and the means thereto. Thomas began by addressing rational arguments to non-Christians, but the discourse is brought to the place where the Christian doctrine of revelation through Christ is considered to be necessary for the completion of creation's plan.

Thomas, having laid the rational groundwork for considering the nature of Jesus, turns to consider various theories of Christology and their adequacy. Revelation through an agent of God himself is necessary to the fulfillment of this rational plan, and now everything depends upon describing Jesus' nature so that we see him as fulfilling this role successfully. No one needs to be converted to Christianity by this means, but at least its rational basis

can be examined. Thomas rejects Arian and Sabellian views as heretical, as orthodox Christians have done, and goes on to discuss each person of the Trinity and to work out a theory of their functions and relationships. Next, a theory of the incarnation is developed. The human nature assumed by the Word (Christ) must be perfect in soul and body in every respect and from the instant of conception.

The need for sacraments and the doctrine of original sin are discussed. Since Thomas concludes with a discussion of the office of the minister and the resurrection of the body, one might almost forget that the *Contra Gentiles* was written for non-Christians. But its non-Christian basis still remains: it aims to present Christian doctrine on the basis of arguments and materials which do not themselves depend for their validity on the prior acceptance of authority. Thomas Aquinas had no intention of avoiding specifically Christian doctrines, but what he meant to do, and did, was to present them in the form of rational discourse, moving on from a theory of God and the nature of man to show the consistency of Christian doctrine with such a rationally developed view. Taking in as it does nearly every major metaphysical, theological, and ethical question, this work is truly a vast *summa*, written to present Christian doctrine upon the basis of rationally structured argument.

320

SUMMA THEOLOGICA

Author: Thomas Aquinas (c.1225-1274)
Type of work: Metaphysics, theology
First transcribed: c.1265-1274

PRINCIPAL IDEAS ADVANCED

Man requires more than philosophy in his search for truth; certain truths are beyond human reason and are available only because of divine revelation; theology, which depends on revealed knowledge, supplements natural knowledge.

The existence of God can be proved in five ways: by reference to motion (and the necessity of a first mover), by reference to efficient causes (and the necessity of a first cause), by reference to possibility and necessity, by reference to the gradations of perfection in the world, and by reference to the order and harmony of nature (which suggests an ordering being who gives purpose to the created world).

God alone is the being whose nature is such that by reference to him one can account for the fact of motion, efficient cause, necessity, perfection, and order.

God's principal attributes are simplicity (for he is noncorporeal and without genus), actuality, perfection, goodness, infinitude, immutability, unity, and immanence; but the created intellect can know God only by God's grace and only through apprehension, not comprehension.

It is a difficult task to comment on Thomas's *Summa Theologica* briefly; it has meant and can mean many things to many people. Partly this is due to its length; it runs to many volumes. And partly it is due to the scope of the questions considered; they range from abstract and technical philosophy to minute points of Christian dogmatics. The situation is further complicated because of Thomas's style. Such works were common in his day, and his is only one of many which were written in this general form. The work consists entirely of questions, each in the form of an article in which the views Thomas considers important are summarized and then answered. Objections to the topic question are listed, often including specific quotations, and then an equal number of replies are given, based on a middle section ("I answer that") which usually contains Thomas's own position; but this, in turn, is sometimes based on some crucial quotation from a philosopher or theologian.

Out of this complexity and quantity many have attempted to derive Thomistic "systems," and both the commentators and the group of modern Thomists form a complex question in themselves. Thomas was considered to be near heresy in his own day, and his views were unpopular in some quarters. From the position of being not an especially favored teacher in a very fruitful and exciting era, he has come to be regarded as perhaps the greatest figure in the Catholic philosophy and theology of the day. His stature is due as much to the dogmatization and expansion of his thought which took place (for example, by Cardinal Cajetan and John of St. Thomas) as it is to the position Thomas had in his own day. Without this further development his writing might have been important, but perhaps it would be simply one among a number of significant medieval works. The Encyclical Letter of Pope Leo XIII, "On the Restoration of Christian Philosophy," published in 1879, started the Thomistic revival. The modern developments in philosophy had gone against the Church of Rome, and Thomas Aquinas was selected as the center for a revival and a concentration upon Christian philosophy. Since that time Thomas has been widely studied, so much so that it is sometimes hard to distinguish Thomas's own work from that of those who followed him.

Part I contains 119 questions, including treatises on creation, on the angels, on man, and on the divine government. The first part of Part II consists of 114 questions, including treatises on habits and law, and in general it covers ethical matters as against the metaphysical and epistemological concentration in Part I. The second part of Part II is made up of 189 questions, and Part III contains ninety. These cover laws, the ethical virtues, and questions of doctrine and Christology. Taken as a whole, it is hard to imagine a more comprehensive study, although it is important to remember that Thomas wrote a second *Summa*, "against the Gentiles," which was intended as a technical work of apologetics for those who could not accept the premises of Christian theology. The works overlap a great deal, but a comparative study cannot be made here. The *Summa Theologica*, then, has as its unspoken premise the acceptance of certain basic Christian propositions, whereas the *Contra Gentiles* attempts to argue without any such assumptions.

The influence of any single philosopher or theologian on Thomas's thought is difficult to establish, and probably too much has been made of Thomas's use of Aristotle. It is true that Aristotle is quoted in the *Summa Theologica* more than any other pagan author and that Thomas refers to him on occasion as "the philosopher." The availability of Aristotle's writings in fairly accurate translation in Thomas's day had a decided influence upon him and upon others of his era. Plato's works as a whole were still unrecovered, so that Aristotle is one of the few outside the Christian tradition who is quoted. Particularly in psychology and epistemology Thomas seems to have followed at least an Aristotelian tradition, if not Aristotle himself. But the authors Thomas quotes with favor cover a wide range, including frequent citations of the Neoplatonic pseudo-Dionysius and Augustine. Moreover, in a theologically oriented *summa*, the Bible and church tradition must play a major role, so that to sort out and label any strain as dominant is extremely difficult in view of the peculiar nature of a *summa*. There are positions which can clearly be recognized as Thomas's own, but the real perplexity of understanding Thomas is to grasp the variety of sources blended there and to hold them altogether for simultaneous consideration and questioning as Thomas himself did.

The first question, consisting of ten articles, is Thomas's famous definition of the nature and the extent of sacred doctrine or theology, and it opens by asking whether man requires anything more than philosophy. Thomas's con-

322

tention that the Scriptures are inspired by God and are not a part of philosophy indicates the usefulness of knowledge other than philosophy. Scriptural knowledge is necessary for man's salvation, for Scripture offers the promise of salvation and pure philosophic knowledge does not. Philosophy is built up by human reason; certain truths necessary for man's salvation, but which exceed human reason, have been made known by God through divine revelation. Such knowledge is not agreed to be reason; it is by nature accepted only on faith.

Now the question arises: Can such revealed knowledge be considered as a science (a body of systematic knowledge) along with philosophy? Of course, such a sacred science treats of God primarily and does not give equal consideration to creatures. This means that it is actually a speculative undertaking and is only secondarily a practical concern. Yet it is the most noble science, because of the importance of the questions it considers, and in that sense all other forms of scientific knowledge are theology's handmaidens. Wisdom is knowledge of divine things, and in that sense theology has chief claim to the title of "wisdom." Its principles are immediately revealed by God, and within such a science all things are treated under the aspect of God.

Naturally there can be no argument on these terms with one who denies that at least some of theology's truths are obtained through divine revelation, for such a person would not admit the very premises of theology conceived of in this fashion. That is the sense in which this *summa* is a *summa* of theology intended for Christians. Since its arguments, at least in some instances,

involve a claim to revealed knowledge, the *Summa* may be unconvincing to the non-Christian. Thus, the reception of grace, sufficient to become a Christian, is necessary to understand the arguments. In the Christian conception, the reception of grace enables the receiver to accept the truth of revelation. But Thomas's famous doctrine here is that such reception of grace does not destroy nature (natural knowledge) but perfects or completes it. Nothing is countermanded in philosophy's own domain; grace simply adds to it what of itself could not be known.

As compared with other classical theologians Thomas believed in a fairly straightforward approach to questions about God. However, Thomas did admit the necessity of the familiar "negative method," since where God is concerned what he is *not* is clearer to us than what he is. The proposition "God exists" is not self-evident to us, although it may be in itself. The contradictory of the proposition "God is" can be conceived.

In this case Thomas seems to oppose Anselm's ontological argument, although the opposition is not quite as straightforward as it seems. Thomas denies that we can know God's essence directly, even though such vision would reveal that God's essence and existence are identical and thus support Anselm's contention. But the ontological argument, he reasons, is built upon a kind of direct access to the divine which human reason does not have.

The existence of God, then, needs to be demonstrated from those of his effects which are known to us. Thomas readily admits that some will prefer to account for all natural phenomena by referring everything to one principle, which is nature herself. In opposition he asserts that God's existence can be proved in five ways: (1) the argument from motion, (2) the argument from the nature of efficient cause, (3) the argument from possibility and necessity, (4) the argument from the gradations of perfection to be found in things, and finally (5) the argument from the order of the world. Without attempting an analysis of these arguments individually, several things can be noted about them as a group. First, all are based on the principle that reason needs a final stopping point in any chain of explanation. Second, such a point of final rest cannot be itself within the series to be accounted for, but it must be outside it and different in kind. Third, in each case it is a principle which we arrive at, not God himself, but these principles (for example, a first efficient cause) are shown to be essential parts of the nature of God. God's existence is agreed to by showing reason's need for one of his attributes in the attempt to explain natural phenomena.

It is probably true that Thomas's five proofs have been given a disproportionate amount of attention, for following them Thomas goes into elaborate detail in a discussion of the divine nature and its primary attributes. Simplicity, goodness, infinity, and perfection are taken up, and then the other chief attributes are discussed before Thomas passes on to the analysis of the three persons of the trinitarian conception of God. Taken together, these passages form one of the most elaborate and complete discussions of God's nature by a major theologian, and it is here that much of the disagreement about Thomas's philosophy centers, rather than in the more formal and brief five proofs.

In spite of Thomas's use of Aristotelian terms, he indicates his affinity with the Neoplatonic tradition by placing the consideration of "simplicity" first. This is the divine attribute most highly prized and most stressed by Neoplatonists, and Thomas concurs in their emphasis. God's simplicity is first protected by denying absolutely that he is a body in any sense, since what is corporeal is by nature subject to division and contains potentiality, the opposite of God's required simplicity and full actuality. Nor is God within any genus, nor is he a subject as other individuals are. The first cause rules all things without commingling with them.

God's primary perfection is his actuality, since Thomas accepts the doctrine that a thing is perfect in proportion to its state of actuality. All created perfections preëxist in God also, since he is the source of all things. As such a source of the multitude of things in this world, things diverse and in themselves opposed to each other preëxist in God as one, without injury to his simplicity. This is no simple kind of simplicity which Thomas ascribes to his God as a perfection. God is also called good, although goodness is defined primarily in terms of full actuality, as both perfection and simplicity were. Everything is good insofar as it has being, and, since God is being in a supremely actual sense, he is supremely good. An object can be spoken of as evil only insofar as it lacks being. Since God lacks being in no way, there is in that sense absolutely no evil in his nature but only good.

When Thomas comes to infinity he

is up against a particularly difficult divine attribute. By his time infinity had become a traditional perfection to be ascribed to God, but Aristotle had gone to great lengths to deny even the possibility of an actual infinite. Without discussing Aristotle's reasons here, it can be noted that Thomas makes one of his most significant alterations at this point in the Aristotelian concepts which he does use. Aristotle had considered the question of an actual infinite in the category of quantity. Thomas agrees with him: there can be no quantitative infinite and the idea is an imperfection. Form had meant primarily limitation for Aristotle, but here Thomas departs. The notion of form, he asserts, is not incompatible with infinity, although the forms of natural things are finite. In admitting the concept of the form of the infinite, Thomas departs from Aristotelian conceptions quite markedly and makes a place for a now traditional divine perfection. Nothing besides God, however, can be infinite.

Turning to the question of the immanence of God in the natural world, Thomas makes God present to all things as being the source of their being, power, and operation. But as such, God is not in the world. For one thing, God is altogether immutable, whereas every natural thing changes. He must be, since he is pure act and only what contains potentiality moves to acquire something. It follows that in God there is no succession, no time, but only simultaneous presence. God's unity further guarantees us that only one such God could exist. Of course a God of such a nature may not be knowable to a particular intellect, on account of the excess of such an intelligible object over the finite intellect;

but, as fully actual, God is in himself fully knowable. The blessed see the essence of God by grace; for others it is more difficult. However, a proportion is possible between God and man, and in this way the created intellect can know God proportionally. This is not full knowledge, but it established the possibility for a knowledge relationship between God and man.

The created intellect, however, cannot fully grasp the essence of God, unless God by grace unites himself to the created intellect, as an object made intelligible to it. It is necessary in the case of God only that, for a full grasp, the natural power of understanding should be aided by divine grace. Those who possess the more charity will see God the more perfectly, and will be the more beatified. Here is Thomas's statement of the famous goal of the beatific vision. Even here God is only apprehended and never comprehended, since only an infinite being could possess the infinite mode necessary for comprehension, and none is infinite except God. God alone can comprehend himself, yet for the mind to attain an understanding of God in some degree is still asserted to be a great beatitude. God cannot be seen in his essence by a mere human being, except he be separated from this mortal life. Thomas here follows the famous Exodus XXXIII:20 passage: "Man shall not see Me, and live."

For Thomas faith is a kind of knowledge, since we gain a more perfect knowledge of God himself by grace than by natural reason. Such a concept of faith has had wide implications. That God is a trinity, for instance, cannot be known except by faith, and in general making faith a mode of knowledge has opened to Christianity the claim to a more perfect comprehension than non-Christians possess.

Names can be applied to God positively on Thomas's theory, but negative names simply signify his distance from creatures, and all names fall short of a full representation of him. Not all names are applied to God in a metaphorical sense, although some are (for example, God is a lion), but there are some names which are applied to God in a literal sense (for example, good, being). In reality God is one, and yet he is necessarily multiple in idea, because our intellect represents him in a manifold manner, conceiving of many symbols to represent him. However, univocal predication is impossible, and sometimes terms are even used equivocally. Others are predicated of God in an analogous sense, according to a proportion existing between God and nature.

In the first thirteen questions Thomas considers God as man approaches him. He then considers the world as it is viewed from the standpoint of the divine nature. Even the attributes of perfection which Thomas discussed, although they truly characterize God's nature, are not separate when viewed from the divine perspective. Now we ask how God understands both himself and the world, and the first thing which must be established is that there actually is knowledge in God. This might seem obvious, but the Neoplatonic tradition denies knowing to its highest principle as implying separation and need. Thomas admits a mode of knowing into the divine nature but he denies that God knows as creatures do. God understands everything through himself alone, without dependence on external objects; his intellect and its object are altogether the same and no potentiality is present. God's knowledge is not discursive but simultaneous and fully actual eternally. This is true because of God's role as the creator of the natural world; God's knowledge is the cause of things being as they are. God knows even some things which never were, nor are, nor will be, but it is in his knowledge not that they be but that they be merely possible.

God knows future contingent things, the works of men being subject to free will. These things are not certain to us, because of their dependence upon proximate, contingent causes, but they are certain to God alone, whose understanding is eternal and above time. There is a will as a part of God's nature, but it is moved by itself alone. The will of man is sometimes moved by things external to him. God wills his own goodness necessarily, even as we will our own happiness necessarily. Yet his willing things apart from himself is not necessary. Supposing that he wills it, however, then he is unable not to will it, since his will cannot change. Things other than God are thus "necessary by supposition." God knows necessarily whatever he knows, but does not will necessarily whatever he wills. And the will of God is always reasonable in what it wills. Yet the will of God is entirely unchangeable, Thomas asserts, since the substance of God and his knowledge are entirely unchangeable. As to evil, God neither wills evil to be done, nor wills it not to be done, but he wills to permit evil to be done; this is good because it is the basis of man's freedom. We must say, however, that all things are subject to divine providence, not only in general, but even in their own individual selves. It necessarily follows that everything which happens from the exercise of free will must be subject to divine providence. Both necessity and contingency fall under the foresight of God.

It should not be overlooked that Thomas devotes considerable time to a consideration of the nature and function of angels. Part of his reason for doing so, of course, is undoubtedly their constant presence in the Biblical record. Part of his interest comes from the necessity of having intermediary beings between God and man. Having assigned to God a nature so different from man's nature, beings who stand somewhere in between are now easy to conceive. When Thomas comes to describe the nature of man, he follows much of the traditional Aristotelian psychology, which he finds more amenable to Christianity than certain Platonistic theories. Angels are not corporeal; man is composed of a spiritual and a corporeal substance. The soul has no matter, but it is necessarily joined to matter as its instrument. The intellectual principle is the form of man and in that sense determines the body's form. Since Thomas claims that the intellect in each man is uniquely individual, he argues against some Arabian views of the universality of intellect. In addition to a two-fold intellect (active and passive), man has appetites and a will.

The will is not always moved by necessity, but in Thomas's views it is subject to the intellect. When he turns to the question of free will, Thomas's problem is to allow sufficient causal power to man's will without denying God's providence and foreknowledge. His solution to this problem is complicated, but essentially it involves God's moving man not directly and by force but indirectly and without doing violence to man's nature.

To obtain knowledge the soul derives intelligible species from the sensible forms which come to it, and it has neither innate knowledge nor does it know any forms existing independently from sensible things. The principle of knowledge is in the senses. Our intellect can know the singular in material things directly and primarily. After that intelligible species are derived by abstraction. Yet the intellectual soul cannot know itself directly, but only through its operations. Nor in this present life can our intellect know immaterial substances directly. That is a knowledge reserved for angels, but it means that we cannot understand immaterial substances perfectly now (through natural means). We know only material substances, and they cannot represent immaterial substances perfectly.

The soul of man is not eternal; it was created. It is produced immediately by God, not by any lesser beings (as is suggested in Plato's *Timaeus*, for instance). Soul and body are produced simultaneously, since they belong together as one organism. Man was made in God's image, but this in no way implies that there must be equality between creator and created. And some natures may be more like God than others, according to their disposition and the direction of their activities. All men are directed to some end. According as their end is worthy of blame or praise, so are their deeds worthy of blame or praise. There is, however, one last fixed end for all men; and man must, of necessity, desire all that he desires for the sake of that last end. Man's happiness ultimately does not consist either in wealth, fame, or honor, or even in power. Thomas never doubts that the end desired is to be happy, but he does deny that the end can consist of goods of the body. No created good can be man's last end. Final and perfect happiness can consist in nothing else than the vision of the Divine Essence, although momentary happiness probably does depend on some physical thing.

Now, it is possible for man to see God, and therefore it is possible for man to attain his ultimate happiness. Of course, there are diverse degrees of happiness, and it is not present equally in all men. A certain participation in such happiness can be had in this life, although true and perfect happiness cannot. Once attained, such happiness cannot be lost since its nature is eternal, but man cannot attain it by his own natural powers, although every man desires it.

Next Thomas considers the mechanics of human action, voluntary and involuntary movement, individual circumstances, the movement of the will, intention and choice. His discussion forms an addition to his psychology and a more complete discussion of the ethical situation of man. When he comes to good and evil in human action, Thomas easily acknowledges that some actions of man are evil, although they are good or evil according to circumstance. As far as man's interior act of will is concerned, good and evil are essential differences in the act of will. The goodness of the will essentially depends on its being subject to reason and to natural law. The will can be evil when it abides by an erring reason. The goodness of the will de-pends upon its conformity to the divine will.

In his more detailed psychology, Thomas discusses the nature and origin of the soul's passions, joy, sadness, hope, fear and then love and hate. Pleasure, pain or sorrow, hope, despair, and fear all are analyzed in a way that anticipates Spinoza's famous discussion of the emotions. When Thomas comes to virtue, his opinion is largely based on Aristotle's. There are intellectual virtues and moral virtues, and to these he adds the theological virtues of faith, hope, and charity. Moral virtue is in a man by nature, although God infuses the theological virtues into man. For salvation, of course, there is need for a gift of the Holy Ghost.

Thomas continues with a discussion of sin, its kinds and causes. Such discussion has been extremely important both to church doctrine and in church practice. Not all sins are equal; therefore, sins must be handled in various ways. The carnal sins, for instance, are of less guilt but of more shame than spiritual sins. Mortal and venial sins are distinguished, but the will and the reason are always involved in the causes of sin. "Original sin" as a concept is of course extremely important to Christian doctrine, and Thomas discusses this in detail.

The treatise on law is one of the more famous parts of the *Summa Theologica*, for it is here that Thomas develops his theory of natural law. First, of course, there is the eternal law of which natural law is the first reflection and human (actual legal) law is a second reflection. The eternal law is one and it is unchanging; natural law is something common to all nations and cannot be entirely blotted out from men's hearts. Human law is derived from this common natural law, but human law is framed to meet the majority of instances and must take into account many things, as to persons, as to matters, and as to times.

A brief survey such as this cannot do justice even to the variety of topics considered in the *Summa Theologica*, nor can it give any detailed description of the complex material presented or of the views Thomas distills from them. The impression which the *Summa Theologica* gives is that of an encyclopedia to be read and studied as a kind of source book for material on a desired issue. In fact, the only way for any reader to hope to understand Thomas and his *Summa Theologica* is to become engrossed and involved in it for himself—undoubtedly what Thomas intended.

A TRACT CONCERNING THE FIRST PRINCIPLE

Author: John Duns Scotus (c.1265-1308)
Type of work: Theology
First transcribed: c. 1300

PRINCIPAL IDEAS ADVANCED

God, the First Principle, is the most perfect Being, that which causes but is not itself caused, that which is independent and on which everything else is dependent.

The First Principle is possible since an infinite series of causes is impossible; such an uncaused being must be necessary in itself.

There is but one First Principle, for multiple first principles are not necessary.

The First Principle is simple, infinite, wise, indefinable, intelligent, and endowed with will.

God created the natural order by a free act of will.

With so little of Duns Scotus's writing translated into English, we are fortunate indeed that A *Tract Concerning the First Principle* has been made available. Scholars admit that Scotus's Latin is difficult. Sometimes it is said that he represents scholastic subtlety at its height (implication: at its most obscure). However, such an estimate represents more a lack of sympathy with the mode of Scotus's thought than it does any extraordinary obscurity. It is true that Duns Scotus is aptly called

the "subtle doctor," but the technical philosophy of any age is couched in specialized terms. Scotus belongs with the host of those before him whose central concern is metaphysics; and, like his profound compatriots, his writing reflects the difficulties inherent in such interests.

Scotus wrote in conscious opposition to Thomas Aquinas, as Ockham did after him. Both of these later men felt that there were certain deficiencies in Thomas's position, especially as it related to Christian doctrine. Both were somewhat more avowedly philosophical than Thomas, and both preferred to separate more radically philosophy and theology as disciplines, although Ockham is the real innovator here. The appearance of Aristotle in translation was new in Thomas's day; and both of these later writers actually seem closer to Aristotelianism than does Thomas, since the Aristotelian corpus had had more time to be appraised, with erroneous impressions corrected and Platonic glosses removed.

The study of Thomas Aquinas received papal encouragement in Leo XIII's encyclical of 1879. The result has been a widespread concentration upon Thomas, together with a much more general acquaintanceship with his work in non-Catholic philosophical circles. The philosophical and theological descendants of Scotus are equally vigorous today but less numerous, although many signs point to an increasing revival of interest in his thought. A critical edition of his work is under way and some additional English translation ought to follow. When this is done, we may find Scotus to be a much more modern thinker than has been generally recognized, rather than the last and most ponderous of the Scholastics. If traditional metaphysical and theological interest is due to be revived in our own day, Scotus may very well prove to be the modern starting point for such a revival.

Even a brief glimpse of the *Tract* will tell us that it is not in any sense a devotional work, even though its subject is God. Nor are any practical or religious goals specifically in view. "God" is mentioned only occasionally. Instead, Duns Scotus prefers an abstract title, the "First Principle." This piece of writing is a technical consideration of metaphysical structure and attributes, and it deals directly with the central speculative questions that surround the divine nature. Theory of knowledge and arguments for God's existence are present, but they are a side issue and a by-product of this straightforward metaphysical analysis of the First Principle of all things.

Systematically speaking, Scotus does not consider man and nature first but rather God. In the solution to questions about the natural order, Scotus holds to the classical belief that an analysis of the divine nature is central in determining the outcome of all such discussion. But this treatise is not long. To discuss man and the world and historical events would require a system and volumes of books. In something like seventy-five pages, on the other hand, an entire theory of the central characteristics of God is outlined. From there Scotus could go on to use his theory both as a fixed point of reference and as a fulcrum in the discussion of the wider range of philosophical and theological issues.

Despite this unapologetic approach to a direct discussion of the First Principle, there is a decidedly non-dogmatic flavor to Duns Scotus's writing. His own opinion is clear and is elaborated technically, but one never gets the impression that he considers his to be the only possible theory or to be binding upon the reader. Here is an exploration simply offered for discussion.

Since no consideration of God can begin from an observed fact, it must receive its focus from some suggested theory, and it is in this spirit that Scotus seems to write. To be sure, the scholastically elaborate form in which the discussion is couched gives the modern reader some initial difficulty in extracting a straightforward statement. But Scotus, like many classical metaphysicians, seems to rely more upon the presence of a single significant statement than on structural simplicity of style or upon the modern directness of the essay form.

Although Scotus's *Tract* has fewer religious overtones than, say, Anselm's *Proslogion*, he still begins with the traditional prayer for divine assistance in his task. Then he turns to Moses and the Old Testament and opens with a brief consideration of the famous "I am Who am" passage (Exodus III:14). But this leads him immediately to a consideration of "being" as the primary name for God, which shifts the discussion on to a metaphysical plane from which it seldom returns. Now comes the traditional "division of orders," a discussion of the various meanings for and divisions of "being."

Eminence versus dependence is the first and traditional division. Whatever is perfect and more noble in its essence is prior, according to Scotus. That which causes but is itself uncaused is first, and everything of a more dependent nature is posterior. The prior is whatever is able to exist without the posterior, whereas the posterior cannot exist without the prior. And this division is accurate even if the prior produces the posterior orders necessarily. After this first and essential division of being, the posterior orders may then be subdivided.

Duns Scotus goes on to quote Augustine with approval: there is not anything at all which brings itself into being. Nothing which we know from its nature to be an effect can be its own cause. A circle is impossible in casual relations. And some aspects are ruled out as being incidental. Only certain crucial relations and orders are to be considered, not all data (as some nineteenth century views attempt to encompass). The goal of such a delimited investigation is an understanding of the first cause in causing, although in addition to this, myriad efficient causes are needed to account for the majority of temporal events. An efficient cause acts for the love of some end; a first cause produces from itself without ulterior motive. No causation, therefore, is perfect other than that which comes from a first cause itself uncaused; lesser causes necessarily have some imperfections connected with them. Of course, in any individual case an analysis may find all levels and modes of causation to be in operation.

Scotus departs from Aristotle in making "matter" prior according to independence, whereas Aristotle completely subordinates matter to form. However, Scotus reasserts with Aristotle the priority of form according to eminence, because it is more perfect. Turning then to Plotinus and to the Neoplatonic tradition, he affirms the traditional preference for unity: plurality is never to be posited without necessity. Actually, this is the classical form of what was to become known as "Ockham's razor." Order is due to simplicity. It is really the preference for simplicity which dictates that the fewest possible principles should be introduced, and this is one of the strongest arguments for positing only a single first principle.

Then Scotus offers his version of the traditional "proofs" for God's existence, phrasing it as being a demonstration "that some one nature is simply first." But Scotus prefers to couch his argument in terms of "possibles," rather than to argue from the nature of the actual natural world. If his reasoning holds for all possible states, he argues, then it would hold for whatever set of states happens to be actual, whereas an argument based on actualities need not hold necessarily for possible states. With Scotus, and later with Ockham, an increasing stress is laid upon simply considering the order of possible entities as something prior to (and thus nearer to God than) the actual order of nature.

Scotus follows the traditional view that an ascent through an infinite series of prior levels or causes is impossible. All he concludes here is, not the assumed existence of a God, but merely that it is possible that some single causal principle should be simply first. As a preliminary step, and as the limit of philosophical argument, God is proved simply to be possible, and then only in the form that "an efficient causality simply first is possible." Metaphysics explores possible arguments; it does not support dogmatic conclusions.

Furthermore, Scotus never attempts to prove that such a cause which is simply first is necessarily itself uncaused. He simply goes on to argue that this is possible, since it is not affected by anything else and yet it affects other things independently. A first cause in the possible order is then shown to be required to bring some set of possibles into actual existence. From this point on, such a being can be examined as to its nature, although it is merely a being whose possible existence (although perhaps it has now become probable) has been established. Scotus reasons: such an uncaused being must be necessary in itself, since it

depends upon no prior causes. Of itself, it is impossible for such a first cause not to be. Such is Scotus's line of contingent reasoning.

Considering such a principle, it becomes evident that there could be only one being of such a nature, since the kind of necessity which belongs to a being that owes its existence to no outside cause cannot be shared. Since there cannot be multiple beings all of whom derive the necessity of their existence from themselves, the unique perfection of such a single and preëminent nature is insured. Arguing like a mathematician for the elegance of simplicity, Scotus turns from the internal consideration of such a first principle to argue that, moreover, there is nothing about the multiple entities in the world which requires more than a single first principle for their explanation. And since multiple first principles are not necessary, it would be foolish to posit more than the single first cause which the explanation requires.

A multitude cannot be from itself; a first cause is required to explain such existence. A unitary and unique being requires no previous cause; it can explain multiple beings without itself requiring explanation. Explanation ends when simplicity is reached. In the essential orders an ascent is made toward unity and fewness. So, there is a stop in one cause. Such a first efficient cause is actual because it contains every possible actuality. No possible entities can be conceived of as being outside its nature. Thus it is perfect, as containing every possible goodness within itself.

Nothing shares perfectly unless it shares, not of necessity, but from the liberality of its nature. Such a consideration of what perfection means leads Duns Scotus on to consider the divine will. If such a first principle must share its being with other beings, due to its natural liberality, then "will" must have an important place in such a nature as essential to its perfection. Along with this necessary endowment of will, Scotus describes his God as being simple, infinite, and wise. Such essential simplicity excludes all possible composition in the divine nature. It is not a being made up of parts as other beings are. None of its perfections are really distinct from the others, although our language and the process of analysis force us to consider each perfection as if it were in some way separate and distinct.

Scotus repeats the phrase common in medieval theology: the First Nature does not fall under a genus. The First Principle is unique and not subject to description according to any ordinary classifications. Normal discussion proceeds by classifying but this principle alone fails to fit the pattern for normal relations or to fall under any of the standard categories. Opinion among metaphysicians is divided as to just how radical this difference is, as to just how inadequate our normal language might be. Scotus falls among those who feel that common terms may be used to describe God if they are properly qualified to fit the special situation.

It seems perfectly acceptable to Duns Scotus to say that the First Efficient is intelligent and endowed with will, although such assertions require special argument to support them and special qualifications to accept them. For instance, most intelligence looks to some end outside itself, but Scotus's First Efficient is made unique by being said not to love any end different from

itself. Thus the traditional categories are used to describe such a First Principle, but they are qualified in a way that makes their application nevertheless unique. However, it is when Scotus turns to the question of contingency that he becomes his most radical and the most subject to innovations.

The First Cause causes contingently, Scotus asserts; consequently, it causes freely. The classical tradition had been united in making the creation of lesser orders in nature necessary and in viewing necessity often as the very hallmark of the perfection characteristic of a First Principle. Christian theologians in considering God and his creative activity had modified this somewhat, although necessity still seemed to be preferred. Scotus for the first time raises contingency to a central place in the divine nature and designates the creation of the natural order as a free act.

What is most important here is that Scotus sees that, if any freedom of action is to be preserved for man, some freedom of action must first be found to be possible in God. For if the First moves necessarily, every other cause is moved necessarily and everything is caused necessarily. The locus of the problem of freedom is not in human nature; it really revolves around an issue concerning God's initial action. If God's creative act is necessary, if he has no freedom of movement in originating the natural order, then it is hardly likely that men could move contingently or freely when even God cannot.

Now Scotus turns to the question of human will. If there is to be freedom in man's causal activity, then he must act contingently. If such contingent action is to be possible, God must first of all have been open to such possibilities in his initial creative act. But nothing, says Scotus, is a principle of contingent operation except will. And this is the source of Scotus's famed "voluntarism." Anything other than an action which is contingent upon the will is a necessary action, so that the possibility of allowing for contingency depends upon upholding a doctrine that gives a primary place to the will, both in men and in God. Contingency means that the act is dependent upon the will's direction. Any view which wishes to preserve at least some human actions as being free must begin with the divine nature and preserve will as an independent power within that nature. Will can give rise to contingent actions and opens a freedom to man, through the similarity discovered between the activity of man's will and God's.

Then Scotus carries the argument for contingency and the primacy of will one step further. There is something evil among us, and this, he feels, argues for the First Efficient's causing through contingency. If contingency (and thus the operation of will) is not present in his action, then every evil factor in nature becomes a necessity, and he becomes directly responsible for every evil act. A perfect First Principle, he argues, that operated necessarily would create a world lacking no perfection. Due to the presence of evil, our world is by no means such a perfect place. As a lesser world, our order must have been selected freely as something below the optimum possible. Reversing Leibniz, Duns Scotus argues from the fact that we do not live in the best of all possible worlds to prove

that we can account for this deficiency only through contingent causation on the part of the First Efficient Cause. Necessity did not force him to create the best possible world; the operation of will allowed the contingent choice of a natural order containing some evil.

The First Principle wills nothing outside his nature of necessity; consequently neither does he cause any effect necessarily. There could be no contingency in any second cause in causing unless there were contingency in the First Principle in willing. The presence of evil demands that God be free either to will or not to will this less perfect order into existence. Thus his freedom in willing also allows us a similar freedom in willing and opens the way for contingent causation by men (second causes). Every effect in nature is contingent, because it depends upon the efficiency of the First Principle, whose efficiency is contingent.

Will becomes identical with the First Nature although no act of his understanding can be an accident for him. Thus, God's understanding of all things is necessary, but the action of his will in causing is not. Necessary cognition of everything whatsoever is a part of the divine nature, which means that God understands everything continually. Thus God must understand everything he wills, and this removes the possibility of a blind action by the divine will. With men, no such necessary understanding exists, so that with them ignorant action is always possible. God is unique in this respect.

No act or intellection in the First Principle is an accident. Men, on the other hand, come by a great deal of their information accidentally; the human act of will often depends either on accidental or incomplete information; with the divine will such is never the case. God's understanding is always perfect, whereas man's is not. Both, however, may cause contingently through an act of will. God's contingent volition is necessarily based on knowledge; man's is not.

Every intelligible concept was understood distinctly and of necessity by the First Principle prior to its existence within the natural order, and also prior to the natural order itself. Every possible state God now knows and always knew. The actual state of affairs in the natural order is subject to contingent volition, first by God and then by men. From this eternal understanding of every intelligible concept Scotus goes on to argue for the necessity of God's being infinite. The possible intelligible concepts are infinite and God must actually understand them all eternally and simultaneously. An intellect capable of such comprehension must itself be infinite and in turn must reside in a nature also actually infinite. God's infinity is claimed as a consequence of the infinity of possible objects of understanding and of his necessary grasp of them all. An intellect which is applicable to an infinity of objects must itself be altogether unlimited.

In a way which would seem strange to Plotinus, Duns Scotus ties simplicity and infinity together. If a being is infinite, then Scotus argues that its various aspects are not formally distinct. Since simplicity must be predicated of God as a primary perfection, Duns Scotus concludes that God must be infinite. Only an infinite principle seems to be free of the distinctions within its nature which cause disruptive multiplicity. A finite entity is subject to division whereas one characterized by infinity holds all of its attributes together in an essential unity. Scotus's argument at this point is both interesting and unusual.

If such arguments appear subject to many objections, it must be remembered that what is most characteristic of Scotus's *Tract* is a certain tentativeness about his reasoning. The spirit which seems to pervade it is that of a speculative intellect testing interesting forms of argument. Scotus is serious about his topic, but the reader nowhere gets the feeling that he expects it necessarily to compel anyone else. His reasoning is more suggestive than logically foolproof. Not every sentence is equally essential to the reasoning, but during the course of it all Scotus obviously thinks that some important things have been discovered and announced. It is hoped that the reader will similarly share his moments of insight.

How can we understand the infinite? Scotus answers that it is through the finite, for the infinite can be defined only through the use of the finite. The meaning of the infinite is grasped negatively, as that which exceeds any given finite limit. Since finiteness itself does not belong essentially to the meaning of being, the natural intellect can easily come to see that "being" may be classified as either finite or infinite. This means that the human intellect apprehends being in general as neither finite nor infinite and then goes on to see whether the particular being it is dealing with is or is not actually finite

335

(subject to limits) or whether it is to be understood negatively as exceeding all finite limits. Such a doctrine allows a much more direct and natural understanding of the divine nature than is usual among theologians.

What is infinite can also be a being, although other beings are finite. The natural intellect finds nothing repugnant or difficult about understanding the concept of an infinite being. On the contrary, "infinite being" seems to be the most perfectly intelligible concept. This is the beginning of the new-found ease of the modern metaphysician in dealing with the infinite, which is an almost complete reversal of the classical fear of the infinite as being an unintelligible object. Traditionally, the human intellect seemed specifically adapted to finite objects; now, as Scotus begins the modern era, infinity becomes the hallmark of perfect intelligibility and is easily grasped.

The argument for the intelligibility of infinity for the human understanding again comes from the will. When we examine our human will, what we see as most characteristic about it is that it is never satisfied by any finite object. It is always restless, always seeking something greater than any finite end. After understanding this, our intellect can then pass on to understand what infinity means: a lack of any specifiable limit or end. In comprehending the phenomenon of will, our intellect grasps what infinity connotes, and recognizes the ease with which it

grasps the concept of infinity. The stress upon will makes infinity an easy and a natural concept.

God has the power to actualize all possible states simultaneously, but he does not choose to do so. Some states mutually exclude one another at any given moment, and other possibilities his will does not choose to actualize. If all possible states existed simultaneously, our world would be absolutely unlimited. Scotus believes the natural order to be finite, its limits representing the original self-restraint of the divine will in creating.

Thus Scotus's First Principle comes to have some of the attributes (will, contingent choice, freedom) which we usually associate with human activity; although in other respects (power, unlimited knowledge, infinity) it belongs to no natural genus. Here is a view which, in certain respects, makes the First Principle very much like man and in other respects distinguishes it radically. Yet more important than this is the overall modernity of Scotus's thought. "Freedom" and "will" predominate in these considerations, and a tentative quality pervades the argument as a whole. The metaphysical framework of most medieval theology is basically classical. Duns Scotus represents, not so much the decline of medieval theology as the beginning of a modern metaphysical spirit, much of which remains as yet essentially unexplored.

WILLIAM OF OCKHAM: SELECTIONS

Author: William of Ockham (c.1280-c.1350)
Type of work: Logic, epistemology
First transcribed: Early fourteenth century (Selections from his writings)

PRINCIPAL IDEAS ADVANCED

All abstractive cognitions (knowledge derived from experience, made possible by reflection upon experience) depend upon prior intuitive cognitions (sense experience of things).

Our knowledge of the existing world is contingent upon God's will, for he can affect our intuitive cognitions whatever the facts may be.

Predication occurs only if the predicate term of a sentence refers to the object referred to by the subject term, and if the predicate term refers to the object not by naming it, but by referring to some feature of it.

Universals are not single properties common to many things, but signs which have application to a number of things.

An explanation involving fewer assumptions than an alternative explanation is preferable to the alternative. [Ockham's "razor."]

William of Ockham was born at Ockham, Surrey, became a Franciscan, attended Oxford, and taught there for several years until he was summoned to the papal court at Avignon to answer charges of heresy arising from his writings and teaching. He was not formally condemned, but during his stay in France he became embroiled in a controversy that split his order into bitter factions, a controversy over the ideal of poverty espoused by its founder, St. Francis. After strenuously opposing both the Pope and the majority of his order on this issue, he and several others found it expedient to flee to the court of the Emperor of Germany, who had just installed an anti-Pope and who was glad to accept their assistance in his battle with the Pope. Excommunicated by the Pope and his own order, Ockham lived in Munich until his death. In his last years he was trying to reconcile himself with his order, but apparently he died before he was

successful. Ockham wrote a great deal, but very little of it is available to the reader of English. Such a reader is limited to several books of selections: *Ockham: Philosophical Writings,* by P. Boehner; *Ockham: Studies and Selections,* by S. C. Tornay; *Selections from Medieval Philosophers,* by R. McKeon; and T. B. Birch's translation of *De sacremento altaris.*

Ockham is known for his famous "razor," for his logic, and for his nominalistic and empirical viewpoint. Living in the fourteenth century, he was the dominant figure in the movement away from Albertus Magnus, Thomas Aquinas, and John Duns Scotus, the great system builders of the thirteenth century. He was the inspirer of an empirically and nominalistically inclined movement that contended with the Thomistic, Albertist, Scotist, and Averroistic schools of the next several centuries. Although he has been called the Hume of the Middle Ages, Ockham was not a skeptic. Negatively, he undermined and rejected most of the metaphysics and a good deal of the natural theology of his contemporaries, but positively, he was a theologian who accepted the traditional Christian dogmas on faith and who preferred to accept them on faith alone rather than to argue for them on dubious philosophic grounds.

His basic inclination toward empiricism is revealed in the distinction between intuitive and abstractive cognitions. When we are looking at Socrates, he says, we can see that he is white. In this case we are aware of the existence of Socrates, of the occurrence of the quality, and of the fact that this individual, Socrates, is white. That is, the senses enable us to know with certainty a contingent fact about the world. This is an instance of what Ockham calls *intuitive cognition*. But we can think of Socrates when he is not present, and of white when we are not seeing it, and we can think of Socrates as being white. In this case we are cognizing the same things, Socrates and white, and we are entertaining the same proposition, but we do not know that Socrates still exists or that the proposition is true. This is an instance of what Ockham calls *abstractive cognition*, abstractive not because the terms are abstract, but because we have abstracted from existence.

The terms of the intuitive cognition are sensed and are particular, while the terms of the abstractive cognition are not sensed and are common. In intuitive cognition the cognition is caused in us by action of the object on our sensory and intellectual faculties, a process that culminates naturally, without any initiative on our part, in the knowledge that Socrates is white. No judgment, at least no explicit one, is involved here, for we simply see that Socrates is white. On the other hand, in abstractive cognition the cognition is not caused by the object, for either the object is absent or, if present, it is not sufficiently close to produce a clear sensation. Under such circumstances we scrutinize the data given by memory or sensation and, perhaps, go on deliberately to judge or refrain from judging that something is the case.

In abstractive cognition an apparently simple idea, such as the concept "Socrates," must be understood as a complex of common terms, for neither Socrates nor any other individual is operating on us to produce the cognition of him. In such a cognition we are entertaining such common terms as "intelligent," "snub-nosed," "white," and "Athenian" which, when taken together, constitute a complex abstractive term limiting our attention to the one desired individual.

By contrast, in intuitive cognition we apprehend Socrates in a different manner, for in this case the object itself is producing in us a simple noncomplex idea of itself. Indeed, we obtain the terms appearing in abstractive cognitions only by attending to and separating in thought the various features of the sensation. Thus, Ockham concludes, all abstractive cognitions depend upon prior intuitive ones, and intuitive cognition must be the source of all our knowledge about the world. Furthermore, Ockham says that we intuit or sense nothing but individual things, and these are either sensible substances such as Socrates, or sensible properties such as the sensed whiteness of Socrates. Even relations are regarded as properties of groups of individuals.

338

When we add to all these considerations Ockham's famous "razor"—"What can be explained by the assumption of fewer things is vainly explained by the assumption of more things"—his nominalistic and empiricistic views follow immediately, for now we have an epistemology that not only makes us start with the senses but also prevents us from going very far beyond them. The senses reveal to us a multitude of sensible individuals and provide us with a great deal of information about them and about their temporal and spatial settings, but they do not reveal any necessary connections, causal or otherwise—and the razor prevents us from assuming any. This epistemology obviously limits the scope of metaphysics but does not quite eliminate it, for the metaphysician can still tell us a little about God. Given the terms "being," "cause," and "first," all of which are derived from experience, and assuming that they are univocal terms, as Ockham does, we can form the complex idea of a being who is a first cause. Furthermore, given intellectually self-evident principles such as "Every thing has a cause," we can demonstrate the existence of a first cause that exists necessarily and which, as the most perfect existent, has intellect and will. However, we cannot prove that there is only one such God or that there might not have been a greater God, and we cannot demonstrate that he has the various features required by Christian dogma.

The sort of world suggested by Ockham's epistemology is also required by his theology. Like Scotus before him and Descartes after him, Ockham emphasizes God's will rather than his intellect. God can do nothing that is contradictory, but this fact does not limit his will, for his ideas are not of his essence and are not exemplars between which he must choose. They are his creatures and the world is whatever he has cared to make it. Consequently, the world does not exist necessarily, and within this world nothing follows necessarily from anything else and nothing requires the existence of anything else. This radical contingency stems from God's complete power over the circumstances in which things shall or shall not come into existence. God ordinarily uses instruments to produce in us the experiences we have, but he could, if he wished, dispense with them and operate on us directly. For instance, Ockham says, it would require a miracle but God could make us see a star even where there actually is no star. That is, we could have exactly the same cognition that is normally caused in us by the star even if there were no star or any other physical cause. Since the seeing of the star is one distinct event and the star itself is another, it is not impossible that either should exist independently of the other.

The possibility of cognition without a corresponding fact reveals a limitation of intuitive cognition, for even though such a cognition makes us certain that something is the case, we could nevertheless be mistaken. Ockham skirts around the threat of skepticism by remarking that although an error of this sort can occur if God interferes with the natural order, miracles are rare. Consequently, the probability of error is insignificantly low. Yet, he acknowledges, it is still the case that our knowledge of the existing world is contingent upon God's will.

There is a remarkable agreement between Descartes and Ockham concerning the contingency of our knowledge.

Because Descartes held a more extreme doctrine about the power of God, he took skepticism more seriously, but, of course, he believed he could escape by using reason. On the other hand, Ockham regarded the risk of empiricism as slight and claimed that it is better to exercise a little faith than to accept the grave risks of rationalism.

In his writings, Ockham, who was probably the best of medieval logicians, commences his discussion of logic by considering the nature of terms. First, he distinguishes between written, spoken, and conceptual terms. The latter are mental contents that function as private signs of things. Since these mental signs are not deliberately produced by us, but come about naturally through the operation of the object on us, they are called *natural signs*. Since spoken signs, on the other hand, are sounds which have been conventionally attached to particular mental signs, they are *conventional signs*. They denote the same object as the associated concept, thus enabling us to communicate what would otherwise be private. Written signs have a similar relation to spoken signs. Ordinarily, when Ockham speaks of terms he has in mind such terms as "man," "animal," "whiteness," and "white," which signify or denote things and which can function as the subject or predicate of a proposition. These terms, which he calls *categorematic* terms, are to be contrasted with *snycategorematic* terms such as "every," "insofar as," and "some," which do not denote anything when they stand by themselves. He also distinguishes between concrete terms such as "white" and abstract terms such as "whiteness," and between discrete terms such as "Socrates" and common terms such as "man."

A more important distinction is that between absolute terms and connotative terms. An *absolute term* is one that denotes directly, whereas a *connotative term* is one that denotes one thing only by connoting another. "Socrates," "man," and "whiteness" are absolute terms for they are used to point to, respectively, a specific individual, any one of a number of similar individuals, or to a property. A connotative term such as "white" is not used as a label, for there is no such thing as white. When it is used in a proposition such as "Socrates is white," it denotes the same object as does the subject term, but it does so by connoting a property of the object; namely, whiteness. The distinction can be formulated in another way. At least some absolute terms, such as "man," have real definitions in which each term, such as "rational" and "animal," can denote the same objects as the defined term. Connotative terms have only nominal definitions, for the definition will require a term in the oblique case that cannot denote the same object as does the defined term. Thus "white" may be defined as "that which has the property whiteness," but "whiteness" does not denote the white thing. In certain definitions connotative terms may occur, but these can always be defined in turn until we reach definitions that contain absolute terms only. That is, language is grounded in terms that denote only, and cognition is basically a matter of being aware of objects and features of objects by intuitive cognition.

This distinction also bring us back to Ockham's epistemology by indicating the way in which a proposition is related to the world. Since there are only particulars in the world, each term of a true proposition, such as "Socrates is white," can refer only to one or more individuals. Such a proposition does not assert that two different things are identical, nor that the subject and predicate are one and the same thing, nor that something inheres in or is part of the subject. In our example, "white" is not another name for Socrates, it is not the name of another individual, and it is not the name of the property *whiteness*; but it must denote something. It can only denote Socrates, but not, of course, as "Socrates" does. That is, it denotes him indirectly by connoting his whiteness. Predication occurs only if (1) the predicate term denotes the very same object as the subject term, and (2) the predicate term denotes the object not by naming it but by connoting some feature of it.

In the above discussion we have mentioned abstract terms such as "whiteness" that are absolute and that denote properties rather than substances. Lest it seem that Ockham was a realist after all, we must turn to his discussion of universals. He denies emphatically that there are universals of either Platonic or Aristotelian varieties, for both doctrines require that something simple be common to many things. This state of affairs, he says, is impossible unless that simple something be plural, a condition which itself is impossible. Furthermore, he says, the problem should be turned around, for since the world is composed of particulars only, the problem is not the way in which some universal thing becomes particularized, but our reason for attributing universality to anything in the first place. The only thing to which we can attribute it is a sign, and even here only by virtue of its function as a sign, for as a mere existent it is as particular as anything else. Thus a universal is a sign or concept that has application to a number of things.

The nature of this universal concept, or common term, can be understood better by considering what it is and how it is produced. First, as a result of intuitive cognition there occurs in sensation, and then in memory, sensations or images that function as natural signs of the individual objects that cause them. Now, through the medium of these images the intellect notices the similarity of the objects so signified and notes that there could be still other entities similar to them. In noting these similarities it produces naturally another entity that resembles the particulars in such a manner that it might very well be used as an exemplar for the construction of similar things. Ockham is not clear about the nature of this new entity, but he says that it is produced by ignoring the differences between the similar particulars. The new sign, or universal, is an indeterminate image that could represent any of the determinate particulars that fall under it. But whatever it is, since it is a natural rather than a conventional sign, this resemblance has come into being as a sign that denotes indifferently any of the particulars it resembles. Ockham says this entity is a fiction only, for since it is not a particular sign produced in us by a particular object, it has no literal counterpart in the world. In Ockham's terms, if we say "Man is a universal," and insist that we are saying something is common to many things, then in this proposition the concept "man" refers to itself (it has "simple *suppositio*") and not to men (it does not have "personal *suppositio*"), and the concept "univer-

341

sal" is of the second intention (it refers to a mental sign) rather than of the first intention (it does not refer to something other than a sign). That is, the universal "man" is only a concept that can be applied to many things; in the world there are only men.

It is to be noted that Ockham is not a nominalist of the Berkeleian-Humean sort, for his general ideas are not particulars standing for other particulars. Perhaps it would be more accurate to say that he holds to a kind of conceptualism. It is to be noted also that later in his life he applied his razor to his own doctrine to eliminate the fictitious entity we have just described, for he then argued that since the act that produces the generalized picture must be able to generalize without the assistance of such a picture, such pictures must be superfluous. In the end, then, universals turn out to be acts of the intellect; the other features of his earlier doctrine are retained.

Finally, it is to be noted that though they have different grammatical functions, concrete substantives and their abstract counterparts (such as "man" and "manness") denote exactly the same things (men). Nonsubstantive qualitative terms such as "white" denote indifferently individuals such as Socrates and this piece of paper; and their abstract counterparts, such as "whiteness," denote indifferently similar features of individuals, such as a certain sensible feature of Socrates and a similar sensible feature of this piece of paper. In these ways all common terms, whether they be concrete or abstract, denote particulars and particulars only.

Ockham discusses terms in greater detail than this summary statement suggests, and he goes on to discuss propositions and arguments. He was concerned primarily with formal syllogistic reasoning, but he did make a number of observations which impinge on the areas we know in symbolic logic as the propositional calculus and modal logic. Among other things he discussed the truth conditions of conjunctive and disjunctive propositions, reduced "neither-nor" to "and" and "not," discussed valid arguments of the form "p and q, therefore p," "p, therefore p or q," and "p or q, not p, therefore q," pointed out the related fallacies, and stated Augustus De Morgan's laws explicitly. At the end of his treatment of inference he discussed some very general nonformal rules of inference. Assuming in appropriate cases that we are speaking about a valid argument, they are as follows: (1) if the antecedent is true the conclusion cannot be false; (2) the premises may be true and the conclusion false; (3) the contradictory of the conclusion implies the contradictory of the premise or conjunction of premises; (4) whatever is implied by the conclusion is implied by the premises; (5) whatever implies the premises implies the conclusion; (6) whatever is consistent with the premises is consistent with the conclusion; (7) whatever is inconsistent with the conclusion is inconsistent with the premises; (8) a contingent proposition cannot follow from a necessary one; (9) a contingent proposition cannot imply a contradiction; (10) any proposition follows from a contradiction; and (11) a necessary proposition follows from any proposition. He illustrated the last two with these examples: "You (a man) are a donkey, therefore you are God," and assuming God is necessarily triune, "You are white, therefore God is triune." Ockham concluded his discussion by saying that since these rules are not formal they should be used sparingly.

OF LEARNED IGNORANCE

Author: Nicholas of Cusa (Nicolaus Cryfts or Krypffs, c. 1401-1464)
Type of work: Metaphysics, theology
First transcribed: 1440

Principal Ideas Advanced

God is the absolute maximum and also the absolute minimum; he is in all things, and all things are in him.

If man makes his own ignorance the object of his desire for knowledge, he can acquire a learned ignorance; although God cannot be comprehended, some knowledge of him can be acquired by reflection on our limitations.

The absolute maximum (God) is absolute unity, for unity is the minimum (and God is the absolute minimum); God, as a unity excluding degrees of more or less, is infinite unity.

The visible world is a reflection of the invisible; man mirrors the eternal and the infinite by his conjectures.

God is best studied through the use of mathematical symbols.

In the Providence of God contradictories are reconciled.

The world is the absolute effect of the absolute maximum; it is a relative unity.

Jesus is the maximum at once absolute and restricted; He is both God and man brought to perfection.

Nicholas of Cusa (Nicolas Cusanus) was both a man of action and a man of speculation. He spent his years as a churchman in the cause of reform and ecclesiastical diplomacy; he was a Cardinal and Bishop of Brixen. As a metaphysical theologian he synthesized the ideas of such predecessors as John Scotus Erigena, Eckhart, and pseudo-Dionysius the Areopagite. His work had a considerable influence on Giordano Bruno, particularly on the latter's *Dialogues Concerning the Cause, Principle, and One* (1584). *Of Learned Ignorance,* Nicholas' most important treatise, is particularly interesting as an attempt to reconcile the Neoplatonic ideas prevalent in the Middle Ages with the growing confidence in empirical inquiry and the use of the intellect. The reconciliation is only partly successful from the logical point of view, and it involves an appeal to the revelatory power of mystical intuition. But for those who sought to understand the possibility of unifying an infinite God and an apparently finite universe, and who were disturbed by their learned ignorance, the efforts of Nicholas of Cusa were a godsend.

The work is divided into three

books and is unified by a concern with the *maximum*, the greatest. The first book is a study of the "absolute maximum," or God, the being who is greatest in the sense that he is one and all, all things are in God, and God is in all things. Nicholas describes this study as one "above reason," and as one that "cannot be conducted on the lines of human comprehension. . . ."

The second book is concerned with the maximum effect of the absolute maximum. The maximum effect is the universe, a plurality which is, nevertheless, a relative unity.

The third book is devoted to the maximum which is both relative and absolute, the perfect realization of the finite plurality of the universe; this maximum is Jesus.

Nicholas begins his work by explaining that men have a natural desire for knowledge but are frustrated in their desire to know by the enduring fact of their own ignorance. Men strive to understand what is not understandable—for example, the infinite as infinite, which is beyond comparison. The only solution, then, is for men to seek to know their own ignorance, even as Socrates advised; if a man makes his own ignorance the object of his desire for knowledge, he can acquire a learned ignorance. The suggestion is that from reflecting on his limitations man can, in knowledge, surmount his own ignorance, at least to some extent.

Finite intellects proceed by comparisons, according to Nicholas; and it is on that account that the Pythagoreans came close to the truth in saying that it is by numbers that all things are understood. But if the effort is to understand the absolute infinite, the means of comparison will not work, for the absolute infinite is beyond comparison. To realize that the quiddity of things, the absolute "whatness" of them, is beyond our intellects—and that, in regard to the truth about ultimate being, we must be ignorant—is to draw closer to truth.

But if we cannot comprehend the absolute maximum (which is God), then what is the point of working out the implications of the conception of the absolute maximum? Nicholas argues that although we cannot comprehend the absolute maximum, nevertheless we can have some knowledge about it; we can know, for example, that the precise nature of the absolute maximum is beyond our powers of understanding. But there is more than that which we can know.

We can also know that the absolute maximum is also the absolute minimum. Nicholas proves this point in an engaging and simple argument: "By definition the minimum is that which cannot be less than it is; and since that is also true of the maximum, it is evident that the minimum is identified with the maximum." There is another good reason for supposing that the maximum and the minimum are synonymous: since the absolute maximum is actually all that it can be, it is both as great as it can be and as small as it can be; and since it is the absolute, it can be absolutely minimum as well as absolutely maximum, and since it can be, it is. Furthermore, the maximum considered in itself, not as the maximum of a certain matter or quantity, is the infinite; but, then, so is the minimum; since both the maximum and the minimum are the infinite, they are one.

The maximum is absolute unity, for unity is the smallest number, or the minimum; God is a unity which "excludes degrees of 'more' or 'less,'" and is, consequently, an infinite unity.

Nicholas introduces his version of the cosmological argument: finite beings are effects which could not have produced themselves; therefore, there must be an absolute maximum, not itself dependent on causes, without which nothing else could exist.

The conception of the Trinity is introduced by an elaboration of the Pythagorean idea that unity is a trinity. Diversity involves unity (two, for example, is two ones); inequality depends upon equality (and, therefore, upon unity); connection depends upon unity, for division is a duality or involves duality. Diversity, inequality, and division, then, necessarily involve unity, equality, and connection; and the latter three are all unities, but unity is one. Unity is a trinity, since unity means non-division, distinction, and connection.

According to Nicholas of Cusa, the visible world is a reflection of the invisible. By the use of conjectural images man can, at least to some extent, mirror the eternal and infinite. The images most helpful to man are mathematical images, for, as Pythagoras pointed out, "the key to all truth [is] to be found in numbers. . . ."

The symbols which Nicholas found most useful in suggesting the nature of the absolute maximum are the line, the triangle, and the circle. An infinite line, according to Nicholas, would be at once a straight line, a triangle, a circle, and a sphere. He argues, for example, that as the circumference of a circle increases, the line becomes less curved; and he concludes that the circumference of the absolutely greatest possible circle would be absolutely straight, the smallest possible curve. (Although logically there is an essential difference between a curve, however slight, and a straight line, Nicholas' figure, considered as a metaphor, achieves the purpose of suggesting that entities disparate in character are nevertheless such that, when taken to infinity, they are indistinguishable.)

A finite line can be used to form a triangle, he argues, by keeping one end fixed and moving the line to one side. (Actually, the figure so formed is not a triangle, but a segment of a circle, a pie-shaped segment.) If one continues the movement of the line (so that it functions as an infinite number of radii), the figure formed is a circle. Half a circle, if turned in three dimensions on its axis, forms a sphere.

An infinite triangle would have three infinitely long sides; infinitely extended, the triangle would finally be indistinguishable from a line. Such a triangle would have three lines in one and in that respect would resemble the infinite absolute maximum (God). (Apparently Nicholas conceived of a triangle's sides as increasing and its base angles, say, as becoming more acute, the apex as becoming more and more obtuse, until finally there would be no triangle distinguishable from a straight line. But he need not have conceived of it this way. He could have conceived of a triangle expanding while its angles remain constant. Part of Nicholas' argument, however, depends upon the assumption that there cannot be more than one infinite. To maintain this point involves a peculiar use of the term "infinite.")

Having demonstrated to his satisfaction that an infinite line is a triangle, a circle, and a sphere, Nicholas de-

345

velops the image to suggest by analogy the relationship of the absolute maximum to all things: the infinite line is to lines what the absolute maximum is to things. The analogy is developed at great length, but the most important features are these: an infinite line is not divisible; it is immutable and eternal; and, oddly, it shares its essential features with finite lines—for finite lines, for example, cannot be divided into anything other than lines and are, in that sense, indivisible. Just as the essence of an infinite line is the essence of all finite lines, so the essence of the absolute maximum is the essence of everything. This point is developed by reference to beings who have only a participation in being; since the essence of such beings is the essence of the absolute maximum, once the feature of participation is eliminated, the distinction between beings who participate in being and the being in which they participate disappears.

Again, by mathematical analogy, Nicholas argues that there could not be four or more divine persons; there must be a trinity. A four-sided figure is not the smallest, simplest measure of things, as is the triangle.

A circle, having neither beginning nor end, being perfect, possessing unity, and so forth, is an ideal figure of the divine.

Nicholas thus comes to one of his characteristic contentions: "In the Providence of God contradictories are reconciled." God's Providence includes all that shall be together with all that shall not be. He has foreknowledge of everything, for he foresees opposites. The absolute maximum is in all being, and all beings are in him.

By the analogy of the infinite sphere Nicholas argues that God is the "one infinitely simple, essential explanation of the entire universe." He is the final cause of everything, the determiner both of existence and of end.

All names attributed to the infinite absolute maximum are anthropomorphic; none is adequate as a name, for God is beyond distinctions. Only the four-letter word "ioth-he-vau-he," one which is unspeakable, is a proper name for God.

Since God is ineffable, negative propositions are truer than affirmative ones. It is better to count on learned ignorance, as enlightened by God, than to count on positive knowledge.

Nicholas proceeds, in the second book, to demonstrations of the absolute effect of the absolute maximum; the unity and infinity of the universe are shown to be a consequence of that infinitude of matter which arises from its incapacity to be greater than it is. Since God is not jealous, and since the essence of every created thing is his essence, and since he is essentially perfect, every thing is, in its way, perfect. The universe (and everything in it) is a principle and a maximum, but in a restricted sense; the absolute maximum brings the universe into existence by emanation (a timeless outpouring of its essential nature).

Thus, everything is in everything, as Anaxagoras said. Since God is in all things by medium of the universe, "all is in all, and each in each." Of course, the universe is in each thing only in a contracted or restricted manner; in fact, the universe is contracted, in each thing, to whatever the thing is. The unity of the universe, which comes from the absolute unity of God, is a unity in plurality; the unity of the universe, then, is not an absolute, but a relative, unity.

The universe is also a trinity as well as a unity, but just as it is a relative unity, so it is a relative or contracted trinity. The unity of the universe is a trinity in the sense that contraction involves a limitable object, a limiting principle, and a connection—or potency, act, and the nexus.

There are four modes of being: the absolute necessity, or God; the mode of being of things according to natural necessity or order; the mode of being of individuals; and the mode of being of that which is possible.

The Soul of the World is a universal form which contains all forms, but it has only a contracted existence; forms are actual only in the Word of God. However, it is possible to use the term "Soul" in such a way that the Soul and God are one. Every possibility is contained in the Absolute Possibility, God; every form (or act) in the Absolute Form, the Son of God; and every connecting harmony in the Absolute Connection of the Holy Spirit. The Father is potency; the Son, act; and the Holy Ghost, connecting movement. Thus, God, who is unity as well as trinity, is the efficient, formal, and final cause of all things; and the movements of the earth and stars are attributable to him, who is the center and circumference. In reflecting on the world and on the wonder of its arrangement, one cannot hope to understand God's reasons; but in the wonder of him and in our learned ignorance we find intimations of his light.

Jesus Christ is "the maximum at once absolute and restricted," and to the defense and clarification of this description Nicholas devotes the third book. Human nature is peculiarly suited to provide God with the possibility of a maximum which reconciles the infinite and the finite by being at once absolute and contracted. As sensible and intellectual, human nature is a microcosm, a world in miniature. Unlike other things which, raised to perfection, could easily become greater because of the inferiority of their natures, man is such that, if perfected, he reveals the nature of all things as perfected. By joining the nature of humanity to the divine nature God made possible the union of the absolute maximum and the nature of all things. In Jesus, God is both God and man.

The remainder of Nicholas' work is a defense, in terms of his mystical metaphysics, of familiar dogmas: that Christ was conceived of the Holy Ghost and born of the Virgin Mary, that He was resurrected after the Crucifixion, that He ascended into heaven, that He is the judge of the living and the dead, that He redeemed all mankind. In this account Jesus is God utilizing the nature of humanity and bringing it to perfection; Jesus is man made perfect in the image and essence of God. Because of Jesus the Church comes into being, the fullest possible realization of the unity of the many "with the preservation of the personal reality of each, without confusion of natures or degrees." And by Jesus the union of the subjects and the Church is resolved into the divine unity. Thus, for Nicholas of Cusa, as for Bruno of Nola, God is the cause, the principle, and the One.

UTOPIA

Author: Sir Thomas More (1478-1535)
Type of work: Political philosophy
First published: 1516

PRINCIPAL IDEAS ADVANCED

Philosophers ought not to advise princes, for rulers are not interested in advice, but would much prefer to have others assent to their fixed policies.

An economic system which allows private property drives the poor from the land and thereby creates thieves whom the existing laws require to be hanged: such a system and policy is neither just nor expedient.

In opposition to the former ideas which are defended by Raphael Hythloday, a world traveler, Thomas More (as a character in the conversation) argues that a nonspeculative, prudential philosopher might be useful in politics, but Hythloday is skeptical.

More objects to Raphael Hythloday's call for the abolition of money and private property by arguing that unless men have the profit motive, they will not work.

Hythloday describes Utopia, a carefully organized state in which the citizens engage in scientific farming according to assignments from magistrates and then return to the cities; they work a six-hour day and spend their leisure moments reading, attending lectures, and conversing on academic subjects.

In Utopia gold has no worth, marriages are regulated, work is coöperative, and pleasure in accordance with virtue is the aim of life.

Unlike men who treat human beliefs and institutions as if their simple persistence were evidence of their truth and unalterability, there are writers who judge the actual in terms of the possible, the real in terms of an ideal. Such men usually object passionately to the evils of existing customs and habits. Many consume their energies in important practical efforts to achieve social and political reforms. But only a few possess the knowledge, sustained moral dedication, and literary ability to produce books which—however radical and even sometimes absurd some of their views about organized social life may appear—confront their readers with ideal maps of the political countryside against which to measure actually existing states. The great ancient classic which fashioned such a mirror toward which men might direct their vision is Plato's *Republic*, a book inexhaustible in imaginative suggestions and incomparable for the range of subject matter treated. An important modern work reflecting the influence of Plato's thought, written during the turbulence of sixteenth century English political strife, is Thomas More's *Utopia*.

The English word "utopia" derives its meaning from a Greek term which can be translated "nowhere." To this day, a scheme called "utopian" suggests the idea of nonexistence. Thomas More invented the term and applied it to a mythical community, and then used his account of this community as a means of criticizing certain European social and political practices which he considered unreasonable.

More's own life lends interest to the contents of his famous book, for More served Henry VIII, the strong-willed English king, in a number of important political capacities. In 1535 he died on the block for resistance to the monarch's policies in a power struggle between the English nation and the Roman papacy. In spite of his humanistic leanings, More stood firm in refusing to recognize Henry's claim to the title which in fact made him head of the Church in England. As an adviser to the monarch, More became a tragic figure caught between opposing institutional pressures which played a unique role in shaping modern English history.

In form, More's *Utopia* is quite simple. Two separate books comprise its contents. Book II (which contains an elaborate description of the Utopians) was written first, in 1515, a year before the completion of Book I (which discusses several general political questions, including whether philosophers ought to advise princes). The latter portion of the *Utopia* introduces the primary figures in the work, who include More himself, presented as having heard the ensuing account of social affairs while serving his monarch on state business in Antwerp (Belgium); a gentleman named Peter Giles; who is said to have introduced More to the leading participant in the written work; and a stranger named Raphael Hythloday, a world traveler widely acquainted with political matters, who shows impatience with several customs then little questioned in European social and political life. Raphael Hyth-

loday is a spokesman for what must have been More's own critical opinions about contemporary practices.

The early discussion centers on whether philosophers ought to advise rulers—a question provoked by Giles's and More's suggestion that Raphael's extensive knowledge could be put to such use. Raphael shows little interest in attempting to advise rulers. At the same time, he argues that the social arrangements of the Utopians (whom he discovered somewhere below the equator) would serve well as a basis for "correcting the errors of our own cities and kingdoms." He is nonetheless convinced that to serve a king in an advisory capacity would make him miserable. "Now I live as I will," Raphael argues—illustrating the tension existing between private and public demands on a person—"and I believe very few courtiers can say that." Raphael insists that princes do not want advice from philosophers, that what they seek is agreement with their fixed policies of waging constant, aggressive warfare. Princes ignore sound advice and refuse to tolerate any posture except that of absolute agreement among their counselors. "They are generally more set on acquiring new kingdoms rightly or wrongly, than on governing well those that they already have." Raphael illustrates his viewpoint by recounting an episode which had occurred at a dinner given by a famous Cardinal. At this affair Raphael became entangled in a discussion when another person present praised some judicial practices which Raphael thought foolish.

What astounds a twentieth century reader is the modernity of the reported discussion. What Raphael advocates during the discussion is something like a reformist as opposed to a retributionist theory of punishment for wrongdoing. He also seeks a general theory which will explain why so many individuals (Englishmen, in this case) risk the death penalty by stealing. Raphael Hythloday wants to understand the causes of thieving. Here he presents a crude yet clear economic thesis, arguing that the land enclosures in sixteenth century England create economic conditions which increase the compulsion to steal. The existing practice of hanging culprits who steal deals only with the symptoms and not with the causes of that unfortunate practice. Unable to gain a fair hearing for their economic situation, the poor are finally driven from the land. "They would willingly work," Raphael insists, "but can find no one who will hire them." Glaring social extremes tend to develop, such as abject poverty existing side by side with extreme luxury. Raphael presents a bald and bold environmentalist theory about the origins of criminal activities. His views condemn the legal and judicial customs of the day. The economic situation inevitably produces the thieves whom the existing laws then require to be hanged. This policy is neither just nor rationally expedient.

Raphael then proceeds to sketch a wiser policy respecting theft and its legal treatment. Citing the Roman practice of employing thieves to work quarries, he mentions the procedures of the mythical Polyerites (meaning "much nonsense") who require apprehended thieves to make full restitution. Thieves convicted of their crimes must work at public services, under state supervision, thus producing some social benefit. They are dressed in a common uniform and distributed in different regions of the country to prevent possible formation of rebellious political groups. Each year some are pardoned. This picture of penal procedures suggests the practices of a number of twentieth century states as opposed to the generally cruel systems prevalent in More's century.

Having heard Raphael's account, the Cardinal admits that such procedures might well be tried. By this admission he introduces a note of experimentalism into the discussion. The Cardinal concludes that if, on trying such means, the thieves were not reformed, one could then still see them hanged.

Thomas More is described as wanting to hear even more from the interesting stranger, Raphael Hythloday. He reminds Raphael that Plato thought that political wisdom could never prevail until philosophers became kings, or kings became philosophers. Raphael replies to this argument by setting up imagined cases in which a philosopher attempts to advise an actually existing ruler—say, the French king, in one instance. Raphael attempts to show that if he asserts that the king, as shepherd of his people, ought to care more for the welfare of the sheep than for himself (an obvious borrowing from Plato), he will be ignored by the royal council. His conclusion is that the philosopher should never give advice when he knows it will fall on deaf ears. Raphael also refers to the practices of mythical peoples like the Achorians (a word which means "no place") and the Macarians (meaning "blessed"), the latter of whom permit their king to possess only a thousand pounds in his treasury at any time. The point of these cases is that Raphael wants to convince the participants in the discussion that "there is no place for philosophy in the councils of princes."

To this somewhat cynical position Thomas More makes a significant counterargument. More admits that speculative philosophy is unhelpful to practical princes. But he argues that there exists another kind of philosophy. This practically useful philosophy "is more urbane" and "takes its proper cue and fits itself to the drama being played, acting its part aptly and well." Thus, More reveals himself as a believer in nonspeculative, prudential philosophizing able to adjust to changing circumstances. For this reason he cautions Raphael: "Don't give up the ship in a storm, because you cannot control the winds." The prudentially oriented philosopher must seek to guide policy-formation in an indirect manner. Raphael's response includes the argument that the prudential philosopher must "rave along with them" (meaning the ruling council). He insists that even Christ's teachings run counter to many existing customs, even in England. Even Plato, Raphael reminds his listeners, advised outstanding men to refuse to meddle in politics.

Raphael returns to his economic thesis—that the chief cause of evil customs is the existence of private property. Only among the Utopians has he found a social system making virtue the primary goal of living. Other nations seeking to create sane institutional arrangements undermine their own efforts by maintaining private property and a money economy. Their laws hopelessly try to protect for the individual what, by the nature of private property, must always stand under threat. Raphael advocates the total abolition of money and privately held property.

To this view More objects, although he shows interest in a fuller description of the Utopians while insisting that absolute equality of possessions means that many will cease working. Men need the incentive of the hope of gain, according to More. From a policy enforcing equal possessions in cases when all men experience extreme want, only warfare and constant factionalism can ensue. Men require authority over themselves based on some distinction in abilities and worth. To More's objections Peter Giles adds his own view that other men are not better governed than the English. His reason for so thinking is that the abilities of English and European rulers are equal to those of other persons. European governmental practices also rest on long historical experience. Raphael replies that the Utopians also possess a long history—that their peculiar success in managing their affairs results from their willingness to learn. His associates in the discussion ask Raphael to provide more information about the Utopians.

In Book II three aspects of Utopian civilization receive consideration under a number of separate headings. There is, first, a description of the island where Utopia exists as well as of the number, distribution, and geographical arrangements of its cities. Next are described the social and political institutions of Utopia. Finally, Raphael discusses the ideas and moral norms by which the Utopians live.

Each city in Utopia is divided in a manner to require several magistrates. From the body of these magistrates, three representatives are chosen to meet in the capital city once a year.

Individual cities contain households fixed in number and built on a planned model, thirty households requiring one magistrate in a given district. Agricultural pursuits aiming at economic self-sufficiency require existence of country households containing forty men and women each. These households receive their members on a rotational basis from the cities. Each Utopian must take a turn at farming and related forms of labor, thus spreading the burden of physical work; but individuals particularly fond of country life and work may remain longer than the otherwise stipulated two-year period. Something very much like scientific farming operates in Utopia.

A wall surrounds each city. Its inhabitants work only six hours each day (an astounding suggestion in More's time). The remainder of a citizen's time is devoted to private pursuits. These pursuits indicate that Utopia is a society composed of professorial humanists or transcendentalist moral philosophers who enjoy academic talk. The citizens are well read. They also attend a wide variety of public lectures. Raphael claims the Utopians undertake these surprising intellectual pastimes on a voluntary basis. The six-hour day in Utopia produces no idlers or maladjusted persons. Apparently, though a Christian, More could picture a human society in which evil does not exist. His Utopia fails to discuss the problems associated with possible misuses of leisure time.

Living in a balanced, well-planned society, the Utopians wear casual, common dress (indicating that More's humanism reflects also some puritanical dislike of color and variety). Gambling, drinking, and related activities do not occur. Good teaching leads Utopians to ignore the usual allure of gold and precious stones. Gold is used for children's ornamentation and, in the adult world, for the making of chamber pots. The Utopians thus learn that gold has no intrinsic worth. Indeed, as Raphael points out, most of the genuinely valuable elements in nature, like air and water, exist in plentiful quantities. In Utopia marriages are also regulated. Children and parents dine in common halls (suggesting some of the practices of organized camplife). The Utopians live moderately, each doing his share of work—including coöperative building and repair of roads.

Social habits in Utopia remind one of aspects of Plato's ideal state, which also emphasized communal domestic life. The general picture reveals a society which trains men so as to minimize cupidity, channeling strenuous energies to productive community ends. Yet each Utopian retains a large share of time for private pursuits. More's ideal society combines a moderate Puritanism with a humanistic stress on learning and moral development. Nowhere in More's Utopia is there a discussion concerning the realism or lack of realism of the humanistic social image presented.

More then considers the Utopians' moral philosophy, their marriage customs, the unique love of learning displayed by the citizens, their bondmen (who seem to do a large amount of bothersome menial labor), care of the sick, legal procedures and punishments, warfare, foreign relations, and religion. The Utopians seek knowledge without requiring irate schoolmasters or crass materialistic inducements. They are an admirably tolerant people, as consideration of a few of their beliefs will indicate.

Happiness (defined as pleasure in accordance with virtue) stands as the Utopian moral ideal. This shows the influence of Epicurean and Aristotelian ethical notions on More's humanism. In fact, the Utopians possess books given to them by Raphael on a return voyage he made to their island —philosophical works by Plato and Aristotle; literary productions by Aristophanes, Homer, Sophocles, and Euripides; historical narratives by Herodotus and Thucydides. The Utopians are a rather philosophical people able to make fairly sophisticated ethical judgments based on reason. As More describes them, the Utopians "discriminate several kinds of true pleasure, some belonging to the mind, others to the body. Those of the mind are knowledge and the delight which comes from contemplation of the truth; also the pleasant recollection of a well-spent life and the assured hope of future well-being."

Bodily pleasures are classified in accordance with the way they produce some immediate sense effect or turn the senses inward (as in the case of the enjoyment produced by hearing music). The Utopians debate aesthetic issues and seek to find delight in "sound, sight and smell." They guard and nourish the mental and physical capacities.

Utopia does enforce some rigid sexual rules. Marriage occurs only when a male reaches twenty-two years and a female, eighteen. Premarital sexual experience leads to severe punishment. Indeed, in the Utopian scheme, those who are caught in illicit affairs forfeit the right to marry for a lifetime unless pardoned by a prince. A few divorces are permitted, but only on the authorization of the senate.

More's account of the religious beliefs of the Utopians provides an interesting instance of tolerance. Different religious systems exist in Utopia, including Christianity—the latter a rather recent missionary introduction meeting with favorable reception. Dogmatic fights over doctrines and creeds are outlawed. Respect for views other than one's own prevails and is defended by the laws. Priests must be elected and are kept relatively few in number. All Utopians must accept belief in an afterlife as well as the view that God punishes in accordance with one's conduct in this life. No one may challenge these beliefs in public. The common element shared by all religions in Utopia affirms a providential order which reasoning about nature can discover. Some priests are celibate while others marry. The different religious worshipers call the object of their devotions Mithra. They pray for guidance in moral endeavors and ask for an easy death. Nowhere does More explain how Christianity manages to exist side by side with so diversified a group of religious systems. Reason rather than revelation seems adequate to determine religious beliefs and practices.

Raphael Hythloday (as More's spokesman) ends his account of Utopia with a criticism of man's essential weakness: pride. Only human pride keeps the world from adopting the sensible laws and customs of the Utopians. Reason shows that class distinctions, property rights, and human anxiety exist only in societies which fail to

353

curb pride. More writes that Raphael's picture of society fails fully to satisfy him, yet he concludes: "I must confess there are many things in the Utopian Commonwealth that I wish rather than expect to see followed among our citizens."

THE PRINCE

Author: Niccolò Machiavelli (1469-1527)
Type of work: Political philosophy
First published: 1532

PRINCIPAL IDEAS ADVANCED

In order to win and retain power a man is fortunate if he is born to power, for a man who rises to power by conquest or treachery makes enemies who must be eliminated.

If a prince must be cruel—and sometimes he must to retain power—he should be cruel quickly, and he should cause great injuries, for small injuries do not keep a man from revenge.

A prince should be concerned for the people he governs only to the extent that such concern strengthens his hold on the state.

Although a prince can sometimes afford to be virtuous, flattery, deceit, and even murder are often necessary if the prince is to maintain himself in power.

Great political thinkers often write about specific historical situations and yet succeed in making recommendations which apply to times other than their own. Niccolò Machiavelli must be numbered among such thinkers. An Italian patriot deeply involved in the diverse political maneuvers of sixteenth century Italy, he addresses advice to Lorenzo de' Medici which, first written in 1513 and later published as *The Prince* five years after his death, marks him as one of the most controversial, enduring, and realistic political theorists of the modern world.

In this short book Machiavelli undertakes to treat politics scientifically, judging men by an estimate of how in fact they do behave as political animals rather than by ideal standards concerned with how they ought to act. The hard-headedly consistent refusal of the author to submit political behavior to moral tests has earned the named "Machiavellian" for amoral instances of power relations among nation states and other organized groups. The power divisions of Machiavelli's Italy are now seen to have been prophetic of the massive national rivalries which followed in the Western world. The problems encountered by Renaissance princes endured long after the princes themselves fell before more powerful enemies. Machiavelli understood how success is always a minimal condition of political greatness. In *The Prince* he presents a manual of advice on the winning and retention of power in a world containing extensive political factionalism and lust for dominion.

Critics who are clearly aware of the amoral aspects of Machiavelli's political recommendations sometimes attempt to gain him a sympathetic hearing in unfriendly quarters. They do so by placing *The Prince* in its limited historical setting and relating its contents to certain biographical facts about the author. They tell us how Machiavelli longed for one ultimate goal—the eventual political unification of Italy as an independent state under one secular ruler, strong enough to rebuff the growing might of powerful neighbors like Spain and France. The armies and policies of these neighboring countries had already seriously influenced internal affairs even in Machiavelli's beloved Florence. Critics often suggest that Machiavelli's subordination of religion to the temporal aims of princes followed from his hatred of the political machinations of the Roman Catholic Church, which, by maintaining a series of temporal states, helped to keep Italy divided. The Church situation also invited foreign intrigues and corrupted the spiritual life of the Italians. In this context, another peculiarity of *The Prince* deserves mention. It is its total unconcern for forms of government other than monarchical ones. This might suggest that Machiavelli favored the monarchical form over the republican form. But such a view would be false. In the *Discourses on the First Ten Books of Titus Livius,* Machiavelli openly expressed preference for republics whenever the special conditions for their existence could be obtained. He tells us, in *The Prince,* that he has discussed republics elsewhere.

Such historical insights help to gain for *The Prince* a more understanding reading by those who reject its sharp separation of politics from morals. Yet the fact is clear that—whatever the author's motives—*The Prince* does ignore all moral ends of organized life and rather emphasizes the need to maintain sovereignty at all costs. Coldly, calculatingly, Machiavelli tries to show princes the means they must use in seeking power as an end-in-itself. He does not discuss moral rules. Discouraging to unsympathetic critics is the extent to which actual political life often seems to fit Machiavelli's somewhat cynical model.

Machiavelli classifies possible governments as either republics or monarchies. In *The Prince* he confines his analytic attention to the latter. Any monarch with a legitimate inheritance of power and traditions is most favored. The reason is that, unlike newly risen rulers, he need offend the people less. Established rulers reap the benefits from forgotten past abuses which led to the established system. Men who rise to power by virtue of conquest or favorable circumstances must confront incipient rebellions. They must also make more promises than the established ruler, thus falling under various obligations. Machiavelli believed newly created rulers must perform their cruelties quickly and ruthlessly. They must never extend cruelties over a long period of time.

Machiavelli insists that if a prince must cause injuries, he should cause great injuries, for small injuries do not keep a man from revenge. In any case, what the prince does must fit the circumstances and the nature of his particular dominion. Not all princes should attempt to use the same methods. All princes must act, however. For example, they should never postpone war simply to avoid it. In political conflicts, time is neutral regarding the participants; it produces "indifferently either good or evil."

Newly created monarchs often find themselves involved with members of a mixed state. Extreme difficulties confront a ruler in such situations. Mixed monarchies usually require rule over possessions whose citizens either share the monarch's language or they do not. A common language and nationality help to make ruling easier for the monarch, especially if his subjects' experience of freedom has been a limited one. There are two general ways in which to treat subjects who lack the monarch's nationality and language. One is that the monarch can take residence among the subjects. To do so permits a ready response to contingent problems and allows the subjects to identify themselves with the person of the ruler. The other is for the ruler to establish select colonies at key positions in the subjects' territory. Such colonies cost little. Their injured parties are also often scattered, thus proving easier to handle. If he maintains such colonies, the monarch should use diplomatic maneuvers aimed at weakening the stronger neighbors and protecting the less powerful ones. Machiavelli uses historical examples here, as he does elsewhere in *The Prince*. For example, he admires the manner in which the Romans anticipated contingencies in governing their colonies and acted promptly, if sometimes brutally, to meet them. On the other hand, Machiavelli asserts that Louis XII of France made basic blunders in a similar situation.

There will be times when the ruler must govern subjects accustomed to living under laws of their own. Machiavelli coldly suggests three methods of ruling these. First, the ruler can totally despoil them, as the Romans did to certain rebellious cities. Second, he can make his residence among the subjects, hoping to keep down future rebellions. If he chooses neither of these alternatives, the ruler must permit the subjects to live under laws of their own. In this event he must exact tribute from them. If possible, he should also put control of the laws in the hands of a few citizens upon whose loyalty he can count. It is dangerous to ignore the activities of men accustomed to living in freedom if they are part of one's sovereign state. The reason is that "in republics there is greater life, greater hatred, and more desire for revenge; they do not and cannot cast aside the memory of their ancient liberty, so that the surest way is either to lay them waste or reside in them."

Machiavelli shows great interest in how men acquire their rule over possessions. Methods of ruling must be made adaptable to differences in manner of acquisition. For example, a ruler may obtain his power as a result of someone else's abilities; or he may win power by his own abilities. Machiavelli judges the "do it yourself" method as the surest. There is no substitute for princely merit. Also, the prince should command his own military forces without depending too heavily on aid from allied troops. The wise prince will imitate great personal models, since life is primarily a matter of imitative behavior. The prudential prince must show careful regard to the right circumstances for seizing power. Once in power, he can use force if he possesses soldiers loyal to himself. Machiavelli warns princes to beware the flattery of their subjects. Especially should they show suspicion of the flattery of their ministers, who are supposed to advise them. Machiavelli's model of the state seems to be the Renaissance city-state—small in population and territorial extent. As an example of a ruler who arises by virtue of talent, he mentions Francesco Sforza, of Milan. Cesare Borgia is used to illustrate the nature of successful ruling by a prince whose power initially results from conditions created by others.

In all, there are four ways in which a prince can attain to political power. These ways are: by one's own abilities; by the use of fortunate circumstances (wealth or political inheritance); by wicked conduct and outright crime; and by the choice of one's fellow citizens. Machiavelli does not condemn the ruler who succeeds by using criminal techniques. Thus, Agathocles the ancient Sicilian used such methods in rising from a military rank to kill off the rich men and senators of Syracuse. Yet Agathocles used such excessive cruelty that Machiavelli warns scholars not "to include him among men of real excellence." Instances of power criminally seized and successfully held lead Machiavelli to suggest that cruelty is intrinsically neither good nor bad. Cruelty must be said to have been used well "when all cruel deeds are committed at once in order to make sure of the state and thereafter discontinued to make way for the consideration of the welfare of the subjects."

Nonetheless Machiavelli never asserts that cruelty is the best means of attaining to power. His judgment here as elsewhere is a hypothetical one: if the situation is one requiring cruelty for the realization of power, then the prince must do what is necessary. Thus, although Machiavelli prefers methods which do not involve cruelty, he refuses to condemn the prince who uses cruelty.

The conditional nature of Machiavelli's recommendations about seizing power becomes evident when he discusses the case of the prince who rises by the consent of his fellow citizens. This makes the most promising situation for a prince. But it rarely happens. Thus, this case cannot serve as a universal model. Chosen in such a manner, a prince need not fear that men will dare to oppose or to disobey him. "The worst a prince can fear from the people is that they will desert him." On the other hand, if his power stems from the nobility, the prince must fear both their possible desertion and their possible rebellion. In order to prepare for a rebellion the people obviously require trained leaders. Thus, a prudent ruler supported by the people must attempt to retain their favor. A prince initially supported by the nobles can win over the people by making himself their protector. If he succeeds, he may end up stronger than the prince originally chosen by the people; for the people will appreciate the benefactor who guards them against internal oppression. Machiavelli is never so cynical as to argue that a wise prince can endlessly ignore the needs of his own people. Yet he justifies a concern for the people solely in terms of its value toward guaranteeing a continuing rule. Realistically, Machiavelli insists that the prince must lead an army. This is true even of churchmen who manage ecclesiastical states. Force or the threat of force serves as the basis of the state. Times of peace should never be permitted to divert the ruler's

357

mind "from the study of warfare." In peaceful times the prudent ruler estimates future events. By thought and preparation he gets ready to meet such events.

A morbid sense of the contingency of human events runs through the book. Any ruler must show concern for changes of fortune and circumstance. The prince should show caution in delegating any of his own powers. Machiavelli hardly ever discusses economic or ideological problems. Normally, the prince of whom he writes is a single man bent on political self-preservation and the quest for methods by which to coerce his enemies into submission or inaction. The picture is one of a ruler feverishly studying the histories and actions of great men to be ready for the possible day when relatively stable conditions may alter for the worse. The reader concludes that, in Machiavelli's view, stability in politics is extremely rare.

Yet Machiavelli understands that no prince can stand completely alone. Some powers must be delegated. Some men must be favored over others. How the prince treats his friends and subjects will always influence future political events. The prince should work to create a character able to make sudden adjustments in terms of his own self-interest. The most successful ruler must "be prudent enough to escape the infamy of such views as would result in the loss of his state." He must never cultivate those private virtues which, in a public man, can prove politically suicidal. He should develop vices if these will help to perpetuate his rule.

Generosity is a value in a prince only if it produces some benefit and no harm. A wise ruler will tax his subjects without becoming miserly. Yet he should prefer the name "miser" to a reputation for generosity which may prevent him from raising monies needed to maintain security. Generosity can more easily lead to the subjects' hatred and contempt than can miserliness. The prince can even show mercy if it is not interpreted as mere permissiveness. The cursedly cruel Borgia proved more merciful than the Florentine rulers who lost the city to foreigners. As long as he keeps his subjects loyal and united the ruler may sometimes act strenuously against them. Especially is this necessary in newly created monarchies. Machiavelli's advice goes something like: try to be both loved and feared, but choose being feared if there is no other alternative. The subjects obey a prince who can punish them.

In maintaining order the prince has some rule-of-thumb rules to follow. He should keep his word unless deceit is specifically called for. He should use admired private virtues if they do not interfere with the play of political power. A conception of human nature operates here. Machiavelli thinks the plain man is capable of some loyalty to a ruler. But such a man is easily led. "Men are so simple," Machiavelli writes, "and so ready to follow the needs of the moment that the deceiver will always find someone to deceive." A prince must know how and when to mingle the fox's cunning (the ability to avoid traps) with the lion's strength (capacity to fight the wolves). He should often conceal his real motives. Internally, he must avoid conspiracies. Externally, he should keep enemies fearful of attacking. Against conspirators the prince always has an advantage. Conspirators cannot work in isolation; thus they fear the existing laws and the threat of detection. Only when the population shows some open hostility need the prince genuinely fear conspirators.

Machiavelli realizes that men seldom get to choose the circumstances most favorable to their political hopes. They must settle for what is possible rather than for the ideal. Princes must avoid the lures of utopian political constructions—"for how we live is so different from how we ought to live that he who studies what ought to be done rather than what is done will learn the way to his downfall rather than to his preservation." Machiavelli regards men as weak, fickle, and subject to changing loyalties. These psychological traits are the bedrock on which a wise prince must build his policies.

Nonetheless the author of *The Prince* understands that success in politics, however rationally pursued, is beyond the complete control of any man. The Renaissance worry about "Chance" and "Fortune" haunts the final pages of Machiavelli's book. Large-order events in the world often seem to drive men onward much like "the fury of the flood." Yet not all events happen fortuitously. Men are half free to shape their political lives within the broader forces of the universe. That prince rules best, therefore, whose character and conduct "fit the times." It will be better for the ruler to be bold rather than cautious. Fortune is like a female—"well disposed to young men, for they are less circumspect and more violent and more bold to command her." Thus Machiavelli argues for a partial freedom of will and action within a world largely made up of determined forces.

The Prince stands as a classic example of realistic advice to rulers seeking unity and preservation of states. Its picture of human nature is somewhat cynical, viewing man as vacillating and in need of strong political direction. Yet the work is not modern in one sense; namely, it fails to discuss ideological aspects of large-scale political organization. Machiavelli's prince is one who must learn from experience. His conclusion is that ruling is more like an art than like a science. What is somewhat modern is the realistic emphasis on tailoring political advice to the realization of national ends whose moral value is not judged. *The Prince* is therefore a fascinating if sometimes shocking justification of the view that moral rules are not binding in the activities of political rulers.

APOLOGY FOR RAIMOND SEBOND

Author: Michel Eyquem de Montaigne (1533-1592)
Type of work: Skeptical criticism of theology
First published: 1580

PRINCIPAL IDEAS ADVANCED

True religion must be based on faith; but, given faith, reasons can be used to strengthen faith.

Rationality is a form of animal behavior; in many respects animals excel men, and in comparison to animals, men seem to be vain, stupid, and immoral.

The Greek skeptics, the Pyrrhonists, were sensible in doubting everything, contesting all claims, and living according to nature and custom.

Scientists, philosophers, and all others who seek knowledge—including those who seek knowledge of probabilities—fail in their efforts.

We depend on sense experience for our knowledge of the world, but we do not know whether five senses are adequate, nor can we determine how accurately the senses represent the real world.

This essay, the longest of all of Montaigne's writings, sets forth the reasons for the great French humanist's belief in skepticism. It is the work which was most influential in reviving and popularizing the Greek skeptical theory Pyrrhonism, during the Renaissance and in the seventeenth century. Montaigne's followers based their arguments upon this essay, and many important philosophers, including René Descartes, Pierre Gassendi, Blaise Pascal, and Nicolas Malebranche studied it and used some of Montaigne's ideas in developing their own philosophies. The essay is also one of the first writings which discuss philosophical issues in a modern language. It had a tremendous vogue in the seventeenth century. Late in the century it was put on the Index of prohibited books. It has remained one of the major classics of French literature and thought, and is one of the richest examples of Renaissance humanism and skepticism.

The essay was apparently begun in 1575, when Montaigne was studying the recently translated (into Latin) writings of the Greek skeptic, Sextus Empiricus, a third century writer. These works so impressed Montaigne that they caused him to doubt all of his previous views and led him to go through his own personal skeptical crisis. During the period of this crisis, he sought to show that the knowledge which men claimed to have gained through the use of their senses and their reasoning capacities was all open to doubt.

The *Apology for Raimond Sebond* purports to be a defense of the views of the fifteenth century rationalist theologian from Spain, Raimond Sebond. At the outset, Montaigne tells us that he had published a translation of Sebond's *Natural Theology* (which appeared in 1569) shortly after his father's death because of his father's wish that he do so. His father had received the work much earlier from a French theologian who reported that he had been saved from Lutheranism by studying Sebond's rational arguments in favor of Christianity. After Montaigne's edition of Sebond appeared, he found that many of the readers (especially, he tells us, the ladies) required assistance in comprehending and accepting Sebond's message. Objections had been raised against Sebond's audacious contention that all of the articles of the Christian faith can be proved by natural reason. Because of the difficulties that readers were having with the work, and because of the objections, Montaigne reports that he undertook the task of writing an "apology"—a defense. Because of the character of the *Apology,* scholars have debated and are still debating the question of Montaigne's real intent in publishing this essay. Was it to defend Sebond (which seems quite unlikely in view of the contents of the essay)? Was it to offer a different defense of Christianity through skepticism—or was it to employ skeptical thought to undermine all beliefs, including those of Christianity? The essay can be, and has been, read in both the latter two ways, and it has greatly influenced the fideists (those who base their religious beliefs on faith alone) and those who are skeptical of all religious beliefs.

The *Apology* is written in Montaigne's inimitable rambling style. It presents a series of waves of doubt, with occasional pauses to reflect on these. The various skeptical themes are interwoven with the recurring note that faith and revelation are the only unquestionable sources of any truth.

Montaigne begins his serious discussion by considering two kinds of objections that have been raised against Sebond's views, one that Christianity should be based on faith and not on reason, and the other that Sebond's reasoning is not sound. In discussing the first point, Montaigne develops his fideistic theme, and in discussing the second, his skepticism. He alleges to defend Sebond by contending first that Christianity is founded solely on faith, and then that, since all reasoning is unsound, Sebond should not be singled out for blame on this score.

Early in the essay, Montaigne excuses Sebond's theological rationalism by stating that there is nothing wrong with using reason to defend the faith, as long as we realize that faith does not depend upon reasons, and that our rational capacities are unable to attain supernatural and divine wisdom. As far as Montaigne can see, true religion must be based on faith given to us by the grace of God. Our purely human capacities are too weak to support divine knowledge. When we rely on human faculties to find and accept the true religion, we end up by accepting religions because of custom, habit, or geographical location. If, however, we have the real light of faith, then reasons like those Sebond offers can be employed as aids to our faith, although not as proofs of it.

To "defend" Sebond on the second charge—that his arguments are too weak—Montaigne begins a general attack on all human reasoning by arguing that no one can attain certainty by rational means. The first level of skepticism offered purports to show that man's capacities are unimpressive when compared with those of animals. Man, egotistically, believes that he, and he alone, can comprehend the world, which was created and which operates for his benefit. But he cannot tell that this is the case. And when he compares his capacities with those of animals, he finds that he possesses no faculties or capacities that beasts lack; in fact, the beasts excel man in many respects. Montaigne introduces various examples from the writings of Sextus Empiricus to show that rationality is just a form of animal behavior. Montaigne insists that even religion is not a unique human possession, for even elephants seem to pray. When man's behavior is carefully contrasted with that of animals, man is seen as rather vain, stupid, and immoral. With all of our alleged superior faculties, we are not able to live as well or as happily as the animals. The illustrative material presented by Montaigne is supposed to have the cumulative effect of making us doubt our superior wisdom and knowledge. We think we know the truth, but our knowing is only a form of animal behavior, and it does not enable us to achieve even as much as the rest of the animals can and do. Hence, Montaigne insists, our disease is our belief that we can know something. And this is why our religion recommends a state of ignorance to us as most proper for belief and obedience.

Montaigne continues this attack on our intellectual pretensions by comparing the wisdom of the educated European of his day with the ignorance of the "noble savages," the recently discovered inhabitants of Brazil. The latter are portrayed as living a far superior life, because "they pass their lives in an admirable simplicity and ignorance, without any learning, laws, kings, or any religion whatsoever."

Christianity, according to Montaigne, teaches us to acquire a similar ignorance in order that we may believe by faith alone. Whatever truths we know are gained not by our own abilities, but by God's grace. Even our religion is not acquired through our reasoning and comprehension. Instead, we receive it only by God's revelation to us. Our ignorance is an asset in this regard, in that our own inability to know anything leads us to be willing to submit ourselves to God's will, and to accept what teachings He gives us. To show that Christianity is based on an awareness of our ignorance, rather than on any knowledge we might have, Montaigne quotes one of his favorite texts from the Bible, the attack on rational knowledge that appears at the beginning of St. Paul's first letter to the Corinthians.

Next, Montaigne presents a more philosophical basis for his complete skepticism in the form of a description and defense of the ancient Greek skeptical view, Pyrrohonism, as well as an explanation of the value of this theory for religion. The Pyrrhonists doubt and suspend judgment concerning any and all propositions whatsoever, even the claim that all is in doubt. They contest every assertion that is made. If they are successful, they exhibit their opponents' ignorance. If they are unsuccessful, they show their own ignorance. While they are doubting everything, the Pyrrhonists live according to nature and custom. Montaigne tells us that this attitude is both the finest of human achievements and that which is most compatible with religion. The Pyrrhonists show man naked and empty, a blank tablet, ready to receive any message that God wishes to write on it. The Pyrrhonists expose man as he really is, in his total ignorance. This exposé should make man humble and obedient, ready to receive divine truth.

The ancient Pyrrhonists not only reached the summit of human wisdom in seeing that all is in doubt, but also, Montaigne and his disciples insisted, provided the best defense of Catholicism against the Protestant Reformation. The complete skeptic would have no positive views and, consequently, no incorrect ones. He would accept only the laws and customs of his community. Hence, in sixteenth century France he would accept Catholicism. Further, by being in doubt about everything, the Pyrrhonist would be in the perfect state to receive the revelation of the true religion. Thus, if God so willed, Montaigne tells us, the skeptic will be a Catholic by both custom and tradition, and by faith also.

Montaigne next compares the achievements of the ancient Pyrrhonists with the failings of the more dogmatic philosophers. The latter have quarreled over every possible question without coming to any definite conclusion. In the end, the dogmatic philosophers have had to admit their failure to attain any indubitable knowledge in any field whatsoever. A survey of the attempts of philosophers throughout history to achieve any true knowledge only leads one to the conclusion that "philosophy is only sophisticated poetry." All that philosophers ever offer us are theories that they have invented, not truths about the world. Some of these theories become accepted at various times, and are regarded as authoritative and unquestionable. But there is no more evidence that these theories are true than that they are false. The only true principles that men possess, Montaigne insists, are those that God has revealed to us. All other alleged truths are nothing but dreams and smoke.

The debacle of human intellectual undertakings is so complete that even the Pyrrhonist is unable to survive unscathed. If the Pyrrhonist declares, after looking at the sad history of man's intellectual achievements, that all is in doubt, then he has asserted something positive and is no longer in doubt about everything. The Pyrrhonist, Montaigne says, cannot state his doubts without contradicting himself. The fault lies with our language, which is basically assertive. Only a negative language would allow for a genuine statement of the Pyrrhonian view.

After making all these points, and digressing in many different directions, Montaigne, toward the end of the essay, finally states the evidence offered by the Pyrrhonists to show that all is in doubt. We do not seem able to gain any knowledge either from our experience or from our reasonings. We appear to be unable to tell what it is that we experience, and whether we actually experience the things we think we experience. We cannot, for example, ascertain the true nature of heat or of any other experienced quality. Similarly, we cannot tell what our rational faculty is, or even, where it is. The experts disagree about everything, and when we look at their various opinions, we are led to realize how uncertain they *all* are. From these considerations, we come to the conclusion once more that our only genuine understanding comes from God, and not from any of our information or faculties.

Some philosophers, after seeing how everybody disagrees about everything, have come to the conclusion that nothing can be known, either about ourselves or anything else, but that some opinions are more probable than others. This view, developed by the Academic skeptics in antiquity, Montaigne maintains, is more unsatisfactory than the complete doubt of the Pyrrhonists. If we could reach any agreement about probabilities, then we should be able to come to agreements concerning the probable characters of particular things. But, as a matter of fact, our judgments change constantly with our various bodily and emotional states; we do not find one view more probable than another, except at specific times and under specific conditions. As our views change, we find that we disagree with what we formerly thought was probable and with what others think is probable. Thus, we cannot take probabilities as guides to truth, but can only fall back on the Pyrrhonian view that everything can be doubted, and on the truths that God gives us.

When we examine the scientific achievements of mankind, we find these as dubious as anything else, since in every science the experts disagree, and what is accepted as true at one time is rejected as false at another. For example, Montaigne points out, earlier astronomers said that the heavens moved around the earth, and now a new astronomer, Nicolaus Copernicus, says that the earth moves. Perhaps centuries from now another astronomer will disprove all of them. Prior to Aristotle, other theories seemed acceptable. Why should we now accept Aristotle's as the last word? Even in a science as apparently certain as geometry, there are difficulties which render it dubious. Paradoxes, like those developed by Zeno of Elea in the fifth century B.C., indicate that geometry is not completely certain. The recent discoveries in the New World indicate that the accepted beliefs about human nature are not so certain. (Montaigne was perhaps the first to realize the extent to which the information about the cultures in America indicated that the beliefs of Europeans about human nature were relative to their own experience and civilization.) Similarly, information about ancient Greece and Rome, as well as about the various cultures in Europe itself, shows that views about law, religion, social customs, and the like change all the time, and that what has been accepted as true in one culture has been rejected by another.

From here, Montaigne moves on to the theoretical basis of the Pyrrhonian position, the critique of sense knowledge, "the greatest foundation and proof of our ignorance." All of our knowledge appears to come from sense information, but there are certain basic difficulties with regard to this information which cast it in doubt. First of all, we do not know whether we possess all the necessary senses for obtaining true knowledge. We have five senses, but it may require ten to see nature correctly. Our sense information may be as far removed from the truth as a blind man's view of colors. Second, even if we possess all the needed senses, there is the possibility that they may be deceptive. The occurrence of illusions gives us some grounds for distrusting our senses. Further, our sense experience seems to vary according to our emotional state. Besides the many reasons that Sextus Empiricus offered for distrusting our senses, there is also the problem that we cannot tell whether our sense experience is part of a dream or a genuine reflection of what the world is like. When we consider all the Pyrrhonian arguments about sense knowledge, we realize that we can know only how things appear to us, and now how they are in themselves.

Besides, Montaigne argues, for all that we know, the senses may distort what we perceive, in the same way that certain kinds of lenses do. The qualities we perceive may be imposed upon objects rather than actually being in them. What we experience differs with our condition, our location, and so on. Unless we possess some standard by which to judge when we have the right experience, we have no way of distinguishing true information about the world from false information. But this raises the classical skeptical problem of the criterion—how do we tell what standard is the true one? To answer this question we need another standard. If we try to use our reason to decide, we will need further reasons to justify the ones we have employed, and so on to infinity.

Hence, if our senses are the sources of all of our ideas, we can be sure of nothing. We have no completely certain standard to use to judge when or if our ideas or sense impressions correspond to the real objects outside of us. We are forever in the position of the man who tries to determine whether a picture of Socrates is a good likeness, when he has never seen Socrates.

These successive waves of skepticism leave one finally with the realization that trying to know reality is like trying to clutch water. It cannot be done. Until God decides to enlighten us, all of our supposed knowledge will remain uncertain. It is only through the grace of God, Montaigne concludes, that we can ever achieve any contact with reality.

Montaigne's *Apology* introduces, in its unsystematic way, many of the traditional arguments of the Greek skeptics. Throughout the essay, Montaigne couples the argument for complete skepticism with an appeal to faith as the way out of doubt. For some of his readers, his important message is that human beings cannot be certain of anything, including the truths asserted by traditional religions. For other readers, both his doubts and his fideistic solution were equally important. For them, Montaigne showed that human beings by their own devices could not find any certain knowledge; they could find it only through faith.

The *Apology for Raimond Sebond* is one of the works which was most important in setting the stage for the beginning of modern philosophy, for it provided a series of doubts about all previous theories. The new philosophers of the seventeenth century had either to find a way of answering the many skeptical arguments of Montaigne, or to accept his skeptical conclusion. In the *Apology*, Montaigne provided the starting point for "the quest for certainty," as well as a skeptical resolution of the problems he considered.

DIALOGUES CONCERNING CAUSE, PRINCIPLE, AND ONE

Author: Giordano Bruno (c.1548-1600)
Type of work: Metaphysics, theology
First published: 1584

PRINCIPAL IDEAS ADVANCED

Knowledge of the first cause and principle of the universe can be acquired only with difficulty through the study of remote effects.

God is the first principle of all things in that, as world soul pervading all nature, his nature is the nature of all things.

God is the first cause of all things since all things have being as the result of the informing action of the world soul.

There is but one substance; but one may distinguish form, the power to make, from matter, the power to be made.

Matter is passive potency in that it can be more than it is; but it is also act in that it contains the forms which, given the efficient cause, it unfolds.

The universe is one, infinite, immobile; all multiplicity is in appearance only.

Bruno's *Dialogues Concerning Cause, Principle, and One* is the work of one of the most brilliant and courageous philosophers of the Italian Renaissance. He was a man of faith with an independent and creative mind. His views did not win favor with the Dominicans with whom he had allied himself, and he was forced to leave the Order. He moved from place to place, provoking criticism wherever he settled. In France and England he produced some of his most famous works, but he finally had to move on. He spent some time in Germany and Switzerland. When he went to Venice in 1591 he became a victim of the Inquisition. He was tried, imprisoned in Rome, and finally burned at the stake because of his refusal to retract.

His philosophy of the universe is in the grand tradition of metaphysics and theology in that it describes an infinite universe which is God, and it attempts to explain how a world which presents a bewildering number of aspects to those viewing it from various perspectives can nevertheless be regarded as a unity. Perpetuating Neoplatonic ideas, and showing the influence of Plotinus, Bruno used his philosophic and poetic resources to build an image of a universe made perfect by the light of God which affects the existence and nature of everything. God is the principle, the cause, and the unity of the infinite universe.

Like Leibniz, whom he influenced, Bruno used the idea of the *monad*, unity of body and soul, and a manifestation of divine energy. The *Cause, Principle, and One*, an earlier work than the *De Minimo* in which the monad conception is developed, prepares the way for the new idea by describing God as the World Soul pervading all being.

The first dialogue of the work introduces Filoteo, a philosopher who serves as the figure of Bruno. It presents a good-humored defense of philosophy, but not without suggesting the difficulties which come to one who has the courage of his convictions. The conversation is with two friends, Heliotropio and Armesso. Bruno, in an "Introductory Epistle," describes the first dialogue as "an apology, or something else I know not what, concerning the five dialogues of 'Le cena de le ceneri,'" one of his satirical dialogues.

With the second dialogue the proper body of the work begins. The interlocutors are Alexander Dixon, described as having proposed the subject matter to Theophilus, who is Filoteo (or Teofilo), or Bruno; Gervasius, not a philosopher, a person who "neither stinks nor smells" and who "makes

366

jokes of the things that Polyhymnius says"; and Polyhymnius, a "sacrilegious pedant . . . one of the most rigid censors of philosophers. . . ."

Theophilus (the lover of God) explains to the others that it is only with the greatest difficulty that the first cause and principle is known; the divine substance, because of its infinitude and distance from its effects, can be known only through traces, the remote effects of its action. To call God first principle and first cause is to say the same thing from different points of view; God is first principle "inasmuch as all things are after him . . . either according to their nature, or according to their duration, or according to their worthiness." God is first cause "inasmuch as all things are distinct from him as the effect from the efficient. . . ." Theophilus explains that the term "principle" is more general than the term "cause": a point is the principle of a line, but not its cause. Principle has to do with the nature of a thing, cause with its production.

God is then described as "universal physical efficient cause" and as "universal intellect." In response to a question from Dixon, Theophilus explains what he means by "universal intellect." The intellect is the most real and proper faculty of the world soul; it illumines the universe and is the mover of all things; it is the "world architect"; it is what the Magi regarded as the seed sower, what Orpheus called the eye of the world, what Empedocles regarded as the distinguisher, what Plotinus called the father and progenitor, the "proximate dispenser of forms," and what Theophilus himself calls "the inner artificer."

Dixon wonders what the formal cause (the idea, the plan) of the universe is, if God, or the universal intellect, is the efficient cause (what brings things to existence); he ventures the answer that the formal cause is the "ideal concept" in the divine intellect. Theophilus agrees, and he supplements Dixon's remark that the final cause (the purpose) of the universe is the perfection of it by saying that the final cause, as well as the efficient cause, is universal in the universe.

A problem disturbs Dixon: he wonders how the same subject can be both the principle and the cause of natural things.

Theophilus answers that although the soul informs the entire universe and is an intrinsic and formal part of it—the principle of the universe—nevertheless, considered as governor and efficient cause, it is not a part.

Theophilus then comes forth with an idea that startles Dixon; it is the claim that the forms of natural objects are souls and that all things are animated. Although Dixon is willing to concede that the universe is animated, he has not considered that Theophilus would regard every part as animated, and he protests, "It is common sense that not all things are alive." Theophilus is insistent; everything has a vital principle. This claim is too much for Polyhymnius: "Then my shoes, my slippers, my boots, my spurs, my ring and my gloves will be animate?" Gervasius assures him that they are because they have within them "an animal such as you." Theophilus finally reassures them by saying that tables as tables, glass as glass, and so forth, are not animate, but as composites of matter and form they are all affected by spiritual substance and in that sense are animated by spirit. But not everything having soul is called animate. There is an intrinsic, formal, eternal principle in all things; it is the One in all things, the world soul in every part, the soul of all parts. Although distinctions can be made between forms, all forms are finally unified in one substantial ground. But the world soul is not present corporeally; it does not stretch out to cover the universe; rather, it is present in its entirety in every part as the formal principle of every part.

When the discussion is resumed (in the third dialogue), Theophilus mentions philosophers who have taken matter as primary and as the only reality. Confessing that he himself once held this view, he adds that he has come to the opinion that there are two forms of substance in the world: form and matter, active potency and passive potency, the power to make and the power to be made. Neither matter nor form can be dissolved or annihilated, although changes of form are common. There is, then, the one soul and formal principle that is the cause and principle of all things; there are the forms supplied by that principle; and there is one matter, the "receptacle of forms."

Matter is regarded as a potency and as a substratum. Potency is either active or passive. Passive potency is common to all matter; it is the capacity to be other than in actuality it is. Only the One is all that it can be, for it contains all being; consequently it contains all that which is passively potent as well as all other being. But death, corruption, vices, and defects, according to Theophilus, are neither act (actively potent) nor passively potent. God is both absolute act and absolute potency, and he cannot be apprehended by the intellect except in a negative way.

After some jesting between Polyhymnius and Gervasius—the theme being that matter is like woman, stubborn, inconstant, never satisfied with its present form, and so forth—Theophilus resumes (in the fourth dialogue) his discussion of matter, arguing that matter is the substratum of all beings, both corporeal and intelligible. He quotes Plotinus's remark that "if this sensible world is the imitation of the intelligible world, the composition of this is the imitation of the composition of that." Other reasons are offered in support of the thesis that there is only one matter. Matter in itself has no determinate dimensions and is indivisible; it is only in virtue of form that what is capable of receiving dimension actually acquires it. But matter, even when deprived of form, is not pure potency; matter as deprived of form is not like darkness deprived of light, but like "the pregnant . . . without its progeny, which she sends forth and obtains from herself. . . ." Matter is that which unfolds "out of its own bosom" that which it has enfolded; it contains within itself all the forms which it is capable of taking on; it is not a pure nothing, but a subject. Form could not arise to inform the matter which enfolds it were matter pure potency.

The fifth dialogue begins with the words of Theophilus: "The universe is, then, one, infinite, immobile." The multiplicity in the universe, the change, the diversity—all this is in appearance and relative to the senses; properly considered, every part of the universe is, in its mode of being, the One. Despite the existence of particular things, everything is one in substance, being, form, and matter; and there is but one cause and principle of all things. Properly speaking, there are no distinctions if one considers the substance of things; for there is but one substance, the infinite, the world soul, the divine intellect. To Polyhymnius, who hears but does not understand and begs for an example, Theophilus explains how a unity can account for apparent multiplicity; he uses an example from arithmetic: a decade is a unity, but is embracing; a hundred is more embracing, although

still a unity; a thousand is even more embracing. But the one is the highest good, the highest beatitude, perfection; it is "the unity which embraces all."

Theophilus, having faithfully served as the apologist of the philosophy of the Nolan (Bruno of Nola), closes with words of praise: "Praised be the Gods, and extolled by all the living be the infinite, the simplest, the most unified, the highest, and the most absolute cause, principle, and the one."

THE ADVANCEMENT OF LEARNING

Author: Francis Bacon (1561-1626)
Type of work: Epistemology, philosophy of science
First published: 1605

PRINCIPAL IDEAS ADVANCED

Scholars should free themselves from bondage to the past; Europeans should cease being awed by the accomplishments of Greece and Rome.

Practical investigation should be emphasized, and scholars should cease wasting their time with vain speculations.

Modern history should be studied with as much enthusiasm as ancient, and there is a need for new sciences: a science to study races in relation to climate, geography, and natural resources; a science of education, a history of mechanics, and sciences having to do with business and diplomacy.

Scientific invention is encouraged by attention to negative instances and to exceptions to rules; calendars of doubts and problems should be kept, and nature should be studied inductively, not deductively.

Human learning has three main parts corresponding to the three capacities of the human understanding: history, based on memory; poesy, based on the imagination; and philosophy, based on reason.

In this, his first major philosophical work, Francis Bacon was directly concerned to influence King James I and the Court in favor of a new concept of learning. The reign of the Tudors (1485-1603) had seen great changes in

the Church, in government, and in the economy of England, but not in the universities. Fired with the same spirit of adventure which had motivated the explorations of Sir Francis Drake and Sir Walter Raleigh, Bacon undertook in this work to make "as it were a small globe of the intellectual world, as truly and faithfully as I could discover; with a note and description of those parts which seem to me not constantly occupate, or not well converted by the labor of man."

Because Bacon believed that the enterprise of exploring and conquering new realms of knowledge would have more appeal to the men who directed the nation's affairs than to sequestered scholars, he wrote the book in English. When his belief proved mistaken, he published a revised edition in Latin to make it uniform with his other philosophical writings, and gave it the name *De Augmentis Scientiarum* (1623). Bacon's effort was wasted on the court of King James, but by the middle of the century independent scholars had made his book the banner of a major crusade; they hailed its author as "the secretary of nature" and the "architect" of the new learning. The Royal Society of London for Improving Natural Knowledge, founded in 1660, is an example of his influence.

In our eyes, it is a fault of *The Advancement of Learning* that it contains so much shameless flattery of King James. Besides beginning each of the two parts of his book with a dedication to the king, Bacon especially praised James's notorious tract called "The True Law of Free Monarchies" (1603) as being "a work richly compounded of divinity, morality, and policy, with great aspersion of all other arts; and being in mine opinion one of the most sound and healthful writings that I have read." But as if the only true flattery were imitation, Bacon seems deliberately to have composed the first book of *The Advancement of Learning* in the pedantic fashion that his monarch esteemed, citing Adam and Moses, Alexander and Caesar and a host of others to prove the excellency and worthwhileness of learning and knowledge. What saves the first book from utter tedium is the sharp criticism which now and again he let fall upon divines, politicians, and scholars for bringing learning into stagnation.

Bacon had two main faults to find with the learning of his day. The first had to do with its bondage to the past. In this respect, he considered Renaissance humanists and Protestant theologians worse offenders than the schoolmen, because they gave far too much attention to the ancient languages, to style and phrase, to the correction and annotation of texts. In his opinion, it was time for scholars to wake up to the age in which they were living. No longer need Europeans feel overawed at the achievements of Greece and Rome. What we call antiquity was in fact the youth of the world. "These times are the ancient times, when the world is ancient, and not those which we account ancient by a computation backward from ourselves."

The second main fault was in mistaking the goal or purpose of knowledge. Too great precedence had, he thought, been given to intellectual activity and not enough to practical investigations. Bacon pleaded for scholars to lay aside "vain speculations" and to turn to "the contemplation of nature and the observation of experience." Contemplation, he said, should ever be conjoined with action and should be pursued not out of mere intellectual curiosity or for the honor or gain of the scholar, but for its utility to civil society.

It is instructive to note how closely

Bacon's strictures on the learning of his times agreed with those of his younger contemporary, Descartes, in his *Discourse on Method* (1637). A modern parallel is found in John Dewey's *The Quest for Certainty* (1929).

In the second and more substantial part of the book, Bacon turned his attention from the scholars to the matter of their scholarship. His purpose was to point out areas of study that had not received sufficient attention, and in passing to note those that had not been neglected. Among the latter he placed mathematics and physics, grammar and eloquence, ancient and ecclesiastical history. This was not to say that he considered them in a satisfactory condition. "I am not now," he noted, "in hand with censures, but with omissions." Of physics, for example, which he did not report as deficient, he nevertheless noted: "In what truth or perfection [its branches] are handled, I make not now any judgment; but they are parts of knowledge not deserted by the labor of man."

Bacon's originality appears in the number of new sciences which he envisaged a place for, and the gaps he saw in the old ones. For example, he urged that modern history should be studied with the same zeal as ancient, and he called for a new science that would study human races in connection with climate, geography, and natural resources. There was need for a science of education and for books on practical morals which would deal with ways of improving the mind and cultivating virtue. A history of mechanics and inventions was needed to parallel the history of thought. And handbooks were needed in the fields of business and diplomacy, comparable in "form of writing" to Machiavelli's works on government. Theology might seem to be overcultivated, but Bacon suggested two new areas—one dealing with the limits of human reason in speculating about divine things, the other defining the latitude which ought to be allowed for theological differences. Medicine, Bacon thought, was in a particularly deficient way, being "a science which hath been more professed than labored, and yet more labored than advanced; the labor having been in my judgment, rather in a circle than in progression." He complained that Hippocrates' method of keeping case histories of his patients had fallen into disuse. He argued for the reinstitution of vivisection, particularly of beasts, in order that anatomy might again go forward. And he wished that physicians would give more attention to searching out specific medicines and less to compounding confections for ready sale.

As would be expected, Bacon gave special attention to the arts of reasoning, anticipating many of the themes of his famous *Novum Organum* (1620). He argued that invention has been far too much the sport of chance rather than the child of intelligence. "Hitherto men are rather beholden to a wild goat for surgery, or to a nightingale for music, or to the ibis for some part of physic, or to the pot-lid that flew open for artillery, or generally to chance or anything else than to logic for the invention of arts and sciences."

Bacon recommended several new angles of approach. He pointed out the importance to invention of the negative instance and the exception to the rule; consequently, he strongly recommended keeping calendars of doubts and problems and popular errors, together with a history of the wonders and monstrosities of nature. He mentioned the need of putting nature to torture in order to make her answer our questions. He criticized the adequacy of syllogistic reasoning for the investigation of nature, and he urged a more particular induction. Also, he pointed to characteristic fallacies which he was later to call the "idols" of the mind.

Perhaps more important than any of these details is the new principle of "the classification of the sciences" which Bacon employed in this work, several features of which deserve notice. In the first place, he drew a sharp division between human learning and divine, the obvious purpose of which was to set human reason free from the authority of revelation. In the second place, he divided human learning into three main parts, paralleling the "three parts of man's understanding": *memory* he saw as the basis for all kinds of history—natural, civil, ecclesiastical; *imagination*, as the basis for poesy—narrative, representative, and allusive; and *reason*, as the basis for philosophy—divine, natural, and human.

Bacon's emphasis upon the divisions within philosophy has been influential in empirical circles to this day. He deprecated the generalized kind of thinking which schoolmen called "philosophy" and parceled out its matter to special sciences. It was, he thought, rather a depradation of other sciences than anything solid and substantive itself. In its place, he proposed a new discipline under the name of "first philosophy," which would be a receptacle for axioms and rules which are valid for several parts of knowledge. Such a science, were it cultivated, would prove a fruitful fountain from which all might draw.

Of special interest is the account he gave of the relation between physics and metaphysics. Both, in his view, are branches of natural science, the former dealing with material and efficient causes, the latter with formal and final causes. Physics, in his estimation, stands above natural history in that it is explanatory and not merely descriptive; but it is below metaphysics, in that it sees causes in their particularity. For example, if the cause of whiteness in snow or froth is inquired, physics will explain that it is due to the subtle intermixture of air and water. Metaphysics must explain it in terms of the "form of whiteness" and show why this particular intermixture of elements is united with this universal character. Bacon said he was not surprised that little progress had been made in metaphysics understood in this way, because men had not paid enough attention to particulars. But he also let escape the doubt that much could ever be accomplished in this direction. Natural philosophy, he said, is like a pyramid, with natural history as the base, physics as the middle, and metaphysics as the vertical point. But "as for the vertical point, the summary law of nature, we know not whether man's inquiry can attain to it."

It is not difficult to see that behind the new division of the sciences lay Bacon's complete rejection of the medieval synthesis of Aristotle and St. Augustine. Without repudiating theology, he sealed it off, restricting "divine knowledge" to faith, manners, liturgy, and church government. As for Aristotelianism, while Bacon preserved much of its terminology, he rejected its fundamental tenets and turned to

Democritus, the materialistic atomist, for his model of the world. (Compare in this respect his younger friend, Thomas Hobbes.)

The new system of classification also points up the anthropocentric ("humanistic" in the twentieth century sense of the word) character of Bacon's thinking. Bacon did not accept Copernicus' theory of the heavens, but the kind of "Copernican revolution" which Kant claimed to have brought about was incipient in Bacon's decision to abandon the traditional division of the sciences based on nature, and to reorganize knowledge according to the faculties of the mind. For example, Bacon brought botany and the rise and fall of civilizations together as branches of a single kind of inquiry: one is "natural history," the other "civil history"; what they have in common is the fact that they are both founded in man's memory and observation, rather than in imagination or reason.

Bacon made no secret of his conviction that all knowledge has for its end the use and benefit of man. This attitude is evident from what has appeared already in what has been said about the necessity of combining contemplation with action and in the deficiency he reported in respect to mechanical and practical knowledge. He was the champion of the kind of learning we associate with polytechnic colleges, business schools, and research institutes. His bias is underscored by the disproportion in the amount of space which he devotes to "human" philosophy (fifteen chapters) as against "natural" philosophy (two chapters). "Know thyself," he said, following the ancient oracle; for the knowledge of man is the "end and term" of human learning, notwithstanding the fact that it is but a portion of "the continent of nature."

Bacon thought of himself as standing on the threshold of a new age. Among its harbingers he mentioned the vivacity of the "wits" of that time, the improved knowledge of the past, the invention of printing, world-wide navigation, the increase of leisure, and political stability. He spoke of the period as constituting a third great age in the history of the world, which he hoped would far exceed in glory and achievement the days of Greece and Rome. Of his own writings, he said that men could say of them what they wished, as long as they observed and weighed them. He suggested that it was comparable to the "noise or sound which musicians make while they are in turning their instruments: which is nothing pleasant to hear, but yet is a cause why the music is sweeter afterwards."

NOVUM ORGANUM

Author: Francis Bacon (1561-1626)
Type of work: Philosophy of science
First published: 1620

To acquire knowledge about the world one must interpret the particulars given in sense experience.

Various false ideas and methods have handicapped man in his attempt to study nature impartially; they are the Idols of the Tribe (conventional beliefs which satisfy the emotions), the Idols of the Cave (erroneous conceptions resulting from individual predilections), the Idols of the Market Place (confused ideas resulting from the nonsensical or loose use of language), and the Idols of the Theatre (various systems of philosophy or other dogmatic, improperly founded assertions).

The discovery, investigation, and explanation of Forms (the properties of substances) by controlled observation and experimentation, utilizing tables of instances by reference to which inductive generalizations can be made, is the philosophical foundation of all knowledge.

This important work in scientific methodology was part of a larger work, *The Great Instauration*, which was proposed in six parts (the *Novum Organum* to be the second) but never completed. Even this work itself is partial, as is indicated by the fact that the author listed in Aphorism XXI of Book II a number of topics which he proposed to discuss, but never did, either here or in his other works. The content of the book clearly indicates that he considered it to be a correction of, or a supplement to, Aristotle's logical writings, the *Organon*. A large portion of Bacon's text is devoted to a demonstration of the futility, if not the error, of trying to understand nature by the deductive method. We cannot learn about the world, he insists, by arguing, however skillfully, about abstract principles. On the contrary, we must *interpret* nature by deriving "axioms from the senses and particulars, rising by a gradual and unbroken ascent, so that the method arrives at the most general axioms last of all. This is the true way, but as yet untried." It was a new "inductive logic" whose rules Bacon proposed to disclose.

The work is divided into two Books,

the first concerned mainly with setting down the principles of the inductive method and the second with the method for collecting facts. Book I is further divided into two parts, of which the first is designed to purge the mind of the wrong methods (Aphorisms I-CXV), while the second is planned to correct false conceptions of the method which Bacon is proposing (Aphorisms CXVI-CXX).

He begins by showing that the relation of man to nature is such that man can know the world only by being its servant and its interpreter. In man knowledge and power meet, for man can control nature only if he understands it; "nature to be commanded must be obeyed." Man can modify nature only by putting natural bodies together or by separating them. Moreover, his control over nature has been very much limited because man has chosen to spend his time in "specious meditations, speculations and glosses," which are well designed to systematize the knowledge which he already has but poorly designed for the discovery of new ideas. The syllogism, for example, serves only to give stability to the errors of tradition; it deals with such unsound notions as substance, quality, action, passion, and essence, rather than with those which have been abstracted from things by the proper inductive methods.

Bacon writes that there are three methods commonly employed for understanding nature. He describes these metaphorically in Aphorism XCV as those of the ant, the spider, and the bee. The ant is an experimenter, but he only collects and uses. The spider is not an experimenter, but he makes cobwebs out of his own inner substance. The bee takes the middle course; he gathers material from the flowers but transforms and digests this by powers of his own. Natural philosophy is exemplified neither by the ant nor by the spider; it does not gather material from natural history and from mechanical experiments and store it away in memory, nor does it rely solely on the powers of the mind. It alters and digests the particulars which are given in experience and then lays them up in memory.

In further clarification of his method Bacon suggests that there is an important distinction between the *Anticipation of Nature* and the *Interpretation of Nature*. *Anticipations* are collected from very few instances; they are sweeping generalizations which appeal to the imagination and thus produce immediate assent. Indeed, if all men went mad in the same manner they might very well agree on all anticipations. But *Interpretations* are obtained from widely dispersed data; they cannot produce consent since they usually disagree with accepted ideas. *Anticipations* are designed to be easily believed; *Interpretations* are designed to master things.

One of the contributions to scientific methodology for which Bacon has become most famous is his doctrine of the *Idols*. These are false notions and false methods which have taken possession of our minds, have become deeply rooted in them, and strongly resist our efforts to study nature impartially. Bacon believes that we can guard against these only if we are aware of what they are and how they mislead thinking. He calls them the *Idols of the Tribe, the Idols of the Cave, the Idols of the Market Place,* and *the Idols of the Theatre*. The first have their foundation in human nature itself, the second in the individual man, the third in the vagueness and ambiguity of language, and the fourth in the dogmas of philosophy and the wrong rules of demonstration.

The *Idols of the Tribe* are exemplified in the following: the beliefs that all celestial bodies move in perfect circles, because we are predisposed to find more order and regularity in the world than we actually find; superstitions, which are accepted because we are reluctant to abandon agreeable opinions even when negative instances arise; unwillingness to conceive of limits to the world, or of uncaused causes, and the resulting eternal search for principles which are ever more and more general; the swaying of our beliefs by emotions rather than by reason; the deceptions which arise because of the dullness and incompetency of the sense organs; and our proneness to prefer abstractions to the concrete realities of experience.

The *Idols of the Cave* are due to the mental and bodily peculiarities of the individual. Men become attached to certain beliefs of which they are the authors and on which they have spent much effort. Some men see resemblances and overlook difference; others reverse these; both err by excess. Some men worship the past and abhor novelty; others reverse these; truth, however, is to be found in the mean between these extremes. Similar examples are to be found in the respective overemphasis on particles as against structure, both of which distort reality. The *Idols of the Market Place* are the most troublesome of all. They are of two kinds: words which are names of things that do not exist (Fortune, Prime Mover, Element of Fire), and words which are names of things that exist but which are vague and confused in their meanings. The latter can be exemplified by the word *humid*, which may apply in its many meanings to flame, air, dust, and glass.

The *Idols of the Theatre* are subdivided into those of Systems of Philosophy and those of False Arguments. Among the former are the *Sophistical* (exemplified by Aristotle, who corrupted philosophy by his logic and his theory of the categories), the *Empirical* (exemplified by the alchemists and all those who leap to generalizations on the basis of a few, "dark" experiments), and the *Superstitious* (exemplified by those who employ their philosophies to prove their theologies). The False Argument idols are found when men improperly extract the forms of objects from the objects themselves, and when, in a spirit of caution, they withhold judgment even though a truth has been well demonstrated, or dogmatically assert a conclusion without sufficient grounds. The only true demonstration is experience, not by means of careless experiments, or experiments in play, or experiments performed repeatedly with only slight variations until one wearies in the process, but by planned and controlled experiments whose motive is true understanding rather than an "overhasty and unreasonable eagerness to practice."

Bacon shows that if we examine the traditional natural philosophy we can easily see why it has not met with success. In the first place, it was largely disputational—a feature which is most adverse to the acquisition of truth. It was primarily dialectical, described by Dionysius as "the talk of idle old men to ignorant youth." Much of it was argued by itinerant scholars, who put their wisdom up for sale and were primarily concerned with defending their own schools of thought. In addition, these men had the disadvantage of there being no historical knowledge, other than myths, on which they could base their conclusions, and they had very limited geographical knowledge. Furthermore, such experimental knowledge as existed was largely a kind of "natural magic" which had almost no utility, philosophy not having realized, apparently, that it, like religion, must show itself in works. Indeed, it proved sterile, not only of mechanical progress but also of theoretical development; it thrived under its founders, remained stagnant for a few years, then declined and disappeared. As a result, many of its advocates not only apologized for the limited character of their knowledge by complaining of the subtlety and obscurity of nature, and of the weakness of the human intellect, but also argued defensively that nature was completely beyond the reach of man and essentially unknowable. To claim that the soundness of Aristotle's philosophy has been demonstrated by its long survival is fallacious, Bacon argues; it has survived not because of the consensus of the judgments of free minds (the only real test of truth), but only because of the blind worship of authority. "If the multitude assent and applaud, men ought immediately to examine themselves as to what blunder or thought they have committed."

Why, then, has science not progressed more rapidly in the long period of its history? Bacon argues that several reasons may be advanced. In terms of the total history of the race, of course, the few centuries which have elapsed since the Greeks is not a long period; we should therefore not be too hasty in disparaging the meager results of man's attempt to understand the world. The poverty of results in natural philosophy can be explained by the great concentration of effort on study in the other areas of thought—religion, morals, and public affairs. Furthermore, the sciences have failed to progress because the natural philosophy on which they must be based for sound support has not been forthcoming; astronomy, optics, music, and the mechanical arts lack profundity and merely glide over the surface of things. In addition, the sciences have remained stagnant because their goal has not been clearly formulated, and the method for attaining this goal has not been stressed; men have tended to rely mainly on their wits, on an inadequate logic, and on simple experiment (which is like a broom without a band). "The true method of experience first lights the candle, and then by means of the candle shows the way; commencing as it does with experience duly ordered and digested, not bungling or erratic, and from it educing axioms, and from established axioms again new experiments; even as it was not without order and method that the divine word operated on the created mass."

Any tendency to praise the accomplishments of the mechanical arts, the liberal arts, and alchemy should be tempered by the recognition of how ignorant we still are in these areas; we know much, but there is so much that we do not know. Much of which poses as knowledge, Bacon insists, has been set forth with such ambition and parade that one easily comes to feel that it is more nearly complete and perfect than it really is; its subdivisions seem to embrace all fields, but many of these fields prove to be empty and devoid of content. Even worse, much of what is practiced in the arts is pure charlatanism, claiming without grounds to prolong life, alleviate pain, bring down celestial influences, divine the future, improve intellectual qualities, transmute substances, and much more. The main defects of such arts are to be found in their combination of littleness of spirit with arrogance and superiority; they aspire to very little, but claim to accomplish very much; they engage in trifling and puerile tasks, but claim to solve all problems.

On the positive side, Bacon believes that there are strong grounds for hope. Knowledge is so obviously good that it bears the marks of Divine Providence on its surface. All that is required is that men should realize that we need a new science, a new structure built on a new approach to experience. The old science is inadequate. "Nothing duly investigated, nothing verified, nothing counted, weighed, or measured, is to be found in natural history: and what in observation is loose and vague, is in information deceptive and treacherous." Accidental experiments must be replaced by controlled experiments—

"of light" rather than "of fruit," which are designed simply for the discovery of causes and axioms. Data should be arranged in *Tables of Discovery* (which Bacon discusses in Book II), and from these we should ascend to axioms educed from these particulars by a certain rule, and then descend again to new particulars. In this activity the understanding, prone to fly off into speculation, should be hung with weights rather than provided with wings. The induction which is based on simple enumeration of accidentally gathered data is a childish thing; it should be replaced by one which examines the axioms derived in this way to see whether they are applicable to new particulars not included in the original enumeration, and whether they should be extended to wider areas or modified and restricted to what the new experience discloses.

The second section of Book I is devoted to a correction of the misconceptions of the Baconian method. Bacon assures the reader that he is not trying to set up a new sect in philosophy and not trying to propose a new theory of the universe. He is not even willing to promise any new specific scientific discoveries which may occur as a result of the introduction of the new method. He grants that his method probably contains errors of detail, though he believes these to be minor in character. Among the results which he is able to show, some will be claimed by others to be trivial, some to be even mean and filthy, and some to be too subtle to be readily comprehended. In reply to these charges Bacon repeats the statement of the poor woman who, having asked for a grant from a haughty prince and been rejected on the grounds that such an act would be be-

neath his dignity, replied, "Then leave off being king." If Bacon is criticized on the grounds that his method is presumptive, since he claims with one blow to have set aside all previous sciences and all earlier authors, his reply will be that with better tools one can do better things; thus, he is not comparing his capacities with those of his predecessors, but his skill at drawing a perfect circle by means of a compass with that of his predecessors who would draw a less perfect one without this instrument. And to the charge that in urging caution and suspension of judgment he is really denying the capacity of the mind to comprehend truth, he can answer that he is not *slighting* the understanding but *providing for* true understanding, not taking away authority from the senses but supplying them with aids.

Book II is concerned with the method for collecting facts. In order to explain this method Bacon first shows what he means by *Forms*. Every body may be regarded as a collection of "simple natures." Gold, for example, is yellow, malleable, heavy, non-volatile, non-combustible. These constitute the Form of gold, for in gold these properties meet. Anyone who knows what these properties are, and is capable of transforming a body which does not possess these properties into one which does, can create gold. The Form of gold can therefore also be called the "law" of gold, for it is a description of the nature of this substance and of the various ways in which it may be created or generated. While it is true that in the world itself there exist only bodies, not empty Forms, nevertheless the discovery, investigation, and explanation of Forms is the philosophical foundation of all knowledge and all operations on objects. There is in the world a limited number of "simple natures," or Forms, and every body can be understood as a compound of such natures.

"The Form of a thing is the thing itself, and the thing differs from the Form no other wise than as the apparent differs from the real, or the external, or the thing in reference to man from the thing in reference to the universe." In view of this fact we must set up procedures which will enable us to distinguish the true Form from the apparent Form. These procedures are employed in the setting up of *Tables and Arrangements of Instances*. These are obtained by the collection of particulars discovered in nature. "We are not to imagine or suppose, but to discover, what nature does or may be made to do." But since nature is so various and diffuse it tends to distract and confuse us as it presents itself. Consequently the particulars must be arranged and organized in order that understanding may be able to deal with them. In this way it is able to use induction and to educe axioms from experience. There are three kinds of such tables. *Tables of Essence and Presence* consist of collections of all known instances of a given nature, exhibiting themselves in unlike substances. As an example, Bacon gives a long list of instances of heat—in the sun, in meteors, in flame, in boiling liquids. A second kind of collection is a *Table of Deviation, or of Absence in Proximity*. These instances are cases where heat is absent; for example, in moonlight, light from the stars, air on mountain tops, and so on. Fi-

nally, there are *Tables of Degrees* or *Tables of Comparisons*. These involve noting the increase or decrease of heat in the same substance, or its varying amount in different subjects. For example, different substances produce different intensities of heat when burned; substances once hot, such as lime, ashes, and soot, retain their former heat for some time; dead flesh, in contrast to living flesh, becomes cold. These three *Tables* are devices by which we assure ourselves that where the nature is present the Form will be present, where the nature is absent the Form will be absent, and where the nature varies quantitatively the Form will vary quantitatively. On data thus arranged we go to work by the inductive process. If we proceed simply on the basis of affirmative cases, as we are naturally inclined to do, the results will be fancies, guesses, and ill-defined notions, and the axioms must be corrected every day. God and the angels may have the capacity to extract Forms solely from affirmative cases; but man must proceed by affirmation, negation, and variation. What we obtain by this process, however, is only the *Commencement of Interpretation* or the *First Vintage*. Bacon presumably means by this what present-day scientists would call a "hypothesis"; that is, a tentative interpretation which we employ as a guide to the selection of further instances (such as *Prerogative Instances*, which he discusses in great detail). On the basis of the hypothesis we then proceed either to collect the instances by controlled observation or to produce them by experimentation.

DISCOURSE ON METHOD

Author: René Descartes (1596-1650)
Type of work: Philosophy of philosophy, metaphysics
First published: 1637

PRINCIPAL IDEAS ADVANCED

The proper method for philosophy is as follows: Never accept any idea as true which is not clearly and distinctly beyond doubt; divide each complex question into simple, basic questions; proceed from the simple to the complex; review all steps in reasoning.

If this method is put into practice, there seems to be no proposition that cannot be doubted except the following: I think, therefore I am. (Cogito, ergo sum.)

As thinking substance, I have the idea of God; and since the idea of a perfect being could not have been derived from my own experience or being, God must exist as the source of my idea.

Furthermore, imperfect and dependent beings could not exist unless there were a perfect being, God, who made their existence possible; in addition, God by his very nature exists, for if he did not exist of necessity, he would not be perfect.

Since God exists, he provides the ground for our knowledge about the external world provided that we are careful to accept as true only those ideas which are clearly and distinctly beyond doubt once the reliability of the senses and of the reason can be seen to be derived from God.

In 1633, the year of Galileo's recantation, Descartes was just finishing his first major scientific treatise, *The World.* Because he made use in it of the Copernican theory, prudence dictated that the work be withheld from publication. But a strong sense of the importance of his discoveries prevailed upon him to issue three token essays as samples of what he was doing, and to compose a kind of prospectus of his work to date for publication under the same cover. This latter is the *Discourse on Method.* Besides explaining the author's method and reviewing his labors, it summarizes his metaphysical reasoning and sketches the plan of the larger, unpublished volume.

Strangely, perhaps, for one whose declared intention was to set all human knowledge on impersonal foundations, the *Discourse on Method* is a highly personal communication. It begins with a biographical reminiscence.

Familiar with books from childhood, the young Descartes had entered the new Jesuit College of La Flèche with high expectation; but he early fell victim to the skepticism which attended the passing of the Renaissance. The study of ancient tongues, of classic treatises on morals and philosophy, and of jurisprudence and medicine were excellent for ornamenting the person and preparing him for a life of riches and honor, but he decided that they yielded nothing that could be called knowledge. The only good to come from the revival of learning, so far as truth is concerned, was the rediscovery of mathematics, which, however, he was inclined to take without the Pythagorean mystifications which so delighted Kepler. The thing that pleased him in mathematics was the certitude and evidence which accompanied its demonstrations; and he was surprised to find that no higher science had been erected on such solid foundations. By contrast, philosophy, on which so much had been based, could exhibit no single claim that was not in dispute.

The young graduate had no further incentive toward books or toward the past. On the hunch that practical men might be wiser than scholars, in that they cannot entertain follies with impunity, he resolved to see the world and talk with men of every rank and occupation. He soon found, however, that practical men disagree as much as do philosophers; and, as for the experience of traveling in foreign lands, nothing so quickly undermines one's confidence in the judgment of one's fellow men.

Then came the turning point in Descartes' life. While he was still in his early twenties, he made the discovery—for which he is celebrated in the history of mathematics—that it is possible to bring geometry and algebra together into a single science by plotting equations along rectangular axes. This startling discovery encouraged him to look into his own mind for still more fundamental truths. "I resolved at length to make myself an object of study, and to employ all the powers of my mind in choosing the paths I ought to follow." The time was the winter of 1619-1620; the place was Germany, where he was serving in the army. He was barely twenty-three when these new prospects opened before him. For another nine years he was content to travel, assuming the role of spectator rather than actor in the affairs of the world. But he was not wasting his time. Part of his program consisted in systematic doubt; by painstaking reflection upon every matter that could be a source of error, he deliberately attempted to destroy beliefs which were not certainly true.

At the end of this period, he retired to Holland. He was then ready to undertake the recovery of truth. The first step was to replace the old metaphysics with one founded on his newly found principles. This task he accomplished in his book *Meditations on First Philosophy*, written in 1628-1629 (but not published until 1641). When this was out of the way, he was free to set about the main enterprise, which was to lay bare the secret laws which govern the world of matter. In the eight succeeding years his progress was astonishing. But the innumerable experiments which kept suggesting themselves required many hands. His motive in presenting the summary of his ideas in the *Discourse* was to recruit workers.

There is evidence independent of the *Discourse on Method* that the first powerful conviction which lifted Descartes out of skepticism and set his feet upon the rock of certitude was the discovery of certain rules for the direction of the mind. In the *Discourse* he associates this phase of his development with the winter in Germany when he was twenty-three. It antedates his enterprise of systematic doubt and, indeed, is presupposed by it, the doubt being but the first step toward carrying through the rules.

The brilliant young mathematician was led to conclude that just as the most difficult demonstrations in geometry can be arrived at easily by a long chain of simple steps, so "all things, to the knowledge of which man is competent, are mutually connected in the same way, and . . . there is nothing so far removed from us as to be beyond our reach, or so hidden that we cannot discover it, provided only we abstain from accepting the false for the true, and always preserve in our thoughts the order necessary for the deduction of one truth from another." These were intoxicating thoughts. What he had discovered, he believed, was a key that would open for mankind all the doors to knowledge. For it was no new power of insight or of reasoning that was needed—every man, essentially, has as much insight and reason as any other. The failure of previous inquirers stemmed from no natural deficiency, but from clumsiness and inexperience. Chiefly, man had been seduced by the powerful claims of his senses and imagination, so that the sober witness of reason had been obscured. What men needed was a set of rules which would help them to keep faithfully to truths which, once the debris had been removed, would shine upon the mind with a natural light.

Descartes was, therefore, a bold exponent of what is known as the deductive or *a priori* method. Still, his approach must not be confused with the scholasticism which, in Bacon's words, "flies from the senses and particulars to the most general axioms, and from these principles, the truth of which it takes for settled and immoveable, proceeds to judgment and to the discovery of middle axioms." The fault of the Aristotelian syllogism, Descartes said, was that, although it helps us to reason persuasively about things we already think we know, it is of no help in investigating the unknown. Thus,

Descartes' method was more radically *a priori* than Aristotle's, which drew its premises from induction. Turning his back on traditional logic, and taking his cue from geometry, he envisaged a chain of linear inferences which would progress from an initial truth so simple and obvious as to be self-evident, to a second which would be seen at once to be included in the first, and thence to a third, and so forth. In practice, the problem would always be to find the simple truth to which the chain could be anchored; afterward, all that would be necessary would be to preserve the true order. Each particular truth along the way would be entirely obvious to anyone who understood what was being affirmed—just as in arithmetic, a child who understands a sum fathoms everything that is within reach of the greatest genius who contemplates the same set of figures.

For convenience, Decartes summed up his principles in four rules, abridged as follows:

(a) Never accept any idea as true which is not so clearly and distinctly true as to be beyond all possibility of being doubted.

(b) Divide each complex question into simple ones.

(c) Order one's thoughts from the simplest to the most complex.

(d) Review the series of inferences to make sure there are no breaks or false links in the chain.

If these rules were rigorously followed, an obscure matter, such as the function of the lungs in the body, would be rendered perfectly intelligible. Such, at least, was the promise that inspired the youthful Descartes and launched him on his great career.

The biographical narrative and the exposition of method make up the first half of the *Discourse*. Part IV is an abridged version of the *Meditations on First Principles*, a work composed in Holland at the end of the nine-year period during which Descartes had sought to uproot all erroneous and unfounded opinions from his mind. Sensing Descartes' preëminently scientific interests, one may be surprised to find that he plunged into a metaphysical work. But, as he explained, to have ventured at once into the difficulties of the sciences would have been contrary to right order, since he regarded all such particular truths as dependent on principles borrowed from philosophy.

The investigation of these First Principles was "so metaphysical and uncommon" that the author questioned whether his readers would find it acceptable. It is, in fact, the only part of the *Discourse* which makes serious demands upon the intelligence. Yet, because the *Meditations* had not been published in 1637, he felt obliged to include a précis of that work. The chief advantage to us, who can read the *Meditations*, of having the argument reviewed in the *Discourse* is that we can see it in its proper perspective—on the one hand, as the first serious attempt to make use of the method of doubt, and, on the other, as being not an end in itself but the foundation for physics and physiology. Lacking this perspective, we might suppose that his preoccupation with God and the soul stemmed from a religious interest. His scholastic-styled proofs suggest to the twentieth century reader that he is laboring to shore up traditional beliefs. Quite the contrary! If we reflect that when Descartes speaks of soul he means "thinking" (and ideally "reasoning," for all the rest of the conscious life is illusion), and that when

he speaks of God he means the "ordered necessity" against which all apparent "contingency" is rendered intelligible, it will appear that, far from seeking to preserve the Christian view of the world, he is substituting for it an uncompromising formulation of the presuppositions of modern (seventeenth and eighteenth century) science. Just how far his philosophical work strengthened the cause of science and speeded its development is impossible to say, but it seems likely that his metaphysics was more useful than his method.

The method required that Descartes discover a truth so simple and self-evident that it could not be further reduced and yet would verify itself. Yet every belief he considered seemed to him to be a possible error. He supposed that even his strongest convictions might have been planted in him by a malevolent and deceiving god. But finally it struck him that even though his beliefs were mistaken, even though he could not go beyond the activity of doubting, the doubting itself existed; thinking existed; and if thinking, then he, as thinking substance, also existed. He expressed his conclusion in the triumphant words, *"Cogito, ergo sum"*: "I think, therefore I am."

When he sought to discover the ground of his certainty, he found nothing that guaranteed the truth of the proposition, "I think, therefore I am" other than his seeing "very clearly that in order to think it is necessary to exist." He thus took as a general rule for further philosophical investigations the principle "that all the things which we very clearly and distinctly conceive are true. . . ." At the same time, he admitted the difficulty of deciding which of the objects of thought were being conceived "clearly and distinctly."

Descartes then realized that he, as one who doubted, was not perfect—and yet he had the idea of perfection and of a perfect being. He found nothing in his own experience to account for his having arrived at the idea of perfection; and he finally concluded that the idea must have been placed in him by a being possessing all the perfections he conceived; namely, by God himself. Descartes was thus led to a renewed conviction in God's existence.

Other arguments in support of the belief in God's existence were quickly generated. All imperfect bodies and intelligences show by their imperfection their dependency on the perfect, on God; hence, God exists. Furthermore, the idea of a perfect being entails the idea of the existence of such a being; for if a being otherwise perfect did not exist, he would lack an essential perfection. (This ontological argument, reminiscent of St. Anselm's more famous version, was regarded by Descartes as having the same rigorous character as a geometric proof.) Finally, Descartes decided that no belief whatsoever could be accepted as a "metaphysical certitude" except by presupposing the existence of God. Even the principle of clarity—that clear and distinct ideas are true—depended for its certainty upon God's perfection and existence.

It has seemed to many critics of Descartes that to prove the certainty of a principle by reference to a God whose existence is proved by the use of that very same principle is certainly a circular procedure. But Descartes probably would have argued that clear and distinct ideas are certainly true whether we know the ground of our certainty

that such is the case. He presumed that by his arguments he revealed the ground of all certainty: God, the perfect being, the independent support of all dependent beings and of all truths endorsed by reason.

Having reassured himself and his readers of the reliability of reason and of the method he had outlined, Descartes then proceeded to summarize the conclusions of his unpublished treatise. According to his account, the treatise was a comprehensive work containing "all that . . . I thought I knew of the nature of material objects." Beginning with light, it touched upon the sun and the stars, on the heavens, the planets, the comets, and the earth, upon terrestrial bodies, and finally, upon man considered as organized matter. Out of caution, the author adopted the device of speaking about an imaginary world rather than about one created as described in the Bible. Suppose that there be matter "without form and void" in some imaginary space; if it is governed by the laws which God's perfection has established and fixed in our minds, it must work itself out of its initial chaos and arrange itself in a manner like our heavens and our earth. Tides, air currents, mountains and seas, summer and winter, minerals and vegetables are all accounted for in terms of fixed laws of nature. One has to turn to the original work to find the laws stated. Perhaps the most significant point Descartes communicates in his summary of *The World* is the important principle that the nature of anything is more easily conceived when understood in terms of its origin than when viewed simply in its completed state.

The greater part of the summary is given to human physiology. Continuing his hypothetical mode of argument, he asks us to think of God as forming the body of a man exactly like ours, but without a rational soul. This being granted, Descartes undertook to show how, according to the same laws as obtain everywhere else in nature, all the internal and external motions of the body must take place exactly as we observe them to, with the exception of intelligent speech and certain inventive actions. The circulation of the blood is taken as an example. Its motion through the body, as Descartes explains it, is the result of the presence in the heart of one of those fires-without-light (the kind present in processes of fermentation). The heat purifies the blood, and the resulting expansion and contraction drives it through the cavities of the heart. Hot blood warms the stomach, enabling digestion to take place. The lungs serve as condensers which cool the blood before returning it to the left ventricle. This cooling releases the animal spirits which are the "most agitated" part of the blood. These go to the brain because the arteries leading in that direction are nearly straight, and "according to the rules of Mechanics, which are the same with those of Nature . . . the weaker and less agitated parts must necessarily be driven aside by the stronger which alone in this way reach" their destination.

Surely this one example is sufficient to make clear the character of Descartes' scientific work. Nothing seems so dated as the scientific theories of yesteryear, but this fact should not obscure for us the original quality of Descartes' purely mechanistic account of vital phenomena. While he continued to hold that man's mind is perfectly adjusted to the body (our feelings and appetites are evidence of this), he was careful to stress their complete mutual independence. And as for animals other than man, they are simply very cunningly contrived machines without any kind of mind or soul.

The modern reader who has followed Descartes' account of nature to this point is impatient to ask whether observation and experimentation have no place in scientific work. Could Descartes' armchair method discover the circulation of the blood? The answer, obviously, is that it could not. (He learned it from the physician William Harvey.) Like everyone else, Descartes had to combine experiences and inference in order to obtain knowledge of the existing world. But Descartes' view of the relation between these two ways of knowing is peculiar. He thought that it is a mistake to begin with experiment. Our ordinary observation provides adequate material to arrive at the laws of nature, provided only that we reflect on it, for the germs of the most general truths exist naturally in our minds. Thus, he found no special observation necessary to account for the gross aspects of the universe—the motions of the heavenly bodies, the properties of the elements which make up the earth. But when he came to particular problems, the situation altered. There are so many ways God might have worked that it is impossible for us to infer which is the case. We know in general the laws by which a clock measures time, but we have to look behind the face of a particular clock to see what combinations of wheels and weights or springs the mechanic has employed. Similarly, in the case of the motion of the blood: once we have observed the arrangement of the heart with our eyes and felt the temperature of the blood with our fingers, we are in a position to understand the method which God has employed, and we can then demonstrate by the laws of physics why the motion must take place as it does.

Experimentation became increasingly important to Descartes the further he progressed in scientific studies. But we must not suppose that his youthful preference for demonstrative knowledge was laid aside. His program for future studies, as he hinted at the close of the *Discourse*, was to devote himself exclusively "to acquire some knowledge of Nature which shall be of such a kind as to enable us therefrom to deduce rules of Medicine of greater certainty than those at present in use. . . ."

MEDITATIONS ON FIRST PHILOSOPHY

Author: René Descartes (1596-1650)
Type of work: Metaphysics, epistemology
First published: 1641

Principal Ideas Advanced

Perhaps everything we believe is false.

There seems to be no way of avoiding the skeptical consequences of systematic doubt.

But if one is doubting, one exists.

This is the starting point for a philosophy based on certainty.

But if one exists, one is a thinker, a mind; and since one conceives of a God whose conception is beyond one's powers, there must be such a being.

But if God exists, then we can count on our sense experience and our reason, provided we are careful to believe only what is clearly and distinctly true.

The complete title of this work, *Meditations on the First Philosophy in Which the Existence of God and the Distinction Between Mind and Body Are Demonstrated,* prepares the reader for an essay in metaphysics. And we shall not accuse Descartes of mislabeling his product. But in order to understand Descartes' interest in these questions, and therefore the fuller import of the work, one must be prepared to find that he is actually reading an essay in epistemology, or the theory of knowledge. Is there such a thing as knowledge? If so, what distinguishes it from opinion? How is error to be explained? Such questions as these seem to have been uppermost in the author's mind. But in order to answer them, to validate knowledge, to lay hold on the necessity which to Descartes (quite in the Platonic tradition) was the mark of truth, it was necessary to raise the fundamental questions of Being.

In choosing to set down his thoughts as meditations, Descartes shows the greatest consideration for his reader.

386

He represents himself as seated before a fire in a cozy Dutch dwelling, wrapped in his dressing gown, freed from worldly care, and devoting himself to a task which he had for some time looked forward to—a kind of mental house-cleaning. On six successive days he pursues his meditation, taking us with him step by step. He pursues the task of clearing his mind of all error.

From *Discourse on Method* we learn that the work was actually composed in circumstances much like those here alleged. In 1628 Descartes was in his thirties and living in Holland, to which he had withdrawn from the more active life for the special purpose of carrying on his philosophical and scientific investigations. The *Meditations* was circulated in manuscript, and when it was published (1641) it included a lengthy appendix composed of objections by leading philosophers—including Thomas Hobbes and Pierre Gassendi—together with Descartes' replies.

The "First Meditation" is, in a way, distinct from the rest. It describes Descartes' effort, which in fact engaged him for many years, to accustom himself not to think of the world in the imagery of the senses or according to the notions of common sense and the traditions of the schools.

Can it be, Descartes wonders, that all beliefs which he had formerly held are false? Perhaps not: but if he is to achieve his goal of building up a body of incontrovertible truth, he must exercise the same rigor toward beliefs that are merely uncertain as toward those which are demonstrably untrue. That is to say, he must make *doubt* his tool. Instead of allowing it to hang over him, forever threatening, he must grasp it firmly and lay about until he has expunged from his mind every pretended certainty.

The first to go are those beliefs that depend on our senses—notably our belief in the existence of our own bodies and of everything that appears to our sight and touch. Our habitual judgment protests. What can be more certain, Descartes asks himself, than that I am seated by the fire holding this paper in my hand? But, he writes, when we reflect that our dreams are sometimes attended with equal confidence, we are forced to conclude that there is no infallible mark by which we can know true perceptions from false.

Of course, what one doubts is, in this case, only that one's ideas *represent* something beyond themselves. Descartes is one of the first philosophers to use the word "idea" in the modern sense. He means by it "whatever the mind directly perceives." But he distinguishes between the idea taken only as a mode of thought, and the idea as a representation of reality. Even in dreams we cannot deny the former of these. What we challenge is the "truth" of the ideas—Descartes calls it "objective reality"—and of judgments based on them. And his question is, whether there is anything in our sense-images that testifies unmistakably to the truth of what they represent. Obviously not, in those that we ourselves initiate in dreams and fantasies. But no more, in those that come from without, through the senses —else how could we make mistakes as to sounds and sights?

There is, he says, another class of ideas which we seem neither to originate ourselves, nor to receive from without, but to be born with—those, for example, which make up the sciences of mathematics. Two and three are five even in dreams: for this sum does not require material counters to make it true. Yet, the ideas of numbers profess to be something besides modes of thought. They do have "objective reality." Moreover, we have been mistaken about mathematical matters. No more than sense-images are they self-authenticating. Our habitual trust in them is not unlike that which we place in our senses, and has the same foundation, namely, that we are creatures of a benevolent deity who would not deceive us. Suppose that this is not the case, and that mathematics is merely a fancy of my mind. Or, worse, suppose it is an illusion deliberately imposed upon us by a malicious demon who has access to the workings of our minds. This is not unthinkable.

These are the thoughts with which the "First Meditation" leaves us. Instead of supposing that the good providence of God sustains his thinking, Descartes resolves to hold fast to the hypothesis that he is constantly being deceived by an evil spirit, so that all his ordinary beliefs are false. In this manner, while he seems to make no progress in the knowledge of truth, he at least habituates himself to suspend judgment concerning things that he does not certainly know. But this is not easy. Descartes pleads with his readers (in the replies to his objectors) not merely to give the exercise such time as is required for reading the meditation through but to take "months, or at least weeks" before going on further. How loath one is to break old habits of thinking he suggests in the figure of a slave who, when sleeping, dreads the day, and conspires to weave the sounds of gathering dawn into his dreams rather than to embrace the light and labors which it brings.

The daylight enterprise that lies before him in the "Second Meditation" is to discover, if possible, some foundation of certainty which doubt is powerless to assault. He has doubted the reality of the world presented to him through his senses. Shall he affirm that some God (or devil) must exist to put these ideas into his mind? That hardly seems necessary, for perhaps he has produced them himself. One thing, however, seems now to loom up in Descartes' mind: "I myself, am I not something?" Suppose all my ideas are hallucinations, whether self-induced or planted in me by some God or devil: in this, at least, I cannot be deceived: "I am, I exist, is necessarily true each time that I pronounce it, or that I mentally conceive it."

Here, then, for the first time, we have encountered a self-validating judgment. It is the unique instance in which man immediately encounters the existence which is represented to him by an idea: I have an idea of "myself." Like other ideas, this one claims to have objective reality. But unlike other ideas, this one's claim is open to inspection—by me. Both the idea and the existence which it represents are present each time I think them. In a simple act of "mental vision" (to use Descartes' expression) I know that I exist. As Locke will say, I know my own existence intuitively.

With this certitude to serve as a cornerstone, Descartes proceeds to raise his palace of Truth. Let man explore the structure of his own inner consciousness, and he will find the clue to universal Being. For instance, we can ask the question, "What am I?" And the answer lies at hand. "I am a thing that thinks." For was it not in the act of thinking (taken broadly to include all conscious activities) that I found the reality of the idea of myself? Contrast with this the traditional view that man is a body indwelt by a subtle essence—a very fine grade of matter—known as spirit. What confusion surrounds the whole conception! There is nothing certain, or even intelligible, about it. In fact, we have only to press ahead with our methodical doubt to discover that most of the ideas which we habitually associate with matter are illusory. Take a piece of wax fresh from the comb: we think of it in terms of color, taste, odor, texture. But none of these is essential to the wax. Place it near the fire, and all the qualities which engross the imagination are altered. All that remains unchanged, so that we can call it essential to the wax, is "something extended, flexible, movable"— properties that are knowable to the intellect and not to the senses. In any case, whether I have a body, it is not as body that I know myself when I behold myself as existing. The realm of being which I discover there has nothing about it of extension, plasticity, mobility. I am a thinking being, Descartes concludes, a mind, a soul, an understanding, a reason: and if the meaning of these terms was formerly unknown to me it is no more.

These are very important results of the second day's meditation, especially when we remember that the forward progress was all made along the path of doubt, for it was the act of doubting that gave Descartes both the certainty that he existed and that his nature was mind. But we have not yet exhausted the implications of his consciousness of doubt. Does not doubt carry with it, and actually presuppose, the idea of certainty, just as error carries with it the idea of truth? Descartes finds in his mind the idea of a perfect being by comparison with which he is aware of his imperfections, a self-sufficient being by which he knows that he is dependent. Following this lead, he proceeds in his "Third Meditation" to demonstrate the existence of God.

His argument takes two forms. First, he asks directly concerning the *idea* of a perfect being, whence it could have come into his mind: From some other creature? From himself? Or must there exist a perfect being to originate the idea? His answer is obscured for the modern reader by the late-medieval philosophical framework in which it is expressed. The idea of God contains more "objective reality" than any other idea (including my idea of myself). But a more perfect idea cannot be generated by a less perfect being. Therefore, the idea of God in his mind must have been placed there by God himself.

The second form of the argument proceeds from the contingent quality of his own existence, made up as it is of fleeting instants, no one of which is able either to conserve itself or to engender its successor. Much in the argument reminds one of the traditional Aristotelian proof; but there is this difference, which makes it clear that the new argument is only another version of the first—it is not merely the existence of a contingent being that has to be explained, or of a thinking being, but of "a being which thinks and which has some idea of God." Thus, the principle that there must be at least as much reality in the cause as in the effect precludes the possibility

389

that any being less perfect than God could have created Descartes—or any man.

The argument here abbreviated is of scarcely more than historical interest. And the same is true of the further argument (from the "Fifth Meditation") that, since existence is a perfection, the idea of a Perfect Being entails the existence of that Being. But we would not be just to Descartes if we did not point out that behind the framework of traditional theistic proof lies a claim which rationalistic philosophers have found valid even in our own time. "I see that in some way I have in me the notion of the infinite earlier than the finite—to wit, the notion of God before that of myself. For how would it be possible that I should know that I doubt and desire, that is to say, that something is lacking to me, and that I am not quite perfect, unless I had within me some idea of a Being more perfect than myself, in comparison with which I should recognize the deficiencies of my nature?" Here, in effect, is a new kind of reasoning. The scholastics were committed to demonstrate the existence of God by syllogisms; and, whether through expediency or inadvertency, Descartes makes a show of doing the same. But in Descartes a new, quasi-mathematical way of reasoning was pushing the syllogism to one side, as the quotation (which could be matched with several others) makes clear. His true ground for affirming the existence of God was not that it *follows from* but that it is *implicit in* his consciousness of himself.

Pascal's famous memorial which insists that the God of the philosophers is not the God of faith is a useful reminder to the general reader. There is no need, however, to suppose that Descartes needed it. The certainty of God's existence is a great triumph —but for scientific, rather than for religious, reasons. It is the *sine qua non* of all further knowledge, since "the certainty of all other things depends on it so absolutely that without this knowledge it is impossible ever to know anything perfectly." We saw earlier that such obvious mathematical truths as two plus three equals five are not self-validating, because they bear no evidence of the competency of our thought. An atheist cannot be sure; hence his knowledge cannot be called science, Descartes tells us in replying to his objectors: doubt may never rise to trouble him; but if it does, he has no way of removing it. But the doubt is removed when a person recognizes that his mind owes its constitution and working to the creativity of God, and that God is no deceiver.

For the rest, the *Meditations* is chiefly devoted to determining just how far man can trust the faculties which the beneficent Deity has implanted in him.

First, one must distinguish between impulses which incline us to belief (such as "the heat which I feel is produced by the fire") and insights into necessary truths (such as "a cause must be as great or greater than its effect.") Both are natural, and owing to the good offices of our Creator. But the former can be doubted, even after we have discovered the truth about God; the latter, which Descartes speaks of as "the light of nature," cannot be doubted at all. They are the principles of reason in our minds by which we arrive at knowledge. We have no other means of distinguishing between true and false.

Second, one must consider the causes of error. It is axiomatic that God can never deceive us and that if we make proper use of the abilities he has given us we can never go wrong. Yet obviously, he has chosen to make us fallible. How does this happen? From the fact that our intellects are finite, together with the fact that our wills (as free) are infinite. One can see why both these things must be and how, as a consequent, man does not easily stay within the narrow realm of truth. The crux of the matter is that, for Descartes, judgment involves the will (in the form of "assent" or "dissent"). It is within our power to withhold judgment when convincing evidence is wanting, and to give it only when the light of reason demands. Indeed, as Thomas Huxley and William Kingdon Clifford were to say again in the nineteenth century, Descartes held that we have a duty to bring judgment under this rule. Failure to do so involves not merely error but sin.

Third, we come to a nest of problems having to do with our knowledge of the external world. We have mentioned the famous passage in which Descartes examines a piece of wax in order to find what constitutes the essence of matter. He observed that the sensible qualities which we most readily believe to be in matter are not part of the nature of wax, as are such attributes as extension, figure, and mobility, which are not properly sensible but intelligible. Comparing the two ways of thinking about things in nature, Descartes concludes (following the lead of Galileo) that by the senses we have only the most confused notions of matter—they arise from the influence upon the mind of the body to which it is united rather than from the mind's apprehension by its own light of the necessary attributes of being. It is by the latter that we obtain true knowledge of nature, which henceforth is seen to possess only those qualities which can be described in mathematical terms. In other words, the physical world has to be envisaged as a vast, complicated machine—but not (let us remind ourselves) the way our senses view machines, rather the way they are viewed on the drawing-board and in the mind of the engineer.

So far reason leads us, Descartes says. If we are correct in supposing that there is a material world, its nature must be as classic mechanics conceives it. But it does not follow that a material world actually exists. It is conceivable that each time I receive and recognize the idea of a body, God himself impresses it upon my mind. Nothing in the idea of matter is inconsistent with its non-existence. All that I can discover which inclines me to assent to its existence is an instinctive impulse such as attaches to all our sense perceptions: and this, of course, is no reason.

Descartes' only recourse is to appeal to the good faith of God. Thus, he writes that if God were the cause of our ideas of matter, he would undoubtedly have given us the means of knowing that this is the case, for he is no deceiver. In granting us free wills, he has, indeed, opened the door to falsity and error: but he has not permitted any error without placing within our reach the means of avoiding it, or, at least, correcting it once it has been made. The claims of our sense-images, which reason disproves, is an example. But no analysis disproves the natural inclination which we have to be-

391

lieve that corporeal objects do exist. Hence, we are justified in affirming, along with the existence of finite mind (one's own) and infinite Being, the actuality of the material world. (Apparently, for Descartes, the existence of other minds is never more than an inference.)

The upshot of the *Meditations* is, then, to replace the common sense picture of nature with one that is amenable to rational investigation. The new cosmology which was being shaped by men such as Kepler, Galileo, William Gilbert and others rested upon fundamental assumptions which were not clear to the investigators themselves. It was the task of Descartes to give these principles their classic formulation.

LEVIATHAN

Author: Thomas Hobbes (1588-1679)
Type of work: Political philosophy
First published: 1651

PRINCIPAL IDEAS ADVANCED

A man is a group of material particles in motion.

The state—the great Leviathan—is an artificial man in which sovereignty is the soul, officers the joints, rewards and punishments the nerves, wealth its strength, safety its business, counselors its memory, equity and law its reason and will, peace its health, sedition its sickness, and civil war its death.

Reasoning is the manipulation of names; truth is the correct ordering of names.

Desire is motion toward an object, and aversion is motion away; the good and bad are understood by reference to desire and aversion.

In a state of nature there is a war of every man against every man; to secure peace men make contracts establishing a sovereign power who is not subject to civil law since by his will he creates law.

Of the three forms of sovereignty, monarchy, aristocracy, and democracy, monarchy is the most effective in securing peace.

The *Leviathan* (*Leviathan, or the Matter, Form, and Power of a Commonwealth, Ecclesiastical and Civil*) is primarily a treatise on the philosophy of politics. It also contains important discussions, some brief, some extended, on metaphysics, epistemology, psychology, language, ethics, and religion. Hobbes develops his views from a metaphysics of materialism and a mechanical analyogy in which everything is a particle or set of particles moving in accordance with laws. Though he was at one time secretary to Francis Bacon, English philosopher and essayist, his inspiration came from Galileo Galilei, Italian mathematician and physicist. Hobbes was unusual in being an early

392

empiricist who recognized the importance of mathematics.

In the *Leviathan* the realism of Niccolò Machiavelli, Florentine man of affairs and political writer, the emphasis on sovereignty of Jean Bodin, French legalist and politician, and the attempt of Hugo Grotius, Dutch jurist, to modernize the conception of natural law by relating it to mathematics and the new science are combined and developed with great originality, clarity, and flair for pungent statement to constitute one of the masterpieces of political philosophy.

Hobbes divides all knowledge into two classes, Natural Philosophy and Civil Philosophy. The former is the basis for the latter and consists in turn of two parts, First Philosophy, comprising laws of particles in general such as inertia, causation, and identity; and Physics, which deals with the qualities of particles. These particles, singly or in combination, may be permanent or transient, celestial or terrestrial, with or without sense, with or without speech. A man is a group of particles that is permanent, terrestrial, sensible, and loquacious. Physics contains not only optics and music, which are the sciences of vision and hearing in general, but also ethics, which is the science of the passions of men, poetry, rhetoric, logic, and equity. The four last are respectively the study of man's use of speech in elevated expression, in persuading, reasoning, and contracting. Civil Philosophy deals with the rights and duties of the sovereign or of subjects.

Hobbes makes extensive use of the mechanical model in constructing his system. Life is motion. Therefore, machines have artificial life. The heart is a spring, the nerves are strings, the joints are wheels giving motion to the whole body. The commonwealth is an artificial man in which sovereignty is the soul, officers are the joints, rewards and punishments are the nerves, wealth is its strength, and safety is its business; counselors are its memory, equity and law are reason and will, peace is its health, sedition is its sickness, and civil war is its death. The covenants by which it comes into being are the counterpart of the fiat of creation.

It is apparent that the model is highly oversimplified. This is, in fact, the basis for much of the force it carries. Hobbes does not hesitate to ignore the model if ill-suited to his purpose, as it is in many cases where he has to deal with the details of psychology, religion, and social and political relations.

The simplest motion in human bodies is sensation, caused by the impact of some particle upon a sense organ. When sensations are slowed by the interference of others they become imagination or memory. Imagination in sleep is dreaming. Imagination raised by words is understanding and is common to man and beast.

Ideas ("phantasms" for Hobbes) proceed in accordance with laws of association or of self-interest, as in calculating the means to a desired end. Anything we imagine or think is finite. Any apparent conception of something infinite is only an awareness of an inability to imagine a bound. The name of God, for example, is used that we may honor him, not that we may conceive of him.

Hobbes considered speech the most noble of all inventions. It distinguishes man from beast. It consists in the motion of names and their connections. It is a necessary condition of society, contract, commonwealth, and peace. It is essential to acquiring art, to counseling and instructing, and to expressing purpose. It is correspondingly abused in ambiguity, metaphor, and deception.

When a man manipulates names in accordance with the laws of truth, definition, and thought he is reasoning. Truth is the correct ordering of names; for example, connecting by affirmation two names that signify the same thing. Error in general statements is self-contradiction. Definition is stating what names signify. Inconsistent names, such as "incorporeal substance" signify nothing and are mere sounds. The laws of thought are the laws of mathematics, exemplified best in geometry, generalized to apply to all names. Reasoning is carried on properly when we begin with definition and move from one consequence to the next. Reasoning is therefore a kind of calculating with names. According to Hobbes everything named is particular but a general name can be imposed on a number of things that are similar. He anticipated fundamental distinctions of Hume, Scotch philosopher and skeptic, and later empiricists in maintaining that conclusions reached by reasoning are always conditional.

Hobbes extended the mechanical model in his discussion of the passions by holding that endeavor begins in the motions of imagination. Desire, which is the same as love, is motion toward an object which is therefore called "good." Aversion, which is the same as hate, is motion away from an object which is therefore called "bad." Other passions are definable in terms of these two. Fear is aversion with the belief that the object will hurt; courage is

aversion with the hope of avoiding hurt. Anger is sudden courage. Religion, a particularly important passion, is publicly allowed fear of invisible powers. When the fear is not publicly allowed, it is superstition. The whole sum of desires and aversions and their modifications carried on until the thing in question is either done or considered impossible is deliberation. In deliberation, the last appetite or aversion immediately preceding action is will. In searching for truth the last opinion is judgment.

Since desires are endless, happiness is not a static condition but a process of satisfying desires. All motivation is egoistic. Man's basic desire is for power which, like all other desires, ends only in death.

Hobbes completes the foundations for the development of his political theory with an analysis of religion. It is invented by men because of their belief in spirits, their ignorance of causes, and their devotion to what they fear. This explains why the first legislators among the gentiles always claimed that their precepts came from God or some other spirit, and how priests have been able to use religion for selfish purposes. Religion dissolves when its founders or leaders are thought to lack wisdom, sincerity, or love.

Hobbes develops his political theory proper in terms of the time-honored concepts of equality, the state of nature, natural law, natural rights, contract, sovereignty, and justice. In his hands, however, they receive treatment that is very different from his predecessors, the Greeks, St. Thomas Aquinas, Jean Bodin, and Hugo Grotius, as well as from his successors, John Locke, English philosopher, and his followers in the liberal tradition.

Machiavelli's views on egoism and the need for absolute power in the sovereign anticipated Hobbes, but were not worked out in detail as a general political philosophy.

In their natural state, according to Hobbes, men are approximately equal in strength, mental capacity, and experience, and everyone has an equal right to everything. If they were without government the conflict arising from their desires, their distrust, and ambition would lead to a state of war of every man against every man. In it there would be no property, no justice or injustice, and life would be "solitary, poor, nasty, brutish and short." Fortunately, both passion—in the form of fear of death, desire for a long and reasonably pleasant life, and hope of achieving it—and reason—in the form of knowledge of the articles of peace in the form of the laws of nature—combine to provide a basis for the establishment of civil society and escape from universal strife.

The first law of nature is to seek the peace and follow it. The second, a necessary means to the first, is *that a man be willing, when others are so too, as farre-forth as for Peace and defence of himself he shall think it necessary, to lay down this* [natural] *right to all things; and be contented with so much liberty against other men as he would allow other men against himselfe.*" This is to be done by making contracts with others. A necessary condition for the operation of the second law of nature is that men perform their contracts, which is the third law of nature. For contracts to be valid it is necessary, in turn, that a sovereign power be established who will make it more painful to commit injustice, which is the breaking of a contract, than to live justly, which is the keeping of contracts. Contracts without the sword, Hobbes reminds us, are only words which guarantee no security. The first three laws of nature, then, combined with the nature of man as a complex set of particles moving in accordance with various sets of laws—not only strictly mechanical laws, but also what might be called egoistic and hedonistic laws—are the source of society, sovereignty, and justice.

Further laws of nature, subordinate to the first three, or special cases, though not specified as such by Hobbes, require the practice of fidelity, gratitude, courtesy, forbearance, fairness, justice, equity, the recognition of natural equality, and the avoidance of contumely, pride, and arrogance. The whole doctrine of natural law, called by Hobbes a "deduction," can be summarized in the general law: do not unto another what you would not want him to do to you. Hobbes considers these laws of nature "eternal and immutable," because breaking them can never preserve the peace. The science of laws is true moral philosophy. He concludes this discussion of natural law with a remark whose significance has usually been ignored, but which must be appreciated if Parts III and IV of the *Leviathan* are to be understood. These "laws," so far, are not properly named; they are only theorems, binding to be sure, *in foro interno*, that is, to a desire they should be effective; but not *in foro externo*, that is, to putting them into practice. If, however, it can be shown that they are delivered in the word of God, who by right commands in all things, then they are properly called laws and are in fact binding.

In working out the details of the second and third laws of nature Hobbes maintains that to achieve peace, contentment, and security it is necessary that men agree with one another to confer their power upon a man or group of men of whose acts each man, even a member of a dissenting minority, will regard himself the original author. "This is the Generation of that great LEVIATHAN or rather (to speak more reverently) of that *Mortal God*, to which wee owe under the *Immortal God* our peace and Defence." We may consequently define a commonwealth as *"One Person, of whose Acts a great multitude, by mutuall Covenants one with another, have made themselves every one the Author, to the end he may use the strength and means of them all, as he shall think expedient, for their Peace and Common Defence."* This person is sovereign. All others are subjects.

The covenant generating the sovereign is not between the sovereign and the subjects, but only between subjects that they will obey whatever ruling power the majority may establish. The covenant may be explicit, actually written, or it may be implicit, for example, by remaining in a conquered country. The covenant is an agreement to refrain from interfering with the sovereign's exercise of his right to everything. The concept of consent is not present, at least not in the sense it carried later with Locke. Making the covenant is the one political act of subjects. Their proper role is to obey as long as the sovereign is able to protect them, unless he should order them to kill, wound, or maim themselves or to answer questions about a crime they may have committed. Even these are not restrictions of the sovereignty of the ruler, but only liberties that subjects retain under the laws of nature. Politically and legally, in Hobbes's system, there is and can be no legal limitation on sovereignty. There is no right of rebellion, for example, since the sovereign is not bound by any contract, not having made one. Subjects have only the legal rights granted them by the sovereign. The sovereign is the only legislator; he is not subject to civil law and his will—not long usage—gives authority to law.

More specifically, the sovereign must have the power to censor all expression of opinion, to allocate private property, to determine what is good or evil, lawful or unlawful, to judge all cases, to make war or peace, to choose the officers of the commonwealth, to administer rewards and punishment, to decide all moral or religious questions, and to prescribe how God is to be worshiped.

There are, says Hobbes, only three forms which sovereignty may take, monarchy, aristocracy, and democracy. Other apparent forms merely reflect attitudes. For example, if someone dislikes monarchy, then he calls it tyranny. Although his arguments would support any absolutism, Hobbes shows a strong preference for monarchy in claiming that it is the best means of effecting peace. The interests of the monarch and his subjects are the same. What is good for the monarch is good for the people. He is rich, glorious, or secure if they are, and not if they are not. He will have fewer favorites than an assembly. He can receive better advice in private than any assembly. There will be no argument and disagreement in making decisions and they will stand more firm. Divisive factionalism and the consequent danger of civil war will not arise. Hobbes admits that monarchy has some problems about succession but says they can be met by following the will of the sovereign, custom, or lineage.

Hobbes maintains that a commonwealth established by acquisition in acts of force or violence differs from one established by institution, peaceably and with something approaching explicit covenant, only in having its sovereignty based upon fear of the sovereign rather than upon mutual fear of the subjects.

No matter how established or what its form, however, there are certain causes of dissolution which Hobbes warns must be avoided: insufficient power in the sovereign to maintain peace, permitting subjects to judge what is good or evil, considering violation of individual conscience a sin, considering supernatural inspiration superior to reason, considering the sovereign subject to civil law, permitting subjects absolute property rights, dividing sovereign power, regarding tyrannicide as lawful, permitting the reading of democratic books, believing there are two kingdoms, spiritual and civil.

The all-important task of showing that there are not two different kingdoms and at the same time showing that the theorems of the first two Parts of the *Leviathan* are in fact laws and as such binding obligations, are Hobbes's main points in discussing the nature of a Christian commonwealth. The essential mark of a Christian is obedience to God's law. God's authority as lawgiver derives from his power. His laws, which are the natural laws, are promulgated by natural reason, revelation, and prophecy. In the first two Parts of the *Leviathan* knowledge of natural laws and their implications have been found out by reason. Laws are, therefore, only conditional theorems. To be shown to be unconditional laws they must be shown to be the will of God. In fact, Hobbes argues, using extensive quotation and acute, though one-sided, analysis of terms in Scripture and in common speech, all theorems of reasoning about the conduct of men seeking happiness in peace are to be found in Scripture. He concludes that there is no difference between natural law known by reason and revealed or prophetic law. What is law, therefore, depends upon what is Scripture.

Scripture, Hobbes argues, again with extensive quotation, analysis, and interpretation, is what is accepted as Scripture in a commonwealth and is nothing apart from its interpretation. If it is interpreted by conscience, we have competition and a return to the state of nature with its war made fiercer by religious conviction and self-righteousness. All the same arguments for commonwealth apply in particular, therefore, more strongly to the generation of a Christian commonwealth. This is a civil society of Christian subjects under a Christian sovereign. There is no question of opposition between church and state because there is no distinction between them. There are not two laws, ecclesiastical and civil —only civil. There is no universal church since there is no power on earth to which all commonwealths are subject. Consequently, obedience to civil law is necessary for man's admission into heaven. Even if a sovereign is not Christian, it is still an obligation and law for a Christian to obey him, since those who do not obey break the laws of God.

When these truths are obfuscated by misinterpretation of Scripture, demon-

397

ology, or vain philosophy then, says Hobbes, a kingdom of darkness arises. He applies, in some detail, the test of asking, "Who benefits?" to a number of doctrines in each category and concludes that the Presbyterian and Roman clergy, particularly the Popes, are the authors of this darkness, for they gain temporal power from its existence. Hobbes adds that the errors from which the darkness arises are to be avoided, in general, by a careful reading of the *Leviathan*. Some of the darkness arising from vain philosophy, for example, can be remedied by more careful attention to Hobbes's doctrines of language. These will show that the function of the copula can be replaced by the juxtaposition and ordering of words, thus removing the darkness that arises from the reification of "esse" in its counterparts "entity" and "essence." These words, says Hobbes, are not names of anything, only signs by which we make known what we consider to be consequences of a name. Infinitives and participles similarly are not names of anything. When men understand these and other facts about language they can no longer be deluded by mistaken interpretations of Scripture, demonology, or vain philosophy. In this instance they will no longer be deluded by the doctrine of separated essence and consequently will not be frightened into disobeying their sovereign.

There are flaws in Hobbes's philosophy. He is often crude in his vigor, achieving a logical solution of a problem by omitting recalcitrant details. His errors, however, are usually due to oversimplification, not to being muddle-headed, superstitious, or unclear.

No matter how wrong, he is never unintelligible. Moreover, he could not in his own day, and cannot now, be ignored. Puritans and Cavaliers could both condemn him but both Cromwell and Charles II could draw on his doctrines. Abraham Lincoln appealed to his doctrines of covenant and unity of the sovereign power to justify the use of force in dealing with secession.

His philosophy, in its outline, development, method, and logic, very strongly affected the later developments of political and ethical thought. It is doubtful that anyone has stated so strongly the case for political authority or more strongly supported the thesis that unity, not consent, is the basis of government, and conformity to the sovereign will is its strength. His influence is clearly apparent in the doctrines of sovereignty and civil law formulated by John Austin, English writer on jurisprudence. His methods of argument about the nature of law prepared the way for Jeremy Bentham, English ethical and social philosopher, and the movement for scientific legislation based on pleasure, pain, and self-interest. In moral philosophy it is not too much to say that the subsequent history of ethics would not have been the same without Hobbes. Reactions by Richard Cumberland, British moralist and quasi-rationalist, and the Cambridge Platonists on the one hand, and by Lord Shaftesbury, English essayist, and Francis Hutcheson, British moralist and empiricist, on the other, developed into the eighteenth century opposition between reason and sentiment which is reflected in many of the problems occupying moral philosophers in the twentieth century.

DE CORPORE

Author: Thomas Hobbes (1588-1679)
Type of work: Philosophy of philosophy, metaphysics
First published: 1655 (Part I of *Elementa philosophiae*)

PRINCIPAL IDEAS ADVANCED

The subject matter of philosophy is bodies in motion.

Philosophy is the knowledge of effects acquired by ratiocination from the knowledge of causes, and of causes from the knowledge of effects.

Ratiocination is a kind of computation, the adding and subtracting of notions.

Our knowledge is derived from our definitions and theorems or from our sense experience.

Bodies have no dependence upon thought.

Philosophy, to Hobbes, is simply science. "Philosophy" is defined as *"such knowledge of effects or appearances, as we acquire by true ratiocination from the knowledge we have first of their causes or generation: And again, of such causes or generations as may be from knowing first their effects."* Since God has no cause, and what is known by revelation is not acquired by ratiocination, theology is excluded from philosophy by definition. All that is left to be the subject matter of philosophy is "every body of which we can conceive any generation, and which we may, by any consideration thereof, compare with other bodies, or which is capable of composition and resolution; that is to say, every body of whose generation or properties we can have any knowledge." There are two kinds of bodies, "one whereof being the work of nature, is called a *natural body,* the other is called a *commonwealth,* and is made by the wills and agreement of men." The study of the former is natural philosophy, that of the latter civil philosophy. But ethics, "which treats of men's dispositions and manners," is prerequisite to civil phi-

losophy. There are in consequence three main divisions of philosophy. The *Elements of Philosophy,* which Hobbes projected as the most comprehensive and systematic of his works, was in three volumes corresponding to this division: Part I, *On Body;* Part II, *On Man;* and Part III, *On the Citizen.* Part III was written first, and Part II last.

"The end of knowledge is power," Hobbes declares, following Bacon. The usefulness of natural philosophy lies ultimately in its technological applications, "but the utility of moral and civil philosophy is to be estimated, not so much by the commodities we have by knowing these sciences, as by the calamities we receive from not knowing them." The chief of these is war, of which civil war, the worst kind, comes from the "not knowing of civil duties."

Because Hobbes conceived of *De corpore* not as a self-contained work but as the first division of a comprehensive treatise, he begins with a discussion of philosophy in general.

According to Hobbes, philosophy is ratiocination about causes and effects,

399

and by *ratiocination* Hobbes meant *computation*; that is, adding and subtracting of notions. Magnitudes, bodies, motions, times, proportions, and degrees of quality are computables in an obvious sense, since they can be represented numerically. Hobbes extends the idea of computation to conceptions, speech, and names: for example, "man" is the sum of "body, animated, rational. . . ." It must be emphasized that it is only the *notion* that is thus a sum; a particular man is also a sum, but of arms, legs, and so forth. In modern parlance, "body," "animated," and "rational" are determinables (Hobbes calls them *universals*), while "this body," "this animated thing," (which Hobbes calls *particulars*) are determinates. Only determinates exist; the universe consists of particular bodies.

Hobbes proceeds to develop these conceptions into what is in effect a short textbook of semantics and formal logic. These chapters contain little that is distinctively Hobbesian. He concludes with an important section on scientific method. For Hobbes, method *"is the shortest way of finding out effects by their known causes, or of causes by their known effects."* There are two kinds of methods, corresponding to the fundamental operations of addition and subtraction. One is compositive, or synthetical. By this method one is able to proceed from first principles (which are definitions) to a knowledge of some complex thing. Geometry is entirely synthetical, and so is syllogistic reasoning. The other method is resolutive, or analytical. Here we attain understanding of a thing by resolving the notion into its constituent universals the causes of

which are plain, embodied in first principles.

Hobbes's descriptions of these two methods are obscure, and his examples do not help much. But his conceptions of scientific method can be paraphrased in this way: science is a body of organized knowledge, for which geometry provides both the model and the starting point. In geometry we begin with axioms, which according to Hobbes are definitions. We then deduce the consequences of these definitions; that is, we "add" them, in Hobbes's broad sense of addition. Now geometry is, for Hobbes, the most abstract science of *motion*; he always thinks of a line, for instance, as the path of a moving point, not as a given (static) extension. Hence, geometry is closely related to science of mechanics, though the latter science requires some additional principles—definitions—of force, of quantity of matter, and of other concepts not part of traditional geometry. As there is nothing in the world but matter in motion, if we know the laws of motion, science is then *complete* as far as its theoretical principles are concerned. The sciences of man and his behavior ("ethics") and society ("politics") are in theory only further applications of mechanics to particular groups of bodies. Ideally, science from geometry to politics, if completed, would be *presented* in a deductive system, in which the progress from definitions to conclusions would be "synthetical."

Hobbes was well aware, though, that the discoveries which advance science are not (for the most part) made in this way. The crucial points come in the adoption of "definitions." Since everything is to be deducible from the definitions, and science must give causal explanations, *the definitions must include causes.* So the central question of scientific method becomes one of securing adequate definitions. *These* definitions cannot, of course, be merely arbitrary; we are not at liberty to define force, or quantity of matter, in any way we like. Wherever the concept we are dealing with is complex, we must *analyze* it *correctly.* The way to tell whether a proposed analysis is correct is to deduce (by means of the "synthetical method") the consequences of our tentative definition. These deductions yield certain *theorems* which ought to be descriptions of what happens in certain circumstances. By *observation* we find out whether what, according to our definitions, ought to happen does happen. If so, well and good; if not, we must try again.

Thus Hobbes's "definitions" turn out to be what are now called *hypotheses,* and this method, which Hobbes calls the "combined synthetical and analytical," is in fact the hypothetico-deductive method of science. Hobbes was the first philosopher to grasp the essentials of this very important conception.

So much for ideally complete science. It is not much help in practical affairs. We cannot in practice deduce the principles of psychology and sociology from the laws of motion. Nor does Hobbes recommend that we wait until the science of motion is completed before we begin the social sciences. The impasse is to be broken by an application of the "analytical method" to produce principles (axioms) of human behavior. (Further treatment of these subjects is to be found in Hobbes's political writings.)

Finding causes is the crux of all science. A cause is "the sum or aggregate of all such accidents [characteristics], both in the agents and the patient, as concur to the producing of the effect propounded; all which existing together, it cannot be understood but that the effect existeth with them; or that it can possibly exist if any one of them be absent." In other words, the cause of anything is the necessary and sufficient condition of its production. According to Hobbes, "in the searching out of causes, there is need partly of the analytical, and partly of the synthetical method; of the analytical, to conceive how circumstances conduce severally to the production of effects; and of the synthetical, for the adding together and compounding of what they can effect singly by themselves." In the subsequent discussion it becomes clear that Hobbes grasps the notions later formulated by Mill as the canons of agreement and difference; but his philosophy is superior to Mill's (as well as to Bacon's) in that in emphasizing the "need of the analytical method" he is in effect recognizing the indispensability, for scientific *discovery,* of fruitful "working hypotheses."

Hobbes regarded certain concepts in philosophy as basic, simple, and unanalyzable. We cannot therefore give causal definitions of them. However, clarity about them is essential and is to be achieved by stating definitions which *explicate* them for "by speech as short as may be, we raise in the mind of the hearer perfect and clear ideas or conceptions of the things named." Such are place, time, body, accident. motion, power.

Hobbes asks the reader to suppose all things annihilated, save one philosopher. What would be left for him to "ratiocinate" about? His memories, Hobbes tells us. He could think about those just as if nothing had happened. Indeed, this is what is actually done here and now: "For when we calculate the magnitude and motions of heaven or earth, we do not ascend into heaven that we may divide it into parts, or measure the motions thereof, but we do it sitting still in our closets or in the dark." The memory of just one thing as having existed outside the mind would yield the philosopher the conception of space; hence "space" is defined as *the phantasm of a thing existing without the mind simply.* Likewise *time* is *"the phantasm of before and after in motion."* (What Hobbes had in mind in calling space and time "phantasms" is not entirely clear, except that he wanted to deny that they were either bodies or accidents of bodies. Perhaps he meant that our concept of space is an idea concerning "where there could be a body." Hobbes held that in fact there is no vacuum, though he denied that vacuum is inconceivable.) Hobbes's definition of spatial and temporal infinity is very good; he writes that *"infinite in power* is that space or time, in which a greater number of the said paces or hours may be assigned, than any number that can be given." He argues, correctly, that to say that space is infinite does not commit one to the view that there must exist two places separated by an infinite distance; it entails only the idea that however great a distance separates two places, there are other places more distant still. (Kant never grasped this point.)

Suppose now that one additional thing were created. Under these circumstances, there would be one thing *independent of the philosopher's mind.* Hence *"a body is that which, having no dependence upon our thought, is coincident or coextended with some part of space."* It is important to take this definition strictly and not read into it more than Hobbes intended. If the body in question were (say) a tomato, all that would be "out there" would be an independent something occupying a certain region of space. (How a "phantasm" can be occupied by something independent of the mind is not explained.) Such characteristics as the redness, juiciness, and taste of the tomato are not parts or constituents of the body but *accidents,* an accident being "that faculty of any body, by which it works in us a conception of itself," or "the manner of our conception of body." Redness is not in blood as blood is in a bloody cloth.

"Bodies are things, and not generated; accidents are generated, and not things." Any accident of a body can be destroyed, without the body's being destroyed. The essence or form is only the accident in virtue of which a name is given to a certain kind of body.

All mutation is motion. (Though Hobbes may be right about this, his proof of the proposition is fallacious.) Since every motion has a cause which determines it to be the motion it is, everything is determined, and "contingency" is only a subjective notion, signifying our ignorance. Everything that is possible will, at some time or other, come to pass. (Hobbes errs here in company with St. Thomas Aquinas.) All causation is efficient causation. So-called "formal causes" or essences are only causes of our knowledge, while "final causes," which occur only in beings endowed with sense

402

and will, are likewise really efficient causes.

Hobbes has an astute section on the "principle of individuation," which is the criterion of the identity of anything. He shows that neither matter, nor form, nor aggregate of accidents will do as a *general* criterion of identity. The solution is pragmatic: "We must consider by what name anything is called, when we inquire concerning the *identity* of it. . . . That man will be always the same, whose actions and thoughts proceed all from the same beginning of motion, namely, that which was in his generation; and that will be the same river which flows from one and the same fountain, whether the same water or other water, or something else than water, flow from thence." (Hume's philosophy would have been very different if he had taken this section to heart.)

In Part III, concerning the proportions of motions, Hobbes endeavors to work out, in some detail, the principles of the science of mechanics, as he had learned it from Galileo. The discussion is marred by the notorious "squaring of the circle," which led to the long and unseemly controversy with John Wallis, Professor of Mathematics at Oxford. Mainly on this account, scholars have paid little attention to this part of Hobbes's work. This is unfortunate, for the discussion contains statements (more or less) of all three of Newton's laws of motion, as well as anticipations of the differential and integral calculus.

In Part IV, "Physics, or the Phenomena of Nature," Hobbes writes, "I now enter upon the other part; which is the finding out by the appearances or effects of nature, which we know by sense, some ways and means by which they may be, I do

not say they are, generated." The first chapter of this part, "Of Sense and Animal Motion," is the only one of philosophical interest. In it Hobbes presents his theory of perception.

"Of all the phenomena or appearances which are near us, the most admirable is apparition itself . . . ; namely, that some natural bodies have in themselves the patterns almost of all things, and others of none at all." We are to find out the causes "of those ideas and phantasms which are perpetually generated within us whilst we make use of our senses." Now, since all change is motion of bodies, it follows that "sense, in the sentient, can be nothing else but motion in some of the internal parts of the sentient; and the parts so moved are parts of the organs of sense." When we look at an object, what happens is that motion from its surface is communicated through the medium to the eye. The pressure thereon is communicated through the humors and retina to the optic nerve and the brain. Everywhere in the line of propagation the actions produce reactions, opposite in direction; the last of these reactions in the brain is the phantasm. Since this reaction is an "endeavour" *out*ward, the object *appears* to us to be outside us, not inside (where the physical occurrence that *is* the perception *really* occurs). Hearing is similarly explained, while the three non-distance senses are easily accommodated to this type of theory. (But Hobbes, strangely, considers and rejects explanation of odors by "effluvia.")

Hobbes defines "sense" as *"a phantasm, made by the reaction and endeavour outwards in the organ of sense, caused by an endeavour inwards from the object, remaining for some time more or less."* By the "remaining for some time" phrase Hobbes attempted to counter the objection that according to his mechanical theory even stones should have sensations, since they react to pressure. They have no memories, and sensation without memory would be in effect no sensation at all! Imagination is "decaying sense." The train of ideas in the mind is not random, but governed by laws of association. (These principles, which are the foundations of associationist psychology, were developed further in *Leviathan* in 1651.) Appetite and aversion are the first endeavors of animal motion. Deliberation is an oscillation between appetite and aversion; the last appetite in deliberation is the "will," which is subject to laws. "And therefore such a liberty as is free from necessity, is not to be found in the will either of men or beasts. But if by liberty we understand the faculty or power, not of willing, but of doing what they will, then certainly that liberty is to be allowed to both."

The book dies out, rather than concludes, in a miscellany of attempts at explaining various interesting natural phenomena. Such was not Hobbes's forte. His strong points were intelligent receptiveness to the new scientific thought of his day and the ability, unhampered by prejudice or sentimentality, to grasp the broad philosophical implications of it. He has received due recognition as the author of the first scientific social philosophy. That he was also, and preëminently, the first thinker to break completely with the Middle Ages in pure philosophy and philosophy of science, has hitherto not been adequately acknowledged.

SYNTAGMA PHILOSOPHICUM

Author: Pierre Gassendi (1592-1655)
Type of work: Logic, epistemology, philosophy of nature, ethics
First published: 1658

PRINCIPAL IDEAS ADVANCED

Between skepticism and dogmatism there is a third possibility: constructive skepticism, the theory that although certain knowledge of nature is not possible, a useful but limited type of knowledge is within our grasp.

By cautious evaluation of our sense experience we can reach conclusions which can be tested by future experience.

Epicurus was correct in maintaining that the universe is composed of atoms moving in empty space; atoms are solid, with figure, weight, and extension; changes in nature are the result of collisions of the downward coursing atoms.

The primary cause of atomic motion is God; he is the great designer of the universe.

Unlike the animal soul, which is wholly corporeal, the human soul is only partly corporeal or material; the rational part of the soul is immaterial, derived from God, and immortal.

Our ideas are not innate, but come either from the senses or from intellectual activity.

Pierre Gassendi was one of the foremost philosophers and scientists of the early seventeenth century. He was the most important rival and critic of René Descartes, and he had a crucial role in the revival of the ideas of the ancient Greek skeptics and atomists. Gassendi began his intellectual career as a skeptic, a stanch follower of Sextus Empiricus, a Greek writer of the third century, and of the French essayist Michel de Montaigne. Gradually he mitigated his skepticism in the face of the scientific revolution of the time, in which he played a major role, and he adopted more and more of a materialistic explanation of the world based on the ancient theory of Epicurus. Though a prominent Catholic priest of his day, Gassendi developed one of the first completely mechanistic and materialistic theories of modern times.

The *Syntagma philosophicum*, the most complete exposition of his mature views, was published only after his death. The work is enormous, containing sixteen hundred folio pages, printed in double columns. It is divided into three general sections, the first dealing with logic and theory of knowledge, the second with the natural world, and the third with ethics. Because of his skepticism, Gassendi did not regard metaphysics as a serious subject and so he omitted it entirely from his book.

At the outset, Gassendi seeks to establish a way to knowledge that is between the doubts of the skeptics and the complete assurances of the dogmatists. Neither the view that we can

know nothing nor the view that we can know everything is tenable. The skeptics admit that we can know how nature appears to us. But they deny that we can know more than this. The dogmatists, on the other hand, claim that we can know the real natures of things which are not apparent to us. This, Gassendi contends, is exaggerating the power of the human mind. However, between skepticism and dogmatism there is a third possibility, which has been called "constructive or mitigated skepticism," an acceptance of the thesis that although in a fundamental sense we cannot gain certain knowledge of the nature of reality, we can nevertheless gain a type of knowledge which we need have no reason to doubt, and which will suffice to enable us to understand the world.

This limited knowledge is obtained first by accepting what is obvious to us, our sense experience, plus certain obvious conclusions from it, such as that things exist. Signs found in sense experience enable us to know about other matters not immediately obvious to the senses. The ancient Greek skeptics had admitted that, on the basis of the constant conjunctions found in experience, we could judge that certain things temporarily not apparent to us were the case, such as when we see smoke, we can judge that there is a fire. In addition, we are also able to judge, by means of our reasoning ability, that particular sense experiences indicate that the world has certain features, even though we are never able to perceive these features. Thus, we can judge from the appearance of sweat on the skin that it has pores. Long before the invention of the telescope, Democritus was able to judge from the white color of the Milky Way that it is composed of an innumerable quantity of stars. This type of reasoning, which leads us to knowledge about the world, is based upon a careful and cautious evaluation of our sense information by our reason, plus inferences, made from this information, based on careful reasoning and on certain general principles that we have learned from experience. The conclusions we reach in this way about the nature of the world are beyond doubt, and are ultimately evaluated in terms of future information gained from experience (as in the case of the Milky Way) and by the usefulness of these conclusions in explaining the course of our experience. We do not discover the absolute truth in this way, but only a faint shadow of it. This faint shadow will turn out to be the most satisfactory scientific explanation that can be given of experience in terms of the hypothesis (confirmed by experience and reasoning) that the world is composed of atoms in motion.

In terms of this theory of knowledge, Gassendi examines various logical systems, ancient and modern, in order to state the best method for attaining limited knowledge. Many of the classical devices, Gassendi finds, are practically useless. The philosophies of Francis Bacon and Descartes have serious defects, Gassendi claims. Our senses can err, and we cannot, no matter what we do, attain real knowledge of the inner nature of things. But a logical method that is based upon sense information carefully analyzed and upon general, unquestionable principles gained from experience and careful reasoning, constantly checked and verified, can serve as the instrument for attaining what truth is possible.

According to Gassendi, what we can know about the world consists of a modified form of the atomism of Epicurus, modified in terms of the science of the time and the religious principles Gassendi maintained that he accepted. (Whether Gassendi was a sincere Christian has been, and still is, debated among scholars.) After surveying and criticizing the view of various philosophers about the nature of the world, Gassendi offers as the most probable theory (but not as the necessarily true one) the view that the actual components of the universe are indivisible atoms, moving in empty space. Appealing to the recent findings of scientists such as Evangelista Torricelli and Blaise Pascal, Gassendi insists that the essential feature of atoms is solidity. In addition, they have the properties of extension, figure, and weight. The atoms vary in shape and size. They are conceived of as having the kinds of configurations found in ordinary experience, like those of wagon wheels and houses, rather than mathematically describable sizes and shapes. (Gassendi had a distrust of those who maintained that nature was to be described in mathematical terms, since he felt that they were probably advocating some type of Platonic metaphysical theory about the nature of reality.)

God has created the atoms and given them an impulse to move downward. They move at different rates of speed, and for this reason they collide with one another. The collisions change the courses of the atoms, causing still further collisions, and so on. The various changes that take place in the world, both on the apparent and on the nonapparent level, can be accounted for by the movements of the atoms, their collisions, and their combinations. Thus, the real world is conceived as a mechanism made up of small moving parts, the atoms. The qualities and movements of the atoms suffice to account for changes in the real world and the way in which the world appears to us. The qualities that we perceive, the colors, sounds, tastes, smells, and so on (the so-called "secondary qualities") are not actually properties of real objects. Instead, they are the ways we perceive various atomic movements when they affect our sense organs.

Gassendi begins to modify his Epicurean theory when he discusses the cause of the movement of the atoms. He accepts the Scholastic thesis that the primary cause of motion is God. The evidence that God exists is the almost universal natural belief in a deity, and the conclusion drawn from observing the order in the universe, namely, that there must be an Orderer or Designer of the world. The fact that there are some atheists is dismissed by Gassendi as similar to the existence of blind people. The fact that a few people lack the normal, natural human faculties and beliefs is no reason to doubt the reliability of the faculties and beliefs of the rest of mankind. Both the senses and our reasoning ability give us an adequate basis for accepting the view that there is a God. Our conception of God is that of an omniscient and omnipotent Being who is all-wise and all-good. He is the author and providential guide and cause of everything that exists and everything that happens in the world.

Gassendi specifically rejects Epicurus' view that everything can be explained and accounted for solely in terms of the atoms and their motions. Where, he asks, do the atoms come from, and what makes them move? Further, if the world were produced only by "the fortuitous concourse of atoms," why is it that the atoms never, by themselves, make a house, or a temple, or a book? Each of these seems to require a designer to organize the atoms in a specific way, and so does the universe in general.

If God is the primary cause of motion, the secondary cause is the atoms themselves through their collisions. God, having created the atoms and implanted in them their downward motions, allows them to move one another through contact. The laws of atomic movements will provide the bases for scientific explanations of all natural occurrences, whether on the atomic level or on that of human sense experience.

Turning from physical events to mental ones, Gassendi attempts to give an atomic explanation of the nature of the soul. First, he exhibits his vast erudition by examining the opinions of many different ancient philosophers on the subject. Then he offers the theory which seemed most probable to him; namely, that the animal soul is a material object. Though we cannot see the soul, reason convinces us that it must exist. The various processes that occur in living beings, such as nutrition, sensation, and movement, could not take place were there not a soul. But what is the soul like? It is very tenuous material substance existing in the body. It is like a very subtle fire, giving life to corporeal things somewhat as fire warms objects.

The human soul, however, is more complex than the animal soul, being composed of two parts. The first is the irrational soul, which is material and is like the soul of any other living thing. It accounts for the vegetative and sensitive processes that go on in man. This part of the human soul comes to us from our parents. In addition to this, we possess another feature of our souls, the rational element which, Gassendi insists, contrary to Epicurus' view, is not corporeal and is not derived from other human beings, but only from God. The rational part of our soul, which is responsible for our higher intellectual activities, is also immortal. Epicurus had argued for the mortality of the soul, but Gassendi strongly insists that only the animal soul is mortal. As evidence for his belief in the immortality of the rational soul, Gassendi contends that the fact that it is immaterial suffices to show that it is immortal. Further, the universal agreement of mankind on this point is offered as another proof, as well as the view that the divine and just government of the world would seem to require human immortality in order for a proper system of rewards and punishments to function.

In his discussion of human psychology Gassendi presents a theory to explain how the various mental processes take place. This section culminates with an examination of the sources of all of our knowledge, which, to some extent, anticipates the views that appear in John Locke's *An Essay Concerning Human Understanding* (1690).

The faculties of sensation and imagination are common to man and animals. (Gassendi even asserts that sensation occurs to some extent in plants and minerals.) Sensation occurs by means of a physical process involving material particles affecting a sense organ and causing a sensation, which is a physical event in the brain. The faculty of the imagination, which includes the memory as well, operates on traces or remains of the physical sense impressions. These traces are conceived of as waves in the brain which are actuated by other motions in the body and then cause further movements in the brain, giving rise to sensations or feelings similar to the original sensation which caused the wave. (Much of the account offered by Gassendi is close to that presented by his contemporary, the materialistic philosopher Thomas Hobbes.)

The imagination has three functions: apprehension, judgment, and reasoning. We can apprehend, as a result of the wave motions, the exact experiences and sensations that have occurred. Because of movements inside and also outside us, the various waves can be agitated at later times, so that we can now be aware of what we experienced yesterday. Also, different features of different experiences can be apprehended at the same time, giving rise to apprehensions of objects that have never, as such, been experienced. Thus, for example, our apprehension of a centaur results from our previous sense experience of a horse and a man, plus the simultaneous activation of part of the remaining wave that came from each of them. Judging and reasoning, which Gassendi insists takes place in both men and beasts, involves comparing apprehensions and associating them together according to their relations in actual experience. The faculties of judgment and reasoning put various apprehensions into an ordered sequence based on the experienced sequences of sensations, plus the natural instinct which makes us expect certain consequences to follow from what we have experienced.

Up to this point, the detailed psychological theory that Gassendi presents is much like that later developed by the British Empiricists from John Locke to John Stuart Mill. But Gassendi also insists that there is another mental faculty that exists in men, but not in other animals, that of intelligence or understanding, which belongs to our rational souls. By means of intelligence we are able to know things that cannot be experienced in sensation, such as God, space, and time. By this faculty we are also able to know the abstract essences of things, which transcend the powers of the imagination. Thus, for example, the imagination can know what "man" is, in terms of the sensations received. But, the essence of man, what it is that makes him what he is, can be known only by the intelligence. Lastly, this highest mental faculty is capable of self-consciousness. It can reflect on its operations and those of the imagination, and make us aware that we see, we think, and so on.

In terms of this theory of the nature of the soul, Gassendi next offers his opinion about the origin of our ideas. He repudiates completely the theory of Descartes and of Herbert of Cherbury that we possess innate ideas. Instead, Gassendi insists on the principle accepted by Aristotle and Epicurus, that there is nothing in the understanding which was not first in the senses. At the outset, the mind is a *tabula rasa,* a blank tablet. All of the particular ideas that the mind ever knows, such as that of the sun, either come directly from sense experience or result from combination of elements furnished by the senses. General or abstract ideas are formed by the intelligence from the collection of sense materials. In this case, the sense information is necessary, but not sufficient to account for general ideas, such as that of "man." The intelligence goes beyond the actual sense data in forming a unique idea from all the particular sensations. With regard to ideas of incorporeal things, which cannot be known by the senses, sense experience and the imagination furnish the occasion for the understanding to gain this knowledge. Because of certain experiences the understanding thinks, reflects, and abstracts and arrives at ideas, such as that of God. The senses provide some of the basic materials for these ideas and provide the context in which the understanding reasons in order to reach a conception of an incorporeal being.

Thus, all of our ideas either come from the senses or result from intellectual activities which are either caused or occasioned by sense information. However, in the cases of abstract ideas and ideas of incorporeal things, the actual content does not derive from any particular sense experiences. General principles, such as "The whole is greater than the part," are formed by induction from various particular experiences. When all of our experiences exhibit the same characteristics, we reach a general conclusion, which then becomes the basis of all further reasoning.

The last part of the *Syntagma* deals with ethics. Gassendi's theory is only a slightly modified version of Epicurus' hedonism. Gassendi holds that every pleasure, considered in itself, is a good and that all things that are considered good have value only in terms of the pleasure they produce. A completely pleasurable life is one without pains and troubles. Ultimately, for Gassendi, such a life can be achieved only by God. We can mitigate the pains in our lives as much as possible and thus attain a relatively good life.

Gassendi's philosophical system was one of the dominant theories of its time. It represented a cautious and careful attempt to explain the world in keeping both with the results of the new science and with the official views of the Catholic Church. Gassendi adapted various features of the philosophy of Epicurus to the state of knowledge of his day, and he modified certain portions of Epicurus' theory that were not in keeping with the Christian religion. The result was a semiskeptical, semiempirical theory which portrayed the world in terms of an atomic structure. Gassendi's philosophy remained important throughout the seventeenth century and was the chief modern alternative to Descartes'. It began to lose its appeal and importance after the development of the scientific theories of Sir Isaac Newton. Many of the basic elements of later English philosophy appear in Gassendi's views, and he probably had great influence on such thinkers as Hobbes and Locke.

PENSÉES

Author: Blaise Pascal (1623-1662)
Type of work: Theology
First published: 1670

PRINCIPAL IDEAS ADVANCED

There are two essential religious truths: there is a God, and there is a corruption of nature which makes men unworthy of him.

Reason is of little use in showing either the existence or the nature of God, but it does reveal man's finiteness and his separation from God.

It is a reasonable wager to stake everything on God's existence, for God either exists or he does not; if God is, then the man who believes in him wins everything, while if God is not, the man who believes in him suffers only a finite loss.

In knowing that he is miserable, man achieves greatness.

Since man's will is subject to his passions, it is important for men to obey custom simply because it is custom, and to obey the law in order to avoid sedition and rebellion.

Pascal's reflections on religion make up a large body of notes, written between 1654 and his death in 1662, intended to form a never-finished work to bear the title, *Apologie de la Religion Catholique*. Composed at different times after a moving mystical experience, the contents of the *Pensées* appeared in print posthumously. These reflections reveal Pascal as belonging to the group of fervently Christian writers who reject the usual claims of natural theology in order the more sharply to separate faith from reason.

Pascal's thought expresses the influence of the Jansenists, a seventeenth century Catholic order indebted to the theological views of John Calvin, one of the Protestant reformers. A group in conflict with the Jesuits, the Jansenists lived at Port Royal, near Paris, where they taught several central beliefs: man's total sinfulness, salvation through God's predestination, grace as sole means to salvation, and the need of the faithful to hold to a Christian belief which can never be proved by reason.

Though never an official member of the Jansenist community, Pascal visited them frequently (his sister belonged) and wrote in their defense in a bitter controversy with the Jesuits. Pascal was a brilliant mathematician as well as a religious writer, aware of the significant mathematical developments of his day. Living an austerely self-disciplined life, he gave away his wealth in an effort to exclude all pleasure and vanity from his practices.

The *Pensées* express numerous reflections concerning a few central themes. The Christian religion as known by Pascal teaches men two essential truths: "that there is a God, to whom men may attain, and that there is a corruption of nature which renders them unworthy of him." Pascal insists that if men deny either of these truths, they must fall into atheism, end up with the philosophers' god so popular among deistic thinkers of his time, or find themselves reduced to a complete pessimism. The Christian God wor-

shiped by Pascal does not require a philosopher's proof of existence, and he writes, "It is a wonderful thing that no canonical author has ever made use of nature in order to prove God." Pascal argues that man's miserable state does not justify total pessimism for the reason that the God worshiped by Christians, as by Abraham, Isaac, and Jacob, is one of love and consolation.

Pascal claims that God becomes available to men only through the mediation of Jesus Christ. Although Pascal makes clear that man is a "thinking reed," man's thinking capacity can nonetheless function religiously only to make clear his absolute finiteness, his total separation from God's actual infinity. In writing about faith, Pascal stresses the utter uselessness of reason for religious purposes. "Faith is a gift of God," he insists. "Believe not that we said it is a gift of reason." Yet reason is never to be disparaged, since it performs its own important functions and provides the key to whatever dignity man may achieve.

Nonetheless, Pascal sometimes does come close to a kind of reasoning about God—as in his famous wager argument for belief in God's existence (although this argument was intended primarily for skeptics who deny the importance of religious belief). In another place Pascal treats the relation of man's miserable condition to his finitude in such a way that he gives something resembling an argument for the necessity of God's existence. This latter argument rests on the awareness that the "I" of Pascal is really a thought. Had Pascal's mother died before his birth, the "I" of Pascal would never have existed. The conclusion is that Pascal is clearly not a necessary being. Pascal sees also that he is neither eternal nor infinite. He asserts that "I see plainly that there is in nature one being who is necessary, eternal, and infinite." This approximation to one of the classical demonstrations of God's existence indicates that Pascal was more concerned to argue that proofs cannot induce one to accept the Christian faith than to claim that proofs are unqualifiedly impossible of formulation. Such proofs, even if possible, turn out to be religiously useless and unimportant.

Pascal contends that men know *that* there is a God without knowing *what* God is. (In this claim he is inconsistent; he also asserts in one place that man can never *know* God's existence.) He insists that men also can know there is an infinite while remaining ignorant of its nature. Numbers cannot be brought to an end. This means simply that men can never mention a number which is the last one. So number must be infinite. Similarly, aware of the infinite's existence and unable to know its nature, men fail to know God's nature and existence because God lacks extension and limits. Men have absolutely no correspondence with the God which Christians worship in faith. The Christians who refuse to give reasons for their faith are essentially right, according to Pascal. They present their God as a "foolishness" to a world which often complains because the Christians cannot prove this God's existence. Some critics reasonably criticize Christians for holding beliefs which are beyond proof. Pascal attempts to reply to these critics by arguing that it is reasonable to believe. This he does primarily by producing his famous wager argument.

The stakes are clear, in Pascal's view. "God is, or He is not." The agnostic can argue that, since reason is unable to decide the issue, one need make no choice either way. Pascal insists that this will not do—that men must wager. They must choose. "It is not optional; you are committed to it." Pascal claims that men own two things as stakes in such a wager: their reason and their will (blessedness). They have two things to lose: the true and the good. Man's nature involves also two things to avoid: error and misery. Now, according to Pascal, since reason is unable to make the decision, the issue must turn on man's blessedness. How is this to be decided? The answer is that if man wagers on God's existence, he stands to win everything, losing nothing. Thus, to wager for God's existence means either the possibility of finite loss (if God does not exist) or infinite gain (if God does exist). Man's wager stakes a possibility of finite loss against one of infinite gain; namely, happiness. Man can therefore make only one wager—that God does exist.

What Pascal set out to prove was not that God exists, but that men *ought to believe* in God's existence. Once made, however, the wager does not necessarily bring one to the Christian God, as Pascal was clearly aware. Yet the wager is a fruitful beginning. The doubter who makes the wager can still use the possible way of "seeing through the game" associated with the reading and study of Scripture. He can also seek to control his passions. In this present life the man who wagers will be better off for having made the wager. Such a man will be driven to associate with others who have already been cured of their malady. Like them, he must act as if he believed. According to Pascal, no harm can come to such a man, for he will be "faithful, honest, humble, grateful, benevolent, a sincere and true friend."

To read Pascal as if he sought to debase the functions of human reason would be to read him wrongly. Because reason is incapable of knowing what God is does not alter the fact that man's greatness is tied to reason. Pascal insists that thought is not derived from body. Thought is its own kind of entity. Reason alone permits man to know the misery which marks his condition, but this very knowledge accounts for his dignity: "To be miserable is to know one's self to be so, but to know one's self to be miserable is to be great." Only man can possess this kind of knowledge which is denied to the other elements in nature. What makes Christianity the solely adequate religion, in Pascal's view, is that Christianity teaches the otherwise peculiar doctrine that man's misery and his greatness are inseparable. Men need to come to terms with their miserable condition, though they cannot fundamentally alter it. This gives both men and religion something important to accomplish. The central religious problem is to learn to control the human will rather than to pile up theological knowledge by reasoning. To cure pride, lust, and ego-centered aggressiveness remains the fundamental task of the Christian religion.

Concern about human willfulness occurs in numerous passages in the *Pensées*. Unlike the reasoning powers, the will operates according to man's perspective. Man finds himself in bondage to his passions. For this reason, custom is a most important necessity of any possible social existence. Against Montaigne, Pascal argued that men should obey custom simply because it is custom and not because it is

reasonable. Men should also obey law as law in order to avoid sedition and rebellion. Pascal insists that classical philosophers such as Plato and Aristotle wrote about politics with many reservations. "If they wrote of politics, it was as if to regulate a hospital for madmen." Pascal could not believe that such men thought reasoning about politics the most serious business of life.

Though he understood the limited possibilities of reasoning, Pascal never degraded reason. Reasoning allows men to encircle the universe in certain ways, but "instinct" and "the heart" are essential allies. "How few demonstrated things there are!" Pascal laments in one place. Men are as much automata as minds. No one should ridicule custom in view of this fact. Agreeing with a philosopher such as David Hume, Pascal says it is custom which permits men to believe that tomorrow will dawn and that men must die. Custom influences men to act, while reason directs only the mind. Habit, including religious practice, remains a routine needed in every day and age. "We have to acquire an easier credence, —that of habit,—which without violence, art, or argument, makes us believe things and inclines all our powers to this belief, so that our mind falls into it naturally." Pascal claims that life would be easier for men if reason were unnecessary; but since nature has not so arranged matters, men need to supplement intuited first principles with limited demonstrations.

Pascal makes a distinction between knowledge and judgment. For example, geometry is a matter of the mind, while subtlety is a function of intuition. Men must judge things either literally or spiritually. Honoring reason, men should accept its limits, knowing what it can and cannot accomplish. Although there is criticism of the Pyrrhonists (skeptics) for some of their beliefs, Pascal shows that he was favorably disposed to a partial skepticism concerning the powers of reason. Men can at most achieve a "learned ignorance." Different from the natural ignorance of all men at birth, a learned ignorance is gained by a few "lofty souls who, having traversed all human knowledge, find that they know nothing. . . ." This is a self-aware ignorance. Between these two kinds of ignorance dwell the great numbers of the intelligent who "disturb the world and judge wrongly of everything." Genuine philosophers are those who learn how to laugh at philosophy.

The imagination and human sickness are two important elements which shape man's constant susceptibility to deception. The wisest men can hope only to modify, never to eradicate these two sources of illusion. Man tends naturally towards wrong judgment. He finds it difficult, if not impossible, to escape the binding conditions of his own vanity. His actions are motivated by self-love. What makes the Christian view of Incarnation important is the radical cure it suggests for man's pridefulness. Men must hate religion as long as it teaches what it must—that the misery of man is objective and absolutely ineradicable except by God's grace. This side of Pascal's thought shows a relation to the long tradition in Western thought concerned with the numerous psychological and cultural obstacles in the way of genuine discovery of self-knowledge. These obstacles are, for Pascal, as much connected with the human will as with the mind. It is as if men want,

in some deep and buried way, to judge things wrongly.

Pascal mentions atheism and deism as the greatest competitiors of a genuine Christian faith. He understands how atheism may be a mark of a strong intellect, though only up to a point. The atheist has blind spots when he comes, say, to the notion of immortality. Pascal asks why the atheist should deny dogmatically the possibility that a man might rise from the dead. He wants to know which is the more remarkable—that a living being should appear at all, or that a once-living being should be reborn. By custom the atheist accepts the fact that there are living beings and then seems astounded by the religious notion of rebirth. Here the atheist puzzles Pascal. On the other hand, the deist seeks to know God without revelation, meaning without the mediation of Jesus Christ. The deist thus misunderstands Christianity, ending with the philosopher's God of proofs and first principles rather than with the God of redemption. Pascal clearly aligns himself with those who assert that the Christian faith cannot fully be translated into philosophical terms.

Affirmation of the original sin of all men is a necessity for Pascal. The evidence for this affirmation is that all men are born disposed to seek their own interests, a disposition which runs counter to the necessary conditions of order. Wars and revolutions arise from the individual's pursuit of self-interest even when his reason tells him that he should attend to the needs of a commonwealth. Men should usually seek the general as opposed to the particular interests of a community, but most often they do not. Facts like these Pascal takes as indicative of some basic flaw in human willing. The glory of the Christian religion stems from its insistence on man's inherent sinfulness. "No religion but ours has taught that man is born in sin," Pascal writes; "no sect of philosophers has affirmed it, therefore none has spoken the truth." This dark doctrine, so stressed by Pascal and borrowed from contemporary Calvinism, helped to bring him into disrepute among the Jesuits, who thought he emphasized it disproportionately. Yet he was quite aware of the nonrational nature of this doctrine and made no effort to prove it.

What makes Pascal's *Pensées* an enduring work is the classical manner in which one aspect of the Christian tradition in theology receives forceful and passionate presentation. Its confessional and personal nature also makes it a work which can help individuals who, like Pascal, find themselves caught up in a struggle to make sense of Christian faith once they have abandoned belief that natural proofs of God's existence are possible. One-sided in emphasis, Pascal's work tries to show that Christian faith is reasonable on its own terms even though not susceptible of rational proofs divorced from reasons of the heart. No matter how extremely emphasized, Pascal's views about the depravity of the will help to counterbalance the more optimistic humanistic conceptions of human perfectibility.

Through the *Pensées* runs a sense of the fragility of human life—a constant reminder of something most men know when they think about it but which they often wish to forget. A sense of the contingency of life, of uncertainty about its duration, pervades Pascal's writings. A mystical sense that there is more to finite existence than meets the finite eye drives Pascal to fall back on intuition and feeling when reason proves unable to establish the kinds of certainty many religious persons hope to find.

Pascal's portrait of man's misery involves a kind of metaphysical sickness. Reasoning man is caught between the finite and an infinite whose nature he can never hope to fathom. He owns a will to self-deception, marked by an endless pursuit of means by which to divert attention from this very fact. On the other hand, a critic may well say that Pascal is too much a puritanical thinker—unwilling or unable to point out the genuinely redeeming features of natural processes. The Pascalian picture of man illustrates the more somber side of puritan thought and feeling. "Imagine a number of men in chains, and all condemned to death, of whom every day some are butchered in sight of the others, those remaining seeing their own fate in that of their fellows, regarding each other with grief and despair while awaiting their turn; this is a picture of the condition of man."

Obviously, some of Pascal's thoughts reflect events of his own biography. He shunned pleasure and picked up the radically austere notions of the Jansenists. Nonetheless, his version of Christian faith remains a recurring theme in the long, unresolved competition between those who argue for a natural theology and those others who insist that revelation is not to be explained in philosophical terms. Pascal's *Pensées* is the expression of a troubled man who seemed to need this specific version of Christian faith to find life itself a meaningful affair. Man's very misery made sense out of the Christian promise, according to Pascal. Unlike many other writers, Pascal attempted to live according to his beliefs. Many men in the twentieth century, including those who would disagree with Pascal, are finding that to live according to one's beliefs is no small achievement.

ETHICS

Author: Benedictus de Spinoza (1632-1677)
Type of work: Ethics, theology
First published: 1677

PRINCIPAL IDEAS ADVANCED

Whatever is the cause of itself exists necessarily.

Only substance is self-caused, free, and infinite; and God is the only substance.

God exists necessarily, and is possessed of infinite attributes.

But only two of God's infinite attributes are known to us: thought and extension.

Since thought and extension are features of the same substance, whatever happens to body happens also to mind as another phase of the same event.

A false idea is an idea improperly related to God; by achieving adequate ideas we become adequate causes of the body's modifications: this is human freedom, freedom from the human bondage to the passions.

The highest virtue of the mind is to know God.

Spinoza's *Ethics* is a truly amazing work. In a field which is subject to great differences of opinion, it has always been recognized as a classic by people of most diverse interests. While other philosophers come and go in popularity, Spinoza maintains a stable place, always attracting the interest of serious students. He did not write a great deal, and of his works, few receive much attention except the *Ethics*. It stands as a single work exacting a place of influence usually reserved for a more extensive collection of philosophical writings.

The figure of Spinoza has often attracted as much attention as his work, and he stands, along with Socrates, as one of the few genuine heroes in a field not much given to hero worship. A Jew, ostracized by his own people and excluded from his homeland, he insisted on following his own ideas despite their heretical tendencies. Moreover, the *Ethics* remained unpublished in Spinoza's lifetime. Upon this single posthumous work his great reputation and reservoir of influence depend. Hegel and many of the later romantics acknowledge Spinoza as the modern thinker whose thought suggests the direction for their later developments.

Widespread interest in Spinoza remains even today, despite his central theological orientation and the recent unfashionability of such an approach. Many men who find traditional religious beliefs unacceptable discover in Spinoza a rational and a naturalistic form of religion. His views on God, man, and the human emotions have widespread popular influence. Although Spinoza is sometimes called "the philosophers' philosopher" because of the abstract and technical nature of the *Ethics*, it is still true that few philosophers' general views are more widely known than are his among the non-philosophical public. It is true that his views are often oversimplified, but it is also true that they are circulated extensively.

A great deal of argument has been generated by the style or form in which Spinoza chose to write the *Ethics*. The Continental Rationalists (Descartes, Liebniz, and Spinoza) were all much impressed by the exciting developments in mathematics, and all of them reflect something of the geometric temper in their writings. Spinoza elected to write the *Ethics* as a geometrical system—definitions, axioms, propositions, and all. Some argue that this form is essential to Spinoza's doctrines; others feel that the *Ethics* can just as easily be read in essay style. All seem agreed that the work does not really have the full deductive rigor of geometry; yet the form indicates Spinoza's desire to be clear and simple in his expression, to be straightforward in his assertions, and to connect the various parts of his thought systematically. All this he achieves with the barest minimum of explanation and with little external reference.

Fortunately we do not need to understand fully Spinoza's own attitude toward this geometrical method of philosophizing, or to appraise its success, in order to grasp the central features of Spinoza's thought. It is true that the geometrical method represents an attempted revolution in philosophical thought. In his unfinished *On The Improvement of the Understanding,* Spinoza agreed with the other modern revolutionaries of his era in stressing methodology and the need for a thorough reëxamination of traditional philosophical and theological methods. His break with the scholastic method of the *Summas* is complete. Spinoza firmly believed that the human intellect can be carefully examined and improved and thereby made able to produce a more rigorous and more complete understanding of things—all this through its own strengthened power.

Properly corrected, reason is self-sufficient, its own guide and its own judge. And this is, for Spinoza, as true in ethical affairs as in speculative matters. He does not belong in the class of dogmaticians; there is no indication that he believed his own views to be either complete or final. What is evident is his trust in the human intellect to work out an acceptable and a comprehensive schema. Spinoza depended heavily on previous theological views, but his modern temperament transformed them by placing them in a new humanistic perspective.

The five parts of the *Ethics* take up in order God, the nature and origin of the mind, then the emotions, and finally the twin questions of human bondage and human freedom. In beginning with a consideration of the divine nature, and then developing all other theories in this light, Spinoza was influenced by medieval theology. Theory of knowledge and attention to human powers of knowing received a more prominent place with Spinoza, but systematically speaking a theory of the divine nature is still first. Spinoza called his first principle sometimes God, sometimes substance. Aristotle had defined "substance" as that capable of independent existence. Spinoza interpreted this with absolute rigor and asserted that only God, a substance of infinite attributes, could fulfill this definition exactly.

The *Ethics* opens with the traditional distinction between that which requires no external cause to account for its existence (cause of itself) and that which owes its existence (causally) to another being. That which is the cause of itself exists necessarily and needs nothing other than itself to be conceived. This Spinoza calls substance. On the other hand, what is finite is what is capable of being limited by another thing of its own kind, whereas substance is absolutely infinite, in that it possesses infinite attributes.

Spinoza defines an "attribute" as that which the mind sees as constituting the essence of substance. A "mode" is some modification of substance. "Freedom" means to exist from the necessity of one's own nature alone (only substance as cause of itself fulfills this requirement) and to be set in action by oneself alone. Only substance, or God, is perfectly free, dependent on nothing else for its existence or action; it is absolutely infinite and thus one of a kind.

From here Spinoza turns to a classical definition of knowledge: we can say we know something only when we understand it through its causes. After this he begins his famous proof that there could be only one substance which would be absolutely infinite and thus be its own cause. These "proofs" are simply a modern version of the traditional arguments for God's existence, although in the *Ethics* they take a novel form. The burden of Spinoza's point is that either nothing exists or else a substance absolutely infinite exists. Something does exist, and the presence of such an absolutely infinite substance precludes the existence of more than one such, and it includes everything else as part of itself.

Since God, or substance, consists of infinite attributes, each one of which expresses eternal and infinite essence, God necessarily exists and excludes the existence of anything else not a part of it. Spinoza goes on to argue that such a substance cannot be divided, nor can the existence of a second such substance even be conceived. From this Spinoza turns to the statement of perhaps his most famous doctrine: whatever is, is in God, and nothing can either be or be conceived without God. Popularly this belief is called "pantheism," but such a doctrine (that the world taken as a whole is God) is too simple to express Spinoza's view. It is not enough to say that the natural order as a whole is God, for what really is true is that Spinoza takes all of the usual transcendental qualities of a traditional God and, combining them with the natural order, calls the sum of these God or substance absolutely infinite.

Spinoza's famous doctrine of the infinite attributes of God is easy proof against a simple label of pantheism. In addition to God's infinity in each kind (in thought and extension), Spinoza posits an infinity of attributes as belonging to God, only two of which (thought and extension) are known directly in our natural world. Thus God, as Spinoza conceives him, is infinitely larger than our natural order, since the world we are familiar with actually represents only a very small part of his vast nature. This is a speculative doctrine, as intriguing as it is baffling.

Since everything must be conceived through, and has its existence in, God, the knowledge of any natural event requires a reference to the divine nature. It is for this reason that Spinoza begins the *Ethics* with a discussion of God's nature, since the understanding of everything else, including man's ethical life, depends upon this. Nothing can be understood in isolation, and all adequate understanding involves locating the particular events and their immediate causes within the larger scheme of a substance absolutely infinite. God in traditional theology was used to explain the natural world as a whole; now every phenomenon is to be seen as a part of him and is to be explained on a part-whole analogy. What it is true to say about the divine nature, then, is also in some sense true of every part of the natural world.

Nothing remains unrealized in such a divine nature. Infinite numbers of things in infinite ways will all become real in the course of time, and time is without beginning or end. Rejecting medieval theories of creation, Spinoza returned to a more classical view of the world as eternal. The natural order is equal in duration with God. One side of his nature is timeless, but the side which includes the natural order is temporal. Time applies to God, but only to one aspect. And there are no alternatives to any natural fact, since infinite possibilities will all be realized eventually. God's existence is necessary and so is his production of the natural order as a part of his nature.

Although this production of the natural order is necessary and its pattern without alternative, nothing outside God's own nature compels him to act, and in that sense God's activity is free. Yet God is absolutely the only genuinely free agent; in nature there is nothing contingent, but everything is determined necessarily in whole or in part by factors and causes outside its own nature. "Will" had been stressed as a causal agent by Duns Scotus; again Spinoza reverts to a more classical doctrine and denies that will can be a free cause. Will, he says, is nothing other than reason's tendency to recognize and to accept a true idea. Things could have been produced, by God or by man, in no other manner and in no other order than they are and were.

In the appendix to Book I, which contains the discussion of God's nature as it includes the world as a part, Spinoza goes on to elaborate his famous refutation of teleology. Christian doctrine necessarily depicts God as acting to achieve certain ends, or otherwise the drama of sin, atonement, and salvation would be difficult to present. God acts to accomplish his purpose, according to the orthodox conception. All of this Spinoza denied. According to the *Ethics*, thought is only one of God's infinite attributes, so that although he is a personal being in some sense, he is so only in part. Will has been denied and thought is not dominant; such a being cannot be said to act purposefully to attain an end unachievable without his conscious action. What happens in nature is simply the necessary outpouring of the divine, absolutely infinite substance, to which there is no alternative conceivable. Although Spinoza's first principle is different, he is very close to the traditional Neoplatonic theories of the necessary (although good) emanation of the world from God.

In Book II, Spinoza begins to trace the nature and the origin of the mind, one of the infinite things which necessarily follow from the nature of God. Although the mind is only one attribute among an infinite number, Spinoza readily admits that it concerns us most and is vitally important for ethical conduct. First he must distinguish between an idea (a concept of the mind) and an adequate idea (one which has all the internal signs of a true idea). Such a distinction is extremely important, since from it will come the whole of the later ethical theory.

For more traditional thought, God alone was considered perfect and all the natural order somehow less perfect (as is implied by a doctrine of original sin). Spinoza takes a radical position here and actually equates reality with perfection. This departure is perfectly understandable. Nothing in nature has an alternative or can be different from what it is, and all things are a part of God and follow necessarily from his nature. God could not be complete without the whole natural order. Thus, it is logical that each part of God (each aspect of the natural order) should be just as perfect as it is real.

Then Spinoza turns to another radical idea: God is extended, or material things are a part of his nature. Christian views had had to make God responsible for the creation of the physical world, but none had made God himself material even in part. Within Spinoza's view, the material world is no longer somehow less perfect, and so it can be made a part of God without lessening his perfection.

And every material thing has an idea paralleling it, although ideas affect only other ideas and physical things affect only things physical. The attribute of extension is reflected fully in the attribute of thought, although the two are only parallel and do not intersect each other. Substance thinking and substance extended are one and the same substance, now comprehended under this attribute, now under that. Nothing can happen in the body which is not perceived by the mind, and the essence of man consists of certain modifications of the attributes of God. We perceive all things through God, although some perceptions may be confused.

How is such confusion as does arise to be corrected? All ideas, insofar as they are related to God, are true. Thus, correct understanding means to take the idea and to place it in its proper locus within the divine nature, rather than to treat it as an independent phenomenon. No idea in itself is false; it is simply improperly related to other ideas if it is confused. For instance, men are sometimes deceived in thinking themselves to be free, but this simply reflects their ignorance of the total causal chain within the divine nature of which their actions are a part. When actions are viewed in isolation, such confusion is possible, although no idea in itself is false.

It is the nature of reason to perceive things under a certain form of eternity and to consider them as necessary. Temporal viewpoints and a belief in contingency simply reflect an unimproved reason, unable to assume its natural viewpoint. For the human mind is actually able to possess an adequate knowledge of the eternal and

420

infinite essence of God. In many previous theological views, the human mind was thought incapable of comprehending God. For Spinoza the human mind is to be seen as a part of the divine intellect, and as such it has within its own nature the possibility for grasping the whole of the divine mind, although to do so requires a great deal of effort.

When Book III begins to discuss the emotions, we begin what ordinarily we would call the ethical part of the work proper. Even here, however, Spinoza's approach is not standard; he claims that no one before has determined both the nature and the strength of the emotions or has treated the vices and follies of men in a geometrical method. And the emotions (hatred, anger, envy) follow from the same necessity as do all other things in nature. Aristotle and others thought that conduct was not amenable to scientific knowledge, but Spinoza's natural necessity, plus the connection of every event with the divine nature, subjects the emotions to the same laws as those which govern all natural phenomena.

Spinoza says that we act when we are the adequate cause of anything; we suffer when we are the cause only partially. An emotion is a modification of the body's power to act. The emotion is an action and the body's power is increased when we are the adequate cause of the modification; the emotion is passive and the body's power of acting is decreased when we are only partially the cause. Our mind acts when it has adequate ideas; it suffers necessarily when it has inadequate ideas.

The law of existence, Spinoza tells us, is that everything should do its utmost to persevere in its own mode of being. This striving is the very essence of every living thing. We feel "joy" when we are able to pass to a higher state of being; we feel "sorrow" when through passivity and suffering we pass to a lower state. Joy, sorrow, and desire are the primary emotions. Love attaches to the things which give us joy (an active and a higher existence); hatred attaches to what gives us sorrow (a passive and a lowered existence). Naturally we endeavor to support those things which cause joy, and just as naturally we tend to destroy whatever we imagine causes us sorrow. Love can overcome hatred and thus increase our joy, and Spinoza recommends that we attempt to return love for hate for that reason. On the other hand, Spinoza feels that the traditional Christian virtue of humility produces impotence and sorrow and is to be avoided for that reason.

Spinoza is often thought of as an unrestrained optimist concerning the powers of human reason, but his treatment of human bondage in Book IV should correct any such impression. In one of the longest books in the *Ethics*, Spinoza outlines in detail the inevitable causes which bind men to the blindness of their emotions and work against any attempted liberation. Good and evil are defined here as, respectively, what is useful to us and what hinders us from possessing something good. Appetite is what causes us to do anything, and virtue and power are defined as being the same thing. Here we have a classical definition of a naturalistic ethical theory.

If our only virtue is whatever power we possess naturally, and if good means only what is useful to us, what on earth could bind men? Spinoza says that there is no individual thing in nature not surpassed in strength and power by some other thing, which means that our power is always threatened and our current well-being always subject to loss. Other things are stronger than we are and continually challenge our powers, which places us in bondage to the passive emotions (sorrow) which necessarily accompany any such threat. The force which we have at our disposal is limited and is infinitely surpassed by the power of external causes. We suffer insofar as we find ourselves to be merely a part of nature surpassed in power and thus threatened by the other parts.

An emotion can be restrained or removed only by an opposed and stronger emotion. Thus our ability to withstand the pressures around us, to prevent sorrow, depends upon our natural power to oppose the emotions surrounding us with an equal vigor. Such a task never ceases and any victory is constantly in danger of being reversed in a weak or lax moment. Yet the highest virtue of the mind is said to be to know God. Why? Simply because such knowledge renders our ideas more adequate; and, as our ideas become more adequate, our power of action is increased. Men disagree as far as their ideas are disturbed by emotions; when guided by reason they tend to understand and thus to agree.

In Book V Spinoza turns finally to an appraisal of the powers of the intellect which make it free, since freedom comes only through the possibility of increased understanding. The primary fact upon which he bases his hope for human freedom is that an emotion which is a passion, and thus destructive of our power, ceases to be a passion as soon as we form a clear idea of it. Thus, we cannot prevent the constant challenge to our power to continue our existence, but we can come to understand all the causes which play upon us. To the extent to which we understand the causes impinging on us, just to that extent we can successfully oppose any threat to our freedom or our power.

There is nothing of which we cannot, theoretically speaking, form an adequate idea, including of course God himself. The way toward increasing freedom is open and is identical with an increased understanding. Such striving toward an increase of our understanding has for its object all or part of God. This is the highest effort of the mind and its highest virtue, since it is the source of the individual's increased power of existence. Such understanding is rarely achieved and is exceedingly difficult, but its unobstructed possibility is a challenge to men and is the source of such freedom as man may have.

DIALOGUES ON METAPHYSICS AND ON RELIGION

Author: Nicolas de Malebranche (1638-1715)
Type of work: Metaphysics, theology
First published: 1688

Human beings exist as thinking beings; they are not material bodies.

The only world we know is an intelligible world, the world of our ideas; but since the ideas have an eternal, infinite, necessary character that is independent of our conception, they must be features of an intelligible extension.

Intelligible extension has its locus in God, but it should not be identified with God.

We understand certain truths only because God illuminates the ideas.

When an event involving the body occurs, an event involving the soul occurs as a result of God's action; in this manner human beings have feelings. [Occasionalism.]

The universe contains three types of beings: God, mind, and body; of the three, God alone is an active agent in the universe.

Father Nicolas de Malebranche was the chief Cartesian philosopher of the late seventeenth century. He was a member of the Augustianian religious order of the Oratory in Paris, where he originally devoted himself to the studies of ecclesiastical history, Biblical criticism, and Hebrew. At the age of twenty-six he came across a work by René Descartes and was so impressed by its method and the theory it contained that he devoted the next several years to studying Cartesian philosophy and mathematics. The first fruits of these studies appeared in 1674-1675 in his famous work *The Search After Truth* (*De la recherche de la vérité*), in which he developed his modified version of Cartesian philosophy. The work was immediately successful and was translated into several languages, including English. It was studied and discussed by major thinkers everywhere and soon led to a series of polemical controversies between Malebranche and his opponents. His *Dialogues on Metaphysics and on Religion* presents a more literary and definitive version of his theory, as well as answers to many of his critics. It has remained the most popular expres-

sion of Malebranche's theory of knowledge and his metaphysics.

Malebranche's views were tremendously influential in their own day. For a period, he was the most important metaphysician in Europe, providing the theory that was debated everywhere. Among the thinkers who were greatly influenced by Malebranche's views were the Irish philosopher George Berkeley and the Scottish skeptic David Hume. Though his works were severely criticized by the Jesuits, and some of his writings were placed on the Index, Malebranche had, and continues to have, an enormous influence among French philosophers.

The *Dialogues* is written more in the style of St. Augustine than of Plato. It presents a statement of Malebranche's theories rather than a discussion of philosophical issues. In it two spokesmen for Malebranche expound his views to a student, Aristes, and correct the latter's misunderstandings.

The first dialogue begins with Theodore instructing Aristes in the method of finding philosophical truth. Understanding should be gained through reason. Hence, for the time being, faith is not taken as a source of knowledge. The sensuous or material world should be ignored, so that the senses and the imagination will not interfere with the pursuit of rational knowledge. With this much in mind, the analysis of what rational truths we can possess is begun.

Since nothing, or non-being, can have no qualities, I, who think, must exist. (I have at least the quality of thinking; hence, I cannot be nothing, or nonexistent.) But what am I? I am not a body, because a body is only a piece of extension. When I examine my idea of a body, the only properties that I find belonging to it are extensional ones, relations of distance. Thought is not a property or type of extension, since thoughts cannot be defined in terms of distances, and since they can be conceived without reference to any properties of extension. Hence, our conception of ourselves is totally different from our conception of bodies. (Malebranche offers these considerations as evidence that we are not material bodies.)

When we examine our ideas, we find that what we are directly acquainted with is an intelligible world, and not a material one. We know ideas, and not physical things. Even if all material objects disappeared, our ideas might remain the same. Since everything that we can know is an idea, it is only the intelligible world that directly concerns us. When we inspect this intelligible world of our ideas, we find that it has an eternal, immutable, and necessary structure that is not in any way dependent on our thinking about it. Truths, such as 3 times 3 equals 9, are always true and

they must be true. I do not decide or will that they be true; instead, I am forced to recognize and accept their truth. Further, the truths of the intelligible world are infinite, in that they apply to an infinite number of objects. Hence, these necessary and unchangeable truths must apply not just to the limited, finite number of things in my mind, but to what Malebranche calls "intelligible extension"—the entire rational world of concepts.

All of this is intended to show that the world of intelligible extension, the realm of true ideas, cannot be a feature of my mind. Intelligible extension has a structure unlike that of myself, in that it is eternal, infinite, immutable, and necessary. Hence, though I am aware of certain aspects of intelligible extension, it must be located elsewhere, in something that possesses the actual characteristics of the intelligible world; namely, God.

The second dialogue deals with the nature and existence of God. Malebranche emphatically denies that intelligible extension is God. Such a view would be similar to that held by Benedictus de Spinoza. Instead, Malebranche contends that the recognition of intelligible extension makes us realize *that* God is, since he alone can be the locus of intelligible extension. But this does not tell us *what* God is. In fact, we know of God only in relation to what he makes us know, or by what he illuminates for us. Any time that we have any knowledge, we know that God exists, but we never know his nature.

To clarify this point, Malebranche argues that God is unlimited Perfection or Being or Infinite Reality. No idea of mine can represent such a Being, since all of my ideas are determinate. In this lifetime, we cannot attain a clear idea of what God is. We can only see that he is, and how he is related to everything that we know. We realize that the proposition "There is a God" is obviously true, and that God's essence includes his existence, but we cannot understand what his nature really is.

According to Malebranche, "We see all things in God," but we do not actually see him. The ideas we have that constitute knowledge do not properly belong to our own minds, but rather to intelligible extension. Because of the characteristics of intelligible extension, it must be located in God. Hence, whenever we know something, we are seeing a truth in God, and seeing it because he illumines it for us. In this respect, Malebranche's theory of knowledge differs sharply from Descartes'. According to the latter, we establish truths about reality from the clear and distinct ideas in our own minds. Descartes contended that since God gave us these ideas, and since he is no deceiver, whatever is clear and distinct about our ideas must be true of the real universe as well. Critics have noted that Descartes never succeeded in building a bridge from his ideas of reality. Malebranche removes the need for bridge-building by insisting that the ideas are not located in *man's* mind, but are in God's Mind. A truth is a direct observation of intelligible extension in God, and we see what is God's Mind because he illuminates the ideas and enables us to see them. Thus, Malebranche's theory is a type of direct Platonic realism. The only truths are truths about the world of ideas, and these are known not by inference from the contents of our minds, but by direct vision of the Divine Mind.

In the third, fourth, and fifth dialogues, Malebranche discusses the relation of ideas to sense information. Ideas are intelligible. This means that they can be defined, so that we can understand why they have the characteristics they do. In terms of this conception of "ideas," the only ideas we have are divine ones. We do not have an idea of ourselves because we do not know our own natures completely, and we cannot make ourselves know ourselves. We do not have ideas of our sense experiences, which Malebranche calls "feelings," since we cannot give clear definitions of them.

In a famous passage, Aristes and Theodore appropriately illustrate this point by discussing music. When one tries to make intelligible the real reason why we hear the sounds we do, the explanation is in terms of the mathematical relationships of vibrating strings, and not in terms of experienced qualities. The mathematical relationships can be defined in terms of the ideas involved in intelligible extension. But the sounds cannot be defined, only "felt." Also, we can discover no intelligible connection between the vibrations and the felt sounds. (Does a certain sound experience *have* to be the result of vibrations of a certain frequency?)

What we can understand relates only to the realm of ideas, the realm of intelligible extension. Sense qualities are not features of our mathematical ideas, for, as far as we know, they are only feelings in us. There is nothing in the mathematical relationships that we can understand about moving bodies that explains the occurrence of these feelings. The ideas that we have of bodies allow us to understand them in terms of the principles of mathematical physics without reference to our feelings.

Then, what accounts for our having feelings, and experiencing them in some orderly relation to physical events? In giving his answer, Malebranche presents his theory of "occasionalism." Bodies cannot cause feelings, since bodies are only extended objects moving. We cannot be the cause of our feelings, since we have no control of them. God, then, must be the cause, giving us a certain set of feelings whenever certain physical events occur. There must be laws of the conjunction of the soul and the body by which God operates on both substances, so that when an event happens to one, a corresponding event happens to the other. Each of these events is the "occasion" but not the cause of the other's occurrence. There is no necessary connection between a physical event and a mental event. God, acting according to general laws he has laid down, causes two independent sets of events, the physical ones and the feelings and ideas. The mind and the body have no contact with each other. But God wills incessantly and produces a sequence of physical events that are correlated with a conjoined series of mental events. By means of the system God employs, we ascertain, through discovering the general laws God provides, what is necessary for our self-preservation. Our feelings alert us to our bodily needs, so that we seek food when we have the feeling of hunger, and so on.

The sense "feelings" that God gives us serve not only as warning signs for the care and maintenance of our bodies (which we would otherwise know nothing about, since our knowledge is only about ideas), but also as the occasions for our becoming aware of truths about ideas. The diagrams employed in mathematics, which are only sensations, cannot teach us since they do not contain the pure ideas. But, they can function as cues, attracting our attention to the truths we can learn from reason. Learning actually consists of our being made aware of some fact about the intelligible world, and of being made aware of this fact by God, who alone has the power to make us think and know.

The sixth and seventh dialogues bring out the crucial characteristics of Malebranche's metaphysical theory, showing why God is the sole causal agent in the universe. The universe contains three types of beings: God, whose existence can be demonstrated from his definition; mind, which can be directly apprehended through its mental processes, though it cannot be clearly known; and bodies, whose existence is known only by Revelation. The last point startles Aristes, and so Theodore examines the evidence available for the existence of bodies.

We do not know bodies by ideas, since our ideas are of intelligible extension, and not of physical extension. We do not feel bodies, since our feelings are only modifications of our own souls, caused by God in consequence of his general laws. In terms of what we know and feel, it is quite possible that bodies do not exist at all. Our knowledge and our experience could be exactly the same, since God directly causes all, whether bodies exist or do not exist. In fact, Malebranche goes on to argue, we cannot show that bodies must exist, but we can show that God need not create bodies. If God is infinitely perfect, there is no reason why he has to create anything. It is compatible with God's nature either that he has created a physical world or that he has not. If it could be shown that he had to create a physical world, then God would not be perfect (and, as Malebranche interprets this term, self-sufficient). He would require something other than himself; namely, what he had to create. Since, by definition, God is dependent on nothing, if he created a physical world, he did it arbitrarily and not necessarily. What Malebranche, in effect, claims is that no necessary conclusion about the nature of created things follows from the concept of an all-perfect, omnipotent deity.

If all of this is accepted, then is there any reason to believe that bodies do, in fact, exist? First, there are some proofs which are convincing but not conclusive. The constancy of our experience, along with our natural inclination to attribute our experiences to bodies, persuades us that there are bodies. But this persuasion could be erroneous, since we know that we could have the experiences we do, together with an inclination to believe certain things about these experiences, without there being any bodies—God could produce all such effects in us. The decisive evidence, according to Malebranche, is given by faith, in the statements that appear in the beginning of the book of Genesis, where we are told that God created heaven and earth. (Bishop Berkeley later disputed whether the text in question says anything about whether God created a physical world, or whether it refers only to a world of ideas.)

In the seventh dialogue, the climax of this metaphysical view is reached. A third character, Theotimus, is introduced, who is a spokesman for Malebranche's theological views. Theodore and Theotimus together defend the theory that God alone is an efficacious agent in the universe. It had already been shown that unaided minds have no power, but receive only those ideas and feelings that God wills to give them. Now it is argued that bodies are also powerless, since their sole defining properties are extensional, that is, relations of distance. Bodies exist only because of God's will, and their particular location at any moment must also be due to God. If all this is the case, then obviously bodies cannot be the cause of their own motions, or of the motions of each other. Only God can be. The same point can be brought out from God's side. If he is omnipotent, then nothing besides God can have any power to act. If it did, then there would be something God could not do, namely, control the actions of a particular object. God's omnipotence implies, according to Malebranche, that God is the only possible active agent in the entire universe. This point is made in the striking assertion that not all the angels and demons acting together can move a bit of straw unless God so wills.

Then, what makes the world operate? In general, God's will. In particular, the world proceeds according to general laws that God provides. Malebranche insists that God wills according to the principle of economy that the smallest set of fixed laws should be employed. God can change everything at any moment, since he is the only active agent. But, because he wills in keeping with his principle of economy, effects continue to occur in lawful sequences, which we can learn through the study of nature. The world as we know it, since it is the effect of God's will, can only be described, never explained. We never know any reason *why* events happen, beyond the general formula that God so wills them. There is no necessary connection between events. Hence, the created world must be known descriptively, not logically.

The remainder of the *Dialogues* deals with Malebranche's theology, in which the author tries to show that his version of Cartesian philosophy is in accord with Christian doctrine and in which he attempts to answer some of the theological objections that had been raised.

To an extent, Malebranche's theory represented the culmination of the grand tradition of seventeenth century metaphysical inquiry. Starting with Descartes, the "new philosophers" had tried to explain why the world discovered by modern science must have the characteristics it does. Malebranche, by consistently following out some of the main themes of Descartes, reduced the hope of reaching a rational explanation of the world to nothing, leaving only theology, instead of philosophy, as the source of knowledge about the world. Berkeley and Hume then followed out some of Malebranche's insights, after which Hume reduced the theological vision of Malebranche to a complete skepticism.

AN ESSAY CONCERNING HUMAN UNDERSTANDING

Author: John Locke (1632-1704)
Type of work: Epistemology
First published: 1690

PRINCIPAL IDEAS ADVANCED

At birth the mind is a blank tablet; no one is born with innate ideas.

All of our ideas come from experience, either from sensation or by reflection.

All simple, uncompounded ideas come from experience; and the mind, by combining simple ideas, forms new complex ideas.

The qualities of objects are either primary or secondary: primary qualities—solidity, extension, figure, mobility, and number—are inseparable from objects; but secondary qualities—such as colors and odors—are in the observer.

The substance of objects is a something—we know not what—which we have to assume as the support of an object's qualities.

Locke's *Essay Concerning Human Understanding* is the first major presentation of the empirical theory of knowledge that was to play such an important role in British philosophy.

The author had studied at Oxford, and later he became a medical doctor. Although he did not practice much, he was greatly interested in the developments current in medical and

428

physical science, and there is some evidence that he first began to formulate his theory of knowledge in terms of considerations arising from medical researches of the day. Locke was a member of the Royal Society of England where he came into contact with many of the important experimental scientists, such as Robert Boyle and Sir Isaac Newton. A discussion with some of his friends seems to have been the immediate occasion of the writing of *An Essay Concerning Human Understanding*, in which Locke attempted to work out a theory of knowledge in keeping with the developing scientific findings and outlook. The completed version of the work dates from the period when Locke, along with his patron, the Earl of Shaftesbury, was a political refugee in Holland. After the Glorious Revolution of 1688, Locke returned to England, and was quickly recognized as the leading spokesman for the democratic system of government that was emerging in his homeland. The *Essay*, first published in the same year as Locke's famous work in political philosophy, *Two Treatises of Government*, quickly established the author as the foremost spokesman for the new empirical philosophical point of view that was to dominate English philosophy from then on.

The question to which Locke addressed himself in his essay is that of inquiring into "the original, certainty, and extent of human knowledge, together with the grounds and degrees of belief, opinion, and assent." By using what he called "this historical, plain method," Locke hoped to discover where our ideas and our knowledge come from, what we are capable of knowing about, how certain our

knowledge actually is, and when we may be justified in holding opinions based on our ideas. The value of such an undertaking, Locke asserted, is that one would thus know the powers and the limits of the human understanding, so that "the busy mind of man" would then restrict itself to considering only those questions with which it was actually capable of dealing and would "sit down in a quiet ignorance of those things" which were beyond the reach of its capacities.

Before commencing his investigations, Locke pointed out that human beings do, in fact, have adequate knowledge to enable them to function in the condition in which they find themselves. Therefore, even if the result of seeking the origin, nature, and extent of our knowledge leads us to the conclusion that we are unable to obtain complete certitude on various matters, this should not be grounds for despair, for skepticism, or for intellectual idleness. Too much time, Locke insisted, has been wasted by men in bemoaning their intellectual situation, or in disputing in areas in which satisfactory conclusions are impossible. Instead, he said, we should find out our abilities and our limitations, and then operate within them.

The first book of the *Essay* deals with one theory about the origin of our ideas, the thesis that our knowledge is based upon certain innate principles, which are supposed to be "stamped upon the mind of man." Locke severely criticized this theory, especially in the form in which it had been presented by thinkers such as Herbert of Cherbury (1583-1648). Adherents of this theory of innate ideas had maintained that the universal agreement of mankind regarding certain principles showed that these must be innate. Locke argued in opposition that the fact of universal agreement would be insufficient evidence as to the source of the principles in question. He also argued that, in fact, there actually are no principles that are universally agreed to, since children and idiots do not seem to know or believe the principles that are usually cited as examples of innate ideas. The way in which children acquire knowledge about the principles in question, through the learning process, further indicates that they are not born with innate ideas.

After having criticized the innate idea theory, Locke turned next to the positive side of his investigation. We do have ideas (an idea being defined as whatever is the object of the understanding when a man thinks); this is beyond any possible doubt. Then, if the ideas are not innate, where do they come from?

The second book of the *Essay* begins the development of a hypothesis about the origins of human knowledge; namely, the empirical theory. Let us suppose, Locke said, that the mind initially is just a blank tablet (a *tabula rasa*). Where, then, does it obtain its ideas? From experience, Locke proclaimed. Experience comprises two sources of ideas, sensation and reflection. We receive many, if not most, of our ideas when our sense organs are affected by external objects. We receive other ideas by reflection when we perceive the operations of our minds on the ideas which we have already received. Sensation provides us with ideas of qualities, such as the ideas of yellow, heat, and so on. Reflection provides us with ideas such as those of thinking, willing, doubting,

and so on. These two sources, Locke insisted, give us all of the ideas that we possess. If anyone has any doubts about this, let him simply inspect his own ideas and see if he has any which have not come to him either by sensation or reflection. The development of children also provides a further confirmation of this empirical theory of the origin of human knowledge. As the child receives more ideas from sensation, and reflects on them, his knowledge gradually increases.

Having thus answered the question concerning the origin of our ideas, Locke proceeded to investigate the nature of the ideas that we possess. All of our ideas are either simple or complex. A simple idea is one that is uncompounded, that contains nothing but one uniform appearance, and that cannot be distinguished into different ideas. An example of a simple idea would be the smell of a rose. A complex idea, in contrast, is one that is composed of two or more simples, such as a yellow and fragrant idea. The simples, Locke insisted, can neither be created nor destroyed by the mind. The mind has the power to repeat, compare, and unite the simples, thereby creating new complex ideas. But, the mind cannot invent simple ideas that it has not experienced. The simples, in the Lockian theory of knowledge, are the building blocks from which all of our complex and compounded ideas can be constructed and accounted for.

Many of the simple ideas are conveyed by one sense, such as the ideas of colors, sounds, tastes, smells, and touches. One crucial case that Locke argued for is the idea of solidity, which he claimed we receive by touch. This idea is that of a basic quality of bodies. It is not the same as the space that bodies occupy, nor is it the same as the subjective experience of hardness that we receive when we feel objects. Instead, for Locke, solidity is akin to the fundamental physical notion of "mass" in Newtonian physics. It is that which makes up bodies. To anyone who doubts that he is actually acquainted with such an idea, Locke suggested that he place a physical object, such as a ball, between his hands, and then try to join them. Such an experience, presumably, will give one a complete and adequate knowledge of solidity or, at least, as complete and adequate an idea as we are capable of obtaining of any simple idea. The importance of this idea in Locke's theory will be seen shortly with regard to his theory of primary and secondary qualities.

Some of our ideas are conveyed by two or more senses. Locke included in this group the ideas of space or extension, figure, rest, and motion, which, he said, we receive by means of both sight and touch. Other ideas come from reflection. And still others are the result of both reflection and sensation. Included in this later group are the ideas of pleasure and pain, and the idea of power (which we gain from reflecting on our experience of our own ability to move parts of ourselves at will).

If these are the types of ideas that we possess, classified according to their sources, can we distinguish those ideas which resemble actual features, or qualities of objects, and those which do not? The qualities of objects are divided by Locke into two categories, the primary and the secondary ones. The primary ones are those that are inseparable from bodies no matter what

state the object may be in. This group includes solidity, extension, figure, mobility, and number. In contrast, the secondary qualities "are nothing in the objects themselves, but the powers to produce various sensations in us by their primary qualities," as, for example, the power of an object, through the motion of its solid, extended parts, to produce sounds, tastes, and odors in us when we are affected by it. Thus, on Locke's theory, objects possess primary qualities, the basic ingredients of Newtonian physics, and they possess secondary ones, which are actually the powers of the primary qualities to cause us to perceive features, such as colors, odors and so on, which are not "in" the objects themselves. In terms of this distinction, we can say that our ideas of primary qualities resemble the characteristics of existing objects outside us, whereas our ideas of secondary qualities do not. The primary qualities of things are really in them, whereas the secondary qualities, as perceived sensations, are only in the observer. If there were no observers, only the primary qualities and their powers would exist. Hence, the rich, colorful, tasteful, noisy, odorous world of our experience is only the way *we* are affected by objects, not the way objects actually are. This distinction between our ideas of primary and secondary qualities led Locke to argue that some of our ideas give us genuine information about reality, while others do not.

In the remainder of the second book of the *Essay*, Locke surveyed the various other kinds of ideas that we possess, those gained by reflection, those that are complexes, and so on. The most important, in terms of his theory, and in terms of later philosophy, is the complex idea of substance. The idea of substance originates from the fact that in our experience a great many simple ideas constantly occur together. We then presume them to belong to one thing, since we cannot imagine how these simple ideas can subsist by themselves. Therefore, we accustom ourselves to suppose that there must be some *substratum* in which the ideas subsist, and we call this substratum a substance. When we ask ourselves what idea we actually have of a substance, we find that our idea is only that of a *something* which the constantly conjoined ideas belong to. When we try to find out what this something is, we discover that we do not know, except that we suppose it must be a something which can support or contain the qualities which could produce the collection of simple ideas in us. If we attempt to find out something more definite about the nature of substance, we discover that we cannot. What do color and weight belong to? If we answer, to the extended solid parts, then to what do these belong? It is like, Locke suggested, the case of the Indian philosopher who said that the world is supported by a great elephant. When asked what supported the elephant, he replied that it rested on a great tortoise. And, when asked what the tortoise rested on, he conceded and said, "I know not what." This, Locke asserted, is all that can finally be said of the nature of substance. It is something—we know not what—which we suppose is the support of the qualities which we perceive or which we are affected by.

Each constantly conjoined group of qualities we assume belongs to some particular substance, which we name

"horse," "gold," "man," and so on. We possess no clear idea of substance, either in the case of physical things or of spiritual things. But, we find that we cannot believe that either the physical qualities or the mental ones which we always experience together can exist without belonging to something. And so, although we have no definite ideas, we assume that there must be both bodies and spirits underlying and supporting the qualities that give rise to our ideas. Our inability to obtain clear ideas of substances, however, forever prevents us from gaining genuine knowledge about the real nature of things.

At the end of the second book of the *Essay*, Locke evaluated what he had discovered about the nature of our ideas. This evaluation commences the examination of the problem of the extent and certitude of our knowledge, which is developed at length in the fourth book. Our ideas are real, Locke contended, when they have a foundation in nature and when they conform with the real character of things. In this sense, all simple ideas are real, since they must be the result of genuine events and things (since the mind cannot create them, but receives them from experience). But not all real ideas are necessarily adequate representations of what does in fact exist. Ideas of primary qualities are both real and adequate. Ideas of secondary qualities are real, but only partially represent what is outside us. They represent powers that exist, but not corresponding features to the ones that we perceive. The ideas of substances that we have are very inadequate, since we are never sure that we are aware of all of the qualities that are joined together in one substance, nor are we sure of why they are so joined. Hence, some of our ideas tell us what is really outside us whereas other ideas, caused by what is outside us, or by our reflection on our ideas, do not adequately represent "real" objects. Later philosophers, such as George Berkeley and David Hume, were to argue that once Locke had admitted that some of our ideas were neither representative of reality nor adequate to portray reality, he could not then be certain that *any* of our ideas actually correspond to real features of the world. Hence, they contended that Locke, in trying to build from an empirical theory of knowledge to genuine knowledge of reality, had actually laid the groundwork for a skeptical denial of the contention that man can know anything beyond the ideas in his own mind. Locke's theory rested on maintaining that our ideas of primary qualities resemble genuine characteristics of reality. But, the opponents argued, primary qualities are really no different from secondary qualities, as we know them, and hence we have no assurance from the ideas themselves that some are real and adequate and others are not.

The third book of the *Essay* appears to deal with some unrelated topics, those concerning the nature of words and language. This book, which has begun to evoke more interest in recent years because of the present-day concern with linguistic philosophy, covers problems normally dealt with in anthropology, psychology, linguistics, and philosophy.

Two points that are raised are of central importance to Locke's main theme of the nature and extent of our knowledge, and played a role in the later history of empirical philosophy.

One of these is Locke's theory concerning the meaning and referent of general terms, such as "man," "triangle," and so on. All things that exist, Locke asserted, are particular, but by abstracting from our ideas of things, by separating from them particular details or features, we finally form a general idea. In this way we arrive at the general abstract ideas that we reason about. Berkeley and Hume both challenged Locke on this point and insisted that we do not, in fact, possess any abstract general ideas. Hence, they insisted that an empirical account of our ideas of so-called general terms must be developed from the particular ideas that we have.

One of the general terms that Locke claimed gained some meaning from the abstracting process is that of "substance." But, when he analyzed what we might mean by the term, Locke distinguished between what he called "the nominal essence" and "the real essence" of a substance. The nominal essence is that abstract general idea of a substance formed by abstracting the basic group of features that constantly occur together. The real essence, in contrast, is the nature of the object which accounts for its having the properties that it does. The nominal essence describes what properties a substance has, whereas the real essence explains why it has these properties. Unfortunately, Locke pointed out, we can never know the real essence of anything, since our information, which we abstract from, deals only with the qualities that we experience, and never with the ultimate causes which account for the occurrence of these properties. Thus, our knowledge of things is sure to be sharply curtailed because of the fact that we will never discover the reasons why things have the character-istics that they do.

The fourth and last book of the *Essay* deals with knowledge in general, with the scope of knowledge, and with the question as to how certain we can be of such knowledge. Our knowledge deals only with ideas, since these are the only items that the mind is directly acquainted with. What constitutes knowledge, according to Locke, is the perception of the agreement or dis-agreement of two ideas. Ideas may agree or disagree in four ways. They may possibly be identical or diverse. They may be related in some respect. They may agree in coexisting in the same subject or substance. And, fourthly, they may agree or disagree in having a real existence outside the mind. All of our knowledge, Locke in-sisted, falls under these headings. We know either that some ideas are the same or different, or that they are re-lated, or that they always coexist, or that they really exist independently of our minds.

If these are the kinds of items that we can know about, how can we gain such knowledge? One source of our knowledge is intuition, the direct and immediate perception of the agreement or disagreement of any two ideas. The mind "sees" that black is not white and that a circle is not a triangle. Also, "this kind of knowledge is the clearest and most certain that human frailty is capable of." Anyone who demands more certainty than that gained by in-tuition "demands he knows not what, and shows only that he has a mind to be a sceptic, without being able to be so." All certain knowledge depends upon intuition as its source and guar-antee.

We acquire knowledge not only by directly inspecting ideas, but also through demonstrations. According to Locke, when we know by demonstra-tion, we do not see *immediately* that two ideas agree or disagree, but we see *mediately*, by means of connecting two ideas with others until we are able to connect them with each other. This process is actually a series of intuitions, and each step in a demonstration is therefore certain. However, since the steps occur successively in the mind, error is possible if we forget the pre-vious steps, or if we assume that one has occurred which actually has not. Intuition and demonstration are the only two sources of certain knowledge.

However, there is another source of knowledge that has a degree of cer-titude assuring us of truths about particular experiences. This kind of knowledge goes beyond bare probabil-ity but does not reach genuine cer-tainty. It is called "sensitive knowl-edge," which is the assurance that we have on the occurrence of specific ex-periences, that certain external objects actually exist which cause or produce these experiences. We cannot reason-ably believe, Locke insisted, that all of our experiences are imaginary or are just part of a dream. Hence, we have sensitive knowledge, a degree of assur-ance that something real is going on outside us.

In terms of these kinds of knowl-edge, types of sources, and degrees of certainty, it is now possible to outline the extent of human knowledge and to evaluate what we can actually know about the real world. We can gain knowledge only to the extent that we can discover agreements or disagree-ments among our ideas. Since we can neither intuit nor demonstrate all the relations that ideas can have with one another, our knowledge is not even as extensive as our ideas. In almost all cases, we can determine with certainty whether our ideas are identical or different from one another. We can tell if our ideas are related to others only when we can discover sufficient intermediary ideas. In fields such as mathematics, we keep expanding our knowledge as more connections between ideas are intuited or demonstrated. The areas in which we seem to be most limited in gaining knowledge are those dealing with the coexistence and real existence of ideas. Since we can never know the real essence of any substance, we can never know why any two ideas must necessarily coexist. We never discover why particular secondary qualities occur when a specific arrangement of primary qualities exists. We are aware of the fact that certain ideas occur over and over again in combination, but we do not know why they do this. With regard to real existence, we are, Locke maintained, intuitively certain of our own existence and demonstratively certain that God exists. We are only sensitively certain that anything else exists, which means that we have serious assurance that objects other than ourselves and God exist only when we have experiences which we feel must be caused by something outside us. Our assurance in these cases is limited to the actual moment when we are having these experiences. Once an experience is over, we have no certitude at all that the object which caused the experience still continues to exist. All that we can know about an object when we know that it exists is that at such times it actually possesses the primary qualities that we perceive, together with the power to produce the other effects that we experience.

This assessment of the extent of our knowledge indicates, according to Locke, that we can never know enough to develop a genuine, certain science of bodies or of spirits, since our information about their existence and their natures is so extremely limited. Since we can, however, obtain sufficient knowledge and probable information to satisfy our needs in this world, we should not despair or become skeptical just because investigation has revealed how limited our knowledge actually is and how uncertain it is in many areas.

Locke's *Essay* represents the first major modern presentation of the empirical theory of knowledge. In developing an account of human knowledge in terms of how it is derived from experience, what its nature is, and how limited it is, Locke provided the basic pattern of future empirical philosophy. In attempting to justify some basis for maintaining that we can have some knowledge of some aspects of reality, Locke raised many of the problems that have remained current in philosophical discussions up to the present time. Empiricists after Locke, such as Berkeley and Hume, showed that if one consistently followed out the thesis that all of our knowledge comes from experience, one could not be certain that substances exist or that anything exists beyond the ideas directly perceived. Locke's *Essay* is the source of many of the methods, ideas, and problems that have prevailed in philosophy, especially in British and American epistemology, ever since its first publication.

OF CIVIL GOVERNMENT: THE SECOND TREATISE

Author: John Locke (1632-1704)
Type of work: Political philosophy
First published: 1690

PRINCIPAL IDEAS ADVANCED

In the state of nature all men are free and equal; no man is by nature sovereign over other men.

The law of nature governs the state of nature; reason reveals the law of nature, which is derived from God.

In a state of nature no one ought to harm another in his life, health, liberty, or possessions—and if anyone does harm another, the one he harms has the right to punish him.

By his labor a man acquires as his property the products of his labor.

In order to remedy the inconveniences resulting from a state of nature in which every man is judge of his own acts, men enter into a contract, thereby creating a civil society empowered to judge men and to defend the natural rights of men.

If a government violates the social contract by endangering the security and rights of the citizens, it rebels against the people, and the people have the right to dissolve the government.

The "glorious revolution" of 1688 saw the expulsion of James II from the throne of England and the triumph of Whig principles of government. James had been accused of abandoning the throne and thus violating the original contract between himself and his people. Two years later, Locke's *Of Civil Government: The Second Treatise* came out and was looked upon by many as a tract which justified in philosophical terms those historical events. The first *Treatise* had been an argument against the view that kings derive their right to rule from divine command, a view held by the Stuarts, especially James I, and defended with no little skill by Sir Robert Filmer in his *Patriarcha* (1680). From a philosophical point of view it is of little consequence whether Locke intended his defense of the revolution to apply only to the events in the England of his day or to all men at any time; certainly we can study his principles for what they are and make up our own minds as to the generality of their scope.

After rejecting Filmer's thesis, Locke looked for a new basis of government and a new source of political power. He recognized that the state must have the power to regulate and preserve property; that to do so it must also have the right to punish, from the death penalty to all lesser ones. In order to carry out the laws passed, the force of the community must be available to the government, and it must also be ready to serve in the community's defense from foreign injury. Political power by which the government performs these functions ought to be used only for the public good

436

and not for private gain or advantage. Locke then set out to establish a basis for this power, a basis which he considered moral and just.

He turned to a concept used by political theorists since the time of the Stoics in ancient Greece: natural law with its concomitants, the state of nature and the state of war. The state of nature has been objected to as a concept by many because history does not indicate to us such a state existed. In this treatise Locke tries to answer this sort of objection by pointing to "primitive" societies known in his day, the nations of Indians living in the New World. But this is not a strong argument and was not really needed by Locke. The concept of the state of nature can be used as a device to set off and point up the difference between a civil state in which laws are enacted by the government and a contrasting state in which either these laws are absent in principle or another set of laws prevails. In this way the basis of civil enactments and the position of the individual within society may be better understood. This applies also to the other concepts mentioned, the state of war and natural law. At any rate, Locke holds that in the state of nature each man may order his own life as he sees fit, free from any restrictions that other men might impose; in this sense he and all others are equal. They are equal in a more profound sense from which, as it were, their right to act as independent agents comes; that is, as children of God. By use of his reason, man can discover God's commands by which he should order his life in the state of nature. These commands we call the "laws of nature." Thus, although one is free to act as he pleases in the state of nature,

he is still obligated to act according to God's commands. This insures that his actions, although free, will not be licentious. The basic restriction that God's laws place upon an individual is that he treat others as he himself would like to be treated. Since men are equal and independent, they should not harm one another regarding their "life, health, liberty, or possessions. . . ."

Man's glory as well as his downfall has been free will, whereby he may choose to do or not to do what he ought to do. To preserve himself from those who choose to harm him, one has the right to punish transgressors of the law. Reparation and restraint are the two reasons that justify punishment when an individual by his acts has shown that he has agreed to live by a law other than that which common reason and equity dictate; that is, he has chosen to violate God's orders. The right to punish is thus a natural right by which men in the state of nature may preserve themselves and mankind from the transgressions of the lawless. This right is the basis for the right of governments to punish lawbreakers within the state; thus Locke provides a ground for one aspect of political power which he had noted earlier.

When an individual indicates through a series of acts which are apparently premeditated that he has designs on another's life or property, then he places himself in a state of war, a state of enmity and destruction, toward his intended victim. In the state of nature men ought to live according to reason and, hence, according to God's commands. Each man must be the judge of his own actions for on earth he has no common superior with authority to judge between him and another when a question of aggression arises, and when relief is sought. His conscience must be his guide as to whether he and another are in a state of war.

In The Declaration of Independence, the American colonists proclaimed that men had natural rights granted them by their Creator, that governments were instituted by men with their consent to protect these rights. Locke, as pointed out, held these rights to be life, liberty, and property, whereas the Declaration proclaims them to be life, liberty, and the pursuit of happiness. It is interesting that Jefferson pondered whether to use "property" or "pursuit of happiness" and in an early draft actually had the former set down. Much of Locke's discussion in this treatise influenced the statesmen and leaders of the Colonies during the period of the American Revolution.

Locke seems to use various senses of "property" in his discussions. Speaking quite generally, one might say that whatever was properly one's own (this might mean whatever God had endowed an individual with or whatever the legislature of the commonwealth had declared as legal possession) no one else had a claim to. In spelling out this idea, Locke starts first with one's own body, which is God-given and which no one has a claim upon; a man has a right to be secure in his person. Included in this idea, of course, is the fact that life itself is a gift to which no one else has a claim, as well as the freedom to move about without restriction. There is next the more common use of "property," which is often rendered "estate" and which refers to the proper possessions which one gains in working the earth that God has given man to use for the advantage of his life and its convenience. Since working for one's own advantage and convenience involves the pursuit of happiness, it can be seen in what way the terms "property" and "pursuit of happiness" are interchangeable. This more common use of "property" is, nonetheless, related to the first use in Locke's theory. What is properly a man's own may be extended when, with regard to the common property that God has blessed men with for their use, a man mixes his labor with it and makes it his own. Divine command prescribes, however, that he take no more than he needs, for to take more than one's share may lead to the waste of God's gift and result in want for others. Locke believed that there was more than enough land in the world for men but that it should be used judiciously; he does complicate matters, however, by stating that disproportionate and unequal possessions may be acquired within a government through the consent of the governed. Locke's embryonic economic theory may be looked upon as an early statement of the classical or labor theory of value. This is especially so if we remember that aside from the "natural" or God-given articles of value that man has, he creates objects of value by means of his own labor; more succinctly, labor creates value. This view was held by such influential thinkers in economic history as Adam Smith, David Ricardo, and Karl Marx. Before we leave this aspect of Locke's theory we should note that he has again provided a ground for the use of political power to regulate, preserve, and protect property in all its aspects by establishing its place in the state of nature prior to the institution of the commonwealth.

Locke has shown that although men ought to live according to divine commands, some do not and thus they turn the state of nature into one of war. Since there is no common superior on earth to whom one can turn for restitution, men are often left helpless. It is obvious that not every injury imagined is a wrong, that two individuals in conscience may disagree, that those instances of obvious wrongs are not always rectifiable when men have only their own judgments and strength to depend upon. A disinterested judge supported by more power than a single person has alone may provide people with a remedy for the insecurity that exists in the state of nature. In the most general sense of "property," a commonwealth may provide the solution to its preservation and security by making public the laws by which men ought to live, by establishing a government by which differences may be settled through the office of known and impartial judges who are authorized to do so, and by instituting a police force to execute the law, a protection absent in the state of nature. Men give up their rights to judge for themselves and to execute the laws of nature to the commonwealth, which in turn is obligated to use the power which it has gained for the ends which led to the transference of these rights. In giving up their rights, men consent to form a body politic under one government and, in so doing, obligate themselves to every member of that society to submit to the determinations of the majority. Note that everyone who enters into the society from the state of

nature must consent to do so; hence, consent is unanimous and anyone who does not consent is not a member of the body politic. On the other hand, once the body politic is formed, its members are thenceforth subject to the vote of the majority.

In discussing consent and the general question, "Who has consented and what are its significant signs?" Locke uses the traditional distinction between tacit and express consent. Although he is somewhat ambiguous at times, his position is apparently as follows. There are two great classes or categories of individuals within society, those who are members and those who are residents but not members. (A convenient and similar distinction would be those who are citizens and those who are aliens.) Both these two groups receive benefits from the government and hence are obligated to obey it. By their presence they enjoy the peace and security that goes with a government of law and order, and it is morally and politically justifiable that that government expect of them that they obey its laws. Those who are merely residents may quit the body politic when they please; their tacit consent lasts only as long as their presence in the state. Members, however, by their express consent create and perpetuate the society. They are not free to be or not be members at their whim, else the body politic would be no different from the state of nature or war from which its members emerged, and anarchy would prevail. Citizens usually have the protection of their government at home and abroad, and often, at least in the government Locke preferred, a voice in the affairs of their nation. Locke points out, however, that the people who form the commonwealth by their unanimous consent may also delegate their power to a few or to one (oligarchy or monarchy); but in any case it is their government.

There are certain aspects of government which Locke believed must be maintained to insure that it functions for the public good. (1) The legislative, which is the supreme governmental power, must not use its power arbitrarily over the lives and fortunes of the people. The law of nature still prevails in the governments of men. (2) Nor should power be exercised without deliberation. Extempore acts would place the people in as great jeopardy as they were in the state of nature. (3) The supreme power cannot take from a man his property without his consent. This applies also to taxation. (4) The legislative power cannot be transferred to any one else, but must remain in the hands of that group to which it was delegated by the people. In so acting, the legislature insures the people that political power will be used for the public good.

Locke believed that the interests of the people would be protected more fully in a government in which the three basic powers, legislative, executive, and federative, were separate and distinct in their functions. The legislature need meet only periodically, but the executive should be in session, as it were, continually, whereas the management of the security of the commonwealth from foreign injury would reside in the body politic as a whole. Strictly speaking, the federative power —treaty-making and so forth—need not be distinguished from the legislative. It is interesting that the three branches of government in the United States include the judiciary rather than the federative, which is shared by the executive and legislative branches of government. This shows that Montesquieu as well as Locke influenced the Philadelphia convention.

Government, which is made up of these three basic powers, of which the legislative is supreme, must not usurp the end for which it was established. The community, even after it has delegated its power, does not give up its right of self-preservation, and in this sense it retains forever the ultimate power of sovereignty. This power cannot be used by the community which is under obligation to obey the acts of the government unless that government is dissolved. It must be pointed out that the community is for Locke an important political concept. The exercise of its power after the dissolution of government is as a public body and does not involve a general return to the state of nature or war by its members. But in what way is a government dissolved?

When a government exercises power beyond right, when public power is used for private gain, then tyranny prevails. Such acts set the stage for the dissolution of government. It should be pointed out that in forming a community and in delegating power to a government, the people, especially in the latter case, enter into an agreement or, analogously, into a social contract with their government to provide them with security, preservation, and those conveniences that they desire, in exchange for the transference of their rights and the honor, respect, and obligation which they render to the government. The violation of their part of the contract leads government to declare them (as individuals) outlaws, to use its police force to subdue them, and its courts to set punishment for them.

In discussing dissolution in general, Locke points out that it can apply to societies and communities as well as to governments. It is seldom that a community is dissolved. If it does happen, it is usually the result of a foreign invasion which is followed by the utter destruction of the society. Governments, on the other hand, are dissolved from within. Either the executive abandons his office (as was done by James II) and the laws cannot be carried out, or the legislative power is affected in various ways which indicate a violation of trust. If, for example, the property of the subjects is invaded, or if power is used arbitrarily, then government is dissolved. Obviously, it falls upon the community to judge when this power is being abused. Generally, Locke holds, the people are slow to act; it takes not merely one or two but a long series of abuses to lead them to revolution. In fact, he points out that the term "rebellion" indicates a return to a state of war and a denial of the principles of civil society. But when this happens in the dissolution of government, it is the government that has rebelled and not the community; it is the community that stands for law and order and puts down the rebellion. Thus Locke rather cleverly concludes his treatise, not with a justification of the right of rebellion but, rather, with the right of the people to put down unlawful government, unlawful in that it violates the trust and the law of nature, leading to tyranny, rebellion, and dissolution.

THE HISTORICAL AND CRITICAL DICTIONARY

Author: Pierre Bayle (1647-1706)
Type of work: Skeptical criticism of theology
First published: 1695-1697

PRINCIPAL IDEAS ADVANCED

Since reason is useless, man should turn to faith.

The traditional philosophical and theological arguments prove nothing; skeptical criticism can demolish any theory.

By consistently employing the arguments of philosophers we find that we can no longer be certain even of the existence of external objects, to say nothing of their qualities.

Such Christian doctrines as those concerning the Trinity, the Fall, Transubstantiation, and Original Sin, if self-evidently true, contradict other propositions that are also self-evidently true.

There is no faith better established on reason than that which is built on the ruins of reason; the true man of faith accepts beliefs for which he can give no rational justification.

441

Bayle's *Historical and Critical Dictionary* is a compendium of arguments, tending toward a skeptical view, for and against almost every theory in philosophy and theology. It was called in the eighteenth century the "Arsenal of the Enlightenment," and it played a very important role in intellectual discussions throughout the first half of the eighteenth century. Significant criticisms of the major and minor philosophers and theologians of the time appear throughout the *Dictionary*. Thinkers such as George Berkeley, David Hume, and Voltaire used the work as a source of arguments and inspiration. Remaining in vogue until it was no longer useful as a reference work, the last edition appeared in 1820.

The author was one of the most interesting critical figures of his time. He was born in southern France, the son of a Calvinist pastor. He was sent to a Jesuit school in Toulouse, where he was converted to Catholicism. Shortly thereafter he was reconverted to Calvinism, after which he fled to Geneva to avoid being persecuted. He studied at the Calvinist university there, and then returned to France incognito. For a time he was professor of philosophy at the Calvinist college at Sedan, but when the final persecutions of the Huguenots took place in France, he fled with many of his coreligionists to The Netherlands, where he remained for the rest of his life. He taught first in a high school in Rotterdam and then devoted himself to editing one of the first learned journals, the *Nouvelles de la Republique des Lettres*. He became embroiled in one controversy after another, with the liberal Calvinist theologians, with the orthodox ones, with Catholic spokesmen in France, and with philosophers of every school. During the last twenty years of his life, he was a central figure in almost every intellectual debate. He insisted that he was a Protestant in the true sense of the word; he protested everything that was said and everything that was done. He fought against religious intolerance and philosophical dogmatism, and he died with pen in hand, writing another blast against some hapless opponent. His death was mourned by friend and foe alike, for he had contributed much to the learned world through his polemical publications and with his critical acumen, his many and varied interests, and his many friendships throughout the intellectual world.

At once the greatest and the most notorious of Bayle's achievements is his *Dictionary*. It was begun as a series of corrections to a previous biographical dictionary, but it grew until it became an enormous work in its own right. It consists, formally, of a series of articles in alphabetical order, giving biographical information and historical data about all sorts of people, places, and things, some historical, some mythological. Many of the people discussed are obscure theologians, or philosophers with strange theories. The meat of the *Dictionary* appears primarily in the footnotes, which occupy most of the space, appearing below the text on the huge folio pages in double columns of small print. Many of the footnotes contain digressions which allow Bayle to bring up all of his favorite disputes. An important, interesting, or exciting digression can appear almost anywhere. In the article on "Rorarius," for example, Bayle launches into one of the first and most significant criticisms of

442

Leibniz. The footnotes are also interspersed with spicy tales about the love lives and sexual practices of various famous people, and with profane versions of Bible stories. In the course of the thousands of footnotes, virtually every theory ever propounded is attacked, and a recurring theme appears —man, realizing the uselessness of rational endeavors, should turn to faith.

When the work first appeared, it was immediately attacked and banned in France for its anti-Catholic, anti-religious, skeptical views, as well as for its obscene content. It was similarly criticized in Holland by Bayle's own church, the French Reformed Church of Rotterdam, which demanded an explanation for the material contained in the *Dictionary*. The author insisted that he had been misunderstood. The obscenities, he said, represented reports of actual historical facts, and he could not be held responsible for the actions of historical personages, many of them long dead. As to the other charges, he insisted that they were entirely without foundation. His intention was to support the faith of his church by exposing the weaknesses of all rational theories, so that people, seeing this, would turn away from philosophy and science, to faith. His opponents contended that Bayle had made such a mockery of the faith that he could not possibly be seriously advocating it. To answer the charges, Bayle wrote some appendices to the *Dictionary*, plus additional footnotes, and incorporated them into the next edition, that of 1702. These additions were considered so much more dangerous and heretical than his original work that they produced another storm of attacks, as well as a series of answers on Bayle's part. For the rest of his life, Bayle fought to vindicate his contention that his general, overall view was the same as that of John Calvin and of all of the most orthodox theologians. The liberal and the orthodox Calvinists fought against this claim and tried to unmask their opponent as a true heretic. Bayle kept pointing out that his most extreme orthodox opponents really said the same things as he did. But, as one of them observed, "When I say it, it is serious. When he [Bayle] says it, it turns out comical."

Bayle has been interpreted, by most critics, as being the earliest figure in the Enlightenment to use his scholarship and his critical abilities for the purpose of destroying all confidence in religion, both through undermining the reasons given by theologians for the faith, and through making the faith appear ridiculous. On the other hand, some scholars have argued that Bayle was sincere, that he was actually defending religion rather than opposing it, using the same sort of irrational "defense" later employed by Søren Kierkegaard. Neither the information about Bayle's life, nor an analysis of his writings, results in a definitive solution of the mystery of his *real* intentions. But, regardless of what he may have thought he was trying to accomplish, the impact of Bayle's thought in the eighteenth century caused many thinkers to doubt traditional philosophical and theological arguments, and to doubt the philosophies and religions as well. Bayle also supplied much of the ammunition used by the skeptical philosophers of the Age of Reason.

In the wide range of articles and issues dealt with in the *Dictionary*, some deserve special notice because of either their influence or their content. The longest article, on Spinoza, was notorious in its day because it presented the first defense of Spinoza's character as a saintly human being, in contrast to the grim rumors of the time that Spinoza must have been a villainous person to have advocated the philosophy that he did. But while defending Spinoza's character, Bayle also engaged in his favorite sport, that of decimating other people's theories. The article on "Rorarius" presents the first serious discussion that had appeared in print of Leibniz's novel metaphysical theory. (When Leibniz wrote a lengthy response, Bayle enlarged the footnotes in "Rorarius," in the second edition, to discuss Leibniz's defense as well as some new criticisms of his own.) The philosophies of Father Malebranche, John Locke, and Sir Isaac Newton are all subjected to devastating criticisms in the article on Zeno of Elea. Two of the articles on early religious groups, one on the Manicheans and the other on the Paulicians, deal with the problem of evil, arguing that it is not possible to disprove the Manichean theory that there is an evil as well as a good God, or the theory that God is author of evil. These two articles unleashed a storm of controversy and led to the writing of two famous answers, that of Leibniz, in his *Theodicy* (1710) and that of William King, Archbishop of Dublin, in his *Origins of Evil* (1739). Both Hume and Voltaire used Bayle's arguments on the subject of evil in their attacks on traditional theology.

In the article on Zeno of Elea, especially in the famous footnotes G and H, Bayle levels his attacks on the modern metaphysical systems. He tries to show that, on the basis of the premises of a philosopher such as René Descartes, no satisfactory evidence can be offered to show that an external world exists, or that it can be consistently described in mathematical terms. First, Bayle argues that the same sort of skeptical evidence that led modern philosophers to doubt that real objects possess the secondary qualities that we perceive, such as color, smell, heat, and so on, should also lead these philosophers to doubt whether real objects possess the primary, mathematical qualities, such as extension. The reality of secondary qualities is denied by almost all seventeenth century philosophers. They all point out that because these qualities are perceived differently at different times, under different conditions, and by different people, the real object cannot possess these variable properties. Bayle then contends that if this argument is considered adequate, it should also be applied to a quality such as extension. The same object appears big to one at one time, small at another. One's perception of its size differs from that of other persons. Hence, extension, like color, is no more than an idea in my own mind, and is not a characteristic of real objects. Further, Bayle gathers together all the arguments from philosophers such as Malebranche to show that there is no genuine evidence that real objects even exist. It cannot be demonstrated that they do. All of the information that is offered as evidence could be due to the actions of God upon us, without requiring the actual existence of objects corresponding to our ideas and feelings, or causing them. If it is answered that God would be deceiving us if he made us believe in the existence of real objects when there really were none, Bayle answers, in the article on Pyrrho of Elis, that God makes peasants think that snow is white, and the philosophers claim this is a delusion, so why cannot God also delude the philosophers into thinking objects exist? To conclude this subject, Bayle endorses Malebranche's view that it is faith only, and not reason, that can justify our beliefs about the real existence of things. Hence, we ought to be content with the light of faith, and give up the hopeless pursuit of truth by means of reason.

The longest and most explicit statement of this theme (and the one that was most often debated in the eighteenth century) occurs in footnotes B and C of the article on Pyrrho. The discussion begins as a comment on the observation in the text that it is fitting that Pyrrhonian skepticism is detested in the schools of theology. Bayle points out that Pyrrhonism, complete skepticism, is a danger only to theology, not to science or politics. Practically every scientist *is* a skeptic, since scientists doubt that it is possible to discover the secret causes and springs of nature. Instead, the scientists look only for descriptive information and probable hypotheses about nature. Regarding politics, the skeptics are not dangerous since they are always willing to follow the laws and customs of society because of the fact that they have no dogmatic moral or legal principles. But skepticism can be a great danger to religion, because religious doctrines should be completely certain. If not, there will be no firm conviction. Fortunately, however, Bayle points out, skepticism has little

effect on people, either because of the Grace of God, their education, their stupidity, or their natural inclinations.

To show the merits or the dangers of skepticism, Bayle tells a story about a discussion between two abbots. One asserts that it is incomprehensible to him that there are still any skeptics around, since God has given us the Revelation. The other replies that both the "new philosophy" and Christian theology provide excellent ammunition for any skeptic. The philosophy of thinkers such as Descartes leads, as the article on Zeno shows, to a complete skepticism about the nature and existence of the real world. By consistently employing the arguments of seventeenth century philosophers we can no longer be sure whether objects possess *any* qualities, including those of extension and motion, and we cannot even be sure that there are any objects.

Further, Bayle insists, we cannot even be sure of the dogmatic philosophers' contention that something is true, because we cannot be certain of the criterion of truth. Philosophers have said that self-evidence is the sure mark of truth. But, the skeptical abbot declares, if Christianity is true, then there are self-evident propositions which must be false, and so, self-evidence cannot be taken as the standard for measuring what is true. Bayle then argues that the Christian doctrines of the Trinity, Transubstantiation, the Fall, and Original Sin contradict various self-evident propositions of philosophy such as that two things not different from a third are not different from each other, that a body cannot be in several places at the same time, that

445

one ought to prevent evil if one can, and so on. In passing from the shadows of paganism to the light of Scripture, the abbot points out, we have learned the falsity of a great many self-evident notions.

Then the skeptical abbot answers the possible objection that all of the evidence against the criterion of truth depends upon evaluating God and his actions by human standards, and these may not be the correct criteria for some judgments. If this objection is taken seriously, then we are again led to complete skepticism because we are then unable to know what is true in God's world if we cannot employ our own standards to judge by.

The arguments of the skeptics, Bayle contends, cannot be answered by human reason, and they expose the weakness of our rational faculties. Thus we are made to feel the need for a guide different from reason; namely, faith. In footnote C, this point is explored further, first by pointing out that complete skepticism is the greatest achievement of human rationality, but that even so, it is completely self-defeating. One cannot even believe that skepticism is true without ceasing to be a skeptic. The attempt to become completely dubious about everything by means of reason finally leads one to give up reasoning entirely, and to turn to a more secure guide, faith. Skepticism is portrayed as the best preparation for religion because it reveals the total and hopeless inadequacy of reason as a means for finding truth. One is then ready to accept Revelation without question. In a later defense of this theory, Bayle asserts that there is no faith better established on reason than that which is built on the ruins of reason.

This total irrationalism and acceptance of religion on blind faith was bitterly attacked by theologians everywhere. In the second edition of the *Dictionary*, Bayle added a more detailed (and more anti-rational) exposition of his views in the appendix explaining the article on Pyrrho. Here, he argued that the world of reason and the world of faith are two totally different and opposing realms. If one looks for evidence, one cannot have faith, and the search for evidence will end only in complete skepticism. If one completely abandons the quest for evidence, then faith is possible. In fact, the more irrational one's beliefs are, the more this means that such beliefs cannot be based on any evidence whatsoever (otherwise, there might be some reason for them). The true and complete man of faith, then, according to Bayle's rendition of the case, is the person who accepts a belief for which he can give no justification and no reason of any kind. Bayle, in keeping with the other French skeptics from Montaigne onward, cites as his Scriptural authority for this interpretation of religion St. Paul's anti-rational pronouncements in the first chapter of his first letter to the Corinthians.

Opponents immediately pointed out that this irrationalism would destroy religion rather than defend it. There would be no reason left for accepting a religion, no standards by which to tell what is true or false, and no way of distinguishing the true religion from all the others. In fact, the critics claimed, Bayle's religion without reason would actually be a form of madness, or superstition, which neither Bayle nor any other "reasonable" man could possibly accept. Bayle fought back during the last years of his life.

attacking the reasons his opponents offered for their religious views and for their criticisms, and insisting that all of the most orthodox theologians had said exactly the same thing as he was saying.

Whether Bayle was sincere or not, the arguments he presented to show that religion could not be based on reason became basic ingredients in the deistic, agnostic, and atheistic views developed in the course of the Enlightenment. His arguments against modern philosophy became crucial themes in the theories of Berkeley, Hume, and Voltaire. The *Dictionary* was all-important in transforming the intellectual world from its metaphysical and theological phase to the skeptical and empirical phase of the Age of Reason.

A TREATISE CONCERNING
THE PRINCIPLES OF HUMAN KNOWLEDGE

Author: George Berkeley (1685-1753)
Type of work: Metaphysics, epistemology
First published: 1710

PRINCIPAL IDEAS ADVANCED

The belief in abstract ideas had led to the supposition that material objects are quite different from sensations; the fact is that material objects are nothing but collections of sensations given a common name.

Esse is percipi; to be is to be perceived—this is a truth concerning all material objects.

If it be argued that ideas are copies of material objects, consider whether anything could be like an idea but an idea.

The distinction between primary and secondary qualities (between such structural properties as figure, motion, and shape, on the one hand, and color, odor, and sound, on the other) on the ground that the former are objective, the latter subjective, cannot be maintained: the primary qualities depend on the secondary; they are equally subjective.

There is no independently existing material substratum; a distinction between the world of illusion and the world of reality can be maintained by realizing the greater vividness and coherency to be found in veridical sensations.

The order in nature is created and maintained by God, who secures the reality of all things by his perception.

The idea that "all those bodies which compose the mighty frame of the world, have not any subsistence without a mind—that their *being* is to be perceived or known" will hardly seem obvious to anyone unfamiliar with Bishop Berkeley or with idealism. This startling statement has considera-

447

ble shock value, but it is true to Berkeley's bold metaphysical thesis that reality is mental or spiritual in nature.

The statement's emphasis on perception reveals its author's epistemological and methodological approach: empiricism. While not all empiricists would accept Berkeley's conclusions and not all metaphysical idealists would accept his method, none would deny his importance in the traditions of both empiricism and idealism. That his method and even his immaterialism have influenced some modern physicists and that his analytical technique is valued even by such antimetaphysicians as the logical positivists are proofs of the classical status Berkeley's work still enjoys.

His aims, however, were primarily those of a metaphysician and theologian; he wished to undermine skepticism and atheism by refuting materialism, to demonstrate God's existence and immateriality, to show the immortality of the soul, and to clarify current scientific and philosophical confusions. The latter are due, he claimed, not to inherent defects in man's mental faculties, but to their use: "we have first raised a dust and then complain we cannot see." Berkeley intended to settle this dust and to destroy materialism.

A chief cause of obscurity, he begins, is the doctrine of abstract ideas, the theory that the mind can abstract from particular qualities a clearly conceived notion of what is common to them, but which itself is otherwise like none of them, or that the mind can separate in thought what cannot be separated in reality. An example of the first abstraction would be a notion of color which is neither red, blue, green, and so forth, or of exten-

sion which has neither size, shape, line, plane, nor surface; an illustration of the second would be an abstract idea of color or motion without extension.

Berkeley finds such abstraction psychologically impossible and challenges the reader to conceive such an idea as that of a triangle with all of the general and yet none of the specific characteristics of triangles. But must Berkeley then deny the universality of ideas essential to rational demonstration such as geometrical proofs relevant to all triangles? No—ideas may be general without being abstract; we generalize particular ideas by temporarily disregarding their unique features, while our demonstrations concern only features shared. But this universality in *function* must not be mistaken for abstract *conception*; the latter is actually without content and unintelligible.

Berkeley claims that the confused belief in abstract ideas arises from language; we have assumed that general names signify precise abstract ideas indispensable to thinking and communication, but these assumptions are false. Let us then attend not to words but to ideas themselves; since these are perfectly transparent, being known directly, we can avoid merely verbal controversies and errors springing from abstraction. Thus, we will be prepared for a most far-reaching application of the above conclusions to an analysis of the nature and existence of the objects of knowledge.

The objects of knowledge, Berkeley writes, are ideas of three kinds: sensations; ideas originating in the mind's own passions and activities; and those of memory and imagination. Our immediate concern is with "sensible" objects. Through sight we know color;

through sight and touch we know size and shape; through touch, hardness; through smelling, odors. Certain constant collections of such ideas are considered one object or thing and accordingly named, such as "apple" or "tree." But obviously perceived ideas require a perceiver, and this is spirit or mind, not itself an idea. Careful examination shows that thoughts and ideas have no existence external to minds; hence "sensible" things or physical objects do not exist apart from their perception in minds—their very *esse* is *percipi*; for them to *be* is to be perceived.

The typical reaction to this conclusion is to accuse Berkeley of denying the reality of the physical world and even the evidence of his senses. But Berkeley explains that when we say that a table *exists,* this means that we or some other spirit sees and feels it, or will do so on occasion. The very meaning of "existence" or "being" applied to perceptible objects is exhaustively described in terms drawn from perception—nothing else can meaningfully be said about them. To think that sensible objects or their alleged metaphysical substratum, matter, exist "without" (external to) the mind is to entertain an unintelligible abstraction and a clear contradiction. People commonly think that houses or mountains exist unperceived. But what are these but objects of the senses? Is it not self-contradictory to think that sensations or ideas exist unperceived? When we imagine that we can think of unperceived objects we are merely thinking of objects while forgetting the perceiver, but meanwhile we *are* perceiving or thinking of them. We cannot conceive the inconceivable.

But the common belief that matter exists even when it is unperceived will not die easily, so Berkeley tries to anticipate every possible objection. One of the first arises from the "representative" theory of perception, which grants that ideas occur only in minds but holds that they represent or copy things outside minds. Berkeley's most direct answer is that ideas can resemble nothing but other ideas. How could a color represent something uncolored, or a sound something inaudible?

Both rationalists and empiricists such as Descartes and Locke held that in describing our knowledge of the physical world we must distinguish sensed qualities which are mostly subjective from others which are wholly objective. These philosophers argue that "primary" qualities such as figure, motion, spatial location, and shape inhere in objects themselves and are perceived without distortion or addition by the observer. But "secondary" qualities such as color, sound, and taste are so obviously variable they must be contributed by the subject's mind, though of course originally caused by action upon him of the primary qualities. Thus color qualities are subjective but caused by motion of light—color is "in the mind" but motion is "out there." Since qualities must qualify something (it was assumed), the primary qualities subsist in matter, the reality of which they are the appearances. Thus primary qualities really do represent or copy the external world.

But this theory is fallacious, Berkeley holds; if it admits that secondary qualities are in the mind, it must concede that primary qualities are also, since both types are inseparable actually and conceptually. Can one conceive of an extended, moving body which has no color or temperature? Too, the arguments from their relativity proving that secondary qualities are subjective apply equally to the primary. Consider size; our estimate of size depends on the nature and position of our sense organs. Berkeley's *Three Dialogues Between Hylas and Philonous* (1713) makes this point by noting that what will seem minute to a man may appear mountainous to a mite. Even number varies with point of view, as when a given length is considered as one, three, or thirty-six (yard, feet or inches). But finally, the copy theory leads to utter skepticism by insisting that ideas represent something wholly unlike ideas, and by distinguishing between "mere appearance" and "reality," for it thus posits an external world forever unknowable.

Still, belief in a material substratum or support of sensed qualities will persist. Yet matter cannot literally "support" qualities, since "support" is itself a spatial term and space is perceptual. Even if there were such a substance, the problem of knowledge would remain. Knowledge stems from either sense or reason; the former yields only immediate objects of perception, or ideas, as even the materialist hold. But reason cannot bridge the gap between ideas and matter, since it would then have to argue from what we know—ideas—to something quite alien; and materialists themselves admit no logically necessary relationship between ideas and matter. Furthermore, it sometimes happens, and conceivably always could happen, that we entertain ideas when no external bodies are supposed present, as in the case of dreams. Finally—and here Berkeley broaches a problem Descartes could not solve—how could matter possibly act on spirit to produce ideas? The more one insists on their substantial differences, the less conceivable is causal interaction.

But if we deny the reality of external bodies, will it not sound very odd to say that we eat and drink ideas? Of course, agrees Berkeley; but his argument is about truth, not terminology. We may use common speech, even the term "matter" itself, as long as we refer only to the sensible world. If an opponent boasts his senses' superiority to any argument whatever, Berkeley is only too glad to join him, for he denies nothing actually perceived. "It were a mistake to think that what is here said derogates in the least from the reality of things." Berkeley intended to refute skepticism and atheism not by denying reality but by showing the impossibility of the materialistic account of it.

Yet if his theory is true, can it distinguish reality from illusion—for example, real from merely imaginary fire—since everything perceived consists only of ideas? If there is any doubt, Berkeley answers, put your hand in the real fire, and you will sense a pain lacking in the imaginary one—but can you suppose pain existing externally to a mind? We differentiate fantasy and illusion from the real world by obvious differences in their ideas; those of the latter are more vivid, constant, and coherent; their regular, predictable order constitutes the laws of nature, and they are independent of our wills as imagination is not. In fact, this independence marks the one legitimate sense in which we speak of "external objects"; sensed qualities are external to finite spirits' wills but not to that of the

450

eternal Spirit, God, of whose will they are a perceptible expression.

Almost every reader objects that if the existence of things depends on perception, they will exist and cease to exist with the occurrence and cessation of perception, and that this theory is absurd. Berkeley counters by asking whether the statement that a table continues to exist when everyone leaves the room means anything more than that *if* one were still there he would perceive it, or if he were to return, he would once again see it. From the reliability of nature's order we can both reconstruct the past and predict the future, in neither of which are there *present* finite minds as perceivers, but this is wholly consistent with saying that objects and events are only what they are perceived to be (in past, present, or future). If no finite minds existed at all, whatever remained would nevertheless be perceived by the omniscient, eternal Spirit. Clearly, the strength of Berkeley's arguments here lies in the difficulty of *describing* an existent known to no mind whatever.

But is this really a plausible account of nature? Must not any scientific explanation of natural events presuppose causal efficacy resident either in matter itself or in primary qualities such as extension and motion? Berkeley says no, he has shown already that the notion of matter explains nothing at all, since it is incomprehensible and the primary qualities are ideas. Ideas are inert or inactive, having no causal power; there is no *idea* of causation in addition to those of successive events. Yet we gain a *notion* of causality from our own volition; we find that we can produce and manipulate some ideas at will. But if action is

the prerogative of spirit, and if finite minds could not possibly produce the vast and intricate system of ideas we call "nature," it follows that nature is the work of the infinite Spirit.

Suppose, however, that we grant both the existence of this Spirit and the extremely complicated mechanism of nature. To what purpose did God create such a powerless machine if he wished merely to communicate with finite minds? Why not do it directly? Berkeley meets this cavil by observing that if anything were superfluous, it would be an unknowable, ineffectual corporeal substance; it is possible, on the other hand, to give a rationale for nature.

Its orderly mechanism, while not indispensable to God, is still instrumental to man's learning and profit. Observing the conjunction of fire and heat, man learns not that the idea of fire *causes* the idea of heat, but that the former *signifies* that the latter will follow. Single ideas are like words, and the laws of nature like the grammar of a language; however, just as it is unwise to study only grammar and neglect meaning, so it is folly for science to concentrate only on mechanical laws and neglect the final causes (purposes) they express, those determined by God's wisdom and goodness. This does not derogate from science, but redirects it to explication of phenomena as signs rather than as effects of physical causes. Thus the hypothesis of matter is unnecessary even to physics.

Why, then, is belief in matter so pervasive? Partly because men found that objects of sensation seemed to be independent of themselves and thus supposed that such ideas exist externally. Philosophers saw the error of this supposition, but in trying to correct it by positing the external existence of matter they substituted another mistake, unaware of the internal contradictions involved. Furthermore, the operations of the eternal Spirit are so lawful that it was not imagined they were those of a *free* spirit rather than those of rigidly mechanical causes; and while they clearly point to his being, still there is no collection of sensed qualities making God visible or tangible as men are.

In the foregoing considerations the existence of spirit has been assumed on the basis of only one argument—that since ideas are not self-subsistent and matter is a nonentity, ideas can exist only in a different substance, spirit. But if they are inactive and we can thus have no ideas of spirit, how do we *know* that spirit exists? Berkeley says that we have a *notion* of spirit because we understand the terms describing it and its activities, a notion we get "by inward feeling or reflection." Other spirits are known by reasoning from analogy with our own; we perceive their effects and infer other minds as causes. A spirit's existence consists not in being perceived but in perceiving; it is "one simple, undivided, active being—as it perceives ideas it is called the *understanding,* and as it produces or otherwise operates about them it is called the *will.*" No more than a notion of matter can be abstracted from sensed qualities can the existence of spirit be abstracted from its cogitation.

An interesting consequence follows from this in conjunction with Berkeley's analysis of time; time cannot be abstracted from the succession of ideas we experience, and so the duration of a spirit depends on the ideas and activities occurring within it. Therefore, Berkeley concludes, the spirit always thinks, the notion of a literally thoughtless mind being unintelligible. He asserts, "*Spirits* and *ideas* are things so wholly different. . . . There is nothing alike or common in them. . . ." Since spirits are indivisible, incorporeal, and unextended, it follows that they are not subject to the laws of nature and hence enjoy immortality.

Berkeley's arguments for God's existence have been given in part; the eternal Spirit must exist as the only sufficient cause of nature. When we consider the lawfulness, perfection, beauty, and design of the whole system, it is obvious that the characteristics of nature suggest the character of God. God's existence is in a sense known more certainly than that of any other spirit, since we constantly perceive his effects, even those ideas by which we communicate with other men. If we do not realize this fact fully, it is because we are "blinded with excess of light."

But granted the existence of God, Berkeley is still faced with the problem of evil. Why does God's universe contain pain, monstrosities, sorrow, death? And is the cumbersome machinery of nature very obviously turned directly by the hand of God? Berkeley answers that natural events occur according to rules of the greatest simplicity and generality; without such regularity there could be no human foresight. What seems like waste from man's viewpoint—countless blighted plants, little fish devoured by parents, and so forth—can be understood as necessary to the riches of God; the apparent defects of nature really augment its beauty, and seeming evil conttributes to the good of the whole. Even the mixture of pain with pleasure is necessary for man's guidance. Clear understanding of these truths instills in us that holy fear which is the chief motive to virtue, and indeed "consideration of God and our duty," was Berkeley's chief aim in writing the book.

To what extent did Berkeley achieve his announced aims? The complete answer cannot be given in brief, just as Berkeley himself could not make all the grounds and implications of his philosophy clear at once. Many readers find themselves unable to refute Berkeley's arguments, yet they remain unconvinced by them; and many professional philosophers have given long and profound attention to the problems he raises. A great merit of this book and of the *Three Dialogues* is that Berkeley was thorough and clever in foreseeing and forestalling possible objections. Yet there are criticisms which, while insufficient to prove a diametrically opposite position such as materialism, or even a more moderate realism, nevertheless show that Berkeley's conclusions do not necessarily follow from his premises.

He was probably correct in his insistence on the dangers of abstraction, although he sometimes seems to have confused conception with visualization. Many thinkers today would agree also with his demand that terms and statements describing the physical world be defined and verified by reference to sensory experience. But can one infer from this experience that the world is ultimately mental or immaterial in nature? Berkeley's argument seems either to beg the question or to depend on ambiguous terms. A fair but condensed statement of it

seems to be this: (1) Physical objects are objects of knowledge. (2) Objects of knowledge are ideas or sets of ideas. (3) Ideas and sets of ideas are in the mind, or mental. (4) Therefore, physical objects are in the mind, or mental. But "objects of knowledge" is ambiguous, unless one already grants that the world is mental; in the first sentence, it means "nonmental things," but in the second it means "constituents of knowledge." Of course, the constituents of knowledge are ideas by definition, but this fact does not bestow upon knowledge the power to *constitute* the real nature of what would not otherwise have been considered ideal or immaterial. Whether we do or do not perceive or conceive a "physical" object is actually irrelevant to the object itself.

Still, this criticism does not prove that physical objects are independently real or that the term "matter" has a meaning describable in terms not ultimately derived from perception. Berkeley has a strategical advantage in the fact that all men are caught in what Ralph Barton Perry called "the ego-centric predicament": in a sense we are forever imprisoned within our own consciousness, since we must always use thought as a bridge to the "outside." But this advantage can also be a liability, for Berkeley's skepticism about external reality can be turned against our knowledge of other minds, the eternal Spirit, and even our own minds considered as substantial entities. Hume and subsequent philosophers, for example, have not agreed that an indivisible, incorporeal self can be discovered by inward reflection. Many of Berkeley's conclusions, such as his account of the self's continuity by saying that the spirit

453

always thinks, have the appearance of absurdities demanded by his premises rather than of facts verifiable by experience. Hence, "spirit" itself may turn out to be an abstraction to be relegated to the company of "matter."

In Berkeley's later writings the purity of his empiricism is diluted by noticeable amounts of rationalism, and even in the present work there are assumptions hardly empirical in origin or confirmation, such as his facile acceptance of the traditional attributes of God—eternal, infinite, omniscient—as obviously pertaining to that Spirit. Berkeley's arguments for God's existence, which are the traditional cosmological and teleological "proofs," would have to meet the devastating criticisms produced by such philosophers as Hume and Kant before they could be acceptable to a modern reader. But even were the being of an infinite, omnipotent, omniscient Spirit granted, the traditional problem of evil posed by comparison of such a Creator with the created universe is one to which Berkeley offers only the usual but ineffective answers. Hume showed in the *Dialogues Concerning Natural Religion* (1779) how ill such answers suit even an empirical theism.

While it is thus doubtful that Berkeley accomplished some of his chief aims, it is certain that he achieved much by the method of his efforts. If he unintentionally undercut his own metaphysics by settling the dust of materialism, philosophy since has been able to learn from his experience.

THEODICY

Author: Gottfried Wilhelm von Leibniz (1646-1716)
Type of work: Theology, metaphysics
First published: 1710

PRINCIPAL IDEAS ADVANCED

The truths of philosophy and theology cannot contradict each other.

If God is all-good, all-wise, and all-powerful, how did evil come into the world?

The answer is that some error is unavoidable in any creature less perfect than its creator; furthermore, all possible worlds contain some evil, and evil improves the good by contrast.

Since man has free will, he is responsible for his acts; God's foreknowledge of the course of man's inclinations did not involve predestination.

The soul is coördinated with the body by a preëstablished harmony.

In some philosophical circles Leibniz's *Theodicy* has been much neglected. This fact is not strange in view of the lack of interest, until recently, in traditional theological questions. It is strange, however, in view of the centrality of the *Theodicy* in Leibniz's own thinking. A good case could be made out that in his own mind it represented his most important, as well as his most characteristic, work. Without it there is much of importance left to Leibniz, to be sure: the pure metaphysician, the logician, the epistemologist, and the mathematician. Yet a balanced view of Leibniz's thought demands that the *Theodicy* be restored to its rightful place as central in his systematic effort.

For all of the continental rationalists (Descartes, Spinoza, and Leibniz), God occupied a large and a systematic place. Much could be made of all that these men owe to medieval theology, but the point is that all these men were centrally interested in the nature of God and his relationship to the natural world. The way in which this problem is worked out by Leibniz has a great deal to do with his solution to other problems. Moreover, there is evidence that Leibniz looked upon himself (to a considerable extent) as a theologian and was most proud of his contributions there. He wished to bring peace between Catholics and Protestants, and his writing has had some effect along this line. Particularly, Leibniz wanted to give rational solutions to traditional theological issues, and more than almost any other man he made it his major goal to provide a reconciliation between traditional religious views and philosophical thought, through demonstrating their essential harmony.

The *Theodicy* has a unique place among the classical writing in philosophical theology, for it is one of the first attempts to "justify the ways of God to man" in straightforward and philosophical terms. All theological views, to be sure, had dealt with the issue of God's choice and his creation of this particular natural order; but many had bracketed the question as being beyond rational scrutiny, and few had set out to answer it directly and in detail. Theodicy, the discussion of God's orderings in so far as they concern man's purposes, became a major part of philosophical theology after Leibniz's treatise.

Leibniz was among those of his age who considered Christianity's merit to be its rational and enlightened nature, as contrasted with at least some other religions. Along with rationalism went a tendency to minimize the differences in nature between God and man. Leibniz shared in this tendency, stating that the perfections of God are those of our soul, even though he possesses them in boundless measure. Leibniz was also an optimist about the essential goodness of man and the possibility of his perfection, and it is probably this view of the nature of man which more than any other single factor led Leibniz into his "best of all possible worlds" doctrine.

The freedom of man and the justice of God form the object of this treatise, and Leibniz's aim was to support both while minimizing neither. To do this would justify God's ways to man; man would be more content to receive what God has ordained, once the logic and harmony of God's plan were grasped. God does whatever is best, but he does not act from absolute necessity. Nature's laws allow a mean between absolute necessity and arbitrary decrees. In this way both God's and man's actions were to be explained and reconciled.

God (for Leibniz) is deeply involved in the affairs of men, continually creating them, and yet he is not the author of sin. Evil has a source somewhere other than in the will of God; God permits moral evil, but he does not will it. Leibniz hoped that this view would offend neither reason nor faith. Consciously, Leibniz set out to modify the strictness of the necessity he found in Hobbes, Spinoza, and Descartes. These philosophers had not been interested in a Christian doctrine of evil, for such a doctrine requires that man be given greater freedom in order to remove evil from God's immediate responsibility.

In the *Theodicy* Leibniz assumes that the truths of philosophy and theology cannot contradict each other. God acts in creation according to general rules of good and of order. Mysteries may be explained sufficiently to justify belief in them, but one cannot comprehend them. In explaining this, Leibniz distinguishes between logical or metaphysical necessity (whose opposite implies contradiction) and physical necessity. Even miracles must conform to the former although they may violate the latter. Reason is the ultimate norm: no article of faith must imply contradiction or contravene proofs as exact as mathematics.

When we come to consider evil, we do so by asking what just reasons, stronger than those which appear contrary to them, may have compelled God to permit evil. God is subject to the multitude of reasons and is even "compelled" by them. Leibniz infers that God must have had innumerable considerations in mind, in the light of which he deemed it inadvisable to prevent certain evils, for nothing comes from God which is not consistent with goodness, justice, and holiness. God must have been able to permit sin without detriment to his perfections; the weight of the reasons argues for it. Men are essentially in the same circumstance in which God was in finding it necessary to permit certain evils.

Since reason is a gift of God even as faith is, Leibniz argues, contention between them would cause God to contend against God. Therefore, if any reasoned objections against any article of faith cannot be dissolved, then the alleged article must be considered as false and as not revealed. Reason and faith can be reconciled. Yet reason is still faced with its central problem: How could a single first principle, all-good, all-wise, and all-powerful, have been able to allow evil and to permit the wicked to be happy and the good unhappy? Since Leibniz's time, philosophical inquiry into theological problems has often begun with this question.

Leibniz did not attempt to make the connection between God and moral evil an indirect one, which has been the traditional method. An evil will, he says, cannot exist without coöperation. An action, he asserts, is not for being evil the less dependent on God. Thus, Leibniz makes the solution to the problem of evil directly a matter of accounting for God's action, since nothing can come to pass without his permission. God is the first reason of things.

The cause of this world, Leibniz writes, must be intelligent, for the first cause has to consider all possible worlds and then fix upon one to create. Such an intelligence would have to be infinite and, united to a goodness no less infinite, it cannot have chosen other than the best of all possible worlds.

It may be, for instance, that all evils are almost as nothingness in comparison with the good things which are in the universe. Whence did evil come then? We must consider that there is some original imperfection, due to the creature's limited nature, in the creature before sin. Leibniz adopts this view of "original sin," that some error is unavoidable in principle in a creature which must be less perfect than the being who creates it.

Other reasons for evil may be given: There is evil in all of the possible worlds, and so no choice could avoid it entirely. Evil often makes us savor good the more because of it— evil in that sense being necessary to any good. Man's will is responsible for its own actions; but this explanation simply leads Leibniz into a consideration of the divine foreknowledge and the question of divine predestination. Here Leibniz indulges in hairsplitting, distinguishing between what is certain and what is necessary. The will is inclined toward the course it adopts, and in that sense its action is and always has been "certain" in God's knowledge. But the action of man's will is not "necessary," although this means merely that its opposite does not involve a logical contradiction. Such "contingency" Leibniz allows to remain.

God always chooses the best, but he is not constrained so to do. This is the extent of his freedom. Another natural sequence of things is equally possible, in the logical sense, although his will is determined in the choice it makes by the preponderating goodness of the natural order he chose; that is to say, the natural order that we actually have. Everything is certain and determined beforehand in man's action, although this is not the absolute necessity which would find any

alternative logically contradictory. The necessity comes from the goodness of the object chosen.

The prevailing inclination always triumphs. In that sense Leibniz cannot conceive of either God or man acting irrationally, and hence the actions of both God and man are necessary. The whole future is doubtless determined. But since we do not know what it is, nor what it is that God foresees or has resolved, we must still do our duty, according to the reason God has given us and the rules he has prescribed. In the midst of an expansive metaphysical doctrine of possible worlds and the infinity of possible choices open to God, Leibniz adopted as conservative a theological view of predestination as the tradition has seen. A radical in metaphysics, he was almost a reactionary in his view of the fixed relation of God to the world.

Like many conservatives, Leibniz tried—and believed that he had succeeded—to reconcile absolute foreknowledge on God's part with human freedom. His answer is as old as Augustine's. We are free in that our actions flow from our own will, but the action of the will in turn is dependent upon its causes, which ultimately run back to God. Notwithstanding this dependence of voluntary actions upon other causes, Leibniz still believed that the existence within us of a "wonderful spontaneity" is not precluded. This makes the soul independent of the physical influence of all other creatures, although Leibniz was careful not to say that it is also independent of God.

The doctrine of preëstablished harmony is introduced to reconcile the difficulty. It was predestined from the beginning that God's design and man's volition should coincide: to Leibniz this seems to be a satisfactory solution. It is the typical solution of the rationalist. A reason has been given, and the whole scheme is seen to fit into a logical framework in which there is no contradiction or ultimate disharmony. Whereas a contemporary might begin with the premise that human freedom must at all cost be allowed for, Leibniz begins with the idea that all factors should be accounted for by a rational framework.

Preëstablished harmony again accounts for the coördination of the soul and body. Like Spinoza's "parallel attributes," God ordained at the time of creation a logical ordering in which the soul's actions coincide with the body's movements. Like Descartes and Spinoza, Leibniz was thoroughly convinced that there is no interaction but there is a rationally determined plan of agreement. God has arranged beforehand for the body to execute the soul's orders. God has accommodated the soul to the body. Actually, the design of the world is simply an extension of God's perfection. Just as the rationalists of this era saw God and the human soul as being very close by nature, so also they viewed the natural order as an extension of the divine nature through creation. Although it is less than God, the created order essentially exhibits the same qualities as does divinity itself.

God is inclined toward every possible good, in proportion to the excellence of that good. God, before decreeing anything, considered among all the possible sequences of things that one which he afterwards approved. God grants his sanction to this sequence (our present natural order) only after having entered into all its detail. From such a description of God's rational selective activity comes the doctrine of the best of all possible worlds.

In most traditional accounts of ultimate origin (as, for example, in Plato's *Timaeus*), the first cause moves because he is good and outgoing, not grudging. But in all classical and in most medieval schemes such a god has no real choices to make. Leibniz presents a modern metaphysical framework in that he stresses the infinitely wide range of alternatives open to God's choice. The philosophical solution, however, is traditional. God selects according to fixed norms. It makes sense to say that classical thinkers also considered this world to be the best possible, but they believed that God had no alternatives. Leibniz simply set classical theory into a wider context of possibilities, but continued to agree to God's fixed goodness and to his necessary selection and creation.

In the *Theodicy* Leibniz also takes up traditional and primarily theological questions concerning Christ and salvation. His answers here are not startlingly novel, except that Leibniz transferred miracles, belief in the nature of Christ, and a Christian doctrine of salvation into a thoroughly rational framework. Leibniz wanted the doctrines of traditional Christianity to be amenable to his philosophical scheme of metaphysics. In the process of demonstrating this mutual harmony, like all philosophical theologians, he was pushed into giving some rather far-fetched accounts of some rather difficult religious notions —for example, the assertion of the existence of all human souls in seed in their progenitors since the very beginning of things. Obviously such an idea would be helpful in establishing a religious notion of original sin in Adam; but it is hardly likely to be confirmable by the microscopic observations Leibniz's rationalism suggests.

It is not in the slightest an exaggeration to say that both Leibniz's questions and his answers are repetitious. The *Theodicy* sets out to refute certain doctrines which Leibniz opposed (particularly those of Pierre Bayle). Leibniz did this partly by reference to and elaboration of certain of his famous theories (preëstablished harmony, the essential goodness of God's choice), but primarily his weapon was the repetition of his own position. As a rationalist Leibniz evinced the traditional irritation at finding that someone else did not find his reasoning as persuasive as he himself did and that his opponent continued to hold different theories. Despite this defect, the *Theodicy* illustrates how important works do not always have the technical rigor and logical tightness that one might suppose. Leibniz repeats his maxims and principles; he does little to explore them in detail. Yet Leibniz is dealing with questions of great moment and common interest, and his proposed solutions are interesting and suggestive. More precise and cogent pieces of philosophical analysis have proved to be less interesting over the years, but Leibniz's sometimes tedious and often loose reflections on the crucial issues of theology are still very much alive.

CHARACTERISTICS

Author: Anthony Ashley Cooper, Earl of Shaftesbury (1671-1713)
Type of work: Ethics
First published: 1711

PRINCIPAL IDEAS ADVANCED

Metaphysics has little to offer man either in regard to a proof of the nature of the self or concerning his morality; in such matters it is better to count on common sense.

True philosophy is the search for what is just in society and beautiful in nature.

Nature is orderly, and virtue for men consists in following nature and in enthusiastically seeking out the true, the good, and the beautiful.

Conscience and aesthetic judgment are alike in being faculties for the discovery of the beauty of nature, the reflection of an order given to nature by God.

Man must exercise his reason by discussing opinions and by examining himself.

Anthony Ashley Cooper, third Earl of Shaftesbury, was a grandson of the famous Whig statesman of that name. When his own career in politics was

459

cut short by ill health, he turned his liberal and humanitarian efforts into literary channels, bringing to the task, besides a puritan sense of moral responsibility, an aesthetic sensibility disciplined by the study of Greek and Roman models. His assorted essays, published under the title of *Characteristics of Men, Manners, Opinions, and Times,* develop the ideal of man working out the purposes of God through moral and spiritual striving. He opposed the dehumanizing tendencies of the Cartesian and Newtonian philosophies, much in the same way that Socrates had opposed the naturalism of an earlier day, and, like the famous Athenian, he taught his age that man should know himself.

John Locke, who was for many years secretary to the elder Shaftesbury, was tutor to the author of the *Characteristics* and may be credited with imparting to him a liberality of spirit and a general trust in reason. But Shaftesbury rejected Locke's theory of ideas and the whole philosophical enterprise which, beginning with Descartes, pursued the ideal of certitude based on self-evident truths.

Far from putting a stop to skepticism, said Shaftesbury, the attempt initiated by Descartes to demonstrate the rationality of nature and morality played directly into the hands of sophists and triflers. The famous *Cogito, ergo sum* merely stated a verbal identity. It left untouched the real problems, "what constitutes the I," and "whether the I of this instant be the same with that of any instant preceding or to come." We have nothing but memory, he said, to warrant our belief in our own identity; and if one wishes to play the metaphysical game, the question about the "successional

I" must remain undecided. ". . . I take my being upon trust. Let others philosophise as they are able: I shall admire their strength when, upon this topic, they have refuted what able metaphysicians object and Pyrrhonists plead in their own behalf."

Indulging the irony or "wit" with which, according to Shaftesbury, persons of breeding habitually respond to the pedantry of scholars, Shaftesbury constructed a metaphysical theory of morals which showed, after the fashion of the Stoics and of Spinoza, that, if one accepts the theory of ideas, man's well-being consists in learning to entertain only those thoughts which will not disappoint. This excursus into "dry philosophy" and the "rigid manner" of metaphysical disputes was, however, only half serious. It was useful, he said, to be able to argue in this way with "moon-blind wits . . . who renounce daylight and extinguish in a manner the bright visible outward world, by allowing us to know nothing beside what we can prove by strict and formal demonstration. . . ." And, in any case, "it is in a manner necessary for one who would usefully philosophise, to have a knowledge in this part of philosophy sufficient to satisfy him that there is no knowledge or wisdom to be learnt from it."

Because it had become engrossed in introspection, Shaftesbury said, philosophy had fallen into ill-repute among men of judgment. The philosopher was now what was formerly intended by the word "idiot"—a person who can attend to nothing except his own ideas. Persons concerned to bring honest reason to bear upon the affairs of life stood "to gain little by philosophy or deep speculations of any kind." "In the main," said Shaftesbury, in a passage which was often appealed to during the eighteenth century, " 'tis best to stick to common sense and go no farther. Men's first thoughts in this matter [morals] are generally better than their second: their natural notions better than those refined by study or consultation with casuists." For, he added, "Some moral and philosophical truths there are withal so evident in themselves that 'twould be easier to imagine half mankind to have run mad, and joined precisely in one and the same species of folly, than to admit anything as truth which should be advanced against such natural knowledge, fundamental reason, and common sense."

But Shaftesbury was unwilling to give up the word "philosophy." A person does not become a philosopher by writing and talking philosophy, he said. In reality, a philosopher is one who reasons concerning man's main interests, and there are good and bad philosophers according as one reasons skillfully or unskillfully. In Shaftesbury's hands, therefore, the bald contrast between philosophy and common sense was not a philistine repudiation of the life of reason but an attempt to vindicate a venerable tradition against the pretensions of "the new learning." Although committed to the political ideals of the rising bourgeoisie, Shaftesbury was alarmed at what appeared to be its want of sound moral foundations. For the greater glory of God, the followers of Luther and Calvin repudiated nature; and for the greater glory of man, the followers of Bacon and Descartes repudiated the past. To remedy these defects, Shaftesbury turned to Plato and Aristotle and to the living tradition of Renaissance Platonism. The aim of philosophy is "to learn what is just in society and beautiful in Nature and the order of the world," and this with a view to enabling man to realize the highest ideal of manhood—what the Greeks called *aner kalos k'agathon,* and the Italians *uomo virtuoso.*

The starting point of Shaftesbury's moral philosophy was the conception of nature as an orderly whole. The daylight philosopher, in contrast to those who fumble among ideas in the cellars of their own minds, recognizes with Plato that nature is a system in which each part is ordered with a view to the perfection of the whole. Shaftesbury was no less impressed than were his contemporaries by the regular motion of the heavens. But even more remarkable, in his opinion, was the microscopic life revealed by the new biology The latter, in particular, suggested that the world is a self-sustaining whole composed of subordinate wholes, each having a life and nature of its own but so adjusted that while it pursues its private end it also functions in the interest of the systems that comprehend it.

From this point of view, all excellence consists in following nature. Shaftesbury said that he was a realist, holding that virtue or excellence is "really something in itself and in the nature of things; not arbitrary or factitious; not constituted from without, or dependent on custom, fancy, or will; not even on the supreme will itself, which can no way govern it; but being necessarily good, is governed by it and ever uniform with it." The breeder of animals knows what is natural and what is unnatural behavior in a dog or in a horse; he knows a good animal from a mediocre one, and wherein the excellence of the former

461

consists. So it is with men. By a native endowment, each of us knows what is just, fair, and honest in men's character and conduct.

The human soul, as Shaftesbury represented it, is like every other living form in that it has a natural constitution. Within the systems of nature and society, each human being is himself a system in which passions, inclinations, appetites, and affections have their place. Some of these are purely local, such as the appetite for food; others are more comprehensive, such as pride, embracing the individual's general interest; others, such as parental love and friendship, bind the individual to society. Each is good in its proper place. And man is endowed with reason to regulate them.

According to Shaftesbury, reason or reflection is that faculty by which man reviews his mind and actions and passes judgment upon them, either approving or disapproving. It manifests itself in two quite different ways, which may be designated "prudence" and "conscience" By the former, man judges what is to his advantage; by the latter, what is proper and right. Shaftesbury denied that prudence gives adequate direction for a man's life. For this purpose, we have been given conscience. It follows, according to Shaftesbury, that the goal of life does not lie in happiness, whether in this world or that to come, but in the perfection of the soul itself and its harmony with the total order of things.

In opposition to the religious doctrine of human depravity, Shaftesbury maintained that all men are endowed with a sufficient sense of right and wrong to enable them to achieve virtuous lives, and that the only obstacles are passion and vice. Appetite or passion he described as the elder brother of reason, striving to take advantage of reason; but when reason grows strong enough to assert itself, appetite, "like an arrant coward . . . presently grows civil, and affords the younger as fair play afterwards as he can desire." Vicious habits and customs presented a more difficult problem. One source of these, according to Shaftesbury, is "corrupt religion and superstition," which teaches men to regard as praiseworthy practices which are "most unnatural and inhuman." Another is idleness, such as befell the "superior" classes in his day. Without a proper goal in life, men fall, he said, into a "relaxed and dissolute state" in which passions break out.

As Shaftesbury pictured it, conscience or moral insight is all of a piece with aesthetic judgment. There is a "natural beauty of figures," for example, which causes a mere infant to be pleased with the proportions of a ball or a cube or a dye. And if, in more intricate cases, where color, texture, motion, sound, and the like are involved, there is room for dispute as to which is the finer fabric, the lovelier face, the more harmonious voice, it remains as a fundamental assumption "that there is a beauty of each kind." "All own the standard, rule, and measure; but in applying it to things disorder arises, ignorance prevails, interest and passion breed disturbance." Nor is it otherwise, Shaftesbury continues, in matters of conduct. That there is a "fitness and decency in actions" can never be denied as long as men preserve the distinction between "that which interests and engages men as good," and "that which they admire and praise as honest."

Ultimately, for Shaftesbury, the beautiful and the good are the same. If we are speaking of a building or of a picture or of the human body, we call it beautiful. If we are speaking of action, life, or operation, we call it good. There are, according to Shaftesbury, three degrees of beauty. The first is the beauty of "dead forms" —of pictures and statues—which exhibit harmony and proportion, but have "no forming power, no action or intelligence." The second, which possesses all that the former lacks, is a double beauty: it is the beauty of "forming forms"—of artists and craftsmen. But there is a third order of beauty—that which forms the "forming forms." Principally, this is the beauty of nature itself, or of the Mind which informs it. This parent-beauty, because it fashions men's minds, "contains in itself all the beauties fashioned by those minds, and is consequently the principle, source, and fountain of all beauty," even including "architecture, music, and all which is of human invention."

The admiration which we owe to this highest beauty was, for Shaftesbury, the foundation of true religion. He raised no opposition against Christianity, except to question whether it conduced to true worship and piety to dwell upon the evil of creation as contemporary divines were wont to do. He thought of himself as a deist, but he denied that the world is like a machine which the Maker, having completed, could leave to its own operation. He rejected the usual "proofs" of God based upon the necessity for a first cause and he appealed rather to the immanence of a continuing Providence which orders all things well.

Thus, Shaftesbury held morality to be the foundation for belief in God, rather than the contrary. But carried further, true religion, or the apprehension of the divine creativity in nature, raises man's eyes to a higher vocation for himself than he would otherwise know. As the offspring of divinity, he is himself divine and is called upon to be himself a creator—not merely in the sense of imposing form upon matter, but in the sense of forming his own nature and that of other rational creatures. In this way he participates in the highest beauty: "He only is the wise and able man who, with a slight regard to [bodies and outward forms] applies himself to cultivate another soil, builds in a different matter from that of stone or marble; and having righter models in his eye, becomes in truth the architect of his own life and fortune, by laying within himself the lasting and sure foundation of order, peace and concord."

Such wisdom comes only to those who exercise their reason in an extraordinary degree. Mere knowledge of the world does not suffice, nor do ordinary deliverances of conscience. A man must find ways of examining opinions which seem true to himself and his generation in order to pass from ignorance into knowledge. Shaftesbury recommended "soliloquy" as the best way for a person to rectify his opinions, especially for those addicted to being "talkers or haranguers" in public. "'Tis the hardest thing in the world," he said, "to be a good thinker without being a strong self-examiner. . . ." For the same reasons, Shaftesbury wished for more honest discussion "in the way of dialogue, and patience of debate and reasoning, of which we have scarce a resemblance left in any of our conversations at this season of the world." Philosophy, or wisdom, as he conceived it, is not the sort of thing that can be transmitted as information. It is a discipline of the mind, a step beyond good breeding.

Shaftesbury's reaffirmation of design in the world raised in an acute form the problem of evil. His answer was similar to that given by the Stoics and by St. Augustine. Suffering and loss are bound to appear evil to the individual because of his limited perspective. When better instructed, we find cause for admiration in the arrangement by which the individual sacrifices his life for the species, and even in the relentless force of earthquake and fire. Monstrous and abnormal births, he said, do not mitigate against the design of nature, since they result not from any natural failure but from the natural conflict of forces. "'Tis good which is predominant," says one of the characters in his dialogue; "and every corruptible and mortal nature by its mortality and corruption yields only to some better, and all in common to the best and highest nature which is incorruptible and immortal."

The optimism of Shaftesbury was far from being forced. As opposed to materialists, such as Thomas Hobbes, he found in the conception of nature as a system grounds for rejecting the doctrine of egotism and the war of each against all. He contended that besides the self-regarding passions man also has passions which impel him to act for the interest of others. Both kinds are necessary in the economy of things. Private affections are necessary, not only because they assist the survival of the individual, but also because they contribute to the public

good. Similarly, social affections, such as parental love and friendship, further the interests and fill out the happiness of the individual. Shaftesbury argued that the purely selfish man does not, in fact, serve his own interest. On the other hand, it is possible for a person to be too much affected with the needs of others for even the public good. Thus, the happy life coincides with the life of virtue, in which reason is allowed to prevail over impulse.

The foundations of art, like those of morals, must, according to Shaftesbury, be laid in natural harmonies and proportions which the styles and humors of a particular age cannot brush aside with impunity. True beauty, he said, is not that which appeals to the senses, but that wherein the rational mind may come to rest. Its enjoyment is a disinterested contemplation, totally different from the pleasures which have their seat in desire. Hence the artist should not aim to represent objects which men find enjoyable, but to create new unities analogous to those which make up the fabric of nature. True beauty lies deep. Many things which seem shocking and offensive at first are later known and acknowledged as the highest beauties.

The influence of Shaftesbury's thought was far-reaching. The French Encyclopedists and the early German Romantics were in his debt no less deeply than the moral philosophers of England and Scotland. The fact that in the Age of Reason "philosophy" freed itself from the knottier problems of metaphysics and epistemology, and engaged the attention of poets and economists, statesmen and propagandists, was in the main his doing.

FIFTEEN SERMONS PREACHED AT THE ROLLS CHAPEL

Author: Joseph Butler (1692-1752)
Type of work: Metaphysics, philosophy of mind
First published: 1726

PRINCIPAL IDEAS ADVANCED

An examination of human nature reveals not only how man behaves, but also how he ought to behave.

Human nature, according to God's plan, is expressed properly when the passions are controlled by self-love and benevolence, and when the latter are controlled by conscience.

Desires have external objects—such as building a house; the theory that all men act to secure their own happiness is mistaken, for men often desire particular external objects without considering the satisfaction to come from securing such objects.

The fact that pleasure is often the consequence of achieving what we desire does not imply that pleasure is the object of desire.

The claim that even though men desire objects other than pleasure, they are all basically selfish, is in error; it depends on identifying compassion with fear, but experience shows no necessary correlation.

If self-love is enlightened, the course of action it prescribes will coincide with that of benevolence.

Joseph Butler, an Anglican clergyman who was a contemporary of George Berkeley and David Hume, a protégé of Samuel Butler, a favorite of Queen Caroline, Dean of St. Paul's, Clerk of the Closet to George II, Bishop of Bristol at the time John Wesley defected, and Bishop of Durham, and who was not Archbishop of Canterbury because he rejected the office, was the most influential Anglican theologian of the eighteenth century. During his own time and for some time thereafter, his fame as a religious philosopher rested primarily on his very influential book, *The Analogy of Religion,* in which he argued for an enlightened theology designed to woo the deists back into the fold of the church. But his enduring philosophi-

cal reputation rests upon his *Fifteen Sermons Preached at the Rolls Chapel* and *A Dissertation upon the Nature of Virtue,* in which he expounds his views about human nature and morality. Indeed, his refutation of psychological egoism, the doctrine that man is always motivated by his own self-interest, is a classic of its kind. This summary will concentrate on this refutation and the analysis of human nature on which it is based. Butler's views on these topics are contained in the preface to the *Sermons,* in Sermons 1, 2, 3, 11, and 12, and in the *Dissertation.*

Butler's analysis rests upon the thesis that an examination of human nature will reveal not only how man does behave, but also how he ought to behave. This thesis, in turn, rests upon the assumptions that God wants man to act in certain ways, that he has given man such a nature that he will naturally act in these ways if that nature is not corrupted, and therefore, that these ways can be discovered by examining his handiwork. This examination will reveal that human nature has a hierarchical structure, with our many impulses, passions, and desires providing the base, the more general and reflective concerns for ourselves and others providing the intermediate level, and the supreme faculty of conscience providing the apex. Consequently, our nature is expressed fully and properly, not in a life dominated by our impulses, but in one in which these are exercised under the guidance of self-love and benevolence, and in which the latter are controlled in turn by conscience.

This summary will examine each of these levels, starting with the one that provides the basis for the other two. Prior to the exercise of rational control man is a creature of impulse, appetite, passion, and desire, acting in a multitude of ways. Without direction, he seems to be impelled by a host of specific desires to a host of specific and unrelated ends. These desires, or affections, as we shall call them, seem to have several important characteristics that distinguish them from the higher principles. On their first appearance, and usually thereafter, they occur spontaneously, without premeditation or deliberation. As far as the structure of human nature is concerned, they exist prior to any control or regulation the mature personality may later exercise over them. Again, they tend to move spontaneously toward particular goals. It is true that, given the affec-

tion, the goal could be sought deliberately, but it is not true that it is chosen deliberately. Finally, Butler says, affections have external objects such as eating food, kicking someone, or building a house—objects external in the sense that they are not states of the agent. That is, for instance, the object of hunger is the consumption of food, and not the relief of a feeling of discomfort, or the production of a pleasant sensation. It is to be noted that when Butler speaks of hunger he is not speaking of a state of metabolism or of a feeling in the stomach, but of a desire for something, the desire for food.

Butler overstates his case when he insists that the object of every affection is external, but his major point is sound. The point is this: the crudest form of psychological egoism is false, for in many, if not most, cases, when a man desires something he does not have in mind his own welfare. If a man who is angered springs up and attacks his persecutor, he would not ordinarily be thinking that this is the thing to do in order to maximize happiness. If asked what he wanted, he might reply that he wished to get even, or to save face, or to kick the other person; these are the things he intends to accomplish; these are the objects of his anger.

Of course, Butler agrees, many of our impulsive or passionate acts do bring pleasure to ourselves or to others, whether we had this result in mind or not. Indeed, affections can be classified according to whether they promote the private or the public good. Thus, the desire for food does tend to keep one alive, even though this is not usually what one has in mind; and the desire for esteem does lead one to treat

466

others considerately, even though the object of one's desire is not their welfare. We might expect that the intelligent agent will recognize these tendencies of the affections to augment either his own or another's general welfare, come to value these two wider possibilities as ends in themselves (if he does not already), and hence be led to satisfy his affections as a means to the achievement of these ends. This, says Butler, we find to be a fact. Emerging from this heterogeneous group of affections are two more general and comprehensive desires: the desire to maximize our own happiness and the desire to maximize that of others. These two desires are present in every normal man.

We do desire our own welfare, but this desire is not to be classified with the affections we have spoken of so far; it is not a passion or an appetite that arises spontaneously and drives impulsively toward a specific goal only to die away when it has been satisfied. Rather, it is a deliberately cultivated, long-enduring desire whose object is such that it cannot be satisfied once and for all at any given time or through the occurrence of any particular event. Furthermore, it functions not merely as a psychological drive, but as a principle according to which we deliberately plan which particular ends we shall pursue in order to enhance our overall welfare. Finally, as experience shows, it is a very powerful motive that exerts a natural authority over the affections; the affections ought to be subordinated to it.

Nevertheless, while it is superior to affections, self-love cannot achieve its object unless they achieve theirs, for pleasures occurs only as a by-product of the pursuit and satisfaction of affections. While Butler is not specific, he has in mind such things as the pleasure we experience in pursuing our objective, the satisfaction we experience because we have attained it, and any other pleasures that may follow upon its attainment. Thus, while one goes to the fields because of a desire to obtain food, one may enjoy the walk, enjoy digging in the earth, enjoy the satisfaction of gathering the number of potatoes intended for the meal, and enjoy the physical satisfaction that follows the meal. Though an affection and self-love may seek the same thing, the one seeks it for itself, whereas the other seeks it insofar as its pursuit and attainment bring pleasure to the pursuer. Self-love can attain its own end only by letting selected affections pass into action.

Butler suggests that the intimate relationship between self-love and the satisfaction of affections has led some noted egoists, such as Hobbes, into the error of identifying the particular affections with the principle of self-love, or of regarding them as just so many particular expressions of it. But the fact that our actions do lead to enjoyment and the fact that this fact is exploited by self-love do not indicate at all that the only thing we seek is such enjoyment, or that because such enjoyments do occur we must have been seeking them. Indeed, if we did not seek something other than pleasure we would experience no pleasure. The conclusion that we must be egoists does not follow from the fact that all affections belong to the self, from the fact that we never act unless we have such affections, or from the fact that all satisfied affections bring pleasure to the self.

However, for all that has been said

so far, there is still room for a subtler egoism, for the egoist might admit that the object of an affection is not the welfare of the agent but insist that insofar as the affections are under the direction of self-love the overriding consideration is always our own welfare. Insofar as man acts reasonably he acts prudently. This type of egoism can be refuted only if there are actions that are not subsumed under the principle of self-love, or subsumed under it alone.

But there are such actions, Butler says, for most men do act part of the time in a genuinely benevolent fashion. He realizes that he will have to defend this position against the most sophisticated egoist. Hobbes had argued, and many were prepared to believe, that what appears to be benevolence is really subtly disguised selfishness. Thus Hobbes claimed that when a man feels pity for another he is really feeling thankful that he has escaped the calamity and fearful lest such a thing should happen to him in the future. A man feels more "sympathetic" toward his unfortunate friend than he does toward strangers because his friend's life is much more like his own and therefore the probability of a similar calamity befalling him is higher. Butler admits that such selfish reflections might occur, but he insists that they must be distinguished from genuine compassion. Hobbes' view requires that we equate compassion with fear, an equation that any man can see to be mistaken. If it were correct, then the more compassionate a man is, the more fearful he would be, but this is simply not the case. In the second place, the more compassionate a man is, the more we admire him; but the more fearful he is, the less we admire him. In the third place, while it is true that the sight of friends in distress evokes greater compassion than the sight of others in distress, it is quite questionable whether the sight of friends in distress raises in us greater fear for ourselves than does the sight of others in distress. This is the classic refutation of Hobbes' doctrine, a refutation that was accepted and polished by men such as David Hume and Adam Smith.

Butler supports his position, not simply by criticizing his opponents, but by drawing our attention to the way people do behave. Human behavior will show, he says, that we do have a propensity to help each other, a propensity that cannot be confused with self-love. He offers examples to support this view. Granted that in some cases an apparently benevolent action may be performed solely for the satisfaction it gives the agent, or for the sense of power he experiences. Yet, has the reader never known of a man who was not in a position to help another but who nevertheless rejoiced when a third party assisted the second? And has the reader never known a man to assist one person rather than another where the choice between the two could not be accounted for in terms of the sense of power? Are there not cases where the choice is made in terms of need? And if you examine your own behavior, will you not find it ridiculous to try to explain your benevolent behavior entirely in terms of your love of power, of being dominant, or of hoped-for reciprocation? Nor will it do to reply that acting benevolently gives you pleasure. Of course it does, but first, this does not mean you sought that pleasure; and second, the action would not have given you pleasure unless you had a concern for the other person. In this way Butler answers the more sophisticated egoist.

Although Butler clearly maintains that there is genuinely benevolent action that cannot be explained away, he is not as clear as he might be about the status of benevolence. There are some passages in which benevolence is spoken of as an affection, but there are many others in which it is spoken of as a rational principle. It is true that benevolence is not as strong a motive as self-love and it is also true that the scope of its application is more restricted, for whereas every affection has consequences that affect the agent, not every affection has consequences that affect others. Most of the passages in which Butler speaks of benevolence as an affection occur when he is making these contrasts, and consequently they seem designed to emphasize the contrasts rather than to express his full view about benevolence. In view of the numerous passages in which benevolence is spoken of as a principle, it seems reasonable to conclude that Butler was not being inconsistent, that he meant that insofar as benevolence transcends spontaneous compassion it becomes a principle functioning as a guide and having a relationship, like that of self-love, to a multitude of affections. Because it is psychologically weaker it needs to be fostered and cultivated in a manner in which self-love does not, but it has a similar function and enjoys the same sort of authority over the affections.

Since these principles are coequal in authority, one might expect conflicts in interest between them, but Butler believes that if self-love is really enlightened, the course of action it prescribes will coincide with that of benevolence. No one who is callous to his fellows will be really happy, not only because this involves thwarting natural affections of sympathy and the like, but also because such behavior invites a similar reaction on the part of those so treated. Furthermore, even though it should appear that the selfish will prosper more on this earth than the benevolent, one should not overlook the fact that there is an afterlife in which God will at least compensate for the earthly imbalance. Once again, because two different motives suggest the same actions we must be wary of falling into the error of identifying them or repudiating one of them. Butler sometimes leaves himself open to misunderstanding on this point when he writes that we are never required to act against our own self-interest. However, when he said this he was pointing out to his worldly and sophisticated congregation that benevolent action does not have consequences that are incompatible with those pursued by self-love. He was not suggesting that benevolence should be placed under the dominance of self-love, but, rather, that if there is a conflict, we had better check to see if we really have discovered what is to our self interest, for the conflict provides *prima facie* evidence that we have not.

So far we have discovered two principles in addition to the basic affections, but neither of these has to do with duty as such. Consequently, as an examination of our nature will show, there is a faculty whose function it is to point out what is right and wrong, the faculty of conscience. It should be noted that we must distinguish between action motivated by compassion or benevolence on the one hand and that motivated by a sense of duty on the other. Of course, benevolence and conscience may, and frequently do, suggest the same course of action, but the motivation is different. As the supreme faculty, conscience should stand above and coördinate the activities of the other principles. Its supremacy does not rest upon its power, for impulse and self-love often override it, but it carries upon itself the mark of authority, as is evidenced by the feeling of wrongdoing or guilt we experience when we do not heed it. "Had it strength as it has right, had it power as it has manifest authority, it would absolutely govern the world." Of course, it need hardly be mentioned that the existence of conscience indicates in yet another way the inadequacy of the egoist's position.

Conscience is not a criterion used in reaching decisions or planning courses of action, as are the rational principles of benevolence and self-love, but a faculty that makes pronouncements about what is right or wrong. It tells us *what* to do and *what* to approve of, but not *why*. Butler suggests that God might be a utilitarian, but he insists that we cannot be, for certain things are simply seen to be praiseworthy or unpraiseworthy quite apart from any tendency they might have to further or hinder the public welfare. Thus, for instance, conscience reveals the baseness of treachery and the meanness of a small mind as well as the praiseworthiness of fidelity, honor, and justice. Conscience does not proceed by reasoning, nor does it seek to justify its deliverances in terms of some underlying principle; it simply pronounces on specific matters and does so with authority. It functions in all "plain honest men" as the vice-regent of God, cutting in a direct and simple manner through the moral perplexities of their daily lives.

Butler believed not only that there is no conflict between conscience and benevolence, but also that there is none between conscience and self-love. There cannot be if we are clear about what is to our self-interest. After all, God intends that we should be happy, and conscience is the faculty he has given us to ensure that we do as he intends. Consequently, as Butler saw it, human nature exhibits a complexly structured system of motives, resting upon the affections which are controlled by the principles of self-love and benevolence and capped by the faculty of conscience which has authority over all. When developed as God intended it should be, it is a nature in which these various factors supplement and complement one another to produce an integrated and harmoniously organized life.

Butler did not develop his views as fully as we could wish, but he traced out in bold outline a view that embodies the classic refutation of psychological egoism, ancient or modern; a view that had a profound effect upon Hume and Smith insofar as it stresses compassion and benevolence; and a view that has influenced such recent philosophers as H. A. Prichard, W. D. Ross, and C. D. Broad insofar as it brings conscience and duty to the fore. Butler is one of the most important moral philosophers of the eighteenth century.

A TREATISE OF HUMAN NATURE (BOOK I)

Author: David Hume (1711-1776)
Type of work: Epistemology
First published: 1739

PRINCIPAL IDEAS ADVANCED

All of our knowledge comes from impressions and ideas; the impressions are more forceful and lively than the ideas.

By the use of memory and imagination we preserve and arrange our ideas.

We have no abstract, general ideas but only ideas of particular things which can be considered collectively by the use of general terms.

Certainty comes from the intuitive recognition of the similarity or differences in ideas, or from the demonstrative process of connecting a series of intuitions —as in arithmetic and algebra.

Our knowledge of causal relationships is simply the habit of expecting events of one kind to follow events of another kind with which they have been observed to be conjoined; there are no necessary relationships between events.

We have good reason to be skeptical about all conclusions reached by the use of reason or on the basis of sense experience.

Hume's *A Treatise of Human Nature* is his earliest philosophical work and the one that contains the most complete exposition of his views. Apparently it was planned when he was in his early twenties, when he claimed to have discovered a "new scene of thought." The work was composed during a sojourn in France from 1734 to 1737 and was revised shortly thereafter in an unsuccessful attempt to gain the approbation of Bishop Joseph Butler. The first book of the *Treatise* was published in 1739, and the other two the next year. Hume had hoped that his views would attract a great deal of attention; instead, the work "fell dead-born from the presses." His novel theories did not attract attention until after he had published a more popular version in *An Enquiry Concerning Human Understanding* in 1748. The *Treatise* was subjected to a full-scale attack by Thomas Reid in 1764. By this time, Hume was so successful as an author, especially on the basis of his essays and his *History of England* (1754-1762), that he refused to defend his first book, and called it a juvenile work. Over the years it has become more and more important as the fullest and deepest statement of Hume's philosophical views; in fact, Book I of the *Treatise* has come to be regarded as one of the finest achievements of English philosophy.

On the title page of Book I, Hume announces that the *Treatise* is "an attempt to introduce the experimental Method of Reasoning into Moral Subjects." In the preface, he explains that he intends to develop a "science of man" by applying Sir Isaac Newton's experimental method to human mental behavior. Following in the footsteps of various English and Scottish moral philosophers, and of the French skeptic Pierre Bayle, he hoped to discover the limits of human knowledge in such areas as mathematics, physics, and the social sciences (the moral subjects). By scrupulously observing human life, Hume thought he could discover certain general laws about human thinking and behavior. He admitted at the outset that it was probably not possible to uncover "the ultimate qualities of human nature," but he thought it should be possible to learn something about the origin and nature of what we think we know.

All of our information, Hume writes, is composed of impressions and ideas. The only difference between these is that the former strike us more forcefully and with greater vivacity than do the latter. Ideas and impressions can be simple or complex, the simple ones being those which cannot be divided into parts or aspects, while the complex ones are composed of simples. There is a great deal of resemblance between the impressions and the ideas. The simple ideas, in fact, exactly resemble simple impressions in all respects except with regard to their force and vivacity. Further, in terms of their appearance in the mind, the simple impressions always precede the simple ideas (except for one unusual case that Hume brings up). The complex ideas are composed of simple parts which are exactly like the simple ingredients of impressions that we have already experienced, though the complex idea itself may not actually be a copy of any complex impression. These discoveries about impressions and ideas indicate, Hume says, that all of our ideas are derived from experience (the world of impressions), and that we have no innate ideas in our minds; that is, ideas that are not based on what we perceive.

In the first part of the *Treatise*, Hume proceeds to explore the bases of our knowledge. We possess two faculties, memory and imagination, for dealing with the ideas that we receive. The memory preserves the ideas in the exact order in which they entered the mind. The imagination, on the other hand, is free to arrange the ideas in any manner that is desired. But, contrary to what might be expected, our imaginations do not function at random. Instead, we imagine ideas in ordered sequences, so that whenever a particular idea comes to mind, other related ideas automatically follow it, according to certain principles of the association of ideas that Hume calls "a kind of ATTRACTION, which in the mental world will be found to have as extraordinary effects as in the natural." Ideas tend naturally to be associated when they are similar, or contiguous in time or space, or when they stand in the relation of cause and effect. The importance of association is brought out when Hume comes to discuss causality in Part III.

Before applying these "discoveries" about the way we think, Hume takes up a few other questions. He argues first for a point Bishop Berkeley had previously made, that we possess no abstract general ideas, but only ideas of particular things. General terms, such as "man" or "triangle," designate the collections of similar particular ideas that we have acquired from experience.

Hume then tries to explain mathematics as being about particular experiences. He knew relatively little about mathematics and based many of his views on comments in Pierre Bayle's *Dictionary* (1695-1697). Hume's empirical mathematical theory has gen-

472

erally been regarded as, perhaps, the weakest part of his book, though he was always proud of having shown that mathematics is "big with absurdity and contradiction." Hume conceived of arithmetic as being a demonstrable science dealing with relations of quantity, whereas geometry was thought of as an empirical science dealing with observable points. Because of the limitation of our ability to see and count the points, the theorems in geometry are always to some degree uncertain.

The most famous part of the *Treatise* is the third part of Book I, which treats "Of Knowledge and Probability." Genuine knowledge is gained by an intuitive inspection of two or more ideas to see if they stand in a particular relationship to each other. We can be completely certain by intuition that two ideas do or do not resemble each other, or that they differ from each other, or that one has more or less of a given quality than another, as, for instance, that one is darker than another. Such knowledge is certain in that it depends solely on what one "sees" when two or more ideas are brought together by the imagination, but it gives us relatively little information. By connecting a series of intuitions, we gain the sort of demonstrative knowledge that occurs in arithmetic and algebra. Intuition and demonstration are the sole sources of complete certainty and knowledge.

Our information about the causal relation of ideas does not arise from an intuitive examination of our ideas, and almost all of our information about what is happening beyond our immediate experience is based upon causal reasoning. How do we decide which ideas are causally related? When we examine two ideas, or two impressions

that we think are so related, we find that we do not perceive any necessary or causal connection between them. We perceive only that the ideas are contiguous and successive. We do not, however, perceive that they are necessarily connected in any way, although we do feel that there must be more to the sequence than merely one idea following after another. We believe that one of the ideas must make the other occur. But, Hume asks, what evidence do we have for such a belief, and where do we acquire the belief? If we admit that we do not perceive any necessary connection between events, then Hume suggests that we ought to ask ourselves why we believe that every event must have a cause and why we believe that particular causes necessarily must have certain effects.

When the first problem is examined, we discover something that is surprising. Even though we all believe that every event must have a cause, this proposition is not intuitively obvious, nor can it be demonstrated. When we conceive of events, we neither see them as caused, nor necessarily think of them in terms of their causes. Because of the freedom of our imagination, each event can be thought of separately and independently. If events can be thought of as uncaused, it is also possible that they occur uncaused. If that is a genuine possibility, then there can be no valid demonstration proving the impossibility of uncaused events. The demonstrations that had been offered by previous philosophers, Hume believed, are all unsatisfactory. They beg the question in that they assume what they are attempting to prove; namely, that every event has a cause. Apparently, the causal principle, which is not self-evident nor demon-

473

strable, is so basic that we all accept it for reasons that seem to be unknown.

To explore the matter further, Hume turns to the other problem: What is the basis for our belief that particular causes have particular effects, and how do we infer one from the other? The actual constituents of our causal reasoning, he asserts, are a present impression of sense or memory, an imagined idea of a related event, and an unknown connection between them. When we hear a certain sound, we think of somebody ringing the doorbell. Why and how do we infer from the impression to its supposed cause? Many other ideas might have come to mind. When we hear the sound, we do not, at the same time, experience its cause, yet we implicitly believe that said cause must also be occurring to produce the perceived effect. This reasoning process is not a logical one, Hume maintains, since there is no *reason* for us to think of one idea rather than another when a particular experience takes place.

If reason cannot be what makes us connect events causally, perhaps experience is responsible. We find that when a sequence of events is constantly repeated in our experience, and when the events are conjoined, we tend to associate ideas about them in our minds. Then, when we experience just one of the events, we also think of the other. One of them we call the cause and the other, the effect. What is there in the fact that certain events have been constantly conjoined in the past that leads us to think of them as being causally related? Hume points out that if the process involved were a rational one, we would have to presuppose that the principle of the uniformity of nature was true. This principle asserts

"that instances, of which we have had no experience, must resemble those, of which we have had experience, and that the course of nature continues always uniformly the same."

Hume next questions whether we possess any evidence that this principle is true, or that it has to be true. Since we can readily imagine that the world might change in many respects in the future, it is not possible to demonstrate that nature must be uniform. Our experience up to the present moment does not constitute evidence as to what the future course of nature will be, or must be. Just because the sun has risen every day up to now does not prove that it has to rise tomorrow. We can only judge the future if we know that nature is uniform. But our information up to this point is only that, so far, nature has always been uniform. Experience can provide us with no clue about what has to be the case in the future. Hence, we can neither demonstrate nor prove from experience that the all-important principle of the uniformity of nature is true, even though much of our reasoning about the world depends upon it.

The acceptance of this principle, Hume contends, is a fundamental characteristic of human nature. We have a habit or custom that operates upon us for unknown and unknowable reasons. After we have experienced the same sequence of conjoined events several times, then, when we perceive one of the conjuncts, habit or custom leads us to think of the other, and to think of it in a lively and forceful way. Although we are able to think of any idea we wish, we are led psychologically to think only of a particular conjoined idea and to conceive of it with some of the force and vivacity of its

474

conjoined impression. Such force and vivacity constitute our belief in the actual occurrence of the conjoined item. In terms of this explanation, the principle of the uniformity of nature is more a principle about how we think and feel than it is one about the order of events in the world.

Hume uses his discovery of the psychological origins of our belief in the uniformity of nature to explain the basis for our conviction that there is a necessary connection between events. The necessary connection is never perceived, no matter how often the same sequence is observed. But, after a constant conjunction of events has been perceived many times, we then feel that one of the conjuncts causes or produces the other. It is not any discoverable fact about the events that makes us believe this, but rather our psychological attitude toward the events. We possess a fundamental propensity or determination of the mind to think of a conjoined idea after experiencing the conjunct or thinking of it, once we have perceived the constant conjunction of the two in our experience. This determination, which is a strong feeling, is the necessary connection that we think exists between events. Although it is felt in us, we have a tendency to conceive of it as existing in the events themselves. This idea is actually a feature of the way we think about events, rather than a feature of them. Thus, the term "cause" can be defined as *"An object precedent and contiguous to another, and so united with it in the imagination, that the idea of the one determines the mind to form the idea of the other, and the impression of the one to form a more lively idea of the other."*

In Hume's explanation of causality, he joins Father Nicolas Malebranche's contention that there is no necessary connection between events with his own psychological account of how we react to the uniformities in experience. Because of our habits, we expect the future to resemble the past, and we feel that when we observe certain events, their constant conjuncts must also be taking place, even if we cannot observe them. We have no actual knowledge of what is taking place, but only beliefs. Since we can never be completely sure that our beliefs correspond to the actual state of affairs, our causal information is always, at best, only probable.

Hume sees the task of the sciences as that of carefully establishing bases for "reasonable belief" by collecting data about the constant conjunctions that occur in human experience, and organizing such data in terms of scientific laws. These laws provide a form of rational expectation, in that they allow us to predict the future course of events on the basis of detailed information about what has happened up to now. The scientist, like anyone else, expects, because of his habits and propensities, that the future will resemble the past. Science, for Hume, is not the search for the "real" cause of events, but for the best available probable predictions about the course of nature, founded on correlations of constant conjunctions of events and the psychological habits of human beings.

After presenting his explanation of the source of our information, the nature of our beliefs about the world, and the character of scientific "knowledge," Hume turns in Part IV of the *Treatise* to the full statement of his skeptical views. He first presents a series of reasons to show why we should be doubtful of the conclusions that we come to because of our reasoning, and those that we come to because of our sense experience and our attitudes towards it. Then Hume contends that though there are basic difficulties with regard to both our reason and our senses, we still have to believe many things because of our psychological structure. Unfortunately, what we believe is often either indefensible or contradictory.

The argument offered to engender a "scepticism with regard to reason" purports to show that even the most certain conclusions of reasoning are actually only probable and that their degree of probability diminishes the more that we examine them. Since we all make mistakes, every time we reason there is a possibility that we may err. When we check our reasoning, it is still possible that we have erred in our checking, and that we will err in checking our checking, and so on. Each judgment that we make about the merits of our reasoning is merely probable, and the combined probability, Hume says, will get smaller and smaller the more we judge our judgments of our judgments of our judgments. Hence, if this checking process were carried on indefinitely, we should begin to lose confidence even in our most certain reasonings in arithmetic or algebra.

With regard to our sense information, Hume insists that we are naturally convinced that the objects we observe exist continuously and independently of us. But as soon as we begin to examine this belief we find that it is completely unjustified and that it conflicts with what we know about our impressions. Neither sense information nor valid reasoning can supply any basis for concluding that there are independent and continuous objects. If our imaginations, through some propensities, supply us with this belief, it is still "contrary to the plainest experience." All that we ever perceive are impressions which, as far as we can tell, are definitely dependent on us. An alteration in our sense organs, or in the state of our health, changes what we perceive. In view of this, we should not think that our perceptions are things that exist independently from us, continuing to exist even when not perceived. But, Hume observes, no amount of argument on this subject makes us give up our natural belief in the existence of the external world.

The discussions of the bases for skepticism indicate that for Hume even complete skepticism is impossible because of the force of natural belief. "Nature, by an absolute and uncontrollable necessity has determin'd us to judge as well as to breathe and feel." Nature forces us to accept certain views, in spite of the evidence for or against them. Philosophy, Hume said elsewhere, would make us into complete skeptics, were not nature so strong. Philosophy would make us completely skeptical about the status of the objects that we perceive with our senses, but, nature prevents us from taking the philosophical arguments seriously.

In his discussion of our knowledge of ourselves, Hume brings out a similar point. We all believe that we possess a personal identity that continues throughout our lives. But when we try to discover the entity we call "ourselves," we discover that all that we are acquainted with is the succession of impressions and ideas. By certain psychological habits and propensities, we have created a fiction which makes us believe that we are also aware of an identical self that perseveres through all our various experiences.

Hence, there is a type of complete skepticism that results from a careful and profound study of human nature. In theory, we realize that there is inadequate evidence to support the bulk of what we believe about the world. Our reasoning and our senses are too unreliable to support these beliefs, which are due to our psychological character and not to any legitimate conclusions of rational processes. Some of these natural beliefs conflict with one another. Hume contends that the factors which make us connect events causally in our experience should make us disbelieve in the continuous and independent existence of sense objects. The more we examine human nature, the more we should realize how dubious and unreliable human opinions are. In the conclusion to Book I of the *Treatise*, Hume points out that his skepticism even undermines his faith in his psychological findings.

But nature prevents us from carrying out this skeptical attitude to its final destructive conclusion. Regardless of the difficulties, in practice we find that we have to believe all sorts of things, even incompatible things. When we go out in the world, the skeptical doubts lose their force; we are overwhelmed by our natural feelings and beliefs, and we act and live in the same way as anyone else. Hume's final advice is that one should be skeptical when one has to be, and be a natural believer when one must, while realizing that neither of these attitudes has any final justification. In periods when doubts are not being taken seriously, one can go on and examine other aspects of the human world, as Hume does in Books II and III of the *Treatise*, and seek for laws about human passions. (One of his findings in this regard is that reason is, and ought only to be, the slave of the passions.)

The *Treatise* has been a rich source of many contemporary views. The more empirical side of it has greatly influenced the logical positivists and the language analysts. Some of the psychological analysis of human belief and behavior has influenced the pragmatists and instrumentalists. The extreme skepticism and irrationalism have had some impact on Neoörthodox theologians. It is for these reasons that *A Treatise of Human Nature* is regarded by many as perhaps the best philosophical work in the English language.

THE NEW SCIENCE

Author: Giovanni Battista Vico (1668-1744)
Type of work: Philosophy of history
First published: 1744 (Definitive edition; earlier edition, 1725)

PRINCIPAL IDEAS ADVANCED

The only way to know man is in terms of his own creations—language, history, law, and religion.

477

The new science consists of reasoning (philosophy) and investigation (philology, considered as the empirical study of language, history, and literature).

After the Deluge the world was dominated by giants; the giants lived like wild animals until storms turned their eyes toward heaven and led them to invent gods; this is the origin of religion.

Because of his fear of the gods man became ashamed of himself; in acting accordingly he created morality.

The practice of burying the dead, undertaken for sanitary reasons, led to the belief in the immortality of the soul.

All cultures must pass through three stages: the age of gods, the age of heroes, and the age of men; corresponding to these stages are three kinds of customs, three kinds of laws, commonwealths, and religions.

Like many an eighteenth century scholar, Giovanni Battista Vico was in agreement with Alexander Pope's slogan, "The proper study of mankind is man." But whereas the typical representative of The Enlightenment thought that the way to study man was to apply to him the principles of Newtonian mechanics (for example, David Hartley, *Observations on Man*, 1749; Julien La Mettrie, *L'Homme Machine*, 1748), Vico maintained that the only way to know man is in terms of his own creations—language, history, law, religion—in short, through the study of civilization.

Vico professed to be carrying on the work of Descartes, and he took sharp issue with both the Cartesians and the Newtonians for supposing that nature is properly understandable by man. Is it not true, he asked, that we can know only what we make? Then only God can understand nature, because it is his creation. Man, on the other hand, can understand civilization, because he has made it. This was Vico's Archimedean point, a truth beyond all question: "that the world of civil society has certainly been made by men, and that its principles are therefore to be found within the modification of our own human mind."

Vico professed, at the same time, to be an adherent of the method of Francis Bacon; he claimed that he was merely carrying over into the study of civil affairs the method Bacon had applied to the study of nature. What he seems to have borrowed from Bacon, however, is not the inductive principle which most people associate with the English thinker, but the practice of turning to sensible evidence to verify one's theories. Vico explained that his science consisted of two parts, reasoning and investigation. The former, which he called "philosophy," had to do with the development of theories on the basis of axioms, definitions, and postulates. The latter, which he called "philology," was the empirical study of language, history, and literature. He maintained that because these latter are founded on memory and imagination and are mixed with emotion, they do not give us the truth; but when they are consulted by an intelligent investigator, who has a theory to test, they are of paramount importance and make possible a science of man.

Vico's central thesis was that modern civilized man has come into existence through a process which is intelligible in terms of certain tendencies inherent in the human constitution. He conceived that initially men roamed the forest like wild beasts, giving no evidence of reason or compassion or any of the traits which have come to distinguish them. Only gradually did man modify his passions and discipline his powers, learning reverence and devising the institutions and inventions with which he has subjugated the earth. Vico did not regard the process as accidental in any sense: it was all part of God's design. But the elements which Divine Providence made use of were, in his opinion, simple and understandable, and finding them was the aim of the "new science." He emphasized the role of providence in history, in order to guard against the belief in fate and chance of the Stoics and Epicureans. In his view, however, providence was a rational principle immanent in the world, rather than a mysterious will transcendent over it.

His work opens with a long list of axioms and corollaries, which should be studied carefully before one reads the rest of the book. They purport to give the fundamental traits of human nature that provide the dynamism for cultural evolution, together with the traits which determine the habits of poets and chroniclers whose creations must serve the scientist as sources. For example: "Because of the indefinite nature of the human mind, wherever it is lost in ignorance, man makes himself the measure of all things." "It is another property of the human mind that whenever men can form no idea of distant and unknown things, they judge them by what is familiar and at hand." "When men are ignorant of the natural causes producing things, they attribute their own nature to them."

When, on the basis of such axioms,

Vico turned to study the myths and legends of the past and with their help to reconstruct the prehistory of the race, the results were hardly in agreement with the assumptions of the eighteenth century drawing room. It was the fashion to think of primitive man as a tender, rational creature, who spontaneously worshipped the God of Nature and knew none of the prejudices or vices of artificial civilizations. Moreover, men took it for granted that Homer was a cultivated philosopher and gentleman, well suited to be a tutor of their youth—except they could not understand why he attributed such scandalous behavior to his heroes and his gods. In Vico's opinion, however, Homer was sublime as a poet in virtue of the fact that he was no philosopher, but a poet with a childlike mind, the product of a childlike age. We must read Homer with this in view and make allowances when we use his material in any attempt to understand his times. Similarly, his gods and heroes must not be judged by our moral standards. They echo the memories of an age when reason and morality had scarcely begun to tame the savage spirit or soften the features of the gods men feared.

Ransacking the myths of pagan peoples, and fitting what he found into the Biblical tradition, Vico constructed the following account. First, there seemed among all peoples to be a recollection of the Deluge; second, all traditions mentioned a time when the world was dominated by giants. Vico argued that God took the children of Shem to be the people of the Promise and conducted their development along supernatural lines which science was not designed to explain. But the descendants of Ham and Japheth were permitted to wander abroad, unattended by divine grace, and to develop the civilization which was Vico's concern. They became a gigantic folk, said Vico, from the fact that after their mothers had weaned them they left them to draw their nourishment from the earth. They became fierce and wild, cohabiting like beasts, and fighting for their food. So it continued until climatic changes, which followed the drying out of the earth, brought thunderstorms into being. The lightning and roar of thunder astonished these savages, causing them to lift their eyes to heaven; and the fear which was in their hearts caused them to invent the first gods. Thus, according to Vico, religion came into being—the first step toward civilization.

The fear of the gods made man take a look at himself and made him ashamed of some of the things he did, particularly concerning matters of sex. When he took his woman into a cave, however, he initiated a series of consequences which he could never have anticipated. In a word, he created morality, the second great principle of civilization, and by bringing his passions one by one under control he liberated his higher capacities, notably reason.

The third principle of civilization recognized by Vico is witnessed by the universal practice among early men of burying their dead. Occasioned at first by the offensiveness of decaying corpses, it came to be the basis of his belief in the immortality of the soul.

In opposition to the orthodox views of his day, Vico held that civilization originated independently in many different lands—a principle which had importance for the study of etymology, to which he gave so much attention. Since each language had a separate origin, it was useless to try to find common roots. On the other hand, different languages could be expected to show parallel developments. For example, because law originally came from God, the Greeks, who called God *"Dios,"* called divine things *"diaion"* and law *"dikaion."* Correspondingly, the Romans called God *"Jove,"* and law *"jus,"* which is a contraction of *"jous."*

It was a general principle with Vico that, on account of the unity of human nature, all cultures must pass through identical stages, namely, the age of gods; the age of heroes; and the age of men. He found their existence attested not merely in mythology and epic poetry, but also in the history of religion, in compilations of laws, and, above all, in etymologies. For, following these three ages, there are three kinds of natures characteristic of men, three kinds of customs, three kinds of laws, commonwealths, religions, and so forth. Thus, in the first age man's nature was fierce and cruel, in the second noble and proud, in the third benign and reasonable. Again, customs of the first age were tinged with religion, those of the second with punctilio (for example, Achilles), those of the third with civic responsibility.

It was Vico's ambition to develop his science along seven different branches. First, he proposed to make it a "rational civil theology of divine providence." He was not alone, in the eighteenth century, in marveling at the "divine legislative mind" which fashions private vices into public virtues. "Out of ferocity, avarice and ambition, the three vices which run through the human race, it creates the military, merchant, and governing classes, and thus the strength, riches and wisdom of commonwealths. Out of these three great vices, which could certainly destroy all mankind on the face of the earth, it makes civil happiness."

Second, his science was to be a "philosophy of authority." In place of the usual speculation about social origins, contracts, the beginnings of property, and so forth, it offered a framework within which to trace the development of sovereignty and right—from the time when authority first sprang from the will of the gods, through the age when it was lodged with princes whose might obligated those who came to them for asylum, to the time when free men concluded by means of reason that authority resides in laws of nature.

In the third place, it was to be a "history of human ideas." Poetry, for Vico, was the wisdom of the heroic age, when men thought in images and confused fancies with memories. It was, however, the beginning of "the knowledge of good and evil," and all the ideas which speculative science was later to bring to refinement were present there in the rough.

The remaining four branches of the new science led to a speculative reconstruction of world history, including such matters as the span of time required for each period, the courses the nations run, the common elements of law and custom among the peoples, and, finally, the principles of universal history.

Because Vico came to his investigations through the study of jurisprudence, he developed the implications of the new science more completely in

that direction and in the field of political thought than in most others He maintained that civil societies evolve through three stages. All begin as aristocracies, which come into being because of the tendency of the weak to seek asylum at the altars of the strong. The peace and prosperity which result from this arrangement gradually strengthen the productive classes, who demand guarantees from their superiors. In time, a republic of free men, governed by law, replaces the aristocracy. But wealth and leisure breed effeminacy and greed. Citizens grow careless, and lawlessness prevails. Deliverance comes when a strong prince establishes order and takes authority into his hands. In Vico's words, "Since in the free commonwealths all look out for their own private interests, into the service of which they press their public arms at the risk of ruin to their nations, to preserve the latter from destruction a single man must arise, as Augustus did at Rome, and take all public concerns into his own hands, leaving his subjects free to look after their private affairs. . . . Thus are the peoples saved when they would otherwise rush to their own destruction." Vico regarded aristocracies and republics as unstable, and maintained that states normally "come to rest under monarchies."

In the century of Frederick the Great, it was nothing unusual for an enlightened thinker to argue in favor of an absolute monarchy. Voltaire did also. But the development which we have so far described was, in Vico's view, only half a cycle. A nation might flourish for some time under a prince, as did Imperial Rome; but the fate of Rome serves notice that the irresponsibility of civilized men in an

481

"age of reason" may pass all bounds and bring about the destruction of everything that had been built up through the centuries. And such was, in Vico's opinion, the eternal law of history. He saw civilization as a fragile achievement which Divine Providence frames out of violence, greed, and pride; but when the zenith has been passed it is destroyed by these same forces. No need, with Gibbon, to place the blame on alien influences and external barbarians! A new "barbarism of reflection" turns civilized men into worse than beasts. Reason disintegrates into skepticism: "learned fools fall to calumniating the truth." Civic loyalties forgotten, the restraints of morality are turned into jests. Men throng together in cities and jostle each other at public festivals, but they live in deep solitude of spirit: under soft words and polite embraces they plot against one another's lives. Their factions grow into civil wars, which decimate the land and let their cities return to forests. Those who survive are reduced again to "the barbarism of sense," until they learn once more the things necessary for life. "Thus providence brings back among them the piety, faith, and truth which are the natural foundation of justice as well as the graces and beauties of the eternal order of God."

Vico gained only a limited fame in his own time. The curious manner in which many twentieth century points of view are anticipated in his work has, however, brought him belated recognition. Pragmatists can see their doctrine of knowledge in his contention that we know only what our minds contrive. Humanists find much wisdom in his account of civilization. Persons concerned with history as a science admire the way in which he combined hypothesis and investigation, and those whose interest is in plotting the cycles of cultures find frutiful suggestions in his work. James Joyce did much to popularize his name among students of literature. And, inevitably, his account of the early giants creating their gods and fleeing in shame to caves has caught the attention of some existentialists.

MAN A MACHINE

Author: Julien Offray de La Mettrie (1709-1751)
Type of work: Metaphysics and natural philosophy
First published: 1748

PRINCIPAL IDEAS ADVANCED

Both animals and men are machines that feel.

The soul is a material part of the brain, as is shown by the fact that when the body is diseased, so is the soul.

Man is distinguished from other animals by his larger brain and by his ability to use language.

Descartes had declared that all animals except men are "machines": very complicated automata, responding to external stimuli in a mechanical way. Thus, man alone, because he possesses an immaterial soul, is conscious and endowed with free will, hence capable of being virtuous or sinful. La Mettrie's leading idea was the denial of any sharp distinction in kind between man and other animals. In his *Natural History of the Soul* (1745) he put this in the form of a strong objection to Descartes' calling brutes "machines," thereby denying that they think and feel. But three years later he changed his terminology (not his doctrine) and argued that animals are machines that feel, and so is man. "The human body is a machine which winds its own springs; . . . the soul is but a principle of motion or a material and sensible part of the brain."

(It is unfortunate that *Man a Machine* has become traditional as the translation of *L'Homme machine,* for in English, unlike French, it is absurd on grounds of usage to call a man or a dog a *machine,* though it makes sense to speak of them as *mechanisms* —which is what La Mettrie meant.) *Man a Machine* is for the most part a treatise on physiological psychology, containing also certain ethical and antitheological reflections. It is in the form of an oration, without subdivisions.

La Mettrie begins with a defense of experience and observation as foundations of knowledge even about the soul, as against the claims put forward for revelation as a source superior to reason. "If there is a God, He is the Author of nature as well as of revelation; . . . if there is a revelation, it can not contradict nature." To be sure, nature stands in need of interpretation; but so does the Bible. Concerning the soul, the requisite "experience and observation . . . are to be found throughout the records of the physicians who were philosophers, and not in the works of the philosophers who were not physicians. . . . Only the physicians have a right to speak on this subject." Theologians have the *least* right.

What experience and observation show the philosopher-physician about the soul is that its character is patently dependent on bodily conditions. When the body is diseased, so is the soul: a genius may be reduced to idiocy by a fever; it sometimes happens, conversely, that "the convalescence of an idiot produces a wise man." Extreme bodily fatigue produces a sleep amounting to the temporary extinction of the soul. The effects of opium, wine, and coffee are cited. Diet influences character: the English are savage because they eat their meat red and bloody. In La Mettrie's opinion the English diet accounts for their vices of "pride, hatred, scorn of other nations, indocility and other sentiments which degrade the character"—but education can counteract this. Extreme hunger, and prolonged sexual abstinence, can produce raving maniacs. When the body degenerates in old age, so does the soul. Female delicacy and male vigor correspond to the different bodily constitutions of the sexes. When you look through a gallery of portraits "you can always distinguish the man

483

of talent from the man of genius, and often even an honest man from a scoundrel." Differences in national characters correspond to differences in climate. In sum, "the diverse states of the soul are always correlative with those of the body."

Comparative mammalian anatomy, especially brain anatomy, bears out and explains this conclusion. Man is the most intelligent animal because he has the largest and most convoluted brain; the descending order of intelligence—monkey-beaver-elephant-dog-fox-cat—is also the descending order of brain size and complexity. La Mettrie makes three generalizations about animals: "1st, that the fiercer animals are, the less brain they have; 2d, that this organ seems to increase in size in proportion to the gentleness of the animal; 3d, that . . . the more one gains in intelligence the more one loses in instinct." But among men, brain defects are not *always* gross: "A mere nothing, a tiny fibre, something that could never be found by the most delicate anatomy, would have made of Erasmus and Fontenelle two idiots."

The higher animals can do surprising things when properly trained. It would be interesting to attempt to teach an ape to speak by application of the method that Amman has used so brilliantly with deaf-mutes. If one chose a fairly young ape, "one with the most intelligent face, and the one which, in a thousand little ways, best lived up to its look of intelligence," the experiment might well succeed. Then the ape "would no longer be a wild man, nor a defective man, but he would be a perfect man, a little gentleman, with as much matter or muscle as we have, for thinking and profiting by his education." For man is not

distinguished qualitatively from the other animals except in possessing language. And language itself is not an inherent possession of the human species as such, but must have been invented by certain geniuses who taught it to the others.

Knowledge consists in the comparison of the sensory ideas (images) produced in the brain, and this comparison can hardly proceed without language, a system of symbols for classifying. This comparison La Mettrie calls "imagination," and he asserts: "All the faculties of the soul can be reduced to pure imagination. . . . Thus, judgment, reason, and memory are not absolute parts of the soul, but merely modifications of [the] medullary screen upon which images of the objects painted in the eye are projected as by a magic lantern." Hence, all talent and genius, whether of Newton or of Corneille, is fundamentally the same thing: lively imagination.

"Man's preëminent advantage is his organism. . . . An exaggerated modesty (a rare fault, to be sure) is a kind of ingratitude towards nature." There is nothing wrong with taking pride not only in skill, learning, and virtue, but even in mind, beauty, wealth, nobility; these, "although the children of chance, all have their own value."

It is wrong to try to distinguish man from other animals by the former's alleged exclusive acquaintance with natural (moral) law. Natural law is "a feeling that teaches us what we should not do, because we would not wish it to be done to us." It manifests itself to *me* when, for example, I feel remorse after bad conduct; my belief that *you* have a similar experience can only be based on my inferences from your behavior. But we see the same signs in animals, such as the "crouching and downcast air" of a dog who has offended his master. La Mettrie cites the story of Androcles and the lion to prove that animals feel gratitude. If, however, it is maintained that despite appearances animals do not really have any awareness of natural law, then it follows that men do not either, for "man is not moulded from a costlier clay; nature has used but one dough, and has merely varied the leaven." But in fact, remorse and gratitude are universal, even among the most hardened criminals. These persons commit their atrocities from morbid impulses and they are punished adequately by their consciences. It would be better to hand them over to doctors than to burn them or bury them alive, as is the custom.

It is clear that for these reasons virtue is its own reward, and that "Nature has created us all solely to be happy—yes, all of us from the crawling worm to the eagle lost in the clouds." (La Mettrie developed the ethical implications of this doctrine in his *Discourse on Happiness*, 1748.)

La Mettrie next turns his attention to religion. It is highly probable, he says, that a supreme being exists; but this is "a theoretic truth with very little practical value." It does not follow that a highest being ought to be worshiped just because he exists; nor does religion (as everyone knows) insure morality, any more than atheism excludes it.

The "zealous writers" who pile up evidences of design in nature to prove the existence of an intelligent Creator are misguided. "Either the mere structure of a finger, of an ear, of an eye, a single observation of Malpighi proves all, . . . or all the other evidences prove nothing." For even if it be admitted that these facts rule out the possibility of a merely "chance" universe, the existence of a supreme being is not thereby proved, "since there may be some other thing which is neither chance nor God—I mean, nature." All we know is that there is an infinite variety of ingenious mechanisms in nature; we know nothing of their ultimate causes; in this situation recourse to God is a mere disguise of ignorance. "The weight of the universe therefore far from crushing a real atheist does not even shake him."

At this point La Mettrie writes (more astonishingly than convincingly): "Such is the *pro* and the *contra*, and the summary of those fine arguments that will eternally divide the philosophers. I do not take either side." A friend of his, however, "an abominable man," maintained to him that "the universe will never be happy, unless it is atheistic." The extirpation of religion would put an end to religious wars; "Nature, infected with a sacred poison, would regain its rights and its purity. Deaf to all other voices, tranquil mortals would follow only the spontaneous dictates of their own being, the only commands which can never be despised with impunity and which alone can lead us to happiness through the pleasant paths of virtue."

Returning to the subject of the soul, La Mettrie next shows that it is not necessary to postulate the soul as a principle or cause of motion of the body, since muscular fibre is inherently motile. He offers ten observations and experiments in proof. One is that portions dissected from polyps regenerate into whole polyps; the other nine are concerned either with spontaneous motions of parts of organisms severed from bodies or with the motion of parts of the body after death. "The soul is therefore but an empty word, of which no one has any idea, and which an enlightened man should use only to signify the part in us that thinks."

La Mettrie describes at considerable length the physiology of reflex and involuntary movements to illustrate the mechanical nature of the body. (He cites, among other things, the phenomena of erection. This and all other references to sex, as well as whole pages on pre-natal influence, embryology, and heredity, are omitted in the Open Court translation, which was made in 1912 by a committee of learned ladies. Oddly, or perhaps not, the one really indecent *double entendre* in La Mettrie's text escaped their vigilance. See pp. 95ff.) The bodily effects of emotional states show moreover that there is no sharp division between what is under control of the will and what is not. Though La Mettrie does not deny (or even discuss) the "freedom of the will," he remarks that the will "can not act save by permission of the bodily conditions." But having shown (to his satisfaction) that the body is self-moved, and that consciousness is a property of its organized matter, not an independent substance, La Mettrie confesses that he can go no further in explanation. "The nature (origin) of motion is as unknown to us as that of matter."

Descartes is praised for having proved that animals are machines. His insistence on the distinctness of mental from material substance was, says La Mettrie, a ruse to throw the theologians off the scent; for the analogy of men with animals is so striking that it could only be overlooked by "animals and machines which, though upright, go on all fours." There is no contradiction in the notion of a thinking, feeling, moral animal-machine. "Thought is so little incompatible with organized matter, that it seems to be one of its properties on a par with electricity, the faculty of motion, impenetrability, extension, etc."

Only pride and prejudice lead men to resist these conclusions. But "matter contains nothing base, except to the vulgar eyes which do not recognize her in her most splendid works."

We are told (again to our surprise) that immortality is not impossible. To suppose it out of the question would be to reason like caterpillars who can have no conception of their coming metamorphosis. We should admit that we are invincibly ignorant in this domain, and will remain so.

La Mettrie concludes by picturing the wisdom, justice, tranquillity, reverence (for nature), gratitude, affection, tenderness, kindliness, pity, and forgiveness—in a word, the happiness —of the materialist. "Convinced, in spite of the protests of his vanity, that he is but a machine or an animal, the materialist will not maltreat his kind, for he will know too well the nature of those actions, whose humanity is always in proportion to the degree of the analogy proved between human beings and animals; and following the natural law given to all animals, he will not wish to do to others what he would not wish them to do to him.

"Let us then conclude boldly that man is a machine, and that in the whole universe there is but a single substance differently modified. . . . Such is my system, or rather the truth, unless I am much deceived. It is short and simple. Dispute it now who will."

Two centuries after La Mettrie one is likely to smile wryly at the pretty picture of grateful lions regulating their conduct by the Golden Rule, and at the conviction that once religion is got rid of, all will be well—as if religion were something imposed on men from outside, contrary to "the spontaneous dictates of their own being"! But these are amiable eighteenth century-isms which should not deceive us into supposing that La Mettrie was a naïve thinker. He deserves the credit (or blame) for many insights usually attributed to such men as Rousseau, Condillac, Helvétius, and Holbach. His brief remarks on the relation of evidence to conclusion in the design argument for the existence of God penetrate to the essential logical point in a manner not inferior to the more celebrated critiques of Hume and Kant.

Materialists, at least since Lucretius, argued that no chasm separates man from the rest of nature and that the soul must be material, or a property of matter, because mental states obviously vary with the condition of the body. La Mettrie did not have a new argument; he only added to the old one such evidence as was available to him from recent investigations of brain anatomy. But just as La Mettrie questioned the relevance of piling up evidence for design in nature for the purpose of proving a Great Designer, so here also one can ask whether more and more detail about the *dependence* of soul on body strengthens the conclusion that soul *is* body. Except for theological considerations (which La Mettrie justifiably ignored), philosophers who were well aware of all the facts concerning the effects of bodily constitution on the soul still upheld the separateness of body and soul for three reasons: (1)

Our thoughts and feelings, of which we are directly aware, are obviously not bodies, nor properties of bodies, since it makes no sense to raise such questions about them as where they are, or how big they are. (2) We know (again immediately) that the self has an identity that no material thing, or property, could have: for anything spatial can be divided, whereas we have no notion of what it would be like to split one self into two selves. (3) Matter is essentially inert; if it moves, there must be a cause of its motion; and our experience reveals that volition, which is mental, is capable of moving the body. (Note that all these purport to be deductions from "experience and observation.")

It is incumbent upon materialists at least to cope with these objections. Now La Mettrie paid attention to the third, and he gave good reasons for denying the inertness of matter especially organic matter. An answer to the second is implicit in his writing: the unity of the self is only a unity of functions, and when the organism is malformed (as in congenital idiocy or deafness) the corresponding functions ("faculties") are absent.

There is discernible in La Mettrie the bare beginning of a materialist reply to the first objection. He says, in the passage already quoted above, that "judgment, reason, and memory are not absolute parts of the soul, but merely *modifications* of [the] medullary screen upon which images of the objects painted in the eye are projected as by a magic lantern." (Emphasis supplied.) That is, when an image is formed on the retina, it is transmitted by the optic nerve to the visual cortex, and the visual sensation *is* the resulting "modification" or "brain-event." This doctrine requires considerable argumentation and explication before it becomes plausible, and La Mettrie provides none. However, he has at any rate progressed beyond the childish view of Descartes, according to whom the immaterial soul somehow "inspects" (directly, infallibly, and unintelligibly) the "medullary screen." In any case, it would be unreasonable to complain of La Mettrie that he did not, once and for all, explain how one is to conceive the identity of thought and brain process—that is, solve the mind-body problem, still the most vexed question on the philosophical agenda despite well-meant attempts to dismiss it as nonsensical.

La Mettrie was the first, the most consistent, and the most extreme of the eighteenth century French materialists. He was a thinker of great originality who insisted on saying what he thought, in print, well knowing that to do so would expose him to the rage of fanatical obscurantists. In fact, he was

forced to flee from France to Holland, thence to Prussia, where Frederick the Great granted him asylum. In Potsdam he resumed the practice of medicine. He enjoyed but two years of security and prosperity; he died at the age of forty-one. (The pious claimed that Epicurean gluttony was the cause of death.) Frederick himself composed his eulogy, saying of him (with justice that the much-maligned philosopher has yet to receive from the historians, with the honorable exception of Lange): "La Mettrie was born with a fund of natural and inexhaustible gaiety; he had a quick mind, and such a fertile imagination that it made flowers grow in the field of medicine. Nature had made him an orator and a philosopher; but a yet more precious gift which he received from her, was a pure soul and an obliging heart. All those who are not imposed upon by the pious insults of the theologians mourn in La Mettrie a good man and a wise physician."

AN ENQUIRY CONCERNING THE PRINCIPLES OF MORALS

Author: David Hume (1711-1776)
Type of work: Ethics
First published: 1751

PRINCIPAL IDEAS ADVANCED

The purpose of ethical inquiry is to discover those universal principles on which moral praise and blame are based.

Benevolence is approved partly because of human sympathy and partly because of its social utility, but justice is approved for its utility alone.

Utility accounts for the worth of such virtues as humanity, friendship, integrity, veracity—and it is by its utility that government is justified.

Theories which attempt to explain all human conduct as springing from self-love are mistaken.

Whatever is worth while is so in virtue of its utility or its agreeableness.
Moral judgment is essentially a matter of sentiment, not reason.

Hume's *An Enquiry Concerning the Principles of Morals* is a philosophical classic which grows older without aging, which remains lively with a wisdom that speaks to the present. It is not the most profound of Hume's works or the most original, being to some extent a revision of Book III of Hume's masterpiece, *A Treatise of Human Nature.* But its author considered it the best of his works, and many critics have agreed with this judgment.

Dealing decisively with major ethical issues, the *Enquiry* presents in clear, carefully organized form an analysis of morals. It continues the attack begun by Bishop Butler against the self-love theory (psychological egoism) of Hobbes, and in so doing achieves a measure of objectivism frequently either overlooked or denied by Hume's critics. On the other hand, after preliminary recognition of the significant but auxiliary role of reason in moral judgment, Hume sides with the eighteenth century school of sentiment against the ethical rationalists, on grounds shared today by those who regard ethical judgments as emotive utterances. But while Hume is frequently cited as a predecessor of the latter philosophers, he avoids the utter relativism and moral nihilism frequently, but erroneously for the most part, attributed to them. Hence, although it would be worth while to read the *Enquiry* for its historical importance alone, it also has a unique relevance to some fundamental problems of mid-twentieth century ethical philosophy, particularly to those concerning the nature of moral judgment.

While the *Enquiry* can be clearly understood without previous reading of Hume's other works, it is an application to ethics of the theory of knowledge and methodology presented in *A Treatise of Human Nature* and *An Enquiry Concerning Human Understanding,* and its interest is enhanced by familiarity with these books. Like them, the present *Enquiry* contains a measure of skepticism which, while fundamental, has been greatly exaggerated and widely misunderstood. Indeed one of the chief merits of Hume's philosophy lies in the "mitigated" skepticism which recognizes the limits of human reason without succumbing to what he calls "Pyrrhonism" or excessive skepticism, which in practice would make belief and action impossible. But those who accuse Hume of the latter skepticism must ignore one of his chief aims: to apply the Newtonian method of "philosophizing" to a study of human nature.

The object of the study is to trace the derivation of morals back to their ultimate source. Hume's proposed method was to analyze the virtues and vices of men in order "to reach the foundation of ethics, and find those universal principles, from which all censure or approbation is ultimately derived." Since this was a factual matter it could be investigated successfully only by the experimental method, which had proved itself so well in "natural philosophy," or physical science.

This "scientific" approach will appeal to many modern readers, but herein lies an ambiguity which, in spite of the clarity of Hume's style, has misled some critics. One must realize that

Hume was at this point writing of ethics as a descriptive study *about* morals —about acts, characters, and moral judgments. In this sense ethics is a behavioral science and its statements are either true or false. This may suggest what today would be called an objectivist position, but Hume was not describing the way in which moral attitudes are affected; moral judgments, strictly speaking, are matters of sentiment, although before they can properly occur reason must furnish all the available relevant information. To avoid misinterpretation, it is hardly possible to overemphasize this distinction between inductive conclusions *about* moral acts and judgments, on the one hand, and moral approvals and disapprovals themselves, on the other.

Hume's analysis begins with an examination of the social virtues, benevolence and justice, since their explanation will have relevance to other virtues as well. Such benevolent sentiments and characters as are described by words like "sociable" or "good-natured" are approved universally. But it is not the mere fact of approval but the principle underlying it which is the object of investigation. We approve benevolence in part because of the psychological principle of what Hume calls *sympathy*, an involuntary tendency in an observer to experience the same emotions he observes in a fellow man, but the more immediate reason for such approval is that we perceive the utility (usefulness, conduciveness to happiness) of this virtue. When we praise a benevolent man, Hume says, we always make reference to the happiness and satisfaction he affords to society. Since benevolence is regarded as one of the highest virtues, it reflects in turn the fundamental importance of utility. Even in our nonmoral judgment of value, usefulness is a paramount consideration.

In cases of uncertainty about moral questions, Hume adds, there is no more certain way of deciding them than by discovering whether the acts or attitudes involved are really conducive to the interests of society. Hume describes several reversals in the estimation of practices, such as generosity to beggars, when it was seen that their tendencies were harmful rather than helpful, as had been supposed at first.

Whereas benevolence is approved partly but not exclusively for its beneficial consequences, justice has merit for no other reason. (One must realize that Hume conceives justice as concerning only property relations, thus omitting "fair play" and equality, ordinarily considered essential to the concept; actually he accounts for impartiality by his account of truly moral judgment, as is shown below.) To prove this apparently controversial claim, Hume cites a number of cases in which the connection of justice and utility is demonstrated by their joint occurrence or nonoccurrence, increase or diminution. Too many and too lengthy to admit adequate recapitulation here, Hume's arguments may be suggested briefly by a few illustrations: In situations of superfluity or of dearth of material goods, the observation of property distinctions becomes useless and is suspended; a virtuous man captured by outlaws flouting justice would be under no restraint from justice if the opportunity to seize and use their weapons arose, since regard for ownership would be harmful; societies suspend international justice in times of war because of its obvious disadvantages.

Examination of particular laws confirms this explanation of justice; they have no other end than the good of mankind, to which even the natural law theorists are forced to appeal ultimately. Particular laws would in many cases be utterly arbitrary and even ridiculous, were it not that the general interest is better served by having specified rules rather than chaos. In individual cases the fulfillment of justice may even be detrimental, as when an evil man legally inherits a fortune, and abuses it, but consistent observance of the law is ultimately more useful than is deviation.

Were individuals completely self-sufficient, again justice would not arise, but actually men mate and then rear children; and subsistence of the family requires observance within it of certain rules. When families unite into small societies, and societies engage in commerce, the domain of utilitarian rules of property enlarges accordingly. Thus the evolution of social groups shows a direct proportion between utility and the merit of justice.

In finding the essence of justice and its moral obligation in utility alone, thus making it of derivative rather than intrinsic value, is Hume degrading this virtue? Not so, he insists: "For what stronger foundation can be desired or conceived for any duty, than to observe, that human society, or even human nature, could not subsist without the establishment of it; and will still arrive at greater degrees of happiness and perfection, the more inviolable the regard is, which is paid to that duty?"

At the end of his section on justice he repeats his conclusion that utility accounts for much of the merit of such virtues as humanity, friendship, and public spirit, and for all that of justice, fidelity, integrity, veracity, and some others. A principle so widely operative in these cases can reasonably be expected to exert comparable force in similar instances, according to the Newtonian method of philosophizing. Hume then finds utility to be the basic justification for political society or government, and he notes that "the public conveniency, which regulates morals, is inviolably established in the nature of man, and of the world, in which he lives."

But is utility itself a fundamental principle? We may still ask *why* utility is approved, to what end it leads. The alternatives are two: it serves either the general interest or private interests and welfare. Hume recognizes the plausibility of the self-love or self-interest theory holding that all approvals are ultimately grounded in the needs and passions of the self, but he claims to prove decisively the impossibility of thus accounting for moral judgments.

The skeptical view that moral distinctions are inculcated through indoctrination by politicians in order to make men docile is very superficial, Hume says. While moral sentiments may be partially controlled by education, unless they were rooted in human nature the terminology of ethics would awaken no response.

But granted this response, must it still be traced to self-interest, perhaps an enlightened self-interest that perceives a necessary connection between society's welfare and its own? Hume thinks not. We often praise acts of virtue in situations distant in time and space, when there is no possibility of benefit to ourselves. We approve some virtues in our enemies, such as courage, even though we know that they may work to our harm. When acts praised conduce to both general and private welfare, our approbation is increased, but we still distinguish the feelings appropriate to each. Now if the first two considerations are rejected by arguing that we approve what is not really to our own interest by imagining our personal benefit had we been in the situation judged, Hume replies that it is absurd that a real sentiment could originate from an interest known to be imaginary and sometimes even opposed to our practical interest.

Even the lower animals appear to have affection for both other animals and us; surely this is not artifice, but rather disinterested benevolence. Why then deny this virtue to man? Sexual love produces generous feelings beyond the merely appetitive, and common instances of utterly unselfish benevolence occur in parent-child relationships. It is impossible, Hume holds, to deny the authenticity of such affections as gratitude or desire for friends' good fortune when separation prevents personal participation.

But if the evidence is so clear, why have self-love theorists been so persistent? Hume blames a love of theoretical simplicity. The self-love theory, as Butler forcibly argues, mistakenly attempts to reduce all motivation to this one principle, and so is psychologically false. Man has physical appetites each having its own object; that of hunger is food, that of thirst is drink; gratification of these needs yields pleasure, which may then become the object of a secondary, interested desire—self-love. Unless the primary appetites had occurred, there could have been no pleasures or happiness to constitute the object of self-love. But the disinterested primary passions also include benevolence or desire for others' good, satisfaction of which then similarly yields pleasure to the self. Hence self-love actually presupposes specific and independent needs and affections, which complexity is again shown by occasional indulgence of some particular passion, such as the passion for revenge, even to the detriment of self-interest.

Since self-love cannot account for our moral approval of utility, then the appeal of the latter must be direct. In any theoretical explanation some point must be taken as ultimate, else an infinite regression occurs; hence we need not ask why we experience benevolence—it is enough that we do. Actually, however, Hume further explains it by reference to sympathy, the almost inevitable emotional reaction to the feelings of others. Yet Hume is careful not to claim that "fellow-feeling" is necessarily predominant over self-love; both sentiments vary in degree. But in normal men there is close correlation between strong concern for one's fellows and sensitivity to moral distinctions. Benevolence may not be strong enough to motivate some men to *act* for the good of another, but even they will feel approval of such acts and prefer them to the injurious.

Having admitted not only interpersonal differences in sympathy, but acknowledging also intrapersonal variations of feeling for others, how can Hume account for any uniformity and objectivity in our moral judgments? Here he offers one of his most significant contributions to ethics. Even while our sentiments vary we may judge merit with practical universality, analogously to judgmental correction of variations in sensory perception. Though we do not all, or always, perceive the same physical object as having the same color, shape, or size, as when we approach an object from a distance, we do not attribute the variations to the object; instead we imagine it to have certain stable, standard qualities. Such adjustment or correction is indispensable to mutual understanding and conversation among men.

Likewise, men's interests and feelings vary. Thus, moral discourse would be impossible unless men took a general rather than a private point of view: "The intercourse of sentiments . . . in society and conversation, makes us form some general unalterable standard, by which we may approve or disapprove of characters and manners." Although our emotions will not conform entirely to such a standard, they are regulated sufficiently for all practical purposes, and hence ethical language becomes meaningful: "General language . . . being formed for general use, must be moulded on some more general views, and must affix the epithets of praise or blame, in conformity to sentiments, which arise from the general interests of the community." In order for this standard to be effective there must of course be a sentiment or emotion to implement it, and here again Hume produces a telling argument against the self-interest theory. Self-love is inadequate to the prerequisites of the concept of morals, not from lack of force, but because it is inappropriate. Such a concept as this implies (1) that there be in existence a universal sentiment producing common agreement in approving or disapproving a given object, and (2) that this sentiment comprehend as its objects actions or persons in all times and places. None but the sentiment of humanity will meet these criteria. Hume's account of a "general unalterable standard" based principally on social utility and hence on benevolence is strongly objectivistic and balances subjectivistic strains in his ethics; it also provides the impartiality apparently neglected by his definition of justice.

Having thus accounted for our approval of qualities conducive to the good of others, Hume continues his analysis of virtues and finds three other classifications. "Qualities useful to ourselves" ("ourselves" here meaning persons exhibiting the qualities) may be approved also for general utility, but primarily for benefit to the agent; examples are discretion, frugality, and temperance. Now a second major division and two other categories of virtues are added: the "agreeable" (pleasant or enjoyable) to their possessors or to others. "Qualities immediately agreeable to ourselves," approved primarily for the satisfying feelings aroused, are such as greatness of mind and noble pride, though some like courage and benevolence may also be generally useful. Good manners, mutual deference, modesty, wit, and even cleanliness illustrate "qualities immediately agreeable to others."

Only when the analysis is almost completed does Hume offer the first formal definition of "virtue" as *a quality of the mind agreeable to or approved by every one who considers or contemplates it.* A second definition, better summarizing the *Enquiry's* results, is that "Personal Merit consists altogether in the possession of mental qualities, *useful* or *agreeable* to the *person himself* or to *others*." A definition of value in general follows: "Whatever is valuable in any kind, so naturally classes itself under the division of *useful* or *agreeable, the utile* or the *dulce*. . . ."

Readers familiar with the history of ethics will thus see hedonistic and utilitarian themes which received subsequent expresssion in Betham and Mill. The only goal of Virtue, Hume says, is cheerfulness and happiness; the only demands she makes of us are those of careful calculation of the best means to these ends and constancy in preferring the greater to the lesser happiness. Such an obligation is *interested*, but the pleasures it seeks, such as those of peace of mind, or awareness of integrity, do not conflict with the social good, and their supreme worth is almost self-evident.

Having discovered what he calls the true origin of morals through the experimental method, Hume is now ready to return to the Reason vs. Sentiment issue he mentions at the beginning of the *Enquiry* but defers for settlement until the end. Throughout the book statements occur which indicate his final position, but unfortunately there are also a number which appear to make moral judgment a matter of reason. This ambiguity is dispelled by Hume's final treatment showing that moral judgment proper is noncognitive and affective in nature. It is true that reason is indispensable to approval or disapproval, for it must provide the facts which pertain to their objects. Very detailed and precise reasoning is frequently required to determine what actually is useful in a given case; nothing other than reason can perform this function. In view of the importance of the question, of whether moral judgment is rational or sentimental (affective), to both the eighteenth century and ours, Hume's full recognition of the auxiliary role of reason must be kept in mind. But he cannot agree with those rationalists who hold that moral judgments can be made with the same mental faculties, methods, and precision as can judgments of truth and falsity, and who frequently make comparisons between our knowledge of moral "truths" and those of mathematics and geometry.

Besides the evidence of the origin of moral sentiment from benevolence, there are perhaps even more cogent arguments based on comparison of the two types of judgment. The judgments of reason provide information, but not motivation, whereas blame or approbation are "a tendency, however faint, to the objects of the one, and a proportionable aversion to those of the other." That is, moral "judgment" is essentially affective and conative, while rational judgments are neither. Although reason can discover utility, unless utility's *end* appealed to some sentiment the knowledge would be utterly ineffective.

Rational knowledge is either factual or relational (logical or mathematical) in nature; its conclusions are either inductive or deductive. But the sentiment of blame or approbation is neither such a conclusion nor an observation of fact; one can examine at length all the facts of a criminal event, but he will never find the vice itself, the viciousness, as another objective fact in addition to those of time, place, and action. Neither is the vice constituted by some kind of relation such as that of contrariety, for example, between a good deed and an ungrateful response, since an evil deed rewarded with good will would involve contrariety but the response then would be virtuous. The "crime" is rather constituted such by the sentiment of blame in the spectator's mind.

In the process of rational inference, we take certain known facts or relations and from these deduce or infer a conclusion not previously known; but in moral decisions, says Hume, " . . . after every circumstance, every relation is known, the understanding has no further room to operate, nor any object on which it could employ itself. The approbation or blame which then ensues, cannot be the work of the judgement, but of the heart; and is not a speculative proposition or affirmation, but an active feeling or sentiment." This is one of the clearest and most definitive statements of Hume's position on moral judgment.

Finally, reason could never account for ultimate ends, as can be shown very shortly by asking a series of questions about the justification of an act. For example, if one says he exercises for his health, and is asked why he desires health, he may cite as successive reasons its necessity to his work, the necessity of work to securing money, the use of money as a means to pleasure. But it would be absurd to ask *why* one wished pleasure or the avoidance of pain. Similarly we have seen that virtue appeals to sentiments which neither have nor require any further explanation. Whereas the function of reason is to discover its objects, that of moral (and aesthetic) sentiment (or taste) is to confer value.

Hence, in a radical sense, moral distinctions are subjective, but the subject from which they derive is the whole human race, and individual subjectivity is corrected by the general unalterable standard. The *Enquiry* thus affords both a naturalistic, empirical description of the origin of moral values and a persuasive account of an ethical norm by which consistent judgments may be made, without appealing to a doubtful metaphysics. It is in this eminently sane recognition of the functions and limits of both reason and emotion that modern readers can learn much from David Hume.

THOUGHTS ON THE INTERPRETATION OF NATURE

Author: Denis Diderot (1713-1784)
Type of work: Philosophy of science, epistemology
First published: 1754

PRINCIPAL IDEAS ADVANCED

The rationalistic approach to nature is useless; to study nature one must proceed from facts by the use of methods of inference.
Inferences should be checked by experiments; reflection and observation should supplement each other in empirical inquiry.

By acts of interpretation one succeeds in becoming more than a mere observer of nature; by drawing general conclusions from the order of things one arrives at an understanding of the world's order.

There is one causal principle operative in the world, but there are numerous elements, divisible into molecules themselves indivisible.

Experimental physics is the basis of all true knowledge.

A small book consisting of fifty-eight numbered paragraphs, Diderot's *Thoughts on the Interpretation of Nature* was composed with a view to arousing young men's interest in scientific experimentation. It did not propose to instruct them, but to exercise them. "A more capable one than I will acquaint you with the forces of nature: it is sufficient if I have made you employ your own," he wrote in his dedicatory epistle, "To Young Men who are Disposed to Study Natural Philosophy."

That an essay of this sort was called for in France as late as the middle of the eighteenth century was not entirely due to religious censorship. Quite as much as scholastic metaphysics, the rationalistic temper of Cartesian science had prejudiced French thinkers against the experimental methods which had been in vogue for a century in England. Voltaire's *Letters Concerning the English Nation* (1732), written after two years spent in exile in that country, had endeavored to acquaint the French people with such thinkers as John Locke and Isaac Newton. Diderot's *Thoughts on the Interpretation of Nature*, although not expressly mentioning the British authors, had a similar intention.

At a time when ability to read English was as rare among Frenchmen as ability to read Russian is among Americans today, Diderot mastered the language and employed himself in translating English works for publication. The present work is clearly an echo of Francis Bacon, whose *Novum Organum* (1620) bore the subtitle, "True Directions Concerning the Interpretation of Nature."

Diderot was convinced that the rationalistic approach to nature, which supposed that there is an exact correspondence between the processes of logic and the laws of the universe, held little promise. The followers of Descartes were accustomed to regard geometry as the only true science because of the certitude of its results. They left to experimenters only the task of deciding which mathematical expression happened in fact to fit the order of nature. In Diderot's opinion this plan reversed the true procedure. Insofar as it merely elaborates the connection between ideas, mathematics is, he said, merely a branch of metaphysics. It is a kind of game which does nothing to increase our understanding of the world. He acknowledged that mathematics had been put to good use by astronomers, but he believed that there was little more to be hoped for in that direction. He predicted that mathematics had reached its zenith and that a hundred years hence there would not be three great geometers in the whole of Europe.

On the other hand, Diderot found no promise in the methods employed by "naturalists" such as Carolus Linnaeus, whose system of classification he ridiculed because it placed man in the class of quadrupeds and (admittedly) lacked means of distinguishing him from apes. He called such investigators "methodists," on the ground that they revised the world to fit their method, instead of revising their method to fit the world.

The proper method for studying nature, according to Diderot, was to proceed from facts by way of inference to further facts Thoughts, he said, are significant only insofar as they are connected with external existence, either by an unbroken chain of experiments, or by an unbroken chain of inferences which starts from observation, or by a series of inferences interspersed with experiments "like weights along a thread hung by its two ends." He favored the latter. "Without these weights, the thread will be the plaything of the least breath of air."

Diderot distinguished three stages of experimental reasoning. First is the observation of nature, by which one becomes acquainted with the facts; second is reflection, by which the facts are combined in the mind; third is experiment, by which the combination is tested with reference to further facts. In a simile reminiscent of Bacon, he said that the scientist is like a bee: he must constantly pass back and forth from reflection to the senses. The bee would wear out its wings to no purpose if it failed to return to the hive with its burden; but it would accumulate only useless piles of wax if it were not instructed how to fashion its harvest into honeycomb.

In contrast to the facile optimism with which many enthusiasts for science have written about method, Diderot recognized that the path of the experimenter is straight and narrow and that there are few who find it. The mysterious combination of gifts which makes up "creative genius" intrigued him. Men who combine the insight necessary for fruitful observation with powers of reflection and with the skill and patience required for fruitful experiment are exceedingly rare, he said; and he saw nothing that could be done about it. Like a maladroit politician who finds it impossible to take hold of a situation, the average person can spend his whole life observing, say, insects, whereas another takes a passing glance and discovers a whole new order of life.

It was the hope of Diderot that experimenters could learn a lesson from skilled craftsmen, who, without any formal teaching but purely as a result of long experience in handling materials, are able to "smell out" the course of nature and adapt their methods to its ways. As the son of a master cutler, Diderot retained throughout his life a high regard for technical skills, as numerous articles and engravings in the famous *Encyclopédie* (1751-1766), which he edited, attest. The workers themselves, he said, believe that they divine the ways of nature through a kind of "familiar spirit." But he explained their gift as being no more than the faculty of perceiving analogies between the qualities of objects which have certain things in common and a massive knowledge of the ways things affect one another when brought into combination. With this insight into the workings of the craftsman's mind, the experimenter should be able not merely to equal but to surpass him in ability.

Diderot would have some sympathy with the man who said that genius is ninety-nine percent perspiration and only one percent inspiration, and he recognized that discoveries are often happy accidents, in which error and folly have a share. To make his point, he adapted the story of the man who on his deathbed told his lazy sons that there was treasure buried in the orchard. They spent the summer digging it over. Though they failed to find the object of their greed, they did receive an unusually good crop of fruit. So, said Diderot, experimentation commonly fails to unlock the secrets of pragmatic truth.

But Diderot continued the parable. The next year one of the boys told his brothers that in the course of digging over the orchard he had noticed a peculiar depression in one corner. With his mind still on treasure, he convinced them that since the prize did not lie near the surface it must have been hidden in the bowels of the earth. In this way he persuaded them to join him in the strenuous task of sinking a deep shaft. After many days, they were at the point of abandoning the project when they came upon, not the treasure which they had hoped for, but an ancient mine, which they began to work with profit. "Such," concluded Diderot, "is sometimes the outcome of experiments suggested by a combination of observation with rationalist theories. In this way chemists and geometers, while trying to solve problems which are probably unsolvable, arrive at discoveries more important than the solutions which they sought."

The strength and originality of Diderot's book has sometimes been said to lie in his own peculiar ability to "smell out" directions which were far beyond the intellectual horizon of the typical eighteenth century *philosophe*. This gift appears not only in his insights into experimental method, but also in his own "interpretation of nature." For Diderot was not a positivist and had no intention of limiting human knowledge to the results of observation and experimentation. "One of the main differences," he said, "between the observer of nature and the interpreter of nature is that the latter takes as his point of departure the place where the former leaves off. He conjectures from that which is known that which is yet to be known. He draws from the order of things conclusions abstract and general which have for him all the evidence of sensible and particular truths. And he arrives at the very essence of the world's order."

Thoughts on the Interpretation of Nature includes several paragraphs devoted to Diderot's own "conjectures" as to the direction that science should take—suggestions such as "that magnetism and electricity depend upon the same causes." It also includes an ironical analysis of the philosophy of Pierre de Maupertuis, whose *System of Nature* had recently appeared (Latin, 1751; French, 1753). Diderot agreed, on the whole, with Maupertuis' position, and he assumed a critical air in order to develop further implications of the theory while professing to be scandalized at the outcome. Diderot had already spent three months in prison for advanced thinking and had learned to envelop his speculations in studied ambiguity.

Perhaps the "thought" which governs all the rest of Diderot's "interpretation of nature" is that when man has discovered that every event must have a cause, he has reached the frontier of metaphysical knowledge. There is no point in speculating about any higher cause, nor in asking "why" things are constituted the way they are. At an earlier stage of his development, Diderot had embraced the deistic account of origins which he found in Shaftesbury's *Characteristics* (1711). In the present work, he took his stand on the side of what today would be called naturalism, which at that time was called Spinozism.

It seemed to Diderot that the possibility of experimental science rested upon the assumption that there is only one causal principle operative in the world. But he was so much impressed by the variety which nature exhibits at every level that he shied away from the view that the world is made of a uniform substance. Instead, he favored the materialistic version of Leibniz's philosophy suggested in Maupertuis' book. In this view, every "element" that goes to make up nature is essentially different from every other. Each element is divisible into molecules, themselves incapable of further division. Moreover, the molecules must be thought of as "organic," endowed with the rudiments of desire and aversion, of feeling and thought. Only thus could the whole range of nature be accounted for.

In his oblique fashion, Diderot gave thanks for the Biblical account of creation. For, he said, if we had been left to our own speculations, the best we could do would be to infer that the elements of living beings had been mingled with other elements from all eternity in the total mass, and that they have joined together to form beasts and men "merely because it was possible

for it to happen!" He allowed himself to speculate that a species of animals might come into being, reach maturity, and perish—just as we observe happens in the case of individual members of a species. And, giving full rein to his imagination, he suggested that living beings must have passed through infinite stages of development, acquiring in turn "movement, sensation, imagination, thought, reflection, consciousness, sentiments, passions, signs, gestures, sounds, articulate sounds, speech, laws, sciences, and arts," with millions of years between each of these acquisitions—that perhaps still other developments are yet to come, of which we are ignorant; that the process may come to a standstill, and that eventually the product of these transformations may disappear from nature forever. "Religion," he said, "spares us all these wanderings and the mental labor which it would require to follow them out."

Diderot's interest in biological evolution was not merely of this speculative sort. Familiar with comparative anatomy, he observed that every one of the quadrupeds is patterned on the same "prototype," that nature merely lengthens, shortens, modifies, or multiplies the same organs. "Imagine the fingers of a hand bound together and the material of the nails increased to envelop the whole: in place of a man's hand you would have a horse's hoof." Such considerations led him to conclude that there is no real division between the animal kingdoms. Nature, he said, is like a woman who loves to vary her costume. She does not require many different outfits because she knows how, by varying a sleeve or a collar, adding a pleat or letting down a hem, to achieve an infinite number of effects while using the same pattern.

Diderot's greatest boldness, however, lay in the view which he took of man's role in nature, and of the role of science in human affairs. The Copernican revolution had convinced enlightened thinkers that the earth is not the center of the universe, but the majority of them continued to think of man as occupying a favored position. In rejecting Deism and turning back to the more expansive tradition of Bruno and Spinoza, Diderot sharply challenged the optimism of his day, particularly as it pertained to the advancement of learning.

In principle, Diderot admitted that, just as mathematicians, in examining the properties of a curve, find the same properties present under different aspects, so experimental physicists may eventually find a single hypothesis which covers such different properties as weight, elasticity, electricity, and magneticism. But how many intermediary hypotheses, he exclaimed, had to be found before the gaps could be filled in. Nor could there be any short cut, such as exists in mathematics, where intermediary propositions can be arrived at by deduction. On the contrary, he saw a deplorable tendency for various branches of science to build mutually exclusive systems of explanation. Classic mechanics was such a system. Diderot said it was a labyrinth in which men must wander without hopes of every reaching understanding with other sciences.

Diderot expressed most vividly the disparity between our fragmentary knowledge and the vastness and variety of nature. "When one begins to compare the infinite multitude of the phenomena of nature with the limits of our understanding and the weakness of our faculties, can one be surprised that our work lags and frequently drags to a halt, and that all which we possess is a few broken and isolated links of the great chain of being?" Suppose that experimental philosophy should continue for several centuries. Where is the mind that could take it all in? How many volumes would be required to record it? And how far would any one person be able to read? Are we not, he asked, "as foolish as the men of Babel? We know the infinite distance that separates earth from heaven, yet we do not cease to build the tower." A confusion of tongues is bound to result which will lead to men's abandoning the effort.

This pessimism was directed against barren intellectualism, the attempt to understand the world in abstract terms, and finds its counterpart in Voltaire's *Candide* (1759), where wisdom is said to consist in cultivating one's garden instead of speculating about matters too high for us. Diderot complained that men are content to live in hovels while raising uninhabitable palaces which reach to the clouds. It was his hope that experimental science would alter that condition and would bring into being vast stores of knowledge which would allieviate man's condition. But he predicted that when this change had come about men would lose interest in science just as they had (in his opinion) already lost interest in geometry. "Utility circumscribes everything. It is utility which, in a few centuries, will set the limits to experimental physics as it is on the point of doing to geometry. I accord several centuries to this study because the sphere of its utility is infinitely more extensive than that of any abstract science, and because it is un-

deniably the basis of all true knowledge."

FREEDOM OF THE WILL

Author: Jonathan Edwards (1703-1758)
Type of work: Metaphysics, theology
First published: 1754

PRINCIPAL IDEAS ADVANCED

The will is the ability men have of choosing one course of action rather than another.

The will is determined when, as a result of certain actions or influences, a decision is made.

The will is always determined by the greatest apparent good.

To be free is to be able to do as one wills.

Freedom is compatible with determination of the will; if the will were not determined, there would be no possibility of moral motivation and no sense in praise or blame.

The Arminians claim that the will is self-determining and that it wills indifferently and without cause; but this idea is inaccurate and self-contradictory; furthermore, it makes virtuous action impossible and moral injunctions senseless.

The problem of the freedom of the will, like many of the traditional philosophical problems, remains a problem for many philosophers because of the manner of its formulation. Even to consider the title of the problem is to be led astray. "The Freedom of the Will"—*what* is the problem? Is it *whether* the will is free? Or is it *how* the will is free? Or is it a question as to *what* the will is? Or freedom? Does it even make sense to talk about the will as free? A man can be free, but what is the sense of saying that the *will*—whatever that is—can be free? Or is the question the familiar question as to whether the will is free or determined?

Jonathan Edwards, the great Puritan philosopher of the eighteenth century, the first significant creative mind in American philosophy, taking his cue from John Locke, whose *An Essay Concerning Human Understanding* (1690) he much admired, recognized the difficulties involved in the formulation of the problem. Consequently his careful study of the problem begins with explanations of the terms involved in discourse concerning freedom of the will; he begins with "will," proceeds to "determination," "necessity," "liberty," and to other terms whose ambiguity and vagueness have made the problem a particularly troublesome one for philosophers. And un-

501

like many philosophers, Edwards did not use the occasion of definition as an opportunity for framing the problem to suit his own purposes; with an analytic acumen which would do credit to twentieth century semanticists, he hit upon the meanings relative to common use; and he clarified those meanings without neglecting consideration of the function of terms in conventional discourse. Thus, in considering "liberty," he noted that, in common speech, "in the ordinary use of language," the words "freedom" and "liberty" mean the "power, opportunity, or advantage, that anyone has, to do as he pleases." "To *do* as he pleases"—in recognizing that to be free is to be able to do as one pleases, Edwards prepared the way for his next point: that it is nonsense to talk about the will as free. It is nonsense because the will is not an agent, not a person who is somehow able to do as he pleases! Thus, Edwards wrote, "it will follow, that in propriety of speech, neither liberty, nor its contrary can properly be ascribed to any being or thing, but that which has such a faculty, power or property, as is called 'will.'" It makes sense to talk about a free *person,* for a person can be in a condition of being able to do as he pleases; but it violates "propriety of speech" to talk about a free *will,* as if a will could do as it pleased, could act as *it* wills.

If, then, to have a free will is to be able to do as one wills, and if the will, the power of choice, is determined by the apparent values of the alternatives brought to the attention of the person, it follows that a free will is determined: a man, who is able to choose, is *free* if, when his choice is *determined* by various considerations, he *can do as he pleases.* If this is the resolution of the

problem—and, except for introducing the careful definitions, the arguments, and the qualifications, this is the essential resolution as Edwards presents it— then it is apparent that the formulation of the problem is misleading. It is misleading to consider the "freedom of the will," as if the will were an agent, capable of doing as it willed; and it is misleading to take the problem as the one put by the question, "Is the will free *or* is it determined?"—as if the alternatives were incompatible. Jonathan Edwards deserves credit not only for resolving the problem in a manner that continues to win the admiration of professional philosophers, but also for making his method clear: the method of destroying a problem by clarifying its formulation.

Jonathan Edwards was a vigorous defender of Calvinism, a minister who was an effective combination of intellectual and emotional power. As minister at Northampton, Massachusetts, he argued for predestination, the depravity of man, and the doctrine of irresistible grace. He held with Puritan fervor to the conviction that God is unlimited in his use of grace; he can save whomever he chooses. In support of these hard doctrines he employed a remarkable talent for developing, defending, and propounding ideas. But he did not expect to win anything by the use of intellect alone; although he disdained religious emotionalism, he declared the necessity of conversion and faith. His extraordinary personality brought about an enthusiastic movement in support of the faith he defended; the church at Northampton became the origin and center of religious revival which came to be known as "The Great Awakening." His strict Calvinism eventually had its effect; as

502

a result of an argument concerning the qualifications for communion, probably only the focal point of a number of doctrinal quarrels, he was dismissed in 1750 from the ministry of Northampton. He moved to the Indian mission at Stockbridge and continued work on the problem of the freedom of the will, an enterprise undertaken sometime in 1747. Written in support of the Calvinistic doctrine of predestination and of the necessity which it entails, the resultant work is nevertheless philosophically relevant to the general problem of the freedom of the will. The full title of the study, which is Edwards' masterpiece, is *A Careful and Strict Enquiry into the Modern Prevailing Notions of that Freedom of Will which is Supposed to be Essential to Moral Agency, Virtue and Vice, Reward and Punishment, Praise and Blame.*

The Freedom of the Will, which Edwards referred to as the *Inquiry*, was Edwards' answer to Arminianism, a doctrine based upon the ideas of Jacobus Arminius, a sixteenth century Dutch Reformed theologian. To Edwards the most objectionable feature of Arminianism, which was a view calling for a moderation of Calvinist doctrine, was the claim that divine grace is resistible. Arminianism, in advocating a less strict conception of election and redemption, prepared the way for an increasing emphasis on the moral and the human, with decreasing emphasis on the divine and on the absolute dependence of man on God. The "modern prevailing notions" to which the title refers are the Arminian notions, in particular the Arminian idea of the liberty of the will. According to Edwards, the Arminians regarded the will as acting contingently,

not necessarily, and without cause—a conception often referred to as indeterminism of the will.

The work has four major parts and a concluding section. The first part defines the terms of the inquiry and explains the problem. Part II considers the Arminian conception of the freedom of will, inquiring whether there is any possibility that the will is indifferent; that is, free from any influence by causal or determining factors. Part III deals with the question whether liberty of the will in the Arminian sense is necessary to moral agency. Part IV continues the criticism of the Arminian conception of the freedom of will by examining the reasons offered in support of that conception. The conclusion reaffirms the basic Calvinistic doctrines: universal providence, the total depravity and corruption of man, efficacious grace, God's universal and absolute decree, and absolute, eternal, personal election.

Edwards begins his treatise with an analysis of the meaning of the term "will." He quite sensibly reminds the reader that definition would probably not be necessary had not philosophers confused the issue. The will, then, is "that by which the mind chooses anything"; it is the power to choose. There is no suggestion that the will is a substantial entity of some sort, an internal mechanism that hands out decisions; the will is what common discourse makes it to be: simply the faculty that a man has of choosing to do one thing rather than another. Where there is no inclination one way rather than another, there is no act of will, no volition.

Next, he considers what is meant in talking about the "determination" of the will. The answer is that the will is

503

"said to be determined, when, in consequence of some action, or influence, its choice is directed to, and fixed upon a particular object." To say that the will is determined, then, means simply that choices are caused.

The "good" is defined as the agreeable, whatever wins acceptance or "tends to draw the inclination. . . ." Thus, Edwards points out, "the will always is as the greatest apparent good is." In other words, if the will is the power to choose, and if choices are inclinations toward some alternatives at the expense of others, and if the greatest apparent good is what most of all provokes the interest, the inclination, of the person, then what is chosen, in every case, is whatever is the greatest apparent good. The factors affecting choice are several: they include the apparent characteristics of the object considered (allowing for the possibility that the object is not precisely what it appears to be), the apparent degree of difficulty involved in attaining the object, and the apparent time it would be before the object was attained. The apparent good, according to Edwards, is a function not only of the apparent character of the object considered, but also of the manner in which the object is viewed or considered, and the circumstances of the mind that views. There is no objection to saying that the greatest apparent good *determines* the will—indeed, that is a proper way of speaking—but to say that the will "is" as the greatest apparent good "is" serves to emphasize the point that an object's appearing most agreeable and its being chosen are not two distinct acts.

The term "necessity" is critical in the problem of the freedom of the will. Edwards states his intention of show-

ing that necessity is not inconsistent with liberty. He rejects several customary definitions of necessity, showing that either they say very little or else they ignore the relativity of necessity: anything which is necessary is so *to us* "with relation to any supposable opposition or endeavor *of ours.*" The necessity relevant to a consideration of free will is philosophical necessity, defined as "the full and fixed connection between the things signified by the subject and predicate of a proposition which affirms something to be true."

A distinction is then drawn between natural necessity and moral necessity. Natural necessity is the result of natural causes other than such moral matters as habits, dispositions, motives, or inducements. Thus, by a natural necessity falling bodies move downward. We are naturally unable whenever we cannot do something, even if we will it; we are morally unable when we are not sufficiently motivated to do a particular act.

"Freedom" or "liberty," as we have noted, signifies the power to act as one wills.

Having completed the definition of crucial terms, Edwards turns to an explication and criticism of the Arminian conception of the free will. According to the Arminians, the will is self-determining. Edwards points out the impropriety of saying that the *will* determines its own choices; after all, the will is not an agent. But even if it be contended that not the will, but the soul, determines the will, and does so without causal influence of its action, the further difficulty remains that every act of choice would be determined by a preceding act of choice. If a first act of choice, in a series of acts, is self-determined, it must be the consequence of a previous choice and, thus, be not first: a contradiction. If, on the other hand, it is not self-determined, then it is not free in the Arminian sense. In either case, the Arminian notion is self-defeating.

The next important consideration is whether it would be possible for an event to occur (say, an act of volition) without a cause of its occurrence. Defining a cause as any antecedent on which the existence or nature of something depends, Edwards claims that no event could occur without cause. He affirms the principle of universal causation as one on which all reasoning about matters of fact depends, and he adds that no proof of the being of God would be possible without that principle. If no event could occur without a cause, then no act of volition could occur without a cause.

The argument that the will has the freedom of indifference; that is, that the will can choose any course indifferently, on its own, without being influenced—or that the soul's power of choice is in that way indifferent—is rejected by Edwards because of the contradiction involved in the implicit claim that the soul, while indifferent (in a state of *not* being inclined one way rather than another), chooses (is in a state of being inclined one way rather than another).

Referring to the Arminian contention that the will is contingent in the sense that acts of will are free from all necessity, Edwards argues that there could not be any act free from both cause and consequence. He adds that, even if an act could in this way be free from necessity, it could not be an act of volition, for acts of volition are *necessarily* connected with motives. To will is to be moved to action by the

greatest apparent good; volition, then, necessarily involves being moved, or motivation; consequently, an act entirely unnecessary could not be an act of will.

In order to strengthen further his point that volitions are not contingent, in the sense of being without necessity, Edwards maintains that God's foreknowledge of events is possible only because of the necessity of those events, a necessity he recognizes.

In Part III, Edwards argues that the Arminian notion of an indifferent will, a will free from all causal necessity, is not only not necessary to moral virtue; it is inconsistent with it. To establish his point, he first of all advances a number of considerations to show that necessity is not incompatible with virtue or vice. God's moral excellence, the holiness of Jesus' acts, the sin of man—these are all necessary, but surely God's nature is virtuous and praiseworthy, as are Jesus' acts; and the acts of the sinner, although morally necessary, are nevertheless instances of vice and blameworthy.

Having argued that necessity is not incompatible with virtue, Edwards then maintains that freedom of indifference is not compatible with virtue, for virtue cannot reside in a soul which is indifferent; what common judgment requires is that a person commit himself, that he be inclined toward commendable action.

The conclusion is that virtue depends upon necessity; if the person could not be moved by exhortations, considerations, and inducements, neither virtue nor vice would be possible, and neither praise nor blame would be sensible. Even the commands of God would have to be acknowledged as senseless, if a virtuous soul could not be moved by those commands without losing its moral freedom.

In Part IV, Edwards considers, among other objections to the doctrine he proposes, the claims that if choices are determined, men are machines; if choices are necessary, fate rules men; the doctrine makes God the author of sin and (ironically) encourages atheism; and, finally, the doctrine is metaphysical and abstruse.

Answering the charges, Edwards argues that men are entirely different from machines in that men are able to reason, to will, to do as they will, to be capable of moral acts, and to be worthy of praise, love, and reward. On the Arminian conception, however, men would be worse than machines, the victims of "absolute blind contingence." If fate, as conceived by the Stoics, involves any limitation of human liberty, as Edwards has described it, then he rejects that notion of fate. It is misleading, Edwards continues, to argue that God is the author of sin, for even if God permits sin and so orders events

that sin occurs, he does so for holy purposes and must be distinguished from the human agents who are the actual sinners. If atheists have embraced the doctrine of the determined will and have used it to defend their ways, Edwards argues, that in no way implies that the view is to blame. To the charge that his philosophy is metaphysical and abstruse, Edwards replies that it seems to be the other way about: the Arminian philosophy depends upon vague and undefined ideas and self-contradictory suppositions.

Edwards concludes by claiming that the chief objections to Calvinism have been met by his discourse. The principal objections against the notions of God's universal and absolute decree and the doctrine of personal election are that they imply a necessity of human volitions and of the acts of men; but the argument has shown that unless choices and acts are necessary, in the causal sense described, no volition is possible, and no judgment of moral action is justifiable.

THE THEORY OF MORAL SENTIMENTS

Author: Adam Smith (1723-1790)
Type of work: Ethics
First published: 1759

PRINCIPAL IDEAS ADVANCED

The origin of moral sentiments is sympathy, placing oneself imaginatively in the situation of another in order to realize the passions which affected him.

We approve the passions of another and regard them as suitable if, imagining ourselves in like circumstances, we find that we would have similar feelings.

The amiable virtues of condescension and indulgence stem from sympathy; and the respectable virtues of self-denial and self-command arise in those who are the objects of sympathy.

The unsocial passions, hatred and resentment, are disagreeable; the social pas-

sions such as generosity, kindness, compassion, are agreeable; and the selfish *passions are mixed, neither as disagreeable as the unsocial passions nor as agreeable as the social.*

The propriety of an action is the fitness of its motivating feeling to the cause of that feeling; the merit or demerit of an action rests upon the character of the consequences of the action.

Conscience is the faculty of judgment of the man within the breast, the inward man who knows the actual motivations of his actions.

Adam Smith was a professor of moral philosophy in the University of Glasgow. He is perhaps better known for his work in economic theory, *An Enquiry Concerning the Nature and Causes of the Wealth of Nations* (1776), than for this, his other major publication. Smith was a contemporary and friend of David Hume. Accepting Hume's moral doctrines on the whole, he offered the theory of moral sentiments as a treatment of an area Hume left only vaguely outlined. Smith considered the science of ethics to have as its business the description of the moral rules with a justness and nicety which would both ascertain and correct our ideas of proper conduct.

Smith was close on the heels of the "moral sense" philosophers, Shaftesbury and Francis Hutcheson. Unlike them, however, he did not ascribe moral perception to an inner sense like the exterior senses, a sense capable of recognizing moral quality in a manner analogous to the way the eye perceives color and shape. Smith asserted that philosophers should give greater attention to the causes of the passions, along with the due heed paid to their consequences.

Smith regarded the origin of the moral feelings to be in the process of sympathy with the passions. This consists of placing ourselves in imagination in the place of another, of conceiving ourselves as undergoing the same events and, consequently, having the same feeling as the other person. We do not have *his* feelings, which is simply impossible; but imagination copies our own feelings upon earlier occasions and supplies them anew to our minds. Thus, a sympathetic feeling could be one of compassion for the misery of an unfortunate person, or also the joy of one delivered from danger. And since we are not actually, but only imaginatively, in the situation of the other, we can never have feelings in such great strength as he. Furthermore, some passions do not arouse fellow feeling but rather act as stimuli to some opposing feeling. Sometimes when we perceive a person's anger, we are aroused against him rather than against those toward whom his anger is aimed; or we may experience fear of him rather than anger. A sympathetic response is aroused more by the knowledge of the situation in which the other's feeling first arises than it is by the perception of the other's feeling. This is shown when we occasionally sympathize with the dead, who can actually have no feeling at all.

The exercise of sympathy brings a pleasure both to him who gives and to him who receives it. The pleasure of receiving sympathy in the disagreeable passions is more intense than in the agreeable, and may serve as a measure of relief.

The basis of our approval of the

507

feelings of another man is whether there is perfect concord between our own sympathies and his, when we are aware of his situation. We determine in this way that his passions are suitable and proper to their objects. Just as to have the same opinion as another is to approve of his having it, so with the feelings; we approve the other's feeling if we, in like circumstances, would have the same feeling. Even in cases in which we do not actually have sympathetic feeling with another, experience leads us to learn the nature and the amount of feeling appropriate to his circumstances, and thus to approve of his feelings.

Our natures are so constituted that we can be at variance with our fellows in our feelings, yet tolerate or even enjoy one another's company, as long as the matters which arouse them are items of indifference to our particular lives. But when an event touches us directly, we hope for the greatest possible concord of the spectator's feeling with ours, and we are likely to select our company only from those who display it. Yet recognizing that no other can feel precisely what we feel, since he cannot imagine to himself all the conditions which stir the feeling in us, we restrain and moderate our own feeling to a degree which those around us can attain when it arises in them upon our behalf. Thus, our desire for their approval and the satisfaction we expect from it act as a curb on the extremes of our feelings, and the society of those who have fellow feeling with us aids in restoring and preserving the tranquillity of our minds.

Two classes of virtues follow from these tendencies. The *amiable* virtues of "candid condescension and indulgent humanity" stem from the sympathy of the spectator, and the *respectable* virtues of self-denial and self-command come from the moderation of passion in the person involved. "To feel much for others and little for ourselves . . . to restrain our selfish, and to indulge our benevolent affections, constitutes the perfection of human nature; and can alone produce among mankind that harmony of sentiments and passions in which consists their whole grace and propriety." The *propriety* or the impropriety of an affection consists in the "suitableness or unsuitableness, in the proportion or disproportion which the affection seems to bear to the cause or object which excites it." Certain qualities are favorable but not necessarily admired; those which excite not only approbation but also wonder and surprise are the admirable qualities. This is true of our actions. Many, perhaps most, actions exhibiting propriety do not require virtue; but those which arouse our admiration at their uncommon delicacy of feeling or strength of self-command are signs of the admirable degree of the amiable or respectable virtue.

Passions originating with the body, such as hunger or pain, are objects more of disgust than of sympathy, since the onlooker can enter into them only to a very low degree. But those which take their origin from the imagination can readily take on the configuration of the imagination of the person affected. Such would be the loss of one's fortune or the frustration of an ambition. A tragic drama may fitly turn on such an event, but not even on so great a physical loss as the loss of a leg.

The passions fall into a set of classifications. The *unsocial* passions are hatred and resentment, with their variations. They arouse in the spectator rival feelings, which must work against each other, for he has as much tendency to sympathize with the person hated as with the person showing hatred. These passions are disagreeable alike to the spectator and the person feeling them. They tend to drive men apart and destroy society. The *social* passions, such as generosity, humanity, kindness, compassion, friendship, and all the benevolent affections, are felt with enjoyment; they bring men together and cement society. We enter into the feeling of satisfaction both of him who shows them and of him who is their object. Finally, the *selfish* passions take a middle place between the others. They are grief and joy when arising over the particular good or bad fortune of the person by whom they are felt. These become neither as disagreeable as the unsocial passions, for there is no rival to arouse a contrary sympathy, nor as agreeable as the social passions, for there is no additional beneficiary in whose satisfaction also we would share.

The qualities of merit and demerit are the qualities of deserving reward or punishment, distinct species of approbation and disapprobation. Whereas the propriety of an action is the fitness of its motivating feeling to the cause of that feeling, the merit or demerit of the action rests upon the beneficial or hurtful effects which the action tends to produce. An action appears to deserve reward which is the proper object of gratitude. Similarly, an action appears to deserve punishment which is the proper object of a fitting resentment. These passions of gratitude and resentment, like every other, "seem proper and are approved of, when the heart of every impartial spectator entirely sympathizes with them, when every indifferent bystander entirely enters into, and goes along with them."

In one passage, Smith refers to the impartial spectator as "every human heart," but again he modifies this to "every body who knows of it." While he thus apparently sets up a standard of popular approbation, he seems to regard its basis—"the impartial spectator" —as an abstraction from instances of the human heart, rather than as a census by count. Thus it is possible to have moral judgments in a case in which no feelings, or the "wrong" feelings, have been stirred; it is possible to judge of the demerit of an injury to a person who is unaware he has been injured; and it is possible to alleviate the apparent demerit of an act which is accidental rather than springing from an improper resentment. Judgments of merit are based on direct sympathy with the agent, through which we approve or disapprove the affection giving rise to the action, and upon a sympathy, indirect but no less strong, with the recipient affected. Smith's view makes retaliation a natural impulse and incorporates it, in due degree, into the body of proper actions.

But the standard of the impartial spectator undergoes a further transformation. "I divide myself, as it were, into two persons; . . . I, the examiner and judge, represent a different character from that other I, the person whose conduct is examined into and judged of. The first is the spectator . . . The second is the agent, the person whom I properly call myself. . . ." The first of these persons Smith refers to again and again as "the man within the breast." Thus imagination and sympathy become the account of conscience or the voice within.

Man naturally desires not only to be approved of by society but also to be what ought to be approved of, to be worthy of approbation. Therefore, the "man within the breast" has a powerful voice in determining one's actions, so much so that in many cases inward approval may completely replace that of actual fellow men. The inward man knows one's inmost secrets of motivation and is not contented to approve merely external appearances of rightly motivated actions.

The general rules of morality are formed inductively upon instances of what our moral faculties approve or disapprove. These rules, together with good habits of action, serve as guides to our conduct when our involvement is great and our passions violent, conditions in which the "ideal man" within is deceived or haste prevents his being consulted. Our sense of duty is our regard for these general rules. Some actions, such as marks of gratitude, are of course better when they are prompted by an immediate feeling than when done solely from a sense of duty. The commandments of justice are the most exact duties; they admit of only such exceptions as may also be derived from the same just principles and with the same precision. Justice is an ordinary virtue, largely negative because on most occasions it only avoids harm rather than doing positive good. Nevertheless, it is the foundation of society, for where men are ready to do each other harm without restraint there can be no society. On the other hand, benevolence, which is free and never required, is the ornament of society and often an admirable virtue.

Nature has made every individual concerned first of all for the preservation and health of his body. Men soon learn to transfer their diligence in these regards toward obtaining social desires, such as the respect of our equals and credit and rank in society. The care of such objects as these, upon which one's happiness depends, is the virtue called prudence. It is perfectly respectable, yet neither endearing nor ennobling. Insofar as our actions may injure or benefit others, the character of the individual may affect the happiness of others. The concern for others prompts the virtues of justice and benevolence. The only motive which can justify our hurting or interfering with the happiness of our neighbor is proper resentment for injustice attempted or actually committed; and the punishment should be more aimed at making him aware of the hurt he has done, and at drawing his disapproval toward the motive of it, than at inflicting harm upon him. While prudence, justice, and benevolence may often summon the approval of a man, his passions may yet mislead him. Therefore, still another virtue is needed, that of self-command. Its best form shows greatness and steadiness of the exertions over self-love, with the strong sense of propriety needed to make and maintain that exertion. The degree of self-estimation, neither too high nor too low, which the impartial spectator would approve, is the same as that which will secure for the individual himself the most happiness.

Smith sharpens the outlines of his doctrine by adding, as the final part of his book, an examination of various systems of moral philosophy. He divides his subject according to two questions: (1) Wherein does virtue consist? (2) By what power or faculty of the mind is this character of virtue recommended to us? These represent the traditional questions, respectively metaphysical and epistemological, around which the philosophy of morals has centered in Western thought. Smith recognizes three possible answers to the first question: (1) Virtue consists either in propriety, the "proper government and direction of all our affections," which considered singly may tend either toward good or toward evil; or (2) virtue consists in prudence, the pursuit of one's own happiness; or (3) it consists in benevolence, the promotion of the happiness of others.

Smith places the ethical systems of Plato, Aristotle, and the Stoics within the group making the first answer. He claims the consistency of Plato's system with his own description of propriety. Aristotle differs in having virtue consist in habits of action rather than sentiments and judgments. The Stoics, he insists at some length, mistake entirely the kind of a system Nature made for man, for they reduce to nothing the importance of what we have the most power over, our immediate circumstances; and they would deaden the sentiments which are the very basis of moral judgments. Smith adds to the group the systems of Samuel Clarke, William Wollaston, and Shaftesbury, remarking that they fail to supply what he has provided, the element of sympathy on which morality is based.

Smith finds Epicurus giving the second answer, that virtue is in prudence. Epicurus, however, was too eager to rest everything on a single principle, bodily pleasure and pain; he failed to notice the powerful satisfactions which we take in the approval of our fellow man.

Philosophers proposing the third answer, regarding the principle of benevolence as the primary virtue, included Ralph Cudworth, Thomas More, and John Smith of Cambridge, but most especially Francis Hutcheson, "the soberest and most judicious." Smith commends these philosophies of benevolence as nurturing the most agreeable and noblest affections, but he objects that Hutcheson and the others fail to provide an adequate account of the real worth of the lesser virtues, such as prudence. Their works in that respect are not true to human nature. Bernard Mandeville, who urges that all society and all virtue are founded on self-love, also did men an injustice, for he presents any passion which is ever vicious as always vicious, and to the utmost degree.

For Smith, the problem of the knowledge of moral worth is the problem of approbation. The three possibilities to him seem to be self-love, reason, and sentiment. Against Hobbes, Puffendorf, and Mandeville, he argues that society cannot have been founded simply as a means of furthering private interest because sympathy is not a selfish principle; rather, a sympathetic feeling arises entirely on account of the other individual. Cudworth and other opponents of Hobbes advanced reason as the source of moral knowledge. Smith agrees that reason gathers the moral rules inductively, but that we must have some source, some "first perceptions," from which the reason gathers its instances. Smith commends Hutcheson for first seeing to what extent moral distinctions arise in reason, and to what extent they are founded on immediate sense and feeling. But, on grounds of the nature of experience, he opposes

Hutcheson's claim to have discovered an inner moral sense. The inner sense, said to have as its sole purpose the judging of the rightness of actions, could not function as claimed because right actions do not always have the same appearance or form. Further, sentiments, whether proper or improper, feel inwardly the same. And if the inner sense is devoted to identifying proper approbations, a species of moral feeling, it is superfluous, for we do not require particular inner senses to account for other species of feelings which are unrelated to the moral. Still further, the inner moral sense is never detected operating apart from allied feelings such as sympathy or antipathy, and there is therefore no evidence of its existence such as its single operation would afford.

Finally, Smith affirms that the ancient sort of moralist, who delineated characters in general, in accordance with recognizable virtues, were much superior to later writers, such as the casuists, who attempted to lay down particular rules covering human conduct in advance of the fact. For conduct will always be various, and systems of human law will never be equal to natural justice, made known to man by his sympathies.

The moral system of Adam Smith stands at an interesting place in the development of ethics. It was not a brilliant constructive performance in itself, being here and there imprecise, and advancing very few grounds for the claims made. It did, however, serve to ameliorate some of the more extreme views of its time by helping to emphasize the complexity and subtlety of human experience and conduct. While it was among the last of the works to found morality upon a plan of virtues, it was among the early efforts to provide a sound psychological basis for choices of conduct. While we can see in it clear glimpses of the narrowing influence of the author's own temperament and of the culture and times in which he lived, we can also discover acute and instructive interpretations of human motives. Despite its copious didactic passages, the work shows a hearty desire not to let our wishes for the moral elevation of man get in the way of our seeing the facts of man's actual moral life.

THE SOCIAL CONTRACT

Author: Jean Jacques Rousseau (1712-1778)
Type of work: Social philosophy
First published: 1762

Principal Ideas Advanced

Whatever rights and responsibilities the rulers and citizens have in a state are derived from some agreement; no social right is derived from nature.

In a state of nature men live to preserve themselves; to make coöperation possible and to assure common security, states are instituted by social contracts.

According to the contract, when a man places himself under the control of a sovereign, he is placing himself under the control of himself and his fellow citizens, for a sovereign exists in order to safeguard the citizens.

The sovereign is limited to the making of general laws; he cannot pass judgment upon individuals.

As a result of the joining of wills by the social contract, a general will, distinguishable from a collection of individual wills, comes into being.

The ideal government is a small, elected group; and the ideal state is small enough to allow the citizens to know one another.

Jean Jacques Rousseau is the most interesting and the most important political thinker of the eighteenth century. He is known for his famous *Confessions* (1784) and for his discussion of education in *The New Héloïse* (1760) and *Émile* (1762), but he is best known today, in philosophical circles at any rate, for *The Social Contract*, which is one of the great classics in the field of political philosophy. Rousseau was very much concerned with the relationship between the state on the one hand and the individual on the other. He recognized that the state has tremendous power over the individual, that it can command him, coerce him, and determine the sort of life he is to live, and also that the individual makes many demands on society, even if he does not have the power to back them up. But surely, he insisted, the relations between the state and the individual cannot be simply those of naked power, threats, coercion, arbitrary decrees and fearful or cunning submission, for we do speak of justified authority, the legitimate exercise of force, the rights of citizens, and the duties of rulers. The big question, then, is this: What is the source of the rights and responsibilities of both the citizen and the ruler?

In *The Social Contract*, Rousseau repudiates those who argue that the stronger have the right to rule the weaker, insisting that strength as such amounts to coercion and not justified coercion. If a highwayman brandishing a pistol leaps at me from a thicket and demands my purse, I am forced to hand it over, but his strength does not justify his act and my weakness does not make my reluctance blameworthy. Nor does this right of society over the individual flow from nature. True, the simplest social group, the family, does rest upon the natural requirement that the parents care for the child—survival is the first law of nature—but since the family usually holds together much longer than is needed to satisfy this requirement, it is evident that the rights and obligations that continue to exist within the family organization are not supported or required by nature. Rather, these obligations and rights depend upon tacit agreements between parents and children that certain relationships shall be maintained and respected within the group, agreements tacitly admitted when the son chooses to stay within the family and the father welcomes his continued presence. Agreements of this sort mark the transition from the amoral state of power and submission to power to the moral state of acknowledged rights and responsibilities. What is true of the family is also true of that larger society, the state, for whatever rights and responsibilities the rulers and citizens possess could only have evolved as the result of some agreement among men. Rousseau insists, like Thomas

Hobbes, John Locke, and many others, that society is based upon some implicit contract.

This contract delivers us from a prior state of nature. Before men lived in societies they were motivated primarily by the basic urge to preserve themselves, an urge that manifested itself in physical appetites and desires and released itself instinctively through actions designed to satisfy these. Man was not governed by reason or by moral considerations, for there were no rights or moral relationships to be respected. Rousseau does not claim that pre-societal man was vicious or the natural enemy of every other man, or that he had no gregarious instincts at all, but he does claim that the life of the individual was dominated by the amoral, unreflective pursuit of his own welfare. As a result of this marked individualism and the rude circumstances of nature, life was uncertain and precarious, coöperation impossible, and aggression common. Such a state could be transcended only by instituting, by common consent, some sort of body politic within which cooperation would be possible and security guaranteed.

According to Rousseau, the society instituted by the contract brings about a marked transformation in man, for rational behavior replaces instinct, a sense of responsibility replaces physical motivation, and law replaces appetite. Latent capacities and faculties finally flower, and out of "a stupid and dull-witted animal" there emerges "an intelligent being and a man." In these respects Rousseau differs from Locke and Thomas Jefferson, who maintained that prior to the contract man is already rational and moral and already possesses rights. The contract does not change man or affect his rights; it only safeguards what he already has. But for Rousseau man's debt to society is far greater, for rights, morality, and his very status as a man are consequences of his being a member of a body politic. Rousseau also differs from Hobbes, not about the nonexistence of morality in a state of nature, but about human nature. The Hobbesian man is so egoistic that he can only be restrained, not transformed. For Hobbes, Locke, and Jefferson, man is essentially individualistic, whereas for Rousseau he is essentially a social creature. This view leads to two different conceptions of the function of political society. In the former, social institutions have only the negative function of securing what man already has by controlling excessive individualism, whereas in the latter, social institutions have the positive function of enabling man to fulfill his nature. In the former, political institutions are a necessary evil, but for Rousseau they are a blessing.

In the contract that establishes the state, men agree with one another to place both themselves and their possessions under the complete control of the resultant body politic, and to give to it the power and responsibility of safeguarding them and of providing the framework within which they can jointly pursue their common welfare.

It may sound as if Rousseau were advocating a rather extreme despotism, but this is not so. In the first place, according to the terms of the contract, civil power and responsibility are not turned over to a king or to some small group of persons, but are kept in the hands of the contractors themselves who thus become jointly sovereign. Consequently, when a man contracts to place himself under the control of the sovereign, his action means only that he, like every other person, places himself under the control of himself and his fellow citizens.

Secondly, while the state shall have control over the individual, the scope of its control is limited to matters pertaining to the preservation and welfare of all. If it transgresses these limits, the contract is void and the citizen is released. Thus, for instance, while the new citizen hands all his possessions over to the state, the state immediately hands them back and, by giving him title to them, institutes property rights as distinguished from mere possession. According to the contract, the state retains control only in the sense that it has the right to appropriate the individual's property if the public interest should require that it do so. Similarly, the state can command the individual only to the extent that control is needed for the public welfare. At all other times and in all other respects it guarantees his freedom from the encroachment of the government and of other individuals. In this way the contract brings human rights into being and specifies their scope.

Again, the individual is safeguarded insofar as the function of the sovereign group is restricted to the making of laws and insofar as the object of the law is always general. The sovereign power can pass laws attaching rewards or punishments to types of action and privileges to certain offices, but it cannot pass judgment upon individuals. The latter is the function of the executive or administrative branch, not that of the legislative. Rousseau maintains emphatically that the legislative and administrative functions shall not be discharged by the same group.

The transformation wrought in the individual and the nature of the sovereign act are both expressed in what is perhaps the most nearly basic of Rousseau's concepts, that of the "general will." Even though man is initially motivated by self-interest, the awareness that a contract is desirable forces him to think about others and their interests. Once the contract is made and the mechanism of democratic assemblies put into practice the individual will be forced to consider those other interests more seriously than ever before. This consideration may result from prudence alone in the first place, but the deliberate joining of lots, the debating, the compromises to accommodate others, and the conscious recognition that they have common ideals cannot fail to encourage a genuine concern for the welfare of all. Man becomes a social creature with a social conscience, and what would otherwise have been a mere collection of individuals with individual goals and individual wills becomes a collective person with a single general will and a single goal. There comes into being a *res publica*, a republic, a body politic with many members.

Rousseau stressed the point that man is not really a citizen so long as he accepts society from prudence alone, that he becomes a real citizen only when he develops a genuine concern for the welfare of all. There is an emphasis here that is not found in the English and American social contract writers. Of course, Rousseau does not write that man's interest in himself will disappear; he claims, rather, that a new dimension has been added. Insofar as he is still self-centered, man must be a subject, but insofar as he is a socially conscious person he can assume

515

his responsibilities as a sovereign.

Rousseau insists that the general will must be distinguished from the many individual wills. If the citizens jointly form a body politic, the general will is the will of that body, a will that comes into being when they jointly concentrate their attention on the needs of that body. This will exercises itself through democratic assemblies of all the citizens and lets its intentions be known through the decisions of such assemblies. An assembly expresses the will of the whole people and not that of a part, but it requires only the voice of the majority *if* the views of the minority have been fairly heard and fairly considered. The general will cannot be ill-intentioned; it is concerned with the good of all, and it cannot be mistaken unless it is ill-informed. Simple, unsophisticated men are quite capable of exercising sovereign power provided that they are socially conscious, and well-informed, and provided further that they act after full discussion, and are not subject to pressure groups. Since sovereignty is the expression of the general will, and the general will is the expression of the will of all, sovereignty cannot be alienated by anyone or delegated to anyone—king or elected representative.

While he sometimes spoke in a rather idealistic manner, Rousseau could also be rather hard-headed. He was quite aware that the conditions just mentioned are not always fulfilled. Pressure groups do occur; citizens become so indifferent or so preoccupied with their own concerns that they fail to discharge their civic responsibilities, and administrators seek to control those they are supposed to serve. In these and other ways sovereignty can be destroyed. No human institution, he writes, will last forever. In addition, it is not likely that simple men can themselves establish the proper kind of state. Some well-intentioned and exceedingly gifted lawgiver is needed to provide a constitution, help establish traditions, and guide the fledgling state with a hidden but firm hand until the people have developed the ability, stability, and desire to carry on for themselves.

Through the expression of their general will, then, the people exercise the sovereignty which they have and must retain in their own hands, but as we have already noted, they do not administer the resultant laws. To do so they establish an executive branch that functions as their agent. The form and structure of the administration will depend upon the size of the state, and, other things being equal, the number of rulers tolerable for efficiency will vary inversely with the number of citizens. This is so since a larger state will require the tighter administrative control that can be achieved only if the executive power is restricted to a small number of administrators. On the other hand, a very small state might get along by allowing all the citizens to take part in the administration. Having in mind a moderately sized city-state, such as his native Geneva, Rousseau suggests that the ideal government would be a small elected group. He says that the function of the executive is restricted to the support and administration of the law and to the preservation of civil and political liberty, and that the sovereign assembly is restricted to legislating, but he does not specify these functions in detail nor does he discuss the relationship between them. Furthermore, he does not discuss a judiciary, but this is presumably included in the administrative complex.

He is clear, though, in his insistence that the administrator be the servant of the assembly. To ensure that this be so, the people enter into no contract with their administrator and, unlike the Hobbesian contractors, transfer no rights to him. They extend to him nothing more than a revocable commission, thereby retaining control over him without being bound by him. When the sovereign assembly meets, as it does very frequently, all commissions granted by it at previous meetings become void until they are renewed.

Rousseau favors a moderately sized state something like the communes of Switzerland wherein every citizen can come to know all the others, for in the large state relations between citizens become impersonal, and their interests, problems, and fortunes become diversified. If there are many provinces, mores will not be uniform and one body of law will not be sufficient. The number and levels of subordinate government will multiply, and as the cost increases liberty will decrease. Chains of command become attenuated to such an extent that administration at the bottom levels becomes indifferent, weak, or corrupt, and supervision from the top becomes difficult. The control of the government by the people becomes impossible, as does the democratic legislative process. Indeed, a very large state cannot avoid being a dictatorship both legislatively and administratively, and that is the best form of government for it. If a state is to be a democratic state it must be small, as small as it can be without inviting encroachment by its neighbors.

It is interesting to speculate about what Rousseau would say of modern democracies which have millions of citizens and embrace hundreds of thousands of square miles. He would perhaps admit that contemporary means of communication obviate some of the difficulties he had in mind, and that security usually requires a considerably larger state than was necessary then. Quite possibly he would admire many of the ingenious ways by which we have delegated both legislative and administrative powers and controlled these powers, but he might argue sadly that we are bedeviled by many of the difficulties inherent in size. Gone forever is the small autonomous political group with its intimacies, its personal concern, its shared interests and problems, and its joint endeavors.

Rousseau's views have influenced many thinkers and political movements, partly because of the central problem with which he was concerned and partly because of the vigor and clarity with which he wrote. But his influence is due also to the fact that unresolved tensions in his thought have permitted partisan readers to place rather different interpretations upon him. On the one hand, his emphasis on equality, liberty, and the supremacy of the citizen made him a favorite author among the leaders of the French Revolution, and these emphases plus those on democracy and the control of the administrators have always made him attractive to those who have supported a republican form of government. On the other hand, his claim that man realizes his full nature only by participating in the life of a society has impressed those who believe that the state should play more than a negative regulatory role. This claim, along with his assertion that the individual is under the complete control of the sovereign power, and his some-

517

times near reification of the general will have seemed to others to foreshadow the engulfing national spirit of Hegel and his followers and to be congenial to the recent German and Italian cult of the Fatherland. The truth, of course, is that each of the above views requires that the interpreter select his passages and, in some cases, stretch them considerably, whereas in fact, Rousseau presents us with a rich array of ideas that are not worked out completely or consistently. These fresh ideas are what make *The Social Contract* one of the great classics of political philosophy.

NEW ESSAYS ON THE HUMAN UNDERSTANDING

Author: Gottfried Wilhelm von Leibniz (1646-1716)
Type of work: Epistemology, ontology
First published: 1765

Principal Ideas Advanced

Locke was mistaken in thinking that at birth the mind is like a blank tablet; certain ideas are innate, but they rise to consciousness only when the mind is provoked by experience.

Sense perception is active, not passive.

Locke's conception of simple ideas ignores such physical phenomena as the color spectrum and light waves; and his distinction between primary and secondary qualities is not necessary since it is possible to qualify perceptual generalizations carefully enough to allow for individual differences.

Locke's suggestion that substance might be nothing but a collection of properties cannot be tolerated, for reason has difficulty in accepting the idea of properties which are not the properties of anything.

External spatial and temporal relations cannot guarantee identity; it is by the internal modifications of substance that an individual acquires its identity.

An exact analysis of the signification of words would show us the workings of the understanding.

In 1707 Leibniz wrote to a friend concerning his *New Essays on the Human Understanding*: "My purpose has been to throw light upon things rather than to refute the opinions of another." He had undertaken this work in response to the criticisms of Cartesian rationalism appearing in John Locke's *An Essay Concerning Human Understanding* in 1690. It was completed about 1707, but Leibniz hesitated to publish it because of Locke's death in 1704; consequently, it did not appear in print until Leibniz himself had been dead for almost half a century. A study of the *New Essays* not only bears out the author's contention that his aim was constructive rather than merely critical, but also makes clear to the reader that Leibniz was one of the ablest and most universal thinkers of all time. Certainly European rationalism at that time had no better exponent than this thinker who combined a deep appreciation of past accomplishments in philosophy with a penetrating originality of his own.

The argument of the *New Essays* follows faithfully Locke's *Essay* and so is itself divided into four books dealing first with the question over innate ideas and truths, second with perception and ideas in general, third with the cognitive use of language, and fourth with the different kinds of cognitive statements and reasoning in which they appear.

The question of the existence of innate ideas and truths arose when Locke compared the human mind at its inception to a blank sheet of paper upon which experience alone wrote. In order to support the Platonic and Cartesian view that certain ideas and truths are innate and not inscribed by experience, Leibniz changed similes and compared the mind to a block of marble whose veins require the accommodation of experience—a view which was to become the foundation of Kant's theory of knowledge. Locke's objections to the contrary, ideas and truths did not have to be consciously entertained by all men, let alone enjoy universal assent, to be regarded as innate. They arose in consciousness and became known only when the mind was provoked by experience to reflect upon the necessary principles underlying the sensible world. Such reflection was not always easy and not all men were capable of it, for it required great powers of analysis and inventiveness in addition to the presentation of sense-experience. To illustrate his point Leibniz fondly recalled Socrates' mid-wifery in extracting from an ignorant slave boy knowledge of certain necessary and rather complicated geometrical relations (in Plato's *Meno*).

Though experience was often helpful to rational activity in bringing to light innate ideas and truths, Liebniz went on, the validity of such ideas and truths was certified by reason alone. The Pythagorean Theorem, he pointed out, established a necessary relationship of equality between the sum of the squares of the sides of a right-angled triangle and the square of its hypotenuse, but it was a proposition whose truth did not depend upon the empirical findings of surveyors. Ancient Egyptians discovered empirically that a corner of land whose sides measured three and four units would measure five units along its hypotenuse, but they never perceived the general and necessary truth behind this discovery. Their observation yielded to them what Leibniz called a truth of fact, but it was Greek geometers who perceived the truth of reason implicit in the factual discovery.

Leibniz, then, in defending the theory of innate ideas and truths was making an important epistemological distinction between those truths whose validity rested upon sense-experience and those truths whose validity did not; contingency earmarked the former and necessity the latter. Leibniz stole a march on Hume in claiming that the fact that things have been observed to happen in a certain way in the past is no guarantee that they will always happen that way. But he associated with this epistemological view the psychological proposition that innate ideas and truths existed in the mind prior to reflection or analysis as dispositions or preformations of their post-analytic emergence in consciousness. This theory was a modification of Plato's doctrine of reminiscence, though it is still unacceptable to some who however accept Leibniz's epistemological distinction. Perhaps still less generally acceptable is the metaphysical thesis Leibniz associated with the foregoing to the effect that truths of reason are identical with the timeless truths of nature which state what is always the case because they are ultimately the principles by which Supreme Reason or God has ordered the world for the best.

This intrusion of psychology and metaphysics into his theory of knowledge was regarded as quite natural by Leibniz, who did not believe it possible to separate epistemology altogether from psychological and metaphysical considerations. He was concerned throughout his philosophizing to exhibit the systematic interdependence of such various considerations and to find illumination in their interplay.

In the second book of the *New Essays* Leibniz turned his attention to Locke's theories of perception, of ideas in general, of substance, and of qualities and relations. He not only disputed Locke's contention that all ideas originate in either sense-experience or introspection—for Leibniz believed that such ideas as God, Being, Unity, and Substance, for example, cannot be traced either to sense-experience or to introspection and so are innate—but also the thesis that sense-perception is a purely passive affair. According to Locke and his successors, our senses are presented with clearly defined phenomena; different colors, shapes, sizes, feelings salute our senses and reveal their identity as they parade by. But Leibniz was convinced that this con-

cept was a myth (now called by Kantians the myth of the given) and held it to be a gross oversimplification of what goes on in sense-perception. He said we must distinguish between what we now call subliminal perception—which is relatively passive but at the same time indistinct—and apperception, which is the attention paid to things within our range of perception in order to determine what kinds of things they are. One can see, for example, that something is actually a whirring hummingbird by attending apperceptively to it. But the terms "attending to" and "noticing" connote activity and not lazy passivity, and it is just such intellectual activity, according to Leibniz, which gives us clear and distinct ideas of what we perceive.

Together with this criticism Leibniz expressed doubt concerning the reality of Locke's simple ideas of such primary qualities as motion and rest and such secondary qualities as colors and tastes. Is the idea of motion really simple and unanalyzable, asked Leibniz? Do we not have to understand the motion of an object in terms of time spent and space covered by the moving object as well as by its relation to other objects? And is not any color to be understood as part of a color spectrum in which it is sometimes difficult to tell where one color leaves off and another begins, and are not all colors, moreover, reducible to different wave lengths of light? Such questions concerning these and other so-called simple ideas led Leibniz to reject their existence.

He was also unable to accept Locke's distinction between primary and secondary qualities, which was based upon the dependence of the latter upon conditions of perception. Honey might taste sweet, for example, to someone in good health but quite bitter to someone who was not. But what this and other examples of the vagaries of perception show, said Leibniz, is that although sensible qualities are indeed relative to the senses, there is nothing to prevent us from making an objective classification of such qualities on the basis of what normal percipients experience under normal conditions of perception. On this basis, he concluded, there is little point in distinguishing between primary and secondary qualities.

Here Leibniz anticipated Berkeley's rejection of this distinction, though, unlike Berkeley, he continued to believe in the real existence of an external physical world and did not erase the distinction between qualities and our ideas of them. Rather, he held with Descartes and Locke that the evidence of our senses faithfully represents the actual qualities of the physical world —though both Descartes and Locke made this claim only of primary qualities and not of their alleged secondary qualities.

To understand the doctrine of representation in the history of the theory of perception we should perhaps bear in mind that the thinkers we have been discussing were attempting to assimilate the physical hypotheses of their age concerning the role of light waves or corpuscles in making objects visible and concerning the reducibility of matter to colorless, tasteless atoms. Such hypotheses did not agree with common sense-experience, and the necessary but difficult task of drawing careful distinctions between the presuppositions of ordinary discourse on the one hand and scientific discourse on the other was only begun by such thinkers as Locke and Leibniz. Neither was entirely free of the confusions which result from failing to make such distinctions; but neither are many present-day philosophers and scientists.

Talk of qualities naturally leads to talk of substances, and indeed Leibniz's concern was with Locke's analysis of the presumably complex idea of substance. Gold, said Locke, is said to be a physical substance. Analyze it, however, and what does one find? Only, Locke argued, an assemblage of qualities such as yellowness, solidity, heaviness, fusibility, malleability, and dissolvability in *aqua regia*, but apart from such qualities one can discover nothing answering to substance as such. Deprive gold of these and its other properties and nothing remains. Thus, for Locke, the idea of substance either signified collections of qualities only or stood for something unperceivable— "a something, I know not what."

Leibniz agreed with Locke that to deprive a material object of all properties would be to leave nothing, the reason being that such properties are determinations of the object and one can more readily imagine an object losing some of its properties than one can imagine properties that are not properties of something. Had Leibniz been a contemporary of Lewis Carroll he might have pointed out that the Cheshire cat is not ridiculous when it ceases to grin, but that something is awry when it departs leaving its grin behind—something that could happen only in Wonderland. Leibniz was therefore more at home with the idea of concrete substances than with the idea of qualities abstracted from such substances, and unlike Locke he regarded the idea of substance as perfectly clear and distinct. He acknowledged that it was not an empirical notion, but held it to be a product of reason instead, and

521

thus he laid the groundwork for Kant's analysis of substance as a category of knowledge.

It is, moreover, just this idea of substance, said Leibniz, which provides the key to the vexing problem of individuality. In Locke's view, no two entities could ever be confused with each other because they could never occupy the same point in space at the same time. All objects are externally related in time and space; since no two of them can have exactly the same temporal and spatial relationships to any other, they are each assured of separate numerical identity. But Leibniz argued that external relations could not of themselves guarantee separate identity, not only because it is far from clear that no two objects can occupy the same position in time and space (he challenged Locke's theory of the impenetrability of things and cited the possibility of two rays of light coinciding in time and space), but also because location in time and space is determined by reference to concrete physical objects in the first place; and so one cannot use time and space determinations to establish the identity of things without begging the question.

Leibniz therefore countered with a doctrine of internal relations to satisfy the requirements of physical and personal identity according to which individual substances affect and are affected uniquely by their environment. A person, for example, as a substantial being in interaction with the universe through ceaseless activity of body and mind (subliminally as well as consciously) has been undergoing internal modification from the moment of his inception. It cannot suffice to say, Leibniz declared in opposition to Locke, that personal identity is assured by the qualitative patterning of his life, since on the level of qualities and external relations only, in abstraction from the substances they qualify and relate, personality development is in principle duplicable over and over again. It is only when personality development is seen as involving the evolution of mind and body substances that genuine individuality is assured.

In this subtle line of argument the application of Leibniz's principles of natural continuity and the identity of indiscernibles is apparent, as was the application of his famous (and contentious) principle of preëstablished harmony in his espousal of the representational theory of perception. The application of such principles is worth noticing because it illustrates once more Leibniz's eagerness to apply metaphysical principles to the solution of philosophic puzzles.

Human beings use language to express their ideas, and though language has more than one use its cognitive employment is extremely important. Thus, it became the subject of the third book of the *New Essays* where we find Leibniz contending against Locke's nominalistic tendencies. Such tendencies manifested themselves in the belief that only particular objects enjoy actual existence and that the essences, species, and genera debated by medieval philosophers are only abstract ideas existing in the human understanding. Nothing in the real world corresponds to such ideas, and Locke therefore wanted to treat them as somewhat arbitrary inventions. Leibniz sided with the realists and argued that talk of different species and genera as well as of the essential properties of things answered very definitely to reality. Was not discourse about species and genera founded upon undeniable and actual resemblances between, let us say, individual tigers on the one hand and tigers and other members of the cat family on the other? And do not all tigers have certain properties in common which make them what they are rather than something else, and do not all felines have certain properties which distinguish them? How can such talk be avoided, asked Leibniz, in giving a factual account of nature? And if it cannot be avoided, there is nothing arbitrary about it.

It is furthermore a *non sequitur,* he went on, to argue as Locke did from the difficulty we sometimes encounter in defining the essential characteristics of natural kinds to the conclusion that there are no such characteristics. All definitions are provisional or hypothetical and subject always to revision, but it does not follow that they are therefore vulnerable to subjective caprice; what it does mean, however, is that the search for the distinguishing characteristics of natural kinds is continuous, as is all scientific inquiry.

But we do not define only for purposes of natural classification, Leibniz pointed out. For other purposes we may give different connotations to general referring terms, but when we do so we should call such definitions logical in order to distinguish them from physical definitions grounded upon natural resemblances between objects. We might, for example, define "mate" for legal purposes more strictly than we do for biological purposes, but it would not follow that the legal term would then designate individuals not designated by the biological term and would thus unnaturally increase the world's membership. If we understand our varied aims in constructing defini-tions—biological, legal, and otherwise—we shall not be tempted to overpopulate the universe. There is fetching irony in the fact that Leibniz's realism permitted him to match Locke's concern for the possible abuses of words, and yet to warn against ungrounded mistrust of language and to conclude with what could well serve as the clarion call of modern linguistic analysis in philosophy: "I truly think that languages are the best mirrors of the human mind, and that an exact analysis of the signification of words would show us better than anything else the workings of the understanding."

In the remaining book of the *New Essays* Leibniz undertook to correct such Lockian impressions as that the laws of logic are trivial and unessential, that the family of cognitive statements includes only those that are either self-evident or follow from self-evident truths, and that deduction is the only accredited form of reasoning. He strongly defended the importance and utility of such intuitive general logical principles as those of identity, contradiction, and excluded-middle as well as other self-evident principles involved in formal reasoning such as the rules of syllogistic deduction. Appeal to such principles was useful in establishing the validity of deductive arguments even if it were true, as Locke maintained, that in common argumentation such principles were not explicitly mentioned. They did not have to be mentioned, said Leibniz, or even clearly recognized by men to count as the principles of correct reasoning and be relevant to logical appraisal. It was, moreover, in accordance with such principles that important theorems of mathematics and formal logic were derived. Leibniz therefore agreed with Locke that self-evident propositions and demonstrated theorems as found in mathematics and logic must be regarded as cognitive statements, but he rejected Locke's characterization of the general principles of logic as rather unnecessary to rational discourse. In so doing he anticipated well in advance the emphasis of our own day upon formal logic as an indispensable tool of inquiry.

Leibniz also went beyond Locke in stating that deductive reasoning is by no means the only acceptable mode of reasoning and that self-evident and demonstrated truths are not the only cognitive statements. He proposed that inductive reasoning and the statements found in the empirical sciences receive accreditation from the logician and epistemologist; he not only expressed the hope that a logic of probability and induction would receive speedy recognition and attention, but went further in suggesting that other modes of logic, such as judicial process, be investigated. It is interesting to note that Leibniz's far-sighted advice in these respects went largely unheeded by logicians until quite recently.

We may also discover in Leibniz's views on logic and scientific method the outline of what has come to be called the hypothetico-deductive or explanatory-inductive method of modern science, according to which hypotheses are suggested by reason to account for an accumulation of empirical data; further consequences are then deduced from such hypotheses in order that they may be tested by sense-experience. Leibniz appreciated the importance of this method of scientific inquiry, and also saw clearly that modern scientific theory is a function of both empirical discovery and deductive theory. That is why he wanted to make room for "mixed" truths alongside straightforward truths of reason and truths of fact. Mixed truths would be those propositions derived from empirical hypotheses in accordance with the rules of deduction, enjoying no greater probability than their contingent empirical premises but yet entitled to cognitive status as probable truths. Leibniz even allowed for the possibility of certainty in the empirical sciences where there was sufficient confirmation for empirical propositions, but he carefully distinguished such practical or physical certainty from rational or metaphysical certainty.

What all this strongly suggests to the reader of the New Essays is that its author had a profound insight into the principles of human knowledge (including those of modern science), perhaps exceeding that of the author of the first Essay. Certainly the acceptance of many of Leibniz's insights into the theory of logic and knowledge by empiricists and rationalists alike is good evidence of the basic soundness of his ideas, or at least of their precious ability to stimulate further inquiry in these important areas of philosophic concern. No better tribute is possible to Leibniz's amazing stretch of mind and originality.

DIALOGUES CONCERNING NATURAL RELIGION

Author: David Hume (1711-1776)
Type of work: Philosophy of religion
First published: 1779

PRINCIPAL IDEAS ADVANCED

The argument from design is an argument which attempts to prove God's existence on the basis of signs of adaptability in nature, but it is an unsatisfactory argument because, although plausible, it does not demonstrate with logical certainty the truth of the claim that the universe was designed.

Furthermore, if we try to deduce the nature of God from the characteristics of nature regarded as his handiwork, God must be finite, imperfect, incompetent, and dependent.

It is possible that order in nature is the result of a natural generative process.

A priori arguments designed to prove God's existence are inconclusive and establish only that something, not necessarily God, may have been a first cause.

Although the cause of order in the universe probably bears some resemblance to human intelligence, nothing can be concluded concerning the moral character of such a cause.

Hume's *Dialogues Concerning Natural Religion* is one of the most famous works criticizing some of the arguments offered by philosophers and theologians to establish the existence and nature of God. Hume, who was known as the "Great Infidel" in his own time, began writing the *Dialogues* around 1751. He showed the manuscript to several of his friends, who dissuaded him from publishing it because of its irreligious content. Over the years, he revised the manuscript many times and finally, just before his death in 1776, he made his final revisions. He was very much concerned to make sure that the work would be published shortly after his death. In his will, he first requested his friend, the economist Adam Smith, to arrange for the publication of the *Dialogues*. When Smith refused, Hume next tried to get his publisher to do so, and when he

also refused, Hume altered his will, instructing his nephew to take charge of the matter if the publisher had not done so within two years of his death. Finally, in 1779, the work appeared, gaining both immediate success and notoriety. It has remained one of the classic texts in discussions about the nature of the evidence presented to prove the existence of God and the character of his attributes.

The *Dialogues* are patterned after Cicero's work on the same subject, *The Nature of the Gods*, in which a Stoic, an Epicurean, and a Skeptic discuss the arguments about the nature and existence of the gods. Both Cicero and Hume found that the dialogue form enabled them to discuss these "dangerous" subjects without having to commit themselves personally to any particular view. They could allow their characters to attack various accepted arguments and positions, without themselves having to endorse or reject any specific religious view.

Hume begins the *Dialogues* with a letter from Pamphillus, a young man who was a spectator at the discussion, to his friend Hermippus. Pamphillus explains that the dialogue form is most suitable for discussing theology, because the subject, on the one hand, deals with a doctrine, the being of God, that is so obvious that it hardly admits of any dispute, while on the other hand, it leads to philosophical questions that are extremely obscure and uncertain regarding the nature, attributes, and decrees and plans of God. The dialogue form, presumably, can both inculcate the "obvious" truth, and explore the difficulties.

After having Philo and Cleanthes debate the merits of skepticism in Part I, Hume presents Philo and the orthodox Demea as agreeing that human reason is inadequate to comprehend divine truths. They concur in the view that there is no doubt concerning the existence of a deity, but that our natural and rational information is insufficient to justify any beliefs concerning the nature of the deity. Philo sums up the case by asserting that our ideas are all based upon experience and that we have no experience at all of divine attributes and operations. Thus, the nature of the Supreme Being is incomprehensible and mysterious.

Cleanthes immediately objects and states the theory that Hume analyzes in great detail throughout the *Dialogues*. The information and evidence that we have about the natural world, Cleanthes insists, enable us to infer both the existence and nature of a deity. He then presents what is called "the argument from design," an argument that had been current in both ancient and modern theological discussions, but which had become extremely popular in the form in which it was stated by Sir Isaac Newton. Look at the world, Cleanthes declares, and you will see that it is nothing but one vast machine, subdivided into smaller machines. All of the parts are adjusted to one another, so that the whole vast complex functions harmoniously. The adaptation of means to ends through all of nature exactly resembles the adaptation which results from human design and intelligence. Since natural objects and human artifacts resemble one another, we infer by analogy, that the causes of them must also resemble one another. Hence, the author of nature must be similar to the mind of man, though he must have greater faculties, since his production is greater.

Philo proceeds to criticize the argument from design by pointing out first that the analogy is not a good one. The universe is unlike a man-made object, such as a machine or a house. Also, we discover causes only from our experience; for example, from seeing houses being built or machines being constructed. We have never seen a universe being produced, so we cannot judge if it is made analogously to human productions. We have perceived many causal processes other than human design, processes like growth, attraction, and so on. For all that we can tell from our experience, any of these may be the cause of the natural world.

Cleanthes insists, in Part III, that the similarity of the works of nature to the works of human art is self-evident and undeniable. When we examine various aspects of nature in terms of the latest scientific information, the most obvious conclusion that we come to is these aspects must be the result of design. By citing several examples, Cleanthes tries to show the immense plausibility of the argument from design. (In other works such as the *Natural History of Religion*, 1755, Hume always stressed the fact that a reasonable man could not help being impressed by the order and design in nature, and could not avoid coming to the conclusion that there must be some sort of intelligent orderer or designer of nature. However, Hume also insisted, as he did over and over again in the *Dialogues*, that no matter how convincing the argument may be, it is not logical, and can be challenged in many ways.)

To counterattack, Hume has Demea point out another failing of the argument from design. If we gained knowledge about God by analogy with the human mind, then we would have to conclude that the divine mind is as confused, as changeable, as subject to influence by the passions, as is man's. Such a picture of God is incompatible with that presented by traditional religions and by the famous theologians. In fact, as Philo and Demea point out in Parts IV and V, if the argument from design is accepted, then strange theology will ensue. Since man's mind is finite, by analogy so is God's mind. If God's mind is finite, he can err and be imperfect. If we have to judge God's attributes from the effects that we are aware of, what can we actually ascertain about God's nature? We cannot determine, from looking at the world, whether it represents a good achievement, as we have no standards of universe-construction by which we can judge. We cannot tell if the world that we perceive was

made by one God or by many deities. If one takes the analogy involved in the argument from design seriously, all sorts of irrelevant conclusions are possible and any conclusion about the type of designer or designers is pure guesswork. "This world, for aught he [man] knows, is very faulty and imperfect, compared to a superior standard; and was only the first rude essay of some infant Deity, who, afterwards abandoned it, ashamed of his lame performance; it is the work only of some dependent, inferior Deity; and is the object of derision to his superiors: it is the production of old age and dotage in some superannuated deity; and ever since his death, has run on at adventures, from the first impulse and active force, which it received from him. . . ." These and all sorts of other hypotheses are all possible explanations, by means of the argument from design, of the order in the universe.

Philo, in Parts VI-VIII, maintains that other explanations can be offered to account for the order in the world besides the explanation of a designer, and that these alternatives can be shown to be at least as probable. Two theories are considered, one that order results from a generative or growth process, and the other, that order is just the chance result of the way material particles come together. Over and over again we see order develop in nature as the result of biological growth. Seeds grow into organized plants. We do not see any outside designer introduce the order. Hence, if we judge solely by our experiences, one genuine possibility is that order is an unconscious result of the process of generation. The world, for all that we can tell, generates its own order just by developing. Since every day we see reason and order arise from growth development, as it does in children maturing, and never see organization proceeding from reason, it is a probable as well as a possible hypothesis to suppose that the order in the world comes from some inner biological process in the world, rather than from some designing cause outside it.

Even the ancient hypothesis of Epicurus, that the order in the world is due to "the fortuitous concourse of atoms" and that there is no external or internal designing or organizing force, suffices to account for the world as we know it. From our experience, it is just as probable that matter is the cause of its own motions as that mind or growth is. Also, nothing that we perceive proves that the present order of things did not simply come about by chance. Philo concludes the discussion on this point by asserting that an empirical theology, based solely on information gained from experience, would be inadequate to justify acceptance of any particular hypothesis about the source or cause of order in the world, or any particular religious system about the nature of the force or forces that govern the universe.

Demea, the orthodox believer, who has agreed with Philo's attack up to this point, now contends, in Part IX, that there are rational *a priori* arguments, not based on any empirical information whatsoever, that show that there must be a divine being. Demea states the classical theological argument that there must be a first cause, or God, that accounts for the sequence of causes occurring in the world. Hume has Cleanthes challenge this argument by introducing some of the skeptical contentions about causality and the inconclusiveness of *a priori* arguments that Hume had presented in his *A Treatise of Human Nature* (1739) and his *An Enquiry Concerning Human Understanding* (1748). Further, Hume points out that even if the *a priori* were legitimate, and even if it actually proved that there must be a first cause, or a necessarily existent being, it still would not show that this being had to be God. Perhaps the material world is itself the first cause, the cause of itself.

With this criticism, Hume concludes his considerations of arguments purporting to establish the existence of God, and turns to what can be known about God's nature or attributes. At the beginning of Part X, Philo and Demea rhapsodize about the misery and weakness of man, which Demea presents as the reason why man must seek God's protection. Philo uses the same information about man's plight to indicate that we cannot infer moral qualities of a deity from what is going on in the human world. If we knew what the deity is like, we might be able to explain, in terms of his perfect plan, why the evils of this world occur, and why there is so much human misery. But, since we do not know God's nature, we are not able to infer that he is perfect, wise, and good, from our limited knowledge of man's dismal and painful existence. Demea offers a religious explanation of the evils; namely, that our present existence is just a moment in the course of our existence. The present evil events will be recompensed and rectified in another realm, in an afterlife. But, Cleanthes insists, if man is to judge of divine matters from his experience, he has no information to support this religious supposition. The only way in which man can accept

528

a belief in a benevolent deity is to deny Philo and Demea's thesis that human life is absolutely miserable. To this, Philo replies that the occurrence of any evil, any misery, any pain, no matter how small a part of human life it might be, raises difficulties in ascertaining if God has the moral attributes accepted by traditional religions. If God possesses infinite power, wisdom, and goodness, how does anything unpleasant happen?

Cleanthes argues, in Part XI, that if one goes back to his analogy between man and the deity, an explanation can be offered. If the author of nature is only finitely perfect, then imperfections in the universe can be accounted for as being due to his limitations. Philo, in turn, argues that present experience provides no basis whatsoever for any inference about the moral attributes of the deity, and that the more we recognize man's weaknesses, the less we are capable of asserting in support of the religious hypothesis that the world is governed by a good and benevolent deity. If we knew that a good and wise God existed, then we might be able to account for the evils in this world by either the theories of Demea or Cleanthes. But if we have to build up our knowledge and our hypotheses from what we experience, then we will have to admit that there are four possibilities concerning the first causes of the universe: that they are completely good, that they are completely bad, that they are both good and bad, and that they are neither good nor bad. The good and the evil events in human experience make it difficult to conclude from our experience alone that one of the first two possibilities is the case.

As Philo explores the four possibilities and seems to be leaning toward the last, Demea realizes with dismay that he and Philo are not really in accord. Demea stressed the incomprehensible nature of God, the weakness of man's intellectual capacities, and the misery of his life as the basis for accepting orthodox theology. Philo employs the same points to lead to an agnostic conclusion, that we cannot know, because of our nature and God's, what he is actually like, and whether there is any explanation or justification for the character of the experienced world. Demea apparently accepted revealed information as the basis for answering the questions that man, by his own faculties, could not, while Philo turned only to man's experience for the answers and found that no definite ones could be given. As soon as Demea sees how wide the gap is between them, he leaves the discussion, and Philo and Cleanthes are left on the scene to evaluate the fruits of their arguments.

In the last part, XII, Philo offers what has been taken as a summary of Hume's own views about religion. Everywhere in nature there is evidence of design. As our scientific information increases, we become more, rather than less, impressed by the order that exists in the universe. The basic difficulty is that of determining the cause or source of the design. The difference between the atheist and the theist, and between the skeptic and the dogmatist, on this matter, is really only a verbal one. The theist admits that the designer, if he is intelligent, is very different from a human being. The atheist admits that the original principle of order in the world bears some remote analogy to human intelligence, though the degree of resemblance is indeterminable. Even a skeptic like Philo has to concede that we are compelled by nature to believe many things that we cannot prove, and one of them is that there is in the universe order which seems to require an intelligent orderer. And the dogmatist has to admit that there are insoluable difficulties in establishing any truths in this area as well as in any other. The skeptic keeps pointing out the difficulties, while the dogmatist keeps stressing what has to be believed.

When these arguments are taken into account, Philo points out, we are still in no position to assess the moral character of the designer. The evidence from the observable world is that works of nature have a greater resemblance to our artifacts than to our benevolent or good acts. Hence, we have more basis for maintaining that the natural attributes of the deity are like our own than for maintaining that his moral attributes are like human virtues. As a result, Philo advocates an amoral, philosophical, and rational religion. In 1776 Hume added a final summation: "the whole of natural theology . . . resolves itself into one simple, though somewhat ambiguous, at least undefined proposition, *that the cause or causes of order in the universe probably bear some remote analogy to human intelligence.*" Nothing more can be said, especially concerning the moral character of the cause or causes.

The dialogue concludes with two perplexing remarks. Philo announces as his parting observation that "To be a philosophical sceptic is, in a man of letters, the first and most essential step towards being a sound, believing Christian." This contention, which was made by all of the Christian skeptics from Michel de Montaigne to Pierre Bayle and Bishop Pierre-Daniel Huet, may have been a sincere conviction on their part. In Hume's case, there is no evidence that his skepticism led him to Christianity, but rather that it led him away from it.

At the very end, Hume has Pamphillus, the spectator, evaluate the entire discussion by saying that "PHILO'S principles are more probable than DEMEA'S; but . . . those of CLEANTHES approach still nearer the truth." Critics have variously interpreted this ending, pointing out that Pamphillus and Hume may not agree, and that this conclusion may have been intended to quiet possible critics. Others have held that Hume himself may have felt, in spite of his devastating criticisms of Cleanthes' position, that it contained more truth than Philo's almost complete skepticism.

The *Dialogues Concerning Natural Religion* has been a central work in discussions about religious knowledge ever since its publication. It is generally recognized as presenting the most severe criticisms of the argument from design, in showing its limitations as an analogy and as a basis for reaching any fruitful conclusions about the nature of the designer of the world. Since Hume in the *Dialogues* discusses only the natural evidence for religion, some later theologians, especially Søren Kierkegaard, have insisted that Hume's arguments only make more clear the need for faith and revelation as the sole basis of religious knowledge.

CRITIQUE OF PURE REASON

Author: Immanuel Kant (1724-1804)
Type of work: Metaphysics
First published: 1781

PRINCIPAL IDEAS ADVANCED

To establish the possibility of metaphysics as a science, it must be shown that synthetic a priori truths are possible.

Synthetic a priori truths are universally and necessarily true (hence, a priori), but their necessity cannot be derived by analysis of the meanings of such truths (hence, they are synthetic).

The two sources of knowledge are sensibility and understanding.

Space and time are the a priori forms of sensibility (intuition); we are so constituted that we cannot perceive anything at all except by casting it into the forms of space and time.

The a priori conditions of our understanding are called the categories of our understanding; the categories of quantity are unity, plurality, and totality; of quality: reality, negation, and limitation; of relation: substance and accident, cause and effect, and reciprocity between agent and patient; of modality: possibility-impossibility, existence-nonexistence, and necessity-contingency.

The principles of science which serve as presuppositions are synthetic a priori; the possibility of such principles is based upon the use of a priori forms of intuition together with the categories of the understanding.

Immanuel Kant's *Critique of Pure Reason* is an established classic in the history of epistemology. First published in 1781 and then revised in 1787, it is the fruit of Kant's later years and as such clearly reflects the insight and wisdom of a mature mind. It is a work in which the author attempted to conciliate two conflicting theories of knowledge current at his time—British empiricism as represented by Locke, Berkeley, and Hume; and Continental rationalism as represented by Descartes, Leibniz, and Wolff. The latter theory maintained that important truths about the natural and the supernatural world are knowable by pure reason alone, independently of perceptual experience, whereas the former held that percep-

tual experience is the source of all our legitimate concepts and truths of the world. Kant believed that both these doctrines were wrong, and he tried in the *Critique of Pure Reason* to correct the pretensions of each while saving what was sound in each. We can best see to what extent Kant succeeded in this undertaking by reviewing the main arguments of this great work.

Kant began his inquiry by asking why metaphysics had not kept pace with mathematics and natural science in the discovery of facts about our world. Celestial mechanics had been developed by Kepler at the beginning of the seventeenth century and terrestrial mechanics by Galileo later in the same century, and the two theories were soon united into one by Newton. These developments represented astonishing progress in natural science, but Kant could detect no parallel progress in metaphysics. Indeed, in metaphysics he saw only interminable squabbling with no apparent method for settling differences. So he asked whether it is at all possible for metaphysics to be a science.

Metaphysics can be a science, Kant reasoned, only if there exists a class of truths different in kind either from the straightforward synthetic truths of nature discoverable through sense-experience or from the straightforward analytic truths which owe their validity to the fact that the predicate term is contained in the subject term of such judgments—in other words, to the fact that they are true by virtue of the meanings of their terms, true by definition. This distinction is illustrated by the statements "Peaceful resistance is effective" (synthetic) and "Peaceful resisters shun violence" (analytic). This distinction had been recognized by Hume, who regarded it as exhausting the kinds of statements that can be true or false. But Kant believed that there are statements neither empirical nor analytic in character—synthetic *a priori* statements. These are statements which are true neither by definition nor because of facts discoverable through sense-experience. Rather, they can be seen to be true independently of sense-experience; in this sense they are *a priori* and necessarily true since no sense-experience can possibly confute them. Kant believed that all mathematical statements are of this sort—for example, "Seven plus five equals twelve." He also believed that synthetic *a priori* truths constitute the framework of Newtonian science, as we shall see shortly. But if such truths

exist, Kant next asked himself, how are they possible?

They are possible, he said, if it can be shown that human knowledge is dependent upon certain concepts which are not empirical in origin but have their origin in human understanding. But even before he revealed the existence of such concepts he attempted to show in the first major division of the *Critique of Pure Reason,* entitled the "Transcendental Esthetic," that *a priori* considerations form the basis even of human perception or sensibility. This view was important to Kant, for in his proposed Copernican revolution in epistemology the two sources of knowledge are sensibility and understanding working in inseparable harness together. He had already written in the introduction to the *Critique* that all knowledge begins with experience, but it does not necessarily arise out of experience.

What are these *a priori* foundations of sensibility? According to Kant they are space and time. He reasoned that all objects of perception are necessarily located in space and time. Such objects may vary over a period of time in color, shape, size, and so on and still be perceptible objects, but they cannot be deprived of space and time and still remain perceptible. Even to establish ourselves as perceivers, and objects in our environment as objects of perception, requires the use of spatial and temporal terms; hence, the concepts of space and time. As percipients we regard perceived objects as separate from or distant from us; and we realize that our perceptions themselves, whether of external objects or of our own thoughts and feelings, succeed one another in time. We cannot represent them otherwise and still sensibly preserve the meaning of the terms "perceiver" and "object of perception." In this sense space and time deserve recognition as presuppositions of sense-experience. All our empirical, descriptive characterizations of perceptible objects take for granted their fundamental nature as objects in space and time. This is why Kant calls space and time *forms of intuition* in order to distinguish them from the *contents* of sense-experience. To be sure, portions of space and moments of time can be perceived, but such parts must always be understood as forming parts of an underlying continuum of space and time. (British phenomenalists like Berkeley and Hume were not in agreement with this interpretation of space and time, but whether we can agree with Kant in the details of his argument, we probably can agree with him that the perception of anything presupposes the existence of space and time.)

Believing that he had already exhibited the dependency of human knowledge upon conditions prior to immediate sense-experience, Kant next proceeded to a consideration of the *a priori* conditions of human understanding. We saw above that, in Kant's view, all knowledge is the product of human understanding applied to sense-experience. Does the understanding organize the contents of sense-experience according to its own rules—rules which must originate elsewhere than in sense-experience if their function is to categorize it? Such rules exist indeed, declared Kant, and he called them the *categories of the understanding*. He argued that there are twelve such categories and that they can be discovered and classified by careful scrutiny of the logical forms of the judgments we characteristically make about the

world. For example, if we look at our categorical judgments we see that they contain a referring expression which we call the grammatical *subject* and a characterizing expression which we call the *predicate*. In "Beethoven was a great composer" the referring or subject term is of course "Beethoven," and our characterizing or predicate term is "great composer." Now a tremendous number of the factual claims we normally make are of this same basic form—*substance* and predicated *property*—and for Kant, therefore, the concept of substance deserves the status of a category of knowledge. Under it are subsumed all the substance-words in our conceptual scheme of things, such as "table," "tree," "moon," "nail," and so on, which denote material objects in our environment. It is thus a family-like concept denoting all those objects which have *substantiality* in common, something which none of the individual terms in this category does.

Much the same point can be made about the concept of *causality,* to take another of Kant's categories, which he derived from the form of hypothetical or conditional judgments—our "if . . . then" judgments. "If water is heated under normal atmospheric conditions to 212°F, it will boil" and "If one suppresses his guilt-feelings he will become neurotic" are examples of hypothetical judgments which assert a causal connection between the states of affairs mentioned by the antecedent and consequent of such judgments. Such judgments also appear frequently in our factual reports on the world and suggest that the concept of causality is an important and fundamental concept in our way of recording experience. It is a concept embracing numerous words in our language, such

533

as "create," "produce," "bring about," "make," and so forth, all of which are causal terms. By virtue of designing such a large family of terms the concept of causality must be regarded as one of the relatively few root concepts or categories at the basis of our conceptual scheme which give this scheme its flavor by influencing it throughout. The importance of causality is something which Kant clearly saw, even though it had been missed by the British phenomenalists.

Many philosophers have disagreed with Kant over his number and selection of categories as well as his method of arriving at them, but they have not taken issue with him as to the existence of categories in our conceptual framework and their importance in any account of human knowledge. But many others have rejected Kant's major contention that human knowledge is dependent upon such categories as substance and causality and so have sided with Hume, who, not finding anything answering to such categories in immediate sense-experience, proceeded to dismiss them as fictitious. Kant, of course, agreed with Hume that substance and causality are not to be found *in* sense-experience, but he insisted nevertheless that they are necessary ingredients in a world about which we can hope to have knowledge. The Kantian point is sometimes made by saying that unless one assumes that the general features referred by one's judgments persist in time and are public entities independent of any particular percipient, there can be no confirmation judgments and consequently no knowledge at all. Kant saw this simple but essential point when he stated that the categories are necessary conditions for our having any knowledge whatsoever.

He also saw that categories such as substance and causality are by no means arbitrary impositions upon sense-experience, as is sometimes implied by Hume and his followers, but are useful concepts since sense-experience testifies to a great amount of orderliness in the world rather than to a befuddling chaos. It is the presence of order observable by all which vindicates the use of such ordering principles as substance and causality—they would have no utility whatever in a chaotic world.

It is chiefly as ordering principles that Kant viewed the categories. What they order or synthesize in his partly phenomenalistic theory of knowledge are the items of experience—colors, shapes, sizes, sounds, tactile impressions, odors, and so on. But Kant believed that there is a problem in showing how such *a priori* principles can be applied to empirical data, and he thought that the answer to this problem is to be found in the mediatory power of time which, as seen above, is an *a priori* ordering form which is a necessary condition of sense-experience. Kant proceeded to relate the categories to the concept of time, and it was this merger of the concepts of substance, causality, and time which paved the way to his discussion of the presuppositions of Newtonian science. Kant believed that there are three such presuppositions; namely, the principles of the conservation of matter, of universal causality, and of the universal inter-relation of all things making up the natural world. (We recalled that in the Newtonian view of the universe all objects were considered to be made

534

up of material particles governed in their behavior by the universal laws of motion and attraction.)

Such principles are not analytic truths, according to Kant, since their denials are not self-contradictory, nor are they empirical generalizations since we know them to be necessarily true, and no empirical generalization is ever necessarily true. They must therefore be genuine synthetic *a priori* truths, and their possibility arises from the fact that they utilize *a priori* concepts whose use is indispensable to human knowledge and yet whose only sanctioned cognitive use is in relation to the objects of sense-experience in the manner dictated by the principles in question themselves.

Kant's argument in this respect is somewhat circular, though it has been defended as illuminating by thinkers who believe that any examination of basic principles must inevitably be circular in that they must be elucidated in terms of one another. But his argument has not been convincing to many others who, although granting that Kant isolated the main presuppositions of the scientific thinking of his day, do not concede that the presuppositions are synthetic *a priori*. Such critics argue that it is one thing to show that certain concepts are not empirical in origin and another to show that the judgments in which they figure are *a priori*. Concepts such as substance and causality may indeed underlie our factual discourse about the world and so be necessary and ineradicable concepts to intelligible and informative discourse, but it is not at all evident that the principles in which they occur—such as that the quantity of substance remains invari-

ent throughout all physical transformations—are necessarily true. Such principles may be fruitful guideposts in scientific inquiry, yet not be true or false judgments at all, merely heuristic rules in the way that Kant himself was to regard certain metaphysical concepts as we shall see shortly.

Up to this point Kant's concern was to explore the foundations of scientific knowledge and to disclose the dependency of such knowledge upon a handful of forms, concepts, and principles. In this exploration he clashed sometimes head-on, sometimes obliquely, as we have seen, with accounts of human knowledge provided by British empiricists. But his conclusions thus far were also brewing trouble and embarrassment for Continental rationalism as well. For what follows from showing that concepts such as causality and substance are presuppositions of empirical knowledge? It follows, Kant said, that their use independent of sense-experience is illegitimate and can only result in conceptual difficulties and empty noise. We recall that Kant's initial concern was to determine whether men can fruitfully engage in metaphysical speculation. In his time such speculation chiefly revolved around such matters as the immortality of the soul, the origin and extent of the universe, and the existence and nature of God. Was a science of such matters really possible? In the third and concluding portion of his inquiry, called the "Transcendental Dialectic" (that dealing with the categories and principles he had termed the "Transcendental Analytic"), Kant's answer to this burning question was an unequivocal "No!"

Kant identified the main concepts

of the above-mentioned metaphysical issues as the psychological idea, or *soul;* the cosmological idea, or *world;* and the theological idea, or *God;* and he considered the author of such ideas to be human reason rather than human understanding or sensibility. But why is human reason unable to develop these ideas cogently and scientifically? Kant's chief explanation for this debility was that nothing in sense-experience corresponds to the ideas of pure reason and thus there can be no control over their speculative use.

Cartesians and Leibnizians, for example, argued that the soul was an immaterial, simple, therefore indestructible substance. But where is the empirical support for such claims? It does not exist, said Kant, and furthermore the reasoning leading up to such conclusions is wholly fallacious. These Cartesians and Leibnizians have treated the "I think" or *cogito*—that is presupposed by all acts of knowing—as the logical subject of our judgments analogous to the way in which "Beethoven" is the subject of the judgment "Beethoven became deaf in his later years"; further, Cartesians and Leibnizians have argued that just as "Beethoven" designates a real person, so does the knowing subject of the *cogito.* Kant's rebuttal to this argument consisted of saying that it is an analytic truth that acts of knowing presuppose a knower, but the existence of the knower is an empirical question which cannot be inferred from an analytic truth whose validity is founded upon the meaning of terms. The existence of the soul as well as its properties must remain an empirical question, and the concept of substance is properly applied only to the self

that is the object of empirical psychology.

Kant next turned to metaphysical speculation about the universe at large. Men have always asked themselves with respect to the universe whether it had a beginning in time or has always existed, whether it is finitely or infinitely extended in space, and whether it was created. Kant showed that no definitive answers are possible to such questions. Indeed, he argued that reasoning can establish with equal cogency alternative answers to such questions. His explanation for such a disconcerting and paradoxical state of affairs in metaphysics was that one cannot regard the universe as a substance or given entity in the way a desk, for example, can be so regarded. It is of course meaningful to ask when a certain desk was made, how it was made, and what its spatial boundaries are. Such questions can be settled empirically, for we can trace the history of the desk and have it before us to measure. But this investigation of the properties of the desk and the countless ones like it which we undertake in our daily lives occur within the framework of the universe, so that the questions that can significantly be raised about things within the universe cannot significantly or profitably be asked of the universe itself. If the categories of substance and causality have as their proper epistemic function the characterization of given and possible objects of perception, it is an improper use of such categories to apply them to what is neither a given nor even a possible object of perception such as the universe. Because it is not such an object, the universe cannot serve as a check or control upon

536

our speculations about it; and it is this basic consideration again which explains reason's incompetence in this area.

Can human reason do any better, then, in the area of theological speculation? Can it, in the absence of empirical evidence, produce convincing arguments for God's existence, his benevolence, omniscience, and so forth? Kant surveyed the standard arguments or alleged proofs for the existence of God and concluded that none of them have any real force. He found that arguments which use the facts of existence, design, and causality in nature to support claims on behalf of divine existence not only make an unwarranted leap from the known to the unknown, but also fall back on the ontological argument for the existence of God as propounded successively by Saint Anselm, Descartes, and Leibniz. This famous and captivating argument begins with the premise that God is the being greater than which nothing is conceivable, and with the help of a subordinate premise to the effect that existence in the real world is better than existence merely in idea proceeds to the conclusion that God must exist, for if he did not he would not then be the greatest conceivable entity.

Kant's rebuttal of the ontological argument consists of saying that all existential statements of the form "X exists" are synthetic *a posteriori* and must be established on empirical grounds. If the major premise of the ontological argument is analytic, then existence is included in the definition of "God" and one has in effect defined God into existence. But, Kant asked, can we by definition define anything into existence, or must we not look beyond our concept of something in order to determine whether it genuinely exists? Kant added that it is in any case a mistake to view existence as a predicate like any other, since in all statements in which referring expressions such as "God" occur as subject terms the existence of the denoted object(s) is not asserted by such statements but rather taken for granted in order to see what is attributed truly or falsely to the denoted object(s). But if existence is taken for granted in this way, then as far as the ontological argument is concerned one has assumed the very point in question and the argument is question-begging.

The results of Kant's inquiry into classical metaphysics prompted him to reject the view that the leading concepts of such speculation have any constitutive place in human knowledge at all. Such concepts do not enter into the weblike structure of our knowledge of the world, as do the categories in his view. But Kant did not progress further to the Humian conclusion that metaphysical works containing these concepts should therefore be consigned to the flames. On the contrary he argued that although such concepts do not have a constitutive role in human knowledge, they nevertheless have a vital regulative function in the scientific quest, for they posit a systematic unity to the world and so stimulate scientists to look for connections in nature, even between such diverse elements, say, as falling apples and orbiting planets. It is pure reason with its concept of an ordering, purposeful and wholly rational God, for example, which proposes for investigation the idea that the world created by God must be rationally constructed throughout and so reward experimental inquiry by men similarly endowed with reason. No other faculty of the mind was for Kant capable of such a stirring vision.

In this remarkable conclusion to his inquiry into the contributing factors of human knowledge, Kant plainly conceded enormous importance to pure reason, although not that exactly which rationalists defended. He therefore no more appeased the rationalists than he did the British empiricists.

Many philosophers since Kant have appreciated his middle road between rationalism and empiricism, even if they have not been able to accept the details of this reasoning, and they have credited Kant with the rare ability to raise problems worthy of philosophical investigation.

But other philosophers have not been impressed by Kant's strictures against rationalism and empiricism, and they have borrowed from his meticulous genius (happily wedded to broad vision) what suits their purposes while ignoring what does not. Thus Hegel, for example, was stimulated by Kant to seize upon pure reason's dialectical tendencies—so futile on Kant's view—and erect upon such tendencies a complete picture of history and the world—quite often at the expense of empirical facts. And latter-day phenomenalists such as John Stuart Mill and Bertrand Russell have persisted in the search for the foundations of human knowledge among sense-data (more lately in conjunction with formal logic), which in all their fleeting transiency are so much unlike Kant's enduring and causally ordered substance.

But most philosophical critics assent to the rich stimulation of Kant's eversurprising fertile mind and rank him among the great philosophers of all time.

ESSAYS ON THE INTELLECTUAL POWERS OF MAN
ESSAYS ON THE ACTIVE POWERS
OF THE HUMAN MIND

Author: Thomas Reid (1710-1796)
Type of work: Epistemology, ethics, philosophy of mind
First published: Intellectual Powers, 1785; *Active Powers,* 1788

PRINCIPAL IDEAS ADVANCED

There is no intermediate between the mental act and the object of knowledge; perception is the direct experience of things present to the senses.

All the intellectual powers involve apprehension of some content and judgment.

We have immediate experience of spatial extension and of temporal duration, and this intuitive knowledge supplies first principles.

Through perception and memory we acquire probable knowledge; through conception and abstraction, knowledge of necessary truths.

538

God has supplied men with consciences which provide intuitive knowledge of the right and the wrong; in following his moral sense no man need fear a conflict of interest and duty.

At the age of seventy-one, Thomas Reid resigned from his University of Glasgow professorship to prepare for publication his celebrated classroom lectures on mental and moral philosophy. The intellectual world already knew the general thrust of the new Scottish Realism through his *Inquiry into the Human Mind* (1764). But the full articulation and defense of the system awaited the appearance of his two books of *Essays,* works so lucid and so plausible that they became almost at once the basis of the orthodox philosophy of the English-speaking world. Reid's philosophy is everything that a "public philosophy" should be. While it lacks the graceful style of certain eighteenth century philosophers, it has a masculine strength and a directness which still arouses admiration.

The *Essays on the Intellectual Powers of Man* contains eight essays of rather unequal length, each (except the Introduction) given over to one of man's intellectual powers or faculties. It is characteristic of Reid's philosophy that, like those of Joseph Butler and Francis Hutcheson, it makes no effort to reduce the different activities to a common denominator. Sense-perception, memory, conception (imagination), abstraction, judgment, reason, and taste are so many distinct and irreducible activities, although they may also occur in combination. Reid begins each essay by identifying the power in question and explaining its typical features. There follows a historical account telling how other philosophers have dealt with the subject.

Often, in addition, one of the British empiricists is selected for quotation and detailed refutation—not the least profitable part of the work.

Reid was a conscientious empiricist, pledged to carry out the program of Francis Bacon for the mental and moral sciences. By observation and investigation he hoped to arrive at fundamental laws comparable to those which Newton had found in natural philosophy. His method is basically introspective: one can learn to attend to one's own mental activities, describe them, and relate them to one another. In this manner we can map out the "human constitution." But description is all that we can attain to, since to man it is not given to know the causes of things. In fact, with Reid, as with most of his contemporaries, the underlying assumption (as basic to them as evolution was to the late nineteenth century) was that by a perfect wisdom all the parts of the world are adjusted to each other.

Besides introspection, Reid makes frequent appeal to common speech to support what he takes to be the witness of man's constitution. An example: Is beauty properly said to be an emotion in the mind of the perceiver, or a property of the object viewed? Language witnesses the latter. Again, are heat, hardness, and the like perceived as ideas in the mind or as qualities in bodies? Our speech testifies that they are perceived as qualities.

Reid's attitude toward the history of philosophy (which he regarded as the history of error) is central to his own common-sense point of view. He shared the optimism of the eighteenth century which held that the truth is always near at hand and that the first step toward enlightening mankind is to clear away ignorance, prejudice, and artificiality. In Reid's view, all the complications in mental philosophy stem from the very old error of thinking of the mind after the analogy of body. Men observe that, in the physical world, there is no action at a distance, and they suppose that similarly the mind can act and be acted upon only by what is immediately present to it. The ancient philosophers taught that bodies give off films which, passing through the sense organs, leave impressions on the mind. The moderns, following Descartes, have refined their doctrine, but have retained the old "phantasms" under the new name of "ideas." These ideas are "hypothetical" in the bad sense of the word which Newton implied when, setting aside the entities of the schoolmen, he said, *"non fingo hypotheses."* According to Reid, the progress of philosophy is assured if the "ideal hypothesis" (which remains to plague the writings of Cartesians and Lockians alike) is relegated to the rubbish heap along with other scholastic notions.

In Reid's theory of knowledge there is no intermediate between the mental act and the object of knowledge. Perception is the direct experience of things present to the senses; memory, of things past; consciousness, of the mind's own activity; and sensation and emotion are pure states of consciousness. It is characteristic of all these powers that they include (1) a notion or apprehension of some content and (2) a judgment or belief about existence. Reid is full of scorn for Hume's suggestion that belief is simply a degree of the vivacity of an object.

He makes use of the distinction between primary and secondary qualities of things, even though he does not hold to the existence of ideas. Perception is a complex act which includes sensation but is not reducible to it. Thus, says Reid, when I touch the table I have a sensation which, however, I do not ordinarily attend to, the mind passing over it to attend to the quality of the thing—that is to say, hardness, smoothness. There is, according to Reid, a natural symbolism here which we cannot understand: the Creator has attached the perception of the quality to the particular sensation, and this is a mystery—just as it is a mystery that certain vibrations in the brain are regularly attached to certain sensations. The case is otherwise with secondary qualities. When we smell an odor, Reid says, the sensation is likely to be mistaken for the physical object, although introspection reveals that when we smell, say, a rose, all that is really attested is the existence of some external cause of the characteristic sensation: we learn to connect the odor with the object of our other senses. Partly this is true also of vision, where, however, the purely mental experiences of color are inseparably blended with spatial properties.

Perception and memory, besides the notion of and belief in the object toward which they are directed, carry with them other truth. As Reid says, I know that I exist as knower, and that some external cause exists adequate to give rise to my perceptions and memories. Through perception I come to know the reality of space, and through memory I know the reality of time— these are presupposed by extension and by duration of which we have immediate experience. Here are examples of what Reid calls intuitive truths. They serve as first principles for our knowledge of the world and man. Other truths follow from them by reasoning or demonstration; but the first principles (requisite to every science) must be known immediately.

The principles so far mentioned all have to do with existence. By means of conception and abstraction it is possible for the mind to invent objects of a different order. These could be called "ideas" without offense—Platonic, rather than Cartesian ideas. They are objects of the mind, and do not represent anything beyond themselves. They do not, as Plato supposed, exist apart from the mind, but are pure essences completely discerned by the mind. Among these theoretical objects, axioms of a different sort are discovered. We call them intuitive also; but they differ from those axioms which deal with contingent truths in that they are seen to be necessary.

The two kinds of principles just mentioned yield two kinds of knowledge—necessary truths (for example, mathematics) yield demonstrative knowledge; contingent truths (astronomy) yield probable knowledge. Reid is dissatisfied with Hume's suggestion that probable knowledge is less certain than demonstrative, and accuses that philosopher of using the word "probability" in a strange fashion. One's knowledge, for instance, that the capital of France is Paris is no less certain than a demonstration in geometry.

Discussing demonstrative knowledge, Reid takes issue with Locke's contention that moral judgments are of this sort since the terms of moral judgments are not real essences but nominal ones. According to Reid, moral judgments are judgments about contingent matters, and flow not from definitions but from intuitions. They depend on moral axioms, more or less clearly discerned by all civilized peoples. And they are properly discussed under the actual rather than the intellectual powers of the mind.

Problems of taste, however, which very much interested the eighteenth century, are dealt with under intellectual powers. Reid is interested in the power of the mind to combine images in meaningful patterns—he is dissatisfied with the purely mechanistic account of thinking expounded under the name of associationism. Here, in the broadest sense, is the basis for art: purposiveness. We not only invent meaningful combinations; but we recognize them and rejoice in them in the handiwork of other men and in nature.

Reid follows the usual division of aesthetic objects into those of curiosity, grandeur, and beauty. The perception of any of these is a complex act involving on the one hand an emotion and, on the other, a notion and judgment respecting the object. There is an analogy between this and his analysis of sense-perception: as sensation is to physical quality, so emotion is to aesthetic quality. Curiosity (like smell, for example) is almost entirely subjective. Not so with grandeur and beauty where we are aware of a property in the thing. It may be that the property is "occult"—in which case our judgment of beauty is like our perception of color, and we do not understand what it is in the object that gives rise to our pleasant emotion. But sometimes the property is perfectly intelligible—in which case our judgment of beauty is analogous to our perception of primary qualities.

541

Reid's philosophy radiates confidence and good will. He is not nervous about his position, and although he indulges in ridicule (he justifies it as one of the ways in which common sense asserts itself) it is never cruel or malicious as is so much eighteenth century wit. Nevertheless, Reid has a genuine enemy: it is skepticism. He thanks Hume for carrying the "spirit of modern philosophy" (Reid's own expression) out to its logical conclusion: if one hypothesizes "ideas" skepticism is inevitable. But skepticism, in Reid's eyes, is merely defeatism of the sort that prevailed in natural philosophy until the miasmas of peripateticism were cleared away by such men as Galileo and Newton. Happily, a return to common sense makes possible new experimental gains in mental and moral philosophy also.

The *Essays on the Active Powers of the Human Mind* carries the investigation from mental philosophy into the field of moral philosophy. This work is only half as long as the former, and hence we rightly infer that it was not Reid's major field of interest, but not that he considered the active life less important than the speculative one. On the contrary, he glows with enthusiasm for those remarkable endowments which set man above the other animals and give him the means of remaking the world in the interests of human happiness. The intellectual powers are only instruments in the service of man's active powers.

Moral philosophy, until almost our own time, included the psychology of motives as well as the principles of normative action. In Reid's philosophy these can scarcely be disjoined. The clue to his system may be found in Pope's *Essay on Man* (1734) as well as in Joseph Butler's *Sermons* (1726). It lies in the belief that man's constitution has been fashioned by a wise and benevolent Creator who always orders the part with a view to the perfection of the whole. There are many motives in man and, though often they seem to be at odds, careful examination reveals a hierarchy among them. Every motive is good at the right time and place: and there are superior principles which determine when and where the inferior are intended to function. Thus, a purely descriptive account of human nature contains by implication a moral code. But in practice man has a readier guide. One of the higher principles with which he is endowed is conscience, which gives him an intuitive sense of right and wrong. Since it is bestowed upon him by the Architect of his being, it can be trusted to lead him toward his proper end.

By the same token, interest and duty are seen to be complementaries. It is part of the office of reason to judge between desires and to steer the course which promises to be good for man on the whole. The man who follows reason is said to be prudent, and insofar as he is successful he achieves a happy life. But such intelligence never extends very far; and for mankind as a whole it is not an adequate guide. In addition to calculating his interest, man should study duty, disclosed to him through the moral sense. Here he is not merely provided with moral truth, from which he may infer his obligation; but the deliverances of conscience are also attended with strong feelings of approval and disapproval, which add greatly to its effectiveness as a guide. While there can be no opposition between these two principles, the rule should be to follow duty rather than interest, on the reasonable presumption that under a wise and benevolent Administration it is impossible that the issue of doing what is right should ever be anything but happy.

In somewhat the same way, egoistic and altruistic motives are proved not to be in conflict. Our animal impulses, whether appetites or desires, by themselves are neither selfish nor unselfish, neither bad nor good. It is only with reference to larger considerations that they become one or the other. Rightly ordered, they both promote our own happiness and serve our fellow men. Reason would, if it were perfect, so regulate them. But because of the limits of man's reasoning power, God has taken the precaution of undergirding his intention and, to secure our social well-being, has implanted in us certain affections which are above the particular desires but beneath reason and conscience. Benevolence, the first of these, is the source of such affections as filial love, gratitude, compassion, friendship, and public spirit. But there is also malevolent affection, which manifests itself in emulation and resentment. (Reid is not sure that they should be called "malevolent.") In themselves they are not evil, being the basis for such honest attitudes as the desire to excel and the disposition to resist and retaliate injury. If they are not brought under the government of reason or conscience they become evil; but this is also true of our benevolent affections.

The question of moral liberty inevitably finds a place in Reid's discussion. The problem, as he sees it, is not whether a man has power to act, but only whether he has power to will.

Hobbes, who defined the question in the former manner, equated liberty with freedom from external impediment; at the same time he held that all man's actions are causally determined. For Reid, it is this last contention which needs to be examined. The matter is complex. Reid holds it to be a self-evident truth that every event in the material world, including the motion of a man's body, must have an efficient cause, but that the nature of the causal nexus is mysterious. Presumably the divine Spirit is the source of the motions in nature at large. The question in hand is whether the human spirit has received a somewhat analogous power. Reid holds that it has, else all our notions of duty and responsibility, praise and blame would be without foundation. As he looks for the source of this freedom in the human constitution, it seems to him to lie on the side of reason as opposed to passions. The latter are impressions upon the mind which have their origin in matter; but the former seems to be independent of these motives and free to direct its attention from one object to another, to weigh their respective merits, to select a goal, and to plan a course of action. Insofar as it is externally motivated, the things that influence reason are final (not efficient) causes, together with such considerations as truth and duty.

Although Reid regards the active powers as a natural endowment, he does not suppose that they occur full-blown in any person. Conscience is a good example. It does not make itself felt at all in infants or in imbeciles. And even in the adult it is extremely subject to education, both for weal and for woe. In this respect, moral competence is like other natural endowments

—like the ability to dance or sing, or to reason logically. The unpleasant fact is that the great part of mankind in every age is sunk in gross ignorance and fettered to stupid and unprofitable customs. But even as the intellectual powers have a natural affinity for truth, so the active incline man toward virtue and well-being. This is manifest in the institutions of all civilized people and in the Law of Nature and of Nations widely recognized as the foundation of political rights and duties.

Reid distinguishes between the moral judgment and the theory of morals. Just as a person may have a good ear which has been improved by practice in the art of music, and still be ignorant of the anatomy of hearing and the theory of sound, so one may have exact and comprehensive knowledge of what is right and wrong in human conduct and yet be ignorant of the structure of our moral powers. Moral theory is important as a part of the philosophy of the human mind, but not as a part of morals.

It is usual to think of Thomas Reid as the apostle of "common sense." The term occurs frequently in his writings, not always with the same meaning. In some places it means "good sense"— that degree of reason which makes a man capable of managing his own affairs and answerable in his conduct toward others. In other places it refers to the opinions of the man in the street. But in the technical sense which came to characterize the system of Reid and of the Scottish school, it stands for that part of man's mental constitution by which he knows the truth of the principles or axioms which, underlying all experience and all inference are the indispensable foundations of science and morality.

"We ascribe to reason two offices, or two degrees. The first is to judge of things self-evident; the second to draw conclusions that are not self-evident from those that are. The first of these is the province, and the sole province, of common sense; and, therefore, it coincides with reason in its whole extent, and is only another name for one branch or one degree of reason."

The most obvious difference between the two kinds of reason mentioned here is that, whereas the second is "learned by practice and rules," the first is "purely natural, and therefore common to the learned and the unlearned, to the trained and the untrained." Whatever the difficulties of formulating its deliverances, there is, native to man's mind, a capacity to grasp the essential truths concerning human existence.

Common sense, so understood, underlies the realism of Scottish philosophy. In his analysis of experience, Reid avoided sensationism and nominalism only because, at each critical juncture, he refused to wear the blinders of technical reason. He professed to repudiate metaphysics, and agreed with his age that man ought to content himself with observed laws and phenomena. But he was little disposed to measure heaven with a span.

"A man who is possessed of the genuine spirit of philosophy will think it impiety to contaminate the divine workmanship, by mixing it with those fictions of human fancy, called theories and hypotheses, which will always bear the signature of human folly, no less than the other does of divine wisdom."

CRITIQUE OF PRACTICAL REASON

Author: Immanuel Kant (1724-1804)
Type of work: Ethics
First published: 1788

PRINCIPAL IDEAS ADVANCED

Morality can claim objectivity and universality only by being founded on pure reason itself.

Moral laws are universal and categorical because of their form, not their empirical content.

The fundamental law of the pure practical reason is so to act that the maxim of the will could always function as a principle establishing universal law.

Were it not for the moral law, man could never know himself to be free; for man, "thou ought" implies "thou canst."

The rational postulates of the practical reason are that man is free, that the soul is immortal, and that God exists.

None of Kant's writings can be understood without a clear recognition of the "Copernican revolution" in philosophy effected by his first critique, the *Critique of Pure Reason* (1781). Previously, the predominant rational tradition in Western philosophy was founded on the assumption of reason's capacity for discovering the forms or essential structures characterizing all things. Whether the form of "tree-ness" was an innate aspect of every existent tree (as Aristotle believed) or a transcendent form in which each existent tree participated (as Plato held), the capacity of reason for perceiving such forms was not doubted. The medieval controversy over "universals" centered not in reason's ability for such perception, but in the nature of this rational activity.

From the first questioning of the nominalists, however, through the break between self and "exterior world" in Descartes, doubt as to the precise authority of rational apprehension increased. Human error and empirical deception began to be seen as intervening between perceiver and perceived, thus raising powerfully the question of the criteria for truth. The Aristotelians, especially from the time of St. Thomas Aquinas on, affirmed that knowledge begins with sense perception; however, because of reason's capacity for extracting forms, human knowledge possessed not only the qualities of necessity and universality, but made possible an inductive knowledge of trans-empirical realities. It was the empiricists, especially David Hume, who provided the most serious challenge to this rationalist claim. Centering his attack on the problem of universal causality (cause and effect as universally operative), Hume raised the question of necessity. On what grounds, he asked, can one insist that, *of necessity,* all "effects" have causes and, similarly, that such causes *necessarily* produce identical effects? Hume's conclusion was that the category of causality, like all human ideas, is derived from sense impressions, having the status simply of a habitual assumption and expectation; human ideas are forever bereft of necessity.

It was Kant who saw the seriousness of this empiricist challenge. Reason was bankrupt as an agent of knowledge if it could no longer claim necessity and thus universality for its findings. Man and the world had been severed, and skepticism seemed the inevitable result.

The answer provided by Kant's first critique was a revolution, a complete reversal of the previous conception of the knowing process. If human knowledge cannot claim a necessity which is resident within the empirical world itself, it is possible, nevertheless, to claim universality for it if the locus of necessity is within the universal operations of human reason. With this new conception of rational necessity and universality, Kant proceeded to exhibit what he conceived to be the necessary operations of rational apprehension, the manner in which the understanding, by its very structure, has and of necessity will always perceive and organize whatever realities encounter it.

As Kant interpreted it, Hume's error was in seeing subjective necessity as grounded only in habit instead of being a result of the *a priori* structure of reason. If the latter is the case, rational necessity and universality are guaranteed, although on a far different basis from before. For Kant, the forms perceived through sense experience are the product of the categories of the human mind, but now the externality so encountered is never known as it is in itself (as "noumenon"), but only in its relation to man (as "phenomenon").

While reason attempts to complete this knowledge by bringing it into a comprehensive unity, it is barred from success in this speculative operation by certain antinomies, both sides of which are in harmony with man's phenomenal knowledge. In the area of speculative psychology, these antinomies make it impossible to affirm a soul existing apart from the physical. In the area of speculative cosmology, the consequence of the antinomies centers in the impossibility of establishing man as free of the determined processes of cause and effect. And in the area of speculative theology, the antinomies negate the possibility of proving the existence of God. In all cases, the antinomies defy resolution of these questions *either* positively or negatively.

As a result, reason, in its theoretical function, is barred from any cognitive penetration into the noumenal. This does not mean that the noumenal realm is necessarily unlike man's phenomenal knowledge of it and that human categories do not apply there; rather, the problem is that pure reason can provide no guarantee of any correspondence.

What is most significant about the first critique is that while Kant revives the old Platonic distinction between noumenon and phenomenon, in exploring reason along the narrowly Aristotelian lines of his day (as a strictly cognitive activity), the Platonic distinction became a severe human limitation. Plato had stressed the noetic aspects of reason, which was deeply imbued with an intuitive or mystical quality. But in the preface to the second edition of the first critique Kant gave indication that he was moving toward a broader, or more Platonic, conception of reason: "I have found it necessary to deny *knowledge* [of supersensible reality] in order to make room

546

for *faith*." Although "faith," for Kant, was to be understood largely in moral terms (stemming from his pietistic background), we have here a beginning indication of his recognition of modes of human apprehension far broader than simply discursive or cognitive reason. Much of the impetus for exploring this possibility came from Kant's tremendous interest in ethics, made urgent by the seemingly undermining affect of his first critique upon this realm. His understanding of the experience of the form of duty, like Plato's experience of the form of the good, has about it a near mystical quality.

The *Critique of Practical Reason* is of major importance not only as the attempt to create a purely rational ethic, but also as a defense of a non-discursive mode of apprehension, as an insistence that the "rational" is not restricted in meaning to the "cognitive." It is this point which Kant develops further in the third critique, the *Critique of Judgment* (1790), in terms of beauty and the purposiveness of nature. In order to understand these points, one must beware of the misleading title of the second critique. In distinguishing between *pure* reason and *practical* reason, Kant is not speaking of two human agents or loci of activity; in both critiques he is speaking of pure reason as such, but in the first he is concerned with its theoretical or speculative function, in the second with its practical or ethical function. For Kant, this second function is the activity known as will. It is his purpose to show that will is not divorced from reason, controlled internally by drives or impulses, or externally by pleasure stimuli. In its fulfilled operation it is a purely rational

enterprise; it is pure reason in its practical operation which must *control* drives and *determine* external ends.

Likewise, in this realm it was Hume who haunted Kant, for Hume understood reason as being the pawn of passions, and morality as being rooted in subjective feeling. Just as Kant's answer in the cognitive realm depended on exhibiting the *a priori* or categorical laws of man's cognitive activity, so his answer in the second critique depended on discovering the *a priori* or categorical laws of the rational will. Morality could claim objectivity and universality only by being founded not on experience, but on pure reason itself. The task of the second critique, then, is to discover the *a priori* or necessary principles of the practical reason.

At the heart of the problem of ethics is the problem of freedom; without freedom, morality is an impossibility. But according to the first critique, since all things are seen, of necessity, under the category of causality, all things are seen as determined. Yet, Kant insists, the same noumenon-phenomenon distinction applying to the object of such knowledge also applies to the subject as well. It is man as phenomenon who is seen under the category of necessity, but the nature of the noumenal man remains unknown. Although the speculative function of reason strives for an understanding of the human "soul," the antinomies, as we have seen, left the matter of freedom for the noumenal self as "problematic but not impossible." If Kant can exhibit the will as free, he believes, he can also show the capacity of pure reason to determine the will's total activity.

If there is to be an objective ethic, an ethic based on freedom, the only possibility for it can be reason presupposing nothing else but itself, for a rule can be objective and universal only if it is not subject to any contingent, subjective conditions. Thus, moral *laws* cannot be based on the pleasure principle, for the objects of pleasure and pain can only be identified empirically, thus having no objective necessity. Further, hedonism can make no legitimate distinction between higher and lower pleasures; only if reason is able to determine the will can there be a higher faculty of desire than base feeling. Likewise, there is no objective, universal basis for an ethic of happiness, for happiness is simply the general name for satisfaction of desire.

Consequently, maxims (subjective, personal principles) of man's commonplace activity can claim the ethical status of law not according to their content, which is always empirically gained, but only according to their form. Every maxim can be tested for such universality of form by inquiring whether that maxim, if made a universal law, would negate itself. For example, all men seeking only their own happiness would soon render happiness impossible; thus, the goal of individual happiness is judged to be lacking the universality required of a moral law.

Now, since it is only the form of the maxim which makes objective claim upon the will, the will must be seen as independent of the natural law of cause and effect; that is, we have here a case in which the will operates in isolation from the phenomenal realm. The act is rooted totally in reason itself. This is the heart of Kant's ethic— "freedom and unconditional practical law imply each other." Since freedom

cannot be known through the theoretical function of reason, its objective reality is discovered by experiencing the moral law as duty, as a rational necessity. This means that the pure practical laws are discovered in the same manner as the pure theoretical laws, by observing what reason directs in indifference to empirical conditions. Without the moral law, Kant insists, man would never know himself to be free—"thou ought" implies "thou canst."

For Kant, the fundamental law of the pure practical reason is this—"So act that the maxim of your will could always hold at the same time as a principle establishing universal law." Such rational control of the will is objective, for the legislation is made in indifference to any contingencies. Yet a distinction must be drawn between a *pure* will and a *holy* will; although the moral law is a universal law for all beings with reason and will, because the free man has wants and sensuous motives, he is capable of maxims which conflict with the moral law. Thus, this law comes to man as a "categorical imperative." It is categorical because it is unconditioned; it is an imperative because it is experienced as "duty," as an inner compulsion provided by reason. Holiness is above duty, but in this life it remains the ideal to be striven for, but never reached. Each maxim must strive for unending progress toward this ideal; it is such progress that deserves the name "virtue."

Kant's formulation of the moral law is, in effect, a philosophical statement of the "Golden Rule." As Kant says, the moral law of universality alone, without the need of any external incentive, arises as duty "to extend the maxim of self-love also to the happiness of others." Or, put on a common-sense level, Kant's moral formula is rooted in the integrity required by reason. It is self-evident that reason, to be rational, must operate in complete self-consistency; since the rational is the universal, reason qua reason must consent to will only that which can consistently be willed universally.

For Kant, the demand of duty is unmistakable and can, without difficulty, be perceived by the simplest person. Where the difficulty arises is in following the imperative. Kant's estimate of man is such that he goes so far as to maintain that the good act is done only when duty and inclination are in conflict. What he really means here is that aversion is a sign that the individual has gone beyond self-interest to real duty. It is necessary to insist, Kant maintains, that satisfaction follows but does not precede awareness of the moral law; there is certainly a "moral feeling" that should be cultivated, but duty cannot be derived from it.

Kant's rejection of all ethical theory but his own formal principle provides a helpful summary of alternative ethical systems. He sees six types. Of the subjective type, there are two kinds—external and internal. In the former, men like Montaigne root ethics in education, while others, such as Bernard Mandeville, see its basis in a civil constitution. Of the internal variety, Epicurus sees physical feeling as central, while Francis Hutcheson grounds ethics in "moral feeling." There are likewise internal and external types within the objective ethical systems. The former is the ethic of perfection, held by Christian von Wolff and the Stoics; the latter is the "will of God" ethic of theological morality. The subjective group Kant quickly discards as empirically based, thus, by definition, failing to meet the requirements of universal morality. Also, the objective types, though rational, depend on a content which, within the confines of Kant's first critique, can be gained by empirical means only; consequently, these too must be disqualified as being neither universal nor necessary.

Man's capacity for obeying the moral law in independence of empirical conditions establishes, for Kant, the objective fact of man's free, supersensible (noumenal) nature. As Kant puts it, the necessity of the practical reason makes freedom a rational postulate. Freedom is not known, in the theoretical sense, but it must be subjectively affirmed as necessary. This does not mean that freedom is simply subjective, but that its objectiveness is perceived through reason's practical rather than theoretical operation. Moral need has the status of law, while the antinomies render the completions of speculative reason hypothetical or arbitrary. Thus, the former provides the certitude which the latter lacks, establishing the factuality of freedom as valid for both the practical and pure reason. Here we see the breadth of Kant's conception of reason —such a moral postulate is both objective and rational, even though it is not cognitive.

Since it is Kant's concern to show that it is pure (speculative) reason itself which is practical, the postulates of reason in its practical function become objective for reason as such. In actuality, the practical function is prior and the speculative function must submit to it, for "every interest is ultimately practical, even that of speculative reason being only conditional and reaching perfection only in practical use." The result of this insight is that the agnosticism of the first critique is transcended by the second, for while still insisting upon his former severe limitations on speculative reason, Kant here provides an alternative mode for metaphysical affirmation. This is most apparent in the two additional moral postulates that Kant draws from the postulate regarding freedom. What is required by the moral law is complete "fitness of intentions," which would be holiness. But since this is impossible for finite man, the practical reason requires that one affirm an "endless progress" in which such fitness can be completed. And since such progress requires the immortality of the soul, this affirmation becomes an objective postulate of the practical reason. Such a proposition is not demonstrable, but is "an inseparable corollary of an a priori unconditionally valid practical law." Thus the second antinomy of speculative reason is practically resolved.

Likewise, a third postulate is involved. The postulate of immortality can be made only on the supposition of a cause adequate to produce such an effect; thus, one must affirm as an objective postulate the existence of God, an affirmation sharing the same necessary status as the other two moral postulates. A further basis for this postulate rests in the fact that although finite existence supports no necessary connection between morality and proportionate happiness, such a connection is morally necessary.

The affirmation of such postulates Kant calls the activity of "pure rational faith," for although they are objective (necessary), freedom, the soul, and God are not known as they are in themselves. This, he affirms, is in truth the essence of "the Christian principle of morality." It is from morality that religion springs, for religion is nothing more than "the recognition of all duties as divine commands."

Since morality has to do with the moral law, with the form of an action, it follows that no "thing" is good or evil; such designations properly apply only to an acting will. Good and evil are defined only after and by means of the moral law; to reverse this procedure is to develop an empirical, subjective ethic. It is the practical judgment which determines the applicability of a universal maxim to a concrete act. To make an application such as this is very difficult, for it is here that the laws of freedom (the noumenal realm) are applied to the laws of nature (the phenomenal realm). Such a meeting is possible because the moral law is purely formal in relation to natural law. That is, it raises this question: if this proposed act should take place by a law of nature of which you were a part, would your will regard it as possible? The center of the moral act thus rests in one's intentions, not in consequences. If the right act occurs but not for the sake of the moral law, it is not a moral act. The only incentive which is valid is the moral law itself.

For man as he is, his natural feelings of self-love are ever at war with the moral law. The very fact that morality resides in law reveals the severe "limitation" of man. The moral law is victorious only if all inclinations and feelings are set aside out of respect for the moral law, in and of itself. An act not performed out of such a sense of duty is inevitably tainted with the self-pride of believing goodness to be a spontaneous reflection of one's nature.

Perhaps the major difficulty in Kant's ethic is the problem of application. There are few acts which a performer would not defend as universally valid if the hypothetical performer and situation were in every way identical with those of the actual performer. Every evil has been defended by the exigencies of person and circumstance. Kant's moral formula is designed to eliminate all such individualized decisions. Yet to the degree that the formula is interpreted, not in such a particularized fashion but in an absolutely universal sense, its inadequacy becomes evident. Total truthtelling, total promise-keeping, and the like, all have obvious moral exceptions. Likewise, how is one to resolve conflicts between these objective duties? And further, law for its own sake tends to be elevated above the individual men between whom moral relations arise.

Kant's moral position has stimulated generations of heated conflict. For certain theologians, Kant's ethic seems to be only an ethic of the fall and not a redemptive ethic; for others, it is a classic Protestant ethic, judging human pretension and incapacity. For philosophers, the difficulty, as with Anselm's ontological argument, rests in its deceptive simplicity (despite the difficulty of its expression). Such a position is uncomfortable in its rather wholesale rejection of consequences, moral incentives, absolute good, and the like. But there is no denying Kant's realistic appraisal of human capacity, the absolute quality of moral activity and yet the relativity of concrete ethical situations. It may be that Kant's ethic is too simple, discards too much, and is too uncompromising, but consequent ethicists have found it impossible to bypass this second critique.

In regard to their larger ramifications, Kant's critiques have been a powerful damper on speculative metaphysics. Philosophically, they have stimulated an exploration of non-cognitive modes of human apprehension; theologically, they have encouraged exploration of the moral dimensions of religion and of theological method.

AN INTRODUCTION TO THE PRINCIPLES
OF MORALS AND LEGISLATION

Author: Jeremy Bentham (1748-1832)
Type of work: Ethics
First published: 1789

PRINCIPAL IDEAS ADVANCED

The first principle of moral philosophy is the principle of utility which states that every man is morally obligated to promote the greatest happiness of the greatest number of persons.

The principle of utility takes account of the fact that all men are governed by an interest in securing pleasure and in avoiding pain.

Only the consequences of acts are good or bad; intentions are good or evil only insofar as they lead to pleasure or pain.

Since suffering is always bad, all punishment is bad; but punishment must sometimes be administered in order to avoid the greater suffering that an offender against society might bring to others.

Bentham's aim in writing *An Introduction to the Principles of Morals and Legislation* was to discover the foundations for a scientific approach to penal legislation. Because he found these in human nature, rather than in statutes and precedents, his work is also a book on morals.

Two distinct elements appear in Bentham's theory. The first is a psychology of motivation according to which all the actions of men are directed toward pleasures or away from pains. The second is a principle of social ethics according to which each man's actions ought to promote the greatest happiness of the greatest number of persons. That the two principles are independent in their origin and application is not altered by the fact that happiness, according to Bentham, consists in nothing other than pleasure and the avoidance of pain.

The obligation to promote the happiness of the greatest number Bentham called *the principle of utility*. In the manner of the eighteenth century, he frankly admitted that this first principle of his philosophy cannot be proved, because a chain of proof must begin somewhere, and there can be no principle higher than a first principle. The principle, he said, is part of "the natural constitution of the human frame," and men embrace it spontaneously in judging others if not in directing their own actions. Bentham believed that, in addition to this prin-

ciple, there are in man social motives, including "good-will" or "benevolence," which work in harmony with the principle of utility; but the inclination to kindness is one thing, and the principle of utility something else. The latter is an intelligible rule which lies at the foundation of all morals; hence, also of legislation.

What chiefly distinguished Bentham from other eighteenth century moral philosophers was, first, that he recognized only one ultimate principle of morals and, second, that the principle which he maintained was one which admitted of empirical application. The "Age of Reason" commonly appealed to a whole array of self-evident principles, intuitive convictions, and laws of nature. But Bentham complained that none of them provided an external standard which men could agree on. In many instances, the alleged truths of nature were an expression of the principle of utility: but at other times they were nothing but expressions of private feelings, prejudices, and interests. The principle of utility, on the other hand, made it possible to define good and evil, right and wrong, in terms which everyone understood and accepted. "Nature has placed mankind under the governance of two sovereign masters, *pain* and *pleasure*. . . . The *principle of utility* recognizes this subjection, and assumes it for the foundation of that system, the object of which is to rear the fabric of felicity by the hands of reason and of law."

These fundamentals having been laid down, Bentham devoted the remainder of his work to detailed analyses of the psychology of human behavior, chiefly as it bears upon problems of social control. His aim was to find the natural divisions of his subject and to arrange the matter in tables which would be of help in drawing inductions.

First, he treated of pleasures and pains. The legislator, he said, has a two-fold interest in these. Inasmuch as the general happiness consists in pleasure and the avoidance of pain, the legislator must consider these as ends or final causes; but since, as legislator, he has to employ motives, he must also consider them as instruments or efficient causes. It is the latter consideration especially that makes it necessary to consider the *sources* of pain and pleasure. The legislator is advised that, in addition to such internal motives as men have toward benevolence, there are several external forces or "sanctions" which reinforce virtue and right. The physical sanction is the pain and loss which nature attaches to certain imprudent acts; the religious sanction is fear of divine displeasure or hope of divine favor; the popular sanction is the favor or disfavor of our fellow men. Political sanction is a fourth source of pain and pleasure, being the rewards and punishments which the ruling power of the state dispenses in cases where the other sanctions are not effective.

The *value* of particular pains and pleasures is obviously relevant in connection with the ends of legislation, but not less so in connection with the means, since the deterrent must be made to outweigh the temptation to crime if it is to serve its purpose. Bentham believed that it is possible to estimate the amount of a pain or pleasure, and he suggested seven calculable factors: intensity, duration, certainty, propinquity, fecundity, purity, and extent. Besides the quantitative side of pain and pleasure, Bentham recognized that there are different kinds of pains and pleasures, and he devoted a chapter to tabulating them. Perceptions, he held, are usually composite, made up of more than one pain or pleasure or both. He undertook to analyze them into their simple parts, and to enumerate these. Besides pleasures of the senses he noted pleasures of acquisition and possession, of skill, of friendship, of a good name, of power, and even of malevolence. Besides pains of the senses, he recognized the pains of privation (desire, disappointment, regret), and the kinds of pains that are opposite to the pleasures listed above. The lawmaker, according to Bentham, must have all these in view. When he considers an offense, he must ask what pleasures it tends to destroy and what pains to produce in order, on the one hand, to estimate its mischief to the public, and, on the other, its temptation to the wrongdoer. Furthermore, when he considers the punishment, he must take into account the several pains which it is in the power of the state to inflict.

Besides these accounts of the general value of pains and pleasures, a special chapter is devoted to individual differences. Bentham listed thirty-two factors which influence men's sensibilities to pain and pleasure, reminding lawmakers that there is no direct proportion between the cause of pain or pleasure and its effect, since differences of health, sex, education, religion, and many other conditions must be taken into account.

Bentham then considered human *action*. The legislator is interested in acts in proportion to their tendency to disturb the general happiness; hence, his judgment has regard only to consequences, not to motives. Bentham distinguished carefully between the intention of an act and its motive. The intention of an act, he maintained, may have two things in view, the act and its consequences, but not equally: one must intend at least the beginning of the act, as, for example, when a person begins to run; but he may have none of the consequences in view, and rarely does he have more than a few. To make his point, Bentham took the story of the death of William II of a wound received from Sir Walter Tyrrel when they were stag-hunting, diversifying it with different suppositions. Had Tyrrel any thought of the king's death? If not, the killing was altogether unintentional. Did he think, when he shot the stag, that there was some danger of the king's riding in the way? If so, the act was intentional but obliquely so. Did he kill him on account of hatred and for the pleasure of destroying him? If such was true, the deed was ultimately intentional. Such examples show that intention involves, besides the motive or will to act, an understanding of the circumstances in which the action takes place. It is the latter which, according to Bentham, must chiefly be taken into account when an intention is praised or blamed, for it is the consequences which are properly good or evil; the intention is good or evil only in so far as the consequences were in view from the start.

Bentham maintained that the will or motive of an intentional act is neither good nor evil. One desire is as legitimate as another, and the pleasure which a man receives from injuring an enemy is, considered by itself, a good, however we may judge the act in terms of its consequences. Bentham was alert to the role which fictitious entities play in human discourse, and noted the difficulties which they place in the way of exact analysis. For example, "avarice" and "indolence" are supposed to act as motives, although they correspond to nothing in the heart of man. Similarly, real motives, such as the pleasure of eating or of sexual satisfaction or of possession are obscured by calling them "gluttony," "lust," and "covetousness." To help clear up the confusion, Bentham went over the whole catalog of kinds of pleasures and pains, and noted how many of them have several names. Thus, pleasures of wealth are called "pecuniary interest" (a neutral term), "avarice," "covetousness," "rapacity," "lucre" (terms of reproach), and "economy," "thrift," "frugality," "industry" (terms of approval), according to the circumstances and our estimate of their consequences. But the motive, in each case, is the same, and may neither be praised nor blamed.

Nevertheless, some motives are more harmonious with the principle of utility than others. Bentham classified the motives as *social* (good will, love of reputation, desire for friendship, and religion), *dissocial* (displeasure), and *self-regarding* (physical desire, pecuniary interest, love of power, and self-preservation). But not even the purest social motive, good will, always coincides with the principle of utility, particularly when it confines itself to the interests of a limited set of persons.

Bentham recognized that when a man is contemplating an act, he is frequently acted on by many motives which draw him in different directions. Some of them are more likely to prompt mischievous acts, others to oppose them. The sum of the motives by which a man is likely to be influenced make up his disposition. "Disposition" was, in Bentham's view, another fictitious notion which represents no more than one man's estimation of how another man is likely to behave. Nevertheless, so far as it can be estimated, the disposition of an offender is important to know. And Bentham admitted that judgments of good and bad do apply to dispositions, as they do not to single motives. He suggested that the degree of depravity of a criminal's disposition is inversely proportional to the strength of the temptation needed to prompt him to a mischievous act.

True to the principle of utility, however, Bentham maintained that, strictly speaking, only the *consequences* of an act are good or bad. Pleasures and pains are real, as dispositions are not. And acts and intentions, which are internal to the doer, are good or evil only as they attach to consequences. Bentham devoted approximately the last half of his book to distinguishing and classifying mischievous acts. The main division is between primary mischief, which is suffered by one or more individuals whose happiness is directly affected by the offense, and secondary mischief, which is the alarm or danger apprehended by the citizenry from the presence of the offender at large in their midst. Penal legislation must take ac-

count of both, since the latter diminishes the general happiness (by disturbing men's sense of security) no less than the former.

Bentham's principles for penal legislation are frankly calculative. The lawmaker must estimate the strength of temptation to do mischief, and make the punishment sufficiently severe to act as a deterrent. Bentham argued that there is no kindness in making the punishment light because if it is strong enough persons disposed to crime will not have to endure it, whereas if it is too light, they will. Severity, of course, is not the only thing to be considered. Applying his method of calculating the amount of pleasure and pain, Bentham argued that the certainty and proximity of the punishment must also be taken into account, as well as its appropriateness.

There is no detailed account in the *Introduction* of the purposes of punishment. But in a footnote, referring to a separate work called *The Theory of Punishment,* the author explains that the principal end of punishment is to control action, whether that of the offender or of others who might be tempted to similar misdeeds. It may work through reformation of the man's disposition, through prohibiting action, or through making him an example. Bentham recognized that vindictive pleasure is also a good, but he could not tolerate making it a basis for punishment.

Like his liberal disciple John Stuart Mill (as in *Essay On Liberty,* 1859), Bentham held that all punishment is mischief and to be admitted only for the exclusion of greater evil. In many cases, to use his words, "punishment is not worth while." This is the case when the act was freely entered into by the party injured, or when the penalty cannot be efficacious (for example, when it comes too late), or when the evils of detecting and prosecuting the crime are more costly than the evils they are intended to prevent. In some cases the mischief is better countered in other ways—for example, the disseminating of pernicious principles should be overcome by educating people in wholesome ones.

The limitations of effective penal legislation were a matter of primary concern to Bentham. He emphasized private ethics and education as more important than legislation. His view of ethics is usually designated "enlightened self-interest" because he maintained that in most instances a man's motives for consulting the happiness of others are dictated by his own inter-est. But he conceded that there are occasions when social motives act independently of self-regarding motives. Private ethics he called the art of self-government; education, the art of governing the young. Admittedly these do not always achieve their full intention; but it is dangerous and unprofitable to try to make up for their defects by criminal procedures.

Bentham was especially critical of the jurisprudence that existed at that time, and he distinguished his approach to the subject by coining a new name. A book on jurisprudence, he said, could have one of two objects: to ascertain what the law is, or to ascertain what it ought to be. Most books are devoted to the former—he called them "expository"; his was devoted to the latter—he called it "censorial" jurisprudence, or the *art of legislation*.

CRITIQUE OF JUDGMENT

Author: Immanuel Kant (1724-1804)
Type of work: Aesthetics, metaphysics
First published: 1790

PRINCIPAL IDEAS ADVANCED

Judgment in general is the faculty of thinking the particular as contained under the universal; if a judgment brings the particular under a given universal, it is determinant, and if it discovers a universal by which to judge a given particular, it is reflective.

Taste is the faculty of judging an object by a satisfaction (or dissatisfaction) which is not dependent on any quality of the object itself; the satisfaction is a subjective response to the mere representation of the object; hence, it is disinterested.

Even though beauty is subjective, it is universal; the beautiful is that which pleases universally because it satisfies the will as if it served a purpose.

The sublime is found when a formless object is represented as boundless, even though its totality is present in thought.

Since its publication the *Critique of Judgment* has been of highest importance to the philosophy of art and of religion. It met opposition as radically skeptical and destructive of theology; indeed, Kant intended to set limits on religious thinking. It opened promising new pathways in aesthetics, still found highly worthy of exploration.

The work is based wholly on the psychology of faculties and the logic Kant adopted in the *Critique of Pure Reason* (1781) and the *Critique of Practical Reason* (1788). The former treats the faculty of *understanding*, which, presupposing natural law, brings us our knowledge of nature. The latter treats *reason* ("practical" reason, will, or desire), which presupposes freedom and legislates for us in accordance with moral law. While writing the first two critiques, Kant believed that the faculty of pleasure and pain could have no critique, being passive only. But he came to regard this faculty to be the same as the judgment, which subsumes representations under concepts, always accompanied by a feeling-response. He declared finally that judgment could have a *regulative* critique of its own, showing its functions and limitations, even though the faculty brings us no objective knowledge. Indeed, the *Critique of Judgment* would show the ground of union between understanding and reason, although their presuppositions had seemingly forced them irrevocably apart.

The desire or will when realized is actually a natural cause, specifically that cause which acts in accordance with concepts. Concepts are of two kinds, natural concepts and concepts of freedom. The understanding carries on a theoretical legislation through natural concepts resulting in knowledge; the practical reason carries on a moral legislation through precepts resulting in choices of actions. Understanding and reason legislate over the very same territory of experience, yet without conflicting. However, the practical reason presupposes a *supersensible substratum*, which cannot be experienced but which is necessary as a condition of freedom of choice. The understanding can give knowledge only through intuition, which can never reach the *thing-in-itself*; the concept of freedom, on the other hand, represents its object as a *thing-in-itself* but cannot give it in intuition. The region of the thing-in-itself is supersensible; but while we cannot *know* it, we can *impute* reality to it. This must be a *practical* reality founded on our necessity of acting, not on any source of substantive knowledge concerning it. To postulate such a substratum enables us to transfer our thought between the realm of nature and the realm of freedom and think according to the principles of each in turn.

The deduction of the principle of judgment is crucial to the book. "Judgment in general," says Kant, "is the faculty of thinking the particular as contained under the universal." Either the universal or the particular might be given. If the universal, then the judgment which brings the particular under it is *determinant*; the judgment brings knowledge according to *a priori* law and with finality. But if the particular is given, then the judgment must find for itself a law to judge by, in the absence of a concept. Hence it is *reflective*; and if the judgments delivered are to be regarded as laws this must be on the assumption of some underlying unifying principle.

The principle must be this: as universal laws of nature have their ground in our understanding (as shown in the *Critique of Pure Reason*), particular empirical laws must be considered in accordance with such a unity as they would have if an understanding had furnished them to our cognitive faculties, so as to make possible a system of experience according to particular laws of nature. The concept of an actual object contains its purpose; the principle of judgment which we take, then, on these suppositions, is *purposiveness* in nature. (For nature to realize a purpose would be to carry out a "particular law of nature.") *If* nature were guided by an understanding, then purposiveness would underlie its variety as the unifying factor. This concept of purposiveness is *a priori*—it provides a principle for reflecting upon nature without needing specific experience of nature. Yet we can never prove real purpose in nature; we only justify our way of thinking about it.

The faculty of judgment functions also as the faculty of pleasure and pain. When the understanding shows us an order of nature and the judgment apprehends it under the aspect of purposiveness, we feel a pleasure, since the attainment of any aim is bound up with the feeling of pleasure. Because the ground of this feeling is a principle *a priori,* the judgment is valid for every man. The *imagination* is the faculty of *a priori* intuitions; our pleasure arises when the judgment of purposiveness places the imagination in agreement with the understanding—shows a form such as an understanding would furnish.

The judgment of taste represents purposiveness without mediation of a concept. But purposiveness may also be represented objectively as the harmony of the form of an object with the possibility of the thing itself according to some prior concept which contains the basis of this form. In two ways a concept of an object may be realized: a person may make an object which fulfills his preconceived concept; or nature may present an object realizing a concept which we supply. Thus we can regard *natural beauty* as the presentation of the concept of subjective purposiveness, and *natural purposes* as the presentation of the concept of an objective purposiveness. Hence, the *Critique of Judgment* is divided into the Critique of the Aesthetical Judgment (considering the former) involving the feeling of pleasure, and the Critique of the Teleological Judgment (treating the latter) involving the understanding and reason, according to concepts. While the aesthetical judgment is the special faculty of taste, the teleological judgment is not a special faculty but only the reflective judgment in general, judging of certain objects of nature according to reflective principles.

True to his critical logic, Kant considers in turn the quality, quantity, relation, and modality of the judgment of taste, in a subdivision called the "Analytic of the Aesthetical Judgment." Then in its "Dialectic," he resolves an antinomy or contradiction which arises in aesthetics.

By the *aesthetical* Kant means that element whose determining ground can be no other than subjective. Consequently, the aesthetic apprehension does not depend on existential relations of the judged object with other things (its usefulness, for example) but only on the relation of the *repre-*

sentation of the object to the observing subject. In contrast, the pleasant and the good always involve a representation not only of the object but of some connection of the judging subject with that object; hence, they bring an interested rather than a free satisfaction. Taste is the faculty of judging of an object, or of the method of representing one, by a satisfaction (or dissatisfaction) which as to quality is entirely disinterested. The object of such satisfaction is called beautiful.

Since the satisfaction does not depend on a particular relationship with a particular subject, it may be thought of as resting on something present in everyone and hence binding universally. Since this element inheres in the subject, not in the objects judged, the quantity is a "subjective universality." What we postulate is that all rational minds are constituted alike in the relation of their cognitive faculties. For a representation to be capable of becoming a cognition at all requires *imagination* for bringing together in ordered fashion the manifold of phenomena, and *understanding* for providing a concept under which the representations may be united. But this requires as its condition a free play in the action of imagination and understanding. Aesthetic pleasure must be communicable among all minds so constituted. What the judgment of taste asserts as universally valid is not some attribute of the object (as in the claim that something is pleasant or good), but rather the claim of our presupposition of the communicability of aesthetic pleasure among subjects. As to quantity, then, the beautiful is that which pleases universally without requiring or providing a concept.

A purpose is a concept of an object insofar as the concept is regarded as the cause of the object. When we can think of an object only as though caused by a concept, *for us* that object has purposiveness, even though we cannot know whether it has purpose. That is, it has *purposiveness without purpose.* The mere form of purposiveness is given, and it is that in which we take pleasure. As to relation, beauty is the form of the *purposiveness* of an object, so far as this is perceived in it *without any representation of a purpose.*

The modality of the judgment of taste is necessity. It is, however, neither objective necessity nor practical necessity, like those respectively of understanding and reason, but *exemplary* necessity. It requires the assent of all "to a judgment which is regarded as the example of a universal rule that we cannot state." This assent may be expected only on the assumption introduced above, the communicability of our cognitions. Under this presupposition, an individual has a right to state his judgment of taste as a rule for everyone and thus assert of all subjects the particular judgment arising from his own experience. The beautiful, then, is that which without any concept is cognized as the object of a *necessary* satisfaction.

The judgment of the sublime has the same quality, quantity, relation, and modality as that of the beautiful, but there are important differences. The beautiful pleases through its form and its bounds; but the sublime is found when a formless object is represented as boundless, even though its totality is present in thought. Hence while beauty is a satisfaction in quality, the sublime is a satisfaction in respect to quantity. Furthermore, in the

559

sublime the form may seem to violate purposiveness and be quite unsuited to our presentative faculty. It rather should be said that the object is fit for the presentation of a sublimity found in the mind, producing in us a feeling of purposiveness of our powers, independent of nature.

The sublime has two kinds: the mathematical, and the dynamic. Whereas that of the beautiful is restful, the judgment of the sublime stirs a movement of the mind which is judged as subjectively purposive and is referred either to the cognition, generating (A) the mathematically sublime, or to the will, generating (B) the dynamically sublime.

(A) We can always think something still greater than whatever the senses give us. While we cannot have an intuition of the infinite, which is absolutely great, we can comprehend it logically. To do this without contradiction presupposes a supersensible faculty. Thus we refer to the ideas of reason (God, freedom, immortality). Comparing the objects of nature, however grand, with these ideas, we gain a feeling of respect for our own destination according to the law of reason. (B) On observing in nature mighty objects from which we are in no danger, if we can think of a case in which we would fear them, we feel the emotion of the sublime. It calls up a comparison with our own power, which is small physically but which in our *rational* faculty has a superiority to nature even in its immensity, in the sublimity of the mind's destination. The judgment of either kind of sublime is thus not so much upon the object but on our state of mind in the estimation of it. Like the judgment of the beautiful, the judgment of the sublime postulates a common faculty among men, in this case the feeling for the legislation of reason, that is, for what is moral.

Kant considers it requisite to provide a *deduction* or proof of its grounds for any judgment claiming necessity. But since the judgment of taste is neither cognitive nor practical, it can draw its necessity from no concepts. Rather, it has a twofold peculiarity: (1) it claims the universality of a singular, not a universal, proposition; and (2) it claims the necessary assent of everyone *a priori*, but cannot depend on *a priori* grounds of proof for doing so. And because of what they are, Kant asserts, the explanation of these peculiarities suffices as a deduction. As to the necessity, although the judgment of each individual improves with exercise, at each stage it claims the necessary assent of others. It claims autonomy. If it submitted to external principles, it would be something other than taste. As to quantity, since it judges without a concept, this must always be singular: "This tulip is beautiful," never "All tulips are beautiful," since the universal subject term of the latter is a concept and brings the understanding into the process. Obviously, then, no objective principle of taste is possible, and no rule can be given to art. Rather, the principle of taste is the subjective principle of judgment in general, operating on the condition solely of the faculty of judgment itself.

Unlike mere labor, or science, or commercial handicraft, beautiful art is free. Yet we must be conscious of it as art and not nature, to keep it within the framework that will allow it to please in the mere act of judging. Beautiful art is the work of genius, which is the "innate mental disposition (*ingenium*) *through which* nature gives the rule to art." Genius is an original productive talent, not a capacity for following rules. Its products serve as examples setting standards for others. Natural beauty is a beautiful thing, but artificial beauty is a beautiful representation of a thing. In some beauties, such as the latter, inevitably a concept enters, and enjoyment through reason as well as aesthetic judging enters with it. Taste, but not genius, is a requisite for judging works of beautiful art. Genius is a faculty of presenting *aesthetical ideas,* representations of the imagination which occasion much thought where no one thought is adequate. This is a particular kind of the play which harmonizes the imagination and the understanding. It goes beyond the limits of experience to find presentations of such completeness that they have no example in nature, presentations which will communicate the aesthetic pleasure to others.

The chief aesthetic problem of Kant's times was how to controvert seriously matters of taste as though taste had an objective standard, when we also assert that there is no disputing tastes. Kant cast the problem as an antinomy in the "Dialectic of the Aesthetical Judgment." The thesis is "The judgment of taste is not based upon concepts, for otherwise it would admit of controversy (would be determinable by proofs)." The antithesis is "The judgment of taste is based on concepts, for otherwise, despite its diversity, we could not quarrel about it (we could not claim for our judgment the necessary assent of others)." The apparent contradiction is resolved when we recognize that "concept" has a different reference in each proposition. A concept may be either determinable or not. The thesis refers to determinable con-

cepts; the antithesis refers to the one indeterminable concept, the supersensible, on which the faculty of judgments rests. So understood, both are true, and the contradiction disappears.

The beautiful is the symbol of the morally good, in that it gives pleasure with a claim for the agreement of everyone else. It makes the mind feel an elevation of itself above mere pleasantness of sensation, and enables it to estimate the worth of others in this regard also. For just as the reason does in respect to the practical, the judgment gives the law to itself with respect to objects of pure aesthetic satisfaction. The propaedeutic to the beautiful arts lies in humane studies, not in precepts, and it reaches art through the social spirit and the communication of men which is distinctive of humanity. Taste "is at bottom a faculty for judging of the sensible illustration of moral ideas. . . ."

The sequel of the study of purposiveness in nature without purpose is the study of the basis of judging nature as having purpose—the "Critique of the Teleological Judgment." We have absolutely no grounds to ascribe purpose objectively to nature, but must regard purpose as a principle supplied by ourselves for bringing this phenomena of nature under rules wherever the laws of mechanical causality do not suffice to do so.

A purpose is a concept which functions as a cause of that of which it is the concept. In order to see the possibility of a thing as a purpose, it is a requisite that its form is not possible according to natural laws and that the empirical knowledge of its cause and effect presupposes concepts of reason. The things regarded as natural purposes are organized, living beings. The understanding takes causes to be immediate preceding conditions (efficient causes) of their effects, but the reason can think a final cause. For a thing to be a natural purpose, its parts must be possible only through their reference to the whole, and they should so combine in the unity of the whole that they are reciprocally cause and effect of each other. Thus nothing is in vain in it. The being so constituted may be regarded as the product of both efficient causes and final causes, an organized and self-organizing being —in a word, a *natural purpose.* Organized beings give the basis for teleology, as they first afford objective reality to the concept of a natural purpose. From regarding them, we are carried farther, reflectively to regard the mechanism of all of nature as subordinated according to principles of reason.

The reflective judgment must subsume presentations under a law not yet given; hence, it must serve as principle for itself. Therefore it needs maxims for its reflection, so as to attain to concepts and cognize nature even according to empirical laws. Among its maxims the following antinomy arises. Thesis: All production of material things and their forms must be judged possible according to merely mechanical laws. Antithesis: Some products of material nature cannot be judged to be possible according to merely mechanical laws. But these are maxims, not substantive propositions. The concepts involved in maxims of the judgment (including "mechanical laws") are not accorded objective reality but are merely guides to reason. Now the thesis may be acceptable as a maxim of the determinant, and the antithesis of the reflective judgment. Hence, no contradiction in fact exists between them.

To unite the mechanism of nature and the principle of purposes, teleology places the supersensible tentatively at the basis of phenomenal nature, but of it we can have no theoretical knowledge whatever. We should explain everything in nature by mechanism as far as this is in our power. But we should acknowledge that some things, which we cannot even state for investigation without a concept of a purpose of reason, must finally be accounted for by purposes.

For anything in nature, if we ask why it exists, the answer is either that it rose solely out of nature's mechanism without design, or else that it has somewhere a designed ground as a contingent being. And if the latter, we can say either that its purpose lies in itself —a final purpose—or that the ground of its existence is external to it in another natural being. Apparently, man is the only being we can regard as the ultimate purpose of creation here on earth, for he is the only creature "who can form a concept of his purposes and who can, by his reason, make out of an aggregate of purposively formed things a system of purposes." That within him which is to be furthered as a purpose must be either what nature could perhaps satisfy, his happiness, or else his aptitude and skill with which he can turn nature to all kinds of purposes, his culture. But if man makes happiness his whole purpose, a purpose dependent upon nature, this renders him incapable of positing his existence as a final purpose and of being in harmony with it. The culture of skill, and particularly of the will, of discipline, makes us receptive of higher purposes than nature itself can supply. Through culture of the beautiful arts and the sciences we are prepared for a reign in which reason alone shall have authority.

The moral law, as the rational condition of the use of our freedom, obliges us *a priori* (as shown in the *Critique of Practical Reason*) to strive for the highest good in the world possible through freedom. The highest physical good is happiness. But the reason supposes virtue to be the worthiness to be happy; and it is impossible to represent virtue and happiness as connected by natural causes or as harmonized in life. Thus, in order to represent to ourselves a final purpose consistent with the moral law, we must assume a moral world cause. While the final purpose cannot be regarded as having objective reality, it has subjective practical reality by being embodied in our actions toward the highest good. Through it we gain the possibility of thinking the world as a

purposive order, although we gain no proof of the existence of its original Being. "For the existence of the original Being as a Godhead, or of the soul as an immortal spirit, absolutely no proof in a theoretical point of view is possible. . . ." Faith (as *habitus* or disposition, not act) is the moral attitude of reason toward belief in something unattainable by theoretical cognition. The mind assumes that, since it is so commanded, the duty to attain the highest good is possible to fulfill. It has grounds for such a faith in the faculty of the reason freely to legislate in accordance with the moral law. Only freedom, among the three pure rational ideas—God, freedom, and immortality—proves its objective reality by its effects in nature; and thus it renders possible the reconciliation in thought and nature of God, immortality, and freedom.

A VIEW OF THE EVIDENCES OF CHRISTIANITY

Author: William Paley (1743-1805)
Type of work: Theology
First published: 1794

PRINCIPAL IDEAS ADVANCED

Either no religion is true, or Christianity is true because it is superior.

Once believe there is a God, and miracles are credible; revelation is a miracle, and through revelation God's will is made known to man.

From historical evidence contained in pagan and Christian writings the truth of Christianity is borne out.

The auxiliary evidences of the truth of Christianity are the prophecies of the Old and New Testaments, the morality of the Gospels, the consistency of the various accounts concerning the life and character of Christ, and the rapid growth of Christianity.

Although there are inconsistencies in the Gospels, they are attributable to historical errors or to the effect of different perspectives.

William Paley is the last of the important English theologians to write on the philosophy of religion without taking seriously the views of David Hume and Immanuel Kant. When he published his *Evidences* in 1794, all three of Kant's great *Critiques* and Hume's *Dialogues Concerning Natural Religion* had appeared within the previous fifteen years. Paley's writings sum up an era in theology. His literary style is clear but uninspired; his doctrine is unoriginal.

His principal works, he argued, form a system which establishes Christianity on a firm and reasonable basis. He has written on the evidences of natural religion, the evidences of revealed religion, and on the duties that result from both. Paley argues that by the argument from design one can prove that there is a God. That this God is the Christian God can be inferred from the excellence of his teachings which are true because they are confirmed by evidence within the Bible and by external accounts of historians. Having accepted in general outline the Christian documents as true, one must then accept the details which, supplemented by the natural light of reason, delineate one's Christian duties. In cases where the moral precepts of the Bible seem not to fit a particular problem, one may use as a basis for moral decision God's general purpose in the universe, which is that he wishes men to be happy. To provide the greatest happiness for the greatest number is an essential property of any moral act, is consistent with the explicit morality of the Bible, and is an infallible test of any moral precept.

A View of the Evidences of Christianity, by dealing with the evidences for revealed religion, holds a central place in his scheme. A typical eighteenth century work in theology, it is divided into three books which reveal in their titles Paley's plan of organization. Part I he calls "Of the Direct Historical Evidence of Christianity, and Wherein It is Distinguished from the Evidence Alleged for Other Miracles." Part II has the title, "Of the Auxiliary Evidences of Christianity," and is concerned with Christ's moral character. Part III, "A Brief Consideration of Some Popular Objections," deals with the discrepancies in the Gospels and with the effects that the spread of Christianity has had in history.

Part I opens with a statement of the position from which Paley will argue. Either no religion is true, he believes, or Christianity is true because from every point of view it is far superior to any other. To prove that Christianity is true is to prove in this sense the very possibility of religious belief. Christianity is in part a revealed religion, and one can be convinced by an examination of the nature of man that revelation is necessary. God intends in his plan of creation that through moral obedience to him man will gain happiness in this world and in the world to come. But man must know a precept in order to obey it, and it is incredible that God should demand obedience without supplying the rules for man to obey. These rules could be supplied to all men only through revelation because reason is too weak to be a sufficient guide. But a revelation requires a miracle; and consequently, miracles are as credible as is the fact of revelation. But if miracles are credible, then some proof of their actuality is at least possible.

The only human evidence that a miracle has occurred is the testimony of witnesses. An objection to this argument, Paley points out, had been made by David Hume. He had maintained that miracles would be contrary to experience and that therefore testimony of witnesses could not be credible. "Contrary to experience," Paley thinks, must mean either contrary to the experience of a particular witness, or contrary to the general or usual experience of witnesses. Miracles have never been thought to fall into either category. Thus, to say that they are "contrary to experience" is not to state an objection to their credibility but to state a fact about them. Hume, Paley argues, has confused miracles with occurrences due to natural law. An event in accord with natural law can recur time after time in the presence of a diversity of witnesses, but miracles by their very nature are unique or nearly so. Hume's criticism is not to the point. The laws of nature are laid down by an intelligent being. However, we are justified in expecting that these laws would be suspended on occasions of particular importance, but infrequently, and only in the presence of a few people. "In a word, once believe that there is a God, and miracles are not incredible." Here lies Hume's error, Paley writes, that he did not first assert the existence and power of God for, in consequence, he maintained that miracles would be incredible to the believer and the unbeliever alike.

Paley shows to his own satisfaction that Hume is wrong and that miracles can be substantiated by the testimony of reliable witnesses. His first argument in support of the truth of Christianity and of the genuineness of miracles is that those who attest genuine miracles would not have acted in the way that they acted, according to the Bible, unless the miracles were genuine. The very fact that Christianity became an established religion is testimony to the effectiveness of miracles and the authenticity of Christ. The exponents of Christianity at its beginnings fought the state and its established religion; they were punished by torture and death; but still Christianity prevailed. It demanded a morality which was contrary to that of the dissolute, pagan age; and yet it was accepted by the people. These paradoxical facts can be explained only by admitting the truth of Christianity and the genuineness of miracles.

Many pagan writers such as Tacitus, Suetonius, Juvenal, and Pliny the Younger testify to the spread of Christianity and to the tenacity with which its adherents believed. In addition to pagan sources, we have four histories of Jesus Christ, the Gospels of Matthew, Mark, Luke, and John. We have also the Acts of the Apostles and a collection of letters written by adherents to the faith.

From this material we learn that the faith had certain characteristics which distinguish it from all other religions. It is an exclusive religion in that it denied every article of heathen mythology, says Paley. It went to the common people and preached renunciation of the world around them and pursuance of the world to come. Containing a system of values that was alien to the pagan world, it exposed its adherents to ridicule and violence. Christianity separated church and state in a way that no pagan religion had. The Gospels foretell the harassment and persecution that the propagators of the new religion had to suffer. That its adher ents persisted in the face of all their difficulties is ample evidence of the strength of their belief in the truth of their preaching that Christ is the Son of God. Paley avers that one must either think of their belief as true or think of their account of it as a vast conspiracy entered into by pagans and Christians alike.

Paley now turns to the question of whether the New Testament gives an accurate account of the activities of Christ and the early Christians. Here again he finds corroborative evidence. There is no trace of an alternative story, although in ancient history we often find conflicting accounts of a single incident. Josephus in his *Antiquities* mentions John the Baptist; James, the brother of Jesus; and, though the authenticity of this passage has been questioned, the facts of Christ's own life. Tacitus, Suetonius, and Pliny, all anti-Christian writers, give us details of the story consistent with the New Testament.

If the Gospels are regarded as separate accounts by different historians, they substantiate one another; and thus the probability of their truth is higher than if there were only one account. We have the same reasons for believing that the Gospels were written by their reputed authors as we have that Caesar wrote his *Commentaries* or that Vergil wrote his *Aeneid*. The Gospels are quoted by Christian writers, beginning with those who were contemporary with the apostles. Paley cites Polycarp, the first bishop of Smyrna, who in a short letter includes forty clear allusions to the New Testament. This is evidence that he had the same books that we have and that he accepted them as the word of God. About the year 170, Hegesippus trav-

eled from Palestine to Rome, visiting churches on the way. He remarks that "in every succession, in every city, the same doctrine is taught . . . which the Lord teacheth." The earliest Christian writers refer to the Scriptures as we have them, and later writers prove that they never lost their authority as canonical books.

Justin Martyr, writing in the year 140, tells us that the Scriptures were read in the churches. In this early period when some living Christians must have spoken with the apostles, the Scriptures were accepted as the authentic word of Christ. Indeed, the high regard in which they were held explains their survival to the present day.

Paley selects, as the three most important controversies among the early Christians, the relation of the Old Testament to the New, the origin of evil, and the nature of Christ. Many opinions were advanced and many opinions were defended, but all the disputants agreed on the same Scriptural canon. Paley quotes Saint Augustine on the Donatists that they ". . . produce some proof from the Scriptures, whose authority is common to us both." The same can be said of quotations in anti-Christian writers such as Celsus, Porphyry, and the Emperor Julian.

In the first centuries of Christianity, as Paley admits, there was some controversy about certain parts of the canon of the New Testament. But, in general, questions of authenticity were raised only about minor Epistles.

To sum up this part of the *Evidences,* Paley writes that he has shown that the account of the life of Christ and the apostles which we have is true, and that the lives of the early exponents of Christianity prove it to be true as do the writings of the early Church Fathers. He believes that if we bring the same tests of authenticity to the Christian texts that we bring to ancient secular texts, then the proof that the Christian texts are genuine is stronger than that for any secular work.

Paley's next general point concerns the credibility of Biblical miracles. He throws doubt on a number accepted by the Roman Catholic Church and discusses the three miracles mentioned by David Hume in Chapter 10 of his *An Enquiry Concerning Human Understanding* (1748). In all of the cases that Paley cites, the alleged miracles will not stand under the tests that prove the Biblical miracles. These tests are that the miracle is unequivocal, that it overthrows established persuasions, that it is contrary to secular authority, that it is believed by many, and that this belief leads men "to a life of mortification, danger and sufferings."

In Part II of the *Evidences*, Paley begins his discussion of prophecy, of Christ's character, and of his resurrection. A prophecy is a statement describing an act before it takes place, before it can be foreseen by natural means. The coming of Christ was foretold in the Old Testament, for example, in Isaiah LII:13-LIII:12. These intentionally prophetic words are fulfilled by the life of Christ. Jesus himself made prophecies. He predicted the destruction of Jerusalem, an event which occurred thirty-six years after his death and under the circumstances he described.

The morality of the Gospels is an argument for their truth. Paley says that morality is not the main object of Christ's mission, which is the redemption of the world, but that it is a secondary object and that Christ put morality on a sound and effective basis. Christianity shifts the emphasis in ethics from acts to intent; and "a moral system which prohibits actions but leaves thoughts at liberty will be ineffectual and is therefore unwise." Christianity gave men a reason for doing their duty, assurance of the reality of the future existence of the soul. The Gospel omits as moral injunctions some of the qualities which other moral systems accept; for example, patriotism, friendship, and active courage. The Gospels stress certain virtues which had been overlooked but which possess high intrinsic value. These are passive courage, patience, humility, and the like. "No two things can be more different than the heroic and the Christian character," Paley points out. However, Christian virtues are those that contribute most to the happiness of society. This stress on happiness is in keeping with Paley's ethical theory as expressed in his *Principles of Moral and Political Philosophy* (1785). This moral doctrine, the Sermon on the Mount, and the Lord's Prayer are without equal or rival and could only have their source in an inspired religion, promulgated by someone with the character of Christ.

Although the four Gospels were written by different people, there is a consistency in the character of Christ which could only have come from acquaintance with the same real person. There is a similarity of phrases in all the Gospels. To give one example, Christ applies the name "Son of Man" to himself seventeen times in Matthew, twelve times in Mark, twenty-one times in Luke, and eleven times in John. The Jewish concept of the Messiah had been primarily political. A fabricated story of the Messiah would have made Jesus a political figure. But his message was in fact original and unique, almost the opposite of political.

Continuing his argument for the truth of the New Testament, Paley now turns to the references to historical facts that can be confirmed by independent accounts. These show that the Biblical narrative was composed by people living at the time and who were familiar with what was happening around them. To select one example from many, in Acts XVII:23 Paul, preaching in Athens, says, "For as I passed by, and beheld your devotions, I found an altar with this inscription, 'TO THE UNKNOWN GOD.' Whom therefore ye ignorantly worship, him declare I unto you." This inscription is referred to by Diogenes Laertius, Pausanius, Philostratus, and Lucian.

The New Testament canon contains thirteen letters ascribed to Saint Paul and an account of his ministry in the Acts of the Apostles. Careful examination had convinced Paley that these two accounts of Saint Paul were independent and in consequence guaranteed each other's authenticity. His elaborate proof of this point had appeared in the book, *Horae Paulinae, or the Truth of the Scripture History of Saint Paul*, published in 1790.

Every part of the New Testament affirms the fact of the Resurrection, and all of the early teachers of Christianity agreed upon it. Saint Matthew relates that the Jews accused the followers of Christ of stealing his body. Paley replies, "It is impossible our Lord's followers could believe that he was risen from the dead, if his corpse was lying before them." But the fact is that they did believe.

Paley argues that the wide and immediate spread of Christianity is evidence of the authenticity of the Scripture. A short time after Christ's ascension, there were about three thousand Christians (Acts II:41). A little time later this number had increased to five thousand (Acts IV:4). The next chapter of Acts records that multitudes of both men and women had joined the new religion. In Chapter VI the number has increased still more—all this within a year of the ascension and in one city, Jerusalem. Four years later there were churches throughout Judea, Galilee, and Samaria. About seven years after the ascension a great number of Gentiles were converted. Eighteen years later the faith had spread through Greece, the coast of Africa, Rome, and into rural Italy. Non-Christian authors attest this spread. Only thirteen years after the ascension, Nero accused the Christians in Rome of burning the city. Tacitus refers to them as a vast multitude. Clement of Alexander, writing one hundred and fifty years after Christ's ascension, said that Christianity had spread throughout the whole world, and he was seconded by Origen about thirty years later. In eighty more years the Roman Empire had become Christian under Constantine.

This spread of Christianity is remarkable, Paley asserts. We are not watching the spread of an idea or an opinion but of a new religion, a new way of life, of thinking, and of acting. If we compare the spread of Mohammedanism with that of Christianity, it is possible for us to better appreciate the marvelous success of early Chris-

568

tianity. Since the later history of Christianity is not marked by such rapidity of conversion, the early Church must have had some means of conviction that we lack. This means could only have been the constant occurrence of miracles.

In Part III of *Evidences of Christianity*, Paley considers some of the objections that might be made to his historical argument for the truth of Christianity. The first of these is the contention that the Gospels disagree among themselves. Paley's answer is that the disagreements can be accounted for by the fact that the same story is being told from different points of view. For example, Saint Matthew's account of Christ's appearance in Galilee differs from that in the other Gospels, but none of the other accounts contradicts his.

It is sometimes argued that the apostles held erroneous opinions, that they misquoted the Old Testament or used material out of context to make dubious points, that they believed in the imminence of the Day of Judgment. These objections can be met by distinguishing Christ's revelation from extraneous matter in the New Testament. In no case will inconsistencies be found in his religious doctrine, and the errors in extraneous matter can be accounted for as historical errors.

Christianity cannot be held responsible for every error in the Old Testament. It recognizes as divine the origin of the Jewish religion, but not of every institution that it gave rise to. Attacks on the New Testament through the Old, such as those of Voltaire and his followers, depend on the mistaken belief that every point in the Old Testament is binding on Christians—an absurd contention.

Paley next tries to account for the fact that Christianity has not been universally convincing. Some people have heard the Christian message and yet have rejected it. For people living in a Christian nation, the acceptance or rejection of Christianity depends on one question, "whether the miracles were actually wrought." Paley argues that "from acknowledging the miracles, we pass instantly to the acknowledgement of the whole." However, we find from reading the New Testament that some Jews could accept the fact of the miracles and yet not accept Christ as the Messiah. Many Jews fancied that the Messiah would have a political mission that Jesus did not fulfill and rejected him for this reason. To heathens Christianity comes with its demand that they change their whole way of life. Many men of arrogant character would rather ignore the Christian evidence than yield to its reform. God could have formed men so that the evidence of Christianity would have been immediately apparent to them; but he did not, and thus it is consistent with his plan that some for a variety of reasons might continue to reject the truth.

Although the evidence for Christianity may not convince every mind, there is sufficient to convince the reasonable mind. God has created a world whose order is beneficent, a nature marked by goodness both of design and effect. It is a nature which bears strong marks of its origin in God. Here is evidence, convincing to the fair mind. Suppose that the evidence were unavoidable; suppose that rain fell whenever it was needed or on the just alone. Men, then, would have no freedom of choice. But free will is an essential part of God's benevolent plan.

Too much evidence would be as harmful as too little; the fact is that God has supplied enough.

This argument of Paley's is an interesting use of the argument from design which he developed at length in his book, *Natural Theology, or Evidences of the Existence and Attributes of the Deity, Collected from the Appearances of Nature.* This book, its title explaining its content, was published in 1802, eight years after the *Evidences.* In it Paley argues that just as one could reason from examining a watch that it is a human contrivance, so by examining the nature of the world one can infer that it was created by God.

Paley next takes up the problem of the effects of Christianity. It has been argued that although Christianity advocates high moral standards, its actual practice has been detrimental to morality. Paley answers that Christianity could not be expected to eliminate every act of immorality. He believes that in the course of history one cannot help being conscious of a gradual improvement. Not everyone who cries, "Lord, Lord," is acting in his name. So not everyone who persecutes in the name of Christ is acting in the spirit of Christian morality.

In conclusion, Paley repeats that there is evidence to support the leading facts of Christianity. However, he warns us not to forget that Christianity is also a revelation and an act of belief.

THE VOCATION OF MAN

Author: Johann Gottlieb Fichte (1762-1814)
Type of work: Epistemology, ethics
First published: 1800

PRINCIPAL IDEAS ADVANCED

Each self appears to be a self-conscious, intelligent, willing element in a rigidly determined system which results from a fundamental forming power in nature.

But the world of experience (together with the causal laws which appear to govern it) is a construction by the self.

The self, therefore, is free and morally responsible.

By faith the self is assured of the existence of other selves; and by action man fulfills his moral obligation: to act, to do—this is man's vocation.

Johann Gottlieb Fichte is a transitional figure in the history of German philosophy. His philosophical impetus came from Kant, and his work began the modifications of Kant which ultimately resulted in the Absolute Idealism of Hegel. He had some trying experiences as a young man, finding himself in financial want during the latter days of his formal education and during the five years that passed between his engagement to his future wife and their marriage. He was forced to scrape along as a tutor during his early career, work that was not always satisfying and rewarding. But during these early years as a private tutor he came across the writings of Kant, and these provided him with background and inspiration for his career as a philosopher. In fact, his emergence from obscurity to national recognition almost overnight resulted from his being mistaken for Kant. A book of Fichte's on philosophy of religion was published without his name appearing as author. The literary world assumed the book had been written by Kant himself. Kant then made it known that the book was from Fichte's pen, not his own, and he also praised the work, thereby immediately making Fichte a national figure.

Fichte was attracted most strongly to the ethical views of Kant. He saw himself in his youth as a Spinozist, but he was not happy with Spinoza's rigid determinism. He had considerable passion and enthusiasm, and he apparently also had a need to feel that his acts were subject to ethical appraisal in that he himself was a free and responsible ethical agent. In the Spinozistic world, of course, all acts followed from their causal antecedents in a necessary way. This view comforted Spinoza, but it was too somber for Fichte. Kant's conviction, expressed in the *Critique of Practical Reason* (1788), that men are free ethical agents, opened a new philosophical possibility for Fichte. But even Kant was not strong enough for Fichte, since Kant did not begin his philosophy with the free ethical agent but with an account of the world of experience which the scientist investigates. Kant's metaphysics and epistemology only made it *possible* that there are free, ethically responsible selves; proof that such is indeed the case was not given. Since Fichte wanted a firmer base than this for his own philosophy, he introduced modifications which, although they seemed innocent enough at first, ultimately resulted in a noticeably different kind of idealism from that of Kant. Kant was moved by both the heavens above and the moral law within; Fichte was too much involved with the moral law within to pay much attention to the heavens.

On the epistemological side, Fichte dropped out the Kantian *ding an sich*. For Kant, the world of experience is a world constructed out of the sensuous material given in the manifold of intuition as ordered by the forms of space and time, a construction which is ordered by the categories. But the manifold of sense is caused by the un known and unknowable *ding an sich*, things in themselves. We can know only the world of our experience; we cannot know anything of the things *in themselves*. (Except, perhaps, that they cause the sensuous manifold out of which we produce the world of our experience.) Things in themselves, then, initiate a process which ultimately yields the world of our experience, but the world of experience, as we are able to know it, includes no things in themselves, and it is, furthermore, something which we ourselves unconsciously construct. We do not experience things in themselves; we cannot know them. It is a short step from this idea of things-in-themselves to saying that we do not need them and that they are therefore not real. This is the step Fichte made. The world of experience was for Fichte, as it was for Kant,

571

a construction made unconsciously by the self. But while Kant saw this construction as a kind of response to the stimulus of an unknown and unknowable thing in itself, Fichte did away with the thing in itself and merely said that the world of experience is an unconscious construction by the self.

Fichte, however, did offer a causal account to explain how the world of experience comes to be constructed, an account which results from his fundamentally ethical orientation. At the base of Fichte's system is the self as an ethical agent. The self, in becoming aware of itself, sees itself as a free ethical agent, and therefore posits the Ego. The self, or Ego, posits its own existence. It is as if Fichte were offering a variation of Descartes' "I think, therefore I am" argument; we might paraphrase Fichte's starting point as "I am obligated, therefore I am." It is not the knowledge problem with which Fichte begins, but the ethical problem. But after the Ego posits itself, it finds that there is need for an additional posit. One cannot be ethical in a vacuum; there must be an arena of action —one must be obligated to other persons. It is this circumstance that produces the world of experience. The Ego, having posited itself as ethical agent, also posits the Non-Ego as a world of experience (which includes other selves) in order that the Ego may have an arena in which to perform its tasks and discharge its obligations. The world of experience is not fundamental in its own right in Fichte's philosophy as it is in Kant's. Rather, the world of experience exists in order that a man can be ethical.

It is against this background that *The Vocation of Man* must be viewed. It is less technical than most of Fichte's writings, and it is addressed to the ordinary reader rather than to the professional philosopher. Fichte says in the preface that the book "ought to be intelligible to all readers who are able to understand a book at all." He therefore avoids the words "Ego" and "Non-Ego," as well as other technical terms which appear elsewhere in his writings. Nevertheless, the position is the same. This avoidance of technicality is one of the considerable merits of this book as contrasted with Fichte's *The Science of Knowledge.* The latter is liberally sprinkled with technical terminology and arguments which Fichte himself thought important and sound, but which recent philosophers have judged to be almost the opposite. *The Vocation of Man* is thus the most understandable and the most popular statement of Fichte's position.

The book has three divisions which are entitled "Doubt," "Knowledge," and "Faith." Roughly, they may be said to represent the Spinozistic, the Kantian, and the Fichtean positions, at least as Fichte understood them.

Book I, "Doubt," has the tone of Descartes' *Discourse on Method* (1637) or his *Meditations* (1641). Fichte writes in the first person and addresses himself to the problem of discovering what he can know about himself and the world in which he lives. He considers the information he gets from sense experience and draws conclusions about what the world is like. He accepts the view that there are independently real objects, each occupying a place in a system which is connected throughout by necessary causal relations. Each object or each event in nature is what it is and is what it must be. Nothing could possibly be other than it is. Removing even a single grain of sand, Fichte says, would change the entire structure of nature; all past and future history would be different.

Each man, including Fichte himself, is, of course, "a link in this chain of the rigid necessity of Nature." There is a "forming power" in nature, or perhaps better, behind or lying under the nature we observe, which gives rise to all the objects and events that make up the system of nature. Fichte himself was produced by the forming power. And as he becomes aware of this power, he says, he feels himself sometimes free, sometimes restrained, and sometimes compelled. Yet this is merely Fichte's awareness of how the underlying power operates in his own existence and consciousness. It explains his own consciousness, his awareness of himself as a discrete item in the system of nature. But this self-consciousness of the forming power as manifested in himself provides the ground from which he infers that the forming power also manifests itself in other objects in nature. There are varieties of individual selves, each resembling Fichte. Finally, the summation of the self-consciousnesses of these selves makes up the "complete consciousness of the universe." Fichte, as a self, then, is one element—a self-conscious, intelligent, willing element —in a rigidly determined system which is the result of a fundamental forming power in nature.

Yet this Spinozistic system of nature fails to satisfy Fichte. There is no freedom in it. If Fichte, together with all his acts, is merely a set of necessary consequences in a rigidly determined system, then he is not an ethical agent. Whatever he does, he necessarily has to do, and his conduct is therefore not subject to ethical evaluation or to praise and blame. This is the outcome of his reflection. But what he desires, on the other hand, is to know that he is free and ethically responsible. He wants to be, in some sense, himself the cause of his behavior, instead of feeling that his behavior is merely the effect of external causes.

The conclusion reached in Book I of *The Vocation of Man,* then, is this: Fichte has stated two possibilities: either he is merely one element in a rigidly determined system, or else he is a free moral agent. One view, he says, satisfies his heart, while the other destroys his own sense of worth. Which view should he adopt? This is the issue he must resolve, but he is left, at the end of Book I, in doubt.

Book II, "Knowledge," is a dialogue, not unlike Berkeley's *Three Dialogues Between Hylas and Philonous* (1713). Fichte writes that he is tormented by the doubt which issued from the first attack on the problem, and he awakens in the night, his sleep interrupted by the unresolved problem. A Spirit then comes to him to lead him out of doubt and into knowledge. The knowledge offered is subjective idealism, and Book II is as fine a statement of the position as is generally available.

The Spirit begins by questioning Fichte about how he knows objects in the external world, to which Fichte replies that he knows them by sensation. But the sensations are merely modifications of Fichte himself, the Spirit points out, and so Fichte has knowledge only of his own condition —not knowledge of the independently real, external world. "In all perception," the Spirit points out, "thou perceivest only thine own condition."

Fichte is not yet convinced, however. The argument moves on to consider the ordinary belief that sensations are caused by independently real, external objects. But such independent objects cannot be known by sense, for if Fichte has sensations, they are merely modifications of Fichte himself, not characteristics of independent objects. If there are external, independent objects, they cannot be known by sense, at any rate. They can only be known in virtue of applications of the principle of causality. But how can the principle of causality itself be justified? Certainly not by appealing to the fact that sense objects are causally connected, for that would be to argue in a circle. The argument would then go: I know there are independent objects because of the principle of causality, and I know the principle of causality because independent objects are examples of it. Such an argument fails to do the required job. The principle of causality must, therefore, be justified in another way. The alternative taken is that the causal principle is a statement of how men really do interpret experience; that is to say, the principle is contributed by the knower, not by the objects known. The principle is thus another modification of Fichte himself, not a feature of the world he believes is external to himself. If this is the case, however, the justification previously given for believing that there are independent objects which cause sensations collapses, and Fichte's world of experience loses all of its independent status. Kant's things in themselves are removed from the philosophical terrain since they are erroneously inferred from an inadequately formulated version of the causal principle. The world of experience is not a response to a set of stimuli from independently real things in themselves; instead, it is from beginning to end a projection of, or a construction out of, the self's own modifications. The "object" of knowledge is only a modification of the knower, and, as such, is (in Fichte's terminology) a "subject-objectivity." Subject and object merge into the subjectivity of the knower.

Such is the subjective idealism developed in the second book of *The Vocation of Man*. His subjective idealism was developed by Fichte in order to settle the doubt which marked the outcome of Book I. Fichte wanted to reject rigid determinism but needed a ground which would justify the rejection. He saw subjective idealism as providing such a ground. If the world of experience is constructed freely by the self, then the self need no longer labor under the onus of rigid determinism. The Spirit tells Fichte that he need "no longer tremble at a necessity which exists only in thine own thought; no longer fear to be crushed by things which are the product of thine own mind."

But other selves, the necessary additional elements which make the ethical situation plausible, do not have fundamental reality in the subjective idealism which is presented in Book II. The doubt of Book I is replaced by knowledge, yet this knowledge does not assure a fundamental reality for other selves. To get full reality for other selves Fichte must go still further; he must go beyond knowledge. If knowledge must be transcended, it is inadequate. This opinion is what lies behind the strikingly strange statement Fichte makes near the end of Book II, that "knowledge is not reality, just because it is knowledge." Knowledge does not disclose reality, according to Fichte. Its function differs from this commonly held view. Really, knowledge is less powerful. Fichte writes that "it destroys and annihilates error," but it "cannot give us truth, for in itself it is absolutely empty." Knowledge is not the avenue to reality. It must make way for a higher power; it must make way for faith, the subject of Book III. Faith assures the self that there are really other selves.

Book III opens with Fichte's dissatisfaction at the outcome of Book II. If all there is to the world is the construction Fichte himself unconsciously makes out of the modifications of his own self, then the world is empty. Yet this is all one can get from knowledge. But knowing does not exhaust human life; there is more to it than just that. "Not merely TO KNOW, but according to thy knowledge TO DO, is thy vocation," Fichte declares. And the "doing" here is clearly an *ethical* doing; it is striving, achieving, fulfilling obligations. Fichte regards himself as under an immediate and underived sense of obligation to act; this is his, it is all men's vocation. Yet if one is to *act*, there must be an arena in which to act; there must be an externally real world to act in and to act on. To justify such a world on the basis of knowledge is not possible. One must transcend knowledge and place his reliance in faith. Early in Book III Fichte resolves to do just this. He turns from knowledge to faith, from intellect to will, and thus he arrives at a real, external world which is populated with other selves related to Fichte and to one another by mutual ties of ethical obligation.

This discussion brings to a conclusion the strictly philosophical segment of *The Vocation of Man*. Fichte goes on for quite a time, however, into what is really more religion than philosophy. Once he has established his own existence and the existence of a world in which he can strive, he sermonizes about fulfilling his obligations. If Book I is similar to Descartes, and Book II is similar to Berkeley, it can be said with equal justice that Book III resembles a sermon enjoining strenuous ethical striving. Fichte tries to sound a clear call to plain living and high thinking, and his fervor, if not the details of his message, cannot fail to strike the reader.

Essentially the position he took is a mystical one. Somehow or other, according to his account, Fichte's own ethical will merged with the Universal Will, a kind of metaphysical ultimate that functioned as Fichte's God. He seemed to feel affinities with St. John's Gospel, but he insisted on de-anthropomorphizing God, and he thus lost what has always been at the center of the devotional life of the saints. Fichte had much of the emotion of the Christian mystic, but little sympathy for the object of Christian devotion. He replaced St. John's incarnate Word (Jesus Christ) with a pantheistic extension of his own ethical sensitivity. The result is quite a frightening projection of Fichte's own passions set up as God. The control exercised over the saint by his worship of a truly transcendent God is missing in Fichte; he remained an egocentric German romantic.

The Vocation of Man is a kind of guided tour beginning with Spinoza, leading through Kant, and ending in a subjective ethical idealism with deep romantic footings. It is an excellent introduction to the philosophy of nineteenth century Germany, and it shares with that general movement its characteristic strengths and weaknesses. The logic is often unsound, feeling often overrules reason, selfish concerns are sometimes read out as the Will of God. Yet the Romantics generally, and Fichte among them, certainly were ethically concerned; they were trying to spell out the moral ideal and to set men moving toward a better world.

However, while *The Vocation of Man* is a fine example of romantic idealism, it is at the same time, paradoxically, a work which foreshadows significant developments in philosophy of a sort opposed in spirit and method to much of what Fichte endorsed. In rejecting the *ding an sich* of Kant, in emphasizing the role of the self in the effort to know reality, in basing his philosophy on the self's declaration of its own existence, and particularly in urging the definitive importance of action, Fichte suggested the basic ideas of later pragmatic and existentialistic philosophies. Of course, Fichte remains a subjective idealist, and he never developed the pragmatic and existentialistic features of his thought; philosophically speaking, he remains a nineteenth century German idealist. But the resolution of the paradox of moral action—the paradox in which man as a free moral agent finds himself involved because of his presence in a causally determined universe—is similar to the resolution achieved by the existentialists, Christian and atheistic alike. To begin with the striving self, to regard man as what he can become as a result of his moral efforts, to take his moral "vocation" as prior to his essence—all of this is strikingly similar to the ideas later to be defended by such radically different philosophic personalities as Søren Kierkegaard and Jean-Paul Sartre.

It is the emphasis on will which makes a philosopher such as Fichte a transitional figure, borrowing from the old idealistic philosophy and suggesting the lines of development of the new pragmatic-existentialistic philosophy. A thinker who extends the principle of the will to the entire universe, deifying will and rejecting all else on its behalf, exhibits a metaphysical radicalism that is today's philosophical conservatism. But one who regards will, the striving of the stubbornly independent self, as definitive of self, of man, but not of all reality—such a one may very well oppose himself to the idealist while, at the same time, refusing to commit himself to realism; he remains pragmatic, testing not only his own nature, but the nature of everything else, in terms of action and consequences.

In arguing that the moral will involves the assumption of a moral law that admits no exceptions, and in regarding the Infinite Will as that law— "a Will that in itself is law"—Fichte shows that he is in the great tradition of idealistic philosophy; but in arguing that it is "the vocation of our species to unite itself into one single body" through the moral striving of the free self, and in suggesting that "All my thoughts must have a bearing on my action," Fichte passes from the metaphysical to the moral, and from moral to the pragmatic and existential. In his philosophy, then, the old and the new combine, neither one in a pure state but each aspect enlivened by the presence of the other.

LOGIC

Author: Georg Wilhelm Friedrich Hegel (1770-1831)
Type of work: Logic, metaphysics
First published: 1812–1816

PRINCIPAL IDEAS ADVANCED

What is real is rational, and what is rational is real.

Logic, which is a systematic creative process, has three stages: the abstract stage, the dialectical stage, and the speculative stage.

In the abstract stage terms of thought are considered separately; in the dialectical stage one realizes that for something to exist it must be, not separate, but in relation to others; and in the speculative stage one understands the unity of opposites in their opposition.

There are three subdivisions of logic: the Doctrine of Being, the Doctrine of Essence, and the Doctrine of Idea—by which being is known not only for itself and for another, but in-and-for itself.

Hegel is in the idealist tradition that evolved in Germany in the late eighteenth and the nineteenth centuries. Kant and the post-Kantians felt that the empirical philosophy of Hume, with its skeptical consequences, was inadequate; that mind through intuition, understanding, and reason could discover the grounds of experience either in an *a priori* categorical structure or in experience itself, if that experience were looked upon as primarily rational. Kant took the first alternative and argued that although events in themselves are unknowable (thus, keeping an element of Humean skepticism), as phenomena which we perceive they are constructed according to the categories of the understanding and the forms of intuition. As such they have their intelligible basis in mind, although there is an empirical content given from the external world. Hegel believed that the categories and forms are as much a part of reality as anything else, that the dichotomy between mind and its objects is a false

one, and, hence, that reality is as rational as thought itself. He expressed this view in his famous statement, "What is real (actual) is rational; what is rational is real (actual)."

How is thought to express the nature of reality? Philosophy from Hume through Kant (and earlier) held that the agreement of thought with reality is the criterion of truth. But Hegel claimed that thought alone brings to light the nature of things; this is the true sense of thought and reality being in agreement.

Like all idealists, Hegel maintained that since reality is known by means of ideas, and since the only thing that can agree with an idea is something like an idea, reality must be mind-like. In seeking to know the nature of things via reflection the individual concentrates upon the universal character of things. But thought so directed loses its individual character, for in proceeding in this way a person reflects as any other individual would who was in pursuit of the truth. Reflective thought thus loses its subjective aspect and becomes objective; thought and reality become one.

As is well known, Hegel held that thought expresses itself in triads, each of which usually has its own triadic structure, a structure which often has a triadic structure of its own. Thus, logic has three stages; its subdivisions are three, and each of these has a triadic structure. It is interesting that Hegel apparently did not use the expression, "thesis-antithesis-synthesis," which has been correctly used to characterize his position. At any rate the emphasis upon the development of thought in terms of a point of view, its negation, and the reconciliation of the two is reminiscent of the dialectical procedure of Socrates and Plato. Hegel, keenly aware of this resemblance, used the term "dialectical" for his own philosophy.

Hegel uses the word "logic" in somewhat the same sense that St. John spoke of "logos." That is, the word refers to a systematic creative process rather than to an analysis of language and argument. For him there are three stages of logic: (1) the abstract stage, or that of the understanding, (2) the dialectical stage, or that of negative reason, and (3) the speculative stage, or that of positive reason.

In the *abstract* stage every term or product of thought appears separate and distinct from one another. The understanding believes that they exist on their own account. What Hegel is saying is that on reflection the individual initially considers the elements of his thought—that is, whatever he is reflecting upon—as taken from the context of experience (or abstracted) and as having an existence of its own independent of anything else. This stage in

thinking occurs throughout the history of thought; so that in each stage of philosophical development, men begin by abstraction. Thus the first stage has its own abstract beginning, but that stage itself, when compared to the next stage, will be seen as abstract.

As an illustration, consider the philosophical view called "empiricism." In the abstract stage of empiricism only the immediately given, that which is presented here and now, has ultimate reality. These data, usually called "impressions," turn out to be bare "givens" devoid of relations and predicates and hidden in a skeptical mist, yet held to be separate and distinct and existing on their own account. But as we read the empiricist, he seems to pass from this "reality" about which he can say nothing, to his ideas about which he says everything that he can say. But his ideas belong to a different level of knowledge; memory and reflection are involved, and thus the empiricist passes from the stage of abstraction to that of dialectic wherein mediate thought is now the subject matter.

The *dialectical* stage is one in which the understanding views the elements in their separate and distinct capacity and as such recognizes that no more can be said of them. (In Hume's work this stage can be seen in his denial of necessary connection in experience and in his skepticism regarding reason and the senses.) There is a "positive" side to dialectic, however, in its indication that whatever is finite, when seen as separate and distinct and as free from all relations to others, ceases to exist. To be one without others is impossible. Existence involves a relationship between at least two entities.

The last stage of logic is the *specu-*

lative, in which reason is wholly positive. For Hegel, the contradictory character of certain metaphysical principles is finally reconciled. In the concept of causation it is argued that for every effect there must be a cause, and that every cause is an effect for which there is yet a cause. This concept is such that the notion of a first cause is untenable, since it too would have to have a cause. But, since causation which has no limits leaves any system of philosophy incomplete, such a concept is repugnant to reason. The same sort of analysis may be made with regard to time as a sequence of events which can have neither a beginning nor an end but still must have both. These paradoxical philosophical problems which Hegel argued had not been solved are reconciled by speculative reason which apprehends the unity of the categories in their very opposition.

As noted earlier, the subdivision of logic has three parts also. These are the Doctrine of Being, the Doctrine of Essence, and the Doctrine of Notion or Idea. Let us first indicate briefly the sense of each doctrine before discussing them in more detail. It should also be pointed out that in these doctrines Hegel intended the sort of development that we mentioned earlier; that is, implicit in the exposition of each is to be found the grounds for the next. Although each may be taken as a doctrine in itself, each would then be an abstraction (another instance of the first stage of logic) and hence untrue as well as incomplete.

In the doctrine of Being we are faced with an analysis of the given in its immediacy. In the history of philosophy there have been innumerable ideas concerning the nature of Being advanced by philosophers claiming to have identified the basic ontological stuff. The One of Parmenides, Aristotle's primary substance, and Hume's impressions are all candidates wearing the label of "Being." Under this doctrine Hegel analyzes the full meaning and consequences of the immediately given and indicates wherein he thinks it false.

The doctrine of Essence takes up where the failure of Being as a satisfactory philosophical doctrine occurs. If the immediate nature of things cannot reveal their essential characteristics to thought, if the search for them forces us to mediate knowledge—that is, to look for intervening features, to wonder how the given came to be as it is—then we can no longer consider the given in itself, but only in its relation to an other. (The other need not be an entity in addition to the immediately given; it may simply be the recognition that the given has limits, a recognition which Hegel believed takes us beyond the immediate.) It is here that the doctrine of Essence enters, for in order for the essential features of a thing to be known by thought, it must be seen in its relations to an other. The doctrine of Essence, however, is concerned in itself with an exclusive analysis of the mediate; hence it, too, is incomplete.

The doctrine of Notion or Idea is that in which the inadequacy of the previous two is reconciled. Being must be known not only for itself and for an other, but in-and-for itself. (We noted that "for an other" need not imply a second given, that it might indicate the limits of the given, its finiteness, and hence refer to itself. In its immediacy nothing can be said about Being.) But when seen in this way,

Being is understood as a Notion or Idea, and the truth of the given is grasped by reason.

In discussing the doctrine of Being, Hegel attempted to accomplish two things: to present the totality of Being and to abolish the immediacy of Being. There are three grades to Being which are necessary to our discussion of it: quality, quantity, and measure. Here we are concerned not only with the history of philosophic thought, but also with the evolution of thought itself.

In the bare beginnings of thought we have, as it were, an indeterminate something from which something determinate is to come; Hegel calls this bare beginning "Being." This impression of which there is not yet an idea cannot be talked about. It is taken as a here-now; in order to talk about it, think about it, predicate anything of it, we would have to take it out of the here-now and make of it something determinate, but as something determinate it would have a quality. A bare datum is without distinction, without time, and to say of it that it is here in a specified way is already to take it out of the immediate and determinate it.

The bare beginnings then pass to a stage in which the given is qualified, is made something; it is saved from not being anything. That it is something and not others, that it has a distinct character which differentiates it from others, subjects it to change and alteration. No longer indeterminable (Being itself) or nothing (not-Being), it stands between the two in the world of becoming.

Perhaps Hegel's discussion will be easier to follow if a philosophical illustration is considered. Impressions may be regarded as similar to indeterminable Being. Impressions are sensations below the level of consciousness, about which we can say nothing because of their fragmentary, fleeting nature; they are gone before they can be talked about. Consciousness arises concomitantly with the birth of ideas. From the fleeting impressions, mind selects and holds for observation—determines, as it were—one of these, and thus ideas are born. In the analysis of ideas, mind finds qualities, time, cause, change. So for Hegel, Being is quality—that determining characteristic without which the given would cease to be.

If we consider a determinate entity, we observe that it is what it is independently of any increase or decrease of its quantity, since a qualitative characteristic defines it. Quantity is both discrete and continuous, for it rests upon a unit construction which is exclusive and which is equalized. Numbers, for instance, fulfill this requirement and may be used to determine both discrete and continuous magnitudes. Yet quantity itself cannot be considered as an absolute notion, for as an object is decreased or diminished, eventually a quantitative difference will make a qualitative one.

Generally, Hegel views change of quantity in terms of absolutes; that is, he conceives of increase or decrease to the infinitely large or infinitesimally small; the one approaches the entire universe, the absolute; the other approaches nothing, not-Being. A house may be a house no matter how large or small; but "no matter how" must be taken relatively, a house cannot be nothing or everything. Hegel considers this an instance of the dialectical at work in quantity, making it what it is not; that is, quality.

Thus, we arrive at the third grade of Being, a quantified quality, or measure. In measure we attain the knowledge that everything is not immediate, but relative or mediate. For everything has its measure, its proper qualitative and quantitative range, as it were, beyond which it cannot remain the same. To know the proper measure of a thing, of Being, is to know its Essence.

Hegel thus accomplished what he set out to do; that is, he presented the totality of Being by analyzing its three grades, quality, quantity, and measure, and he abolished the immediacy of Being by showing that its Essence, whatever makes it what it is, rests not upon its immediately given appearance, but upon its measure, which is a mediate or relative concept demanding that the given be seen in terms of an other. This analysis depended not upon mere perception of the immediately given, but rather upon reflective thought. Thought and its object are progressing together. Being is the immediate appearance of reality; through reflection the philosopher has proceeded to the mediate aspect of reality, its Essence. Neither Being nor Essence is more real than the other; reflective thought has gone from one to the other to give us a greater insight into reality.

In the doctrine of Essence we also find three grades; identity, diversity and ground. We have seen that an analysis of a thing is such that it is conditioned by, and conditions, something else. In order to be determinate, not only are the boundaries of the thing needed, so that it can be defined as a finite object, but in its very definition it is distinguished from what it is not. Thus, not only is it related to itself in terms of its identity, but also it is related to others in terms of its difference.

Hegel's argument is reminiscent of Plato's analysis of the One and the Many in the *Parmenides*. Plato showed that the paradox of the One— that it is and yet that it is not—can be resolved if we introduce the concepts of identity, difference, and other than. The One is (identical with itself) and the One is not (others); that is, the One is other than or different from. Hegel's work contains a similar (although in many ways different) analysis. In order to understand the essence of a thing we must grasp the apparently contradictory characteristics of identity and diversity in some sort of unity. Unity is found in the concept of the ground. In order for a thing to be, that is, to exist, there must be more than its self-identity. For self-identity when not contrasted with what the self is not would once more lead to an indeterminate, abstract Being. On the other hand, there must be more than the mediating relations which indicate that there are others than the self. That is, we cannot concentrate only upon what the self is not. In the concept of a ground Hegel finds the proper meaning of Essence, for the thing is seen in its inward relations (its self-identity) *and* in its relations to an other also; but this is the concept of the ground.

The final sub-division in Hegel's logic is that of the doctrine of Notion or Idea. (Hegel's term in the German is "Begriff"—a term which, replete with difficulty, has the conflicting shades of meaning alluded to earlier and, as it were, all present at the same time.) The three grades of this doctrine are universal, particular, and individual.

Having presented two aspects of reality, its immediate and mediate appearance, its Being and its Essence, Hegel was ready to consider reality in its totality. The movement from Being to and through Essence is a dialectical process involving reflection, a process by which the nature of the given is revealed. The doctrine of Idea emphasizes for us that the only way in which we can discover the nature of a thing is to proceed through this kind of process. Hegel points out in the doctrine of Idea that in the process of development the thing is revealed to reflective thought in the aforementioned grades. In its bare beginnings as immediate Being, it is an indeterminate, undefina-

ble thing in itself—the very *ding an sich* that Kant spoke of. It is an undeveloped universal. From the immediately given, one proceeds to a consideration of the thing as a differentiated something. (Hegel refers to this as the particularizing phase of development.) Finally, in reflecting upon the further development of the thing into a Being which is both immediate and mediate, identical and different, universal and particular, the individual is realized. But to see the individual as it is, it must be understood in terms of its process from undifferentiated universal to differentiated particular to individual. If the parts are to be understood, we must understand the process as a whole. Thus, for Hegel, the process of knowledge and that which is known, Being, ultimately are one. Reality and rationality are interchangeable.

THE WORLD AS WILL AND IDEA

Author: Arthur Schopenhauer (1788-1860)
Type of work: Metaphysics
First published: 1818

PRINCIPAL IDEAS ADVANCED

The world is my idea—this is a truth for every man, since the world as it is known depends for its character and existence upon the mind that knows it.

By his understanding man forms the world of phenomena, and by his reason he achieves harmony in a world of suffering.

The entire world of phenomena, including the human body, is objectified will.

The will is a striving, yearning force which takes various forms according to its inclinations.

By losing oneself in objects, by knowing them as they are in themselves, one comes to know the will as Idea, as eternal form.

In his preface to the first edition of *The World as Will and Idea*, Scho-

penhauer states that his chief sources are Kant, Plato, and the *Upanishads*.

He does indeed blend these three into his own philosophical system, but he gives the whole his own philosophical interpretation.

The opening book is entitled, "The World As Idea," and in it Schopenhauer presents his modified scheme of Kant's "Copernican Revolution" in philosophy. Kant had held that the world of phenomena which we perceive is to be understood as a world which is made known to us through various features of our understanding. Events appear to us as in space and time; for Kant these were ultimately to be understood as forms of intuition or perception which, as it were, gave to events their spatial and temporal characteristics. In his famous analogy, the forms of intuition are the spectacles through which we view the world in its spatial and temporal aspects. In addition, we know the world in terms of traditional categories among which cause is a primary one; for Kant these categories are also of the understanding. Thus, the world of appearances is in the final analysis one in which undifferentiated "stuff" is formed in space and time and categorized by the understanding into the related events that science studies. But, to repeat, at bottom it is a mind-formed world. Schopenhauer accepted the Kantian view of the world, and rather brilliantly reduced the twelve categories of the *Critique of Pure Reason* to one, that of the principle of sufficient reason (causation). This principle, with its four-fold root in science, logic, morality, and metaphysics, formed the basis of Schopenhauer's analysis of the world of phenomena.

"The world is my idea" means, then, that the world of objects that I perceive depends for its existence as a perceived system of things upon the mind of consciousness that perceives it. Schopenhauer follows Kant in that he distinguishes mere sense impressions from perceptions (or ideas). Sense impressions are received by the mind from the external world; through the forms of space and time and the principle of sufficient reason, the understanding gives form to sensations, making them into ideas. Since it is the understanding which makes ideas what they are, perception is essentially intellectual. The subject or conscious mind becomes aware of object or body first through sense knowledge of its own body. Schopenhauer believed that the subject infers from sense effects immediately known to the self's body and to other bodies. It is in this way that the world of ideas is constructed. The world of ideas may be considered in two ways. The understanding itself contains the potentiality to form a world of perceptions. But it would remain dormant, as it were, did not the external world excite it. In this sense, then, there is an objective side to the possibility of knowing the world; the world must be capable of acting upon the subject to make perceptions possible. The subjective expression of the world, however, actually converts this possibility into a world of phenomena, for the law of causality springs from and is valid only for it. This means that the world of events as existing in space and time and causally related to one another is formed by the understanding. Additionally, as we noted, the sensibility of animal bodies makes possible the body as an immediate object for the subject.

Although the understanding makes

meaningful the world of objects (there would be but undifferentiated sensations otherwise), there is yet another aspect of mind which has an important role to play, and that is reason. Reason distinguishes man from other animals in that by its use he is able to deal in abstract ideas or concepts, and thus to plan, choose, and build—in general, to act prudently. If he merely perceived the world of objects through his understanding he would never be able to transcend and contemplate it. In the quiet life of contemplation, he rises above the hustle and bustle of everyday activities; he can achieve stoical calm, peace, and inner harmony in a world of pain and suffering.

In the second book, "The World as Will," Schopenhauer considers the reality behind the world of appearances, what had been for Kant unknowable, the thing-in-itself. It is traditional for philosophers to speculate upon the why of things, to try to understand what makes things what they are. For Schopenhauer, this question cannot be answered by searching within the world of phenomena, but only beyond that world. The key is to be found in the subject himself who, as an individual, has knowledge of the external world rooted in the experience of his body—object to his self. Body is given to the individual in two ways. As we have seen, it is given (1) as an idea; an object among objects subject to the law of objects, that is, to the law of cause and effect. It is also given (2) as an act of will; when the subject wills, the apparent result is a movement of the body. This aspect of Schopenhauer's philosophy can also be found in Kant. Kant had held that for morality to be possible, the will must be autonomous and not subject to the same laws as phenomena. Otherwise our actions would be causally explainable, and hence no more morally responsible than a rolling stone's action. As autonomous, the will is part of the noumenal world of things in themselves and is thus free. The result of willing, for Kant, was a physical movement subject to scientific laws, part of the world of phenomena. The cause of the movement was not itself part of the world of phenomena; hence, not a cause in the scientific sense, it was thus morally free.

We must understand that the term "cause" has a curious history in philosophical works. There is the sense of cause which we might term the creative sense, that which brings an event into being and keeps it existing. In this sense the word is often used to refer to something outside the world of events (usually a being such as God) regarded as responsible for the creation and continuity of that world. But there is another sense of "cause" which while not original with David Hume has since his time been in more popular use among many philosophers. That is cause as a constant conjunction of events within the world of phenomena; what there might be outside that world as a cause of it is held to be subject not to knowledge, but perhaps to faith. It is a religious sense of cause. When Kant refers to the autonomous action of the will, he refers to an action that is not part of the world of events, yet one which has a consequence there—a bodily movement. The sequence of bodily movements is a sequence of events (or ideas) that is subject to causal analysis in the second sense mentioned above; but since the will is

584

not part of the world of phenomena its activities are free from scientific analysis, and thus responsible. It is this sense of the Kantian notion of will that Schopenhauer accepts.

Since an act of will is known as a movement of body which is itself an idea, Schopenhauer regards the body as objectified will. He states also that the entire world of ideas, the realm of phenomena, is but a world of objectified will. For Schopenhauer, the world of noumena is nothing but a world of will, that which is "beyond" the world of events, yet its very ground. We also have knowledge of the noumenal world; there is a unique relationship between the subject and his body in which he is aware of his "noumenal" willing and the resulting physical movements. It is possible to look upon the entire world of events, including other subjects known only as ideas, as one's own world. But Schopenhauer would not be satisfied with solipsism.

In holding that body is but objectified will, Schopenhauer argues that the various parts of the body—for example, teeth, throat, and bowels—are but expressions of will, in this case of hunger. For Schopenhauer, there is a force in all things which makes them what they are: the will. Recall, however, that phenomenally this force is not perceived; since all we know are events subject to the principle of sufficient reason, the will here is groundless. But in self-consciousness the will is not hidden but is known directly, and in this consciousness we are also aware of our freedom. We are aware of an activity that cannot itself be part of the world of events that follows from that activity.

Although it has been customary in the history of philosophy for philosophers to raise questions concerning the purpose or end of existence, of creation, Schopenhauer claims that such questions are groundless. In effect they refer to the activity of the will; but the will has no purpose. It moves without cause, has no goal; it is desire itself, striving, yearning, wanting without rhyme or reason.

The third book of Schopenhauer's work is also entitled, "The World as Idea," but "idea" is now seen as a product of reason rather than as a perceptual event. It is here that Plato's concept of the idea or form is used by Schopenhauer, and his prime purpose is to develop his theory of art by means of it. He begins by pointing out that the will is objectified not only in the many particulars that we come to know as events in space and time, subject to change and, hence, explainable under the principle of sufficient reason; but it also manifests itself in universals, which are immutable and thus not susceptible to causal analysis. Schopenhauer holds that the will as universal presents us with a direct objectification, a Platonic form, whereas as a particular it is indirect.

How is the individual to know these direct objectifications? He may gain knowledge of them by transcending the world of events, of space and time and causality, and looking at things as they are in themselves. He does so by losing himself in the object, by giving up his own subjectivity and becoming one with that which he perceives. In such a state, Schopenhauer holds, the individual becomes the pure will-less, painless, timeless subject of knowledge. He becomes a knower of ideas or forms, and not of mere particulars; the object to him is now the

Idea, the form, of the species. This seems to be something like the sort of knowledge that has been attributed to the mystic, and, no doubt, the influence of the Far East upon Schopenhauer can be seen here also; but he likens the apprehension of forms to art. The artist repeats or reproduces Ideas grasped through pure contemplation; knowledge of the Ideas is the one source of art and its aim is the communication of this knowledge. With this in mind we can see that Schopenhauer's definition of "art" fits closely with his views. It is the way of knowing things independently of the principle of sufficient reason. The man of genius is he who by intuition and imagination most completely frees himself from the world of events to grasp the eternal present within it.

Schopenhauer writes that the aesthetic mode of contemplation involves two features: (1) the object known as a Platonic idea or form and (2) the knowing person considered not as an individual in the ordinary sense, but as a pure, will-less subject of knowledge. When the knower gives up the four-fold principle of sufficient reason as a way of knowing things and assumes the aesthetic mode of contemplation, he derives a peculiar pleasure from that mode in varying degrees depending upon the aesthetic object.

Ordinarily it is difficult and, for most persons, impossible, to escape from the world of desires and wants, the world which gives rise to our willing and which can never be satisfied. Our wants are without satiation; thus, suffering, frustration, and a sense of deficiency are ever-present to us. But if by some external cause or inner disposition we are raised above the cares of the daily world, our knowledge is freed from the directives of will and the temporal aspects of events, and we can achieve that transcendent state of peace, the painless state that separates the world of forms from that of suffering. This is the state of pure contemplation that the great Greek philosophers spoke of.

The artist who has attained this state and then represents it to us in his works allows us to escape the vicissitudes of life and to contemplate the world of forms free from the machinations of the will. His work of art is a means by which we can attain his heights. Nature, too, in certain circumstances, can present us with her objects in such a way that we transcend the world about us and enter into the realm of forms. But the slightest wavering of attention on our part once more returns us to the world of phenomena; we leave contemplation for desire. Aesthetic enjoyment can also be obtained in the remembrance of things past. Schopenhauer points out that the individual in contemplating his memories finds them freed from the immediate tinges of suffering and pain that events often have. Generally speaking, aesthetic pleasure arises whenever we are able to rise above the wants of the moment and to contemplate things in themselves as no longer subject to the principle of sufficient reason; pleasure arises from the opposition to will; it is the delight that comes from perceptive knowledge. When a contemplated object takes on the Idea of its species, we hold it to be a beauty. The nineteenth century aestheticians were concerned with the sublime also; Schopenhauer sees it in the exaltation which arises when one forcibly and consciously breaks away from the world of events and enters the world of forms. The object transfigured in this contemplative act yet carries an aura of its existence as an event created by will. As such it is hostile to the perceiver, yet in being "made" into a form it is the object of pleasure and beauty. If the hostility crowds out the beauty, then the sublime leaves. When the sublime is present we recognize our own insignificance alongside that which we perceive, yet, Schopenhauer feels, we also recognize the dependence of the object upon us as one of our ideas. We are both humble and monumental in its presence.

Tragedy is the summit of poetical art; it presents the terrible side of life, the pain and evil, the want and suffering. We see in nature the all-consuming war of will with itself. When we learn of this inner struggle through tragedy, we are no longer deceived by the phenomena about us. The ego which is so involved in the world of events perishes with that world as we see it for what it is. The motives which keep the will striving are gone; they are replaced by knowledge of the world. This knowledge produces a quieting effect upon the will so that resignation takes place, not a surrender merely of the things of life, but of the very will to live. (This is not to be confused with a "desire" to commit suicide, which is a definite, if ill-advised, act of a will tormented by the world of events; rather, it is a renunciation of all desire as one becomes one with the eternal.)

The last book is also entitled, like the second, "The World as Will," but in the second aspect of will Schopenhauer further examines the renunciation of the will to live. In this particular book, Schopenhauer emphasizes the Eastern religious and philosophical view of denial and renunciation. He also concentrates on the idea of life as tragic. It is interesting that Schopenhauer develops a theory of the act of generation as an assertion of the will to live. His discussion is reminiscent of Freud's account of the libido as a general drive manifesting itself throughout mankind and accounting for much, if not all, of human behavior. Freud is supposed to have been shown the passages in Schopenhauer which were similar to his. He claimed not to have read Schopenhauer, but he did acknowledge the similarity of the views.

Schopenhauer believed that in each phenomenal object the will itself is present fully, in the sense that the object is the reification of the will. But the will in its noumenal nature is most real; in inner consciousness the individual, as we noted, is directly aware of the will. The individual within the world of events, aware of pure will in himself, desires everything for himself. Schopenhauer believed that in this way selfishness arises. Recall that each has within himself, for himself, the entire world of phenomena as ideas as well as the world as will. Recall, too, that all other selves are known by the individual as his own ideas—thus he hopes to have all, to control all. His death ends all for him, although while he lives he seeks the world for himself. In this eternal war with one another men deserve the fate which the world as will has for them: a life of tragedy, of want, of pain and suffering. Ultimately, also, the will, in trying to express itself at the expense of others, punishes itself.

As we saw, only those who can rise above their principle of individuation,

587

above the world of cause and effect, who can see the world as one of woe and suffering, can triumph over it. Once one has seen the world for what it is, there is no need to go on willing and striving. One renounces the world of ideas and of will; knowledge quiets the will. This freedom found outside the world of necessity is akin to grace; therein, believed Schopenhauer, lies one's salvation.

COURSE ON THE POSITIVE PHILOSOPHY

Author: Auguste Comte (1798-1857)
Type of work: Social philosophy
First published: 1830-1842

PRINCIPAL IDEAS ADVANCED

Social dynamics is the science of history; the positive philosophy provides a law of three stages to make historical facts significant.

In the theological stage of a society, men invent gods and arrange society accordingly: the priests rule; in the metaphysical stage, intellect deifies itself, authority is challenged, religion becomes sectarian, and individuals abandon their social responsibilities; in the positive stage, the positive sciences provide certainties which make order possible, inspire a moral regeneration, and make social concerns primary for all.

Sociology completes the body of philosophy by tracing out the unity to be found in the various sciences.

The natural sciences, like the societies of men, and like men themselves, have passed through the theological, metaphysical, and positive stages.

The various sciences can be arranged according to their degree of complexity and their dependence on others; beginning with the most general (after mathematics, which is not a natural science), the order is: astronomy, physics, chemistry, biology, physiology, and sociology.

Comte had two distinct aims in writing *Course on the Positive Philosophy.* The first and "special" aim was to put the study of society on a positive foundation, comparable to that at which one by one the natural sciences had arrived. The second and "general" aim was to review the natural sciences, with a view to showing that they are not independent of one another but, as it were, "all branches from the same trunk." As we shall see, the two aims are inseparable.

Comte divided the study of society—sociology or "social physics," as he called it—into two parts, following a distinction which he believed runs through all the sciences: social statics, and social dynamics. The former seems not to have interested him especially. He maintained that in its broader aspects, at least, it was deducible from human physiology, which demands that men live in society, that they form families, and that they obey political authorities. On these grounds, he held that woman is inferior to man and bound to subservience, and that some men and races are constitutionally suited to obey and others to command.

But Comte dealt with these matters only in passing. His interest was not so much in the generic traits which are found in all human societies, as in the laws which govern the transition of a society from one condition to another. This is what he intended by the term "social dynamics." His work was to be nothing less than a science of history. History, said Comte, had compiled many facts but had been unable to contribute anything of importance to understanding man's condition because, like the data of meteorology, its facts needed a law to become significant. Comte thought that he had discovered that law; he called it the "law of the three stages."

In the first, or *theological stage*, according to this law, man invents gods in order to explain the world to himself, and in so doing he creates the conditions which make possible the specifically human kind of society; for belief in gods gives him some purpose in living beyond the satisfaction of mere bodily wants. At first, the gods are merely tribal fetishes, which do not demand much by way of social organization. But as these are exchanged for astral deities, and eventually for a single god, discipline and order are imposed upon the whole community. Authority characteristically comes to be vested in a priesthood. But a military caste arises, with responsibility for defense, and agricultural labor becomes

the foundation of the economy. From the sociological point of view, it is a happy, prosperous condition. A common faith and goal give coherence and strength to the community.

But there is a serpent in the garden. The intellectual turn of mind which made man invent the gods is never content with its creation. Turning critical, it denatures divinity into a set of first principles and eternal essences. Comte called this the *metaphysical stage*. Intellect practically deifies itself, owning allegiance only to truths of reason. Not only theological beliefs, but theological institutions come under criticism. The principle of authority is challenged, and notions of equality and popular sovereignty are offered in its place. As the new attitude permeates the masses, individuals abandon their social responsibilities, and compete with one another to improve their private conditions. Religion becomes sectarian; peasants drift to the cities; military might declines. Sociologically, it is a negative moment, a time of dissolution and decay.

According to Comte, these two stages have appeared again and again in the history of the world, and hitherto there has been no way of saving a society which has passed into the metaphysical stage. But modern Western civilization has the means of breaking out of the old cycle. The negative moment, represented in European history by the Reformation, the Renaissance, and the Enlightenment, has marked the end of a Catholic-dominated culture, and of itself promises nothing but moral and political chaos. Coincident with the rise of libertarian thinking and laissez faire economics and politics, however, the positive sciences have

589

also made great gains. It is the assured results of these latter which, according to Comte, provide a remedy for metaphysics and make it possible for the mind of man to move forward into a new *positive stage*. Like the theological stage, it will be a time when men will know what to believe; only, this time, there will be no illusion about it—and no chance that the certainties will be overthrown. The new certainties will make possible a reorganization of society, provide a rational system of command, and inspire complete devotion in the hearts of the people. A moral regeneration will make coercive government almost a superfluity. Such regulation of life as the new society requires will rest with a managerial class arising out of industry, while ultimate authority will reside in a new spiritual class, the positive philosophers. Meanwhile, men will have cast away private ambition and personal rivalry, and will have learned to consider all functions as social. They will see the "public utility in the humblest office of coöperation, no less truly than in the loftiest function of government," and will feel "as the soldier feels in the discharge of his humblest duty, the dignity of public service, and the honor of a share in the action of the general economy."

Comte devoted hundreds of pages to the analysis of Western history along the lines indicated. His work is, from one point of view, a speculative undertaking. He considered that he had put history on an indisputably scientific foundation. He wrote: "It certainly appears to me that the whole course of human history affords so decisive a verification of my theory of evolution that no essential law of natural philosophy is more fully demonstrated.

From the earliest beginnings of civilization to the present state of the most advanced nations, this theory has explained, consistently and dispassionately, the character of all the great phases of humanity; the participation of each in the perdurable common development, and their precise filiation; so as to introduce perfect unity and rigorous continuity into this vast spectacle which otherwise appears desultory and confused. A law which fulfils such conditions must be regarded as no philosophical pastime, but as the abstract expression of the general reality."

But from another point of view, this Herculean labor was a blueprint for a Brave New World. A youthful disciple of the utopian socialist, Claude Saint-Simon (1760-1825), Comte had as his ultimate purpose in developing the positive philosophy the moral and spiritual regeneration of the West. He believed that by providing an infallible system of truth he was doing the one thing which could bring this regeneration to pass.

With this view of the new science of social dynamics before us, we turn to consider the second aspect of Comte's philosophy, namely, his review of the natural sciences. All the sciences, with the exception of sociology, had already achieved the status of positive knowledge in Comte's time, but their true significance could not be discerned without sociology because, according to Comte, it was a function of the positivist philosopher (himself a sociologist) to trace out the unities and analogies of the sciences. Thus, sociology completes the body of philosophy, not merely as being the last of the sciences, but as "showing that the various sciences are branches from a single trunk; and thereby giving a character of unity to the variety of special studies that are now scattered abroad in a fatal dispersion." Had man been endowed with an angelic intelligence, all the sciences would have sprung into being at the same time, and their hierarchical relation would be evident in an *a priori* fashion. But because man has slowly and painfully arrived at the truth, the only intelligible account of the relationship between the sciences is the empirical one which traces their development. Thus, "all scientific speculations whatever, in as far as they are human labors, must necessarily be subordinated to the true general theory of human evolution," which, being the proper study of sociology, is the warrant for "the legitimate general intervention of true social science in all possible classes of human speculation."

As we have seen, Comte's science of history declared that the social evolution of man is a function of his intellectual evolution and that, broadly speaking, the knowledge of man has passed through three states—theological, metaphysical, and positive. It is not surprising, therefore, that the same cycle governs the development of particular sciences as governs the evolution of knowledge as a whole.

According to Comte, this development is clear on empirical grounds. Every science which has reached the positive state bears the marks of having passed through the others. Astronomy, for example, became truly scientific in Hellenistic times, when observations of the heavens were first coördinated by means of geometrical principles. But myth and astrology are reminders of times when celestial phenomena were explained in terms, first of divine will, and afterwards of impersonal fate. In fact, the more primitive beliefs linger on among less progressive parts of the population; and, according to Comte, they are recapitulated in the development of the mind of each civilized man, who in childhood is a theologian, in youth a metaphysician, and in manhood a natural philosopher.

But Comte held that the empirical account could be supported by reflection, and that it is *a priori* evident (*post factum*) that knowledge must pass through three stages. With Francis Bacon, he held it as a fundamental principle that mere facts are not sufficient to arrive at truth—the mind must form theories; but because intelligent theories cannot be formed without facts, one seems to be confronted with a vicious circle. At least, according to Comte, here is the reason why primitive man did not arrive at scientific truth. Caught, as it were, "between the necessity of observing facts in order to form a theory, and having a theory in order to observe facts, the human mind would have been entangled in a vicious circle but for the natural opening afforded by theological conceptions." Granted that primitive man's speculations owed more to imagination than to experience and reason —what matters is that, by hypothesizing about the gods, he was launched on the intellectual enterprise which could not have been started in any other way. Similarly, according to Comte, the metaphysical stage is necessary before the positive stage can be reached: its abstract and impersonal conceptions prepare the mind for positive knowledge, which is too radically different from theological beliefs for man to accept it immediately.

Comte maintained that different kinds of knowledge have passed through the three stages at different paces. Astronomy became a science before terrestrial physics, physics before chemistry, chemistry before biology, and biology before sociology. According to Comte, it had to be this way. Not only is physics simpler than sociology—it is more general, and hence more fundamental. Here we are introduced to Comte's celebrated hierarchy of the sciences and to the principle upon which it was based. The principle is essentially that of nominalistic logic, according to which the extension of a term is inversely proportional to its intension. Physics has greater extension than biology; that is, more objects of different kinds come under its laws, including both living and non-living bodies. In Comte's language, physics is more general than biology. Conversely, biology has greater intension than physics; that is, although its laws apply to objects of only one kind, they comprehend more of their aspects. In Comte's language, biology is more complex than physics.

On this principle, Comte arranged the sciences in hierarchical order. Mathematics he placed first, because it is the most general, simple, and independent of all, and serves as the basis of all others. But because of its abstract character, Comte did not regard mathematics as a "natural science." Natural sciences he divided into inorganic and organic. That the latter are more complex than the former is self-evident, inasmuch as organization is a complexity. So, within the two divisions, on the inorganic level, astronomy is less complex than physics, and physics than chemistry; likewise, on the organic level, physiology, which relates to individuals, is less complex than sociology, which relates to aggregates. It

may be observed that Comte did not leave a place for psychology in the hierarchy, a notable omission in view of the fact that J. S. Mill, in his *System of Logic* (1843), was to maintain that associationist psychology is as fundamental to all the human sciences as mechanics is to all the physical sciences. Comte argued, however, that because psychology proceeds by the method of introspection and assumes the actuality of the self, mental states, ideas, and the like, it is a relic of the metaphysical stage. Its counterpart in the positive system is cerebral physiology, which had newly come to the fore. In fact, Comte held that it was the discovery of the physiology of the brain which brought biology to perfection and made possible for the first time the new science of sociology.

Comte said of his classification of the sciences that, although it is artificial, it is not arbitrary. It is artificial because it marks out boundaries where none exist in the actual sciences. One of Comte's deepest concerns was to preserve the unity and integrity of man's intellectual pursuit, which he considered threatened to the point of sterility by increasing specialization in his day. He favored the development of a new kind of scientific worker whose task it would be to formulate the general principles of the respective sciences and to connect new discoveries with known truth. By making it possible to keep the whole structure of knowledge in view, these scientific workers would lay a new foundation for education. At the same time they would further research by serving as consultants; for, according to Comte, investigators are often handicapped by their ignorance of what is well known by specialists in other fields.

But while Comte was eager to preserve the unity of knowledge, he maintained that the special sciences are essentially autonomous. Therefore, he insisted that the classification was not arbitrary, and he opposed the view that the sciences can eventually be reduced to one master science and all phenomena explained by a unitary law. "Our intellectual resources," he said, "are too narrow, and the universe too complex, to leave any hope that it will ever be in our power to carry scientific perfection to its last degree of simplicity." The only real unity to science, he said, is that of the positive method, which spurns the idea of asking questions about origins and ends (theological questions) or about essences and causes (metaphysical questions), and settles down to the business of analyzing the circumstances of phenomena and connecting them by the relations of succession and resemblance. It is this method which has led to the division of knowledge into several specialties, so that, in delineating the divisions, positive philosophy was following the requirements of the method itself.

Comte's book derives much of its bulk from the detailed account he gives of all the natural sciences at that time. But he said that it was not his aim to teach the sciences as such: to do so would be endless and would demand more knowledge than one person could hope to muster. In any case, it would miss the point, which was "only to consider each fundamental science in its relation to the whole positive system, and the spirit which characterizes it." He said that his book was a course, not in positive science, but in positive philosophy. In his view, however, positive philosophy was "a whole, solid and entire." From the time of Francis Bacon it had been slowly forming until, in the nineteenth century, only one major gap remained—social physics—which was about to be filled.

THE PHILOSOPHY OF HISTORY

Author: Georg Wilhelm Friedrich Hegel (1770-1831)
Type of work: Philosophy of history, metaphysics
First published: 1832

PRINCIPAL IDEAS ADVANCED

Spirit is freedom and self-consciousness acting to realize its own potentiality.

The real is the rational, and the rational is the real; Idea or Reason is the formative principle of all reality.

The goal of history is the liberation of Spirit from its confinement in Nature in order that Spirit might be reunited with its essence as Idea.

The Spirit could not realize its reunion with Idea were it not for the force of Will, as derived from human passions.

The individual as individual is unimportant; only the historically decisive actor, the hero, makes a significant difference in history; but whether a man be a

593

conventional citizen, a courageous person, a hero, or a victim, he is nothing but the Spirit's instrument.

The embodiment of the Spirit's freedom is the State; the State is the concrete unity of freedom and passion.

History is understood by Hegel as the movement of Spirit toward the attainment of self-consciousness. To comprehend world history as the progress of the consciousness of Spirit it is necessary to arrive at a conceptual grasp of the three constitutive elements which structure historical movement: (1) The Idea of Spirit, (2) the means of actualization, and (3) the State as the final and perfect embodiment of Spirit. Hegel begins his discussion with a formulation of the abstract characteristics of the Idea of Spirit. The peculiar quality of Spirit is grasped when it is seen in contrast with its opposite—matter. The essence of matter is gravity, which means that it has its center outside itself and thus is dependent upon a central point toward which it tends. The essence of Spirit is freedom, which designates a self-contained existence.

Another characteristic of Spirit is self-consciousness. It is of the essence of Spirit to know itself or be conscious of itself. The self-contained existence of Spirit as freedom is thus self-consciousness. Now in the phenomenon of self-consciousness two modes must be distinguished—the fact *that I know* and *what I know*. There is the self which is conscious, and there is also the self of which the self is conscious. Insofar as in self-consciousness the self is conscious of itself, these two modes are merged into a unity. The self has itself within itself. Self-consciousness is a unity, but it is a unity which expresses a reduplication. I can know myself, I can love myself, and I can hate myself. Spirit as freedom is self-reflexive or self-reduplicative. As it is the nature of Spirit to know itself, so also it is the nature of Spirit to actualize itself. Spirit forever drives beyond that which it is *potentially* to make itself what it can become *actually*. Spirit yearns for actualization. "The very essence of Spirit is activity; it realizes its potentiality—makes itself its own deed, its own work—and thus it becomes an object to itself; contemplates itself as an objective existence."

Hegel's definition of Spirit must be understood in its context of a rational philosophy which proclaims an identification of reason and reality. In the Hegelian system the laws of logic are at the same time the laws of being. This undergirding principle of Hegel's philosophy was first formulated in his *Phenomenology of Spirit* (1807), and he expressed it thus: the real is the rational and the rational is the real. This principle also governs his interpretation of history. In *The Philosophy of History* he writes: "The only Thought which Philosophy brings with it to the contemplation of History, is the simple conception of *Reason;* that Reason is the Sovereign of the World; that the history of the world, therefore, presents us with a rational process. . . . That this 'Idea' or 'Reason' is the *True,* the *Eternal,* the absolutely *powerful* essence; that it reveals itself in the World, and that in that World nothing else is revealed but this and its honor and glory—is the thesis which, as we have said, has been proved in Philosophy, and is here regarded as demonstrated." Idea or Reason thus constitutes the primary formative principle in Hegel's philosophical system. This Idea expresses itself first in Nature but also in Spirit. The triadic unity of Idea, Nature, and Spirit thus defines the whole of Hegel's system. Expressed in terms of his dialectical logic, Idea is the thesis, Nature the antithesis, and Spirit the synthesis. Nature exhibits the emergence of the Idea in space; Spirit exhibits the actualization of the Idea in time and history. The primary category for Nature is space. The primary category for Spirit is time. Through the workings of Spirit the Idea is wrested from its localization in space and becomes temporized and historicized. Both Nature and Spirit are subject to a development under the impetus of the Idea; but the development in Nature is that of a quiet and subdued unfolding, whereas Spirit expresses a dynamic self-realization in which conflict and alienation are integral movements. "Thus Spirit is at war with itself; it has to overcome itself as its most formidable obstacle. That development which in the sphere of Nature is a peaceful growth, is in that of Spirit, a severe, a mighty conflict with itself. What Spirit really strives for is the realization of its Ideal being; but in doing so, it hides that goal from its own vision, and is proud and well satisfied in this alienation from it." Spirit is alienated from the Idea in its subjugation or bondage to Nature, but in the process of self-realization through which it attains self-consciousness Spirit becomes sovereign over Nature, subordinates Nature to its purposes, and thus drives to a reconciliation of itself with the Idea. It is in the historical consciousness of the Hebrew people, as we shall see later,

that Hegel finds the first liberation of Spirit from Nature. In the Hebrew doctrine of creation Nature is understood as a creature and a servant, and Spirit appears as the creator and the master.

The aim or goal of history is the actualization of Spirit as freedom, wresting itself from its confinement in Nature, and seeking reunion with itself as Idea. This aim or goal defines at the same time God's purpose for the world. Hegel's philosophy of history thus takes on the function of a theodicy—a justification of the ways of God. God's providential activity in the world is the self-realization of Spirit. Hegel converts the truths of religious myth into the truths of philosophical categories and seeks to establish a conceptual justification for the suffering and sacrifices which occur in the course of world history. "Itself is its own object of attainment, and the sole aim of Spirit. This result it is, at which the process of the World's History has been continually aiming; and to which the sacrifices that have ever and anon been laid on the vast altar of the earth, throughout the long lapse of ages, have been offered. This is the only aim that sees itself realized and fulfilled; the only pole of repose amid the ceaseless change of events and conditions, and the sole efficient principle that pervades them. This final aim is God's purpose with the world; but God is the absolutely perfect Being, and can, therefore, will nothing other than himself—his own Will. The Nature of His Will—that is, His Nature itself— is what we here call the Idea of Freedom; translating the language of Religion into that of Thought."

The second constitutive element of the world-historical process is that of

595

the means of actualization. The Idea of Spirit, as the aim or goal of history, as such is merely general and abstract. It resides in thought as a potentiality which has not yet passed over into existence. We must thus introduce a second element—actualization. The source of power which drives Spirit from its potential being into actuality is Will. The author defines Will as "the activity of man in the widest sense." In this definition he seeks to keep the ranges of meaning sufficiently broad so as to include the needs, instincts, inclinations, and passions of men. "We may affirm absolutely," asserts the author, "that *nothing great in the World* has been accomplished without *passion*." Two elements are thus disclosed as essential for an understanding of history. The one is the Idea of Spirit; the other is the complex of human passions. Hegel speaks of the former as the warp and of the latter as the woof of the cloth of universal history. The concrete union of these two provides the third and final element of world history—freedom embodied in the State. The means or material of history is thus the passions and interests of men, used by Spirit for the attainment of its end. Individual men, activated by their inclinations and passions, constitute the power plant for the world-historical process. But these individuals are, in the final analysis, sacrificed for the end or goal of history. History is the slaughter bench at which the happiness and welfare of each individual is sacrificed. The individual constitutes but a moment in the vast general sweep of world history. He remains historically unimportant. "The particular is for the most part of too trifling value as compared with the general: individuals

are sacrificed and abandoned. The Idea pays the penalty of determinate existence and of corruptibility, not from itself, but from the passions of individuals." Spirit uses the passions of men to attain its final self-consciousness. It sets the passions to work for itself. This integration of human passions with the aim of Spirit is accomplished through the "cunning of Reason." The cunning of Reason weaves together all the expressions of passion and makes them contributory to the final goal.

The passions which are put to work by the cunning of Reason arise from the wills of particular individuals, as they play their diversified roles and carry out their variegated functions. These particular individuals are classified by Hegel into four distinct, yet interrelated, historical categories: the citizen, the person, the hero, and the victim.

The *citizen* is subject to what the author calls customary morality. The determinant of action for the citizen is the will of society, the will of a nation-state, or the will of a religious institution. The citizen has not yet apprehended his subjective existence, and consequently has no consciousness of freedom—neither personal nor universal.

The *person* is the individual who can transcend the morality of his particular society and act on the basis of a morality grounded in subjectivity. It is in the person that subjective freedom makes its appearance. The morality of the person is not subordinate. It is determined by a personal consciousness of freedom. The person exhibits an implicit awareness of the Idea as Spirit, and thus drives beyond the static customary morality of the citizen. Hegel

596

finds in Socrates the example *par excellence* of the person who has been liberated from the confining morality of the citizen. "Though Socrates himself continued to perform his duties as a citizen, it was not the actual State and its religion, but the world of Thought that was his true home."

But it is only when we come to the *hero* that we find the "world-historical individual." The hero is the historically decisive actor. Like all other men, he is motivated by private gain and interest, but his actions express at the same time an attunement with the will of the World-Spirit. His own particular will involves at the same time the larger issues of world history. The heroes of history are practical and political men. They are neither philosophers nor artists. They have no theoretical understanding of the Idea which they are unfolding. But they have insight into what is timely and needed, as well as courage to act decisively on the basis of their convictions. They know what their age demands, and they commit themselves to its challenge. Caesar, Alexander the Great, and Napoleon were such men. They responded to the requirements of their times and shaped the history of the world through their decisive action. After seeing Napoleon ride through the streets of Jena, Hegel retired to his study and wrote: "Today I saw the World-Spirit riding on horseback." Napoleon was an instrument, used by the cunning of Reason, in the actualization of the self-consciousness of freedom. To become heroes or world-historical individuals these men had to sacrifice personal happiness. "If we go on to cast a look at the fate of these World-Historical persons, whose vocation it was to be agents of the World-Spirit—we shall find it to have been no happy one. They attained no calm enjoyment; their whole life was labor and trouble; their whole nature was nought else but their master-passion. When their object is attained they fall off like empty hulls from the kernel. They die early, like Alexander; they are murdered, like Caesar; transported to St. Helena, like Napoleon."

The *victim,* who comprises the fourth category, moves solely in the realm of private desires and inclinations. He has no interest in and offers no contribution to the customary morality of the citizen, nor to the subjective morality of the person, nor to the march of universal freedom exhibited by the hero. He is abandoned to his private situation. His goal is private success and happiness. Hegel has few good words for this type of individual. Obviously, he cannot become historically decisive. In a sense history moves on without him, but in another sense he remains part of the historical pattern insofar as the cunning of Reason must use all the material which passion provides. In the final analysis Spirit makes use of the hero and victim alike. There is a real sense in which both the hero and victim are "victims." The victim is a "victim" of the hero and the age; the hero in turn is a "victim" of the World-Spirit. In all this we see the emergence of the implicatory principle of Hegel's philosophy of history that the individual *as* individual is unimportant.

As Kierkegaard, the chief of all critics of Hegel, has later demonstrated, the existential significance of the individual is sacrificed to the universal and the general. A frank admission of this disregard for individuality is expressed when Hegel writes: "The His-

597

tory of the World might, on principle, entirely ignore the circle within which morality and the so much talked of distinction between the moral and the politic lies—not only in abstaining from judgments, for the principles involved, and the necessary reference of the deeds in question to those principles, are a sufficient judgment of them —but in leaving Individuals quite out of view and unmentioned."

The third constitutive element of world history is the State. The aim or goal of history is Spirit as freedom; the means of actualization are the passions of mankind; the embodiment or fulfillment of this freedom is found in the State. The State, as understood by Hegel, is the concrete unity of universal, objective freedom and particular, subjective passion. Thus the State synthesizes at one and the same time freedom and passion, the universal and the particular, the objective and the subjective. In the State universal freedom becomes concretized and is given substance. The freedom of subjective passion is mere arbitrariness and caprice. The actualized freedom of universal history, on the other hand, is *organized* liberty, or freedom structured by a State.

In the final analysis, the entities which are under consideration in Hegel's philosophy of history are "peoples" or cultural totalities. The State rather than the individual embodies universal freedom. The State does not exist for its subjects—it exists for its own sake. It is its own end. The subjects of a State are means towards its end. It is important not to confuse Hegel's definition of the State with an individual bureaucratic political organization. Such a political organization— British Monarchism, French Constitu-

tionalism, American Democracy—may express the will of a State, but the two are not identical. The State, for Hegel, designates a cultural complex which integrates the art, religion, politics, and technology of a people into a unified self-consciousness. The Third Reich of Hitler, for example, according to the Hegelian philosophy, must be understood as a ghastly distortion of the true meaning of a State. Nazism constituted a pseudo-state—a State without cultural content. The State, for Hegel, becomes the foundation for any organization—political or otherwise. The State is responsible for all cultural activities. The implication of this is the subordination of personal morality, personal religion, and political self-determination to a corporate or group substance. This group substance or State, insofar as it provides the foundation for all of man's temporal activities, is understood as an expression of God's purpose for the world. The State is thus defined to be the divine Idea as it exists on earth. There is no room for personal religion and personal morality in Hegel's system. The individual as individual stands outside morality, and outside history itself. Only as a moment in the march of universal freedom, embodied in the State, does the individual become significant. The State or the culture, rather than the individual, is, for Hegel, the bearer of history.

In formulating his philosophy of history Hegel traces the development of the consciousness of freedom as it moves from Eastern to Western civilization. History travels from East to West. Oriental civilization is the childhood of history. Greek civilization marks the period of adolescence. In Roman civilization history develops to manhood.

Germanic civilization appears as the fourth phase of world history—old age. The Orientals had acknowledged only *one* man as being free—the despot. And insofar as the freedom of the despot expressed itself in the recklessness of passion, it must be accounted as mere caprice; hence, in Oriental civilization we do not yet find freedom, properly understood. In Greece and Rome, the consciousness of freedom manifested itself in the acknowledgment that *some* men are free. Slavery, with its restriction of freedom, was an accepted institution in both Greece and Rome. It is not until we come to the Germanic nations that we find the acknowledgment that *all* men are free. Germanic civilization, under the influence of Christianity, attained the consciousness of universal freedom.

Among the peoples of China and India, who comprise Oriental civilization, we find only the first glimmerings of a historical consciousness; history as such does not begin until the rise of the Persians. In China and India, the Idea remains bound to Nature. The peculiar determinants of Spirit are lacking. In China, morality is equated with legislative enactments, individuals are stripped of personality, and the will and the passions of the emperor constitute the highest authority. The emperor as the supreme head of political affairs is also at the same time the chief priest of religion. Religion is thus subordinated to the despotism of a particular bureaucratic organization. Such an organization, according to Hegel, is the very negation of a historical State as a cultural unit. The civilization of India exhibits a similar bondage to Nature. This is expressed particularly in the institution of the caste system. The individual does

not choose his particular position for himself. He receives it from Nature. Nature is the governing power. Thus, in Oriental civilization the universal Idea emerges in Nature, but it does not drive beyond itself to the self-consciousness of Spirit.

The Persians are the first historical peoples. This historical consciousness is expressed in their use of Light as a symbol for the Good (*Ormuzd*). Light provides the condition for the exercise of choice, and it is precisely choice, action, and deeds which constitute the stuff of history. Historical states are what their deeds are. The Persians understood history as a struggle between Good and Evil, in which the actors were confronted with the inescapability of choice. There is a deficiency, however, in the historical consciousness of the Persians. They failed to grasp the higher unity in which the antithesis of Good and Evil is synthesized. Judaism, which took its rise in the same geographical and cultural milieu, provides a further advance in the progressive development of the consciousness of freedom. In Judaism, Spirit is liberated from Nature and is purified. Both the individual man and Israel as a nation come to a consciousness of themselves as distinct from Nature. Jehovah, as the quintessence of Spirit, is understood as the Lord of Nature. Nature is subordinated to the role of creature. Spirit is acknowledged as the Creator. "The idea of Light has at this stage advanced to that of 'Jehovah' —the *purely One*. This forms the point of separation between the East and the West; Spirit descends into the depths of its own being, and recognizes the abstract fundamental principle as the Spiritual. Nature—which in the East is the primary and fundamental existence—is now depressed to the condition of a mere creature; and Spirit now occupies the first place. God is known as the creator of all men, as He is of all nature, and as absolute causality generally."

Judaism thus marks the transition from East to West. Spirit is acknowledged in its separation from Nature, but neither Spirit nor Nature are yet fully comprehended. In Greek civilization another advance becomes apparent. Greece, as the adolescent period of the historical process, introduces the principle of subjective freedom or individuality. This principle is expressed both in the personal or subjective morality of Socrates (as contrasted with the customary morality of society), and in the rise of Athenian Democracy. As despotism was the peculiar characteristic of the political life of the Orient, so democracy is the peculiar characteristic of the political life of Greece. Spirit becomes introspective and posits itself as particular existence, but it posits itself precisely as the ideal and thus suggests the possible triumph over particularity through a comprehension of universality itself. But the universals of Greek thought are fixed and static essences; hence they are still fettered by the limitations of Nature. They still remain dependent upon external conditions. Therefore, the new direction projected by the consciousness of the Greek Spirit still retains natural elements. A concrete expression of this principle is the continued practice of slavery, which grants freedom to some but not to all. In Rome, in which history attains its manhood, an advance is made from democracy to aristocracy. The institutions of the people are united in the person of the emperor. In the will of the emperor the

principle of subjectivity, enunciated in Greek thought, gains unlimited realization. The will of the emperor becomes supreme. But insofar as subjectivity is universalized and objectivized at the expense of the claims of art, religion, and morality, the State which emerges in Roman civilization is still an inferior State, lacking in cultural content.

The State, understood as the concrete embodiment of subjective and objective freedom, comes to its full realization in the German Spirit. The German Spirit, like the Greek, apprehended the principle of subjectivity, but unlike the Greek it became the bearer of the Christian ideal and thus universalized the principle to mean that *all* men are free. The Greek and Roman Spirit still kept some men (the slaves) in chains. The individual interests and passions of men thus find their fulfillment only in the German Spirit. This fulfillment is the unification of the objective Idea of freedom, as the aim of history, with the particular and subjective passions of mankind, in the concrete embodiment of a cultural whole. Subjective freedom, without objective order, is mere caprice—expressed either in the will of a despot or emperor, or in the chaos of anarchy. Thus, subjective freedom cannot be realized until it finds its place within a structured whole—the State. "This is the point which consciousness has attained, and these are the principal phases of that form in which the principle of Freedom has realized itself; —for the History of the World is nothing but the development of the Idea of Freedom. But Objective Freedom—the laws of *real* Freedom—demand the subjugation of the mere contingent Will—for this is in its nature formal. If the Objective is in itself Rational, human insight and conviction must correspond with the Reason which it embodies, and then we have the other essential element—Subjective Freedom—also realized."

MONADOLOGY

Author: Gottfried Wilhelm von Leibniz (1646-1716)
Type of work: Metaphysics
First published: 1840 (Written in 1714)

Principal Ideas Advanced

Monads are the elements of all things; they are simple substances, created all at once out of nothing; they can neither be altered in quality nor changed internally by any other created thing.

No two monads are perfectly alike; for every individual monad there is some internal difference which accounts for its particular nature.

Perception and apperception are the two chief types of activities by which monads exhibit their natures.

Men are distinguished from the animals by their knowledge of necessary and eternal truths; man reasons according to the principles of contradiction and sufficient reason.

Only through God's mediation is interaction or knowledge of any sort possible; although the monads are isolated, they function and perceive according to God's preëstablished harmony.

This is the best of all possible worlds, for God's goodness made him choose it from the infinite number of possible universes.

The *Monadology* is undoubtedly Leibniz's best-known work. Since it is a condensed statement of his main philosophical principles, written late in life, there is good reason for this popularity. On the other hand, its popularity is somewhat strange, since Leibniz himself gave no title to the manuscript and it was published neither by him nor during his lifetime. Written in French, it appeared first in a German translation in 1810. Not until 1840 did the original French version appear, and the title "La Monadologie," given to the work at that time, has remained. Although the *Theodicy* (1710) represents Leibniz's philosophical and theological interests more directly, and his *New Essays* (1765) undoubtedly provoked more immediate interest, the importance of the *Monadology* as a brief metaphysical sketch remains.

The *Monadology* has been called an "encyclopaedia of Leibniz's philosophy," and one of its drawbacks is that in a strict sense the reader needs to know Leibniz's other writings in order to understand its contents properly.

Support can be found for considering the *Theodicy* to be a more central work from the fact that Leibniz himself added references in the margin of his manuscript (later named the *Monadology*) referring particularly to passages in the *Theodicy* where the views were more fully expressed. Yet the *Monadology* can be, and usually has been, read alone. As such, it stands in a tradition of brief yet comprehensive metaphysical expositions which have an influence out of all proportion to their length.

Particularly in view of the fact that Leibniz did not himself title the *Monadology*, the work could just as easily be called *On Substance* or *On the Modes of Being*. In subject matter the *Monadology* follows the great tradition of metaphysics in trying to define what the ultimate substance of the world is and in trying to arrange a hierarchy to account for all of the different modes of existence which are possible. The *Monadology* is divided into ninety brief paragraphs, each summarizing some fundamental point. The first paragraph opens with a description of a "Monad," thus introducing Leibniz's most famous doctrine and the single principle in terms of which his entire metaphysics is developed.

Like Spinoza, whom he knew and admired, Leibniz was impressed with mathematical rigor, and he reflects this love of simplicity and brevity in his philosophical writing. The *Monadology* is not an intricately structured work like Spinoza's *Ethics* (1677), but the same love of clarity and of a single first principle is clearly evident in both. Leibniz, who was equally famous as a mathematician, still enjoys the almost unique position of being read by mathematically and logically inclined philosophers as well as by speculative metaphysicians and theologians.

A monad, he tells us, is a simple (indivisible) substance which enters into compounds, and a compound is an aggregation of simple things. Monads are the elements of all things, the atoms of all nature; they are indestructible, since no such simple substance can be destroyed by natural means. Nor can they come into existence artificially within natural limits, since they could not, by their very nature, be formed from anything else. Spinoza's "substance" was so large that it became absolutely infinite and included both God and the world as ordinarily conceived. Leibniz's substances, on the other hand, are the smallest and simplest conceivable entities.

Creation and annihilation are the means of entrance and exit for monads, and here Leibniz's theological dimension is most evident. They are, Leibniz says, created "all at once," which is a condensed reference to the traditional doctrine of creation *ex nihilo*, just as "annihilation" has similarities to traditional eschatological views. Since monads are conceived as having such extra-mundane means of entrance and exit, it is not really surprising that Leibniz asserts that the monads cannot be altered in quality or changed internally by any other created thing. This has overtones of traditional doctrines of predestination, but Leibniz puts it in his dramatic and famous phrase that the monads "have no windows" through which anything could come in or go out. Each is a self-contained, self-developing entity. The means of their coördination will be explained later.

602

But if monads cannot be altered from without, they would all be identical and indistinguishable were it not for internal differences in quality. The monads derive the qualities they have from internal differences. This is another way of saying that Leibniz denies that there is any general or external principle of individuation. Leibniz then reverses the emphasis from trying to account for a principle of individuation and difference among monads to asserting, in a more radical note, that every monad is absolutely different from every other. No two are perfectly alike; in even the most similar some internal difference of intrinsic quality can be found.

Having covered the basic questions concerning monads as such in eight brief paragraphs, Leibniz then sets forth more general metaphysical principles, built upon the doctrine of the monads as the ultimate simple components of all things. Every created being (and the monad itself is a created thing) is subject to change. All natural changes of the monad come from an internal principle, and the pattern of change which a group of monads characteristically exhibits is its nature. The nature of a thing is its pattern of activity. Perception and apperception (or consciousness) are the two chief types of activity of a monad or of a group of monads, and all activity may be divided under these two headings. The activity which produces change from one perception to another is what Leibniz calls "appetition," and nothing but perceptions and their changes can be found in a simple substance like a monad.

Monads have a kind of self-sufficiency, an internalized and purposeful plan of activity, which is what makes them their own source of their internal activities. Since they have this self-directive action as well as perceptions and desires, they may be called souls, although this title is to be reserved only for those whose perception is distinct and is accompanied by memory.

One perception comes only from another perception, as a motion comes only from another motion. Thus every present state of a monad is a consequence of its preceding state. So understood, any present moment has within it much more of the future than either the past or the present. Leibniz's theory of monads, although in a sense deterministic, is a view which is directed primarily toward the future. Certainly all activity and perception have this orientation. However, men are unique and are to be distinguished from the animals, despite the basic similarity between our component parts and theirs. Such a distinction of man from animal must be based on a distinction of degree; men have knowledge of necessary and eternal truths, but animals do not.

Leibniz began in his theory of monads with a description of a common nature which all things share. Beginning with this separation of men from animals in virtue of man's knowledge of eternal truths, Leibniz concentrates primarily on man and God and for this reason, the common substance we all share receives less emphasis. For man's knowledge of necessary and eternal truths raises him to a knowledge of himself and of God. Reflective self-consciousness has been introduced. Men have a knowledge of necessary truths, and they may think about God's nature—all of which requires a unique type of reasoning.

Man's reasoning is founded on two great principles: the principle of contradiction, which separates the true from the false, and the principle of sufficient reason. The latter tells us that for every fact there is a reason sufficient to account for the fact regardless of whether the reason can be known. Truths in turn are to be divided into two kinds: those of reasoning and those of fact. Truths of reasoning are necessary, and their opposite is impossible; truths of fact are contingent, and their opposite is possible.

Leibniz then offers his arguments for God's existence. The sufficient or final reason for things must be outside the sequence or series of particular contingent things, however infinite the series may be. Thus the final reason for all things must be a necessary substance, and this substance we call God. There needs to be only one God, since this God is sufficient to account for the variety of particulars.

Such a God is absolutely perfect, since perfection as Leibniz defines it is nothing but the presence of positive reality, and God, as an unlimited sequence of possible beings, must contain as much reality as possible. To separate man from God, Leibniz asserts that created beings derive their perfections from God but their imperfections from themselves, since God is infinite but man must be limited. God's infinity seems to be the chief source of his perfection and is the quality which separates him most radically from man, since both are composed of basically similar monads.

Leibniz modifies Anselm's ontological argument for God's existence. Instead of using Anselm's phrase, "necessary existence," Leibniz writes, "He must necessarily exist, if He is possible." This changes Anselm's point and shifts the question of God's existence to one of demonstrating the possibility of a God. Nothing can interfere with the possibility of an infinite God's existence (this part of the reasoning is traditional), but the possibility of a God must first be established (this is new).

One of Leibniz's most famous, and disputed, doctrines is that of the creation of monads. He has asserted that none can be brought into being or destroyed by natural causes, but this leaves open the question of a divine origin. God, it turns out, is the only uncreated monad; all the rest are created or derivative. This process Leibniz calls "fulguration," and it seems to be not a single act but an activity of the Divinity continued from moment to moment. Since no further explanation of this important doctrine of the origin of monads is given, nor any further definition of the key term "fulguration" (except a reference to the *Theodicy*), this theory of Leibniz has been the source of much discussion.

Only through the mediation of God can one monad affect another; and one affects another only in the sense that, in predestinating things from the beginning, God may have considered one monad in determining the activity of another in relation to it. God is said to have a "will" which regulates things according to a principle of the best, but this does not allow him any alternatives in design. Here we discover Leibniz's most famous doctrine, that God has in fact created the best world which it was possible for him to devise.

God does have an infinite number of possible universes to choose from, it is true, but only one of them could become actual through his creative activity. Fitness, or degree of activity in perfection, determines him, so that in that sense his activity in creation is not really free. When all that must be considered and balanced is included, there are no alternatives to the world he did create. His goodness makes him choose it, and his power makes him produce it.

We are not at all cut off in this world. Each living thing is a perpetually living mirror of the universe. It sometimes seems as if we all live in many different worlds, but these are in truth nothing but aspects of a single universe, viewed from the special point of view of each monad. Being joined in this way, we are not really independent. Everybody feels the effect of all that takes place in the universe. Each created monad thus represents the whole universe within itself. All nature shares in this interconnectedness, down to matter itself. There is nothing fallow, nothing sterile, nothing dead in the universe, no chaos, no confusion save in appearance.

God alone is completely without body, although this means merely to be a monad of a special type. The births and deaths of natural bodies are not abrupt transitions (no transition for Leibniz is abrupt). Birth and death are gradual changes. Body and soul both follow their own laws (no soul is without body except God). The body and soul of any entity agree, despite their variant laws, through the "pre-established harmony" of all substances which God has arranged. This is a modern metaphysical version of the traditional theological doctrine of fore-ordination. Souls act according to the laws of final causes through appetitions, ends, and means. Bodies act according to the laws of efficient causes or motions. Through God's original design, the two realms are in harmony with each other.

Minds are able to enter into a kind of fellowship with God. The totality of all such spirits composes the City of God, and this is the moral world within the natural world. This moral world and natural world are, like body and soul, in perfect harmony. God as architect satisfies in all respects God as lawgiver. The world exceeds all the desires of the wisest men, and it is impossible to make it better than it is. On this high note of optimism, the *Monadology* ends.

One thing which should be noted is that the famous doctrine of the monads occupied only the first part of the unnamed treatise, and in the later sections the traditional theological problems are taken up with less and less mention made of the theory of the monads. The *Monadology* is not the tightly knit and interlocking statement of doctrine it is often thought to be. Within this brief treatise many important theories are merely mentioned; few are argued at all. More independence probably exists between the various theories here than is often recognized, and certainly other of Leibniz's writings need to be studied (primarily the *Theodicy*) before any appraisal at all can be made. What is to be found within the ninety brief paragraphs of the treatises is, without question, a reflection of Leibniz's attempt to meet and to deal with every major philosophical and theological problem.

A SYSTEM OF LOGIC

Author: John Stuart Mill (1806-1873)
Type of work: Logic, philosophy of induction
First published: 1843

PRINCIPAL IDEAS ADVANCED

Terms denote only particulars, and the only particulars we can speak of significantly are those we are acquainted with.

The syllogism is not a form of proof which allows inference to particular statements from general statements, but a form of argument which relates inductive conclusions to present inductive generalizations.

Mathematical propositions are synthetic and empirical (not analytic and verbal), and the only necessity attaching to them is a psychological necessity.

By the methods of agreement, difference, residues, and concomitant variation inductive generalizations are possible.

Inductive inference is based on the principle of the uniformity of nature—which is itself a principle established by inductive argument.

John Stuart Mill is the best known of the English Utilitarians. Educated almost entirely at home—as the heir apparent of the movement—he became fully conversant with the philosophic, social, political, and economic views of James Mill (his father), Jeremy Bentham, David Hartley, and David Ricardo, and through them he received the heritage of Locke, Berkeley, and Hume. While he was not a great original thinker, he assimilated all that was presented to him, analyzed and developed it, made some important changes, and presented it to the world in such a forceful manner that he became the most influential of the Utilitarians. He wrote a number of works ranging from semipopular ethical and social essays to criticisms of the logicians and metaphysicians of his time. He is best known today for *Utilitarianism* (1863), *Essay On Liberty* (1859), and various doctrines presented in his *A System of Logic,* the work that immediately established his

reputation among his contemporaries, that had to be reckoned with by any logician during the remainder of the century, and that was still being reprinted in its entirety in the early years of this century.

In Book I, Mill discusses words and propositions with the intention of indicating the limits of meaningful discourse. In defending the traditional doctrine that simple propositions are composed of two names linked by the copula, he makes a number of distinctions, the most important of which are as follows. He distinguishes between *general* names such as "man," which are used to refer to any of an indefinite number of similar things, and *singular* names which are used to denote one specific thing. Singular names may be either *proper* names such as "Peter" or *complex names* such as "the man standing on the step." He also distinguishes between *concrete* terms such as "man" and "white" (that is, "white object") and *abstract* terms

606

such as "humanity" ("manness") and "whiteness." The latter are names of properties. Finally, he distinguishes between *connotative* and *non-connotative* terms. In the sentence "Peter is white," both terms refer to, designate, or denote Peter, but they do so in different ways. "Peter" functions as an arbitrarily assigned mark used to identify the person, but "white" or "white thing" denotes him by calling attention to or connoting a property he has, the property that is denoted by the abstract term "whiteness." Only proper names and some abstract terms such as "whiteness" are non-connotative.

If we could not make this last distinction we would be forced to conclude that all propositions are identity statements in which we are asserting only that one thing is denoted by two names. Given the distinction, we can say that we are asserting that whatever is denoted by the subject term has the property connoted by the predicate term. The "is" of predication, which is thus distinguished from the "is" of identity, expresses time through its tenses and expresses denial through the addition of "not," but strictly speaking, it does not assert existence. Hence, we need yet another "is" for this. But since these three uses exhaust the functions of the verb, a simple statement is meaningful only if it asserts an identity, makes a predication, or asserts existence. Of course, we can make statements about causes and about relations, but since causes can be explained as causal relations and since all relations can be regarded as relational properties, these are no more than special cases of predication.

Mill claims that the account given so far is a philosophically neutral one, but he pushes the analysis further in an empirical direction. In the first place, while Mill does not make clear the exact nature of general ideas, his conception falling somewhere between Locke's and Hume's on this matter, he is clear about the denotation of terms: they denote particulars only. Thus, a general name like "man" does not denote a class that is some sort of entity in addition to the individuals that compose it. There are only men, and "man" denotes them. Again, while all men are classified as such because each of them is rational, the abstract term "rational" does not denote a Platonic universal. Rather, it denotes indifferently any of a number of similar properties characterizing different individuals.

The particulars of which we can speak significantly are those we know; these are not the underlying material and spiritual substances of the metaphysician. Mill allows us to speak of causes and relations, but he argues that these can be reduced to predication. He allows us to speak of predicates and of substances, but he insists that all we really know of them are their sensible effects, and therefore that we must restrict ourselves to what is immediately given; namely, to the content of sensation, emotion, and thought. Consequently, to predicate a property of a substance is to say no more than that a phenomenon or set of phenomena denoted by the predicate term accompanies, precedes, follows, or is included in the phenomenon or set of phenomena denoted by the subject term. To assert the existence of anything is to assert the occurrence of some phenomenon, and to assert identity or difference is to compare phenomena.

In Book II, in his discussion of deduction, Mill argues not only that the

607

power of syllogistic reasoning has been greatly overrated, but also that its nature has been misunderstood. He insists that as a method of proof it always begs the question. This is obvious, he says, in the case of the syllogism "All men are mortal, Socrates is a man, therefore Socrates is mortal," for we know that all men are mortal only because we know that Socrates, Caesar, Henry VIII, and others have died. Yet, since we can frame parallel syllogisms in which the person referred to is a living person, the generalization that "All men are mortal" cannot be regarded simply as a summary of facts. Yet, these latter syllogisms are questionable too if they are thought to prove their conclusions, for it is still the case that we have mounted up from the mortality of Socrates, Caesar, and others to the generalization, and have descended from it to the mortality of, say, the United States President. We can think of this sequence as a complex inference in which an inductive inference is followed by a deductive one, but we do not need to, for we might just as well argue directly that because Socrates died, Caesar died, Henry VIII died, and the Duke of Wellington died (among others), so also the said President will die. Since it is superfluous, the syllogism is not the form of the inference, or even of a part of the inference— strictly speaking, the argument is an inductive one. Mill believed this to be true in general: particulars are not inferred from generals, but only from other particulars.

Since Mill did not deny the usefulness of generalizations or of the syllogisms they make possible, he had to reinterpret the function of the major premise. This he did by maintaining in *A System of Logic* that the major premise itself asserts an inference, an inference from particulars to the general, and that it functions as a guide for making inferences, inferences from particulars to particulars. It can function as such a guide because the inference from particulars to a particular is essentially the same as the inference from these particulars to the general statement. Strictly speaking, this guide is superfluous, but it is useful insofar as it reminds us of a valid type of inference, provides supplementary assurance that the present inference is valid, and fosters consistency by leading us to draw inferences in accordance with those we have drawn earlier. The syllogism, then, is not a form of proof in which something is derived from a general premise, but the machinery through which the relevance of earlier inductions is brought to bear upon a present one.

In Book II, Mill also makes his well known assertions about the nature of mathematics. He recognized that the truth of some propositions follows logically from the meanings of the words contained in them, but that these truths are truths only about words. He agreed with the Kantians of his day in claiming that the propositions of mathematics are synthetic propositions about the world of measurable and countable things, but as an empiricist he could not accept their claim that such propositions express insights into conditions imposed on experience by the knowing mind. They must, then, be experimental truths of a very general and pervasive sort. Strictly speaking, insofar as they refer to magnitudes they are only very close approximations and therefore not literally true —do the measured angles of actual triangles always total 180 degrees?—but the facts agree with them so closely that for all practical and scientific purposes they can be regarded as exceptionless truths. To the objection that they cannot be empirical statements because they are necessarily true, he writes that they are necessarily true only in the sense that it is psychologically impossible to conceive of their falsity. Carrying his position to its conclusion, he insists that even the laws of contradiction and excluded middle are empirical generalizations based upon such facts as that belief and disbelief displace each other, light and darkness exclude each other, and so on. For a number of reasons, this analysis of mathematics and logic has been rejected by almost all serious students of the subject.

In Book III, Mill discusses induction, which is obviously the basic form of reasoning for him. Almost every student of elementary logic is familiar with his four canons: the canon of *agreement* which states that if cases in which a phenomenon occurs have in common only one thing, then that thing is the effect or the cause or part of the cause of the phenomenon; the canon of *difference* which states that if cases in which the phenomenon occurs differ from cases in which it does not in only one respect, that respect, or its absence, is the effect or cause or part of the cause of the phenomenon; the canon of *residues* which states that if we subtract from a phenomenon the effects we know to be due to certain antecedents, then the remainder is the effect of the remaining antecedents; and the canon of *concomitant variations* which states that when one phenomenon varies whenever another does, then either

there is a causal relation between the two or they are both related causally to a third thing. Mill regards these methods as ways of both discovering and testing causes. He says that the method of difference is the most important of the four, because it lends itself to experimental applications; of all the purely inductive methods it alone reveals or establishes causes with a high degree of probability. The method of residues requires some deductive steps, the method of concomitant variations is basically but a less useful variation of the method of difference, and the method of agreement is not very effective since we cannot exclude the possibility of plural causes.

Mill believed that inductive inference is based on the principle of the uniformity of nature, the assumption that everything has a cause and that causal laws are invariant. He also believed, and this is more interesting, that this principle itself is established by induction. Having already discovered a good number of empirical laws, such as that fire burns and water drowns, we generalize on the basis of them to attain the principle. We subsequently use the principle when we are making inferences in less obvious situations. To the objection that he begs the question, Mill writes that the principle was not used in the induction that established it or in inductions leading to the laws from which it was induced. While Mill is unclear about the details of his defense, it is clear that to avoid an outright contradiction he would have to modify his earlier assertion that every inductive inference presupposes the principle. Perhaps he would have done this, for he indicates in various ways that he intends to claim only that inductions based on the four methods presuppose the principle. First, these four types of induction are said to comprise "scientific" inference in contrast to induction by simple enumeration, which Mill regards as a much less reliable form of inference. The inductions that precede and establish the principle of the uniformity of nature are "non-scientific" inferences. Again, the four methods are supposed to enable us to detect and test causes, whereas it is not the case that induction by simple enumeration is expected to do so. Consequently, the former is thought to presuppose the principle of universal causation, whereas the latter is not. Furthermore, since the whole point of the principle is that it enables us to recast our inferences in a deductive form, its role is exactly that of the major premise of a syllogism. Consequently, it is not involved as a premise at all. It functions as a guide that is not logically required but which does support the induction insofar as it makes it clear that this induction is similar to ones that are acceptable. Furthermore, Mill writes, once we know that the event does have a cause—and the principle assures us that it does—we have an additional reason for thinking that runs of favourable instances, concomitant variations, and other relationships are more than mere coincidences. In these ways inductions that rise above the "loose and uncertain" status of induction by simple enumeration presuppose the principle.

But if this is what Mill meant, he still leaves us with certain puzzles. For instance, the difference between unreliable inferences of the "All crows are black" type and reliable ones such as "Fire burns" is not at all clear. According to Mill, the difference is that although in the case of fire we have discovered a causal law, in the case of crows we have not. But the introduction of causes raises a number of difficulties. First, there is the difficulty of specifying how we identify a causal relationship, for—as the case of the crows indicates—it cannot be on the basis of the presence of a large number of favorable instances and the absence of any instance to the contrary. Second, the term "cause" must refer to more than Humean conjunctions. Mill asserted that some sort of necessity is presupposed in the assumption that nature will repeat herself, but his reluctance to go beyond Hume prevented him from giving a clear or consistent account. Third, if "All crows are black" is not a reliable scientific inference because, as Mill claimed, the principle of the uniformity of nature is not applicable to it (it is not a causal law), then Mill should have concluded that the generalizations on which the principle rests and the principle itself are similarly unreliable. At least, he should have done so to maintain his own assertion that the question has not been begged because the principle was not involved in the earlier inferences. If the principle is to be reliable and is to be a statement about causality, then the earlier generalizations, such as "Fire burns," must be regarded as reliably confirmed causal laws, but in this case the question has been begged. He equivocated between the positions, but in either case Mill failed to show how the principle can bestow a higher degree of reliability on inferences made in accordance with it. His discussion is confused in part by his failure to distinguish clearly between psychological and logical matters.

Mill himself realized as well as many of his critics that his four methods cannot be applied easily, mechanically, or universally, and that we do, as a matter of fact, hold well-established beliefs that have not and could not have been discovered or tested by the methods alone. Perhaps the most important fact that thwarts the application of the methods is that of the composition of causes. As in the case of the compositon of forces in physics, a number of causes can combine to produce one effect and this effect can be such that an inspection of it will not reveal the effect of any one of the component causes. While we cannot apply the methods to such a phenomenon we do have another way of proceeding. For if we know what sorts of causes might, if combined properly, produce this kind of composite effect, and if we know the laws of these causes, we can calculate the net effect of various combinations of these possible component causes until we find one that agrees with the observed complex effect. Thus we have a technique which enables us to explain complicated phenomenon in terms of more general laws. If we are successful, there is no reason why we could not apply a similar procedure to these laws to obtain intermediate laws, and to these in turn to obtain yet more basic laws. In this way it is theoretically possible to reduce a whole science to a small set of basic principles from which all the rest can be inferred. This has actually been done for mechanics and astronomy by Newton's laws and for chemistry by Dalton's atomic theory. These intermediate and basic laws are what we call theories.

In discussing the first level explana-tion of complex phenomena Mill frequently wrote as if we have an exhaustive knowledge of the possible causes and as if the discovery of the correct combinations requires no ingenuity but only the straightforward examination of the possible combinations. The technique of proceeding in this manner is called the "deductive method." But he was well aware that many possible causes and their laws are not known and that in the case of the lower level ones they can never be discovered by any mechanically applicable procedure. In these cases we have to make assumptions as to what the causal laws might be, just as Newton did when he speculated that the gravitational force varies inversely with the square of the distance and not with the cube. These suppositions, for which we have little or no evidence at the outset, are "hypotheses," and the modified technique is the "hypothetical method." In some of its applications we are looking for basic laws, but in others we are concerned with finding intermediate level laws that will enable us to infer known empirical laws from accepted principles. The use of this method requires ingenuity, and success is by no means antecedently guaranteed. Since a hypothesis cannot be verified directly, the establishment of its truth depends upon the verification of facts or laws inferred from it. Since two hypotheses might very well be elaborated to explain the same phenomenon, a hypothesis is not really established unless unanticipated consequences that follow from the one hypothesis, but not from the other, are also verified.

Hypotheses and deduction become more and more indispensable as a science develops, for the more inclusive a theory becomes the less likely it is that it can be discovered by a direct examination of the facts. Mill believed that by themselves the four inductive methods will not take us very far, for the first two steps of the required hypothetical method—those of propounding hypotheses and elaborating their consequences—are beyond their scope.

Turning to the social sciences, Mill wrote that experimentation is largely impossible, that the method of agreement is not widely applicable because many phenomena are produced by different causes, and that the method of difference is of little use both because situations are too complex and because many effects are the composite effects of several causes. Consequently, the hypothetical method is even more indispensable in this area. We cannot hope for as high a degree of certainty here because it is usually possible to elaborate different intermediate hypotheses linking basic principles with empirical laws, and there is no convenient way

of distinguishing between them. The basic laws are presumably the laws of associational psychology. We encounter additional difficulty when we deal with human beings; man reacts to changes in his environment in such a way that the conditions to which men are subject at one time are not these to which they are subject at another. As a result there is a historical development, even in human nature itself, so that the empirical and intermediate laws are not invariant. Man's changing state of knowledge is the principle factor in this progressive development.

A System of Logic concludes with some remarks that every reader of his *Utilitarianism* should consult. Mill argues that morality is essentially a matter of rules and that consequently moral statements are imperative rather than indicative statements. Since they express precepts and not matters of fact they lie beyond the province of science.

EITHER/OR

Author: Søren Kierkegaard (1813-1855)
Type of work: Existential metaphysics
First published: 1843

PRINCIPAL IDEAS ADVANCED

The aesthetical mode of existence is exemplified by both romantic hedonism and abstract intellectualism; both the sensualist and the intellectual fail to commit themselves decisively and thereby to achieve existence and selfhood.

Only through choice is authentic selfhood attained; life is a matter of either/or. The aesthetical way leads to boredom, melancholy, and despair.

In turning toward decision and commitment because of despair, the self passes from the aesthetical stage to the ethical.

In the ethical stage, in virtue of having chosen itself, the self becomes centralized, unified, and authentic.

The third stage of development is the religious; but no stage is sufficient by itself; the ethical stage transfigures the aesthetical, and the religious transfigures the ethical.

Either/Or is a two-volume work in which the author seeks to elucidate the contrasts and interrelationships between the aesthetical and the ethical modes of existence. As with most of the writings of Kierkegaard, *Either/ Or* was not published under his own name. The elucidations are penned under various pseudonyms. The first volume contains an analysis and description of the territory of the aesthetical. The literary style is heterogeneous. Use is made of lyrical aphorisms, orations, psychological analyses, drama reviews, and philosophical formulations.

The aestheticist, expressing his views through these various literary forms, is designated as A. The ethical thinker in Volume II, bearing the pseudonym of Judge William, is designated as B. In one of his later works, *Concluding Unscientific Postscript,* Kierkegaard has explained the central theme of *Either/Or* by informing the reader that A is an existential possibility, superior in dialectics and highly gifted in the uses of wit and poetic style, who nevertheless remains unable to commit himself in decisive action, and thus never exists in the true sense at all. B, on the other hand, represents the ethical man whose whole life is transformed into inwardness, passion, and commitment.

Judge William elucidates the content of the ethical in the form of a letter addressed to A. The communication of ethical truth demands a form or style which is commensurate with it. Ethical truth is existential and concrete, as contrasted with the theoretical and abstract, and consequently requires for its expression a form which has the personal quality of a dialogue or a letter. This constitutes the form of indirect communication. At the outset Judge William reminds the aestheticist of the Biblical story of the Prophet Nathan and David as a supreme example of this form of communication. King David listened attentively to the prophet's parable but remained in a state of theoretical detachment. He intellectualized the parable as an objective story which applied only to the mythical stranger. Not until the Prophet Nathan made the application explicit in his statement, "Thou, O King, art the man," did David apprehend the existential relevance of the parable. The Prophet Nathan used the form of indirect communication. This is also the form used by Judge William.

The aesthetical mode of existence has two primary expressions—romantic hedonism and abstract intellectualism. Mozart's *Don Giovanni* is depicted as the classical representative of the sensual or hedonistic view of life, and Goethe's *Faust* expresses the aesthetical personality of abstract intellectualism. Kierkegaard's archenemy, the Hegelian rationalist, also falls victim to the latter expression. For both the sensualist and the intellectualist inward existence and commitment are accidental and remain a matter of indifference. Neither is able to shoulder his responsibility and commit himself in action. They lack the ethical pathos which characterizes B.

The view of life which characterizes

the hedonist is portrayed by the young lover in the "Diary of a Seducer," who carries through his seduction with a diabolical cunning. The young lover is a prototype of Mozart's *Don Giovanni;* he experiments with numerous possibilities but never commits himself to the responsibility of actualizing any particular one in earnestness and seriousness. He experiments with the techniques of seduction but never commits himself in a promise. He experiments with love but never commits himself in marriage. In his aesthetical experimentation the young lover retains the proper abstractness and indifference about him. Every girl is, for him, a *woman in general.* Insofar as the young lover has a guiding principle, it is the hedonistic principle that enjoyment or pleasure constitutes the only end of life. The necessary internal conditions for the attainment of this life of pleasure are physical beauty and health; the necessary external conditions are wealth, glory, and high status. But these conditions provide no ethical pathos for a committed life, and it is precisely a committed life which the young lover seeks to avoid. He lives only in the moment, utilized as an erotic present in which the satisfaction of a desire is maximized. But then the moment passes and a new desire asserts its claim to thrive. His whole life becomes a discontinuous succession of passing from one moment to the next. His personality thus lacks unity and continuity. He has dispersed or lost himself in the present to the neglect of his past and his future. He no longer retains his past in memory, and he retreats from his future which confronts him with the responsibility of decision.

The speculative intellectualist suffers the same loss of selfhood as the romantic hedonist. Whereas the hedonist loses himself in the immediacy of the erotic present, the speculative thinker loses himself in the immediacy of his thought. The speculative thinker seeks to comprehend the whole of reality through the categories of a universal logic. But in such a system the concretely existing subject really does not matter. Just as for the sensualist every girl is a woman in general, so for the intellectualist all reality is dissolved into general categories. Speculative thought sees only the general movement of history, explained through the mediation of logical categories, but forgets the individual who apprehends himself within his particular and concrete history. Thus, both the hedonist and the speculative thinker evade the responsibility of decision. Both flirt with the realm of possibility but neither makes the leap into existence. The hedonist escapes from the future and responsibility by dispersing himself in momentary pleasures. The speculative thinker evades choice by playing the role of a detached observer who speculates about the general movements in world history, but who never participates in his own inner history with pathos and inwardness. Expressing the Socratic irony of which Kierkegaard was a master, his pseudonym is made to say: "To the philosopher world history is concluded, and he mediates. Hence, in our age as the order of the day we have the disgusting sight of young men who are able to mediate Christianity and paganism, are able to play with the titanic forces of history, and are unable to tell a plain man what he has to do in life, and who do not know any better what they themselves have

614

to do." The speculative thinker reduces existence to thought, sacrifices involvement for detached observation, and substitutes a reflective deliberation on universal history for the responsibility of concrete, personal decision. The common denominator of both expressions of aesthetical existence is a retreat from the reality of choice. In both cases the self has not yet found itself. Only through choice is authentic selfhood attained. This demands an awareness that life is a matter of either/or. But the either/or is a matter of indifference for the hedonist and the intellectualist alike. The aestheticist moves in a realm in abstraction from inwardness and existence.

The aesthetical mode or stage of existence leads to boredom and melancholy, and finally to despair. *Either/Or* and the writings of Kierkegaard as a whole contain graphic descriptions of the enveloping character of the moods of boredom, melancholy, and despair. Boredom is depicted as an aesthetical determinant which has plagued man from the very beginning. "The gods were bored, and so they created man. Adam was bored because he was alone, and so Eve was created. Thus boredom entered the world, and increased in proportion to the increase of population. Adam was bored alone; then Adam and Eve were bored together; then Adam and Eve and Cain and Abel were bored *en famille;* then the population of the world increased, and the people were bored *en masse."* The aesthetical life of pure pleasure, as well as that of pure thought, leads to an abyss of boredom and tedium. Now it is necessary to distinguish two forms of boredom. In one form boredom is apprehended as an intentional

mood which is directed toward a particular object, event, or person. One is bored with a book, a movie, or a boorish conversant. This form of boredom is merely a surface phenomenon which does not yet disclose man's true situation. In the second and more genuine form of boredom one is bored not with an intentionally specified object or person—one is bored with oneself. Man is confronted with a nameless emptiness which threatens life itself with a loss of meaning. This form of boredom brings man to a more intensified awareness of his predicament.

The enigmatic, nameless emptiness which characterizes genuine boredom is also an existential determinant of the melancholy individual. If the melancholy individual is asked what it is that weighs upon him, he is prone to reply, "I know not, I cannot explain it." Melancholy is a "spiritual ailment" or a "hysteria of the spirit" which confronts man with the abyss of emptiness and meaninglessness, and reveals the disquietude and discontinuity of his existence. But for the most part the individual who is subject to the disquieting moods of boredom and melancholy refuses to accept his condition, and seeks to conceal it through various diverting activities.

Like Blaise Pascal, Kierkegaard saw profoundly how man seeks to escape from himself through diversions which provide momentary distraction. The continuing search for diversion is descriptively characterized in the concept of the "rotation method" elucidated in Volume I. Man is bored with life in the country, so he moves to the village; he becomes bored in the village, so he moves to the city; he then becomes bored with his homeland and travels abroad; he becomes bored with life in a foreign land and then entertains the possibility of an endless journeying to alleviate his boredom. So also the melancholy individual engages in a self-defeating and frustrating search for diversion. It is in Nero, says the author, that we find the example *par excellence* of a melancholy nature that had given itself over to an endless search for diverting distractions. Nero sought to divert himself through an immersion into pleasure. He appointed "ministers of pleasure" who were entrusted with the task of finding novel ways to satisfy his desires. Only in the moment of pleasure could Nero find distraction from his melancholy. "Then he grasps after pleasure; all the world's cleverness must devise for him new pleasures, for only in the instant of pleasure does he find repose, and when that is past he gasps with faintness." When the instant of pleasure passes, Nero again plunges into melancholy. Hence a new desire must be created so that another momentary gratification may occur. But there is no end to this sort of thing, and Nero finds himself sucked into an abyss of meaninglessness and emptiness. Finally in his need for pleasure-producing distraction he orders the burning of Rome, but when the last embers die, he again gyrates into an appalling melancholy. This description of Nero's nature, we are reminded by the author, has not been undertaken as an occasion to thank God along with the Pharisee that we are different from Nero. Nero is "flesh of our flesh and bone of our bone," which is to say that in Nero a universal determinant of human existence becomes transparent.

Despair is the most intensive expression of the threat of meaninglessness and emptiness; it constitutes the culmination of the aesthetical mode of existence. The aesthetical life proves itself to be despair. In despair the self experiences a loss of hope because diversion no longer provides its momentary satisfaction. The aestheticist now realizes that he cannot find himself outside of himself—neither in his hedonistic and sensual pursuits nor in the abstractions of his speculative thought. To discover his genuine selfhood he must turn inward. He must turn toward earnestness, passion, decision, commitment, and freedom. Only in this movement will he be able to collect himself out of his dispersed and dissipated existence and become a unified and integrated self. Despair is thus an intensification of subjectivity which constitutes the gateway to authentic or genuine selfhood. In "choosing" despair the self gives birth to itself and passes from the aesthetical stage of indecision to the ethical stage of decisive commitment.

The ethical stage is the stage of decision and resolute commitment. The act of choice is an intensification of the ethical. Even the richest personality, writes the author, must be accounted as nothing before he has chosen himself. On the other hand, the poorest personality is everything for having chosen himself. Choice liberates the self both from the immediacy of pleasure and from the immediacy of reflection or pure thought, and makes possible the discovery of genuine selfhood. Through decision and commitment the self becomes integrated and "centralized." The aestheticist is always "eccentric" in that he seeks the center of his self in the periphery of hedonist or intellectualistic concerns—which means that he has lost his self. The ethical man, by virtue of having shouldered his responsibility in decision, has his center within himself. His life is centralized and unified. The unity of the ethical self is not a unity which is anchored in some residual ego or abiding substratum. The self is not an object which can be abstractly defined as having a permanent nature or a substantial fixity. Unity is achieved, not given. The self achieves or attains its unity and integrity through choice.

Choice thus becomes the central category for the ethical thinker. This is the category which lies closest to the heart and thought of Judge William. Not being a logician, he has no lengthy and impressive list of abstract categories—he has only one concrete denomination: choice. Now choice involves freedom, an either/or, and it is in this that we find the greatest treasure which man can possess. Judge William explains to the reader the central intention of his ethical elucidations when he writes: "For freedom, therefore, I am fighting. . . . I am fighting for the future, for either/or. That is the treasure I desire to bequeath to those whom I love in the world; yea, if my little son were at this instant of an age when he could thoroughly understand me, I would say to him, 'I leave to thee no fortune, no title and dignities, but I know where there lies buried a treasure which suffices to make thee richer than the whole world, and this treasure belongs to thee, and thou shalt not even express thanks to me for it lest thou take hurt to thine own soul by owing everything to another. This treasure is deposited in thine own inner self: there is an either/or which makes a man greater than the angels.'"

Judge William's central intention of calling the aestheticist to an awareness of his freedom and the importance of choosing is understood as an expression of the Socratic task of attaining self-knowledge. "Know thyself" and "Choose thyself" are conjunctive rather than disjunctive tasks. The knowledge which was the concern of Socrates was an ethical knowledge, and ethical knowledge can be achieved only through choosing. The self becomes transparent to itself only in decisive action.

In the person of Judge William we find the concrete exemplification of the ethical mode of existence. He is a married man who has commited himself in conjugal love. As such he is contrasted with the young lover of the "Diary of a Seducer," who dissipates himself in his various experiments with romantic love. Romantic and conjugal love are thus understood as existential qualities which differentiate the aesthetical and the ethical. Romantic love is experimental and nonhistorical, lacking continuity. Conjugal love expresses an inner history which gives it constancy and stability. The romantic hedonist lives in the present, and this present he experiences in abstraction from existence. The present becomes an instantaneous now, defined as the occasion for enjoyment. The past loses its existential significance and the future is never really faced. The young lover seduces a girl, and after the moment of seduction passes, all is over. The moment then becomes part of an abstracted past which has significance only as an object for melancholy recollection. Romantic love knows no repetition. The romantic hedonist lives his life as though it were a discrete succession of instantaneous nows, each now coming to be and passing away into a past which is bereft of existential importance. Everything is concentrated in the present, which is apprehended as embodying full reality. Conjugal love, on the other hand, strives for repetition. The ideal husband is one who is able to repeat his love every day. The married man thus carries within himself the memory of his past, anticipates his future, and undertakes his daily tasks and decisions in the context of his integrated wholeness. His past, future, and present are unified. It is thus that time and history become of paramount importance for conjugal love. The constancy and continuity of conjugal love are made possible through a unification of the self in its inner history.

In distinguishing between romantic and conjugal love Judge William does not intend an absolute disjunction. He speaks of marriage as the true transfiguration of romantic love. Marriage is its friend, not its enemy. Romantic love is not left behind in the transition to the ethical sphere. It becomes transfigured through the constancy of conjugal love. In the ethical stage romantic love is historicized and apprehended in terms of its temporal significance. The aesthetical always remains in the ethical, but it remains as a *relative* and *dependent* mode of existence. "By the absolute choice the ethical is always posited, but from this it does not follow by any means that the aesthetical is excluded. In the ethical the personality is concentrated in itself, so the aesthetical is absolutely excluded or is excluded as the absolute, but relatively it is still left." The romantic hedonist absolutizes the aesthetical as the final and self-sufficient dimension of

existence. The ethical man appropriates the aesthetical in its relativity and transforms it by the existential determinants of choice and commitment. At one point in his letter Judge William speaks of the three stages (aesthetical, ethical, and religious) as "three great allies." The spheres or stages of existence are not temporally successive levels of development, excluding each other in a hierarchical ascent. They are modes of existence, always in some sense present, penetrating the personality in its process of becoming. They constitute the existential cross section of the self and coexist interdependently throughout its history. No sphere is sufficient by itself. The absolutization of one of the three spheres brings about a suffocation of the self.

The phenomenon of time, which plays such an important role in ethical existence, is the focus of a profound analysis of Hegel's teaching on the alienated or unhappy consciousness. Hegel had already taught that the alienated consciousness is the self that is never present to itself, being absent from itself either in the past or in the future. The author agrees that Hegel was right in thus defining the realm of the unhappy consciousness, but argues that he was wrong in understanding it abstractly rather than existentially. Hegel "beheld the kingdom from afar off." The author understands himself to be a native inhabitant of the realm. Consciousness is alienated from itself when it is severed either from its past or from its future. The alienated consciousness has lost the memory of its life and has nothing for which to hope. Thus, it culminates in despair. The unified consciousness has within it both pastness and futurity. Memory and hope are unified in the center of personality. The ethical man attains this unified consciousness in the moment of decisive action. In the act of choice the past is taken up, the future is acknowledged and faced, and the self is centralized.

The touchstone of the decision through which the self achieves its unity and integrity is inwardness. An authentic choice is a choice made inwardly in passion and earnestness. The accent falls on the *way of choosing* rather than on *what is chosen*. In the ethical sphere man is educated in *how* to choose. His first concern is not with the choice of the "right," but with the earnestness and inwardness which determines the movement of choice. This does not mean that the ethical thinker has no interest in the moral content of choice. It does mean, however, that the moral content cannot be abstracted as a *what*—as an objectively determined and legislated moral standard. An action made solely because of external standards is bereft of moral content. Only that action which proceeds from the depths of inwardness qualifies the self as ethical. Judge William has little interest in a table of virtues which delineates abstract moral requirements. Ethical action is not a matter of following virtues. It is a matter of self-knowledge and self-commitment. Like Nietzsche's strong man, Kierkegaard's ethical man exists "beyond good and evil."

Either/Or concludes with a prayer and a sermon. This is a reminder to the reader that the ethical stage is not the final dimension of existence, but is itself transfigured by a religious state. As the ethical stage transfigures the aesthetical, so the religious transfigures the ethical by introducing the existential determinants of suffering, guilt, sin, and faith. But *Either/Or* does not carry the existential elucidation beyond the ethical. One of the reasons why Kierkegaard wrote his book, *Stages on Life's Way* (which appeared two years after *Either/Or*) was to give proper due to the religious stage.

PHILOSOPHICAL FRAGMENTS

Author: Søren Kierkegaard (1813-1855)
Type of work: Existential theology
First published: 1844

PRINCIPAL IDEAS ADVANCED

Men can be separated into three groups, depending on the values they hold: the aesthetes want entertainment, pleasure, and freedom from boredom; ethical men live for the sake of duty, taking on obligations in order to be bound to discharge them; and religious men live in order to obey God.

The Socratic idea of religious truth is that truth in religious matters is not unique, that one learns religious truths by recollection of what one has learned in the realm of Ideas.

The alternative position (the Christian view) is that God in time (Jesus Christ) is the teacher of men, that faith is an organ of knowing, that knowledge comes through the consciousness of sin, and that in a moment of decision a man's life can be changed.

Søren Kierkegaard's *Philosophical Fragments* is the central work in a series of books which are marked by a consistent theme, a most unusual manner of presentation, pervasive irony, and a single-minded effort to present Christianity in a fashion which requires the reader to reach some sort of decision about it. The irony of Kierkegaard is evident even in the title of the book: *Philosophical Fragments*. Very few philosophers would entitle their main work a "fragment," or try to present in less than one hundred pages the core of their position.

In order to read Kierkegaard with some degree of understanding, it is necessary (for most readers, at any rate) to have some knowledge of the general plan of his literary work. One of the essential features of his philosophical position is the doctrine of the "Stages." Kierkegaard believed that men can be separated into three groups, depending on what values they hold as fundamental. He calls these three groups "aesthetes," "ethicists," and "religionists."

The *aesthete* is a person who lives for the interesting; he wants entertainment and variety in his life, and he seeks to avoid boredom as the worst evil that can overtake him. He lives to find immediate satisfactions and he avoids making any long-term commitments. All men have the aesthetic as the basic material of their lives; many remain in the aesthetic stage throughout life. But some men move into another sphere, the ethical.

The *ethicist* lives for the sake of doing his duty; he replaces the interesting versus the boring with the good versus the bad. The kind of man Immanuel Kant had in mind when he urged us to do our duties rather than follow our inclinations is the kind of man Kierkegaard called the ethical man. The ethicist's life is successful if he takes on as many obligations to other men as possible and does his best to discharge these obligations.

Kierkegaard contrasted the ethical man with the aesthete in his first book, *Either/Or* (1843), by posing the question of love and marriage. The aesthete falls in love, lives for a multitude of engagements (but no marriages), wants romance in the Hollywood sense. The ethical man does not fall in love, but rather chooses to love, wants a short engagement so that he may enter the state of being married (and thereby become duty bound to another person for the remainder of his days), and finds his romance in the daily routine rather than in secret, passionate moments.

A great many persons with this kind of ethical concern base the ethical rules which govern their lives in God's will. For such persons, there is no difference between being ethical and being religious. However, Kierkegaard felt that the Christian religion demanded a different orientation from that which characterizes the ethical man. Kierkegaard did not believe that the Christian concept of sin could be explained by saying that to sin is to break an ethical rule. Sin is not violation of a rule, but violation of the person of God. Kierkegaard contrasted the ethical man's orientation with the *religious* man's orientation in his book *Fear and Trembling* (1843), where he considered the problems arising out of Abraham's intended sacrifice of his son, Isaac. As Kierkegaard saw it, Abraham had to choose between the ethical demand to avoid murder and the religious command from God that he sacrifice his son. Kierkegaard raised the question whether it might not be the case that religious commitment sometimes requires a man to suspend his ethical concern. The religious man may at times face the temptation to be good rather than holy.

Such is the doctrine of the stages in Kierkegaard's philosophy. There is one other feature of Kierkegaard's writing that should be pointed out before considering *Philosophical Fragments* in more detail. It is the technique Kierkegaard called "indirect communication." Considerable time might be spent elaborating it, but for the present purpose it will be sufficient to point out that the technique implied that the doctrine of the stages should not be stated directly. The representatives of the various stages should not be described from the point of view of an external observer, but presented "from within," so to speak. To this end, Kierkegaard often adopted pseudonyms in his books. He felt he could best present the aesthetic stage by imagining an aesthete, then writing out what such an aesthetic man would say. *Either/Or,* for example, is an extended correspondence between "a young man" and his older friend, "Judge Wilhelm." Kierkegaard does not directly enter the picture at all, and he offers no judgment between the two views of life presented by the young man and the judge; the reader is left to decide. Kierkegaard was quite successful in this matter, even presenting the imaginary characters with different writing styles. The young man writes beautifully, is poetic, sensitive, and lyrical; the judge writes in a pedestrian style, lecturing as he goes, paying little attention to literary graces.

The pseudonymous author of the *Fragments* is Johannes Climacus—one who is writing about something which is at the climax of the total problem that concerned Kierkegaard throughout his entire literary and philosophical production. Climacus is detached, ironic, and supposedly uncommitted on the immediate problem he is considering; namely, the possibility of giving a different view of religious truth from that presented by Socrates. Socrates is used in the book as a foil, as a man holding a position against which an alternative view can be seen more sharply. Christianity, as Kierkegaard understood it, is the alternative, of course, but, although the reader understands this quite early in the book, the position is not called Christianity until the last paragraph of the book.

The "Socratic" position which Climacus assumes in the book is a rather common interpretation of the Socrates of Plato's dialogues. It may be put briefly as follows: Truth in religious matters does not differ from other kinds of truth. The point of religion is to hold true beliefs about God and to act in accordance with them. Coming to hold true beliefs, in religion as in other areas of human concern, is essentially a matter of recollection, of remembering what a man knew in the realm of the Ideas before birth but forgot when the soul was imprisoned in the body. The teacher, in this case, does not introduce anything new to the learner, but merely serves as mid-wife, helping the learner to recall what he once knew. After the recollection occurs, the learner adjusts to the true propositions, and the teacher drops out of the knowing relation. The teacher is an occasion, but not a condition, for knowing.

The essential elements in the (Christian) alternative position regarding religious truth are set forth quite openly by Kierkegaard's pseudonym in the "Moral" which he appends to the *Fragments*. The Christian "hypothesis" (as Climacus calls it) differs from the Socratic position, as sketched above, in assuming *faith* as an organ of knowing, in presupposing that there can be in men a *consciousness of sin*, in supposing that there can be a *moment of decision* which changes the course of a man's life, and in assuming a different kind of *teacher* from Socrates —namely, God in time (that is, Jesus Christ). The detachment of Climacus can be seen in the fact that he states these new assumptions so clearly in this "Moral," thus enabling the reader to reject Christianity simply and yet with understanding, if he so desires. Furthermore, Climacus merely states that the hypothesis he has been elaborating differs from Socrates' position in these respects. The question of which hypothesis is true is an entirely different question, he says, and he makes no effort to settle this latter question.

Now if Socrates is right, Climacus argues, the truth is within a man. The teacher merely helps the pupil to realize what he had known all along. In such a case, a man is in the truth rather than in error. In addition, the teacher is not important, since he does not remove the learner from error

nor does he introduce him to new truth. Further, the time at which a learner recalls the truth is not important. All in all, the situation is similar to what happened with most, if not all, of us when we learned the basic elements of arithmetic; we can no longer remember who taught them to us or when we were taught. The important thing is that two and two make four, and they always have and always will.

The alternative to this view obviously involves assuming that man is not naturally in the truth but is naturally in error. If this is the case, then the teacher must first give the learner the condition for leaving error and apprehending truth. Then the teacher must provide the truth for the learner to apprehend. The moment at which the learner leaves error and apprehends truth is now quite important and decisive for the learner. And the teacher must be more than an ordinary man, since he is essential to the learner's apprehension of the truth. Indeed, the teacher is so crucial that he is even necessary in order that the learner may recognize that he is in error. Such a teacher, Climacus says, we could appropriately call "Savior."

These elements in Climacus' alternative hypothesis are obviously elements in the traditional Christian account. The fact that one is naturally in error rather than in the truth and also that one does not even recognize such a condition clearly refer to the Christian doctrine of sin, and Climacus does call being in error "sin." The truth that one gains from the teacher is just as obviously the faith that Christians possess. The very unusual teacher who is essential to coming into the truth is, as Climacus calls him, "God in time"; that is, Jesus of Nazareth. And the crucial moment in which a man leaves error for truth is the conversion experience that is the object of so much preaching in the Christian churches. Climacus leaves no doubt that these identifications are appropriate, since he often speaks to the reader about what he has written, citing the original sources of the "hypothesis" he is developing.

In outline, then, the account in the *Fragments* is a very familiar one, differing from the usual Christian account only in the words used to express it and in the reference to the Socratic alternative. There are, however, some implications of Climacus' simple account which are deserving of further treatment. Two matters should be looked into further here: Climacus' account of "the Absolute Paradox," and the question of the "disciple at second hand."

The Absolute Paradox is a discussion of the philosophical significance of the Christian claim that God was incarnate in Jesus of Nazareth. One of the implications of the Socratic view that the truth is somehow within man and needs only to be drawn out by a skillful teacher such as Socrates is that the human mind is adequate for knowing the truth, even religious truth. If, on the contrary, man does not have the truth within himself in some sense, then what a man ought to know or needs to know is beyond man himself —it is the unknown. Or, as Climacus calls it, it is "the other," the absolutely other. But if it is the absolutely other than man, then man's reason is not competent to know it. Yet man, if he is to achieve the truth, must come to know this absolutely other. To this end, so Christians hold, God—the absolutely other—became incarnate in man;

that is to say, the absolutely other became not absolutely other. This requires us to say, then, that the Unknown (God) is both absolutely other and not absolutely other than man. And this statement, clearly, has the form of a self-contradiction.

One of the senses of the word "paradox" is such that a paradox is an apparent contradiction which is seen, on examination, not to be a contradiction. Thus, it is paradoxical to say of a certain member of a group, who is very talkative, that he says less than anyone else in the group. Here, at first glance, it looks as if we are saying that the person both talks a great deal and does not talk a great deal. But the puzzle is resolved quickly when attention is called to the way the words "talk" and "say" are used; namely, although he *talks* a great deal, he *says* very little. Most of his talk is insignificant, it is idle chatter. Such a paradox, then, can be resolved by making some kind of distinction between the apparently incompatible predicates.

In saying that his paradox is "Absolute," however, Climacus seems to be saying that it cannot be resolved. The reason the paradox cannot be resolved lies in the uniqueness of the particular paradox in question. It is essential to Climacus' paradox that the word "absolutely" be included. God both is and is not *absolutely* other than man. If we said of Jones that he is other and not other than Smith, we could go on to specify the similarities and differences between the two men: both are philosophers, but one is interested only in logic, while the other is interested only in ethics. They are alike, yet they differ. But if Jones were said to be *absolutely* other than Smith, then no comparisons could be made at all. When we use the expression "totally different" in ordinary speech, we usually mean to emphasize strongly a difference which is really only partial. We mean that two things differ fundamentally in *some* (but not all) respects. But Climacus is using "absolutely other" in a rather strict way, and this means that even to express the total difference is to go beyond the strict limits of language and understanding. Strictly speaking, we cannot even mention a total difference between two things; the very mention of them indicates at least one respect in which they are not totally different; namely, they are alike in that they can be talked about.

If this is the case, however—that God or the unknown is both totally like and totally unlike man, and yet that we should not even be able to state this—then the paradox Climacus is expressing cannot be resolved. It cannot be resolved because the very language of this paradox, in one sense at least, does not have meaning. The paradox is absolute. Yet we must express ourselves. Or at least Christian men feel that they must express themselves. There is an urge in men, Climacus feels, which drives them to try to express the inexpressible. (Reason, Climacus says, seeks its own downfall.) To come at this point in a somewhat different way, most men can remember trying to express the uniqueness of their beloved in a language which has its power in virtue of expressing the common features, the repeatable elements, the universally instanced qualities of experience. We try to express the unique in terms of the common, and the result is often the paradoxical or the trite. This is why the modern suburbanite's calling his wife "Honey" is at once so full of significance for him, and yet so trite to his neighbors.

If Christianity is true, then its central claim—that God was incarnate in Jesus of Nazareth—leads to a paradox, a paradox which cannot be resolved as paradoxes usually are. But there is also another sense of the word "paradox" which is involved in the discussion in the *Fragments*. Another meaning of the word (its etymological meaning) is "contrary to the received opinion." The Absolute Paradox is paradoxical also in this sense, and this leads to another point Climacus makes in connection with the paradox. Climacus' discussion of the Absolute Paradox is followed by a section in which he claims that man's response to the paradox is to be offended. The religious man, when he has passed through the "moment" and has changed from being in error to being in the truth (to having faith), has his ordinary value commitments upset. Some of Jesus' remarks, at least as they are reported to us in the Christian Scriptures, surely run counter to the prevailing values of everyday life. Common sense—perhaps we have a sample of it in Polonius' advice to his son Laertes in Shakespeare's *Hamlet:* "This above all, to thine own self be true . . ."—surely does not suggest that we turn the other cheek when a man strikes us, nor does it agree that the meek shall inherit the earth. What men usually adopt as a pattern for life is in conflict with the pattern set forth in the Christian Gospels. Men usually want "success" rather than "peace" (in the Christian sense). And so the Christian recommendation, based on its being a revelation from a transcendent God, offends man. Why should one love his neighbor rather than sell to him at a profit? Because God says so.

But this recommendation is unreasonable. True enough, but who is to say that God is reasonable? Did not God reveal himself in a most unexpected way? Namely, as the apparently illegitimate son of a poor Nazarene woman, born outside wedlock and in the ancient equivalent of a garage? The Christian account is so contrary to the received opinion of what is of real value that it offends the hearer. Such is Climacus' observation.

Another consequence of the Christian account is that if God revealed himself in Jesus of Nazareth, then it seems he gave special advantages to those men who were contemporary with Jesus and knew Jesus personally, advantages which are denied to the rest of us who are not contemporaries of Jesus. Climacus argues that the immediate followers of Jesus, the "contemporary disciples," enjoyed no advantage over the non-contemporary, the "disciple at second hand." The paradox is the key to Climacus' position here. What the contemporary *saw* was not God, but the man Jesus. It was not apparent or obvious to a normal observer that Jesus is or was more than simply a good man. The divinity which Christians attribute to Jesus was not evident to the senses, but represented an additional characteristic about Jesus which men recognized only in the light of what traditionally has been called the gift of grace from God. Men did not naturally look at Jesus and see His divinity; they beheld only His manhood. Only if God granted grace to the observer, did the observer "see" the divinity of Jesus. Again using the traditional Christian terminology, we can say that even the Apostles could not recognize the divinity of Jesus without having been enlightened

by the Holy Spirit. Thus, the contemporary disciple enjoyed no advantage over the disciple at second hand insofar as Jesus' divinity is concerned. The only advantage the contemporary enjoyed concerns Jesus' manhood, His historical existence. Indeed, if there is any advantage, it is the advantage which the disciple at second hand enjoys in having the testimony of several generations that the man Jesus is also God. The reiteration of this claim brings it home as a possibility in a way that the contemporary disciple did not experience.

Such, then, is the position set forth by Kierkegaard, through the pseudonym "Johannes Climacus," in the *Philosophical Fragments*. It is what is at the heart of the (religious) "existentialist" position Kierkegaard gave the name to. The position is elaborated, by the same pseudonym, in a much longer and more involved book, *The Concluding Unscientific Postscript to the Philosophical Fragments* (1846)—which runs to 550 pages as compared with the ninety-three pages of the *Fragments*— but it is the same position nevertheless. It is stated clearly and succinctly in the *Fragments* as a hypothesis; in the *Postscript* an attempt is made to discuss what would happen to a sophisticated person were he to attempt to put into operation in his own life what is discussed merely as a possibility in the *Fragments*. In *The Concluding Unscientific Postscript to the Philosophical Fragments* Climacus concerns himself with the personal question: How do I become a Christian? But the *Postscript* depends upon the *Fragments,* and the *Fragments* is really the central statement of Kierkegaard's position. Rarely does one find such an important question as the philosophical account of

Christianity stated with the precision, clarity, and wit which Kierkegaard exhibits in the *Fragments*. Kierkegaard was possessed of a keen intellect, a logical passion, and an ability to give expression to one of the most significant

alternatives in Western Civilization in a manner that retains the kernel of Christianity yet makes possible its discussion in the modern milieu. To have done this is a philosophical and literary achievement of the first order.

CONCLUDING UNSCIENTIFIC POSTSCRIPT

Author: Søren Kierkegaard (1813-1855)
Type of work: Existential theology
First published: 1846

PRINCIPAL IDEAS ADVANCED

The subjective thinker is an engaged thinker, one who by his activity commits himself to an understanding of the truth which, by the manner of his existence, he is; he seeks to comprehend himself, not as an abstraction, but as an ethically engaged, existing subject.

Only individuals matter; existence is individual in character.

An existent individual is one in the process of becoming; he moves into an uncertain future.

Since death is imminent every choice has infinite worth, and every moment is a unique occasion for decisive action; each individual achieves his being through decision.

In his development the thinker may pass through the aesthetical stage (in which he experiments but does not commit himself), the ethical stage (in which he acts decisively and commits himself), to the religious stage (in which his sin is acknowledged and he commits himself to God).

Kierkegaard has been called the "Danish Socrates." The *Concluding Unscientific Postscript to the Philosophical Fragments,* which is the central point of his whole authorship, bears out Kierkegaard's legitimate claim to this title. In the *Postscript* Socrates is acknowledged as the illustrious Greek who never lost sight of the fact that a thinker remains an existing individual. The Socratic maieutic method, with its use of ignorance, irony, and dialectics,

pervades the whole work. The Athenian gadfly reappears in these pages in a modern counterpart.

The Socratic method is used by Johannes Climacus (Kierkegaard's pseudonym) to elicit from the reader an awareness that truth is subjectivity. The doctrine of "the subjective thinker" stands at the center of this classic, and it provides the pivot point around which all the themes revolve. The subjective thinker is the *engaged* or *involved* thinker whose thought, directed toward a penetration of his inner consciousness, moves in passion and earnestness. He finds in the theoretical detachment of objective reflection a comic neglect of the existing individual who does the reflecting. Objective reflection tends to make the subject accidental and transforms his existence into something indifferent and abstract. The accent for the subjective thinker falls on the *how;* the accent for objective reflection falls on the *what.* Objective truth designates a "what" or an objective content that can be observed in theoretical detachment. Subjective truth is a "how" that must be inwardly appropriated. Truth as subjectivity thus becomes inward appropriation. Truth, subjectively appropriated, is a truth which is *true for me.* It is a truth which I *live,* not merely observe. It is a truth which I *am,* not merely possess. Truth is a mode of action or a manner of existence. The subjective thinker lives the truth; he *exists it.*

One need not proceed far into the pages of the *Postscript* to become aware that Kierkegaard's arch enemy, against whom his Socratic, ironical barbs are directed, is Hegel. Johannes Climacus finds in the systematized, objective and theoretical reflection of Hegel's philosophy a fantastic distortion of truth and an ingenious system of irrelevancy. Climacus never tires of harpooning the System. The Hegelian, in neglecting the crucial distinction between thought and reality, erects a system of thought which comically excludes his own existence. He seeks to comprehend himself as an expression of abstract, universal, and timeless categories; thus he loses himself as a concrete, particular, and temporal existent. "One must therefore be very careful in dealing with a philosopher of the Hegelian school, and, above all, to make certain of the identity of the being with whom one has the honor to discourse. Is he a human being, an existing human being? Is he himself *sub specie aeterni,* even when he sleeps, eats, blows his nose, or whatever else a human being does? Is he himself the pure 'I am I?' . . . Does he in fact exist?" The Hegelian affords an instance of philosophical comedy in which we have thought without a thinker. He erects a marvelous intellectual palace in which he himself does not live. The subject, in Hegel's objective reflection, becomes accidental, and truth as subjectivity is lost.

Descartes shares Hegel's fate of falling under the Kierkegaardian irony and devastating intellectual harpooning. It was Descartes who provided modern philosophy with the *cogito, ergo sum* for its foundation. Now either the "I" which is the subject of the *cogito* refers to a particular existing human being, in which case nothing is proved (If I *am* thinking, what wonder that I *am!*) or else the "I" refers to a universal pure ego. But such an entity has only a conceptual existence, and the *ergo* loses its meaning, the proposition being reduced to a tautology. The attempt by Descartes to prove his existence by the fact that he thinks leads to no real conclusion, for insofar as he thinks he has already abstracted from his own existence. Descartes had already prepared the stage for the later Hegel's identification of abstract thought and reality. Contra Descartes, Climacus is ready to defend the claim that the real subject is not the cognitive subject, but rather the ethically engaged, existing subject. In both Descartes and Hegel he finds that cognition and reason have been viciously abstracted from the concrete particularity of existence.

The subjective thinker emphatically rejects the rationalists' reification of reason, but he in no way denies the validity of thought so long as it is existentially rooted. The subjective thinker is indeed a thinker who makes use of thought in seeking to penetrate the structures of his subjectivity and so to understand himself in his existence. The nobility of the Greek thinker (particularly Socrates) is that he was able to do this. He existed in advance of speculation and the System. The subjective thinker is at the same time a thinker and an existing human being. This is a truth, says Climacus, a statement which, deserving emphasis, cannot too often be repeated, and the neglect of which has brought about much confusion. Kierkegaard was by no means an opponent of thought. He insisted only that thought be placed back into existence, following its vicious abstraction by Hegel. "If thought speaks deprecatingly of the imagination, imagination in its turn speaks deprecatingly of thought; and likewise with feeling. The task is not to exalt the one at the expense of the other, but to give them an equal status, to unify them in simultaneity; the medium in which they are unified is *existence*."

When the subjective thinker thus makes the movement of understanding himself in his existence, he discovers that in the order of reality (as distinct from the order of abstract thought) individuals—and individuals alone—exist. Existence is indelibly individual in character. Kierkegaard's philosophy is a crusade for the reality of the concrete individual. "The individual"

(*Enkelte*) was Kierkegaard's central category. It is in this category that he saw bound up any importance that he as a subjective thinker might have. This category was so decisive for his whole literary efforts that he asked that it be inscribed on his tombstone (and it was). The human self is not humanity in general. Humanity does not exist; only individual human beings exist. Existential reality resides not in the genus or in the species but in the concrete individual. Universals, like crowds, are abstractions which have neither hands nor feet.

To exist means to be an individual, but to exist also means to be in the process of becoming. "An existing individual is constantly in process of becoming; the actual existing subjective thinker constantly reproduces this existential situation in his thoughts, and translates all his thinking into terms of process." Although Hegel in his *Logic* had much to say about processes in which opposites are combined into higher unities, his doctrine of becoming is ultimately illusory because it does not understand process from the point of view of concrete existence. Logic and pure thought can never capture the existential reality of becoming, for logical entities are *states of being* which are timeless and fixed. In the moment that Hegel wrote his *Logic*, with the intention of encompassing the whole of reality, he forfeited the concrete becoming in which the subjective thinker finds himself disclosed. But this intractable reality of concrete becoming remains as a source of profound embarrassment for the Hegelian—particularly when he is ready to write the last paragraph of his system and finds that existence is not yet finished! Kierkegaardian irony reaches its height when Climacus undertakes to satirize the System. "I shall be as willing as the next man to fall down in worship before the System, if only I can manage to set eyes on it. Hitherto I have had no success; and though I have young legs, I am almost weary from running back and forth between Herod and Pilate. Once or twice I have been on the verge of bending the knee. But at the last moment, when I already had my handkerchief spread on the ground, to avoid soiling my trousers, and I made a trusting appeal to one of the initiated who stood by: 'Tell me now sincerely, is it entirely finished; for if so I will kneel down before it, even at the risk of ruining a pair of trousers (for on account of the heavy traffic to and fro, the road has become quite muddy),'— I always received the same answer: 'No, it is not yet quite finished.' And so there was another postponement— of the System, and of my homage." System and finality are correlative concepts. But existence, which is constantly in the process of becoming, is never finished. Thus, an existential system is impossible. Reality itself is a system—but a system only for God. There can be no system for an existing individual who always stands in the throes of becoming.

As existence involves individuality and becoming, so assuredly does it involve the future. One exists in a process of becoming by facing a future. The subjective thinker is passionately and earnestly interested in the time of immediate experience as it qualifies his existence. Time for the existing subject is not a time in general—an abstract, cosmic time which is spatialized through objectivizing categories. His interest has to do with the time of his inner experience—time as it is concretely lived rather than abstractly known. In the subjective thinker's immediate experience of time, the future has priority. His life is lived primarily out of the future, for in his subjectivity he understands himself as moving into a future. This future generates uncertainty and anxiety. Tomorrow may rob me of all my earthly goods and leave me desolate. The subjective thinker, when he penetrates to the core of his subjectivity, thus finds the uncertainty of life itself. Wherever there is subjectivity, there is uncertainty.

Death is one of the most ethically significant uncertainties of life. Subjective thought discloses death as an imminent possibility. But for the most part man devises means of concealing this imminent possibility. He approaches the fact of death through the eyes of objective reflection and thus conveniently transforms it into something in general. Viewed *objectively*, death is a general and universal occurrence which befalls all forms of life. Viewed subjectively, death is an imminent uncertainty which pertains to my particular existence and which makes a difference for my individual decisions. Death is thus apprehended not as a generalized empirical factuality, but as a task or a deed. "If the task of life is to become subjective, then the thought of death is not, for the individual subject, something in general, but is verily a deed." Death, subjectively understood, becomes a task in that it is defined in terms of its ethical expression. It is experienced and appropriated in an anticipatory conception in such a way that it transforms the whole of man's life. When death is existentially appropriated, then every decision receives a singular importance. If death is imminent every choice has infinite worth, and every moment is a unique occasion for decisive action. Death makes a difference for life.

In the subjective movements of his engaged existence the subjective thinker discloses his existence as qualified by individuality, becoming, time, and death. Already in these movements the pathway is opened for decisive action. The category of decision becomes a centralizing concept for the subjective thinker. In facing a future the existing subject is called to decision. Thus the subjective thinker is at the same time an ethical thinker. He understands his personal existence as a task and a responsibility. He must choose in order to attain his authentic selfhood. His essential humanity is not given. It is achieved through decision. The greatness of man is that he has an *either/or*. This either/or becomes a matter of indifference for the Hegelian. In Hegel's timeless categories there is no place for decisive action or ethical commitment. "Ethics has been crowded out of the System, and as a substitute for it there has been included a something which confuses the historical with the individual, the bewildering and noisy demands of the age with the eternal demand that conscience makes upon the individual. Ethics concentrates upon the individual, and ethically it is the task of every individual to become an entire man; just as it is the ethical presupposition that every man is born in such a condition that he can become one." The objective reflection which is so peculiar to the System transforms everyone into an observer. But existing individuals are actors as well as observers. They make choices which affect the whole of their lives. They are engaged in action which is decisive for themselves as well as for others. The ethically existing subject is thus of utmost importance; but for the Hegelian, who is concerned with the general developments of world history and the meditation of opposites in this world history, the ethical subject remains unacknowledged.

Kierkegaard regarded the existentially decisive act for the ethically engaged subject as not an external action but rather as an internal decision. It is inward passion rather than external consequences which constitutes the criterion of ethical action. The person who does not own a penny can be as charitable as the person who gives away a kingdom. Let us suppose, says Climacus, that the Levite, who found the man that had fallen among thieves between Jericho and Jerusalem, was inwardly concerned to help sufferers in distress. Let us suppose further that when he met the victim he was frightened at the possibility of robbers near by and hastened on lest he also become a victim. He failed to act, giving no help to the sufferer. But after having left the victim he was overcome by remorse, and hurried back to the scene, but arrived too late. The Samaritan had already helped the victim in his distress. If this were the sequence of events would one not have to say that the Levite acted? Indeed he acted, says Climacus, and in an inwardly decisive sense, even though his action had no external expression.

Much time is devoted in the *Postscript* to a delineation of the "stages" or "existence spheres"—a delineation which Kierkegaard had already undertaken in two of his earlier works, *Either/Or* (1843) and *Stages on Life's Way* (1845). However, for the first time in his writings we have an analysis and description of irony and humor as transitional stages between the aesthetical and the ethical, and the ethical and the religious, respectively. The aesthetical stage is the stage of experimentation. The aestheticist is one who experiments with various possibilities but never commits himself in passionate choice. He experiments with love but never commits himself in marriage. He experiments with thought but never commits himself in action. A constant flight from the responsibility of decision characterizes the aestheticist. Thus he lacks the decisive content of subjectivity—inwardness, earnestness, and passion. It is only in the ethical stage that these decisive determinants appear. The transition to the ethical stage is by way of irony. Climacus speaks of irony as the "boundary zone" between the aesthetical and the ethical. The purpose of irony is to rouse man from his unauthentic aesthetical floundering to an ethical consciousness. Irony elicits the discrepancy between the inward and outward, as this discrepancy is expressed in the life man. Irony makes man aware of the discrepancy between his inward lack of wisdom and his outward claim of its possession. It makes man aware that his outward profession of virtue betrays an inward lack of it. Irony constitutes the first awareness of the ethical, seeks to bring these suppressed discrepancies to light, and thus drives beyond itself to the next stage.

The ethical stage is the sphere of decisive action and self-commitment. The ethical man has resolutely chosen himself and exists in passion and in inwardness. The personality of the aestheticist is dispersed because of his floundering in possibilities. The personality of the ethical man is unified or centralized because he has been able to commit himself in definite modes of action. But the ground of this unification and the ultimate source of this commitment is not disclosed until the self apprehends itself in the movements of the religious sphere. Although in tension, the ethical and the religious are so close, says Climacus, that they are in constant communication with one another. It is for this reason that the two stages are often hyphenated and designated as the ethico-religious sphere. The "boundary zone" between the ethical and the religious is humor. The ethical thinker drives beyond the ethical to the religious through the expression of humor, in which there is a protest against the externalization of ethical norms and standards. The humorist is aware of this externalization, which tends to become identified with the religious, contests it as the proper measure, but still is unable to establish a God relationship in terms of religious passion *stricte sic dictus*. (Kierkegaard's provocative book, *Fear and Trembling*, 1843, incomparably expresses this suspension of an externalized ethics through the movement of faith, exemplified by Abraham in the intended sacrifice of his son Isaac.) Only when the existing subject has apprehended his relationship to God as a relationship qualified by inwardness and passion does he proceed to the religious stage.

The new determinant which is introduced in the religious stage is the determinant of suffering. Suffering is the highest intensification of subjectivity. In it we see the fullest expression of inwardness. The suffering which is acknowledged in this stage, however, must not be confused with

631

the poetic representations of suffering peculiar to the aesthetical stage, nor with the reflection *about* suffering which is always qualitatively different from the fact of suffering, nor with suffering as a simple outward ethical manifestation. Religious suffering is an expression of an inward God-relationship, like that of Job, which remains opaque to the aesthetical and ethical consciousness.

The religious stage is internally differentiated by two levels of existence—religiousness A and religiousness B. Religiousness A is the religion of immanence. Religiousness B is the "paradoxical religiousness," that in which the qualitative distinction between God and man is disclosed, and God's presence in time is revealed in the paradox of Christ. The distinction between A and B also expresses the corresponding distinction between guilt-consciousness and sin-consciousness. Guilt, properly understood, is a determinant of religiousness A; sin is a determinant of religiousness B. Guilt is a disrelationship of the subject with himself. It points to an internal fissure within consciousness which results because of an alienation from his absolute *telos*. It is still a movement within immanence. In religiousness B guilt becomes sin. The disrelationship of the subject with himself is now apprehended as a disrelationship with God. The existing subject can acquire a guilt-consciousness through the purely human movement of dialectics in which he understands himself as alienated from himself in the process of becoming. But sin-consciousness requires a disclosure by God so as to reveal to man that his guilt is at one and the same time an implication of sin. The pagan can have no consciousness of sin. Sin-consciousness emerges only in the subject's awareness of himself as existing in a disrelationship with God. This God is a God who has entered time and history. It is thus that religiousness B finds its supreme expression in Christianity, with its teachings of the "Absolute Paradox" or "Deity in time." As the "paradoxical religiousness," religiousness B affirms a qualitative distinction between God and man. God is wholly and utterly transcendent to the temporal order. Thus, religiousness B breaks with religiousness A. There is no natural kinship between the eternal and the temporal. And so the advent of eternity in time is disclosed as a paradox. Christ is the absolute paradox who reveals God in time, makes man aware of his sin, and calls him to faith and decisive commitment through which sin is overcome.

In his analysis and description of the religious stage as the crown and culmination of the three stages (which must be understood not in terms of temporal sequences of successive development, but rather in terms of copresent qualifications of subjectivity), the author makes his central intention quite apparent. The leading question which concerns Climacus is already put to the reader in the introduction. "The subjective problem concerns the relationship of the individual to Christianity. To put it quite simply: How may I, Johannes Climacus, participate in the happiness promised by Christianity?" It is significant that in the appendix, "For an understanding with the reader," the question is reiterated: "Now I ask how I am to become a Christian." This is indeed Kierkegaard's central question, posed not only in the *Postscript*, but in all of

632

his other writings. Explaining his own perspective as an author, Kierkegaard informs his readers in his book *The Point of View* (1849) that underlying the whole of his literary work is the central concern of how to become a Christian—a task which is extremely difficult in Christendom.

FORCE AND MATTER

Author: Friedrich Karl Christian Ludwig Büchner (1824-1899)
Type of work: Metaphysics, natural philosophy
First published: 1855

PRINCIPAL IDEAS ADVANCED

There is no force without matter, and no matter without force.
Matter is immortal, and the laws of nature are immutable.
Everything in nature is the result of a natural evolution, not of some creative supernatural force; and there is no evidence of design in nature.
The soul and the brain are inseparably connected.
There are no innate ideas.
There is no strict distinction between organic and inorganic matter, and the soul of man differs only quantitatively from the souls of brutes.

"No force without matter—no matter without force!" This is Büchner's thesis, from which he concludes that there is not and cannot be such a thing as completely inert matter, nor disembodied force. Hence it is impossible for there to have been a creative power that produced the universe out of itself or out of nothing; the universe is eternal. In any case, since a disembodied creative power would exist only when active, it could not have antedated the universe.

The immortality of matter is (presumably) proved by chemistry. "There exists a phrase, repeated *ad nauseam,* of 'mortal body and immortal spirit.' A closer examination causes us with more truth to reverse the sentence." Force is likewise immortal, according to Büchner: "We call the truth simple and self-evident, because it results from a simple consideration of the relation of cause and effect." The eight different forces—gravitation, mechanical force, heat, light, electricity, magnetism, affinity, cohesion—are interconvertible, but their sum is constant.

Matter is very finely divisible, as the microscope shows; Büchner doubts whether there is any limit to divisibility. Space is infinite, and matter is distributed, on the whole, evenly through it; if it were not, the universe would have a center of gravity, and would collapse. (Büchner was unaware of Olbers' proof (1825) that if the universe were infinite and homogeneous the light at the earth's surface would have an intensity 40,000 times that of sunlight.)

633

The laws of nature are immutable; there are no miracles. In any case, if there were miracles, their existence would afford an argument *against* the theological conception of God as the Perfect Being: "If the world has been created by God perfect, how can it require any repairs?" One ought not to lament natural necessity, since the conception emancipates man from the degraded state of "a puppet in the hands of unknown powers." Since the natural laws that hold in this part of the universe are in effect everywhere, it is possible, or even probable, that there is life and thought like ours throughout the universe.

The heavens have been formed by the action of gravitational forces on diffuse matter. The whole process is mechanically explicable; "nowhere is there a trace of an arbitrary finger, which has ordered the heavens, or pointed out the paths of comets." The earth is immensely old (more than a billion years); it has evolved from an incandescent state to its present condition gradually, under the influence of forces still operative. To suppose that the whole process is a manifestation of the work of a creative power is "whimsical," for why should such a power have need of "all these roundabouts?"

The fossil record proves an evolution of life also, from simple forms of sea and plant life through gigantic reptiles to mammals and, ultimately, man. (In editions before 1860, Büchner's speculations about the processes of organic evolution are vague and fantastic; after 1860, he writes approvingly of Darwin's work.) Despite the failure of science to exhibit convincing instances of spontaneous generation now, such *must* have occurred at some time in the earth's history when conditions were right; or else the earth was seeded by means of meteorites, some of which have been shown to contain organic compounds. It is probable that the human species is not descended from one original pair, but rather the races arose independently. Evidence for such a theory is provided by the fact that there exist unrelated families of languages. The hierarchy of organic life is continuous. The fossils fill up some of the apparent gaps, and besides, at the present time the Negro is intermediate between man and ape. (Büchner's views about Negroes are all based on citations from "authorities"; it does not seem that he had ever actually seen a Negro. Thus, his views—absurd today—reflect a prejudice sometimes associated with purely speculative reasoning.)

To impute design to nature, Büchner argued, is to "admire a wonder which the intellect has created itself." "The stag was not endowed with long legs to enable him to run fast, but he runs fast because his legs are long." Diseases, monstrosities, and other imperfections of nature (including the inadequate velocity of light) refute a teleological conception of the universe. "What are the life and the efforts of man, and all humanity, compared wth the eternal, inexorable, irresistible, half-accidental, half-necessary march of nature? The momentary play of an ephemeron, hovering over the sea of eternity and infinity."

"The brain is the seat and organ of thought; its size, shape, and structure, are in exact proportion to the magnitude and power of its intellectual functions." Büchner bases his proof on observation of persons who have suffered brain lesions, and on the results of vivisection: "Can we desire any stronger proof as to the necessary connection of the soul and the brain than that afforded by the knife of the anatomist, who cuts off the soul piecemeal?"

Büchner does not explain the nature of the connection of brain and soul; he explicitly refuses to speculate on this matter, contending that having established the *fact* of connection, the "How?" of it can be disregarded. However, he takes to task Vogt, who had said: "To express myself rather coarsely, thought stands in the same relation to the brain, as bile to the liver, or urine to the kidneys." This is wrong because "thought, spirit, soul, are not material, not a substance, but the effect of the conjoined action of many materials endowed with forces or qualities." But of course Vogt was right to stress the *dependence* of thought on the brain.

All our feelings are in the brain, as we demonstrate by cutting nerves and finding that sensations cease in the parts of the body on the other side of the cut from the brain. "Habit and external appearance have led to the false notion, that we feel in places subjected to external irritation. . . . We falsely attribute the feeling perceived in the brain to the place where the impression is made."

Mediumism and spiritualism are in principle impossible according to Büchner; all mediums and clairvoyants are charlatans.

It is very mistaken and pernicious to despise matter, Büchner wrote—particularly one's body. *Mens sana in corpore sano* should be the ideal of every rational person.

Defenders of body-soul dualism assert that the soul is endowed with certain aesthetic, moral, and metaphysical innate ideas—a false claim, as is shown by the absence of these putative conceptions among deaf-mutes and feral children, and by the facts discovered by anthropologists, who have found the greatest variety of ideas among different peoples, including moral notions the opposites of those entertained in Europe. There is, in any case, no universal standard of morality, whether universally acknowledged or not. "It is well known that the notion of good cannot be defined. The theologians help themselves by saying, that is good which agrees with God's commands. But the commands of God are made by the theologians themselves." Even the conceptions of mathematics originate in sense-perception. Here Büchner's vigorous flogging of the dead horse of innate ideas has led him into absurdity.

In particular, there is no innate idea of God. History shows that the so-called gods of the heathen have nothing to do with the notion of God as a supreme personal being; and many peoples have been discovered who are entirely devoid of religious sentiments. When Moffat, the missionary, explained the tenets of Christianity to "the Bechuanas, one of the most intelligent tribes of the interior of South Africa . . . there only escaped from them exclamations of great surprise, as if these things were too absurd to be listened to by the most stupid." Religion is in fact (as Feuerbach said) human self-idealization.

"Whilst the visible and tangible matter sensually exhibits its indestructibility, the same cannot be asserted of spirit or soul, which is not matter, but merely an ideal product of a particular combination of force-endowed materials." Death is eternal sleep; there is nothing in it to be afraid of. Few people who profess belief in immortality really so believe; and if the soul were immortal, there could be no greater calamity. Büchner praises Buddhism for its denial of God and immortality.

No strict distinction between organic and inorganic is possible; there is no such thing as a vital force. Physiological chemistry does not differ in principle from any other kind; more and more vital processes are being duplicated in the laboratory. "The doctrine of vital power is now a lost affair."

The soul of man differs only quantitatively, not in kind, from the souls of brutes. So-called instinct is only a lower degree of intelligence: "It is not a necessity inborn in themselves and their mental organisation, nor a blind, involuntary impulse, which impels animals to action, but deliberation—the result of comparisons and conclusions." Büchner's evidence for this assertion is anecdotal, as is also his proof that brutes (specifically bees, chamois, baboons, swallows, and storks) have languages. Again, savage races are intermediate with respect to language: "That of the Bushmen is, according to Reichenbach, so poor in words, that it consists mostly of harsh, throat sounds, and clicks, for which we have no representatives in our alphabet, so that they communicate with each other much by signs."

"Free will, to the extent to which man *believes* he possesses it, is a mere chimera. . . . No one . . . who searches beneath the surface can deny that the assumption of a free will must, in theory and practice, be restricted within the narrowest compass." Men's actions are almost entirely determined by their characters, and these in turn are the resultant of external circumstances,

particularly climatic. "Deficiency of intellect, poverty, and want of education, are the chief causes of crime. Criminals are rather deserving of pity than of disgust. 'Therefore,' says Forster, 'it were best to judge and to condemn nobody.' " This is not, however, to deny that there is such a thing as crime, nor to object to society's right of self-defense. "What is true is that the partisans of these modern ideas hold different opinions as regards crime, and would banish that cowardly and irreconcilable hatred, which the state and society have hitherto cherished with so much hypocrisy as regards the malefactor."

To the complaint that "modern ideas" if adopted by the populace would lead to moral breakdown and the subversion of society, Büchner replies that "these ideas of God and the world, or moral motives, in so much danger of being wrecked against naturalism, exercise but a very imperceptible influence on the ordinary march of human society." Furthermore, actual European society is egotistical, hypocritical, and rotten: "A society which permits human beings to die of starvation on the steps of houses filled with victuals; a society whose force is directed to oppress the weak by the strong, has no right to complain that the natural sciences subvert the foundations of its morality." A more widespread diffusion of the scientific attitude would make possible a rational reconstruction of society on a humanitarian basis. (Büchner provides no details.) Finally, "truth is above things divine and human; there exist no reasons strong enough to cause us to abandon it."

"The following pages," Büchner wrote in the preface to the first edition, "pretend neither to establish a system nor to be exhaustive. They are merely scattered, though necessarily connected, thoughts and observations, which, on account of the difficulty of mastering all the facts of empirical and natural science, may perhaps meet with some indulgence on the part of the scientific critic." Such an avowal may serve in some measure to disarm criticism; further, much ought to be forgiven the author for having produced a book that is (as its subtitle promises) "intelligibly rendered"—not a common phenomenon in nineteenth century Germany. Nevertheless, the book has some notable shortcomings.

In the first place, Büchner was a doctor of medicine, which at his time and place was not at all the same as being a man of science. Thus, despite the parade of toughmindedness, Büchner was insufficiently skeptical—a fact which becomes glaringly apparent in his anthropological passages, where the reports of miscellaneous travelers are set out quite uncritically whenever they serve his purpose; and in his animal lore, where one point may be supported by reports of careful research, while the next is "proved" by a recital of a single anecdote the source of which is not stated.

Nor was Büchner trained as a philosopher. The modern reader may feel that this was all to the good, in view of the condition of German academic philosophy in mid-nineteenth century. However, such give-away remarks as "we might as well say, the dog barks, therefore the dog exists" (which, Büchner naïvely thought, disposed of the Cartesian "I think, therefore I am" and, in consequence, of all objections to Descartes' position based on the primacy of consciousness) reveal

how inadequately prepared Büchner was to cope with the two central problems of materialism: consciousness and free-will. One is not surprised to find that the brief passages bearing on these matters scarcely show awareness of the difficulties.

It might be said in Büchner's defense that despite the reputation of *Force and Matter* as the bible of what is (in some quarters) disparaged as "old-fashioned materialism," the author was not committed to any official creed; and indeed in the preface to the ninth edition he stated expressly: "Science or positive philosophy *per se* is neither idealistic nor materialistic, but realistic; all it aims at is to apprehend facts and their rational connection, without first adopting some particular system." In the same writing he spoke approvingly of the positivism of Comte, and averred that "we can know nothing about the *Why?* all we can ascertain is the *How?* of things, and the laws discovered in this manner are final solutions." However, if Büchner's philosophy was not materialism, neither was it really positivism. It was eclectic, in a bad sense; for he availed himself of positivism to excuse his refusal to treat the mind-body problem seriously, while at the same time, as a materialist, he ignored the complexities of theory of knowledge which beset positivism and push it into phenomenalism and idealism. This is not to say that a consistent philosophy embodying Büchner's point of view is impossible; it is to say that Büchner did not even begin to work it out, evidently on account of unawareness of any (even apparent) difficulties in his position. For instance, he was able to say, quite blandly, that we "perceive feeling in the brain" and "falsely attribute it to the place where the impression is made"—and then to drop the subject!

But it is ungrateful, and perhaps irrelevant, to castigate Büchner for lack of philosophical subtlety. *Force and Matter* was designed as a bludgeon, not as a scalpel, and a very effective bludgeon it was. The modern reader is more likely to be bored than shocked by it, a good indication that its battle has been won. As the review of its subject matter has indicated, there is little in it (barring some unfortunate details) that is not today commonplace among literate persons in general. But such was decidedly

not the case when it was published. Büchner was, predictably, ejected from his professorial chair; he was denounced throughout Germany; yet his book went through ten editions in fourteen years.

The evaluation by J. F. Collingwood, the editor of the English edition, is still just: "Its subject-matter may not be new to well-informed persons, as it does not aim at original scientific investigation; but the manner of treatment adopted by its accomplished author will be highly appreciated by those who wish for the advancement of mankind through the free exercise of thought."

MICROCOSMUS

Author: Rudolf Hermann Lotze (1817-1881)
Type of work: Metaphysics
First published: 1856-1864

PRINCIPAL IDEAS ADVANCED

The physicists are right in claiming that the universe is made up of atoms, but the atoms are sentient and they influence one another in a causal fashion predictable according to natural law.

The sentient atoms, or monads, may be considered causally from without, but internally they are the expressions of will.

All nature, which is a mechanism directed by purpose, is the expression of the creative will of God.

Man is unique because of his mind; although, like the other animals, man evolved in the struggle for existence, his history cannot be understood in purely mechanical terms.

Man, who is himself a unity, brings unity to existence by the use of ideas and ideals; wholes in nature are products of mind.

When he selected the title *Mikrokosmus* for his book, Rudolf Hermann Lotze drew upon the ancient tradition, still strong in the eighteenth

and nineteenth centuries, which taught that in the little circle of his activities man recapitulates the plan and purpose of the whole world. "As in the great fabric of the universe the creative spirit imposed on itself unchangeable laws by which it moves the world of phaenomena, diffusing the fulness of the Highest Good throughout innumerable forms and events, and distilling it again from them into the bliss of consciousness and enjoyment: so must man, acknowledging the same laws, develop given existence into a knowledge of its value, and the value of his ideals into a series of external forms proceeding from itself." A few years before, the celebrated naturalist Alexander von Humboldt had begun the publication of a panoramic work entitled *Kosmos* (5 volumes, 1845-1862), designed to exhibit in an imaginative synthesis all that was known about the physical world. Lotze's *Microcosmus* sought, in a manner, to redress the balance by focusing attention on man and his achievements. Volume One is an account of the human constitution in its physical, vital, and psychical aspects; Volume Two deals with the physical evolution of man and his mental and social development; Volume Three discusses the meaning of history, not neglecting its metaphysical and theological presuppositions.

For this grandiose undertaking, Lotze was well qualified. To his philosophical labors he brought the prestige of a man of science, reminding us in this respect as in others of the philosopher and mathematician Alfred North Whitehead. The same year that he took his doctor's degree in philosophy he received the degree of doctor of medicine; and his writings on metaphysics and logic were interspersed with works on physiology, pathology, and medical psychology. *Microcosmus* exhibits the results of his labors in these fields.

Lotze's purpose in writing *Microcosmus* was to adjust the differences which divided the educated world of his day into two warring camps, naturalists and humanists, materialists and spiritualists, or what Willliam James was later to call the "toughminded" and the "tender-minded." Like James, Lotze believed that the truth lies somewhere between the exclusive claims of these parties. He blamed the former for making an idol of truth and renouncing human interests which no man has the right to renounce. But he lamented the irrationalism in which romantic defenders of art, morality, and religion were accustomed to wrap themselves. It was his opinion that the philosophy which takes the realm of value as its starting point is able to frame a consistent and intelligible account of the world by tracing things back to their origin in the purpose of a personal God. And he further argued that the scientific view of the world is not fully intelligible except on this same assumption.

The key to Lotze's proposal for bringing the world-view of science into harmony with the world-view of aesthetics, morals, and religion is his attitude toward the principle of mechanism. He maintained that the universe is indeed made up of atoms and that these act upon one another in a regular and necessary fashion that can be described in terms of mechanical law. He saw no necessity for limiting or qualifying this causal principle. Some philosophers, in order to preserve freedom and responsibility for man, had set up a dualism of body and soul, arguing that mechanism holds for the former but not for the latter; others had declared for a spiritual monism, maintaining that matter is merely phenomenal and that

639

the chain of causation which appears to determine its movements has no reality in things themselves. Lotze rejected both of these views. He did accept a kind of spiritual monism; the atoms known to physics he held to be actually sentient, like the monads in Leibniz's system. Leibniz, however, had denied that one monad really influences another, explaining their apparent interconnection by his theory of "pre-established harmony." Lotze held that they do influence each other and that their behavior is predictable in terms of law. At the time he wrote, many biologists were contending that mechanistic determinism does not apply to living things. Lotze maintained in his works on physiology that it does, and he did not hesitate to speak of the "mechanism of life."

To that extent Lotze accommodated himself to the views of science. But having admitted that mechanism is universal, he went on to argue that it is everywhere subordinate to purpose. If we consider the atom not from the outside but from within, causality appears in a different aspect. Its essence may be described as feeling, and its activity toward other atoms as excitation and impulse. Nineteenth century materialists were divided into two groups—those who maintained that atoms are qualitatively homogeneous and those who maintained that they are heterogeneous. Lotze took the latter position. He held that each monad or particle has a determinate essence which draws along with it a definite series of possible changes. As it comes into relation with other things it responds in specific ways. Viewed from without, its behavior may be described in terms of law; viewed from within, it is the realization of inclination or will. Like Leibniz,

Lotze required a principal monad to complete the picture. Existing things, each ceaselessly acting to realize its own satisfaction, are joined and fitted into harmonious wholes, which in turn go to make up one concordant system, the expression of the creative will of God. It is in the notion of a whole that Lotze found the complement to mechanism which, without subverting causal necessity, subordinates it to an *idea*. The upshot is that mechanism is everywhere operative, but, as is the case with the artifices of men, the laws of nature serve to realize ends.

Lotze's reason for believing that there are unities in the world derives from the peculiarity of mental phenomena. The customary reason given for distinguishing between mind and matter is, according to Lotze, that the one exercises freedom of self-determination which is forbidden to the other. This theory he found inadequate because there is no evidence that conscious choices are determined. Our feeling of freedom could be misleading if it is true that even material particles share with minds the attribute of excitability. The true ground for distinguishing between mind and matter lies in the unity of consciousness, which is totally unlike the kind of unity that we encounter among natural phenomena. On the material plane, two forces, when they combine to produce a third, merge so as to become indistinguishable. But consciousness keeps its objects separate at the same time that it combines them. In this way it gives rise to genuine wholes. Lotze held that it is only in virtue of consciousness (God's or man's) that wholes exist. Moreover, he argued from the fact that minds perceive unity to the unity of minds themselves. It may not appear to us that consciousness is anything but an unconnected plurality; but the very fact that anything which appears does so to *us*, or that the world appears to us as made up of *unities*, is proof incontestable. For only that which is itself a unity can unify manifold phenomena.

Lotze regarded man as occupying a unique status in the world. He is "a phenomenon in space, a connected organism, the head of the animal kingdom," but at the same time he is set off from the rest of creation by "the addition of a wholly new germ of development," namely, the rational *mind*. Writing before the publication of Darwin's *On the Origin of Species* (1859), he laid the groundwork for a mechanistic theory of evolution, including the notions of variation and the selection of existing varieties through the struggle for existence. Nor did he except man from this scheme. But he discerned a deep abyss between the natural history of animals and the intellectual and moral history of the human species. The former can be adequately accounted for in mechanical terms, the latter not by those means at all. *Microcosmus* is the account of man's peculiar development within creation, the story of a creature made in the image of God.

Lotze did not deny that animals have souls, but he did claim that we know too little about animals to speak intelligently on the subject. Their outer lives are all we have to go by. Presumably they experience sensation and desire much as man does, and they cannot be without a kind of intelligence. But, as far as we can tell, they stop short of attaching significance to their experiences and their actions. A dog may find a morsel pleasant to the taste without attaining to a recognition of sweetness; he may bury a bone, but without the thought of providing for tomorrow's need. Man, on the contrary, lives by taking thought, by bringing to bear upon the manifold content of sensation and desire an architectonic structure which transforms the raw product of psychic stimulation into "an organically utilizable thought-atom." Only in view of this creative (or re-creative) function can human phenomena be explained. The bird's song, the beaver's dam, the monkey's capers can all be understood in terms of mechanistic principles. But failure awaits the attempts of materialists (for example, Ludwig Büchner's *Force and Matter*, 1855) to explain the achievements of man by appealing to natural laws. A second principle of explanation must be employed, which takes account of ideas and wholes.

From this latter point of view, Lotze surveyed the whole range of human culture. The structure of language, with its parts of speech and rules of syntax, is the first embodiment of thought, closely following its natural forms. Man's intellectual life, as observable in science and abstract reasoning, further discloses the unique formative activity of the mind as it compares and distinguishes impressions and uncovers relations and connections which it did not originate, lifting out of their spatio-temporal context orders and patterns and beholding their timeless essence. Morality shows similar features, inasmuch as man, unlike the lower creatures, is motivated by ideal principles of duty and obligation and not merely by animal impulse.

In all his specifically human achievements man reveals the presence of mind. Not, indeed, to the exclusion of his body and its laws! Sensation, according to Lotze, is caused by physiological stimulation: the chemical reactions in the brain affect the soul in specific ways, giving rise there to color, taste, and sound impressions. Impressions such as these are the basis for its perceptions. Language originates in spontaneous physiological movements of the respiratory system. Morality is rooted in feelings of pain and pleasure, and when man formulates ideal ends, he is still motivated by antipathy and desire. Lotze claimed that it was proof of the correctness of his theory that it brought together the "theory of an ideal unity in mental life" and the "theory of its mechanical realization." And if his work was directed in the first instance against crude materialism and its attempts to explain civilization in mechanical terms, it was also intended as a corrective of Absolute Idealism, which, he said, "makes the significant Idea float in isolation as a boundlessly shaping power above the low sphere of the ordinary psychic mechanism."

It may be gathered from this quotation that Lotze would not be in sympathy with Hegel's philosophy of history. And this was, indeed, the case. Instead of conceiving history as the logical unfolding of an idea, Lotze viewed it as an interaction between man and his environment. The human mind does not work in a vacuum. In fact, it does not work at all except under the stimulating and guiding influence of various external causes. We may view human activity as an attempt to realize the good, the beautiful, and the just—for these are the ends which man comes to respect; but these goals would never have been sought for themselves, apart from man's bodily and communal needs. And in this con-

nection, such unspiritual factors as climate and rainfall have to be considered, as well as the claims of the ideal.

Lotze saw a development in history. Because of favorable circumstances or because of the possession of peculiar genius or a specially pregnant idea, certain peoples, at least, have developed forms of life which far transcend organic needs; and, in the West, particularly, an overlapping of cultures has permitted later ones to build upon their predecessors' achievements. But Lotze was not greatly impressed with the doctrine of progress as such. In mechanical arts, he granted, it is not difficult to improve upon the achievements of one's predecessors. But he doubted whether there is any progress in art or in the depth and character of mental life from one civilization to another.

Lotze found special difficulty in another feature of the progress-doctrine. It seemed to him irreconcilable with any consistent scheme of values to argue that countless generations of individuals should serve as means to the happiness of those who should come after. On the contrary, he maintained that the life of any generation in any culture has the same intrinsic worth as that of any other. That the whole of history makes up a pattern and has a meaning he was far from denying; but he held that only God knows what it is or can have any satisfaction from it. In fact, Lotze applied the same principle to the cosmos that he applied to history, and one of the reasons which inclined him to view the elemental parts of nature as sentient was his unwillingness to suppose that the vast proportion of the world has no enjoyment of it and exists only for the satisfaction of men.

The arguments by which Lotze arrived at his conception of God as a personal creator are of such a subtle and metaphysical order that it is unprofitable to try to summarize them. Lotze was prepared to prove that the notion of causation presupposes a more fundamental being underlying the interacting particles. His background in chemistry and biology led him to repudiate the notion that atoms are inert extended bodies which interact on one another through external collision; he favored a dynamic conception which explained causation in terms of the internal constitution of things. This led to his discerning patterns or wholes in nature, which, he held, can have no existence apart from a mind which thinks them. The notion that the world is called into being by a purely ideal necessity, as Hegel had suggested, seemed to him inadequate to account for the actuality which things possess and the real causality which they exert on one another. To account for the active quality of existence, he believed it was necessary to hold to an active God, who wills and enjoys, as well as thinks.

When Lotze turned from physical causation to the consideration of value, he found further arguments for a personal creator. He opposed Kant's contention that the highest good is a will determined purely by duty. To make an abstract relation a good seemed to him altogether contrary to experience. In reality, nothing is good except self-satisfaction. A benevolent act is good only if it brings happiness to some other being. And to Lotze, since values are as much a constituent part of the world as existence and law, it was necessary to think of the creator as the one for whom things have preëminent worth. He ventured, with these thoughts before him, to trace the origin of our world to God's eternal love, which, rejoicing in the goodness of his own thoughts, willed that they should have their own existence. Because creation was an act of love, it was not enough that God should enjoy it, but the parts themselves, each in its determinate measure, must know the self-satisfaction of being what they are.

Lotze's philosophy has many loose ends. He reminds himself repeatedly that the finite mind of man, while it can trace the general features of the world, cannot expect to see its ultimate necessity. No philosopher was ever more sophisticated than Lotze—that is to say, less naïve. If he returns to an essentially religious tradition, he does so with due deliberation. It might be true of Kant that his philosophy was an elaborate rationalization of his pietistic faith. This was hardly the case with Lotze, who saw the nihilistic implications in official nineteenth century philosophies and was impelled to take a longer look. He concluded, on the one hand, that our science can never be more than fragmentary, and he warned against exaggerating its findings into systems which impoverish faith without enriching knowledge. On the other hand, he held fast to "the old-fashioned conviction" that there are ways leading to fuller light and that it is man's duty to follow them as far as he can.

ESSAY IN LIBERTY

Author: John Stuart Mill (1806-1873)
Type of work: Political philosophy
First published: 1859

PRINCIPAL IDEAS ADVANCED

An individual's liberty can rightfully be constrained only in order to prevent his doing harm to others.

Certain areas of human freedom cannot rightfully be denied: the freedom to believe, the freedom of taste, and the freedom to unite (for any purpose not involving harm to others).

Open expressions of opinions should not be repressed, for if the repressed opinion is true, one loses the opportunity of discovering the truth; while if the repressed opinion is false, discussion of its falsity strengthens the opposing truth and makes the grounds of truth evident; furthermore, the truth may be divided between the prevailing opinion and the repressed one, and by allowing expression of both, one makes recognition of the whole truth possible.

Important political thinkers often write like men who are convinced that a bedrock of significant issues underlies the otherwise multitudinous details of human political life. How such men estimate the nature of that bedrock accounts for the important differences of viewpoint among the great political philosophers from Plato to contemporary minds. John Stuart Mill thought long and hard about the theoretical and the practical problems connected with liberal democratic government. Actual service in the British Parliament brought him into intimate contact with applied politics. Beneath the surface of nineteenth century British political experience Mill came upon the one problem he considered central to all men's long-range interests. The clarity with which he stated this problem in the *Essay on Liberty* has earned for him a justified reputation as defender of the basic principles of Liberalism. "The struggle between Liberty and Authority," he wrote in

that work, "is the most conspicuous feature in the portions of history with which we are earliest familiar, particularly in that of Greece, Rome, and England." The individual's relation to the organized power of state and popular culture requires that men draw the line between what in principle rightly belongs to each. The liberal task concerns how men are to meet the necessary demands of organized life without destroying the rights of the individual.

Mill mentions two ways in which men gradually subdued sovereign power after long and difficult struggles. First, select groups within a given political domain worked to compel the rulers to grant them special immunities. Second (and historically a later phenomenon), men managed to win constitutionally guaranteed rights through some political body which represented them. These historical tendencies limited the tyrannical aspects of sovereign power without raising questions about the inherited right of the sovereign to rule.

A later European development involved the replacement of inherited rulers by men elected for periodic terms of governing. This was the aim of popular parties in modern European affairs, according to Mill. Men who once wanted to limit governmental powers when such government rested on unrepresentative principles now put less stress on the need of limitation once government received its justification by popular support—say, through elections. "Their power was but the nation's own power, concentrated, and in a form convenient for exercise." Yet Mill criticizes European liberalism for failing to understand that popularly supported governments may also introduce forms of tyranny. There can be what Mill's essay refers to as "the tyranny of the majority." The earlier question went: Who can protect men from the tyranny of an inherited rule? Modern Europeans can ask the question: Who will protect men from the tyranny of custom? The individual citizen's independence is threatened in either instance. He needs protection from arbitrary rulers and also from "the tyranny of the prevailing opinion and feeling." Even a democratic society can coerce its dissenters to conform to ideals and rules of conduct in areas which should belong solely to the individual's decisions.

The chief concern of modern politics, then, is to protect the individual's rights from governmental and social coercion. Mill argues that the practical issue is even narrower—"where to place the limit" which liberal minds agree is needed. Mill understands that organized life would be impossible without some firm rules. Men can never choose to live in a ruleless situation. "All that makes existence valuable to anyone, depends on the enforcement of restraints upon the actions of other people." But *what* rules are to prevail? To this important question the satisfactory answers remain to be realized. Existing rules, which will vary from one culture and historical epoch to another, tend to become coated in the clothing of apparent respect through force of custom; they come to seem self-evident to their communities. Men forget that custom is the deposit of learned ways of acting. Few realize that existing rules require support by the giving of reasons, and that such reasons may be good or bad. Powerful interest-groups tend to shape the prevailing morality in class terms. Men also often act servilely toward the rules created by their masters.

Mill credits minority and religious groups, especially Protestant ones, with having altered customs by their once heretical resistance to custom. But creative groups out of step with prevailing modes of action and thought often sought specific changes without challenging in principle the existing rules of conduct. Even heretics sometimes adopted a bigoted posture toward other theological beliefs. As a result many religious minorities could simply plead for "permission to differ." Mill concludes that religious tolerance usually triumphed only where religious indifference also existed side by side with diversified bodies of religious opinion.

A criterion by which rightful interference in a man's personal life can be determined is offered by Mill. Individuals and social groups may so interfere only for reasons of their own self-protection. Society has a coercive right to prevent an individual from *harming* others, but it may not interfere simply for the individual's own physical or moral good. In this latter domain, one may attempt to persuade but not to compel an individual to change his views or his actions. Mill adds a further qualification; namely, the individual must possess mature faculties. Children, insane persons, and members of backward societies are excluded from the use of the criterion. Moreover, the test whether interference is proper can never involve abstract right but only utility—"utility in the largest sense, grounded on the permanent interests of man as a progressive being." Failures to act, as well as overt acts causing harm to others, may be punished by society.

The question is then raised as to how men are to interpret the notion that unharmful acts belong solely to the agent. What are the rights belonging to a man which can never lead to harm to others? There are three broad types of such rights, according to Mill. The types are: one, "the inward domain of consciousness"; two, "liberty of tastes and pursuits"; three, "freedom to unite, for any purpose not involving harm to others." Mill insists that no society or government may rightfully deny these areas of fundamental human freedom. Men must be permitted and even encouraged to seek their good "in their own way." This means that the repressive tendencies of institutions, including churches and sects, must continually be curbed. Mill points out how even August Comte, the famous French sociologist, encouraged a form of despotism over individuals in society in the name of a positivistic rationality. Mill insists that any successful resistance to the individual's coercion by opinion or legislation requires defense of the right to think and to express one's views in the public marketplace.

Mill's famous book addresses several aspects of the problem concerning the relation of authority to the individual: first, the nature of man's freedom of thought and public discussion of controversial ideas; second, the ways in which human individuality is a necessary element in man's well-being; third, the limits of society over the individual. There is then a concluding chapter which shows some practical applications of the liberal principles which Mill has defended.

The first argument against repression of open expression of opinion is that the repressed opinion may be true. Those who silence opinion must act on the dogmatic assumption that their own viewpoint is infallible. But if a given opinion happens to be true, men can never exchange error for its truth so long as discussion is curtailed. On the other hand, if the controversial opinion is false, by silencing discussion of it men prevent more lively truths in existence from gaining by the healthy collision with error. No government or social group should be permitted to claim infallibility for the limited perspective which any given group must inevitably hold toward events. "The power itself is illegitimate," Mill argues, insisting that "the best government has no more title to it than the worst."

Mill lists a number of possible objections to his first argument in defense of free discussion: One should not permit false doctrines to be proclaimed; men should never allow discussion to be pushed to an extreme; persecution of opinion is good in that truth will ultimately win out; and only bad individuals would seek to weaken existing beliefs which are useful. None of these objections proves persuasive to Mill. He answers by asserting: There exists a difference between establishing a truth in the face of repeated challenges which fail to refute it and assuming a truth to prevent its possible refutation; open discussion holds significance only if it applies to extreme cases; many historical instances show that coercive error can interfere with the spread of true opinions; and, finally, the truth of an opinion is a necessary aspect of its utility. Mill reminds men how very learned persons joined with those who persecuted Socrates and Jesus for holding opinions which, later, won many adherents. Such persecution often involves the bigoted use of economic reprisals in many cases, about which Mill says: "Men might as well be imprisoned, as excluded from the means of earning their bread."

Mill's second argument for open discussion concerns the value it holds for keeping established truths and doctrines alive. Such discussion challenges men to know the reasons for their beliefs—a practice which forms the primary basis of genuine education. Without challenge, even accepted religious doctrines become lifeless, as do ethical codes. Discussion of false opinions forces those holding existing truths to know *why* they hold the opinions they do. Mill points out that even in the natural sciences there are instances when alternative hypotheses are possible. Experience indicates that in religious and moral matters one should expect a great range of viewpoints. Organized intolerance of opinions which conflict with the official views kills "the moral courage of the human mind." Mill agrees with the critics who assert that not all men can hope to understand the reasons for their received opinions, but he reminds the critics that their own point involves the assumption that someone is an authority regarding those reasons. Consolidation of opinion requires open discussion. Mill's judgment is that with no enemy at hand, "both teachers and learners go to sleep at their post."

The third argument for free discussion rests on the possibility that competing views may share the truth between them. Even heretical opinions may form a portion of the truth. To the objection that some opinions are more than half-truths, like those associated with Christian morality, Mill replies by stating that this morality never posed originally as a complete system. Christian morality constituted more a reaction against an existing pagan culture than a positive ethical doctrine. Men's notions of obligation to the public stem from Greek and Roman influences rather than from the teachings of the New Testament, which stress obedience, passivity, innocence, and abstinence from evil. Mill's conclusion is that the clash of opinions, some of which turn out to be errors, proves helpful to the discovery of truth.

The question about how freely men may act is more difficult. Mill agrees with those who insist that actions can never be as free as opinions. Actions always involve consequences whose possible harm to others must receive serious consideration. Men need long training in disciplined living in order to achieve the maturity required for a responsible exercise of their judg-

647

mental capacities. Yet individuality constitutes an inescapable element in the end of all human action, which is happiness. For this reason men must not permit others to decide all issues for them. The reasons are that others' experience may prove too narrow or perhaps it may involve wrongful interpretations; prove correct and yet unsuited to a given individual's temperament; or become so customary that men's passive acceptance of the experience retards their development of numerous unique human qualities. The man who always acquiesces in others' ways of doing things "has no need of any other faculty than the ape-like one of imitation."

What concerns Mill—a concern prophetic of contemporary difficulties in organized social life—is that society shows a threatening tendency to curb individuality. The pressures of social opinion lead to a deficiency of individual impulses, a narrowing of the range of human preferences, and a decline in spontaneity. At this point Mill, who usually speaks favorably of Protestant resistance to earlier orthodox doctrines, singles out Calvinism for harsh criticism. Modern society evinces dangerous secular expressions of the earlier Calvinist insistence that men perform God's will. The emphasis was on strict obedience. So narrow a theory of human performance inevitably pinches human character. As an ethical teleologist and a Utilitarian, Mill holds that the value of human action must be determined by its tendency to produce human self-realization. Obedience can never be an adequate end of human character.

Mill insists that democratic views tend to produce some conditions which encourage the loss of individu-

ality. There is a tendency "to render mediocrity the ascendent power among mankind." Political democracy often results in mass thinking. To protect human individuality, men must show a great suspicion of averages; for the conditions of spiritual development vary from person to person. In fact, Mill argues that democracy needs an aristocracy of learned and dedicated men who can guide its development along progressive paths. What Mill calls "the progressive principle" is always antagonistic to the coercive stance of customary modes of thinking and acting. Such a principle operates only in contexts which permit diversity of human types and a variety of situations. Mill laments that the latter condition seems on the wane in nineteenth century England. He suggests, also, that the slow disappearance of classes has a causal relation to the growing uniformity in English society. His general conclusion, expressed as a warning, is that the individual increasingly feels the compulsions of social rather than governmental coercion.

To what extent may society influence the individual? Mill asserts that society can restrain men from doing damage to others' interests as well as require men to share the burdens of common defense and of protection to their fellows' rights. Society may rightfully establish rules which create obligations for its members in so far as they form a community of interests. Education aims at developing self-regarding virtues in individuals. Individuals who are persistently rash, obstinate, immoderate in behavior, and filled with self-conceit may even be subject to society's disapprobation. But society must not punish a man by legal means if the individual acts in disapproved ways regarding what he thinks to be his own good. "It makes a vast difference both in our feelings and in our conduct towards him," Mill warns, "whether he displeases us in things in which we think we have a right to control him, or in things in which we know that we have not." Mill rejects the argument that no feature of a man's conduct may fall outside the area of society's jurisdiction. A man has the right to make personal mistakes. Finally, Mill argues that society will tend to interfere in a person's private actions in a wrong manner and for the wrong reasons. Religious, socialistic, and other forms of social censorship prove unable to develop adequate self-restraints. A full-blown social censorship leads, in time, to the very decline of a civilization.

Mill concludes his work by pointing out the circumstances under which a society can with justification interfere in areas of common concern. Trade involves social aspects and can be restrained when it is harmful. Crime must be prevented whenever possible. There are offenses against decency which should be curbed, and solicitation of others to do acts harmful to themselves bears watching. Mill writes: "Fornication, for example, must be tolerated, and so must gambling; but should a person be free to be a pimp, or to keep a gambling-house?" The state may establish restrictions of such activities, according to Mill. Finally, Mill argues that the state should accept the duty of requiring a sound education for each individual.

FIRST PRINCIPLES

Author: Herbert Spencer (1820-1903)
Type of work: Philosophy of nature
First published: 1862

PRINCIPAL IDEAS ADVANCED

The business of philosophy is to formulate the laws concerning phenomena common to all the branches of scientific knowledge.

From the principle of the persistence of force can be derived the other principles of natural philosophy, among them the principles of the uniformity of law, the transformation of forces, and the line of least resistance.

The Principle of Evolution and Dissolution is the dynamic and unifying principle of nature; evolution is an integration of matter and a dissipation of motion, during which matter passes from homogeneity to heterogeneity; dissolution occurs when resistance overcomes equilibrium and a system loses its force without adding to its organization.

Society is a kind of super-organism which exemplifies the same principles of differentiation.

Reality is unknowable; we know only appearances.

649

Spencer intended the *First Principles* to be an introduction to his comprehensive study of the world, entitled *Synthetic Philosophy*. But he made it an independent work, complete in itself, which not merely announced the principles of evolutionary naturalism but illustrated them amply from all fields of knowledge. For good measure, he also raised the issue of science and religion and proposed an amicable solution.

Spencer shared the classical positivist conviction that knowledge consists solely in empirical generalizations or laws. Particular sciences, he held, have the task of formulating the laws which govern special classes of data; but, inasmuch as there are phenomena common to all branches of knowledge, a special science is needed to gather them up into laws. This, he claimed, was the business of philosophy. In his view, that business was now completed. The synthetic philosophy included not only general laws but also one law from which all other laws, both general and specific, could be deduced *a priori*. He therefore offered a new definition of philosophy: it is "completely unified knowledge."

Two highly general principles of natural philosophy were already well-established in Spencer's day; namely, the continuity of motion and the indestructibility of matter. Work in the field of thermodynamics had more recently shown that matter and motion are, in fact, different forms of energy, making it possible to combine these principles into one, which Spencer called the principle of the persistence of force. Here, in his opinion, was a fundamental truth from which all other principles could be deduced. The first principle which Spencer inferred from it was that of the persistence of relations of force, more commonly known as the uniformity of law. The second was that of the transformation of forces; namely, that every loss of motion is attended by an accretion of matter, and vice versa. The third was that motions follow the line of least resistance.

None of these principles, however, sufficed to explain the origin and structure of the ordered world of our experience. What Spencer needed was a unifying principle that applies equally to the burning candle, the quaking earth, and the growing organism. All these events he saw as instances of one vast "transformation." The problem was to find the dynamic principle which governs this metamorphosis as a whole and in all its details. The answer he found in the Principle of Evolution and Dissolution.

Spencer regarded it as his special contribution to philosophy that he was able to show deductively what others (notably the embryologist K. E. von Baer, 1792-1876) had concluded experimentally and on a limited scale; namely, that change is always from a state of homogeneity to a state of heterogeneity. According to Spencer, it is self-evident that homogeneity is a condition of unstable equilibrium. At least this is true of finite masses—though if centers of force were diffused uniformly through infinite space, it might possibly be otherwise; but Spencer held such a state of affairs to be inconceivable. It follows that, because of the inequality of exposure of its different parts, every finite instance of the homogeneous must inevitably lapse into heterogeneity.

Primarily, according to Spencer, evolution was a passing from the less to the more coherent form of energy: for example, the formation of the solar system out of a gaseous nebula. But because the same instability is found in each part of the universe as is found in the whole, the differentiation process will be recapitulated within each new aggregate, giving rise to a secondary evolution: for example, the stratification of the surface of the earth. Primary evolution is a process of integration, the passage from a less to a more coherent form with the dissipation of motion and the concentration of matter. Secondary evolution adds to this a process of differentiation, in the course of which the mass changes from a homogeneous to a heterogeneous state.

But not all heterogeneity is constructive: for example, a tumerous growth. Thus, Spencer had further to qualify his law of change: evolution is change from the indefinite to the definite, from the confused to the ordered. Finally, the same process which has hitherto been stated in terms of matter might equally well be stated in terms of motion: evolution is a concentration of molecular motion with a dissipation of heat.

In sum: *"Evolution is an integration of matter and concomitant dissipation of motion; during which the matter passes from an indefinite, incoherent homogeneity to a definite, coherent heterogeneity; and during which the retained motion undergoes a parallel transformation."*

It was clear to Spencer, however, that evolution cannot go on forever. The redistribution of matter and motion must eventually reach a limit beyond which a simplification takes place: lesser movements are integrated into greater ones, as when the secondary gyrations of a spinning top subside into the main motion. Spencer called this tendency "equilibration." In a harmonious environment, suitably integrated motions continue indefinitely without undergoing noticeable change. Nevertheless, a change is taking place. Resistance, ever so minor, must in time produce its effect upon the system, wearing it down, causing it to dissipate its force without adding to its organization. Even the solar system, which is nearly a perfectly equilibrated system, is losing its energy and must continue to do so until in the distant future it no longer radiates light or heat.

Evolution, therefore, according to Spencer, is only one aspect of the process; it is paralleled by its opposite, dissolution, about which, however, he had little to say because he found it lacking in the interesting features that attend evolution. Still, it is not to be ignored, nor is it a stranger to us. The death of any living organism is "that final equilibration which precedes dissolution, is the bringing to a close of all those conspicuous integrated motions that arose during evolution." And the process of organic decay is dissolution. Particular systems decay while more general systems are still in the state of integration, and Spencer was far from being of the opinion that the evolution of our planetary system has reached its height.

This bare skeleton of Spencer's argument must remain unconvincing without the illustrations which he used to fill it out. To show that the principle of coherence governs even such matters as the evolution of human speech, he pointed out that the primitive Pawnee Indians used a three syllable word, "ashakish," to designate the animal which the civilized English call by the one-syllable word "dog." The history

651

of the English language offers illustrations of the same tendency toward coherence and integration: witness the passage from the Anglo-Saxon "sunu" through the semi-Saxon "sune" to the English "son"; or, again, from "cuman" to "cumme" to "come." Other examples are taken from politics, industry, art, religion—not to mention the physical sciences. A characteristic one is the following, which shows the change toward heterogeneity in manufactures: "Beginning with a barbarous tribe, almost if not quite homogeneous in the functions of its members, the progress has been, and still is, towards an economic aggregation of the whole human race; growing ever more heterogeneous in respect of the separate functions assumed by separate nations, the separate functions assumed by the local sections of each nation, the separate functions assumed by the many kinds of makers and traders in each town, and the separate functions assumed by the workers united in producing each community."

It was in connection with his argument that homogeneous masses are always unstable that Spencer gave his most explicit account of biological evolution. Given a homogeneous mass of protoplasm, the surface will be subject to different forces from those of the interior, and consequently the two will be modified in different ways. Moreover, one part of the surface is exposed differently from another, so that the ventral features will differ from the dorsal. Again, two virtually identical blobs of protoplasm which chance to arise in different environments—for example, moist and dry— will be modified in different ways. Spencer's theories in these matters had already been published before Dar-

win's *On the Origin of Species* (1859) appeared, and he saw no reason to change them afterwards. In his view, the real cause of differentiation between species lay in the environmental influences. He thought it probable that modifications in the parent are transmitted through heredity to their offspring. But, in any case, it *must* sometimes happen "that some division of a species, falling into circumstances which give it rather more complex experiences, and demand actions that are more involved, will have certain of its organs further differentiated in proportionately small degrees. . . . Hence, there will from time to time arise an increased heterogeneity both of the Earth's flora and fauna, and of individual races included in them." No doubt Darwin's principle of "natural selection" facilitates the differentiation, he explained in a footnote, but the varieties can be accounted for without it; and without the changes caused by the environment, natural selection would accomplish little.

Spencer's theory of social evolution paralleled his account of biological origins. In his view, society is a kind of superorganism, which exemplifies the same principles of differentiation as those that appear on the inorganic and the organic planes. His was a system of strict determinism which explained social dynamics in terms of universal laws and denied any role to human purpose or endeavor. His guiding principle was the formula that motion follows lines of least resistance. Thus, migrations and wars result from the reaction of societies to climate, geography, and the like. Likewise, internal movements, such as the division of labor and the development of public thoroughfares, arise from the effort to fulfill man's desires in the most economical manner. To the objection that this was only a metaphorical way of viewing social change, Spencer replied that it was not: men are, he said, literally impelled in certain directions, and social processes are in fact physical ones.

Psychology provides further instances. What we think of as mental processes are, from a more fundamental point of view, material ones. Spencer cited as an example the processes of thought engaged in by a botanist who is classifying plants. Each plant examined yields a complex impression; and when two plants yield similar impressions, this "set of molecular modifications" is intensified, "generating an internal idea corresponding to these similar external objects." It is a special case of the general principle called by Spencer "segregation," which states that like units of motion will produce like units of motion in the same or similar aggregates, and unlike will produce unlike.

Such is the tenor of Spencer's system. Philosophy in the traditional sense hardly concerned him. His objective, like that of Descartes, was to put all knowledge on a deductive basis, and his *First Principles*, like Descartes' *Meditations* (1641), merely laid the foundation for the superstructure which was to follow. Unlike Descartes, however, Spencer pleaded ignorance of the underlying nature of things. Following Hume and Kant, he professed that what we know are only appearances, ideas or impressions in the mind. Reality is unknowable.

Spencer had no intention of wasting his energies on the transcendental problems which concerned Kant and the German speculative philosophers. But he did devote the first hundred pages

of his book to "The Unknowable." Here he dealt, very much in the manner of T. H. Huxley, with the limits of human understanding, especially with the claims of revealed religion and of scientific metaphysics. He found it conveniently admitted by Canon H. L. Mansel (1820-1871) of the Church of England that the object of religious devotion cannot be thought. In Mansel's opinion, this belief was due to the relativity of human knowledge, whereas God is, by definition, Absolute. Of course, said Spencer, it is not merely the object of religion that is unknowable. The reality which science describes is also unknowable, if one tries to think of it absolutely. Kant's paralogisms and antinomies make it clear that such concepts as space, time, motion, consciousness, and personality have meaning only in the limited world of experience and tell us nothing about reality.

Nevertheless, said Spencer, the notion of the Absolute is not entirely negative: there is something which defines and limits the knowable; we have a vague, indefinite notion of a being more and other than what we know. Perhaps our closest approach to it is by analogy to the feeling of "power" which we have in our own muscles. The true function of religion is to witness to nature from its mysterious side, as the true function of science is to discover its knowable side. Here as elsewhere Spencer discerned a process of differentiation. The conflict within culture between science and religion is due to "the imperfect separation of their spheres and functions. . . . A permanent peace will be reached when science becomes fully convinced that all its explanations are proximate and relative, while religion becomes fully convinced that the mystery it contemplates is ultimate and absolute."

But, according to Spencer, writing and talking about the problem will not do any good. Cultural changes are not furthered by taking thought concerning them. As presently constituted, men are not ready morally or socially

to do without theology: they still need to believe that the Absolute is a person like themselves in order to strengthen their resolve to act rightly. By the time science and religion have differentiated themselves completely, men will presumably have evolved morally to the point that they do good spontaneously.

UTILITARIANISM

Author: John Stuart Mill (1806-1873)
Type of work: Ethics
First published: 1863

Principal Ideas Advanced

Those acts are right and good which produce the greatest happiness for the greatest number of persons.

An act derives its moral worth not from its form but from its utility.

Although it is the intrinsic worth of pleasure which gives value to acts conducive to pleasure, some pleasures are better than others in quality.

The proof of the value of pleasure is that it is desired, and the proof of the claim that some pleasures are better than others is that experienced, rational men prefer some pleasures to others.

Justice is the appropriate name for certain social utilities by which the general good is realized.

The central aim of John Stuart Mill's *Utilitarianism* is to defend the view that those acts are right and good which produce the greatest happiness of the greatest number. This ethical position did not originate with Mill. An influential predecessor, Jeremy Bentham, earlier championed pleasure and pain as the sole criteria for judging what is good and bad. The utility yardstick measures goods by asking: Does an act increase pleasure, and does it decrease pain? Bentham's crude "Push-pin is as good as poetry" interpretation of the yardstick led to numerous criticisms. Therefore, Mill states the principle of utility in its most defensible form both to counter some specific criticisms of it and to make clear what are the sanctions of the principle. He also offers a proof of the principle. The work concludes with a discussion of the relation of utility to justice.

The ethics of Utilitarianism influenced a large number of public men and helped to shape important reform legislation in nineteenth century British political life.

Utilitarianism opens with the author's lament that little progress has occurred through centuries of ethical analysis. Ethical philosophers seeking to define the nature of "good" have left a number of incompatible views to their intellectual posterity. Mill admits that history of scientific thought also contains confusion about the first principles of the special sciences. Yet this is more to be expected in the sciences than in moral philosophy. Legislation and morals involve practical rather than theoretical arts. Since such arts always aim at ends of action rather than thought, they require agreement about a standard by which the worth of those ends can be evaluated. There is greater need of fixing the foundation of morals than of stating the theoretical principles underlying bodies of scientific knowledge. The sciences result from accumulation of many particular truths, but in moral philosophy "A test of right and wrong must be the means, one would think, of ascertaining what is right or wrong, and not a consequence of having already ascertained it."

Ethical intuitionists insist that men possess a natural faculty which discerns moral principles. Against them, Mill argues that appeal to a "moral sense" cannot solve the problem of an ultimate ethical standard for judging acts. No intuitionist claim about knowledge of moral principles can provide a basis for decisions regarding cases. Intuitionist and inductive moral theorists usually disagree about the "evidence and source" grounding moral principles. Clearly, then, the main problem facing moral philosophers is that of justifying our judgments in the light of a defensible principle.

Mill asserts that even those philosophers must invoke the greatest happiness principle who wish to reject it. For example, the German philosopher Immanuel Kant claimed that the basis of moral obligation involves a categorical imperative: "So act that the rule on which thou actest would admit of being adopted as a law of all rational beings." Mill insists that numerous, even contradictory, notions of duties can follow from this imperative. Kant's noble effort thus leads to decisions which can be shown to be immoral only because the consequences of some universally adopted acts would be unwanted by most men.

The fact that men tacitly employ the utility yardstick is not the same as a proof of its validity. Mill offers to present such a proof. He makes clear that no absolutely binding proof, "in the ordinary and popular meaning of the term," is possible. To give a philosophical proof means to advance reasons directed at man's rational capacities. Philosophical proofs are their own kind of proofs. It is in this sense of proof that Mill promises to make good after he has first more fully characterized the Utilitarian doctrine.

Mill must first perform an important polemical function in replying to critics who find problems with the Utilitarian doctrine. The polemic is to serve the persuasive goal of winning over critics to a proper understanding of Utilitarianism, whose basic view of life is "that pleasure and freedom from pain are the only things desirable as ends." A corollary to this claim is that all things desirable are so either for the pleasure they can directly produce or for ways in which they serve as means to other pleasures or preventions of pain. Aware that some thinkers view his idea as a base moral conception, Mill states a number of outstanding objections to it. He argues that the objections represent either misunderstandings of the Utilitarian doctrine or, if they contain some truth, views which are not incompatible with it.

Mill rejects the argument that Utilitarianism chooses to picture human nature at the lowest animal level. Clearly, animals are incapable of experiencing many pleasures available and important to men. Every "Epicurean theory of life" also admits that intellectual pleasures are more valuable than those of simple sensation. "It is quite compatible with the principle of utility to recognize the fact that some kinds of pleasure are more desirable and more valuable than others." Pleasures must be judged in terms of quality as well as quantity. Mill suggests a way in which the value of two possible pleasures may be determined. Only that man can decide who, out of wide experience, knows both pleasures and can thus state a comparative judgment. Apparently Mill believed this test is adequate. He assumed that the man of experience actually knows the worth of competing pleasures in a manner which is not simply psychological but objective. Rational beings should choose pleasures of higher quality. Not all men are equally competent to render decisive judgments. In a striking sentence Mill writes: "It is better to be a human being dissatisfied than a pig satisfied."

A summary statement of important criticisms of the Utilitarian doctrine, along with brief descriptions of Mill's replies, is here in order. First, the Utilitarian "greatest happiness" principle is said to be too exalted in expecting human beings to adopt a disinterested moral posture. Mill's reply is that in serving the interests of one's fellow creatures the motive may be either self-interest or duty. The resulting act rather than the motive must be judged, though the motive of duty can influence us to honor also the character of the doer. Men can promote the general interests of society without always fixing "their minds upon so wide a generality as the world, or society at large." Second, to the charge that Utilitarianism will make men cold and unsympathizing, Mill answers that men should show interest in things other than those concerned with standards of right and wrong. Yet it is necessary to emphasize the need of making judgments of right and wrong and to supply moral standards for human behavior. Third, Mill calls simply false the view that Utilitarianism is a godless doctrine. Religiously inclined men can use the Utilitarian standard to determine what in detail the will of God means for human action. Fourth, some critics complain that Utilitarianism will end in expediency. Mill's rebuttal is that the utility principle does not justify acts which result only in the pleasure of the lone individual. The social standard must always operate. Fifth, Mill argues that Utilitarianism can account even for the actions of martyrs and heroes. Heroism and martyrdom involve individual sacrifices whose ultimate aim is the increase in the happiness of others or of society as a whole. Other criticisms—that Utilitarianism overlooks lack of time for men to decide the results of given actions and that Utilitarians may use the doctrine to exempt themselves from moral rules—are shown to apply equally to other ethical doctrines.

Mill goes on to admit that other questions about a moral standard can be raised. For what reasons should any person adopt the standard? What motivates one to apply it? Such quesions about the sanctions of a moral standard Mill treats as if they are meaningful. There are two possible kinds of sanction for Utilitarianism—an external and an internal one. Desire of favor and also fear of displeasure from one's fellows, or from a sovereign God, constitute the Utilitarian principle's external sanctions. Given feelings of affection for other men or awe for a God, men may act also out of unselfish motives which can "attach themselves to the Utilitarian morality, as completely and powerfully as to any other."

Conscience makes up the internal sanction of the principle. Mill defines conscience as "a pain, more or less intense, attendant on violation of duty." This sanction is really a feeling in the mind such that any violation of it results in discomfort. Even the man who thinks moral obligation has roots in a transcendental sphere acts only conscientiously in so far as he harbors religious feelings about duty. There must be a subjective feeling of obligation. But is this feeling of duty acquired or innate? If innate, the problem concerns the objects of the feeling. Intuitionists admit that principles rather than the details of morality get intuited. Mill argues that the Utilitarian emphasis on regard for the pleasures and pains of others might well be an intuitively known principle. Some regard for interests of others is seen as obligatory even by intuitionists who insist on yet other obligatory principles. Mill thought that any sanction provided by a transcendental view of the origin of obligation is available to the Utilitarian doctrine.

Nonetheless, Mill's view was that men's notions of obligation are actually acquired. Though not a part of man's nature, the moral faculty is an outgrowth of it. This faculty can arise spontaneously in some circumstances as well as benefit from proper environmental cultivation. The social feelings of mankind provide a basis of natural sentiment which supports the Utilitarian doctrine. "Society between equals can only exist on the understanding that the interests of all are to be regarded equally." Proper education and social arrangements can encourage the moral feelings toward virtuous activity. By education men can learn to value objects disinterestedly which, in the beginning, they sought only for the sake of pleasure. Mill claims that virtue is one good of this kind.

In *Utilitarianism* Mill raises the peculiar question as to whether the utility principle can be proved. It is difficult to understand what kind of question Mill thought he was asking here. The setting for this question appears to involve something like the following: When someone asks if the principle has any sanctions, it is as if he were to ask: "Why should I seek the good even if the utility principle is sound?" But when someone asks for a proof of the principle, it is as if he were to inquire: "How can I know *that* the utility principle is true?" Strangely, this question comes up only after Mill has already refuted a whole range of criticisms of the Utilitarian doctrine as well as shown the sanctions which support it.

Mill argues that "the sole evidence it is possible to produce that anything is desirable, is that people do actually desire it." One difficulty with this assertion concerns the word "sole." Even if it is true that nothing can be desirable which is not desired by someone, would it follow necessarily that one's desire of an object is sufficient evidence of its desirability? If not, what besides desire would account for an object's desirability? Contextually, it would appear that Mill might have to agree that though everything desirable must be desired, not everything desired need be desirable. This would follow from his earlier claim that some pleasures are qualitatively better than others. A human being who desired to live like a pig would seek to evade realizing the highest kind of happiness available to him. To this argument Mill might have wanted to reply that, in fact, no man really does want to live like a pig. Yet the most controversial aspect of Mill's proof occurs when he insists that "each man's happiness is a good to that person, and the general happiness, therefore, a good to the aggregate of all persons." Some philosophers call this statement an example of an elementary logical fallacy—attribution of a property applicable to the parts of a collection to the collection itself. The Utilitarian stress on men's obligation to seek the happiness of the greatest number raises a question about the relation of individual pleasures to social ones. A man may desire to drive at high speeds as an individual, yet not have grounds for making desirable the changing of the speed rules. What Mill wants to underline is that in conflicts between social and individual interests, the individual interests must often give way.

Ultimately a conception of human nature must serve as justification of Mill's use of the utility principle. The proof runs to the effect that men are, after all, naturally like that. If they do not seek happiness directly, they seek other ends as a means to it. To a skeptic convinced that the principle cannot be proved by an appeal to human nature, Mill might have said: "Obviously, you misunderstand what you really desire." In this case the utility principle is proved in that it conforms to what men are like. On this basis, however, it seems peculiar to want to argue that men *ought* to use the principle in making moral judgments. To say that men ought to act in a given way is to imply that they may not.

The concluding chapter of *Utilitarianism* discusses the relation of justice to utility. The idea of justice tends to impede the victory of the Utilitarian doctrine, according to Mill. Men's sentiment of justice seems to suggest existence of a natural, objective norm which is totally divorced from expediency and hedonistic consequences. Mill's task was to indicate how the Utilitarian doctrine could accommodate this sentiment and nevertheless remain the sole acceptable standard for judging right and wrong.

One must examine objects in the concrete if he wants to discover whatever common features they may contain. This is true of the idea of justice. Several fundamental beliefs are associated in popular opinion with notions like "just" and "unjust." Justice involves respect for the legal and moral rights of other people. It implies the wrongfulness of taking away another's moral rights by illegal or even legal means. There can be bad laws. The notion of desert is also important. This notion entails belief that wrongdoing deserves punishment and the doing of right, reciprocation in good acts. Justice cannot mean doing good in return for evil, according to Mill. Nonetheless men may waive justice when they are wronged. Furthermore, men ought not to break promises which are willingly and knowingly made. This is so even in the case of implied promises. Justice precludes breach of faith. Finally, justice implies impartiality and equality in the treatment of men and claims. This means that men ought to be "influenced by the considerations which it is supposed ought to influence the particular case in hand." Mill concludes that several general features rather than one are common to these opinions about justice. Turning to the etymology of the word, he asserts that the primitive meaning of justice is "conformity to law." The Greeks and Romans, recognizing the possibility of bad laws, came to view injustice as the breaking of those laws which ought to be obeyed. The idea of justice in personal conduct also involves the belief that a man ought to be forced to do just acts.

To say that justice accepts the idea of the desirability of compelling someone to do his duty tells men what justice is about. Yet it does not mark off the peculiar nature of justice from other branches of morality. According to Mill, justice involves the notion of perfect obligation. Duties of perfect obligation imply the existence of a correlative right in a person or persons. "Justice implies something which it is not only right to do, and wrong not to do, but which some individual person can claim from me as his moral right." This view of justice admits a distinction between moral obligation and the domains of beneficence and generosity. In men the sentiment of justice becomes "moralized," spread over a social group or community. Justice then involves the feeling that one ought to punish those who harm members of that community. Men's need of security plays a role here. The idea of right does also. Justice involves a belief that there are rights which morally society must defend. Thus justice is compatible with the utility principle, for "when moralized by the social feeling, it only acts in directions conformable to the general good."

The idea of justice requires belief in a rule of conduct applicable to all men, plus a sentiment which sanctions the rule. This sentiment, which insists that transgressors be punished, is compatible with the utility principle if the idea of justice is taken to refer to special classes of moral rules. These are the rules without which the realization of the general good would be impossible. An important example of such rules would be those forbidding one person to harm another. Such rules presuppose the Utilitarian doctrine that one person's happiness must be considered as important as another's. Mill's conclusion is that "Justice remains the appropriate name for certain social utilities which are vastly more important, and therefore more absolute and imperative, than any others are as a class."

Utilitarianism is a book of significance for thinkers concerned about the problem of moral fairness in a social setting. Mill attempted to show that men's notions of obligation can be made compatible with the utility principle. What animates the work is Mill's clear conviction that even the more exalted moral claims of intuitionists and Kantian moralists make sense only if the Utilitarian doctrine is the true one. Only with justice and binding rules of obligation can man achieve the greatest happiness of the greatest number.

659

THE PHILOSOPHY OF THE UNCONSCIOUS

Author: Eduard von Hartmann (1842-1906)
Type of work: Metaphysics
First published: 1869

PRINCIPAL IDEAS ADVANCED

An unconscious will is the ground and true cause of everything that comes to be.

Morality, history, and the mind of genius all show the unconscious will at work.

The universe is composed of atoms, but the atoms are atoms of force, not matter.

Although the unconscious will never errs, in evolving consciousness, which is its opposite, it shows itself to be irrational in its creative process.

The philosopher, who prizes consciousness and rationality, is the enemy of the will; by being conscious he triumphs over will.

Man reaches "old age," or philosophical maturity, only after passing through the "childhood" stage (in which happiness is sought), the stage of "youth" (in which one counts on the rewards in heaven), and the stage of "manhood" (in which man labors to build a paradise on earth).

Hartmann completed this most celebrated book, of some thirty which came from his hand, before he was twenty-five years of age. More than a thousand pages long (in the English translation), it revived the agnostic spirit of German speculative philosophy to combine it with the findings of empirical science. (It bears the subtitle, "Speculative Results According to the Inductive Method of Physical Science.") Its protest against the mechanistic view of nature and against the liberal and optimistic view of man found a large and appreciative audience. Its appeal to nature ministered to the sentimentality of dying romanticism, and its teleological outlook strengthened religious orthodoxy in its struggle against Darwinism. But it has the more enduring claim of being one of the wellsprings of modern irrationalism as expressed in the literature of

psychoanalysis and in the political theories of right-wing socialism.

At the center of Hartmann's thought is the notion of an unconscious will which is the ground and only true cause of everything that comes to be. He has drawn freely from Fichte, Schelling, Hegel, and Schopenhauer, as well as from Herbart and Fechner. But, broadly speaking, what he has done is to combine the Hegelian notion of the unconscious self-unfolding of the Idea with Schopenhauer's notion of a blind, striving will. In his opinion, Schopenhauer did not do justice to the fact that every act of willing presupposes a purpose. The future state must be contained in the present existing state, and since it cannot be there actually, it must be there ideally, as representation. On the other hand, Hegel did not bring out clearly what is involved in the conception of Absolute Idea which has not yet been externalized in nature or become conscious in mind. If the ideal realm is not thought of as residing in God, considered as conscious and therefore as Spirit (which, for Hegel it was not, since Spirit is the fulfillment of the System), then it remains that it is unconscious and present only as will.

Hartmann's choice of the term "will" to designate his first principle is based on the analogy of conscious activity. Volition is "the form of causality of the ideal with respect to the real." When a man wills, he imagines a future event which he is in a position to bring about, but only through intermediate causes. The infallible mark of will is that it gives rise to preconceived action. But, argues Hartmann, we have only to open our eyes to see that preconceived action is going on all around us, and that conscious willing is only a special case of a universal phenomenon. The only straightforward and intelligible name for this universal cause is "will."

As *The Philosophy of the Unconscious* is divided, the first two parts, which are entitled "The Unconscious in Bodily Life" and "The Unconscious in Mind," are devoted to illustrating the author's thesis that everything in nature and history is the working out of an unconscious purpose. The third part, called "Metaphysic of the Unconscious," traces the evolution of the cosmos out of the unconscious and explores the moral consequences of this knowledge.

Writing only ten years after the appearance of Darwin's *On the Origin of Species*, Hartmann found the theory of natural selection a good target. Not that he repudiated altogether the mechanistic type of explanation—nature does operate to a great extent according to mechanical principles—but these pertain only to means and pay no regard to ends. Hartmann elaborates a proof against the chances of our world's having emerged mechanically by using the well-worn method of mathematical probabilities. For example, the physiology of that day enumerated thirteen conditions necessary for the existence and maintenance of normal vision. All are there at birth, although the occasion for their exercise has never arisen. The material conditions of the blastoderm offer not the slightest probability that any one of the conditions (say, the optic nerve) should develop. Clearly something is missing in a purely mechanical explanation.

From the argument based on abstract probability, Hartmann turns to the ever-startling evidences of teleological behavior in nature. There is, for example, a wisdom of the body not confined to the cortex—the beating of the heart, the rhythm of the stomach-muscles, the minute adjustments commonly referred to as "reflexes." Add to these a catalogue of the curious instincts of spiders and bees, the reparative powers in the limbs of a crab, and the whole science of embryology. Everywhere we meet immanent purpose, or will. Hartmann does not limit himself to such commonplace examples; perhaps much of the excitement which the work held for the nineteenth century reading public lay in the thoroughness of his compilation, which must have cost him many hours with books on nature.

No less comprehensive than his treatment of the inner teleology of nature is his account of the works of the unconscious in the character and conduct of man. For many readers today, Hartmann's chief significance doubtless lies in the manner in which he anticipated depth psychology when he pointed out the obliquely purposive quality of many of our seemingly unintentional acts. But Hartmann's interest in these facts extends merely to the support they lend to his thesis of universal teleology, and he does not linger over them. In fact, he is less concerned with the bizarre behavior which occupies the medical psychologists than with the social and cultural achievements of the race. Thus, speech is originally as unpremeditated as the cry of a bird; but it contains the rudiments of logic and philosophy—a point of his system which he allows was ably developed before him by Schelling. And there is more than an echo of the romantic philosophers in his account of artistic production, where he distinguishes between genius and talent and exalts the products of inspiration (Plato's "divine frenzy") over so-called art which is the product of rules and conscious design. He places taste on the level of instinct, together with morality. His teaching is that moral principles are innate, and that when a people emerges from barbarism to a civilized estimate of moral principles, there is then a coming to consciousness of judgments which were subconsciously present all the time. Not merely the fruits of civilization, but the historical process itself is the working out of a secret plan. History makes sense, and the great upheavals and movements which mark its course give expression to unconscious Ideas. Like Hegel, Hartmann holds that these are sometimes disclosed to masses of men, as when a

new conception takes possession of an entire people without anyone consciously discovering it; but perhaps more often they are revealed through the mind of a single genius, more conscious than his fellows, who serves as a prophet for the coming of the will.

Writing as he did against the background of post-Kantian speculation, Hartmann was especially concerned with the question of the status to be given to the individual in relation to the absolute. The unconscious, in his system, is unity, and for Hartmann, as for his predecessors, the world of appearance is an unfolding of infinite potentialities hidden there. In the last analysis, therefore, everything that comes to pass owes its existence to this Primal Being. But Hartmann tried to overcome the complaints which had arisen since Hegel's time against Idealism on the grounds that it did not do justice to the reality either of nature or of the personality of the individual. Instead of conceiving the world as a purely ideal representation, he thought of it as built up of atoms, very much in accordance with the chemistry and biology of his day. The distinctive thing in his account, which made it possible for him to reconcile scientific realism with his doctrine of the will, was that he conceived of the atoms purely as forces. He distinguished between body-atoms and ether-atoms, representing respectively the forces of attraction and of repulsion; and by the behavior of these, he accounted for the laws of matter. This part of his system he called "dynamic atomism," and he claimed that by atoms of force he could account for anything which more conservative scientists could explain in terms of atoms of matter. At bottom, of course, each of his atoms was thought of as an expression of the unconscious and as fulfilling a unique purpose in the world plan.

From this beginning, Hartmann went on to explain the rise of living creatures, from the simplest organisms to man. A striking feature of his system (which inevitably reminds us of Leibniz's) is the way in which he argues that psychic activity is present in the lowest organisms and that sensibility is present in plants as well as in animals. The natural world, therefore, is as real as anything else. The Neoplatonic prejudice against materiality has no hold here. Higher forms of being have exactly the same kind of reality as lower. For although the world is an ascending evolution in which the potentialities of the unconscious are ever more completely actualized, the higher products are always conditioned by the lower. Even consciousness, which is the goal and end product of the whole development, is bound to physiological conditions. It is found only in higher vertebrates and is absolutely dependent upon the healthy working of a brain and nervous system.

In this way, Hartmann "saves" appearance, preserving for the world of nature the reality demanded by the physical scientists, for the world of economics the reality demanded by political agitators, and for human ambitions and aspirations the reality demanded by moralists and philosophers of religion. They are, in the final analysis, only appearances, because they are really expressions of the sovereign purpose of the unconscious will. They have the only kind of existence that is conceivable to partial and particular things separated from the world ground. They are what Hartmann calls "objectively real phenomena."

Thus, he comes to the border of a still more difficult problem: Why is there something instead of nothing? If the unconscious is the ground of being, why did it extend itself to become something which it was not? Is there a second world principle independent of the unconscious which seduces it out of the eternal night? Is creativity a "fall"? Space has sometimes been thought to function in this way, as the void disturbed the eternal calm of Plotinus' One. But for Hartmann, following Kant, space is itself posited by the unconscious as the theater for its tragic representation. And in any case, a dualistic explanation offends our deepest philosophical instincts. The only possible explanation is that the dynamism which causes the unconscious to unfold itself lies within the original unity itself. This would be the case if, as Hartmann held, the unconditioned is neither the pure Idea of Hegel nor the pure will of Schopenhauer, but will and Idea inextricably combined, an irrational impulse ever stirring itself to accomplish rational ends. According to Hartmann, the unconscious is, from one point of view, perfectly rational. When it comes to realizing its ends, it is infallible. It never hesitates, it never errs, but in virtue of an absolute clairvoyance, it achieves with minimal effort the goal which it has set before it. In this sense, ours is the best possible world, and the eighteenth century was correct in its praises of the wisdom of divine providence. But the other side of the question is whether no world at all would not have been better than this one, whether a fully rational being would have permitted any world to be. The answer is not to be given in terms of our egoistic satisfaction, but from the point of view of reason itself. And the fact that the direction of evolution is toward the production of consciousness, which is the contradictory of its original, makes it clear that creation is irrational and yet, in terms of its own conditions, it should not be. It is self-defeating, hence absolutely bad. Pure, blind chance would not have been evil in any profound sense. But an absolute in which the rational and the irrational are inseparably and eternally one is criminal. It is "willful" in the derogatory sense of that word.

Hartmann's pessimism differed from the *Weltschmerz* of the romantics in that it was theoretically based and not merely an expression of frustrated hedonism. This base accounts for the apparent ambiguities in his attitudes toward evolution and progress. Creation and history are a madman's tale which must be condemned *in toto*. They are also to be condemned from the point of view of the individual ego, which tries to maintain its own private worth and satisfaction. But the tendency of evolution is to produce ever higher consciousness. And insofar as an individual is so fortunate as to be endowed with superior understanding, he can affirm that evolution is progress and that the end result is good. He does so by depending on the inherently contradictory unconscious. For the unconscious tends to destroy itself, and the true philosopher, insofar as he lives on the plane of consciousness, is its nemesis. Knowing this, he affirms rationality and intelligibility wherever these manifest themselves in evolution and history. He can even affirm pain, because that is an ingredient in consciousness and a condition for the emergence of free intelligence.

Consciousness, according to Hartmann, is the emancipation of idea from will, just as unconsciousness is the inseparable unity of idea and will. It extricates the rational elements of being from their native soil, the realizing will, and in this way disarms the cunning of the absolute or diverts it into channels where it can do no harm. Hartmann is, in this respect, on the side of enlightenment and intelligence; he has no patience with those who would make voluntarism an excuse for resigning themselves to the movements of the unconscious. According to Hartmann, man cannot with impunity neglect the use of his higher endowments, for when the unconscious evolves a complicated machine to do a certain work, it makes no provision for that work to be done in other ways. Thus, when man received intelligence, he was deprived of instinct. The unconscious does nothing in vain, and a human being who refuses to think is simply discarded like so much rubbish. Man has to reason, to plan, and to decide. The other side of the issue, however, is that intellect can never cut itself free from the unconscious; and this is particularly true when production and creativity are involved. Reason can impose limits on nature's caprice, preserve and heighten those effects which are harmonious, and weed out those that disturb. By analysis it can anticipate the unfolding of Idea, and speed up the progress of cosmic development. But it must never lose touch with concrete reality or suppose that it can revise the conditions of human existence. In this respect, Hartmann set himself against what he calls the "mock enlightenment" of the eighteenth century and against the rationalist mentality in his own time.

Mankind as a whole, Hartmann believed, is a long way from being able to make any proper use of consciousness. The history of civilization is the record of elaborately cultivated illusions. Such consciousness as man has achieved scarcely has done more than make him aware of the evils of existence and compound them with folly and vice, from which he has fled into worlds of fancy and hope. Several stages are discernible. Ancient man, in the "childhood" stage of the race, supposed that happiness is attained in the present life. He worked, sacrificed, endured disappointment and defeat, believing that wealth, fame, and friendship have the power to bring satisfaction. Disenchanted with the more obvious goals, he tried religion and vice, or turned to art and invention—always persuaded that somewhere the world must offer fulfillment to those who know how to court its favor. But at last experience convinced him of the contrary and led to the conclusion, "All is Vanity."

Hartmann calls the second stage "youth." It is represented in history by the Christian idea which, condemning the present life, promised treasure in heaven where mortal ills cannot prevail. The fancied nearness of the other world taught men to sacrifice present benefits for future gain; but it did little or nothing to weaken the individual's pride and self-will. And when, with further understanding, man found it impossible any longer to keep up the illusion, he turned his hope again to this life.

The post-Christian mind, however, maintains its own illusion. This stage Hartmann labels "manhood." It signifies the stage in which man plans and labors for future generations, persuading himself that he can build a cooperative paradise on earth. Such was the prevailing attitude in Western society when Hartmann was writing his book. It too, according to Hartmann, is an illusion, a life-lie. There is no historical basis for believing that science or education or democratic government contributes anything to social harmony or to private happiness; and thoughtful consideration of the factors which limit human existence shows that under no conceivable circumstances can real pleasure counterbalance real pain. Fortunately, however, in "old age," or philosophical maturity, man finds that when he has cast off illusion, the pain and disappointment of life are not intolerable. He discovers that ego is not ultimately real and that its desires and ambitions are merely part of the primal urge. And in the very act of understanding them, he cuts their nerve and dissipates their forces, while freeing himself for rational and aesthetic satisfactions. Few men, according to Hartmann, have reached this level. And when the race as a whole achieves it, history and civilization will come to some sort of rest. The reader who desires to know how it may work out is advised to read Bernard Shaw's *Back to Methuselah*.

665

A GRAMMAR OF ASSENT

Author: John Henry Cardinal Newman (1801-1890)
Type of work: Metaphysics, epistemology
First published: 1870

PRINCIPAL IDEAS ADVANCED

There is no qualitative break between our knowledge of God and other kinds of knowledge.

Since God is the most concrete and determinate of beings, knowledge of him must be real apprehension—intelligent acceptance through personal, concrete experience.

Assent does not depend on inference, and inference is not always of the formal sort described by logicians.

The right to assent to religious truths comes from personal involvement in the concrete situations in which God manifests himself.

Cardinal Newman may not be thought of by many as a philosopher, possibly because he is a sort of philosophical outsider without specific ancestry or descent; and histories of philosophy, victims of their own schemes of classification, find it difficult to include such individualists. In our own day, however, when men have grown dissatisfied with established traditions and have taken to reviewing the history of thought with a view to discovering where we may have gone astray, Newman's writings have excited a new interest. And this is the case, not primarily among Roman Catholics, whose scholastic revival is quite foreign to Newman's way of thinking, but chiefly among realists and empiricists, who are drawn to him because of his appreciation of the whole person, and his recognition that man's thought processes are complex and cannot be understood apart from the rest of man. Scholars have suggested that he anticipated Bergson in his interpretation of the roles of intui-

tion and intellect, that what he calls a "Grammar" of assent and certitude is a very model of phenomenological analysis, and that his emphasis upon the distinct kind of reality belonging to man and to God (in virtue of personality, concreteness, individuality, and vitality) discloses existentialist insights. Whatever the truth of these claims, they serve to dispel the notion that Newman was primarily an antiquarian. Perhaps as much as any Victorian Englishman, he found himself abreast the stream of post-modern thought.

A Grammar of Assent is concerned with the problem of knowledge, which, like his predecessors of the British school, Newman approaches by analyzing the activity of mind in perception and reasoning. The central problem is that of "assent," and it corresponds to the problem of "belief" in Hume and in Reid. Newman considers it in two relations which give the divisions of his book: assent and apprehension; assent and inference.

The term *apprehension* is standard

in the literature of empirical thought, and there is nothing exceptional in the way Newman defines it: "Apprehension is an intelligent acceptance of the idea or of the fact which a proposition enunciates." We can "assert" a matter without apprehending it, that is, without grasping the significance of what we are saying.

On the other hand, Newman argues that we can apprehend a meaning without "understanding" it in any concrete, experiential sense. Here we sense the special quality of Newman's thinking, which is powerfully inclined toward the concrete and sensible and away from the abstract and intellectual. There are, in general, two ways of apprehending a truth: we may grasp it in a merely "notional" sense, or we may grasp it as a "reality." The former is the work of the intellect. It involves naming, comparing, distinguishing, and classifying. It reduces real things to notions or concepts, to symbols and linguistic signs. The latter way is the work of sensation, imagination, and memory. Only through these do we have experience of the concrete, singular thing. And the more experience we have, the more real our apprehension. For example, a French economist may write about facts well known to himself with a view to being understood by others who are furnished with comparable facts. A bright schoolboy could translate his work into English with but the faintest understanding of what the treatise really maintained; yet his apprehension of all the terms would be correct enough to enable an informed Englishman to understand the French author.

We may now see the relation of apprehension to *assent*. Assent is "belief," but belief as fully specified to fit Newman's observations. He defines it: "the absolute acceptance of a proposition without any condition."

Assent is, thus, a sort of internal assertion. We may assert without apprehending; but if we apprehend what we assert, the assertion is an assent. How much must we apprehend? Merely the predicate term. For example, a child asks, "What is lucern?" If his mother answers, "Lucern is food for cattle," the child apprehends the predicate. He assents to it, even though he has never seen lucern, and he can henceforth go further, even to assenting to propositions where "lucern" is the predicate; for example, "That field is sown with lucern." If, however, his mother were to reply, "Lucern is medicago sativa of the class of diadelphia," he can then assert this; but since he does not apprehend, he cannot assent to it. There is, indeed, an indirect way in which he can assent to this proposition also—if it be given a new predicate such as "That lucern is medicago sativa is true," he can assent to it, which he does because he believes his mother. This latter would be, incidentally, a notional apprehension: and, as we shall see, notional apprehensions lead to assertion only in a conditional or inferential manner; that is, on the basis of some previous assent.

As between real and notional assents, Newman holds that the former are generally stronger because of the vividness with which they strike the imagination. Imagination plays an important role in Newman's thought, not as creating assent (after the manner of Hume) but as intensifying it, giving it body and substance and making it easier for us to hold onto it. This is a "natural and rightful effect of the acts of imagination," and it is important for educators to bear this in mind. Notional assents may become real—for example, a passage of poetry or Scripture, once held only in a notional way, may as a result of some private experience come to "mean more" to us than it did before; it becomes concrete.

We have not yet considered the reasons or grounds of assent. This is the burden of the second part of the work, where Newman comes to treat of the relation between assent and *inference*. In his view, traditional philosophy has taken too theoretical a view of the grounds of assent by consulting an idea of how the mind ought to act instead of interrogating human nature as an existing thing. One would think, from reading Plato or Locke, that there is really no such thing as assent apart from inference, and that our degree of confidence in the truth of a proposition is proportional to the strength of the reasons that can be brought for and against it. Newman shows that there are instances in which correct inference fails to produce assent, and others in which we assent without any inference at all.

There is such a thing as *simple* assent which does not rest on argument. It is "adhesion without reserve or doubt to the truth of a proposition." Ordinarily it follows automatically from real apprehension: from what I see, what I remember, what I have on good authority. But it is possible to pass from simple assent to *complex* assent, based on inference. For example, I may believe the proposition "Great Britain is an island," without any thought of the reasons on which this belief is established. This is simple assent. But if called upon to do so, I could call up the reasons, and do this without any suspension of the belief while I was thinking of them. When it is done, however, the assent is in a manner altered. I now assent deliberately, hypothetically, conditionally. In fact, it will be observed, I am now asserting a new proposition, namely "That Great Britain is an island is true." This act of the mind is reflexive. Newman distinguishes it from the other by calling it "certitude." It is more than assent as "following on investigation and proof, accompanied by a specific sense of intellectual satisfaction and repose, and [in] that it is irreversible."

Certitude, according to Newman, is essential to the whole pursuit of knowledge. Without it, truth would still be truth; but knowledge of truth would ever be beyond us and unattainable. Philosophers, with their preconceptions of how the mind should work, have contradicted the plain facts of experience. We do know many things for certain; and, as a general rule, certitude does not fail us. The fact that sometimes we are mistaken does not destroy other certitudes any more than the fact that clocks are sometimes wrong destroys our confidence in clocks. "No instances of mistaken certitude are sufficient to constitute a proof that certitude itself is a perversion." Newman seriously considers the case against this position, showing that we often have a conviction of certainty and are proved wrong. But in at least some instances where this seems to be the case, we have been careless about the distinction between propositions which we hold for certain and those of which we are strongly persuaded but not certain. If we bother to keep these apart, Newman thinks, it is rare that a certainty has to be given up. We are made for truth, can attain it, and having attained it can keep it, recognize it, and preserve the recognition. Though errant, the mind is capable of discipline, of progress, of approaching by practice to perfection.

Newman's analysis of inference may be said to put logic in its place. Reasoning, he maintains, is as spontaneous to man as are perception and memory. "By means of sense we gain knowledge directly; by means of reasoning we gain it indirectly." But there is too strong a tendency in western intellectual history to restrict inference to the *formal* process. The Aristotelian syllogism is merely an attempt to analyze a natural process of the mind and "invent a method to serve as a common measure between man and man." It succeeds so far as words can capture the subtleties of thought; but its inability ever to do this completely should make us cautious about taking the syllogism for a norm.

Here is the place to speak of the role of intelligence in Newman's philosophy. Its world of abstractions and symbols makes possible the whole realm of human science—mathematical, physical, biological. But it has serious limits, and is far from being the whole of mind. The great vice of the Enlightenment, the Age of Reason, was to suppose that all truth is of this conceptual order, and that in ordering and judging among its notions we are dealing with reality. "Science in all its departments has too much simplicity and exactness from the nature of the case to be the measure of fact. In its very perfection lies its incompetency to settle particulars and details." The hu-

man mind includes more than can be described by the syllogism or by the most refined mathematical calculus. Consider any actual problem—for example, one in literary criticism. "How short and easy a way to a true conclusion is the logic of good sense; how little syllogisms have to do with the formation of opinion; how little depends upon the inferential proofs, and how much upon those preexisting beliefs and views, in which men either already agree with each other or hopelessly differ, before they begin to dispute, and which are hidden deep in our nature, or, it may be, in our personal peculiarities."

Besides considering formal inference, Newman analyzes what he calls *informal* inference. It is carried out in the concrete, is largely implicit, and is chiefly an accumulation of probabilities. There is, in addition, what he calls *natural* inference, which is the immediate perception of relations without proof, granted to spirits of high genius. Examples: Napoleon's disposal of troops in battle, or Newton's rule for discovering imaginary roots of equations.

To designate the normative processes of inference, Newman uses the term "illative sense," which he justifies by setting it alongside the parallel faculties by which we judge duty and taste. He remarks its similarity to the *phronesis* (judgment) by which Aristotle said that we have our perception of the "mean." He points to the taste of a Phidias or a Raphael, which is more subtle and versatile than any treatise on art could ever grasp. Corresponding to these special senses is the "illative sense," which deals with truth. It is the same for all kinds of subject matter, although one individual may by endowment or training be skilled in applying it in one area and not in another; and because it proceeds always in the same way, its processes may be described by logic and extended in mathematical calculus. But in no case is there any test of the truth beyond the trustworthiness of the illative sense just as there is no other test of beauty or morality beyond their special senses.

Man's business, Newman says, is not to justify this illative sense, but to use it. We are in a world of facts: it would be out of place to demand the credentials of earth, air, fire, and water. So of our own mental capacities: "Our being, with its faculties, mind and body, is a fact not admitting of question, all things being of necessity referred to it." This common-sense remark could have been made by Reid; but note that Reid and his followers never actually made it. They took their stand within the circle of consciousness and had the problem of breaking out and establishing the not-self. Newman took his stand on the world as a whole; he regarded man's existence as something that was certainly known. From his point of view, he had more in common with the Greeks than with his own age, dominated as it was by subjectivism. "My first disobedience," he says, in a pointed criticism of the spirit of modern philosophy, "is to be impatient at what I am and to indulge an ambitious aspiration after what I cannot be, to cherish a distrust of my powers, and to desire to change laws which are identical with myself."

A larger proportion of the *Grammar* is given over to the discussion of religion than this review has indicated. But the application of Newman's general principles to religion can be quickly shown. For Newman, there is no qualitative break between our knowledge of God and other kinds of knowledge. Man requires no special faculty by which God comes to be known to him, no special feeling of dependence, or sense of the numenous. We know reality at any level in the degree that we have concrete, personal, living experience of it. We know our old clothes, our customary surroundings, our familiar acquaintances in a peculiarly solid and satisfactory way. Our knowledge of our friends illustrates this very clearly. The first meeting leaves us with scarcely more than a silhouette. It is as we renew the impression in a variety of ways that it begins to take on depth and fullness. The roles of sensation and imagination are more important in this getting acquainted than our abstractive powers which, in a sense, are the enemy of true knowledge—there is a kind of routine familiarity that is compatible with profound ignorance. Now, God being the most concrete and determinate of all beings, our knowledge of him must be just as particular.

For Newman, religion consists in real apprehension, and theology in merely notional. The true religion commands *assent* because God has manifested himself in tangible and imaginable forms—through the lives of holy men, the liturgy and hymns, and the sacraments. Its *certitude*, when that is called for, is founded on the witness of conscience, and upon the evidences of history and anthropology. Like the Thomists, Newman argues from natural revelation to special: but instead of appealing, as they do, to philosophical proofs (natural theology), he argues from sacrifice and prayer among primitive peoples (natural religion). "Revelation begins where Natural Religion fails. The Religion of Nature is a mere inchoation, and needs a complement—it can have but one complement, and that very complement is Christianity."

In Newman we are dealing with an authentic person: his whole life bears the stamp of autonomy and self-determination. What is impressive in his account of religious truth is that in listening to his presentation of it, we are not listening to a mere philosopher who is trying to fit religious phenomena into a satisfactory world view, but to a religious genius who is at the same time a profound and disciplined thinker. A Grammar of Assent is not an attempt to prove religion, or even to expound a doctrine. It is an attempt to render intelligible the actuality of a life (Newman's own) founded on the knowledge of God. In this province, he says that "egotism is true modesty. In religious inquiry each of us can speak only for himself, for for himself he has a right to speak."

THE METHODS OF ETHICS

Author: Henry Sidgwick (1838-1900)
Type of work: Ethics
First published: 1874

PRINCIPAL IDEAS ADVANCED

Modern man uses three different methods of ethics, three ways of resolving moral problems: egoism, intuitionism, and utilitarianism.

Egoistic hedonism, the theory that one ought to seek his own pleasure, is one of the natural methods of ethics; its primary disadvantage is the difficulty of measuring and evaluating pleasures.

The ethics of right and duty employs an a priori method, utilizing intuition, or direct cognition, as a way of discovering duties; but it is difficult to find moral principles that do not need qualification and that do not admit exceptions.

Certain moral principles are manifestly true: the principle of impartiality, the principle of prudence, and the principle of benevolence.

Utilitarianism is true to the principles of impartiality and benevolence; but it is difficult to reconcile egoism and utilitarianism.

Henry Sidgwick held that ethics has to do with the reasons which men use in deciding between two courses of action and that the study of ethics is the attempt to bring these reasons together in a coherent system. Modern Western man uses three different "methods" of ethics; that is, three different ways of answering the question, "Why should I do such and such?" He may reason with a view to self-interest; he may ask what his duty is; he may try to estimate the effect of the action in question on the general well-being. Sidgwick held that the ordinary man does not find it necessary to choose

671

between these methods: on some occasions he uses one, and on other occasions another.

Professed moralists, however, have condemned this slackness and have insisted that all ethical reasoning should proceed from one principle and employ one method. Some have maintained that ethics is the reasoned pursuit of happiness, whether one's own or that of all mankind. Others have denied this and maintained that man's reason knows immediately what acts are right and what are wrong. In Sidgwick's view, neither of these approaches could be carried through consistently without unduly constraining the moral intention of ordinary men. He accepted the ideal of unity and consistency which governs all theoretical inquiry; but he was wary of Procrustean solutions, and thought it better to leave certain questions unresolved than to do violence to important aspects of moral experience. Thus, instead of championing only one method, he sought to find a higher unity in which the distinctive contribution of each of "the methods of ethics" is preserved.

A work with such a thesis might have turned out to be a tiresome piece of eclecticism. Actually, it is a masterpiece in philosophical analysis, a pioneer work which set the style for philosophy at Cambridge University for at least two generations afterwards. Sidgwick aimed at synthesis, but his conclusions were modest and imperfect. The strength of his work lies in the sympathetic treatment which he accorded each method, the care he expended in defining and testing claims, and the hopeful and tentative manner in which he developed rival positions. Sidgwick broke with the practice, which had prevailed in English philosophy before his time, of treating moral philosophy as an adjunct of metaphysics, or of divinity, or of psychology. Whether moral law has its foundation in the will of God or in the evolution of society, whether the will of man is an efficient cause, whether man is naturally selfish or social are questions which do not enter into ethical inquiry. Ethics is a search for "valid ultimate reasons for acting or abstaining." Problems concerning God, Nature, and Self belong not to ethics but to general philosophy. "The introduction of these notions into Ethics is liable to bring with it a fundamental confusion between 'what is' and 'what ought to be,' destructive of all clearness in ethical reasoning."

Limiting his field, therefore, to what would today be called "the phenomenology of morals," (see Husserl, *Ideas*), Sidgwick brought under review three methods of ethical reasoning and their corresponding principles. He called them, for brevity, egoism, intuitionism, and utilitarianism. British ethical opinion, when his book first appeared, could fairly well be summed up in these three positions. The neo-Hegelian position, represented by T. H. Green and F. H. Bradley, had not yet challenged the "national philosophy." When it did, beginning with the publication in 1875 of Green's *Introduction to Hume's Treatise,* the picture was no longer so simple. In subsequent editions (the sixth appeared posthumously in 1901), Sidgwick undertook to refute the new philosophy. But historians question whether he could have conceived and written the kind of book he did if idealism had taken root in England a decade earlier.

The first method discussed by Sidgwick is egoistical hedonism. We have

672

mentioned Sidgwick's concern to separate ethical questions from psychological ones. But historically, ethical hedonism has always been closely connected with psychological hedonism and has been thought to draw support from it. For example, Jeremy Bentham maintained that "the constantly proper end of action on the part of any individual" is his own happiness. This is an ethical proposition. But Bentham also said that "on the occasion of every act he exercises, every human being is inevitably led to pursue that line of conduct which, according to his view of the case, taken by him at the moment, will be in the highest degree contributory to his own greatest happiness." This is a psychological proposition. Sidgwick said that, if the psychological statement be construed strictly, the ethical statement is meaningless: there is no point in maintaining that one "ought" to pursue the line of conduct which will bring him the greatest happiness if he is incapable of following any other line. But even if the psychological law is taken in a weak and approximative sense, "there is no necessary connection between the psychological proposition that pleasure or absence of pain to myself is always the actual ultimate end of my action, and the ethical proposition that my own greatest happiness or pleasure is for me the *right* ultimate end."

Ethical hedonism does, however, deserve consideration as a method of ethics apart from the alleged psychological law. When a man makes "cool self-love" the ordering principle of his life, he is, according to Sidgwick, using one of the "natural methods" by which men judge between right conduct and wrong. And the philosophical egoist who defines the good in terms of pleas-

ure is doing no more than state this view in clear and meaningful terms.

One problem, for example, that is implicit in the popular conception of estimating satisfactions—say, the relative value of poker and poetry—is to find a common coin by which they can be measured. Pleasure, conceived of as "the kind of feeling that we seek to retain in consciousness," serves as that coin. To give the theory further applicability, pain may be regarded as commensurable with pleasure, along a scale on either side of a "hedonistic zero."

Sidgwick submitted these notions to searching criticism, the most damaging of which, in his estimation, was that methodical and trustworthy evaluation of the pleasures involved in two different courses of action is impractical. He did confess, however, that "in spite of all the difficulties that I have urged, I continue to make comparisons between pleasures and pains with practical reliance on their results." But he concluded that for the systematic direction of conduct other principles were highly desirable. He thought that this would be recognized by the man who is concerned only with his own happiness.

Common morality, however, although it allows a place for reasonable self-love, does not admit that a man has the right to live for himself alone. This brings us to the second "method" of ethics, which Sidgwick called intuitionism. From this point of view, right conduct has very little to do with desires and selfish enjoyment. What matters to it is duty and virtue.

Sidgwick held that the notions of "right" and "ought," which are fundamental to the intuitionist point of view are "too elementary to admit of any formal definition." They cannot be derived from the idea of the good, if this is understood to consist in happiness. If, on the other hand, it is understood to consist in excellence, this is merely another way of referring to what ought to be. The judgment that a certain course of action is right presents itself as a direct cognition. It may be accompanied by feelings, such as sympathy or benevolence, but it is itself a dictate of reason. Unlike egoistic hedonism, which reasons *a posteriori* in its effort to estimate future good, the ethics of right and duty employs an *a priori* method, reasoning from self-evident truth. Sidgwick called it, therefore, the method of intuition.

Sidgwick maintained, however, that it is one thing to recognize the *prima facie* claims of moral insight—that they are simple and categorical—and something else to grant that their claims are veridical. The point he wished to make is that man would not have the notions of morally right and wrong (as distinct from instrumentally right and wrong and logically right and wrong) except for some kind of direct moral insight.

The systematic moralist soon discovers that not all moral intuitions are trustworthy. There are, said Sidgwick, three levels on which the claims of obligation present themselves to man's conscience. First, there is the kind of judgment ordinarily referred to as the voice of conscience, which functions after the analogy of sense perception and testifies to the rightness or wrongness of single acts or motives. But the slightest experience with men is enough to convince us that conscience, in the sense of an intuitive perception, is not infallible. Virtuous men differ in their judgment of a course of action. In

their effort to persuade one another, they appeal from the particular instance to general rules which seem to be self-evident. This is the second level of intuitive moral reasoning. It comprises rules such as these: that we govern our passions, obey laws, honor parents, keep promises, and the like.

To the unreflective mind, these rules seem unexceptionable. But a serious attempt to give them precise meaning and application discloses at once their ambiguity. For example, it is said to be intuitively certain that "the promiser is bound to perform what both he and the promisee understood to be undertaken." But on examination, all sorts of qualifications come into view, which are just as obviously reasonable as the original principle. The promisee may annul the promise if he is alive; and there are circumstances in which it seems that promises should be annulled if the promisee is dead or otherwise inaccessible. Again, a promise may conflict with another obligation. Or, a promise may have been made in consequence of fraud or concealment. Sidgwick explored these and other possibilities in detail, and concluded "that a clear consensus can only be claimed for the principle that a promise, express or tacit, is binding, if a number of conditions are fulfilled," and that "if any of these conditions fails, the consensus seems to become evanescent, and the common moral perceptions of thoughtful persons fall into obscurity and disagreement."

Recognizing the weakness of common moral axioms, philosophers, ancient and modern, have sought to raise the principle of intuition to the level of an axiomatic science by formulating abstract principles of morality so clearly that they cannot conceivably be doubted or denied. For example, "we ought to give every man his own," and "it is right that the lower parts of our nature should be governed by the higher." These alleged axioms are self-evident, but only because they are tautologies. Sidgwick called them "sham axioms." They are worth even less than popular moral rules.

It might seem, from this analysis, that the entire attempt to base ethical reasoning upon intuition was a mistake and should be abandoned. Such, however, was not Sidgwick's contention. "It would be disheartening," he said, "to have to regard as altogether illusory the strong instinct of common sense that points to the existence of such principles, and the deliberate convictions of the long line of moralists who have enunciated them." And if the "variety of human natures and circumstances" is so vast that rules are not helpful in determining particular duties, there are, nevertheless, "certain absolute practical principles, the truth of which, when they are explicitly stated, is manifest."

The first such principle is that of justice or impartiality. It states that "if a kind of conduct that is right for me is not right for someone else, it must be on the ground of some difference between the two cases other than the fact that I and he are different persons." Sidgwick saw this as an application of the principle of the similarity of individuals that go to make up a logical whole or genus.

The second principle is that of prudence. It states "that Hereafter *as such* is to be regarded neither less nor more than Now." In other words, a man ought to have a care for the good of his life as a whole, and not sacrifice a distant good for a nearer one. Sidg-

wick said that this was an application of the principle of the similarity of the parts of a mathematical or quantitative whole.

The third principle is that of benevolence, and follows from the other two. If we combine the principle of justice (equal respect for the right of every man) with the principle of the good on the whole, we arrive at "the notion of Universal Good by comparison and integration of the goods of all individual human—or sentient—existences." "I obtain the self-evident principle that the good of any one individual is of no more importance, from the point of view of the universe, than the good of any other. . . . And it is evident to me that as a rational being I am bound to aim at good generally."

In Sidgwick's opinion, these formal principles of intuition are an indispensable part of systematic ethics, providing the rational necessity on which the whole structure is based. Egoistic hedonism would have no kind of rational foundation apart from the axiom of prudence here expressed. Nor would universal hedonism, or utilitarianism, without the other two axioms, those of justice and benevolence.

But the axioms of intuition do not offer practical guidance by themselves. They must be given content and direction in terms of the good—not merely in terms of the formal concept of the good as "excellence," but in terms of the material concept of the good as "happiness," that is, "desirable consciousness." We have seen the validity of this concept in connection with egoism. All that remains is to accept it as the ultimate criterion or standard which ought to govern our actions toward our fellow men.

Sidgwick's discussion of utilitarianism, the third of his three "methods," is brief. It need not be extensive because its main principles have already been stated—that the good is pleasure was shown under egoism and that the right action has regard to the happiness of the whole was shown under intuitionism. As we have seen, Sidgwick does not try to base our duty to mankind at large on "feelings of benevolence," or "natural sympathy." It rests on a moral cognition, as Jeremy Bentham, because of his affinities with the Age of Reason, saw better than John Stuart Mill. Sidgwick declared that utilitarianism requires a man to sacrifice not only his private happiness but also that of persons whose interests natural sympathy makes far dearer to him than his own well-being. Its demands are sterner and more rigid than traditional notions of duty and virtue. And the Utilitarian who follows his principles will find the whole of organized society rising up against him "to deter him from what he conceives to be his duty."

The fact that he found the rationale of utilitarianism implicit in the axioms of intuitionism was, for Sidgwick, a great step toward bringing the diverse methods of ethics into a higher synthesis. That egoism finds its rule of prudence among them was also encouraging. But one fundamental breach remained to be healed. How to reconcile egoism with utilitarian duty?

Theologians have resolved the prob-lem by the doctrine of immortality and eternal rewards. But Sidgwick refused that solution in the interests of preserving the autonomy of ethics. He did not deny the desirability of such an arrangement but he saw no rational evidence for it. "It only expresses the vital need that our Practical Reason feels of proving or postulating this connection of virtue and self-interest, if it is to be made consistent with itself. For," he says, "the negation of this connexion must force us to admit an ultimate and fundamental contradiction in our apparent intuitions of what is Reasonable in conduct."

That would be tatamount to admitting that rational ethics is an illusion. It would not mean abandoning morality, "but it would seem to be necessary to abandon the idea of rationalizing it completely." And this, in turn, would have the practical consequence that in a conflict between duty and self-interest, the conflict would be decided by "the preponderance of one or other of two groups of non-rational impulses."

Sidgwick's conclusion has about it the inconclusiveness of many a Socratic dialogue. He suggested that we may be faced with the alternative of accepting moral propositions "on no other grounds than that we have a strong disposition to accept them," or of "opening the door to universal scepticism."

ETHICAL STUDIES

Author: Francis Herbert Bradley (1846-1924)
Type of work: Ethics
First published: 1876

To be morally responsible a person must be intelligent, capable of making moral distinctions, uncoerced, and actively involved in a situation in which not all of his behavior is predictable in advance.

To ask, "Why should I be moral?" is to ask a senseless question, for it presupposes the instrumentality of moral action.

The sense in which morality as an end in itself is an end for man is that through moral action man realizes himself.

Self-realization is a creative process whereby a self, which is a unity, aims at the higher unity made possible through social coöperation with others.

In *Ethical Studies,* F. H. Bradley did not attempt to delineate a complete system of moral philosophy; rather, this book contains a discussion of problems in ethics which seemed to Bradley to be of particular importance. He believed that the function of ethics "is not to make the world moral, but to reduce to theory the morality current in the world." Consequently, the discussion begins with a consideration of the facts of ordinary morality.

What does the average person mean when he says that someone is morally responsible? Moral responsibility means that a person must answer for some or all of the things that he has done, that he must answer to some moral authority, and that it is right that he should so answer if called upon. He must be the same person when he committed the deed as when he is called upon to answer for it; he must have a certain amount of intelligence; he must be capable of making moral distinctions.

A person is not responsible for every act. For example, he may be forced to do something that is contrary to his desire. He might even know what he is doing in the sense that an insane man knows and still is not responsible. But if a person wills an act, even though he is persuaded to will it, the persuasion alone does not relieve him of moral responsibility.

An ethical act must be in some sense freely done. What meaning can we attach to freedom? It is sometimes said that freedom means liberty to do what a person wills to do and liberty to choose what he wills to do. However, to be free to choose does not mean that the choice is not motivated. A choice without motives is no choice at all; one must choose something on some grounds. But if every act of a person could be predicted in advance, we would be unlikely to say that he was free at all. The truth is that some prediction is compatible with freedom, while some is not. We must know how a moral person will act under certain circumstances, but it does not follow that we can know how he will act under all circumstances. The first sort of prediction is founded on knowledge of character; the second sort, the prediction of all his acts, annihilates him as an individual, denies him a character and a self. The character of a man is not made, but makes itself out of the man's disposition and environment. Thus the ordinary person does not believe that mind can be explained in terms of purely physical laws.

The unsophisticated person believes that there is a necessary connection between punishment and guilt. Punishment is the penalty that someone pays because he owes it. He merits the punishment because he has done wrong, and the wrong exists in the self or in the will of the doer. Punishment is thus an end in itself. Its purpose is not to correct the criminal nor is it to protect society. It is the denial of wrong by the assertion of right.

If I am responsible, if I am free, if I have a theory of punishment, I might still ask the question, "Why should I be moral?" Before this question can be answered, its meaning must be made clear. Bradley points out that this is a strange question. Usually when one asks, "Why should I do it?" one is asking for information concerning the value of the act. But it seems odd to ask, "What is morality good for?" The answer seems to be that morality is good for its own sake. If this is not the answer, then we seem to imply by the question that only means are good and that there is some end beyond morality. But where every good is a good *for*, everything is good because everything can be a means to something else. However, no one would ask, "Why should I be moral?" and then accept the answer, "You cannot be otherwise."

What, then, can the question mean? It may mean, "What should I get by being moral?" This question rests again on the assumption that there is an end in itself that is not morality. But Bradley believes that he has shown that morality cannot be concerned merely with means. He concludes that a genuine ethical theory must be concerned with ends. Therefore, the *"Why?"* in "Why should I be moral?" asks nothing, has no meaning.

There is one other possible interpretation of the question. One might ask, "What does it mean to say that morality as an end in itself is the end

for man?" The term which comes closest to expressing the end for man is self-realization. What can this term mean? To understand its meaning clearly, Bradley thinks that we must understand the meanings of *"self,"* *"real,"* *"realize,"* and *"end."* These terms can be understood only within a system of related meanings and such a system would be in the area of metaphysics, with which this book by Bradley is not concerned.

What we can show is that when we act morally, we do try to realize ourselves. We act to secure some end or object that we desire, and "all we can desire is, in a word, self." A desired object is a thought of an object as desired by the individual. What we aim at is the object as desired; that is, at the self in the object. But do we aim at a series of states of the self, discontinuous and fragmented? No, we aim at the sum of these states, a sum to which this particular state contributes. "The question in morals," Bradley says, "is to find the true whole."

If we ask ourselves what it is we most wish for, we shall answer with some general term such as "happiness," "security," "position." This is the whole toward which we intend our acts to aim. Every choice that we make is a choice relative to the self which stands above the particularity of the choice. This self is a unity in a diversity. It is not merely unity, which is static, nor yet merely diversity, which is chaotic; but it is both realized in one infinite whole. Bradley affirms, " 'Realize yourself as an infinite whole,' means, 'Realize yourself as the self-conscious member of an infinite whole, by realizing that whole in yourself.' "

But why aim at self-realization when one can aim at some specific thing such as happiness? A concern with happiness is central in the utilitarian theory of ethics. Bradley wishes to dispose of this theory. He answers his question by saying that happiness is not a specific thing. It is what everyone wants but wants in a thousand different ways. Most agree that happiness is not the search for pleasure. Pleasure, when achieved, is found as an accompaniment of some other goal. But suppose that pleasure for pleasure's sake were a workable goal. Would it be a moral goal? To say that my aim is to feel pleased as much as possible and as long as possible seems to be contrary to every notion of morality that a person could have unless he accepted the theory. A goal must present itself as a concrete whole which we can realize by our acts. But pleasure is never realized in this way. It is a momentary internal state of an organism, various and perishing. When the pleasure is gone, we are no longer satisfied. But the goal of the theory is to achieve a sum of these momentary pleasures. Such a goal is impossible, Bradley believes. No organism ever reaches the end of possible pleasures until it is dead. Further, past pleasures are not pleasures but only ideas of pleasures, and they cannot be added to real pleasures.

The hedonist tells us that we should not aim at pleasure but at some reasonable course of action that will bring pleasure. What guarantee is there that any such course will result in pleasure? In whose pleasure will it result? What is pleasure to one may be pain to another. The injunction to act so as to achieve one's own personal pleasure is neither a general rule nor a moral mandate. Also, Bradley says that "to aim at pleasure is not to get it, and yet the getting of it is a moral duty." The seeking of personal pleasure gives no practicable end to life.

Most moralists have believed that judgments must be made as to the goodness of means as well as of ends. They believe that a good end does not justify evil means. Bradley believes that the hedonist cannot, on his own theory, be concerned with the ethics of means. If the end increases happiness, any means is justified as a means. Is prostitution an evil? The question for the utilitarian is, "Does it increase the general happiness?" There is no way in which an answer to this question could be found; and even if one were found, it could hardly be relevant to the moral problem.

What does it mean to say that pleasure is a moral end? John Stuart Mill wrote in *Utilitarianism* (1863), "Each person's happiness is a good to that person, and the general happiness, therefore, a good to the aggregate of all persons." Bradley replies that the conclusion does not follow. A person desires his own happiness on psychological grounds, and he desires the happiness of others either as a means to his own happiness, or on some non-utilitarian moral ground such as unselfish duty toward others. Because my own happiness is desired and the happiness of others is desirable, it does not follow that the combination of both is desired and desirable. Bradley concludes this phase of his argument by remarking that Mill's argument "is not a good theoretical deduction, but it is the generation of the Utilitarian monster, and of that we must say that its heart is in the right place, but the brain is wanting."

The argument stemming from the question, "Why should I be moral?"

679

has shown that the moral good as an end in itself must be sought for its own sake. One theory which stresses this view is the duty for duty's sake ethics of Immanuel Kant. Briefly, Bradley's cricitism of Kant's ethical theory is that the theory is too abstract to be used as a guide for practical action. To do a duty is to do a specific act; but the reason for doing it, duty's sake, gives no specific object for the act. Duty's sake is an abstract concept. One can give this concept meaning, but one cannot deduce any concrete meaning from it.

The moral end for Bradley is self-realization, not the isolated self as with the utilitarians, not the abstract self acting for the sake of duty as with the Kantians, but a self having a relation to other selves in a community. Only individuals are real, but they become real through relations with other individuals in families, states, and nations. These communities are the means through which the individual can realize his real self. He has a place in a system of selves which requires that he act in certain ways in relation to the whole and to the other selves which are parts. The obligation that he has in relation to this system is summed up by Bradley as follows: "In short, man is a social being; he is real only because he is social, and can realize himself only because it is as social that he realizes himself." It is true that a person can choose his station within certain limits, but everyone has a station and duties pertaining to it. Certain circumstances and a certain position require certain acts. The theory establishes a relation between the subjective person and the objective world which is the society in which he lives. When a person wills to act morally, he wills to fill an objective place in the concrete world. When he succeeds, that is, realizes himself morally, something which ought to be in the world is in it. Then the person is what he ought to be, and he is content and satisfied.

The next problem is to determine how a person can know what particular act is right or wrong. This is an important question, but for Bradley it is not the function of philosophy to answer it. Philosophy does not deal with particulars. This is the area of common sense, science, and other fields of practical action. Philosophy tries "to understand what is."

Within Bradley's self-realization theory of ethics, we can still raise the question as to whether morality and self-realization are the same thing. A person may realize himself through his work, but we would not be inclined to say that he was moral just because he was a good scientist or a good artist. On the other hand, we would not be inclined to call a person moral if, although he failed to transgress any moral rules, he had done nothing at all. The moral man seems to be one who tries to do well in everything that he attempts. The moral demand is that one do his best both in work and in play. Of course, there are courses of action which are not moral choices. One may go to another city by train, car, or bus and the choice need not be a moral one (although it could be), even though the act of going is morally desirable.

If a moral act is a good act, and if a moral act is one which realizes the self, we may say, according to Bradley, that morality is coextensive with the realization of the ideal self. What is the ideal self? It is both a social and a nonsocial idea. As a social ideal it is realized in society, in one's station and its duties. But one also has duties to oneself, duties beyond the station. A good man is a man who strives for good whether he achieves it or not. Not all goods will be realized; much that is striven for will not be attained. One's good in one's station is a good made visible in the world; the good beyond is the good of the ideal self.

Morality is self-realization insofar as this may be taken as an expression of the will for good. It is a devotion to what seems best as against what we happen to like. Its achievement is the compatibility of reason and passion, of demand and accomplishment. It is the state in which all individual acts are subsumed under one collective end. The nature of this end is the subject of metaphysics.

In contrast, the bad self is one that has no coherence. It acts on no principle; it acts toward no coherent end. It turns away from its social dimension, contradicting and opposing the good self. Acts that accord with the good self give us pleasure because they accord with our real being and that of the world, but the bad self is self-contradictory; it has no center to which its acts are related. It is driven by lust from one course of action to another, from one supposed end to some different one. The bad self is not self-conscious. If it were, it would become the good self by selecting some unifying ideal for self-realization. Nor can the bad self be desired for its own sake. An evil act may be desired but not insofar as it is evil. If morality is self-realization, then to desire evil would be to hate the self.

Reflection on morality leads us beyond it. On the one hand, it demands that we explain the self as a metaphysical entity. On the other, it leads us into a philosophy of religion to answer the question of the connection between religion and morality. One fact is clear—that the person who is religious and does not act morally is an impostor. Religion requires some act, and that act is a moral one. But morality is not religion. Mere morality is an ideal; religion is belief in a real object.

An ideal, something only in our imagination, cannot be the object of religion. Faith is the recognition of one's true self in an object. It includes the belief that the course of the world converges on some purpose and that the real human self and the divine self are one. Justified by faith, the ideal self, through religion, finds its objective realization in God.

PROLEGOMENA TO ETHICS

Author: Thomas Hill Green (1836-1882)
Type of work: Ethics, metaphysics
First published: 1883

PRINCIPAL IDEAS ADVANCED

Nature is dependent upon a self-distinguishing consciousness that is prior to finite minds.

Human consciousness stands between nature and the divine consciousness; man is free because he has understanding and the capacity to will.

The Utilitarians are mistaken in claiming that pleasure is the greatest good; man's good is whatever satisfies man when, as a moral being, he is motivated by the ideal of realizing his capacities, the divine in him.

Virtue, rather than pleasure, is the moral good.

What Green called "the national philosophy" of Britian was represented in the nineteenth century of J. S. Mill, T. H. Huxley, and Herbert Spencer. It was rooted in materialism and sensationism and found its political and ethical expression in altruistic hedonism. In the universities, to be sure, a more classical, theologically grounded tradition remained; and such British men of letters as S. T. Coleridge and Thomas Carlyle had, through their writings, familiarized the literate public with the flavor of German Transcendentalism. But "the national philosophy" was effectively challenged for the first time by a group of academic philosophers, chiefly at Oxford, who fell under the spell of Kant and Hegel. It has been said that they invented the "Hegel-myth" in order to counteract the "Darwin-myth" which Huxley was so successfully propagating at the time, which may indicate that important elements in the British religious and moral heritage were not adequately represented in "the national philosophy."

Such, at any rate, is the contention of Green in his *Prolegomena to Ethics*, originally given as lectures at Oxford. The work falls naturally into two parts, of which the first is concerned with the metaphysical foundations of moral and the second with moral principles and their application. But both parts are developed in antithesis to traditional British philosophy; they point out in turn the failings of naturalism as metaphysics and of Utilitarianism as ethical theory. Under the impetus of Darwinism, according to Green, empiricism had come near to explaining morality out of existence. Newly enlightened, the moralist could no longer mock the misery of the poor or flatter the complacency of the prosperous by speaking of obedience to law, because it had been demonstrated to him that laws were not the sort of things that could be disobeyed, and that it was laws that had brought the poor their misery and the others their prosperity. The charm of this discovery was that it removed much that had previously seemed mysteriously beyond human comprehension; but when its implications had had an opportunity to sink in, a reconsideration had to come. Nothing, Green maintained, could be more contrary to the ideals of enlightened reason.

Green begins his reconsideration by raising the question "whether a being that was merely the result of natural forces could form a theory of those forces explaining himself." If not, if science presupposes a principle which is not one of the facts which it explains, then we shall have learned that, at least in respect of knowing, man is not merely a child of nature but is possessed of a principle that is higher than nature. Green argues that because the data of the natural sciences are all given within consciousness, the latter is the prerequisite for our knowledge of nature and cannot conceivably be the by-product of material forces, as Huxley was maintaining. Not merely are the data known through consciousness —they are constituted by it. Motion, for example, "has no meaning except such as is derived from a synthesis of the different positions successively held by one and the same body." We cannot think of it without engaging mental processes which give continuity and form to a manifold of sense impressions.

But, as the argument develops, man's knowledge of nature is only an instance of the wider principle that consciousness is prerequisite to the existence of nature itself. By nature we mean "a system of unalterable relations." Now, any relation involves the familiar problem of unity in diversity. But the source of unity and connection cannot be inside nature, for nature is a process of change, and that which gives the world its permanent character cannot itself be subject to change. Intelligence, however, readily accomplishes that which in nature is inconceivable. A multiplicity of feelings and sense impressions is ordered and unified at every moment of our experience. This is the way the world becomes one for each individual. But, since nature is obviously not dependent on particular human intellects for its existence, there must be a unifying factor prior to our finite minds. It must be the common source of the relations which constitute nature and our conception of it; and, "because the function which it must fulfil . . . is one which, on however limited a scale, we ourselves exercise in the acquisition of experience, and exercise by means of such a consciousness," we are justified in concluding that it, too, is "a self-distinguishing consciousness."

For Green, human consciousness stands between the divine consciousness and nature. Man exists in time: his bodily changes are causally related to everything else in nature. And his kinship with the latter is not limited to his body: his sensations are connected with changes in the brain, which in turn are influenced by light and motion. From this side, the mind may well be thought of as "a stream of consciousness." That, however, is only half the truth, for if consciousness were merely a stream it would never arise to self-awareness. Only because man is able to take a stand outside the stream, to find a point unmoved by change, does he know anything. In this aspect, his thought transcends nature and is related to the eternal consciousness. According to Green, the relation is peculiarly intimate: the divine consciousness "reproduces itself" in man, using feeling and sensation to objectify itself there. The reproduction takes place piecemeal and by degrees because its vehicle is part of nature, because it takes up into itself the "constant succession of phenomena in the sentient life." But though our knowledge is partial, it is nevertheless identical in essence with the eternal consciousness which it reproduces.

Herein lies the secret of man's freedom. He alone of all natural creatures is a self, able to stand apart from the world and, by virtue of the fragment of divinity which is in him, subdue nature and have dominion over it. In addition to understanding he has the capacity to will, and the world appears to him not merely for what it is but also for what it should be.

Just as analysis of knowledge made it necessary to distinguish a *punctum stans* over the flux of sensation by means of which sensations were integrated into facts of nature, so the analysis of volition presupposes, as standing over our feelings, appetites, and desires, a conscious moment in virtue of which these impulses are converted into motives. Wants are natural: man shares them with other animals. But, properly speaking, a want becomes a desire only when it is present to consciousness as an object; that is to say, as an ideal end. There is no desire apart from intellect. But knowing a want involves comparing it with others, preliminary to deciding whether it is to be satisfied. The choice between desires is determined by volition; that is, by the character of the individual. Green opposed the contention of empirical psychology that man's actions are determined by the strongest desire. Desires only condition our choices, which are determined by the self. And a man's self, as Green has maintained, is only partially contained in nature.

On the strength of these metaphysical considerations, Green was prepared to challenge the naturalistic theory of morals and to develop an idealistic one. Both parties—the naturalists and the idealists—were agreed that insofar as man acts morally he seeks self-satisfaction. They were also agreed that intellect plays an important role in determining which acts are good and which are bad. The difference between them lay, as we might anticipate, in whether man's satisfaction is to be found on a purely natural level, or whether it involves an ideal that transcends nature. It should be noted that in practice Green was closer to his opponents than their theories might suggest. Both were progressive and humanitarian in outlook, condemning heartless ambition and lazy indulgence. Both were active and optimistic in politics, sharing the vision of peace and brotherhood among men. The problem was to provide the correct theoretical account of what morality consists in. And each side believed that theory matters and that wrong thinking is likely to lead to evil conduct.

In its simplest form, the question was: Is a maximum of pleasure what man always desires? Green maintained that it is not—that the object chosen is always the satisfaction of some specific desire and never pleasure on its own account. The thought of the pleasure which accompanies the realization of the object may increase our eagerness for the object; but desire defeats itself if pleasure becomes the chief object of our striving. There is, moreover, a logical contradiction in maintaining that the *summum bonum* is the greatest sum of pleasures. Pleasures are instantaneous, and the sum of pleasures is not a pleasure but an intellectual abstraction, according to Green. To say that we seek the sum of pleasures is to abandon hedonism and to admit that man finds his satisfaction on an ideal plane. Green pointed to J. S. Mill's *Utilitarianism* (1863) as an example of the inconsistencies into which hedonism leads. Mill had amended the doctrine of earlier Utilitarians in conceding that pleasures vary in quality, and he tacitly admitted that what properly motivates man is a sense of his own dignity. Nature does not provide us with any such ideal: we are thrown back, as in the case of knowledge, upon the notion of a divine consciousness present to man's mind and working there for its own fulfillment.

For Green, therefore, the moral good must be distinguished from good in general as "that which satisfies the desire of a moral agent, or that in which a moral agent can find the satisfaction of himself which he necessarily seeks." The practical definition of that good admittedly presents some difficulties. Man is bent on realizing to the full extent his moral capacities; but he cannot know those capacities until he has realized them. Nevertheless, in the moral struggle for the better life in which men through the centuries have been engaged, the direction is evident. It has become clear, on the one hand, that the life of intemperance and self-indulgence is no way to realize the good; nor, on the other, is the life of ruthless self-seeking. We have no difficulty, therefore, in marking out certain general lines of moral advance. The good is *personal* and it is *social*.

Although the divine plan is for all humanity, it can be realized only when individual men freely submit to the direction of the eternal consciousness as it is manifest in their lives. In different historical settings, the ideal appears to change; but the formal element in every moral situation is the same. The good for man is never anything but loyalty to the ideal. Suspended as he is between nature and divinity, man is ever compelled to choose whether he will identify himself with his physical appetites or with that which stands to him as a divine command. His realization of selfhood demands that he choose the latter. In Kant's language, he must follow duty for duty's sake.

But it is not possible to respect the demands of reason in one's own person without respecting them in all others. On this Kantian axiom, Green developed his account of the common good, once again finding himself in opposition to "the national philosophy,"

which, although it had recognized the principle of benevolence or altruism, had never been happy in its attempts to show why a man should sacrifice his own happiness for that of others if he were not inclined to do so. The fact is, according to Green, the "better reason" which presents itself as a law to the individual also presents itself as a law to every man and for the same reason, "as prescribing means to the fulfilment of an idea of absolute good, common to him with them."

Virtue, then, instead of pleasure is the good which man ought always and everywhere to pursue; and, according to Green, the course of moral progress is best traced in terms of the extent to which men were interested in the cultivation of virtue rather than in material prosperity. Reviewing the history of Western morality from the Greeks to the present, he maintained that while Plato and Aristotle adequately understood the personal aspect of moral goodness, they were deficient in their appreciation of its scope—a defect supplied by Christianity. If modern morals are superior to those of the Greeks, it is in the greater renunciation which they impose upon the individual—a self-denial which, however, is not mistaken for a good in itself, but as a means to assisting "in the struggle upward of the many."

The final portion of the book concerns the question of the value of moral theory in helping persons know their duty. In Green's opinion, theory is important because the moral ideal is to make men aware of their true natures, which requires that they reflect on their conduct and on the adequacy of accepted standards. As between the "greatest happiness" theory and that which finds man's good in "self-realization," the former appears to provide the clearer criteria; and Green credited the leaders of the Utilitarian movement with important moral and political gains. But, inasmuch as the hedonistic theory gave no adequate account of duty, it seemed to Green to pose a threat to moral initiative and, indeed, dangerously to weaken the individual's ability to resist evil. Green's own the-ory, as he acknowledged, offers no tech-nique for making moral choices—the philosopher's judgments, like those of other men, being largely an intuitive application of the ideal. But it has the advantage of keeping uppermost the claims of the ideal, and in cases of moral conflict it may help the individ-ual choose "the higher but more pain-ful good."

THUS SPAKE ZARATHUSTRA

Author: Friedrich Wilhelm Nietzsche (1844-1900)
Type of work: Ethics
First published: Parts I and II, 1883; III, 1884; IV, 1885

Principal Ideas Advanced

Life is the will to power, and he who would truly live must overcome the beliefs and conventions of common men; he must become an overman (or "super-man").

Those who teach the Christian virtues of pity and meekness seek to corrupt man, to destroy his will to power, and to make him submit to those who prosper from the conventional way.

Men who do not have the courage to live seek to escape by sleeping, by prizing the soul more than the body, and by seeking peace instead of war.

The overman is virtuous when he frees himself from the belief in God and from the hope of an afterlife; he is nauseated by the rabble, and his joy comes from surpassing those who live by false hopes and beliefs.

Worship of any sort is a return to childhood; if men must worship, let them worship donkeys if that suits them.

It is difficult to decide whether Nietzsche is greater as a literary figure or as a philosopher. He was a literary master of the German language. He in-fluenced such writers as Bernard Shaw, H. L. Mencken, Theodore Dreiser, Robinson Jeffers, Frank Norris, and Jack London. He is neither a system-atic philosopher in the sense of Hegel, nor a meticulous critical philosopher in the sense of Ernst Mach, the philos-opher of science. Nietzsche belongs rather to the tradition of philosophers who wished to tell men how to live. His injunction is for one to become an individual, and to follow one's own de-sires—if necessary, through the de-struction of others.

Nietzsche is often inconsistent, some-times contradictory; but he is almost

686

always provocative. His criticisms of nineteenth century institutions remind the reader of those of his contemporaries, Søren Kierkegaard and Fyodor Dostoevski, and like theirs often seem to apply to our own century. His positive doctrine is rejected by most people and is accepted not, as Nietzsche had hoped, by potential leaders but by those hopelessly defeated by modern civilization.

There are three principal themes in *Thus Spake Zarathustra*: the will to power, the consequent revaluation of values, and the doctrine of eternal recurrence. Life is essentially a will to power, the feeling that one is in command of oneself and of the future. In controlling the future, one finds that the values which most people accept are inadequate and that one must adopt a new, in many cases opposite, set of values. But neither power nor the new set of values is desirable for its consequences. If one were to use power to accomplish some final end, one would no longer need it; if one were to realize the new values, one would no longer need them. For Nietzsche there are no final ends. Power and the revaluation of values are good in themselves; and, consequently, there is no millennium, nothing but an eternal recurrence of people, things, and problems.

These three themes are developed carefully in *Thus Spake Zarathustra*. This exposition will follow Nietzsche's manner of development which is both self-conscious and purposive.

The main theme in Part I is that the individual stands alone with his fate in his own hands. He can expect no help from others either in this life or in some imagined future life. He must "make himself" to use the phrase of the modern existentialists. As Part I opens we find that Zarathustra has spent ten years on a mountain in meditation. His companions have been his eagle, a symbol of pride, and his serpent, a symbol of wisdom. He has just decided to go into the world of men to teach some of the wisdom that he has acquired during his period of meditation.

On the way down the mountain, he meets a saint who tells him that the way to help men is to stay away from them and to save them through prayer. Here Nietzsche announces one of his important ideas, that the individual can expect no supernatural help because God is dead.

Zarathustra reaches a town where, finding a crowd engaged in watching a tightrope walker perform his act, he says to them, "I teach you the overman. Man is something that shall be overcome." He explains that man has evolved from apes but that he is still apelike. Man is poisoned by those who teach that salvation is found not in this world but in the next, and by those who teach the Christian ethics of virtue, justice, and pity. But the people in the crowd are not ready for Zarathustra's message. They think that he is announcing the tightrope walker's act. He reflects that they cannot be taught since they are not ready to take the first step toward learning by recognizing that their present beliefs are false. What Zarathustra must find is those "who do not know how to live except by going under, for they are those who cross over."

The tightrope walker falls and is killed. Zarathustra and the corpse are left alone in the market place. Zarathustra then realizes that one of his great problems will be to communicate his message to people too indifferent or too stupid to understand him. But his purpose remains firm, "I will teach men the meaning of their existence— the overman, the lightning out of the dark cloud of man." Since he cannot teach the multitude, he decides that he will have to select a few disciples who will follow him "because they want to follow themselves. . . ."

Throughout the rest of Part I, Nietzsche expresses a series of more or less disconnected criticisms of the men of his time. Most people are sleepers because sleep robs them of thought, makes them like inanimate objects, and imitates death. Man uses sleep as a means of escape, just as God created the world as a diversion, as an escape from himself.

Another sort of escape is found by accepting the injunction to renounce the body and love the soul. But the soul is only a part of the body; and one must love the whole more than one loves any part. Love of the soul to the exclusion of the body is a kind of renunciation of life. Another is the belief that life is full of suffering. So it is, but the overman will see to it that his is not one of the sufferers. War brings out many of the best qualities in men, Nietzsche argues. "You should love peace as a means to new wars—and the short peace more than the long. . . . You say it is the good cause that hallows even war? I say unto you: it is the good war that hallows any cause."

The state, another escape from reality, is one of the greatest enemies of individualism. It tells the citizen what to do, how to live; it replaces his personality with its own.

Another renunciation of life is dedication to the ideal of chastity. To deny the lust of the flesh is often to affirm the lust of the spirit. Why deny lust?

Nietzsche asks. Women are only half human at best, more like cats or cows. What is great is the passion of love between men and women, for all creation is the result of passion. The solution to all of women's problems is childbearing; and this is the only interest women ever have in men. A man needs two things, danger and play. His interest in woman is that she is "the most dangerous plaything." She is "the recreation of the warrior. . . ." Her hope should be that she will bear the overman. Men are merely evil, but women are bad. That is why they are dangerous. Men can overcome them only by subjugating them completely. An old crone agrees with Zarathustra and adds her advice, "You are going to women? Do not forget the whip!"

How should one die? Only when one has perfected his life; but if one cannot live a perfect life, then it is best to die in battle. Death must come because one wants it.

Part I ends with the injunction that through Zarathustra's teaching one should not become merely a disciple and imitator of the prophet, but should learn through him to understand oneself. The section ends on a note that has become familiar: " 'Dead are all gods: now we want the overman to live'. —on that great noon, let this be our last will."

In Part II Nietzsche develops the notion of the will to power. The first part is largely negative, but the second part provides the positive doctrine. It begins with the idea that the conjecture of God is meaningless because it defies the imagination. However, the conjecture of the overman is within the scope of the human mind if one first eliminates error. One cause of error is pity; but the overman is willing to sacrifice himself, and so he is willing to sacrifice others. Priests cause error. They have taken death as their God's triumph; they need to be redeemed from their Redeemer. They are virtuous because they expect a reward in the afterlife, but there is no reward. For the overman, to be virtuous is to be true to oneself and to follow where the self leads. The mass of people want power and pleasure too, but they want the wrong kinds. The overman must seek the higher powers and pleasures. He must be nauseated by the rabble that is around him.

This category of nausea is also found in works by Dostoevski and Jean-Paul Sartre. In *Notes from Underground,* the sickness is caused by the loathsomeness of life; in Sartre's *Nausea,* it is caused by the meaninglessness of existence. For Nietzsche, the malaise comes from seeing the rabble as one would see a field of dead, decaying animals, from seeing their "stinking fires and soiled dreams. . . ."

Nietzsche's statement of his positive doctrine is often interrupted by fell criticisms. The contrast between the desires of the masses and those of the overman reminds him of the belief that all men are equal. But if men were born equal, there could be no overman. Those who have preached equality have told the people what they wanted to hear rather than the truth. The truth can be discovered only by the free spirit that wills, desires, and loves. Such a free spirit finds that not all things can be understood, and that some must be felt. The will to truth is just one aspect of the will to power. Such a will carries the free spirit beyond truth and falsity and beyond good and evil as well. The slave thinks that he can conquer his master by his servility; he has the will

to power, but in its lowest form. The forerunner of the overman has the will to be master, the will to command, the will to conquer. Since he is incapable of positive action, the slave can do neither good nor evil. The master with his capacity for evil has a capability for good. If the good requires positive action, so does the beautiful. Zarathustra asks, "Where is beauty?" and answers, "Where I must will with all my will; where I want to love and perish that an image may not remain a mere image."

If one cannot find truth among those who tell the people what they want to hear, still less can one find it among the scholars, who have removed themselves from the possibility of action and who "knit the socks of the spirit." Neither can one turn to the poets. They know so little they have to lie to fill the pages they write. They are the great myth-makers; they created God. Zarathustra's mission is to lead men away from myths toward an assertion of the will. Men who accept the myths are like actors who play the parts assigned to them but who can never be themselves. The man who exercises the will to power can do so only by being himself.

The Third Part of *Thus Spake Zarathustra* introduces the theme of eternal recurrence, but it is almost obscured by other themes. The main question is: What does one experience when one travels? Zarathustra decides that no matter where one travels one can experience only oneself. But if this is the case, then the individual is beyond good and evil, both of which require some absolute standard or criterion of judgment. There is none. Man lives in a world, not of purpose, knowledge, law, and design, but of accident, inno-

689

cence, chance, and prankishness. "In everything, one thing is impossible: rationality." Of course one may use a little wisdom, but only as a joke.

But what of people who cannot accept this doctrine because they are weak in body and in mind? They cannot be expected to accept the truth; they talk but cannot think. They ask only for contentment and refuse to face life. They expect teachers of contentment, flatterers who will tell them they are right. They want those who will condemn as sins the acts that they never commit, and who will praise their small sins as virtues. But Nietzsche continues, " 'Yes, I *am* Zarathustra the godless!' These teachers of resignation! Whatever is small and sick and scabby, they crawl to like lice, and only my nausea prevents me from squashing them."

Although much that Nietzsche says is negative and critical, he constantly warns the reader that criticism should be given only out of love and in preparation for a positive doctrine to follow. Condemnation for its own sake is evidence only of an interest in filth and dirt.

If God is dead, how did he die? Here Nietzsche cannot resist a criticism of the musician Wagner, with whom he had been closely associated and with whom he had finally quarreled. Wagner had written an opera, *Götterdämmerung* (*The Twilight of the Gods*). It is a highly dramatic story of the destruction of the Norse gods. Nietzsche says that the gods did not die in the way that Wagner describes. On the contrary, they laughed themselves to death when one of their number announced that there was only one god. This jealous god had lost his godhead

by saying the most godless word; and the other gods died laughing.

What are often considered evils turn out on close examination by Nietzsche to be goods. Sex, which is cursed by "all hair-shirted despisers of the body," is a virtue for the free and innocent. Lust to rule, which destroys civilizations, is a fit activity for the overman. Selfishness, a vice only of masters as seen by their slaves, is a necessary virtue of great bodies and great souls. The first commandment is to love yourself; the great law is *"do not spare your neighbor!* Man is something that must be overcome."

Nietzsche turns at last to the doctrine of eternal recurrence. The theory that history repeats itself in identical cycles is familiar to us through Plato, who derived it from the writings of Egyptian and Babylonian astronomers. It requires a concept of time that has not been congenial to Western thought ever since it was attacked by Saint Augustine. For us, time seems to move in a straight line that has no turnings. Nietzsche, knowing that his doctrine would not be well received, stated it first of all as coming from Zarathustra's animals: "Everything goes, everything comes back; eternally rolls the wheel of being." Whatever is happening now will happen again and has happened before. The great things of the world recur, but so do the small. The recurrence of the small things, of the men farthest removed from the overman, seems at first impossible for Zarathustra to accept. That the return is exactly the same—not that the best returns, not that the part returns, not that all except the worst returns, but that *all*, best and worst, returns—is difficult for him to acknowledge. But at last he is willing to abandon the doctrine of progress for the truth of eternal recurrence.

The fourth part of *Thus Spake Zarathustra*, not intended by Nietzsche to be the last, is concerned with the consequences of accepting some portion of Zarathustra's teaching without accepting the whole. One must take all or none. Much of this part consists of parodies of Christian views—for example, that one must become like a little bovine to enter the kingdom of heaven.

Zarathustra, who is still concerned with the overman, wonders what he will be like. As he goes from place to place in the world, he sees that man is fit only to be despised unless he is the prelude to the overman. Man is not to be preserved; he is to be overcome. Man must be brave even though there is no God; man must be strong because he is evil; and he must hate his neighbor as a consequence of the will to power.

But once more, this doctrine is too strong for the people who listen to Zarathustra. Although God is dead, it is necessary for them to make a god of their own; and this time they choose a donkey. The animal fulfills all of the requirements for a god. He is a servant of men. He does not speak and therefore is never wrong. The world, created as stupidly as possible, is in his own image. Everyone is able to believe in the donkey's long ears. Zarathustra, after upbraiding the people for worshiping a donkey, is told by them that it is better to worship some god, even a donkey, than no god at all. At least here is something that the worshiper can see, touch, hear, and even smell and taste if he wants to. God seems more credible in this form. The first atheist was the man who said that God is spirit.

Zarathustra replies to this plea for the donkey by pointing out that worship of any sort is a return to childhood. The overman has no wish to enter the kingdom of heaven; he wants the earth. However, if the people need to worship, let them worship donkeys if such a belief helps them.

No man except Zarathustra has seen the earth as it is. But the overman will come, and he will see it. He will command the earth and it will obey. With this vision in mind, Zarathustra turns again to the world to search for and bring into perfection the overman.

THE ANALYSIS OF THE SENSATIONS

Author: Ernst Mach (1838-1916)
Type of work: Philosophy of mind, epistemology
First published: 1886

PRINCIPAL IDEAS ADVANCED

The special sciences are systems of symbols by means of which man orders the facts immediately given in experience; the world is the sum of all phenomena.

Since physical objects, bodies, and sensations are all phenomenal in character, it is possible that sensations are connected with physical events.

Our perception of dimensional space represents the experience of countless generations; the conceptions of our bodies as moving and of the environment as fixed are fixed in racial memory.

The common sense, realistic view of the world is a product of nature developed in the course of evolution.

The concepts of science are useful fictions, names for complexes of phenomena.

The ostensible purpose of Mach's *Contributions to the Analysis of the Sensations* was to report certain experiments which he had made on the relationship between sensations and neural physiology. But the permanent interest of the book is due less to the experiments themselves than to the radically empirical standpoint which the author adopted in the exposition of his findings. Setting aside the traditional mind-body problem as "metaphysical," he proposed that psychology and physiology alike be restricted to describing facts and their connections. These two sciences, he argued, do not treat of different kinds of facts but of the same kind of facts in different relations. More generally, he maintained that all facts are of the same kind, namely, what is immediately given in experience, and that the special sciences are systems of symbols by means of which man orders the facts to suit his several interests.

Mach did not claim to be a professional philosopher. As a worker in the field of science, he was compelled to raise philosophical questions in order to overcome difficulties which confronted him when he tried to move from one scientific discipline to another. "I only seek to adopt in physics a point of view that need not be changed the moment our glance is carried over into the domain of another science; for, ultimately, all must form one whole." Is the world an electromagnetic field, or is it a swarm of molecules which in turn are composed of indestructible atoms? Too much intellectual energy, said Mach, was being diverted from real problems in an effort to resolve pseudo-problems such as these.

The gulf that separated physics from psychology was one of these pseudo-problems. In order to help bridge it in an intelligible manner, Mach had adopted Leibniz's theory of monads. But he soon concluded that he was giving too prominent a place to the "artificial scaffolding" as distinguished from "the facts which really deserve to be known." He therefore discarded "this cumbrous artifice" and turned to a simpler view—one which had intrigued him almost from childhood; namely, the view that the world consists solely of sense-impressions.

Educated in the German tradition, Mach approached empiricism through the philosophy of Kant rather than through the English or French sensationalists. He was only fifteen when he read Kant's *Prolegomena to any Future Metaphysics* (1783). Of it, he said, "The book made at this time a powerful and ineffaceable impression upon me, the like of which I never afterward experienced in any of my philosophical reading." However, some two or three years thereafter he detected Kant's blunder in introducing the "thing in itself." "On a bright summer day under the open heaven, the world with my ego suddenly appeared to me as *one* coherent mass of sensations, only more strongly coherent in the ego. Although the actual working out of this thought did not occur until a later period, yet this moment was decisive for my whole view." The reason it did not work itself out at once lay, he said, in his scientific training. "With the valuable parts of physical theories we necessarily absorb a good dose of false metaphysics." Only as he alternated his scientific studies with readings in the history of science, and his physical investigations with psychological research, did he see his way clear to break with tradition and reconstruct his scientific views along the bold lines suggested by his youthful vision.

In this view, the world is the sum of all phenomena, that is, of all sounds, colors, smells, and so on, that ever did or will exist, together with the connections which tie them into parcels and link them into chains and meshes. Initially, Mach spoke of them as "sensations," in a manner that resembled Hume (without his being acquainted at the time with Hume's writings); but he later determined to call them by a neutral term, "elements." He did this because it was essential to his theory that the same elements which are called sensations when joined together to make up what we know as consciousness are called physical properties when they are joined together to make up what we know as the world, or that singular border-territory between consciousness and the world which we call "our body."

Mach adopted the following kind of schematism, which he used throughout the book to illustrate his meaning. Let *ABC* represent elements in nature; let *KLM* represent elements in "our body"; and let *abc* represent elements in our mind. *ABC*, *KLM*, and *abc* are all phenomenal in character. But *ABC* might stand for the sensible qualities of an apple; *KLM* for the observable properties of my digestive system; and *abc* for my sensations of red, juicy, sweet. For even though the elements are interchangeable, my vital interest compels me to distinguish the apple from my digestive system, and both of them from my feelings or sensations.

Here is the first merit which Mach claimed for his philosophy. Whereas common sense regards the complexes of elements as forming more or less permanent entities ("bodies" and "souls"), and metaphysics goes further and invents eternal substances ("matter" and "mind"), Mach reverted to pure experience and acknowledged the existence only of what is immediately given. By abolishing metaphysics, he claimed to have rid mankind of numerous "suppositious" problems, and by illuminating common sense, he prepared the way for the unification of the sciences.

The application to problems of physiological psychology lay immediately to hand. On Mach's assumptions, it is not necessary to show how matter can influence mind and vice versa. The ego or soul has only that existence which belongs to individual elements

693

of consciousness and their connections; and the same is true of nerves and muscles. Moreover, since the elements we have designated *abc* are no different essentially from those we have designated *KLM*, and since the connection which joins *a* to *b* is no different in kind from that which joins *K* to *L*, there is no reason why combinations of the sort *KLa*, and *ÀKa* may not exist. In other words, sensations may be connected with physical events quite as plausibly as with other sensations.

The experiments in psycho-physics which Mach's book was designed to give to the public were an attempt to show that such sensations as those by which a person judges distances in space or intervals of time are functions of his nervous and muscular activities. One of his simpler experiments consisted of attaching putty to his eyeballs and noting his sensations as he tried to use his eyes in gauging distances. "The will to perform movements of the eyes, or the innervation to act, is itself the space-sensation," he concluded. Time-sensation, he conjectured, is probably "connected with the organic *consumption* necessarily associated with consciousness. . . . The fatiguing of the organ of consciousness goes on continually. . . . The sensations connected with greater expenditure of attention appear to us to happen *later*."

A question which has long interested philosophical empiricists is whether we have a sensation of distance. The eighteenth century followers of Locke were of the opinion that we do not—that judgments of this sort are the product of experience and have to be learned by practice, possibly requiring two different senses, vision and touch. Mach's analysis might have led him to similar conclusions if it had not been for the theory of evolution, which dominated his thought. Mach agreed that our perception of dimensional space is learned—but he held that it represents the experience of countless generations of men, not to speak of their subhuman ancestors. In other words, it is firmly established in the racial memory and is to be explained in terms of its biological value. A simple experiment was used to prove his point. When a person's body is in motion on a turntable or on a moving train, his eyes do not sweep the environment in a continuous motion, but move in jerks from one fixed point to another. This is true even of small children, proving that it is not the result of individual learning but of racial evolution. The conception of our bodies as moving and of the environment as fixed has impressed itself upon the memory of mankind because of its utility. "We understand why it is that, in our numerous turnings and ramblings in the streets and in buildings, and in our passive turnings in a wagon or in the cabin of a ship—yes, even in the dark—we do not lose our sense of direction. . . ."

Like Kant, therefore, Mach held that man brings to his experience the forms of intuition of space and time, although, unlike Kant, Mach explained these as the product of human evolution. In the same way he explained other basic notions and beliefs with which the ordinary mind is endowed. Man brings with him a ready capacity, which he easily perfects by practice, of seeing, not unrelated colors and forms, but solid objects. Likewise, he has a strong disposition to interpret certain sequences as necessarily (we say, "causally") related. In short, the whole common sense or "naïvely realistic" view of the world "has arisen in the process of immeasurable time without the conscious assistance of man. It is a product of nature, and is preserved and sustained by nature."

Mach attributed the highest importance to this natural inheritance in which we all share. Nothing which man's conscious art and reflection have added to it by way of philosophy and science can begin to compare with it. Nor can we ever leave it behind, but, having made our flights into higher mathematics and speculative physics, we must return "to the universal point of view held by all men in common." And if these common sense beliefs are "true" only in the sense that they have biological value and are "formed for special, practical purposes and with wholly provisional and limited ends in view," exactly the same is true of our sophisticated theories.

We come now to the second merit which Mach claimed for his philosophy. While showing that the concepts of science (electricity, atoms, forces, laws, and so forth) are fictions, it also was able to show why fictions are necessary. They are labor-saving devices by which the mind brings under surveillance and control vast numbers of facts which otherwise would be unmanageable. If we had the kind of omniscience which would make it possible to grasp in detail the phenomena which go to make up an earthquake, for example, we would not require a scientific account of it. But because we would lose ourselves in the literal description, we observe complexes of phenomena and give them names— such as "fault" and "volcano." To mistake these concepts for entities and

causes would be to lapse into the ways of metaphysics. But if we recognize them for what they are, "indirect descriptions" and "intellectual abridgements," we can use them just the same and not prejudice the advance of knowledge or prevent other scientists from developing alternative symbols to describe the same phenomena.

Mach recognized the contribution which felicitous images have made to the advancement of science. For example, the Scottish chemist Joseph Black supposed heat to be a fluid substance which passes from one body to another. This was a useful concept. On the other hand, this image prevented Black's successors from using their eyes, and they overlooked an important group of phenomena where heat is produced by friction. Hence, Mach warned investigators not to be led astray by their representations.

A theory, according to Mach, is always a "representation." It "puts in the place of a fact something *different*, something more simple, which is qualified to represent the fact in some *certain* aspect, but for the very reason that it is different does *not* represent it in other aspects." Scientific concepts, theories, and laws, because they are representations, exist in the mind only. For this reason, Mach's studies in psychology were finally determinative of his attitude toward all the other sciences. Either for practical ends or for theoretical ("removing intellectual discomfort"), the mind evolves new ideas which will represent old ones in a more satisfactory fashion. To quote Mach's schematic language again, "Science arises where in any manner the elements *ABC* . . . or the elements *KLM* . . . are reproduced or representatively mimicked by

695

the elements *abc* . . . or the latter by one another. For example, physics (in its broadest signification) arises through representatively reproducing by *abc* . . . the elements *ABC* in their relations to one another; the physiology or psychology of the *senses*, through reproducing in like manner the relations of *ABC* . . . *to KLM* . . . ; physiology, through reproducing the relations of *KLM* . . . to one another and to *ABC* . . . ; while the reproducing of the *abc* . . . themselves by other *abc* leads to the psychological sciences proper."

In speaking of concepts as representations, Mach did not, however, intend to imply that they outline or copy phenomena in any literal sense. In language which is similar to that employed by pragmatists, Mach emphasized the "operational" role of scientific terms. "In using a word denot-

ing a concept," he said, "there is nothing involved in the word but a simple *impulse* to perform some familiar *sensory operation*, as the *result* of which a definite sensuous element (the mark of the concept) is obtained." Elsewhere (*Popular Scientific Lectures,* 1894), he used the striking analogy of musical notation: "The concept is to the physicist," he said, "what a musical note is to a piano-player."

Mach had an important part in popularizing the positivist view of knowledge. But his views were in various degrees paralleled by the writings of other scientists and mathematicians of his day, such as Karl Pearson and Henri Poincaré. As Professor of the History and Theory of Inductive Science at the University of Vienna, he particularly influenced the men who came to be known as the Vienna Circle of Logical Positivists.

BEYOND GOOD AND EVIL

Author: Friedrich Wilhelm Nietzsche (1844-1900)
Type of work: Ethics
First published: 1886

PRINCIPAL IDEAS ADVANCED

Ideas which preserve life and add to a man's power are more important than ideas sanctioned by logicians and seekers after the absolute.

The metaphysical interest in the freedom of the will should give way to an interest in the strength of the will.

Men must turn conventional values upside down in order to live creatively; the established values of society were invented by the weak to enable them to triumph over the strong.

Scientific minds are weak when they fail to pass judgment; whoever denies the will denies the power of life.

Progress in life is possible only if there are men of action who have the courage

*to trust will and instinct; new values arise which go beyond conventional good
and evil when the will to power asserts itself.*

Friedrich Nietzsche holds a commanding historical significance in modern thought in spite of a continuing controversy about his stature as a philosophical mind. Many scholars refuse to judge Nietzsche's brilliant writings as serious philosophical contributions. They prefer to view him as a poet, or as a critic of culture and religion, or even as a superb master of the German language. Yet some contemporary scholars insist on Nietzsche's importance as a genuine philosophical figure—a lonely, disturbed thinker who anticipated contemporary criticism of the classical ideal of a rigorously deductive model of philosophical knowledge and of the accompanying belief in the possibility of a completed metaphysics. Nietzsche felt keenly the impact of Darwinian evolutionary views which so stirred many nineteenth century thinkers in a number of intellectual fields. As a philosopher, he must be included in that group of thinkers for whom the philosopher's primary function is to lay bare the unexamined assumptions and buried cultural influences lurking behind supposedly disinterested moral and metaphysical constructions.

Symptomatically, *Beyond Good and Evil* begins with a chapter entitled "About Philosophers' Prejudices." Written during Nietzsche's intellectual maturity, hard on the heels of a lengthy literary development yet prior to the tragic illness which ended his career and made him a mental case, this book reflects the many important central tendencies of his thought. Its contents illustrate the surprisingly wide range of Nietzsche's intellectual interests—the origin and nature of moral valua-

tions, the history and psychology of religion, the psychology of human motivation, and the relation of man and historical processes. Nietzsche often uses aphorisms (as he does in the fourth section of *Beyond Good and Evil*) which, though unsystematic from a logical point of view, manage to express a tolerably consistent philosophical viewpoint.

Nietzsche's writings contain numerous passages which suggest similar positions worked out in greater psychotherapeutic detail by Sigmund Freud. Frequently he shows greater interest in the question, "What are the motives of philosophizing?" than in "What do philosophers say?" When he turns to an analysis of moral judgments, Nietzsche worries about what may hide submerged in such valuations —much as a student of icebergs wants to discover what exists beneath the surface. Perhaps the valuations produced by moralists always represent a perspective on things in the sense that there may exist no final metaphysical standpoint from which to render such valuations. In a similar manner, the philosophical quest after truth may peculiarly express what Nietzsche terms the "will to power" rather than a disinterested description of things. Even assuming that genuine truth can be obtained in principle, Nietzsche points out that the value of an idea has greater significance than the truth of the idea. The value perspectives by which individuals live may be necessary and yet not objective. "Un-truth" may carry greater value than "truth" in many situations. Such perspectives must be judged in terms of the degree to which they are life-furthering. "Even behind logic and its apparent sovereignty of development stand value judgments," Nietzsche suggests early in *Beyond Good and Evil*; "or, to speak more plainly, physiological demands for preserving a certain type of life." On this supposition, a psychologist would ask of any belief whether it is conducive to sound health (a therapeutic matter) rather than whether it is true. "True" and "health-producing" become synonymous in Nietzsche's treatment of ideas.

Nietzsche criticizes a philosopher like Immanuel Kant for having assumed existence of an unknowable "thing-in-itself" behind the phenomenal universe available to science. Similarly, he shows scorn for Hegel, who sought to find in the antithetical aspects of existence (passions, ideas, moral valuations) the expressions of a more fundamental rational reality. The tendency toward dualism, by which the "I" as subject stands independent of that which is perceived (as well as logically distinct as "subject" over against "object"), receives criticism as a possible grammatical prejudice erected into a false and misleading metaphysical argument. Rather than philosophizing in "the grand manner," Nietzsche encourages piecemeal treatment of a host of specific, clearly stated problems. Physiology may hold the key to solution of a number of old and baffling questions, including moral ones.

A philosophical investigator must forego easy solutions happening to fit his prejudices—just as physiologists must cease thinking that the basic drive behind organic life is that toward self-preservation. The will to power may prove more fundamental than desire of self-preservation. The will to power expresses an expansive, assimilating, positive, value-creating tendency in existence, nonhuman as well as human. There may also be no immediate certainties like the philosopher's "I think" or "Schopenhauer's superstition, 'I will.' " The older superstition that thinking activity results from a human will requires sophisticated and subtle analysis, for "A thought comes when 'it' and not when 'I' will." Indeed, even to say, "*It* is thought," instead of "I think," may cause another set of misleading metaphysical puzzles to arise. Nietzsche also argues that the metaphysical question about freedom of the will results from misuses of terms like "cause" and "effect," which are simply concepts. These concepts are fictions useful for the facilitation of common understanding but not as explanations. Men must stop creating myths about an objective reality based on pure concepts useful for other ends. There is neither "free" nor "non-free" will, according to Nietzsche, but simply "strong will and weak will."

Psychological investigations done previous to Nietzsche's day are found suspect because of the subtle ways in which their conclusions reflect human prejudices and fears. This theme sounds constantly throughout Nietzsche's writings. Nietzsche wanted a new kind of psychologist able to resist the unconscious forces in himself influencing him to accept conclusions dictated by his "heart." The evidence is what must count in such investigations. He asks his readers to imagine an investigator in physiology-psychology who possesses the courage to believe that greed, hatred, envy, and such passions are "the passions upon which life is conditioned, as things which must be present in the total household of life." So, too, the new philosophical breed will approach the study of the origins of morals with a ruthless honesty.

In a later book, *Toward a Geneology of Morals* (1887), Nietzsche in practice attempted the kind of historical-genetic investigation his *Beyond Good and Evil* recommends in principle. In the former book it is suggested that the concepts "good" and "bad," as well as "good" and "evil," arose out of a spiteful transvaluation of classical values by the meek and the lowly. "Bad" is the valuation placed on acts previously termed "good" in an aristocratic, healthy culture. Jewish and Christian priests, expressing their hatred of life, described as "evil" those biological functions fundamental to creation and healthful strength.

The central suggestion in *Beyond Good and Evil* is that another transvaluation of human values must now follow from the evolutionary notion of the will to power—that the cultural standpoint of western Europe so influenced by Christian valuations must undergo a deep change certain to usher in gigantic, even sometimes cataclysmic, alterations in the table of values. Man is seen as a being who must "get beyond" existing valuations in order to live creatively and even dangerously. A culture whose established values are foundering, in which the faith in metaphysical absolutes wobbles unsteadily on aging legs, throws up the question whether the belief in the possibility of an objectively justifiable morality is not an illusion. Never does Nietzsche say that men can live without making valuations. Nor does he argue that moral valuations are unqualifiedly relative—one as good as another. His point is psychological and critical. Nietzsche believed that man's nature, a product of evolution, demands the constant creation of new valutions even in the face of the absence of absolute standards. This aspect of his thought brings to mind contemporary existentialist thought which, however differently expressed by numerous existentialist writers, responds to the anguish of the human situation by making value judgments possible even though absolutes are lacking.

Nietzsche warns that the new philosopher must guard against some of the characteristics of the "intellectuals." This is a theme expressed early in his literary life (in *The Use and Abuse of History*, 1874, for example), when Nietzsche cautioned against bringing up a German generation so preoccupied with history that the *value* of those things whose history is studied could receive neither affirmation nor denial. Intellectualistic pursuit of objective knowledge tends to weaken the critical and evaluative capacities needed by men as a basis for living. Nietzsche never ridicules the scientific quest after objective knowledge as such. What he warns against is the production of scientific minds unable to make judgments about better and worse. Objective knowledge functions valuably only as a means to some other end or ends, like those which actualize human potentiality in all its possible varieties. Scientific knowledge fails to show men what things they should say "Yes" and "No" to from a valuational standpoint. Judgment is a function of the will—something which the scientific man can never determine.

For long centuries men decided on the value of actions by reference to their consequences. Nietzsche calls this the *pre-moral* period. Since he else-

699

where caricatures English utilitarian thought, one must assume that Nietzsche thinks little of a value standard based on the tendency of acts to produce pleasure rather than pain. A second period, lasting for the past ten thousand years (according to a Nietzsche who made no anthropological survey of such an enormous space of historical time), is marked by a predominant tendency to judge the value or worthlessness of an act by its origins. "The origin of an action was interpreted to rest, in a very definite sense, on an *intent*." Such an intentional yardstick for judging actions reflected an aristocratic stance. In his own time, Nietzsche believed neither the intent nor the consequences of an act would play the crucial role. This would be the *amoral* period. In a famous passage, Nietzsche characterizes the nature of the philosophers who would conduct new amoral analyses of human valuations: "A new species of philosopher is coming up over the horizon. I risk baptizing them with a name that is not devoid of peril. As I read them (as they allow themselves to be read— for it is characteristic of their type that they wish to remain riddles in some sense), these philosophers of the future have a right (perhaps also a wrong!) to be called: *Experimenters*. This name itself is only an experiment, and, if you will, a temptation." These thinkers will view pain and suffering as the necessary pre-conditions of any new valuations. They will also issue commands rather than simply describe or explain.

Nietzsche's treatment of what he calls "the peculiar nature of religion" bears a crucial relation to his prophesied transvaluation of existing values. According to Nietzsche, a student of religious phenomena should develop that kind of malicious subtlety which the moral investigator needs in all times and places if he is to succeed in his work. Although he despised the moral values taught by traditional Christianity, Nietzsche nonetheless admired the psychological self-discipline of the Christian saints. Religious phenomena fascinated him. The faith demanded of early Christians, a rarely attained reality, provides an example possessing peculiarly tough and lasting appeal. Nietzsche writes that contemporary men lack the corresponding toughness to appreciate the paradoxical statement of faith: God dies on a cross. Early Christian faith demanded qualities found in a modern Pascal, according to Nietzsche. In Pascal this faith "looks in a horrible way like a continuous suicide of the reason, a tough, long-lived, worm-like reason which cannot be killed at one time and with one blow." Nietzsche believed that such a faith would require careful study if the new experimenters were to learn how to succeed in their own transvaluation of Christian values. Especially intriguing are the three restrictions associated with what Nietzsche calls "the religious neurosis"—solitude, fasting, and sexual abstinence. For a student to understand the earlier historical transvaluation which occurred he must answer the question: "How is the saint possible?" Genuinely to understand how from the "bad" man one gets, suddenly, a saint requires one to compare Christianity's valuations to the lavish gratitude characteristic of earlier Greek religion before fear made Christianity a possibility.

Nietzsche argues that the study of moral and religious phenomena can never be the work of a day or a brief season. Modern thinkers can hope only to assemble the necessary evidence, slowly and painstakingly. Their first concern is the statement of a morphology of morality rather than the former ambitious attempt to give a philosophical justification of the derivation of a morality. Only "the collection of the material, the conceptual formalization and arrangement of an enormous field of delicate value-feelings and value-differences which are living, growing, generating others, and perishing" is possible at the present time along with some observations about recurrent features of these value growths. Investigators must know where to look for the proper evidence. For this task, the scientific man lacks the capacities needed for directing the investigations. The scientific man functions best as an instrument—an enormously valuable one. Yet the instrument "belongs in the hands of one who has greater power"— one who commands what uses the instrument shall be put to. Most philosophers also fail to qualify for this kind of moral analysis. The reason is that they have reduced philosophizing to theory of knowledge, which produces a value skepticism when what is required is action—value-commanding and value-judging.

The whole problem of understanding moral valuations is reminiscent of the older Faith versus Reason controversy in theology. Does "instinct" (the tendency to act creatively without always knowing how to give reasons for one's actions) hold a more important place in the subject matter of moral analysis than reasoning (the capacity to give reasons for one's valuations)? This problem emerges early in the character of Socrates—a philosopher whom Nietzsche admires for his magnificent irony and dialectical skills even though Nietzsche denounces "Socratism," the dogma that beliefs are valuable only in so far as they are capable of logical justification. Nietzsche considers Socrates a much greater figure than Plato. Socrates knew how to laugh at himself, realizing that his superior powers failed to discover the means by which to justify many beliefs he held important. Plato was more naïve than Socrates. Plato left a moral prejudice which Nietzsche simply rejects: the view that instinct and reason ultimately seek the same end— "God" or "the Good." Plato, in thus dissolving all that Nietzsche finds fascinating in the Faith-Reason controversy, made possible a later Christian institutionalization of herd-morality.

Fundamentally, Nietzsche distrusted individuals who venerate reason and deny the value of instinct. He insists that men of action illustrate the gap that exists between those who merely know (intellectually) and those who act. Any existing morality needs a horizon provided by men of action who say: "It shall be thus!" This command source of any morality must itself go unjustified and unquestioned. Any existing morality is in this sense always "problematic." By this Nietzsche probably meant that after reasons for the existing valuations have been given, there must remain, at last, a self-justifying command for which no further reasons are possible. Indeed, all morality containing progressive aspects stems from an aristocratic type of commanding. Every command requires a commander, some individual who supplies the necessary value horizon which others must simply accept. There can be no objectively grounded perspective of all perspectives. Life as an expanding process requires the cutting off of deliberative procedures at some point.

Nietzsche was willing to accept some of the painful consequences of this view of the command origin of all moral valuations. One consequence is that any existing morality requires sacrifice of numerous individuals and of many nuances of feeling and human tendency. Morality requires the application of command in such a way that not all legitimately natural instincts can find total expression at any one time. It also rests on exploitation as a necessary element in the creation of values. Some instincts must give way to others—and the commanding ones ought to be domineering and aristocratic. There must occur "the forcing of one's own forms upon something else."

Nietzsche's analysis of morality led him to dislike equalitarian democracy and herd-utilitarianism ("the greatest happiness of the greatest number"). An order of rank must exist. Between commander and commanded must arise a social distance based upon the former's greater value. The new philosopher seeking to transform valuations must stand "against his own time"—finding a value standpoint "beyond" the accepted valuations of his own era. To do so requires hardness and patient waiting. Philosophical success is thus partly a result of circumstances beyond any individual philosopher's control. *What* his creative response shall be is a function of what the situation is in which he finds himself. In this sense the philosopher must always be a lonely man, "beyond" the good and evil of conventional morality. This loneliness will produce anguish.

In *Thus Spake Zarathustra* (1883-1885), Nietzsche describes the anguish which results from the discovery that no God is found beyond good and evil. Nor is there a higher, more ultimate Platonic harmony. The new philosopher must learn to embrace existence for its own sake. Nietzsche attempts to express the nature of this love of existence through a doctrine of "eternal recurrence," which seems sometimes to function even mystically in his thought. The philosopher of existence must say "Yea" to reality while knowing that "God is dead." Any new values which arise in the evolutionary process do so as expressions of man's self-commanding capacity. Error and pain inevitably and necessarily are aspects of existence. "That everything recurs, is the very nearest approach of a world of Becoming to a world of Being: the height of contemplation," he wrote in the second volume of *The Will to Power* (a work published by Nietzsche's sister, 1901-1904, from remaining notes). The new philosopher of "beyondness" needs this doctrine of eternal recurrence, since he must command new values in an existence which expresses the will to power rather than a rational scheme of things.

In Nietzsche's style one finds a brilliance to match his intellectual daring—a wealth of suggestion, irony, maliciousness, a fine balancing of value antitheses, and playful criticism coupled with the most serious intention. The understanding of Nietzsche's works requires that one attempt to read them sympathetically, returning to them again and again. If he is to be judged severely for his unsystematic methods and for the disordered expression of his complex anxieties, his age and culture must also be so judged. Nietzsche was (as he says all men are) a philosopher who worked from an inner necessity to achieve self-under-standing. Of philosophers he wrote: "But fundamentally, 'way down below' in us, there is something unteachable,

a bedrock of intellectual destiny, of pre-destined decision, of answers to pre-destined selected questions."

TIME AND FREE WILL

Author: Henri Bergson (1859-1941)
Type of work: Metaphysics
First published: 1889

PRINCIPAL IDEAS ADVANCED

It is inappropriate to limit thought to spatial concepts; time, in particular, should not be conceived of as extension.

It is misleading to conceive of dynamic matters by the use of static concepts.

In giving accounts of aesthetic feelings or sensations, philosophers often attempt to describe qualitative changes in a quantitative fashion.

Space is the material with which mind builds up the conception of number, but the sensations by means of which we form the idea of space are themselves unextended and qualitative, not quantitative.

Time is duration, and duration may very well be nothing but a succession of qualitative changes permeating each other.

A self of pure duration is not subject to the distinctions which are imposed upon the self considered symbolically; the self is free when its acts spring from the whole personality.

Bergson stands as one of the great names in late nineteenth and early twentieth century philosophy, and the question of the freedom of the will is one of philosophy's classical problems. However, it is interesting to note that Bergson's little book is one of the few which treat this problem directly. Plato, Aristotle, and Augustine give classical analyses of time, but these come about in the course of the development of larger works. The problems which surround freedom of the will are numerous, but few have attacked the problem directly. In fact, it is probably safe to say that the focus upon freedom

of the will as a central issue is a development of modern philosophy. Theology developed this as a major part of the question of God's foreordination. Classical philosophy dealt with freedom only incidentally. Modern philosophy singled it out as a major issue, and Bergson wrote one of the few direct and systematic treatments of the issue.

The approach in this work is through psychology and particularly through an analysis of psychic states. Not only had philosophy not yet been separated in Bergson's time from psychology as a discipline, but the interest in psychology had really only begun to grow within philosophy. The empirical psychology, and the interest in sense perception so typical of British empiricism, combined with continental phenomenology to bring psychology to the foreground in philosophy, and this is Bergson's approach. As a Frenchman, the introspective analysis of Descartes has left its mark, although Bergson is noted as the great opponent of the strict Cartesian rationalism. The author is adept at detecting approaches which are inadequate to their subject matter, and so here he starts out by noting the inappropriateness of always thinking in spatial concepts. His problem (free will) is common to both metaphysics and psychology, and he begins by trying to point out a confusion of duration with extension, which has complicated the treatment of the problem of free will.

The first of the three chapters discusses the intensity of psychic states. In considering intensity in relation to extension, Bergson finds that intensity contains the image of something virtually extended. As is so often the case with Bergson, he breaks down barriers and finds in two apparently different phenomena elements of similarity and aspects of community. Again, Bergson considers the reflective consciousness as a way of looking at things and finds that it is repelled by the wholly dynamic way of perceiving. Such static-dynamic oppositions are Bergson's prime target, and he makes the case for dynamic views without surrendering more traditional approaches.

As an example of gradual transition which results in change in kind, Bergson cites aesthetic feelings as a striking example of the progressive intrusion of new elements, which in reality are merely altered emotions and not an increase in magnitude as they appear to be. In an aesthetic feeling we sympathize with the feeling that is expressed. Art aims at impressing feelings on us rather than at expressing them. The feeling of the beautiful is no specific feeling, but every feeling experienced by us assumes an aesthetic character, if it has been suggested and not caused.

Bergson continues with his analysis of sensations, emotions, and muscular effort after finishing his discussion of feeling. The magnitude of a representative sensation, he concludes, depends upon our transferring the cause into the effect. The intensity of the affective element depends, on the other hand, on the more or less important reactions which prolong the external stimulations and find their way into the sensation itself. We promote the changes of quality into variations of magnitude.

Bergson opposes some postulates of what he calls a psycho-physical interpretation, on the grounds that they cannot be verified unless the postulates are first granted. He resists the reduction of all psychological phenomena to physical states, and he insists that there is no point of contact between the unextended and the extended, between quality and quantity. There is no radical opposition; both arise as resultant variations in degree and are not disparate in nature.

Conscious states should not be considered in isolation from one another. Their proper context is in concrete multiplicity, for they unfold themselves in pure duration. Then you have to go on to inquire what the multiplicity of our inner states becomes, what form duration assumes when the space in which it unfolds is eliminated. The usual radical opposition has been broken down by Bergson, and now the problem becomes one of giving an adequate account of duration as the source.

In the second long chapter Bergson studies duration and begins by breaking down the concept of number into a synthesis of the one and the many. The idea of number implies the simple intention of a multiplicity of parts or units, which are absolutely alike. Every clear idea of number implies a visual image in space. For counting material objects means thinking of these objects as being together, thereby leaving them in space. Space is, accordingly, the material with which mind builds up number, the medium in which the mind places objects.

Ultimately, Bergson finds two kinds of multiplicity: that of material objects, to which the conception of number may be applied; and the multiplicity of states of consciousness. The latter cannot be thought of as numerical without the help of some symbolic representation, and in this a necessary element is space. But now we ask, has duration anything to do with space? It could be that space comes in as a later addition. The sensations by means of which we form the notion of space are themselves unextended and simply qualitative—this is the most likely hypothesis.

In actuality, space is what enables us to distinguish a number of identical and simultaneous sensations from one another. It is a principle of differentiation but not a qualitative one. Consequently, it is a reality with no quality. The mind perceives under the form of extensive homogeneity what is given it as qualitative homogeneity. There are two kinds of reality, one heterogeneous (that of sensible qualities), the other homogeneous (space). Because the latter is clearly conceived by the human intellect, we are able to use clear-cut distinctions, to count, to abstract, and also to speak. However, we still regard time as an unbounded medium, different from space but, like it, homogeneous. We can thus conceive of succession without distinction, and think of it as a mutual penetration, as interconnection and organization of elements. Each one represents the whole and cannot be distinguished or isolated from it except by abstract thought.

Pure duration might well be nothing but a succession of qualitative changes which melt into and permeate one another without precise outline. Yet it is extraordinarily difficult to think of duration in its purity. The real concrete self is made of such pure duration; its symbolic substitute has all of the artificial distinctions, and thus contradictions, implied in the problems of freedom, causality, and personality. An inner life, it is true, with well-distinguished moments and with clearly characterized states will answer better the requirements of social life. But a self of pure duration overcomes problems of freedom and causation by not being subject to their distinctions.

Dynamism is what Bergson prefers, and this starts from the idea of voluntary activity, given by consciousness. (Mechanism takes the opposite path.) The self experiences a first feeling and, according to the dynamic theory, has already changed to a slight extent when the second feeling takes its place. In this way a dynamic series of states is formed which permeates and strengthens the feeling states which are its members. Freedom depends on such a series. We are free, Bergson says, when our acts springs from our whole personality. Our acts express our personality. They have that indefinable resemblance to it which one sometimes finds to exist between an artist and his work. The believer in free will assumes that the same series of antecedents could issue in several different acts, all equally possible.

For Bergson freedom must be sought in a certain shade or quality of the action itself and not in the relation of this act to what it is not or to what it might have been. There are two ways of assimilating antecedent events, the one dynamic and the other static. Yet we still cannot analyze the outcome of a free action, for we cannot know the value of the antecedents without knowing the final act, which is the very thing that is not yet known. The question is whether the definite regularity of antecedent to consequent is found in the domain of consciousness, too. That is the whole problem of free will.

Of course, if we stand by experience, then we would say that we feel ourselves free, that we perceive force (rightly or wrongly) as a free spontaneity. The relation of inner causality is purely dynamic and has no analogy with the relation of two external phenomena which actually condition each other. Freedom is the relation of the concrete self to the acts which it performs, "This relation is indefinable, just because we are free." Every demand for an explanation of freedom comes back to the question: Can time be adequately represented by space? If you are dealing with time flow, then the answer is yes. Freedom is therefore a fact, among the facts which we observe; there is none which is clearer.

Bergson thus used his famous doctrine of conscious time as flowing from a primitive apprehension of undivided duration. By his doctrine he attempted to release causal action from the grip of mechanical regulation and to place the source for free acts in a consciousness ultimately free from space and its rigid divisions. In *Time and Free Will* Bergson thus argues for an undivided duration behind conscious states and normal distinctions and thereby leaves an area for spontaneity and free decision in psychic states if not in physical matter.

APPEARANCE AND REALITY

Author: Francis Herbert Bradley (1846-1924)
Type of work: Metaphysics
First published: 1893

PRINCIPAL IDEAS ADVANCED

The distinction between primary (sensed) qualities of physical objects and secondary (structural) qualities is based on appearance; in reality there is no such distinction.

Upon analysis it turns out that space, time, objects, and selves are appearances, not realities; the concepts do not stand up because alleged differences vanish when it is discovered that definitions are circular, empty, or inconsistent.

706

The logical character of reality is that it does not contradict itself; the metaphysical character of reality is that it is one; and the epistemological character of reality is that it is experience.

Reality, or the Absolute, must be because appearances are the appearances of reality.

In judgment, an idea is predicated of a real subject; a judgment is true insofar as it predicates harmonious content, removing inconsistency—but since predicates are ideal, every truth is but a partial truth, every error but a partial error.

F. H. Bradley wrote with the confidence of a leader in the main stream of British philosophy between the 1870's and the 1920's. His speculation, strongly influenced by Hegel, was highly metaphysical; and his intention was to arrive at ultimate truths about the universe as a whole. His general method was to show that the world regarded as made up of discrete objects is self-contradictory and, therefore, a world of appearances The real is one, a world in which there are no separate objects and in which all differences disappear. Curiously enough, Bradley's conclusions about reality have not been of primary interest to contemporary philosophers. It is, rather, his critical method that they have found important, his destruction of the world of appearance.

In his preface to *Appearance and Reality*, Bradley describes metaphysics as "the finding of bad reasons for what we believe on instinct, but to find these reasons is no less an instinct." He warns the reader that many of the ideas he presents must certainly be wrong; but since he is unable to discover how they are wrong, others will have to be critical of his conclusions.

If metaphysics is so liable to error, why should Bradley bother to study it, much less write over six hundred pages about it? He reminds us that we have all had experiences of some-

thing beyond the material world and that we need metaphysics to understand these experiences, at least insofar as they admit of being understood. Metaphysical speculation on its constructive as well as on its critical side protects us from the extremes of crass materialism and dogmatic orthodoxy. We learn from the study of metaphysics that either of these solutions is too simple, that both are peremptory. "There is no sin, however prone to it the philosopher may be," Bradley says, "which philosophy can justify so little as spiritual pride."

Appearance and Reality is divided into two parts. In the first part, "Appearance," Bradley deals with some of the recurring problems of philosophy, such as quality, relation, space, time, causation, and self. His general intention was to show that these problems have been formulated in such a way that no determinate solution can be found for them, that the world viewed from their perspective is contradictory and, therefore, appearance.

The first problem with which Bradley deals is the division of the properties of objects into primary and secondary qualities. Those who maintain this division mean by primary qualities those spatial aspects of things that we perceive or feel. All other qualities are secondary. Primary qualities, these advocates hold, are constant, permanent, self-dependent and real. Secondary qualities, such as color, heat, cold, taste, and odor are relative to the perceiver.

In one of his arguments against this view, Bradley grants that secondary qualities are mere appearances because he wishes to show that the same thing is true of primary qualities. If an object has secondary qualities, even though they are relative to the perceiver, they must have some ground in the object. A thing can be relative only if the terms of the relation are real. For example, in the sentence, "The table is to the left of the chair," the relation, "to the left of" can hold only if there are a table and a chair. Consequently, to show that a quality is relative is to show that it is grounded in an object. The ground or terms of the relation must be real for the relation to hold. Consequently, secondary cannot mean unreal, as some proponents of the theory seem to argue that it does. Again, primary qualities must also be perceived and would be relative for the same reason given for secondary qualities. The division of the properties of objects into primary or secondary qualities turns out on close examination to be mistaken. This division, which has seemed real to many philosophers, is merely an appearance.

The structure of Bradley's argument, which often recurs in this section of the book, might be stated as follows: Some opponent maintains that x is different in kind from y, but both x and y are seen to depend on a. The opponent takes a as the defining property of x; therefore he is inconsistent in not taking it as the defining property of y. Thus x and y are not different in kind. The opponent defined them from different points of view and con-

cluded that they were different in kind from his difference in definition. The alleged difference is merely one of appearance.

Metaphysicians are often quoted as saying that space is unreal. One of Bradley's arguments that space is unreal or an appearance involves the question of whether space has an end. If one thinks of a small portion of space, one thinks of it as bounded. The space between the table and the chair is bounded by the table and the chair. But space itself cannot be bounded. What would be outside it? However, precise boundaries determine space. This difficulty arises from regarding space first of all as a relation with the table and chair as its terms and then regarding it as a quality which is unlimited. Space cannot be a relation because any space can be divided into smaller spaces, But to divide space is to have a relation with another relation as its terms. "Space," says Bradley, "is essentially a relation of what vanishes into relations. which seek in vain for their terms. It is lengths of lengths of—nothing that we can find."

But what of space as a quality? If it is a quality, it must have limits because it is a quality in contrast to some other quality. But there is no such other. If there were, space would be a relation. According to Bradley, the philosophers who have thought of space as real have wanted to think of it both as infinite and ideal and as limited and experienced. Neither of these views by itself is enough, but one can be maintained only at the expense of the other.

A similar argument applies to time. Suppose that time is composed of units; then it has no duration. Suppose it has duration; then it has no units and no before or after. As he had said of space, Bradley avers, "Time . . . must be made and yet cannot be made of pieces."

The world seems to be made up of things or objects. But what is a thing? A minimum qualification for being a thing is to be located somewhere and probably at some time. But we cannot make clear the notions of spatial or temporal location. Not only must a thing be located but also it must have qualities; yet here again is a notion to which we cannot give any determinate meaning. In Bradley's analysis the world of this and that has disappeared.

But if the external world is appearance, what of the self? Surely here is a constant point of reference. However, the word "self" has many meanings. If the self is defined in terms of what is not self, that is, the external world, then this external world must have some meaning. If the self is understood by self-examination, then it is at once subject and object—an impossibility.

Now that objects and selves have become appearances, Bradley has only the world of things-in-themselves to deal with. But if things-in-themselves are absolutely unknown, then their existence itself is unknown; and to the extent that things-in-themselves are known, they are not things-in-themselves.

Here we come to the end of Bradley's section on appearance. What conclusion are we to draw from this part of *Appearance and Reality?* Whatever we have examined has turned out to be appearance, to be inconsistent with itself. But we have not proved that these inconsistent entities have no connection with the real. Reality com-

pletely divorced from appearance would have no meaning. We must look for some way in which appearance and reality can be joined, and it is to this problem that the second part of the book, "Reality," is devoted.

Bradley maintains that there are three fundamental properties of reality, one logical, one epistemological, and one metaphysical. The logical character of reality is that it does not contradict itself. This immediately differentiates reality from appearance. The metaphysical property is that reality is one, another characteristic to be contrasted with appearance. The epistemological property is that reality is experience. This is Bradley's way of putting the central doctrine of philosophical Idealism that the real is the rational. For him, to be rational is to be in some mind. A rational, nonmental world could at best be merely potentially rational. But to be in some mind is to be experience. These three principles, as Bradley develops them, are seen to be constitutive of all reality and, as such, are metaphysical principles.

Reality, taken as the totality of all that exists, Bradley calls the Absolute. There must be such a reality because something can be an appearance only if it is the appearance of something. The problem now is to show how such things as appearance, evil, finite objects, error, time, and space are related to and are compatible with this Absolute.

Before the question of the Absolute can be settled, we must have a definition of truth. What is a real object? Bradley says that every real thing has at least two properties, existence and characteristics. We have to be able to say that the entity *is* and *what* it is.

But to be able to say something is to have ideas, and through judgment an idea is predicated of a real subject. Existence, then, is contained in the subject, and the predicate contains an ideal character which it relates to the real subject. We are now ready for Bradley's definition of truth: "Truth is the object of thinking, and the aim of truth is to qualify existence ideally." Furthermore, "Truth is the predication of such content as, when predicated, is harmonious, and removes inconsistency and with it unrest." But a truth is never wholly adequate. The predicate is only ideal, not real. Therefore, every truth is a partial truth and is capable of being expanded and extended indefinitely towards more truth.

If one can account for truth, one must also account for error. The Absolute exists and what is not a part of the Absolute does not exist. Error seems to be an exception. It cannot exist as part of the Absolute because it is in contradiction with it and is hence, error. It cannot be nonexistent because people really do make errors. It is as naïve to think that there is no error as it is to think that there is no evil in the world. On the other hand, there is a sense in which error is a partial truth. The subject and predicate refer to real things and the relation asserted between them does exist. But this partiality is also the source of error. It is a partiality which must be supplemented to become truth. Its error is in its one-sidedness; but in spite of that, it expresses one side or aspect of the Absolute.

If solipsism were true, it would be a forceful argument against the Absolute. The argument in favor of solipsism may be stated as follows: Whatever I am conscious of is an experience. But every experience is my private experience. Therefore, all I can know are various states of my own mind. Bradley's answer to this view is through definitions of the term "experience." There are two meanings that the term may have. One is that experience is a succession of bare mental states, unrelated to one another. This meaning of experience is not enough for the solipsist because he must be able to talk about a self or mind which is the agent or subject of the experiences. Thus the experiences on which solipsism is based must be more than bare mental states. They are experiences that go beyond the moment of feeling. But the solipsist may say that experience in going beyond the present moment stops short at the self. Even for him this self must have a past and a future, which are constructed by inference from the present self. But in the same way that he infers the existence of other states of his own self, he could infer other selves. The truth in solipsism is that one can know the universe only through one's own experiences and sensations. Its falsity is that it wishes to stop the expansion of experience at an arbitrary point. For Bradley, the expansion of experience, once begun, cannot stop short of the Absolute.

Are things more or less real and statements more or less true? Bradley says, "The Absolute considered as such, has of course no degrees; for it is perfect, and there can be no more or less in perfection." But if the Absolute is perfectly real and statements of it perfectly true, then true statements of any thing other than the Absolute must be less true and refer to something less real. It seems odd to say that one thing is less real than another. One would be inclined to think that a thing is either real or not: this chair is real; ghosts never are. But it is easy to see Bradley's difficulty. Either every statement must be of the Absolute or some must be less true than others. The same consideration must be applied to existence. Properly speaking only the Absolute exists, and you, I, and the gatepost exist only partially.

No propositions are adequate to the Absolute; and Bradley must say, "There will be no truth which is entirely true, just as there will be no error which is totally false. With all alike, if taken strictly, it will be a question of amount, and will be a matter of more or less." But even this doctrine must have a proviso: "Our thoughts certainly, for some purposes, may be taken as wholly false, or again as quite accurate; but truth and error, measured by the Absolute, must each be subject always to degree."

Bradley discussed morality in his *Ethical Studies* (1876). In *Appearance and Reality,* he treats goodness as a metaphysical category. One might ask the question, "Is the Absolute good?" The answer is that good is an incomplete category, simply one aspect of perfection. Beauty, truth, and so on are good, but they are something else besides. Good is limited in its scope; but, limited, it cannot be a property of the Absolute. "Goodness, as such, is but appearance which is transcended in the Absolute."

Surely, then, the Absolute must be God. But the God of religion must be an object to man. The God of religion must be available. But if he has these properties, then he is appearance. The logic of development in Bradley's metaphysics cannot be suspended even for God. If God is another name for the Absolute, then he is unavailable to man. But if he is not the Absolute then he is subordinate to it. The God of religion must remain in the world of appearances.

Thus religion would have little to recommend it if it were knowledge. The essential factor in religion is not knowledge. It is, Bradley says, "the attempt to express the complete reality of goodness through every aspect of our being."

Most of the doctrines that we have attributed to Bradley have been negative. Many of the things in which we most firmly believe have turned out to be appearances, half-truths at best. But only the Absolute is true. What can we say about it? We can only approach a description of the Absolute because no statements are infinite as statements of this sort would have to be. The Absolute is perfection. Insofar as a statement approaches perfection, insofar as the system approaches completeness, our statements become more nearly true. A statement will be more nearly complete to the extent that its opposite is inconceivable. A statement is inconceivable when its truth would falsify a system of truths. Thus a true statement is one related to other truths within a system, and the more comprehensive the system, the more nearly true the statement.

Truth about the Absolute is only one part of the Absolute itself. Truth refers to statements that are abstract, but the Absolute itself is reality and concrete. Philosophy, the concern of which is truth, can only hope to be partial at best. Bradley says, "Truth, when made adequate to Reality, would be so supplemented as to have become something else—something other than truth, and something for us unattainable." But there are degrees of truth; and insofar as their limits are determined, truths are genuine.

In an early chapter of *Appearance and Reality*, Bradley tells us that "what is *possible*, and what a general principle compels us to say *must be*, that certainly *is*." There is some sense in which this statement is the key to what Bradley does in *Appearance and Reality*. His sharp, critical mind led

him to reject much of what common sense would admit. The few principles that remain he accepted reluctantly because they seemed to him impervious to attack. What could he contruct with the material that he had left? Logical necessity led him into a world in which none of us can feel at home, a world which transcends the scope of philosophy and even of language.

COLLECTED ESSAYS

Author: Thomas Henry Huxley (1825-1895)
Type of work: Epistemology, ethics, philosophy of science
First published: 1893-1894 (in nine volumes)

PRINCIPAL IDEAS ADVANCED

Not only has science had practical benefits, but also it has brought about a revolution in man's conception of man and of his place in the universe.

Education is learning the rules of the game of life; the educated man possesses skills, a trained intellect, and knowledge of facts; but he is no ascetic.

There is but one kind of knowledge, and that is to be found in the verifiable conclusions of the natural sciences.

Although all life has a protoplasmic basis, it is an error to conclude that materialism is superior to spiritualism; the fact is that both theories involve empty and unverifiable conceptions.

It is wrong for a man to say that he is certain of the truth of a proposition unless he can produce evidence, and it is wrong to demand belief from others when evidence is not available to substantiate the belief.

Nature is nonmoral; to make progress man cannot count on evolutionary processes; he must use his best energies and his intelligence.

Huxley was a surgeon by profession, whose original investigations into natural history led to his election in 1850 to the Royal Society and to his appointment in 1854 to a lectureship at the School of Mines. But after the publication of Charles Darwin's epoch-

making work in 1859, Huxley renounced whatever ambition to scientific fame he might have cherished in order to devote himself to the task of promoting a general increase in scientific knowledge, "to the popularization of science; to the development and or-

712

ganization of scientific education; to the endless series of battles and skirmishes over evolution; and to untiring opposition to that ecclesiastical spirit, that clericalism, which . . . is the deadly enemy of science." The papers which make up the *Collected Essays* were written over a period of thirty years and were brought together by their author near the close of his life.

Undoubtedly Huxley's fundamental motivation was humanitarian. He believed that man ought to take an active part in improving his own condition, and it was plain to him that the increase of natural knowledge was the only effective means. But he rejected the view that science is merely "a sort of comfort-grinding machine." In an early essay entitled "On the Advisableness of Improving Natural Knowledge," he maintained that science "has not only conferred practical benefits on men, but, in so doing, has effected a revolution in their conceptions of the universe and of themselves, and has profoundly altered their modes of thinking and their views of right and wrong." The vision of the infinite magnitude of space and of the endless modifications of life, with every atom determined in a fixed order by an unchanging causation, satisfied Huxley's "spiritual cravings"; and the stern demands imposed upon man's intellect by the increasing hazards of the human condition seemed to him "the foundations of a new morality." With it all, there was a note of sadness, but, according to Huxley, such is the essence of all religion—"this consciousness of the limitation of man, this sense of an open secret which he cannot penetrate."

It was clear to Huxley that science had opened the door to a new era in human history. He saw, moreover, some of the perils which technological advancement holds for nations which are not sufficiently matured in spirit to assume the responsibilities which material progress brings in its train. In his view, compulsory primary education was an imminent necessity. It was needed in order to prove trained leadership in proportion to the increased demands of the new age. But it was also needed in order to save society from the danger of revolution by a miserable and ignorant proletariat.

When the Education Act of 1870 was being debated, Huxley wrote an essay entitled "Administrative Nihilism," in which he argued against laissez faire individualists who were opposed to involving the state in education. He quoted John Locke (*Of Civil Government*), who had said, "The end of Government is the Good of Mankind," and he went on to maintain that the general welfare demands new kinds of legislation to meet changing times. "I take it," he said, "that the good of mankind means the attainment, by every man, of all the happiness which he can enjoy without diminishing the happiness of his fellows." He admitted that it is unnecessary and undesirable for the state to undertake directly to increase either the material prosperity of its people or their personal happiness. But he thought that, just as there are indirect ways in which legislation aids industry and commerce, so there are indirect ways in which it can aid the improvement of morals and the advancement of art and science, among the most patent of which is the education of the young.

Huxley was not merely concerned to make education more widely ac-

713

cessible. It seemed to him that in the age of science important revisions had to be made in what is taught. In this connection, he undertook to redefine "A Liberal Education." Life, he said, is like a game in which every man's happiness depends upon knowing the rules. "Education is learning the rules of this mighty game. In other words, education is the instruction of the intellect in the laws of Nature . . . and the fashioning of the affections and of the will into an earnest and loving desire to move in harmony with those laws." He explained that when he spoke of the laws of Nature, he included those which govern the behavior of men, so that he was not to be understood as favoring the physical sciences to the exclusion of the social. Moreover, as a man of great breadth and depth of "culture," in Matthew Arnold's sense of the word, he insisted on the importance of literature and history, and sanctioned what is called the "education of taste." He saw the educated man as one possessing bodily skills, a trained intellect, a mind well supplied with facts—"one who, no stunted ascetic, is full of life and fire, but whose passions are trained to come to heel by a vigorous will, the servant of a tender conscience; who has learned to love all beauty, whether of Nature or of art, to hate all vileness, and to respect others as himself." Such, he said, was the goal of a "liberal education."

To the view, prevalent in literary and academic circles, that a liberal education is synonymous with instruction in humane letters, Huxley opposed two propositions. The first was that knowledge of Greek and Roman antiquity does not have as much direct value, either in terms of its subject matter or in terms of the mental discipline which it demands, as a comparable training in the physical sciences. The second was that, supposing one must choose between an exclusively scientific education and an exclusively literary education, the former is at least as effectual as the latter "for the purpose of attaining real culture." In fact, Huxley saw no need of making education so exclusive. The omission of the classical languages, said he, is not incompatible with the mastery of the mother tongue and the reading of the Bible, Shakespeare, and Milton, whom he thought not inferior to Homer and Vergil. Huxley rejected the distinction between pure and applied science, maintaining that the latter is "nothing but the application of pure science to particular classes of problems." He did not envisage the new scientific colleges, which were then coming into existence, as narrow trade schools. "Industry," he said, "is a means and not an end." And he saw it as one of the main functions of education to enlarge men's minds, so as to ennoble their aspirations and enhance their capacities for higher goods, notably the pleasures of the mind. But, he argued, in the age of Newton and Darwin the mind which is not trained to think scientifically is more impoverished than one which is ignorant of Greek.

Classical education, however, had not formed the mind of the larger British public. And in Huxley's view, the most serious obstacle to intellectual and social advance came not from traditional education but from popular religion. The issue, for all practical purposes, was the conflict between naturalism and supernaturalism. In an article called "The Progress of Science," Huxley maintained that there is only one kind of knowledge—the kind shared by the physical sciences, namely, physics, chemistry, and biology. These all have the same objective, "the discovery of the rational order which pervades the universe," and the same method, that "of observation and experiment for the determination of the facts of Nature; of inductive and deductive reasoning for the discovery of their mutual relations and connections." Furthermore, they rest on the same three assumptions which, strictly speaking, are indemonstrable, but which have vindicated themselves in terms of the results they make possible. These are the existence of an "extended, impenetrable, mobile substance" termed matter; "the universality of the law of causation"; and the eternal validity of the "laws of Nature." Natural sciences, said Huxley, deserve the name of knowledge because their findings are verifiable. And he pleaded with his age to lay aside the consideration of any hypotheses which are unverifiable.

Although Huxley spoke the language of materialism, he preserved a sophisticated attitude toward this language, which he saw as being merely symbolical, "the aid by which Nature can be interpreted in terms apprehensible by our intellects." In an essay entitled "On the Physical Basis of Life," he said that, judging from the direction biology was taking, he saw no alternative to concluding that all life has a protoplasmic basis. At the same time, he protested that he himself was not a materialist. He believed that materialism is a grave error because it involves an unverifiable, empty conception of matter. "What do we know," he asks, "about this terrible 'matter,'

except as a name for an unknown and hypothetical cause of states of our own consciousness? . . . And what is the dire necessity and 'iron' law under which men groan? Truly, most gratuitously invented bugbears." The argument for using "materialistic terminology" is that this way of thinking of the world has made possible the discovery of truths of Nature, "whereas the alternative, or spiritualistic, terminology is utterly barren, and leads to nothing but obscurity and confusion of ideas."

Huxley's position was essentially the same as that which Herbert Spencer had outlined under the heading of "The Unknowable," in his *First Principles*. By suspending judgment about ultimate being, Huxley avoided systematic materialism, with its implicit threat to moral responsibility. At the same time, he was delivered from the necessity of admitting spiritual entities into the naturalistic account of the world. If our minds are not capable of knowing ultimate being, he argued, we are no more justified in calling it spirit than in calling it matter. Let it remain out of bounds for human inquiry, particularly in view of the fact that the kind of knowledge which science gives us is ample for our needs.

These views Huxley shared with many nineteenth century positivists. His characteristic contribution was to grace them with a name—agnosticism. In a piece by that name, he gave an amusing account of the origin of the word. When he was accustomed to attend meetings of a certain Metaphysical Society, where everyone else was an-*ist* of one kind or another, he felt like the proverbial fox which had lost its tail. "So I took thought, and invented what I conceived to be the appropriate title of 'agnostic.' It came into my head as suggestively antithetic to the 'gnostic' of Church history, who professed to know so much about the very things of which I was ignorant; and I took the earliest opportunity of parading it at our Society, to show that I, too, had a tail like the other foxes." In a later article, "Agnosticism and Christianity," he went on to explain precisely what the term stands for. An agnostic, he said, is not simply an unbeliever, much less one who from indifference or sloth has not troubled to inform himself about higher matters. His is the ethical or intellectual principle "that it is wrong for a man to say that he is certain of the objective truth of any proposition unless he can produce evidence which logically justifies that certainty." Huxley was more cautious, in this respect, than Spencer and many of the positivists, inasmuch as he did not wish to lay it down as a dogma that no knowledge of ultimate reality is possible. However, he confessed that knowledge of ultimate reality was beyond him, much though he regretted it, and he was tolerably certain that it was beyond everyone else. Huxley was especially vexed with ecclesiastics who maintained that it is wrong not to believe certain dogmas, no matter what evidence science brings against them, and he saw it as compounding the "abomination" when they further declared that their doctrines must be taught, even if they are not true, on the grounds that they are necessary for morality. "Surely the attempt to cast out Beelzebub by the aid of Beelzebub is a hopeful procedure as compared to that of preserving morality by the aid of immorality. . . . The course of the past has impressed us with the firm conviction that no

good ever comes of falsehood."

In the popular mind, the great issue between science and religion in Huxley's day centered about evolution. Huxley was unambiguously on the side of the latter. He had rejected pre-Darwinian theories of evolution as being purely speculative, but when Darwin brought forward the theory of natural selection, Huxley embraced it as providing for the first time a hypothesis which made evolution scientifically verifiable. Still, he was never completely convinced that Darwin's hypothesis was correct. In 1892, he wrote, "That the doctrine of natural selection presupposes evolution is quite true; but it is not true that evolution necessarily implies natural selection." What stood out in his mind at that time was not any particular explanation as to the origin of species, but a great body of facts all tending to the same conclusion: embryology attested that the evolution of individual plants and animals is taking place every day; and paleontology attested that species arose in just those morphological relations in which they would have arisen supposing that evolution had taken place. To these facts, he said, "all future philosophical and theological speculations will have to accommodate themselves."

With the example of such men as Herbert Spencer and Ernst Haeckel before him, Huxley repudiated anything that could be called a "philosophy of evolution." Attempts to construct such a philosophy might be admirable but, in his opinion, they were premature. In particular he opposed attempts to give an evolutionary account of ethics, as Spencer and others were doing.

Nature, Huxley insisted, is nonmoral. When we study it with our minds, we find cause for admiration; but when we view it in terms of our moral sympathies, we can only shudder. The Mother-goddess of middle Eastern cults, in whom were combined the attributes both of generation and of destruction, seemed to him a fairly accurate representation of nature. This conception preserved a healthy balance between the optimism which supposes that the world exists to make man happy, and the pessimism which concludes that it makes happiness impossible.

According to Huxley, man, in becoming civilized, has ventured on an undertaking for which he alone is responsible and for which he can expect no help or sympathy. Everywhere in nature, the struggle for existence goes on, unrelieved by generosity or scruple; and originally the human species, like every other, must have been engaged in "a Hobbesian war of each against all." But civilization, or what we call society, is man's attempt to escape from that condition by setting limits to the struggle. In return for exercising self-restraint and coöperating with his fellows, man not merely satisfies his biological needs more adequately than he could do in a savage state; entirely new dimensions are opened to him. But, in Huxley's view, of these the cosmos knows nothing. He rejected the argument that moral propensities are the result of evolutionary processes, pointing out that immoral propensities are no less so. And to the supposition that the struggle for survival, if permitted to continue, will automatically bring men to ethical perfection, he replied that the kind of fitness which enables an organism to survive bears no relation to the human ideal.

If men want to preserve civilization, Huxley argued, they must devote to it their best energies and intelligence. Distinguishing evolution from progress, he deplored the mental confusion of persons who made the principle of survival of the fittest an argument for competition within society. In his view, man's survival demands more coöperation and more planning; and he declared his faith that "intelligence and will, guided by sound principles of investigation, and organized in common effort, may modify the conditions of existence. . . . And much may be done to change the nature of man himself." One of the problems which he said demanded attention was that of overpopulation. Nature overpopulates itself, and this is one of the causes of the struggle for survival. If man is to eliminate war and famine, he must take in hand the problem of stabilizing the population.

In the end, Huxley admitted, the cosmic process must defeat the human enterprise. Like Spencer, he held that evolution is conterbalanced by dissolution. Civilizations rise and fall. So do planetary systems. To this grander prospect Huxley responded in Stoic fashion. "We should cast aside the notion that escape from pain and sorrow is the proper object of life." It is time, he said, to put away youthful confidence, but without plunging, like so many nineteenth century men of letters, into "the no less youthful discouragement of nonage." As mature men, strong in will, we must cherish the good that falls our way, and bear the evil "with stout hearts set on diminishing it."

717

THE SENSE OF BEAUTY

Author: George Santayana (1863-1952)
Type of work: Aesthetics
First published: 1896

PRINCIPAL IDEAS ADVANCED

Our preferences are ultimately nonrational; things are good because they are preferred.

Beauty is pleasure objectified; when a spectator regards his pleasure as a quality of the object he sees, he calls the object "beautiful."

Form pleases when in perception the excitation of the retinal field produces a semblance of motion while the mind synthesizes the elements perceived.

The aesthetic component "expression" is the result of the emotional associations excited by contemplation of the aesthetic object.

George Santayana is one of the few philosophers whose writings have a beauty of style which can be appreciated independently of their philosophical worth. Literary ability should not be taken as a substitute for clarity in presenting ideas; but at his best Santayana had the fortune of combining both well. In this early work not only does he present a provocative account of aesthetics in what may be called a "naturalistic" vein, but in addition he gives an insight into the development of his later metaphysics and ontology.

The Sense of Beauty is divided into four parts. In the opening part Santayana discusses the nature of beauty. He points out that the term "aesthetics" originally meant "perception" and that it was associated, by use, with a particular object of perception and its study, that which we call "the beautiful." This can be put in a different but related manner if we speak of a perceptual quality which we are to analyze; namely, "beauty." Here one should remind himself of words which make use of the "perception" meaning of "aesthetics"; for example, we use the

term "kinaesthesis" to refer to a certain sense which our muscles have, and we speak of "anaesthesis" as the loss of our sensations.

To return to the sort of perceptive activity with which this analysis is to be concerned, it should be pointed out that we are not examining the world of facts considered independently of any observer. Such a world is neutral as far as value is concerned, for it is not good (or evil) for any one. Herein we see a basis for Santayana's naturalism. The existence of worth or value depends upon the presence of somebody's consciousness; nature has purpose or growth only in that one values what nature exhibits. Nature is not itself aware of the changes. Since the consciousness that observes must also appreciate if it is to hold patterns of value, there is a nonrational as well as a rational basis for our judgment of the world as one in which phenomena are loved or hated. Santayana lays bare his indebtedness to Spinoza and Hume when he proclaims that our preferences regarding the events of the world are ultimately nonrational.

Things are good because we prefer them; they are not preferred because they are good.

One should point out, however, that Santayana's view that values must be separated from facts rests upon a distinction which is false in fact. It is not meaningless to contend that we are creatures who have desires because objects in the world provoke our interests; in this sense, it is as much true that we desire things because they are good as that they are good because we desire them. Either philosophical view, the one that says that values are independent of consciousness and intrinsic to the world (the so-called "absolutist position"), or that which claims values wholly dependent upon and relative to the attitudes of subjects, is incomplete and only part of the story.

Santayana goes on to discuss the difference between moral and aesthetic values. The analogy that he draws is between work and play, between duty and amusement. Morality prepares us for the serious aspects of life: death, disease, passion, and, only against the background of these, the possibility of salvation. To seek pleasure, to enjoy experience—these are but futile pursuits, trivial and potentially dangerous against the stark reality of existence. Actions are looked upon in terms of the consequences they will have in preparing us for our stern lives. There is no time to give oneself to the pleasure of an experience enjoyed for its own sake, which aims at nothing else. This attitude toward the world is akin to the Biblical attitude toward work; one must labor by the sweat of his brow because of man's first disobedience, which brought death and disease into the world. As the pressures upon a society lessen and it becomes more secure in its struggle with its environment, the seriousness of life lifts and individuals are more likely to take on a holiday air; play and freedom go together and with them the love of immediate pleasures for their own sake, free from fear and independent of consequences. In the distinction between duty and pleasure, work and play, constraint and freedom is to be found the difference between moral and aesthetic values.

In defining beauty, Santayana points out that as a pleasure it has certain peculiar characteristics which allow us to distinguish it from other pleasures. Most pleasures that we get from perceiving (in the wide sense of the term) can be distinguished from the object perceived. We usually go through certain actions before the pleasure is felt. In eating, drinking, inhaling, the activity is entered upon and thereby pleasure follows. There are certain pleasures that seem to occur in the process of perception itself; when this happens to us we then intuit the pleasure as a quality of the thing perceived. Santayana holds that the very mechanism or structure of the mind by which we perceive various qualities as one homogeneous object also objectifies this type of pleasure, as it were, so that it, too, is felt as an integral part of the object. This is the kind of pleasure that is considered to be intrinsic, enjoyable in itself, and, of course, of positive value in the sense that it belongs to the play, holiday, free class rather than to the moral one. For Santayana, beauty is *positive, intrinsic, objectified pleasure* or *pleasure regarded as the quality of a thing*.

Although some hold that in nature we can find such aesthetically pleasant objects, generally speaking it is to

719

man and his creations that we look for objects in which we can take some contemplative pleasure. Santayana has a problem, however, in considering beauty as he does; for if we identify those objects as works of art, we then have the problem of tragedy and of painful works of art. We shall later see how he meets this challenge.

In "The Materials of Beauty," Santayana discusses the substance of beauty—sound, color, and fragrance—as well as other topics concerned with the appeal of our lower senses in relation to the total aesthetic experience. There are those who have argued that the experiences which we must have by *direct* contact with an object (because of the structure of certain parts of our sensorium) cannot be of the beautiful. The bouquet and taste of wine, the touch of brocade, of marble, or sandalwood, are pleasant yet do not seem to be beautiful. Santayana claims, however, that all contribute to the ultimate experience of beauty in that they teach us to appreciate the pleasant, to delight in things sensuous. Those who find the height of aesthetic experience in objects appealing to eye and ear through their formal structure must recognize that form and meaning can be presented only in something sensible. To divorce content from a work of art is to present something utterly barren.

In the third part of his work, Santayana analyzes form as a main aspect of beauty. In the previous section we noted that certain elements presented to the senses charm or please in themselves. We need look no further than the coolness of a summer breeze to explain the pleasure we feel in its company. But there is a pleasure we encounter which, although immediate and intrinsic, is yet puzzling and perhaps mysterious when we come upon it. There are presented to us objects which have elements none of which is particularly pleasing yet which, because of their arrangement, combination, or pattern, are pleasing. The *form* of the object is the aesthetician's name for it, and he insists that to reduce it to its elements destroys its distinctive, pleasing effect, although without those elements there could not be form.

Santayana turns to the psychology of perception to explain, hypothetically, the pleasure which one derives from form in its various manifestations, as well as to indicate why some forms are either boring or incomplete as visual wholes. (He concentrates on visual form and specifically omits auditory form as too technical to analyze in this work, although he indicates that in principle it should be the same.) Briefly, he claims that the visual image is gathered as a series of sensitive points about the center of the retina. These points or spots each have their peculiar quality of sensation and are associated with the muscular tension and relaxation that occurs with the turning of one's eyes. As the associations are formed they establish a field which is such that when certain elements (or perhaps a single element) are presented to the eye the entire field is excited. The excitation produces a semblance of motion; there is a radiation about the points that tends to re-create the associated image, so that the point leads the mind to the possible field. Various geometrical figures affect the eyes in ways that lead to a graceful and rhythmic completion by the mind (depending to a certain degree, if not entirely, on the figure given) which is pleasing. The muscular movement is not itself smooth, but rather a series of jerks; the visual effect, however, is one of movement full and graceful, combining actual and possible (or perhaps imaginary) rays.

The form presented does not automatically produce a pleasing effect. Because of their gross or tiny size some forms fail to excite the eye and its muscles significantly.

Symmetry is a good example of aesthetic form, where it is an aid to unification, where it helps us to organize, discriminate, and distinguish—in other words, to bring a semblance of harmonic order to a confused or chaotic jumble—the effect is pleasing. Form then may be looked upon as the perception of unity in variety, where by a conscious and attentive effort, we are able to bring comprehension to what might otherwise not be understood. In this sense, it is an activity of mind as well as of perception. The elements may stimulate and excite, but it is the mind that synthesizes, that has an insight into the order of the elements.

Santayana goes on to discuss various aspects of form which illustrate both its aesthetic value and its dangerous (from an aesthetic point of view) possibilities. There is unity in variety, as noted, but also there is multiplicity in uniformity. The starry skies present to us a picture of an infinite number of similar bodies. The field that is the sky is peppered by a multiplicity of objects that is overwhelming, yet they do not blend into one, for each retains (or at least enough do) its individuality. In its presentation to us the heavens' beauty is increased by the very material composing it—the blackness of the heavens glittering with the light of the stars—so that form and substance are blended in perfect union.

It should be noted that multiplicity as an aesthetic component may lead to boredom and disinterest if not properly presented. The attention span of the individual and his ability to synthesize may be brief when the same elements are given repeatedly. Just as sheer variety becomes another name for confusion, so multiplicity is synonymous with dullness when presented for its own sake.

Aestheticians have long pondered the question, "Are all things beautiful?" Santayana addresses himself to this question, and it is not difficult, cued as we are by what has been presented of his system so far, to guess what his reply would be. Since the world independent of consciousness and will would be valueless, and since what is good (or beautiful) depends upon our desires, nothing in principle can be ruled out as a possible object of beauty. One makes a mistake, however, if one concludes from this possibility that everything is equally beautiful. As Santayana states: "All things are not equally beautiful because the subjective bias that discriminates between them is the cause of their being beautiful at all. The principle of personal preference is the same as that of human taste; real and objective beauty, in contrast to a vagary of individuals, means only an affinity to a more prevalent and lasting susceptibility, a response to a more general and fundamental demand. And the keener discrimination, by which the distance between beautiful and ugly things is increased, far from being a loss of aesthetic insight, is a development of that faculty by the exercise of which beauty comes into the world."

The most important aspect of form, and the one which best expresses Santayana's view, is that in a neutral universe there are elements which are susceptible to the imaginative activity of our mind. By means of such activity the world is constructed by reference to ideals into unities from elements which are diverse in themselves. In this activity lies the basis for the life of reason and contemplation and for the discovery of the world of phenomena which we know and the beauty which it has. Although a naturalist in his outlook on value, Santayana comes close to a variety of Kantian idealism in his consideration of the imaginative, synthesizing character of mind by which the world of objects and the beauty therein is constructed.

In the final section of *The Sense of Beauty* the aesthetic component called "expression" is discussed. In the presence of beautiful objects the mind is affected by and contributes to both the material and the formal aspects of the aesthetic object. There is an additional feature, however, which, given the object and the mind's activity, must be mentioned. There is present, both with the immediate perception of the object and after it is no longer perceived, an emotional overtone which colors the sensation and our memory of it. This aura is the result of associations which we have made and which affect our memory as well as our immediate perceptions; this quality we call "the expression of the object."

Form and substance constitute aesthetic value in the first term, whereas expression is value in the second term. The latter value is found in the associations, the moral values, the history, the accouterments—all of which may go with the presentation of a work of art. These, accompanying the work itself, are raised to the level of beauty, when in themselves they present a joy and sweetness which transcends the utilitarian or functional character that they ordinarily have.

The difficult question which was raised earlier as to the place of tragedy as an aesthetic object in a theory which emphasizes that pleasure is beauty when seen as the quality of a thing can now be answered. It is by expression that tragedy is beautiful. The events of *Hamlet* or *Oedipus* can be imagined as reported in a newspaper; in this context they would hardly constitute that which we would call "beautiful." Moral and pathetic, perhaps, if written well, but the utility of the journalistic presentation would doubtless preclude any feeling of pleasure. The horror, the pain, the sadness of life would come through; the world of moral value, of duty, of work, and, rather than that of beauty, of play and of joy would be given to us. But these events can, when placed in the context of the theater or treated under the brush of the painter or pen of the composer, take on a positive value and thus move, as it were, to a new plane. The moral, negative in itself, may then take on the character of a first term value and become positive.

In this way we turn the evil in life into a good; we see in the tragic lesson something to be learned, something which makes us better for it, something which points toward a possible and, we hope, realizable perfection. And in the transference of the negative value into something good we prepare the way for the events to be a source of pleasure. The tragic elements are there, but through their expressiveness they have been made by mind into a thing of beauty. It is in this way that Santayana analyzes the object of beauty into its material, formal, and expressive aspects and prepares the way for an analysis of the life of reason through which man raises the world which is given, a world of no value, into one in which, ultimately, good is supreme.

WHAT IS ART?

Author: Leo Tolstoy (1828-1910)
Type of work: Aesthetics
First published: 1896

PRINCIPAL IDEAS ADVANCED

Art is the intentional communication of feelings.

The artist uses colors, sounds, words, or other materials to create an object which will provoke in the spectator the feeling the artist himself once had and which he intends to pass on to others.

True art is not only sincere, but infectious; the more widespread the appeal and effectiveness of the work as a means for the communication of feeling, the better the work is as art.

The highest art is that which communicates the feeling of brotherhood and the love for one's neighbor.

Tolstoy, like Plato, believed art too important to be judged in terms of art alone. Since art is capable of making men better or worse, better citizens or worse citizens, better men or worse men, the social and ethical consequences of art must be considered in judgments about art. Tolstoy denied that a work of art can be great but corrupting, artistically good but morally evil.

Tolstoy was sixty-eight when he published *What is Art?* thirty years after the completion of *War and Peace,* nineteen years after the completion of *Anna Karenina.* However, Tolstoy's longstanding concern with the nature and function of art is revealed by "Schoolboys and Art" (1861), an account he wrote of discussions with his pupils thirty-five years prior to publication of *What is Art?*

The answer Tolstoy finally found to the question "What is art?" is very simple. Art is the intentional communication of feelings. In a work of art the artist creates something which calls up, first in the artist and then in others, a feeling experienced by the artist. According to Tolstoy, the creation of a work of art proceeds along the following lines. First, the artist has an experience or feeling, such as fear, joy, grief, anger, hope. He then desires to share this feeling with others, to infect them with it, to give them this same feeling, to make them fearful, joyous, griefstricken, angry, or hopeful. In order to communicate his feeling to his fellow men he creates a work of art, a story, a song, a poem, a play, a painting. If he is successful, if he has created a genuine work of art, his creation will give him again his original feeling, but —and this is more important—it will give other men this same kind of feeling. Art is essentially a means of communication; it is the most direct and immediate form of communication since the very feeling which led the artist to create his work of art is experienced by his audience. The artist does not merely describe his feeling of joy or grief, nor does he merely reveal or show his feeling of anger or fear; the artist shares his feelings with other men by creating something which makes them feel joy, grief, anger, or fear.

It is not very surprising that Tolstoy rejected as pseudo-art much of what is usually accepted as art. Art must originate with an experience or feeling of the artist. Much pseudo-art comes from insincerity, or the attempt to create a work of art which does not grow from an actual experience or feeling. The aspiring artist, lacking any feeling which could be conveyed by a genuine work of art, tries to imitate the accepted artists. In his effort to achieve recognition the artist who has nothing to communicate tries to give the public what they want by copying the popular fashions or by following the formulas learned in school. Tolstoy denies that anything created in answer to an external inducement rather than to an inner need can be genuine art.

Nevertheless, sincerity, however necessary, is not sufficient. Even if an aspiring artist is sincere, he may fail in his effort to create a work of art. The attempt to communicate the genuine feeling may be ineffective. An artist is judged not by his feelings but by his creation. Good intentions are not enough. In addition to feeling, a work of art requires adequate form. However, Tolstoy recognizes only one measure of adequate form, infectiousness. A work of art must infect the audience it must compel the audience to feel what the artist felt. Adequate form requires individuality rather than imitative repetitiousness, brevity rather than bulkiness, clarity rather than obscurity, simplicity of expression rather than complexity of form. The adequate form of a genuine work of art is shown by the universality of its appeal. A genuine work of art does not need an interpreter. A genuine work of art is not restricted to an elite, to the happy few. A genuine work of art directly and immediately creates in other men the feelings of the artist.

Art, then, demands the adequate expression of genuine feeling. However, Tolstoy adds yet a third requirement, not a requirement which determines whether something is art, but a requirement which determines whether something is good art—morally good, worthy of support and encouragement. Tolstoy recognizes that art can be morally corrupting, that art which is good art judged by the sincerity of the artist's feeling and the successful communication of this feeling might still be undesirable. The feeling communicated is also important. If the feeling or the experience which the artist is communicating is evil or perverse or trivial or silly, it is possible for the work of art to be artistically good but morally bad. Tolstoy says that art demands sacrifices not only from the artist but also from other men. The artist is a member of society; his efforts must be supported in many ways by his fellow men. The question of what kind of art is worth the sacrifice demanded is a moral question; Tolstoy's answer to this question is clearly a moral answer. The feelings communicated by a work of art are not relevant when we are trying to decide whether it is a work of art, but they are relevant when we are trying to decide whether it is good, whether it is worthy of support and encouragement.

Tolstoy rejected orthodox Christianity; he was excommunicated by the Synod of the Russian Church in 1901 and after his death in 1910 was interred without Christian burial. Tolstoy attacked Church Christianity as a corruption of the original teaching of Jesus. The brotherhood of man, the golden rule, the turning of the other cheek, love for all men, including those who hate you, are the essential teachings Tolstoy sees in the New Testament but not in the Church. There is a very close connection between Tolstoy's views on art and on religion. Art is the handmaiden of religion. The feelings communicated by the artist to his fellow men by the work of art will in the case of the best art be feelings which unite men, which increase their love for each other. The final judgment on a work of art must be a moral judgment as well as an aesthetic judgment. Tolstoy writes, "The estimation of the value of art (or rather, of the feelings it transmits) depends on men's perception of the meaning of life; depends on what they hold to be the good and evil of life."

The connection between art and religion, the service art is expected to give religion, the consequences for art of Tolstoy's perception of the meaning of life are clearly stated in the closing paragraphs of *What is Art?* "The task for art to accomplish is to make that feeling of brotherhood and love of one's neighbor, now attained only by the best members of society, the customary feeling and instinct of all men. By evoking under imaginary conditions the feeling of brotherhood and love, religious art will train men to experience those same feelings under similar circumstances in actual life; it will lay in the souls of men the rails along which the actions of those whom art thus educates will naturally pass. And universal art, by uniting the most different people in one common feeling by destroying separation, will educate people to union and will show them, not by reason but by life itself, the joy of universal union reaching beyond the bounds set by life."

Tolstoy saw in the art of the Middle Ages an example of true art. In that period religion provided a basis common to the artists and the mass of the people, so that the feelings experienced by the artist could be communicated to the mass of the people. This true art, shared by the whole community, ended when the people who rewarded and directed art lost their religious belief. The universality of the art of the Middle Ages was followed by a split between the art of the upper classes and the masses of the people. The development of an exclusive art, incomprehensible to most men, seriously weakened and almost destroyed art itself. The subject matter of art became impoverished; the only feelings acceptable for communication were pride, discontent, and sexual desire. The artist became a professional, living by his art, creating counterfeits of art rather than genuine works of art. Critics, perverted but self-confident, took away from plain men the valuation of art.

Genuine art, Tolstoy argues, needs no critics. If the work succeeds in transmitting the feeling of the artist, there is nothing for the critic to do. If the work fails to transmit the feeling of the artist, there is nothing the critic can do. The final perverted and perverting consequence Tolstoy ascribes to the reduction of art to an amusement for the upper classes is the establishment of art schools. Tolstoy, a teacher as well as an artist, denies that a school can evoke feeling in a man, or teach him how to manifest his feeling in a way which will transmit his feeling to others. Art schools destroy the capacity to produce real art in those who have the misfortune to enter them; they do nothing more than train imitators of artists, professionals who produce on demand the counterfeits of art which amuse the perverted upper classes, provide the critics with an excuse for their activity, and debase the taste of the masses.

If there is any danger that admiration for the artistic achievements of the author of *War and Peace* and *Anna Karenina* will lead to uncritical acceptance of Tolstoy's theories about the nature and purpose of art, it is more than balanced by the danger that contempt for Tolstoy's critical judgments will lead to uncritical rejection of these theories. It is quite possible that judgments of Tolstoy's point of view as perverse and even stupid (as in F. M. Cornford's introduction to Book IX of Plato's *Republic*) are caused by Tolstoy's judgments on particular works of art rather than by his theories as to the nature and purpose of art. *War and Peace, Anna Karenina,* and in fact all of his own work except the stories, *God Sees the Truth but Waits* and *A Prisoner of the Caucasus,* fall, in Tolstoy's eyes, into the category of bad art. Included with the Psalms, the writings of the Jewish prophets, the *Iliad* and *Odyssey, Don Quixote,* and *The Pickwick Papers* as examples of genuine art are Dickens' *A Christmas Carol, Uncle Tom's Cabin,* and Millet's drawing "The Man with the Hoe." Tolstoy praises as true art Pushkin's short stories and poems, but calls *Boris Godunov* "a cold, brain-spun work" produced under the influence of false criticism. Sophocles, Euripides, Aeschylus, Aristophanes, Dante, Milton, Shakespeare, Goethe, Raphael, Michelangelo, Bach, Beethoven, Wagner—these are among the artists judged and found wanting by Tolstoy. Michelangelo's "Last Judgment" is called absurd; Beethoven's piano sonata in A major, Opus 101 (Hammerclavier) is bad art because it "artificially evoked obscure, almost unhealthy, excitement"; Beethoven's Ninth Symphony is bad art because it neither transmits the highest religious feeling nor unites all men in one common feeling; from *Hamlet* Tolstoy received "that peculiar suffering which is caused by false imitations of works of art." Baudelaire is criticized on two counts: the feelings transmitted are "evil and very base" and these feelings are expressed with "eccentricity and lack of clearness," in fact with "premeditated obscurity." Baudelaire is judged lacking in "naïveté, sincerity, and simplicity," but overflowing with "artificiality, forced originality, and self-assurance."

Tolstoy directs his most detailed and extensive criticism in *What is Art?* against Wagner's operas. He describes a performance of *Siegfried.* Tolstoy calls this a "model work of counterfeit art so gross as to be even ridiculous." He was unable to sit through the entire performance and "escaped from the theatre with a feeling of repulsion." Tolstoy sees in *Siegfried* almost everything he detests in pseudo-art. It would be incomprehensible to a peasant with unperverted taste; it is accepted because fashionable by the "cream of the cultured upper classes"; it requires a great deal of wasted labor; it provides the art critics with an excuse for their activity; and it perverts and destroys the capacity to be infected by genuine art.

It would be a mistake to judge Tolstoy's view on art by the examples he chooses. Tolstoy himself says that he does not attach great importance to his selection since he believes he is among those whose taste has been perverted by false training. Since the examples appear to be chosen to illustrate or ex-

plain Tolstoy's theory, they are less important than the theory itself.

Others have agreed that art is the language of emotions, that art expresses or communicates feelings. But the distinctive feature of Tolstoy's theory is his claim that the actual experience is communicated by art. We do not merely recognize that the poem is an expression of grief; we do not merely recognize that the author was moved by an authentic feeling of grief. If the poem is a genuine work of art, we grieve. The connection between art and life cannot be made closer. Tolstoy, like Plato, denies the autonomy of art, the uniqueness of aesthetic experience.

THE WILL TO BELIEVE

Author: William James (1842-1910)
Type of work: Ethics, philosophy of religion
First published: 1897

PRINCIPAL IDEAS ADVANCED

Decisions between hypotheses proposed to our belief are genuine options when they are living (of vital concern to us), forced (no third alternative is possible), and momentous (presenting a unique opportunity of considerable importance).

Whenever a genuine option cannot be settled on intellectual grounds, it is right and necessary to settle it according to our passional inclinations.

The religious option concerning the belief in God is a genuine option which promises most to the person who has the passional need to take the world religiously.

Men possess free wills which are not determined; determinism—the theory that decisions are causally determined—fails to account for the sense of human freedom.

Now a classic, this work takes its title from the first of ten separate essays written at different times. Originally presented as lectures to academic

clubs, these essays express "a tolerably definite philosophic attitude" which James named *radical empiricism*—an ordinary man's empiricism which takes experience as it comes, "seeing" even matters-of-fact as subject to possible future reinterpretation; yet radical for its rejection of dogmatic monism in the face of the obvious plurality of the things making up the universe. James also wanted to make a case for the right of men to believe some moral and religious postulates for whose certainty the evidence can never fully be on hand. Sympathetic to a wide range of philosophical viewpoints, James sought to give intellectual significance to the role of the emotions in specified contexts. He also criticized the prevailing academic opinion that only scientific methods can produce an adequate understanding of the human condition.

The first four essays ("The Will to Believe," "Is Life Worth Living?", "The Sentiment of Rationality," and "Reflex Action and Theism") are concerned directly with religious problems. Two others ("The Dilemma of Determinism" and "The Moral Philosopher and the Moral Life") also give some attention to religious aspects of ethical problems. A final essay ("What Psychical Research Has Accomplished") defends scholars who inquire into the possibility that mental life may involve phenomena which escape our ordinary scientific criteria. The remaining essays ("Great Men and Their Environment," "The Importance of Individuals," and "On Some Hegelisms") show James's concern to find common-sense facts philosophically interesting; to criticize some unexamined assumptions of rationalism; and to resist the spread of absolutist and totalist theories which swallow up the individual in an "environment," overlook human differences by stressing only similarities, and ignore diversity in emphasizing unity.

Three broad types of subject matter receive treatment in James's book. These are the nature and motives of philosophizing, the justification of religious and moral beliefs, and the nature of the moral enterprise. A common theme also runs through what would otherwise be a collection of unrelated essays. This theme is the problem of the relation of evidence to specific human beliefs. If the book has a positive thesis, it is that men may rightfully hold certain religious, moral, and metaphysical beliefs even when conclusive evidence for their adequacy is absent. James resists the positivistic tendency of his age to assume that scientific methods will prove able to decide all important questions about existence. Similarly, he expresses criticism of any extreme rationalistic reliance on logic as the sole criterion of philosophical adequacy. There are some beliefs which are truths-in-the-making. "And often enough our faith beforehand in an uncertified result *is the only thing that makes the result come true*," he writes. One comes to understand that James is moved to philosophical activity by a desire to justify the rightness of certain beliefs —that God exists, that men possess free will, that moral effort represents a genuinely objective worthiness, that pain and evil cannot justify suicide, and that practical as well as theoretical needs ought to influence one's philosophical outlook.

The book's historical influence partly stems from the nature of the problems addressed by the author. Most of these problems are close to ordinary human experience. James also reassures those thinkers who, unconvinced that a completed metaphysical system is really possible, want to resist making a forced choice between philosophical certainty and philosophical skepticism. Philosophical argument can take place fruitfully somewhere on this side of certainty, according to James. Yet such argument need not lapse into arbitrariness. Logic is a subservient instrument. It is subject to the felt needs of religious, moral, and practical demands. James argues that a qualified moral idealism need not lead to sentimentalism in escaping the twin threats of pessimism and nihilism. Some philosophical viewpoints are relatively more adequate than others even though no one viewpoint can hope to exhaust the whole domain of reality. Such a generous spirit animates James's essays that even critics who are unpersuaded by some of the arguments nonetheless recognize in them the evidences of a rare and gifted philosophical mind.

The book's opening essay is crucial for the broad way it sketches the nature, purposes, and possibilities of philosophizing. Written in 1879, "The Sentiment of Rationality" states convictions which are presupposed in James's more restricted discussions of topics in religious and moral philosophy. A number of basic questions caused James to write this essay. What is the philosophic quest really about? What are the conditions which any philosophy must meet if it is to be accepted? How can one know that the philosophic demand for a peculiar kind of rationality has been satisfactorily met?

Philosophic pursuit of a rational conception of existence marked by universality and extensiveness succeeds whenever a feeling of intellectual "ease, peace, rest" is the result. Any adequate philosophy must satisfy two kinds of human distress. One is theoretical—the intellectual concern to form a general conception of the universe. The other is practical—the moral and religious desire to include men's passional natures in any philosophical consideration of how men are to act and what they should believe.

Two cravings gnaw at the philosopher. Intellectual simplification is always one philosophic need. Simplification requires reduction of the world's numerous details to fewer significant abstractions which stress similarities. Theoretical life would be an impossibility without such abstractions. The other need is the clear demand for recognition of the perceived differences among things. Philosophic rationality results only when each of these competing impulses receives serious consideration. James insists that philosophizing involves a continuous, yet never fully successful, synthesizing of these two cravings—a mark of whose successful handling is the feeling that some original puzzlement no longer proves irritating to the mind. As an activity, philosophizing must involve the whole man. Philosophizing must therefore often give way to hosts of other intellectual quests since its own unique function is to discover a general picture of "the hang of things."

An important conviction operates at this point in James's development. It is that any metaphysical conception must remain open to future possible theoretical anxiety. Man's need of a philosophic view of the nature of things results only in partial and temporary satisfaction. Any instance of the feeling of rationality can itself founder on the shoals of the question about its justifiability. Even if the world *is* a certain way, it *might* yet be otherwise. Thus the worry about "nonentity" arises, named by James "the parent of

729

the philosophic craving in its subtilist and profoundest sense." Through awareness of a possible other state of affairs, men can lose the feeling of rationality once gained. No single logically consistent system can still man's theoretical demands when he is faced by the query: Why just this sort of world and no other? "Every generation will produce its Job, its Hamlet, its Faust, or its Sartor Resartus." Mystical ecstasy can realize the psychological equivalent of the feeling of rationality when logic proves inadequate. Yet "empiricism will be the ultimate philosophy," for even the mysteriousness of existence depends on an irreducible fact about a universe which is dissatisfying to our theoretical demands.

Exclusive concern with the theoretical impulse leads men to skepticism or to a sense of wonder about the universe. One or the other arises when a completed metaphysical system begins to wane. Does the matter end here? Denying that it does, James argues that now the practical life acquires a heightened rational significance. Practical demands play a role in one's choice of a philosophy when systems exist whose logical methods are equally sound. Men's belief that their wills can influence the future must receive justification in any important philosophical system. Men can adopt that philosophy which most fully satisfies certain moral and aesthetic requirements of human nature.

The better philosophy is always relevant to men's expectations about the future. Yet there is no one, final, "better" philosophy. For example, a philosophy which retains the notion of substance will remain a perennial contender for human acceptance. Similarly, idealism will remain a challeng-

ing possibility for thinkers requiring an identification of the universe with our personal selves, materialism for thinkers wanting an escape from selves. James concludes that temperamental differences are important in the quest after the sentiment of rationality. To be humanly acceptable, a philosophy must limit moral skepticism and satisfy men's belief that they "count" in the creation of a future world. According to James, no philosophy can succeed which ignores the practical craving after a world which is partly responsive to men's future expectations, their human faiths, and their common-sense conviction that moral striving genuinely counts for something.

Take the question: Does God exist? James rejects the agnostic argument that one ought never to hold beliefs for which conclusive evidence is lacking. Reasonable persons seek both to avoid error and to attain the maximum amount of truth. Yet there may be questions such that neither "yes" nor "no" replies are justified by existing evidence but to which men may rightfully give an affirmative belief-response. James insists that the matter of God's existence is such a question, as are questions about the importance of the individual, the value of life versus suicide, and the possible existence of human free will. *How* men treat such questions is important. James argues that men may believe certain statements for reasons of the heart when conclusive evidence is lacking and the beliefs help to initiate future discoveries of a practical kind. This thesis forces James to consider the problem of the relation of evidence to belief.

Belief involves a willingness to act on some hypothesis. James insists that any proposition may serve as a hypothesis—though he is not always clear about the form of such a hypothesis. Ordinarily, a proposition like "This litmus paper is blue" is not considered a hypothesis because it lacks a proper hypothetical form. A proposition of the form: "If this litmus paper is put into a given solution, it will turn red," is a hypothesis capable of some testing provided the proper details are supplied. But James had in mind statements of moral and religious belief whose adoption by men might result in bringing about a desired truth. One may help to make another person's attitude friendly towards himself by adopting a believing attitude toward the statement: "X is friendly towards me." Belief in some propositions is a requirement of their future possible verification. According to James, religious beliefs may often be of this kind. Religious beliefs involve one in assenting to statements for which conclusive evidence is absent. James wants to defend the right of men to hold such beliefs if they meet specified conditions. A man has an option to believe certain hypotheses in religion and morals if the hypotheses are living rather than dead, forced rather than avoidable, and momentous rather than trivial.

What makes a hypothesis "living," "forced," and "momentous" is its relation to a thinker's interests. The test here seems to be predominantly psychological and cultural, for an individual's interests are what they are, however caused. James admits that not all men will find the same hypothesis living, forced, and momentous—giving the example of a Christian confronted with the command: "Be a Theosophist or be a Mohammedan." Yet James insists that the God-hypothesis confronts men with a genuine "option," meaning that such an option is living, momentous, and forced. He argues that the agnostic who neither affirms nor denies God's existence has already decided against such an existence. The agnostic decides to give up all hope of winning a possible truth in order to avoid a possible error in a situation for which evidence must in principle be inconclusive. The agnostic's right to disbelieve in this case is no greater than the religious man's right to believe.

A critic may say at this point that James's way of arguing may encourage men to choose their beliefs by an individualistic criterion of psychological comfort—something on the order of the command: "Believe what you need to believe." James warns his readers that he is countering academic people's disregard of the passional aspects in human decision-making and that the right to believe occurs only in a matter which "cannot by its nature be decided on intellectual grounds." James apparently thinks the genuine religious option concerns the *thatness* of God's existence rather than the choice of an existing institutional means for expressing one's decision to believe in God's existence. Yet he does seem to argue, on the other hand, that those who are agnostics choose to treat the God-hypothesis as a dead one. Moral and religious options are such that, if the believer takes an affirmative stance regarding a belief, they promise that the better aspects will win out in the universe and a man will be better off for believing. One might put even the God-hypothesis in a psychological form: "If you believe that God exists, even now you will be benefited." Yet it is not clear that

James would wish to regard the force of the central religious hypothesis as purely psychological.

In discussing features of the moral landscape, James once again shows his distrust of intellectual abstractions and generalizations. He is convinced philosophers can never produce an airtight, finished moral system. Nor can moral philosophers dogmatically solve all issues in advance of actual situations. Yet James openly defends two general moral notions. One is that human demands and obligations are coextensive. The second is that men have a right to believe they are free. Any genuinely moral philosopher places his own cherished ideals and norms in the scales of rational judgment even as he realizes that no one standard measure is attainable which will apply to all occasions. The moral philosopher holds no privileged status for deciding concrete instances of conflict in human demands. James insists that the moral philosopher "only knows that if he makes a bad mistake the cries of the wounded will soon inform him of the fact."

James advances the thesis about coextensiveness of demands and obligations in the essay "The Moral Philosopher and the Moral Life." There are no intrinsically "bad" demands, since demands are simply what they are. Without them, there could be no basis of moral life. Here James seeks to give due recognition to biological and psychological facts. He wants an "ethical republic." Terms like "good" and "bad" —whose meanings constitute the metaphysical function of moral philosophizing—refer to objects of feeling and desire. Only "a mind which feels them" can realize moral relations and moral law. James insists that the moral philosopher must "vote for the richer universe"—that which can accommodate the widest possible range of human wants. Yet James fails to make clear how the philosopher may determine what should pass as the richer universe if all demands have equal status in principle. On this issue James seems to appeal to intuition, for he argues that "the nobler thing *tastes* better"—indicating that he recognized that some demands are more appealing than others.

The most suggestive essay concerned with a moral issue is "The Dilemma of Determinism," in which James argues that, though no proof is possible, man does possess free will. This is a unique defense of indeterminism which presupposes a metaphysical position; namely, that the universe is in reality a pluriverse containing objective possibilities of novelty. The problem which concerns him is that of the relation of freedom to chance rather than of freedom to cause. "Chance" is a relative word which tells one nothing about that of which it is predicated. "Its origin is in a certain fashion negative: it escapes, and says, Hands off! coming, when it comes, as a free gift, or not at all." James disliked the contemporary distinction between "hard" and "soft" forms of determinism. The "soft" form of determinism argues that causality is quite compatible with responsible action and ethical judicability. What James wanted to discover is the metaphysical view necessary to determinism. He concluded it is a view which takes possibilities never actualized as mere illusions. James insists that determinism is unable to give adequate account of human feelings about possibility—the feeling that the universe contains genuine choices or alternatives, objectively real risks. Indeterminism insists that future volitions can be ambiguous, and "indeterminate future volitions *do* mean chance."

According to James, determinism results in an unavoidable dilemma. It must lead either to pessimism or to subjectivism. Men share a universe which daily calls for judgments of regret about some things happening in it. But if events are strictly necessitated, they can never be otherwise than what they are. Taken seriously, human regrets suggest that though some feature of the universe could not have been different, yet it would have been better if it were different. This reasoning leads to pessimism. James argues that men can give up pessimism only if they jettison their judgments of regret. Men can perhaps regard regrettable incidents—including the most atrocious murders—as teleological links in a chain leading to some higher good. Murder and treachery then cease to be evils. But a definite price must be paid for such a teleological optimism. The original judgments of regret were themselves necessitated, on the determinist's position. Some other judgments should have existed in their place. "But as they are necessitated, nothing else *can* be in their place." This means that whether men are pessimists or optimists, their judgments are necessitated.

One escape from this pessimism-optimism impasse is to adopt subjectivism. The practical impulse to realize some objective moral good can be subordinated to a theoretical development of an understanding of what is involved in goodness and evil. The facts of the universe can be valued only insofar as they produce consciousness in men. Subjectivism emphasizes the knowledge of good and evil in order to underscore the nature of human involvement. Experience rather than the objective goodness or badness of experience becomes the crucial factor for any moral subjectivism. But the indeterminist must reject subjectivism because it fails to do justice to men's empirical notions of the genuinely *moral* significance of human experiences. In addition, subjectivism leads to mere sentimentality and romanticism.

James concludes that common sense informs men that objective right and wrong involve real limits. Practical reason insists that "conduct, and not sensibility, is the ultimate fact for our recognition." Only indeterminism can make sense out of this practical insistence on objective right and wrong. Yet indeterminism does not argue that Providence is necessarily incompatible with free will. In an example involving chess, James shows how Providence can be like a master chess player who, though knowing the ultimate outcome of the game, must face unpredictable moves by an amateur player. On the other hand, James concludes that indeterminism gives men a special view—"It gives us a pluralistic, restless universe, in which no single point of view can ever take in the whole scene." James concludes that men have a right to be indeterminists and to believe in free will even in the absence of a persuasively final proof.

THE RIDDLE OF THE UNIVERSE

Author: Ernst Heinrich Haeckel (1834-1919)
Type of work: Philosophy of nature
First published: 1899

PRINCIPAL IDEAS ADVANCED

A scientific philosophy must join experience with speculation.

The greatest triumphs of science, including the cellular theory and the theory of evolution, are philosophic achievements.

In a scientific age a monistic philosophy is necessary, one in which matter and spirit are abstractions from a single physical nature, attributes of the universal substance.

Man is distinguishable quantitatively, but not qualitatively, from the lower animals.

Haeckel was one of the leading biologists of the nineteenth century, best known today for his formulation of the "Biogenetic Law": "Ontogenesis is a brief and rapid recapitulation of phylogenesis." That is, the embryo of an animal in its developments passes successively through stages in which it resembles adult forms of its evolutionary ancestors. He was the first German biologist who wholeheartedly supported Darwin's theories, in the popularization of which he did for Germany what Thomas Henry Huxley did for England. In *Die Welträtsel* (literally, "The World-Riddles"), which was an enormously popular book, he attempted to present an overall picture of the universe and man's place therein, in accordance with the new insights of evolutionary theory.

Despite the suggestion of mystery in its title, the work is emphatically not skeptical. As far as Haeckel was concerned, the world-riddles had been solved. In 1880 the eminent physiologist Emil Du Bois-Reymond enumerated seven enigmas: (1) The nature of matter and force, (2) the origin of motion, (3) the origin of life, (4) the (apparently preordained) orderly arrangement of nature, (5) the origin of simple sensation and consciousness, (6) rational thought and the origin of speech, and (7) the question of the freedom of the will. Du Bois-Reymond declared the first, second, and fifth to be utterly "transcendental" and insoluble; the third, fourth, and sixth to be possibly soluble; and he professed ignorance as to which group the seventh belonged. On the contrary, wrote Haeckel, the "transcendental" problems are settled by the monist conception of substance; the third, fourth, and sixth are already "decisively answered by the theory of evolution"; while "the freedom of the will is not an object for critical, scientific inquiry at all, for it is a pure dogma, based on an illusion, and has no real existence."

The nineteenth century, drawing to its close as Haeckel wrote, was the century of science. It saw great advances in chemistry, particularly in the chemistry of carbon; in physics the unity of forces in the entire universe was at last established, as well as the highly important Law of Substance —encompassing the principles of conservation for energy and matter. The greatest discoveries were in biology: the cellular theory and organic evolution. Technical progress in every field was immense.

All this should have effected a revolution in philosophy, but it did not. Because of churchly opposition to enlightenment, in conjunction with the political policies of ignorant and reactionary lawyers, the progress of science has not been equaled in moral and social life. "And from this obvious conflict there have arisen," Haeckel wrote, "not only an uneasy sense of dismemberment and falseness, but even the danger of grave catastrophes in the political and social world." Anthropism, "that powerful and worldwide group of erroneous opinions which opposes the human organism to the whole of the rest of nature, and represents it to be the preordained end of the organic creation, an entity essentially distinct from it, a godlike being," still reigned. It could be overthrown only by a scientific philosophy.

In his scientific philosophy Haeckel intended to join experience with speculation. Plato and Hegel on the one hand, Bacon and Mill on the other, were too one-sided. "The greatest triumphs of modern science—the cellular theory, the dynamic theory of heat, the theory of evolution, and the law of substance—are *philosophic achievements*; not, however, the fruit of pure speculation, but of an antecedent experience of the widest and most searching character."

At the time there were two prevailing kinds of philosophy: dualistic (or supernatural) and monistic. Monism, in the tradition of Spinoza and Goethe, held that "matter cannot exist and be operative without spirit, nor spirit without matter." It was therefore distinct from materialism. (But Haeckel, of course, regarded the classical and nineteenth century materialists as allies against supernaturalism.) A monistic world-view was inevitable once the implications of the laws of substance and of evolution had been grasped.

The place of man in nature had to be clearly specified. Haeckel expounded the facts of comparative anatomy to show that man is a vertebrate, a tetrapod, a mammal, a placental, a primate, a catarrhine, and, among the catarrhines, much more closely allied to the anthropoid apes than the latter are to the cynopitheci on the next rung down. He outlined the evolutionary explanation of this classification.

According to Haeckel, if man is continuous physically with the rest of nature, so is he also in soul. For ". . . we consider the *psyche* to be *merely a collective idea of all the psychic functions of protoplasm*. In this sense the 'soul' is merely a physiological abstraction like 'assimilation' or 'generation.'" Psychology is "a section of physiology." In accordance with this conception, Haeckel presented a mass of data (of the sort later emphasized by the behaviorist psychologists) in the attempt to show that gradations of sensibility, spontaneous movement, reflex action, and memory correspond in their complexity to the degrees of organization of the evolutionary scale. Man is not distinguishable qualitatively, only quantitatively, from the lower animals with respect to intelligence, emotions, and even language. Indeed, Haeckel argued, there is a greater difference between Goethe and an Australian than between an Australian and a dog. (We are not told why this alleged fact is not a counter-instance to the correlation of bodily structure and mental ability.)

The Riddle of the Universe states that psychic qualities, like bodily ones, are inherited; they are determined at the moment the sperm cell penetrates the ovum. (But Haeckel agreed with Chevalier de Lamarck that acquired characteristics can to some degree be passed on to descendants; he was aware of, but rejected, August Weismann's theory of the continuity of the germ plasm.) In an individual, "psychic life runs the same evolution—upward progress, full maturity, and downward degeneration—as every other vital activity in his organization."

For Haeckel, the will, as simply one mode of psychic activity, is thoroughly determined by heredity and adaptation. Consequently, there could be no question of exceptions from the iron laws of nature.

Consciousness, which Haeckel distinguished from sensibility, is described as "the central mystery of psychology." Haeckel pointed out that much psychic life—in man as well as in other animals—is unconscious, and that the higher animals are obviously conscious too, as the comparative physiological effects of narcotics, anaesthetics, and hypnotism demonstrate. But where consciousness begins on the scale of animal life is impossible to determine. Perhaps the centralization of the nervous system is a prerequisite. Haeckel did not believe that consciousness is an inherent property of all matter, but he argued that unconscious sensation and will do pertain essentially to matter. In man and the higher animals, at any rate, brain physiology has succeeded in locating the actual seat ("or preferably the organ") of consciousness.

Belief in the immortality of the soul, "that highest point of superstition," is not universal, not occurring in Buddhism, Confucianism, or early Judaism. The "typically Christian idea is thoroughly materialistic and anthropomorphic," being that of the resurrection of the body. The more metaphysical conception, stemming from Plato, really amounts to the theory that the soul is a gas. But if it were (Haeckel observes, with ponderous Teutonic *Witz*), "we could then catch the soul as it is 'breathed out' at the moment of death, condense it, and exhibit it in a bottle as 'immortal fluid' (*fluidum animae immortale*). By a further lowering of temperature and increase of pressure it might be possible to solidify it—to produce 'soul-snow.' The experiment has not yet succeeded." And in any case, he wrote, it would be a dreadful thing if the soul *were* immortal.

So much for man. As for the universe at large, the fundamental principle for its understanding is the law of substance, which "in the ultimate analysis is found to be a necessary consequence of the principle of causality." Taking energy to be the same as Spinoza's "thought," Haeckel declares: "To this profound thought of Spinoza our purified monism returns after a lapse of two hundred years; for us, too, matter (space-filling substance) and energy (moving force) are but two inseparable attributes of the one underlying substance." Matter is of two sorts: the ordinary kind, and ether, "the existence of which as a real element is a *positive fact*, and has

736

been known as such for the last twelve years." The relation of these two is, Haeckel admits, obscure. Perhaps matter is a sort of "condensation" from ether. Empedocles was right, in principle, in making Love a cosmic force; for there is a *unity of affinity in the whole of nature,* from the simplest chemical process to the most complicated love story."

The universe is a perpetual-motion machine, infinite in extent and duration. Processes within it are cyclic. "Hence the theory of *entropy* is untenable," because if it were true, the universe would have a beginning and end, a state of affairs "untenable in the light of our monistic and consistent theory of the eternal cosmogenetic process. . . ."

Haeckel outlines the history of the earth (in accordance with the nebular hypothesis of Kant and Laplace), of life (though he holds that living creatures must have originated spontaneously at some time, he does not speculate on the details of this), and of man. Teleology, Haeckel observes, has long been banished from the inorganic sciences, which are consequently atheistic. Darwin banished it from biology too. It is not only fruitless but in error ever to regard evolution as a purposive process, as is shown by instances of dysteleology such as the survival of the vermiform appendix. Haeckel put himself in opposition to all "philosophy of history." The phrase "survival of the fittest" carried no moral implications for him. While all processes are rigidly determined, they are at the same time subject to "chance" in the sense of absence of aim or purpose.

The Riddle of the Universe deals with theory of knowledge, but somewhat sketchily. Sensations, synthesized by association in consciousness, produce presentations—"internal pictures of the external objects given us in sensation." By comparison we know that there is a consensus of normal observers. The presentations of normal observers "we call *true,* and we are convinced that their content corresponds to the knowable aspect of things. We *know* that these facts are not imaginary, but real." Skeptical objections that "the brain, or the soul, only perceives a certain condition of the stimulated nerve, and that, consequently, no conclusion can be drawn from the process as to the existence and nature of the stimulating environment" are dismissed by arguing that in the evolutionary process the different sense-organs have developed their specificity to various classes of stimuli by adaptation from originally undifferentiated sense-cells.

"The presentations which fill up the gaps in our knowledge, or take its place, may be called, in a broad sense, 'faith.'" For Haeckel a conception of knowledge (such as positivism) attempting to dispense with theories and hypotheses is impossible. Religious faith, however, is quite a different thing from scientific hypotheses, since the former is incompatible with the facts of observation.

The remainder of the book is devoted mostly to a polemic against Christianity in general and Roman Catholicism in particular, and to an outline of monist religion and ethics. (In this section occurs the famous description of the God of popular religion as a "gaseous vertebrate.") The world-system of the modern scientist is pantheism. Atheism is "only another expression for it, emphasizing its negative aspect, the nonexistence of any supernatural deity." The three goddesses of the monist are truth, beauty, and virtue. Goodness consists in charity and toleration, compassion and assistance. Ethics can be scientific, for science shows that the feeling of duty rests "on the solid ground of *social instinct*." Egoism and altruism are both natural laws and equally indispensable. The Golden Rule (found in many cultures antedating Christianity) is the supreme principle. While Christ was an admirable man, "the noble prophet and enthusiast, so full of the love of humanity," he was far below the level of classical culture, even though his father was Greek (so Haeckel informs us). Even purified Christianity is ethically objectionable in despising egoism: " 'If any man will take away thy coat, let him have thy cloak also,' translated into the terms of modern politics, means: 'When the pious English take from you simple Germans one after another of your new and valuable colonies in Africa, let them have all the rest of your colonies also—or, best of all, give them Germany itself.' " In despising the body Christianity leads to dirtiness; in denying souls to animals it condones cruelty; in despising earthly goods it is inimical to civilization; in deprecating sex it dishonors love and the family. But Haeckel believed that science was on the march and would someday supercede much of Christian dogma. The "free societies" of monists, he predicted, would decorate not with madonnas and crucifixions but with paintings of the beauties of nature, such as the radiolaria, the thalamophora, and the medusae.

Haeckel had the type of mind to which broad outlines are more con-

genial than fussy details; this was evident even in his biological researches. And though throughout his life he served honorably, even heroically, in the forefront of the battle for freedom of thought and liberal politics against entrenched reaction and bigotry, he was nevertheless tenacious, even vain, of his own opinions, tending always to answer criticism with abuse. In consequence, even the biological sections of *The Riddle of the Universe* present as settled facts many theories which were exploded, or at least qualified, at the time of writing. Outside biology Haeckel had no competence at all, as his ludicrously dogmatic remarks on ether and the law of entropy make painfully clear.

The "monism" that Haeckel served up as the new philosophy is almost too vague for criticism. To say merely that entities so *prima facie* disparate as sensation, will, and life are inherent properties of "one substance" is not to produce a philosophy, much less a "monistic" one, in any but a trivial verbal sense.

The main objection to Haeckel as a philosopher is that he fails to come to grips at all with those problems that are incumbent upon a thinker of his point of view to treat: principally the well-known epistemological objections against identifying consciousness with brain activity. It is not enough just to show, however elaborately, that without a brain there is no thought.

Nevertheless, to show the absolute necessity of the brain itself to thought *is* the indispensable first step to a satisfactory philosophy of mind. And if today we can take it for granted and pass immediately to (perhaps) subtler theorizing, we can do so only because Haeckel (among others) in the nineteenth century transformed into solid fact what from Lucretius to Dietrich von Holbach had been only speculation.

In this and other respects Haeckel deserves some sort of praise or homage for having helped to create the general climate of opinion in which a more satisfactory scientific philosophy can be worked out. That man, including his "soul," is a part of nature, and not exempt from scientific study, is now an axiom of educated thought everywhere except in a few citadels of medievalism. It was not so when Haeckel wrote—when Darwin was forbidden to be mentioned in the German schools, and had not even been heard of in Tennessee.

The modern reader may find it quaint that Haeckel argues so solemnly for conclusions that are now commonplace. His boisterous attacks on religion may even be deemed offensive, being contrary to the amiable doctrine that there has never been a war between science and religion. But there was, to paraphrase Galileo; and even those who find it convenient to assume that at any rate the war has been terminated should not be so ungrateful as to refuse Haeckel some gratitude for this happy state of affairs.

THE WORLD AND THE INDIVIDUAL

Author: Josiah Royce (1855-1916)
Type of work: Metaphysics
First published: Vol. I, 1900; Vol. II, 1901

PRINCIPAL IDEAS ADVANCED

Being can be understood as an absolute system of ideas which embody the fulfillment of purposes.

All knowledge is of matters of experience.

The individual self must be defined in ethical terms by reference to a life plan.

As a free individual each person by his will contributes to the world and to God's will.

Although no perfection is to be found in the temporal world, the Eternal Order is perfect.

Because we are finite, union with the infinite God is realized.

Professor Josiah Royce of Harvard University has proved to be the most durable American proponent of what is, for the most part, an outworn metaphysical creed: Absolute Idealism. *The World and the Individual* is composed of two series of Gifford Lectures delivered before the University of Aberdeen in 1899 and 1900, the first entitled "The Four Historical Conceptions of Being," and the second, "Nature, Man, and the Moral Order." In

739

these lectures Royce developed, with some significant changes, earlier ideas which he had presented in such works as *The Religious Aspects of Philosophy* (1885) and *Studies of Good and Evil* (1898).

A statement of the core of Royce's philosophical position appears in the last lecture of the second volume: "The one lesson of our entire course has thus been the lesson of the unity of finite and of infinite, of temporal dependence and of eternal significance, of the World and all its Individuals, of the One and the Many, of God and Man. Not only in spite, then, of our finite bondage, but because of what it means and implies, we are full of the presence and the freedom of God."

This is a truly revealing statement considered not only as a condensation of Royce's central claim, but also as indicating the characteristic mode of argument which gives Royce's philosophy its individual content and flavor, distinguishing it from other Hegelian idealisms. For what does Royce maintain?—That from man's finitude, God's infinite presence and freedom follow. Royce supposed that the finite, the limited, is conceivable only by comparison with an actual infinitude. It is as if he had argued that man, in virtue of his limitations, suggests the actual unlimited, the Absolute—otherwise, there would be no sense in saying that man is "limited," that he does not come up to the mark. We are reminded of Descartes' argument that knowledge of man's imperfection leads to knowledge of the actuality of God's perfection and, hence, of God's existence.

If we consider the general character of Royce's argument, we can see that it takes the form of the claim that from imperfection, knowledge of perfection follows. Hence, from knowledge of purpose, knowledge of fulfillment follows; from knowledge of error, or of its possibility, knowledge of the actuality of truth follows; from knowledge of the partial, knowledge of the Absolute; from knowledge of the individual, knowledge of the community —and from knowledge of the unfulfilled and finite individual and community, knowledge of the fulfilled, infinite, "Individual of Individuals," God himself, follows.

To appreciate the character of this argument, used by Royce in these several ways, we have only to turn to an earlier essay, "The Possibility of Error." In this essay, a chapter from *The Religious Aspect of Philosophy*, Royce argued that the possibility of error implies the actuality of "an infinite unity of conscious thought to which is present all possible thought." Royce suggested that an error is a thought which aims at being a complete thought in regard to its chosen object, and it is only by comparing the incomplete or inadequate thought with a complete or adequate thought that the incomplete thought can be known to be erroneous. Furthermore, not only could the error not be *known* to be erroneous were there not a complete thought present to a thinker who could compare the complete thought with the erroneous thought, but the error could not even be an error were there not such an actual complete thought and actual, knowing thinker. For how could the idea be incomplete by reference or comparison to *nothing*, or by reference to something other than a thought; no, for an error to be an error, an actual, adequate thought (and thinker) must exist. Since "there must be possible an infinite mass of error," there must be *actual* an infinite, all-knowing thought.

A pragmatist such as William James or Charles Sanders Peirce would say that a belief can be understood to be erroneous *if* what one *would* receive in the way of experience, *were* one to act appropriately, *would* run counter to one's expectations. But the mere *possibility* of a more satisfactory and adequate experience was not enough for Royce. Unless there were *actually* a complete idea, no belief could possibly be erroneous, for no belief could fail to measure up to a complete idea unless there actually were such a complete idea.

In the Preface to *The World and the Individual* Royce writes: "As to the most essential argument regarding the true relations between our finite ideas and the ultimate nature of things, I have never varied, in spirit, from the view maintained in . . . *The Possibility of Error*. . . ." He goes on to refer to a number of books in which the argument was used, and then states that "In the present lectures this argument assumes a decidedly new form. . . ." The argument in its new form is presented in Chapter VII of the first volume of *The World and the Individual*, the chapter entitled "The Internal and the External Meaning of Ideas." Here the argument concludes with the fourth (and final) conception of Being considered by Royce: "*What is, or what is real, is as such the complete embodiment, in individual form and in final fulfilment, of the internal meaning of finite ideas.*" The three conceptions of Being which Royce examined and rejected prior to settling upon this final idea were those of realism, mysticism, and critical rationalism. The fourth conception of Being, for all of the novelty of its presentation, is fundamentally that with which readers of Royce's earlier works are familiar; and the argument in its support is, strictly speaking, not a new argument distinguishable from the one to be found in "The Possibility of Error" and *The Conception of God* (1897), but—as Royce himself wrote —the argument in "a decidedly new form."

To understand the argument in its new form a distinction must be drawn, in Royce's terms, between the "internal and external meaning" of ideas. According to Royce, an idea "is as much an instance of will as it is a knowing process"; that is, an idea is a partial fulfillment of the purposive act of desiring to have an adequate conception of something. By the "internal meaning" of an idea Royce meant the "conscious embodiment" of the purpose in the idea. If I try to get a clear idea about someone, then to the extent that my thoughts are directed by that interest and come to have something of the content they would have were I entirely clear in my conception, then to that extent my idea has internal meaning. Unless to some extent I fulfill the purpose of my thought by thinking accurately, I cannot be said to have an object of thought: in thinking about someone, I have to think accurately enough, at least, to identify him as the object of my conception. Internal meaning, then, is a function of, and consequence of, human will and purpose.

But ideas refer beyond themselves to something external, not part of their content. And Royce asks, "How is it possible that an idea, which is an idea

741

essentially and primarily because of the inner purpose that it consciously fulfils by its presence, also possesses a meaning that in any sense appears to go beyond this internal purpose?" The answer is that the external meaning of an idea is the "completely embodied internal meaning of the idea." Or, in other words, a finite thought fulfills itself to some extent by managing to be *about* something; but what the thinker aims at is a more complete and adequate idea, a fuller conception, one that fulfills his purpose in thinking. Yet unless there is such an adequate idea, such an external meaning, then the incomplete thought, the unfulfilled idea, the partial conception, aims at nothing; and if it has no objective, it cannot fail; and if it cannot fail, it cannot be incomplete or partial. Hence, the possibility of unfulfilled internal meanings implies the actuality of external meanings; and the totality of external meanings is God. God is the "Other," the fulfillment of purpose, which alone can be the object of thought. An idea is true to the extent that it "corresponds, even in its vagueness, to its own final and completely individual expression."

Royce built his conception of God in such a manner that God, or that Being which is the absolute fulfillment of all individual wills, "sees the one plan fulfilled through all the manifold lives, the single consciousness winning its purpose by virtue of all the ideas, of all the individual selves, and of all the lives."

Another insight which serves to illuminate Royce's philosophy and his method is the realization that for Royce, "the world is real only as the object of true ideas." This proposition is not peculiar to us because we tend to interpret the word "object" as we choose in order to adjust the claim to our own philosophies. But realize that, for Royce, to be the "object" of an idea is to be that at which the idea aims, its objective; and the objective of the idea (of the thinker) is a completely adequate thought, one that fulfills his original purpose in thinking. Hence, if "the world is real only as the object of true ideas," the world is real only as an absolutely adequate thought, itself an expression of will. The consequence is that God alone is real—but, then, in so far as any individual or any thought fulfills the purpose which has being because of the finite individuals and wills, then just to that extent the finite individual or thought has Being, is part of Being. Thus, unity is achieved despite the variety and finitude of things. The individual contributes to the Being who fulfills the purposes of the individuals.

With the final conception of Being, the first volume of *The World and the Individual* comes to a close. In *Nature, Man, and the Moral Order*, the second volume of these Gifford Lectures, Royce worked out the implications of his conception in order to present an idealistic theory of knowledge, a philosophy of nature, a doctrine about self, a discussion of the human individual, a portrait of the world as "a Moral Order," a study of the problem of evil, and some conclusions concerning the bearing of these matters on natural religion.

Royce's idealistic theory of knowledge is a reaffirmation of his central predisposition to accept as real only that which fulfills the purpose of an individual will. Realists talk about "hard" facts, he writes, but analysis shows that "hard" facts are understandable as facts which enable us "even now to accomplish our will better than we could if we did not acknowledge these facts." A fact is *"that which I ought to recognize* as determining or limiting what I am here consciously to do or to attempt." A distinction is drawn between the ethical Ought, definable by reference to a more rational purpose than our own, and a theoretical Ought, definable by reference to a world of recognized facts which embodies and fulfills purposes. To know, then to apprehend a fact, is to come to have the thought which the present thought would be were its purpose (its internal meaning) fulfilled by further considerations (the external meaning); to know is to think what you *ought* to think relative to the purpose of your thought. Facts are *objective* in that they are *"other than"* the present, incomplete thoughts; our grounds for acknowledging facts are *subjective* in that they are related to our purposes, the intentions of our wills; but the objective and subjective are synthesized by "the essential *Teleological* constitution of the realm of facts . . ."—a teleological constitution which is understood once reality or Being is recognized as absolutely ordered and fulfilling will.

Royce argues that to us who see the reality in a fragmentary fashion, facts appear to be disconnected; but there is, he claims, a linkage of facts which illuminates the particular character of each fact. Analogously, through temporal failures and efforts the reality of eternal fulfillment is won.

To Royce it appears that our wills are such that they cannot be satisfied by the mere addition of content, additional facts; for the full expression of will, other wills are necessary. Finally, fulfillment comes only from a system of wills which is such that Being is a unity, a one out of many, a will (the Individual of Individuals) which is the infinite, eternal embodiment of individual wills which, by their temporal efforts, have contributed to the reality of the whole.

According to Royce, the idea that nature is hopelessly divided between matter and mind is itself the product of a scientific enterprise motivated by social concerns. The fulfillment of that social concern is best served by recognizing the unsatisfactory character of a conception which maintains a diversity in nature, an irreconcilable tension between matter and mind. The conception of the natural world "as directly bound up with the experiences of actually conscious beings" is more in accord with the Fourth Conception of Being which the first series of lectures was designed to advance. The idea of a nonconscious, nonliving, nonwilling reality is unacceptable, for to *be,* to be *real,* is to be the conscious fulfillment of purpose. Thus, if nature is real, nature is the conscious fulfillment of purpose.

The idea of the human self is constructed not by reference to any "Soul-Substance" but, as we might expect, by reference to an "Intent always to remain another than my fellows despite my divinely planned unity with them. . . ." There is no conflict between individual selves and the Divine Will, "for the Divine Will gets expressed in the existence of me the individual only in so far as this Divine Will . . . includes within itself my own will, as one of its own purposes."

In order to justify the claim that reality exhibits a moral order, Royce insists that every evil deed must sometime be "atoned for" or "overruled" by some individual self; in this manner, perfection of the whole is realized. The evil of this world is in its incompleteness, its partial fulfillment of purposes—but since the incomplete, the unfulfilled, make sense only by reference to an actual Absolute, by being incomplete they make Being possible as an ordered whole.

Royce regarded God, or Absolute Being, as a person, that is, as "a conscious being, whose life, temporally viewed, seeks its completion through deeds. . . ." God is the totality of all conscious efforts, but viewed eternally, God is an infinite whole which includes temporal process. Man is also a person, but not absolute; his reality finally consists in God's reality—God and man are one.

Since the self possesses individuality, a uniqueness of purpose, it can be satisfied only by what is Other, by what fulfills that purpose, namely, God. But God is eternal. Consequently, the immortality of self is assured.

One can come to understand, provided he views Royce's arguments with sympathetic tolerance, how if the self is realized only in God, there is a sense in which the self (the individual) and God are one—although viewed from the varying perspectives of time and purpose, they are distinct. But if the self and God are one, then, in the respect in which they are one, they are alike: God's eternity, then, is man's; and this is man's immortality. Although the individual self, in being distinguished from other selves by his peculiar purposive striving, is only par-

tial; yet, in contributing to the reality of the Absolute and in becoming unified with the Absolute, it is itself absolute. The part is equal to the whole, even though, considered otherwise than by reference to the final unity, the part is distinguishable from the whole.

One cannot fail to be persuaded of Royce's moral sincerity and intellectual acumen for *The World and the Individual* is eloquent witness to both. Fantastic as the idealistic image is to the realist who presupposes an unconcerned and unconscious material world as the barren scene of his pointless adventures, it has a certain intellectual charm and moral persuasiveness to one who is willing to sympathize with the interest that leads a man such as Royce to fail to understand how anything could be *real*, could be worthy of the honorific name "being," which did not show itself to be a conscious effort to go beyond the limits of fragmentary knowledge and experience to a recognition of and identity with the whole of such effort. If such a proposition as, "All Being is the fulfillment of purpose," is taken not as a description of the facts of the matter in regard to the kind of world the physicist studies, but as a suggestion that all human effort be directed to the ideal coöperation of all seekers after truth and goodness, *The World and the Individual* comes to be recognizable as a revolutionary manifesto directed to the human spirit— something quite different from the naïve speculative expression of an idealistic philosopher remote from the world of hard facts and hard men.

AESTHETIC

Author: Benedetto Croce (1866-1952)
Type of work: Aesthetics, metaphysics
First published: 1901

PRINCIPAL IDEAS ADVANCED

Art is intuition, and intuition is the expression of impressions.

A sense impression or image becomes an expression, or intuition, when it is clearly known as an image, and when it is unified by the feeling it represents.

The externalization of works of art by the fashioning of physical objects which will serve as stimuli in the reproduction of the intuitions represented is not art.

Art is not concerned with the useful, the moral, or the intellectual.

The fanciful combining of images is not art.

Intuitions are of individuals, not universals.

The theoretical activity of the spirit has two forms: the aesthetic and the logical; the practical activity is composed of the economic and the moral.

The aesthetic values are the beautiful (the expressive) and the ugly; the logical values are the true and the false; the economic values are the useful and the useless; and the moral values are the just and the unjust.

Benedetto Croce's *Aesthetic as Science of Expression and General Linguistic* is the first of three volumes comprising Croce's *Philosophy of the Spirit;* the other two volumes are the *Logic* and the *Philosophy of the Practical.* Croce is generally regarded as an inspired proponent of the idealist strain in philosophy, and the *Aesthetic,* the introduction to his theory, continues to be the work for which he is known; and, it is by his aesthetic theory that he is judged.

The entire thesis of the *Aesthetic* rests on the concept of intuition, and because of the ambiguity of that term, Croce's work has never received the critical attention which is possible for those capable of reading the work in the original Italian. No English term, used without careful qualification, has enough levels of meaning, enough systematic ambiguity, to carry the burden of Croce's central idea. If, in addition,

as may very well be the case, one must bring to the reading of the *Aesthetic* a certain tolerance of mind which the prevailing empiricist temper makes difficult, it becomes even more evident that one must resist the temptation to understand Croce all at once; the idea, however deceptively direct its initial expression, must be built with great care, according to Croce's plan.

With this warning in mind, it becomes possible to take certain phrases as initial statements of Croce's position, retaining them as expressions to be illuminated by further discussion and reflection, for otherwise they are practically meaningless. Thus, for Croce, art is intuition, intuition is expression; art is the expression of impressions, and expression is the objectification of feelings by way of representative images. Many negations follow from these affirmations; of them, the most important, for those who would understand Croce, is the denial that the work of art is a physical object.

Croce begins the *Aesthetic* with a careful elaboration of the distinction between intuitive and logical knowledge; it is a distinction which bears some resemblance to Bergson's distinction between intuitive and scientific or conceptual knowledge, but there is a difference. Bergson seemed to be concerned to argue that certain matters cannot be understood analytically or by classes; they must be *felt*, in their internal particularity; to know by *being*: that is intuition. For Croce, the distinction between the object as known from the outside and as realized by itself is not the critical distinction, although it is encompassed by the distinction he does stress; for Croce, intuitive knowledge is the possession of images, but of images clarified by the attention of spirit, freed of all vagueness by the act of apprehension. The idea is remarkable enough to need and deserve amplification, and fortunately there are examples by the use of which Croce's idea of intuition becomes clear.

He asks how a person can be said to have an intuition of a geometrical figure, or of the contour of the island of Sicily, if he cannot draw it. The notion that the artist is skilled in the act of transferring an image from the mind to some physical surface, as if his peculiar gift were in the handling of a pencil or brush, is repudiated by Croce. Unless one possesses a sensation or impression contemplatively, realizing it as an individual image, expression has not taken place; under the influence of sentiment one may suppose that he intuits, but unless he knows an image as an expression, he deceives himself.

To enforce his point, Croce points out that the term "expression" is generally limited to verbal expression, but he uses it to cover nonverbal expressions of line, color, and sound.

Apparently, for Croce, expression is not merely the clear apprehension of an image; the image is expressive of the feeling which it evokes, and it is as expressive of feeling that it becomes full expression or intuition. Thus, in the *Breviary of the Aesthetic* (1913, like the *Aesthetic*, translated by Douglas Ainslie) Croce writes that "what gives coherence and unity to the intuition is feeling: the intuition is really such because it represents a feeling, and can only appear from and upon that." He then goes on to affirm that "Not the idea, but the feeling, is what confers upon art the airy lightness of the symbol: an aspiration enclosed in the circle of a representation —that is art. . . ."

The *Breviary*, which is in many respects a superior expression of Croce's aesthetic theory, is interesting because of the series of denials by which the positive import of Croce's idea is brought out by contrast. To claim that art is intuition, that the artist produces an image which is expressive of feeling, and that he realizes this image in its full individuality, involves the denial that art is a physical fact (for physical facts, according to Croce, "*do not possess reality*"); it also involves the denial of the claim that art is concerned with the useful, with pleasure and pain; it denies that art is a moral act (for art, unlike morality, "is opposed to the practical of any sort"); and, finally, it denies that art is conceptual knowledge (for intuition is unconcerned with the distinction between reality and unreality).

Croce distinguishes between "fancy," which he describes as "the peculiar artistic faculty" and "imagination"; unfortunately, the translation of this passage of the *Breviary* is misleading, for by "imagination" Croce meant the fanciful combination of images, while by "fancy" he meant the production of an image exhibiting unity in variety. The distinction can be grasped by reversing the terms: the mere fanciful handling of images is not art, and the composite image thereby produced is not a work of art; but if the imagination holds on to a sense impression, realizing its presence, taking an interest in it because it serves as the embodiment of feeling, then the image is a work of art.

The esoteric character of Croce's central idea diminishes as one realizes that Croce was concerned to emphasize the artist's ability to see more clearly what others only vaguely sense. "The painter is a painter," he writes in the *Aesthetic*, "because he sees what others only feel or catch a glimpse of, but do not see."

Having argued for the claim that art is intuition, and that intuition is expressive knowledge, Croce considers the critical rejoinder that, although art is intuition, not all intuition is art. He rejects the sophisticated notion that art is the intuition of an intuition—that is, the expression of intuitions. He argues that there is no such process and that what critics have regarded as the expression of expression is, as intuition, the expression of a more complex field of impressions than is ordinarily covered by intuition.

He goes on to suggest that the word "art" is often used to call attention to intuitions more extensive in their scope than ordinary intuitions. But from the philosophical point of view—which is concerned with essence and not with quantity—all intuition is art.

If the question arises as to whether content or form is the distinctive aesthetic element in intuition, and by content is meant impressions and by form, expression, then the aesthetic fact, the distinctive aesthetic element, is form.

Because art is the elaboration of impressions, the unifying of impressions into a single, intuited image expressive of feeling, it is a means of liberation for man; the objectification of the passions frees man from their practical influence. The artist is a man of passion who is nevertheless serene; that is because he utilizes sentiment in the intuitive activity, and by that activity he liberates and purifies himself. The paradox of the artist is resolved once it is realized that sensation is passive, but intuition, as the contemplative and creative activity of realizing images as expressive symbols, is active; through activity the artist dominates what would otherwise dominate him.

Art is intuitive knowledge and not conceptual knowledge because knowledge by concepts, according to Croce, is knowledge of the relations of intuitions. Thus, conceptual knowledge depends upon the intuitive, and the latter cannot be reduced to the former. Furthermore, concepts are universals; an intellectual conception is concerned with what is common to a number of things, or intuitions. But intuitions are of particulars; individual images become expressions and serve as works of art. Croce concludes his discussion of this point with the remark that "The intuition gives the world, the phenomenon; the concept gives the noumenon, the Spirit." But this statement is misleading unless we remember that the world presented in intuition is one in which distinctions between actual and possible, true and false, pleasant and unpleasant, and good and bad are irrelevant.

Croce passes from a positive statement of his aesthetic theory to a criticism of rival theories. He considers briefly and in turn the theories that hold art to be an imitation of nature, the representation of universals, the presentation of symbols or allegories, or the portrayal of various forms of life. All such theories commit the fallacy of mistaking the intellectual for the artistic, confusing the concept with the intuition. Once a person concentrates on the *type* of subject matter, the *mode* of treatment, the *style* exhibited, he loses the aesthetic attitude; he has passed on to the scientific or intellectual activity, the exercise of logic, which is concerned with concepts, or universals. "The science of thought (Logic) is that of the concept," he insists, "as that of fancy (Aesthetic) is the science of expression."

As the criticism continues, the outlines of Croce's philosophy of spirit become better defined. The theoretical activity of the spirit has two forms: the aesthetic and the logical; the practical activity also has two forms: the useful or economical, and the moral. "Economy is, as it were, the Aesthetic of practical life; Morality its Logic." Economy is concerned, then, with the individual and his values (just as aesthetic is concerned with the individual intuition and its value), while

morality is concerned with the general, with the values of the universal. Nevertheless, the economic will (the practical will) is not the egoistic will; it is possible to conduct oneself practically without being limited to a concern for self. To act morally, one must act economically; but the reverse is not necessarily the case. To conduct oneself economically is to adjust means to ends, but to conduct oneself morally is to adjust means to *ideal* ends, to what the spirit would desire were it rational, aiming at the noumenon, the spirit, of the self. Just as aesthetic is concerned with phenomena, and logic with noumena, so the economic is concerned with the phenomena and morality with the noumena, the ideal.

The beautiful, considered as aesthetic value, is defined by Croce as *"successful expression,"* but, realizing that expression which is not successful is not expression, Croce concludes by writing that beauty is expression. Consequently, the ugly is unsuccessful expression, or the failure to achieve expression.

Corresponding to the polar values of beauty and ugliness in the aesthetic are the values of truth and falsity for the intellectual, the useful and the useless for the economic, and the just (or good) and unjust (or evil) for the moral. In every case, the positive value results from the successful development of spiritual activity.

Croce's central criticism of any form of aesthetic hedonism—of any theory which regards art as the production of the pleasurable—is that aesthetic hedonism fails to distinguish between the beautiful, which is the pleasurable as expression, and other sources of pleasure. He scornfully rejects any theory which finds the source of artistic activity in the sexual, in the desire to conquer. He admits that "one often meets in ordinary life poets who adorn themselves with their poetry, like cocks that raise their crests," but he argues that such a man is not a poet, but "a poor devil of a cock or turkey."

For Croce, the physical reproduction of intuitions, the making of physical objects that will stimulate those who experience them to the activity of recreating the intuitions, is an aid to memory, or a way of preserving intuitions. Physical reproduction is called "externalization," and it is defined as the activity of producing stimuli to aesthetic reproduction.

In ordinary language, the physical objects found on the walls of art museums, the statues of stones or metal that stand in gardens, and other such physical, created objects are works of art; but for Croce only intuitions are works of art; the inner image guides the production of the physical "reproduction," but the physical object is never the aesthetic fact. To confuse the techniques necessary for the externalization of art with the art activity itself is to confuse "Physic" with "Aesthetic." Externalization is a practical activity, while aesthetic is a theoretic activity. Art is thus independent not only of the intellectual, the useful, and the moral; it is independent of the activity of externalization (which is one kind of useful activity). The effort to reproduce the expression by means of the physical object involves the effort to restore the conditions under which the physical object was produced by the artist; works that are to serve as stimuli to expressions are *"historically conditioned."*

Croce concludes his *Aesthetic* with a chapter in which he explains why he chose to add the words *"and General Linguistic"* to the title *Aesthetic as Science of Expression.* Aesthetic is the science of expression since, for Croce, art is expression (intuition), and aesthetic is the systematic attempt to acquire knowledge about expression. But Croce claims that aesthetic and linguistic are a single science; philosophical linguistic is aesthetic; "Philosophy of language and philosophy of art are the same thing." Aesthetic is the science of general linguistic, then, because language is expression, and aesthetic is the science of expression. The defense of his thesis depends upon Croce's decision to mean by "Linguistic" a rational science, the pure philosophy of speech, and by "speech," any mode of expression.

AN INTRODUCTION TO METAPHYSICS

Author: Henri Bergson (1859-1941)
Type of work: Epistemology
First published: 1903

Metaphysics is the science which uses intuition.

Intuition is a kind of intellectual sympathy by which one understands an object by placing oneself within it.

Intuitive knowledge is superior to analytic knowledge for intuitive knowledge is both absolute and perfect, while analytic knowledge is relative and imperfect.

Science depends on symbols and employs the analytic method; consequently, science deals with classes rather than with individual objects; it can grasp time, motion, change, and the self only by reducing the fluid to the static.

Intuition, on the other hand, reveals reality as a changing, restless flux—a kind of creative mobility that can never be understood by the use of static concepts.

This famous essay first appeared in the *Revue de Metaphysique et de Morale* in January 1903. Published in book form in 1912, it has been translated into many languages and constitutes what many philosophers consider to be the best introduction to Bergson's philosophy. Strictly speaking, the title is misleading. The book is not an introduction to metaphysics but rather an introduction to the *method* of metaphysics: *intuition*. While there is a close relation between Bergson's view of the world and his conception of the intuitive method, the emphasis in this book is predominantly on the latter. Metaphysics, in fact, is *defined* by Bergson as the science which uses intuition.

Neither the term "intuition" nor the conception of a direct and immediate way of knowing objects was original with Bergson. A number of rationalists had used the word to describe the awareness of certain basic notions which exhibit a kind of transparency as to their truth and are commonly spoken of as "self-evident." The mystic has often described the culmination of his mystic experience, in which he sees God face to face, as an intuitive experience. Many philosophers have

recognized, as Bergson did, the need for a direct, as well as an indirect, way of knowing and have variously characterized intuition as "acquaintance," "sensation," "introspection," "instinct," "feeling." To Bergson goes the credit for extracting what is common to all of these conceptions of immediacy and for portraying the intuitive method in a clear and forceful manner by means of a wide range of vivid examples.

Intuition is defined by Bergson as "the kind of intellectual sympathy by which one places oneself within an object in order to coincide with what is unique in it and consequently inexpressible." In contrast, the method of analysis attempts to grasp the object by portraying the features which it possesses in common with other things. Analysis, therefore, always sees an object partially—from a certain perspective—rather than in its individuality and in terms of its peculiar properties. Intuition gives us what the object is in itself; analysis provides only the shell or the husk.

Of all the metaphors which Bergson uses to contrast the method of intuition with that of analysis, the spatial one is perhaps the most frequent. Consider the contrast between entering into an object and moving around it. Because of spatial perspective an object appears different from various points of observation—larger or smaller, of different shapes, sometimes of varying colors. To identify the object with any one of these appearances would be a mistake. All such knowledge is relative and partial. But the object has a true character of its own; otherwise it would not be capable of exhibiting itself in these many ways. We could not determine this character merely from the many appearances, for there would be an infinity of such manifestations, and we could not create the object by merely adding them together. But if we can intuitively grasp the object by "entering into it" we can see its essential nature and we can then predict what the various perspectives will be. This knowledge does not depend on a point of view, nor does it use any symbols. Hence it is *absolute* rather than *relative*.

Bergson illustrated the difference between intuition and analysis by examining the two methods by which we come to know a character whose adventures are portrayed in a novel. After the author has portrayed the hero through his speech and behavior we feel that we understand him. But this knowledge is superficial and unreliable unless we can succeed at some time in identifying ourself with him, unless we *become* the hero and experience his feelings and drives. Once we have done this we can see that his speech and behavior flow naturally from his personality; we are able, having seen him from the inside or absolutely, to account for his actions relative to varying situations. Having grasped his unique nature we are able to recognize what he has in common

with other people—what may be known of him through descriptions, symbols, and analysis.

Intuitive knowledge, according to Bergson, is not only absolute but *perfect*, whereas analytic knowledge is *imperfect*. Try to ascertain what the inner meaning of a poem would be by examining its translations into all possible languages, each with its own shade of meaning, and each correcting the other. The individual translations would be only symbolic representations and could never add up to the true meaning of the poem; they would all be imperfect because partial, and even their sum could not give the intended meaning.

Analysis and intuition are the respective methods of positive science and metaphysics. Science works with symbols—words, numbers, diagrams, graphs. It makes comparisons between forms and reduces complex forms to simple ones; it deals with *classes* of things, not with the *individual objects*. Metaphysics, on the other hand, attempts to grasp the world without any expression, translation, picture, model or symbolic device. It is the study which claims to dispense with symbols.

From the many illustrations which Bergson gives of the contrast between the intuitive and the analytic methods three may be selected for special emphasis. These are to be found in our knowledge of the *self*, of *duration*, and of *motion*.

According to Bergson, as I first look at myself I see three things: a series of perceptions of the external world, a group of memories which adhere to the preceptions, and a crowd of motor habits or urges. But as I examine these elements more carefully they seem to recede from my true self, which be-

751

gins to take on the character of the center of a sphere with the perceptions, memories, and tendencies radiating outward toward the surface. The self which I discover here is not like any flux that I know, since the successive stages merge into one another, each retaining something of what has just passed and each giving a hint of what is still to come. It is not like a series of discrete elements but more like the unrolling of a coil or the rolling up of a thread on a ball. Or it can be compared to a spectrum of colors, with insensible gradations from one hue to the next. But none of these metaphors is quite adequate. The spectrum, for example, is something which is ready made, while the self is a living, growing, developing being, with retentions of what has taken place in its past existence and expectations of what is to come. The inner life of the self has variety, continuity, and unity —yet it is not merely the synthesis of these, for they are themselves abstract and static concepts, while the self is characterized by mobility.

Both empiricists and rationalists miss the real self, for they try to find it in its *manifestations,* which they mistake for its *parts,* not realizing that these are really *partial expressions* of a *total impression* obtained through intuition. The empiricist can find in the personality nothing but a series of psychical events, which he calls "states of the ego." But the ego eludes him because he has only a very confused notion of what it is that he is looking for; he is seeking an intuition but he is using in this search the method of analysis, which is the very negation of it. However closely the states are joined, and however thoroughly the intervals are explored, the ego escapes.

We might as well conclude that the *Iliad* has no meaning because we fail to find it in between the letters of which it is composed.

Rationalism is no more successful. It, too, begins with the psychical states. But it realizes that the unity of the personality cannot lie merely in the series of percepts, images, and feelings. Hence, it concludes that the self must be something purely negative—the absence of all determination, form without content, a void in which shadows move. Small wonder that the rationalist finds it hard to distinguish Peter from Paul; if the ego itself is devoid of determination, the individual self must be also. Thus the empiricist tries to construct the unity of the self by filling in the gaps between the states by still other states, while the rationalist tries to find the unity in an empty form. The empiricist reduces the string of beads to the unstrung beads; the rationalist to the unbeaded string; *both* lose the reality with which they began. What is needed is a new empiricism which will define the self through an intuitive examination of the self. This definition can hardly produce a concept at all, since it will apply to only one object. But certainly no concept of the self can be reached by taking sides with empiricism or with rationalism. Only from an intuition of the self in its uniqueness can we descend with equal ease to both philosophical schools.

Bergson offers the idea of duration as another illustration of what happens when we try to understand the world through analysis. From one point of view duration is *multiplicity;* it consists of elements which, unlike other elements, encroach on one another and fuse. If we try to "solidify" duration by adding together all of its parts we fail; we find that we get not the mobility of the duration but the "frozen memory of the duration." From another point of view duration is *unity*. But it is a moving, changing, and living unity, not at all like the abstract and empty form which pure unity demands. Shall we then try to get duration by combining multiplicity and unity? But no sort of mental chemistry will permit this; we cannot get from either of them or from their synthesis the simple intuition of duration. If, however, we start with the intuition, then we can easily see how it is unity and multiplicity, and many other things besides. Unity and multiplicity are only standpoints from which we may consider duration, not parts which constitute it.

Here again Bergson shows the error in trying to understand the world through analysis. Movement can be considered as a series of potential stopping-points; these are points through which the moving object passes, its positions at various times during its motion. Now suppose there were an infinite number of such potential stoppages. Would there be motion? Obviously not. If the object were judged to be *at rest* at each of these positions, no sum of them—finite or infinite— would constitute motion. If the object were judged to be *in motion* at each of these positions, then we should not really have analyzed motion; we should only have broken up a long motion into a series of shorter ones. Passage is movement, and stoppage is immobility, and the two have nothing in common. We try to get mobility from stoppages by increasing the number of stoppages to infinity, and then, when this fails to give us what we want, we add a mysterious "passage from one stoppage to another." The trouble is, of course, that we have supposed rest to be clearer than motion, and the latter to be definable from the former by way of addition. What we should recognize is that mobility is simple and clear, and that rest is merely the limit of the process of slackening movement. Given an intuition of motion, rest becomes easily understood; without this intuition the motion can never be grasped, whether approached from rest or from any of the other points of view which constitute notes of the total impression.

Through the intuition of movement we can know it *absolutely* rather than *relatively*. Here again Bergson uses the spatial "inside" and "outside" distinction to sharpen the contrast between the two methods of knowing. When we know motion absolutely we insert ourselves into the object by an act of imagination. When we know it relatively we see it only as a function of coordinate systems or points of reference, or as dependent on our own motion or rest with reference to it. The only way really to understand motion is to move. Motion has an interior (something like states of mind), and when we intuit motion we sympathize with this inner nature. We no longer view the motion from outside, remaining where we are, but from within, where the movement really is.

Bergson admits that there are certain difficulties in accepting the intuitive method. Two of these may be mentioned.

One difficulty is that the adoption of the intuitive method requires a change in our ordinary habits of thinking. When we try to understand an object we customarily pass from the concept to the thing, rather than the reverse. Now concepts are abstractions and generalizations; they portray only what is common to objects, not what is peculiar to them. If, then, we try to capture an object by putting concepts together we are doomed to failure. For a concept can only circumscribe around an object a circle, which is too large and does not fit exactly. Realizing this in the case of any one concept, we add another concept, which is also too large but which partially overlaps the previous circle and thus cuts down the area within which the object is to be found. Then we continue the process to infinity, confidently believing that we shall finally reach an area so small that it will contain *only* the object, will characterize it uniquely, and thus will coincide with it. But while the area does coincide with the *properties* it does not coincide with the *object*; the identity of the properties and the object can be grasped only if we start with the object, not if we start with its properties. If we know the thing we can understand its properties, for from a unity we can proceed to the various ways of viewing that unity; but once the unity has been divided into many symbolic expressions, it can never be restored. There will ever remain a gap between the object which is a unique member of a class and the class of which object is the only member. To avoid this predicament we have only to reverse the usual methods of thinking. Instead of starting with concepts and trying to get objects we should start with intuitively grasped objects and then proceed to symbolize their aspects and properties. Only in this way can inconsistent concepts be harmonized, and only in this way can

concepts be molded to fit their objects.

A second difficulty in accepting the intuitive method is that it seems to displace science and render all of its conclusions worthless. But Bergson cautious against this inference on the grounds that both science and the analytic method have an important practical role to play. To illustrate, let us return to the concept of *motion*. We saw that motion cannot be grasped in its essence by thinking of it as an infinite series of positions occupied by the moving object. But now suppose we wish to stop a moving object—as we might well wish to do for certain practical reasons. It will then be very important for us to know where the object is at this precise moment. Science, by the analytic method, can provide us with this information. Indeed, the need for this kind of information accounts for the exactness and precision of science, for its well-defined concepts, and for the method of inductive generalization which it so effectively employs. Through the centuries increased emphasis on the techniques of logic has brought about great improvement in the scientific method. This, in turn, has increased our control over the world. But we do not thereby penetrate deeper into the heart of nature. We can use nature better; we can see better how it will behave toward us and how we should behave toward it, but we do not have the intellectual sympathy which is identical with true understanding. Every concept is a *practical* question which we put to reality. Reality replies in the affirmative or in the negative. But in doing so it hides its true identity.

What sort of a world is it that is revealed by intuition? For an answer to this question we must go to Bergson's other works. Here he states only a few conclusions which can be drawn. Reality is external, but it can be directly experienced by mind. It is characterized primarily by such words as *tendency, mobility, change, flux*. It is a world *being made* rather than a world *ready-made*. It is better understood as a "longing after the restlessness of life" than as a "settling down into an easy intelligibility," as a world of Soul than as a world of Idea.

In this way Bergson tells us about intuition. His success in this attempt, however, leads us to wonder. Has he not in the achievement of his goal destroyed the very thesis of his book; namely, that the true nature of intuition cannot be communicated by means of abstract, general, or simple ideas? For he has used ideas to communicate successfully the nature of intuition. Perhaps his reply would be that he has not really analyzed intuition. What he has done is to select illustrations of intuition so skillfully that we have been able in each case to identify ourselves with intuition and thus to receive an intuition of intuition.

PRINCIPIA ETHICA

Author: George Edward Moore (1873-1958)
Type of work: Ethics
First published: 1903

PRINCIPAL IDEAS ADVANCED

The adjective "good" names an indefinable, unanalyzable, simple, unique property.

The term "naturalistic fallacy" is applied to any theory which attempts a definition of good, for if good is simple, it has no parts to be distinguished by definition.

Sometimes the value of a whole is not simply the sum of the values of its parts. [*The Principle of Organic Unities.*]

One's duty, in any particular situation, is to do that action which will cause more good than any possible alternative.

The ideal good is a state of consciousness in which are combined the pleasures of aesthetic contemplation and the pleasures of admiring generous qualities in other persons.

That G. E. Moore's *Principia Ethica* has attained the status of a modern classic is amply attested by the number of references made to its central concepts and arguments. Moore's central contention is that the adjective "good" refers to a simple, unique, and unanalyzable property. He claims that propositions containing value terms and ethical predicates are meaningful and can be found to be either true or false, even though the word "good"

755

names an indefinable property knowable only by intuition or immediate insight. Moore also argues that the truth of propositions predicating intrinsic goodness—that is, that something is good on its own account, quite without reference to its value as a means—must likewise be seen immediately and without proof. The term "naturalistic fallacy" is proposed to name the error of mistaking some property other than goodness for goodness itself. Any definition of "good" would involve reference to something having distinguishable aspects or parts—hence, not simple; but since goodness is simple, any such definition would be false, an instance of the naturalistic fallacy.

The failure of previous systems of ethics, Moore alleges, is attributable to their imprecise formulations of the questions peculiar to ethics. His objective is to discover and lay down those basic principles according to which any scientific ethical investigation must proceed. Ethics should be concerned with two basic questions: "What kinds of things ought to exist for their own sakes?"—which presupposes knowledge of good—and "What kinds of actions ought we to perform?"

The first task of ethics, then, is to determine what "good" means. The only relevant type of definition is not a verbal definition but one which describes the real nature of what is denoted by stating the parts constituting the whole referent. But in this sense of "definition," "good" cannot be defined. It is a simple notion, not complex. The word "good," like "yellow," refers to an object of thought which is indefinable because it is one of many similarly ultimate terms presupposed by those complex ones which can be defined. True, one can give verbal equivalents of these notions; for example, yellow can be described in terms of light vibrations of certain frequencies—as the physicist might describe it —but light waves are obviously not identical with yellow *as experienced*. One either knows yellow in his experience or he does not, for there is no substitute for the visual experience. Likewise, while there are other adjectives, such as "valuable," which can be substituted for "good," the property itself must be recognized in an act of direct insight.

With respect to the notion of good (as a *property* indicated by the adjective—not as a substantive, "a good" or "the good"), and to propositions predicating intrinsic goodness, Moore is an intuitionist. Such propositions are simply self-evident; proof is neither possible nor relevant. But in other respects Moore rejects intuitionism; he denies that such propositions are true *because* they are known by intuition. Holding that this, like any other way of cognizing, may be mistaken, he also denies that propositions in answer to the second basic question—concerning what *ought* to be done—can be known intuitively, since it is a question of means involving intricate causal relations and variable conditions and circumstances. Judgments about intrinsic goodness are true universally if true at all, but in order to know what we ought to do, that is, to know that any given action is the best, we would have to know that the anticipated effects are always produced and that the totality of these reflect a balance of good superior to that of any alternatives. Such judgments can be only probable, never certain. Thus, both types of ethical judgment presuppose the notion of good, but in ways not always clearly distinguished. The situation is complicated because various combinations of intrinsic and instrumental value and disvalue or indifference may occur. Obligatory acts may have no intrinsic value at all, and acts which are impossible and thus not obligatory may have great intrinsic goodness.

But things having this simple, unique quality of goodness also have other properties, and this fact has misled philosophers into what Moore terms "the naturalistic fallacy." To take any other property, such as "pleasant" or "desired," no matter how uniformly associated with good, as *definitive* of "good," is to make this error. These other properties exist in space and time, and hence are in nature; on the other hand, good is nonnatural; it belongs to that class of objects and properties which are not included in the subject matter of the natural sciences. Thus, when someone insists that "good" *means* "pleasant," or in the substantive sense, "pleasure," he is defining good in terms of a natural object or property; that this is fallacious may be seen by substituting for the meaningful question, "Is pleasure good?" the question implied by such a definition: "Is pleasure pleasant?" Clearly we do not mean the latter, Moore insists, or anything like it, and can by direct inspection see what we do mean—we are asking whether pleasure is qualified by an unanalyzable and unique property. That we can have this notion of good before our minds shows that "good" is not meaningless. The idea that it names a complex which might be analyzed variously must be rejected because we can always ask about any proposed definition of good as complex, "Is X good?" and see that the subject and predicate were not identical. For

example, suppose "good" were defined as "that which we desire to desire." While we might plausibly think that "Is A good?" means "Is A that which we desire to desire?" we can again ask the intelligible question, "Is it good to desire to desire A?" But substituting the proposed definition yields the absurdly complicated question, "Is the desire to desire A one of the things which we desire to desire?" Again, obviously this is not what we mean, and direct inspection reveals the difference between the notions of good and desiring to desire. The only remaining alternative is that "good" is indefinable; it must be clear, however, that this condition applies only to what is meant by the adjective "good," not to "*the* good"; were the latter incapable of definition and description, ethics would be pointless.

Moore calls attention to another source of great confusion, the neglect of what he calls the "principle of organic unities." This is the paradoxical but most important truth that things good, bad, and indifferent in various degrees and relationships may constitute a whole in which value of whole and parts are not regularly proportionate. Thus, it is possible for a whole made up of indifferent or even bad parts to be good, or for one containing only good parts to be indifferent or bad, and in less extreme cases, for parts of only moderate worth to constitute wholes of great value. Crime with punishment may make a whole better than one of these two evils without the other; awareness of something beautiful has great intrinsic goodness, but the beautiful object by itself has relatively little value, and consciousness may sometimes be indifferent or bad. The relationship of part to whole is not that of means to end, since the latter consists of separable terms, and upon removal of a means the same intrinsic value may remain in the end, which situation does not obtain for part and whole. Failure to understand the principle of organic unities causes erroneous estimation of the value of a whole as equal to that of the parts.

The foregoing principles and distinctions form the core of Moore's ethics and underlie both his criticism of other views and the final elaboration of his own. He argues that naturalistic theories which identify good with natural properties must either restrict the sense of "nature" if they define "good" in terms of the natural, since in other respects the evil is just as "natural" as the good, or else must select some special feature of nature for this purpose, as does Herbert Spencer in describing the better as the more evolved. In any case the naturalistic fallacy occurs. Hedonism, the view that "pleasure *alone* is good as an end . . . ," is by far the most common form of ethical naturalism, and it receives more detailed treatment. Hedonism is initially plausible, Moore concedes; it is difficult to distinguish being pleased by something from approving it, but we do sometimes disapprove the enjoyable, which shows that the predicate of a judgment of approbation is not synonymous with "pleasant." But most hedonists have fallen into the naturalistic fallacy. John Stuart Mill furnishes a classic example when he asserts that nothing but pleasure or happiness and the avoidance of pain are desirable as ends, and then equates "desirable" with "desired." Actually Mill later describes other things as desired, such as virtue, money, or health; thus, he either contradicts his earlier statements or makes false ones in attempting to show that such things as virtue or money are parts of happiness. He thus obliterates his own distinction—and one upon which Moore insists—between means and ends.

Moore writes that of the hedonists only Henry Sidgwick recognized that "good" is unanalyzable and that the hedonistic doctrine that pleasure is the sole good as an end must rest on intuition or be self-evident. Moore here freely admits what others might regard as a serious limitation in the intuitionist method—that Sidgwick's and his own intuitions conflict and that neither is able to prove hedonism true or false. But this is disturbing primarily because of the disagreement rather than the lack of proof, Moore adds, since ultimate principles are necessarily incapable of demonstration. The best we can do is to be as clear as possible concerning what such intuited principles mean and how they relate to other beliefs we already hold; only thus can we convince an opponent of error. Mill had rejected Jeremy Bentham's view that the only measures of value in pleasure are quantitative, and he had suggested that there are differences in kind; we learn these by consulting competent judges and discovering their preferences. But if pleasure is really the only desirable end, differences in quality are irrelevant; thus, Sidgwick reverted to the simpler form of hedonism, but specified that the ultimate end is related essentially to human existence. Moore submits reasons for rejecting Sidgwick's intuitions. The first objection is that it is obvious that the most beautiful world imaginable would be preferable to the most ugly even if no human beings at all were there to contemplate either. It follows that things separable from human existence can be intrinsically good. But pleasure cannot be good apart from human experience; it is clear that pleasure of which no one was conscious would not be an end for its own sake. Consciousness must be a *part* of the end, and the hedonistic principle is thus seen to be false: it is not pleasure alone but pleasure together with consciousness that is intrinsically good.

The importance of this conclusion lies in the method used to achieve it—that of completely isolating the proposed good and estimating its value apart from all related objects—for the same method shows that consciousness of pleasure is not the only good. Surely no one would think that a world consisting of nothing but consciousness of pleasure would be as good as one including other existents, and even if these were not intrinsically valuable, the latter world could be better as an organic unity. Similar methods of analysis refute other forms of hedonism—egoistic and utilitarian; Moore concludes that, at best, pleasure would be a criterion of good were pleasure and the good always concomitant, but he regards this as very doubtful and supposes that there is no criterion of good at all.

The chief remaining type of ethics Moore criticizes is what he calls "metaphysical ethics" positing some proposition about a supersensible reality as the basis for ethical principles. He admits that the metaphysicians are right in thinking that some things that *are* are not natural objects, but wrong in concluding that therefore whatever does not exist in nature must exist elsewhere. As noted above, things like truth, universals, numbers, and goodness do not exist at all. But metaphysi-cal ethicists such as the Stoics, Spinoza, and Kant have tried to infer what is good from what is ultimately real and thus have committed a variant of the naturalistic fallacy, for whether the reality involved is natural or supernatural is irrelevant. To the second basic ethical question, "What kind of actions ought we to perform?" a supersensible reality might be relevant, but typical metaphysical systems have no bearing on practice. For example, if the sole good pertains to an eternal, perfect, Absolute Being, there is no way by which human action can enhance the goodness of this situation.

Perhaps the metaphysical ethicists have thus erred through failing to notice the ambiguity of the question, "What is good?" which may refer either to good things or to goodness itself; this ambiguity accounts for the inconsistency between such propositions as that the only true reality is eternal and that its future realization is good, when what is meant is that something like—but not identical with—such a reality would be good. But in this case it becomes clear that it is fallacious to define good as constituted by this reality. While "X is good" is verbally similar to other propositions in which both subject and predicate stand for existents, it is actually radically different; of any two existents so related we may still ask, "Is this whole good?" which again shows the uniqueness of the value predicate.

Because of Moore's precise analytical method, the details of his criticism of other positions cannot be treated adequately here, but they are in principle germane to the lines suggested above, as is also his account of practical ethics. It is essential to remember that in answering the question as to what we

759

ought to do once we know intuitively what things are good as ends, a different method must come into use. Since practical ethical judgments assert causal relations between actions and good or bad effects, the empirical method affording probability, never certainty, is indicated. Thus, Moore differs from traditional intuitionists both in his definition of "right" and in his account of how it is known. Right is not to be distinguished from the genuinely useful, and duty is "that action, which will cause more good to exist in the Universe than any possible alternative." In practice our knowledge of right and duty is most limited, so we must consider as duties those acts which will *usually* yield better results than any others. Such limitations do not excuse individuals from following the general rules, but when the latter are lacking or irrelevant, attention should be redirected to the much neglected intrinsic values of the foreseeable effects. It follows, of course, that virtue, like duty, is a means rather than an end, contrary to the views of some Christian writers and even of Kant, who hold inconsistently that either virtue or good will is the sole good, but that it can be rewarded by something better.

It remains to state Moore's conception of "*the* good" or the ideal. He notes that he will try to describe the ideal merely as that which is intrinsically good in a high degree, not the best conceivable or the best possible. Its general description follows: "The best ideal we can construct will be that state of things which contains the greatest number of things having positive value, and which contains nothing evil or indifferent—*provided* that the presence of none of these goods, or the absence of things evil or indifferent, seems to diminish the value of the whole." The method of discovering both the intrinsically valuable and its degrees of value is that previously mentioned: the method of isolation. It will show that "By far the most valuable things, which we know or can imagine, are certain states of consciousness, which may be roughly described as the pleasures of human intercourse and the enjoyment of beautiful objects." Moore stresses the point that it is these wholes, rather than any constituents, which are the ideal ends.

In aesthetic appreciation there are cognition of the object's beautiful qualities and also an appropriate emotion, but neither of these elements has great value in itself compared to that of the whole, and to have a positive emotion toward a really ugly object constitutes a whole which is evil. Beauty is thus not a matter of feeling: "the beautiful should be *defined* as that of which the admiring contemplation is good in itself," and whether an object has true beauty "depends upon the *objective* question whether the whole in question is or is not truly good, and does not depend upon the question whether it would or would not excite particular feelings in particular persons." Subjectivistic definitions of beauty commit the naturalistic fallacy, but it should be noted that beauty can be defined as it is above, thus leaving only one unanalyzable value term, "good." Consideration of the cognitive element in aesthetic appreciation shows that knowledge adds intrinsic value; aside from the value of true belief as a means or that of the actual existence of the object, it is simply and clearly better to know it truly rather than merely to imagine it. Thus appreciation of a real but inferior object is better than that of a superior but imaginary one.

The second and greater good consists of the pleasures of personal affection. All the elements of the best aesthetic enjoyments plus the great intrinsic good of the object are present here. Part of the object consists of the mental qualities of the person for whom affection is felt, though these must be appropriately expressed in the bodily features and behavior. Since "Admirable mental qualities . . . consist very largely in an emotional contemplation of beautiful objects . . . the appreciation of them will consist essentially in the contemplation of such contemplation. It is true that the most valuable appreciation of persons appears to be that which consists in the appreciation of their appreciation of other persons . . . therefore, we may admit that the appreciation of a person's attitude towards other persons . . . is far the most valuable good we know. . . ." From these assertions it follows that the ideal, contrary to tradition, must include material properties, since both appreciation of beauty and of persons

requires corporeal expression of the valuable qualities.

Since the emotions appropriate to both beautiful objects and to persons are so widely varied, the totality of intrinsic goods is most complex, but Moore is confident that "a reflective judgment will in the main decide correctly . . ." both what things are positive goods and the major differences in relative values. But this is possible only by exact distinction of the objects of value judgment, followed by direct intuition of the presence, absence, or degree of the unique property, good.

Twentieth century students of ethics have benefited immeasurably from Moore's attempt to be clear and precise in the analysis of ethical principles and from his redirection of attention to the really basic questions. Some critics cannot accept certain major conclusions concerning the indefinability of "good," its presence to intuition, its objective status, and the consequent treatment of the "naturalistic fallacy," but even the nature and the extent of the disagreement he has aroused testify to Moore's stature as a philosopher of ethics.

THE LIFE OF REASON

Author: George Santayana (1863-1952)
Type of work: Metaphysics, philosophy of history
First published: 1905-1906

Principal Ideas Advanced

The philosophy of history is an interpretation of man's past in the light of his ideal development.

The life of reason, which gives meaning to history, is the unity given to existence by a mind in love with the good.

By the use of reason man distinguishes between spirit and nature, and comes to understand his own wants and how to satisfy them.

Instinct which originally showed itself only in animal impulses takes on ideal dimensions and leads man into service for society and God.

Finally, in art, which is the imposing of form on matter, but most of all in science, which puts the claims of reason to the test of fact, the life of reason reaches its ideal consummation.

In his autobiography, Santayana says that *The Life of Reason* had its origin in a course which he gave at Harvard University entitled "Philosophy of History." It drew heavily from Plato and Aristotle, but also from Bacon, Locke, Montesquieu, and Taine. We may add Schopenhauer (who was the subject of Santayana's Ph.D. dissertation), and his professor William James, whose biologically oriented psychology left a strong impression on Santayana.

For Santayana, the philosophy of history implies no providential plan of creation or redemption but is simply "retrospective politics"; that is to say, an interpretation of man's past in the light of his ideal development. It is the science of history which deals with events inferred from evidence and explained in terms of causal law. But not content with a mere knowledge of what has happened, man has a strong propensity toward trying to find meaning in events as if history were shaped to some human purpose. Admittedly, it is not; still, the exercise is profitable, for it is one of the ways in which we discover what goals we wish to pursue in the future. The failures and successes of our forebears, as their acts will appear when measured by our ideals, can help us to appraise our standards, as well as to enlighten us with respect to how far they

can be attained. But it can serve its function only if we remember that it is ideal history—an abstract from reality made to illustrate a chosen theme —rather than a description of actual tendencies observable in the world.

The theme which Santayana selects as giving meaning to history is the rise and development of reason. Unlike his idealistic counterparts, who think of nature as the product and embodiment of reason, he conceives reason as a latecomer on the evolutionary scene and very much dependent upon what has gone before. This is not to say that there is no order in nature prior to the dawn of consciousness in man. Santayana's contention, on the contrary, is that reason, which is too often thought of in the abstract, schoolmasterly fashion, is in reality an extension of the order already achieved in organized matter. In its earliest phase, it is nothing more than instinct which has grown conscious of its purposes and representative of its conditions. For in the dark laboratories of nature, life has already solved the hardest problems, leaving to its strange child, reason, nothing to do at first but amuse itself with the images which drift through the mind while the body goes about its accustomed business. We can scarcely call it reason until, distinguishing these mental states from objects, reason gradually sees what the

762

parent organism is about, what it runs from, what it pursues, and how it manages each new eventuality. Then it begins to play its role. Where instinct is dependent on present cues, reason can summon thoughts from afar, suggest short cuts, and balance likelihoods. Often its well-meant suggestions lead to destruction; but, on the other hand, its occasionally fruitful counsels tend to perpetuate themselves in habits and customs, as a shelter of branches which, devised for one night's protection, remains standing and becomes a rudimentary home. It is in this way that reason, an adjunct of life, comes to have a "life" of its own.

Reason, by this accounting, is the servant of will or interest. It is these that determine what is good. Santayana calls the Life of Reason the unity inherent in all existence.

Santayana traces reason's career through five phases. He devotes one book to each.

Reason in Common Sense may be regarded as introducing the other books. It outlines the origins of the two realms, nature and spirit, whose fortunes are followed through the rest of the work. Out of an originally chaotic experience, man learns to distinguish first the stable, predictable realm of nature. Regularity and order are present there; and things occurring repeatedly can be identified and their habits noted. But in a great part of experience, images come and go in no discernible pattern, and combine in innumerable ways. This remainder we come to designate as spirit: it is the seat of poetry and dreams, and later of philosophy and mathematics.

Human progress may be viewed as the gradual untangling of these two realms. The rich garment of sight and sound under which nature appears to our senses conceals its structure and beguiles man into supposing that trees and rivers have spirits and pursue purposes not unlike his own. It is practical experience—fishing and agriculture—that gradually teaches him otherwise, enabling him to strip off irrelevant qualities, and discern the mechanical process underneath. Not surprisingly, he is sometimes reluctant to leave behind the more congenial picture of poetry and myth. But insofar as he becomes aware of his advantage, he learns to prefer things to ideas, and to subordinate thinking to the arts of living.

Almost as difficult as discerning nature is the task of deciding what is good. Before consciousness awakened, instinct guided the body toward the satisfaction of genuine, if partial, needs. But when ideas appeared, impulse was diverted, and moral perplexity began. False gods arose, which exist only in imagination, and these must be set aside in favor of ideas which live up to their promises. And there is the further problem of subordinating the claims of competing goods under a common ideal. Reason has not to go beyond human nature to discover the truth and order of values. By understanding man's wants and the limits of his existence, it points him toward his highest fulfillment, that is, his happiness—than which he has no other end.

Viewed in these larger aspects, the rational life is sanity, maturity, common sense. It justifies itself against romanticism, mysticism, and all other-worldliness which betoken a failure to distinguish between ideal and real, or a misguided flight from nature to the world of dreams.

Reason in Society follows the course

of man's ideal attachments from the passionate love of a man for a maid to the fancies of a man of taste and finally to the devotions of a saint. The instincts which unite the sexes, bind parents and offspring, and draw the lonely from their isolation into tribes and cities, when illuminated with the flame of consciousness, take on ideal dimensions and give rise to love, loyalty, and faith. It is the mark of love to combine impulse and representation; and no one who has truly loved can be entirely deaf to the voice of reason or indifferent to the liberal life toward which it calls.

Santayana groups societies into three classes. The first, which he calls *natural* societies, includes not merely the family, but economic and political groups. In these, association is more instinctive than voluntary: but they serve reason well when the regimen that they prescribe becomes the means of fashioning strong, reliant individuals who, without disloyalty to their origins, form *free* societies based on mutual attachments and common interests. Such persons, in possession of their own wills, may go further and create *ideal* societies, which is what we do when, forsaking the company of men, we make beauty or truth our companion.

In its social expressions, perhaps more than anywhere else, reason has to draw the fine line between crude fact and irresponsible fancy. Somewhere between the shrewd materialism of Sancho and the lofty madness of Don Quixote, there is a way of living which incorporates the ideal in the actual, whether in love or in politics. Therein lies the liberal or free life for man.

Reason in Religion develops the view, which is perhaps as characteristic of Comte as it is of Hegel, that religion is a half-way station on the road from irresponsible fancy to verifiable truth. It is neither to be rejected out of hand as imbecile and superstitious, nor rationalized and allegorized until it agrees with science. In the story of human progress it fulfills a civilizing function, but under serious disabilities: for although it pursues the same goal as reason, it relies upon imagination instead of logic and experiment. On the positive side, its occasional profound insights into moral reality have spurred mankind to needed reforms; but this gain is offset by its stubborn adherence to an anthropomorphic view of nature which closes the way to systematic advance.

A lifelong student of the religions of the West, Santayana illuminates his theme with detailed criticisms of the major traditions. The Hebrew religion gets high marks for its wholesome emphasis upon morals, but is censured for its dogmatic and intolerant spirit. The Christian gospel, which dramatizes man's efforts to transcend his nature, is an important step toward the goal of freedom; but it needs to be blended with pagan ritual if man is not to lose sight of his moral dimensions. Along the Mediterranean shores, such a paganized Christianity developed. But it remained strange to its converts in the northern forests. Gothic art, philosophy, and chivalry are, by contrast, a barbarized Christianity, and have as their proper motif the native religion of the Teutons. This it was that, coming of age, threw off the world-denying gospel and emerged in its proper sublimation, first as Protestantism, then as romanticism and Absolute Egotism. Less mature, and further divorced from reality than Catholicism, Gothic Christianity lingers on in various idealisms—moral, political, philosophical—obscuring the path of reason.

Reason in Art is broadly conceived to include every activity which "humanizes and rationalizes objects." For Santayana, with his classical bias, artistic activity consists in imposing form upon matter. Like religion, art is preoccupied with imagination; but its concern is more wholesome because, instead of mistaking fancies for facts, it fashions facts according to its ideal preferences. Thus, each genuinely artistic achievement is a step forward toward the goal of rational living.

Man's earliest constructions must have been clumsy and unprepossessing, not even rivaling the spontaneous products of nature. Compared, for example, with the prancing of a stallion, the movements of a savage in his dance are crude and ridiculous. But when art frees the dance from the excitement of war or courtship, and makes the intention its study, a new form of discipline and social control appears which purges the soul. So man tames his own spirit and gladdens it with sights and sounds.

The advance of civilization is not always friendly to free creation. Customs, acquiring almost the force of instincts, stifle invention; and products have a way of enslaving their producers. A society which looks upon art as truancy from business condemns the artist to vagrancy and robs his genius of its normal incentive. It has entered a post-rational phase because it has lost touch with man's genuine needs. Art is no mere pleasurable accessory to life. Man is engaged in liberal and humane enterprise in the measure that, transcending his animal needs and vulgar ambition, he becomes the master of the conditions of his existence, visits on them his kind of perfection, and renders their tragic aspects endurable by clothing them in intelligible and regular forms.

Reason in Science brings the Life of Reason to its *logical* conclusion; for, as Santayana defines science, it is the consummation of the rational ideal in the light of which the other phases of human life have been interpreted and alongside which they have been judged. Insofar as the standard has been presupposed all along, this final volume is somewhat anticlimactic. What saves it from this lot is the feeling of contemporaneousness that goes with the word "science," together with the belief (characteristic of the period in which the work appeared) that mankind has *actually* entered the scientific era for which all previous history was but the prelude. Science, says Santayana, is practically a new thing: only twice in history has it appeared— for three hundred years in Greece and for a comparable time in the modern West. Art and religion have had their day—nothing more is to be expected from them. They bow before the new techniques of measurement and verification. The fruits of science, however, have scarcely begun to appear; and the morrow is sure to bring many surprises.

Santayana's purpose, however, was not primarily to trumpet the dawn of a new day. Optimism with respect to the future was never one of his characteristics. But he was concerned to defend tough-minded naturalism against tender-minded idealism and against all kinds of compromise. Perhaps we might say that his trumpet blast is an effort to frighten off the enemies of science who, he thought, would yet have their way.

To this end, he stresses the sharp distinction between the realm of nature and the realm of spirit. There is a science corresponding to each of these which, using classic terms, he designates respectively as *physics* and *dialectic*.

The ideal expression of physics is mechanics, because the laws governing the behavior of matter are there made perfectly intelligible. But mechanics is exceptional, true only in the gross. The forms and repetitions of nature are never simple and never perfect. Nevertheless, all knowledge which has to do with facts must adopt a mechanical principle of explanation. This is true, Santayana insists, even in the sciences that treat of man—notably history and psychology. There are no special "historical forces," such as idealists are wont to suppose: historical causation breaks up into miscellaneous natural processes and minute particular causes. Similarly, there are no "moral causes," such as biographers and literary psychologists presume: the part of psychology which is a science is physiological and belongs to the biology of man.

As physics comprehends all sciences of fact, dialectic includes all sciences of idea. Its perfect expression is mathematics, which makes possible the deductive elaboration of hypotheses in physics. But another branch of dialectics elaborates the relationship between conflicting human purposes or ideals. Socrates, who pioneered in its development, first established rational ethics. Purely a normative science, it sheds great light on human undertakings, and is presupposed in any study (such as the present one) which attempts to deal intelligently with problems of good and evil. But it is limited to ideas, and cannot take the place of observation and experiment in questions that have to do with existence.

As between questions of fact and questions of purpose, the latter are by far the more fateful, since it is within their domain to decide whether the Life of Reason is to be pursued. Here Santayana considers at length the subject of post-rational ethics and religion. The age of the Greeks passed. In mathematics, physics, and medicine, knowledge continued to progress; but meanwhile a sense of world-weariness descended upon men's minds, causing them to turn their backs on worldly enterprise and seek consolation in pleasure or compensation in ecstasy, or to deaden disappointment by asceticism and obedience. The humanism of Socrates gave place to Stoicism, Epicureanism, Skepticism, and to a revival of pagan cults, all founded on personal or metaphysical despair. In Christianity a similar experience of disillusion forced the imagination to take wings and seek its hope beyond the clouds.

In Santayana's judgment these post-rational systems are not to be condemned. They witness to the fact that life is older and more persistent than reason and knows how to fall back on more primitive solutions to its problems when its bolder experiments fail. And, even in retreat, they hold on to certain conquests of reason, which they fortify and furnish in rare fashion. So, true sages can flourish and true civilizations can develop in retrogressive times, and supernaturalism can nourish a rational and humane wisdom.

This, however, is not to admit that the post-rational systems are an advance over the rational even in the solution of man's spiritual enigmas.

And when the same despair breeds arbitrary substitutes for physical science, it is time to cry alarm. Santayana's final chapter, "The Validity of Science," is devoted to criticisms of science, particularly from theologians and transcendental philosophers. The former wish to combine scientific explanation with relics of myth, and so preserve a sanction over moral and political behavior. What the latter seek is less clear. Their attack consists in showing (what was never in doubt) that the findings of science are relative; such philosophers, apparently, aim at freeing their minds of intelligible notions so that they can swim in the void of the vegetative and digestive stage of consciousness.

Science is not beyond criticism. A healthy skepticism respecting the claims of reason is ever in order. It is an integral part of science to review its findings, and purge itself of arbitrariness and bad faith. For its whole aim is to free the mind from caprice by bringing it under the control of objective principles. Santayana quotes Heraclitus' saying, "Men asleep live each in his own world, but when awake they live in the same world together." Religion and art are too much like dreaming; when man brings his dreams under the control of the real world, on the one hand, and the principle of contradiction, on the other, he passes from mere faith and aspiration to knowledge and expectation.

CREATIVE EVOLUTION

Author: Henri Bergson (1859-1941)
Type of work: Metaphysics
First published: 1906

PRINCIPAL IDEAS ADVANCED

The attempt to understand the self by analyzing it in terms of static concepts must fail to reveal the dynamic, changing character of the self.

There is an interesting force that shows itself in living things, an élan vital that has endured through the ages, accounting for the creative evolution of life and of instinct and intelligence in living things.

Instinct is limited in that although it grasps the fluid nature of living things, it is limited to the individual; but intellect is limited in that although it constructs general truths, it imposes upon life the static character of concepts.

But by the capacity of intuition, a disinterested and self-conscious instinct, a kind of knowledge is made possible which is superior to that provided by either instinct or intellect working separately.

At the time of his death in 1941, in the France dominated by the Nazis, Bergson was a relatively forgotten man, forgotten by the cultivated public and given little attention by the professional philosopher. Yet in the first two decades of this century he was lionized by the former and respected and often received enthusiastically by the latter. His fame was made by his immensely popular *Creative Evolution*. In this book he engages in metaphysical speculation on the grand scale, projecting his views back into the remote past and forward into the future. He speculates about matters that are difficult to speak about and impossible to verify in any of the traditionally accepted ways. Indeed, he mounts a concerted attack on traditional philosophic assumptions and techniques, insisting in particular that the dominant mechanistic and materialistic approach can lead only to a gross misrepresentation of reality. The chief villain here is intellect itself, for it can operate only through the use of concepts, and concepts are fixed, static categories that cannot contain fluid reality. There was a strong strain of anti-intellectualism in Bergson.

These basic views are expressed first in his discussion of the self. Perhaps the most noteworthy feature of our own inner life is the unceasing change that occurs there, the unceasing flow of thoughts, feelings, perceptions, and volitions. It is quite natural to think of this change as a succession of states in which each state holds the stage for a while before it is followed by its successor. Pursuing this analysis, we are led to think of the states themselves as internally static and changeless, for change is just the replacement of one state by another. Similarly, we are led to think of time as a succession of moments within which temporal change does not occur. Having cut the self into a collection of independent and static atoms of experience, we then wonder how this

collection can constitute a unified, dynamic self, but we solve this difficulty by postulating the existence of an unexperienced mental substance that supports them, holds them together, and accounts for the manner of their succession.

We have gone astray, Bergson says, because we have tried to describe the dynamic, pulsating self by using concepts that inevitably impose their foreign rigidity upon it. Change in the self is not a process in which unchanging blocks are successively cast into and out of existence. Rather, it is a continuous process occurring in a self in which "states" (if we must use this term) are not units demarcated by sharp lines, but are at most centers of intensity trailing off indefinitely within the unbroken fabric of experience. Because it is growing, the self is changing in a direction that cannot be reversed, the past accumulating around the present as snow accumulates around a rolling snowball. To be such a changing thing is to be a self, and to experience such irreversible change is to have a history. This dynamic snowballing time, this time that counts, is real time or "duration," as Bergson calls it to distinguish it from the conceptualized, static, essentially reversible time of the mathematician. Memory is not the recalling of experiences that have long departed, but is the past living on in the present, affecting our present behavior. Consequently, in the self there is no exact repetition of past patterns, and novelty is the rule. Man is free, for in using the past he creates the future. We can discover all this for ourselves if we attend to our own inner life and are not misled by the concepts intellect would like to impose. Duration is not to be thought about; it is to be experienced, for only experience can reveal it to us.

Compared with the self, physical objects do not grow and change, they do not have memories, they do nothing new, they do not have histories, and they do not endure, for time makes no difference to them. The planets revolve as they always have, and they will continue to do so, except insofar as they are subject to changing external forces. The static concepts of mathematics and physics apply quite appropriately to them because they lend themselves to description in just such terms. These differences between physical objects and the living self indicate the presence of something in the latter that is not in the former, some dynamic element that makes the difference between the accumulative, purposeful, creative behavior of the one and the passive, repetitious, monotonous existence of the other. If we turn to biological phenomena and especially to the evolution of living things, we will discover overwhelming evidence in support of this thesis. One of the main examples is that of the evolution of the eye. Both the complex arrangement of otherwise useless components and the long history of increasingly complex sensory organs cannot be explained plausibly unless we assume some sort of integrating force that is moving in a definite direction.

Bergson cites the biological evidence that supports the fact of evolution, but we are not concerned with the fact itself as much as we are with what it presupposes. Darwin's theory of the survival of the fittest is all right as far as it goes, but it does not explain why mutations should occur in the first place or why many of them survive when they have no immediate survival value.

Bergson rejects three theories before he offers his own. First, he says that no mechanistic or materialistic account will do, for such an account forces the dynamic processes of life into the strait jacket of physical concepts and, in insisting that the future is determined completely by the past, repudiates the duration, freedom, and creation that are evident in the realm of living things. Second, Bergson rejects any finalistic view that describes the world as being attracted or directed toward some future goal, some end it cannot avoid, for such a view replaces one form of determinism by another. Finally, he repudiates the vitalism that was current in the biology of his day, for the postulation of a vital principle whose function is restricted to explaining the organization of parts and drives within the individual does not explain the fact of evolution.

Bergson's own view is a sort of cosmic vitalism in which the vital principle or *élan vital*, as he calls it, is life itself as it has endured through the ages, and evolution is the history of the effort of life to free itself from the domination of matter and to achieve self-consciousness. Beginning as the dimmest spark distinguishing the living from the dead, thrusting itself out in various directions, the *élan vital* has tried one by one the experiments represented by the divergent branches of the evolutionary tree. Many of the resultant forms have long ago been rejected as unsuitable, and others have been allowed to stagnate as the *élan* has continuously diverted its energies into the more promising ones. It pushed out into the vegetable and animal kingdoms and found that the latter allowed it greater scope. It discovered that the storage and explosive release of energy lead to freedom, that motion and consciousness are better than a sedentary torpor, that defense through high mobility and dexterity is better than that of armor, and so on through a host of minor and major alternatives. The most significant dichotomy of all has been that between the arthropods which have developed through the various insect forms to culminate in the hymenoptera, and the vertebrates which have diversified but culminated in man. This dichotomy is significant because the culminating species embody the best solutions the *élan* has yet found in its long struggle to emancipate itself from the matter that drags it down, the solutions represented by instinct and intelligence.

Both instinct and intelligence emerged as instruments for manipulating matter. Intellect fulfills this function through its ability to apprehend problems and to produce the mechanical devices needed to solve them. In fact, according to Bergson, intelligence is the faculty of making objects—such as tools to make tools—and of varying the manufacture at will. Arising from the animal's hesitation in a dilemma, intelligence expresses itself in thought rather than in action; developing the technique of language, it can operate when the original stimulus is no longer present; becoming aware of this subjective process it develops self-consciousness; concentrating on relations and forms, it frees itself from matter and develops the ability to generalize; and finally, using these resources and indulging its aroused curiosity, it turns from practical to theoretical matters. Instinct, too, operates through the use of tools, but the tools in this case are

integral parts of the body, tools designed for a specific use and limited to that use. The instinctive reactions of the insect are sure and precise, but their scope is both limited and invariant. Instincts are released directly in action and function unconsciously. Yet they do involve an important kind of knowledge—not knowledge *about,* but an unconscious empathy with their object.

Both intellect and instinct have their advantages as well as their disadvantages. Among the great advantages of intellect are its consciousness and its ability to discover general truths, but it has disadvantages stemming from its inability to grasp things except through forms that are suggested to it by the object but crystallized into sharply defined concepts by itself. Thus, it is limited in two respects; it can grasp only the external form of a thing, and it cannot avoid seeing in the thing the static nature of the concept through which it is seen. Instinct has the advantage of grasping the fluid nature of living things, but it is limited to the individual and has not attained consciousness.

The production of instinct and intelligence is an experiment in which the *élan* has been articulating divergent but complementary tendencies that have lain dormant in it from the beginning. Through the resultant clarification it is readying itself to combine the desirable features of each in a new capacity that will transcend both. This new capacity already appears fleetingly in man. It is the capacity of intuition, a capacity that may be described briefly as instinct that has become disinterested and self-conscious. Artists to a greater extent, and most men to a lesser, are able to place themselves in a sort of divining sympathy with things and with other people. Intuition manifests itself in situations in which men are not dominated by disinterested thought—in the crises of life where problems press in and drastic action is required, and in moments of intense joy, sadness, or commiseration. In such cases and for a brief time we know our own inner being and that of others in a much more intimate fashion than we do when we sit in our studies and describe ourselves. Life then becomes aware of itself, of duration, and of the world, not through the distorting mediation of concepts, but directly and immediately. Man in his present state cannot maintain such insight for long, but if the *élan* is successful it will develop beings who can. What the nature of that intuition will be, and whether the *élan* will attain its goal of complete self-consciousness and complete dominance over matter, we cannot tell. We cannot tell for we are manifestations of the *élan*, and it does not know. It is striving less blindly than it did in past ages, but still, it does not know.

In the first half of his book, when he pits the *élan* against matter, it appears as if Bergson were maintaining that the world is composed of two radically different and independent principles. But in the latter half he makes it clear that he does not maintain such a metaphysical dualism. The distinction he has made between the *élan* and matter shares the defect of all distinctions made by the intellect —it is overdrawn. On the one hand the physical world around us is not quite as static and inert as it appears in the enclosed systems of the physicist, for if we regard it over long periods and great expanses we will find that it does not repeat itself quite as monotonously as we sometimes think it does. On the other hand, the self is not a continuously creative, pure-burning center of energy, for it can lapse into periods of lethargy during which it approaches the status of a physical thing. This is not to deny that there is a big difference between *élan* and matter, but it is to deny that the difference is an absolute one. It has the signs of being a difference in degree rather than one in kind.

If we retrace our steps in time we will find that the difference was even less long ago. Did the first organic things differ radically from the inorganic compounds from which they arose? Did not their emergence presuppose some prior creative activity? Indeed, Bergson speculates, life and matter stem from a common inarticulated source that contained neither as we know them, even though it did contain the tendencies from which they have evolved. Feeling dimly a need for creation, the primal substance began to stir, and gathering strength erratically but gradually, it generated life and matter by processes that are the inverse of each other.

Sometimes Bergson writes as if the quickening in the original indeterminate source has led to its articulation into parts that vary in their vitality, the less vital lapsing into relatively passive matter that resists the efforts of the more vital to move it or to move through it. At other times he writes as if the resistance to life stems from life itself. It is pictured as a frail element that overextends itself, that depletes itself, and that lapses into lethargy before it can gather itself together for another spurt. Matter is tired life. If the *élan* is a flowing current, then

771

matter is a congealing of it. If the *élan* is a cosmic tension, then extension is the interruption or disappearance of that tension.

Bergson expresses himself in two particularly vivid metaphors. The first is that of a vessel of steam from which live jets escape, travel through space, lose their energy, condense into water and fall, only to provide a cooling medium that saps the energy of the jets that in penetrating it try to carry it with them in their upward thrust. Thus, through the ages, both life and matter have come from an inexhaustible reservoir, generated by processes that are the inverse of each other, and having inverse effects upon each other. The other, and perhaps better, metaphor is that in which the emerging *élan* is likened to a series of skyrockets. Imagine an original skyrocket that rises, slows down, and bursts, scattering its exhausted fragments through the sky. Imagine also that as it bursts it releases a number of rockets that gather speed and mount upwards in various directions through the debris. Some of these, retarded by their own weight and slowed by the resisting ashes of their predecessors, will simply fizzle out, doomed to do no more than scatter debris yet higher in the sky. But, in a final burst, some will release still others that will probe the upper reaches before they too die, barrenly or fruitfully. In this fashion the original urge to life has climbed through the ages, fighting its own lethargy, thrusting through or by the static remnants of its past endeavors, gathering strength to go off in new directions, sometimes succeeding and sometimes failing in its attempt to attain higher levels of consciousness.

Bergson's reliance on vivid metaphors of this sort accounts in part for the immediate impact the book had, but it also gives rise to some of the more severe criticism leveled at him. Metaphors are suggestive, but they are not accurate. Time and the self may both be like a rolling snowball rather than like a series of beads on a string; matter may be like congealing jelly or life like a river seeking the easiest path through the constraining land, and the *élan* may be like steam or skyrockets, but such suggestions should be followed by hard-headed, nonmetaphorical analyses. Although Bergson was often a good critic of others' speculations, the exposition of his own doctrine remains both ambiguous and vague. The concepts of duration, matter, *élan vital*, and intuition are never entirely clarified, and different images of them are not really reconciled. Furthermore, the distinction between epistemological and metaphysical considerations is not maintained, particularly in the discussion of matter where it is often unclear whether the villain is our concept of matter or matter itself. His criticism of the mathematician's account of space and time is based on an inadequate knowledge of the mathematics of the continuum, for apparently he believed all series must be discrete series. Finally, his attacks on the extent and accuracy of intellectual knowledge, and in particular his assumptions that the intellect must distort and that it is the blind captive of its own distortion, seem too extreme.

Perhaps Bergson would reply that although the intellect is capable of giving us knowledge of a sort, better knowledge may be achieved by intuition. Perhaps he would defend his use of metaphors in this way also, arguing that in using them he deliberately intends to lead us away from conceptual analysis, which must fail, toward intuition which alone can succeed. Intuition, duration, the self, or the *élan* cannot accurately be described simply because they are indescribable; he can only point to the sort of experience in which they are immediately known, and urge us to discover them for ourselves.

THE NATURE OF TRUTH

Author: Harold Henry Joachim (1868-1938)
Type of work: Epistemology
First published: 1906

PRINCIPAL IDEAS ADVANCED

An idea is true if it fits in with other ideas to form a coherent whole.

To conceive something clearly and logically involves more than recognizing logical relationships; it involves achieving a coherency in one's judgments that goes beyond abstraction to material considerations.

Error is the distortion that results from a partial view of things; truth is the ideal of achieving a structure of judgments that fits the totality of all experience.

Joachim's short treatise, *The Nature of Truth*, has come to be regarded as the classical statement of the coherence theory of truth. The book is modest in size (180 pages), sticks closely to the point, and is written in that lucid style which often graces the writings of British philosophers. It is a work that philosophers can read with ease and profit.

Joachim divides the work into four chapters as follows: (1) Truth as Correspondence, (2) Truth as a Quality of Independent Entities, (3) Truth as Coherence (with a section on The Coherence-Notion of Truth, and a section on Degrees of Truth), and (4) The Negative Element and Error. The first two chapters are statements and criticisms of alternative views which prepare the way for the positive statement of the coherence theory in Chapter III. In the last chapter Joachim further supports the coherence theory by arguing that the problem of error cannot be accounted for as satisfactorily within the alternative theories as it can within the coherence theory.

Joachim begins by considering the view that correspondence means that *for a mind* two "factors" (Joachim's word) correspond in their structures and purposes. This is a very general and abstract conception of correspondence, and it applies to such things as portraits and photographs as well as to descriptions in words. The fundamental notion involved is that of copying. A portrait or a photograph or a description is faithful if it conveys, as a whole, the same sense of purpose or significance as does the original of which it is a copy, and if it is such a faithful copy we say it is *true*. But, Joachim argues, the concern with a *whole* having a purpose or significance indicates that the faithfulness of the copy is a symptom rather than the fundamental characteristic of truth. It is the systematic coherence of the whole that makes it a faithful copy (if it is), and therefore the important element in the truthfulness of the copy is its coherence.

From this abstract version of the correspondence theory, Joachim moves on to consider the correspondence that supposedly holds between a judgment and the referent of the judgment—the fact to which it refers. Here he rests his case on the claim that both the judgment and the referent of the judgment are finally mental. Both the judgment and its referent are elements in "experience," and experience for Joachim, as for all idealists, is finally mental. The correspondence is a correspondence (or identity) of structure between two kinds of experience. However, Joachim balks at abstracting a structure or form in such a way as to neglect the matter or material which exhibits the structure. At stake here is the doctrine of internal relations, to which we must shortly turn for a more detailed discussion. The point can be made here, however, that Joachim refuses to compare the form of the judgment with the form of the experienced fact. Thus, both the judgment and the experienced fact which is the referent of the judgment remain embedded in experience. Experience, furthermore, is a totality containing the judgment and the experienced fact as elements. Both have significance, for Joachim at any rate, within this wider context of experience, and if they are abstracted from the concreteness of experience

they lose their significance. Experience, finally, is the coherent whole which gives significance to both the judgment and its referent. Again, coherence seems to be the key to truth.

In his second chapter, "Truth as a Quality of Independent Entities," Joachim states and rejects what he understands to be the position taken by G. E. Moore and the early Bertrand Russell, the Russell of *The Principles of Mathematics* (1903). Two assertions are the object of Joachim's concern here: (1) There are simple facts which can be experienced or apprehended without being affected in any way by this experiencing or apprehending. (2) There are logical entities, called "propositions," which are the proper subjects of the predicates "true" and "false." Joachim disagrees with both assertions. With regard to the first assertion—namely, that there are facts which are unaffected by men's experiencing of them—Joachim points out that there is certainly a difference between a complex which is a fact, but which is not an *experienced* fact, and a complex which is a fact, but which is also experienced. This line of reasoning, of course, would not distress either Russell or Moore in the least. But Joachim seems to believe that this difference implies that experiencing a fact somehow changes the fact. However, to say this is to misrepresent Joachim (and other idealists as well), for he does not admit that there are any such things as unexperienced facts. To be a fact is to be experienced—in this regard Joachim stands in the same position as did Berkeley.

Part of what is involved in Joachim's rejection of the view that experiencing facts does not change them is the parallel case regarding judgments as opposed to propositions. Just as there are no unexperienced facts for an idealist, so there are no "propositions," where by "proposition" is meant the content of a judgment considered as apart from the assertion of it by some person. These propositions are the "independent entities" which the chapter heading refers to. Russell, Joachim claims, regards truth and falsity as predicates of independent logical entities called propositions. If there are propositions which can be considered in abstraction from their being asserted by some person, and if there are facts which can be apprehended without that apprehension changing them, then there are two "factors" which can be examined in order to see whether or not they correspond. For a coherence view to stand, then, it is important to reject this possibility decisively. Joachim tries to do this by arguing that it makes no more sense to talk about facts which are not experienced than to talk about propositions which are not asserted by someone. Here it becomes obvious that the earlier inclusion in the statement of the correspondence view of the words "for a mind" is crucial for Joachim. Facts are all *experienced* facts, and propositions are all *asserted* propositions (that is, judgments). But the premise Joachim offers—namely, that we always deal with experienced facts and asserted propositions—does not support his conclusion—namely, that we cannot speak of facts and propositions in abstraction from some mind which experiences the facts and asserts the propositions.

The inference just mentioned rests, for Joachim, on the doctrine of internal relations. We should look at this doctrine before proceeding. It is not elaborated by Joachim in *The Nature of Truth,* but he admits that he is assuming it, and it provides the background and real motivation for the rejection of Russell's position.

Essentially the doctrine of internal relations is a denial, a denial that relations are real entities having any status or meaning apart from the situations in which they are exemplified. There is a certain plausibility in this view. It seems, *prima facie,* that we come to speak of relations as a result of interpreting our experience. We may, for example, come into a room and have a complex, but unitary, experience which includes seeing a dog under the table, smelling the fragrance of a vase of flowers, hearing the radio playing a popular song, and so forth. Our unreflective apprehension of the room may be such that these elements are not distinguished, but rather are experienced as an undifferentiated totality. However, in interpreting our experience, we analyze and describe and classify the unity into a multiplicity of things having qualities and standing in relations. Joachim takes the usual idealist view that in moving from the unitary experience of such a totality to the reflective interpretation of it we abstract from the real. Therefore, although it is true that we must talk of relations (and qualities and terms as well, because they are similar to relations in this respect) in describing our experience, these relations are abstractions, and hence they are unreal—partially unreal at best, perhaps totally unreal. Certainly they do not have status as independent entities. When we say that "the dog is under the table," we are abstracting from the unity of our experience, and if we go further and think about the relation of "being under" by itself and apart from its exemplifications, we have performed still another act of abstraction. But these abstractions have taken us out of the immediacy and concreteness and unity of the experience itself, and they have given us instead something formal and unreal.

Nevertheless, idealists such as Joachim make a concession to the fact that we do use relations in describing our experience. Our knowledge structure, according to idealists, is constructed out of immediate experience by means of judgments, judgments which do assert relations. Thus, in spite of our recognition of the undifferentiated totality as something without relations (so says the idealist), our knowledge construction out of this experience does contain judgments which assert relations. To this extent, relations do have a status and function. Still, relations, if they are regarded as something independent of their concrete manifestations in experience, are abstractions out of experience and are thus not genuinely real. The proof of this is that there is no way of compounding the concreteness of our experience out of the judgments asserting relations (or qualities). We cannot synthesize our experience out of the descriptions or judgments we make; to do so would give us a mere aggregate of formal characteristics and not concrete experience. We simply cannot achieve the individuality and uniqueness of experience by compounding judgments. Nevertheless, we are forced to use relations, so our best course is to recognize that we have abstracted and are therefore speaking of the only partially real.

Thus, the doctrine of internal relations really consists of two assertions: (1) Relations are not independently real, and they have no significance apart from the situations in which we judge them to be present. (2) Relations are arrived at by abstracting from concrete experience and thus, although necessary in judgment, they have only a partial and derivative reality. It is this doctrine that lies behind Joachim's rejection of the Moore and Russell position. The doctrine of internal relations rests on the conviction that abstraction from the immediacy of experience is falsification, but certainly the independent facts and propositions of Russell are abstractions from experience; therefore, such independent facts and propositions must be rejected by Joachim.

In his third chapter Joachim takes up the positive exposition of the coherence theory. The doctrine of internal relations also provides a fine background for this theory, for, as we shall see, the coherence theory is really one way of expressing the doctrine of internal relations and its implications.

Joachim offers as an abbreviated formulation of the coherence theory the following: "Anything is true which can be conceived." He continues by explaining what he means by the term "conceive." He points out that he does not mean "image" or "imagine." What he does mean by "conceive" is "think out clearly and logically." But here it is important to bear in mind the distrust of abstraction which we saw manifested in the doctrine of internal relations. For most contemporary philosophers, "to think out clearly and logically" suggests drawing the implications of a set of statements. To do so would be possible also in the case of false statements or fictional statements, and there is even a sense in which a set of truth functions or propositional functions could be elaborated deductively. We would say that we are thinking out clearly and logically the implications of "All men are mortal" and "X is a man" if we draw the conclusion that "X is mortal," yet it might be false that all men are mortal, and it certainly is neither true nor false that X is a man. We seem to have something less than truth in this case. But for Joachim we are not able to think something out clearly and logically if we abstract in such a manner from the fullness and concreteness of immediate experience. Thus, the coherence theory reveals again the usual idealist rejection of any kind of formalism. It is this rejection which scuttles the misunderstanding of the coherence theory which takes it to be the view that whatever is logically consistent is true. It is not uncommon to hear that the coherence theory is refuted by the fact of alternative geometries, each logically consistent, but incompatible with the others. If Euclidean geometry is true (so this argument goes), then non-Euclidean geometries are false, since they are inconsistent with Euclidean geometry. Thus, we would have something consistent but false, and the coherence theory is therefore false. But this identification of "coherence" with "consistency" is rejected explicitly by Joachim. He states that whatever is true will certainly be consistent, but he denies that bare consistency is a sufficient condition for truth. Consistency is a formal characteristic; coherence is a richer notion which includes material considerations as well.

But let us turn to giving a positive account of coherence. It does seem to make sense to say that the totality of our experience is some sort of system. For one thing, our experience seems to be temporally organized; our memories refer to past events, our expectations have a future reference. There also seem to be repeatable elements in our experience; every twenty-four hours I go to sleep, eat food, and drink water. At regular intervals I go to work and return home again. But within *my* experience, at any rate, certain other possibilities are not genuine. I cannot, for instance, play first base on a major league baseball team. To say that yesterday I hit a home run for the Giants in their game with the Braves simply does not fit in with the rest of my experience. Thus, by the time I fill in *all* the elements of my experience, certain possibilities are ruled out, while others are unmistakably included. As I proceed to interpret the totality of my experience by making the judgments that comprise my knowledge structure, I come closer and closer to reflecting the richness and fullness of this totality. The goal I strive for is a complete recasting of my experience in a set of judgments. The nearer I come to achieving this complete account of my experience in a system of judgments, the nearer I approach truth.

This endeavor to reach truth as the reconstruction of the totality of my experience leads naturally to some other features of the coherence theory. It is quite consistent with saying that the more complete my structure of judgments, the nearer I approach truth, to say also that truth is properly reserved as a predicate for the total structure of judgments. Truth, for Joachim, is not a predicate of particular propositions or judgments; it is rather a predicate of the total system of judgments. Furthermore, absolute truth is an unrealizable goal. The best I can ever come up with is partial and incomplete truth. Nor is this all, for there is a sense in which I might say that a certain specific judgment which I now make is partially true because it occupies a place in the total structure of judgments which I have developed as of this date. But as the days and years go by I will be adding to this structure of judgments, making it more adequate and more complete. But if I retain the original judgment in the wider and more adequate structure, it becomes more and more true. As the knowledge structure expands and comes closer to completion, any given judgment in it becomes more true. Joachim points out that a simple mathematical relation, such as 3 squared equals 9, is truer for the skilled mathematician than it is for the boy in grade school who has just committed it to memory. Truth, on this view, admits of degrees.

What "think out clearly and logically" comes to, then, is this: We must see the judgments as elements in a rational structure which is constantly being enlarged and therefore is approaching ever closer to a complete account of the totality of our experience. Truth is the ideal of the complete faithfulness of such a structure of judgments to the totality of experience.

The last section of Joachim's book deals with the problem of error. He points out that the correspondence theory is unable to handle the matter of error as adequately as the coherence theory. Essentially, the coherence theory of error is that error represents a partial truth which is superseded as the system of judgments becomes more complete. I may make a judgment now that the moon is made of green cheese, and this may cohere with the limited set of judgments I now have. However, as I fill in the gaps in my structure of judgments, I recognize that the judgment that the moon is made of green cheese does not cohere with the remainder of my judgments. I therefore replace this judgment with one which fits in better with the other judgments I have made. Error is thus a kind of stage we go through on the way to fuller truth. Error is the distortion that results from a partial view.

It has been fashionable in recent decades to smile indulgently at the foolishness of idealism generally and the coherence theory of truth specifically. It seems fair to say, however, that recent philosophizing about the relation between meaning and use probably has raised questions that suggest a reexamination of what the great idealists such as Joachim had to say about truth as coherence. For certainly it can be said that before a statement's truth value can be determined, its meaning must be understood. But if meaning is related to use, and use is related to a context in which terms and statements occur, then some of the points raised by the coherence theorists seem to have relevance again. If the coherence theory can enlighten some contemporary philosophical disputes, then a classic statement of it, such as Joachim's *The Nature of Truth*, deserves careful study once again.

PRAGMATISM

Author: William James (1842-1910)
Type of work: Epistemology, philosophy of philosophy
First published: 1907

PRINCIPAL IDEAS ADVANCED

Pragmatism is both a philosophical method and a theory of truth.

As a method, it resolves metaphysical disputes by asking for the practical consequences of alternative resolutions.

Once a distinction of practice is made, theoretical difficulties disappear.

As a theory of truth, Pragmatism claims that ideas are true insofar as they are satisfactory; to be satisfactory, ideas must be consistent with other ideas, conformable to facts, and subject to the practical tests of experience.

Occasionally a book succeeds in giving influential expression to an attitude and a set of principles which eventually make up a historically important philosophical movement. This is the case with William James's *Pragmatism*. Borrowing the term from his philosophical contemporary, Charles S. Peirce (1839-1914), James attempts in a series of published lectures to popularize and defend "a number of tendencies that hitherto have lacked a collective name." Pragmatism came to dominate the American intellectual scene for more than two decades as well as to gain recognition as a uniquely American philosophical position. To this historical phenomenon of the pragmatic movement James's book still serves as a sympathetic if sometimes polemical introduction. Its eight related essays discuss the origin and meaning of Pragmatism as well as suggest how the pragmatic method can be applied to troublingly perennial problems in metaphysics and religion. The contents give evidence of James's belief that philosophizing, as a technical concern, must always involve consequences for the life of common sense and common men.

Given the question: Can a philosopher settle all philosophical disputes disinterestedly?—James replies in the negative. The point here is not that philosophers ought to ignore claims of logic and evidence. Rather, the point is that philosophical "clashes" involve more than logic and evidence. James insists that no philosopher can wholly "sink the fact of his temperament," however responsibly he seeks to give "impersonal reasons only for his conclusions." A philosophical attitude necessarily becomes colored by a man's temperament. In "The Dilemma in Philosophy," which opens *Pragmatism*, James argues that a fundamental opposition in temperament has marked the history of thought—that between rationalism and empiricism. The rationalist values "abstract and eternal principles"; the empiricist, "facts in all their crude variety." Aware that so hard and fast a distinction can serve only a rough-and-ready use, James suggests that clusters of traits tend to distinguish the rationalist from the empiricist. Rationalists are "tender-minded," "intellectualistic," "idealistic," "optimistic," "religious," "free-willist," "monistic," "dogmatical." Empiricists are "tough-minded," "sensationalistic," "materialistic," "pessimistic," "irreligious," "fatalistic," "pluralistic," "skeptical."

This rule of thumb distinction between two attitudes James applies to his view of the existing philosophical situation. This situation is one in which even children "are almost born scientific." Positivism and scientific materialism tend to dominate the scene, favoring the empirically minded outlook. Yet men also seek to preserve an element of religiousness. James insists that a philosophical dilemma arises which is unacceptable to his contemporaries: adopt a positivistic respect for empirical facts which ignores religion or keep a religiousness which is insufficiently empirical. James will settle for neither alternative. He asserts that "in this blessed year of our Lord 1906" the common man as philosopher demands facts, science, and religion. The ordinary man cannot find what he needs in the philosophical country store. Materialists explain phenomena by a "nothing but" account of higher forms in terms of lower, while religious thinkers provide a choice between an empty transcendentalist idealism (whose Absolute has no necessary relation to any concretely existing thing) and traditional theism (whose compromising nature lacks prestige and vital fighting powers). Rationalist elements in idealism and theism emphasize refinement and escape from the concrete realities of ordinary, everyday life. The result is that for the common man's plight "Empiricist writers give him a materialism, rationalists give him something

religious, but to that religion 'actual things are blank.' "

For this dramatically staged intellectual predicament James has a philosophical hero ready in the wings. It is "the oddly-named thing pragmatism." Pragmatism is offered as a philosophy which can salvage the religious values of rationalism without perverting man's many-sided awareness of facts. It can also take account of the way temperamental demands inevitably affect foundations of philosophical systems. What James promises for his generation is a kind of philosophical synthesis which locates personal ways of seeing things squarely in the heart of philosophical subject-matter. What this involves he describes in two essays: "What Pragmatism Means" and "Pragmatism's Conception of Truth."

Pragmatism is both a method and a theory of truth. The method can be used by men holding widely different philosophical persuasions. Its function is chiefly that of settling metaphysical disputes which seriously disturb men. Metaphysical arguments involve "notions" about which one can always ask whether the notions lead to any practical consequences. Such notions must be shown to make a difference in human conduct if they are to prove meaningful. Two Jamesian examples can illustrate what is meant here. One example concerns an argument about whether, if a man circles a tree around whose trunk a squirrel is also moving, one can say the man "goes round" the squirrel. James shows how the answer depends on what is meant by "round." Mean by "going round" that the man is in successive places to north, east, south, and west of the squirrel, then he does go round the animal. Mean, on the other hand, that the man is behind, then to the right of, then in front of, and then to the left of the squirrel, then the man may not actually go round the squirrel—since the animal may move simultaneously with the man's movements. James concludes that an argument of this kind, if analyzed, turns out to be a verbal one.

Another example illustrates how the pragmatic method is compatible with many possible results. James asks his readers to view the method as being like a corridor in a hotel, whose doors open into many rooms which contain thinkers involved in a variety of intellectual pursuits. These pursuits may be metaphysical, religious, or scientific. Metaphysically, one room may harbor a man working out an idealistic system, while another may shelter a thinker attempting to show that metaphysics is an impossibility. James insists that the pragmatic method is neutral regarding the kinds of thought going on in the rooms. Nonetheless, he insists that as a theory of truth Pragmatism favors the nominalist's preference for particulars, the Utilitarian's stress on what is useful, and the positivist's dislike of metaphysical speculations and merely verbal solutions of problems. James believes men wanting to employ words like "God," "Matter," "the Absolute," "Reason," and "Energy" should use the pragmatic method in seeking to show how such notions can have practical effects.

As an instrumentalist theory of truth, Pragmatism views sharp distinctions between logic and psychology with great suspicion. Ideas are instruments which help to dispel doubt when inherited bodies of opinion no longer produce intellectual ease. Belief means the cessation of doubting. But what makes a belief true? James asserts that an idea is true if it permits the believer to attain "satisfactory relations with other parts of our experience." This genetic conception of truth—influenced by Darwinian biology—sees ideas as true for specified situations, always in principle subject to change and reëvaluatoin. Some critics interpret James's emphasis on the contextual truth of an idea as meaning a man may believe whatever happens to make him comfortable. James rejects any wish-fulfilling conception of pragmatic truth. He states conditions which any idea must satisfy to qualify as workable. These conditions are quite conservative: Ideas must prove consistent with other ideas (including old ones) conformable to existing facts, and subject to experiential corroboration and validation.

James is mostly critical of rationalistic metaphysical ideas leading to no observable differences in domains of human conduct. He rejects claims about *the* Truth. Nonetheless he will consider even theological ideas as possibly true as long as their proponents can show them to affect some actual person's behavior. "Truth lives, in fact, for the most part on a credit system." Truth concerns matters of fact, abstract things and their relations, and the relations of an idea to the entire body of one's other beliefs. Ideas unable to conform to men's factual knowledge simply cannot have what James calls "cash-value."

James's relevant essays about truth sometimes raise questions which they do not satisfactorily answer. Some critics accuse him of advocating a subjectivist theory of truth. Elsewhere,

James defends his views by suggesting two kinds of criteria for testing the meaning of any sentence. First, a sentence has meaning if it leads to observable consequences in experience. Second, a sentence is meaningful if someone's belief in it leads to behavioral consequences. James seems to employ the first view when he writes about scientific and factual knowledge. He uses the second view when discussing certain moral and religious beliefs. It is the second view which worries some critics, who think that—if taken literally—it can justify as true any psychologically helpful belief.

The bulk of the remaining essays in *Pragmatism* seek to illustrate how the pragmatic method and theory of truth may be applied to specific problems. These are predominantly philosophical rather than scientific problems. In "Some Metaphysical Problems" and "The One and the Many" he applies the generous theory of meaning to such problems as the meaning of substance, the relative values of materialism and spiritualism, the problem of evil, the debate about freedom of the will, and the merits of monism and pluralism as cosmological notions. "Pragmatism and Common Sense" discusses three kinds of knowledge whose truth-claims are perennial. "Pragmatism and Humanism" and "Pragmatism and Religion" indicate how Pragmatism can mediate in disputes among hard-headed empiricists and abstract rationalists.

Taking the traditional puzzles about substance. design in nature, and free will, James argues that such metaphysical issues often lead to no genuine consequences for action if treated in solely intellectual terms. "In every *genuine* metaphysical dispute some prac-

tical issue, however conjectural and remote, is involved." Metaphysical arguments thus concern something other than what seems the case. Influenced by the thing-attribute aspect of grammar, men worry about substance because they suppose a *something* must support the external and psychological objects of our perceivable world beyond what these objects are experienced *as*. James asks us to imagine that a material or spiritual substance undergoes change without altering our perceptions of its supposed attributes. In such a case our perception of the properties would be the same as before. It follows that the notion of substance as standing for something beyond perceived qualities of objects can add nothing to our actual knowledge of the things in the world. Only in the Catholic claims about the Eucharist can the notion of substance have any practical use—a religious one. Similarly, arguments whether God or matter best explains the origin and development of the universe are unimportant so far as the observable facts go. Only one's expectations about the future can make the theist-materialist issue important. The pragmatic method leads to a slight "edge" for theism, according to James, since the belief in God "guarantees an ideal order that shall be permanently preserved." *What* the world is like, even if God created it, remains a matter for patient scientific labors to discover. The theistic conception of the world's origin permits men a kind of enjoyment which materialism excludes. Morally, theism is preferable since it refuses to take human disasters as the absolutely final word, while materialism denies the eternity of the moral order.

The question whether there is de-

782

sign in the world is also pointless if raised with scientific intent. The design issue is really a religious one. It is not open to purely rational solution. The significant aspects of the issue concern *what* that design may be, as well as *what* the nature of any possible designer. James applies a similar treatment to the determinism versus freewill controversy. For him, this is an out-and-out metaphysical issue rather than interesting solely in relation to the discussion of moral judicability. To decide in favor of free will means to accept a faith that the universe can be improved through human effort. James calls this faith in improvability "meliorism." In turn, such a belief requires rejection of any absolute monistic conception of the cosmos. It requires belief in the notion that reality is a multiverse. The universe is neither simply one nor an absolute randomness. It is a pluriverse which contains specific kinds of unity as well as directly experienced "gaps." It is not *now* an absolute unity in light of our experience, but men may hope for such a completed unity as a possible future cosmic event.

James insists on the misleading nature of traditional metaphysical disputes. Metaphysical arguments seem to concern problems which human intellect can solve if only that intellect "gets them right." Yet, they are really practical problems. They are significant only when found to express hidden religious and moral issues. The pragmatist favors a decision for free will, belief in God's existence, faith in an increasing unity in a pluralistic universe, and hope that elements of design exist as grounds for one's belief in meliorism. Faith may rightfully decide when human reason proves insufficient. The reason is that such faith expresses confidence in the promise of the future and results in beneficial consequences for our present living.

James rejects metaphysical monism for moral and religious reasons. Monism implies a certain completedness about the universe even now. This completedness requires the denial of free will and, if God exists, of a worthwhile God. Nonetheless, James's pluralism includes the view that many kinds of unity compose the universe. Intellect aims neither at variety nor unity, but at totality. The world contains important unities but is not a total unity. Some parts of the world are continuous with others, as in spacetime; practical continuities appear (as in the notion of physical gravity); and there are systems of influence and noninfluence which indicate existence of causal unities. Furthermore, there are generic unities (kinds), unities of social purpose, and aesthetic unities. These are experienced. Yet, James says, we never experience "a universe pure and simple." Pragmatism therefore insists on a world as containing just as many continuities *and* disjunctions as experience shows to exist.

The only ultimate unity may be an absolute knower of the system. Even the system may not always be considered to be a necessary unity, since the world may exist as eternally incomplete—actually subject to addition and loss. Our knowledge of such a world grows slowly, through scientific criticism, common sense, and philosophic criticism. No one can demonstrate conclusively which, if any, of these ways of knowing is the truest. Common sense builds up customary ways of organizing the materials of experience. It uses such concepts as thing, same or different, kinds, minds, bodies, one time, one space, subjects and attributes, causal influences, the fancied, the real. Scientific criticism adds more sophisticated notions, like "atoms" and "ether," say, casting some doubt on the adequacy of common sense concepts. The philosophical stage gives no knowledge quite comparable to the other two. Philosophical criticism does not make possible description of details of nature. Our decisions about which philosophical views to adopt must turn on practical rather than theoretical criteria. On the other hand, choice between common sense and scientific notions will rest on existence of kinds of corroboration which, in principle, will always be lacking in the cases of competing philosophical claims.

The essays in *Pragmatism* express a loosely stated yet consistent philosophical viewpoint. Through them runs the excitement of discovery that, if only the pragmatic method be adopted, many old and perplexing issues can be translated into practical ones. James seems eager to help men discover the metaphysical views which will conform to their experienced needs. On the other hand, he wants to insist on binding tests when the pragmatist handles common sense and science. He is less insistent on such tests in religious and moral domains. His major thesis is that "all true processes must lead to the fact of directly verifying sensible experience *somewhere,* which somebody's ideas have copied." His generosity remains attractive even to some critics who reject his philosophical conclusions.

THE MEANING OF TRUTH

Author: William James (1842-1910)
Type of work: Epistemology
First published: 1909

PRINCIPAL IDEAS ADVANCED

An idea is true if it works; truth happens to an idea; the true is whatever is expedient in the way of thinking.

In answer to the objection that such a theory makes truth a function of attitude so that truth has nothing to do with reality, the critics are reminded that knowledge depends on immediate, perceptual experiences (brute facts) and on the satisfactory use of concepts.

A concept (proposition) is true if it is such that, if acted upon, what one would receive perceptually is what one expects; in this sense, a true proposition satisfies an expectation.

No idea is satisfactory unless it works in such a way as actually to put the person who counts on the idea into a harmonious relationship with reality.

Although satisfaction is subjective, it can be a sign of objective truth.

In 1908 William James published his famous volume *Pragmatism,* in which he exposited the pragmatic theory of truth. His views were immediately attacked by a great many philosophers in the United States, England, France, and Germany. James felt that the criticisms were mainly due to a misunderstanding of the views presented in his book and in the writings of his fellow pragmatists. He, therefore, gathered together a group of his articles and papers, dating back to 1884, which he hoped would clarify the pragmatic theory. In addition, he joined to these a series of answers he had previously published against specific objections, plus a few new replies to the most recent criticisms. This collection was published under the title of *The Meaning of Truth* and constitutes the most complete explanation of James's theory of truth.

The general types of objections that James tries to answer are that the pragmatic theory of truth is entirely subjective, and that the pragmatic theory denies that truth has anything to do with reality. In *Pragmatism,* James had presented his famous formulation of the theory—truth is that which works; it is something that happens to an idea. The truth of an idea is the process of verifying it. What is true is what is expedient "in the way of our thinking," just as what is right is only what is expedient in our behavior.

Critics immediately pointed out that if an idea's truth depends merely on its satisfying someone's needs or wishes, then truth is a function of attitude and condition and has nothing to do with reality. In fact, the critics argued, an idea could actually be false in terms of reality, and yet true pragmatically for somebody. Choosing some of James's examples, especially from his *Will to Believe* (1897), opponents pointed out that if somebody believed that God exists, and this belief worked for him and satisfied him, then the belief would be true according to pragmatism, even though it is possible that it is false in fact.

James sought to respond to all of his critics by showing them what he had already said about the psychology of gaining true knowledge, about the reality of what we know, about the objectivity of what we know, and about misunderstandings of the pragmatic method and theory. The first few essays in *The Meaning of Truth,* "The Function of Cognition" (1884), "The Tigers in India" (1895), "Humanism and Truth" (1904), "The Relation Between the Knower and Known" (1904), "The Essence of Humanism" (1905), "A Word More About Truth" (1907), and "Professor Pratt on Truth" (1907), all stress the contention that the pragmatic psychological explanation of truth requires that truths deal with reality and that they must, from their very character, be objective.

The opponents, according to James, all hold to a view that in the knowing process there are three elements: the knower, the object that is known, and a third entity called "the knowing." An idea or belief is true, by this theory, if what is known corresponds to the actual object that is known. This theory creates an "epistemological gulf" between the knower and what he is trying to know. In some mysterious way, James points out, the knower has to leap over this gulf, by means of the process labeled "knowing," and get from his own beliefs and ideas to the objective state of affairs in order to ascertain whether he possesses true knowledge. Various theories of knowledge have been presented to try to explain how the leap takes place. But, James insists, to the extent that these theories ever succeed in illuminating the mysterious process, they turn out to offer portions of the pragmatic account, and they show that a psychological understanding of what occurs in knowing is, in fact, what knowing is.

Knowing consists, in James's account, either of a direct, immediate awareness, such as knowing that this paper is white, or of a conceptual knowledge in which a concept, such as "tigers in India," is connected and employed, in the context of immediate experience which the world supplies, with satisfactory results.

An immediate experience is not a datum which the mind sees and then tries to relate to something "out there." Instead, for James, it is a "brute fact," and the mental content and the perceived object are one and the same thing. It is only later, in terms of other theories we work out, that we develop two different ways of describing this one fact, that the paper is in the mind, or that the mind is "around" the paper. The rock bottom of our world is the experiencing of brute facts. According to James's theory of radical empiricism, these facts occur, they are the basic data of which we are aware, (awareness of them, is, itself, a brute fact), and they occur together with their relations to one another as part of the "given" experiences. (Here, James rejects the classical empirical theory of David Hume and John Stuart Mill, which holds that experience consists of atomic, individual data that are completely separate and distinct.)

These immediate, perceptual experiences are "real" and "objective." What such a proposition meant for James is that in the actual context of life, these experiences provide a hard-core residuum which we cannot alter or ignore and hence must accept. The claim that these experiences are "real" in some further trans-experiential sense James finds difficult to fathom, since, as far as he can see, any attempt that might be made to explain what is real about experience, or how it might be determined that an experience is real, would have to appeal to our direct, psychological acquaintance with the "reality" of brute facts.

Conceptual experience, knowledge of facts not immediately or directly given in experience, is known, and is known to be true, by its relationship to the context of perceptual experience. A proposition makes sense and is true by reference to a sequence of perceptions and a sequence of actions which, if followed out, would terminate in harmonious and satisfactory experience. In the example that James analyzes, that of the tigers of India, this concept points to others, to actions which we might or do perform, and to the context of our experiences, both "real" and "ideal." In terms of our expectations, we would be dissatisfied (surprised) if shown a picture of a jaguar and told it was an Indian tiger. But we would be satisfied if we went to India, or thought of going to India, and perceived, or thought of perceiving, a certain striped animal which was usually called a tiger. The concept, then, of "tigers in India" works harmoniously and satisfactorily within the context of our other experiences, whereas other concepts do not work as well and hence are rejected as untrue. Conceptual experience grows and changes as the experience of harmonious and satisfactory relations betweeen experiences grows and develops. Thus, in keeping with James's doctrine in *Pragmatism*, truth is something that happens to an idea. An idea can become more or less true as it is employed in relation to other experiences. An idea which does not seem to be harmonious or satisfactory in relation to other experiences may become more harmonious as experience changes and grows.

Throughout the essays, James tries to make the notions of "working," "satisfactory," and "harmonious" clearer, since much of what he claims is his opponents' misunderstanding of pragmatism stems from their misinterpretations of these terms. The terms cannot be precisely defined, for there are so many different ways in which ideas may work satisfactorily or harmoniously in our experience. But, in general, in view of the account offered about the psychology of "knowing," ideas can work harmoniously and satisfactorily only insofar as they conform to "reality." Since reality consists of the perceptual and conceptual experiences that we have, an idea that did not conform to, or fit in with, reality, would not be harmonious with the context of our experiences. Hence, ideas work not because we want them to, but because their working is conditioned by the "real" world of our experience.

Further, James insists in several of the essays, working is not merely a practical matter, and satisfaction is not merely a pleasant personal feeling. The terminology employed in *Pragmatism* may have led critics to conceive of an idea as "working" only in terms of physical actions occurring and succeeding in their aim. But, James explains, working is a complex process involving the solving not only of practical problems, but of theoretical ones as well, plus the overall satisfaction that we can gain only by having our conceptual and immediately experienced world form a consistent and harmonious whole. As human beings, we seek and demand more than mere practical or utilitarian satisfaction. We are unable to accept perceptual or conceptual experiences which conflict with others that we have had, or which conflict with concepts or theories that have worked in the past. Whenever we seem to be faced with such discrepancies, we seek other immediate and conceptual experiences in order to overcome the difficulties, so that our entire world of experience and thought will form a harmonious whole. Then, and only then, will our ideas work satisfactorily.

Some of the statements of the pragmatic theory, including some of James's early ones, make it appear that the feeling of satisfaction involved in having a consistent perceptual and intellectual world is a purely subjective and psychological matter. "The sentiment of rationality," as James labels it, is a feeling that normal, reasonable people have when everything they believe and perceive fits together. In *The Meaning of Truth*, James stresses the point that this sentiment of satisfaction is, in fact, actually achieved only through uniting one's conceptual and perceptual experience consistently into one harmonious world. The satisfaction involved may be subjective and psychological, but it requires theoretical effort and logical consistency.

In the eighth essay of *The Meaning of Truth*, "The Pragmatist Account of Truth and Its Misunderstanders" (1908), James reviews his answer to his critics regarding the relation of pragmatic truth to "reality," "objectivity," and "consistency." The opponents have insisted that since, according to the pragmatists, the truth of beliefs consists in their giving satisfaction, and since satisfaction is a subjective condition, then the subject receiving satisfaction can manufacture his own truths when he likes, depending only on what satisfies him, and having nothing to do with "reality" or "objectivity." But, James points out, human being are so constituted that the kinds of satisfactions they actually do find in their beliefs occur as a result of believing that there are independent physical realities, that there are other minds, that there have been past events, and that there are eternal logical relations. And, "Above all we find *consistency* satisfactory, consistency between the present idea and the entire rest of our mental equipment, including the whole order of our sensations, and that of our intuitions of likeness and difference, and our whole stock of previously acquired truths." The pragmatist, James asserts, treats his satisfactions as possibly true guides to reality, and not as guides that are true solely for him. The critics appear to suppose that because "satisfaction" is a subjective feeling it therefore cannot indicate objective truth, while the pragmatist contends that since this feeling is, in fact, our final way for deciding what is, and what is not, objectively true, the feeling of satisfaction is interwoven with "reality" and yields "objective truth."

But the critics object again, pointing out that it is a notorious fact that erroneous views and beliefs are often quite satisfactory to the person who holds them. Hence, the satisfactory feeling cannot suffice to guarantee the objective truth of a belief, its relation to reality. James replies that the pragmatist has said only that the feelings of satisfaction are indispensable for "truth-building." He has not claimed that the feelings themselves are sufficient. The critic criticizes the pragmatic theory by considering feelings of satisfaction out of the actual contexts in which truth-satisfactions occur coincident to our being led to direct experience of reality. If only the feelings took place, we would not actually be completely satisfied, because something, the awareness of immediate reality, would be missing. Therefore, James contends, given the situations in which truth-satisfactions are felt by human beings, the subjective and even solipsistic problems that the critics of pragmatism raise are not really relevant, since one does not and would not feel satisfied unless what one believed led to an awareness of reality—that is, to future experiences of a sort one anticipated.

The remaining seven essays deal with various forms of the same objections that had come up in books and articles that had just appeared in the United States, England, France, and Germany against James's formulation of the pragmatic theory of truth. Though interesting points occur in these essays, they deal, for the most part, with restatements of James's reasons for denying the subjectivist charges of his critics and with reassertions of his contention that the pragmatic theory is realistic and objective. From the present-day perspective, the most interesting of these essays is the one dealing with the objections raised by the English philosopher Bertrand Russell.

In the essay "Two English Critics,"

James deals with criticisms of pragmatism that Russell had presented in his article, "Transatlantic Truth," that had appeared in the *Albany Review* in 1908. Russell argued that according to the pragmatists a true proposition is one such that believing it is worth while. If this be the case, he claimed, anyone who believes that a proposition is true must already have ascertained that its consequences are, in actual fact, good. And, in many instances, it is obviously much more difficult to settle the question of whether the consequences are good than whether the original proposition is true. Hence, the pragmatic test cannot really be applied to tell if any given proposition is true.

James replies that Russell has made the pragmatic theory appear silly by taking the notion of "good consequences" as a sign or criterion of a proposition's truth. Instead, James contends, the potential consequences are the "lurking" motives for the making of truth-claims, though they may also, occasionally, serve as measures or marks of truth. The consequences are not the *logical* premises for beliefs, although they do give intelligible practical meaning to calling a belief true or false. The consequences are the *psychological* reasons for our asserting beliefs and the psychological cues for our acting upon our beliefs.

Russell's attack continues, contending that it follows from the pragmatic definition of "truth," that a proposition can be true even though what it asserts is false. A proposition is true if it works, for the pragmatists, and "it works" means that "it is useful to believe it." Hence, by substituting definitions for the terms defined, one comes to the conclusion that to assert that a proposition such as "Other people exist" is true, means that it is useful to believe that other people exist, even if, in fact, they do not.

James rejects Russell's criticism by insisting that it results from "vicious" abstractions. Russell has abstracted the pragmatic terms from the context in which they occur and has juggled definitions to come to his conclusion. "But may not real terms . . . have accidents not expressed in their definitions?" James asks. Beliefs, James insists, have their objective content, as well as their truth. For this reason, when somebody believes that other people exist, both the consequences and the so-called objective content are involved in his belief. In effect, James denies that the nature of truth can be examined abstractly, in terms of definitions. Instead, it must be examined in the context of the real situations in which it occurs.

The fifteen essays that comprise *The Meaning of Truth*, though extremely repetitious, contain an important exposition of James's pragmatic theory. The work also presents one of the best discussions, from the pragmatic side, of the standard objections that have been and still are being raised to James's theory. In view of more recent considerations of pragmatism, the essays are most intriguing in showing how James tried to establish that his theory does not rest on the purely subjective. Whether one is convinced or not, one is impressed by James's attempt to grapple with the fundamental points raised by his critics.

THE PRINCIPLE OF INDIVIDUALITY AND VALUE

Author: Bernard Bosanquet (1848-1923)
Type of work: Metaphysics, philosophy of value
First published: 1912

PRINCIPAL IDEAS ADVANCED

An individual is not a mere particular, nor is he a personality finding supreme value in experience; an individual is a whole organized from mutually supplementing parts.

The world process is moving in the direction of greater integration of its parts.

The principle of individuality, when viewed in terms of ideas, is the principle of harmony, coöperation, and noncontradiction.

Purpose is secondary to individuality; to understand the world, one must understand it not in terms of purpose but on the principle of individuality.

Value depends on order and harmony; a life acquires value when it contributes to the realization of a larger whole.

The Absolute may be an individual in whom all selves are brought together in a single thought.

In this, his first series of Gifford Lectures, Bernard Bosanquet dealt with the perennial metaphysical problem of how the world can be one and at the same time many. In his day there were were pluralists, who denied that the world is one, and monists, who denied that it is many. In between were dualists, who held that mind, *élan vital,* or some such unifying principle is engaged in eternal struggle against matter and chance. Bosanquet, maintaining that the world is an integral whole, pointed out that it is the characteristic of a whole to bring diverse elements together into a higher unity.

The term "individual," as employed by Bosanquet, is a synonym for "whole." He carefully distinguished his use of the word from other meanings that the word has. Some philosophers have made it synonymous with "particular," in accordance with the logic of classes and members. Useful as the familiar scheme of universal and particular is for many purposes, Bosanquet complained that because it proceeds by abstraction, it leads away from rather than toward ultimate truth. For example, the notion "man" is arrived at by leaving out such characteristics as height, color, musical ability, and the like in order to find those characteristics that are common to all members of the class. When a concrete human being is thought of simply as a particular instance of the class man—as he is likely to be viewed by scientists—everything that makes him an individual is left out. Bosanquet said that it is a misuse of language to call the particular an individual.

Other philosophers have used the term "individual" to stand for human personality in its unique, idiosyncratic aspect. The nineteenth century, with its democratic and romantic sentiments, may be said to have discovered "personality." Every human being, regardless of his status, was said to have

790

infinite value, not so much in his identification with the image of eternity as in virtue of the supreme value attached to each man's "experience." Several schools of thought proclaimed the primacy of consciousness, and declared that novelty is the highest good. Under their influence, the term "individual" came to stand for the fresh, the spontaneous, the original; they did not hesitate to affirm that the only thing of value in the whole universe is the immediate, unrepeatable experience of conscious beings; and that, if there is a God, he must resemble man in these respects.

Bosanquet rejected this account of individuality no less firmly than the other. He maintained that empirical consciousness has so little coherence it is fatuous to think of it as one in any sense. A healthy man has unity when viewed as a physical organism; and when viewed as a moral and spiritual being he has the measure of unity which good habits and knowledge impart to his behavior. But there is no comparable unity in the consciousness of man, which is a tumbling chaos of sensations and fancies. When here and there our experience achieves unity, this comes from the order of the world which is experienced, not from man's fleeting awareness.

True individuals, Bosanquet held, are everywhere around us. A flower is an example; so is a family, a poem, or a machine. Wherever parts fit together in a larger complex and differences mutually supplement each other to form wholes, there the principle of individuality is found. Mostly, said Bosanquet, we are not conscious of it, because, like the air we breathe or the light by which we see, it is too obvious. We become conscious of this principle of individuality chiefly in those situations where we had not expected to find it, as, for example, when through the artist's eye we see a wood where we thought there were only trees, or through the sociologists' investigations we discover that a crowd is something more than the men and women who make it up.

Bosanquet was an idealist, but only in the sense that Plato was, for whom "ideas" were the real determinations of things and not contents of man's mind, as philosophers since Descartes have so often affirmed. He was an "objective" idealist because he held that the relations which determine things do not depend on anyone's awareness of them. To make clear his affiliations, he made bold to say that his philosophy was "materialism or externalism with a difference."

Although many idealists in his day felt it necessary to decry the naturalistic account of evolution which explained the origin of species in mechanistic terms, Bosanquet rather welcomed the stringent impersonalism of the Darwinian world-view. He said that the sciences proceed by abstraction; hence, they leave out much that is important, but this does not mean that their account is false. After all, a mechanism is an individual in which the parts function only because they are mutually adapted to each other. Bosanquet's chief complaint against naturalism was that it misconstrued the principle of the uniformity of nature. He said that the less reflective advocates of mechanism and materialism wrongly supposed this principle to mean that the future will resemble the past, whereas philosophers such as J. S. Mill understood quite well that such resemblance as occurs in nature is a result of the interconnection of its parts. The law of gravity is a good example because it explicitly mentions the mutual attraction of bodies and specifies that it is proportional to the masses and their distance apart. Natural selection is another example: it affirms that those organisms which are suited to their environment tend to survive in the struggle for existence.

Evolution was not essential to Bosanquet's view of the world, inasmuch as his fundamental outlook was one he shared with such nonevolutionists as Plato and Spinoza. But on the basis of scientific evidence he accepted evolution and worked it into his account of the world. In his view, the world-process is moving in the direction of greater integration of its parts. On the lower levels, determination is almost entirely mechanical. Even in living organisms, adaptation is mostly repetitious and associative. But as we follow the process to higher planes, we find more freedom of adaptation and a more explicit determination of the parts by the organism as a whole.

Another aspect of naturalism that vexed many idealist philosophers was the view that mind or consciousness merely reflects bodily behavior and has no power to originate or modify behavior. Against this view, commonly called epiphenomenalism, they advanced the view called interactionism, which contends that mind has an independent existence and is both acted upon by body and acts on it. Here, again, Bosanquet leaned toward the naturalist position. He argued that a man can do nothing merely by entertaining a purpose in his mind. For example, it is easy to propose a charitable undertaking; but carrying it out depends upon skills and habits which require a lifetime to develop and are no part of consciousness at all, having their locus as nearly as we can tell in the brain and nervous system. He did not deny that "higher" mental processes distinguish the conduct of men from that of lower creatures; but he maintained that consciousness is not the workingpart of these higher processes.

This is not to say that he regarded consciousness as playing an unimportant part in the life of man or its emergence as insignificant in the evolution of the world. On the contrary, in its role of spectator, mind has a value of its own. Here the unconscious unities and adaptations of the world appear on a new plane: they are understood, appreciated, enjoyed. In a manner reminiscent of Spinoza, Bosanquet held that there are two ways of viewing the world. If it is viewed as external, it appears to be a texture of conflicting forces seeking to resolve their oppositions in the most economical fashion. If it is viewed from within, it takes the appearance, rather, of conflicting ideas which are seeking logical resolution. Bosanquet's logic, of course, was not the logic of linear inference which Spinoza learned from Descartes, but Hegel's dialectics, which supposes that initial antinomies are reconciled in a higher synthesis. The evolution of the species and the history of man have causal explanations, but they can also be viewed as the working out of the logical principle of noncontradiction. Things can be different, Bosanquet insisted, without being contradictory. Colors, for example, may clash or they may harmonize. The principle of individuality which, viewed in external terms, yields the notion of an organism (a self-maintaining machine), when viewed in terms of ideas is the principle of harmony, coöperation, and non-contradiction.

Bosanquet rejected the view, popular among opponents of naturalism, that the world can be understood in terms of purpose. Purpose, he argued, is always secondary to individuality. Finite wholes, which are never entirely self-sufficient, have wants; and behavior designed to satisfy these wants, by adapting means to the desired end, is what is meant by purpose. Such adaptation, however, is not to be confused with the adjustment of parts within a whole. To achieve a purpose means to remove differences, for, when the want is satisfied, both ends and means cease to exist. It is the mark of an individual, however, that it does not abolish differences but reconciles them in a higher unity. The sentimental novel exemplifies the purposive standpoint: when the lovers are united, after overcoming many obstacles, the novel must end. Greek tragedy exemplifies the principle of individuality: conflicts find their resolution in a transformation of the will of the protagonist. Bosanquet did not deny that there is purpose in the world, on the preconscious as well as on the conscious plane. But he did deny that the notion of purpose has any value for understanding evolution or history, or the destiny of man, or the world as a whole. The reason at work everywhere about us, he said, is not intelligible in terms of means and ends; it is intelligible only on the principle of individuality.

Bosanquet reasoned about value in a similar way. The ordinary nineteenth century understanding of value made it equivalent to satisfaction. But satisfactions, like purposes, exist only in finite individuals, so that to equate value with the satisfaction of wants makes it quite a minor thing. And if, as was commonly maintained, it is not the satisfaction as such that is good but the consciousness which a man has of the satisfaction, it is more minor still. For Bosanquet, not the satisfaction of a purpose but the harmony of a whole is what has value, and the more comprehensive the whole, the greater the value. He maintained, with Plato (*Republic*, Book IV), that society has more value than any of its members, and that the value of personal life and effort derives from the function a man fulfills in the greater whole. Thus, the housewife, the worker, the soldier, the statesman become valuable as they perform the duties of their respective stations.

Bosanquet accepted the dictum of T. H. Green (*Prolegomena to Ethics,* 1883) that there is no value where there is no consciousness; but he urged that consciousness is not valuable by itself—the value lies in that of which we become conscious, and only secondarily, in the quality of mind which is able to appreciate values. These considerations led Bosanquet to set aside the usual moralistic and hedonistic interpretations of man's existence and put in their place an aesthetic one. Appreciation of the order and harmony of the world, whether in terms of science or art or philosophy, was, in his view, the thing for which consciousness is properly suited. Getting pleasure is a function of a healthy constitution; good morals a function of mental hygiene and social discipline. One does not have to take thought about them. Moreover, they hold only limited opportunities for self-realization. Man deepens and integrates his conscious life only as he progresses toward understanding and appreciating the world. By learning to think coherently, improving his judgment, cultivating his taste, he achieves the fullness and freedom which are the prerogative only of conscious selves or souls.

Bosanquet criticized the view that creative excellence in art lies in novelty or in so-called originality. Rather, he said, it consists in the artist's penetration of reality which permits him to reveal treasures beyond the scope of the average mind. In his view, the vision of the artist is closely related to the theory of the scientist: both are expressions of the "logic which lays bare the heart and structure of things, and in doing so purifies and intensifies the feeling which current appearances are too confused and contradictory to evoke."

This vision, Bosanquet said, is impersonal and can be shared. Not everybody shares it equally because of differences in mind due to training and native genius. Moreover, physical circumstances, such as fatigue or illness, limit one's mental power. But the value is there, however completely or partially the empirical consciousness manages to lay hold on it. That what is primary is the object of vision rather than the consciousness which possesses it appears when we observe that our most satisfactory experiences are those in which self-consciousness moves into the penumbra and leaves us aware only of the truth.

The emphasis which modern men have put on self-consciousness and personality favors a pluralistic view of mind. It suggests that minds rise like so many pillars, each isolated from the others. Bosanquet proposed, as a more likely figure, that we think of human minds as ocean waves, some rising to greater heights than others but otherwise occupying the same space. He said that social experience is like a single mind in several bodies —the child, the worker, the statesman each being conscious of the same whole in varying degrees. Finite minds, he said (borrowing an expression from Hegel), are "copulas"; and he added, "Every self is the representative center of an external world." Nature becomes alive in it; the experiences of other selves are shared. In this way each mind "expands from its place in nature to a more or less wide and deep participation in the Absolute."

About the Absolute, Bosanquet was not very specific. In affirming it, he signified his conviction that the world is a whole, that is, a meaningful system. According to Bosanquet, there is nothing strange or extreme in such a view: all meaningful activity, whether devotion to duty or the search for truth, presupposes it. But is the Absolute a mind? Is the Whole conscious of what takes place within it? Bosanquet supposes that it is, not as finite selves are conscious when, as finite, they have the sense of being other than what they know, but in a manner suggested to us by those rare moments in which we come near to losing ourselves in our vision of the world. Such high awareness, said Bosanquet, such "perfect union of the mind and nature" as is exemplified in Dante's great poem, distantly figures a complete experience in which all nature, all selves, are brought together in a single thought. Such, it may be, is the Absolute.

IDEAS: GENERAL INTRODUCTION TO PURE PHENOMENOLOGY

Author: Edmund Husserl (1859-1938)
Type of work: Metaphysics, epistemology
First published: 1913

PRINCIPAL IDEAS ADVANCED

Natural sciences are, by nature, dogmatic; the phenomenologist must under-take a critical study of the conditions under which knowledge is possible.

To distinguish within experience that which experiences from that which is experienced, one must suspend natural beliefs; this suspension of belief is made possible by a method of bracketing by which we talk not about trees and selves as items external to experience but of the "trees" and the "perceptions" of experience.

Noema, that which is perceived, is dependent upon noesis, the perceiving; but noema has the kind of being peculiar to essences.

The absolute forms or essences which owe their actuality in consciousness to acts of perceiving are Eideia, eternal possibilities of quality, related to other Eideia by external relations.

The term "phenomenology," as it is used by Husserl and his disciples, designates first of all a principle of philosophical and scientific method. The usual method of natural science proceeds from a body of accepted truth and seeks to extend its conquest of the unknown by putting questions to nature and compelling it to answer. The phenomenological method adopts a softer approach. Setting aside all presuppositions and suppressing hypotheses, it seeks to devise techniques of observation, description, and classification which will permit it to disclose structures and connections in nature which do not yield to experimental techniques. It has been widely fruitful in psychology and the social sciences, as well as in epistemology and value-theory.

Husserl, in his *Logical Studies* (1900-1901), did much to advance general phenomenological studies. But he had in view a specifically philosophical application of the technique which many of his associates did not completely grasp, or failed to share. *Ideas* was written with a view to clearing up the distinction between phenomenological psychology, which he regarded as a legitimate, but secondary, science, and phenomenological philosophy, which, he was prepared to maintain, is the foundation of all science. When a sociologist or psychologist conducts a phenomenological investigation, he puts aside all the usual theories and assumptions which have governed research in that field: but he cannot rid himself of all presuppositions (such as, for example, the belief in the existence of the external world, the constancy of nature). As Plato saw, every science must proceed upon some assumptions—except philosophy. To fulfill its promise, the phenomeno-logical approach must bring us at last to an absolutely presuppositionless science. Pure phenomenology, or phenomenological philosophy, is, in Husserl's opinion, precisely that. (It has long been the aspiration of philosophers to make their science an absolute one, one that rids itself of all presuppositions and stands with open countenance before pure Being. Husserl stands in this tradition.)

Phenomenology is not to be confused with "phenomenalism," a name sometimes given to extreme forms of empiricism, such as that of Ernst Mach, which maintains that nothing is real except sense data. In fact, this is one of the misconceptions which phenomenology is designed to overcome. If the empiricists are right, the unity and order which we are accustomed to find in the world are not given in experience but put there by the activity of the mind. Genetic psychology, which seeks to explain the origin of our various mental habits and responses, would therefore hold the key to understanding our whole view of the world. A good example is J. S. Mill, who in his *A System of Logic* (1843) undertook to explain the force of syllogistic reasoning in terms of associationist psychology. Other positivists and pragmatists have attempted to give a psychological theory of knowledge and of valuation. Husserl argued, however, that the empiricists were wrong, that they did not come to their conviction about the absence of order and intelligibility in the pure data of experience by examining what is given there, but had it as an Idol of the Theater (to use Francis Bacon's term). It follows that they have misconceived the task of psychology in

supposing that it can discover in the mind laws which give rise to the meaning of the world, and that it is incumbent upon us to set about developing new accounts of logic, knowledge-theory, aesthetics, and ethics which stand on their own evidence. In place of *psychologism* (a misconceived psychology or science of the soul) what is needed, if justice is to be done to experience, is *phenomenology* (science of phenomena, or appearances).

Husserl takes his place, then, in the forefront of those twentieth century philosophers who have sought to reaffirm the autonomy of various philosophical disciplines over against psychology. He was equally concerned to turn back the tide of the popular-scientific view of the world which he called naturalism. The particular sciences, by nature, are dogmatic. That is to say, they proceed without examining the conditions under which knowledge is possible. This is not to be held against them. But when anyone attempts to build a natural philosophy on the findings of the sciences, his uncritical procedure opens the way to skepticism, because the categories in terms of which we grasp natural events are unsuited to take account of conscious events, including the pursuit of scientific truth. It seems innocent enough to explain consciousness in terms of natural causes until we recollect that matter and the laws which govern its behavior are themselves part of our experience. This, according to Husserl, is the point at which the philosopher must step in. His primary task, in fact, will be to distinguish within experience the part that experiences from the part that is experienced.

There are many overtones of Descartes in Husserl's writings. The former philosopher, in order to escape from the ambiguities and uncertainties of our ordinary, natural experience, developed a method of doubting. By bringing under question the whole phenomenal world, he laid bare a world of logical forms which he could not doubt. Husserl adopts a similar method. He talks of "suspending" our natural beliefs, including the fundamental conviction of every healthy mind that there is a world "out there," that there are other selves, and so on. We are asked to "alter" this natural standpoint, to "disconnect" our beliefs about causation and motion, to "put them out of action." This is, of course, only a methodological procedure, in order to help us overcome our animal bias and make it possible for us to take a coolly intellectual view of things. Greek philosophy used the term *epochē* to indicate the suspense of judgment. Husserl presses this term into his service.

To make his meaning clear, he uses the example of looking with pleasure into a garden where an apple tree is blossoming. From the natural standpoint, the tree is something that has transcendent reality in space and time, and the joy of perceiving it has reality in the psyche of a human being. But Descartes has reminded us that perceptions are sometimes hallucinations. We pass, therefore, from the natural to the phenomenological standpoint, bracketing the claims of both the knower and the known to natural being. This leaves us with "a nexus of exotic experiences of perception and pleasure valuation." We can now speak of the content and structure of the situation without any reference to external existence. Nothing is really taken away from the experience, but it is all

there in a new manner. In order to indicate this, the use of quotation marks is helpful. We can now speak of "tree," "plant," "material thing," "blossoming," "white," "sweet," and so forth, and be sure that we are talking only about things that belong to the essence of our experience. Similarly, at the opposite pole, we can distinguish "perceiving," "attending," "enjoying," and other ego-acts. These each have their special characters, and repay analysis.

Husserl was at one time a student of Franz Brentano (1838-1917), who had said that what distinguishes mental acts from non-mental acts is that the former invariably refer to something other than themselves. Drawing from the scholastics, he said that they are "intentional." Husserl makes constant use of this discovery. To designate the ego-acts, which are not limited to cognition but include as well various attitudes such as doubting and supposing, as well as volitions and feelings, he uses the Greek word *noesis* (literally, a perceiving). To designate the corresponding objects, for instance, "tree," "fruitful," "charming," he uses the corresponding word *noema* (literally, that which is perceived). An important part of the analysis of consciousness consists in tracing the relation between these. In each case, the *noesis* is real and fundamental, but *noema* is dependent and, strictly speaking, unreal. In our example, "the perceiving of the tree" is actual and constitutive of "the tree perceived." But conversely, though it does not have reality, *noema* has being, which is lacking to *noesis*: that is to say, it is composed entirely of essences, which are eternally what they are and stand in necessary or *a priori* relations with each other. The same thing is true of volition and other modes. "The valuing of the tree" is a *noesis*. It has the same reality as "the perceiving of the tree." Correspondingly, "the value of the tree" is a *noema*. It does not have reality, but it has the same kind of essential being as the structure and properties have which make up the object of cognition. The value-characters likewise take their place in an *a priori* system together with other values.

As long as our interest, as philosophers, is directed primarily toward the life of the mind, we shall be chiefly interested in exploring the various *noeses*. Husserl's delineation of these is subtle and perceptive, and goes a long way toward persuading the reader of the necessity of this descriptive groundwork, although as is sometimes true of the drawings of a microscopist we may have difficulty in recognizing in it the familiar features of the mind. His account of "meaning," for example, should be studied by those who are interested in semantics, and his analysis of "sentiment" and "volition" provides an instructive approach to the question of the relation between emotions and values. One thing is common to all *noeses*, according to Husserl: all are at bottom *thetic*, or postulational; Husserl speaks of them as *doxa* (Plato's word for "opinion"). This does not imply that some of our *noeses* are not characterized by "certainty," just as others are characterized by a "sense of likelihood" or "doubt." But in any case, it is what we commonly call a "moral certainty." The conviction is a mode of the "perceiving" rather than a function of anything lying in the "perceived."

But in the present work Husserl does not consider mental acts *per se*. He studies them because they provide the key to the various grades and types of objects which make up the *noemata*; for, corresponding to "perception" there is the realm of "colors," "shapes," and "sizes"; and corresponding to "perceptual enjoyment" there are "dainty" pink and "gloriously" scented. These qualities owe their actuality in consciousness to the *noeses*; but they are part of an order of being which is absolute and independent. Husserl calls all such absolute forms or essences *Eideia*, to avoid the ambiguities of such words as Ideas and Essences. They are eternal possibilities, each perfectly definite and distinct from every other, but also linked with every other in a system of eternal relations. Thus, "pink," "white," "green" are species under the genus "color"; and "color" itself stands in a hierarchy of perceptual "qualities." A similar hierarchical structure embraces the *noema* of value.

Husserl, who began his philosophical studies as a logician, was preëminently interested in the grammar of meaning. He claims that, on a very abstract level, all *noema* exemplify universal relations which can be formulated in a *Mathesis Universalis* such as Leibniz conceived. But the theorizing logician does not do justice to the wealth of formal relations which lie before the phenomenologist. "Its field is the analysis of the *a priori* shown forth in *immediate* intuition, the fixing of immediately transparent essences and essential connexions and their descriptive cognition in the systematic union of all strata in pure transcendental consciousness." It begins by distinguishing various regional ontologies—of which the "formal re' gion" exploited by the logician is only one. "Material regions" are numerous. The region of the physical *Thing* will serve as an example. The question presents itself as follows: "How are we to describe systematically the *noeses* and *noemata* which belong to the unity of the intuitionally presenting Thing-consciousness?" Leaving aside the *noetic* factor, the problem is to analyze the essential connections by which "appearances" present themselves as "one and the same thing." The analysis discloses that a mere *res extensa* is conceivable apart from the idea of a *res materialis* and a *res temporalis.* Yet as a matter of fact, a thing as presented to "us humans" involves all three of these. So, there are "strata" and "formations" constituting the thing. And it is necessary to analyze each of these unities in turn. The problem of "presentation in space" has here to be faced. Although, according to Husserl, its meaning has never yet been completely grasped, it now appears in a clear light—namely by "the phenomenological analysis of the *essential* nature of all the noematic (and noetic) phenomena, wherein space exhibits itself intuitionally and as the unity of appearances."

In the present volume, as is proper in an introduction, Husserl is able only to indicate the direction which the investigation must take. And one must look to his other works, and those of his disciples, to see the analyses carried out in detail. While Husserl worked chiefly in the field of epistemology, his disciples carried the method into axiology and philosophical anthropology (Max Scheler), aesthetics (Theodor Lipps), sociology (Karl Mannheim), comparative religion (Rudolph Otto), and ethics (Nicolai Hartmann), not to mention the "existentialism" of Martin Heidegger and Jean-Paul Sartre. For the ordinary reader, these developments are more interesting and fruitful than pure phenomenology. But that is because it is difficult for most people to exercise themselves about the sheer possibility of knowledge. Husserl's significance, as a philosopher, is that, like Descartes and Kant, he appeared at a time when the foundations of science were themselves threatened, and irrationalism, skepticism, and nihilism threatened the very nerve of Western civilization. He sought to revive knowledge, to make possible once again a rational view of the world and of the human enterprise. He was conscious of being the continuer of a long tradition, and with some reluctance admitted to falling under the classification of idealist. He most resembles Kant, and his work can be summed up as the search for the transcendental conditions which make "meaning" (scientific, ethical, aesthetic, religious) possible.

OUR KNOWLEDGE OF THE EXTERNAL WORLD

Author: Bertrand Russell (1872-   )
Type of work: Epistemology, metaphysics
First published: 1914 (Lowell Lectures, Boston, March and April, 1914)

The method of logical analysis makes the resolution of philosophical problems possible by defining the limits of scientific philosophy so as to exclude speculative metaphysics.

We can account for our knowledge of the external world by realizing, through logical analysis, that the world as we know it is a construction from the data given in sense experience; an individual's "private world" is the class of all data within his perspective, and a perceived object is the class of all aspects to be found in all the perspectives which include the object.

The conception of permanent things can be constructed by reference to appearances if points are defined by reference to enclosure series of spaces, and if time is defined by reference to classes of events simultaneous with each other.

Zeno's paradoxes of motion can be resolved by use of the mathematical theory of continuity.

The significance of this book lies in the fact that it proposed a new method for philosophizing. While the method suggested was not strictly novel (it had been previously used by such mathematical logicians as George Boole, Giuseppe Peano, and Gottlob Frege), it was modified by Russell and transferred from mathematical to philosophical subject matter. Russell called it the "logical-analytic" method or the method of "logical atomism." Since the publication of these lectures the method has been taken over and radically modified and broadened by a large school of philosophers who call themselves "analysts" and who constitute an important group in the modern philosophical world.

The analytic method, as Russell formulated it, is less ambitious than that of classical philosophy in that it does not claim to determine the nature of reality or the universe as a whole. What it does is both less speculative and less sweeping, but more scientific. It uses the techniques of modern logic and modern mathematics, and employs such concepts as *class, relation,* and *order* for the purpose of clarifying and

solving some of the perennial problems of philosophy which have not yet yielded to satisfactory solution. There are many such problems, but Russell here considers those concerned with the nature of the external world, with how the world of physics is related to the world of our ordinary sense experience, and with what is meant by space, time, continuity, infinity, and causation. The book consists of illustrations of the application of the logical-analytic method to these problems for the purpose of showing its fruitfulness. Russell insists that his results are to be taken as tentative and incomplete, but he believes that if any modification in his method is found necessary, this will be discovered by the use of the very method which he is advocating.

The philosophies of two typical representatives of the classical school— F. H. Bradley and Henri Bergson— are first examined in order to show the errors which these men made. Bradley found the world of everyday life to be full of contradictions, and he concluded that it must be a world of Appearance only, not of Reality. His error lay in his attempt to determine the character of the world by pure reasoning rather than by going to experience and examining what he found. Bergson believed that Reality is characterized fundamentally by growth and change; he then concluded that logic, mathematics, and physics are too static to represent such a world and that a special method called "intuition" must be employed. His mistake was twofold: (1) He supposed that because life is marked by change and evolution the universe as a whole must be so described; he failed to realize that philosophy is general and does not draw conclusions on the basis of any of the special sciences. (2) His emphasis on life suggests that he believed philosophy to be concerned with problems of human destiny. But such is not the case; philosophy is concerned with knowledge for its own sake, not with making men happier.

One reason why the logical-analytic method was not more widely employed earlier, according to Russell, is that it was new and only gradually replaced some of the earlier and erroneous conceptions of logic. The traditional (syllogistic) logic had been quite generally abandoned as inadequate. The inductive logic of Bacon and Mill had been shown to be unsatisfactory because it cannot really show why we believe in such uniformities as that the sun will rise every morning. Our belief in universal causation cannot be a priori, since it is very complicated when formulated precisely; nor can it be a postulate, for then it would be incapable of justifying any inference; nor can it be proved inductively without assuming the very principle which one is trying to prove. Russell claims that Hegel made the mistake of confusing logic with metaphysics, and that only mathematical logic provides the tool by which we may hope to solve philosophical problems.

Mathematical logic is both a branch of mathematics and a logic which is specially applicable to mathematics. Its main feature is its formal character, its independence of all specific subject matter. Looked at formally, it can be said to be concerned with propositions. The main types of propositions are *atomic* propositions, such as "Socrates is a man"; *molecular* propositions, which are atomic propositions unless connected by *and, if, or, unless*; and *general* propositions, such as "All men are mortal." In addition, there must be *some* knowledge of general truths which is not derived from empirical evidence. For example, if we are to *know* that all men are mortal we must also know that the men we have examined are all the men there are. This we can never derive from experience, since empirical evidence gives us only particular truths. Thus, there are certain general truths which, if they are known, must be either self-evident or inferred from other general truths.

It is obvious that one of the oldest problems of philosophy is the problem concerning our knowledge of the external world. In applying the logical-analytic method to this problem Russell finds that what we have to begin with (something which is always vague, complex, and inexact) is knowledge of two kinds: (1) Our acquaintance with the particular objects of everyday life—furniture, houses, people, and so on; and (2) our knowledge of the laws of logic. These may be called "hard" data since doubt in such cases, while it *could* occur, normally would not, and if it did, would probably be considered pathological. Most of us would be willing to add to these data certain facts of memory, some introspective facts, spatial and temporal relations, and facts of comparison, such as the likeness or unlikeness of two shades of color.

But Russell argues that certain very common beliefs probably should be excluded from our data. One is the belief that objects persist when we are not perceiving them. Another is the belief in the existence of other minds and of things outside our experience which are revealed by history and geography. These should be called "soft" data, since they can be doubted and are actually derived from our belief in hard data. The problem, then, is to determine whether the existence of anything other than our own hard data can be inferred from these data.

In formulating the question by asking whether we can know of the existence of anything independent of ourselves, Russell finds that the terms "independent" and "ourselves" are too vague to determine whatever solution we happen to be seeking. What we *can* show, however, is that the appearances of an object—its color, shape, and size—change as we move toward it or away from it, or around it. Russell calls these appearances "sense-data," and he then defines a "private world" as an object seen from a certain perspective. If we move around an object we shall discover that the sense-data change and that correlated with these changes are the bodily sensations associated with our movements. Then, if we assume the existence of other minds, we can correlate their private worlds and perspectives with ours and define an object as the *class* of all of its perspectives. This is much safer

than inferring a *thing* which exhibits itself in these perspectives. The *perspectives* are certainly real and constitute hard data; the thing is an inference and may be mistaken. A class is merely a logical construction, and we have thus substituted a logical construction for an inferred entity. This explanation fits the facts, has no empirical evidence against it, and is free from logical contradictions. Russell thus regarded himself as having solved the problem of how we know an external world.

Another philosophical problem that yields to Russell when his logical-analytic method is applied to it is that of the relation between the world of physics and the world of sense-data. According to physics, the world consists of material bodies, located in space and time and having a high degree of rigidity and permanence. While the bodies themselves may change, they are made up of particles which are themselves unchanging and indestructible. On the other hand, the world of sense-data for any one of us comes and goes; even such permanent things as mountains become data for us only when we see them; they are not known with certainty to exist at other moments. The problem of "getting these worlds together" involves the attempt to construct things, a single space, and a single time out of the fleeting data of experience.

Permanent things can be constructed if we can find some way of connecting what we commonly call "appearances of the same thing." While some sort of continuity among appearances is necessary, it is not sufficient to define a thing. What is needed in addition is that the appearances of a *single* thing obey certain physical laws which the appearances of *different* things do not.

In much the same way the dimensionless points (no one has ever seen a perfect point) of physics must be constructed out of the surfaces and volumes of our sensory experience. Using the fact that spaces can be observed to enclose other spaces (like Chinese boxes), Russell constructs "enclosure-series" which can be called "point-producers" because points can be defined by means of them. Russell does not, however, define a point as the lower limit of an enclosure-series, for there may be no such limit. Instead he defines it as the series itself; thus, a point is a logical entity constructed out of the immediate data of experience.

It can now be seen how Russell derives the concept of durationless instants of time. Events of our experience are not instantaneous; they occupy a finite time. Furthermore, different events may overlap in time since one event may begin before the other, but there may be a common time during which they both occur. If we restrict ourselves to the time which is common to more and more overlapping events we shall get durations which are shorter and shorter. Then we can define an instant of time as the class of all events which are simultaneous with one another. To state accurately when an event happens, we need only to specify the class of events which defines the instant of its happening.

Russell reminds us that since the days of Zeno philosophers have wondered about the problem of permanence and change, and especially about the apparent paradox of motion. Some motions, such as that of the second hand on a watch, seem to be continuous since we can actually *see* the movement; other motions, such as that of the hour hand, seem to be discontinuous because we can observe only a broken series of positions. Russell's solution to this apparent contradiction in the nature of motion lies in the mathematical theory of continuity.

Continuity is regarded as, first, a property of a series of elements, of terms arranged in an order, such as numbers arranged in order of magnitude. Second, a continuous series must in every case be "compact," which means that no two terms are consecutive and that between any two terms there is always another. If space is thought of as being made up of a continuous series of points, and time as a similar series of instants, then motion will consist of a correlation between a series of different points in space and a series of different instants in time. But Russell cautions us that we must not say that a body moves from one point in space to the next, for if the series is truly compact there is no next point in space, no next instant in time. This takes care of the difficulty we experience in thinking of a continuous motion as consisting of a very rapid series of jumps from one position to another.

Bergson argued that motion is simple, indivisible, and not validly analyzable into a series of states. In replying to him Russell argues that on grounds of physiology, psychology, and logic there is no incompatibility between the mathematical theory of continuity and the evidence of the senses. From physiology we learn that sensations do not cease instantaneously but gradually die away. Thus when we see a rapid motion we do not perceive it as a series of jerks because each sensation blends into its successor. From psychology we learn that there are actually cases of sense-data which form compact series. If a blindfolded person is holding a weight and to this a small additional weight is added, he may not observe the added weight if it is small enough. And if still another weight is added he may still not notice it. But if both weights had been added at once, he might have detected the difference. This proves that weights form a continuous series. Finally, on grounds of logic, Bergson must be mistaken. For if analysis always falsifies, there could never be two facts concerning the same thing, and this would make motion, which depends on the distinction between earlier and later, impossible.

After a discussion of Kant's conception of infinity, Russell turns to an analysis of Zeno's famous paradoxes. Zeno had four arguments designed to show the impossibility of motion—all based on his theory of the infinite divisibility of space and time. His first argument was designed to prove that a runner cannot get to the end of a race course, for if space is infinitely divisible, he will have to cover an infinite number of points in a finite time, and this is impossible. According to Russell, Zeno's error came from thinking that the points must be covered "one by one." This would, apparently, require an infinitely long time, for the series has infinitely many elements. But the series actually has a limit of 1, and this specifies the instant when the runner will complete the race.

Zeno's second argument attempts to show that Achilles can never overtake the tortoise if he gives it a head start, for by the time Achilles reaches the point where the tortoise was at any given time, the tortoise will always be slightly ahead. Achilles must then make up this distance, but again the tortoise will be slightly in advance. Achilles gets always closer to the tortoise but never is able to pass him. Russell claims that Zeno's error here is the same as in the previous case—an infinity of instants does not necessitate an infinitely long time.

Zeno's third argument begins with the claim that whatever occupies a space equal to itself must be at rest. An arrow in flight always occupies a space equal to itself; hence, it cannot move. Here Zeno supposes that the arrow could not move through an instant because this would require that an instant have parts, and this cannot be. But Russell points out that the mathematical theory of infinity has shown that since there are no consecutive points or instants, an instant *can* have parts. When this is realized Zeno's difficulty disappears.

Zeno's last argument attempts to prove that "half the time may be equal to double the time." This is illustrated by a column of soldiers passing another column at rest and a third column marching in the opposite direction. In the first case the soldiers pass only half as many soldiers as in the second case, yet these actions both take place during the same time. The error again disappears for Russell with the recognition that there is no "fastest" motion which requires that slow motion have intervals of rest interspersed.

According to Russell's analysis, infinite numbers differ from finite numbers in two ways: (1) Infinite numbers are *reflexive*, while finite numbers are not, and (2) finite numbers are *inductive*, while infinite numbers are not. A number is reflexive when it is not increased by adding 1 to it. Thus the number of members in the class 0, 1, 2, 3 . . . n is the same as the number in the class 1, 2, 3, 4 . . . *n* plus 1. Even more surprising, the number of even numbers is equal to the total number of numbers (even and odd). It is therefore possible in the case of infinite numbers for a part of a class to equal the whole class.

Infinite numbers are also noninductive. Inductive numbers possess a certain property which can be called "hereditary." This is like the property of being named "Jones," which, if it applies to a man, also applies to all of his male descendants. Every property which belongs to 0 and is hereditary belongs to all of the natural numbers, and we can define the natural numbers as those which are inductive. To all such numbers proof by mathematical induction applies.

Philosophers have tried to define numbers, but without much success. Russell refers to the mathematician Frege, who recognized that numbers are neither physical nor mental but logical—that is, numbers are properties of general terms or general descriptions and thus are applicable to classes, not to things. The author asks: "When do two classes have the same number of members?" and answers "When a one-to-one correlation can be set up between them." This applies both to finite classes which can be counted and to infinite classes which cannot. As an example, Russell refers to monogamous countries where the number of husbands is the same as the number of wives, though we may not know how many of both there are because the relation of marriage is a correlating relation. The number of a class can then be defined as the class of all classes which are similar to it— that is, which have a one-to-one correlation with it. Note that number is not a *property* of a class but is a *class of classes*. This is a valid conception even if classes are considered to be fictions, for there is a method for translating statements in which classes occur to statements in which they do not.

Russell's final application of the logical-analytic method is to the problem of causation and free will. Causation is a complicated relation that must be described by a carefully worded formula: "Whenever things occur in certain relations to each other (among which their time-relations must be included), then a thing having a fixed relation to these things will occur at a date fixed relatively to their dates." The evidence for causation in the past is the observation of repeated uniformities, together with knowledge of the fact that where there appears to be an exception to such uniformities we can always find wider ones which will include both the successes and failures. The only guarantee we could have that such a causal law would continue to hold in the future would be some sort of *a priori* principle. The law of causality is therefore an *ideal* law, possibly true, but not known to be true.

Determinism can be demonstrated, Russell believes, only if we can show that human actions are theoretically predictable from a sufficient number of antecedents. This we cannot do, he claims. In the great majority of cases, volitions probably have causes, but the only evidence for this is the fact of repeated instances. Furthermore, since causes do not *compel* their effects the will is free in the sense that our volitions are the results of our desires, and we are not forced to will something which we would rather not will.

THREE LECTURES ON AESTHETIC

Author: Bernard Bosanquet (1848-1923)
Type of work: Aesthetics
First published: 1915 (Delivered at University College, London, 1914)

PRINCIPAL IDEAS ADVANCED

Aesthetic experience is distinguishable from other experience in that it is pleasant, stable, relevant, and common.

The aesthetic experience is contemplative, not practical; it is organizational, and both personal and general.

The aesthetic response is a response to form and substance in an appearance, requiring the imagination, and resulting in the pleasant awareness of a feeling embodied in the appearance.

The most satisfying asethetic experience is realized when the artist forms his work in harmony with the character of his medium.

In its proper sense, beauty is what is common to artistic products insofar as they are excellent; beauty may be easy or difficult; difficult beauty is characterized by intricacy, tension, and width—that is, it is complex, provokes heightened feelings, and demands breadth of interest.

For Bosanquet there is a significant difference between the philosophy of art and art criticism, art instruction, or the psychology of art. The critic distinguishes good from bad works of art, while the teacher of techniques is concerned with ways of producing beauty. The psychologist explains in terms of causes the feeling of pleasure associated with the work of art. The philosopher's function is to take the facts discovered by others, select those that are relevant, and expand them into ideas which are exhaustive and self-consistent.

According to the philosopher's method, what is an aesthetic experience as Bosanquet explains it? In its simplest form it is a feeling of pleasure distinguished from other pleasant feelings by being *stable, relevant,* and *common.*

The aesthetic experience is *stable* in the sense that it is not satiable. We do not satisfy the need for aesthetic feel-

ing in the way that we satisfy the need for food. We may become physically tired at a museum, but we do not tire of responding to aesthetic objects.

The aesthetic response is to the whole object as sufficient in itself; it is *relevant.* We may receive pleasure from hearing a dinner bell, but it is likely to be in anticipation of dinner, not in the sound of the bell itself.

The aesthetic feeling is *common* because it can be shared and is increased by sharing. It is a product of education. "To like and dislike rightly is the goal of all culture worth the name."

Since the aesthetic experience is a response to an object, it has other characteristics which help to explain it. First, it is *contemplative.* It does not try to alter or use the object. Second, it is *organizational.* To Bosanquet this property of the aesthetic response to the object was of great importance. Through it, he was able to relate the

806

aesthetic experience to the individual who has the feeling and beyond the individual to a type of experience. Thus the aesthetic experience is both personal and general. The individual has his experience of the art object, but his experience can be described so that others can have the experience too. From this property of organization, the value of the aesthetic experience arises.

The object is valued for what it is in itself. One can use an object or have information about it without responding to it aesthetically. One may know its history, market value, cause, and location, for example. The aesthetic experience is a response to what is there, to what the object is in itself, and not to some relation the object has to other things or other people.

Since the aesthetic response is not to some aspect of the object but to its inner organization, it may be described as a response to form. Form is not merely technical form in the sense of sonnet form, not merely shape in the geometric sense. It is the combination of these forms with matter of such a sort that form and matter become one object. The response to form and substance as one is the aesthetic response.

The aesthetic object is an appearance, not a real thing. A poem about love is not love; the painting of a house cannot be lived in. As an appearance, the aesthetic object can be known, but not known about. We know about a painting when we know its history, how it was painted, and by whom. This knowledge is a response to the painting as object, but it is not an aesthetic response to the painting as appearance. Bosanquet writes, "Great objects of art contain myriads of elements of form on different levels, knit together in

more and more complex systems, till the feeling which they demand is such as to occupy the whole powers of the greatest mind, and more than these if they were to be had."

Because we do not regard the aesthetic object as something to be understood or manipulated, because our response is to the appearance rather than to the reality, it is a response that requires the use of the imagination. Imagination is the mind considering possibilities. Its use in practical concerns is limited to the consideration of real possibilities. In aesthetic matters this restriction does not apply; there is no need for agreement with reality. The aesthetic use of imagination has for its end satisfaction through feeling. Although in its practical use the imagination is limited, in its aesthetic use it is set free.

In short, the aesthetic experience is defined by Bosanquet as "the pleasant awareness of a feeling embodied in an appearance presented to imagination." The critic to be a good critic must first be a spectator. He must have the aesthetic feeling and then reflect on it. A good critic is one who leads others to an aesthetic experience of an object. His reflection on his aesthetic feeling, his judgment of how it is furthered by the form of the object, his judgment of where the object fails to give aesthetic satisfaction, should furnish the raw material for his critical pronouncements.

Bosanquet contends that the aesthetic experience can best be understood by considering simple rather than complex examples. He cites as examples easy melodies and dance steps, geometric figures such as the circle and the cube, decorations on the entablatures of some buildings. Each object considered has formal elements and contains the three characteristics of aesthetic objects: stability, relevance, and community. It is important to notice that none of these patterns is representational. Representation introduces a new factor because the thing represented carries the spectator beyond mere pattern to association and toward the problem of the beauty of nature. Poems about events, statues of individuals, pictures of familiar objects bring to aesthetic appreciation the test of facts. But there is the danger of subordinating aesthetic quality to knowledge; that is, of turning an aesthetic object into a representation of facts. However, we cannot and should not ignore factual content. It too is a medium of expression and has aesthetic value. Much of the significance of the work of art may lie in its factual content. Green trees remind us of summer and bare trees of winter; smiles denote happiness and tears sorrow. We have learned these symbols through experience and this knowledge is essential to aesthetic appreciation. The representational work of art is always more than mere pattern in the sense that repeated curves form a pattern, but it is a pattern in the sense that it represents a type or norm. In Bosanquet's words, "Man's mind possesses a magic by which it can extract the soul of the actual thing or event, and confer it on any medium which is convenient to him, the wall of a cave, or a plate of gold, or a scrap of paper."

Since, according to Bosanquet, the artist reproduces the object as type in a different medium, his aesthetic theory would have to be modified to accommodate developments in the fine arts since the appearance of *Three Lectures on Aesthetics*. Nonrepresenta-

tional painting could not be dealt with in terms of Bosanquet's theory as he has stated it. He says, for example, that representation "introduces an enormously larger and deeper world than the world of non-representative pattern-designing." Much of modern art is not pattern-designing, but neither is it representational. It would have to be for Bosanquet like music, which does not represent objects but represents emotions. The beauty of nature presents a similar problem. We must somehow regard it as we would a work of art, as an appearance which we love or admire, not simply as a series of objects to be understood or used. Nature as beautiful is nature as expressive rather than as the content of a rational construction.

How are the arts to be classified? There are different arts and their classification should reveal the roots of the aesthetic experience—that is, of beauty. Bosanquet begins with the fact that different artists may take the same subject and treat it in different mediums and in different ways. This difference in treatment is due in large part to the demands of the medium. The properties of a medium lead the artist to do certain things that another medium would not lead him to do. There is a triadic relation here, a triple interaction of the subject, the artist, and the medium. Clay leads the artist in a different direction from wrought iron, and stone in still another way. Bosanquet says in summary of this point, "The feeling for the medium, the sense of what can rightly be done in it only or better than in anything else, and the charm and fascination of doing it so—these, I take it, are the real clue to the fundamental question of aesthetics, which is 'how feeling and its

808

body are created adequate to one another.'"

Bosanquet is concerned to show that his theory applies to folk arts as well as to fine arts. He was influenced here by Ruskin, Pater, and Morris; and all in turn influenced John Dewey.

The artist idealizes nature. What does this mean for Bosanquet? It does not mean that the artist creates the abstract, general type. He does not paint or describe a tree which is somehow a summary of what all trees have in common. He paints a tree which is particular and individual, but which expresses its ideal type through its individuality. Bosanquet was a philosophical idealist, and it is a part of his theory that the individual can express his place in the total scheme of reality without losing his individuality.

The artist's experience is the source of his subject matter. Some event in the external world, either an objective or subjective happening, is felt in its relations to other events. Through these relations the event takes on a magnitude and importance which are its significance and which are expressed through some medium. The artistic medium communicates just as language communicates. A superb use of medium is like the happy choice of words to express an idea; the idea is enhanced through the choice of words. Subject, artist, and medium are common characteristics of all the arts, and it is through these properties that "all good art is one."

In consequence, the word *beauty* is used in two senses. In one, it refers to what is common to all artistic activity insofar as it produces excellence. In the other sense, it refers to what most people find aesthetically pleasing.

The first sense, which for Bosan-quet is the more correct one, includes art that to ordinary people seems strange, grotesque, or awesome. Certain types of art at a given time will be appreciated only by the aesthetically educated. Beauty in this first and wider sense is of two sorts, difficult beauty and easy beauty. Easy beauty—the simple tune, the rose, the beautiful face— is pleasing to everyone; nevertheless, it can be beauty of the highest type.

Difficult beauty, Bosanquet argues, contains three elements which explain its difficulty. These are *intricacy, tension,* and *width. Intricacy* is the property that many objects have of being analyzable into component parts. A painting may be seen as telling a story, as a juxtaposition of shapes, as a relation of colors and so on. Full appreciation depends on the ability of the spectator to see these elements as related in a harmony. *Tension* is the capacity to provoke heightened feeling which we often associate with tragedy, but which is within the capacity of every art form. It elicits a response to art that many people would prefer to avoid, a complete identification of the individual with the full impact of the work of art. The third dimension of difficult art is *width,* the power of satisfying a wide range of interests. Many people fail to respond to some forms of art, for example to the comic when it makes ridiculous something that they hold dear. But if the spectator has a wide range of interests, he can respond to comedy and to the other demands that the variety of the arts make; he must shift his mood to respond to the mood of the work of art.

Bosanquet's distinction between easy and difficult beauty is not a sharp one, nor was it intended to be. One and the same work of art may be both when

809

seen by the ordinary person and by the connoisseur. His purpose was to extend the meaning of beauty to include all aesthetic excellence and to allow what he considered to be an adequate distinction between the beautiful and the ugly.

What many persons regard as ugly is whatever they are incapable of appreciating. To experience aesthetic pleasure from an object is to respond to its beauty, but to fail to feel this pleasure is not to prove that the object has no real aesthetic quality. True ugliness is a property of an object that no normal imagination could see as beautiful however sensitive this imagination might be. An object expresses beauty, but it cannot express ugliness. To be ugly is to have properties which frustrate the expression of beauty. We expect to receive an aesthetic response from the object, but its properties prevent and nullify our expectation. We find ugliness in insincere art, in art where beauty is attempted and the attempt fails. Thus, for Bosanquet, nature is never ugly, because it lacks conscious intent. Again we see an effect of philosophical idealism. The ugly is an inconsistency in the concept and execution of the aesthetic object. The artist first imagines and then expresses so as to communicate feeling. Aesthetic feelings have their source in every experience of living, but the artist relates his experience to other possibilities of experience, and in this relation is beauty. Beauty is the source of aesthetic pleasure for the artist and for the spectator.

THE IDEA OF THE HOLY

Author: Rudolf Otto (1869-1937)
Type of work: Philosophy of religion
First published: 1917

PRINCIPAL IDEAS ADVANCED

Holiness is the quality unique to religious experience; the presence of the numinous, that which is holy, is universally experienced as a kind of fearful awe in the presence of the mysterious.

The numen, the divine, must be known through the religious feeling; but the feeling itself cannot be described.

In the presence of the holy the human being is aware of his own nothingness, and with the feeling of creature-consciousness he becomes aware of the wholly other, that which overpowers while it charms.

The absolute distinction between numen and creature is overcome by God's grace.

The nineteenth century was marked by a permeation of almost every field by the "scientific methodology" as the one valid method for analysis and interpretation. It appeared that religion, with its supra-sensible object, its competing theologies, its pre-scientific world-view, its emotionalism, and its origins in "superstition," was incompatible with this scientific epoch. In this situation, two possibilities were open—either that science admit the possibility of a universal "nonrational" mode of experience, and thus the possibility of religion as a legitimate human enterprise, or that it insist uncompromisingly on a narrow empiricism, reducing religion to some nonreligious common denominator. Until the last several decades, the latter option was largely chosen.

Anthropologists such as James George Frazer and Émile Durkheim, and psychologists such as Freud, interpreted religion in purely naturalistic terms, as a primitive mentality or immature projection. Philosophers such as Hegel saw it as a symbolic or mythological version of what philosophy better understood logically and conceptually. Such attacks tended to discredit religion as a *sui generis*, unique, and *bona fide* mode of experience, apprehension, and expression.

One of the problems indigenous to a study of religion encouraged such naturalistic reductions—the near impossibility of generalizing concerning the content of religion. To almost any definition of religion offered, there are recognized religions which prove the exception. When one recalls the atheistic branches of Hinduism, the "ritualless" religion of the Quakers, the "nonmoral" aspects of fertility religions, the anti-theological sects in Protestantism, as well as the claims of communism and "the democratic way of life" to religious devotion, one can see how seemingly unmanageable, indeed questionable, is the inclusive entity called religion.

Within the realm of religion itself, however, there had been a continuing attempt from the time of Kant's collapse of the theistic arguments to defend the legitimacy of religion philosophically from a post-Kantian perspective. Kant himself had prepared such a defense when in the second *Critique* he held God, immortality, and freedom to be legitimate postulates from the sense of duty, and in the third *Critique* he saw in the experience of beauty and sublimity a nonrational indication of supra-sensible purposiveness in the universe. Where strict reason ended in antinomies, unique *sui generis* experiences, universal to the human species, provided entry into the realm of the noumenon.

It was Friedrich Schleiermacher (1768-1834) who saw the possibilities for religion here, writing *On Religion: Speeches to Its Cultured Despisers* (1799). Drawing from his own pietist heritage, he rejected religion as dogma, belief, metaphysics, ethics, or a combination of these. Religion is a unique experience belonging to the realm of "feeling" (Gefühl) or "affection." This primal feeling is of a "deeper unity with the whole," a sense of "absolute dependence" upon the Infinite and Eternal; from this sense of utter contingency morality flows as action and doctrine as reflection. Schleiermacher used this understanding as a foundation for interpreting Christianity in *The Christian Faith* (1821-1822), and this classic marked the beginning of liberal Protestant theology. Because this work overshadowed his *Speeches*, few recognized the importance of the latter for the emerging discipline of philosophy of religion.

During the past several decades, there have been increasing attempts by many anthropologists and sociologists to restore religion to integrity. Descriptive, nonvaluational studies of cultures have been rejected in favor of a cultural analysis and interpretation in terms of "cultural universals." Bronislaw Malinowski, for example, understands religion in terms of his "functional anthropology" as the universal and necessary response of man to the crises or mysteries of existence such as birth and death. Psychologists such as Carl Jung, Gordon Allport, and Erich Fromm see religion as a necessary component of harmonic psychic realization. Perhaps the best philosophic attempt in this endeavor, however, is Rudolf Otto's classic work, *The Idea of the Holy*. He stands solidly with Buber, Bergson, Tillich, and perhaps James, in the Kantian approach of Schleiermacher. His is no mere reduction or critique of religion, but an exposition of the universal experience called "religious," carefully documented from anthropology, psychology, and philosophy. It is a monumental apology for "religious experience" as a unique, legitimate, and necessary dimension of human existence.

Otto's work is misunderstood if seen, as some have, as an irrational approach to religion; rather, it is a rational analysis of the supra-rational aspects uniquely characterizing the experience of the Divine. As he says, "This book, recognizing the profound import of the non-rational for metaphysic, makes a serious attempt to analyse all the more exactly the *feeling* which remains where the *concept* fails, and to introduce a terminology which is not any the more loose or indeterminate for having necessarily to make use of symbols." Otto clearly insists upon the necessity of reason, operating through analogy, in predicating attributes of the Divine. But even the most

ardent rational theologians confess that such concepts do not comprehend God's deepest essence, which requires comprehension of a different sort. In forgetting this, Otto claims, orthodox Christians have most often given a one-sided, rationalistic interpretation of God. This has misled most thinkers into failing to see that of all human experience, the religious is "unmistakably specific and unique, peculiar to itself."

"Holiness" is that quality which Otto finds unique to the religious feeling. But since this term has come to mean "moral goodness," he has coined the word "numinous" to designate its original sense. This ingredient cannot be strictly defined, for as a feeling it must be evoked to be known. As a result, Otto's presuppositions are radical— since the religious cannot be reduced to anything but itself, only the person who can recall "a moment of deeply-felt religious experience" is in a position to understand religion, its uniqueness and its validity. Only with this common datum before the reader will Otto suggest continuing.

Schleiermacher's similar attempt to isolate this religious feeling, exhibiting it as "the feeling of absolute dependence," Otto finds inadequate on two counts. First, Schleiermacher's terminology is prone to subjectivism, failing to indicate the qualitative distinction between the religious awareness and analogous experiences between finite creatures. Otto finds the term "creature-consciousness" far more expressive of Schleiermacher's essential meaning— the "emotion of a creature, submerged and overwhelmed by its own nothingness in contrast to that which is supreme above all creatures." But more important, Schleiermacher inferred the fact of God from an experience exhibited as self-consciousness. To this Otto strenuously objects, for "creature-feeling" arises only when something "numinous" which is objective and external to the self is experienced as being present.

Otto's investigation indicates that the presence of the numinous is universally experienced as the "mysterium tremendum." This mysterious object can thus be "known" only by analyzing human feelings when in its presence. Otto's chosen term, "tremor," suggests fear, but his meaning is closer to "dread," "being aghast," or perhaps best, "awe." In primitive religions this element is evinced by "daemonic dread"; we still preserve something analogous in the terms "ghostly," "uncanny," or "supernatural." Old Testament references to divine wrath, jealousy, and anger are all reflections of this quality.

The second ingredient is that of "overpoweringness," "absolute unapproachability," or "majesty." From this awareness of one's nothingness emerges religious humility. Together these qualities produce the feeling of "creature-consciousness." The final ingredient is "urgency," the "energy" of the numinous object, the awareness of the numen as active, living, and willing. As analogies, Otto warns, these symbolic expressions of feeling dare not be taken for rational concepts; they are pointers and not containers of unique religious feeling. This idea is basic for Otto—we can *feel* the special character of the numen while being incapable of adequate conceptualization.

The more difficult aspect of Otto's designation to analyze is "mysterium." Otto's best alternative symbol is "the wholly other," that which is utterly beyond and yet elicits overwhelming astonishment. Here we perceive the basic religious polarity. Not only is there the quality of awe, overpoweringness, that which "repels," but uniquely intertwined with it is that of fascination. This is the Dionysiac element in all religions, the charm, the entrancement, the allurement, indeed, the intoxication, from which the rational qualities of love, mercy, pity, and comfort emerge. Otto's imagination strains here for the precise word; he settles for "grace." It is ironic to Otto that previous analyses have usually not recognized this unique polarity, for without it worship cannot be understood. Dread alone can create only a worship of expiation and propitiation; man's yearning for the numinous object *for its own sake* would be totally inexplicable. Such analyses cannot deal with the intense fascination which is the mystical "moment," the experience of conversion, salvation, redemption. In this basic tension rests the awareness that God is not simply ground of all that can be thought, but is himself subject on his own account.

Otto not only draws from primitive and traditional religions for documentation but also uses analogous feelings from other realms for the sake of clarity. Above all it is Kant's analysis of the sublime which he finds best, for the sublime is likewise beyond adequate conceptualization and exhibits the same dual character. From such feelings, Otto attempts to show that while one feeling can give rise to a similar one, feelings themselves do not change. For example, moral obligation does not evolve from constraint by custom; these are qualitatively distinct. The idea of "ought" can arise only because there is an *a priori* potentially within man. Other feelings may arouse the moral sense, but they are not its explanation or cause. The same, Otto concludes, is true of the numinous feeling—it is *sui generis* and *a priori*, and is not derived from any other, although it may be stimulated.

Although the nonrational numinous feeling is the source of all religion, it is not its totality. As Kant showed Otto, nonrational data is schematized by rational concepts; in the same way a permanent connection is established between religious feeling and analogous feelings through the internal necessity of reason. The higher religions mark the most developed schematization of the universal numinous feeling.

Otto's most suggestive illustration of this view comes from music. At its base is a nonrational feeling, the wholly other aspect of which is schematized by reason according to more commonplace experiences; this schematization can be only partly successful, for its origin is an ever-mysterious, *sui generis* feeling. Here Otto makes an important point which others, like Buber, blur—the nonrational of music and the nonrational of the numinous dare not be confounded, for "each is something in its own right, independently of the other."

Man's response to the numinous is, on the one hand, the concomitant of creature-consciousness—the awareness of uncleanness, of sin, not from consciousness of any definite moral fault, but from a general "disvaluation" in the presence of the holy. On the other hand, there is the feeling of appreciation and praise of the numen in comparison. The holy thus possesses value in two senses: first, appreciation is the awareness of subjective value for the individual; second, the sense of awe is an awareness of objective value which claims homage. So understood, it appears that moral transgression is neither the source of man's search for redemption nor an adequate penetration into the feeling of the God-man relation. What is needed in the presence of the numen is atonement, a covering of nothing in particular but a freeing of the creature from profaneness, a rendering numinous of the approacher himself. The paradox of religion is that the absolute distinction between numen and creatures is overcome by God's admission of the creature into his presence—this is the meaning of grace for Otto.

There are two movements operating in the evolution of religion from its universal basis to its plethora of forms and manifestations. The first is a process totally within the nonrational sphere whereby primitive dread becomes worship and daemonic power becomes divine power. The second, which is subsidiary, is the process of rationalization and moralization on the basis of the primary numinous consciousness. It is this latter which has been traditionally called "the history of salvation." It is here that the holy is completed and filled, for it becomes likewise the good. One of Otto's basic concerns is to exhibit the dogmas of rational theology as simply conceptual attempts to clarify different aspects of this base feeling. Note, for example, one of his typical conclusions—"predestination we have found to be nothing but the intensified 'creature-feeling' in conceptual expression, and to be altogether rooted in the numinous consciousness."

It is helpful here to place Otto's psychological analysis within a philosophic whole. His work is best seen as the development of a fourth Kantian *Cri-*

tique. Throughout he is obedient to the Kantian analysis of reason and the process of knowing. What he is intent on exhibiting is the "objective" datum of the numinous as well as an *a priori* category of the holy within man. Thereby the fact of religious experience is preserved, its universality guaranteed, and the transcendent mystery of the Divine affirmed, while human symbols and concepts of the numinous are given a status commensurate with other modes of human apprehension. All Kantian categories have sense impression as their occasion, but never as their source; so it is with Otto's *a priori* of the holy, that predisposition of the human spirit which differs from both pure and practical reason. This distinction he sees Kant as having made in the *Critique of Judgment* (1790), defending there not "aesthetic" in the sense of "beautiful," but a separate "faculty of judgment based upon feeling of whatever sort from that of the understanding, from discursive, conceptual thought and inference." Religion, being grounded in feeling, shares this "objective validity, universality and necessity" exhibited by Kant.

Otto's "proof" of this is two-fold: the introspective analysis that we have described, and his assumption of the general correctness of the Kantian *Critiques*. What must be seen is the radical difference between a universal potentiality (*a priori*) and a universal possession. The obvious lack of the latter, Otto maintains, has wrongly been seen as a disproof of the former; but maturation of the religious *a priori* has taken a large part of history, commensurate with the time required for the pure and practical realms. This *a priori* nature of the religious Otto applies to its nonrational and rational aspects, and to the inward, necessary interrelation of the two. As long as the numinous experience and its rational schematization occur in vital dialogue, they are true to both the numinous and the human spirit; in fact, this harmony Otto sees as the best criterion of the relative ranks of religion. Conceptualization, although always imperfect (for the experiential ground is ever wholly other), is possible, for the inborn capacity of each man may be aroused to a feeling of the numinous through the rational analogies of another. Schematization both reveals and communicates the feeling that is at its roots nonrational.

What Otto is intent on eliminating is the perennial distinction between general and special revelation, natural and historic religion. History and the individual are always in interrelation, the former providing the stimuli for the development of the *a priori* dispositions of the latter, the latter being thereby attuned to specific portions of history as manifestations of the holy. For Otto, they operate together or not at all.

Otto's work is not the only attempt of this sort; in fact, similar attempts, most of which have emerged from a clearly Christian context, have established the liberal wing of Protestant theology. On the one hand, most of these have failed to do justice to the claims of orthodoxy, and, on the other, they have not sufficiently escaped the narrowly apologetic predilections of that tradition to do justice to the general religious phenomenon. Otto's work more successfully escapes these limitations and comes as one of the best contemporary attempts to restore religion to the status of a *sui generis*, unique, and valid mode of experience and relations to reality.

INTRODUCTION TO MATHEMATICAL PHILOSOPHY

Author: Bertrand Russell (1872-   )
Type of work: Philosophy of mathematics
First published: 1919

PRINCIPAL IDEAS ADVANCED

Mathematics can be shown to be a logical development of certain basic ideas; mathematics can be reduced to logic.

The number of a class is the class of all those classes which are similar to it. (Classes are similar when their members can be put into a one-to-one relation with each other.)

A relation is symmetrical when if one thing has the relation to another, the other has the same relation to it; a relation is transitive when if one thing has the relation to a second, and the second has the same relation to a third, the first has the relation to the third. (Other relations are defined.)

An infinite cardinal number satisfies the equation, n equals n plus 1. (An infinite collection has parts which have as many terms as the infinite collection itself.)

By distinguishing between types of entities it is possible to avoid paradoxes which have perplexed philosophers for centuries.

Mathematical truths are a priori and have nothing to do with facts about the world; they are logical tautologies.

Bertrand Russell wrote three books on mathematical philosophy: *Principles of Mathematics* (1903); *Principia Mathematica* (with A. N. Whitehead, 1910-13); and *Introduction to Mathematical Philosophy*. The last of these is substantially a condensation and simplification of the second, which is a large three-volume work (with a contemplated fourth volume which never appeared), expressed almost wholly in specially devised symbols and containing formal proofs showing that mathematics can be "reduced" to logic. Since these proofs are somewhat formidable for one not versed in mathematics and not having an aptitude for mathematical symbolism, Russell attempted in the present book to acquaint the reader with the main results of the earlier study in a language which, while necessarily technical, does not require either the understanding of formal proofs or the ability to manipulate abstract symbols.

The general thesis of the book is that we can start with the familiar portions of mathematics, say, such a statement as "2 plus 2 equals 4," and go either "up" into higher mathematics, leading to the consideration of fractions, real numbers, complex numbers, infinite numbers, integration, and differentiation, or "down" into lower mathematics, leading through analysis to notions of greater abstractness and greater logical simplicity. The latter route, which is the approach adopted primarily in recent mathematics, and consequently less familiar to non-mathematicians, asks not what can be defined and deduced when we assume that 2 plus 2 equals 4 but what more general ideas and principles can be found in terms of which 2 plus 2 equals 4 can be defined and deduced. In other words, the most obvious and easy things in mathematics do not come logically at the beginning, but somewhere in the middle, just as the bodies which are easiest to see are neither those which are very near nor those which are very far, but those which are at a "moderate" distance. The easiest conceptions to grasp in mathematics are neither the complex and intricate ideas nor the logically simple and abstract ideas, but the common-sense notions involved in the whole numbers.

The reason why such a study can be called "mathematical *philosophy*" is to be found in the fact that although many of the notions considered in this type of investigation—*number, class, relation, order, continuity, infinity*—have been traditionally examined by philosophers, without (according to Russell) very much success, interesting results can be obtained when the methods of speculative philosophers are replaced by the more refined and precise methods of the mathematicians and logicians. In order to stress his point Russell frequently argues that these newer conceptions render the traditional philosophical problems insoluble, or perhaps meaningless.

(Because of the fact that the book is already a condensation of a much larger work, no systematic survey of its contents is possible without reducing the work to a series of more or less meaningless definitions and postulates. The attempt will be made, therefore, in what follows, not to cover the book in its entirety but to extract certain typical problems and show how Russell formulates them and solves them.)

Perhaps the best example of Russell's mathematical philosophy is his definition, following Giuseppe Peano, of the notion of the natural numbers. One could hardly imagine a concept which would seem clearer to the ordinary man than that exemplified by the series:

$0, 1, 2, 3, \ldots n, n$ plus $1 \ldots$ Yet Peano shows that though this notion is familiar it is not understood. It can be reduced, in fact, to three primitive ideas and five primitive propositions. The notion involved in the use of "primitive" must first be explained.

Since all terms that are defined are defined only by means of other terms, we must accept some terms as initially clear in order to have a starting point for our definitions. This procedure does not require that these latter terms be *incapable* of definition, for we might have stopped too soon and we might be able to define them if we go further. On the other hand, there *may be* certain terms which are logically simple in the sense that they cannot be analyzed into any other terms. The decision between these two possibilities is not important for logic; all that is needed is the knowledge that since human powers are finite, definitions must always begin with some terms which are at least undefined at the moment, though perhaps not permanently.

Primitive *propositions* have the same status. Whenever we prove propositions to be true, we do so by reducing them to other propositions, which must themselves be proved by reducing them to still other propositions. Ultimate proof, therefore, presumably cannot be achieved unless we assume certain propositions to be self-evident. But mathematicians have quite generally abandoned the notion of "self-evidence" since it seems to rest on psychological rather than on logical considerations, and permits truth to vary from individual to individual. However, they have granted that there must be in any formal system certain propositions, usually called "postulates," which are unproved *within the system*, though they may be provable by going to still more basic postulates *outside the system*.

Peano's three primitive ideas are "0," "number," and "successor." These ideas can be illustrated, though not defined, in terms of the natural numbers. For example, by "successor" he means the relation which holds between 1 and 0 when we say that 1 is the successor of 0, and between 1 and 2 when we say that 2 is the successor of 1.

Peano's five primitive propositions are:

(1) 0 is a number.

(2) The successor of any number is a number.

(3) No two numbers have the same successor.

(4) 0 is not the successor of any number.

(5) Any property which belongs to 0, and also to the successor of every number which has the property, belongs to all the numbers.

Several remarks about this definition of "number" are in order. In the first place, the five primitive propositions enable us to extend the series indefinitely, since by (2) a number *always* has a successor, and by (3) no new successor obtained can be one of the previous numbers, and by (4) zero can occur only as the first member of the series. Postulate (5) is the familiar principle of mathematical induction which enables us to prove that a certain theorem which is true of 0, and when true of 0 is true of 1, and so on, must be true of all numbers.

In the second place, Peano's system, while it is exemplified by the natural numbers, does not apply to them uniquely. In fact, it proves to be an *abstract* system in the sense that it need have no interpretation at all, or it may have a variety of different interpretations. For example the series,

0, 2, 4, 6, 8, . . .

1, ½, ¼, ⅛, . . .

would exemplify Peano's axioms, though in such instances the notions "0," "number" and "successor" would take on different meanings. Indeed, the Biblical series,

Adam, Cain, Enoch, Irad . . .

would constitute an exemplification of his axioms provided the notion of "successor" is properly defined, and that there are certain hereditary properties which are always transmitted to the male offspring. Any series which possesses the properties defined by the postulates is called a "progression," and there are obviously very many instances of progressions in the world.

In the third place, all traditional pure mathematics may be shown to contain only propositions about the natural numbers. This indicates the fundamental importance of what Peano succeeded in doing.

Finally, since Peano's axioms do not guarantee that there will be anything in the world which exemplifies them, and since we want our numbers to be such as can be used for the purpose of counting common objects, we should supplement Peano's work by making it into a theory of arithmetic. This was done by another mathematician, named Gottlob Frege. It requires the introduction of the notion of "class." A class may be defined in two ways: by enumerating its members—say, Brown, Jones, and Robinson—or by mentioning a defining property, as when we speak of "inhabitants of London." The former is called "extensional," the latter "intensional." The latter is more fundamental, since extension can always be reduced to intension, but intension often cannot, even theoretically, be reduced to extension. This is important for the definition of numbers, for numbers themselves form an infinite collection and cannot be enumerated. Furthermore, it is probably true (though this cannot be demonstrated) that there is an infinite number of collections in the world—for example, an infinite number of pairs. Finally, we wish to define "number" in such a way as to permit the existence of infinite numbers as well as finite ones, and this requires that we be able to speak of the terms in an infinite collection by means of a property which is common to all its members and peculiar to them.

Proceeding in this way, Russell shows how it is possible to demonstrate when two classes "have the same number"—that is, exhibit a property in terms of which their number could be defined. This can be done by showing that the classes are "similar," where "similarity" is defined in terms of having a one-to-one relation to each other. For example, in countries where neither polygamy nor polyandry is permitted, the relation "spouse of" constitutes a relation on the basis of which the class of married men can be shown to be similar to the class of married women. The use of this criterion does not require that we be able to *count* either class, and we can know that the number of married men is the same as the number of married women without knowing the number of either. The notion of similarity is

therefore logically more simple than the notion of counting, though not necessarily more familiar. If we now make a bundle of all pairs, of all trios, and of all quartets, and then extend this to a bundle of all classes that have only one member (unit classes), and to a bundle of all classes that have no members (null classes), we could then go on to say that by "2" we mean the property which is common to all pairs, by "3" we mean the property which is common to all trios, and so on. However, Russell does not choose to do so because he is afraid that if we suppose some property in nature which we call "twoness" we may be unconsciously creating a metaphysical entity whose existence is debatable. Of the class of couples we can be sure, but of the metaphysical 2 we cannot. Therefore, he defines the number "2" simply as the *class* of all couples, not as the *property* which they all possess. And, more generally, *the number of a class is the class of all those classes which are similar to it.* This definition sounds odd, but it is precise and indubitable and can be shown to apply to the world in such a way as to make arithmetic possible.

Another idea which Russell examines is that of "relation." There are many different kinds of relations, each having its own properties and uses. For example, certain relations are *symmetrical*. A relation, R, holding between a and b is symmetrical if when aRb, then bRa. For example, the relation "spouse of" is symmetrical but the relation "father of" is asymmetrical. Certain relations are *transitive*. A relation, R, is transitive if when aRb and bRc, then aRc. For example, the relation "ancestor of" is transitive, but the relation "father of" is intransitive. Certain relations are *connected*. A relation, R, is connected with regard to a class of objects a,b,c,d . . . if taking *any* two terms from the class, say, a and c, then either aRc or cRa. Thus, if I take any two integers, one is smaller and the other is greater, but this is not true of complex numbers; if I take any two *moments* of time, one must be earlier than the other, but of two *events* in time this is not the case since they may be simultaneous.

On the basis of this discussion of the concept of "relation" Russell shows how we can define "order." In a sense "to order" means "to arrange," and all orders, therefore, are as arbitrary as are arrangements. But when we say that we are ordering the natural numbers, we are really looking for certain relations between them, which themselves generate a certain arrangement. "We can no more 'arrange' the natural numbers than we can the starry heavens; but just as we may notice among the fixed stars either their order of brightness or their distribution in the sky, so there are various relations among numbers which may be observed, and which give rise to various different orders among numbers, all equally legitimate." Ordering, therefore, is an operation which is performed on a class when we discover a relation which holds among its members and which has certain characteristics. The notion of *progression*, which was mentioned earlier, is a special case of a class which is ordered on the basis of a relation which is asymmetrical, transitive, and connected.

The notion of "infinity," which has puzzled philosophers since the days of the Greeks, can easily be defined. There are many different kinds and levels of infinite numbers, and only the simplest, the infinite cardinal numbers, are examined. Russell points out that what he had previously called the "natural" numbers can also be called the "inductive" numbers, such usage indicating merely that we are naming the numbers in terms of Peano's fifth postulate rather than in terms of something else. The principle of mathematical induction can be crudely stated in the form, "what can be inferred from next to next can be inferred from first to last."

Suppose that we now take under consideration the collection of the inductive numbers themselves. This collection cannot itself have as its number one of the inductive numbers, for if we suppose n to be any inductive number, the inclusion of zero in our collection compels us to say that the number of such a collection will be n plus 1. Hence, the number of inductive numbers is a new number, which is different from all of them and is not possessed of all inductive properties. This number is called an "infinite cardinal number" and its unusual character is shown in the fact that it satisfies the equation, n equals n plus 1. A class possessing such characteristics is called a *"reflexive"* class (one which is similar to a proper part of itself) and the number of such a class is a reflexive cardinal number. A still more surprising characteristic of an infinite cardinal number is that it satisfies the equation, n equals $2n$. For example, the number of *even* inductive numbers is the same as the number of *all* inductive numbers, both odd and even. Leibniz used this fact to prove that infinite numbers are impossible, but modern mathematical logicians use it only to show that the commonly accepted belief that the whole is greater than

820

one of its parts is really not true and is based on an unperceived vagueness in some of its terms.

Granting the existence of infinite numbers (Russell limits himself to lower-order infinites, that is, infinite cardinals) an interesting question arises: Does there exist in the world a class the number of whose members is infinite? An affirmative answer to this question *appears* to be demonstrable. Assume that the number of individuals (the meaning of the term "individual" is left undefined for the moment) is some finite number, say n. Now there are mathematical truths which inform us, first, that, given a class of n members there are 2^n ways of selecting some of its members (including the extreme cases where we select all or none), and, second, that 2^n is always greater than n. If we now start with a class of n members, then add to this the class of classes that may be formed from n, namely, 2^n, then add the class of classes of classes that may be formed from this, namely, 2^{2n}, and so on, we shall have a total whose number is the infinite cardinal. Hence, the number of "things" in the world is infinite.

Russell confesses that he formerly believed this to be a valid proof. But he now rejects it because it involves what has come to be called the "confusion of types." The fallacy consists in the formation of "impure" classes. If there are n *individuals* in the world, and 2^n *classes* of individuals, we cannot form a new class whose number is n plus 2^n. Classes are logical constructions, not things, and the two "types" cannot be combined. Plato argued that since the number 1 has being, but is not identical with being, 1 plus being equals 2; then 1 plus 2

equals 3; and so on; hence the world is infinite. Two mathematicians, Bernard Bolzano and Richard Dedekind, argued that because ideas of things are "things," and because there is an idea of every thing, the class of "things" is a reflexive class (since it is similar to a part of itself) and its number must be infinite. Russell tries to show not only that these "proofs" have an air of hocus-pocus about them, but also that unless we prevent this confusion of types we shall be able to prove all sorts of self-contradictory statements— for example, that if a class is a member of itself, it is not a member of itself. One way to avoid both the feeling of uneasiness and the paradoxes is to define the word "individual" as referring to an entity of a certain "type," the word "class" as referring to an entity of another type, the word "relation" as referring to an entity of still another type, and so on.

The problem which Russell here formulates has given rise in recent literature to the distinction between languages and metalanguages, a metalanguage being a language which talks about a language. It then becomes important not to confuse these two "types" of language because absurdities and paradoxes may develop if we do.

In conclusion, Russell returns to the general question concerning the nature of mathematical philosophy and its relations to logic and empirical knowledge. Mathematics, formerly defined as the science of quantity, can no longer be so defined. Many branches of geometry have nothing to do with quantity, and even arithmetic, which is commonly thought to deal with numbers, concerns itself rather with the more basic ideas of one-to-one relations and similarity between classes. The generalization of the notion of order also means that mathematics is no longer particularly concerned with the number series.

What, then, is this new study which starts with mathematics and ends with discussions of classes, relations, and series? It may be called indifferently either "logic" or "mathematics"; the choice of name is not important. But its *characteristics* should be clarified.

In the first place, it does not deal with particular things or particular properties. It tells us that 1 plus 1 equals 2 but not that Socrates and Plato are two. A world in which there are no individuals would still be a world in which one and one are two. Traditional logic tells us that "All men are mortal and Socrates is a man," implies that "Socrates is mortal." But it does not tell us that all men *are* mortal or that Socrates really *is* a man. Thus the validity of a syllogism is independent of the truth or falsity of its premises. We try to express this by representing the *form* of the syllogism, independent of its *content*. We say, "No matter what values x and A and B may have, if all A's are B's and x is an A, then x is a B." We realize that the argument is valid for all individuals without the necessity for demonstrating it for Socrates and Plato and all the rest of the individuals, and it is valid for cats and four-legged creatures without demonstrating it for each particular cat. We can say that the "form" of a proposition is that which remains unchanged when every constituent of the proposition is replaced by another. The proposition "Socrates is earlier than Aristotle" has the same form as "Napoleon is greater than Wellington." In every language there are certain words whose function is merely to indicate form. These are called "logical constants." For example, the word "is" in the proposition "Socrates is human" is a logical constant. In pure mathematics the only constants which occur are logical constants. In this sense, therefore, logic and mathematics are one.

But in the second place, both mathematics and logic deal with propositions of a peculiar sort, quite different from those which are commonly called "empirical." They may be called "tautologies," though Russell confesses that he does not know how to define this term. (One of Russell's students, Ludwig Wittgenstein, later did define the term.) They are propositions which we seem to be able to know without any appeal to experience; for example, we know that the syllogism about Socrates is valid merely by examining the argument in its abstract form, not by appealing to experience. But this is merely a fact about the way in which we know such propositions, not about the propositions themselves. Russell admits that this analysis brings him to the very frontier of knowledge, that he cannot give a more precise definition of logical truths. He feels that these propositions are in some sense *a priori*, and that they can be said to be analytic, providing we adopt a new meaning for this term. But he feels that he cannot define them in spite of being quite familiar with the kind of property which he is trying to define. He ends by apologizing for his inability to make the subject matter of the book clear without the use of technical words, but he expresses the hope that readers will not hesitate to acquire the mastery which is necessary for such understanding.

SPACE, TIME, AND DEITY

Author: Samuel Alexander (1859-1938)
Type of work: Metaphysics
First published: 1920 (Gifford Lectures, Glasgow, 1916-1918)

PRINCIPAL IDEAS ADVANCED

Philosophy attempts to identify the generic and specific features of whatever exists.

The ultimate reality is space-time; matter is composed of motions which, in turn, are made up of point-instants.

The categories of being are fundamental properties of space-time; the major categories are identity, existence, relation, and order.

Matter, life, and consciousness are as real as the universal features of reality; they are emergent qualities of the space-time reality.

Deity is the highest order of being, the principle of evolution, the mind of the world.

Samuel Alexander belonged to the generation of English philosophers which found itself in revolt against the neo-Hegelianism of Bradley and Bosanquet. His philosophy shares most of the characteristics of the realism of that period: its conviction that experience can be analyzed into elements which are directly intuited; its insistence that the mental act is a different thing from the object known; and its inclination to account for the order of nature in nonspiritual terms. He went further than many realists in the role which he accorded to the natural sciences in philosophy; and further than most in his optimism respecting the possibilities of an all-inclusive system.

Philosophy, as Alexander understood it, differs from science not so much in method as in content. It has for its subject matter the pervasive aspects of things. In other words, it deals with those features of the world which recur over and over and in a wide variety of contexts. It has to identify these features, but also must discover their interrelations. The undertaking is recognizably Aristotelian, particularly in the contention—basic to Alexander's construction—that nature forms a pyramid, with general features at its base which permeate everything in nature, and successively more special features characterizing those which occur at higher levels. Thus, motion is an extremely basic character; matter is more special; life is more special still. And in each case, the higher presupposes the lower.

Space, Time, and Deity is Alexander's comprehensive work. Many philosophers tell us what they think philosophy should be, then apologize for offering us a mere sketch or sample. Alexander provides us with a finished work which is in many respects a masterpiece. The broad outline is implemented in a manner which shows sound knowledge both of the history of Western philosophy and of the revolutionary developments of contemporary science. Perhaps it does so completely what it sets out to do that nothing remains for the reader but to put it on a shelf and explore new avenues.

In Alexander's system, the ultimate reality from which all things are engendered is space-time. This preëminently modern conception was no doubt suggested to him by the developments of mathematical physics; but it owes at least as much to Bergson's intuition of time as duration. And Alexander, who was first and last an empiricist, although he did not venture to teach physicists their business, thought it important not to confuse geometrical constructions with the world of experience which, as a philosopher, he was bound to describe. For the common conception of a three-dimensional space moving like a column through fourth-dimensional time, he substituted the image of molecules of gas moving inside a closed container. The value of this figure is that it preserves the notion of a space made up of points successively occupied by instants of time. Such is the nature of the world we experience. Its ultimate constituents are events which, besides their location in space, also have a past and a future. What we call matter, Alexander maintained, is composed of many motions, just as motions are made up of events or point-instants.

A prominent feature of Alexander's book is his discussion of the *categories*. These are viewed by him as fundamental determinations of being. They are not to be confused with *qualities*, which in his system are variable and accidental, because the categories are universal and constitutive. They are *a priori* in the sense that they are known in advance to apply to every existing thing. But they are genuine features of reality and not mere dispositions of the mind, as Kant had held. For this reason, Alexander did not pretend to deduce them by any necessity, logical or mechanical. The realists held that the business of the philosopher is not to explain everything but to describe what he finds. And Alexander's procedure was to disclose one after another of the traditional categories of philosophy as fundamental properties of space-time itself.

Thus, *identity* and *diversity* (the first two categories) need not be regarded as peculiarities of man's intellect nor as archetypal forms which determine the limits of all being, but as primary characteristics of the point-instant. Time exhibits sameness as duration; it exhibits difference as succession. Similarly, space exhibits unity as being a continuum, diversity as being composed of parts. The inseparability of space-time is bound up with these features. Alexander argued that space is what gives time its unity and that time is what gives space its diversity; otherwise time would be a mere succession and space would be blank unity.

Being or *existence* is simply another name for identity of place and time. Alexander rejected the notion of neutral being supposedly embracing entities which transcend sense experience. But he did not on that account deny that *universals* are real. On the contrary, he maintained that they are patterns or habits which determine actual events. They are a kind of identity as between different particular happenings. Thus, they exist, have their own efficacy, and may be apprehended directly by minds. A distinction is made between universals and *particulars* and *individuals*.

Relations express the continuity of

space-time. Alexander resisted a physicalism which would reduce all relations to those of space and time, but he held that in the last analysis all relations do depend upon spatio-temporal ones. A relation is a connection in virtue of which two terms enter into a whole. A simple example is an interval of space or of time. A more complex one is the relation of a king to his subjects. In this example, where a set of acts and passions constitute the total situation, the relation is not directly a feature of space and time; but the acts and passions of men are themselves complex patterns of space-time events.

Order is a separate and a major category of its own; identity, existence, and relation complete the class of major categories.

Substance, Alexander maintained, is a relation between the spatial and temporal elements in a definite volume of space-time. It is no "brute senseless somewhat" (Berkeley) which serves as a support for qualities, but the spatial contour within which a particular set of qualities exists. A portion of space-time is a substance in virtue of being the seat of motion, though the motion be as simple as the flight of an electron. Empty space is included in substance at the molecular or atomic level—supposing these to be miniature planetary orbits. But it is not part of the substance on a macroscopic scale. The holes of a sponge, to cite Alexander's example, are not part of the substance of the sponge.

Causality (here treated as a category) is a relation between substances. It spells out the implications of Alexander's fundamental hypothesis that space-time is a continuous system in which every event is related to one which precedes it and to one which follows. The popular notion of causality distinguishes between things and events, which the present view does not. A thing is already a complex of motions, and it becomes a cause when one or more of its constituent motions is continued in a different motion. Alexander greatly simplified a notoriously difficult issue. For him, all causality is *a tergo:* the cause must be adjacent to the effect in space, and immediately prior in time. He rejected the suggestion of Ernst Mach and the positivists that the notion of causality has been rendered obsolete by the progress made by science in the use of mathematical descriptions. For Alexander, a mathematical description, to be relevant, must describe something. If formulae mean anything, they assert a reciprocal determination of two motions, which is what is here understood as causality. *Reciprocity* is a separate, but related, category. *Quantity, intensity, whole, parts, number,* and *motion* complete the categories.

The description of space-time and of the categories takes up the entire first volume of the work. Although the matter is abstract, the method is comparatively simple and straightforward. Categories apply equally to all existents, from a simple motion to a thought. Once the nature of space-time is grasped, the delineation of the particular categories is merely a matter of detail. It is otherwise when we come, in the second volume, to consider *quality.* For one of Alexander's main tenets, which he shared with Moore, Russell, and the American neo-realists, was that empirical objects have real and independent existence. Other naturalists and materialists have held that the categories are sufficient to account for all actual determinations of being. In attempting to maintain that matter, secondary qualities, life, and consciousness are just as real as the universal features of the world, Alexander was confronted with a challenging task. The problem was to conceive of the relation between quality and its spatio-temporal or categorial ground— how, in other words, certain spatio-temporal complexes are correlated with such empirical facts as materiality, vitality, entelechy, and knowledge—ultimately also, with goodness, beauty, and truth.

The method, therefore, in this part can no longer be simple description and analysis. Since what is sought is the correlation between quality and its categorical ground, Alexander looked for an unambiguous instance of this correlation, and proceeded by analogy to apply it through the length and breadth of the world. The instance which he chose as a paradigm is the correlation between *mind* and the *nervous system*. This connection, because it is uniquely open to our inspection, is suited as none other to unlock the mystery. On the basis of the findings of neurology he argued that the mind is something new in life but that it is not a separate entity. There is but one process which, viewed in the context with nutrition, respiration, elimination, is vital; but viewed in its unique aspects (as meaningful) it is of a different order. This theory suggests that when a neural process has a specific complexity, intensity, and connection with other processes and structures, it takes on new characters so that, without ceasing to be vital, it becomes mental.

With this instance before him, Alexander proceeded to generalize. Happily, he could draw upon the work of Lloyd Morgan, the biologist, who had introduced the distinction between additive and *emergent* qualities. Some combinations in nature are purely quantitative, such as molecular weights. But others give rise to qualitative changes, such as the properties of water, which could never be predicted from the properties of hydrogen and oxygen. Alexander cites the famous lines from Robert Browning's poem *Abt Vogler*, which tells the story of a musician who out of three sounds framed, not a fourth sound but—a star! This is what happens in the higher vertebrates when *mind* emerges; and, Alexander suggests, it is our best clue to what happens when certain motions give rise to chemical *matter*, and certain chemical combinations give rise to *life*. The novelty is not something added—Alexander repudiated "vitalism" just as he repudiated "animism." Life is basically chemical, but it is a specific grade of matter which manifests properties that defy description in chemical terms. The same is true of matter: it is motion, and from one point of view "nothing but motion"; still, it has properties (hardness, color, special affinities) which other motions do not have and which, if we were committed to a reductionist logic, must be regarded as "unreal" because they are not categorial.

It is in connection with his discussion of mind and the neural system that Alexander treats the problem of *knowledge*. He regards it as erroneous to suppose, with many modern philosophers, that epistemology is the foundation of metaphysics. Rather, it is a chapter of metaphysics, a special case of the way in which a finite thing, on any level of being, is in rapport with its environment. Any two things which are connected, as mind is with the object of cognition, in the same space-time, interact causally, not only according to their spatial relations but also according to their special natures. The latter introduce a selective factor, particularly important in accounting for perception. A table is differently affected by the wall and by the fireplace; in a similar manner, the optic nerve reacts to some qualities and not to others.

But neural activity as such is not cognition, which comes into being only on the level of consciousness. And it is here that we meet the characteristic epistemological problem: whether the objects of the mind's perception are qualities of the thing or the activity of the brain itself. Alexander maintained that they are both, but in different respects. To make his idea clear he introduced two new terms which have gained a certain currency. The mind's awareness of the neural activity he called *enjoyment*; its awareness of the qualities of the thing perceived he called *contemplation*. The object of perception is not the modification of the nervous system, but the process of knowing is. And it is by living through or enjoying the latter that the mind confronts or contemplates the thing. Alexander saw a similarity between this account and the doctrine of Spinoza, who stated that the mind is the "idea of the body." He also believed that it got at the truth which G. E. Moore elucidated in his "Refutation of Idealism."

Cognition can be understood as analogous to other natural processes, but judgment, necessary to the resolution of value problems, is unique in that it is always a *social* phenomenon. Thus, instead of involving merely the mind and its object, judgment also involves a *norm;* and this norm, Alexander argued, comes into being only through social intercourse. A man who grew up apart from society might form a judgment and later correct it in the interest of efficiency. His mistake would be misadventure, not an error. Only when he found his judgment disagreeing with the judgment of another would he become aware that judgments have a reality of their own. This would put him, for the first time, in the position to distinguish between the judgment and the thing judged, between truth (or error) and reality (or illusion). The same holds true of goodness and beauty, which outside a social context would be no more than volitions arising out of pleasurable anticipations. They take their place as values when judged in accordance with a standard which arises as a result of a meeting of minds.

This is the part of Alexander's philosophy which seems to most students to represent a departure from the strict realist standpoint. He has abandoned the view that values exist in things and has denied that they are given instantly in experience. His realism has, in fact, given place to a naturalistic metaphysics which permits him to "explain" values as real, in the sense that a "whole situation," consisting of knower and known, is real. Values, says Alexander, are not objective in the way secondary qualities are, nor subjective in the way pains and pleasures are. Subject and object mutually determine each other in an organic whole. He reminds us of objective idealism when he goes on to argue that "coherence" is the only criterion, not only of truth but also of goodness and beauty, and he appeals to the larger experience of society to decide what is coherent. But the biological emphasis is never far away. One of his contentions is that knowledge (and *a fortiori* the other values) is fundamentally an expression of will, for "judging is the speculative side of volition, and what is willed in willing is the proposition or object judged." In fact, his account of truth bears many resemblances to pragmatism. He agrees that the test of truth is that it works, but he denies that this is all that can be said about it. It works, he adds, because it is determined by the nature of reality.

But we must return to the broad outlines of Alexander's theory, and in particular to the notion of *deity* with which, in Book IV, he brings his system to its completion. Two main features have been noted so far. The first is that everything in the world is made up of motions, more or less complex; the second is that a particular combination of motions has qualities which are inseparable from it. The former was worked out by Alexander in terms of point-instants and the categories which make up the space-time continuum; the latter, in terms of the theory of emergent characters. The one is *a priori*; the other empirical. But this distinction, important as it is, is not an absolute one. What is lacking so far is the notion of *evolution*, according to which emergence is built into the very stuff of the world itself— the point-instant. Mere points would be static. The point-instant is dynamic. Its spacial component corresponds to the body; it is the "matter" of which the world is formed. Its temporal component corresponds to the mind; it is the "form" which generates qualities in space. Creativity and development are,

in this sense, built into the nature of the world.

This is about as far as Alexander is willing to go in the direction of traditional theology. The religious impulse demands for its object a being which is higher than man. But philosophy wants a principle of explanation which is relevant to the world of its experience. If we combine these two, we arrive at the conception of a universe engendering within itself ever higher orders of being, with deity as the one beyond the human mind. If time is designated as the "mind of Space," deity can be described as the "mind of the whole world." But this would be merely figurative, since deity is nowhere actualized. A stricter account would be to say that God is the "infinite world with its nisus toward deity."

Alexander distinguishes between *deity*—which is a quality higher than but analogous to matter, life, and mind —and *God,* which he defines as "a being which possesses deity." Man has *faith* in God, based upon his *experience* of deity. This latter is a veridical experience and not mere imagination. Deity does not now exist, but as the next order to evolve, it is experienced as future; and in Alexander's system, past and future are just as real as the present. Alexander argues for the autonomy of the religious sentiment through which deity is apprehended. It is a specific kind of consciousness, not reducible to the apprehension of value. For although the religious emotion is likely to be communal, and the God of faith is ordinarily thought of as on the side of the good, the religious emotion is a unique "hungering and thirsting after" the totality of being in its striving toward deity.

When he approached the problem

of religion exclusively in terms of "religious experience," Alexander was in step with the liberal theology of that day. And presumably his own strong empirical bias prevented him from postulating God as a creative agent, in the way that Lloyd Morgan and A. N. Whitehead were to do. This is the more remarkable because several times Alexander points to lacunae in his own system (for example, the existence of emergent qualities) which, on the "principle of sufficient reason" solicit the service of a First Mover. But Alexander declines the gambit. "As being the whole universe," says he, "God is creative, but his distinctive character of deity is not creative but created." As for the mystery of empirical being, he prefers to accept it "with the 'natural piety' of the investigator. It admits no explanation."

TRACTATUS LOGICO-PHILOSOPHICUS

Author: Ludwig Wittgenstein (1889-1951)
Type of work: Logic, philosophy of philosophy
First published: 1921

PRINCIPAL IDEAS ADVANCED

The world is made up of atomic facts; atomic facts are facts which are incapable of analysis into more elemental facts.

Propositions are logical pictures of (possible)facts; what is common to a proposition and the fact it pictures is logical structure.

A proposition does not express the form of a possible fact; it shows it.

To give the general form of proposition is to give the essence of all description and of the world; any proposition whatsoever can be formed by drawing from the class of elementary propositions and using various logical operations.

Philosophy is a process of clarification; the propositions of natural science are meaningful, but the attempt to say something meaningful in ethics, aesthetics, or metaphysics is bound to fail, for any such attempt involves the impossible task of talking about the world from the outside.

This is an unusual book, both in content and in style. In content it is about logic, though the author finds the chance in discussing this subject to say much about the theory of signs, epistemology, metaphysics, and philosophy in general. Furthermore, in talking about logic Wittgenstein indicates that there are many things which we cannot say about logic, not because we do not know them, or even because we do know them but cannot find words by which to express them, but because they are literally *inexpressible* by means of *any* language. Consequently we must remain silent about them.

In style the book is also strange. The sentences (or sometimes groups of sentences) are all numbered in accordance with a plan. For example, a certain sentence has the number 3; this follows sentences 1 and 2 in the order of the natural numbers. But between 2 and 3 are sentences numbered, for example, 2.0122 and 2.151. Sentence 2.0122 is a statement referring to statement 2. Statement 2.151 follows statement 2.1 and is a comment on it; but 2.1, in turn, is another comment on 2, and follows it. All statements are in this way arranged in a unique, linear order based on the decimal notation, and the reader is able to determine by the number attached to each sentence what *general* topic is being considered, what *special* aspect of this general subject is involved, and so on, sometimes to the fourth level of specialization.

Furthermore, because of the unusual meanings associated with many of the terms employed by the author, the editor has chosen to publish on facing pages the original German text and its parallel English translation. This permits the reader who is familiar with German to improve his understanding of the text by checking with the original German and in many cases to detect fine shades of meaning which might otherwise have escaped him. In a book where such common words as "fact," "object," "meaning," and "truth" occur in great abundance and are employed with somewhat unusual connotations, the parallel translation is of great help. The book also contains a valuable introduction, written by Bertrand Russell, which both summarizes the text and criticizes it on some important points.

For convenience of discussion it will be well to combine Wittgenstein's discussion of Proposition 1 and the remarks on it, with Proposition 2 and all of the remarks contained in Propositions numbered 2.0. Proposition 1 states that the world is everything that is the case; Proposition 2 asserts that what is the case, the fact, is the existence of atomic facts. The world, then, is made up of atomic facts and is constituted by them. Atomic facts are facts which are incapable of analysis into more elemental facts. This does not mean that atomic facts cannot be analyzed, but only that they cannot be analyzed into other atomic facts. An atomic fact is itself a combination of objects (entities, things), each of whose essence lies in its being a constituent of an atomic fact. But the objects which are elements of atomic facts cannot themselves be analyzed, since they form the substance of the world. If we take advantage of the illustration of an atomic fact which Russell gives in his introduction (Wittgenstein does not give illustrations of atomic facts), we may say that it is what is asserted by the proposition "Socrates is wise." This contains two objects, *Socrates* and *wise,* each of which, in its own unique way, unites with the other to form the atomic fact. Traditional philosophy would call these objects "substances" and "qualities." Wittgenstein states that however different from the real world an imaginary world might be, it must have something, its form, in common with the real world. Since the form is given by the objects, we may presume Wittgenstein to be saying that any imaginable world would have to contain substances and qualities, however these might differ from those in our real world. The world is the totality of atomic facts; it also determines the nonexistence of atomic facts, for the nonexistence of an atomic fact is a

830

kind of fact. Reality, therefore, is the totality of atomic facts plus the fact that these are *all* the atomic facts.

Beginning with Proposition 2.1, continuing more or less explicitly through Proposition 4, and extending implicitly through the rest of the book, Wittgenstein examines what is meant by saying that a proposition is a picture of a fact. He describes this picturing relation variously as "modeling," "standing for," "representing," "corresponding with," "depicting," and "projecting." We should note, first, that a proposition is itself a fact. By this is not meant the propositional sign which expresses the fact, though Wittgenstein admits that propositions can be expressed perceptibly through the senses, but rather the *sense* of the proposition. The point is, of course, that the proposition is a *logical* picture of the fact, not a *visual* one or an *audible* one. He says that it represents the fact in "logical space"—a metaphor which he uses repeatedly throughout the book. Its representative character lies in its form or structure, which means a coördination of the elements in the picture with the objects in the fact, and an identity of logical form exhibited by both the picture and the fact. Thus the proposition "Socrates is wise" pictures the fact of Socrates' wisdom because "Socrates" represents Socrates, and "wise" represents wisdom, and the form exhibited by "Socrates" and "wise" in the propositional relation is the same as that exhibited by Socrates and wisdom in the fact. That this is a logical form rather than a spatial form is to be seen in the fact that while the sentence "Socrates is wise" has a spatial order of its elements, neither the *meaning* of the sentence nor the *fact* asserted by the

sentence is spatial; what is common to the meaning and the fact is a logical structure.

More precisely, the proposition does not strictly represent the fact, but rather the *possibility* of the fact, the possibility of the existence and nonexistence of atomic facts. A proposition whose expression mentions a complex is not nonsense if this complex fails to exist, but simply false. A proposition represents what it represents independently of its truth or falsity, through its form of representation, through its *sense*. Furthermore, by virtue of the identity of form which runs through various facts, the picture represents every reality whose form it has; thus "Socrates is wise" also pictures that fact that Plato is human.

"The logical picture of the facts is the thought" (Proposition 3). To say that an atomic fact is thinkable means that we can imagine it. And if it is thinkable it must also be logical, for anything which is "unlogical" could not be expressed at all. Language cannot express anything which "contradicts logic" any more than a spatial figure can represent anything which contradicts the laws of space, or can represent the spatial coördinates of a point which does not exist.

The sign through which thoughts are expressed is the propositional sign. Both the proposition and the propositional sign are facts. In the propositional sign the elements (the words) are combined in a definite way so that the objects of the thoughts correspond to the elements of the propositional sign. The simple signs used in propositional signs are called "names." Objects can only be named and spoken about; they cannot be asserted. Names cannot be further analyzed; they are primitive signs. They have meanings only in the context of propositions.

A propositional expression presupposes the forms of all propositions that it expresses, and thus it may be said to characterize a form and a content; the form is constant, and everything else is variable. If every constituent part of a proposition is changed into a variable, the logical form (the logical prototype) remains. Thus, to use an example which Russell gives elsewhere, if we change the proposition "Socrates drank hemlock" into the proposition "Coleridge ate opium," the form of the proposition, "ARB," remains. This may be called a "propositional variable."

In the language of everyday life the same word often signifies in two different ways, and different words signify in the same way. For example, the verb "to be" appears sometimes as the sign of equality, sometimes as the expression of existence, sometimes as an intransitive verb, and sometimes as a sign of identity. Words of this kind are the cause of some of the most fundamental confusions in thought, especially in philosophical thought. The only way to avoid these difficulties is to invent a special symbolism—a symbolism which obeys the rules of *logical* grammar (logical syntax). Such rules follow of themselves if we know only how every sign signifies. Bertrand Russell and the mathematician, Gottlob Frege, have invented such logical symbolisms, but even these do not exclude the possibility of error.

The great advantage of a logical language is that it calls our attention to formal properties of objects and facts. This is not because propositions express the form of facts, but because they "show it" and do not state it. No proposition is capable of representing its form of representation, for this would require something which is impossible—the picture would have to place itself outside its form of representation. "The proposition *shows* how things stand, *if* it is true." The existence of a structure in a possible state of affairs is not *expressed by* the proposition which presents the state of affairs; it is *shown in* the proposition by means of its structure. The identity of form which is exhibited by the proposition and by the fact accounts for the representation of the fact by the proposition, but this does not give the proposition a *formal property* of representing the fact. It would be as meaningless to ascribe a formal property to a proposition as to deny it of the proposition. And it would be equally meaningless to assert that one form has a certain property and another form has a different property, for this assumes that there is sense in asserting that either form has either property. We do not ascribe properties to forms nor do we ascribe forms to propositions or states of affairs. In this respect formal concepts differ from proper concepts. The proper concept "man" can be expressed by a propositional function, for example, "x is a man"; but the formal concept "object" cannot be expressed by "x is an object." In this expression "x" is a sign of the pseudo-concept *object*, and to say that a rose is an object (thing, entity) is to utter nonsense. The same holds true of such words as "complex," "fact," "function," and "number," which should be represented in symbolism by variables, not by proper concepts. Recognizing these as variables shows the absurdity of making such statements as "There are objects" (sup-

832

posedly patterned after "There are books") or "There is only one 1" (which according to Wittgenstein is as absurd as it would be to say "2 plus 2 is at 3 o'clock equal to 4"). To summarize, then, the great advantage of a precise logical symbolism is that it prevents us from talking nonsense. The correct use of the symbols, as was said above, follows immediately if we know how every sign signifies.

A further consequence of the notion that "object" is a pseudo-concept is the impossibility of finding some "property" which all "objects" possess. We have already seen that atomic facts are complex and contain objects as elements of a certain structure. These objects are unanalyzable. Consequently, to name a certain atomic fact is to presuppose the truth of a certain atomic proposition, namely, the proposition asserting the relatedness of the constituents of the complex; and this, in turn, presupposes the naming of the constituents (object) themselves. But now, according to Wittgenstein, since the concept "object" is a pseudo-concept, there is no way by which we can describe the totality of things that can be named. This means that we cannot say anything about the totality of what there is in the world. There is no property, such as self-identity, which all objects possess. To say that if all objects were exactly alike they would be identical, and there could be only one object in the world, is to assert not a logical truth, but an accidental characteristic of the world. Consequently, we cannot use self-identity as a property by which we can "locate" an object. Instead, we signify objects by means of letters, and different objects by different letters.

The simplest proposition, the elementary proposition, asserts the existence of an atomic fact. Such a proposition is a concatenation of names and is incapable of analysis into further propositions. Now it is an important thesis of Wittgenstein that all propositions are truth-functions of elementary propositions and can be built up from them. (An elementary proposition is a truth-function of itself). Truth-functions are obtained in the following way: Suppose all elementary propositions were given. Each of these could be either true or false. Therefore a proposition containing three elementary propositions p, q, r could have a truth-function T,T,F, or T,F,T, and there would be eight such possible truth-functions; in case there were four elementary propositions there would be sixteen truth-functions. Starting with any group of elementary propositions the truth-functions formed from them may be arranged in a series.

Of the propositions, two kinds are particularly important. One of them, called a "tautology," is a type of proposition which is true for all the truth-possibilities of the elementary propositions. The other, called a "contradiction," is a proposition which is false for all the truth-possibilities of the elementary propositions. The truth of a tautology is *certain;* the truth of a contradiction is *impossible;* the truth of all other propositions is *possible.* Here we have the serial arrangement of propositions which forms the basis for a theory of probability. An example of a tautology is "It is either raining or it is not raining"; this is always true regardless of whether the p and the *not-p* which it contains are true or false. A tautology, therefore, "says nothing" about the world, for it is true of all possible states of affairs. An example of a contradiction is "It is both raining and it is not raining"; this is false regardless of whether the *p* and the *not-p* which it contains are true or false. A contradiction therefore also "says nothing" about the world, for it is false for all possible states of affairs. Tautologies and contradictions are without sense. "Contradiction is the external limit of the propositions, tautology their substanceless center."

Logical operations are those which produce propositions from other propositions. For example, "denial" (not), "logical addition" (either-or), "logical multiplication" (and) are all logical operations. Thus, operations do not assert anything; the *result* of an operation, a proposition, does assert something; and what it asserts depends upon the elementary propositions on which it is based. We can thus express the general form of all propositions; this is a propositional variable whose values would be all possible propositions. Wittgenstein states this form in abstract symbols; it means, according to Russell's statement in the *Introduction*, "whatever can be obtained by taking any selection of atomic propositions, negating them all, then taking any selection of the set of propositions now obtained, together with any of the originals—and so on indefinitely."

We saw above that language cannot express anything that contradicts logic. Wittgenstein now resumes the discussion of this topic and points out that we cannot say what we cannot think. We cannot say that there is *this* in the world but there is not *that*, for such a statement would imply that logic can exclude certain possibilities from the world; but in such a case

logic would have to "get outside the limits of the world"; that is, it would have to consider these limits from both within and without the world. However, logic cannot go beyond itself; "logic fills the world: the limits of the world are also its limits." This principle also has applications for solipsism. Solipsism is correct, but cannot be asserted; it can only be "shown." The subject who knows is the limit of the world; he does not belong to it. The best example of this theory is the field of vision: there is nothing *in the field of sight* that permits us to conclude that it is seen by an eye.

Reality, for Wittgenstein, proves to be very loose-knit. No atomic fact contradicts any atomic fact, and no atomic fact can be inferred from an atomic fact. There is no causal nexus in nature, and belief that there is such a thing is superstition. Induction is a process of assuming the simplest law that can be made to describe the regularities of nature. But there is no necessity in this process. The only necessity is a *logical* necessity, and the only impossibility is a *logical* impossibility; and these presumably do not exist in the world.

The *sense* of the world lies outside the world. If there were *value* it would have to "lie outside all happenings and being-so. For all happening and being-so is accidental." As a consequence, ethics and aesthetics cannot be expressed, and are transcendental.

What, then, is philosophy? It seems to have two tasks. One is to show that every proposition is a picture of a fact. This cannot be *said*, for no proposition can say anything about itself. That a proposition has, for example, the subject-predicate form cannot be said in a proposition, and that a proposition has the form *"p or q"* cannot be said in a proposition. Nor can it be said how a proposition pictures reality. A sentence has no *apparent* pictorial character. But neither does a musical score, or a phonograph record; and neither does a pattern of sound waves obviously picture the sound themselves. Yet all of these stand to that which they represent in a relation which can be seen in the similarity of structure holding between them and the facts. There is a "law of projection" which enables us to translate the picture into the fact, though this *law* cannot be stated. And since the law cannot be stated, we should not try to do so. Wittgenstein therefore concludes with proposition 7, "Whereof one cannot speak, thereof one must be silent."

But there *is* another task for philosophy. Philosophy is not a theory, like one of the natural sciences, ending in a series of conclusions which can be called "philosophical propositions." It is an activity, a process of clarification, in which we try to delimit thoughts which are obscure and confused. If philosophy finds that the *answers* to its questions cannot be expressed, it should realize that its *questions* have not been properly expressed, for "if a question can be put at all, then it *can* also be answered." To doubt where there are no questions is absurd. To insist that the problems of life have not been touched by the sciences, and yet to be unable to formulate these problems which remain in a language which is clear enough to permit an answer is really to say that there is no problem left. This is precisely what Wittgenstein says. "The solution of the problem of life is seen in the vanishing of this problem." The right method of philosophy is to turn all of the things which can be said over to the scientists, who will *say* them, and then when anyone asks a metaphysical question, to point out to him that his question is meaningless. Philosophy will then "see the world rightly."

HUMAN NATURE AND CONDUCT

Author: John Dewey (1859-1952)
Type of work: Ethics
First published: 1922

PRINCIPAL IDEAS ADVANCED

Moralities of the past were deficient in that they were based on arbitrary rules rather than on a scientific understanding of human nature as formed within a social environment.

Human nature is continuous with the rest of nature; ethics is thus allied with physics and biology, and with sociology, law, and economics.

Vices and virtues are habits developed during the interaction of the human organism and the social environment.

835

Morals are ways of action invented to meet specific situations; reactions to them become habits and acquire prescriptive character.

Education must enable the organism to modify its behavior in the face of novelty.

Reflection upon conduct has as its objective the satisfying resolution of a problem arising from the incompatibility of various impulses.

In the preface to *Human Nature and Conduct: An Introduction to Social Psychology* Dewey says that his book "sets forth a belief that an understanding of habit and of different types of habit is the key to social psychology while the operation of impulse and intelligence gives the key to individualized mental activity. But they are secondary to habit so that the mind can be understood in the concrete only as a system of beliefs, desires and purposes which are formed in the interaction of biological aptitudes with a social environment."

Thus, to understand ourselves and others in terms of Dewey's theory, we must study human nature and the social institutions in which it functions. Both forces work to shape the individual. Morality is the interaction between the two.

Dewey criticizes the morality of the past as being based largely on arbitrary rules rather than on a scientific understanding of human beings. The few have given and administered rules which the many have obeyed with reluctance, if at all.

Such morality is largely restrictive, concerned with what should not be done. Many people conform, but others circumvent the morality in their practice, while giving lip service to it or by having a theory which avoids it. The romantic device of the glorification of impulse as opposed to knowledge is such a theory. Those who attempt to live by a morality divorced from an adequate theory of human nature inhabit a world in which the ideal and the real are sharply separated. They must renounce one world or live uneasily in a world split in two.

It is Dewey's contention that only knowledge can solve moral problems and that only scientific method holds promise of providing knowledge. The moral life operates in an environmental setting that is both natural and social. Human nature is continuous with the rest of nature, and as a result ethics is allied with physics and biology. Since the activities of one person are continuous with those of others, ethics is allied with such social sciences as sociology, law, and economics. Even the past is not irrelevant. We can study history to understand the present as derived from the past and to help us determine the structure of the future.

The moral acts of a person are closely related to his habits. Habits are compared by Dewey to psychological functions. Both require the cooperation of the organism and its environment. Vices and virtues are not private possessions of a person; they are the result of the interaction of human nature and environment. "All virtues and vices are habits which incorporate objective forces." They can be studied and understood and, as such, can serve as the basis of moral discussion.

Everyone is familiar with bad habits. They are tendencies to action which somehow command us but which we usually have acquired without conscious intent. Since they command, they are will in a clear sense of this word. Since they are demanding, and determine what we regard as significant and what as trivial, they are the self if we are to understand that concept.

Dewey uses this view to replace the belief that will is a separate faculty which, if exercised, can achieve whatever the individual wishes to achieve. A person with a bad habit is not simply failing to do the right thing; he has formed a habit of doing the wrong thing. Habits cannot be dismissed by a simple effort of will any more than rain can be brought on by a simple act of dancing. As one must understand the conditions that cause drought and bring rain, so one must understand the objective conditions which cause and continue habit.

Neither reason nor will can be separated from habit. What one reasons about, what one decides upon, how one acts on decisions is determined by the relation of the human organism to an environment.

Many people have thought that social institutions are the result of individual habits. The contrary is true for Dewey. They are the source of information about habits, in the sense that the individual must acquire habits that conform with those of his social group. This explains the meaning of such terms as group mind, collective mind, and crowd mind. They can mean nothing more than "a custom brought at some point to explicit, emphatic consciousness, emotional or intellectual." Dewey adds, "In short, the primary facts of social psychology center about collective habit, custom."

One might expect that democracy would encourage individuality, but democracy as we live it seems, on the contrary, to encourage conformity. Conformity is due to the unfavorable influence of past custom as it affects beliefs, emotions, and purposes. An education tied to the past "becomes the art of taking advantage of the helplessness of the young; the forming of habits becomes a guarantee of the hedges of custom." But habit is not necessarily conservative. It is any ability formed through past experience. One can acquire the habit to seek new solutions to new problems as easily as the habit to attempt to solve all problems in old ways. Dewey does not describe habit as simply a way of acting it is also a way of thinking, because thinking requires energy and energy is organized by habit.

Dewey's view of habit places him in opposition to a central contention of the great majority of moralists. They have held that ethical decisions can or must be made by the intellect, unencumbered by nonrational dispositions such as habits or customs. Morality involves relating a set of ideal laws to particular situations and deciding on a course of action which resolves the situation and is in accord with these laws. What classical moralists do not account for, Dewey contends, is the source of ideal laws. Such laws do not suddenly appear, fully formulated, carrying with them their own demand for obedience. On the contrary, they grow like language from incoherent mutterings to complex systems of communication, requiring adherence to rules which are a product of after-the-fact reflection and which acquire a prescriptive character. Morals are ways of acting invented to meet specific

837

situations. When these situations are repeated, the reaction to them becomes a habit and acquires a prescriptive character. Morality refers to social institutions to which we must defer if we are to live. But deference is not implicit obedience. Indeed, implicit obedience to any rule of action is impossible. The rule is derived from the environment, and conditions change. In a completely static world, rules might forever remain the same; but our world is not static, and new rules arise from inevitable change.

We must distinguish between impulses and habits. All human beings love, hate, desire, and avoid; and these impulses have been embodied in social institutions. But what variety there is in these institutions! Different societies utilize the same impulses in many ways: the communism of the South Sea islanders, the pacificism of the Chinese (these are Dewey's examples), the militarism of the ancient Persians, the variety of class morality in almost every society.

The infant is largely potentiality. It is born in an adult environment which provides channels for its impulses; indeed, without these channels the impulses have no meaning, because while an activity stems from the impulse, the nature of the activity comes from the social environment. This environment may be intensely tight, narrow, and restrictive or it may be loose, wide, and tolerant. Dewey advocates the latter sort. He says: "With the dawn of the idea of progressive betterment and an interest in new uses of impulses, there has grown up some consciousness of the extent to which a future new society of changed purposes and desires may be created by a deliberate humane treatment of the impulses of youth. This is the meaning of education; for a truly humane education consists in an intelligent direction of native activities in the light of the possibilities and necessities of the social situation."

Dewey describes insistence on conformity as training, not education. Education, properly speaking, must enable the organism to modify its behavior in the face of novelty, rather than to withdraw timidly. Dewey says again and again and in article after article that no old set of habits will ever be adequate to meet new situations. One fact about the future we can be sure of is that it will contain novelty. Old rules sometimes meet new situations but only because the old rules are vague.

By defining human nature as this combination of impulses and social conditioning, Dewey is able to claim that human nature can be changed. As social conditions change, new ways must be devised to meet the change; old impulses are directed into new channels and a new human nature is formed. Indeed, the very words we use to describe human nature—selfishness, greed, altruism, generosity—are social terms and have no meaning apart from our interaction with the environment. A person acts with regard to the consequences of his acts, and a part of these consequences is what others will think of the act.

Instincts provide the motive for action but do not determine the character of the action. To attribute all business activity to the acquisitive instinct is an oversimplification, tending to obscure the study of business enterprise. Another case in point is pleasure. The moral literature of the world is full of tirades branding pleasure as evil. Certainly some excesses of pleasure do harm; but pleasure is as necessary to the human organism as work, which is often taken as its opposite. It is through art and play that new and fresh meanings are added to the usual activities of life. Both have a moral function. Both bring into use the imagination which often finds no part to play in our mundane activities. Both heighten and broaden the meaning of our ordinary concerns. Art and play release energy in a constructive way.

The constructive release of energy is in the direction of meeting new situations by modifying old ways of action. The alternatives are frozen custom or unbridled revolution. What Dewey wants is conscious, reflective reconstruction of society. We must act, but we must act constructively, guided by intelligence.

What, then, is the place of intelligence in conduct? Dewey has already discussed habits. They are related to intelligence in two ways. The first is restrictive. Habits confine intelligence to the problem at hand; but if this were its only function, the goal of intelligence would be mindless action. Intelligence offers the solution; habit takes over and repeats the solution again and again. But habit is not only restrictive. In its second function it presents alternatives. The more numerous our habits, the greater are the possibilities of action. In explaining this second function of habit, Dewey says that we "know how by means of our habits." This means that through habits of inquiry we recognize the novelty in a situation and marshal our previous experience by means of the channels of habit to meet it. This focus of habits on a problem and the solution which results is an essential function of intelligence. Unless we have habits of inquiry, there is no approach to the problem. We must learn until it becomes habit that problems can be recognized and that to solve them we must recollect, observe, and plan.

Some psychologists believe that intelligence and moral conscience are separate faculties which are unconditioned by experience but which operate on the subject matter of experience when it falls within their realm. Dewey does not share this view. For him, both develop in the human organism as the organism develops. The organism grows in height, learns to swim, evinces a desire for knowledge, accepts and rejects. Every habit is an impulse. The child learns something, likes what he learns, and then wants to learn more. That he may want to learn more is no more mysterious than that he may want to swim better or that he may want to act morally.

To act morally is to act in the best or wisest way. Such a course of action requires deliberation. To deliberate is to examine with the mind the possible courses of action and their consequences. The possible courses of action which are considered are the result of habit. The choice of one course rather than others simply means that "some habit or some combination of elements of habits and impulse finds a way fully open. Then energy is released. The mind is made up, composed, unified." Deliberation is always the search for a way to act, not an end in itself.

Dewey disagrees with the Utilitarians. Their theory, he believes, is that the intellect calculates the consequences of various courses of action and then chooses the one that will result in the most pleasure. His first objection to this theory is that it depends on the misapprehension that reason leads directly to action. On the contrary, habit furnishes the force of action, not reason nor yet the anticipation of feeling. Secondly, there is the difficulty of predicting future pleasures. Future pleasures depend on our bodily state at some future moment and on the environment of that state. Both of these are independent of present action. "Things sweet in anticipation are bitter in actual taste, things we now turn from in aversion are welcome at another moment in our career." What makes utilitarianism seem plausible to its advocates is their assumption that the organism and its surroundings will remain constant through time. They project the present into the future.

"There is seen to be but one issue involved in all reflection upon conduct: The rectifying of present troubles, the harmonizing of present incompatibilities by projecting a course of action which gathers into itself the meaning of them all." In this sentence Dewey summarizes his ethical theory as he formulated it in *Human Nature and Conduct*. Good means the unity that the organism experiences in an action which harmonizes incompatibilities. A moral act is the solution to a problem. Moral aims are not expressed in precepts that exist outside action but they are consequences or natural effects of action. Men like some consequences and attempt to achieve them again. In this attempt at realization, consequences function as ends. An end is a dream in which present conflict is ended; the environment is corrected; and the future is seen in terms of a concrete course of action. The dream of fixed ends at which all action should aim is another expression of men's hope for certainty in action. That this hope is vain is the subject of another of Dewey's books, *The Quest for Certainty* (1929).

The function of intelligence is to foresee the future insofar as this can be done by means of principles and criteria of judgment. These principles are like habits. When they become fixed and are regarded as changeless, they can restrict action. However, it must be remembered, Dewey warns, that these principles were derived originally from concrete situations and that they deserve the deference due to any generalization that results from experience. They are hypotheses with which to experiment and whose use is to forecast the consequences of action.

What part does desire play in moral judgment? Most theories evaluate desire in terms of its object. But reflection shows that a desire can have a variety of objects. Psychologically, desire drives the organism forward. It gives activity to life. The projected object of the desire and the attained object never agree, however close they may approach one another. Desire acting without will misses its object because action is not controlled. Desire acting with intelligence, Dewey concludes, is led toward its object.

No person who acts can control the future; his control is limited to the present. He may die before his goal is reached or he may no longer desire it as a goal. Neither can he provide for all contingencies. If he attempts to do so, he will never act at all. He must act in the present. A new house

840

may be a future goal, but it has to be built in some present if it is to be lived in. Future goals are attained by learning through action in the present. Dewey applies these ideas to education. "If education were conducted as a process of the fullest utilization of present resources, liberating and guiding capacities that are now urgent, it goes without saying that the lives of the young would be much richer in meaning than they are now." This principle can also be applied to modern industrial production. The worker confronted with article after article that he will never use soon loses the interest that might motivate him to make his work efficient. His work seems senseless.

For Dewey, the scope of morals extends to all cases in which there are alternative possibilities of action. The word "conduct" covers every act that is judged better or worse. Morality is not to be severed from other life activities. Every type of conduct incorporates value and gives for good or bad a meaning to life.

Any doctrine of moral conduct which replaces adherence to precepts with a naturalistic theory must explain the fact of freedom. Whatever happens in accord with a law of nature is not free; and if morality is not somehow separated as different in kind from natural facts, moral actions will not be free and men will have become automatons. Dewey must meet this problem. To do so, he defines the

person acting freely as having three characteristics: (1) the ability to plan and act in accord with the plan; (2) the capacity to vary plans to meet new conditions; and (3) the conviction that desire and choice are a significant factor in action. The capacity to plan presupposes intelligence, and so intelligence is a precondition to freedom. There are two sorts of freedom, freedom-to and freedom-from. Freedom-from is necessary but restrictive. It must leave room for freedom to act, which requires desire, deliberation, and choice.

For Dewey, we live in a social world. We are conditioned by education, tradition, and environment. The materials on which our intelligence operates come from the community life of which we are a part. Morals are social, and the school as well as other social institutions have a responsibility towards them. The knowledge of how to fulfill moral responsibility must come from the social sciences. Just as a castaway on an uninhabited island has no moral problems, so morality is a natural outgrowth of social living. The question, "Why be moral?" has no meaning in a social context. The moral situation is a part of the social environment in which everyone lives, changing and dynamic, but always present, always presenting its obligations. Morals are actualities. In moral acts we express our awareness of the ties that bind every man to every other.

PHILOSOPHICAL STUDIES

Author: George Edward Moore (1873-1958)
Type of work: Philosophy of philosophy (with examples)
First published: 1922

PRINCIPAL IDEAS ADVANCED

If the language by the use of which philosophical problems and theories are formulated is clarified, the problems often disappear.

There is usually some good reason why the language of common sense is insisted upon, and philosophers would do well to take common sense seriously.

For example, the idealist argues that to be (to exist) is to be perceived, but he fails to distinguish between the awareness of something, on the one hand, and the content of awareness, on the other.

Again, the pragmatists claim that true ideas are simply ideas which work; but this claim is ambiguous, and by a clarification of language it can be shown to what extent it is true and to what extent false.

G. E. Moore was one of the first of a group of philosophers who have since come to be known as the "ordinary language philosophers" or the "Oxford analysts." Moore himself was at Cambridge, closely associated with Russell and Wittgenstein. These three and certain of their followers are sometimes called, by contrast, the "Cambridge analysts," though the distinction between the schools is a fine one and hard to specify. What the analysts have in common is an interest in approaching philosophical problems from the point of view of the language in which they are expressed. The philosophical task, therefore, is characterized by a painstaking analysis of the *formulations* of its problems and the *statements* of its conclusions. Analysis often takes the form of a word-by-word study of a philosophical assertion in the attempt to eliminate vagueness and ambiguity and thus prevent the philosopher from wasting his time by trying to solve pseudo-problems that lead him unconsciously into absurdities and paradoxes.

When clarification has been achieved, what were thought to be genuine problems often disappear completely.

This method is well illustrated in the present book. But there is another method which Moore, in contrast to some of the other analysts, considers to be equally important. This is the appeal to "common sense" as a basis for solving philosophical problems. Moore is convinced that there is usually some important sense in which the ordinary man is right when he insists that tables exist, that other people have being when we are not observing them, and that time is real. Therefore, we have only to determine what this sense is in order to refute those philosophers who argue that tables are "mere ideas," or that other people have only apparent being, or that time is unreal. The determination of this meaning requires a careful analysis of language in order to ascertain what is meant by such assertions. But it also provides, after the analysis, a criterion by which the assertions may be judged to be true or

842

false. Thus it permits problems not only to be clarified but also to be solved, because it is based on the assumption that men could not possibly be deceived in these fundamental beliefs.

Philosophical Studies consists of a collection of essays, most of them published previously in periodicals, and all of them illustrating Moore's approach to certain philosophical problems. They fall into two general classes: (1) *problems*, such as whether there is an external world, whether there are intrinsic values, and whether our feeling of obligation is purely subjective; (2) *claims of certain philosophers* (William James, David Hume, F. H. Bradley) which seem contrary to common sense and which therefore can be shown to be wrong by a careful analysis of the language in which they are expressed.

The first such problem that Moore examines is that of *idealism*. Idealism attempts to prove that the universe is spiritual. One method used for such proof is to argue from the premise that *esse* is *percipi—to be* is *to be perceived*. To refute this statement would not disprove idealism but it would destroy one of its main arguments. Therefore if it can be shown that *esse* is not *percipi*, the idealistic position is considerably weakened.

This can be done, Moore argues, by distinguishing in any perception the *awareness* from the *content of the awareness*. A sensation of blue differs from a sensation of green in that there are different contents, but a sensation of blue resembles a sensation of green in that they are both cases of awareness. Since the awareness and the content always exist together—for we never have an awareness without a content or a content without an awareness—philosophers have tended to confuse the two and have not realized that we can distinguish the awareness from the blue in the same way that we can distinguish the blue from the green. The awareness is something very elusive, and when we try to focus our attention on it, it seems to vanish. But when we finally discover it, we can see that it has a unique relation to the blue which we express by saying that it is *of* the blue. Now the awareness is obviously mental, but there is no reason whatsoever for concluding that the blue must also be mental. This argument provides no ground for concluding that the blue is not mental, but it removes the ground for concluding that it is. Hence it destroys idealism by destroying one of the strongest reasons for believing it.

Moore now turns to a certain belief which is generally held not only by the ordinary man but also by most philosophers. This belief really has two parts which are interconnected. (1) Something other than ourselves and what we directly perceive exists. (2) Among the things other than ourselves and what we directly perceive are persons who have thoughts and feelings similar to our own. The first belief involves certain ambiguities, which the second does not; consequently, Moore decides to examine only the latter.

Certain preliminary points must first be clarified. To ask why we believe this statement is not to imply that we should not believe it; we may believe it without grounds, or on the basis of grounds quite different from those which are commonly accepted. Furthermore, we are not asking how we come to believe in the existence of other people, for there may be many things which cause us to believe this, though they may not be grounds for the belief. Moreover, to ask for reasons is to ask for *good* reasons—reasons which are actually believed and such that we would not believe in the existence of other people unless they were true. (Reasons of this kind may be hard to find since philosophers are often in disagreement as to what *good* reasons are.) Finally, when we ask for reasons for this belief we do not mean reasons which will conclusively demonstrate that other people exist; all that we can hope for is that our belief can be established with a certain degree of probability. Since we have the belief, it is likely that there are other people who have thoughts and feelings similar to ours.

The kind of reason which could support such a belief, Moore claims, must have two properties. In the first place, it must be some sort of *generalization*. A generalization has the form, "When A exists, B generally exists also." In this particular case the generalization would be: "When we hear certain words, someone besides ourselves generally has the thoughts which constitute the meanings of those words." The relation in this case is not such that we can say that A *intrinsically* points to B, but merely that, given A, there is a reasonable probability, based on actual occurrences, that B will occur also. In the second place, the evidence for the generalization must itself be obtained through perception. But in making this knowledge rest on perception we must not be confused as to the meaning of this word. In one sense we may be said to perceive the thoughts of others when we interpret what they are saying; in another sense

the generalization may be said to rest on the perceptions which other people have had. Both of these meanings of "perception" are excluded in this context.

Moore states that when we set up these requirements concerning the kind of reason which would support our belief in the existence of other people we realize that there can be no such reason. We can show only that certain of our perceptions are connected with certain other of our perceptions, not that certain of them are connected with the existence of other people. This does not mean that we cannot prove the existence of other people but only that we cannot prove it by this method.

If we look again at the kind of reason which would prove conclusively the existence of other persons, we can see that all of us actually perceive two different kinds of "things": "sense-contents," such as patterns of colors and shapes, and perceptions themselves. For example, we can perceive *a blue color* but we can also perceive our *perception* of a blue color. When Berkeley said that *to be* is *to be perceived* he evidently meant that for a sense-content to exist it must be perceived, not that for a perception to exist it must be perceived. But if perceptions can exist without being perceived, why cannot sense-contents also exist without being perceived? Certainly there is nothing self-contradictory in the possibility.

This, then, provides Moore with the proof which he requires. He notes that a certain sense-content (his hand suddenly catching hold of his foot in a particular way) is preceded by another sense-content (a particular feeling of pain). Now if he perceives a similar movement in another person he can infer that this individual has similar feelings (which Moore himself cannot perceive but which stand in the same relation to the other person's movements that Moore's do to his own movement). Such arguments establish the likely existence of others who have feelings similar to those of the observer. The belief is grounded on the assumptions that sense-contents can exist without being perceived, and that analogous relations between sense-contents provide a basis for inference from sense-contents that *are* perceived to sense-contents which *are not* actually perceived.

Moore now offers an illustration of the effectiveness of the analytic method when it is applied critically to the views of another philosopher. He examines the claims of William James in his book, *Pragmatism: A New Name for Old Ways of Thinking* (1907). James claims to establish three things: (1) There is some connection between truth and utility, that is, true ideas are those that "work." (2) Truth is in some sense mutable, rather than static. (3) "To an unascertainable extent our truths are man-made."

Moore's scrutiny of James's arguments shows that there is ambiguity in what he says. According to one interpretation James seems to be trying to prove certain things which are really commonplace and would be accepted by everyone. Among these are the following: most true beliefs are useful and most useful beliefs are true; since the world changes, a given statement may be true at one time and false at another; truth, in the sense of our beliefs, does depend on us both be-

cause it depends on our mental history and because we change the world and thus make our beliefs in this altered world true.

But Moore insists that James probably intends to assert something in addition to these truisms, and these further assertions are, according to Moore, quite obviously false. For example: *All true beliefs are useful.* Moore refutes this claim by taking the belief that two plus two equals four, which is obviously true, and then showing that it might be useless—and, indeed, might even get in the way of our solving a problem on which it has no bearing. *All useful beliefs are true.* This is refuted by lies which "work." *Utility is the only property which all true beliefs have in common.* Moore shows that this proposition reduces to an absurdity. For it would require that if on a certain occasion belief in the existence of something were useful, that belief would have to be true even if the thing did not exist. A final example: *Whenever the existence of a belief depends on us the truth of that belief also depends on us.* This statement is ridiculous, for while it may be true that my *belief* that a shower will fall depends on me, the *truth* of that belief does not depend on me, for I do not make the shower fall.

Moore then turns from James to Hume. Hume tries to define the limits of human understanding by examining a certain kind of belief which we all seem to have. This is one concerning "matters of fact" which we have never observed but which are based on past experience; for example, the belief that the sun will rise tomorrow. The results of Hume's analysis, Moore shows, are inconsistent with one another. At one point Hume says that a proposition expressing such a belief can be known, even to the extent of leaving no room for doubt or opposition. At another point he asserts that it cannot be established, since we can never experience external objects directly and cannot therefore know that they exist. In still another place he denies that we can ever know that one fact is causally related with another and consequently that we can ever use past experience as a basis for anticipating future experience. In support of the second and third views Hume uses two arguments—both, according to Moore, invalid. (1) When Hume asserts that we cannot know about external objects he contradicts himself, for he implies that we *do* know that men cannot have this kind of knowledge; but this kind of knowledge *is* knowledge of external objects; namely, knowledge about men and what they can and cannot know. (2) When Hume asserts that from the knowledge that two facts have been causally conjoined in the past we cannot know that they will be causally connected in the future, he is making an unjustifiable assumption—the assumption that because we cannot *prove* a certain statement by means of a certain argument, we cannot *know* that statement to be true. Moore believes that we know many things which do not follow logically from anything else we know, and thus that we *can* know that facts will be causally conjoined in the future even though this latter proposition is not based on what Hume presumes it to be based.

In proceeding to an examination of the problem of perception Moore insists that we need to refine our vocabulary. We must invent a term which will describe what is common to images, dream objects, hallucinations, afterimages, and sensations proper. Let us call these all "sensibles." We must then answer two questions: How are sensibles related to our minds? How are sensibles related to physical objects?

In order to answer the first question we must invent another term. We shall say that sensibles are "directly apprehended" by our minds. Attempts to show that sensibles can have any other relation to our minds have been unsuccessful. Furthermore, attempts to show that sensibles cannot exist *unless* they are directly apprehended have also failed. Berkeley claimed that an unapprehended sensible is self-contradictory. But this is clearly not the case. Others have claimed that we have *a priori* knowledge that sensibles must always be apprehended. This, again, is simply not true.

The second question can be answered only if we assume that there are some beliefs of which we can be quite certain, though we may not know exactly how to interpret them. Such beliefs would be illustrated by saying that when I look at two coins of different size I am *really* seeing two coins, that they are *really* circular even though I see them as elliptical, that the coins *have* an inside (though I don't see it), that the upper side of one of the coins is *really* larger than that of the other, and that both coins *continue to exist* even when I shut my eyes. We must now add to this belief two others, which are equally certain. (1) The upper side of the coin which I am said to *see* is not simply identical with the visual sensible which I directly apprehend in seeing it. (2) My knowledge of the coins is based on the apprehension of sensi-

846

bles. The simplest interpretation of these three beliefs is to say that when I really see the coins I mean that *if* I were to move my body in certain ways I should directly apprehend certain *other* sensibles—for example, certain tactual ones. According to Moore this is what we mean when we say that we *really* perceive the coins.

The assertion of F. H. Bradley that time is unreal provides another challenge for Moore in his role as an analytic philosopher. Careful study of Bradley's attempts to prove this philosophical proposition shows that he apparently thinks of the word "time" as having different meanings in different contexts, and that he presumably is using the word "real" in two different senses. He seems to be saying that time exists but is unreal. But if he is using "time" and "real" in their ordinary senses he would seem to be denying that there are any facts of the kind expressed by saying that something happens before something else, or that something happened in the past. To say that time is unreal in this sense is plainly false, for there *are* happenings of these kinds.

How, then, can his error be explained? Simply in terms of a confusion.

He believes (correctly) that time could be unreal even though we do think about time, just as unicorns could be unreal even though we think about them. But he also believes (incorrectly) that because we do think about time there is such a thing as time. From these two premises (one true and the other false) he correctly infers that the statement, "Time is unreal," must be consistent with the statement, "There is such a thing as time." But he is unsuccessful in showing just *how* these statements can be consistent.

In Moore's essay entitled "Some Judgments of Perception," he returns to the question of the status of "sensibles." The problem is not to determine whether we can ever truly make such assertions as "That is an inkstand"—for we continually make such statements and believe them—but what we *mean* when we make them. Certainly two things which we mean are that the inkstand can be selected from surrounding objects and designated as *the* object which we are perceiving, and that if there is an inkstand it is not given to us in any way independently of any sensibles (sense-data). But to say that the inkstand is dependent on sense-data is not to say that it is dependent in the way in which one object is called to mind by another through associative ties.

The problem is to explain what this relation of dependence *is*. Many philosophers would say that the presented object (the sense-datum) is only a *part* of the *surface* of the inkstand. For we can detect that a presented object sometimes changes, and yet this observation apparently provides no basis for concluding that the surface of the object changes. The reason we have to say that it only *apparently* provides no basis is that we can never be sure that the presented object *does* change perceptibly. This has commonly been assumed, but it may not be true. Perhaps it only *seems* to change. Possibly the sense-datum which I see when I look at a tree a mile off is not *really* smaller than the one which I see when I look at it from a distance of only a hundred yards; perhaps it is only *apparently* smaller. If this is true, then we shall have to admit a special, ulti-

847

mate, not further analyzable, kind of relation expressed by saying that *x seems* blue or *y seems* circular. This kind of relation would have to be sharply distinguished from that expressed in *x is perceived to be* blue or *y is judged to be* circular. Since there seems to be no reason why there could not be such an ultimate relation, Moore concludes that its existence is at least a possibility.

The controversy as to whether value is subjective or objective, Moore says, should be settled by translating it into the problem of whether value is intrinsic or extrinsic. If value is intrinsic it must be objective, but the converse does not hold. When we say that a thing is intrinsically valuable we mean two things: (1) that if it possesses this value at one time, or in one set of circumstances, or to a certain degree, it *must* possess it at another time, and in other circumstances, and to the same degree; and (2) that anything *exactly like* the thing in question *must* possess the value and to the same degree. These statements are not to be understood as using "must" in the sense that there is nothing which is intrinsically valuable and which lacks these characteristics, nor in the sense that an effect must follow its cause. What is meant is that there *could be* nothing which is intrinsically valuable and which lacks these properties, and that a thing which is intrinsically valuable *would have to have* these characteristics even in a universe whose causal laws would be quite different from ours. We can then say that intrinsic predicates and intrinsic values depend on the intrinsic natures of the things which possess them. But yellowness, which is an intrinsic *predicate, describes* the thing which possesses it, while beauty, which

is an intrinsic *value, does not describe* its object.

Moore now returns to his examination of the views of other philosophers. F. H. Bradley asserts that all relations are "internal" to the terms related, meaning by this that they all *affect*, and pass into, the being of their terms. Moore believes this statement to be false if applied to *all* relations. He thinks that there are some relations which are internal and some which are external. In order to show the source of Bradley's error he attempts, first, to clear up an equivocation in the logical expression "follows from," and, second, to reveal an ambiguity in the meaning of the word "internal."

The commonly accepted notion of "follows from" is that which is used by Whitehead and Russell in *Principia Mathematica*. This is called "material implication" and is defined by saying that when P materially implies Q it is not the case that P is true and Q is false. The other meaning of "follows from" can be called "entailment" and is defined by saying that when P entails Q, Q can be inferred from P, or Q is deducible from P. The important distinction is that in entailment the relation exhibits a kind of necessity which is not present in the case of material implication.

Now, says Moore, let us define a relational property as a property which a term possesses by virtue of its relation to something else. For example, a man possesses fatherhood because he has the relation of "father" to someone. If we then gather together all relational properties, there are two things which we may assert about them. (1) All relational properties are such that the possession by *x* of the relational property P *entails* that the absence of this

848

property in the case of *y materially implies* that *y* is other than *x*. (2) All relational properties are such that the possession by *x* of the relational property P *materially implies* that the absence of this property in the case of *y entails* that *y* is other than *x*. These are two ways of stating that if a thing which has a relational property did not have it, the thing would be different. Those who believe in the internality of all relations believe not only that both (1) and (2) are true, but that (2) follows from (1). Neither of these, according to Moore, is correct. (1) is not true of *all* relations, but only of *some*; those of which it is true are internal; those of which it is false are external. Hence, there are some relations which are internal and some which are external. Furthermore, (2) does not follow from (1), as can be seen if we express (1) as

p entails (*q* materially implies *r*)

and (2) as

p materially implies (*q* entails *r*).

The following example will show that (2) does not follow from (1):

Let *p* equal All the books on this shelf are blue.

Let *q* equal My copy of the *Principles of Mathematics* is a book on this shelf.

Let *r* equal My copy of the *Principles of Mathematics* is blue.

If we substitute these statements in (1) and (2) above we can readily see that (1) is true, while (2) is false. Hence, Moore concludes, (2) cannot follow from (1).

Finally Moore examines moral philosophy. This commonly deals with two ideas, the first of which—the idea of *obligation*—is really a moral idea, and the second of which—the idea of the *good*—is commonly talked about by moral philosophers but is not properly a moral idea at all. When we talk about *obligation* we discover that there are two kinds of rules: rules of *duty*, which tell us what we ought to *do*, and *ideal* rules, which concern our inner life and tell us what we ought to *be*. When we talk about the *good* we may mean something such as Aristotle had in mind when he defined the good life as the active exercise of mental excellence.

With regard to both of these ideas, Moore says, certain philosophers have claimed that all we mean to say when we assert that a certain action ought to have been done or that a certain state is better than another, is that some person has a tendency to have a certain feeling towards the action or the state. This view makes moral philosophy and ethics mere departments of psychology, and the strange consequence of the view is that no two people can ever argue about whether an act is wrong or not wrong, for the word "wrong" (since it deals with the speaker's feelings) will mean one thing for one speaker and another for another, just as the pronoun "I" means something different to each person who utters it. Hence there can really be no such thing as a difference of opinion on moral matters. Moore believes this conclusion to be absurd, since people *do* differ in opinion on moral matters. We must conclude, then, that ethics is more than psychology, though Moore admits that he has some difficulty in stating just what this additional element is.

THE PHILOSOPHY OF SYMBOLIC FORMS

Author: Ernst Cassirer (1874-1945)
Type of work: Epistemology, philosophy of culture
First published: 1923-1929

PRINCIPAL IDEAS ADVANCED

The mind creates symbols to interpret the data of experience; to understand knowledge and the significance of science it is necessary to understand the function of symbolic forms in explanations.

Forms of cognition are affected by language and myth; language, myth, and science are all forms of human expression.

Experience begins with the immediacy of feelings; but as living creatures respond in accordance with their needs, certain items in their experience take on sign and symbol functions.

In the phase which follows, the distinction between self and nonself becomes fixed, the flux of sensations is recognized and ordered into things by the use of names, and space and time are conceived.

Philosophy becomes the criticism of language, and religion becomes the criticism of myth.

Ernst Cassirer was one of the few men with sufficient breadth of scholarship to undertake the task of synthesizing the findings of twentieth century science. He wrote authoritatively on the history of ideas and on the methodology of the sciences, as well as on literature, politics, and primitive culture. *The Philosophy of Symbolic Forms* is his masterwork, in which he attempts to give a systematic view of the entire range of human achievement.

Thoroughly at home in the fields of biology and physics, Cassirer nevertheless turned his back on the more unusual type of synthesis (for example, A. N. Whitehead's *Process and Reality*, 1929) which takes nature as ultimate and seeks to interpret man in terms of cosmic evolution. For Cassirer, modern science is more interesting for what it reveals to us about the mind of the scientist than for the information it discloses to us about an alleged material universe. In his synthesis, science is viewed as a cultural phenomenon, the most advanced condition of mind since its emergence from preconscious animal existence. His survey is primarily a philosophy of culture. It traces the evolution of mind rather than the evolution of nature, and indeed gives nature a place among the contents of mind. In short, Cassirer's synthesis is in the idealistic rather than in the realistic tradition.

Cassirer's philosophical lineage is easily traced. He was a member of a group known as the Marburg school (after the university where it flourished), which was dedicated to bringing up to date the philosophy of Immanuel Kant. Kant had never completely broken with the belief that reality is prior to and independent of our knowledge of it. The Marburg group considered this belief inconsistent with Kant's own principles, and carried through the thesis that nothing is real except what is given in experience. They employed Kant's "transcendental method" and sought, by the analysis of perceptions, judgments, and arguments, to uncover the structure of the intellect which makes knowledge possible.

Although Cassirer always worked in this tradition, he went well beyond others of the group in an important respect. It has been characteristic of the successors of Kant to be preëminently concerned with epistemology, or the theory of knowledge. Cassirer came to believe that knowledge is only one aspect of the mind's activity, and he argued that if we are to understand our experience, either our immediate perceptions or our scientific hypotheses, we must familiarize ourselves with the development of language and with mythical thought as well as with the processes of sensation, perception, and judgment. According to Cassirer, language, myth, and knowledge are three distinct but overlapping frontiers on which the human spirit has advanced in its effort to bring under its power the chaos of organic feelings. Forms of perception, such as space, time, and number, together with concepts such as substance, attribute, and causality, all have their origins in primitive symbols, images, and acts. Not only our knowledge of the world, but our consciousness of ourselves as well, presupposes the unfolding and articulation of these "forms"; and such order and intelligibility as we find in our experience is, in actuality, the order which consciousness in its long development has itself created.

In this modified form, the Kantian thesis is no longer dependent on a merely theoretical deduction. As Cassirer has stated it, it is an empirical hypothesis, to be verified by reference to the findings of students in the fields of linguistics and of cultural anthropology. There is, in the three volumes of *The Philosophy of Symbolic Forms* (*Language; Mythical Thought;* and *The Phenomenology of Knowledge*), a minimum of the kind of abstruse reasoning which characterizes the *Critique of Pure Reason*. Instead, the author offers us a compendium of modern knowledge in the three fields.

Cassirer first developed the notion of symbolic forms in connection with his studies in the methodology of the sciences (*Substance and Function*, 1910). He maintained that the ordinary view of knowledge, according to which scientific concepts and laws reproduce the actuality of things experienceable by the senses, is disproved by the developments of modern physics. He agreed with those mathematicians and scientists who said that mathematical symbols and such physical concepts as mass, energy, and the atom are not empirical facts in the same sense that light, heat, and electricity are, but are instruments of the intellect which make it possible for us to correlate and order these more immediate aspects of our experience. The problem for the philosopher, according to Cassirer, is to explore the connection between the scientific explanation and the data which it illuminates. Both the range and the precision of the exact sciences derive from the purely formal character of their constructions. How, then, can we account for the agreement between the theories and our actual experience?

Kant's approach seemed to point to the answer. The mind does, indeed, create new symbols to interpret the data of its experience. But in so doing it only carries further the same activity in which it has been engaging since the dawn of consciousness. All our experience has its structure in virtue of the creativity of the mind. An example is the perception of things in space. The vital feelings of earliest men did not include the notion of three-dimensional or any other variety of space. Even among so-called primitive peoples today, a mythical view of space prevails which lacks the universal, homogeneous character that space has for us. Space, in other words, is a symbolic form by which evolving consciousness imposes unity upon the manifold of concrete intuition. And though the higher geometries seem quite to transcend intuition, still they carry with them something of our common spatial representation. Thus, it is not altogether surprising that they have proved useful for correlating new fields of experimental data.

The exact sciences bring knowledge to its highest perfection and provide a capital instance of the role of symbols. A philosopher with fewer universal interests than Cassirer might have stopped with this insight. But the fact that forms of cognition are intertwined with those of language and myth suggested to him the answer to another longstanding problem of philosophy; namely, that of the relation between man's quest for knowledge and his concern with religion, morality, and art. At this point, the philosophy of symbolic forms ceased to be merely a philosophy of science and was projected into a philosophy of culture, in which language and mythology would be treated not simply as stages on the way to knowledge, but as divergent and independent, though supplementary, ways in which man has raised himself

above the animals and become the monarch of all he surveys.

Cassirer went considerably beyond Kant, somewhat in the manner of Hegel. He spoke of his philosophy as a phenomenology of spirit in the manner of Hegel, to whose *Phenomenology of the Spirit* (1807) he often refers. For both Cassirer and Hegel history is the story of man's emerging awareness of himself and of his growing freedom and autonomy. They differed in that Hegel conceived the essence of spirit to be reason, from which he concluded that all aspects of culture were related to one another in a logical fashion and found their consummation in pure knowledge. For Cassirer, in step with the pragmatic temper of his time, reason took its place as one function among others. Hence, he did not follow the dialectical part of Hegel's philosophy, or suppose that there is any rational or logically necessary connection between language, myth, and science. As a result, he was less tempted than Hegel to sacrifice the autonomy of art, religion, morality, and other aspects of experience to any one master science, and he remained closer to the position of Kant.

Nevertheless, according to Cassirer, there is a fundamental unity running through all modes of experience. Language, myth, and science are all forms of expression; and governing the internal development of each of these is a kind of law of three stages, which Cassirer claimed as the high point of his philosophy. In a way, it too is a kind of dialectic although much less rigid than Hegel's.

As Cassirer viewed it, the first phase in the development of any branch of experience is characterized by *immediacy*, when consciousness has not yet distinguished clearly between subject and object. The symbol by means of which consciousness succeeds in arresting a portion of the flux is as much a feeling as it is something felt. It has not yet become a medium by which the self responds to the environment, because at this level the vital adjustment is so spontaneous and automatic that no distinction is made between one and the other.

Cassirer drew upon the findings of biology and of animal and infant psychology to reinforce the evidences of cultural anthropology in these matters. He was impressed by the view that each animal species lives in a world of its own which is schematized for it in accordance with its particular organic needs. "Function" determines "form"—that is to say, the form under which the world appears to any living creature. The difference between a sign and a symbol, according to Cassirer, is that the former stands in a one-to-one relationship with the thing signified, whereas the latter has achieved a more universal reference. In terms of function, the sign is an immediate stimulus to the organism and normally leads to a specific response, but the symbol breaks the receptor-effector arc and either waylays consciousness or sends it along a detoured route. In either case, a radical innovation has taken place. A particular feeling no longer merely exists—it has become freighted with meaning.

With this change, Cassirer argues, consciousness is on the way to becoming self-conscious. Still, in the first phase, as has been indicated, a large measure of immediacy remains. Gesture, for example, is partly an expression of feeling, partly an imitative act, and partly a conventional designation

of, say, consent. So, presumably, was earliest speech. Such must also have been the condition when myth arose, which has for its province the realm of imagination. The hunter, for example, no longer merely recognized his prey: its image took on magical powers for him; but, as the totemic structure of earlier societies suggests, this occurred without a clear distinction being made between the hunter and the hunted. Knowledge, as distinct from language and myth, is rooted in sensation and properly emerges as the mind gradually discriminates between the external and internal senses and between sense contents and affective tones. In contrast with the usual empiricist account of experience, Cassirer held that sensations are not given as discrete elements of experience, but are abstracted by the mind from a congeries of emotions and feelings. They are, thus, early symbolic forms and are peculiarly immediate, especially those which, like smell and touch, can be identified, even by the sophisticated mind, either with the self or with the object.

Once it has begun the use of symbols, consciousness evolves by a kind of necessity. Since symbols by their very nature introduce a break into the immediacy of the vital activity, it is inevitable that the break will compound itself. The second phase in this development is characterized by *mediacy*. At this stage, the distinction between the self and the nonself becomes fixed. According to Cassirer, the knowledge of objects precedes the knowledge of the self: only after consciousness has succeeded in dividing and ordering the world of things is it possible for it to form any notion of an inner, subjective realm. This is achieved in large measure through the fixation that language

853

and myth make possible. The flux of sensations is ordered into things endowed with independent, substantial existence: this is largely the function of naming. Space and time, which have their origin in mythical imagination, also contribute to the ordering and differentiation of the world. No sharp distinction is made, however, between fact and fancy: mythical images are reified as well as sensible ones.

It was a happy moment in the history of mind when the symbol could be identified with the thing which it symbolized, a kind of honeymoon between life and spirit. But it could not last. With the discovery of the role of mind in creating symbols and the role of symbols in determining any world-representation, man necessarily entered a third level of consciousness. This took place, as far as language is concerned, at the beginning of philosophy, when the magical connection between the thing and its name was dissolved and man's attention directed to the ideal and functional character of speech. A similar process took place in the world of myth. According to Cassirer, religion developed from mythology when the distinction became clear between the sensible image and that which the image reveals—opening therewith a new dimension in which the norms of myth and magic were no longer valid. It is in the realm of knowledge that man has been slowest to recognize the creative activity of the intellect and the symbolic elements in truth. The Pythagorean-Galilean revolution, which overthrew the world of sense perception, only strengthened the conviction that the intelligible aspects of the world are real and eternal. Only the most modern developments prepare us to accept the ideality of space and time

and the functional origin of our concepts of causality and law.

The dialectical movement within the symbol-using consciousness served as the unifying principle for Cassirer's system. Because it is purely formal it enabled him to view experiences of the most diverse kinds as all manifestations of the same fundamental activity. He maintained that this is the basic difference between a critical philosophy, such as his own, and the traditional metaphysical systems which raise one or another objective content of experience to the level of a first principle. The philosophy of symbolic forms does not, like that of Hegel, start with rational necessity, much less, like that of Marx, with material necessity. For Cassirer, rational necessity is itself purely formal: when mind works with logical concepts, it must, to achieve its purpose, follow the connections that are entailed in symbols of this kind. The same thing is true of physical necessity; the kind of order which the mind has imposed on the physical world includes causality. A defect of all metaphysical explanation, according to Cassirer, is that, beginning with an abstract concept of unity, it is compelled to explain all multiplicity, and hence also all knowledge, as illusory. He claimed as the singular merit of his philosophy the fact that it does not suppress any kind of experience. Myth is just as legitimate as mathematics, and aesthetic feeling is not inferior to scientific fact. They merely lie along different axes, and they may represent earlier or later moments in the evolution of form. But one variety of experience is intrinsically no more valuable than another.

On the other hand, though all experiences are, in a sense, equal, they do, on this hypothesis, fit into one another to make up a meaningful universe. And this, according to Cassirer, is something that most empirical and positivist philosophies have not been able to encompass. The mistake he found in these philosophies is their initial claim that experience is composed of discrete sensations and feelings. According to his critical analysis, such is not the case. The least sense content we are capable of discriminating is part of a preformed whole. If this fact is admitted, it resolves the difficulty which has always defeated empiricism's efforts to explain how independent parts can come together to form meaningful unities; how, for example, five separate sounds can form a musical theme or an intelligible sentence. For Cassirer, who has as his starting-point not the contents of the mind but the form of the mind as it expresses itself, the musical theme or the intelligible sentence is given first; and on accurate analysis the structure of the whole is found to be implicit in any of the parts.

Like Kant, Cassirer left his system open. He did not claim that its analysis is able to reduce experience entirely to intelligible components. At the lower end, sense contents always remain as a limit, in spite of the fact that any feeling or content taken up into consciousness is already touched with meaning. At times he was not averse to speaking of the lower limits as life, and he showed some sympathy with Henri Bergson's philosophy. But he regarded as futile all mystical attempts to know this prime condition by direct intuition; and any attempt to inquire about it in terms of higher symbols, such as those employed by biology or sociology, would, on his view, be self-defeating. The most that he claimed for his system was that it provided a morphology of consciousness in the act of expressing itself.

His system was also open in the direction of intellect. While he recognized the need for consciousness to become ever more aware of its own creativity, he did not venture to suggest that the consummation was yet in sight, or indeed that there ever would be a condition of perfectly self-contained consciousness. In this respect, the philosophy of symbolic forms invites contrast with Hegel's philosophy of spirit. The latter was governed by a logical *a priori*, which, when it had once disclosed itself, left nothing further to discover. Thus, Hegel's works all bear the impress of finality. But the *a priori* element in Cassirer's system is multiform and complex. Spirit develops in many directions, each of which manifests its own pattern. All that can be said with assurance is that there is always a tendency toward greater freedom of spirit and form, and away from subservience to matter and sense. For Cassirer, a world of pure form and intelligibility is unthinkable. Symbolic forms range along a scale, some dominantly sensible, others dominantly intelligible; but no form, no object which consciousness can entertain, can be completely without its sensible, existential component, any more than it can be without the structural, intelligible part which gives it meaning.

Cassirer's attempt to account for the evolution of culture without reference to natural events (to such matters as climate, geography, economics, and politics) has brought criticism, much as Hegel's system provoked reaction among some of his followers. But Cassirer did not deny that other things besides consciousness influence man's development—he only maintained that any attempt to know them involves us in the use of a symbolic system which may or may not give a valid account of what comes to pass. With good reason, his philosophy has been hailed as a humanist answer to culturologists and economic determinists who subject man to natural laws. If Cassirer is right, nature holds no domination over man other than that which man thinks it holds. At a certain stage of his intellectual development, he is likely to attribute to objects a reality and independence which they do not possess, and submit himself to their bondage. His hope lies in the fact that, sooner or later, he is bound to throw off this yoke of dogmatism and myth. When he does, and becomes fully aware of the creative uses of symbols, new vistas will open before him. This is not to say that life may not perish before the goal is realized or that, unsettled by advancing knowledge and the loss of earlier certitudes, man may not destroy himself. Two works written by Cassirer in exile from his native Germany during World War II (*An Essay on Man*, 1944, and *The Myth of the State*, 1946) represent civilization as a fragile bark, afloat on stormy deeps, which we must make a positive effort to save. His tone, however, remained hopeful, much like that of the eighteenth century Enlightenment, whose heir he was.

I AND THOU

Author: Martin Buber (1878-   )
Type of work: Theology, epistemology
First published: 1923

PRINCIPAL IDEAS ADVANCED

There is no independent "I" but only the I existing and known in objective relation to something other than itself, an "It," or as encountered by and encompassed by the other, the "Thou."

Just as music can be studied analytically by reference to its notes, verses, and bars, or encountered and experienced in such a manner that it is known not by its parts but as a unity, so the I can relate itself analytically to something other, "It," or it can encounter the other, "Thou," so as to form a living unity.

The "Thou" stands as judge over the "It," but as a judge with the form and creative power for the transformation of "It."

Each encountered "Thou" reveals the nature of all reality, but finally the living center of every "Thou" is seen to be the eternal "Thou."

The eternal "Thou" is never known objectively, but certitude comes through the domain of action.

Since its first appearance in German in 1923, this slender volume has become one of the epoch-making works of our time. Not only does it place within one cover the best thinking of one of the greatest Jewish minds in centuries, but also, more than any other single volume, it has helped to mold contemporary theology. For example, ironically the neoörthodox tradition in recent Protestantism has appropriated in rather wholesale manner Buber's "I-Thou encounter," the "Eternal Subject," and other features. Although such men reinterpret these points from a radical Protestant context, others, such as Tillich, have developed systems that are in fundamental agreement with Buber's fuller understanding. Perhaps at no other point do liberal and orthodox Christian thinkers find so rich a place of meeting.

For Judaism, on the other hand, Buber's writings have been a new leaven. It is not true, as some have maintained, that Buber is a rebel from basic Judaism, that he is simply a Jew by birth and an existentialist by conviction. Rather, Buber is a living mortar for the rich heritage of Judaism, some of it long neglected, and certain insights of contemporary thinking. No other living writer has so shaken Judaism from its parochialism and applied it so relevantly to the problems and concerns of contemporary man.

Buber's writing is often rhapsodic in quality, frustrating the searcher for clear and distinct ideas; his key work has been aptly called a "philosophical-religious poem." Yet this is as it should be, for Buber is no system builder, but the imparter of a way of life. At its center is a unique type of relation, one universally available and yet almost universally neglected. His task is not so much one of detailed and logical exposition, but one of evoking, eliciting, educing this relation which is its own proof.

Quite early, Buber's youthful mastery of Jewish thought, life, and devotion came into tension with European intellectualism, especially the thought of Kant and Nietzsche. Buber's tentative resolution was that of mysticism, particularly as developed by the post-medieval Christian mystics. But a sense of rootlessness drew him back towards Judaism, first in the form of emerging Zionism, not so much as a political movement as a cultural renaissance. Here, in the venerable roots of Jewish religio-culture, Buber found an alternative to man's modern plight of over-commercialism and super-intellec tualism. But it was in Haṣidim, that his answer became crystalized. This pietist conservative Jewish movement, emerging in eighteenth century Poland, moved him to withdraw from active life for five years of intensive study. The teachings stressed not monastic withdrawal, but joyous life in communities of this world, worshiping in every practical activity.

At this same time Buber encountered translations of Søren Kierkegaard's work. Kierkegaard's insistence on total involvement and absolute commitment, on the priority of subjective thinking, on truth as existential or lived truth, and his stress on the centrality of the individual—all of these elements made immediate contact with Buber's new-found religious devotion. The resulting tension of existentialism and Haṣidim was creative for Buber. The emphasis of Haṣidim on the warmth of community tempered the cold stress of Kierkegaard on the lonely and anxious individual; the latter's pessimism concerning man was largely dissolved by the general Jewish confidence in man's God-given potential. On the other hand, the existentialist stress on authentic existence grounded in the totally free and responsible decision of the self transformed Buber's earlier concern with mystic absorption and the illusory nature of the commonplace world. In personal experiences resulting from men's seeking him out for help, Buber learned the utter necessity of religion as a this-worldly faith, as a total devotion transforming every aspect of common life together. The unique "I-Thou" was no longer understood as a state of the absorbed individual in unity with an Absolute, but as a permeating relationship with all life—a lived experience, not of loss, but of transformation and fulfillment in reciprocity. With this key awareness, Buber's religious philosophy was fully formed, and it emerged in his greatest writing, *I and Thou*.

Quite clearly, this work is an essay in epistemology; it is epistemology, however, not simply in the traditional sense of understanding the nature and ascertainable truth of common-sense perception, but in the sense of exploring in sweeping fashion the possible "modes" or types of "knowing." It is Buber's thesis that strict empiricism is only one of several kinds of relation with reality, and that a life founded upon this mode alone is anemic to the core. Although he refuses to argue the point, Buber assumes that the plurality of modes corresponds with dimensions within reality itself. Such a contention stands within a time-honored tradition, whether it be Plato's distinction between sense impression and *noesis* or most recently Teilhard de Chardin's distinction between the "inner" and "outer" aspects of all things. Such a distinction, Buber holds, cannot be logically argued, for logic is simply the instrument of one of these modes and

does not apply to others. Verification is thus intrinsic to the mode itself; it is self-verifying and requires no further "proof."

Buber's key affirmation is this—"To man the world is twofold, in accordance with his twofold attitude." This overarching attitude is expressed in every language by the words indicating "I," "It," and "Thou." "It" and "Thou" do not signify different things, Buber insists, but two different relations possible between the same self and the same "object." This is an interesting contention, first developed in detail by Kierkegaard, for in general parlance the ground for such a distinction is usually held to be within the object itself. Underlying Buber's position here is a radical rejection of Descartes' famed *"Cogito, ergo sum."* There is no such thing as an independent "I" which, internally certain of its own existence, then moves externally to God and the world. Rather, there is no I in itself but only the I existing and known in these two basic ways.

The "I-It" relation is the realm of objectivity, the realm of "experience," which is generally understood as perceiving, imagining, willing, feeling, and thinking. It includes all activities of the "I" in which there is an object, a "thing," whose existence depends on being bounded by other "things." Here one experiences and extracts knowledge concerning the "surface of things." Above all, the "I-It" experience is unilateral; in it the "I" alone is active, and the object perceived has no concern in the matter, nor is it affected by the experience.

This experience, as well as the "I-Thou," occurs in regard to three spheres—our life with nature, with men, and with intelligible forms. For example, to use Buber's most difficult illustration, in an "I-It" experience with a tree, I may look at it, examine its structure and functions, classify it, formalize the laws of its operation, see it in terms of its numerical components or control and shape it by activity. But not only may I experience the tree but I may enter into relationship with it—this is the mode of "I-Thou." Here I am "encountered" by the tree; I become bound to it, for it seizes me with "the power of exclusiveness." Although this relation is totally different in kind from the "I-It" experience, it is not strictly different in "content." In it one does not have to reject or forget the content of objective knowledge; rather, all of the above enumerated components become indivisibly united in the event which is this relation—"Everything belonging to the tree is in this: its form and structure, its colours and chemical composition, its intercourse with the elements and with the stars, are all present in a single whole."

While objective knowledge is always of the past, the relation of the "I-Thou" is always present, a "filled present." Above all, characteristic of this relation is its mutuality. Yet we cannot say that in this relation the tree exhibits a soul, or a consciousness, for of this we can have no experience. The relation is undifferentiated, and to inquire of its constitutive parts is to disintegrate what is known only as an indivisible whole. Such a wholeness is all-consuming and absolute—a "He" encountered as a "Thou" is a "whole in himself" and "fills the heavens." What Buber means is not that the "He" alone is existent but rather that this relation is such that "all else lives in *his* light."

To one not naturally inclined to Buber's way of thinking, the best available illustrations, as Buber's own examples clearly indicate, are from the arts. In fact, Buber maintains that the "I-Thou" relation is the true source of art. Music can be analyzed in terms of notes, verses, and bars; this is the realm of the "I-It." This same music, however, may be encountered in a living relation in which each component is included, yet experienced not as parts but as an inseparable unity. In artistic creativity, a form which is not an offspring of the artist encounters him and demands effective power. This calls for sacrifice and risk—risk, for endless possibility must be ended by form; sacrifice, because the work consumes the artist with a claim which permits no rest. Buber's interpretation of this artistic form is helpful in understanding the "content" of the "I-Thou" encounter. Says Buber, "I can neither experience nor describe the form which meets me, but only body it forth."

Here we begin to see Buber's transition from the exclusive relation of the "I-Thou" to the inclusive, concerned life which Buber espouses, in contrast to the mystic. The "I-Thou" is consummated in activity, activity which inevitably partakes of the "I-It" experience, but activity which is redeemed, for in being the creative and transforming ground of activity, the "I-Thou" relation is exhibited in its fullness. This creative tension of "It" and "Thou" in the practical life is exemplified in such contrasts as those between organization and community, control and mutuality, and individuals and persons. The "Thou" stands as judge over the "It," but a judge with the form and creative power for its transformation. In existential living the fathomless dimension of the "Thou" is creatively incarnated, as it were, into the commonplace world of the "It." As an "It," the created object will be scrutinized with all the instruments of "objectivity," but as a living embodiment of a "Thou" it has the capacity to lift its perceiver from the commonplace to the all-pervasive dimension of the Thou in which all things fundamentally participate. As Buber continually insists, such relation is not simply subjective, for then it could have no mutuality: "To produce is to draw forth, to invent is to find, to shape is to discover." This relation of "I-Thou" is subjectivity and objectivity in a totality which transcends the "I-It" quality of either in isolation.

We begin to see here that Buber is passing inevitably from the field of epistemology to that of metaphysics. If it be true that the relationship of "I-Thou" is a valid mode of apprehending reality, a relationship grounded in the very nature of reality, a further question is unavoidable—what is the relation of "Thou" to "Thou," each of which is apprehended as *the* totality and as *the* illuminator of the whole? It is Buber's answer to this question which distinguishes him from aesthetic philosophers such as Santayana, Jordan, and Bosanquet, and marks him as a religious philosopher. He begins by perceiving love as the unique quality of the "I-Thou" relation, love as a "metaphysical and metapsychical fact." This is the nature of the relationship between "Thou" and "Thou," and the "I" as it participates in that which is the constituting relation of all. At this central point Buber comes intriguingly close to Christianity. "Love is responsibility of an I for a *Thou*. In this lies the likeness . . . of all who love, from the smallest to the greatest and from the blessedly protected man . . . to

him who is all his life nailed to the cross of the world, and who ventures to bring himself to the dreadful point —to love *all men*." Or again, the "I-Thou" relation is one in which man "calls his *Thou* Father in such a way that he himself is simply Son. . . ." There can never be hatred of a "Thou"; hatred can be only against a part of a being. The "Thou," the whole, can only be loved, for this is the very nature of the mutual relation.

Since each encountered "Thou" reveals the inmost nature of all reality, we see that everything can appear as a "Thou." This is so because in the "I" is an "inborn Thou," an *a priori* of relation. We see this, Buber affirms, as the child's fundamental guide to action from the instinct to make contact by touch and name, to its blossoming in tenderness and love, and its perfection in creativity. All of these emerge from the "I's" inherent longing for the "Thou." Throughout life "I-Thou" encounters continue, but they are not ordered, for they are only "a sign of the world-order." Increasingly one sees this to be so, for every "Thou" inevitably becomes an "It"; but man cannot rest content with only a momentary "I-Thou" relation. The inborn "Thou" can be consummated only in a direct relation with the "Thou" which cannot become "It." All lesser "Thou's" whet the soul for the relation which is abiding, for which all others are mere foreshadows. Through them the "I" sees that the "Thou's" are such only because they possess a "living Centre," that "the extended lines of relations meet in the eternal Thou."

Witness to this is exhibited for Buber even in the practical realm. Men can live in mutual relation only when they first take their stand in mutual relation with a living Center. A great culture rests on an original, relational event from which a special conception of the cosmos emerges. Loss of this center reduces a culture to the impotence of a mere "It." Likewise, marriage is consummated by a couple's mutual revealing of the "Thou" to one another; only thereby do they participate in the "Thou" which is the unifying ground in which mutual relations in all realms are possible. Whatever name one gives to this "Thou," if he really has "Thou" in mind, despite his illusions, he addresses the true "Thou" which cannot be limited by another. Even though he regards himself as an atheist, he stands in a relation which gathers up and includes all others.

This meeting of the "Thou" is a matter both of choosing and being chosen. One can prepare, yet since all preparations remain in the realm of "It," the step from that realm is not man's doing. Thus the word "encounter" is the only one appropriate. Epistemologically, the particular encounters are prior; metaphysically, the Central Thou is eternally prior. Through the former we are addressed by the latter; ours is the response. It is here that we reach the apex of Buber's position—"In the relation with God unconditional exclusiveness and unconditional inclusiveness are one." This relation means neither the loss of world nor "I," but a giving up of the self-asserting instinct by regarding all in the love relation of the "Thou." The world of "It" cannot be dispensed with, nor is it evil; it becomes demonic only when the motivating drive is not the will to be related but, for example, in economics is the will to profit, or, in politics, the will to power. Buber's ethic can be clearly stated—man participating in

awareness of the Thou "serves the truth which, though higher than reason, yet does not repudiate it. . . . He does in communal life precisely what is done in personal life by the man who knows himself incapable of realising the *Thou* in its purity, yet daily confirms its truth in the *It*, in accordance with what is right and filling for the day, drawing—disclosing—the boundary line anew each day." Such a life is characterized by action filled with meaning and joy, and possessions radiating with "awe and sacrificial power." These are the truths of primitive man, encountering with wonder the immediacy of life, but now purified of superstition and fitted for civilized community. To hallow life is to encounter the living God; to encounter this "Thou" is to hallow life—this is the paradox which best summarizes Buber's thought.

It is in this relation that Buber sees true theology resting. Its basis is not dogma, a content once and for all delivered. It is a compulsion received as something to be done; its confirmation is its product in the world and the singleness of life lived in obedience to it. This is the meaning of revelation, revelation which is eternal and ever available. It must be completed in theology, in objectification, but the abiding sin of religion is to substitute the objectification for the relation, to make the Church of God into a god of the church, to make the Scripture of God into a god of the scripture. The mystery at the foundation of theology cannot be dispelled, yet language can point in the right direction. For Buber the affirmations "God *and* the world" or "God *in* the world" are still in the "I It" realm; but the declaration "the world in the Thou" points to the true

861

relation. With hesitation, Buber attempts to say more, drawing heavily upon the artistic analogy. The God-man relation is characterized by the polarity of creatureliness and creativity, of being totally dependent upon God and yet totally free. For Buber this tension can only mean that while we need God in order to exist, God needs us for the very meaning of life. That is, "there is a becoming of the God that is" —herein is the eternal purpose of our existence. Mutual fulfillment, which is the "I-Thou" relation, must mean, in the final account, that we are co-creators with God in cosmic fulfillment.

Such declarations will raise immediate questions for the logical philosopher. Is this absolute idealism, pantheism, pan-psychism, or process philosophy? In what sense is this the theistic world-view of traditional Judaism, centered in the God of providence and history? Buber's refusal to be of any help here shows the degree to which he is not a philosophic system-builder but an existentialist and, above all, a religious thinker. The problem for him is not so much to know as it is to act in lived awareness of the omnipresent "Thou."

But at least this much can be said. In Buber we have the general Kantian position taken to a religious conclusion. The realm of the "Thou" is the realm of the noumenon; here is to be found no causality but the assurance of freedom. The realm of "It" is the phenomenal realm, the realm of necessity, causality, and the objectification of all according to finite categories. But for Buber the noumenal is more than a postulate or an inference. Similar to Kant's impact of the moral imperative and the encounter of beauty and sublimity in the *Critique of Judgment,* the noumenon is encountered through the total self. And finally, as in Kant, the eternal "Thou" is never known objectively, but certitude of it comes centrally through the domain of action.

THE MIND AND ITS PLACE IN NATURE

Author: Charlie Dunbar Broad (1887-   )
Type of work: Metaphysics, philosophy of mind, epistemology
First published: 1925 (Tarner Lectures, Trinity College, Cambridge, 1923)

PRINCIPAL IDEAS ADVANCED

Of the three theories advanced to account for differences in material objects— vitalism, the theory of emergence, and mechanism—the emergence theory is the most satisfactory: new wholes are formed in nature the behavior of which could never have been predicted from knowledge of the parts.

The mind-body problem (What are the relations between body and mind?) has been made difficult by confusion concerning the meanings of "mind" and "body"; but the solution probably is that mind affects body, and body affects mind.

There must be a center of consciousness which is more than a mere ordering of sense data, but this center may be nothing more than a mass of bodily feelings. Memory traces are neither purely mental nor purely physiological; they are psychic factors.

C. D. Broad shares the realist standpoint of his Cambridge colleagues, G. E. Moore and Bertrand Russell, and his work combines the former's meticulous habits of analysis with the latter's respect for the findings of the particular sciences. The present volume deals with the problems which confronted the new realism when it had passed beyond its early polemic phase and was faced with the task of formulating the details of its own position. It is a patient, at times wearisome, ransacking of modern knowledge for clues as to the ultimate constitution of the world. From an overall point of view it presents a single, sustained inquiry into the place of mind in nature, concluding in favor of a kind of emergent materialism. But the argument takes second place to the definition and analysis of problems which arise along the way, so that the work may be profitably consulted in a topical manner.

Among the questions dealt with are those pertaining to mechanism and vitalism, mind and body, perception and matter, the unconscious, and the evidence of man's survival of bodily death. Broad makes no claim to give original solutions to these problems. His method, which is more memorable than his conclusions, is to bring the widest possible range of hypotheses under investigation. Some of these he eliminates on the grounds of linguistic confusion and logical inconsistency, others for want of empirical evidence, until only two or three are left. Of these, he observes with diffidence that the evidence slightly favors one above the others.

Broad holds the particular sciences in high regard and believes that our understanding of the world is entirely dependent upon them. But in Broad's view the construction of a philosophy of nature is hampered by the failure of scientists to check their hypotheses with the findings of men in other fields of investigation. Thus, physicists have too long undertaken to give an account of matter without attending to the findings of biologists; similarly, epistemologists have traditionally discussed mind only in the context of knowledge and have neglected its relation to man's bodily life. Broad sees it as the function of the philosopher to take the lead in helping overcome this departmentalism. By formulating precisely what presuppositions and consequences a given explanatory theory entails, the philosopher seeks to help the scientific worker to see the limits of his evidence and thus to save him from committing himself to a more general hypothesis which, although suited to his purposes, may be rendered dubious by findings in another field. The philosopher must often take it upon himself to bring up alternative possibilities which experimenters have neglected, and to focus evidence upon them from widely separate sources. But the test of rival hypotheses is always the available evidence; and where this is inconclusive, the philosopher must be content to leave his questions unanswered.

Since many of the difficulties which

are encountered in explaining "the mind and its place in nature" stem directly from wide-spread preconceptions about unity, substance, and causation, Broad begins his book by considering these matters at what he calls "the level of enlightened common sense."

The argument between *monists* and *pluralists* he finds confused by the failure on both sides to make clear whether their claims apply to substance, differentiating attributes, or specific forms. Spinoza, for example, claimed that there is one substance, but he supposed that there are many differentiating attributes, whereas Leibniz held that there is but one differentiating attribute but many substances. In our day, according to Broad, there is no serious question of our being anything other than substantial pluralists: what is in dispute is whether there is more than one specific form of being.

The issue between the vitalists and mechanists in biology is illustrative. "Are the apparently different kinds of material objects irreducibly different?" As Broad defines it, mechanism, when strictly interpreted, includes four related assumptions: one kind of stuff, one intrinsic quality, one kind of change, and one fundamental law of change. These assumptions provided an adequate framework for Galilean physics, but they have never been quite satisfactory for chemistry or biology, or for recent physics. When a modern scientist claims that he is a mechanist, he uses the term in a modified sense. According to Broad, there are three possible ways of accounting for apparent differences in the behavior of physical bodies: *vitalism* holds

that they are due to a peculiar component, a soul or "entelechy"; *emergence* denies a peculiar component but maintains that new "wholes" are formed in nature the behavior of which could never have been predicted from a knowledge of their component parts; and *mechanism,* denying both of these contentions, holds that there is never anything in the behavior of the "whole" that is not determined by the parts and, in principle, deducible from a knowledge of them. Of these three hypotheses, Broad finds vitalism the weakest, both because of its obscurity and because of its non-verifiability. It was plausible only so long as it was thought to be the sole alternative to mechanism. Mechanism has in its favor the tidiness which it enables us to bring into our view of the world: since it seems highly probable that living cells are composed of chemical atoms, and that atoms are composed of electrified particles, one has only to suppose that these obey the same elementary laws and that they are compounded according to a single law to open up the possibility of a purely theoretical deduction of the behavior of any body from a knowledge of the number and arrangement of the atoms. But in our present state of knowledge, the facts suggest that there is less unity in the world than is postulated under this ideal. All the sciences present instances of wholes which are not intelligible in terms of their elements. For example, vectors cannot any longer be treated as sums in the ordinary sense of the word; organic compounds composed of identical elements in identical proportions are found to manifest distinct characteristics depending on the structure of the molecule; and, most obvious of all, the data of consciousness—colors, smells—have no intelligible relation to the physical vibrations or chemical changes which we take to be their causes. Such considerations weigh in favor of an emergent theory of nature, according to which each level of phenomena must be dealt with in terms of laws peculiar to itself. Broad believes that vitalism arose because of real defects in the mechanistic explanation of biological facts, and that the emergent theory corrects the errors of mechanism with minimum loss to the ideal of unity, order, and law. While continuing to hold to one differentiating attribute, its proponents are pluralists when it comes to the question of special forms, which, they hold, are not illusory.

It is useless to ask whether mental facts are reducible to material or are to be treated as existing in their own right until one has considered what, in the light of current knowledge, these terms can signify. Broad reviews at some length the traditional debate over the *mind-body* question, but expresses grave doubts as to whether the debate serves any useful purpose. The arguments, he says, have been incredibly bad, making it difficult to see how they have imposed on so many learned men. If anything can be concluded from them, it would be in favor of the theory of two-fold interaction, rather than of psycho-physical parallelism or epiphenomenalism—mind and body reflecting each other's activities. But in Broad's opinion, the notions "body" and "mind" are so badly in need of clarification that it is doubtful whether the notion of interaction is suitable to describe the relation between them.

The bulk of the book, therefore, is devoted to investigating the notion of mind in its various contexts.

We can get at it most directly by considering the mind in the *knowledge* situation. Broad enters the contemporary epistemological controversy and devotes separate chapters to perception, memory, introspection, and our knowledge of other minds. Especially important for understanding the constitution of the mind are such questions as: What is the status of sense data? Are they components of the physical object? Are they components of the perceiving mind? Or are they in some way distributed between mind and the physical object? Broad leans away from those theories which regard *sensa* (that is, sense images) as independent of mind and which interpret perception as a selective relation between two physical regions. The difficulty of accounting for illusion on these grounds causes him to favor the view that sensa are peculiarly related to the mind. On this theory, which is closer to critical realism than to neorealism, a distinction must be maintained between the epistemological object and the physical object. The former is made up of sensa—color, size, shape—together with a mass of bodily feelings and quasi-beliefs. The physical object is otherwise determined: extension and geometrical properties actually do characterize it, but they are never more than analogous to the size and figure which, as sensa, are present to mind.

But Broad's problem, in this book, is not primarily to give a theory of knowledge. Rather, it is to single out the elements in the knowledge processes which must be described as mental, and to ask whether these mental events presuppose a single substantive mind. Against the neorealists, Broad holds that there must be a center of consciousness which is more than a mere ordering of sense data in a field; but he leaves open, at this point, the question of whether the center need be conceived as a pure ego and develops the alternate possibility that it is no more than "a mass of bodily feelings." This latter, he believes, is sufficient to account for our conviction that there is a continuing, abiding self which is present as the knower in every cognitive act, particularly if it is allowed that the feelings are "causally dependent on the traces left by past experience."

It is the question as to the nature of these "traces" that opens up the whole problem of *The Unconscious*, to which Broad devotes the third part of his book. His analysis of this ambiguous notion is worthy of being consulted for its own sake. He is not without appreciation for the clinical insights of the psychoanalysts and for the light they have shed upon the existence and activity of traces and groups of traces which are inaccessible to introspection. But he is not so ready to grant the claim that these hidden factors are mental. Two theories balance out about equally at this stage of the investigation: the memory traces which seem called for to explain normal memory as well as aberrant behavior can be interpreted as mental; but they can also be viewed as purely physiological. The fact is, we know nothing about them in detail, and we can predict nothing on one hypothesis that we could not equally well predict on the other; but considerations of simplicity would favor the latter account.

Here we have a further instance of Broad's rule that one must leave open the choice between rival hypotheses until other fields are heard from. If epistemology and abnormal psychology are inconclusive, it remains to consider evidence for human *survival* of bodily death. If the mind or any part of it persists beyond the death of the body, this is important evidence against the physiological explanation of memory traces.

The traditional arguments for immortality, including the one based on moral worth, Broad regards as specious. He is more impressed by the evidence collected by The Society for Psychical Research, particularly accounts of seances which disclose information presumably unknown to any but deceased persons. But granting the facts, it is another thing to conclude that the whole mind survives. The low intellectual and moral quality of the alleged messages weighs against the view that anything comparable to a pure ego survives. Broad thinks that it is sufficient to postulate the persistence for a longer or shorter time after death of a "psychic factor," which is "not itself a mind, but it may carry modifications due to experiences which happened to John Jones while he was alive." This gives us a third hypothesis by means of which to account for the memory traces; they are neither mental nor physiological, but peculiarly psychic. In the normal personality, on this view, the psychic factor combines with neural processes to form the mind. In abnormal conditions, it may be temporarily divorced from the brain, and may (as in the case of multiple-personalities) organize itself into two or more selves which alternately unite with the same brain. In the entranced medium, shreds and snatches of psychic stuff come into temporary union with an otherwise vacant brain and form a "little temporary 'mind'" or "mindkin."

In a final chapter, entitled "Status and Prospects of Mind in Nature," Broad formulates seventeen types of theory combining the various alternatives which he has turned up along the way. All of the principal historical positions, from pure materialism to pure mentalism, appear in this classification, along with some that are of purely theoretical interest. The extreme positions find little to recommend them—neither behaviorism, according to which mind is an illusion, nor mentalism (wrongly called "idealism"), which regards matter with the same disdain. The various intermediate types are necessarily more or less sophisticated, since they have to combine "mentality" and "materiality" in one system. Three of these alone stand up under the crossfire of Broad's examination. The first is Samuel Alexander's theory in *Space, Time and Deity* (1920), which Broad calls "Emergent Neutralism." On this theory, the ultimate reality is neither mind nor matter, both of these being emergent characteristics. The second is Bertrand Russell's theory in *Analysis of Mind* (1921), which Broad calls "Mentalistic Neutralism." It resembles Berkeley's theory in regarding matter as delusive, but rejects Berkeley's mentalism and takes mind as no more than a field of neutral sensa. Broad, while he can find no conclusive reason for rejecting either of these, finds more reason to favor a third theory, which he calls "Emergent Materialism." On this view, reality is thought of as being truly material, and mind as an emergent characteristic depending upon the nervous system. Such a theory is sufficient to account for normal mental activity such as knowing, willing, feeling. The memory traces can be regarded simply as neural patterns, and the notion of unconscious mental states dismissed. But the view can be modified, as we have seen, to take account of abnormal and supernormal phenomena by recognizing, in addition to the neural factor, a distinct psychic factor with its own traits and dispositions. Such a modification of the view can be accomplished, Broad thinks, without abandoning the foundation of materialism, by allowing that the psychic stuff is itself an emergent, and that conscious mind is a compound of neural and psychic factors.

In a brief concluding section, Broad indulges in some speculative flights entitled "The Prospects of Mind in the World." Since mind, as we understand it, exists only in connection with the brain and nervous system, we cannot conceive that it is active in the evolution of the universe or of the human race. The claim of mentalists —that the world is the unfolding of a Cosmic Mind—Broad rejects in favor of the cosmology of modern physics, which conceives of the universe as composed of different systems, some in process of running down and others, presumably, winding up. His rejection of the Cosmic Mind of the mentalists does not rule out Theism, which, he says, is as compatible with materialism as it is with mentalism. But he has nothing to say in its favor, and he concludes with the humanistic refrain, that the prospects are good for man to modify the world favorably by the exercise of his own mental capacities—in the use of which he has barely made a start.

ETHICS

Author: Nicolai Hartmann (1882-1950)
Type of work: Ethics
First published: 1926

PRINCIPAL IDEAS ADVANCED

Ideal principles influence real things; values and obligations have autonomous being in the realm of essence, but provide human beings with the foundations of morality.

Valuational insights are possible to men of moral genius who discern new value complexes.

There is a determinate order among values; although values are relative to persons, they have objective status.

Moral values are realized by seeking to secure such nonmoral values as intelligence, health, and equality.

The three principal branches of the good are the noble, richness of experience, and purity.

Moral law can bind the will without determining it because the will operates under the influence of moral obligation, on a plane between the physical and the ideal.

People who suppose that reading a book about ethics should make one a better person will find that Hartmann's work on the subject (especially Volume Two) fully meets their expectations. Broadly conceived, it has something of the character of Aristotle's *Nicomachean Ethics* in that it discusses actual goods, including human virtues, in a manner that enhances our appreciation of them; but it also resembles Kant's *Metaphysics of Morals* (1785) in the way it elaborates the conditions which make morality possible. One may say that it combines the formal ethics of Kant ("duty for duty's sake") and the material ethics of Aristotle ("the good life"), taking from the former the concept of obligation and uniting it in a novel way with the latter's appreciation for concrete value.

According to Hartmann, a new exigency confronts ethics, one which Nietzsche first made plain. Formerly, it was supposed that man knows what is good and what is evil, so that practical ethics need be concerned only with means for realizing self-evident goals, and theoretical ethics only with fitting moral phenomena into one's larger world-view. In the present crisis, however, as Nietzsche showed, no goals are any longer self-evident, and we must inquire what is good and what is evil. Nietzsche's attempts to answer this question were, in Hartmann's opinion, sadly incomplete. Intoxicated by the view which opened before him, Nietzsche thought that he had comprehended in a glance the whole realm of values, failing to see that he had entered upon "a field for intellectual work of a new kind." Moreover, his celebrated demand for "the revaluation of all values," with its implicit relativism, contradicted his claims elsewhere to have discovered positive goods. Nevertheless, according to Hartmann, our debt to him is immeasurable. He marks the turning point between backward-looking and forward-looking (Promethean) ethics.

It is clear that under Nietzsche's inspiration Hartmann was grappling with difficulties of the same order as exercised Martin Heidegger and the Existentialists. Man, by virtue of his powers of thinking, is a problem to himself. The rift which thought introduces into his soul sets him ever apart from other animals and confronts him with the ceaseless problem of deciding what sort of being he shall become. According to Hartmann, the first and fundamental question is: "What ought we to do?" This is the practical question, and it has become urgent in our day because Western culture no longer provides a convincing answer. But we cannot answer it until we have answered a second theoretical question: "What is valuable in life and in the world?" This is the question to which philosophical ethics must address itself. Hartmann was not swayed by the skeptical demur that there is no answer, nor by the subjectivist claim that any answer must be an expression of man's will. He believed, on the contrary, that an analysis of moral phenomena discloses the principles which we need to make moral decisions and at the same time sheds light upon the nature of man and his place in the world.

Hartmann's preoccupation with the *problems* of human life is seen in his method. He did not take it as the goal of philosophy to solve problems, for he was reconciled to the possibility that reality may not be completely intelligible. In his view, philosophical progress consists in learning to distinguish between what we know and what we do not know, and again, between what is knowable and what is not. Problems serve as instruments or probes for exploring the conditions of our existence. Certain key problems, which he designated by the Greek word *aporiae*, by the very stubbornness with which they resist our systematizing efforts, keep us alert to disparate kinds of being.

Besides his *Ethics*, Hartmann wrote important systematic works in epistemology and metaphysics, in which he defended a realistic theory of knowledge and a pluralistic theory of being. There are, as he conceived being, many kinds or grades of it, each with its own categories and principles. These seemed to him to be arranged in strata, so that the categories of the lower grades of being continue to operate on higher levels, where, however, they are supplemented by new principles. As a result of his probings, he distinguished the following grades of reality: the spatial outer world, which is subdivided into the inorganic and the organic, and the nonspatial inner world, which is subdivided into the psychic

869

and the spiritual. These make up the real world; in addition, there is the realm of the possible, which has its own claims to being and is ruled by its own principles of determination.

Hartmann's philosophy is materialistic in the same sense as that of George Santayana and that of Samuel Alexander. He rejected the personalist argument of Max Scheler, which would make the material world dependent for its existence and order on spirit. Accordingly, he saw no basis for the contention that there is a teleology in nature or that everything in nature is governed by reason. Nevertheless, his *aporetic* forced him to maintain that, in some way not comprehensible to us, ideal entities do manifest themselves in the actual world; besides the categories and laws which belong to matter and mind, there are purely ideal principles, such as those of geometry, which influence real things. Similarly, values and obligations, which have autonomous being in the realm of essence, invade time and space, where they provide a framework for our experience of things as good and bad.

Hartmann ran against the whole tendency of modern philosophy in grounding his ethics in his ontology. But the fact that he was compelled to "return to Plato" was not due to any failure on his part to understand what contemporary thought had to offer. It was, rather, due to his judgment that modern schools (idealism, naturalism, and positivism) have all failed to do justice to the actuality of ethics, being misled by their presuppositions. Although initially a member of the Marburg school (neo-Kantian; see, for example, Ernst Cassirer), he became impressed by the phenomenological movement (Edmund Husserl, Max Schel-

er), which was especially dedicated to the task of rescuing the data of experience from the distortions imposed upon it by theories and hypotheses. Much of Hartmann's *Ethics* is phenomenological research—a painstaking description of morality in all its dimensions. But in Hartmann's view, phenomenology was not enough. Practiced consistently, in accordance with the purpose of its founder, Husserl, it left one the prisoner of his own consciousness, a consequence which, to Hartmann, seemed to contradict the evidence of experience itself. The phenomenology of morals disclosed *aporiae* or problems; and the implications of these led Hartmann to affirm the existence of autonomous values, of conscience, and of free will.

One of the problems which intrigues ethical thinkers is that which commonly goes by the name of cultural relativism. It arises not only in connection with the existence of competing moral systems, but also from the fact that the ethos of any culture undergoes more or less continuous change. Hartmann insisted that this is a real problem. It is not solved by maintaining that values and norms are merely an expression of social needs, because they claim to be much more: we evaluate cultures. On the other hand, to set up one's own scheme of values (say, Utilitarianism) as scientifically founded then judge all others by its standards merely raises the problem anew in a comic way. Hartmann met the difficulty by distinguishing, somewhat as Henri Bergson was to do in *Two Sources of Morality and Religion* (1932), between conventional norms, which are mediated by tradition and fixed by language, and valuational insights, which are immediate and vivid, but difficult to hold and to transmit. Hartmann compared the valuational consciousness to a searchlight moving unpredictably over the realm of values. At a given moment it singles out a particular complex, which it esteems and seeks to realize. Thus it happens that values shift within a culture, so that frequently the values to which it gives lip service have in fact been supplanted by others which have no official sanction and, perhaps, not even names. Rival ethical systems are understood in a similar way, particularly those which can be traced to religious and ethical founders: a prophetic spirit makes "valuational discoveries" which his genius impresses upon the consciousness of a people at a critical moment. Their validity and universal appeal rest upon the fact that they are discoveries of a high order; but no value complex can possibly include more than a segment of the possible—hence, the diversity of moral systems. It is the story of the blind men and the elephant over again.

Another fundamental problem of ethics is the conflict between value and obligation. As has been recognized since the time of Socrates, man never wills anything except what has value; on the other hand, whenever we make a moral choice, we express the conviction that some courses of action are superior to others. According to Hartmann, the problem is at the basis of the argument between the two traditional parties in the history of moral philosophy: eudaemonism (emphasizing the pursuit of value) and formalism (emphasizing obedience to law). Each party claims to have solved the problem. But if, instead of trying to solve it, we keep the problem alive in both its aspects, the matter is more complicated than either party is willing to recognize, although not entirely unintelligible.

First, there is a determinate order among values themselves, on the ideal plane, what Hartmann called a "scale of values." Here, particularly, Hartmann was carrying out the program of the phenomenological school. There is, he believed, an ideal "valuational space" in which values are arranged according to categorical principles of opposition, of subordination, and of dependence. A hint of Hartmann's procedure in this part may be conveyed if we mention the conflict, widely recognized in the history of mankind, between the value of comprehensiveness and that of individuality. Here the opposition is relative (both are good) and not modal (as between pleasure and pain); but the relation is extremely complex and paradoxical. Individuality is bound up with personality, including man's characteristic functions as both subject and object of intentional acts, and his peculiar capacity for discerning and bearing values. Comprehensiveness, when applied to humanity, involves community, and in this way incorporates individuality; but as a whole, the community is also an individual that, although lacking personal characteristics, is the bearer of values on a grander scale. The community is the subject of far-seeing enterprises that are out of the question for a single mortal, and therefore, it is able to make possible many individual values (for example coöperation, devotion, and sacrifice) which otherwise would not exist. According to Hartmann, these relations are purely *a priori*. They hold for the ethical consciousness, quite apart from their actualization in history, just as

871

mathematical reasoning holds whether it is or is not exemplified in space and time.

But this is only part of the answer. An ideal value is only a possibility. The ethical problem has to do with actual values, which have their locus in existing things and are (or may be) the objects of choice. The problem for the analyst is to do justice to the natural and subjective side of goods without losing the autonomy and objectivity which distinguish values from physical properties and from feelings. Hartmann declared that values "exist" only in the world and only for consciousness. And in this sense he spoke of them as relative. A good dinner or a good deed is such only by reference to the situation and only for a person who contemplates its merit. But Hartmann found these considerations no grounds for the relativistic constructions which some (for example, Nietzsche) had placed upon the matter. The same thing that has been said about values might be said about the measurements of surveying or the laws of psychology—they "exist" only in particular media and for trained minds. But this does not mean that they are without objective significance. So, according to Hartmann, the relatedness of values to things and to minds does not warrant our reducing them, after the fashion of naturalism, to lower categories of existence, or, after the fashion of psychologism, to mental attitudes. Our appraisal has as little to do with determining them as the astronomer's measurements have to do with determining the position of the stars.

Hartmann's analysis of values reveals a basic distinction between those that belong to the subject and those that belong to the object. The former are the specifically moral values, dealing with the character, habits, dispositions, and acts of persons. There are personal positive and negative values which are not moral. As an object, man has various kinds of worth to society and to other individuals; moreover, different traits and capacities, both natural and acquired, have conditional value for him as subject. Intelligence and health are nonmoral values which inhere in persons. Justice and courage are moral values.

It is one of the paradoxes of ethics that moral values are not properly to be sought after. They "ride on the back of" situational values, to use the expression which Hartmann borrowed from Max Scheler. The intention of a man's acts always has to do with values in the world about him. Thus, to the question "How can I be just?" the answer is, "Respect the equal rights of all men." Here the value sought is not justice, but equality; but justice comes into being when a man acts in such a way as to respect men's equal claims.

An unusual feature in a book on theoretical ethics is Hartmann's detailed classification and exposition of particular moral values. The first section deals with moral values in *general*, and devotes a chapter to each of the following: the good, the noble, richness of experience, and purity. These form, as it were, a trunk (the good) and three main branches. One can be a good man in different ways—but if he is noble, it must be at the expense of richness of experience and of purity. Hartmann thought that there might be other branches: history has had a great deal to do with determining our moral insight, so that inevitably there are gaps in our understanding of values. This is particularly apparent as we move on to consider *special* moral values, which Hartmann placed in three loose groups. The first includes the values of ancient Greece, with special attention to Aristotle's account. The second group begins with brotherly love and includes the cluster of values which historically grew up in the early Christian community: truthfulness, trustworthiness, humility, and others. A third group is necessary to acknowledge values which "have become accessible to our modern perception," but which were not prominent in other times—the love of the remote, radiant virtue, the value of personality, and personal love. Of these, the first two are due to Nietzsche, whom Hartmann esteemed as a modern prophet, both because of Nietzsche's rare insight into values and because of his ability to give definition to what had hitherto never had a name.

A third major problem which Hartmann considered is the freedom of the will. Not surprisingly, he took as his starting point Kant's famous antinomy between "the causality of nature" and "the causality of freedom." Kant showed, correctly in Hartmann's opinion, that the freedom demanded by our moral consciousness is not freedom "from" causality of nature, but a different kind of freedom that transcends nature. Hence, for Hartmann, the "causal antinomy" is not an *aporia*, not a crucial problem. But other antinomies arise between the will, which is actual, and the realm of value, which is ideal. How is it possible that moral law binds the will without determining it? Evidently, in virtue of an "ought." But the "ought" in man's will must either be the same as that in the law, or different; if the former,

there is no freedom; if the latter, no determination. In discussing this "ought-antinomy" Hartmann distinguished six root-difficulties (*aporiae*) to be clarified. The data of the problem (the consciousness of self-determination, moral accountability and responsibility, the consciousness of guilt) make it clear that the will is not determined purely by moral law, but that ethical life presupposes a partial identity between the two. The term "ought," therefore, includes an equivocation—when applied to moral principles it means "ought to be"; when applied to the will, it means "ought to do." In this light, the moral will appears as a third principle operating on a different plane from the physical, but also on a different plane from the ideal. Hartmann made no claim to have proved the freedom of the will. The skeptical objection, that our consciousness of self-determination and responsibility is merely illusory, is a legitimate one. But Hartmann held that the burden of proof is on the skeptic, and that it is an intolerable burden because it deserts the phenomena. In all theoretical reasoning, according to Hartmann, there is a gap which can never be filled up from reasoning itself; science can go behind some data and find further facts, but there is always a limit. The moral will must be allowed as marking such a boundary beyond which our desire for explanation cannot go.

So much for Hartmann's theoretical ethics. If we return for a moment to the practical problem, and remind ourselves of the concern which Nietzsche raised in Hartmann's breast, we are now in a position to observe the direction which he felt man must take. It was his opinion that in our day ethics can become truly normative, not by telling man what he must do, but by providing him with regulative principles by means of which he can judge between competing goods. Thus it can realize the Platonic "ideal of ruling and moulding mankind spiritually through the power of philosophical perception, through the vision of Ideas." Although he denied divine providence, Hartmann gave a positive sense to the Protagorean saying, "Man is the measure of all things." In virtue of the fact of consciousness, man not only mirrors the outer world but participates in his own being, and is himself both providence and predestination. These are ambiguous powers: there is a danger point beyond which both foresight and purposive efficacy become intolerable burdens. Man has no choice but to live with them. And Hartmann noted the demonic tendency which these gifts arouse in man. "It happens that the gift, the more he is conscious of the power which is in his hands, leads him astray, lures him to ever higher stakes. But in this frenzy he does not become aware of the limits of his strength, until after he has overstepped them and the game is lost for him."

Still, one should not get the impression that Hartmann was a pessimist. Happily, it is not the task of the philosopher to forecast the world's future. His it is to cultivate wisdom, a word which Hartmann identifies from its Latin root (sapientia, from sapere "to taste") with "moral taste." It is not to be confused with knowledge or insight in the intellectual sense—these may well breed pessimism—for it signifies "appreciation of everything and an affirming, evaluating, attitude toward whatever is of value." The wise man is conscious of his own narrowness and at the same time of the boundless resources which surround him. "He sees himself as one who is too rich, who is overwhelmed, and whose power to receive is not equal to the gifts bestowed. His cup is already overflowing, his capacity is exceeded by his possessions. And in that he in this way exercises unintentionally an influence as an example, he is a true educator of men in inner spiritual freedom and in the one true happiness."

GENERAL THEORY OF VALUE

Author: Ralph Barton Perry (1876-1957)
Type of work: Ethics
First published: 1926

PRINCIPAL IDEAS ADVANCED

Any object acquires value when any interest, whatever it be, is taken in it.

If some objects are more valuable than others, it is only because some interests are stronger than others.

Man is distinguished from the other animals in being able to plan ahead in accordance with his interests.

874

There are various kinds of values corresponding to various kinds of interests: values are inherited or acquired, positive or negative, recurrent or progressive, real or playful, aggressive or submissive, subjective or objective.

The highest good is an ideal—a harmonious society of benevolent persons; but the ideal depends upon an interest in working out conflicts coöperatively.

Ralph Barton Perry's theory of value in terms of interest remains one of the most detailed and carefully defended statements of empirical value theory to be found in the history of philosophy. Its very matter-of-fact air and its careful progression from point to point are characteristic of American thought when it is both plain and respectable. There is nothing exciting or revolutionary about Perry's ideas; but what he brings about by his analysis is a new temper of philosophic thought, one in which attention to the facts of the matter takes precedence over recourse to the eternal and elusive realm of ideas. Later philosophers on the subject—such as Charles Leslie Stevenson in his *Ethics and Language* (1944)—may lay stress on the emotive functions of value language, and they may look with forbearance on studies which center their attention on value itself, not on language; but for all that, no significant rebuttal of Perry's theory has been forthcoming or is likely. No rebuttal is likely because the theory that "Any object, whatever it be, acquires value when any interest, whatever it be, is taken in it," is so general, so plausible, so continuously verifiable, that any quarrel about it is likely to be petulant (involving some plaintive appeal to "intuition of the indefinable") or pedantic (reducing itself to quibbles about phrasing or method).

This is high praise for a work of twentieth century philosophy, but the work is worthy of it. It was no easy task for modern thinkers to turn their minds from conceptions, essences, and presumably eternal, immutable, and unanalyzable truths, to those parts of the world of experience that give substance and sense to human discourse. But Perry, together with other empirical and analytic philosophers, has not only pioneered philosophically, but has done so with such diligence and skill that the results of his investigations are worth considering long after we have ceased to be enchanted by the skillful amendments which later philosophers have advanced.

Perhaps it should be made clear that Perry's general theory of value is significant in philosophy not because of its novelty, but because of the novelty of its genesis. The "age of analysis," as Morton White has termed the age of twentieth century philosophy, is distinguished from earlier philosophic periods by its central concern with analysis of some sort as opposed to synthesis, or system-building. Of course, there are living philosophers whose trust is in what is claimed to be the philosopher's peculiar and nonanalytic insight, his intuition, who reject the attempt to explain or dissect value and who prefer to call attention to value as something unique, ultimate, and beyond the possibility of analysis. England's Sir David Ross in his influential *The Right and the Good* (1930) has shown himself to be one of these "old-fashioned" philosophers— "old-fashioned" in the literal sense of holding to the fashion of thinkers in ages prior to our own. But Perry quite aptly terms himself one who tries "to bridge the gap between common-sense and science" and who believes that "philosophy must face the facts of life and nature, taking them as both the point of departure and the touchstone of truth."

Perry's theory is a *general* theory in that it attempts to explain value quite without regard to any question as to whose value is under consideration or as to what kind of value it is. Perry is well aware of the fact—which anyone in his right mind acknowledges, some quite seriously—that *what* is valued differs from place to place and person to person, and that what is valued may be valued in different ways, even by the same person. But what he is concerned, in his theory of value, to explain is precisely what is involved in a situation in which something (it does not matter what) is of value (it does not matter of what kind, or for what reason) to someone (it does not matter who).

Perry is not blind to the relevance of a study of the use of language for one who would identify the subject of his philosophical discourse. "The task of the theory of value . . . may be regarded as the study of the act of *valuing*, or as the study of the predicate *valuable*," he writes. Nor is Perry naïve enough to suppose that by turning to the word "value" all ambiguities are resolved and all data given: "The fact is that the word 'value' instead of having a clear denotation like the word 'house' . . . refers us to a region whose nominal boundaries have yet to be agreed upon." A nice distinction is drawn between the empirical aspect of philosophical inquiry—which involves a "topographical survey" of all to which attention has been called by the use of the term "value"—and the legislative act of deciding to limit the denotation of the term to a certain part of the area surveyed. It is just that distinction, among others, which Wittgenstein was concerned to make and illustrate in his *Philosophical Investigations* (1953).

Before developing and defending at some length the proposal that any object of any interest is valuable, Perry examines and discards the opposed ideas that value is irrelevant to interest, that value is the qualified object of interest, and that value is the object of qualified interest.

In considering value as irrelevant to interest, Perry considers the idea that value is immediately perceived, as G. E. Moore claimed in *Principia Ethica* (1903). Objecting to the view that value is an indefinable characteristic inherent in objects and empirically discoverable there, Perry calls attention to the close relationship between value and the interest in agreeable feelings. He suggests that it is only on the assumption that value is an empirical property that the analogies between value and other properties, such as color properties, have any persuasive force. The claim that value is an indefinable property, present for all to witness, is weakened by consideration of the fact that it is always relevant, in determining the value of an object, to go from one judge to another; the verdicts vary because men vary, as do their interests with their differences. Finally, Perry rejects the identification of value with some such property as fitness or self-realization. He argues that fitness and self-realization, as well as organic unity, are understandable only by reference to interest.

The distinction between the idea that value is the *qualified object* of interest and the idea that value is the object of *qualified interest* is not as subtle as it might at first seem.

According to the first view, "certain objects are preëminently qualified to evoke interest. . . ." Perry reviews the most prominent ideas of this sort: the idea that only those objects which are purposive are truly worthy of interest, the idea that the good is the desirable when "desirable" means that which actually evokes desire, the idea that the valuable objects are those which are *capable* of evoking desire (as distinguished from actually evoking it), and finally the idea that the object which has value is the object which ought-to-be. The errors resident in these various ideas, according to Perry, are either instances of supposing that objects actually have the properties of responses human beings make to objects, or of limiting the area of value to whatever most concerns the philosopher in question.

According to the second view—the view that value is the object of qualified interest—only those objects are valuable which become the objects of an interest in some way distinguishable from other interests that might be taken in objects. For example, it might be held that only an interest or desire which is harmonious with nature or with the will of God is a "real" interest, a value-determining desire. Or it might be maintained that only a rational will can determine value, that an object is valuable only if it *would be* desired, *were* the reason in control of desire. Several other ideas, variants of these, are considered by Perry. He concludes that the various kinds of interests which various philosophers have put forward as authoritative and value-determining are none of them paramount and preëminently value-creative; but they do determine various *kinds* of value.

Having shown what is unsatisfactory in the claim that value is the qualified object of interest and in the claim that value is the object of qualified interest, Perry then put forth his preferred generic theory of value: the theory that value is *any* object of *any* interest—that whatever the interest, desire, concern for or in an object, the fact of that interest's having been taken determines the object as an object of value. "That which is an object of interest is *eo ipso* invested with value," he writes.

After noting that the idea is not entirely novel—since it may be found in the works of Spinoza, Santayana, and Prall—Perry mused: "It may appear surprising that a doctrine so familiar, if not banal, as that just stated, should have received so little authoritative support." The unpopularity of the idea among professional philosophers is attributed to philosophical interest in some specific value to the neglect of generic value; and Perry attributes the interest in specific values to the interest in forcing value theory to support some religious or metaphysical notions which would otherwise collapse.

The obvious weakness in the theory is in its very breadth. If an object is made valuable by an act of interest, how could anyone be disappointed? How could some desires be unworthy of virtuous men? It might seem that Perry's theory involves a truly vicious —since indiscriminate—relativism. But Perry does not evade this criticism; he meets it by declaring that a generic theory of value naturally does not account for organizations of value which result in giving preference to certain interests over others. He does not deny that, relative to a certain interest, another interest might be wrong; but what he insists upon is the revelatory character of his principal thesis: that, *generically* considered, an object has value if some interest has been taken in it. A truly vicious relativism, he declares, is one which fails to recognize the relation of interest between subjects and objects.

This is a point well worth emphasizing. To say, as Perry does, that an object has value if someone takes an interest in it, is not to say that there is no such thing as value, or that value is *not worthy* of consideration (an ironic claim) because, after all, it is merely a function of interest. To realize that there is a sense in which interest confers value on objects is to be liberated from the old, constrictive notion that either values are inherent in objects—in which case we should all agree on value considerations—or all discourse about value is meaningless—in which case all value disputes are senseless. And Perry merits serious attention for his view that emphasis on any one kind of interest, with a subsequent upgrading of some particular species of value, is itself an expression of interest, a dogmatic conferring of value on one attitude to the exclusion of other concerns.

In his analysis of interest Perry refused to limit himself to an examination of introspective data. He preferred to "look for interest in the open—upon the plane and in the context of physical nature." Writing in 1926, Perry hailed the advance of psychology as a result of its behavioristic direction and contended that a thorough study of value involves taking advantage of methods which have proved so useful. Consequently, a chapter is devoted to the biological approach to interest, and another to the psychological definition of interest.

The capacity to act in accordance with one's expectations, the ability to plan ahead and to form plans in the service of present inclinations is what distinguishes man, although not sharply but by degree, from other animals. Having claimed this, Perry offers a definition of interest which fits in with the biological and psychological study of man: "An act is interested in so far as its occurrence is due to the agreement between its accompanying expectation and the unfulfilled phases of a governing propensity." In other words, if someone wants something (a house) and acts (by assembling wood, nails, and other materials) because of his expectation that by following a certain procedure (as outlined in the house plans) he can achieve what he wants—then he is *interested* as he acts. This account of interest in general is carefully elaborated by Perry, and it fulfills his intention of explaining interest without having to assume scientifically inexplicable phenomena or capacities in the human being.

In reading Perry one is reminded not only of Spinoza—whom Perry quotes with favor because of Spinoza's claim that things are good because we like them—but also of Montaigne, who, realizing that the worth of things is more dependent on our attitudes than on the nature of things, urged the good sense of changing our attitudes whenever we are dissatisfied with things. Behind Perry's systematic and pedagogical style one discerns the active and practical interest in using

878

value theory as an instrument of human freedom. In pointing out that adaptability is peculiar to men, he is in effect urging that men use their ability to plan ahead in order to satisfy their interests. Nothing could be farther from the old idea of making life fit patterns of conduct derived deductively from presumed revelations of divine will.

In support of his thesis that there are various kinds of interest and, consequently, various species of value, Perry devotes several chapters to what he calls "modes of interest." His survey encompasses the relations between reflex, habit, and instinct; an account of positive and negative interests in terms of approach and withdrawal; clarification of the distinction between recurrent interest (interest which succeeds itself in relation to objects present in the immediate future) and progressive interest (interest which arises with the coming into existence of a certain object of interest); a study of the difference between "real" interest and play interest; a comparison of aggressive with submissive interest; and, finally, a discussion of those modes of interest involving pleasure, pain, and emotion. Perry concludes that values, like interests—because they are functions of interest—can be categorized as "inherited or acquired, positive or negative, recurrent or progressive, real or playful, aggressive or submissive, subjective or objective."

Perhaps the most helpful part of Perry's defense of his theory is his account of value judgments. Perry shows that although interest can be distinguished from cognition, the two are "intimately interdependent." Interest affects cognition, and cognition affects interest; our interest in moving ourselves results in our acquiring knowledge, and our knowledge of objects has its effect on our interests. It is not surprising, then, that Perry decides that judgments of value are similar to other kinds of judgments; judgments of value "have their indices, their predicates and their objects; they are true or false. . . ." It is this claim—that judgments of value are true or false—which proponents of the theory that value judgments are merely expressions of emotion find so disturbing. But Perry underscores his point by definition and example: "To be valuable is to be object of interest," he writes. "To be judged valuable . . . is to be judged to be object of interest." For example, ". . . the judgment 'peace is good' is true when there is an interest such that peace is its objective. It is not necessary that peace should exist, or that the question of its existence should be raised."

Perry's analysis does not neglect the problems which arise because of the conflicts of interest within an individual or between individuals. He regards apologetic reasoning as the effort to find a common ground for harmonious action. Society is not a person and cannot be treated as a person; it is a "composition or interrelation of men," a composition in which individual men, by their actions, affect and modify each other. According to Perry, interests may be integrated through common objects, or by becoming objects for one another, or through mediating one another. The hope of achieving the constructive integration of the various interests of men in society depends upon benevolent coöperation, a kind of general willingness to utilize the various modes of social integration.

How is a critique of values possible

for one who regards value as a function of interest? Perry answers that an illuminating answer depends upon recognizing the possibility that one interest may become dominant, and relative to that interest an act or object of another interest may come to be rejected. To take a homely example (not the author's): A cake may be a good cake, the very best available; but that means only that as an object of interest in cake, this cake takes precedence over other cakes. But the interest in remaining slim may take precedence over the interest in eating cake, and consequently, relative to that latter interest, eating cake is bad.

If Perry seems to depart at all from his cautious and fruitful value relativism, it is in his concluding chapter, "The Highest Good." Perry endorses an ideal, realizable by men, as the highest good; it is an ideal which presupposes a harmonious society of benevolent persons. But is harmony a value to the man who lives by conflict, who finds satisfaction only in struggle and in the hope and realization of victory? According to Perry's own theory, if conflict is an object of interest, then it is a value. How, then,

account for this concluding endorsement of harmony and benevolence?

Without having to win his point by an awkward calculation of comparative worths, Perry argues that if all would concur in working out a resolution of conflicts coöperatively, the resultant situation would be better for all; and if the resolution of conflicts were such that no greater interest would be elicited by some other resolution, such a state of affairs would be the ideal, the greatest good relative to the interest of each. The highest good, then, is such "as judged by, and only as judged by, the standard of inclusiveness hypothetically applied." Because the value is, in a sense, conditional, no violence is done to Perry's relativism.

As a critically articulated empirical philosophy of value, as an examination of the role of interest in that broad area to which the word "value" in its most general use calls attention, Ralph Barton Perry's *General Theory of Value* remains a provocative statement to be reckoned with by anyone who supposes that value terms are meaningless or that value is an ultimate and unanalyzable aspect of reality.

THE LOGIC OF MODERN PHYSICS

Author: Percy Williams Bridgman (1882-   )
Type of work: Philosophy of science
First published: 1927

PRINCIPAL IDEAS ADVANCED

The concepts of physics should be flexible in order not to restrict the possibilities of future experience.

To provide flexibility, concepts should be defined operationally; the concept is synonymous with the operations by which one determines whether the concept applies, or what the measure of something is.

There is no absolute time; time is measured by reference to clocks of some sort.

Such concepts as causality, identity, force, energy, temperature, and light become useful and meaningful as they are defined by reference to physical phenomena and operations of measurement.

Since the turn of the century increased attention has been devoted to critical examination of the concepts and presuppositions of the sciences. In the case of physics this shift of emphasis from content to methods was largely the result of such revolutionary discoveries as the relativity theory and quantum mechanics. These not only revealed new and unexpected truths which had to be assimilated, but also showed that the old methods of studying the world had proved inadequate. Bridgman's contribution to this problem lay in his formulation and development of the *operational method.* While this method was not new and had been more or less unconsciously employed by physicists for some time, Bridgman argued that a much clearer conception of what it really involved was essential if physics was to avoid some of the difficulties through which it had passed in the preceding halfcentury.

Fundamental to this approach, as far as Bridgman is concerned, is a new emphasis on the empirical character of physics. There must be no *a priori* principles which restrict the possibilities of future experience. Experience is determined only by experience. Since this is the case, concepts must be flexible in order to allow for their modification when experiment is pushed into new domains—smaller particles, higher velocities, greater distances, greater pressures, higher temperatures—where discontinuities may ap-

pear and the world may change character in unexpected ways. Indeed, we even find that concepts sometimes disappear entirely, as in the case of temperature when applied to a single molecule. We cannot therefore predict that nature will ultimately be embraced in a single formula. While such may actually be the case, we should not approach experience with this expectation, for we shall then try to force nature into a preëstablished form and the result may well be that certain of our accepted concepts will become meaningless if we try to use them to interpret the new areas of experience.

The best way to provide for the required flexibility, Bridgman argues, is to define concepts operationally. Let us examine the concept of *length.* Suppose we are trying to determine the length of a house. We apply a measuring rod according to accepted rules and come up with a certain number, say 42 feet, which we say is the length of the house. Now let us attempt to determine the length of a moving street car. Here we cannot proceed as we did before, for the car is moving and we are at rest. We shall have to stop the car, get on it, start it, measure it, stop it, and get off. Since we have used different measurement techniques we are not really entitled to say that by the *length* of the moving street car we mean the same thing as we do in the case of the *length* of the house. For higher velocities, such as that of the stars, this method will obviously not work and another must be devised. This fact will give us a new meaning of *length*. Or suppose we wish to determine the length of a large piece of land. We shall probably establish this by means of trigonometry and a surveyor's transit. If we extend this method to stellar distances, on the one hand, and to the distances separating molecules, on the other, the measuring techniques will once more be changed.

What conclusion can we draw? There is no *one* meaning of length, but as many meanings as there are ways of measuring length. We cannot say what *the* length of anything is. Apart from some operation for measuring length, the concept is meaningless; *the concept is synonymous with the corresponding operations.* If we have more than one set of operations, then, in the interest of precision and in the interest of tying our concept down to the area to which it properly applies, we ought to have a separate concept for each set.

The need for the operational approach is illustrated by the pre-relativity attempts to define *time*. Newton lieved that "Absolute, True and Mathematical Time, of itself, and from its own nature, flows equably without regard to anything external." But Bridgman points out that we can have no assurance that there exists anything in nature which has such properties. Indeed, we can not even assure ourselves that the concept of absolute time has any meaning. Certainly if we were to *measure* time, we should have to employ some sort of clock, and we could have no way of knowing whether the clock "flows equably." All time, then, is relative, and dependent upon measurement. We cannot base physics on any concept of time which excludes this flexibility from its meaning; hence we must abandon absolute time.

Bridgman indicates several consequences of this operational method. In the first place, when we approach a new area where previous operations cannot be performed, we must devise a new set of operations, thus redefining our concept. It may be *convenient* to retain the old concept, but we may have to purchase this convenience at the cost of precision in our language. We must recognize these "joints" in our conceptual structure if we are to simplify the tasks of the unborn Einsteins. In the second place, we may often find that as we extend knowledge into new domains, concepts fuse together, as in the case of length and electric field vector when applied to an electron. In the third place, as seen above, *all* knowledge becomes relative. This does not mean that we can never know nature, for the statement that the length of an object can be ascertained by applying a measuring stick to it is a very important and fundamental truth about nature. Furthermore, a thing may be said to have an absolute property if the numerical magnitudes obtained by all observers who measure the object are the same. Finally, if we accept the operational approach, we readily discover how easy it is to reformulate questions which are meaningless when (as in the case of the question about the flow of absolute time) there are no operations by which they can be answered. Some such meaningless questions are: Was there ever a time when matter did not exist? May time have a beginning or an end? May space be bounded? Are there parts of nature forever beyond our detection? May there be missing integers in the series of natural numbers as we know them? Is the sensation which I call blue really the *same* as that which my neighbor calls blue?

The operational approach involves far-reaching change in our habits of thought. While thinking becomes simpler, since fewer sweeping generalizations become possible, much of traditional philosophy becomes unreadable. One looks continually for operational meanings where there seems to be none. Thinking becomes harder in the sense that the demand for operational concepts is often difficult to meet. Finally operational thinking proves to be an unsocial virtue, for a person finds that he is continually antagonizing his friends by insisting in the simplest conversation that all concepts be operationally defined before they are used.

By "experiment" in physics Bridgman means, from the operational point of view, simply reducing a situation to its elements; that is, discovering familiar correlations between phenomena. He claims that an explanatory sequence extending into new areas may be terminated in three ways: (1) By disentangling complexities. This involves nothing new. The best illustration is found in the explanation of the thermal properties of gas by the kinetic theory. (2) By coming up against situations involving such genuinely novel elements that we are at a complete loss as to how to explain them. Quantum phenomena and relativity exemplify these situations, and they present a real crisis in physics. (3) By devising new elements beyond the range of present experiment, or radically modifying old elements, in the attempt to make them fit the novel area into which we have penetrated. Because of the lack of justification for the belief that as we penetrate deeper and deeper into nature we shall find the elements of experience repeated, this method is opposed to the operational approach. It may be used, however, if we recognize its dangers. The new elements must be considered to be simply mental constructs and their utility to lie merely in the fact that they are working hypotheses which may suggest new experimental truths.

Some of the results of Bridgman's application of the operational method to certain physical concepts are as follows: *Space* as used in physics becomes an empirical concept and is meaningless if separated from physical objects and measuring rods. Geometry, therefore, is not an abstract logical system built up from postulates, but a physical framework made up of bodies in relations to one another. We cannot measure the distance between two points in empty space. *Time,* when restricted to "local" time, can be operationally defined by the use of simple clocks; but when extended to include the remote past, or when extended to the process of synchronizing clocks at distant places, it must be defined through the use of various kinds of records and by means of light signals. *Causality* can be defined only by recognizing that it is relative and involves the whole system in which the causally related events take place. The animistic element, originally associated with the concept, is eliminated as far as possible, and the system in which causal action takes place is assumed to be capable of isolation from disturbing forces, so that repeated experiments can be performed on it. *Identity,* as exhibited by ordinary physical objects, can be detected by continuous observation of those objects and noting the absence of change in properties. But this method does not enable us to determine whether an electron jumping about in an atom preserves its identity. *Force,* exhibited by objects at rest, has its locus in muscular sensations, but when extended to objects in motion must be redefined in terms of mass and acceleration But mass must be capable of measurement independently of force—something which can be done in the ordinary range of experiments with low velocities. However, in the domain of celestial mechanics, where the only thing we can observe about the heavenly bodies is their positions, the concepts of force and mass lose their definiteness and become partially fused. This is characteristic of concepts on the fringe of the experimentally attainable.

Energy is a certain complicated property of a material system, but because of the absence of specifiable operations by which it may be measured, Bridgman believes that it is probably not entitled to the fundamental position that physical thought has been inclined to give it. *Temperature,* basically a physiological concept, is extended by being connected with the physical phenomenon of thermal equilibrium. *Electrical concepts* are defined first in connection with large scale static phenomena. Then they are extended, with proper changes in operations, to high velocities and to very small scales of magnitude. *Light* gets its direct meaning in terms of "things lighted." By experimenting with sources and sinks, with screens placed between a light and an illuminated object, and with rectilinear propagation, we readily conclude that light is a "thing which travels" and has properties analogous to those of all material things which travel. But

there is one important difference. We can have evidence of a ball, for example, at intermediate points in its movement, because we can see it or possibly hear it. But the situation is different with regard to light; we can know of its intermediate existence only by interposing a screen of some kind, and this operation destroys the very beam itself; the light cannot continue to travel beyond that point. Thus the concept of light becomes operationally meaningless when we try to speak of it in an empty space between the initial and terminal phenomena. *Relativity concepts* suffer from the fact that there is still a wide gap between the theory and its physical applications; we have no way of relating our physical measures of *time* to the t in our formulas. *Quantum concepts* border on the meaningless because they seem to require that space and time be essentially discontinuous at the microscopic level, and this cannot be reconciled with the way in which length and duration were originally defined.

Bridgman suggests that in our study of nature we must try to avoid the unconscious intrusion of hypotheses which might restrain possible future experiences. One *general* hypothesis we cannot avoid; namely, that our minds will continue to function in the future as they have in the past. This certainly does not restrict us too seriously. On the other hand, there are three *special* hypotheses whose roles must be examined—the simplicity of nature, the finiteness of nature as we go to smaller and smaller dimensions, and the causal determination of the future by the present. Bridgman examines each of these.

The hypothesis of simplicity claims that nature is completely describable in terms of a few principles of great breadth and simplicity, such as the inverse square law. This hypothesis does not seem to be borne out in our experience. The *time* of relativity is proving to be much more complex than the *time* of Newtonian physics. We have not been able to extend gravitational laws to small-scale bodies, and we have not yet been able to extend electrical laws to large-scale bodies. Thus we seem to be continually discovering new *kinds* of phenomena where the established concepts will not work.

A second hypothesis is that as we analyze nature into smaller and smaller particles we find that the world is constituted by a smaller number of *kinds* of elements; two molecules may differ from each other though they may consist of atoms which are alike. Nature is simple because everything is made up, perhaps, of only two different constituents—positive and negative electric charges. But present experience in physics does not seem to support this hypothesis either. New experiments show that the universe at any given level is becoming increasingly complex and that simplicity is receding. It is very probable that there are structures beyond the electron and the quantum. Indeed, there is no reason to believe that the analytic process will ever be terminated: a drop of water may be infinite.

As a result of this fact the third hypothesis—that of determinism—is considerably weakened. For if even a small part of the universe had an infinite structure, we could never give a complete description of it and consequently we could never know all of the causal factors that would enter into the determination of the future; to predict anything we must know its *complete*

cause. The future would therefore fall into a penumbra of uncertainty—this uncertainty increasing as we pass to finer details of structure. Our belief in causation originates in our experience with mechanical systems, and there is no reason to believe that these systems will still apply when we deal with phenomena of radiation. There is, however, more and more reason for believing that nature is deterministic as far as large-scale phenomena are concerned.

There is still another sense in which the physicist may have a predisposition toward simplicity in the world: he may feel that the universe can ultimately be explained in terms of analysis. This is the thesis that we should start with small-scale things and then proceed to explain large-scale things in terms of these. According to this point of view, the large can be constructed out of the small since the properties of the large are obtained by merely adding the properties of the small. For example, the mass of a very large object is the sum of the masses of its parts. But although a system in which this is true would be one which is easy to handle, we have no assurance that all systems are of this kind. We do not know whether the kinetic energy of a number of electrons making up an electric current is the sum of the kinetic energies of the individual electrons, or whether it is described by means of some nonadditive property. Nor do we know whether the mass of an electron is the sum of the masses of its elements.

In conclusion, Bridgman suggests that if we try to look ahead we can see what we shall require of our methodology in the future. We must make a more self-conscious and detailed analysis of all of our physical concepts with a view to clarifying their operational meanings. We shall probably find that as we penetrate deeper the number of concepts will become smaller. Finally, we must examine our mental constructs in the effort to determine which of them are embodied in reality and which of them are pure

inventions. A good construct is one which possesses a unique correspondence with the data in terms of which it is defined, which is uniquely connected with other physical phenomena different from those which entered into its definition, and which is useful in suggesting new experiments.

BEING AND TIME

Author: Martin Heidegger (1889-   )
Type of work: Existential metaphysics
First published: 1927

PRINCIPAL IDEAS ADVANCED

The world, existentially and phenomenologically understood, is a region of human concern; man is a being-in-the-world, in that by participation and involvement the world becomes constitutive of man's being.

Man has being in an environment; and his world is a world he shares with others.

Man is a creature of concerns; in relation to environment, his concerns are practical; in relation to the communal world, his concerns are personal.

The three fundamental features of man are factuality (he is already involved in the world), existentiality (he is a project and a possibility, that which has been, but also that which can become), and fallenness (he has the tendency to become a mere presence in the world, failing to make the most of his possibilities because of gossip, curiosity, and ambiguity).

Through anxiety man encounters nothingness and becomes aware of his finitude and the necessity of death; but through resolution man, who moves in time from past to future through the present, appraises himself, chooses with the whole of his being, and thereby achieves authentic existence.

The primary philosophical problem for Heidegger is the problem of Being. His major philosophical treatise, *Being and Time,* constitutes an attempt at a formulation of the basic questions and forms of analysis which are to lead to a clarification of the meaning and structures of Being. The form of analy-

sis which peculiarly characterizes *Being and Time* is what Heidegger calls *Daseinsanalytik* (analysis of human being). This form of analysis is adopted because it is believed that man is the portal to the deeper levels of reality, and that only through a disciplined analysis and description of human being can the path be opened for an apprehension of Being itself.

Heidegger, in his analysis and description of human being or presence (*Dasein*), makes use of the phenomenological method. Philosophy thus becomes "phenomenological ontology." The ontological content of philosophy is Being, and the method which is used to clarify and explicate the meaning of Being is phenomenology. Heidegger was a student of Husserl, and at least in part took over Husserl's transcendental phenomenology and its program of a return "to the data themselves." Adherence to this formula, argues Heidegger, will preclude abstract constructions and formulations, sterile concepts, and the adoption of pseudo-questions which tend to conceal the phenomena or the data rather than reveal them. In the use of the phenomenological method Heidegger seeks to get back to the data of immediate experience, and describe these data as they "show themselves" in their primitive disclosure. The word "phenomenon" has a Greek etymological root φαινόμενον (*phainomenon*), derived from the Greek verb φαινεσθαι (*phainesthai*), which means: that which shows itself or that which reveals itself. The original Greek meaning of λογος (*logos*), the second constitutive etymological element in the word "phenonenology," is discourse, which "opens to sight" or "lets something be seen." Thus, phenomenology, properly understood as the *logos of the phenomenon*, is the disciplined attempt to open to sight that which shows itself, and to let it be seen as it is. In using the phenomenological method, one must therefore discard all preconceived logical and epistemological constructions and seek to examine and describe the phenomena as they show themselves.

The application of the phenomenological method in the analysis of human being or *Dasein* discloses first of all the foundational experience of "being-in-the-world." Man emerges in a world of going concerns and initially discovers himself in his engagement and involvement in practical and personal projects. Heidegger's phenomenological and existentialist concept of the world should not be confused with any objective conceptualization of the world as a substance or an abstract continuum of points. It is Heidegger's persistent argument that Descartes' conceptualization of the world as a *res extensa* entailed a phenomenological falsification of the world as a datum of immediate experience. The world is not an extended substance or an objective spatial container into which man is placed. The world, existentially understood, is a field or region of human concern which is never disclosed independent of this concern. There is no world without man. Thus, to say that man's being is a "being-in-the-world" is to describe human reality in terms of a self-world correlation which underlies all concrete participation and engagement. Man is *in* the world in the sense of being *in* a profession, being *in* the army, being *in* politics, being *in* love, and the like. The relationship between man and the world is not that of a coinherence of substances or objects, but rather the relationship of existential participation and involvement. *Dasein* is in the world in the sense of "being preoccupied, producing, ordering, fostering, applying, sacrificing, undertaking, following through, inquiring, questioning, observing, talking over, or agreeing." The phenomenon of "being-in" denotes the intimacy and familiarity of "being-with" as distinct from the objective spatial proximity of "being-besides."

As the phenomenon of world is falsified when understood as a substance or objectivized entity, so also human being or *Dasein* is distorted when interpreted as a substantial self or a self-identical subject. Again, the error of Descartes' isolation of the thinking substance (*res cogitans*) is disclosed, and the spurious character of the epistemological quandaries which such a view entails is made apparent. Man is not an isolated epistemological subject who first apprehends his own existence and then seeks proof for an objective external world. In his primordial experience man already has his world given in his immediate concerns and preoccupations. The world is constitutive of his being. It is in this way that Heidegger's phenomenology undercuts the subject-object dichotomy, bequeathed by the Cartesian tradition to contemporary epistemological theory, and liberates the self from its lonely, worldless isolation.

A phenomenological description of man's being-in-the-world shows that the world is structurally differentiated into various regions or existential modalities. There is the region of the *Umwelt* (environment), initially disclosed through the utensils which *Dasein* uses in his practical concerns. My world is disclosed in one of its modifications as an instrumental world in which utensils are accessible for the realization of my various undertakings. The German word *Zuhandensein*, which can be translated as "at-handness," designates this accessibility of utensils which constitutes an integral part of my world. Utensils are "at-hand" for one's use and application. But my *Umwelt* is also disclosed in the mode of *Vorhandensein* ("on-handness"). This modality lacks the existential proximity of "at-handness," and is epistemologically secondary and derivative. Heidegger's favorite illustration of these two modifications of the *Umwelt* or environment is his example of the hammer and the act of hammering. In man's primitive experience of his world the hammer is an instrument with which he hammers. The hammer is revealed as a utensil or instrument through the act of hammering. On this level of experience, knowledge and action, or understanding and doing, are in an inseparable unity. Action is already a form of knowledge, and knowledge involves action. One can, however, objectivize one's environmental world and view one's hammer as a physical object in abstraction from its instrumental value. When a hammer becomes a mere object or thing we can speak of it only as being "on-hand" as contrasted with being "at-hand." The hammer in the mode of "on-handness" becomes the object of a theoretical, scientific construction, and is defined in terms of the qualities of weight, composition, size, and shape which constitute it as a material substance. When we say that the hammer *as utensil* is heavy, we mean that it will render more difficult the act of hammering. When we say the hammer *as object* is heavy, we mean that it has such and such a scientifically determined weight. The mode of "at-handness" is thus man's existentially primitive mode—the mode through which *Dasein* first encounters his world in his practical concerns. The world as "on-hand" is a later construction

Man's "being-in-the-world" thus includes a relatedness to an environmental region—either in the mode of "at-handness" or "on-handness." But man's environment does not exhaust his world. Coupled with his relatedness to an environmental region is his relatedness to a communal region. The *Dasein*-world correlation encompasses a *Mitwelt* as well as an *Umwelt*. Man's world is a world which he shares with others. Human being is essentially communal (*"Dasein ist wesenhaft Mitsein"*). The communality of human being is a pervasive phenomenon which shows itself in man's experience of aloneness as assuredly as in his experience of being-with-others. Aloneness is itself a deficient mode of being-with. Man experiences aloneness only as a privation of an original communal relatedness. Thus *Dasein* possesses an indelible communal character. In society and in solitude man is structurally a communal creature. Now for the most part man exists in the unauthentic communal mode of the "anonymous one." To exist in the mode of the "anonymous one" is to exist in one's communal world in such a way that man's unique selfness is depersonalized and reduced to the status of an "on-hand" being. In short, man transforms himself and an other self into an object or a thing, thus depriving both of their unique existential freedom which alone makes authentic communication possible.

The movements of the *Mitwelt* are conceptualized in terms of the categories and relations which obtain in the *Umwelt*, and man becomes a tool or utensil which can be used by another, or a mere object or thing. The "anonymous one," thus depersonalized, moves in the realm of the customs, habits, and conventions of everyday life. He succumbs to what Heidegger calls the everydayness of existence. He simply takes on the mechanical habits, the established customs, and the accepted conventions of everyday life. The "anonymous one" is further characterized by an "averageness" in which the average becomes the measure of his potentialities and the final standard for his creativity. He lives by a spurious "golden mean" in which social behavior is calculated on the basis of socially binding "laws of averages." This leads to a leveling process in which all superiority is flattened and all originality trivialized. Publicity is another existential quality of the "anonymous one." He "opens" himself to the public, conforms to its demands and opinions, accepts its standards, and thus retreats from personal commitment and responsible decision. *Das Man* designates that leveled and reduced self which thinks what the public thinks, feels what the public feels, and does what the public does.

In the various projects of his "being-in-the-world" *Dasein* is disclosed to himself as a creature of care or concern. His existential relation to his environmental world is a relation of practical concern, and his relation to his communal world is one of personal concern. Man's engagement or involvement in his practical and personal projects discloses *Dasein* as that being whose movements are peculiarly characterized by the existential quality of concern. Concern is the ground determinant of the being of *Dasein*. Concern permeates every modality of his "being-in-the-world." Heidegger finds it to be significant that this existential self-understanding of human being as concern was already expressed in an old Latin myth attributed to Hyginus, the compiler of Greek mythology:

As Concern was going across a river she saw some clay. Thoughtfully she took a piece of it and began to form it. As she was contemplating that which she had made, Jupiter appeared. Concern begged Jupiter to bestow spirit upon that which she had formed. This wish Jupiter happily granted her. But when Concern wished to give her name to that which she had made, Jupiter protested and demanded that his name be used. While Concern and Jupiter were disputing over the name, Earth arose and demanded that her name be used as it was she who had offered a piece of her body. The disputing parties sought out Saturn as judge, and he submitted the following decision: "You, Jupiter, as you have given the spirit, shall take the spirit at death. You, Earth, as you have given the body, you shall then again receive the body. But Concern, since she has first formed this creature, may possess it as long as it lives. And as there is a dispute concerning the name, so let it be called 'homo' as it has been made out of earth (humus)."

The fable clearly expresses the point that man has his source in concern, and concern will permeate his being as long as he lives. Man's being-in-the-world has the indelible stamp of concern. Also, the fable is explicit in showing that it is Saturn (time) who submits the final decision relative to the nature of man, making it clear that temporality provides the ontological ground and inner meaning of this creature that has been formed by concern.

The peculiar task of Heidegger's phenomenological ontology is that of a delineation of the constitutive features of *Dasein*, who has been defined as Concern. The three foundational features of *Dasein*, all of which have attached to them a temporal significance, are factuality, existentiality, and fallenness.

The factuality of *Dasein* characterizes man's naked "thereness"—his abandonment or "throwness." As he discloses himself in the various concerns of his being-in-the-world, man finds that he has been thrown into a world without consultation and abandoned to the chance factors which have already constituted him. He discovers himself as already brought into being, a fact among facts, part of a going concern, involved in situations which he has not created and in which he must remain as long as he is. In Heidegger's analysis of factuality we can anticipate the significance of temporality as the final ontological meaning of concern. Factuality expresses primarily the directionality of pastness. *Dasein* reveals himself as *already* being-in-the-world. He is already begun and has a past through which he has been defined and shaped. His factuality is his destiny.

The second constitutive structure of *Dasein* is *existentiality*. This structure points to man's disclosure of himself as a project and a possibility. Man is that which he has been, but he also is that which he can become. Man finds himself thrown into the world, but he also experiences freedom and responsibility to transform his world and redefine himself in his concerns with it. This involves an apprehension of human being in terms of possibilities. *Dasein* as possibility is projected into the future. Thus, existentiality is temporally rooted in futurity as factuality is rooted in the past. In a sense existentiality and factuality are polar elements of human being. By virtue of his factuality man is always already thrown into a situation; by virtue of his existentiality he exists as possibility and understands himself as moving into a future.

The third structural element in the ontological constitution of *Dasein* is *fallenness*. Fallennesss points to the universal tendency of man to lose himself in his present preoccupations and concerns, alienating himself from his unique and personal future possibilities. Fallen man exists as mere presence, retreating from his genuine self which always involves his past and his future. He thus becomes a reduced self. The fallenness of human being receives its most trenchant expression in the movements of gossip, curiosity, and ambiguity. Gossip is an unauthentic modification of speech which simply repeats the accepted, everyday, conventional, and shallow interpretations of the public. No decisive content is communicated, because gossip is concerned only with a reiteration of the clichés which reflect the present and restricted world horizons of the "anonymous one." Curiosity, which is always allied with gossip, indicates man's insatiable desire to explore everything in his present environment simply for the sake of discovering novelty—not for the purpose of authentic understanding, but simply to engage in pursuits which will provide momentary distraction. Ambiguity is the lack of comprehension and singleness of purpose which results when the self

has forfeited its unique possibilities in its preoccupation with the present. Thus, factuality, existentiality, and fallenness constitute the three basic ontological structures of human being. These structures are correspondingly rooted in the three modes of temporality—past, future, and present. Factuality qualifies *Dasein* as already-in-the-world, having arrived from a past; existentiality qualifies him as purposive or as existing in-advance-of-himself; and fallenness qualifies him as present with the world in his everyday concerns.

A phenomenological description which seeks to penetrate to the immediate experience of being-in-the-world will need to give disciplined attention to the phenomenon of anxiety. Anxiety is described by Heidegger as a ground-determinant of the human situation. Anxiety is the basic mood which discloses the threatening character of the world by confronting man with his irremovable finitude. Anxiety, first of all, should not be confused with fear. Fear has a definite object which can be specified either within the region of the environmental world or the communal world. A utensil, an object, or a person constitutes the source of fear. But the source of anxiety remains indeterminate. That which threatens cannot be localized or specified. It remains indefinable. The source of anxiety is nothingness. Through anxiety man encounters the nothingness which is constitutive of his finitude. Anxiety, properly understood, is an intentional disclosure. It is an instance of pre-theoretical intentionality, pointing to and revealing a most vital aspect of one's being-in-the-world. The theoretical intentionality of pure thought can never disclose

891

nothingness because thought is always directed to an object, but nothingness can never be objectivized or conceptualized. It can be experienced only on a pre-theoretical and pre-objective level. The interior of human being remains opaque to purely theoretical analysis. It can be penetrated only through pre-objective elucidation and description. This accounts for Heidegger's emphasis on the phenomenological importance of man's "preconceptual understanding of Being." The nothingness, pre-objectively disclosed through anxiety, brings *Dasein* face to face with his radical finitude. The accentuation of the principle of finitude is a theme which runs throughout the whole of Heidegger's philosophy. His *Daseinsanalytik* is in its central intention a philosophy of human finitude. In this disclosure of nothingness and finitude anxiety also reveals the contingency of human existence and the threat of meaninglessness. Anxiety breaks down the superficial, surface realities which conceal man's true predicament and reveals the world as something strange and uncanny. The trusted world of everyday and mediocre concerns collapses. What was previously a refuge of security and contentment now becomes strange and puzzling. The world has nothing more to offer. Its former significance is reduced to insignificance. All protections and supports vanish. Nothing remains.

As anxiety discloses man's finitude, so also it discloses his indelible transitoriness—his "being-unto-death." The death which is examined in Heidegger's phenomenological analysis is not the death of the "death-bed," or death understood as the biological termination of empirical reality. Such a view of death is an objectivized view which can be understood only by the one observing, never by the one who has to die. The "being-unto-death" of which Heidegger speaks is an experience of death which interpenetrates one's subjectivity. It is a death which one understands and appropriates in one's existential concerns. It is a mode of existence which *Dasein* takes over as soon as he is. Death is a phenomenon which embraces the whole of life and entails a responsibility for life. In anticipating his final and irrevocable limit of being-in-the-world, *Dasein* appraises himself in light of the finite possibilities which precede his end, shoulders his responsibility for these possibilities, and authentically chooses himself as a whole. As had already been taught by Kierkegaard, death makes a difference for life. The anticipation of death infuses every choice with existential urgency. Man's possibilities are limited by his final end—which is always imminent. As soon as man is born he is old enough to die. Thus, he must seek to take over his death by affirming himself with the whole of his being in every decisive moment. But for the most part man engages in a retreat or flight from his having to die. He loses himself in an unauthentic being-unto-death, whereby death is objectivized and externalized as an "on-hand" factuality which befalls man in general but no one in particular. This is the death of the "anonymous one." An authentic being-unto-death, on the other hand, is an awareness of death as a unique possibility which I, and I alone, will have to face. Numerous responsibilities are transferable and can be carried out by proxy. But no such transferability is possible for the task of dying. There is no dying by proxy. Every *Dasein* must die his own death.

Conscience and guilt play a dominant role in Heidegger's *Daseinsanalytik*. Conscience is defined as the "call of concern" which summons man to an awareness of his existential guilt. Man as such is guilty. Guilt is an inevitable and irreducible determinant of human being. The guilt which is under discussion in *Being and Time* is quite clearly not a moral quality which man may or may not possess. It is a determinant of his finite existence as such. The concept of guilt in Heidegger's analysis is a trans-moral concept. The moral view of guilt is rooted in an ontology of "on-handness," wherein guilt is externalized and defined as a "thing" or an "on-hand" reality. The common expression of such an unauthentic, external view of guilt is the court scene representation in which man is pronounced guilty by an external judge. The trans-moral concept of guilt understands guilt as a structural implication of finitude and nothingness. *Dasein* as a field of concern is basically a structure of finite possibilities, which he is free to actualize in his concrete choices. These possibilities are primarily rooted in the future. However, the past also holds possibilities which can be repeated. Thus, in his temporal existence *Dasein* is ever projected into one or another of his possibilities, choosing one and excluding another. Choice involves an inevitable sacrifice or exclusion of possibilities. In every choice *Dasein* is "cutting off" possible alternatives which might have been but are not. These nonchosen possibilities remain structurally a part of his being

and constitute one expression of the nothingness of his existence. "The nothingness which we have in mind belongs to *Dasein*'s being-free for his existential possibilities. This freedom *is* only in the choice of one, which means not-having-chosen and not-being-able-to-choose the other." Conscience calls me to my possibilities, but I must always sacrifice some of these possibilities in choosing others. In actualizing one I am not actualizing another, and thereby becoming guilty. Every action implies guilt, but it is impossible to exist without acting. Thus, guilt is an irremovable quality of human being.

One would not be too far amiss in saying that the crowning phenomenological concept in Heidegger's *Daseinsanalytik* is resolution. Anxiety has disclosed nothingness and finitude, and has revealed a world without supports. The existential reality of death has made man aware of his ephemeral or transitory being. Conscience has summoned *Dasein* to an acknowledgment of his inevitable guilt. But man must drive beyond these discontinuities of existence and affirm his being. He does this through resolution. Resolution thus becomes a *sine qua non* for authentic existence. This resolution is given its final meaning in Heidegger's seminal interpretation of the character of human time. Heidegger's analysis of time is in a real sense the focal point of the whole discussion in *Being and Time*. Central to Heidegger's analysis is his distinction between the quantitative, objective, and scientifically measured clock time, and the qualitative, subjective time of human concern. Quantitative time is understood as an endless, passing, irreversible succession of discrete, objectivized nows. Nows are conceptualized as "on-hand" entities, thus betraying the restriction of this view of time to the region of "*Vorhandensein*." In "clock time" present moments are viewed as discrete entities. Some moments have gone by and we call them the past. They are no longer real. Some moments are yet to come and we call them the future. They are not yet real. Only the present is real. Qualitative or existential time, as contrasted with "clock time," understands time as an ecstatic unity. The past, future, and present are inseparable phases of the care-structure of human existence. "Temporality temporalizes itself fully in each ecstasy, *i.e.*, in the ecstatic unity of the complete temporalizing of temporality there is grounded the wholeness of the structural complex of existentiality, factuality, and fallenness, which comprises the unity of the care-structure." In existential time the past is *still* real and the future is *already* real. Whereas quantitative time gives priority to the present, existential time gives priority to the future. Man's concerns are primarily oriented to the future. However, the past retains its significance in an existential view of time. The past is never existentially finished. It holds possibilities which can be repeated. Thus, we find Heidegger insisting on the importance of the notion of repetition—a notion which was introduced into modern philosophy by Kierkegaard.

Existential time provides the ontological horizon for man's self-understanding of his historicity. *Dasein* exists historically, which means that he is always arriving from a past, moving into a future, and deciding in the present what he is to become. The authen-

tic self faces the future in resolution. Man achieves integrity when he apprehends himself in his temporal and historical movements, acknowledges his past and future possibilities, appraises himself in light of his final possibility (death), and chooses in the moment with the *whole* of his being. Such a self is unified or authentic. Authenticity and unauthenticity thus receive their final clarification in Heidegger's discussion of time and history. The unauthentic self of the "anonymous one" is a reduced self—a self which has lost itself by virtue of its fall into the mode of "on-handness" and its consequent sacrifice to the present. The "anonymous one" exists in a depersonalized and objectivized mode, in which he has dispersed himself in present concerns to the neglect of both future and past. The time which becomes normative for the "anonymous one" is the quantitative time of the clock and the calender. But this time applies only to the mode of "on-handness." The final meaning of unauthenticity is thus found in the tendency of man to reduce himself and other selves to "on-hand" reality—to a thing or an object—which has no temporal significance beyond its simple presence as a discrete now. The authentic time of human existence is a unique, qualitative time in which past and future are always co-present. *Dasein* exists authentically when he acknowledges the unique qualitative time of his personal being, and seeks to unify the three ecstasies which are structurally a part of his being as long as he is. These ecstasies are unified in resolute choice. The resolute *Dasein* thus achieves or wins his authenticity when he takes over his unique past, anticipates his unique future, and chooses in such a manner that his past and future are integrated. The past is held in memory, the future is courageously faced, and the moment is creatively affirmed as the "opportune time" for decisive action.

REALMS OF BEING

Author: George Santayana (1863-1952)
Type of work: Metaphysics
First published: 1927-1940 (*The Realm of Essence,* 1927; *The Realm of Matter,* 1930; *The Realm of Truth,* 1938; *The Realm of Spirit,* 1940)

PRINCIPAL IDEAS ADVANCED

There is no logical escape from skepticism; all of our philosophical beliefs are expressions of animal faith in something that makes sense out of experience.

Since essences are merely characteristics considered in abstraction from things, the leap from a consideration of essence to a belief in matter is a leap of animal faith.

Truth is that part of the realm of essence which is realized in the material universe.

Spirit, or conscious intelligence, by going beyond the limits of the present in its operations makes possible a life of reason in which action is ordered for the satisfaction of animal impulse.

Santayana considered *Realms of Being* his magnum opus. It is his most comprehensive work, and may fairly be said to contain his distinctive "system" of philosophy. Here the technical details of his thought are worked out with great virtuosity. But the work was not conceived primarily as a contribution to academic philosophy. Santayana liked to think of himself as representing "human Orthodoxy" in an age that was eager to pursue novelties. He was writing not for the professional philosopher so much as for reflective persons in every walk of life. His teachings were intended to be founded on common sense and upon principles which any mind can discover within itself.

It is characteristic of Santayana, however, that he combines the realism of common sense with a strong dose of transcendentalism. His thought may be said to have two focuses: it originates in questioning and doubt, and in an unmistakable predilection for poetry and imagination; but it is never able to escape the tug of impulse and desire. They bind it to the world and keep skepticism from hardening into dogma. Santayana's writings are a constant dialogue between these two interests or aspects of his thought. By questioning at each stage what they have affirmed, the writings arrive at a view which is neither skeptical nor naïve but combines something of both. His position is accurately indicated

895

when he is classified as a *realist;* that is, as a *critical* realist.

The philosophical implications of this dual starting-point are clearly expounded in *Scepticism and Animal Faith* (1923) which is actually an introduction to the work under discussion. A vast abyss is seen to separate the mind, with its ideas, from the existing world of things. We are reminded of Descartes by the systematic effort which Santayana makes to doubt all existence. But whereas the father of modern rationalism believed that he found in the extremity of doubt a passage from ideas to reality, Santayana freely admits to being unable to span the gulf. Logically there is no escape from skepticism; but logic is not the whole story. Every idea contemplated by the human mind is bound up with bodily impulses; there are some matters which, as animals, we *must* believe. This intentional aspect of experience, which Santayana calls "animal faith," is the basis for our convictions concerning existence. The abyss, however, remains, nor may it be lost sight of. Plato lost sight of it, ascribing reality to ideas; Descartes lost sight of it, affirming rationality of the material world; Hegel lost sight of it, ascribing existence to logic. These errors, which result from confusing the two aspects of experience, are the source of what Santayana calls "metaphysics." Since *Realms of Being* is an attempt to avoid them and their consequences, we are warned not to speak of his system as "metaphysical." (However, as a term of classification, the word fits better than any other; perhaps we can call Santayana's philosophy a *critical* metaphysics.)

When we turn from these methodological considerations to formulate a world-view, two divisions are inadequate to the complexities which unfold. In pure skepticism one is confronted with *essences* which do not exist; but there exists even then something by which they are confronted: mind or *spirit.* And the commerce which we have through animal faith with the flux of things and events demands not merely that we acknowledge the existence of *matter,* but that we make a place in the realm of essence for a special province to be known as *truth*—namely, actualized essence.

Essence, matter, truth, and spirit: these are Santayana's four "realms of being." "Being," for Santayana, is pure essence, and does not, as in popular speech, mean existence. The "realms" of being are, therefore, not four regions within the total order of things, each with a status corresponding to its peculiar kind of reality. Strictly speaking, the realms are not real at all: they are "summary categories of logic, meant to describe a single natural dynamic process, and to dismiss from organized reflection all unnecessary objects of faith."

The Realm of Essence: Santayana relates that an early hint of his "essences" came to him when he heard William James criticizing Spencer for saying that a thing passes from indefinite to definite. "Nothing," said James, "can be indefinite. Make a blot of ink at random on a piece of paper. The spot is not indefinite: it has precisely the outline that it has." This kind of determination, whether of an ink-blot or a copy-book letter, is what "essence" means in modern philosophy. The essence of the color which is before your eyes is precisely *that* kind of color, of the melody which sounds in your ears, *that* kind of melody. Take away from the image every association with its material support or with the mind which attends it: essences are the "characters" which things assume, or which minds contemplate. But, besides these, there are an innumerable multitude of essences which are never actualized either in matter or in thought. Each is individual, concrete, and absolutely and eternally what it is.

The reader, searching for historical analogies, must not think of medieval realists with their Platonizing metaphysics, but of the nominalists and particularly of Berkeley. According to Santayana, each essence is absolutely independent of every other: essences are not subordinated under one another as species and genus. Thus, the "realm of essence" is not to be thought of as a hierarchy of ideas, as an eternal Logos, in which essences are rationally connected and necessarily follow from each other. There is no eternal Reason in heaven or in the earth.

It is true that Santayana stresses with emphasis dialectic and the connections between ideas; but these connections (with the exception of purely analytical ones) are grounded not in the ideas themselves but in the bias of the mind which entertains them. All rational processes have organic roots, are expressions of the same animal intent which affords us our belief in the material world. Thus, the rational processes do not trace eternal truths but human interests. The *a priori* elements of our thought are preformations of the psyche, mental habits which result when an intention becomes settled in the mind. Our efforts after logical cogency are a healthy endeavor after consistency, which is to say, mental

harmony and peace. A finished system is a monument to the spirit which composes it. But since systems of ideas are influenced by traditions of various sorts, different systems have become classic and orthodox. But of these orthodoxies, no one is right against another, for there is no external standard by which they may be judged: the only measure of a system is its overall adequacy.

But just as there is no necessary order in the realm of essence, so things on the plane of existence have no rational connection with each other. They are in flux, and temporarily embody first one essence then another: but between the essence which comes before and that which comes after there is no dialectical relation. Causality is not in the order of logic. Neither is the hierarchy of goods. Every instance of essence in nature perfectly realizes its own essence; if we judge one thing to be more nearly perfect than another, it is again by reference to our interests.

The Realm of Matter: Matter represents the opposite pole to essence. We do not, according to Santayana, have any clear knowledge of what matter is, and when we talk about it we must be careful to distinguish between matter and some conventional idea of it— whether Aristotle's or Democritus' or Descartes' or the modern physicist's. As Santayana conceives it, matter is the "flux of existence." It has no characteristic form, but it is that which is constantly assuming first one essence and then another. We do not know it directly or even by inference, but by a kind of "transcendental reflection" analogous to that used by Kant. That is, in order to make our experience intelligible to us, we must postulate this

897

substance which gives actuality to certain essences and provides a field for our bodily action. Following these hints, we go on to postulate concerning matter that it persists, that its quantity remains the same, that each phase of matter is determined by what goes before. But these are idols of the mind, as is indeed our whole concept of an orderly nature.

Matter, then, is the host of essences. It is in flux, perpetually leaving one essence and taking another. But patterns and rhythms are observable within the change. We distinguish as a "natural moment" the interval during which a given essence is realized, and observe several moments forming configurations that we call "events." The essence which is realized by the total complex event we may call a "trope." Examples of tropes are the vibrations within a molecule, the pulse of a heart, the combination of sounds that make up a spoken word, the life-cycle of an organism, a historical epoch such as the Renaissance. Santayana does not think of tropes as perspectives, relative to an observer: they are actual structures realized in the flux.

One kind of trope has particular interest in a comprehensive work such as the present one: it is the human psyche, which, according to Santayana, is a complex of tropes, partly in conflict, partly in harmony with one another. This is not supposed to be astonishing, as if inert matter spontaneously gives rise to something as alien as life and spirit. On the contrary, we know nothing about pure matter, and must understand it as a very fertile kind of stuff which does all sorts of unpredictable things. The "laws" which we observe in nature are not to be thought of as binding. When-

ever chance produces a trope sufficiently harmonious with itself and with its environment, it tends to survive. In this way complex organisms and even conscious beings have established themselves. The soul or psyche is the sum of vital tendencies which govern the animal. In man, as in the humbler creatures, the soul's activities are almost entirely unconscious and automatic. This is not to deny that man's higher consciousness makes a difference—that it opens up to him vast new possibilities of modifying his behavior and controlling his environment. But always behavior is determined by psyche, a trope in the realm of matter. And this is no less true of intelligent and purposive acts than of instinctive and habitual ones. Consciousness may enlighten our motives, but the motives are rooted in bodily needs, and their execution depends upon adjustments and skills that have already become automatic.

The Realm of Truth: As matter clothes itself in this essence and that, it gives rise to a new realm of being, namely "truth." Truth does not belong to the material world, and it is not to be confused with events or tropes. It belongs to the realm of essence, of which it is a segment—that special segment which comes to have the special dignity of being actualized in matter. In fact, when Santayana began thinking about *Realms of Being* (as early as 1911), there were only three realms—no separate realm of truth. But the distinction between the logical determinations of essence and their material determination is a basic one for an opponent of rationalism. If it is established on the categorical level, many confusions are avoided. Hence, the decision to make truth a separate realm.

The view of truth here held to is, according to Santayana, the view of common sense—presupposed not merely in our pursuit of knowledge but in all our animal striving. The facts of the world are independent of our opinions. The essence which is realized in fact is "truth." The realm of truth is absolute and eternal, comprehending each detail of the world and relating every event to every other.

Truth, then, is not an idea or an opinion, although these share in truth insofar as they correspond to reality. When literal correspondence is out of the question, an idea may be judged true if it rewards the psyche with success in its practical enterprises. However, utility presupposes truth, and therefore must not be regarded as synonymous with it. The notion that truth is a property of ideas and judgments is one of the aberrations of idealism which, because it denies the existence of matter, can think of ideas as being related only to other ideas.

Since truth is bound up with existence, there is no purely logical truth. Mathematics, for example, which concerns only the relationship between essences, is formally cogent, but not true. Only when mathematics is applied to the world of existence is it brought into this new dimension. We have seen that the formal relation that may be traced between essences does not bind the behavior of things in which the essences are embodied. Nevertheless, mathematics has proved a useful fiction in describing the basic rhythms and tropes of the natural world. In this context, its theorems share in the truth. By the same token, the more dramatic images of poetry and myth can sometimes establish the claim to be true: for we must think humanly, and the truth for man often takes on a dramatic quality. Statistics and pointer-readings are inadequate to express the moral reality with which he is always concerned.

And so we come to an important consideration about *knowledge,* which must be carefully distinguished from truth. The latter is comprehensive, impartial, and free from any vagueness or uncertainty. Knowledge, on the other hand, is always limited, biased, and subject to error and doubt. Knowledge, because it aims at truth, makes claims about existence; but, as we have seen, every existential assertion rests at last on animal faith. Faith, therefore, is implicit in knowledge, which, on this account, can never have that certainty, self-evidence, and immutability which Plato and Descartes claimed for it. These high attributes are proper enough to dialectic and intuition, which deal only with essences; but knowledge is the pursuit of truth.

The Realm of Spirit: In introducing the consideration of knowledge and intuition, we have already entered upon the precincts of "spirit," which is Santayana's name for thought or consciousness. As we have seen, psyche is a trope within the realm of matter. It regulates the bodily behavior of the organism according to principles best understood in mechanical terms. Actually, it is a system of tropes which not infrequently are in conflict with each other and at odds with circumstances. These tensions, it would seem, are what generate awareness in the higher animals—pain being the prime example. In man this inner sensibility achieves sufficient steadiness to enter upon a life of its own.

Spirit's attachment to psyche insures that in the first instance it will bring to consciousness the urges, satisfactions, and disappointments of the body. But its spontaneity enables it to go beyond the limits of actual experience, to entertain ideas that are not present, and to invent new ones. Thus, there may grow up between spirit, with its ideals, and the actual world, a conflict which leads to melancholy. When this happens too often, spirit turns out to be a liability to psyche's health. But if spirit submits to the measure of truth, it can become psyche's truest friend, bringing new scope and perspective into man's activity, revealing to him the limits of possible achievement, and prescribing a regimen for his impulses which will lead to harmony and satisfaction. This is what Santayana describes as the "life of reason." Its use is to bring about the best adjustment between the human body and its environment.

But although the spirit renders a service to the organism, it has motives of its own. Even the most harmonious animal existence falls far short of its ideal, and if spirit is to escape from sorrow and discouragement, it must do so by fixing on other goals than those which make up the will of the particular psyche to which it is attached. If we can think of a will running through all existence, we may say that spirit finds its freedom and peace by resigning so far as possible the unique prerogatives which its own will claims, and uniting itself with the will of every struggling thing. Santayana designates this moment of spirit's coming of age by the word *metanoia* ("conversion") and the new frame of mind as *charity*.

The task of delineating this libera-

tion and fulfillment of spirit takes up the greater part of the fourth volume, involving an extended critique of the greatest religions and philosophies of life. Salvation is not to be gained by repudiating consciousness and sinking into an organic stupor, as some mystics recommend; but neither does it consist in a purely intellectual vision of the truth. While spirit must be loyal to its own affinities, which lie in the realm of essence, it cannot repudiate the existing world of which it is a part. Thus, it cannot deny matter and, in particular, the wills of living things. Naturalism and humanism seek to remedy this indifference: but merely bowing down before reality, with Spinoza and the Stoics, involves the denial of will and alienation from the good; while, pledging as one's ideal a merely human good, after the manner of Socrates, involves disloyalty to Truth, since the universe is not governed for man. The ideal to which we most suitably give our allegiance is a comprehensive one, embracing in sympathy and pity the goals of every natural thing. This is what Santayana understands by charity. It is suitably represented in the Christian story of the incarnation of God, where Spirit's scope is as wide as its own life is narrow. Knowing itself as the first-born of all creatures, it does not condemn its brethren for falling short of the ideal but cherishes their good and laments their defeat. This high calling is not beyond the reach of man; for though, on Santayana's accounting, there is no God in the usual sense, and spirit is but an accident in the world, yet the fact remains that a remarkable set of harmonies within the flux of things has preceded its emergence. As nature's highest product, it may in its

900

best moments embrace the universe's whole vast endeavor. In no lesser ideal can it find healing and rest.

The chief characteristic of this work is its catholicity, its faithfulness to the many interests which have a claim upon it. It is humanist, but not at the expense of being uncritical and un-naturalistic; it is other-worldly without ceasing to be this-worldly as well.

The peculiarity of spirit and its good is that, unlike psyche, spirit is not a power. It is not responsible for the world, but merely a guest there; neither can it do anything, only offer suggestions which psyche may or may not be persuaded to adopt.

Santayana never ceased to be inter-ested in the possibilities of bringing intelligence to bear upon moral and political matters. But as a philosopher and contemplative he did not share the enthusiasm of most reformers, both because he held that non-rational fac-tors (passion, tradition, habit) actually direct behavior, and because he knew that as a conscious animal man has problems that can never be resolved on a merely animal level. In other words, he affirmed his naturalism and materi-alism and accepted their deterministic implications, but he did not allow this to rob the spirit of independence or the immediacy of its own good, which is love without either anxiety or desire.

ETHICS

Author: Frank Chapman Sharp (1866-1943)
Type of work: Ethics
First published: 1928

Principal Ideas Advanced

A volition is right if a reflective, benevolent person would desire it to control the actions of men; right action aims at the general welfare.

Morality is a reflective, rational affair; it involves an interplay between what we take to be right at the time and what we learn to be right.

Good will and ill will conflict in moral consideration; men have both selfish and unselfish inclinations, and ethics must take this fact into account.

Objectivity in morality can be gained by relating rightness to values; the for-malists are mistaken in supposing that rightness is a function of universally applicable rules of conduct.

The good is the desirable, and the desirable is what would be desired were one judging reflectively on the basis of relevant information.

Pleasure is always good-in-itself, worth having for its own sake; right action aims at the general happiness.

Frank Chapman Sharp's *Ethics* ex-presses the results of a long and care-ful investigation of morality. It be-longs to the empirical, utilitarian tradition exemplified by Hume, though it seeks to supplement Hume by developing the objective import of moral judgments. In texture, it is both descriptive and normative.

As a philosophical discipline, ethics concerns itself with the attempt to find well-founded principles for morality, principles which can be justified and applied intelligently. Terms must be clarified and defined and as much unity as possible introduced. Ethics is an old subject which goes back at least to Socrates in the Western world and to Confucius in China. It found development in the writings of Plato and Aristotle, the Stoics, and the Epicureans. As Professor Sharp points out, the egoistic utilitarianism of Thomas Hobbes started a revival of ethical theory largely for the purpose of refuting his assumptions. Rationalism and intuitionism were developed as a base for the establishment of objective rules. In contrast, a more universalistic utilitarianism was also worked out. Something of this interplay still operates. It is well to have a book which develops so carefully and in a concrete way the utilitarian perspective. In a small posthumous book, *Good Will and Ill-Will* (1950), we find Sharp's final reply to intuitionism. It is, he argues, meaningless to talk about moral intuition when there is no universal agreement about moral matters.

The primary aim of ethics is theoretical, as in pure science, but this fact does not preclude interest in practice. As a matter of fact, practice feeds into theory and helps to illuminate it. One must, of course, keep the proper balance between them. Few ethicists have made more careful empirical investigations into morality than has Sharp.

It is a little difficult to classify Sharp's outlook in terms of recent controversy. He is certainly not an *emotivist,* for he puts stress on moral judgment. And he cannot be called a deontologist, for the right and duty have, for him, a foundation in values. Yet the larger part of his book is concerned with what is objectively right. It is apparent that G. E. Moore's famous "naturalistic fallacy" had little meaning for Sharp. He was careful to define the meanings of the terms "right" and "good" and to locate them in morality as a human affair. There is much emphasis these days on the logic of moral discourse and on the language of morals, but although Professor Sharp had a keen ear for usage, his approach was more psychological.

As a utilitarian, Sharp's approach stressed values as terminal. Right, duty, and obligation have to do with the reasonable maximizing of values for those concerned. In point of fact, Sharp intimates that, unlike the ancients, modern philosophers have reflected too little upon human values.

An important chapter in the second part of the book deals with "The Best Things in Life," such as knowledge and beauty. We should not be surprised, therefore, to find Sharp saying that his argument is of the nature of a running criticism of formalism in ethics. The center of the stage is, for him, occupied by volitions, with their motives and anticipated consequences. Volitions are natural human acts, not reducible to something else. The job is to get benevolence, or good will, free from diversions in favor of selfishness and shortsightedness. Morality in its normative aspect stands for the broad, searchlight outlook. It is easy to neglect relevant interests from lack

902

of imagination. There are psychological stimulants and depressants which must be recognized.

Sharp agrees with Aristotle in pointing out the need for moral education. Consequently, he refers to a scientific conscience which must be activated as well as a moral conscience. Conscientiousness involves care. In a broad sense, then, Sharp was a cognitivist rather than an emotivist. His concern was with enlightened judgment working with good will. The authentic is the reasonable in the context of benevolence.

One of the contributions of Sharp was his frank recognition of malevolence or ill will in human affairs. There are dysdemonic volitions as well as eudemonic ones. Desire for revenge operates in punishment. There are sadism and also cruelty. Sharp lived long enough to see these at work during the rise of communism and national socialism. As normative, morality expresses the demands of the better side of human nature.

Sharp's forte rests on the broadness of his base. There is detailed knowledge of actual moral judgments gained by the use of the questionnaire method, supplemented by careful, personal interviews. His intention was not so much statistical as a matter of exploring moral tendencies. Professor Max Otto aided Sharp in some of this work. His competence in introspective psychology of the James-Stout variety was also important. His treatment of the self illustrates this method. Desires are intrinsic to the self which, in some sense, is more enduring and of larger scope. The contrast between the desired and the desirable has point here. The element of reflection has entered. It is quite wrong to think of the self as knocked about by desires as separate forces.

Ethics was Sharp's primary interest and he knew the history of the subject thoroughly. One has the impression, in reading this book, that every topic has been mulled over. The collection of notes at the end of the book represents a return to key issues in an attempt to make the author's stand as definite as possible.

Sharp's *Ethics* goes with Dewey's and with Tuft's works as one of the solid American contributions to the subject. Of course, it reflects the period in which it was written. A book written now would probably put more stress on the results of psychiatry and on social ethics in relation to the social sciences. Sharp was a liberal and not a radical, so that what stands out is a strong ingredient of common sense. He refused to be either a pragmatist or an idealist.

Sharp discusses numerous topics of major interest in ethical theory, such as the meaning of *right*, the meaning of *good*, the sources of moral approval and disapproval, the operation of standards or ideals, the role of benevolence and of malevolence, the parts played by egoism and altruism, and the status of pleasure. The consideration of these topics will furnish a base from which to judge subjectivism, rationalism, intuitionism, aestheticism, and Sharp's own universalistic utilitarianism. After that, one can consider with him the relation of responsibility to the traditional alternatives of determinism and indeterminism. Here Sharp stresses causality and causal laws and the importance of character.

Sharp was quite aware of the need to define the term *right*. And he wanted to avoid such a tautology as would result from defining it in terms of some outer result, what the intuitionists would call a "natural property." Thus, to say that right *means* "procuring the greatest happiness for the greatest number" would merely result in repetition: actions procuring the greatest happiness for the greatest number procure the greatest happiness. No—according to Sharp, one must be more concerned with the springs of action, with character and will. The correct approach is to recognize agency and the object of moral judgment. *Right* is a term which applies to volitions that necessarily involve motives and consequences. The inner cannot be separated from the outer or, in the last analysis, the outer from the inner. To call a volition *right* means that I believe it to be such that I, in virtue of my benevolence, desire it to control the actions of men under the given conditions. Note the element of objectivity and universalization. I am thinking in a social way. To call a volition wrong is to assert that I believe it to be in conflict with the demands of good will. Of course, I may be guided largely by the acceptance of sanctioned rules. But when these are questioned, Sharp believed, the next step is an appeal to consequences in the way of general welfare. There is here the recognition of tendencies. It is doubtful that Professor Sharp believed in the Benthamite calculus except as an indication of some kind of summation of factors at work. There is meaning to quantity, fecundity, and intensity of pleasure experiences and their contrary, unpleasantness. One must work with psychologists in this area of ethics.

As has been noted, Sharp recognized the working of malevolence or ill will in human nature. These lead to dysdemonic judgments; that is, judgments deviating from welfare. Tribal morality puts the alien, in large measure, outside the group. Cultural development has meant the enlargement of the range of moral attitudes. It seems to be a historical fact that something of the nature of such an extension took place in the ancient world. It has been called an axial period and has been associated with the rise of ethical religions.

It appears that Sharp tried to avoid sentimentality about human nature by acknowledging the struggle between ill will and good will. Morality is an affair of the dominant motivation of benevolence and the sense of the community and its life, as a larger whole. It is in this fashion that Sharp qualified individualism. His discussion of "natural rights" is guided by the ideal of a balance. Rights are inseparable from duties.

Though in many ways a follower of Hume, Sharp wanted to develop the objective import of moral judgment. A right volition is one that one is ready to universalize in an impartial way. Its validity has about it something of the nature of true and false in cognition. Ideals and standards are developed and operate in moral judgments. Here, of course, is the domain of normative ethics as against merely descriptive ethics. And norms must be backed up by adequate motivation. Character enters here as it is recognized that volitions reflect a continuing source. It is from this angle that character gets its own kind of intrinsic value. An aesthetic quality is usually added as connected with moral admiration, but aesthetic theories of morality overemphasize this quality.

On the descriptive side, Sharp argued, it must be recognized that contradictory moral judgments exist. These are due to the spotlight effects of such factors as the striking good, the good of the nearer, or of what is regarded as the more excellent. These factors introduce bias. The moral job is to see the whole situation in a searchlight way, to keep the general welfare impartially before one's eyes. Apparently, Sharp believed that there are social and personal forces supporting this objectivity and impartiality. These factors work for objectivity and reasonableness. There is the increasing awareness that that volition is right which aims at the general welfare. This standard, in Sharp's opinion, corresponds to the actual working of the moral consciousness of the ordinary mind. In interviews, the searchlight outlook can replace the spotlight distortions.

It is interesting to note that Sharp contends that the sense of the welfare of the group operates in the primitive mind, though unreflectively. One would need to analyze the idea of social pressure rather carefully here. Social anthropologists are doing careful work in this field. There is stress on social pathology as well as on social health. Perhaps the feeling is increasing that mere cultural "relativity" is not the correct answer.

If morality is normative, Sharp continues, subjective valuations with their partiality must be controlled. It is easy to care most of all for what is near and known. That is one of the dangers of the exaltation of nationalism which took place in the nineteenth century and which is still continuing, mingled with ideological fervors. Moral judgment develops best in the cool hour. The Golden Rule is fundamentally correct: one must place onself in the position of others. However, one must not ignore the just demands of the self in the total picture. It is evident that Sharp thought of the ethical imagination as having a social context. There are leaders in what Bergson has called open morality. Hume pointed in this way, for he had a historical sense in his criticism of rationalism. But he was inclined to be conservative. One could consider Sharp a Humian working in another period.

What, then, is a volition for Sharp? It would seem to be a higher level desire which takes into account both *pro* and *con* factors. Morality has learned to stress the importance of what is ignored in motivation as well as of what is dominant. We blame people for what they disregard and seek to call their attention to it. An autoist who drives with great speed through a village is endangering the lives of children. Morality is a reflective, rational affair. It involves an interplay between what we take to be right at the time and what we learn to be right. These do not necessarily coincide. (There are, of course, linguistic difficulties in all this. Words have so many uses.)

Next comes Sharp's discussion of egoism, altruism, and love. Recent social psychology and psychiatry have thrown additional light on these terms. Selfishness is not something innate; it reflects the plasticity of child psychology and the anxieties of adults. Culture has much to do with it. Sharp thought that our American culture is probably too competitive in its texture. He argued for the existence of altruism as a fact. There is more "ready for service" altruism than is often admitted.

Involved in these general principles are supplementary problems. Is there a duty to the self? Sharp argues that there is as regards the future and in a given situation. What we ought not to do is pretty well established. And there is a fair amount of agreement concerning what ought to be done. Praiseworthy conduct and the conduct of the "saint" go beyond ordinary moral expectations.

There is an ambiguity between subjective rightness, which is the sincere volition of a moral agent, and objective rightness, which involves standards and criteria connected with the general welfare. Another ambiguity is that between inner and outer rightness. Inner rightness refers to the will to produce certain results, while outer rightness is a name for the results which a man ought to produce.

As Sharp saw it, there are operative in historical ethical theories varying ideas of the standard of rightness and of the *source* whence comes the standard in the human mind. In modern times, the chief conflict has been between utilitarianism and intuitionism. As in the case of Henry Sidgwick, these can be mixed.

Intuitionism, rationalism, and deontology are closely connected, Sharp believed. He calls them *anaxiotic;* that is, they seek to deny that the rightness of an action has any necessary connection with values. The two central weaknesses in intuitionism are reflected by its failure to account for moral motivation and to explain the lack of agreement on moral matters. But one cannot do justice to this position until one notes that its aim was to supplant egoism and subjectivism. The intuitionists took a short cut from the demand for objectivity to a belief that reason is a faculty for recognizing moral truths directly—in a manner analogous to the recognition of mathematical axioms. But what Sharp wanted was another foundation for objectivity. It is his contention that objectivity can be gained by linking rightness to values. But one must have a satisfactory value theory in order to defend a valve-centered ethics.

Sharp's treatment of the aesthetic approach to morals in Aristotle and the Stoics should be noted. Virtues are attractive and awaken admiration. Sharp agrees that the ideal of the Stoics of self-sufficiency had its appeal, and that Aristotle portrayed the mean between extremes sympathetically. But neither traced out the foundation for the rightness of actions.

Universalistic utilitarianism has a long history. We find something of the kind in Confucius and Mo Ti in China. Richard Cumberland, Francis Hutcheson, and Hume explored its foundations in opposition to rationalism and intuitionism in the debate which followed on Hobbes. As we have noted, Sharp undertook to complete Hume.

Since Sharp's ethics is axiological—value-centered—rather than intuitionistic, it is of interest to examine his conception of the meaning of good, standards of goodness, and the sources of goodness. Sharp's opinion was that we all use the terms "right" and "good," but that their definition requires clarification. Hedonism now comes into the picture. What can we do with what Freud called the pleasure principle?

Early hedonism, Sharp maintained, did not sufficiently recognize the fact that many of our desires are not directed toward pleasure. These are called "anhedonic" desires. Yet it seems to

906

be Sharp's conclusion, from numerous instances, that if pleasure does not finally accompany the attainment of what is desired, desire will wither. We will not then take pleasure even in anticipation. This is the familiar distinction between the idea of pleasure and pleasure in an idea.

We come now to the controversial uestion of the meaning of the term good," when what is meant is intrin-'c goodness and not instrumental alue. One position is that the more re think of intrinsic goodness and leasure, the more we tend to identify .hem. This means that the words acquire the same meaning, become synonymous. Thus, satisfaction is intrinsic value.

Consider the distinction between what is desired and the desirable. The good is the desirable and the desirable is what is reflectively judged to be worthy of desire and, of course, is also desired. Pleasure is intrinsically good, no matter whose pleasure it is. This position is called ethical hedonism and it is to be contrasted with psychological hedonism, which holds that pleasure is the sole object of desire. Since Sharp accepted anhedonic desires, he rejected psychological hedonism.

Like most ethical hedonists, Sharp denied qualitative differences in pleasure as such. Much of the belief in higher and lower pleasures comes from aesthetic attitudes and confusion between pleasure as such and our attitude towards the conditions of its occurrence. We are disturbed when a wicked man derives pleasure from his deeds. But it must be remembered that right has to do with volitions and voluntary actions in the light of motives and consequences. Morality tries to hold dysdemonic desires in check both in primary action and in punishment. Professor Sharp stressed deterrence and reform.

There are incidental issues in the *Ethics*. Sharp was opposed to indeterminism in the classical sense as rejecting causality. Probably he would have been favorable to ideas of levels of causality and some measure of self-direction. He suggests that we can improve our own character. And it should be pointed out that Sharp appeals to the role of the brain. But he rejects materialism on two grounds: (1) Berkeley's argument and (2) the irreducibility of consciousness. Any modern notion of materialism must, certainly, deal with these objections.

THE QUEST FOR CERTAINTY

Author: John Dewey (1859-1952)
Type of work: Philosophy of philosophy; pragmatism
First published: 1929

In the past the quest for certainty, to be achieved by the discovery of eternal truths and ultimate reality, led to the misleading distinction between theory and practice.

Science and philosophy, by becoming experimental and operational, have shown that idea and practice work together as instruments: ideas relate experiences and make predictions possible, and by experience ideas are tested.

Statements about present enjoyments are factual, while value judgments indicate attitudes to be assumed; such judgments are instrumental and corrigible.

The Quest for Certainty, considered against the background of traditional philosophies, is a revolutionary work. In his book Dewey does not claim originality for all of its ideas, but he justifiably asserts that were its program enacted, a revolution comparable to the Copernican would be effected not only in philosophy but also in the moral, social, and economic dimensions of daily life. That this claim is a valid one is partially verified by the pervasive influence of Dewey's teachings on many phases of American culture, especially on education. That Dewey's works should have such an influence is especially appropriate in view of his constantly recurring emphasis upon the importance of an intimate, reciprocal relationship between theory and practice. Whether the reader finds all of Dewey's methods and conclusions acceptable or not, it is undeniable that the author's searching criticism of older theories combined with constructive suggestions of remedial and progressive measures have profound practical import.

The quest about which Dewey writes is an ancient one, originating as a need for security from the perils of primitive life, security sought first, perhaps, by prayers and rites performed in an attitude proper to the holy, or on the other hand, by magical manipula-tions of fortunate or lucky tangible objects. Mystery and glamour attended the former, while the latter were regarded as more amenable to practical control. Gradually this distinction was generalized and abstracted into that between the spiritual and intellectual on the one hand and the material and practical on the other; the distinction was also between superior and inferior respectively, and resulted in an isolation of theory and knowledge from practice which has hampered human progress ever since. Action is notoriously subject to failure or at least unforeseen results; material objects are only partially amenable to man's control. Consequently, man was led to seek certainty in an eternal, immaterial realm of thought not subject to the risks of action. This was conceived as the realm of true Being or ultimate reality, unchanging, thoroughly rational and governed by the laws of logic, and hence alone the object of genuine science. The mundane world, on the contrary, was regarded as infected with non-being, unreality, and change; it was irrational and the object only of belief or opinion, not genuine knowledge. Moreover, the Good was identified with the real so that value was attainable only by knowledge, and both were dissociated from action.

The developments of these distinctions have had ramifications into almost every traditional philosophical theory, Dewey argues; the ideals of certainty in knowledge, various metaphysical views, theories about mind and how it knows—all of these, even when formulated by strongly opposing schools, have stemmed from the jealously guarded barrier between theory and practice erected in the quest for certainty. Since modern philosophy has accepted the conclusions of natural science while retaining doctrines about mind, knowledge and values formulated in pre-scientific ages, it has found itself increasingly isolated from the actual problems and values of contemporary life. Consequently, the basic problem for philosophy today is the integration of our beliefs about existence and those about values, especially since this gap has been widened by misinterpretations of certain developments of modern science.

Greek science, says Dewey, was basically aesthetic in character; its explanatory and descriptive categories, such as harmony, symmetry, and proportion, were used to organize logically the qualitative characteristics of experienced objects into kinds of species. Thus nature, considered only an inferior kind of reality patterned after the eternal forms, was known—insofar as it was an object of knowledge at all rather than of opinion or belief—by reason rather than by experience. Greek natural philosophy was also teleological, holding that things and events tended toward their own proper ends or goods and thus toward the highest and best. This outlook, lasting through the Middle Ages, fostered an attitude of acceptance rather than an art of control such as that made possible by modern science.

Galileo and other founders of the new science effected a revolution by eliminating the qualitative and purposive and by substituting the quantitative interpretation of scientific objects. Rather than classifying things into species defined by and tending toward eternal forms, the new science saw them as reducible, for its purposes, to a few basic categories of space, time, mass, and motion. Phenomena such as heat, light, mechanical motion, and electricity could be converted or translated into one another; homogeneity replaced the heterogeneity basic to the Greek view, and "All that counted for science became mechanical properties formulated in mathematical terms. . . ." The revolution was not completed at once, however. Though Newton ostensibly subscribed to the empirical approach, remnants of the old metaphysics were obvious in his belief that change occurred only in the external relations between particles of permanently fixed natures. This postulate of permanence was really evidence of the longstanding quest for certainty rather than a hypothesis experimentally verified. Even the most avowedly empiricist school showed this same bias; for them, knowledge was founded on sensory impressions given by an antecedent reality unaffected by knowing. Later, objective idealists held that reflective thought merely reproduces the rational structure of a universe constituted by an Absolute Reason. Even now realism holds that valid inquiry apprehends prior existence—it does not modify it. All these views presuppose that inference and judgment are not originative.

As the new science became truly experimental, however, this premise was abandoned; science now *"substitutes data for objects.*" This means that science, instead of taking qualitative objects such as stars and trees as finalities waiting only for logical classification, takes them as problematic, inviting further interpretation and investigation. The latter is undertaken in response to problems and unresolved difficulties which are never wholly theoretical but are always ultimately rooted in need for practical security; these problematic situations determine the lines of inquiry and the criteria of successful solution. Experimental knowledge, inference, or judgment then becomes originative in a very real sense; its "procedure is one that installs doing as the heart of knowing. . . ." Change, once regarded as evidence of the inferiority of the experienced world to the ideal and eternal, now becomes useful: "*The* method of physical inquiry is to introduce some change in order to see what other change ensues; the correlation between these changes, when measured by a series of operations, constitutes the definite and desired object of knowledge." The objects of scientific knowledge are not qualitative entities, but *events,* mathematically formulated relations between changes undergone by experienced objects, and most important for our present purposes, *consequences.*

Dewey takes physical science as a model for experimental philosophy because on the whole the former yields the best authenticated and reliable knowledge we enjoy at present, while at the same time its conclusions are corrigible and its hypotheses subject to revision in the light of future evidence and problems. Besides, in its technological applications it is as a matter of fact already the dominant feature of modern life. Philosophy can learn from it,

Dewey believes, how to approach the basic modern problem of reintegrating beliefs about existence with those about values, as well as how to avoid some of the more technical philosophical problems to which traditional theories inevitably led.

Dewey cites with approval Bridgman's statement in *The Logic of Modern Physics* (1927): ". . . we mean by any concept nothing more than a set of operations; *the concept is synonymous with the corresponding set of operations.*" The philosophical implications of such an experimental empiricism (as distinquished from traditional sensational empiricism), understood at the time by only a few thinkers such as William James and Charles Sanders Peirce, are so far-reaching as to make it "one of three or four outstanding feats of intellectual history." It shows that neither sensational empiricism nor *a priori* rationalism was wholly right or wholly wrong: ideas are empirical in origin, but sensory qualities, to be significant, must be related by ideas; the new method's concepts of scientific objects are neither *a priori* nor reducible to sensation. The object of knowledge is "eventual; that is, it is an outcome of directed experimental operations, instead of something in sufficient existence before the act of knowing." Thus the sensory and rational elements of knowledge do not compete but cooperate; the latter are used to organize and direct, the former to test and verify or correct. Conclusions, not the previously given, are *truly known;* but conclusions of former investigations become in turn instrumental to the achievement of new solutions.

The operational method makes mind a participant rather than a mere spectator in the knowing situation. As

910

is illustrated by the Heisenberg principle of indeterminancy, the act of observation is itself an essential ingredient in what is known. From this point of view, then, nature is neither rational nor irrational as it has been described traditionally, but is, rather, intelligible; it is *to be* known through intelligence. This approach also yields new definitions of intelligence, thought, and mind. Merely mechanical and animal responses to uncertain and perilous situations are reactions or direct actions, but "response to the doubtful as such" is definitive of mind and thinking, and when responses "have a directed tendency to change the precarious and problematic into the secure and resolved, they are *intellectual* as well as mental." Misinterpretations of Newtonian science, by emphasizing the difference between ordinary perceptual experience and the scientific formulation of nature, had reinforced the metaphysical distinction between mind and body, but in Dewey's view, "There is no separate 'mind' gifted in and of itself with a faculty of thought; such a conception of thought ends in postulating the mystery of a power outside of nature and yet able to intervene within it." As defined above, thinking is observable behavior, whereas traditional theories on the contrary tried to explain the more by the less obvious. Now with our greater understanding of the relation between sensory organs and perception we are able to conceive the same relation as holding between the brain and thought.

One stronghold of the rationalistic and mentalistic schools, however, and one not adequately accounted for by traditional empiricism, was the structure of mathematics. Because mathematics seemed to rest on self-evident axioms known intuitively, and because of the universality, immutability, ideality, and logical necessity of mathematics, it was thought to demonstrate the subsistence of a realm of eternal essences and a non-physical reality; the applicability of mathematics to the physical world, moreover, seemed to show a rational element even therein. Does the operational theory of ideas, together with its implications concerning the nature of mind and thought, break down here? Dewey thinks not. We must distinguish between overt and symbolical operations, operations to be enacted and those merely possible but without actual consequences. Just as the concepts of space, time, and motion were finally seen to be ways of correlating observations rather than as reflecting properties of Being, and their worth was found in the former function, so logical and mathematical principles and relationships may be interpreted. They may have arisen from practical needs for manipulation and organization of physical things, later to be developed more fully and independently of immediately instrumental purposes. Men then become interested in such operations as operations which, when symbolized, can be performed without any direct reference to existence. That this is the case seems most clearly illustrated by the history of geometry, which originated in the need for measurement of utilitarian objects. The formal order and internal relations such systems show are analogous to the self-consistent structure of a machine designed for a certain purpose. The means-consequence relation as exemplified in the operation of a machine may be *thought* abstractly as an operation to which the imperfections of actual machines are irrelevant;

so conceived, the function has the ideality, immutability, internal necessity, and universality which characterize the realm of essence supposedly encountered in logic and mathematics.

The worth of a machine is judged by the efficacy with which it performs the function for which it was designed, and the more abstractly this function is conceived—the more it is idealized—the more clearly it can be understood. But in the conception of function ideas for improvement are germinated. Thus, the operational or experimental method is capable of projecting new goals and values and of instituting its own standards. It is imperative that this lesson learned from science be applied in the moral, social, and political life, where it is not yet fully operative. The apparent value-sterility of quantitative and operational science can now be regarded as illusory, the illusion being rooted in the notion that science discloses reality as it is in itself. The experimental method is an effective way of thinking of things, but since it is not the only way to think of them, it is not actually inimical to qualitative experience, and it can make positive contributions to the qualitative aspects of human life by affording means of making values more available and secure. We recall that, according to Dewey, the main problem for modern philosophy is to reintegrate beliefs about existence and those about values. It is obvious now that his purpose in tracing the development of operationalism and instrumentalism is to show their significance for what he calls, typically, the "*construction*" of good, suggesting thereby that values, like objects of knowledge, are not so much given as achieved.

By "value" Dewey means "whatever is taken to have rightful authority in the direction of conduct." But there are still rival theories about the status of values comparable to the traditional epistemological opposites, empiricism and rationalism. Some writers would equate goods with actual enjoyments, while others see them as eternal, universal, absolute. Dewey favors the empirical and subjective theories to the extent that they relate "the theory of values with concrete experiences of desire and satisfaction," but the operational approach again makes a significant emendation: values are not antecedently given, but are enjoyments attained as *consequences*. Previous goods and present enjoyments are problematic, as are immediately experienced qualitative objects in relation to knowledge. The crucial differences here are indicated in the very suffixes of terms such as "the enjoyed and the enjoyable, the desired and the desirable, the satis*fying* and the satis*factory*." This is in no sense to derogate immediate enjoyments and likings, but mere feelings have no claim over us as ideals and future goods, any more than objects as immediately experienced are adequate as scientific objects. Whereas propositions about present enjoyments are factual and may be of instrumental worth, value judgments and appraisals indicate attitudes *to be* assumed and hence do make claims on us. Dewey summarizes this view in what he describes as his main proposition: "*Judgments about values are judgments about the conditions and the results of experienced objects; judgments about that which should regulate the formation of our desires, affections and enjoyments.*"

Value judgments, then, like their counterparts in science, are relational

912

in nature. They, too, are instrumental and never final, and are thus corrigible. There are criteria of goods—for example, genuine goods are not later regretted; in achieving goods concern is centered on the valuable object rather than on the mere feeling of satisfaction—but such criteria are never absolute and fixed. It is thus impossible to set up a detailed catalog of values in hierarchical order. Dewey's approach "would place *method and means* upon the level of importance that has, in the past, been imputed exclusively to ends," for as long as ends alone are considered ideal and of true worth, while means are scorned as merely practical, ends fail to be realized. While failure to achieve the good has been attributed to perversity of will, the real obstacle has been lack of adequate knowledge of means. Hence the traditional elevation of spirit over matter is similarly mistaken, for the material serves as means.

The traditional separation of ends and means, another reflection of that of theory and practice, has left action without the guidance afforded only by knowledge. Consequently, some means, such as material wealth, have been overvalued as ends in the absence of any adequate philosophy of values appropriate to contemporary problems. The technological applications of science have been used selfishly and irresponsibly. Nowhere is the failure properly to relate ends and means more evident than in industrial life, and the resulting tragedy is that enjoyment of the highest social and cultural values, the truly human goods, is dependent on economic conditions ignored by many ethical philosophers. Our economy tends therefore to evade moral guidance as irrelevant and to be frankly materialistic, but the remedy is not to treat economics as beneath the notice of ethics; it is rather to apply here the instrumentalist approach.

Whereas mechanistic philosophy rejected the concept of purpose as explanatory of natural events, the developments of modern science have made clear the role of the observer in knowledge; and Dewey holds that in a significant sense purpose has been restored to nature, since "distinctively human conduct can be interpreted and understood only in terms of purpose." By removing the artificial barriers between knowledge and practice, science and values, and the consequent false problems such as those of the relationships between mind and body, spirit and matter, nature can be regarded as the ultimate source of all ideals and goods. To remove such obstacles, to free men's minds and hearts from slavery to the past, to turn them from the quest for an illusory certainty to discoverable paths to enjoyable goods, is the task of contemporary philosophy. No longer in competition with science through claims to sole superior knowledge of reality, philosophy takes up the task of exploring the richly various ways of putting science to truly human use.

MIND AND THE WORLD-ORDER

Author: Clarence Irving Lewis (1883-   )
Type of work: Epistemology
First published: 1929

PRINCIPAL IDEAS ADVANCED

A priori *truths are definitive in nature; they specify the real because of antecedently determined criteria of what is to be called "real."*

Empirical *truth is never more than probable because descriptions of matters of fact are hypothetical propositons, pragmatic in character.*

Knowledge *is the result of interpreting the sensuously given by means of a priori concepts; thus, there is no contradiction between the relativity of knowledge (to the concepts) and the independence of the object (understood in terms of the given).*

To know *is to have reason to expect that were we to act in certain ways, our experience would present the character we expect.*

The a priori *has its origin in mind, but its applicability is a function of the world order; a world which would not, relative to some interpretative act of mind, exhibit order is practically inconceivable.*

Pragmatism, sometimes called the characteristically American philosophy, is usually considered to have been best exemplified in the writings of William James, C. S. Peirce, and John Dewey. The position is sometimes called "humanism" (for example, the point of view developed by the English philosopher, F. C. S. Schiller) and sometimes called "instrumentalism." Although there were many variations in the specific philosophies of these individuals, they shared a belief in the relativity of truth to the concrete verification processes and to the practical role which man plays in the world. In general they were in agreement also in being more or less hostile towards metaphysics, at least of an absolutistic sort, and feeling that a view of the universe which "made no difference" to the common man, either in the sense that it could not be confirmed or disproved by observable phenomena, or

in the sense that it did not help him to live a better life, was really meaningless, and that indulgence in speculation of this kind was a waste of time.

Except for Peirce, none of this group had any great familiarity either with epistemology or with modern logic and its problems. They approached philosophy largely from the "human" point of view—through ethics, social and political philosophy, religion, education. C. I. Lewis has had many of the same interests that Peirce did, and, like Peirce, he has made important contributions to the fields of the philosophy of science and symbolic logic. Lewis's *Survey of Symbolic Logic* (1918) is one of the standard works in this area. In *Mind and the World-Order*, this broad knowledge of the nature of deductive systems and of the difference between *a priori* and *a posteriori* cognition is used to develop a position which Lewis chose to call "conceptualistic pragmatism." It has much in common with the views of the earlier pragmatists, and Lewis frankly acknowledges his indebtedness to these philosophers; but it also has certain distinctive aspects. For this reason it deserves careful consideration as an important contemporary philosophical position. Posterity will undoubtedly credit Lewis with having modified pragmatism in such a way as to make it compatible with the methodologies of the mathematical and natural sciences.

Lewis attempts to reduce his point of view to three principles: (1) *A priori* truths are not forms of intuition or categories which determine the content of experience; they are, rather, definitive in nature and limit reality only in the sense that whatever is called "real" is selected from experience by means of criteria which are antecedently determined. (2) The application of any *a priori* concepts to a particular experience is hypothetical because it is instrumental or pragmatic; consequently, empirical truth is never more than probable. (3) No belief in the conformity of experience to the mind or its categories is required, for a complete nonconformity of these two aspects of knowledge is inconceivable.

To explain these principles Lewis begins with an analysis of the philosophical method. Philosophy is not "another science," nor is it a substitute for science. It is the critical and reflective application of the mind to experience. It deals with what is already familiar to us, but it analyzes this familiarity into the clear ideas which constitute it. Philosophy begins with the experiences of reality, goodness, and validity, which we all have, and attempts to clarify these notions by critical con-

sideration of what is implicitly in them and therefore does not transcend experience. (A person with no sense of reality will not acquire one by the study of metaphysics.) More specifically, this analysis of experience involves the discovery of *categories*—the formulation of the criteria of reality. Experience does not determine its own categories; *mind* provides these criteria and they are imposed upon the given by our active attitude. Philosophy is not empirical if this claim means that it takes what is merely given to the mind as the totality of experience; nor is it analytic in the sense that it accepts a ready-made experience. Philosophy is not rationalistic if this claim means that it forces reality into a Procrustean bed; but it is rationalistic in the sense that it is particularly concerned with that aspect of experience which the mind contributes by its interpretive act.

Analysis of knowledge reveals two elements: the concept and the sensuously given. The former is the product of thought; the latter is merely presented, and involves no such activity. The conceptual element is *a priori*, and philosophy can be defined as the study of the *a priori* in the sense that it undertakes to define, or explicate, such concepts as the *good*, the *right*, the *valid*, and the *real*. The pure concept and the sensuously given do not limit each other; they are mutually independent. Knowledge is the result of interpreting the given by means of concepts. Consequently there is no knowledge in the mere awareness of the given. Furthermore, all empirical knowledge is only probable because it is based on the application of a temporally extended pattern of actual and possible experiences to something

915

which is immediately given, and this pattern may have to be revised in view of what future experiences disclose. However, the independence of the conceptual and the given in no way prevents us from having valid knowledge. Nor does it in any way restrict the possibility of finding concepts under which any conceivable experience can be subsumed.

There are two theories of experience, Lewis argues, which do not accept the partition of experience into the given and the conceptual. One of these eliminates the conceptual entirely and reduces experience to the given. This theory is exemplified by Bergson and the mystics. Its inadequacy can be clearly seen in its inability to handle the fact of error. If mind is pure receptivity, that with which it coincides in knowledge must always have the same objectivity, and we can never make mistakes. The other theory eliminates the given and reduces knowledge to the conceptual. This is the position of the idealists. Its inadequacy lies in its failure to recognize in knowledge an element which we do not create by thinking, one which we cannot, in general, displace or alter. This element is always ineffable; for if it is describable, concepts must have been brought in. And it is an abstraction, for it never exists in isolation in any experience or state of consciousness. It is given *in,* not *before,* experience. It is made up of "qualia," which are repeatable and recognizable, but have no names. They are fundamentally different from the universals of logic. They may be characterized by such terms as "the given," "the data of sense," "the sensuous," and "the given in its feeling character," provided one

does not in the use of this terminology give the qualia merely a psychological status.

The conceptual element of experience, on the other hand, is quite different from the given. It is the construction, or interpretation, which is put upon the given. It is not to be understood in terms of any imagery or any psychological state of an individual mind. On the contrary, it is defined as "that meaning which must be common to two minds when they understand each other by the use of a substantive or its equivalent." Verifying the commonness of meaning in the case of any concept takes one of two routes: exhibiting the denotation by a behavioral act, or employing a definition. The former is unsatisfactory because it does not enable us to determine *uniquely* the meaning of the concept. The latter specifies the meaning directly in terms of a pattern of other concepts: A is defined in terms of B and C, and these are defined by other concepts. This is obviously a process which is never completed, but it does enable us to ascertain a genuine identity of meaning in two minds. It should not be interpreted as an analysis of meaning in the sense of a repeated dissection of a meaning into other meanings until one is reached which is no longer relational; *every* concept is a pattern of other concepts. To argue this definition of concepts on the grounds (a) that when we use a concept we "seldom have in mind" such a pattern of concepts, and (b) that we may have a meaning which we cannot state in terms of such a pattern without further thought, is to overlook the fact that concepts play a role in knowledge which is primarily practical; meanings may be exhibited implicitly in the consistency of behavior, as well as explicitly in the statement of definitions.

Having indicated that experience consists of two elements, the given and the conceptual, Lewis proceeds to ask what is involved in our perceptual knowledge of objects. His first task is to show that there is no knowledge by mere acquaintance; that is, knowledge *always* transcends the immediately given. This view requires him to distinguish, on the one hand, between qualia and our immediate awareness of them, and, on the other, between objects and our knowledge of them.

Qualia are subjective and have no names in normal language; they can be indicated by such phases as "looks like" or "appears to be." Since they are immediately given they have no need of verification and we cannot possibly be mistaken about them. But if we take the simplest concepts, for example, "blue" or "round," we can see that what they embrace are not qualia but patterns of relations. This is shown by the steps which we would take in order to confirm our judgment that a given penny, say, is round: we might walk around it or view it from a different angle, we might pick it up and turn it in our fingers, we might move toward it or away from it. In each case we are attempting to confirm certain predictions which are involved in the supposition that it really *is* round. If these do not turn out as anticipated, we withdraw our judgment. The objective reality of the property consists in what would verify it and in what would disprove it. Thus the existence of an objective property is not constituted by the presentation of a given quale, but by the presentation of a given quale *plus* the concept of an ordered relation of different qualia tied up with certain conditions of behavior. The concept *means* this pattern of qualia. It therefore extends temporally beyond the given quale, permitting the pattern to be confirmed or disproved as an interpretation of the given, and it always prescribes possible ways of acting toward the presented object. *Without* such a pattern we could never identify an object. But—unfortunately, perhaps—even with such a pattern we cannot surely identify an object because the pattern always contains unrealized future experiences and because a certain pattern may serve to identify different qualia; also, different patterns may be applicable to the same quale. Our perceptual knowledge of an object is consequently more than mere acquaintance with a quale; when we ascribe objectivity to a presentation, the "acquaintance with" changes into "knowledge about" and we have a conceptual interpretation of what is presented. Knowledge consists of that part of the flux of experience which we ascribe to ourselves and which we change by our activities, and of that part which is objective and which we cannot predicate of ourselves. The world is bigger than the content of our direct experience only because we are active beings, only because we can say to what is revealed in our experience, "If we should do this, then we should experience that," and we find that the carrying out of these actions often reveals new truths about the world.

In further elaboration of this theory of knowledge Lewis shows that the examination of the problem of how we know has been guided since Descartes by an erroneous belief in the incompatibility of three alternatives: knowledge is not relative to the mind; the content of knowledge is not the real; and the real is dependent on mind. He proceeds, first, to show that there is no contradiction between the relativity of knowledge and the independence of the object. Indeed, relativity *requires* an independent character in what is thus relative. The fact, for example, that the weight of an object can be determined only relatively to a standard, such as a pound or a gram, does not imply that weight "in itself" has no meaning and that the object is therefore outside the category of weight. The concept of weight is an interpretation which *transcends* this relativity because it is a relational pattern exhibited by the independently real object. Furthermore, one should not, on the grounds that mind cannot be known, argue from the dependence of knowledge on mind to the conclusion that such knowledge cannot be of the real.

For I do know my mind, Lewis argues, though I learn it only in its commerce with real objects. In other words, I can learn the relation between mind and object by varying the object and noting the variation in its appearances and subjective manifestations, and by varying the mind and noting the resulting variations in the object. Finally, the fact that mind may have unrecognized limitations in its capacity to know the real does not imply either that knowledge is deceitful or that we must forever remain ignorant of the real.

Having shown that there is no knowledge without interpretation, Lewis examines the consequences of this fact. One of these is that there must be at least *some* knowledge which is *a priori*. The reasons for this are easy to see.

Interpretation represents an activity of the mind and is always subject to test by future experience. The mere fact that interpretation reflects the character of past experience is not sufficient; there must be an assumed orderliness in experience which will entitle us to *expect* a certain kind of future on the basis of what the past has disclosed. This knowledge that nature is orderly must be *necessarily* true and independent of the particular character of experience. Knowledge of this kind is *a priori*.

After proving that certain historical conceptions of the *a priori*, which identify it with that which is psychologically undeniable, that which is self-evident, or that whose denial implies its affirmation, are erroneous, Lewis turns to an explanation of the *a priori*. The *a priori* has nothing to do with anything which is inescapable; it always permits of alternatives. It has its origin in an act of mind, thus exhibiting mind's creativity and not its dependence on anything inside or outside itself. Mind is, of course, limited in the sense that our perceptual organs are restricted to a certain range of stimuli; dogs can smell things which we cannot smell, and eagles can see things which we cannot see. But these things are not beyond the range of our *conception,* though they are beyond the range of our *perception.* Could there be anything, then, which *is* beyond the range of our conception? Obviously not, for in saying that an object is conceivable we are really saying something whose opposite makes no sense; the alternative to what can be experienced could not even be phrased. But although the range of the *conceivable* cannot be determined by any act of mind, the range of the *real* might be so determined. Science, in fact, does precisely this. It prescribes the character which reality must possess. Consequently, when we say that we experience dream objects, or fairies, or mermaids, science tells us that these kinds of "objects" cannot possibly be real.

A priori principles are required to limit reality; they are not required to limit experience. An interpretation is a priori only in the sense that it prescribes for a particular case and is thus not subject to recall even if the particular should fail to conform to the prescription. On the other hand, an interpretation is a posteriori if it is abandoned when the case does not fit. Let us suppose, for example, that we set up the categorial interpretation of scientific reality as "the realm in which every event has a cause." Now let us further assume that we come upon what is presumably a genuine miracle. We have two alternatives: we can say that the miracle did not really happen, or we can say that real events can happen without any natural causes. If real events must always have natural causes, then the miracle could not have been real; but if real events generally have causes (but might not), then the particular case could constitute an exception to the generalization. In the former case our interpretation is a priori; it can be maintained in the face of all experience, no matter what. In the latter case our interpretation is empirical and subject to disconfirmation in terms of experience. Lewis illustrates his point by the story of the man who boastfully made out a list of the names of all the men whom he could whip. When one burly man, whose name appeared on the list, approached him belligerently and insisted that he could not be whipped, the maker of the list said, "All right; then I'll just rub your name off." His original boast had no a priori character.

The apparent problem, of course, is how to get the empirical and the a priori together. But the real problem, according to Lewis, is not to "get them together" but to discover their co-presence in all cases of knowledge. The analysis of knowledge reveals the following five phases: (1) the immediate awareness of the given, exemplified by "This looks round"; (2) judgments about presented objects, exemplified in "This object is round"; (3) the a priori development of abstract conceptual schemes, exemplified in such mathematical judgments as "In a Euclidean triangle the sum of the angles equals 180 degrees"; (4) the categorial knowledge implied in our interpretation of reality, exemplified in the judgment, "If this is a round object, then if I change my position in a certain way, it will appear elliptical"; and (5) empirical generalizations, such as "All swans are white."

Misunderstanding is sure to arise if we fail to distinguish phase (1) from phase (2). Merely to be aware of an appearance (a quale) is, as we have seen, not knowledge. But to judge that an object is round, rather than appears round, is knowledge. What makes it knowledge is the fact that it rests for its corroboration on a judgment of the kind indicated in phase (4): "If this object is round, then I can expect certain other appearances to reveal themselves." In fact, when I say that it is round, I assert implicitly everything the failure of which would falsify the statement. This is a priori and regulative in character, for it commits me to saying, "If I find that the presented ob-

919

ject does *not* confirm my predictions of its other appearances. I shall deny that it is round." An *a priori* proposition always has this characteristic. For example, the statement "All swans are birds" is *a priori* because if any creature originally designated as a swan were discovered not to be a bird, the designation "swan" would be withdrawn. On the other hand, an empirical generalization, such as "All swans are white," might be contradicted if we found a black swan. Thus, an *a priori* proposition does not assert any limitation of experience; it asserts merely that we are tentatively trying out a certain categorial system which is so compactly organized that if one of its concepts does not fit reality, its other concepts will also not fit, and we should therefore abandon it and try another. Only if we have such a rigid scheme can we have knowledge of reality at all. For if an object is to be identifiable in terms of a certain concept, we must be provided with a criterion by means of which we can decide whether the object exemplifies the concept. If we were to change our criterion whenever an object failed to exemplify it, we could never have any criteria and we could never have knowledge. It *does* follow, of course, that our knowledge of objects can be probable only, never certain, for no matter how many predictions concerning the expected appearances of the object have been confirmed, there is always the possibility that the next one will not be; all verification is partial and a matter of degree. If we demand, therefore, something more than this, and require that in order to save us from skepticism empirical knowledge must be *certain*, we are doomed to disappointment.

Lewis concludes with a chapter entitled "Experience and Order." If all knowledge is in terms of concepts and concepts are of the mind, the application of concepts to experience demands a certain orderliness in the world. The givenness of certain qualia must be a clue to certain expected sequences, and the occurrence of these sequences in the past must be a valid ground for our belief in their occurrence in the future. This is commonly called the "assumption of the uniformity of nature."

Lewis tries to show just what is involved in this necessary "uniformity." It can be expressed in three principles. *Principle A* says that "it must be false that every identifiable entity in experience is equally associated with every other." This assumes merely that there are *some* recurrent sequences in nature; that is, there are things of such nature that concepts can be applied to them. *Principle B* states that whenever we have cases where *Principle A* does not apply (namely, where the sequences seem to be "random"), we can extend these situations through certain identifiable entities in such a way as to make them satisfy *Principle A*. For example, if we can find no order among events, we can pass to simpler elements by deeper analysis, or to a larger whole containing the original constituents, or to a higher level of abstraction by disregarding irrelevant aspects. In each case we will find order where there had previously appeared to be none. *Principle C* affirms that "the statistical prediction of the future from the past cannot be generally invalid, because whatever is future to any given past, is in turn past for some future." This states simply that the person who uses as a basis for prediction a statistical generalization which is continually revised in terms of actual observations cannot fail to make more successful predictions than one who does not. A world which exhibits these principles is certainly not an inconceivable one. Indeed, since all we want to assure ourselves of is the *probability* of our apprehensions and our generalizations, not their *certainty,* we can hardly imagine a world which would *not* provide a basis for such knowledge. For certain modes of cognition an irreducible variety in the world would be completely irrelevant. Moreover, our demand for uniqueness in the individual thing seems to require a world of unlimited variety. But in most modes of understanding the uniformity is not *discovered* in the world, but *imposed on the world* by our own categorial procedure. What we are really saying, therefore, when we assert that the world is orderly is merely that there must be apprehensible things and objective facts—and to this conclusion there seems to be no conceivable alternative except the nonexistence of everything.

PROCESS AND REALITY

Author: Alfred North Whitehead (1861-1947)
Type of work: Metaphysics
First published: 1929

Principal Ideas Advanced

Only a philosophy of organism can describe a universe in which process, creativity, and interdependence are disclosed in immediate experience.

Philosophy involves generalization from the concrete particulars we know to universals; it aims at a description of the dynamic process which is reality.

A philosophical system should be logically consistent and coherent, and it should be grounded in immediate experience.

The categories of this philosophy of organism are the category of the ultimate (creativity), the categories of existence (actual entities, prehensions, nexūs, subjective forms, eternal objects, propositions, multiplicities, and contrasts), the categories of explanation (twenty-seven in number), and the categories of obligation (nine in number).

Everything but God is an actual entity occasioned by something; but God, although an actual entity, is not an actual occasion.

Every event in the creative, interdependent process is qualified by past, present, and future.

Process in reality is a creative advance in which feelings are integrated, actual occasions grow together toward a final phase of satisfaction, and God is conditioned by, and reciprocally affects, events in the temporal world.

The central aim in Whitehead's chief work, *Process and Reality,* is to replace the traditional philosophy of substance with a philosophy of organism. The thesis of the author is that only a philosophy of organism can provide clarification of a universe in which process, dynamic actualization, interdependence, and creativity are disclosed as the primary data of immediate experience.

Although Whitehead expresses some far-reaching reservations regarding traditional modes of thought, he formulates his philosophy of organism through a dialogue with the great logicians, scientists, metaphysicians, and theologians of the past. He finds the thought of Plato more decisive than that of Kant; he considers Bergson more suggestive than Hegel; he contends that Locke was closer to a philosophy of organism than Descartes; and he is ready to choose Leibniz over Aristotle. Western philosophy is defined by the author as a series of footnotes to Plato. Some of these footnotes he wishes to salvage and reformulate; others he is quite happy to see deleted. Of all the philosophical giants in the Western tradition, Kant is the least cordially received. The author makes it clear that his philosophy of organism constitutes a recurrence to pre-Kantian modes of thought. According to Whitehead, the Copernican revolution of Kant was not as revolutionary as many of his followers maintained it to be. Whitehead's philosophy is a speculative philosophy formulated into a coherent and logical system of general concepts which are intended to provide the categorial interpretation for any and all elements of human experience.

In examining the methodological foundations of Whitehead's system, we find first a procedure of descriptive generalization, and second an epistemology which expresses both a rational and an empirical side. Philosophical method involves generalization, in which there is a movement from the concrete particular to the universal. This generalization is based on description rather than deduction. Whitehead considers it to be a mistake that deduction, the primary method of mathematics, has intermittently become the touchstone for philosophical inquiry. Deduction is for the author an auxiliary mode of verification that should never be given primacy in philosophical methodology. Applied in Whitehead's philosophy of organism, this method of descriptive generalization takes the form of a description of *dynamic process* rather than of static structure. Morphological description is replaced by description of dynamic life processes.

Whitehead's epistemology contains both rational and empirical elements. The rational criterion is coherence and logical consistency; the empirical criterion is applicability and adequacy. A philosophical system must be coherent and logical. No entity can be conceived in abstraction from all other entities, nor can an entity be understood as long as its relation to other entities is not specified according to logical rules. But knowledge demands also an empirical justification. Categories must be applicable and adequate. They are applicable when they describe all related experience as exhibiting the same texture. They are adequate when they include all possible experience in their conceptual vision. Whitehead was deeply concerned to maintain an experiential basis for his philosophy: "The elucidation of immediate experience is the sole justification for any thought." Philosophy should aim at generalization, but it should not overreach its mark and lose itself in abstractions that are not grounded in experience. One of the chief errors in philosophy, contends the author, is the "fallacy of misplaced concreteness." This fallacy results when an abstraction becomes an exemplification of the system and replaces the concrete entity of which it is an abstraction. The success of philosophy, continues the author, is commensurate with the degree to which it avoids this fallacy.

Through the implementation of his method of descriptive generalization Whitehead derives a categorial scheme which sets forth the governing concepts of his philosophy of organism. His categories are classified according to a fourfold schematic division: (1) the category of the ultimate; (2) categories of existence; (3) categories of explanation; and (4) categorial obligations.

The *category of the ultimate* is creativity. Creativity is the universal of universals, the ultimate metaphysical principle which underlies all things without exception. Every fact of the universe is in some way or another an exemplification of creativity. Even God is subordinate to the category of the ultimate. As the ultimate metaphysical principle, creativity is also the principle of *novelty*. It provides the reason for the emergence of the new. In its application to the novel situation, of which it is the origination, creativity expresses itself as the "creative advance."

The *categories of existence* are eight in number: (1) actual entities; (2) prehensions; (3) nexūs (plural of nexus); (4) subjective forms; (5) eternal objects; (6) propositions; (7) multiplicities; and (8) contrasts. *Actual entities*, which replace the traditional concept of particular substances,

are the final facts of the universe; they are the real things of which the world is made up. *Prehensions* are the concrete facts of relatedness, exhibiting a "vector character," involving emotion, purpose, valuation, and causation. A *nexus* is a particular fact of togetherness of actual entities. *Subjective form* is the determining or defining quality of private matters of fact. *Eternal objects* are the pure potentials by reason of which facts are defined in their subjective forms. *Propositions* render meaningful the distinction between truth and falsehood; as abstract potentialities they are suggestions about the concrete particularity of actual entities. *Multiplicities* indicate the disjunctions of diverse entities. *Contrasts* indicate the mode of synthesis which occurs in a prehension or a concrete fact of relatedness. Along with these eight categories of existence Whitehead delineates twenty-seven categories of explanation and nine categorial obligations. We shall discuss the explanations and obligations as they become relevant in the development of the author's system.

Actual entities, which constitute Whitehead's first category of existence, are the building blocks of his organismic universe. Here the philosophy of organism inverts Spinoza. For Spinoza actual entities, as particulars, are inferior modes; only the Infinite Substance is ultimately real. In the philosophy of organism actual entities are the ultimate facts. These actual entities are in a process of "perpetual perishing," but as they perish they are somehow taken up in the creative advance, pass into other actual entities through the operation of prehension, and achieve objective immortality. This interpretation of a universe of flux in which actual entities come to be and pass away must be understood, according to the author, as simply an expansion of a sentence in Plato's *Timaeus:* "But that which is conceived by opinion with the help of sensation and without reason, is always in the process of becoming and perishing and never really is." The universe, as it is immediately disclosed, is a universe of becoming, flux, and perishing. The category of actual entities has universal applicability. It applies to nonliving matter as well as to all instances of life. It applies to the being of man as well as to the being of God.

A significant implication of this doctrine is that God, for Whitehead, is not outside the system. He is within the reach and range of the categories. However, God is differentiated from all other actual entities in that he is not occasioned by anything. Thus, all actual entities other than God are also occasions. God is an actual entity but not an actual occasion. Every actual occasion exhibits a dipolar structure consisting of a physical pole and a mental pole. By reason of its physical pole the actual occasion prehends other actual occasions; by reason of its mental pole a prehension of eternal objects is made possible. In this description of the bipolar structure of actual occasions the author formulates an alternative to the Cartesian dualism of mind and body. God also exhibits a dipolar structure. He possesses two natures—a primordial nature and a consequent nature. His primordial nature, which consists of an envisagement of all the eternal objects and an appetition for their actualization, corresponds to the mental pole of actual occasions. His consequent nature, which is the consequence of the reaction of the world

upon God, corresponds to the physical pole of actual occasions.

Actual occasions are grouped into societies or nexūs through the operation of prehension. A prehension, according to the eleventh category of explanation, consists of three factors: (1) the subject which is prehending; (2) the datum which is prehended; and (3) the subjective form which designates the manner in which the subject prehends its datum. A nexus, according to the fourteenth category of explanation, "is a set of actual entities in the unity of the relatedness constituted by their prehensions of each other." By reason of their physical poles actual occasions can prehend each other and form societies or nexūs. There results an organismic coinherence in which every event in the universe is a factor in every other event. All things ultimately inhere in each other. There are no isolated events. For Whitehead the universe is an interdependent universe in which all parts are interrelated. The analogy of the organism replaces the analogy of the machine. Not only, however, do actual occasions prehend each other by reason of their physical poles; they also prehend eternal objects by reason of their mental poles. Eternal objects are permanent and immutable principles of determination, clearly reminiscent of the eternal forms or ideas in the philosophy of Plato. An eternal object is a pure potential which, in itself, remains neutral to any particular fact of ingression in the temporal order. There are no new eternal objects. They are fixed in the timeless primordial vision of God. However, each eternal object is a potentiality in the history of actual occasions. An actual occasion prehends an eternal object and thus

924

the object becomes realized in time and space. Ingression refers to the particular mode in which the potentiality of an eternal object is realized in a particular entity, contributing to the structure and definition of that actual entity. Eternal objects contribute the necessary structure which keeps the organismic process from dissolving into an indeterminate and discontinuous succession. Process does not contradict structure in Whitehead's analysis. Process and structure are interdependent concepts.

Actual occasions, and the societies which they form, are in a process of growing together until they reach a final phase which is called "satisfaction." This process of growing together, in which new prehensions constantly take place, is designated by the author as "concrescence." "In a process of concrescence, there is a succession of phases in which new prehensions arise by integration of prehensions in antecedent phases. . . . The process continues until all prehensions are components in the one determinate integral satisfaction." Each actual occasion as it is objectified in the process of concrescence exhibits a claim upon the future. The future is in some sense constitutive of the being of every actual occasion. Whitehead expresses this when he describes an actual occasion as a "subject-superject." Every occasion is at once the subject experiencing and the superject of this experience; it is the present experiential datum, but it is also the future result or the aim of its present experience. This aim or future project is called the "subjective aim," which controls the becoming of the actual occasion and lures it to its final satisfaction. All becoming thus occurs within a spatio-temporal continuum, in which

all entities experience the bite of time. Each event in the universe is qualified by the past, present, and future. Although actual occasions perish, they enter into the internal constitution of other actual occasions, in which they become objectified. Every present fact of the universe is thus constituted by all antecedent phases. So also is every present fact constituted by its potentialities for future realization by its subjective aim. An actual entity is that which it can become. "That *how* an actual entity *becomes* constitutes *what* that actual entity *is*; so that the two descriptions of an actual entity are not independent. Its 'being' is constituted by its 'becoming.' This is the 'principle of process.'"

That all things flow is the one ultimate generalization around which Whitehead develops his whole system. This doctrine of a fluent, becoming universe, remarks the author, was already suggested in the unsystematized insights of Hebrew literature (particularly the Psalms), as well as in the early beginnings of Greek philosophy (particularly Heraclitus). Coupled with this doctrine of flux, however, is a competing notion—the permanence of all things. These two notions, contends the author, constitute the complete problem of metaphysics. Whitehead does not intend to reject the doctrine of permanence, but rather seeks to adapt it to his ultimate generalization that all things flow. This adaptation is expressed in two implicatory principles of his system—his doctrine of self-constituting identity and his doctrine of cosmic order. In his nine categorial obligations the author formulates the category of objective identity, which asserts the essential

925

self-identity of every actual entity as an individual constituent in the universe. Each actual entity is a cell with an atomic unity. In the process of concrescence actual entities grow together but they do not sacrifice their atomic unity. They retain their self-identity and thus give expression to a life of their own. Viewing the organismic process from the side of the cellular and atomic units which comprise it, we need to acknowledge a self-constituting individuality which indicates a permanence within the flow of all things. As there is objective self-identity in Whitehead's philosophy of organism, so also is there preëstablished harmony or universal cosmic order. The latter aspect of the universe is indicated in the author's seventh category of obligation, the category of subjective harmony. The process of concrescence exhibits a preestablished harmony in which all prehensions are viewed as being contributive to a stable cosmic order, informed by the eternal objects and directed by the subjective aim. Thus does the doctrine of permanence receive another expression in Whitehead's system. His elaboration of the notion of preëstablished harmony has some interesting implications for the author's position on the nature of evil. Although he does not formulate an explicit theodicy, he veers in the direction of a Leibnizian resolution to the problem. Novelty is not to be identified with creativity. The emergence of novelty in the organismic process may inhibit and delay the creative advance and thus provide the condition for the rise of evil. Evil constitutes a real fact in Whitehead's universe. Spinoza's attempt to explain away evil as an illusion arising from our finite, modal point of view is thus rejected. Evil is for Whitehead an *ens reale,* and not simply an *ens rationis.* However, when the creative advance attains its final phase or its satisfaction, the universe is the better off for the fact of evil. The satisfaction or the final phase is richer in content by reason of the particular cosmic disharmonies. All inhibiting novelties are somehow contributive to a greater good. In the creative advance of the world, particular evil facts are finally transcended.

Whitehead's philosophy of organism occupies a unique position in the history of philosophy in that it makes the sentient quality of experience decisive. His theory of prehension and his doctrine of the creative advance are governed by a notion of the pervasiveness of feeling. In the final analysis, prehension involves an objectification of feelings, and the creative advance is a process in which these feelings are integrated in an exemplification of harmony. "In the place of the Hegelian hierarchy of categories of thought, the philosophy of organism finds a hierarchy of categories of feeling." This accent on the sentient quality of experience by Whitehead has both epistemological and metaphysical implications. It entails, first of all, a rejection of the subject-object dichotomy as the foundation for knowledge. Most traditional varieties of philosophy, claims the author, give priority to the intellect and the understanding. In such a view the knowing subject is the primary datum and the philosophical task becomes a demonstration of the validity of propositions about the objects encountered by the subject. It was particularly in the Cartesian tradition that this subject-object form of statement became normative.

In Whitehead's philosophy of organism the subject is an emergent datum, rather than the foundational datum. The complex of feelings constitutes the primitive datum. The primitive element is sympathy, or feeling in another and feeling conformally with another. Intellect and consciousness arise only in the higher phases of concrescence. The universe is initially disclosed as a system of "vector feelings." This primacy of feeling is made explicit in Whitehead's doctrine of "presentational immediacy." In its immediate presentment the world is *received* as a complex of feelings. Primitive experience must thus properly be understood in terms of *sense-reception* rather than *sense-perception*. In sense-reception the interconnections of feelings are simultaneously disclosed. There is thus an internal bond between presentational immediacy and causal efficacy. Both Hume and Kant, in giving priority to the conscious subject, were unable to grasp this point. The sense-perception of the subject was for them the primary fact, and any apprehension of causation was somehow to be elicited from this primary fact. In the philosophy of organism, which gives primacy to sentient experience, causal relations are disclosed on the level of feelings. They are directly felt on a pretheoretical or pre-cognitive level of experience. The types of feeling are indefinite, and depend upon the complexity of the data which the feeling integrates. There are, however, three primary types of feeling which are constitutive of all more complex patterns: (1) physical feelings, (2) conceptual feelings, and (3) transmuted feelings. *Physical feelings* arise for the physical pole of the actual entity and have for their initial datum another actual entity. *Conceptual feelings* arise from the mental pole and have for their datum an eternal object. *Transmuted feelings* are akin to physical feelings in that they proceed from the physical pole, but their objective datum is a nexus of actual entities rather than a single entity. The creative advance integrates these various types of feeling in its progression toward satisfaction. This integration proceeds in such a manner that the earlier phases of feelings become components of later and more complex feelings. Thus, in each phase there is an emergence of novelty. This goes on until the final phase is reached, which is the complex satisfaction in which all earlier phases of feelings are taken up as formative constituents of a final and coordinated whole.

The categories of Whitehead's philosophy of organism receive their final exemplification in his metaphysics of theism. The doctrine of God completes Whitehead's system. In formulating his metaphysics of theism he has no intention of submitting rationally demonstrative proofs for the existence of God; rather, he intends to provide a theoretic system which gives clarification to the immediate facts of religious experience. The touchstone of religious experience is love. The author finds the most decisive expression of this religious attitude in the Galilean origin of Christianity. The theism suggested in this Galilean origin must be contrasted, on the one hand, with the theism of Aristotle, in which God is the unmoved mover who exhibits no concern for his creation and, on the other hand, with the theism of medieval theology, which, according to the author, gave to God the attributes which belonged exclusively to Caesar. The author's intention is thus to formulate a theistic view which arises from a religious experience in which love is the governing datum.

In Whitehead's philosophy this God of love is not to be treated as an exception to the categories and the metaphysical principles which they enunciate. God is the chief exemplification of the metaphysical system. In this role of chief exemplar his nature can be viewed from two perspectives—as *primordial* and as *consequent*. As *primordial*, God is unlimited or infinite potentiality. He is a unity and plenum of conceptual feelings, in abstraction from any physical feelings, and hence lacks the fullness of actuality. God as primordial is deficient in actuality. As a unity of conceptual feelings and operations he is a free creative act. He is in no way deflected by the particular occasions which constitute the actual world. The actual world presupposes the primordial nature, but the primordial nature does not presuppose the actual world. All that the primordial nature presupposes is the general and abstract character of creativity, of which it is the chief exemplification. As unlimited potentiality the primordial nature includes the eternal objects and accounts for the order in their relevance to the process of creation. So also God in his primordial nature is the *lure* for feeling or the "object of desire." He provides the condition for each subjective aim and draws the process to its final satisfaction.

Coupled with God's primordial nature is his *consequent* nature. His consequent nature is derivative. It expresses the reaction of the world upon God. The consequent nature is thus, in part, subject to the process of actualization in the actual world. By reason of his consequent nature God can share in the fullness of physical feelings of the actual world as these physical feelings become objectified in God. God shares with every actual occasion and every nexus its actual world. As consequent, God is conditioned by the world. His nature is consequent upon the creative advance of actual occasions in the process of concrescence. The primordial nature is free, complete, eternal, actually deficient, and unconscious. The consequent nature is determined, incomplete, everlasting, fully actual, and conscious. By reason of his consequent nature God establishes a providential relation to the world. His providential love is expressed through a tender care that nothing be lost. He saves everything in the world and preserves it in his own life. God's providence also manifests itself in the workings of divine wisdom. Through his infinite wisdom he puts to use even that which in the temporal world would be considered mere wreckage. The consequent nature thus makes possible a continuing point of contact and a reciprocal relation between God and the world. The events in the temporal world are transformed through God's love and wisdom, and his love and wisdom then pass back into the world. God thus receives his final definition as the great companion—the fellow sufferer who understands.

THE RIGHT AND THE GOOD

Author: William David Ross (1877-   )
Type of work: Ethics
First published: 1930

PRINCIPAL IDEAS ADVANCED

Rightness and goodness are simple and unanalyzable properties; they cannot be explained in terms of feelings, nor are they scientifically discoverable.

We cannot discover value or rightness by the use of the senses; such properties are discoverable only by intellectual intuition.

Basic moral truths are invariant; they are not products of various cultures.

The claim that "right" means "productive of the greatest possible good" is mistaken, for some acts—such as keeping a promise—are right regardless of whether they are productive of the greatest possible good.

Moral principles, discoverable by anyone who is intellectually mature, fall into a moral order; but the moral order cannot specifically be stated, for the resolution of conflicts between moral principles must be made in the light of particular circumstances.

Sir William David Ross, one of the most influential of recent philosophers, has played a leading role in the development of contemporary ethics. He is the best-known exponent of a nonnaturalistic deontological ethical theory, a type of theory that has been at the center of philosophic controversy during most of the first half of this century.

Like H. A. Prichard and E. F. Carritt, or in an earlier period, Kant and Richard Price, Ross is a deontologist or formalist insofar as he insists that the concepts of "right," "duty," and "obligation" are fundamental concepts that cannot be explained in terms of, or derived from, other value concepts such as "good." In this respect he differs from utilitarians such as J. S. Mill and, recently, G. E. Moore, who have argued that concepts of moral obligation can be derived from "good," the primary notion. However, like Moore, Ross is a nonnaturalist insofar as he insists that properties such as right and good are not to be explained in terms of the feelings or inner states of the judge, nor are they properties that can be detected by the senses or discovered by any scientific procedure. They are, rather, "nonnatural" properties apprehended by intellectual insight. This doctrine places him in opposition to naturalists such as George Santayana, John Dewey, Ralph Barton Perry, C. I. Lewis (to a certain extent), and to a number of sociologically inclined thinkers such as David Émile Durkheim. It also opposes him to emotivists such as A. J. Ayer and C. L. Stevenson, who deny that the ethical significance of terms is cognitive at all. Ross's views are expressed most elegantly in *The Right and the Good*, a book that has become a modern classic in the literature of ethics. They are expanded somewhat in a later book, *The*

Foundations of Ethics (1939), which an interested reader will want to consult.

In this review we shall adopt Ross's order of discussion, starting with right and turning later to good. When he speaks of "right," he has in mind the closely related concepts of "right," "obligation," and "duty" which, he says, with minor qualifications refer to the same thing. He is using the term "right" not in the weaker sense of "not wrong" but in the stronger sense of "wrong not to." The property of rightness, he says, is simple and nonanalyzable, and the concept of "right" is consequently indefinable. Here he is following the pattern laid down by Moore in his *Principia Ethica* (1903), although Moore applied it there to the concept of "good" only. Furthermore, he argues, as Moore did in the case of "good," that in addition to being indefinable, "a word like 'right' . . . does not stand for anything we can point out to one another or apprehend by one of the senses." Rather, it is a property we recognize in certain types of action by an intellectual insight or intuition.

Ross believes that even though "right" is indefinable, most of us will know what it means, for most of us are moral people who constantly make moral judgments quite satisfactorily. If we are not sure, we can always consider particular cases and see that we do distinguish between moral behavior on the one hand and other kinds of behavior on the other. And if we are confused about the relationship between the notion of "right" and value concepts such as "good," once again we can clarify the issue only by attending to, analyzing, and comparing cases. Ultimately each of us must examine his own moral consciousness if he wishes to attain clarity, for, as Ross has already argued, " 'right' . . . does not stand for anything we can point out to one another." The moral insight is private in the sense that we cannot look to make sure the other person is apprehending what we apprehend. This does not mean that communication is impossible, for observation and discussion will reveal that on the whole we agree that there is moral behavior and we agree, also, on the kinds of behavior that are moral.

Ross himself discusses and criticizes several prominent philosophical views that deny one or another of the major points of his own position. Thus he argues against thinkers like Durkheim by claiming that moral insight is not to be equated with or explained away in terms of the mores a culture happens to have at some particular time. The insights men have may vary from time to time, as may the codes men lay down, but basic moral truths themselves are invariant. Against Moore's doctrine in *Principia Ethica,* that "right" means "productive of the greatest possible good," he has two arguments. First, he uses Moore's own open question technique against him, for, he says, it surely is an important question whether actions that produce the greatest good are right. This is not the trivial question it would be if the corresponding statement were analytic, and it would be analytic if the alleged definition were correct. Second, he argues that the rightness of certain actions, such as that of promise keeping, does not depend entirely or essentially upon the good produced by such actions. It is to be noted that later on, in *Ethics* (1911), Moore himself changed his mind and agreed with Ross that "right" is indefinable.

Ross also argues against the view that to say an act is right is to say that it is morally good; that is, that it stems from a morally praiseworthy motive. Here, too, he uses two arguments. First, he says that since motives are feelings or desires that cannot be summoned up at a moment's notice, it would be impossible in many cases to do what is surely our duty. Since *ought* implies *can*, it cannot be our duty to act from a good motive. (This is not to deny that it is our duty to develop our character or that we can act from good motives.) Second, it is not our duty to act from a sense of duty but rather our duty simply to do certain things, such as to return the book we have borrowed. The goodness of the act is important if we are concerned with the virtue of the agent, but this goodness must not be confused with another property the act may have, that of being right or obligatory.

Ross then turns from the question of the meaning of ethical terms to another major question: What is the criterion of right and wrong? Here too he is reacting against Moore and other utilitarians, for regardless of whether they think they are giving a definition of right, they all maintain that the goodness produced by an act is the sole criterion of its rightness. Ross replies that this is not the case with respect to a wide variety of actions. We have already mentioned promise keeping. Ross acknowledges that the consequences of keeping a promise must be taken into account when we consider whether or how we should keep it, and he acknowledges that in some cases these consequences are such that we should not keep it, but he points out that in many cases we are obliged to keep a promise even if it should result in less beneficial consequences than some other action, and that in all cases involving a promise there is a moral consideration present which has nothing to do with consequences. In the case of promises, an obligation arises because of a special sort of action in the past rather than because of future consequences, and it arises because in promising, and by promising, we "create a moral claim on us in someone else." The utilitarian ignores the fact that the act of promising is the source of an obligation. Other things being equal, then, we are obliged to keep our promises, and this obligation is not the obligation to produce beneficial consequences. Ross does assert that we are also obliged to act so as to benefit others, but this is another, quite different, obligation.

Ross maintains that there are still other sorts of obligation. First, there are obligations similar to that of keeping promises in that they stem from the particular actions of men. He writes not only of promises and contracts, but also of cases of fidelity such as the "implicit promise" underlying the understanding that we will tell the truth. Also included in the category of "special obligations" are our obligations to compensate others for the wrongs we have done them (the duty of reparation) and to return the services of those who have helped us (the duty of gratitude). In contrast to these "special obligations" which occur only if one party to the obligation has acted in a particular way with respect to the other, there are the "general obligations" we have with respect to all men simply because and insofar as they are men. In addition to the duty to benefit others, Ross mentions our obligations to distribute happiness according to merit

931

(justice), to improve ourselves, and to refrain from injuring others. Ross believes he has given a complete catalogue of duties, but he is less concerned with defending this contention than he is with emphasizing that there are many types of obligation quite distinct from the obligation to maximize the amount of good in the world. The important point is that not one of these obligations can be explained away in terms of any of the others. The utilitarian is mistaken when he asserts that there is only one criterion of what is right, for there are many, each as fundamental and irreducible as the others.

Each of these is a moral principle, each is a moral truth. Together they express the "moral order" which is "just as much part of the fundamental nature of the universe . . . as is the spatial or numerical structure expressed in the axioms of geometry or arithmetic." Men have not always apprehended these principles, but any who "have reached sufficient mental maturity and have given sufficient attention" to them should recognize their self-evident truth.

Since there will be many particular cases where these principles will clash, it cannot *always* be obligatory to keep a promise, or to rectify wrongs done to others, or to benefit others, and so on. For this reason, Ross says that promise keeping and other kinds of acts which are usually obligatory are *prima facie* right, meaning by this that if no stronger and contrary moral consideration is relevant to the case in point, promise keeping, or whatever it is, is morally obligatory. He draws an analogy with the parallelogram of forces in physics: the fact that one makes a promise "tends" to make a certain action right, but the fact that this same action right, but the fact that this same act will harm another person "tends" to make it wrong. If only the first tendency were present, it would determine the outcome and keeping the promise would be right or obligatory and not merely *prima facie* right. But since there are two opposing "tendencies" actual duty will be determined by the stronger of the two. The weaker tendency is still present, though overcome. It may be wrong to keep the promise in this situation but even so, keeping it is still *prima facie* right. This is Ross's way of maintaining the absoluteness of moral principles in the face of the obvious fact that they clash in particular cases.

Ross does not think these principles can be arranged hierarchically in such a fashion that when any two clash we know beforehand which must take precedence over the other, and he does not believe there is any principle that enables us to resolve such conflicts. He maintains that our moral life is far more complex than the systematizers of ethics imply it is. We must consider cases as they come, weigh the relative strengths of the moral considerations as they occur in the individual cases, and reach our decisions accordingly. As a result, we cannot be nearly as certain about the rightness of particular acts as we can be about the truth of the general principles, for while the latter is self-evident, the former can never be known with certainty.

In his discussion of the good, Ross is concerned primarily with "intrinsic" goodness which he, like many others, distinguishes from "instrumental" goodness. Something is intrinsically good if it is good for its own sake, quite apart from any value it might have as a means of attaining some other good. Ross believes that only states of mind or relations between them can have intrinsic value and, therefore, that anything else has value only insofar as it produces such states or relations. Thus, for instance, the physical painting has instrumental value but only the experience it produces in us has intrinsic value. It follows that a world that contained no conscious beings would be a valueless world.

When we examine our states of mind, Ross says, we will find that only four things are intrinsically valuable. The first three, in increasing order of importance, are (1) pleasure, (2) knowledge and right opinion, and (3) morally good states such as virtuous dispositions and morally good motives. Of the third, sense of duty ranks highest followed by feelings such as sympathy and benevolence. He presents "the apportionment of pleasure and pain to the virtuous and the vicious respectively" as the fourth intrinsic good. To support his view he asks us in each case to consider two universes which are equal in all respects except that the state under consideration is present in one and absent in the other, believing that in each case we will agree that the universe containing the state in question is the better one. If anything other than these four things is intrinsically good, it can only be something exhibiting several of them. Thus, for example, the intrinsic goodness of aesthetic enjoyment involves both pleasure and knowledge.

Ross's analysis of the nature of intrinsic goodness is like that of G. E. Moore, to whom he acknowledges his debt. Good is a simple, unanalyzable property of a state of mind, a property it has in virtue of the fact that it has some other property, that of being pleasant, knowing, or virtuous. Good is not to be confused with these other properties. Good is a "consequential" or "dependent" property insofar as the state of mind has goodness only because it also has some other properties, but good is not a "constitutive" property of the state of mind, as the other properties are, for it does not belong to the essential nature of the state of mind. That is, while a statement such as, "A state of knowing is a cognitive state" is an analytic statement, the statement, "A state of knowing is intrinsically valuable" is synthetic.

Good is a simple property and the corresponding concept, "good," is indefinable. Ross defends this claim by arguing that no offered definitions have been able to survive examination. Some fail because either they exclude actions that are right or include actions that are wrong. And all, even those in which the denotations of the *definiens* and the *definiendum* may coincide, fail because they do not express what we mean by "good." This latter argument is much like Moore's use of the open question technique which we have already mentioned in our discussion of right. Ross does not insist that we can prove that "good" is indefinable, but he does hold that the fact that all proffered definitions have failed is extremely strong evidence, especially when we consider that there is no reason in the first place why we should think that good is a complex property. In brief, Ross ends up as Moore did, by considering good to be a simple, unanalyzable, "nonnatural" property that is present in something because of the presence in it of certain other quite natural properties.

This conception of a nonnatural property and the related notions of intuition and synthetic *a priori* truths lie at the center of Ross's position, and as such have been the targets of most of the criticism directed against him. Nonnatural properties have been especially bothersome. Ross and Moore both maintain that value and moral terms refer to properties of things and actions, and yet both insist that these properties are not sensed and cannot be discovered by scientific means. Consequently, they have the difficult task, which has bothered Moore particularly, of trying to explain what such nonnatural properties are. As Moore's long puzzlement indicates, they have not succeeded even to their own satisfaction. On the other hand, they have refused to abandon the notion because they believe that the consequence would be the destruction of the cognitive significance of moral and value statements, a consequence made all too clear by the work of the later emotivists. The dominating model of significance and truth is that made familiar by empirical propositions: if a statement is cognitively significant, then it must be capable of being true; and if it is capable of being true, then it must refer, correctly or incorrectly, to things and properties. Furthermore, we must be able to observe things and their properties. Applying this model to value statements, we are forced to make a similar series of moves. If the statement "A is good" is true, then there must be such a property as good, A must possess it, and we must be able to examine A and notice that A possesses it. We may be puzzled as to exactly what sort of thing the examination reveals, but if we say that A is good, it seems that we are forced to admit that we have inspected A and have noticed that it has the property we call good.

Very recently writers such as S. Toulmin, P. H. Nowell-Smith, K. Baier, and A. I. Melden have attacked the underlying model of significance, arguing that the concepts of "reasonable," "valid," and "true" have quite legitimate and distinctive uses in moral discourse, uses which vary from the uses of these terms in scientific discourse. Thus, they contend, we can escape the postulation of puzzling nonnatural properties without giving up the contention that moral discourse does differ significantly from scientific discourse, and we can do so without denying that moral statements have cognitive significance. That is, very recent thought has broken out of the bonds indicated by our recent classification of ethical theories as being either naturalistic, nonnaturalistic, or emotivist, a scheme of classification which presupposed the acceptance of the dominant model that has been mentioned.

As for Ross, no matter how severely some of his ideas are being criticized, there is no doubt that he has played a very important role in the development of contemporary ethical theory and that his influence still lives strongly. His insistence that moral and value terms differ from descriptive terms, his insistence on a deontological ethics, and his insistence that morality is far too complex to be contained by any theory which would reduce it to a single principle have been and continue to be very influential. These basic ideas persist even in the views of many who are somewhat unhappy about the epistemological framework within which Ross has expressed them.

PROBLEMS OF ETHICS

Author: Moritz Schlick (1882-1936)
Type of work: Ethics
First published: 1930

PRINCIPAL IDEAS ADVANCED

Ethics is a science in that it is the effort to acquire knowledge about the right and the good.

We use the term "good" to recommend something as desired by society; by discovering what is desired, one is able to define the good.

Human beings choose to perform whatever actions most appeal to them as they consider the possibilities.

Moral valuations are emotional reactions according to normal expectations concerning the pleasant or unpleasant consequences of performing certain acts.

Values and obligations are relative to the desires of persons, and they are objective in the sense that, as a matter of fact, human beings do prefer some things to others.

A free will is not an undetermined will; it is a will which is not compelled.

Schlick's *Problems of Ethics* is one of the earlier ethical works of the school of logical positivism. Readers interested in ethical developments of this general position should consult other works influenced by, but significantly differing from, those of the Vienna Circle, of which Schlick was a founder. Typical of such later works are those of the emotivists, Alfred J. Ayer and Charles L. Stevenson.

Ethics, Schlick holds, is a science in that its object is knowledge. It seeks to understand the right and the good, not to produce them. Contrary to the views of many modern ethicists, its primary task is not to establish a definition of "good," though it must discover the meaning empirically and scientifically. Opposing G. E. Moore's position that "good" is indefinable, Schlick insists that while it cannot be exhaustively defined any more than can the name of a color, it can be defined sufficiently to locate its content accurately, as can

any meaningful word. He then describes the formal characteristic of the good as *its being demanded of us,* its "oughtness." But what is the origin of oughtness? This suggests the material characteristic: we use the term "good" to recommend something as desired by society.

By examining approved acts and dispositions we can find and generalize their common characteristics in a rule of the form, X must have properties A, B, C . . . and N in order to be called "good." (Note that the rule concerns not what *is,* but what is *called* "good.") This rule or norm would thus express a fact, and hierarchical arrangement of such norms would ultimately yield a moral principle or definition of "good." Hence, the usual opposition of factual to normative sciences is false. While ethics does justify particular judgments by reference to rules or norms, such justification is relative rather than absolute; as a science, ethics must still in-

935

vestigate the sources of norms. It cannot ultimately justify or establish the highest norms and values, since to justify is to refer to a higher principle. Instead, "Such norms . . . must be derived from human nature and life as facts." Schlick thus rejects the radical distinction commonly made between the "is" and the "ought" or the factual and the normative. The central task of ethics when it arrives at the highest values is then to seek their causal explanation or factual sources; since the causes of conduct in general are more fundamental than those of moral behavior, the method and materials of ethics must be psychological.

When, then, are the ultimate relevant causes or motives of conduct? Schlick states the law of motivation thus: ". . . the decision of the will proceeds in the direction of the most pleasant end-in-view, in the following manner: of the ideas which function as motives, that one gains the upper hand which finally possesses the highest degree of pleasant emotional tone, or the least unpleasant tone. . . ." Schlick argues that the law needs little proof, being exemplified constantly, although there are apparent exceptions requiring explanation. In cases of self-sacrifice or martyrdom, it might at first seem that the agent was not motivated by pleasure or the avoidance of pain— a false assumption. Unusual conditions change what is ordinarily pleasant and painful, and the goal of the inspired hero appears so desirable that other motives, such as fear of death, are repressed. It is impossible to desire something absolutely unpleasant, since to desire is to entertain an idea with pleasure; hence, the self-sacrificial decision must be motivated by some dominant pleasure even while accompanied by pain. There is no necessary connection between a pleasant idea of a state and an idea of a pleasant state, and thus martyrs may anticipate with pleasure what is usually painful. But overwhelming confirmation of this law of motivation is the fact that institutions of all kinds—religious, educational, and political—apply it as the sole means of controlling conduct.

But the law is insufficient to distinguish good from evil or the moral from the immoral. Schlick solves this problem indirectly by examining the term "egoism," resignating a chief object of moral censure and thus leading to the discovery of what is meant by "immoral" and "moral." Some philosophers describe egoism as the impulse to personal welfare, to pleasure, or to self-preservation, but in context all these terms prove too vague, broad, or inaccurate. The true meaning of "egoism" is "inconsiderateness"; it designates not so much impulses of the self as the manner in which some personal inclinations are fulfilled to the neglect of the social impulses, and therefore egoism is disapproved by society. This suggests ". . . the following law as a fundamental ethical insight: the moral valuations of modes of behavior and characters are nothing but the emotional reactions with which human society responds to the pleasant and sorrowful consequences that, according to the average experience, proceed from those modes of behavior and characters."

Here the affinities of Schlick's views with the social approval theory, psychological hedonism, and utilitarianism become clear. "Approved" in its moral sense means "desired," and pleasure and pain are the governing factors in desire. Schlick significantly emends the utilitarian concept of what is approved, however: he agrees that what is considered morally good is "what advances the pleasure of society," but whereas utilitarians attempted to say what good *is*, Schlick avoids this difficult problem by claiming only that "In human society, that is *called* good which is *believed* to bring the greatest happiness." Similarly the "demand" character of the good stems only from the desires of society reinforced by sanctions. Thus good and obligation are factual as originating in human nature, but they are relative to it rather than absolute or self-subsistent.

The theory of absolute values is that they are wholly independent of human emotion and knowledge and relate to everyday reality only through man's obligation so to act as to bring about the most valuable results. Schlick's first criticism of this theory alleges the impossibility of determining the meaning and truth of its value judgments. What objective criteria might one use? Not concomitant pleasure since the theory itself rejects that: the good may be pleasant, but pleasure is not the good. Not in such a criterion as contribution to upward evolution, since such terms as "upward" are circular in presupposing a meaning of "value." Indeed, the error of this approach is "in seeking value distinctions in the objective facts themselves, without reference to the acts of preference and selection, through which alone value comes into the world."

Are there then subjective criteria? Some absolutists describe a specific experience or intuition of value, comparable to sensory perception of material objects. But unless one has this experience it is difficult to accept the theory, and value judgments do not show the consistency of sensations. To consider comparing value judgments to logical or mathematical statements, as some absolutists do, is unsatisfactory, for such statements are tautological and do not express factual truth. Were value judgments comparable they would be unverifiable and, worse, irrelevant to life, whereas "Judgments about value ought to tell us just what is most important."

The oughtness of good is likewise incapable of an absolute subsistence, contrary to the teaching of Kant. "'I ought to do something' never means anything except 'Someone wants me to do it'" and that reward, punishment, or other consequences will attend satisfaction or neglect of the desire. Kant's description of a categorical or absolute imperative, Schlick adds, is contradictory because it defines "oughtness" without reference to one who demands or desires, while such reference is essential to the concept. The only verifiable experience of the ought is the familiar awareness of compulsion: sanctions have feeling tones which dominate those of other ideas and so determine volition. In this way values and moral law affect conduct, but an absolutist theory cannot show any relationship between values and desire or action.

But if not absolute, to what extent are values relative and subjective? Schlick thinks they are relative to the feelings of the subject, but are not capricious; given certain relations of specific objects and subjects with fixed constitutions and dispositions, the feeling reactions or values will also be determined unambiguously. This is an objective fact; neither the relativity nor the objectivity of value is metaphysical. But value relativity is more complicated than has yet been shown; while the view that pleasure is essentially or frequently worthless is largely prejudice, it is true that sorrow is sometimes valuable. Why? "Happiness" and "sorrow" name indefinite, complex states not identical with pleasure and pain— themselves complex and variable. Pain, for example, can have pleasant components and is sometimes associated with pleasure, as when painful labor produces pleasant effects. Many great pleasures follow great pains according to the law of "contrast." Furthermore, we feel that suffering provides a dimension of depth not otherwise attainable, and is sometimes valuable inherently, rather than by association alone. Schlick explains that we feel pleasure in being stirred to the depths of our nature, but this occurs infrequently; thus, when a partially painful experience moves us deeply, as does emotional involvement in dramatic tragedy, we find it pleasant. Suffering and extreme joy are both expressed by tears, which pure pain does not yield. Great art, one notes, is concerned more immediately with sorrow than with pleasure, and it thus provides further evidence of the heterogeneity of feeling tone.

Schlick then turns to a pseudo-problem which, he insists, was solved long ago by Hume and others; it involves misunderstanding of "freedom of the will" and obscures the genuine but simple problem of moral responsibility. Every science presumes the principle of causality, or that every event is under universal law, but it has been and still is argued that such determinism precludes free will and hence responsibility. This conclusion confuses two meanings of "law": (1) compulsory rule and (2) description of events. To describe nature as governed by univer-

sal law means merely that events occur uniformly and are predictable, not that they are *compelled* in the sense of "forced against the will." Similarly, psychological laws do not compel decisions but merely describe those we do make. The confusion between determinism, or universal causality, and compulsion breeds related confusion between their opposites, indeterminism and freedom, so that the champions of "free will" proceed to confuse freedom with the opposite of causality. Morality requires both freedom, or "absence of compulsion," and responsibility; the latter involves the possibility of changing motives, and hence implies causality. Advocates of "free will" fail to see that a decision without a cause would be a matter of mere chance and utterly irrational, and that it is quite consistent to admit both freedom and determinism in the senses defined. To act from our own desires is not to act without a cause, and it is ridiculous and unfortunate that these confusions have been perpetrated.

Schlick's concluding chapter returns to the main problem of ethics as he sees it: to discover why man acts morally. To answer this exhaustively would be to show how the joys and valuations of morality arise from the most underivative pleasures, and how the latter occur. But we have insufficient psychological knowledge to do so with precision. Besides, the previous discussion has ignored an essential feature of human inclinations—changeability— which has more practical import than does the original problem. Consequently, Schlick substitutes the more pertinent questions: How are moral dispositions strengthened? How do we attain the valuable? The obvious answer is that we do so by suggestion, punishment, and reward—but less primitive and more permanent means are desirable.

These superior means lie in recognizing the distinction between motive pleasures and realization pleasures, those which determine and those which result from an act. (The distinction shows, incidentally, that it is possible for man to seek something other than happiness.) When discrepancies occur, as when anticipated pleasure materializes in pain, the act tends to be eliminated and replaced by one in which motive and realization feeling tones are similarly pleasant. Thus the key to consistent character and behavior is in encouraging those acts for which this relationship is fairly constant. The effects of external compulsion to morality will be weakened unless moral conduct itself leads to pleasure, and the ultimate justification of moral behavior is simply that it yields happiness to the agent. "It follows from the universally valid law of volition that he can will only such ends as are valuable for him. However, he will then distinguish genuine from spurious values: both are real, but the latter can be destroyed by the assimilative process. Spurious values exist by virtue of the pleasure which belongs to the *idea* of the end alone, and not to the end itself; while genuine values consist in those feelings of pleasure with which the end itself is experienced."

The inclinations which best qualify as genuine are the social impulses, in which the idea of pleasant or unpleasant states of others have similar feeling tones for the self. When these states of others are realized as the ends of our conduct, our perception of others' pleasures is also pleasant for us, and thus the motive and realization pleas-ures concur, reinforcing altruistic behavior. Again the insight of Bishop Butler is relevant here: concern for the good of others is not contrary to but rather one of our own interests, and its fulfillment contributes to our own good. Thus, fortunately, the chief motives of morality are these social impulses; virtue and happiness have common causes. There are of course values which are more obviously personal, and differences in rank among these; the so-called "lower" pleasures such as those of the body are not evil, but unrestrained gratification diminishes their realization value, whereas the "higher" pleasures make the subject more susceptible to new joys and thus not only multiply but also diversify accessible goods. The social impulses are in the higher group; in fact, one of them, love, provides the highest happiness possible. Such impulses relate individuals rather than an individual to mankind in general; Schlick rejects the utilitarian goal of the greatest happiness of the greatest number as too abstract.

But when happiness is sought directly, paradoxically it most frequently eludes us; consequently the emphasis should be put on the capacity for happiness. Schlick does not claim that virtue guarantees happiness; the best that man can do is to heed the precepts, "At all times be fit for happiness" and "Be ready for happiness," imperatives which come as close as possible to being moral principles. (Schlick appears to forget here that at first he described moral principles as factual propositions, indicative statements reporting generalizations from particular moral approvals.) Since the greatest capacity for happiness is found in the altruistic impulses, which may seem contradictory to the neophyte in virtue, the earlier stages of morality involve renunciation and compulsion; but as the individual progresses and experiences the joys rewarding these social inclinations, the ethics of duty gives way to the ethics of kindness. To the objection that unmitigated kindness is nothing but misguided weakness, Schlick answers that, of course, correction by intelligence and by insight into the consequences of generous impulses is necessary. But he maintains that if we subsume all altruistic impulses under "kindness" and describe the rational harmony of all impulses as "personality," we will have named the two prerequisites of the good life.

THE DESTINY OF MAN

Author: Nikolai Berdyaev (1874-1948)
Type of work: Theology, ethics, epistemology
First published: 1931

PRINCIPAL IDEAS ADVANCED

Ethical knowledge is a way of being; it is different from scientific knowledge in that it is not knowledge about objects or events.

Freedom is necessary to morality; it is the primeval abyss out of which all distinctions arise; it is the condition of being itself.

Without a theodicy—a justification of God in a universe of which evil is a disturbing part—there can be no ethics: the only satisfactory theodicy is one in which God is shown as subject to an uncreated freedom.

Without an adequate theory of man, there can be no ethics: the only satisfactory philosophical anthropology is one in which man is shown as a personality, a being capable of transcending his natural and social world.

There is an element of the demonic in man; to overcome the demonic, to make creativity possible, man must be deified through the presence of God in time.

In *The Destiny of Man* Berdyaev undertakes the formulation of a philosophico-theological ethics. This ethics is defined both as an ethics of creativeness and as a theo-andric ethics. The treatise begins with a delineation of the foundational principles which undergird such an ethics, proceeds to an elaboration of three distinct but interrelated ethical theories (ethics of law, ethics of redemption, and ethics of creativeness), and concludes with a discussion of the significance of eschatology for ethics. The style is heavy and ponderous and the form is consciously systematic. The author is convinced that ethics, ontology, and theology comprise an interdependent complex of considerations, and his pattern of argument is developed in such a manner that it expresses throughout an attempt at a systematic integration of these three areas.

The foundational principles of Berdyaev's ethical system are explicated in Part I of his treatise. The first principle is an epistemological one, having to do specifically with the nature of ethical knowledge. The author's views on epistemology express a marked existentialist influence. Epistemology is subordinated to ontology. Knowledge is a part of being. The knowing subject is at the same time an existing subject, and all of his reflections arise from, and are rooted in, his project of existing. Kant is credited with having disclosed the irremovable limitations of objective knowledge, and thus his services to epistemology are deemed invaluable. It is impossible, says the author, to return to a precritical form of philosophizing. At the same time, however, Berdyaev is led to reject Kant's transcendental consciousness, because it results in the reflection of an epistemological ego which loses touch with concrete existence. The Kantian epistemology answers the problem of knowledge on the level of abstraction, but has no relation to the concrete man who is the knower. It is for this reason that he chooses the existentialists over Kant. Knowledge, for Pascal, Kierkegaard, and Heidegger is *existentially* determined. It remains a part of concrete life. This existentialist point of departure entails a rejection of the applicability of the subject-object dichotomy to ethical knowledge. Objectivization destroys life and being. The author grants that the subject-object distinction is relevant in natural science, where truth claims are justified through empirical and objective investigations, but least of all can ethical knowledge be objectivized. Scientific knowledge is *"about* something," but not so with ethical knowledge. Ethical knowledge

"is something"; it is not *about* an object which somehow stands over against it. Ethical knowledge is irreducible and immediate. The objectivization of ethical knowledge leads inevitably to "normative" ethics, and for the author all normative ethics are tyrannical.

The second foundational principle is freedom. Morality presupposes freedom. Any ethics of creativeness demands freedom as a pre-condition. Freedom as a philosophical category is for the author a broader designation than simply *human* freedom. Freedom has both a cosmic and a pre-cosmic status. It is pre-cosmic and uncreated in that it is the source of being itself. Being springs from freedom, not freedom from being. Freedom indicates the primeval abyss (the author makes use of the notion of the *Ungrund* to express this primeval freedom—a notion which he takes over from Jacob Boehme), out of which all distinctions of being arise. Freedom as uncreated is the non-being which remains impenetrable even to the being of God. God as the Creator is all-powerful over being, but he has no power in his function of Creator over non-being—the primeval, uncreated freedom. Man is both a child of God and a child of uncreated freedom. The fact of uncreated freedom accounts for the dark side of human nature, out of which arises both creativeness and destructiveness. Freedom provides the condition for a continuing co-creation with God, but it also provides the condition for the rise of evil. Freedom thus accounts for tragedy as an essential element of morality.

Through freedom the distinction between good and evil arises, and thus the problem of theodicy makes its appearance. Without a theodicy, says the author, there can be no ethics. If there is a real distinction between good and evil, then God must be justified, for only in this way can the problem of evil be solved. Berdyaev finds the traditional doctrines of theodicy to be philosophically and theologically impoverished. The traditional theological explanation of evil through a created freedom and a doctrine of the Fall results in a divine comedy in which the only part is a monologue—played by God. Evil cannot be simply explained as being due to the misuse of a freedom with which God endowed his creatures. Hence, the views of both Augustine and Leibniz on theodicy are in the final analysis superficial. The Marcionites, the Gnostics, and the Manichees were more poignantly aware of the tragic character of life, and saw the inadequacy of explaining evil through a freedom which was itself created by God. It is only with a doctrine of pre-cosmic, uncreated freedom that the ways of God can be justified. God himself emerges out of the *Ungrund,* and is subject to a freedom which he has not created. Thus, he cannot be held responsible for the freedom which gives rise to evil.

Such a theodicy leads to a metaphysical dualism, and this conclusion the author is ready to embrace. All monistic systems founder because they are incapable of dealing productively with the problem of evil. A theodicy which is adequately formulated will thus justify God by placing the origin of evil in uncreated freedom. But if God "precedes" the determination of evil, so also he "precedes" the determination of good. It is equally wrong to say that God is bound to will the

good. God is "beyond good and evil." The distinction arises only from the side of man in his fallen existence. God is above good as he is above evil. The highest value thus lies beyond good and evil. Nietzsche saw the full force of this insight. Ethics must at the same time provide a basis for morality and point out its falsity. It is significant that Berdyaev has chosen as the epigraph for his book the lines from Gogol's notebook: "It is sad not to see any good in goodness."

The fourth fundamental principle for ethics has to do with an adequate doctrine of man. The distinction between good and evil arises only through man, hence one is always driven back to the basic question, "What is man?" Ethical inquiry cannot proceed without an adequately formulated philosophical anthropology. In the formulation of his philosophical anthropology, Berdyaev draws heavily from the insights of Max Scheler. It was Scheler, argues the author, who grasped the implications of anthropology for ethics more profoundly than any preceding philosopher. The determinant of personality is central for both Scheler and Berdyaev. True anthropology is personalistic. Personality should not be confused with individuality. Individuality is a naturalistic and biological category, personality is a religious and ethical one. Personality denotes the image and likeness of God in man, by virtue of which he is able to rise above the natural life. As personality cannot be reduced to mere individuality, so also it cannot be reduced to a function of society. As a being with personality man is capable of transcending both his natural and his social world. Personality liberates man from the tyranny of society and public opinion, and makes creativity possible. Society is an object of moral valuation, but never its source. Personality determines the self as unique and irreplaceable, possessing an original freedom, through which alone moral actions can occur.

The author sees clearly that an awareness of personality and moral action presuppose an acknowledgment of other persons (an I-Thou relationship, as Martin Buber would say), but he insists on a distinction between sociality and communalty (*sobornost*). Sociality has to do with customs and manners which are the result of social sanctions, but remains intentionally neutral to moral facts. Communalty is a religio-moral category which expresses a free union of personal selves as they stand in the presence of God. (This distinction between sociality and communalty is also expressed by Scheler when he distinguishes *Gesellschaft* from *Gemeinschaft*). A philosophical anthropology, which remains true to the facts of concrete experience, will need to give due consideration to the element of the demonic in man. Uncreated freedom is the source of man's destructiveness as well as his creativeness. To define man simply as a bearer of a universal reason who strives for order and harmony, is to define man partially. This is to neglect that aspect of human nature which contradicts reason and order. This neglect, according to the author, is the chief weakness in all varieties of idealism. Modern psychopathology has proved to be invaluable for philosophical anthropology by uncovering the demonic tendencies which result from repressed instincts and drives. Psychopathology has shown that man is a creature of unreason as well as reason.

This truth, continues Berdyaev, was already part and parcel of the Biblical doctrine of man, which disclosed the demonic as a structural implication of the Fall. But the Biblical doctrine does not begin, nor does it conclude, with the fallenness of man or the fact of human sin. It begins with man made in the image of God and concludes with God becoming man. Thus the fall must always be understood within the context of Creation and Incarnation. God enters human existence in the person of Christ. The central anthropological idea of Christianity is thus the idea of a divine humanity. The crowning moment in the Christian drama is the deification of humanity. There can be no ethics of creativeness so long as there is a separation between God and man, between the divine and the human. Creativity is made possible only through the presence of eternity in time. It is this which properly defines Berdyaev's ethics as a theo-andric ethics.

In Part II of his treatise the author sets forth a typology of philosophico-theological ethics. Three major types are delineated: ethics of law, ethics of redemption, and ethics of creativeness. The distinguishing mark of the ethics of law is its social character. It legislates for the social rather than the personal conscience, and hence is unable to acknowledge personal freedom, uniqueness, and creativity. It is concerned only with that which is universally binding and thus disregards the element of particularity in moral action. The ethics of law strives for a social homogeneity and cohesiveness, and it can best bring about this end by localizing the source of moral judgment in some centralizing authority—either a clan, tribe, caste, priesthood, or government. Respect for rank becomes the basis for moral action. The head of the clan, the hierarchy of the church, or the ruler of the government legislates the universally binding norms. As respect for rank constitutes the source of law ethics, so fear accounts for its maintenance. An ethics of law inevitably inspires fear. The socially prescribed "oughts" are upheld because of a fear of the consequences which would follow their violation. The tragic implication of an ethics of law is that it degenerates into a herd morality. Personality is dissolved into sociality, the exceptional and the unique are leveled to the average and the standardized, and creativity is curtailed. Quite clearly, Nietzsche, Kierkegaard, and Heidegger are in the background of Berdyaev's critique of law ethics. Reference is made by the author to Heidegger's concept of *das Man,* which indicates the anonymous and depersonalized existence of the individual who has lost himself in the public conventions of a standardized mode of life. An ethics of law reduces everything and everyone to a common denominator and cools the fires of the creative spirit. Yet, Berdyaev's attitude toward an ethics of law is not wholly negative. The ethics of law does provide a positive value. Although it warps personality it still preserves it. In a world into which sin has entered, life itself would be threatened were it not for the protections of social sanctions. Exclusive dependence upon an ethics of grace and an ethics of creativity would endanger the very existence of personality. Man lives in a sinful, fallen world. Hence, the law is needed. The ethics of law must be transcended, but it cannot be abrogated.

The ethics of redemption stands in a paradoxical relationship to the ethics of law. On the one hand redemption presupposes law; on the other hand it implies a liberation from the law. Redemption presupposes law because the world which is redeemed is a sinful world in which relative justice must be safeguarded by legal sanctions—both political and ecclesiastical. Justice is the highest achievement of the ethics of law. The ethics of redemption does not cancel this justice, but transfigures it through love. The highest achievement of the ethics of redemption is love. Thus on the one hand redemption is continuous with law; but on the other hand redemption expresses a movement through which man is freed from the law. The redeemed man is not subject to universally binding norms. He sees every moral problem as one that demands an individual solution. Christianity, as the supreme expression of the ethics of redemption, knows no universally legislative morality. Christian ethics is lost in that moment that it is transformed into a norm. In its liberation from the ethics of law, the movement of redemption transvalues the moral principles which have become standardized by the legal consciousness. The "wicked," the "rebellious," the "adulterers," the "unbelievers" prove to be more acceptable to God than the "good," the "pious," the "just," and the "faithful." Thus, the ethics of redemption becomes a stumbling block for the ethics of law. It teaches that the first shall be last and the last shall be first. The moral judgments of the rationalized and legalized conscience are ironically disclosed as pharisaical vices. The moral ambiguity of the sinful world, which is the condition for the ethics of law, renders impossible a clear demarcation between the evil and the good. Redemptive ethics is disclosed on the other side of the sinful world, as an answer to it, and thus lies beyond the distinction between good and evil. The ethics of redemption transvalues the interpretive moral categories of the ethics of law.

The ethics of creativeness demands three conditions: (1) a primeval, uncreated freedom; (2) gifts or talents bestowed upon man by God; and (3) the world as the field of man's activity. Every act of human creation thus involves a condition which is supplied by God—the gift of genius; but also there is that condition which resides in the abyss of the self and which does not proceed from God—uncreated freedom. Thus, it is first in the ethics of creativeness that we see man in his superlative grandeur and true nobility. Man becomes a veritable co-creator with God. He creates *ex nihilo*—out of the nothingness which resides in the depths of his self. This creativeness has an inner and an outer aspect. The inner aspect is the primary creative intuition which as such is not concerned with realization. It is the energy or the potentiality which makes realization possible. The outer aspect has to do with the realization process, which terminates in the statue, the painting, the book, or the social institution: the created "object." But in this second aspect there is a cooling down of the creative fire. A created "object," by virtue of the fact that it becomes an object, is inevitably less than the creative intuition from which it took its rise. This is the essential tragedy of human creativity. The ethics of creativeness differs from the ethics of law in that it is personal and creative rather than social and legisla-

tive. Creativity can never be confined to universally binding rules. It differs from the ethics of redemption in that its first concern is with values and not with salvation. It presupposes a morality different from that of both law and redemption. The creator engages in a movement of self-transcendence, forgets about himself, and understands all moral progress to be adventitious to the creative vision. No amount of ethical striving for moral edification will enhance his creativity. His creativity has to do with values above man; it strives for the "selfless and disinterested love of God and of the divine life, of truth and perfection and all positive values." It is at this point that the creative and theo-andric aspects of Berdyaev's ethics are harmonized. Creativity, in its final dimension, is a movement expressing a divine humanity.

The third and final part of Berdyaev's philosophico-theological treatise consists of an examination of the relevance of eschatology for ethics. The problems of death and immortality, of hell and paradise are discussed in the light of their ethical significance. The author credits Kierkegaard and Heidegger for having recognized the paramount significance of death for ontological ethics, and his analysis is markedly influenced by the reflections of both the Danish and German existentialist. Death is understood not simply as a biological happening, but as an event which embraces the whole of life. Death penetrates life in every experience of transitoriness and separation. Death is existentialized as a phenomenon experienced in the midst of life. Immortality provides the answer to the anxiety which is created in the encounter with existential death. But immortality, as defined by the author, is not an objectivized and naturalized life beyond the grave. It too is existentialized as a subjective mode of existence which is attained while still in time.

Berdyaev carefully distinguishes objective immortality, which is a peculiar legacy of Greek rationalism, from subjective immortality, or eternal life, which has its roots in the Judaic-Christian tradition. Eternal life is not a life in a future world, but rather a qualification of the present life of man in the creative moment. Eternal life comes not in the future, but in the "depths of an instant of time." Hell and paradise, as the central eschatological symbols of Christianity, can thus never be understood as objectiv-

ized regions of reality. They are symbols of man's spiritual life—of his experience of complete separation from God and his experience of reunion in the creative moment. Hell is the experience of an utter isolation and loneliness, and a final inability to love, in which every instant of time appears as an endless duration. This is the bad infinity of which Hegel had already spoken, and which can properly be thought of as hell. Paradise symbolizes the experience of eternity in time. Eternity becomes present, not in an endless duration, but in the moment of creative inspiration and reuniting love. Berdyaev's theo-andric and creative ethics thus receives its final meaning through eschatology.

THE SPIRIT OF MEDIAEVAL PHILOSOPHY

Author: Étienne Henry Gilson (1884-   )
Type of work: Ontology, theology
First published: 1931-1932

Principal Ideas Advanced

The central idea in medieval philosophy is the idea of Being; in contrast to the Greek conception of being as essentially intelligibility and perfection, the medieval philosophers' conception of being was conditioned by religious belief: God is Being.

According to the medieval philosophy, God is self-sufficient and perfect because he exists.

God created the world ex nihilo (out of nothing), the medieval philosophers claimed; consequently, man's being is the image of Being Itself.

The medieval philosophy regarded ethics as an expression of God's will and man's fulfillment as being in the life following resurrection.

History as having a beginning (the creation), a middle (the incarnation), and an end (the Last Judgment) was the invention of medieval Christians.

Étienne Gilson's book, *The Spirit of Mediaeval Philosophy* (The Gifford lectures for 1931 and 1932), is an attempt to show that medieval philosophy was more original and significant than many contemporary critics believe. Much of what Gilson argues for in the book is not as widely questioned today as it was when the lectures were originally given. And Gilson, probably more than any other single figure, has been responsible for the great change that has occurred concerning this question. Few historians of philosophy today retain the simple erroneous view (stemming originally from the Renaissance humanists) that the Middle Ages, since their culture consisted merely of a misunderstood remnant of classical culture, can safely be ignored in discussing the history of Western philosophy. Anyone who has read even one of Gilson's books knows that this Renaissance view is simply false. Contemporary philosophers are much in Gilson's debt for pointing out so forcefully and so clearly that the medieval period included quite an array of thinkers of a high order, and that modern philosophy has in the medieval tradition roots which are just as significant as the roots it has in Greece and in science as inaugurated by Galileo, Kepler, and Newton.

Gilson recognizes that there were differences between the various medieval philosophers, that between Augustine, Anselm, Aquinas, and Duns Scotus there were genuine differences in philosophical orientation and in philosophical conclusions. But he argues that their differences all occur within a wider framework which these philosophers shared without disagreement. This wider framework is made up of two elements: the Greek metaphysical tradition and the Judeo-Christian religious tradition. The medievals questioned neither the intention of the Greek metaphysicians nor the provisional adequacy of the syntheses the Greeks produced. On the other hand, they were committed on religious grounds to the tradition developed in Palestine as it found expression in the Christian Scriptures and in the writings of the Patristic fathers. The task the medieval philosophers set themselves was to make a synthesis of the two traditions, a task which involved elaborating, complementing, and modifying the Greek metaphysical tradition in such a way that the religious insights of Christianity transformed and gave new life to that same metaphysical tradition.

The central idea in medieval philosophy, according to Gilson, is the idea of Being. The concept of being (a capital "B" indicates the medieval idea and a lower case "b" indicates the Greek concept) was a familiar one to the Greeks, but Gilson argues that the Greek concept of being was radically transformed and reinterpreted in the light of the Christian revelation. In spite of obvious similarities between the Greek concept of being and the medieval idea of Being there are fundamental differences. Gilson's book amounts to an extended treatise on the idea of Being, first contrasting it with the Greek concept of being and then tracing the implications of the medieval doctrine for a variety of philosophical problems.

To the Greek, intelligibility and metaphysical perfection were the essential components in the concept of being; the more intelligibility and perfection (self-sufficiency) a thing had, the more being it had. It is probable that this philosophy found its fullest expression in Plato's doctrine of degrees or reality. As a mind ascends in the Platonic hierarchy from nonbeing through becoming to the realm of being itself, the mind moves from less to greater intelligibility and self-sufficiency. Finally, in the Idea of the Good, the mind reaches the ultimate in intelligibility and self-sufficiency; indeed, the very ground of being itself. Aristotle, too, shared in this interpretation of the concept of being. His unmoved movers were self-sufficient and completely intelligible. They were pure forms and, as such, were preëminently intelligible, and the fact that they were themselves unmoved is equivalent in the Aristotelian scheme to saying that they were self-sufficient. Intelligibility and perfection, then, were the ground of existence in the Greek view of things, so much so, in fact, that even the gods were criticized in the light of this metaphysical persuasion by the philosophers. In Plato's scheme of education as set forth in the *Republic* certain myths and religious poems were outlawed because they were judged inadequate in the light of his metaphysical views.

Things were different for the medieval philosophers. Rather than judging their theological tradition in the light of metaphysical doctrine, they used the theological doctrines to judge the metaphysical tradition. One of Gilson's points illustrates in a very striking fashion the medieval reversal of the Greek attitude toward the interplay of metaphysics and theology and it can serve here to exemplify Gilson's concern, which runs throughout the book, to show that medieval philosophy is something more than just new wine in old bottles. He points out that the Greeks never finally emerged from polytheism in religion. Plato never referred to the Idea of the Good as God, for example, and in spite of the fact

that he often uses the singular term "God," he also uses the plural "gods," indicating that he never advanced to full-blown monotheism. Aristotle, too, remained a polytheist. He was uncertain whether, under his first Unmoved Mover, there were forty-nine or fifty-five subordinate Unmoved Movers. By contrast, the Hebrews had no doubts on this score; at the very core of Judaism is Moses' ringing cry: "Hear, O Israel, the Lord our God is one Lord." (Deuteronomy VI:4.) And Christianity is just as monotheistic, as the opening words of the Nicene Creed proclaim: "I believe in one God. . . ." Thus, in this unmistakable manner the matter was settled for the medievals; there is only one God, and all that remains is to see the implications of monotheism for metaphysics. Never again, Gilson reminds us, was there any serious consideration of polytheism in Western civilization. Even in our day, when attitudes toward religion are considerably more heterogeneous than they were in the medieval period, the question for philosophers of religion is whether God exists —not how many gods there are.

Just as the question of how many gods there are was settled for the medievals by their religious faith, so it was that from their religious convictions they derived their conception of God's nature. It was not because God was self-sufficient and intelligible that he existed, but because he existed in the fullest and most complete sense they knew he was self-sufficient and intelligible. What is God? God is Being, for Moses again had recorded the words that settled the matter, this time repeating the very words of God himself. Moses, while tending sheep in Midian, came upon the burning bush out of which God spoke to him, directing him to lead the Children of Israel out of their bondage in Egypt. Moses himself had no doubt about his divine commissioning, but he wondered what the Israelites would think. He asked Jehovah what he should tell the Israelites when they asked him who sent him to lead them out of captivity—what was God's name? God then answered out of the burning bush: "And God said unto Moses, I AM THAT I AM: and he said, Thus shalt thou say unto the children of Israel, I AM hath sent me unto you." (Exodus II:14.) God's very name, "Jehovah," means (in translation) "I AM." Here, then, out of their religious faith, came the content for the medievals' idea of Being. God's nature is *existence*—not mere intelligibility or perfection; God is Being. Religious faith and metaphysical beliefs meet at the apex of each other; what remains for the philosopher is to elaborate the body of philosophical doctrine which is suspended from the idea of Being as it is thus filled out with a content that has been religiously revealed. The medievals used Greek terminology and Greek thought patterns, since the created world had its (derivative) being from Being Itself, and, furthermore, the reasonableness the Greeks had discovered and formulated was the intrinsic reasonableness of this derivative being. Nevertheless, the medievals did not hesitate to transform or to go beyond the insights of the Greeks, provided this step was necessary to make their philosophy compatible with their religious faith.

From the idea of Being, cast against the background of the Christian Scriptures, Gilson moves on to consider derivative beings. The medieval philosophers differed from the ancients on this question, too. For the Greeks, the world about us is a metaphysical ultimate, or at least the stuff of that world is ultimate. There was no doctrine of creation in Greek philosophy. The nearest approach to a creation doctrine was perhaps Plato's myth in the *Timaeus* about the origin of the world. But in this latter myth the Demiurge (the divine agent) merely forms (or *in*forms) a preëxistent matter. The matter itself is not made; it is an ultimate in the metaphysical picture. Of course, the Christians could not go along with this Platonic or Greek interpretation, for they had all read the opening words of Genesis: "In the beginning God created the heaven and the earth." Just before the beginning—if one overlooks for the moment St. Augustine's observation that it makes no sense to talk this way—there was nothing, nothing in the strictest possible sense. Then God created it all, ordering it both temporally and physically, as is recorded in Genesis.

Certain other elements from the Genesis account are taken into the medieval metaphysical picture. God not only created the world *ex nihilo*, but he "saw that it was good." and Furthermore, he made made, the crown of creation, "in his own image." All this has consequences for metaphysics. In the first place, the world in which we live has a derivative being, a being that is an effect of God's, or Being's, creative activity. The rocks, trees, animals, and the rest have being because they were created by Being. And in a special sense man also has being since he, too, is created, and therefore Being has communicated being to him. But man's being bears on its face an additional mark. Man's being is the image of Being Itself. This idea had an added consequence for the medieval philosophers; an epistemological doctrine was derived which parallels the ontological and anthropological doctrines. In knowing himself man knows an analogue of Being Itself. There is therefore a pathway to knowledge of the divine. Out of the metaphysical emerges the epistemological. Descartes' well-known remark about the mark of the Craftsman, left imprinted on his handiwork, is but a later reflection of this medieval doctrine of the analogy of being and an example of the often overlooked influence of medieval thought on modern philosophy.

The doctrine of the analogy of being is one example of how the idea of Being influenced medieval metaphysics. Gilson considers many other examples of this transformation of Greek metaphysics in the light of Christian belief. Two important areas of medieval philosophical concern which he discusses are ethics and history.

One of the most noticeable differences between the ethical views of classical Greece and Christianity is the presence in the latter of the concept of sin. In Greek ethics and in Greek religion there was no concern with sin in the Christian sense. There were, of course, rules regarding what was proper religious conduct, but they dealt mainly with ritual purity. And in Greek ethics there were general rules of conduct, but they were not interpreted in such a way as to make violations of them sinful acts. The best-known Christian code of conduct, however, the Ten Commandments, was attributed directly to God, and God made it clear that violation of the Commandments was a personal affront to him. ("For I the Lord thy God am a jealous God. . . .") Again, the Chris-

tian God was added to the philosophical tradition by the medievals and a new synthesis emerged. The ethical principles of the Greeks were retained, but they were not merely the deliverances of reason (although the medievals did not deny that reason could, and indeed had discovered them). But the ethical rules were also the expression of God's will regarding man's conduct. Just as man's being was an indelible mark indicating the fact that he was a creature made by God, so man's conscience had written on it God's Law. The Greeks had discovered the Natural Law because God had written that Law on the hearts of all men. The Greeks knew the Law, but they had not known that it was another stamp left on man by his Creator.

But there was still more in the medieval ethical position. The Greek believed that the rules of ethics told him how to live his life most satisfactorily here on earth, but there was no transcendent reference. For the Christian, however, conduct was the key not only to satisfactory living here in this life, but it was also the crucial determiner of his eternal destiny. Man's fulfillment, for the medieval, was not in this life, but in the life following the resurrection. This idea, Gilson argues, introduced two considerations that were lacking in the Greek view: a concern for the individual man as a being of eternal worth, and an attitude toward the physical world which again rested on an affirmation of the everlasting worth of the resurrected body. As another example of the shift from the usual perspective which results from Gilson's sympathetic reading of medieval philosophy, we might note here his observation on medieval monastic asceticism. He points out that it does not originate in a Platonic rejection of the body, as is the usual understanding; instead, it reflects an effort to discipline the body in order to make that very body serve more adequately in its proper spiritual vocation.

These observations about the consequences of the doctrine of the resurrection of the body for ethics lead easily into a consideration of the medieval philosophy of history. Surely the speculations of St. Augustine on time in the concluding books of the *Confessions* and his doctrine of the two cities in the *City of God* insure Augustine's eminence in this area of philosophical inquiry. Gilson merely points out that this philosophy of history is another instance of the pervasive influence of the central idea of Being in the thought of the medieval Christians. The Greeks had only a cyclical view of history, they had no feeling at all for history as the tale of the significance of individual human striving. For St. Augustine in particular, and the medievals generally, however, history had an origin, a direction, and a goal, and was made up of the acts of individual human beings, beings with immortal souls and with bodies which would again be active following the Resurrection. History, as told in terms of human personality and as having a beginning (the creation), a middle (the incarnation), and an end (the Last Judgment), was clearly the invention of the medieval Christians. It resulted from speculation that operated against the background of Christian revelation. Such a conception of history was lacking in the Greek world; it originated in the medieval interval, and remains with us today.

In spite of the many excellences of Gilson's book, and his refreshing refusal to view medieval philosophy as a pointless, logic-chopping debate over silly questions, there are certain inadequacies that remain. Some medieval philosophers are barely mentioned, and their views are slighted. Siger of Brabant, whose Averroistic doctrine of separate truths for faith and reason does not fit in well with Gilson's picture, is an example. The tension at Paris during the thirteenth century between, on the one hand, Siger's emphasis on fidelity to Aristotle's own text, even when it conflicted with Scripture and religious tradition, and, on the other hand, the Thomist concern to accommodate Aristotle to religious orthodoxy is not given the discussion it should receive in a book on medieval philosophy. The realism-nominalism controversy, around which so much philosophical debate centered, is another problem which Gilson treats less fully than one might expect. Ockham, a commanding figure in the late medieval period, is given scant notice. Generally speaking, the Thomist synthesis occupies such a dominant position in the book that many of the rich countermelodies of medieval thought do not emerge.

Finally, the sophisticated Protestant reader cannot help feeling that some of Gilson's incidental remarks about Martin Luther reveal less sympathy for the spirit of the Reformation than they do for the spirit of Thomistic philosophy. It is a rare person indeed who can look at both St. Thomas and the impulsive and often horribly mistaken Luther without feeling that one of them was seriously in error, but one suspects that there must have been in the medieval period a tradition that somehow provided a background for the Reformation. The nominalist Ockham and the philosophers who held that will was superior to intellect in

God provided parts of this background. Gilson leaves the reader with the feeling that these stresses were almost entirely missing in the medieval intellectual milieu.

But these are errors of omission, not of commission. It would be a mistake to make more of them than merely to mention them. And Gilson himself has shown in other of his writings his awareness of the influences which he here neglects. In spite of its shortcomings, Gilson's book remains an excellent interpretation of what is clearly the main current of medieval thought.

It is a book that no historian of philosophy can afford to be without, and it is a book that makes understandable and commendable the current revival of interest in scholastic philosophy generally and in St. Thomas specifically. Neo-Thomists have enriched contemporary philosophy considerably in areas as diverse as philosophy of religion and logic. Professor Gilson's very important role as one of the leaders among this group cannot surprise anyone who reads *The Spirit of Mediaeval Philosophy*.

COLLECTED PAPERS

Author: Charles Sanders Peirce (1839-1914)
Type of work: Logic, epistemology, metaphysics
First published: (1931-1958, eight volumes)

Principal Ideas Advanced

A belief is a habit of action; different beliefs give rise to different modes of action.

Our idea of anything is our idea of its sensible effects; objects are distinguished according to the difference they make practically.

True ideas are those to which responsible investigators, were they to push their inquiries far enough, would finally give assent; reality is what true ideas represent.

Of the four methods of fixing belief—the method of tenacity, of authority, of a priori judgments, and the method of science—the scientific is preferable as providing critical tests of procedures.

By the conceptions of Firstness, Secondness, and Thirdness, a metaphysics of cosmic evolution can be developed; Firstness is the individual quality of a thing, Secondness is the relatedness of a thing to something other than itself, and Thirdness is the tendency to mediate, to contribute to law.

There is chance in the universe (tychism); the universe begins in a chaos of unpersonalized feeling and develops habits or patterns of action (synechism); finally, as laws develop, the universe moves toward a condition of perfect rationality and symmetry (agapasm).

Although it is almost a century since Charles Sanders Peirce—in conversation with William James, Chauncey Wright, Nicholas St. John Green, and Oliver Wendell Holmes at informal meetings of the "metaphysical club" in Cambridge, Massachusetts—developed and brought to clear expression the central ideas which became the core of pragmatism, the pragmatic philosophy continues to prevail as the predominant American philosophy. Of course, if one were to make a survey, it might very well turn out that the majority of American philosophers would deny being pragmatists, although few would deny having been influenced by the ideas of Peirce, James, and John Dewey. But idealism in America is practically dead, despite some isolated champions in its behalf; and the new linguistic empiricism—which represents the emphasis of the Vienna positivists on grounding philosophical claims in experience (and manipulating statements according to an impartial logic), together with the emphasis of the British philosophers on the study of ordinary language in the multiplicity of its uses—comes very close to being a sophisticated, latter-day version of the American pragmatism which Peirce invented and defended.

But Peirce was more than the creator of pragmatism; he was a scientist, mathematician, logician, and teacher —although his career as a professor was limited. He lectured at Harvard and The Johns Hopkins University. Peirce's failure to find, or to be offered, a university position suitable for one of his talents, was a consequence of his independent and undisciplined nature. The result of his being free from academic restrictions was per-

haps both fortunate and unfortunate: as an outsider, his creative powers had no formal limits, but his intellect was brilliant, and he knew where to stop in his inventions and speculations; but because he was an outsider, he had neither the security nor the incentive to fashion his essays into any coherent whole. Although he attempted, in later life, to write a great, single work in which his views on logic, nature, science, man, and philosophy would be developed in some mutually illuminating and supporting fashion, his poverty and isolation—together with his iconoclastic stubbornness—combined to frustrate his great ambition.

The most comprehensive collection of Peirce's papers is the *Collected Papers of Charles Sanders Peirce* (eight volumes, 1931-1958), edited by Charles Hartshorne and Paul Weiss, but other selections from his essays are available, including *Chance, Love, and Logic: Philosophical Essays by the Late Charles S. Peirce* (1923), edited by Morris R. Cohen, and *The Philosophy of Peirce* (1940), edited by Justus Buchler.

Although the critical interest in Peirce's writings is as lively now as it has ever been, and the attention given to the papers has intensified since the publication of the *Collected Papers,* so that new discoveries are constantly being made and new enthusiasms are frequently aroused, most editors of Peirce's essays and most commentators on his work are agreed on the importance of certain essays as being particularly characteristic of Peirce at his best. Among the early essays are "The Fixation of Belief," and "How to Make Our Ideas Clear," and among the later, "The Architecture of Theories" and "The Doctrine of Necessity Examined." Since these essays contain some of the most famous and revealing statements of Peirce's basic opinions, an examination of them will serve as an introduction to other significant essays.

Peirce's thought, varied and original as it was, falls naturally into four categories: the pragmatic, the epistemological, the logical, and the metaphysical. The poles are the pragmatic ideas of meaning and truth, (ideas which condition the epistemological conceptions) and, at the other extreme of his thinking, the metaphysical ideas. The effort to relate these poles to each other rewards the student of Peirce with a synoptic idea of Peirce's philosophy which illuminates the otherwise confusing variety of essays to be found in the *Collected Papers*.

In the essay "How to Make Our Ideas Clear," which first appeared in the *Popular Science Monthly* for January, 1878, Peirce set out to clarify the unclear conception of clarity to be found in Descartes' writings on method. The first step was to clear up the conception of belief. Peirce began by speaking of doubt as a kind of irritation arising from indecisiveness in regard to action; when a man does not know what to do, he is uneasy, and his uneasiness will not leave him until he settles upon some mode of action. Belief is "a rule for action," and as it is acted upon repeatedly, each time appeasing the irritation of doubt, it becomes a habit of action. Thus, Peirce concluded, "The essence of belief is the establishment of a habit, and different beliefs are distinguished by the different modes of action to which they give rise."

In a previous essay, "The Fixation of Belief," which appeared in the *Popular Science Monthly* for November, 1877, Peirce had written of doubt as a state of dissatisfaction from which we try to free ourselves, and of belief as a satisfactory state. The struggle to remove the irritation of doubt and to attain belief, a rule of action, was described as "inquiry," and the settlement of opinion was set forth as the sole object of inquiry.

It was Peirce's conviction that logic, as the art of reasoning, was needed to make progress in philosophy possible; he anticipated logical positivism in urging that only "a severe course of logic" could clear up "that bad logical quality to which the epithet *metaphysical* is commonly applied. . . ."

Thus, the first step in learning how to make our ideas clear is to come to the realization that belief is a habit of action, the consequence of a process of inquiry undertaken to appease the irritation of indecisiveness. Since the entire purpose of thought, as Peirce conceived it, is to produce habits of action, it follows that the meaning of a thought is the collection of habits involved; or, if the question has to do with the meaning of a "thing," its meaning is clear once we know what difference the thing would make if one were to become actively, or practically, involved with it. Peirce's conclusion was that "there is no distinction of meaning so fine as to consist in anything but a possible difference of practice."

As an example, he referred to the doctrine of transubstantiation and to the Catholic belief that the elements of the Communion, though possessing all of the sense properties of wine and wafers, are literally blood and flesh. To Peirce such an idea could not possibly be clear, for no distinction in practice could be made between wine and wafers, on the one hand, and what *appeared* to be wine and wafers, on the other. He argued that no conception of wine was possible except as the object of the reference, "this, that, or the other, is wine," or as the object of a description by means of which certain properties are attributed to wine. But the properties are conceivable only in terms of the sensible effects of wine; "Our idea of anything *is* our idea of its sensible effects. . . ." Consequently, "to talk of something as having all the sensible characters of wine, yet being in reality blood, is senseless jargon." The rule for attaining clearness of thought, Peirce's famous pragmatic maxim, appears in "How to Make Our Ideas Clear" as follows: "Consider what effects, which might conceivably have practical bearings, we conceive the object of our conception to have. Then, our conception of these effects is the whole of our conception of the object."

Peirce's discussion of his maxim, centering about examples, makes it clear that the rule for the clarification of thought was not designed to support a simple phenomenalism. Although Peirce used sentences such as "Our idea of anything *is* our idea of its sensible effects . . . ," he did not use the expression "sensible effects" to mean sensations merely. By conceiving, through the use of the senses, the effects of the action of a thing, we come to understand the thing; our habit of reaction, forced upon us by the action of the thing, is a conception of it, our belief regarding it. The object is not *identifiable* with its effects—that is not even proper grammar, and Peirce was aware of the relation of linguistic practice to philosophical perplexity—but the object can be conceived as "that which" we conceive only in terms of its effects.

Peirce's pragmatic rule should be distinguished from William James's version of the same principle. James stressed an idea's becoming true; he used the misleading expression "practical cash-value" to refer to the pragmatic meaning of a word, and he sometimes emphasized the *satisfactoriness* of an idea, as constituting its truth, in such a way that no clear line was drawn between sentimental satisfaction and the satisfaction of a scientific investigator.

Peirce, on the other hand, in developing the ideas of truth and reality made careful use of the contrary-to-fact conditional in order to avoid any loose or emotional interpretation of the pragmatic method. He wrote, in "How to Make Our Ideas Clear," that scientific processes of investigation "if only pushed far enough, will give one certain solution to every question to which they can be applied. . . ." Again, in clarifying the idea of reality, Peirce came to the conclusion that "The opinion which is fated to be ultimately agreed to by all who investigate, is what we mean by the truth, and the object represented in this opinion is the real." In other words, those opinions to which systematic, responsible investigators, *would* finally give assent, *were* the matter thoroughly investigated, are true opinions. It was Peirce's dissatisfaction with the tender-minded versions of the pragmatic method that led him finally to give up the name "pragmatism," which he invented, and to use in its place the term "pragmaticism."

Peirce's preference for the scientific

method of inquiry is nowhere more clearly expressed and affirmed than in his early essay, "The Fixation of Belief." Regarding the object of reasoning to be the discovery of new facts by a consideration of facts already known, and having argued that a belief is a habit of action which appeases the irritation of doubt or indecisiveness, he went on to examine four methods of fixing belief: the method of tenacity, which is the method of stubbornly holding to a belief while resisting all criticism; the method of authority, which consists of punishing all dissenters; the *a priori* method, which depends on the inclination to believe, whatever the facts of the matter; and, finally, the method of science, which rests on the following assumption: "There are real things, whose characters are entirely independent of our opinions about them; those realities affect our senses according to regular laws, and, though our sensations be as different as our relations to the objects, yet, by taking advantage of the laws of perception, we can ascertain by reasoning how things really are, and any man, if he have sufficient experience and reason enough about it, will be led to the one true conclusion."

Peirce strongly endorsed the scientific method of inquiry. He argued that no other method provided a way of determining the rightness or wrongness of the method of inquiry itself; the test of a procedure undertaken as scientific is an application of the method itself.

In support of the realistic hypothesis on which the method of science is based, Peirce argued that the practice of the method in no way cast doubt on the truth of the hypothesis; fur-

thermore, everyone who approves of one method of fixing belief in preference to others tacitly admits that there are realities the method can uncover; the scientific method is widely used, and it is only ignorance that limits its use; and, finally, the method of science has been so successful that belief in the hypothesis on which it rests has been strengthened proportionately.

These passages should be of particular interest to those who suppose that Peirce, as the founder of pragmatism, was absolutely neutral in regard to commitments ordinarily regarded as metaphysical. He did not claim to know the truth of the realistic hypothesis, but it did seem to him eminently sensible, accounting for the manner in which nature forces experience upon us, and making uniformity of opinion possible. (However, his theory of cosmic evolution, as shall be seen, is a peculiar kind of realism.)

In the essay "The Architecture of Theories," published in *The Monist* in January, 1891, Peirce introduced the critical conceptions of First, Second, and Third, which he described as "principles of Logic," and by reference to which he developed his metaphysics of cosmic evolution. He defined the terms as follows: "First is the conception of being or existing independent of anything else. Second is the conception of being relative to, the conception of reaction with, something else. Third is the conception of mediation, whereby a first and second are brought into relation."

Arguing that philosophical theories should be built architectonically, Peirce offered the conceptions of First, Second, and Third as providing the logical principles of construction. Any adequate theory, he maintained, would order the findings of the various sciences by the use of the principles of First, Second, and Third. Thus, in psychology, "Feeling is First, Sense of reaction Second, General conception Third, or mediation." Significantly, as a general feature of reality, "Chance is First, Law is Second, the tendency to take habits is Third," and, Peirce maintained, "Mind is First, Matter is Second, Evolution is Third."

Peirce went on to sketch out the metaphysics which would be built by the use of these general conceptions. He wrote that his would be a "Cosmogonic Philosophy," and that it would describe a universe which, beginning with irregular and unpersonalized feeling would, by chance ("sporting here and there in pure arbitrariness"), give rise to generalizing tendencies which, continuing, would become "habits" and laws; the universe, such a philosophy would claim, is evolving toward a condition of perfect rationality and symmetry.

Four more papers, all published in Cohen's selection, *Chance, Love, and Logic,* develop the ideas introduced in "The Architecture of Theories." They are "The Doctrine of Necessity Examined," "The Law of Mind," "Man's Glassy Essence," and "Evolutionary Love."

In "The Doctrine of Necessity Examined," Peirce argued for the presence of chance in the universe. But Peirce's conception of chance was not the usual conception of the entirely uncaused and irregular, acting without cause or reason. He wrote of chance as "the form of a spontaneity which is to some degree regular," and he was careful to point out that he was not using the conception of chance as a principle of explanation

but as an element in the description of a universe in which there is the tendency to form habits and to produce regularities. The doctrine of absolute chance was named "tychism," and the doctrine of continuity was named "synechism." The essay "The Law of Mind" develops the latter doctrine.

In "The Law of Mind," Peirce argued that there is but one law of mind, that ideas spread, affect other ideas, lose intensity, but gain generality and "become welded with other ideas." In the course of the article Peirce developed the notion of an "idea" as an event in an individual consciousness; he argued that consciousness must take time and be in time, and that, consequently, "we are immediately conscious through an infinitesimal interval of time." Ideas are continuous, Peirce claimed, and there must be a "continuity of intrinsic qualities of feeling" so that particular feelings are present out of a continuum of other possibilities. Ideas affect one another: but to understand this, one must distinguish three elements within an idea (Firstness, Secondness, and Thirdness make their appearance again); the three elements are, First, the intrinsic quality of the idea as a feeling, its *quale;* Second, the energy with the idea affects other ideas (its capacity to relate); and, Third, the tendency of an idea to become generalized (its tendency to be productive of law). Habits are established by induction; general ideas are followed by the kind of reaction which followed the particular sensations that gave rise to the general idea. Mental phenomena come to be governed by law in the sense that some living idea, "a conscious continuum of feeling," pervades the phenomena and affects other ideas.

Peirce concluded "The Law of Mind" with the striking claim that matter is not dead, but it is mind "hidebound with habits."

In the essay "Man's Glassy Essence" Peirce argued that mind and matter are different aspects of a single feeling process; if something is considered in terms of its relations and reactions, it is regarded as matter, but if it is understood as feeling, it appears as consciousness. (This is a more sophisticated philosophy than James's radical empiricism, which resembles Peirce's hypothesis in some respects.) A person is a particular kind of general idea.

If it seems intolerable to suppose that matter is, in some sense, feeling or idea, one must at least consider that for Peirce an idea must be considered not only in its Firstness, but in its Secondness and Thirdness as well. In other words, an idea or feeling, for Peirce, is not *simply* a feeling as such; that is, a feeling is more than its quality, its Firstness. A feeling is also that which has the tendency to relate to other feelings with which it comes in spatial and temporal contact, and it works with other feelings toward a regularity of development which can be known as law. It does not seem likely that Peirce can be properly interpreted so as to delight a physical realist who maintains that matter is in no way feeling or mind; but his philosophy is much more acceptable, to one concerned with the multiplicity of physical phenomena, than an idealism which regards ideas as static individuals existing only in their Firstness (merely as feelings).

In "Evolutionary Love," Peirce maintained that his synechism calls for a principle of evolution that will account for creative growth. How is it that out of chaos so irregular that it seems inappropriate to say that anything exists, a universe of habit and law can emerge? Chance relations develop, the relations become habits, the habits become laws; *tychism* emphasizes the presence of chance, *synechism* emphasizes the development of relations through the continuity of ideas, and *agapasm* (Peirce's term) emphasizes the evolutionary tendency in the universe. Thus, we discover how the logical (ordering) principles of Firstness, Secondness, and Thirdness make intelligible not only the idea (with its *quale,* its relatedness, and its tendency to contribute to the development of law), but also the person (who is a general idea), matter (which is mind hide-bound with habits), and the character of the universe. The logical principles become metaphysical.

Peirce is important in contemporary thought primarily because of his pragmatic, logical, and epistemological views. There is a great deal of material in the *Collected Papers* that remains to be explored, and those who would picture Peirce as the forerunner of linguistic and empirical philosophy can find much to support their claims in his essays. His metaphysics is regarded as interesting, though as pragmatically insignificant; but this is partly a matter of current taste. When interest in metaphysics revives, and there is no methodological reason why it cannot revive and be respectable, the metaphysics of Charles Sanders Peirce, his theory of cosmic evolution or agapasm, will certainly be reconsidered.

THE TWO SOURCES OF MORALITY AND RELIGION

Author: Henri Bergson (1859-1941)
Type of work: Ethics, philosophy of religion
First published: 1932

PRINCIPAL IDEAS ADVANCED

There are two kinds of morality: compulsive morality and ideal morality.

There are two kinds of religion: popular religion and dynamic religion.

Corresponding to the two kinds of morality and the two kinds of religion are two kinds of societies, the closed and the open, and two kinds of souls, the enslaved and the free.

The two sources of morality and religion are the practical needs of men and societies and the idealistic impulse.

Men rise above the static patterns of compulsive moralities and popular religions, achieving freedom in open societies, when they recapture, through mystical intuition, their original vital impetus.

In no sense was Bergson's philosophy a mere compilation of the scientific findings of his time. Nevertheless, his kind of empiricism required him to investigate on his own principles the subject matter of various sciences. His early works may be viewed as studies in psychology. In *Creative Evolution* (1906) he turned to biology. His last great work, *The Two Sources of Morality and Religion,* took him into the fields of sociology and cultural anthropology. Here he made "vital impulse" the key to understanding morality, religion, and history. The work is admittedly more speculative than its predecessors. Whereas in *Creative Evolution* he had tried to "keep as close as possible to facts," in this later work he permitted himself to argue from "probabilities," on the grounds that "philosophical certainty admits of degrees." Whenever possible, philosophic intuition should be "backed up by science"; but where science falls short, Bergson maintained, it is legitimate to appeal to the testimony of great prophetic and mystical teachers. The author regarded this work as a valuable confirmation of the thesis presented in *Creative Evolution.* Others have found it rewarding for the fresh perspectives it has brought to social studies.

As the title indicates, the author's approach was a genetic one. Understanding of the phenomena under investigation meant seeing how they were necessitated by the evolutionary impulse. Bergson's contribution was to suggest that morality and religion cannot be understood in terms of one kind of explanation only. Followers of Comte, Spencer, and Marx had tried to explain all morality and religion as arising out of the needs of society. Bergson went a long way with them; but he insisted that since some morality and religion are, in the usual sense, antisocial, they must be traced to another source; namely, the spiritual vision of exceptional men. In fact, according to Bergson, all historical systems of morality and religion are blends, combining idealistic with pragmatic elements.

This amalgamation takes place because man's life is so largely dominated by intelligence, which moderates the seemingly extravagant claims of mystical insight even as it relaxes the hold of tradition and habit. Bergson denied that it is possible to explain either moral obligation or religious belief on intellectual grounds: reason is emphatically not one of the two sources from which morality and religion arise. Nonetheless, its presence is felt.

To make his thesis plain, Bergson discussed morality and religion under separate chapters. His argument is that there are two kinds of morality and two kinds of religion. Corresponding to these there are two kinds of souls and two kinds of societies.

The first kind of morality is a *common, compulsive morality* demanded by society for its protection. Bergson regarded social life as a device of the life impulse for increasing its mastery over matter and enhancing its freedom. Social life is an evolutionary advance, for the true individual is found only in society. But there are grades of social life. Insects have purchased their efficient organization only at the expense of adaptability. But it was the gift of intelligence which enabled man to break out of the hard and fast regulations imposed by instinct. The problem for man is that of preserving the social organism. Bergson imagines, as an example, that an ant momentarily endowed with sufficient intelligence asks herself whether it is in her interests to perform the onerous tasks imposed upon her by the group. He concludes that were she to consider long enough, she might at last arrive at the conclusion reached in the history of human thought by John Stuart Mill, and resume her labors, happy in the belief

that her interests are identical with those of the group. Meanwhile, however, she will perish unless instinct draws her back with the imperative, "You must because you must." Such, according to Bergson, is the sense of obligation which lies at the basis of common morality. Closely connected with habit, it is a weakened form of instinct. Intellect, far from providing a basis for moral obligation, is what obligation was designed to overcome. Moral obligation operates impersonally in a compulsive manner, and has its analogies in somnambulistic behavior. But moral compulsion is not natural in the sense that animal instincts are. Bergson denied that acquired characteristics—such as moral compulsions—are inherited. Moral patterns must be learned by each generation from its predecessor and may be modified in the process. Thus, the moralities of civilized nations differ radically from those of primitive peoples. But obligation as such is the same in all societies and everywhere exercises identical control.

Contrasted with morality of this compulsive kind is that which works under the attraction of an *ideal*. For example, an ordinary man feels obliged to render what he thinks of as justice to his friends, such as returning a favor, and to his enemies, such as exacting vengeance. But rare individuals have caught a glimpse of a higher kind of justice, what we call "social justice," that makes no distinction between friends and enemies and treats all men as equals. It is impossible, according to Bergson, to explain the origins of the latter as a development or modification of the former. Customary morality speaks for an existing order which demands to be perpetuated; the higher morality speaks for a vision which inspires in sensitive people a demand that the existing order be changed. It does not ordinarily require great effort either to learn or to practice common morality; but an ideal morality requires constant propaganda even to keep it alive and is practiced only at the expense of personal discipline and self-denial. Accordingly, we have to look not to the mass of men for its origins but to exceptional persons who have had a vision of reality in its unity and striving. Prophets through their preaching and mystics through their example call upon mankind to enter a truer way. And their teaching, not subject to the vicissitudes of history and tradition, is a perennial source of insight and motivation to lesser men.

Analogous to the first kind of morality is *popular religion*, which Bergson calls *static*. Like conscience, by which nature secures the individual's submission to the welfare of the group, religious belief is a protective device, invented by vital impulse to overcome the hazards which attend the use of intelligence in the "human experiment." Instinctive acts are performed without thinking and without any doubt as to whether they will be effective, but intelligent acts are complex; and deliberations concerning means and ends would paralyze human activity altogether if nature did not come to the rescue and teach man to invent necessities where none exist. This is what lies at the bottom of myth. A myth is a kindly hallucination which fills up the gaps left by our understanding, permitting man to act with assurance and ease.

The hunter, facing a beast at bay, needs to believe that his arrow is directed after it leaves his hand; and the farmer is comforted by the belief that there are powers which preside over the seed which he has planted in the earth. Somewhat in the same way, man needs assurance in the face of death, which has never threatened the nonreflective animal as it does man. The belief in an afterlife neutralizes doubt and fear, and provides man with the sense of self-mastery. In these ways provident nature preserves her favorite, man, making it possible for him to benefit by intelligence without being destroyed by it.

In Bergson's view, myth and magic pass over into religion in the same proportion that men accustom themselves to think of environing powers in personal terms. The *mana*, which anthropologists claim is the basis of the religious response, Bergson took to be an expression of purposive activity. In magical practices, man supposes that he employs this mysterious power himself; in religious acts, he seeks the cooperation of unseen beings who, he believes, have even greater *mana* at their disposal. For Bergson, religion is not primarily a matter of knowledge, nor is it based on poetic imagination. It has its origins in practical needs, and it provides a scaffolding for human activity.

Opposed to this static religion, which has no cognitive worth, is the *dynamic religion* which has its source in mysticism. Bergson was sparing in his use of the ambiguous term "mysticism"; like William James, he regarded mystical insight as a definite kind of experience which most of us never directly share. The visions of mystics bypass the constructions of myth and imagination as well as those of rational argument, and yield immediate experience of reality in its character as a whole. Bergson held that the Greeks, because of their intellectualism, never attained to a full-blown mysticism. In India, it developed further, but frequently it was blighted by a speculative tendency or perverted into hypnotic trance. The prophets of ancient Israel contributed the vision of a God as just as he was powerful: but his transcendence above the world and the particularism of his purpose were residues of static belief. Only the Christ of the Gospels—to whom we owe the truth that God is love—was completely open to divine reality. The great mystics of the Church are "the imitators, and original but incomplete continuators, of what the Christ of the Gospels was completely." Christ's influence is also seen, according to Bergson, in the mystics of Islam, and such modern Hindus as Ramakrishna and Vivekananda. (Bergson, it may be noted, was a Jew, although in his latter years he showed sympathy for Roman Catholicism.)

According to Bergson, genuine mysticism is not pessimistic, nor antisocial, nor quietistic. The vision of God as love generates in the beholder charity toward all of God's creatures, stirring in him the desire to lead all men into the higher form of life which has been disclosed to him. Furthermore, it releases energies in him and opens his eyes to possibilities that are sealed off from ordinary men. God works through him. He becomes the agent of the evolutionary impulse in its purpose to transcend the present stage of human like. But, as always, divine freedom must adjust its steps to material conditions. In order to draw men upward to higher freedom, the mystic accommodates his teaching to the capacity of his hearers. To get a portion of the truth accepted, the mystic has

to compromise. For humanity understands the new only as it is incorporated into the old.

Dynamic religion is the result of this compromise. It does not come into being through a natural development of the static, but by the deliberate adaptation of old forms to new ends. Like the higher ethics, dynamic religion requires a constant effort to keep it from lapsing completely into familiar static forms. Indeed, a constant tension exists between the "civic" and "universal" functions which all of the higher religions seek to perform.

The whole problem is illuminated by Bergson's distinction between "closed" and "open" societies, and the types of souls which correspond to them. Natural societies are *closed societies:* examples are families, clans, city-states, and sovereign nations. They exist to serve the interests of their own members and take no responsibility for the rest of man. "Self-centeredness, cohesion, hierarchy, absolute authority of the chief"—such are the features of the closed society. The *open society,* by contrast, is largely an ideal existing in the minds of chosen souls. In principle it embraces all humanity. But in practice the most that ever is achieved is an enlarging here and there of closed societies. Such enlargement, according to Bergson, never takes place of itself but only as a result of propaganda carried on by dedicated men, who may effect more or less far-reaching transformations of the existing order. "But after each occasion the circle that has momentarily opened closes again. Part of the new has flowed into the mould of the old; individual aspiration has become social pressure; and obligation covers the whole." Bergson regarded modern democracy as in principle an "open society," founded as it is on the ideals of liberty, equality, and brotherhood of all men. Thus, it rests on foundations quite different from those of Athenian democracy. Nevertheless, the tensions between the demands of nation-states and the service of mankind remain; in fact, our Western democracies, too, are "closed societies."

In a final chapter entitled "Machanism and Mysticism," Bergson explains the bearing of these investigations on the thesis set forth in *Creative Evolution*: that in man the divine impulse toward freedom is destined to realize itself. Does the history of the human race support this thesis? Bergson's answer was affirmative. But, as we have seen, he had to depart from the simplicities that characterize most theories of cultural evolution. They assume that through intelligence man has progressed thus far toward liberty and justice. Bergson maintained that intelligence was not a sufficient explanation and that had it not been supplemented by a halo of "intuition," it would have proved fatal to man. What enables man to rise above the static, ingrown patterns of natural societies is the capacity, never entirely lost to him, of recapturing in his own self, through the mystic vision, the original vital impetus, and moving forward with it toward higher unity and greater freedom.

Viewing the situation in our times, Bergson lamented the fact that man seems to have fallen slave to the machine. But he was unwilling to subscribe to any kind of economic determinism. Industry, which came into existence to satisfy real needs, has taken a different direction and fostered artificial ones. But this can be corrected, and by simplifying his way of life man can make machines a benefit. "The initiative can come from humanity alone, for it is humanity and not the alleged force of circumstances, still less a fatality inherent to the machine, which has started the spirit of invention along a certain track." Bergson thought that a new mysticism, with an attendant ascetic discipline, might well be in the offing, which would renew in man a sense of his high calling. In view of the breakdown of popular religion, psychical research seemed to him also to bear some promise, by restoring to the masses belief that life is more than meat and the body more than raiment. "Mankind lies groaning," he concludes, "half crushed beneath the weight of its own progress. Men do not sufficiently realize that their future is in their own hands. Theirs is the task of determining first of all whether they want to go on living or not. Theirs the responsibility, then, for deciding if they want merely to live, or intend to make just the extra effort required for fulfilling, even on their refractory planet, the essential function of the universe, which is a machine for the making of gods."

DEGREES OF KNOWLEDGE

Author: Jacques Maritain (1882-   )
Type of work: Metaphysics of knowledge
First published: 1932

Several kinds of knowledge are granted to man, each with its own merit and dignity.

Sensation, reason, revelation, and mystical union all make their contributions.

Apparent conflicts between their respective claims can be adjusted if we rightly distinguish between physics and natural philosophy, metaphysics and theology, reason and the suprarational.

A leading member of the neo-Thomist school, Maritain owes his philosophical outlook to St. Thomas Aquinas, whom he follows closely in the first half of his book, entitled "The Degrees of Rational Knowledge." But in the second half, entitled "The Degrees of Suprarational Knowledge," he goes beyond St. Thomas, and takes as his guide the sixteenth century Spanish mystic, St. John of the Cross.

Maritain calls his philosophy "critical realism," without wishing to be identified with the group usually known by that name. Its claim to be called "realism" follows from its common-sense starting point: with the plain man, Maritain holds that what the mind knows is identical with what exists in the world of things. But it is "critical realism" in that it subjects knowledge to scrutiny, and in so doing avoids the naïve view that the mind literally and materially copies nature. Maritain follows Aristotle in holding that essences can exist both materially in things and immaterially in minds. When the mind knows a thing, it becomes, after its own mode, the thing known—not in every respect, but in respect of the properties apprehended.

Maritain's realism puts him in a strong position with regard to modern physical science, which, he argues, can never be satisfied with the irrationalist and nominalist foundations supplied for it by modern disciples of Hume and Kant. According to these latter, whether positivists, logicists, or pragmatists, universal notions and intelligible necessities are creations of the mind and have no foundation in the world of sensible experience. But science, even in its most sophisticated expression, can never get away from the fundamental intuitions of Euclidean space, of real time, and of causal determination. Following Aristotle, Maritain maintains that science is necessary knowledge, and that those investigations of nature which rise to the level of necessary knowledge presuppose a structural aspect in the world which, though not directly observable, is nevertheless the ontological ground for the stable relations which we discern there.

In this connection, Maritain introduces the scholastic distinction between essences which exist only in the mind (*entia rationis*) and essences which exist in things as well (*entia realia*). The former, which we may call mental fictions, play an important role in all sciences, especially in the earlier inductive phases. Their function is to help the investigator translate observations into manageable form. Notions such as ether and gravity, mass and energy, belong to this order, together with imaginary and irrational numbers and non-Euclidean spaces. They are mere "beings of reason," though insofar as they enter helpfully into scientific theory they presuppose and are

964

founded upon "real beings." Deductive sciences, such as mathematical physics, on the other hand, often attain to the "real being" of things. Real dimensions, real space, real time, real causality, the structure of molecules, and patterns of crystallization are mentioned by Maritain as examples of scientific concepts which are true determinations in nature. In his view, positivists and pragmatists, who treat all scientific concepts as "beings of reason" or fictions, are guilty of overlooking an important distinction which scientists do not overlook.

Maritain does not wish to see natural science handed back to the philosophers. He cheerfully admits that the ancients were asking the wrong questions so far as experimental knowledge was concerned. Physics was on the wrong track when it supposed that bodies have natural places toward which they ascend or descend, and biology had to give up its preoccupation with teleology and eternal species. Modern science, from the time of Galileo and Harvey, has fully vindicated itself in throwing off these Aristotelian notions. The ancients failed, in many instances, to distinguish between philosophy of nature and the special sciences. And now that the distinction is clear, both stand to gain.

For the remarkable progress of the special sciences does not, according to Maritain, do away with the need for philosophy of nature and for metaphysics. The special sciences are never completely intelligible taken by themselves. Not only are their categories and principles in need of clarification, as positivists insist; they need to be fitted into a larger vision if their significance and proportion are not to be lost from view. And here, Maritain

argues, the ancients still have much to teach us. The collapse of "hylomorphism" (Aristotle's famous doctrine that things must be understood in terms of their matters and their forms) as a principle of natural science does not destroy its value for philosophy of nature. Thus, Aristotle's *Physics,* which interprets motion in terms of potentiality and actuality, is no match for Galilean mechanics as a principle of celestial or terrestrial dynamics; but it is not without value for understanding nature in its more general aspects.

Natural philosophy, for Maritain, is a speculative science standing between natural sciences and metaphysics. Natural sciences are closely bound to sense perception; metaphysics is based on pure intellectual intuition. It is essential to the sciences that they concern themselves with special characters of material being, whereas metaphysics deals with being as such, whether material or immaterial, temporal or eternal. Natural philosophy is more specific than metaphysics—it deals only with "nature"; that is to say, with being which is material, spatial, and temporal. It must begin with sense knowledge, but it goes beyond experimental truth to lay hold on the deeper intelligibility of natural processes. In Maritain's terms, mechanistic determinism, vitalism, and emergent evolutionism are attempts at natural philosophy. Working scientists implicitly employ some natural philosophy or other, often without being aware of what they are doing. It is Maritain's purpose to replace lazy, uncritical notions about natural process with true notions which the mind can achieve if it makes natural processes in general the object of inquiry.

Metaphysics, for Thomists, is not a

hypothetical extension of our knowledge beyond the limits of empirical verification, but an intuitive apprehension by the intellect of the essential characters of being. Instead of reasoning by logical inference, as do scientists and natural philosophers—who deal with universals abstracted from sense experience—the metaphysician must reason by analogy because he is dealing with different orders of being—corporeal, spiritual, and divine. Consider the category, *substance*: one can speak of corporeal substance or of spiritual substance, of created substance or of uncreated substance; but inferences cannot be made directly from one to the other. Nevertheless, the intellect discerns certain relations. One can say that spiritual substance is to spiritual being what material substance is to material being. In this way, Thomists believe, it is possible to avoid such dogmatic impasses as Cartesians and Hegelians have encountered, while continuing to affirm that being is always and everywhere rational.

Of special interest to Thomists is the part of metaphysics which concerns divine being, often called natural theology. Thus, true to tradition, Maritain takes a moderate position between those who (like St. Anselm) believe that man's reason can fathom the depths of God's being, and those who (like William of Ockham) believe it can fathom nothing. The attributes under which we represent God to ourselves (the "divine names") do, according to Maritain, tell us something about his nature. When we say that God is One or Good or True, we are not, to be sure, using these words in the same sense they have when we apply them to creatures; but neither are we using them in a completely different sense.

We use them "analogically," understanding that Unity or Goodness or Truth in the divine modality is comparable to unity or goodness or truth in the human. Analogies, according to Maritain, are more than metaphors. The latter are based on extrinsic and accidental resemblances, but the former are based on inherent characters of being and thus form an essential bond between the different modes.

Metaphysics, which is sometimes called speculative wisdom, was thought by Aristotle to be the highest form of knowledge. And Thomists agree that this is true so far as man's natural knowledge is concerned. As Christians, however, they hold that man's capacities are not fully realized on the natural plane. Man's proper end, for which he was created, is the intellectual vision of God in eternity when, according to the Bible, the faithful shall "be like him" and shall "see him face to face." Because of sin, man has lost the vision; but the grace and revelation of God are medicaments for its restoration. Thus there is a higher wisdom, which the pagan Aristotle did not know. Actually, according to Maritain, this higher wisdom is divided into two parts— *theological wisdom* and *mystical theology*.

Theological wisdom is based upon the truth of revelation. It is conceptual knowledge, like metaphysics. But whereas metaphysics knows God from the outside, as it were, viewing him as Perfect Being, theology knows him from within, sharing the mysteries of his Deity. This latter, of course, is possible only to the extent that God has spelled out his secrets in terms suitable to our understanding. For example, the doctrine of the Trinity reveals that there are three Persons in the unity of the Divine Being, and that these are Father, Son, and Holy Spirit. In making known his mysteries, God has employed analogy so that the truth may be suited to our understanding. The metaphysician would never be able to understand divine analogies by his unaided reason. Nevertheless, according to Maritain, they have their basis in the fundamental unity of being which permits divine secrets to be traced out in human lineaments. Maritain speaks of these analogies as "parabolic" analogies, with reference to the use which Christ made of parables. Like the analogies used by metaphysics, they are "proper proportionalities," and express truths in a precise and determinate degree; but they are more fruitful than those of metaphysics, in that they seem to overflow with meaning, and express more than they literally say.

Higher than theological wisdom, however, and the very acme of human knowledge is the beatific vision—assured to all the faithful in heaven, but permitted to a select number while yet on earth. The unitive experience by which God is known is knowledge in the perfect degree, for the mind becomes that which it knows without the mediation of concepts, which are essential on all lower planes. Such experience is, therefore, intimately personal, and involves the infusion of the soul with the special ministrations of the Three Persons of the Trinity. By the same token, it is essentially incommunicable: only indirectly, by metaphors and poetic figures, can the mystic express what he has beheld. Nevertheless, there is a *mystical theology,* a practical discipline, wherein the masters of a wisdom which is itself incommunicable set down counsels and rules for the guidance of others. With St. John of the Cross, whom Maritain takes for his example, mystical wisdom is through and through a practical science, the counterpart on the suprarational level of the "practical reason" of rational philosophy. (See Aristotle's *Ethics,* Book VI.) Maritain stresses emphatically the practical issues of mystical knowledge, agreeing in this respect with the teaching of Bergson in *Two Sources of Morality and Religion* (1932). Mystical knowledge, according to Maritain, renders man ever more perfectly spiritual and, as it does so, enables him to see all creatures in the light of faith and in turn to love all things with divine charity.

Maritain's discussion of mysticism is completely orthodox. He has no use for the "comparative religionist" approach to the subject, which takes a naturalistic view of all such phenomena. Holding fast to the distinction between natural and supernatural knowledge, he will tolerate no account of mysticism which seeks to make it something less than a special manifestation of the Holy Trinity in the heart of man. This view raises a question as to the validity of the mysticism of the non-Christian East. Is one bound to deny that non-Christians have experienced union with God because they are outside the Church and without the means of divine grace? According to Maritain, we would be bound to deny it, if we were sure that they had not received God's grace. He appeals, however, to the Church's doctrine of "spiritual baptism," according to which teaching there are persons outside the pale of the visible Church who, though they have never heard the gospel or received the sacraments, nevertheless have been visited by the grace of God.

Authentic mystical experiences among non-Christians are, in his opinion, to be understood in this way. In place of the usual comparative phenomenalist mysticism, he would like to see a comparative theological mysticism, which would bring some norms to bear upon the confusion that now prevails in the field.

PERCEPTION

Author: Henry Habberley Price (1899-   )
Type of work: Epistemology
First published: 1932

PRINCIPAL IDEAS ADVANCED

Sense-data are the given elements in our sense experience, the colors, odors, noises, and pressures of things as they are met in consciousness; such sense-data are particulars, not universals.

Material objects are spatially complete, three dimensional objects; but sense-data are spatially incomplete and private, and they are free from the causal relations which characterize material objects.

Sense-data which fit together to form solids are said to be constructible, and solids perceptually constructed within a mediate range of vision in which perfect stereoscopy is possible are said to be constructed from perfectly constructible sense-data.

The material object, known by reference to constructible sense-data, has causal properties which could not belong to any family of sense-data; consequently, phenomenalism is false.

In a book which might well be a model of procedure for such special studies, H. H. Price undertakes to examine existing theories of perception, reject what is bad, retain what is good, and by adding original reflections construct a new, more adequate theory avoiding the difficulties of the old. Price phrases the problem of perception in two separate questions: (1) What is perceptual consciousness and how is it related to sensing? (2) What is the relation of "belonging to" when we say a sense-datum "belongs to" a thing?

Consciousness contains givens—color expanses, pressures, noises, smells. These givens are *sense-data,* and the act of apprehending them intuitively is *sensing.* There are other data of consciousness, such as of introspection or memory. Sense-data differ from these solely in that they lead us to conceive of and believe in the existence of material things (whether such things *actually* do exist). By accepting sense-data as given, we do not commit ourselves to believing (1) that they persist when not being sensed (but only that they exist when sensed); (2) that the same sense-datum may be a datum of more than one mind; (3) that sense-data have some particular status in the universe; or (4) that they originate in any particular way.

Price examines and rejects naïve realism, its offshoot termed the selective theory, and the causal theory. He makes some use of the theory of phenomenalism and gathers the apparatus with which to exclude it only after stating most of his own theory. He never loses sight of his two basic questions, and all his very thorough and detailed arguments and rebuttals keep constant contact with them.

Naïve realism asserts that (1) perceptual consciousness is knowing that there exists an object to which a sense-datum now sensed belongs, and (2) for a visual or tactual sense-datum to belong to an object is for that sense-datum to be part of the surface of a three-dimensional object. Those who oppose the naïve realist usually regard hallucinations and perceptual illusions as ample refutation—but they commonly assume in their premises the theory they profess to upset. Price argues that the argument which actually disposes of naïve realism is simply that the many surfaces as seen, if they were really surfaces, simply would not fit together to construct the sort of three-dimensional solid the naïve realist believes in. From the controversy, we can rescue the facts that the *totum datum* (the sum of all the data of all the senses at a particular time) has main parts, the somatic sense-data and the environmental, and that in certain respects these vary concomitantly. They are always co-present and co-variant; that is, the *totum datum* is *somatocentric*. Similarly, from the remains of the effort to establish an improved

form of realism which he names the selective theory, Price draws the lessons that we must account for abnormal and illusory sense-data as well as normal ones; that to various persons the same material thing may be present to the senses in various ways; and that obtainable as well as actual sense-data will have to be provided for.

The causal theory of perception states, as answers to Price's initial questions, that "belonging to" means "being caused by" a material thing, and that perceptual consciousness is fundamentally an *inference* from effect to cause. While Price expects to refute the theory readily, he notes that it seems to be the official foundation for the natural sciences. The only plausible version of the causal theory is, if every event has a cause and if sense-data are events, something other than sense-data must exist: the *causes* of sense-data. But we can know nothing of the character of the causes, and cannot prove them to be material. The fact is that from the first, we are "on the look out" for sets of sense-data of the sort that we already expect to adumbrate solids. We already have a notion of the material thing before being capable of formulating ideas of causality. This notion seems not only innate but *a priori*, a necessary condition of certain kinds of experience. This must be a whole complex notion of thinghood, including the factor of causality.

Price then sets out toward his own theory. Sense-data are not universals but particulars; not redness, but instances of red. They are not facts, but the bases for judging facts. Visual and tactual sense-data are the primary ones for establishing the existence of material things. A visual sense-datum can be called a colored expanse, but to call it a colored surface assumes too much. Sense-data are not substances; when suitable bodily and external conditions are present; they are created out of nothing and, when these conditions disappear, vanish into nothing. They have a finite, usually very small, duration. They take up no space and do not have causal characteristics, such as inertia or impenetrability. They are not so much like mechanical processes as *vital* processes. They are generated in neither the brain nor the mind alone, but in the substantial compound of the two, having certain characteristics which neither would have by itself.

The primary form of perceptual consciousness of our sense-data is perceptual acceptance. With the arising of a sense-datum there also arises a state of taking for granted the material thing to which it belongs. The question whether to believe simply does not enter with the first sense-datum, though it may be introduced later. Other than the datum itself, perceptual acceptance has no content. While I take for granted that the front surface of what I see has a back, I leave it until later to determine the nature of the unseen part. Moreover, the first sense-datum does not completely specify the details of the accessible side, but rather it simply limits the possibilities to some extent. Further observation adds greater detail. I therefore do not actually take my first datum as identical with the front surface of the object, but simply take it that a thing now exists which has a certain general character.

Unlike the transitory sense-datum, a material thing persists through a period before and after the sense-datum. It is spatially complete in three dimensions, whereas a sense-datum is spatially incomplete. It is public and accessible to many minds, whereas a sense-datum, being somato-centric, is private. "Belonging to" it are sense-data of many, usually all, of the different senses. Finally, it has causal relations, whereas the relation between a sense-datum and the awareness of that sense-datum is not causal.

Price accounts for error, illusion, and even mere peculiarities of interpretation by referring to the difference in nature between sensing and perceptual consciousness. Sensing is undoubted and perfectly intuitive reception of the given. Perceptual consciousness is a mode of *taking as* existing a material thing, although that thing is not *necessarily* present; it *seems* intuitive only because it is instantaneous, not discursive, and is yet the raw material of judgment, not the product. But the claim of any ostensibly sensed object to exist, and have a certain character, may be tested and corrected.

The further development of perceptual consciousness is *perceptual assurance*. This leads our primary acceptance through additional perceptual acts to a settled conviction of the existence and nature of the material thing that first gave rise to sense-data. With succeeding acts of perception the mode of reception is no mere acceptance, as with the first. Conditioned by the first sensing, it is now a *progressive confirmation* of the thinghood of what is sensed, a continual further specification of previously unspecified detail and addition of other parts not at first sensed. For we take the initial sense-datum as confirmable by other obtainable sense-data, which will fit together in a unified, enduring something that is spatially complete and

970

has causal characteristics. As further acts of perception provide such confirmations, the existence of the thing and the specifications of its nature become settled rational beliefs. (Those cases with some confirmation but in which the way to adequate confirmation is blocked may be said to bring *perceptual confidence,* our ordinary state regarding most things.)

Price carries out a subtle and complex analysis of the relation of sense-data to one another. From the separate sense-data of sense-fields, as both change, we gain our beliefs in the existence of individual things. The theory that sense-data which resemble one another comprise a class, and that the thing is simply the class of resembling data, is inadequate since many of the data of an individual thing do not resemble one another in any sensible way. A better theory is that of gradual transition, which accounts not only for the changing of sense-data with motion of the observer, but also for distorted data (as in perspective viewing) as well as for changing qualities (while, it is assumed, the thing itself does not change). According to this view, the whole group of changing data gathered as we move about a thing to get further specification of it, "belong to" the particular thing. But shapes, sense-data apprehended as spatial, must be related not only geometrically but also *locally.* We need an account of the manner in which sense-data "fit together" to form a solid. Price calls data which thus fit together *constructible.*

Price cites certain empirical facts. While optical theory has not recognized it, vision has two types of stereoscopy, *perfect* and *imperfect.* The familiar sort associated with perspective seeing is the imperfect; it allows us to construct solid objects from its data, but incompletely. Immediately before the eyes there is a range of depth in which the usual perspective effects are reversed—the parallel edges of a matchbox when held against the nose seem closer together at the nearer rather than farther end. Between this nearest range and the outer one, there is a range of perfect stereoscopy, in which the visual sense-data of any object small enough to lie within it *actually do coincide,* approximately, with the surfaces of the particular thing. In this range, things are seen without distortion. The rectangular sides of the matchbox are seen as rectangular, not trapezoidal, even though the three sides seen at once are facing in quite different directions.

These facts allow Price to conclude that the thing seen within the range of perfect stereoscopy is seen virtually as it is ("as it really is," in common language). The solid perceptually constructed in this range is constructed from *perfectly constructible sense-data.* He calls it a *nuclear solid.* Around it we can arrange all constructible sense-data, in order from the least deviation to the greatest. The variations in perspective order will form a *perspectival distortion series,* and those varying concomitantly with that series from greatest to least specification will form a *differentiation* series. The members limiting these series at the position of the nuclear solid are their *nuclear members.* The nuclear solid provides the ground for uniting both continua, and indeed the continua of all sense-data both of spatial and nonspatial senses. The nuclear members with respect to a single sense are standard forms—the nuclear visual sense-datum, for example, gives the *standard figure* and *standard color*. The nuclear solid constructed from the perspectival distortion series, emended by the best presentation (that with most specific detail) of the differentiation series, gives us the *standard solid*. The collection of all sense-data unified by a standard solid is a *family of sense-data*.

To establish the validity of the construction of material things from sense-data, Price cites three propositions that seem obviously true, although he cannot imagine a way to prove them. First, some sense-fields are not momentary, but have a finite duration; second, some two sense-fields must be continuous, rather than discrete, in time and quality; and third, two successive sense-fields sometimes overlap in time—have a part of their durations in common. These are the logical requirements of three-dimensional construction. If granted that they actually occur, then, given two sense-fields, one containing a pair of sense-data AB and the other containing a pair BC, each pair sensibly adjoining and also arranged in a spatial relation R (such as "to the right of"), we can know that A and C are also related by relation R. This *method of progressive adjunction* is our validation of the "beyond"—the existence of unseen surfaces.

It is easily seen that the non-nuclear data do not exist in space. The table-top which is narrower at the far end exists in sense only, as a member of the family of sense-data of the table, not as a constituent of the standard solid of the table. The nuclear sense-data are not parts or surfaces of the standard solid, but may be said to *coincide* with it. Position in physical space is not a characteristic of a single sense-datum, but rather a *collective* characteristic of a whole group of sense-data constituting a standard solid.

A family of sense-data perhaps should not be said to *exist* in time and undergo change, but to *prolong* itself through time and differ through time. The point of view of the observer, and its motion, are definable in terms of the space of standard solids. Obtainable sense-data are definable in terms of changes of the observer's point of view.

So far, it might seem that the theory of perception Price has offered is an elaborated phenomenalism, identifying a material thing with the family of sense-data. He shows, however, that this is not his theory. A material thing *physically*, as well as sensibly, occupies a space. By this we mean that it manifests in that space certain *causal* characteristics, most notably that of impenetrability. When a chestnut drops on a stone and bounces away, it is a causal characteristic of the stone, not a sense-characteristic, that has acted on the chestnut. An obtainable sense-datum, on the other hand, is not an existent particular, but a fact of the form "If any observer were at such and such a point of view, such and such a sense-datum would exist." Since an individual observer can occupy only one point of view at a time, he can realize only one of the alternatively obtainable sense-data at a time. The family of sense-data thus has a peculiar mode of existence, as a collection of actual sense-data, plus an infinite number of obtainable sense-data existing as contemporary alternatives, centering on a standard solid. This is not the kind of entity to which causal characteristics may belong. Further, in many instances, a family of sense-data is manifested in only one part of a region

972

when a causal characteristic is being manifested in many parts of that region. Again, causes continue to be manifested during times when no sense-data are obtained. There is no necessary concomitance of caused events with sense-data, though there is concomitance among sense-data themselves. Accordingly, the causative physical occupant and the family of sense-data are not identical, and phenomenalism is false.

Now we see that for a sense-datum s to belong to a certain material thing M, first s must be a member of a family of sense-data prolonging itself through time and centering in a standard solid having a certain place in the system of standard solids; and second, that the place must be physically occupied—causal characteristics must be manifested there. This is Price's theory, the Collective Delimitation Theory. It stresses that the primary relation of "belonging to" is between an entire family and a material thing, the relation of a single sense-datum to the thing being derivative; moreover, that the family is related to the material thing by coinciding with the physically occupative portion of the thing.

Probably we get our first hint of the relation of causation to sense-data by observing other people's changed behavior in the face of certain evident changes in their environment. More important is the influence of the fact of our having several senses. By reflection on the data of one, we discern how the data of another sense originate. Concomitant changes in our tactual sense-data, for example, with the introduction of objects of the visual

field to the skin, are a source of knowledge. The *complete thing* is the physically occupative thing with causal properties plus the family of sense-data. A changing complete thing is not the cause of changes in our sense-data, for the data are part of the thing. But a change in the thing *as physical occupant* of space may entail changes in the sense-data that depend upon the presence both of it and its observer. The laws of sense-data are of a different order from ordinary causal laws. We can define a given type of physical occupant only by reference to the kind of family of sense-data it is coincident with and to all those foreign ones whose mode of prolongation it influences. But of the intrinsic qualities of physical occupants, we have no knowledge at all.

Price's *Perception* perhaps represents our farthest point of advance in its area. Whether his position is adopted, his close study of the problems and his careful solutions have much that is useful. For the introspective part of his procedure, Price asks of us only the accordance with our own experience, a reasonable enough request. And he seems to begin with the perhaps intuitive preconceptions which have made us suspicious of some of the stranger theories of perception, and to exhibit and justify these conceptions. Finally, Price's convincing exposition of the differences between the separately certifiable orders, sense-data and the manifestations of causality, seems by correcting the "emptiness" of phenomenalism to be a considerable contribution.

973

AN IDEALIST VIEW OF LIFE

Author: Sarvepalli Radhakrishnan (1888-   )
Type of work: Ethics, metaphysics
First published: 1932

PRINCIPAL IDEAS ADVANCED

The ideal world, which alone is real, lies beyond the phenomenal world of appearance, yet dominates it; the center of the universe is the transcendent, the Absolute, Brahma.

Intuition is the way to an integral apprehension of ultimate reality; it is a knowledge by identity which transcends the distinction between subject and object.

Scientific certainty is not the only kind of certainty available to men; but in considering the mystical revelation as a source of certainty, one must distinguish between the content of the experience and the interpretation of it, for interpretation is historically conditioned and liable to error.

The scientific view of the inorganic world and of life and mind is more compatible with idealism than with naturalism.

An Idealist View of Life has a marked mystical foundation in theory of knowledge. In this regard, it may be said to express the main Hindu tradition in philosophy. This is one reason for its importance. The other is the author's familiarity with Western philosophy and science. Though his general standpoint guides him, there is no turning away from crucial problems.

Sarvepalli Radhakrishnan recognizes that the term idealism needs definition. It is clear that he is not a subjective idealist of the mode of the early Berkeley. Nor does he much concern himself with Hegelian rationalistic idealism. Rather, his emphasis is on the relation of value to reality. The truly real is replete with value. The alignment is with the *Upanishads* in India and the outlook of the Platonists, especially that of Plotinus, the father of the Western tradition of mysticism.

As suggested, the book is peculiarly interesting because it does reflect the meeting of the East and the West along these lines. The broad sweep of Radhakrishnan's thought brings together Hindu classic thinkers with Plato and Aristotle, and with the Anglo-American idealists, Bradley and Royce. As one might expect, less attention is paid to Western naturalism and realism. That is both the strength and the weakness of the book. It stands out as an excellent example of its perspective. And it does have scope and verve.

The general argument is to the effect that the ideal world, which alone is real, lies beyond the phenomenal one of appearance yet is tied in with it and dominates it. Spirit is working in matter that matter may serve spirit. In a sense, matter is an abstraction and not a concrete reality, such as spirit. That is why materialism can be absorbed and transcended. It is doubtful whether Western materialists would accept this thesis; but it goes quite logically with the author's outlook. For him, the center of the universe is the transcendent, the Absolute, Brahma, that which has *aseity*, being. But, despite this assurance—rather, because of it—he is sympathetic with other points of view because they have their partial truth.

The first of the eight lectures concerns itself with the modern challenge to the religious outlook on the universe as a result of scientific and social thought. Here the author confronts Freud, John B. Watson, and Émile Durkheim. The second lecture notes contemporary movements such as humanism, naturalism, and logical positivism. These are tied in with science. In all this, the author is frank and well informed. He is not trying to defend specific orthodoxies. Like the Buddhist, he has no tradition of particular doctrines in geology and biology. Science is to be accepted but has its limits. It is fascinating to note how he draws the line.

It is in the third lecture that Radhakrishnan states the basic claims of the religious consciousness, especially at the mystical level. Here we have the introduction of *intuition* as a way of knowledge other than that of sense perception or discursive conception. He puts forward the claim for an integral apprehension of ultimate reality. It is a knowledge by identity which transcends the distinction between subject and object. Here, of course, is where dispute arises. Those who do not have the mystical vision are likely to deny its significance.

In the fourth lecture, Radhakrishnan develops the idea that scientific certainty is not the only kind of certainty available to us. A query may, of course, be raised as to the scientific claim which is usually more modestly put as an affair of working hypotheses. But the author is ready to admit that, in the mystical revelation, we must distinguish between the kernel of it and the interpretation given, which is historically conditioned. Thus Hindu, Moslem, and Christian mystics have different accounts of the meanings of their experiences.

The fifth lecture takes up the non-conceptual, intuitive, imaginative, and affective ingredients of morality, art, and religion. The element of creativity is noted with reports from mathematicians, scientists, and poets. Just how do new ideas arise? What part does the subconscious play? It is generally agreed that there must be preparation. It takes a trained mathematician to have relevant ideas and to solve mathematical problems. There is a big literature on this question and Radhakrishnan is familiar with it. He is at home in aesthetics and art and quotes freely from Croce, Dante, Keats, Shakespeare, and Browning. The stress, it is to be noted, is on creativity. The suggestion is that this is something higher in nature than perception and conceptual reasoning. Does it link up with his third kind of knowledge?

The sixth and seventh lectures are devoted to a brief formulation of the scientific view of the inorganic world, of life, and of mind. It was written in an era in which Eddington and Jeans were the avowed spokesmen of science. A semi-idealistic, semi-agnostic note was in the air. Relativity and quantum-mechanics were transforming science away from Newtonian mechanics. Scientists were finding the world a more subtle and complex sort

975

of thing than had been supposed earlier. The question at issue was whether naturalism could do justice to this development or whether it implied idealism. If these are the alternatives, there is no question as to which side Radhakrishnan adopts. He sees the development as favoring idealism. And it is well to have this alignment so beautifully carried out.

In the eighth, and last, lecture, the turn comes for metaphysics and its basis in an integral intuition of ultimate reality. Here we have an excellent example of transcendental metaphysics, something to which the logical positivist is so opposed with his insistence that sensory verification is essential for the meaningfulness of empirical statements. It is clear that much depends upon the certainty and value of the mystical experience. It is upon this foundation that Radhakrishnan builds. Nothing could be more desirable than such a confrontation.

Let us now go over the movement of Radhakrishnan's argument in more detail to bring out its scope and its point. Even a person who remains skeptical of the mystical insight will be impressed by the idealism to which it leads. Though Nehru is more of an agnostic, one can note in him something of the same elevation of spirit.

The essential thing, Radhakrishnan argues, is to know what the problem is. Freud's queries help to bring this home. Is religion an illusion? That there have been illusory ingredients is undeniable. Popular religion has been too anthropomorphic and has laid too much stress on special providences. On the other hand, Newtonian rationalism led to deism and the absentee God. But of what use is an absentee God? Surely, that is not the sort of God the religious consciousness requires.

The influential feature of science has been its attack on parochialism and narrow ideas. Watson's behaviorism, for instance, has forced us to think more clearly about mind. These challenges must be met. For instance, the French school of sociology represented by Durkheim stresses the pressure of society but does not do justice to personality and self-consciousness. Again, the study of comparative religions should have the effect of enlarging our horizon. The so-called higher criticism of the Scriptures ought to have the same effect. Such a critical attitude is fairly common among thoughtful Hindus and Buddhists. And it is doubtful that the traditional proofs for theism are convincing. Radhakrishnan stresses an internal religious approach. It would appear that he regards the materialistic atmosphere of technology as the greatest enemy. It is not the mastery of nature as such that is at fault but the industrial and utilitarian climate.

The result of this frank approach is the contention that nothing can be true by faith if it is not true by reason. But then reason must not be taken as limited to deduction from fixed premises. Radhakrishnan believes in a source of insight of a higher order.

But what are the substitutes for religion offered these days? One is an atheistic naturalism. It appears that Radhakrishnan has in mind Russell's early protest against a supposedly alien nature composed of blind atoms ruled by mechanical laws. This would be, in effect, a malign nature which might well be defied. Such an outlook would represent a mixture of naturalism, stoicism, and paganism. The stoicism reflects man's innate dignity.

Humanism is an old tradition which goes back to the Greeks with their doctrine of inner harmony and to the Romans with their sense of decorum. There are elements of it in Chinese thought and in Kant. Such humanism tends to be religion secularized and separated from a larger reality. It lacks *élan*. It sets up boundaries. It is these boundaries which religion oversteps. On the other hand, it cannot be denied that humanism is humanitarian and stresses social reform.

Pragmatism is more an American development which emphasizes will and practice. It is a protest against the separation of knowledge and active planning.

Modernism, on the other hand, is a halfway house. It seeks to revise religious tradition. It is confronted by the revival of authoritarianism. This regards itself as an escape from anarchy. But loyalty to tradition should not involve bondage to it. There is often a secret skepticism in authoritarianism.

All these movements seem to Radhakrishnan to lack something of the spiritual. There is a lack of profundity. What is needed is a synoptic vision.

We come now to the positive position. Religious experience is factual in its own right. Philosophy of religion explores this domain and differs from dogmatic theology. For religion is not a form of knowledge. It is more akin to feeling. It is inward and personal. It is the response of the whole man in an integral way to reality. It expresses an incurable discontent with the finite and seeks the transcendent.

It is now that the Hindu tradition comes to the front, though it is soon connected with the mystical note in the West. The Vedic seers stressed the eternal and sought to raise themselves to this plane. In this respect, Plato, Augustine, and Dante are examples of the same direction. Can this massive evidence be illusory? But it involves a higher kind of knowledge or insight. That is the problem for philosophy of religion. The justification of this claim is taken up in the conclusion. This constitutes the debate with scientific empiricism and naturalism.

One must be very careful here, Radhakrishnan warns us. There is danger in a purely negative approach. It is so hard to translate the mystical experience. Its note is timelessness and unity. When we use language to bring out the contrast, we call this ultimate reality the Absolute. The term "God" is of the nature of a symbol.

There goes with the experience a sense of harmony and unity. Self-mastery is involved. From this flows idealism and denial of what is selfish. The danger in this concentration is, perhaps, disregard of social ties. This should be guarded against.

If all knowledge were of the scientific type, as some empiricists hold, then the challenge to the religious outlook on the world could hardly be met. Hence comes the importance of the question of intuitive knowledge, something which cannot be expressed in propositions, yet is justifiable. It is well to recall that sense qualities are confused and that logic and mathematics are essentially analytic and do not give us factual information.

In Hindu thought, in Plotinus, in Bergson, there is emphasis upon direct intuition. The facts of telepathy, for example, prove that one mind can directly be aware of another's thoughts. It would seem that intuition is the extension of a sort of perception beyond the senses. Bergson sets limits to the intellect. He thinks it useful rather than true. Hegel criticizes immediacy and tends to ignore the importance of feeling and will. Yet he is opposed to the abstractions of the understanding. But is not the unity of nature coördinate with the unity of the self? Kant emphasized the "I think" at the phenomenal level and believed in a noumenal world beyond. Faith and spiritual experience make their demands. It is well to look at the creative spirit in man.

Scientific discovery is more like intuition than people ordinarily realize. Henri Poincaré's account of mathematical imagination is a case in point. There is something creative about it. We prove deductively but invent by intuition. There is here a kind of integrative passivity. Michael Faraday is another case of unpredictable invention. The whole self is involved. When philosophers devote themselves to abstruse analysis, this creative factor may escape them.

If we turn from science to poetry and the plastic arts, intuition stands out even more clearly. The poet feels himself to be inspired. This should not be taken too literally, yet it has meaning. There is emotional value and this has significance. It would seem that Croce connects intuition and expression too closely. There must be room for communication. It is well to recall the testimony of Plato and Carlyle. Emotional intensity goes with a sense of deep insight. Too much modern literature tends to be trivial and to avoid the agonies of spirit. Has it given us one genuine epic?

Creativity is a path to discovery and is to be connected with knowledge. It involves understanding of life and brings us into accord with it. It is true that Juliet dies, but only after making us realize the greatness of love.

If we turn to ethics, Radhakrishnan maintains, we find something similar. The moral hero, or saint, tends to be somewhat antinomian. He does not keep to conventions. It is because of this that moral heroes can make fools of themselves in the eyes of the world.

Modern science stresses abstraction and statistics. For Eddington and Jeans, matter tends to be reduced to thought. In terms of relativity and quantum mechanics, it is a term for a cluster of events possessing habits and potencies. The traditional idea of substance is in abeyance. There is a touch here of the Hindu notions of Samsara. All is becoming. There is another respect in which science suggests idealism. What we know is the effect things produce in us; all is experience and possible experience. This is the idealistic note.

If we turn to life, we find it to be of the nature of a dynamic equilibrium. The theory of evolution developed from Georges de Buffon and Chevalier de Lamarck to Darwin and is still subject to improvement. Natural selection is a sifting process. Herbert Spencer made it too quickly into a philosophy.

Mind is under study in comparative psychology. The nature of nervous integration is under study. Pavlov and Watson were pioneers, but we now

978

have *Gestalt* principles opposed to purely mechanical notions.

Radhakrishnan then turns to human personality. Atomistic psychology is obsolete. The person is a unity and more than the sum of his parts. He is an organized whole. We must give up the notion of a changeless soul. The self is a growth constantly interacting with its environment.

And now we come to the term "subject." William James and James Ward differed in their views on this topic. James thought of it as the passing thought. This concept seems inadequate; there must be something more enduring. The subject, by its very nature, cannot be an object. Why not hold it to be one with the simple, universal spirit? Here we are beyond the lower order of existence and are confronted by such problems as those of freedom and *karma*. Eastern and Western thought have long pondered these problems. It seems to Radhakrishnan that mere predestination is unethical. Freedom is not a matter of caprice nor is *karma* mere necessity. Suppose we take freedom to be a term for self-determination. It is the whole self that is involved in choice. The will is the active side of the self. It is not something in itself. *Karma* means, literally, action or deed. It is the principle of causal continuity. Thus, it is not opposed to creative freedom, unless one takes causality to demand mere identity or repetition.

There is a good side to the idea of *karma* which is not always recognized. It involves sympathy. People may be more unfortunate than wicked. There is tragedy in the world.

While there is a demand for a future life and personal immortality, people hardly know what they want. There are those who hold that immortality is a prize to be won. This is called conditional immortality. But the idea seems to favor the more fortunate and to be semi-aristocratic in motivation. It is certain that the modern mind cannot accept the idea of endless punishment which is not justified by improvement as a goal. Surely, no being is wholly evil. The Hindu idea of rebirth has its biological difficulties but these are not insurmountable. There would need to be some kind of selectivity.

All this leads up to the speculative climax of Radhakrishnan's argument. How are we to envisage ultimate reality? Radhakrishnan summarizes the results of his survey of the world. The world is an ordered whole; everything is an organization with its mode of connection. There is a development in the direction of greater union with surroundings. Nature is a domain of becoming without fixity. Yet these changes are not meaningless. Evolution goes with progress on the whole. And, lastly, the highest kind of experiences and personalities seem to indicate a goal of being.

These principles are opposed to traditional naturalism. It did not have a sufficient place for time. Radhakrishnan aligns himself in some measure with holism and Lloyd Morgan's emergent evolution. But, it would seem, he is most in sympathy with Whitehead's Platonism, with its primordial God and Consequent God. God is the home of universals, of possibilities, and of ideal harmony.

The Eastern note in the conclusion is interesting. The Absolute is also absolute freedom in activity. All else is dependent, created reality, *Maya*. One can speak symbolically of three sides of God's nature. In Hindu tradition, these are Brahma, Vishnu, and Siva. These must not be set apart.

It is clear that Radhakrishnan regards absolute idealism as representing the basis for a fusion of the Vedanta perspective in India and Western thought. It is debatable whether he has done justice to trends towards realism and analysis. But he would be the last to hold that human thought has finished its task. Probably the most intriguing element in his thought is his belief that mystical apprehension is a genuine form of knowledge, though it is evocative and does not lend itself to description. Here, he would hold, we are capable—a few of us at least—of contact with the absolute and the eternal.

THE PHILOSOPHY OF PHYSICAL REALISM

Author: Roy Wood Sellars (1880-)
Type of work: Epistemology and metaphysics
First published: 1932

PRINCIPAL IDEAS ADVANCED

Human beings know external objects by being affected sensibly by them.

By means of the organs of sense the brain is stimulated by objects in such a manner that particular sense-events occur.

The object is disclosed in the act of perception, and human knowledge is not mere inference but actual knowledge.

Only individual things are real; there are no universals.

Substance is a self-existent continuant which can enter into relations with other self-existents.

Consciousness is an emergent feature of a brain-mind process.

Values are understandable in terms of the power of things to become important to human beings.

Despite the fact that in the United States idealism has had a significant role to play in the development of American thought, the philosophy which confines reality to mind and its ideas has never been a direct expression of the American temperament. Pragmatism and realism, on the other hand, appear to be the intellectual equivalents of the frontier spirit, for they take the world as it presents itself, as a problem to be handled by plans of action put to the test. Although pragmatists and realists are not always happy in one another's company, they are alike in turning away from the habit of mind which, putting full faith in the use of reason, calls into question the existence of whatever is most tangible, most recalcitrant, most independent in the world of common sense and action.

980

It is customary to regard the American realists as innovators in epistemology, as philosophers who set out to show that to *know* is to confront the existence and character of something which is in no way dependent for either its existence or its nature on the fact of its being known. Put as directly as possible, a *realist* is one who believes that there are objects, known and unknown, which exist whether or not they are known; the *idealist*, on the other hand, supposes that to be, to exist, is either to be a thinking substance, a mind, or one of its ideas (or perceptions, sensations, emotions, beliefs). The argument between realists and idealists, then, has often taken the form of an epistemological argument: Is the act of knowing an act which involves the independent existence of the object of knowledge? The realists have argued that knowing does involve some kind of transcendence of the object, while the idealists have contended that the attempt to go beyond the mind's own content is not only futile but senseless.

Since it has been customary to regard the realistic account of the knowledge process as an epistemological venture, Roy Wood Sellars' *Critical Realism* (1916) has generally been interpreted as presenting his theory of knowledge, while his later defense of evolutionary naturalism, *The Philosophy of Physical Realism*, has been described as presenting "metaphysical" views. Thus, Joseph Blau speaks of Sellars' "version of the critical realist theory of knowledge," and then refers to Sellars' "metaphysical views to which we may assign such descriptive names as 'physical realism,' 'naturalism,' or 'materialism.'" Professor W. H. Werkmeister, writing in a similar fash-

ion, speaks of Sellars' "evolutionary naturalism" or "physical realism" as "a metaphysical doctrine" developed after "the controversy over epistemological realism. . . ."

Nevertheless, although Sellars himself, in the Preface to the *Philosophy of Physical Realism*, speaks of the book as "an attempt at 'first philosophy,' . . . a development and defense of physical realism," and of critical realism as "an *elucidation of natural* realism in which the mechanism of knowing is studied and certain illusions about the nature of knowing are mastered," and goes on to state that "The epistemological task is not the replacement of natural realism but its development," it may very well be that all of these writers have erred, practically if not theoretically, in attempting to distinguish between critical and physical realism on the ground that the former is epistemological while the latter is metaphysical. Although critical realism presents itself as a theory of knowledge, it proceeds from a limitation of the use of the term "knowledge" to realistic contexts in which it is no longer meaningful to talk about the possibility that physical objects are, after all, merely complexes of ideas or sensations. Yet it is precisely such persistent philosophical restriction of language which justifies the application of the term "metaphysical." If this is so, Sellars' physical realism is best described as the metaphysical addition to his earlier critical realism, itself metaphysical. This is not to deny the value of his effort. It is only from a positivistic point of view—itself metaphysical —that metaphysical commitments are disreputable.

Sellars' philosophy in the volume under review is naturalistic, evolutionary, and critically realistic in its opposition to new or "naïve" realism. To understand these adjectives it is necessary to consider Sellars' philosophy as emerging from the realistic revolt against American idealism.

The New Realism (1912) appeared as a further defense of a program and platform already enunciated and supported by six American realists: E. B. Holt, W. T. Marvin, W. P. Montague, R. B. Perry, W. B. Pitkin, and E. G. Spaulding. As described by Montague in a retrospective essay, "The Story of American Realism," which appeared in *Philosophy* in April, 1937, the new realists supported a realism which was, at once, existential, Platonic, and presentative. It was existential (in a sense having no relation to existentialism) in holding that "Some, at least, of the *particulars* of which we are conscious exist when we are not conscious of them." It was Platonic in claiming that "Some, at least, of the *essences* or *universals* of which we are conscious subsist when we are not conscious of them." And it was presentative in its distinctive assertion that "Some, at least, of the particulars as well as the universals that are real are apprehended directly rather than indirectly through copies or mental images."

Clothed in its technical terminology, new realism is not surprising—nor is it, in any obvious way, a defense of common sense (as it is sometimes purported to be). But if we call the particular sensation we have upon perceiving a physical object a "sense-datum" —what is given to sense—then we may understand the new realist as claiming that sense-data sometimes exist when we are not conscious of them (existential realism), that the characteristics of sense-data (like mathe-

matical relationships) sometimes exist when we are not conscious of them (Platonic realism), and that physical objects (ordinarily understood as complexes of sense-data in abstraction from any act of sensation) can be "apprehended" directly (presentative realism). Reduced to the language of ordinary discourse (thus accentuating the bizarre character of the new realist thesis), the new realism is a philosophy which regards the surfaces of physical objects as directly and immediately seen, smelled, touched, and so forth; colors, for example, are not to be understood as the causes of visual sensations, but as qualities of surfaces seen immediately and precisely as they are. Of course, such a view makes explanation of error or sense differences difficult.

Disturbed by a philosophy which made the naïve faith in the appearances of things a respectable doctrine, a group of American philosophers in 1920 issued *Essays in Critical Realism*. The authors were George Santayana, C. A. Strong, A. K. Rogers, A. O. Lovejoy, Roy Wood Sellars, J. B. Pratt, and Durant Drake. The opposition to new realism had grown in momentum over the years, as a result of work done by Santayana, Lovejoy, D. C. Macintosh, and others. The critical realists contended "that knowledge is *transitive,* so that self-existing things may become the chosen objects of a mind that identifies and indicates them; second, that knowledge is *relevant,* so that the thing indicated may have at least some of the qualities that mind attributes to it." This realism rested on a causal theory of perception which involved the claim that physical objects affect a perceiving subject who takes the content of his ex-

982

perience as an identifying sign of the presence and character of the object. Some realists, like Santayana, supposed it possible that, on occasion, the character (essence) of the object known might be identical with the character of the experience (sense-datum) by which it was known—but most were agreed that identity in character was perhaps limited to certain structural properties. In any case, for most critical realists, to know an object was to identify it by the character of its sensible effect and to be able to anticipate the character of subsequent sensible effects; the notion that objects could be "intuited"—known for what they are by some *immediate* perception, not by the conscious response to the sense stimulation of the physical organism—was rejected as naïve and as making an account of error impossible.

In what sense, then, is such a philosophical realism a metaphysical—and not merely an epistemological—point of view? In the sense that the causal theory of perception was assumed, not proved. But some realists—and Sellars is among them—maintain that we *do know* physical objects, and that we distinguish between the objects we know, which are the causes of our sensations, and the sensations of these objects. But to insist that we know *that* there are physical objects and that we also know *what* they are is to be persistently realistic—dualistically—in one's use of the verb "to know." There is nothing illegitimate or "mistaken" about this procedure; it is the linguistic way of being metaphysical.

The Philosophy of Physical Realism, therefore, may be considered an individual philosopher's extension of a metaphysical thesis which was developed in coöperation with others and in opposition to new realism which was, in turn, a manifestation of a critical opposition to American idealism.

In arguing against new realism and for his own variety of realism, Sellars contends that the proper epistemological method "is to begin with the actual cognitive experience and to examine it carefully in the light of its claims and of the relevant facts." He offers six general principles as the basis of a theory of knowing that would make sense out of the claim that in knowing the knower transcends himself:

"First principle: Human knowing is conditioned in a perfectly natural way as regards both external controls and internal operations. . . .

"Second principle: Though conditioned causally and resting on neuromuscular mechanisms, human knowing is yet knowing. . . .

"Third principle: The causal theory of perception should be restated as the causal theory of sense-data and not of perceiving. . . .

"Fourth principle: Knowing must be studied at its various levels as a characteristic claim of the human knower. . . .

"Fifth principle: The act of cognition is complex and appears in consciousness as an interpretation of an external object in terms of logical ideas. . . .

"Sixth principle: Things are selected as objects by the mind and not in the mind. This signifies that knowing involves a peculiar transcendence."

(In the text Sellars follows each principle with a defense and explanation of the point involved.)

Sellars is careful to point out that in perceiving we are ordinarily convinced that we are "in contact" with the perceived object and that the sensory presentation is the surface of the object—but to suppose this philosophically is to be naïve. Nevertheless, he objects to the claim made by many scientists that since perceiving involves interpretation, the physical object is inferred. He suggests an idea of human knowing "which permits of degrees and approximations."

Sellars' theory of truth is based upon a distinction of three factors: the attitude of belief, the content of the belief, and the external state of affairs which is denoted. The attitude and the content are "features of the knower," but the third element, the external state of affairs, is not. A true idea is a "knowledge-giving" idea in that it discloses (whether or not one knows that it discloses) the denoted object. True ideas are *such that* we can think the object as it is by means of them."

Sellars can be distinguished from some other critical realists by reference to his claim that sensory presentations are *particulars, not* essences. In other words, Sellars supposes that the brain-mind is stimulated by objects in such a manner that particular sense-events occur; these sense-events, or sensory presentations, are not characteristics which can belong to other events in other minds, nor are they predicates which can be attributed to objects. It is not surprising, then, that he rejects the theory of universals (Platonic realism) and accepts a nominalism which takes the form: "Only individual things are real; and these are real in their relations." When it is pointed out that we characterize objects by use of adjectives, suggesting that they are alike in kind, Sellars replies that "Onto-

logically, similarity is sufficient." Human beings make the mistake, he argues, of supposing that since there is organized stability in the world, there is an identity of features corresponding to the logical identities in our language.

The possibility of error is easily accounted for on Sellars' view. He argues that there are two ways of being mistaken in our reference to objects: (1) we may attempt to indicate an object when no object is present, and (2) we may describe an object incorrectly when one is present. To make a claim in regard to an object, to present a proposition concerning it, is to use a sense presentation as the basis of a meaning intended to disclose the object; if there is no object when we suppose there is, or if the object is not disclosed by our proposition, then we are in error, and truth and knowledge have been missed.

With Chapter XI of his book Sellars begins the development of what he calls his "ontology." We are prepared for this by his preface in which he remarks, "I am an unashamed ontologist and a convinced believer in the ontological reach of science. And this in spite of pragmatist, Viennese positivist, or religious personalist." Nevertheless, despite his belief in "the ontological reach of science," Sellars is not inclined to regard the theory of relativity as having ontological significance; that is, he is not inclined to suppose that since, according to the physicist, there can be no absolute simultaneity of events, an account of simultaneity cannot be given. The scientist is interested in discourse that makes sense relative to measurement operations he and others can perform, but the philosopher—particularly when he is a realist—is not inclined to accept any such limitation upon his conception of things. According to Sellars, Newtonian physics confused ontological and operational questions—and to some extent so do modern physicists who take the theory of relativity as a theory having to do with a reality beyond measurement. The proper approach, according to Sellars, is to recognize that there are two approaches: measurement and ontology.

The extent of Sellars' philosophical courage can be seen in his defense of substance. He considers the objections advanced by Berkeley and Hume, and he argues that a cogent reply involves a reformulation of Locke's conception of substance. Like Spinoza, Sellars regards substance as a self-existent continuant, but he does not agree with Spinoza in denying substance the possibility of relations with other self-existents. He rejects the idea of substance as an inert focal "stuff" to which properties are somehow "attached."

In causal theory Sellars allies himself with C. J. Ducasse and others who reject a uniformity theory of cause in favor of a single event explanation. Thus, he opposes himself to Bertrand Russell's idea of cause as involving regular sequence. The point here appears to be that if an event can be known to be related to another event with which it is continuous and contiguous, it can be known to be causally related to that other event whether or not similar pairs of events are observed.

Without rejecting causality Sellars accounts for human freedom and moral import by emphasizing man's existence as an agent, a process, not as a fixed thing. He gives up predestation, but he gives positive content to his philosophy by calling attention to "the capacity of matter to organize into things like ourselves."

Sellars' evolutionary naturalism comes to the fore in his account of consciousness. In response to the question, "How precisely are we to think of consciousness as *in* the brain?" he answers that "Consciousness is in the brain as an event is in the brain, and is as extended as is the brain-event to which it is intrinsic." According to Sellars, judgment is the basic feature of cognition, and in judgment we form predicates based upon sense-data in order to describe objects. The sense-data provide the basis for judgments about objects, but they cannot accurately serve as the basis of judgments about the brain: for example, when an apple is judged to be red in virtue of the presence of a red sense-datum, it would be an error to judge the brain to be red. Throughout his account Sellars makes the effort to analyze consciousness as an emergent feature of a whole process which the brain-mind makes possible; there is no separate "thinking substance."

Sellars offers an objective, capacity theory of value; that is, he claims that the adjectives "good," "bad," "beautiful," and so forth, call attention to the capacity of objects "to enter human life with certain consequence of importance to the self or to a social group." He rejects the possibility of intrinsic value, but mostly because he takes the term "intrinsic" to be synonymous with "non-relational"; and since he supposes that goods are always goods *for* someone, it seems to him that no good could be intrinsic. Since Sellars emphasizes the descriptive use of value terms in propositions having truth-values, he is not sympathetic toward such a theory as Perry's, as developed in the latter's *General Theory of Value* (1926), dismissing it as a study probing "in a behavioristic way into the mechanism of interest and propensities."

Sellars closes grandly with the declaration that "I have tried to show that, with an adequate epistemology and ontology, most of the traditional riddles vanished and that then man could see himself as he is, a creature in one world, a creature strangely gifted to look before and after and to follow his desires and dreams on an earth partly plastic to his power." Although the author may be optimistic in hoping that *The Philosophy of Physical Realism* can lead to elimination of most of the traditional riddles, surely this work deserves reëxamination as a lucid and meaningful defense of a critically responsible realism.

ART AS EXPERIENCE

Author: John Dewey (1859-1952)
Type of work: Aesthetics
First published: 1934

PRINCIPAL IDEAS ADVANCED

When experience is satisfactory, when it combines memory of the past with anticipation of the future, when it is an achievement of the organism in the environment in which it functions, the experience is an experience.

Any experience which is, in this unified and consummatory way, an experience is an aesthetic experience.

Art is to be understood as an experience made possible by the organizing and unifying process in which the artist engages; the spectator meets the interest of the artist with an interest of his own in the reciprocal process of going through a similar operation.

Art supplies mediums of communication, making community of experience possible.

All arts share a common form: they are organized toward a unified experience; they all operate through sensory mediums such as stone, water colors, oil paints, and words; and they are all concerned with space and time.

Art as Experience is the most extensive and, many say, the best book on aesthetics from the pragmatic point of view. Dewey believed that aesthetic theory should attempt to explain how works of art come to be and how they are enjoyed in experience. How is it that something produced to fill a need becomes in addition a source of aesthetic enjoyment? How is it that ordinary activities can yield a particular kind of satisfaction that is aesthetic? These and like questions must be answered by an adequate aesthetic theory.

Dewey's interest in biology influenced his description of the aesthetic experience. An organism lives in an environment through which it fulfills certain needs. The process of fulfilling these needs is called *experience* and may be more or less satisfactory to the organism. When experience seems to be completely satisfactory, when it is a happy experience that combines memories of the past and anticipations of the future, when it is an achievement of the organism in the world of things, Dewey calls it "an experience." *An* experience, realized by a human being, is aesthetic. Thus, there is no sharp line between animal and human experience. Animals could have aesthetic experience, but we simply would not be likely to call it that.

Aesthetic experiences are not found in museums or in libraries alone. As a matter of fact, such settings often make enjoyment impossible by putting works of art beyond ordinary human activities and concerns. For Dewey, an intelligent workman doing his job, interested in it, finding satisfaction in doing it well, is having an experience. He is artistically engaged; he is finding aesthetic enjoyment. Consequently, everyday activities are the ones most meaningful to the average person. To him the most vital arts are popular music, comic strips, newspaper accounts of crime and love, articles on the intimate doings of popular entertainers. These things are a significant part of the concerns of an organized community, just as in the past rug, mat, and cloth making, dancing, music, and storytelling were an integral part of day-to-day living.

Modern museums and institutions segregate art and remove it from the concerns of most people. Dewey criticizes the modern artist for reflecting the view that art is isolated and for not attempting to reach anyone except those whom the artist regards as having a superior cultural status. The object that he produces may be thought of as a work of art, but the actual work of art is to be understood as what affects human experience. The problem of the artist should be to show that his activity can be connected with the actual processes of living.

Dewey points to other properties of the aesthetic experience. In his practical concerns with the real world, a person thinks in terms of effect and cause. He converts these for his own use into ends he wishes to achieve and devices for achieving them; that is, into consequences and means, organizing the world in terms of needs and environment. Art, too, involves organization and may be related to any activity of the living organism. The great work of art is a complete organization; and in this completeness lies the source of aesthetic pleasure.

No experience is a unity, Dewey says, unless it has aesthetic quality. The integrated, the well-rounded, the emotionally satisfying make up the artistic structure of the experience which is immediately felt. Because of its relation to experience, art is always a part of the process of doing or making something. Like all experience, it involves emotion and is guided by purpose. The artist organizes, clarifies, and simplifies his material according to his interest. The spectator must go through these same operations according to his own interests in order to have an aesthetic experience from his relation to the art object. He must be creative when confronted by the art object, just as the artist was creative when he produced it. What the spectator creates is an experience which is enjoyed and is satisfying for its own sake.

What are the characteristics of experience for Dewey? Experience begins with an impulsion of the whole organism, outward and forward. The organism moves to satisfy a need, but the nature of this motion is determined by the environment and the past experiences of the organism. Emotion always accompanies an experience. Without emotion there is no action.

A work of art does not simply evoke an emotion. The material in it becomes the content and matter of emotion when it is a part of the environment which satisfies a need in relation to the past experiences of an organism. Art objects may be inadequate or excessive in relation to the emotional needs of the spectator. Art is not nature; it is nature organized, simplified, transformed in such a way that it places the individual and the community in a context of greater order and unity.

Thus, for Dewey, the work of art represents nature as experienced by the artist. It organizes the public world by taking the scattered and weakened material of experience, then clarifying and concentrating it. But the work of art does not lead to another experience of the world; it is *an* experience. Only secondarily, as it becomes a part of the past experiences of a person does it transform his everyday existence. The painter, for example, perceives the world just as everyone else does. But to him certain lines and colors become important, and he subordinates other aspects of what he is perceiving to relations among them. What he takes as important is influenced by his past experiences, by his theories of art, by his attitudes toward the world, and by the scene itself.

One reason for the importance of art, claims Dewey, is that it supplies "the only media of complete and unhindered communication between man and man that can occur in a world full of gulfs and walls that limit community of experience." Since art communicates, it requires, like language, a triadic relation of speaker (the artist), the thing said (the art product), and the hearer (the spectator). All language involves what is said and how it is said—substance and form. In art, substance is the content of the work itself; form is the organization of this content.

Each art has its own medium, fitted for a particular kind of communication. When there is a complete set of relations within a chosen medium, there is aesthetic form. Form is relation, and relations are modes of interaction: pushes, pulls, lightness, heaviness. In a successful work of art, the stresses are so adapted to one another that a unity results. The work of art satisfies many ends, none of which is laid down in advance. The artist experiments. He communicates an individual experience through materials that belong to the public world. He means the work of art, and the work of art means whatever anyone can honestly get out of it.

In *Art as Experience* there is a difference between the art product and the work of art. The art product—the statue, the painting, the printed poem —is physical. The work of art is active and experienced. When the art product enters into experience it takes part in a complex interaction. It is the work of art with its fixed order of elements that is perceived. But the work of art is like an organism: it manifests movement, it has a past and present, a career, a history. Energy is organized toward some result. The spectator interacts with the work of art so that energies are given rhythmic organization, are intensified, clarified, concentrated.

The fact that art organizes energy explains its power to move and to stir, to calm and to tranquilize. Paintings that seem dead in whole or in part are those that arrest movement, rather than carry it forward toward a dynamic whole. Thus aesthetic perception differs from ordinary perception. The latter results in classification: those are rain clouds, so I must carry an umbrella. Aesthetic perception is full, complete, and rhythmical.

"What properties do all of the arts share?" Dewey asks. In the past it had been argued that they have a common subject matter. But the tendency in the arts is to go beyond limits. New artists have new interests and express them through new uses of material. Yet, the arts do share a common form to the extent that they are all organized toward a unity of experience. Further, all arts operate through sensory mediums. A material such as stone, watercolor, oil paints, or words becomes a medium when it is used to express a meaning other than that of its commonplace physical existence. Different mediums give different qualities to works of art; pastel differs from oil. "Sensitivity to a medium as a medium is the very heart of all artistic creation and esthetic perception." The medium is a *mediator*; it relates the artist and the perceiver. The third property that all arts share is that they are concerned with space and time. The arts are dynamic, and all action must occur in

space and time. Spatiality is mass and volume; temporality is endurance.

The aesthetic experience, Dewey contends, is located in the interaction between the spectator and the art product. Thus, art products cannot be classified into aesthetic categories. There can be as great a variety of works of art as there can be a variety of unified experiences. The work of art comes into existence when a human being coöperates with the art product. This coöperation results in an experience which is enjoyed because of its liberating and ordered properties. Thus, for Dewey, no art is inherently superior to any other. Every medium has its own power, its own efficacy and value. The important thing is that it communicates by making common, related, and available what had been isolated and singular.

Every work of art contains something of the particular personality of the artist. In practical action we must divide reality into subject and impersonal object. No such division characterizes aesthetic experience for Dewey. Art is a unity of subject and object. Like rite and ceremony, it has the power to unite men through shared celebration to all of the concerns and anticipations of life.

Aesthetic experience, indeed all experience, is imaginative. Imagination helps to adjust the old to the new, connecting the new with its physical past and the past of the person involved. Aesthetic experience is the paradigm of experience, experience freed from the factors that would impede and thwart its development.

Thus, if Dewey is right, it is to aesthetic experience that philosophers must turn if they are to understand the nature of experience itself. In the past, philosophers have explained aesthetic experience as but one type of experience. Rather, they should have taken experience in its most complete form, the fusion of the self with the objective order and law of the material that it incorporates, and used this—aesthetic experience—as the model for understanding experience in general.

Dewey uses the principles delineated in *Art as Experience* to solve what he takes to be some of the major problems of aesthetics. Does art express the universal or the unique and particular? In Dewey's opinion it does neither exclusively. It forms a new synthesis which is both. The expression is neither objective nor subjective, neither solely personal nor completely general.

Does art convey knowledge? It is true that it makes life more intelligible, says Dewey; but not through concepts in the way that knowing does. Art clarifies by intensifying experience. Both philosophy and art depend on the imaginative power of the mind. Art is a manifestation of experience *as* experience, of experience unalloyed. Because of this manifestation, it can provide a control for the imaginative ventures of philosophy.

Dewey has much advice for the critic. Criticism is a judgment about art. If we are to understand the nature of criticism in the arts, we must first understand the nature of judgment. The material which judgment uses is supplied by perception. This material in a mature judgment must be controlled and selected. In viewing a work of art, the spectator conducts a controlled inquiry, which requires an extensive background and developed taste. The spectator must discriminate and unify, but unlike the jurist he has no socially approved rules to apply. The law is conservative, but criticism must be sensitive to new forms of expression that stem from spiritual and physical changes in the environment.

At the opposite extreme from Dewey is the impressionistic critic. Mere impression can never organize experience; unification and discrimination always involve reference to some theory. If works of art are not to be judged by impressions, they are also not to be judged by fixed standards. In the primary sense, a standard is a physical object that measures quantitatively. The critic measures qualitatively.

How, then, can the critic make objective judgments? The qualities that he is judging are those of an object, and his judgment requires a hypothesis. It is his hypothesis that provides a criterion for judging him as a critic. His theory of criticism must be adequate to enable him to point to properties of the art object that will evoke an aesthetic experience. He must discuss form in relation to matter, the function of the medium, the nature of the expressive object. He must lead rather than dictate. He must discover a unifying pattern which pervades the work of art, perhaps not the only one, but one that can be shown to be maintained throughout the parts of the art object.

Art as Experience identifies two fallacies of aesthetic criticism. The first of these is reduction. The reduction fallacy occurs when some aspect of the work of art is taken as the whole. The work of art is a self-contained unity; it combines many things, none of which has aesthetic priority. The second fallacy results from a confusion of categories. Works of art provide data for students of art; for example, for the art historian. But to identify the historian's account of the work of art with aesthetic criticism is to be guilty of a confusion of categories.

Another type of category confusion concerns values. The most obvious example is found in moralistic criticism. A work of art may well make moral judgments, but these are not the sole criterion of its aesthetic value. Art is a medium of communication in its own right, not a substitute for religion, science, philosophy, or moral exhortation. The function of the critic is to delineate the aesthetic experience, which has its own inherent value, to reëducate so that others may learn from the criticism to see and to hear.

There is one problem that the artist, the critic, and the aesthetician must face. It is the relation between permanence and change. Human beings and their environments are continually subjected to change operating within a structure of laws. This structure is in turn subject to gradual change. Art must reflect such changes. Artists and critics have only begun to realize that the rise of industrialism is the source of new patterns and of new materials. Art can show that there is permanence in the changing and change in the permanent.

In a broad sense, aesthetic experience reveals the life and development of civilization. Art is a magnificent force that brings together conflicting elements found in every period of history. The customs and rituals of a people, all of their communal activities, unite the practical, social, and educative into an aesthetic unity.

The art of the past must have something to say to the present to be worthy of present consideration. An art can die just as can any other human institution. But great art, for Dewey, is a revelation of self and always has something to say to succeeding peoples under different environments; it tells of the ordered movement of the matter of some experience to a genuine fulfillment.

We often think of ancient civilizations in terms of their art products. To the elements of civilization which the art of the past reveals have been added two in the modern world. These are natural science and its application to industry and commerce through machinery. These new factors have yet to be absorbed into the attitudes of most people. Science has given us a new conception of our environment and of our relation to it. Science tends to show man as a part of nature and gives rational support to his desire to control himself and his environment. It enables him to understand himself in relation to his past, his present, and his future.

Industry creates an environment in which more and more people leave the rural world of nature for the man-made world of the machine. This new setting can have aesthetic quality. Objects with their own internal functional adaptions can be combined with man in a way that yields aesthetic results. The artist can create a physical and moral environment that will shape desires and purposes, that will determine the direction of the interest and attention of human beings. Artistic experience, says Dewey, can and must shape the future.

MIND, SELF, AND SOCIETY

Author: George Herbert Mead (1863-1931)
Type of work: Philosophical psychology
First published: 1934

PRINCIPAL IDEAS ADVANCED

Mind and self can best be understood as emergents from a more basic social process.

There is no absolute separation between the social and the organic, and any pragmatic or behavioral account of human action which fails to recognize this fact is faulty.

Novelty of response is possible for individual selves which, by the use of memory, can take advantage of past experience within society.

How Professor Mead's book came to be published tells one something about the author's unusual stature as a teacher. The book's contents primarily represent the careful editing of several sets of notes taken down by appreciative students attending Mead's lectures on social psychology at the University of Chicago, especially those given in 1927 and 1930. Other manuscript materials also find some place in the book. For more than thirty years Mead taught at the University of Chicago, exerting a powerful scholarly influence on students, colleagues, and professional acquaintances. His written contributions during his lifetime were confined to articles and reviews for learned journals. Nonetheless, as a result of the devotion of some of those he influenced, Mead has left to the learned world four published books which bear his name. All of these appeared after his death. The other three books are *The Philosophy of the Present* (1932), *Movements of Thought in the Nineteenth Century* (1936), and *The Philosophy of the Act* (1938).

Mind, Self, and Society remains cru-

cial for the manner in which its central concerns dominated all of Mead's philosophizing during the first three decades of this century. Its subtitle—"From the Standpoint of a Social Behaviorist"—indicates the theme. Mead thought that all aspects of human conduct, including those so often covered by terms like "mind" and "self," can best be understood as emergents from a more basic process. The four separate but related parts of the book present Mead's defense of a social behaviorism: "The Point of View of Social Behaviorism," "Mind," "The Self," and "Society."

Mead's attempt to state the nature of social behaviorism is related to the specific situation which he found on hand in the intellectual landscape. As a naturalist strongly influenced by the theory of biological evolution, Mead shows the usual suspicion of older dualistic accounts of the mind-body problem. He sets out to explain physical and mental events by one embracing theory. Thus, he rejects the view that a physico-psychological dualism exists which requires a theory to account for supposed differences between mental and nonmental forms of conduct or between human and nonhuman.

Mead's philosophical views are those of the pragmatists, for whom the function of intelligence is the control of actions rather than a supposedly disinterested description of metaphysical realities thought to be independent of experience. But how is the psychologist to avoid a dualist theory if he retains in his vocabulary words like "mind," "consciousness," "self-consciousness," and "self"? This was Mead's initial problem, stated here in the form of a simple question. One answer of the day had come from John B. Watson, sometimes called the father of psychological behaviorism. Watson had argued that the scientific study of human conduct must confine itself strictly to those aspects of behavior which are externally observable. Accordingly, Watson insisted that psychologists give up using terms like "mind" and "self," since what can be observed are brains and nervous systems in response to external stimuli.

Like Watson, Mead claims that any effort to understand human behavior by reliance on introspection of internal mental states produces a theoretical difficulty in that psychological explanations can never be subjected to experimental tests. Mead also insists that earlier philosophers made hasty and often illegitimate metaphysical capital out of the distinction between *external* and *internal* aspects of behavior. Thus, he shares Watson's general scientific aim—the statement of a thoroughly behavioral account of human action. But Mead criticizes Watson's physiological version of behaviorism as resting on too narrow a conception of what makes up

an action. Words like "mind" and "self" must be kept in the psychological vocabulary, but they should never be thought of as referring to entities or processes which stand outside the subject matter of behavioral analysis. Watson's views result from a heavy reliance on mechanical models as well as from too restricted a notion of the nature of reflex activity. By *reducing* experiences of a mental kind to explicitly physiological correlates, Watson produced a psychological behaviorism which "leads inevitably to obvious absurdities."

Mead's claim is that psychologists need not "explain away" those features of conscious life which often prove embarrassing to strictly physiological analysts of conduct. There definitely are minds and selves. The narrow Watsonian model fails to take their existence into account. The reason is that the model depicts conduct as created by an organism (containing a brain and a central nervous system) responding to numerous stimuli (response-provoking objects which are external to that organism). Here lies the source of Watson's incorrect view of what action involves, according to Mead. This view lacks an adequate awareness of the *social* aspect of action, especially human action. To produce an adequate behavioral theory of action one needs a model demonstrating that the social aspects of human action *belong partly to* the organism itself rather than *result from* the relations between atomic organisms and external stimuli. What this means is that, in the case of human action, no absolute separation exists between the social and the organic.

The major problem for Mead is to explain how minds and selves appear in the social process. Minds and selves are exclusively features of human conduct. Mead admits that animals possess intelligence but denies that they have minds, even though animals also function in social contexts. The necessary conclusion is, then, that only social beings can be said to possess self-consciousness. Only human organisms are socially based emergents having this specific kind of mental life. How can this be explained? Mead answers in terms of the emergence in the social process of what he calls *significant* symbols. Such symbols are ultimately linguistic in form, but they evolve from the roles played in all organic conduct by gestures and responses to gestures. Certain gestures become significant symbols when "they implicitly arouse in an individual making them the same responses which they explicitly arouse, or are supposed to arouse, in other individuals, the individuals to whom they are addressed. . . ." Human organisms differ from other animal organisms in their ability to make use of significant symbols. For example, a dog which growls at another dog is making a gesture; but the dog cannot make use of a *significant* gesture since he can never take the role of the "other" in a process of communication the way men can and do. Communication involves this taking of the role of the other, self-consciously in a social context. It is this ability possessed by human organisms which makes language and communication possible.

Meade does not argue that "meaning" exists only in linguistic form, but he argues that language constitutes the most meaningful type of communication. For Mead, meaning is objectively *there* as a feature of social processes.

"Awareness of consciousness is not necessary to the presence of meaning in the process of social experience." Communication involves making available to others meanings which actually exist to be discovered and talked about. Significant symbols function to make the user of them aware of the responses they call out in those to whom he directs them. The significant symbol not only calls out in the user the awareness of others' responses to it; the symbol functions to make those responses serve as stimuli to the user. This gives an anticipatory character to communication. The result is that users of such symbols can respond to them in novel ways, actually introducing changes into the social situation by such responses. In this view, ideas are anticipations of future expected actions made possible by the capacity to use significant symbols.

This capacity of the human organism to use significant symbols is a precondition of the appearance of the self in the social process. The self is not like the body, which can never view itself as a whole. The self emerges from a process of social communication which enables one to view himself, as a whole, from the perspective of others. Mead treats this problem in terms of the phases of the self, the "me" and the "I." His effort is to understand this human capacity to adopt the attitudes of others toward oneself. Each response to a significant symbol presupposes that one can associate himself with the set of attitudes making up the social group ("the generalized other") to which he belongs. In this manner the "me" emerges as a phase of the self, for the "me" *is* that set of attitudes appropriated by the individual. The "I" as a phase of the self is that which makes possible the organism's response. The "I" can respond to the "me" even in novel ways, meaning that, for Mead, social action is never simply imitative or literally repetitive. Mead makes use of the notions of the game and play to illustrate his thesis. Games and play require participants to adopt the roles of the others involved. Just as in a game one can never get beyond the set of attitudes associated with the various roles of the different players, so in the case of the human "mind" and "self" there is no getting beyond the social process which they presuppose. Without society involving a number of different roles there would be nothing in terms of which a self could arise. Without the viewpoints of others which form the "me" there would exist nothing to which the "I" could respond.

Mead's treatment of the nature of the self permits him to take seriously features of "depth" psychology which Watsonian behaviorism overlooks. To understand a self means to understand something about the roles and attitudes of others as productive of that self. Here Mead finds a difference between the social lives of animals and men. Animal and human social communities involve organization, but in human social systems the organization reflects the self-conscious adoption of a number of roles, a thing impossible in animal communities. The strict organizational patterns found in bee and ant societies do not lead to significant communication or to the creation of a language. While social life is necessary as a condition of the appearance of minds and selves, minds and selves do not always exist where there is social life. *What* emerges in the form of minds and selves *from* a social process is

a genuine and an irreducible reality.

Because the self exists only when an individual can know the attitudes of others in a community, it is normal for a multiple self to be present in each person. These attitudes form the possibility of a "me" which can become an object and response-provoking stimulus to an "I." The self can become an object to itself in a way in which a body cannot. The nature of the social community in which the self arises obviously influences the nature of that self. "Normally, within the sort of community as a whole to which we belong, there is a unified self, but that may be broken up. To a person who is somewhat unstable nervously and in whom there is a line of cleavage, certain activities become impossible, and that set of activities may separate and evolve another self."

The pathological aspect of a multiple self concerns the possibility of "forgetting" forms of past experiences from which important elements of the self have emerged. In any existing social community, there must exist some fairly stable attitudes and roles if a self is to emerge at all; and it is the stable elements which permit language to possess a universal significance for communication. The symbols of a language permit a self to respond to the same meaning or object as others in the group using that set of symbols. Linguistic confusions reflect social instability in that meanings are hardly fixed at all. Personality is unable to develop when rapidly altering social attitudes and roles fail to permit language to capture relatively stable meanings. The reason is that there can be no completely individual self. "When a self does appear, it always involves an experience of another; there could not be an experience of a self simply by itself."

In Mead's analysis of the self, the "me" reflects those features which make up the stable habit patterns of an individual's conduct. In a sense, the "me" is the individual's character insofar as it can issue forth in predictable forms of behavior. But how does the "I" arise as a phase of the self which permits some novelty of response? Mead's answer is that the "I" appears only in the memory of what the individual has done. Mead claims that an individual usually knows what he has done and said only *after* he has acted and spoken. There is a retrospective stance to the self-awareness of the "I" which permits novel uses of this memory in new situations. Individuals are not compelled to respond in the same way they formerly did once there is a self. They can react in original ways to the attitudes of other members in the social community. In such reactions the "I" always acts in terms of an appeal to a widened social community if it reacts against the existing practices of the group. Mead claims that the moral importance of the reactions of the "I," as a phase of the self, resides in the individual's sense of importance as a person not totally determined by the attitudes of the others. "The demand is freedom from conventions, from given laws." Such a demand, when it occurs, implies that another community exists, if only potentially or ideally, in which a broader and more embracing self is possible of realization. The complete development of a self therefore requires both phases, the "I" and the "me"—established habits in a social situation which yet leave room for novel responses to new situations.

Each individual in a social community will have some element of a unique standpoint from which to react to the attitudes making up that community. The reason is that each individual can reflect on his own experiences within the social structure supporting his existence. Mead thinks that a rational social community will encourage development of self-responsible action rather than automatic responses by coercive external conditioning. Such a community will provide opportunity for the stereotyped kind of work which each person needs (if he is a healthy individual) plus opportunity for self-expression through unique responses to situations (so that the person does not feel "hedged in" and completely "the conventionalized 'me'"). A rational community differs from a mob or a crowd, for in a rational community the individual can become a determinant of aspects of the environment. Great personalities like Socrates, Jesus, and Buddha were able to influence the communities of their own day and age by their appeals to an enlarged potential community.

Mead's social behaviorism places him in opposition both to the individualistic and to the *partially* social explanations of mind. The individualistic theory argues that mind is a necessary logical and biological presupposition of any existing social process. Its adherents attempt to account for the social aspect of human existence in terms of contract theories of the origin of political and social life. The *partially* social theory admits that mind can express its potentialities only in a social setting but insists mind is in some sense prior to that setting. Mead argues that his social behaviorism is in direct contrast to these competing theories in that "mind presupposes, and is a product of, the social process." For Mead, the forms of social groupings tend either toward coöperative or aggressively competitive ones. Mead favors the former. He believes that the democratic ideal of full human participation in a variety of social situations (involving different roles) can best call out the wide range of human responses which mind makes possible. In a democratic society the twin quests after universality of experience, economic and religious, can best be harmonized. Such a society also makes available a wider range of roles from which an individual can develop a self. It is clear that, for Mead, democracy involves a society which permits a rich variety of primary groups to exist.

Mead's attempt to state a consistent theory of social behaviorism may have failed. In fact, his position is a metaphysical rather than a scientific one. However, his views form a metaphysical defense of the democratic ideal in terms of the behavioral hopes of psychologists to bring human conduct under rational control. Mead is at least on the side of reason and rationality. He is stubborn in his refusal to give up terms like "mind" and "consciousness," and he is equally unwilling to discard the behaviorist model of the psychologists. He tries valiantly to widen men's conception of the human act. The critical question remains, naturally, whether Mead or any man can have the best of two possible worlds.

PHILOSOPHY AND LOGICAL SYNTAX

Author: Rudolf Carnap (1891-)
Type of work: Philosophy of philosophy
First published: 1935

PRINCIPAL IDEAS ADVANCED

Philosophy is the logical analysis of meaningful language.

Meaningful language is either the language of logic and mathematics (involving analytic sentences) or the language of science (involving empirically verifiable synthetic sentences).

Metaphysics and ethics are not legitimate parts of philosophy for their language is meaningless.

Logical analysis is logical syntax, and logical syntax is the study of the manipulation of signs in accordance with the rules of a language.

Rudolf Carnap's *Philosophy and Logical Syntax* is the substance of three lectures which he gave at the University of London in 1934. As a result, the book is short, presenting the essentials of the logical positivism of the Vienna Circle in outline form. It is perhaps as good an outline summary of the Vienna Circle views as is available, coming, as it does, from the pen of the best known—and perhaps the most influential—member of the group.

Logical positivism is certainly not an unknown movement to American and British philosophers. During the 1930's and early 1940's it seemed destined to sweep all other philosophical movements into the forgotten and insignificant areas of the past. Recent days, of course, have seen the movement called into question, but the ghost of the verifiability criterion of meaning and the emotive theory of ethics still stalks the philosophical world.

Logical positivism had its origin in a seminar conducted in the 1920's in Vienna by Moritz Schlick. A number of the members of this group, the original "Vienna Circle," were scientists reacting against those idealist philosophers who pontificated, sometimes in almost complete ignorance, about the aim and function of science. Part of positivism's program was the explicit rejection of this kind of irresponsible philosophizing. Another characteristic concern of the group was a strong interest in logic, an interest which grew out of their admiration for the work which had been done on the foundations of mathematics toward the close of the nineteenth century and in the early twentieth century, particularly the work of Whitehead and Russell in their *Principia Mathematica* (1910-1913). These interests quite naturally led the Vienna group to deliberate regarding philosophy's proper business. They decided that philosophy is properly the analysis and clarification of meaningful language. By meaningful language they meant the language of empirical science together with the language of mathematics; all other language, they held, lacked cognitive meaning. The Vienna Circle philosophers gave expression to this conviction in their criterion of empirical meaning, a widely known and vigorously debated tenet of logical positivism.

Carnap spends the first of the three chapters of *Philosophy and Logical Syntax* discussing the implications of the verifiability criterion. At one point he states that only the propositions of mathematics and empirical science "have sense," and that all other propositions are without theoretical sense. However, he does not do much in the book with mathematical propositions —with "analytic" propositions, as positivists sometimes labeled the propositions of logic and mathematics. He spends most of his time with "synthetic" propositions; that is, with propositions whose truth value cannot be determined simply by referring to their logical form. As examples of this analytic-synthetic distinction we might consider here the two propositions: (1) "The ball is red," and (2) "Either the ball is red or the ball is not red." We cannot know whether the first one is true or false without in fact examining the ball, but we can know that the second proposition is true without looking at the ball. It is true in virtue of its logical form. A sentence which is true or false in virtue of its form alone is analytic; a sentence whose truth value is determined by the (nonlinguistic) facts is synthetic.

Carnap holds the view that the only synthetic propositions which make sense are those propositions whose truth value can be determined by consulting the evidence of sense. And these propositions, he further believes, are all to be found within the domain of empirical science. He uses the word "verification" in the usual logical positivist sense; that is to say, a proposition is verifiable if its truth value can be determined by reference to sense experience. The only synthetic propositions which make sense, then, are verifiable propositions, and these are all scientific propositions. This is the verifiability criterion of empirical meaning.

It is Carnap's view, then, that philosophy is the logical analysis of meaningful language, and meaningful language is restricted either to analytic propositions (logic and mathematics) or to empirically verifiable propositions (natural science). This theory implies that certain traditional areas of philosophy are no longer to be regarded as legitimate. Carnap rejects what he calls traditional metaphysics since it is made up of propositions which he feels are neither analytic nor empirically verifiable. As examples of such illegitimate metaphysical sentences he mentions sentences about "the real Essence of things," about "Things in themselves," about "the Absolute," and "such like." In addition, Carnap rejects traditional philosophical ethics. He believes the usual utterances of ethical philosophers—such as "Killing is wrong"—mislead people in virtue of their grammatical form. They look like propositions, and so philosophers have given arguments to show that they are either true or false. Carnap, however, believes that what is grammatically an assertion, "Killing is wrong," is logically not an assertion at all, but rather a disguised command, "Do not kill." However, commands are neither true nor false and hence cannot be propositions. Ethics, then, is necessarily ruled out of the domain of philosophy.

Ethics and metaphysics are thus ruled out of philosophy proper. But there must be something to them; otherwise why have people been so concerned about them? Here Carnap also has a simple answer. Metaphysical and ethical utterances express deep feelings and emotions. That is why people are so concerned about them. They express our emotions. But this, Carnap points out, is to say that they resemble the utterances of the lyric poet; that is, they express emotion, and they evoke a profound response in the reader, but they nevertheless do not make theoretical or cognitive sense—they are meaningless from a philosophical and scientific point of view.

But not only metaphysics and ethics suffer from Carnap's determination to rid philosophy of the senseless burden it has borne. Epistemology and psychology also suffer as a result of his reforming zeal. Insofar as there is a legitimate area of psychology, it is an empirical science which, as such, is not the philosopher's concern. And epistemology is, Carnap suspects, a hybrid of psychology and logic. Philosophers must continue to do the logic, but they should give over the psychology to the behaviorists. And now, finally, we reach the proper domain of the philosopher, after rejecting metaphysics, ethics, psychology, and epistemology. The philosopher is to do logical analysis on the language of the scientist. There can be no misunderstanding of Carnap's intention here, for he writes: "The only proper task of *Philosophy* is *Logical Analysis*."

We should now try to determine what Carnap means by "logical analysis." As Carnap understands it, logical analysis is a concern with the logical syntax of a language. This claim needs elucidation.

In other of his writings, Carnap has taken some pains to identify what he means by logical syntax. In the *Foun-*

dations of Logic and Mathematics (1939) he has perhaps made the distinctions most clearly. There he distinguishes pragmatics, semantics, and syntax as parts of the general philosophical concern with language which he calls "semiotic." The first distinction which needs to be made here is between language which is about language, and language which is not about language. One might, for example, assert the proposition: "The ball is red." In this case one would be using language to talk about the nonlinguistic world, to talk about a ball. But one might then go on to talk about the proposition which refers to the red ball; one might say: "The proposition 'The ball is red' has four words in it." In this case the proposition is not about objects such as red balls, but about language itself. Such language about language is called "meta-language"; language about objects is called "object language." The general theory of an object language, stated in a meta-language, is what Carnap means by "semiotic." But semiotic has three branches: pragmatics, semantics, and syntax. Pragmatics is an empirical study of three elements which can be distinguished in the use of a language —linguistic signs, the meanings (Carnap calls them "designata") of the signs, and the users of the signs. Pragmatics studies all three elements. Oversimplifying, pragmatics may be likened to the activity of an anthropologist constructing a dictionary for a tribe he is studying. The anthropologist studies and records how the tribesmen use words, how the words are spelled and combined, and what the words indicate.

Semantics is an abstraction from pragmatics. The semanticist (in the Carnapian sense—not to be confused with the so-called "General Semanticist") restricts his concern to the words or signs and their designata, their meanings. He abstracts from users to focus solely on the signs and their designata. There can be two kinds of semantics: descriptive semantics is an empirical study of signs and their matter-of-fact meanings in popular usage; pure semantics, on the other hand, is not an empirical study but a normative one which lays down rules regarding the signs and what their proper designata are. A pure semantical system is an artificial language consisting of rules specifying designata for a collection of linguistic signs. An example of a pure semantical sentence might be: "The predicate word 'large' designates the property of being large in a physical sense." This specifies how the word "large" is to be used in a given artificial language, and it implies that such common language expressions as "That's a large order" are incorrect in the semantical system in which the rule occurs.

Syntax represents yet another level of abstraction. Pragmatics includes signs, designata, and users. Semantics ignores the users and focuses its attention solely on signs and their designata. Syntax ignores the designata of the signs as well as ignoring the users. It is concerned only with the signs and the rules in accordance with which they can be combined and manipulated. Again we may oversimplify and say that the subject matter of syntax is the traditional rules of logical deduction, provided we add that the rules are formulated in a more abstract and formal way than is customary. Very roughly speaking, then, we may say that pragmatics may be likened to making a dictionary of usage, that semantics may be likened to specifying the exact and unambiguous definitions of words in, say, a technical treatise, and that syntax may be likened to constructing a formal set of rules of logic.

In his second chapter Carnap attempts to characterize and illustrate logical syntax somewhat more fully. In the first place, he says, syntax is a "formal" theory. He means by this that syntax abstracts from all concern with the sense or meaning of the signs and confines itself strictly to the forms of the signs or words. It consists entirely of rules specifying how signs—regarded simply as shapes or designs or sounds—may be combined and manipulated. Within this formal theory there are two kinds of rules: formation rules and transformation rules. The formation rules, in effect, define what is to be regarded as a proper sentence. The ordinary man's rejection of Russell's well-known example of an ill-formed sentence—"Quadruplicity drinks procrastination"—is made in virtue of an appeal to the implicit formation rules of the English language. Ordinarily, of course, we all abide by the implicit formation rules of English. Carnap's formation rules are intended to make explicit these implicit rules that we follow. The other group of rules, the transformation rules, specify what manipulations can be performed on the well-formed sentences identified by the formation rules. The transformation rules are the rules of logical deduction expressed in syntactical terms. Carnap states that the two primitive terms in a logical syntax are "sentence" and "direct consequence." That is to say, syntax is concerned to identify what are proper sentences and also to specify how we are to draw their logical consequences.

There are other important syntactical terms in addition to "sentence" and "direct consequence," however. Carnap spends a fair amount of time in the second chapter defining and illustrating these additional syntactical terms. He defines "valid" as the property a sentence has if it is a direct consequence of the null class of premises. Putting this into a different logical terminology, we could say that a proposition which is validly inferred from tautologies is itself a tautology; Carnap means by "valid" what is often called "tautologous." Carnap then defines "contravalid" so that it corresponds to the usual notion of self-contradiction. These two classes of sentences, the valid and the contravalid, make up the class of "determinate" sentences; all other sentences (sometimes called "contingent sentences" by other logicians) are called "indeterminate."

The syntactical transformation rules serve to isolate the valid and contravalid sentences. These rules are called "L-rules" by Carnap. But there are other inferences that may be made which depend, not on these logical rules, but on certain laws of natural science; for example, Newton's laws or the laws of thermodynamics. Scientific laws, such as these, which also serve to justify drawing the consequences of sentences, Carnap calls "P-rules" to distinguish them from the L-rules. Carnap is then able to distinguish additional kinds of sentences; namely, P-valid and P-contravalid sentences.

Other additional terms are defined in this second chapter. Enough have been mentioned here, however, to enable us to see what it is that Carnap is up to. He is making many of the usual distinctions and defining many of the usual terms of traditional logic. But he is doing it in a slightly different way from that characteristic of traditional logic. He has avoided the usual basic logical terms "true" and "false," since they depend on the question of the meaning of the propositions which are said to be either true or false. He has also avoided the usual logical term "implication," and has replaced it with "direct consequence." All of this is intentional and novel. Carnap sees it as being implied by his definition of syntax as a *formal* theory. He can describe a language and lay down rules for manipulating it without ever dealing with the question of the meaning of the words and sentences, and, consequently, without ever worrying about what the subject matter is that the language deals with. He is not doing physics or chemistry or biology; rather, he is manipulating symbols, symbols which might be assigned meanings later on so that they become words and sentences in a theory of chemistry or physics or biology. But, as Carnap sees it, he has sharply separated the work of the philosopher-logician from the work of the scientist. Furthermore, abstracting from the meanings of the words and sentences enables the philosopher-logician to concentrate on the properly logical matters and avoid the tangles that often impede progress in the sciences. Best of all, he has, as a philosopher-logician, a legitimate activity in which to engage, one which benefits the scientist and which also circumvents the morasses of much traditional philosophy.

Just how Carnap feels he has avoided the morasses of traditional philosophy is best seen by looking at his discussion of what he calls "pseudo-object sentences." (In his *The Logical Syntax of Language*, 1934, he calls these "quasi-syntactical sentences.") Carnap feels that many times philosophers have combined syntactical predicates with non-syntactical subjects. The result is neither one thing nor another; they are not statements in the object language, nor are they statements in the meta-language. They are, however, responsible for many of the disputes of traditional metaphysics about the reality or non-reality of entities such as universals. One example will perhaps illustrate Carnap's distinction fairly clearly. He distinguishes three sentences:

(1)	The rose is red.	A real object-sentence in the material mode of speech
(2)	The rose is a thing.	A pseudo-object sentence
(3)	The word 'rose' is a thing-word.	A syntactical sentence in the formal mode of speech

No disputes arise over the first sentence. It is a sensible sentence which everyone understands and knows how to handle. Nor do disputes arise over the third sentence. Most people do not speak this way, but when they do (that is, when they are philosophical syntacticians), they make sense and avoid confusion. Unfortunately, philosophers have too often spoken in the manner of the second sentence. They then believe they are speaking about roses, and they begin debating and defining, getting further and further mired in the morass of bogus entities. One should speak either with the vul-

1002

gar about red roses or with the sophisticated about thing-words. But one should beware of speaking with the metaphysicians about rose-things.

Pseudo-object sentences are likely to give rise to pseudo-questions. This is the burden of the final chapter of Carnap's book. Logical positivism offers hope, he feels, for genuine progress in philosophy because it identifies the errors of earlier philosophies, and it provides a technique for avoiding them. The problem of universals, for example, is not a real problem; it is a pseudo-problem which results from confusing the "formal mode" of speech and the "material mode" of speech, from being deceived by pseudo-object sentences such as "The rose is a thing." We should speak in the formal mode about "predicate words"; we should not speak in the material mode about universals as things.

The position Carnap states in *Philosophy and Logical Syntax* has been stated much more fully in other of his works, especially in his earlier *The Logical Syntax of Language*. In some of his later works he has also modified some of his earlier views—most notably, perhaps, by admitting semantics to philosophical legitimacy along with syntax. But in its essentials the position is as stated in *Philosophy and Logical Syntax*. It is a view which has influenced contemporary philosophy greatly, and it is a view which is genuinely novel—a notable achievement in as ancient a discipline as philosophy.

It probably has not had the influence outside philosophy which the intrinsic merit of the position deserves. This lack of widespread influence is quite probably the result of Carnap's tendency, in his more extended writing, to use a formidable and forbidding battery of technical apparatus including strange terms and Gothic script. He unfortunately has not completely rid himself of a Germanic fascination with architectonic and a tendency to identify the profound with the unfamiliar. He has also suffered from a tendency to oversimplify and trivialize the views he opposes. One can understand his rejection of the excesses of some idealist philosophers, but one finds it hard to move from that to the simple "resolution" of the problems the idealists wrestled with which defines them out of existence as "pseudo-problems." But when all is said about Carnap's lack of understanding and sympathy for any philosophical problems other than his own, one must still acknowledge the great skill he has brought to bear on the problems that did interest him. Carnap is a great innovator and an original thinker of enormous stature; one can forgive him if he is not the best twentieth century historian of philosophy. And when the history of twentieth century philosophy is written, surely Carnap's attempt to develop a logic which does not rest on any prior theory of meaning will be given a most prominent place, and deservedly so.

1003

REASON AND EXISTENZ

Author: Karl Jaspers (1883-   )
Type of work: Existential metaphysics
First published: 1935

PRINCIPAL IDEAS ADVANCED

No description of Existenz is possible; Existenz can be clarified only by reference to concrete situations.

Existenz is the freedom of an individual, the possibility of decision; because man exists in this special sense, he is that which he can become in his freedom.

The Encompassing is that which man encounters; considered as Being-in-itself, the Encompassing appears only in and through the Being-which-we-are. (We know what confronts us only in terms of what we are because of it.)

Reason and Existenz develop mutually and are interdependent.

In existential communication the self first comes to full consciousness of itself as a being qualified by historicity (determination in time), uniqueness, freedom, and communality.

The five lectures which comprise *Reason and Existenz* were delivered at the University of Groningen, Holland, in the spring of 1935. In these lectures the author knits together with a remarkable facility the various themes which are elaborated in his multi-volumed philosophical writings. *Reason and Existenz* is thus both a helpful summary and an excellent introduction to the author's philosophy.

Jaspers defines philosophy as the elucidation of *Existenz* (*Existenzerhellung*). (We retain the term "Existenz" since the English "existence" is not the equivalent.) This elucidation of *Existenz* needs to be sharply contrasted with any attempt at a *conceptualization* of *Existenz* through objectively valid and logically compelling categories. Jaspers denies that a unifying perspective of the content of existential reality is possible. Nonetheless, a clarification of or elucidation of *Existenz* as it expresses itself in concrete situations can be productively undertaken.

According to Jaspers the philosopher is the one who strives for such clarification.

Jaspers finds in the concrete philosophizing of Kierkegaard and Nietzsche a profound exemplification of the philosophical attitude. Both, in their interest to understand existential reality from within, had serious reservations about any program which intended to bring thought into a single and complete system, derived from self-evident principles. Any claim for a completed existential system affords nothing more than an instance of philosophical pretension. *Existenz* has no final content; it is always "on the way," subject to the contingencies of a constant becoming. Kierkegaard and Nietzsche in grasping this fundamental insight uncovered the existential irrelevancy of Hegel's system of logic. It was particularly Kierkegaard, in his attack on speculative thought, who brought to light the comic neglect of *Existenz* in the essentialism and rationalism of Hegel. Kierkegaard and Nietzsche further laid the foundations for a redefinition of philosophy as an elucidation of *Existenz* through their emphasis on the attitudinal, as contrasted with the doctrinal, character of philosophy. They set forth a new intellectual attitude toward life's problems. They developed no fixed doctrines which can be abstracted from their thinking as independent and permanent formulations. They were both suspicious of scientific men who sought to reduce all knowledge to simple and quantifiable data. They were passionately interested in the achievements of self-knowledge. Both taught that self-reflection is the way to truth. Reality is disclosed through a penetration to the depths of the self. Both realized the need for indirect communication and saw clearly the resultant falsifications in objectivized modes of discourse. Both were exceptions—in no sense models for followers. They defy classification under any particular type and shatter all efforts at imitation. What they did was possible only once. Thus the problem for us is to philosophize without being exceptions, but with our eyes on the exception.

At the center of Jaspers' philosophizing we find the notion of the *Umgreifende*. Some have translated this basic notion of Jaspers as the "Comprehensive"; others have found the English term, the "Encompassing," to be a more accurate rendition of the original German. The Encompassing lies beyond all horizons of determinate being, and thus never makes its appearance as a determinable object of knowledge. Like Kant's noumenal realm, it remains hidden behind the phenomena. Jaspers readily agrees with Kant that the Encompassing as a desig-

nation for ultimate reality is objectively unknowable. It escapes every determinate objectivity, emerges neither as a particular object nor as the totality of objects. As such it sets the limits to the horizon of man's conceptual categories. In thought there always arises that which passes beyond thought itself. Man encounters the Encompassing not within a conceptual scheme but in existential decision and philosophical faith. This Encompassing appears and disappears for us only in its modal differentiations. The two fundamental modes of the Encompassing are the "Encompassing as Being-in-itself" and the "Encompassing which-we-are." Both of these modes have their ground and animation in *Existenz*.

Jaspers' concern for a clarification of the meaning and forms of Being assuredly links him with the great metaphysicians of the Western tradition, and he is ready to acknowledge his debt to Plato, Aristotle, Spinoza, Hegel, and Schelling. However, he differs from the classical metaphysicians in his relocation of the starting point for philosophical inquiry. Classical metaphysics has taken as its point of departure Being-in-itself, conceived either as Nature, the World, or God. Jaspers approaches his program of clarification from the Being-which-we-are. This approach was already opened up by the critical philosophy of Kant, which remains for Jaspers the valid starting point for philosophical elucidation.

The Encompassing as Being-which-we-are passes into further internally articulated structural modes. Here empirical existence (*Dasein*), consciousness as such (*Bewusstsein überhaupt*), and spirit (*Geist*) make their appear-

1005

ance. Empirical existence indicates myself as object, by virtue of which I become a datum for examination by the various scientific disciplines such as biology, psychology, anthropology, and sociology. In this mode of being man apprehends himself simply as an object among other objects, subject to various conditioning factors. Man is not yet properly known as human. His distinctive existential freedom has not yet been disclosed. He is simply an item particularized by the biological and social sciences for empirical investigation. The second structural mode of the Being-which-we-are is consciousness as such. Consciousness has two meanings. In one of its meanings it is still bound to empirical reality. It is a simple principle of empirical life which indicates the particularized living consciousness in its temporal process. However, we are not only particularized consciousnesses which are isolated one from another; we are in some sense similar to one another, by dint of which we are disclosed as consciousness as such. Through this movement of consciousness as such man is able to understand himself in terms of ideas and concepts which have universal validity. Empirical existence expresses a relationship of man to the empirical world. Consciousness as such expresses a relationship of man to the world of ideas. Ideas are permanent and timeless. Thus man can apprehend himself in his timeless permanence.

The influence of Plato upon the thought of Jaspers becomes clearly evident at this point. We participate in the Encompassing through the possibility of universally valid knowledge in which there is a union with timeless essences. As simple empirical consciousness we are split into a multi-plicity of particular realities; as consciousness as such we are liberated from our confinement in a single consciousness and participate in the universal and timeless essence of humanity. Spirit constitutes the third modal expression of the Encompassing which-we-are. Spirit signifies the appetition towards totality, completeness, and wholeness. As such it is oriented toward the truth of consciousness. It is attracted by the timeless and universal ideas which bring everything into clarity and connection. It seeks a unification of particular existence in such a way that every particular would be a member of a totality.

There is indeed a sense in which spirit expresses the synthesis of empirical existence and consciousness as such. But this is a synthesis which is never completed. It is always on the way, an incessant striving which is never finished. It is at this point that Jaspers' understanding of spirit differs from that of Hegel. For Hegel spirit drives beyond itself to its own completion, but not so for Jaspers. On the one hand, spirit is oriented to the realm of ideas in which consciousness as such participates, and is differentiated from simple empirical existence; on the other hand spirit is contrasted with the abstraction of a timeless consciousness as such, and expresses kinship with empirical existence. This kinship with empirical existence is its ineradicable temporality. It is a process of constant striving and ceaseless activity, struggling with itself, reaching ever beyond that which it is and has. Yet, it differs from empirical existence in that empirical existence is unconsciously bound to its particularization in matter and life, by virtue of which it can become an object in a determinable horizon. As empirical existence we are split off from each other and become objects of scientific investigation. Spirit overflows every objectivization and remains empirically unknowable. It is not capable of being investigated as a natural object. Although it always points to its basis in empirical existence, it also points to a power or dynamism which provides the impetus for its struggle toward meaning and totality.

It is through the Encompassing which-we-are that one has an approach to the Encompassing as being-in-itself. Being-in-itself never emerges independently as a substantive and knowable entity. It appears only in and through the being-which-we-are. In this appearance it is disclosed as a limit expressing a two-fold modification: (1) the world, and (2) transcendence. The being-which-we-are has one of its limits in the experience of the world. The world in Jaspers' philosophy signifies neither the totality of natural objects nor a spatio-temporal continuum in which these objects come to be. It signifies instead the horizon of inexhaustible appearances which present themselves to inquiry. This horizon is always receding and it manifests itself only indirectly in the appearances of particular and empirical existence. It is never fully disclosed in any one of its perspectives and remains indeterminate for all empirical investigation. The Encompassing which-we-are has its other limit in transcendence. Transcendence is that mode of being-in-itself which remains hidden from all phenomenal experience. It does not even manifest itself indirectly. It extends beyond the horizons of world-orientation as such. It remains the completely unknowable and indefinable,

existentially posited through a philosophical faith.

All the modes of the Encompassing have their original source in *Existenz*. *Existenz* is itself not a mode but carries the meaning of every mode. It is the animation and the ground of all modes of the Encompassing. It is thus only in turning our attention to *Existenz* that we reach the pivotal point in Jaspers' philosophizing. In *Existenz* we reach the abyss or the dark ground of selfhood. *Existenz* contains within itself an element of the irrational, and thus never becomes fully transparent to consciousness as such. Consciousness is always structurally related to the universal ideas, but *Existenz* can never be grasped through an idea. It never becomes fully intelligible because it is the object of no science. *Existenz* can only be approached through concrete elucidations—hence, Jaspers' program of *Existenz-erhellung*. *Existenz* is the possibility of decision, which has its origin in time and apprehends itself only within its temporality. It escapes from every idea of consciousness as well as from the attempt of spirit to render it into an expression of a totality or a part of a whole. *Existenz* is the individual as historicity. It determines the individual in his unique past and his unique future. Always moving into a future the individual, as *Existenz*, is burdened with the responsibilities of his decisions. This fact constitutes his historicity. *Existenz* is irreplaceable. The concrete movements within his historicity, which always call him to decision, disclose him in his unique individuality and personal idiosyncrasy. He is never a simple individual empirical existent that can be reduced to a specimen or an instance of a class; he is unique and irreplaceable. Finally, *Existenz* as it knows itself before transcendence, reveals itself as freedom. *Existenz* is possibility, which means freedom. Man is that which he can become in his freedom.

As the modes of the Encompassing have their roots in *Existenz,* so they have their bond in Reason. Reason is the bond which internally unites the modes and keeps them from falling into an unrelated plurality. Thus Reason and *Existenz* are the great poles of being, permeating all the modes but not coming to rest in any one of them. Jaspers cautions the reader against a possible falsification of the meaning of Reason as it is used in his elucidation of Existenz. Reason is not to be construed as simple, clear, objective thinking (*Verstand*). Understood in this sense, Reason would be indistinguishable from consciousness as such. Reason, as the term is used by Jaspers, is closer to the Kantian meaning of *Vernunft.* It is the preëminence of thought which includes more than mere thinking. It includes not only a grasp of what is universally valid (*ens rationis*), but touches upon and reveals the non-rational, bringing to light its existential significance. It always pushes toward unity, the universal, law, and order, but at the same time remains within the possibility of *Existenz.* Reason and *Existenz* are thus inseparable. Each disappears when the other disappears. Reason without *Existenz* is hollow and culminates in an empty intellectualism. *Existenz* without Reason is blind incessant impulse and irrational striving. Reason and *Existenz* are friends rather than enemies. Each is determined through the other. They mutually develop one another and through this development find both clarity and reality. In this interdependence of Reason and *Existenz* we see an expression of the polar union of the Apollonian and the Dionysian. The Apollonian, or the structural principle, dissolves into a simple intellectual movement of consciousness, a dialectical movement of spirit, when it loses the Dionysian or dynamic principle. Conversely, the Dionysian passes over into irrational passion which burns to its own destruction when it loses its bond with the Apollonian.

The reality of communication provides another dominant thesis in the philosophy of Jaspers. Philosophical truth, which discloses *Existenz* as the ground of the modes and Reason as their bond, can be grasped only in historical communication. The possibility of communication follows from the ineradicable communality of humanity. No man achieves his humanity in isolation. He exists only in and through others, and comes to an apprehension of the truth of his *Existenz* through interdependent and mutual communal understanding. Truth cannot be separated from communicability. But the truth which is expressed in communication is not simple; there are as many senses of truth as there are modes of the Encompassing which-we-are. In the community of our empirical existence it is the pragmatic conception of truth which is valid. Empirical reality knows no absolutes which have a timeless validity. Truth in this mode is relative and changing, because empirical existence itself is in a constant process of change. That which is empirically true today may be empirically wrong tomorrow because of a new situation into which one will have passed. All empirical truth is dependent upon the context of the situation and one's own standpoint within the situation.

As the situation perpetually changes, so does truth. At every moment the truth of one's standpoint is in danger of being refuted by the very fact of process. The truth in the communication of consciousness as such is logical consistency and cogent evidence. By means of logical categories one affirms and denies that which is valid for everyone. Whereas in empirical reality truth is relative and changing because of the multiple fractures of particulars with one another in their time-bound existence, in consciousness as such there is a self-identical consciousness which provides the condition for universally valid truths. The communication of spirit demands participation in a communal substance. Spirit has meaning only in relation to the whole of which it is a part. Communication is thus the communication of a member with its organism. Although each spirit differs from every other spirit there is a common agreement as concerns the order which comprehends them. Communication occurs only through the acknowledgment of their common commitment to this order. Truth in the community of spirit is thus total commitment or full conviction. Pragmatic meaning, logical intelligibility, and full conviction are the three senses of truth expressed in the Encompassing which-we-are.

But there is also the will to communicate Reason and *Existenz*. The communication of *Existenz* never proceeds independently of the communication in the three modes of the Encompassing which-we-are. *Existenz* retains its membership in the mode of empirical existence, consciousness as such, and spirit; but it passes beyond them in a "loving struggle" (*liebender*

Kampf) to communicate the innermost meaning of its being. The communication of *Existenz* is not that of relative and changing particulars, nor is it that of an identical and replaceable consciousness. Existential communication is communication between irreplaceable persons. The community of *Existenz* is also contrasted with the spiritual community. Spirit seeks security in a comprehensive group substance. *Existenz* recognizes the irremovable fracture in being, accepts the inevitability of struggle, and strives to open itself for transcendence. Only through these movements does *Existenz* apprehend its irreplaceable and essentially unrepeatable selfhood, and bind itself to the historical community of selves who share the same irreplaceable determinants. It is in existential communication that the self first comes to a full consciousness of itself as a being qualified by historicity, uniqueness, freedom, and communality.

Reason plays a most important role in existential communication. Reason as the bond of the various modes of the Encompassing strives for a unity in communication. But its function is primarily negative. It discloses the limits of communication in each of the modes and checks the absolutization of any particular mode as the full expression of Being. When empirical existence is absolutized the essence of man is lost; he is reduced to an instance of matter and biological life, and his essence becomes identified with knowable regularities. He is comprehended not in his humanity, but in his simple animality. The absolutization of consciousness as such results in an empty intellectualism. Man's empirical reality is dissolved into timeless truths, and the life of the spirit remains unacknowledged. When spirit becomes a self-sufficient mode the result is a wooden culture in which all intellection and creativity are sacrificed to a communal substance. None of the modes are sufficient by themselves. Each demands the other. Reason provides the internal bond through which their mutual dependence can be harmoniously maintained.

For Jaspers, the truth of Reason is philosophical logic; the truth of *Existenz* is philosophical faith. Philosophical logic and philosophical faith interpenetrate as do Reason and *Existenz* themselves. Logic takes its impulse from *Existenz* which it seeks to clarify. Philosophical logic is limited neither to traditional formal logic nor to mere methodology; it prevents any reduction of man to mere empirical existence or

to a universal consciousness. Philosophical logic is negative in that it provides no new contents, but it is positive in establishing the conditions for every possible content. Philosophical faith, the truth of *Existenz*, confronts man with transcendence and discloses his freedom. Philosophical faith is contrasted with religious faith in that it acknowledges no absolute or final revelation in time. Transcendence discloses a constant openness in which man apprehends himself as an "inner act," more precisely, an act of freedom. Faith is an acknowledgment of transcendence as the source of man's freedom. The highest freedom which man can experience is that freedom which has its condition in a source outside of itself.

LANGUAGE, TRUTH AND LOGIC

Author: Alfred Jules Ayer (1910-   )
Type of work: Philosophy of philosophy, epistemology
First published: 1936

PRINCIPAL IDEAS ADVANCED

Metaphysics is impossible because metaphysical statements are meaningless.

A sentence is factually significant if and only if there is a method of verification an observer could adopt to determine the truth or falsity of the sentence; when experience cannot settle an issue, the issue has no factual meaning.

The propositions of philosophy are not factual, but linguistic; they are not factual reports, but either definitions of words in use or expressions of the logical implications of such definitions.

Value statements and statements declaring duties are neither true nor false; they express the feelings of the speaker.

Alfred Jules Ayer presents here a modified version of logical positivism that he prefers to call "logical empiri-

cism." However, the doctrines, particularly their implications for philosophy, are largely those of logical positivism, and the work serves to bring these together succinctly and vigorously. Therefore, the book has had great importance in the twentieth century, both as a positivistic document and as a center of controversy about positivistic tenets. In it, Ayer offers to solve the problems of reality, perception, induction, knowledge, meaning, truth, value, and other minds. He presents no great new idea; rather, his are solutions others have proposed, but which Ayer has modified and brought into logical consistency. A second edition (1946) enabled Ayer, in a new introduction, to reply to his critics. He provided a further explication and changed a few beliefs, but essentially his position remained unchanged. The reader of *Language, Truth and Logic* who is unfamiliar with the field probably would prefer to reserve reading the new introduction until after examining the text itself.

Ayer attacks the possibility of metaphysics, saying that he will deduce the fruitlessness of attempting knowledge that transcends the limits of experience from the "rule which determines the literal significance of language." The sentences of metaphysics, failing to meet this rule, are meaningless.

The criterion of meaning Ayer finds in the *verification principle.* "We say that a sentence is factually significant to any given person, if, and only if, he knows how to verify the proposition which it purports to express—that is, if he knows what observations would lead him, under certain conditions, to accept the proposition as being true, or reject it as being false." Another possible kind of meaningful sentence is the tautology. But any sentence which is neither a tautology nor a verifiable proposition (by this criterion) is a mere pseudo-proposition, a meaningless sentence.

Certain provisions qualify this tenet. Ayer distinguished practical verifiability and verifiability in principle. Some sentences are not practically verifiable, because of inconvenience or the present state of science and culture. If one could know what observations would decide such a matter if he were in a position to make them, the proposition is verifiable in principle. A further distinction is that between "strong" verifiability and "weak" verifiability. According to the "strong" theory, advanced by the Vienna Circle of logical positivists, a sentence is meaningful only if it is conclusively verifiable empirically; according to the "weak" theory, it is meaningful if experience may render it probable. Ayer chooses the "weak" theory, on the basis that since no empirical demonstration is ever one hundred percent conclusive, the "strong" theory leaves no empirical statement meaningful. By using the "weak" theory, Ayer believes he allows meaning to general propositions of science and to propositions about the past, two types which had given difficulty to previous positivistic writers. The proposed principle rules out such assertions as the statement that the world of sense is unreal, and such questions as whether reality is one substance or many. No experience could decide these issues, so they have no literal significance. The metaphysician has usually been misled by the grammar of his language, so that he posits an entity ("substance," "Being") where grammar requires a noun as the subject of a sentence, even though thought may exert no such requirement.

By the abandonment of metaphysics, the philosopher is freed from the function of constructing a deductive system of the universe from first principles. For first principles cannot come from experience, whose propositions are hypotheses only and never certain. But if they are taken *a priori*, they are only tautologies, which cannot apply to the universe as factual knowledge.

The problem of induction can be set aside as unreal. It is the attempt to prove that certain empirical generalizations derived from past experience will hold good also in the future. It must have either an *a priori* or an empirical solution. But in the first case it is improper to apply tautologies to experience, for they cannot apply to matters of fact; and in the second, we simply assume what we set out to prove. Since Ayer can conceive no test that would solve the "problem" through experience, he concludes that it is not a genuine problem. In actuality, we place our faith in such scientific generalizations as enable us to predict future experience and thus control our environment; there is no general logical problem about this practice.

A common mistake is to assert that without a satisfactory analysis of perception, we are not entitled to believe in the existence of material things. Rather, the right to believe in their existence comes simply from the fact that one has certain sensations, for to say the thing exists is equivalent to saying the sensations are obtainable. It is the philosopher's business to give a correct definition of material things in terms of sensations. He is not concerned with properties of things in the world, but only with our way of speaking of them. The propositions of philosophy are not factual, but linguistic in character—"that is, they do not describe the behavior of physical, or even mental, objects; they express definitions, or the formal consequences of definitions." Philosophy is a department of logic. It is independent of any empirical, not to say metaphysical, assumptions. Often propositions which are really linguistic are so expressed as to appear to be factual. "A material thing cannot be in two places at once" is actually linguistic, recording "the fact that, as the result of certain verbal conventions, the proposition that two sense-contents occur in the same visual or tactual sense-field is incompatible with the proposition that they belong to the same material thing." The question, "What is the nature of x?" asks for a definition, which is always a linguistic statement.

Philosophical analysis essentially provides definitions. But they are not the most frequently occurring kind; that is, *explicit* or synonymous definitions giving an alternate symbol or symbolic expression for the term to be defined. Rather, they are a special sort, *definitions in use*, which are made by showing how a sentence in which the definiendum occurs can be translated into equivalent sentences which do not contain the definiendum or any of its synonyms. An example taken from Bertrand Russell defines "author" in the sentence, "The author of *Waverley* was Scott," by providing the equivalent, "One person, and one person only, wrote *Waverley*, and that person was Scott." Such definitions clarify sentences both where no synonym for the definiendum exists, and also where available synonyms are unclear in the same fashion as the symbol needing clarification. A complete philosophical clarification of a language would first enumerate the types of sentence significant in that language, then display the relations of equivalence that hold between sentences of various types. Such a set of definitions would reveal the structure of the language examined; and any truly philosophical theory would hence apply to a given language.

Some of our symbols denote simple sense-contents, and others logical constructions, the latter enabling us to state complicated propositions about the elements of the logical constructions in a relatively simple form. But logical constructions are not inherently fictions. Rather, material things are among such logical constructions. The definition-in-use will restate the definiendum naming a material thing by translating it into symbols that refer to sense-contents that are elements of the material thing. In other words, roughly, to say something about a table is always to say something about sense-contents. The problem of the "reduction" of material things into sense-contents, long a chief part of the problem of perception, is a linguistic problem readily solved by providing definitions-in-use. To accomplish this reduction, Ayer stipulates that two sense-contents *resemble* each other *directly* when either there is no difference, or only an infinitesimal difference, between them; and *indirectly*, when they are linked by a series of direct resemblances amounting to an appreciable difference. He stipulates further that two sense-contents are *directly continuous* when within successive sense-fields there is no difference, or only an infinitesimal difference, between them, with respect to the position of each in its own sense-field; and *indirectly continuous* when related by an actual, or possible, series of direct continuities. Any two of one's sense-contents, then,

are elements of the same material thing when they are related to each other by direct or indirect resemblance and by direct or indirect continuity.

Ayer assumes that the object of a theory of truth is to show how propositions are validated. Like all questions of similar pattern, the question "What is truth?" calls for a definition. Consequently, no factual theory is needed to answer it. The real question discussed most of the time in "theories of truth" is "What makes a proposition true or false?"

Ayer adopts the distinction between analytic and synthetic propositions. Each has its own validation. "A proposition is analytic when its validity depends solely on the definitions of the symbols it contains, and synthetic when its validity is determined by the facts of experience." While "Either some ants are parasitic or none are," an analytic proposition, is indubitably and necessarily true, it provides no actual information about ants. As a tautology, it has no factual content and serves only to help us understand matters of language. The valid propositions of logic are true by tautology and are useful and surprising in revealing hidden implications in our sentences. They can help us gain empirical knowledge, but it is not the tautologies which render empirical knowledge valid. Whether a geometry actually can be applied to physical space is an empirical question which falls outside the scope of the geometry itself. There is thus no paradox about the applicability of the analytic propositions of logic and mathematics to the world.

Synthetic propositions, Ayer affirms, are validated by experience. Experience is given in the form of sensations. Sensations are neither true nor false; they simply occur. Propositions about them are not logically determined by them in one way or another; hence, while these are perhaps largely dependable, they may be doubted. Similarly, they may be confirmed by additional experience. In other words, "Empirical propositions are one and all hypotheses." And, in fact, whenever a verification is carried out, it is applied to an entire system of hypotheses—a principal one, together with supplementary hypotheses which often are adjusted by the verification rather than by the principal hypothesis. Therefore, the "facts of experience" can never *per se* oblige us to abandon a particular hypothesis, since we may ever continue without contradiction to explain invalidating instances in various ways while retaining the principal hypothesis. We must of course retain a willingness to abandon it under certain circumstances because of experience, or else we make of it not a hypothesis but a definition. It must be granted that we are not always rational in arriving at belief—that is, we do not always employ a self-consistent accredited procedure in the formation of our beliefs. That a hypothesis increases in probability is equivalent to saying that observation increases the degree of confidence with which it is rational to entertain the hypothesis.

The exposition of synthetic propositions, every one of which is a rule for the anticipation of our future experience, constitutes Ayer's validation of the verification principle, for it comes to just what the verification principle states, that the literal significance of an empirical proposition is the anticipated sense-contents entailed in it.

To account consistently for statements of value with empirical principles, Ayer holds that descriptive ethical sentences are empirical statements and that normative ethical sentences are "absolute" or "intrinsic," not empirically calculable, and indefinable in factual terms. The normative symbols in a sentence name no concepts, add nothing to the factual content. Thus, normative sentences are not capable of being true or false. They simply express certain feelings of the speaker. They are not even *assertions* that the speaker has a certain feeling, for such assertions would be empirical and subject to doubt. Thus we remove the question of their having any validity at all.

But how, then, can we dispute about value? Ayer maintains that actually we never dispute about questions of value, but only about questions of fact. The pattern usual in such a dispute is to exhibit to our opponent what we believe to be the facts, assuming a common framework of value statements, and attempt thus to bring him to our way of seeing the facts.

As to religious knowledge, we cannot appeal to tautologies for factual truth about God, for these are mere stipulations of our own. Nor can we have empirical propositions about God, for we can conceive of no experience which would bring us different sense-contents if God exists than if he does not. Hence, the notion is metaphysical and meaningless.

Ayer applies a complete phenomenalism to the traditional problems of the self and knowledge of the world. He denies that the given needs a logical rather than sensory justification. Further, he rejects the pattern of subject-act-object as an account of perception. He defines a sense-content not as the object, but as a part of sense-experience, so that the existence of a sense-content always entails the existence of a sense-experience. Hence, the question of whether sense-contents are mental or physical is inapplicable. Such a distinction can apply only to the logical constructions which are derived from them. The difference between mental and physical objects lies in differences between the sense-contents, or in the different relations of sense-contents that constitute objects.

The self may be explained in similar terms. "It is, in fact, a logical construction out of the sense-experiences which constitute the actual and possible sense-history of a self." To ask its nature is to ask what relationship obtains between sense-experiences for them to belong to the sense-history of the same self. Rather than retain the metaphysical notion of a substantive ego, we can identify personal identity simply in terms of bodily identity, and that in turn is to be defined in terms of the resemblance and continuity of sense-contents. To say anything about the self is always to say something about sense-contents. I know other selves empirically, just as I know physical things and my own self empirically.

Ayer urges the unity of philosophy with the sciences. Rather than actually validating scientific theory, the philosopher's function is to elucidate the symbols occurring in it. It is essential to the task that he should understand science. Philosophy must develop into the logic of science.

As well as providing further exposition, Ayer's introduction to the second edition contains some modifications of doctrine which deserve notice. In the interim between editions, he came to accept a belief of the logical positivists, which he opposed in the first edition, that some empirical statements may be considered conclusively verified. These are "basic statements," referring to the sense-content of a single experience, and their conclusive verification is the immediate occurrence of the experience to which they refer. As long as these merely record what is experienced and say nothing else, they cannot be factually mistaken, for they make no claim that any further fact could confute. But this change makes little difference to the chief doctrine, Ayer maintains, for the vast majority of propositions are not of this sort.

Ayer introduces the term "observation-statement," to designate any statement "which records an actual or possible observation." To remove the objection that, as originally stated, the principle allows any indicative statement whatever to have significance, Ayer amends its expression to say that the principle of verification requires of a literally meaningful, nonanalytic statement that it should be either directly or indirectly verifiable. For it to be directly verifiable it must be an observation-statement or, in conjunction with one or more observation-statements, must entail at least one other observation-statement not entailed by the other observation statements alone. To be indirectly verifiable, first, in conjunction with certain other premises, a statement must entail one or more directly verifiable statements not deducible from the other premises alone and, second, the other premises must include no statement that is not either analytic, or directly verifiable, or indirectly verifiable independently.

Ayer gives up the position that *a priori* propositions are linguistic rules, for they can properly be said to be both true and necessary, while linguistic rules cannot be called true and are arbitrary. Descriptive linguistic statements of contingent empirical fact of language usage are, however, the basis for statements of logical relationships —which are necessary truths. Ayer admits doubts as to whether his account of the experiences of others is correct, yet says, "I am not convinced that it is not." He confesses error in assuming that philosophical analysis consists mainly in providing "definitions in use." Such a result is the exception rather than the rule; and in fact, for statements about material things such definition becomes impossible, since "no finite set of observation-statements is ever equivalent to a statement about a material thing."

Finally, rather than classify philosophical statements alongside scientific statements, Ayer states that "it is incorrect to say that there are no philosophical propositions. For, whether they are true or false, the propositions that are expressed in such a book as this do fall into a special category . . . asserted or denied by philosophers. . . ." The lexicographer is concerned with the use of particular expressions, but the philosopher, with classes of expressions; and his statements, if true, are usually analytic.

PERSONAL REALISM

Author: James Bissett Pratt (1875-1944)
Type of work: Epistemology
First published: 1937

PRINCIPAL IDEAS ADVANCED

Images and symbols are not the objects they refer to; objects exist independently of symbols, and symbols have meanings only because selves endow them with meanings.

In conceiving individual things we may be led, by our knowledge of the respects in which they are similar, to use the same concept for them; Platonism and nominalism are indefensible extreme positions.

Rationalism concerns itself with the characters of things at the expense of the independent existence of things.

A true judgment corresponds to objects in the sense that the objects may be as the judgment describes them as being.

Causation is an objective relation; there are substantial, physical objects which are causal factors in the order of nature.

New realism—realism without dualism—has difficulty accounting for illusions and memory; critical realism, which asserts the independent existence of ontological objects distinct from the epistemological objects by which the former are known, is preferable.

This book is an expression and a defense of Pratt's mature thought on the nature of human knowing and the status of the self in the world. He was

1016

very much concerned with human personality and its moral and religious standing in the nature of things. Pratt was a student of the psychological aspects of religion and well versed in both Eastern and Western religions. Thus, he had a wide perspective and many interests. *Personal Realism* is concerned with the clarification of his ideas on basic themes in contemporary thought. His purpose was to defend critical realism, with emphasis on dualism and transcendence.

Pratt begins by drawing a contrast between rationalism and empiricism, much after the manner of A. K. Rogers. While rationalism stresses the logical coherence of thought and tends to identify thought and existence, empiricism devotes itself to the world of empirical facts, to existence and the various kinds of existent things. Rationalism tends to be abstract and *a priori* in its outlook, while empiricism dwells on concrete experience and beliefs. The influence of his teacher, William James, is shown here in Pratt's thought. He was willing to learn from rationalism all he could but sought empirical probability about basic questions. He argues that philosophy has something to add to the special sciences. It asks unavoidable questions about the general nature of human knowing, about causation, and about the relation of mind to matter, questions which the sciences do not quite broach.

In his discussion of the term "meaning," Pratt refers to the wide extension of the use of the term but chooses two examples apparent in everyday experience as central, namely, pointing, or reference, and the significance of symbols, such as words. The first of these two meanings of "meaning"

comes out in the sentence: "No, I do not mean Rome, N. Y., but Rome, Italy." The proper name denotes, selects, points to an object. The second meaning of "meaning" is apparent when a synonym of a word or phrase is given, as in a definition: " 'Dog' means the animal that barks." While a person can *mean* in the sense of referring to something, a symbol acquires meaning through linkage in experience.

There are, of course, several interesting philosophical points involved. Proper names must be distinguished from general names and both from abstract terms. These items are taken up in logic and are under considerable discussion today. What Professor Pratt chose to stress, as an empiricist, is the point that while symbols have meaning or significance, their objects are only what they are. Objects are independent of symbols; what we seek to do is to characterize objects. This reference to objects and their characterization has been too much neglected by psychologists. It is at this point that Pratt introduces the question of transcendence. The image or symbol used is not the object referred to. It is in terms of this contrast, that Pratt defends critical realism against idealism and various forms of the "new realism." The note of personal realism is struck in the assertion that it is a self which puts meaning into symbols. Pratt argues—against the logical positivism of the time—that statements have meaning apart from their verification. Verification and its methods concern knowledge and truth.

Pratt deals with the perennial topics of terms and relations, universals and existence. He regards relations as internal but not wholly constitutive of

1017

their terms. This is a natural, empirical view. Again, qualitative data are not analyzable into relations. On the other hand, acquired properties do involve relations: a person could hardly be a father apart from paternity. Turning now to universals, Pratt seeks to avoid both Platonism, which tends to reify them, and extreme nominalism, which denies them altogether. We discover character with individuals. In conceiving individuals, we may be led to use the same term for them. Then we have a class and speak of a common connotation. We are also likely to speak of the members of a class as similar, similar with respect to some characteristic. After all, we are thinking about objects, not intuiting them.

This fits in with critical, referential realism. Language and communication support "free ideas" or concepts. We speak both of concepts and of conceiving, just as we speak of percepts and perceiving. We must be careful here and not make unnecessary entities. What do we *grasp* in conceiving? It would seem to be the general properties of things. In grasping these general properties, we have knowledge about the things. But the danger to avoid is that of making entities out of them. To call concepts universals encourages this tendency. Even to speak of *universalia in re* gives them something of this status. Nominalism has wanted to stress individuals and their similarity. Here, it would seem, we have the job of adjusting the mechanism of human knowing with its use of concepts to the ontological situation. So-called psychological nominalism with its stress on sensations and images could not quite do justice to transcendent knowing. We know through and by means of concepts. It might be said that the term universal is tied in with the *function of cognition*. For example, we know that *this* thing is square, and also that *that* thing is square.

Pratt makes much of existence as contrasted with essences or concepts. Here he is arguing against objective rationalism of the Blanshard variety, which is also to be found in Royce and Joachim. He writes that rationalism rules out change, duration, and individuality. He argues that, after all the qualities of things are abstracted, there remains a residue which is not identical with them. Here lies the *that* as distinct from the *what*. As an empiricist, Pratt regarded this distinction as basic.

Inevitably, Pratt was led to defend the correspondence theory of truth, just as the rationalist supports the coherence theory. He argues that since the judgment in an individual mind can refer to objects outside itself, the judgment may correspond to these objects in the sense that as referents they are what the judgment asserts them to be. He claims that the pragmatic theory of truth is not so different from the coherence theory as is usually supposed. He argues that the principles of logic apply to the world, for without them, we could not investigate it.

Professor Pratt uses solipsism as a sort of test. In a way, George Santayana did the same and got animal faith. Pratt, on the other hand, stresses transcendence and communication. Communication, he argues, works through the body and the use of symbols. A letter sent to China is read by the recipient and understood. The panpsychist is a realist of sorts who wants to interpret the material world as ultimately mental in nature. The pragmatist seeks to read everything in terms of an "if-then" relation; observability is substituted for enduring things. Such endurance is considered by the pragmatist as unverified, unnecessary, improbable, and really meaningless. In Pratt's opinion, pragmatism is nearer to solipsism than it admits. We have already noted that Pratt, like A. K. Rogers, found objective idealism or objective rationalism very ambiguous in its claims; such theories confused thought and things.

As one would expect, Pratt takes causation to be an objective relation. It must be distinguished from general causal laws and from mere invariability. Time flow, important for causality, makes it different from logical implication.

In his discussion of the general, realistic hypothesis, Pratt defends the belief in substance and in physical things as factors in the executive order of nature. Later, as we shall see, he supplements it with an appeal to theistic purposiveness. This is prepared for by his dualism and his idea of the self.

Pratt then proceeds to consider the "new realism" or, as he calls it, realism without dualism. He rightly points out that realism had once ruled almost unquestioned but that it was nearly driven from the field by various schools of idealism—Berkeleian, Kantian, neo-Kantian, and positivist. As he remarks, in the last part of the nineteenth century it was about all that a philosopher's reputation was worth to suggest there was anything in realism. In the United States, pragmatism undoubtedly operated as a transition movement. The campaign of logical positivism had much the same context. That is probably why it and pragmatism got along so well together. One

could do without epistemology and ontology if one had colorful slogans praising the unity of science, together with a sufficiency of logical and linguistic puzzles. Often this is the way in which advance is made in philosophy.

Since Pratt lived through this era, it is interesting to note his reactions. The first step was to regard mind as pure activity, a sort of transparent awareness. This gave a form of naïve realism: mind contemplates the nonmental—which may consist of what were called sense-data. British neorealism tended to take this form, while American new realism followed suggestions in William James and ended in a panobjectivism which sought to eliminate "mental awareness" and ally itself with behaviorism. But how deal with illusions and with memory? Pratt expresses the belief that the role of ideas in knowing cannot be avoided and that "ideas" were in some measure invented to supplement naïve realism.

American new realism, or epistemological monism as it was often called, identified thing and idea. The tulip one sees and one's idea of the tulip are identical. But it is hard to carry out this new concept in detail. What was called objective relativism was an attempt to keep presentational, or naïve, realism by introducing relations of percipient organisms as part of the quality of the object. Whitehead explored this scheme. Pratt holds that it simply will not do.

He then gives his version of critical realism, reminiscent of his contribution to Essays in Critical Realism (1920). It is interesting to note that he resorts to Broad's distinction between an epistemological object and an ontological object: the mind does not literally include the objects it knows; and two minds can concern themselves with an identical object. The job, evidently, is to understand what human knowing involves. Pratt's dualism favored his adoption of Broad's terminology, but he had difficulty connecting the epistemological object with the ontological one. Quite rightly, Pratt appeals to psychology against the new realism and quotes Aristotle and C. A. Strong.

The adoption of a mind-body dualism makes *transcendence* something of a mystery. This is the case with Arthur O. Lovejoy as well as with Pratt. But if we can break down transcendence into a reference connected with response and the evidential value of sensory data under the control of external things, transcendence becomes an achievement resting on the "form and to" structure of perceiving. It is the chair, itself, which we are looking at, referring to, and characterizing.

Materialism, parallelism, and interaction remain to be considered. According to Pratt, traditional materialism tended to epiphenomenalism; and it is hard to see how logical implication could be given a base in physical, causal necessity. Pratt agrees with Paulsen that we *mean* different things by the physical and the psychical. But all this may signify that traditional thinking was dominated by wrong assumptions. Pratt is open-minded enough to consider an identity theory along the lines of emergence and double knowledge. His chief objection seems to be that it does not do justice to the self.

Pratt's basic objection to the double-knowledge view would seem to be logical. The "essence," the brain as a structural and moving system, is not identical with the "essence," pain. De

Witt Parker seems to have had much the same logical objection. However, the advocate of the double-knowledge view might well reply that he is not asserting the identity of these two meanings, only that the type of knowledge given in the one, which is knowledge about, does not reach participation in cerebral activity and that, in consciousness, the agent is on the inside of this activity. Pratt recognizes the subtlety of this theory but keeps to his dualism. Certainly, such an enlarged materialism must explore the status and function of awareness and consciousness.

Pratt then proceeds to defend interactionism with dualism of process because of his conviction that complete parallelism would involve an extraordinary series of coincidences.

In introducing the theory of interaction, the author notes that the meaning of mind which identifies it with a stream of consciousness does not do justice to all we actually mean by mind. Consciousness is fragmentary and does not have the substantive unity which reasoning and decision imply. More is needed: there must be agency. The self is such an agent; and it is the self which interacts with the body. Such a self is organic to the body or embodied. The self is the mind as perceiving, conceiving, and willing. Because its unity with the body is so intimate I feel that whoever does things is I. Yet the body is not a part of the self. It is, rather, the self's closest environment or, as W. E. Hocking puts it, a "piece of property," of the self. In perceiving, for instance, the self and the brain act jointly, making up a unitary whole. Pratt is inclined to adopt the theory that the self has the capacity of producing sensations and meanings in response to sensory processes of the brain. This is the logic of animism. Perhaps only an enlarged, evolutionary materialism with a clear epistemology can meet animism.

In the chapter on "Knowledge and the Self," a strong argument is put forward for the purposive and unifying role of the self as a subject. Associationism and even *Gestalt* theories are rejected as not doing justice to activity and organizational power. Thinking, judging, and planning do not terminate in sensations and images. It is the self which refers beyond the given to what is meant. Arguments from Descartes, Kant, Rudolf Lotze, and Franz Brentano are used. There still remains the question of just what the *subject* is. It is not the *I* of self-consciousness with its social overtones, but is presupposed by it. Feelings as subjective point to the self.

The self, then, is a concrete substance exercising capacities. It is an agent and has inherent unity. It maintains itself in and through its experiences. In some sense, it endures through time, but it also changes in it. The question of the nature of self-consciousness has been an important one from the time of the ancient Indian thinkers to Hume. We have knowledge about the self. Do we have also some sort of direct acquaintance with it? Pratt finally takes his stand on a kind of intuition of the self as subject.

In his treatment of the will and its freedom, Pratt rejects indeterminism and supports self-determination. Here, again, the stress is upon activity.

In what sense can there be a science of man? Can psychology formulate laws like those of physics and chemistry? Pratt doubts it. We can have statistical generalizations and types, but it is unlikely that we can make deductive predictions of the sort the inorganic sciences achieve. For Pratt, the nature of the self must be considered. Laws connect events, but selves make decisions.

Pratt's speculations are along teleological and theistic lines. A purpose must be a cause if it is to have an effect. Is there evidence of purpose in nature as a whole? Pratt suggests a kind of immanent teleology in the long development of living things. The analogy between the self and the body is usable for theism. God may act as a musician who improvises on an instrument, but perhaps not all things are under his control. Pratt does not believe in special providences of the popular religious kind; he admits that we are here in the realm of overbeliefs, of speculation.

NATURE AND MIND

Author: Frederick James E. Woodbridge (1867-1940)
Type of work: Metaphysics, epistemology
First published: 1937

Pragmatism is important because of its emphasis on contexts and operations; the pragmatic method is useful for the clarification of ideas.

Despite pragmatism's usefulness as a method of clarification, it errs in rejecting objects antecedent to knowledge to which an idea must conform if it is to be true.

The alternative to a theory of perception which makes ideas the objects of perception is an operational realism, a theory which rejects sensations as myths and which understands perception as a sense operation directed at objects.

A coöperative working of naturalism and humanism, of science and art, is the natural outcome of a theory in which the antithesis between science and metaphysics is regarded as unfortunate.

This collection of essays by Professor Woodbridge was presented to the author on the occasion of his seventieth birthday by Amherst College, The University of Minnesota, and Columbia University, institutions with which he had been associated. He was a graduate of Amherst where his interest in philosophy had been stimulated by a famous teacher of the subject, Professor Garman; and he had taught at both Minnesota and Columbia. The essays were carefully selected to bring out in a unified way Woodbridge's position and its development. Its priority to the work of G. E. Moore and Bertrand Russell is worth noting.

The collection begins with the essay "Confessions," which Woodbridge contributed to the project, *Contemporary American Philosophy*. After this conscientious review of his thought come sections on metaphysics, logic, consciousness, and cognition. The conclusion consists of addresses on various occasions. Taken together, the material gives a clear picture of the man and his work; and anyone who reads these essays carefully is put into touch with philosophy as it was developing in the United States in the first part of the twentieth century.

Woodbridge's reaction to pragmatism is particularly interesting. It was similar to that of the new realists and the critical realists. It is clear that he wanted cognition to be direct, and he was fearful of a subjective consciousness engrossed with "ideas."

Woodbridge had a keen interest in the history of philosophy and a sense for its currents. Of equal importance was his interest in the growth of the positive sciences. In a broad sense he was a realist, as much one of attitude as of specific doctrine. It is said that he was fond of quoting from Matthew Arnold the saying: "Things are what they are and the consequences of them will be what they will be; why then should we wish to be deceived?"

Professor Sterling Lamprecht, one of Woodbridge's students who later taught at Amherst, sums up his teacher's perspective in these words: "This kind of attitude was bound to generate doctrines when it was firmly sustained through a course of philosophic reflections. It was bound to generate metaphysical doctrines." The metaphysical view resulting was analytic in character, and was concerned with nature and man's inclusion in it. There was nothing about this metaphysics of that transcendental import which current positivism has in mind when it rejects metaphysics. Perhaps the term ontology is less misleading. In any case, the Viennese positivists were contending with German idealists and existentialists and had little knowledge of American philosophy.

Both American pragmatism and American realism were, in the main, naturalistic in perspective. While British empiricism tended to link up with Hume, such was not so much the case in American thought. Woodbridge tended to wrestle more with Locke than with Hume. He kept up an interest in Aristotle and sought to revise the ancient categories. It is evident that the parochialism of "Cambridge talking to Oxford" did not dominate his thought. Philosophers who get engrossed in minor technicalities are sometimes led to affirm the incredible, and Woodbridge sensed this danger in connection with traditional idealism. Surely, the world is not mind-dependent. The cure he advocated was ever fresh contact with concrete realities: confront the abstract with the factual, take second thoughts.

In his "Confessions," Woodbridge indicates that Aristotle, Spinoza, and Locke were the philosophers in whom he was most interested. Perhaps Hobbes should be added. When Santayana's *Life of Reason* came out in 1905 Woodbridge reviewed it; it seemed to him a matchless commentary on human thinking, for it exhibited the passage from the natural to the ideal, from common sense to reason. The continued interest in Santayana at Columbia as against his neglect at Harvard perhaps stems from this enthusiasm.

Woodbridge was seeking to revise Aristotle's categories of prime matter and form, in order to substitute structure, behavior, and a natural teleology of sequence. These general characteristics of the world he thought of as metaphysically fundamental. One can note a certain impatience with epistemology, as was the case with Dewey. There was frustration, the feeling that philosophy had become so immersed in the operation of knowing that it had made states of mind their own objects. But was epistemology to blame here? Is not the concentration on states of mind a bad foundation for epistemology? After all, can we have knowledge about our world without cognitive operations? The struggle between pragmatism, new realism, and critical realism in American philosophy was to concern itself with the need for a reorientation in epistemology. Pragmatism, under Dewey, took the path of a logic of inquiry, but Woodbridge wanted to keep ideas and things somehow together. Consciousness, he held, was relational. It seems that he meant by consciousness, cognition or consciousness *of* something. The term is, unfortunately, ambiguous. A stream of consciousness—to use James's expression—is one thing, and an act of cognition, or directed knowledge-claim, is another.

While a little impatient with the *vanities* of epistemology, Woodbridge faced up to unavoidable problems. Somehow, ideas, mind, and the order of things had to be brought together. While Locke stressed ideas, Spinoza emphasized logic and discourse and substance. Here was kinship with Aristotle. In this setting, Woodbridge worked out his analytic metaphysics of structure and behavior and his notion of natural teleology. To Aristotle, he owed his recognition of the importance of language. Truth is not a matter of nature; the *saying* of things is.

Such retrospection enables us to comprehend Woodbridge's intellectual Odyssey. It is clear that he had early rejected subjectivism and idealism because they involved wrong perspectives. But the job was to connect cognition with the natural order of things. What he was after was a *direct realism*. As with the new realists who were becoming vocal at the time, this was taken to involve presentationalism or the givenness of the object. Woodbridge struggled with *sensations* in this connection. Can they be given up and be translated into *sensings*? Dewey faced the same problem in a similar attempt to escape the subjective and the intra-cortical. But cannot we have a direct realism while regarding sensations as guiding perceiving when perceiving is regarded as a referential act concerned with external things? The emphasis, then, is upon cognizing as a mediated achievement.

A good place to begin, if one wants to appreciate Woodbridge's setting in American thought, is with the essays "The Promise of Pragmatism" and "Experience and Dialectic."

Woodbridge believed that the value of pragmatism lay in its stress upon the clarification of meanings, and that the shift to the problem of truth was, in many ways, unfortunate. "When it was claimed that an idea is true because it works, the rejoinder was ready and well-nigh inevitable that an idea works because it is true." As a good Aristotelian, Woodbridge probably took agreement with existence to be the criterion of truth.

The valuable feature of pragmatism was, then, its stress upon context and upon operations. One can understand otherwise cryptic remarks if one focuses on their contexts. Woodbridge's remarks on Whitehead and Sir Arthur Eddington in this connection show robust common sense. What does one mean by society? How could one send out a message tomorrow and receive it today? To answer such questions, any shift in vocabulary should be indicated; what *is* the context of one's remarks? The dogma which denies that ideas could possibly represent, stand for, or duplicate objects might well submit itself to pragmatic analysis.

In the second essay mentioned above, Woodbridge queries Dewey's proneness to dialectical discourse. While granting Dewey's starting point, the need to exercise intelligence in reflective thinking on problems, Woodbridge does not admit that it involves a rejection of objects antecedent to knowledge to which knowledge must conform to be successful. He asks whether Dewey's rejection of antecedent objects follows from his emphasis upon inquiry. He claims that Dewey's statement to the effect that only the *conclusions* of reflective inquiry are *known* begs the question. Really, do what things are and the way they operate depend on the outcome of inquiry? Is there not a touch of anthropomorphism in Dewey's position? Man is a sample of nature but there are many other samples. Dewey seems to argue them into illegitimacy. He expresses a preference for the precarious and incompleted. The outcome is a dialectical playing off of the permanent and the changing in a conceptual way against one another. Dialectic is put in the place of the kind of metaphysics that fits in analytically with investigation. Why did Dewey think in

1024

this fashion? One answer is that he associated permanence with the timeless and eternal of objective idealism. Woodbridge is restrained in his criticisms but they have point. It is unfortunate that so many American philosophers think that they have to choose between Russell's philosophy as inspired by Hume and vitalized by mathematical logic, and Dewey's instrumentalism. Woodbridge was seeking a realistic alternative.

In his criticism of epistemology, Woodbridge had in mind the Lockian interposition of *ideas* as cognitively terminal. He had learned the lesson of Locke's unperceived things and its support for idealism, and thus he thought of epistemology *contextually*.

In his theory of perception, Dewey was motivated, much as Woodbridge was, by the fear of a subjective mind. It would be absurd to end up with cognition terminating on, and concerned only with, mental states *in* the brain. One must firmly reject this cortical and subcutaneous view of the status of mind. What is an alternative? Presentational realism. Things are as they are experienced. It is an affair of behavioral transactions. In many ways, Woodbridge's answer is similar to Dewey's. Eyes and ears are for *sensing* what is out there to be sensed. Sensing is a form of cognition and does not require those peculiar entities which psychologists call sensations.

The interesting fact is that Woodbridge returned to this question again and again. He had a marked feeling for the realities of the situation. Nothing G. E. Moore wrote is superior to Woodbridge's little essay in this book entitled "The Deception of the Senses." As he puts it, our proper question is not "What is the thing?" but "Why does it appear different?" Why does the straight stick in water appear bent? His answer is that the stick must appear bent under these conditions. Science has its explanation in terms of optics. Railroad tracks should look *as though* they converged.

In *Nature and Mind*, Woodbridge does not once refer to Moore. There were at this time two centers of thought in the English-speaking world. The British group gradually edged away from the Americans; and the era of Moore, Russell, and Wittgenstein began. Oxford talked with Cambridge and Americans began to listen in. The whole development is complex, and it must not be oversimplified.

Is there not another alternative to subjectivism? The whole question of the mechanism of perceiving comes up for consideration. May not sensations guide response and be information-carrying? What we really do in perceiving is to refer selectively to the things around us and to characterize them. We develop concepts in touch with the information- carrying sensations, but the import of the concepts is objective and concerns what we are referring to. The unit on which all this is founded is sensori-motor. The brain is not primarily concerned with itself; it is an organ of adjustment.

Having taken the alternative of sensing things and not having sensations and appearances to be used in cognition of a referential sort, Woodbridge argued that consciousness must be relational. Consciousness *of* something is cognitional and makes no difference to things.

Woodbridge argues that sensations, as traditionally conceived, are myths. Gilbert Ryle, in *The Concept of Mind* (1949), has sought to do the same in terms of linguistic behaviorism. What Woodbridge puts in the place of sensations are sensings, operations directed at objects. The operations are the same; it is the objects that differ.

Thus, both Dewey and Woodbridge returned to naïve, or presentational, realism in order to escape subjectivism. Things are as they are sensed, though sensing has its complex, external conditions, as in the case of the stick that looks bent in the water or the case of converging railroad tracks. But could we not equally say that we perceive *through* our sensations, thus conditioned, the things we are looking at? We use the evidence of our senses, a locution which is well founded. In this manner, also, we can escape the influence of the introspective tradition combined, as this was, with the limited, causal approach which neglected response. Sensations are not cognitively terminal, but they are aids in perceiving. It was this line that the critical realists began to explore. So far as cognition is concerned, it is also a form of objective realism; that is, it is the external thing to which we are responding and to which we are referring.

Curiously enough, while the United States has been conventionally a religious area, its social science and philosophy have been dominantly naturalistic, as is recognized abroad. None of the four existentialist theologians, Maritain, Berdyaev, Buber, and Tillich, of whom we hear so much these days, is an American thinker.

Woodbridge, of course, antedated existentialism. He was concerned to qualify traditional naturalism by including man in nature and spelling out a natural teleology. In his view, everything is somehow real and must be taken account of. Perhaps the positive sciences have been too much under the spell of the mechanical, and literary humanism has tended to look backward and exalt the past. But the present alone is actual and creative. It is well to have a long vista, but it should lead up to the situation of the time. Thus the coöperative working of naturalism and humanism, of science and art, is the thing to be desired.

The antithesis between science and metaphysics is unfortunate, Woodbridge believed. While Aristotle had a cosmology which has been outgrown, his metaphysics is concerned with first principles: it emphasizes categories or the general features of being, and it is quite prepared to apply these in the special sciences. In his reformulation of Aristotelianism, Woodbridge wanted to avoid *materia prima* and form and put, in their place, structure and behavior. Nature *is* structure. As a believer in substance, Woodbridge was opposed to an analysis in terms of events alone.

Woodbridge's addresses reveal the man and his outlook. They are sane and robust. In the "Enterprise of Learning" the emphasis is upon knowledge and the "inquisition of truth"—Bacon's phrase. Let us keep the imagination awake and creative, Woodbridge urged; the life of reason is unquestionably the best life for man. Santayana is here allied with Aristotle against any popular form of pragmatism.

In "The Discovery of the Mind" Woodbridge deliberately propounds the belief that the university is the most important of human institutions. It is well to have such a thing said in these days of giant corporations and organizational men. It marks the distinction between pure and applied science. How are these to be ordered? The lecture on "The Practice of Philosophy" has an amusing remark on confessing to other people that one's profession is that of being a philoso-

pher. There is, Woodbridge notes, always surprise. But one is left wondering whether there are not, in addition, disbelief, amusement, and a sense of deep waters.

THE KNOWLEDGE OF GOD AND
THE SERVICE OF GOD

Author: Karl Barth (1886-   )
Type of work: Theology
First published: 1938

PRINCIPAL IDEAS ADVANCED

Christian theology must be Church theology, and it must be centered in Christ; natural theology rests on an error.

The paradox of revelation is that although God reveals himself, he is forever the Hidden God.

History has had two significant phases: the history of Israel, of God's faithfulness despite man's unfaithfulness, and the history of the promise fulfilled, of God's becoming one with man.

Christian truth rests entirely on the fact of the resurrection of Christ.

In the service of God man is saved by Christ from having to justfy himself before the law; but he is therefore bound by gratitude and love.

The current renaissance of Protestant theology, after nearly a century of theological de-emphasis and cultural accommodation, has as its founder Karl Barth and as its date of birth 1918. After Immanuel Kant's destructive interpretation of the Theistic proofs, Protestant theologians concerned with a defense of Christianity against its "cultured despisers" followed the lead of Friedrich Schleiermacher (1768-1834), understanding revelation in terms of a unique, universal experience called "God-consciousness" or "absolute dependence." This "liberal" tradition, continuing

through a diverse line from Adolph Harnack to Paul Tillich, led in its extreme "modernist" forms to teaching, as H. Richard Niebuhr says, that "a God without wrath brought men without sin into a kingdom without judgment through the ministrations of a Christ without a cross." Above all, the unique centrality of Jesus Christ as the incarnate God-man, the impotence of the human will, the centrality of both Cross and Resurrection, tended to give way to a highly optimistic doctrine of man, revelation as universal religious experience, a religion of morality, and Jesus as perfect man. Differences between religions were understood primarily in terms of degree, Christianity being the most morally pure. Increasingly, Christianity was becoming a cultural phenomenon of Western culture.

Into this liberal milieu came Barth, pastor of a small Swiss church and theological advocate of Schleiermacher. As he tells it, with the German guns of the approaching war as threatening background, the weekly ritual of sharing religious experiences became manifestly meaningless. Unless the Divine God of Creation stands in damning judgment over the follies of prideful men, Christianity is simply irrelevant; but if man's rebellion and God's judgment establish as fact Kierkegaard's unheeded "qualitative distinction between time and eternity," God and man, then the message of Christ as Incarnate Mediator becomes the one relevant proclamation.

In exploring the theological profundities of orthodox Christianity from this now existential human predicament, Barth not only began the theological revival termed "neo-orthodox" or "neo-Reformation," but effected a fresh reëxamination of Pauline theology and the thought of Søren Kierkegaard (1813-1855). These three elements converged in 1918 in Barth's theological bombshell entitled *The Epistle to the Romans.* Although the various editions of that volume show increasing movement away from "liberal" tenets, this work from the first was a fresh consideration of St. Paul's doctrine of man from the perspective of Kierkegaard's understanding of despair, original sin, and the absolute centrality of God's unique act in Christ. The theological world was ripe for such a pronouncement of judg-

ment, not only on mankind but also on the Protestant capitulation to culture. Barth likens his effort to that of climbing a belfry at night and, while grasping for support, finding that he has pulled the bellrope and awakened a sleeping city. Barth's "fame" was almost immediate; overnight he found himself in the midst of a wide and vigorous theological debate extending undiminished into the present.

This first major work by Barth was not so much an exegesis of St. Paul as it was a violent challenge to the fundamental tenets of liberal theology, especially those concerning revelation and man's finite condition. Barth's statements were extreme and his judgments uncompromising. The most famous debate to result was that with his early sympathizer, Emil Brunner. In the volume *Natural Theology,* Brunner tried to remain loyal to Barth's basic position while still making contact with the dictates of reason; only by establishing a natural human point of contact upon which Divine Grace may act, Brunner insisted, can there be any truly human response, any answer to revelation which is not simply God's self-answer. Barth's reply was emphatic: "Nein!" God is Subject, never Object; if he is to be known, it can be only when the Divine Subject reveals himself and wills a human response.

From this point the theological vocation of Barth emerged. At first he had understood this central Christian revelation in largely negative terms. He likened revelation to a crater left by a meteor—not the object itself but only the result of the impact was visible. The impact of divine judgment on history was indelible, but God himself remained forever hidden. Gradually Barth's understanding of revelation changed. He remained consistent in his total rejection of the *analogia entis* maintained by Roman Catholics and liberals, for there is no visible analogy between the natural and the supernatural realms. God is "totally other." But Barth came to see an *analogia fidei* (analogy of faith) which gives valid content to revelation, for in Christ the Divine Subject has become Object. For men of faith, operating in the Community of the Holy Spirit, valid communication concerning the divine is possible.

Consequently, Christian theology must have two basic features. It must be *Church* theology—the internal dialogue of the fellowship of believers— and it must be completely Christocentric; every Christian affirmation must have the God-man as both content and norm. The result has been Barth's monumental *Church Dogmatics* (*Kirchle Dogmatik*), still being written. Those volumes of that work which have been finished have already placed Barth in the company of Luther and Calvin as the great theologians of Protestantism.

The best single volume for understanding Barth's position, especially in regard to philosophical inquiry, is his Gifford Lectures of 1937 and 1938, entitled *The Knowledge of God and the Service of God According to the Teaching of the Reformation*. Barth's appearance as a Gifford Lecturer was an oddity requiring justification. The will of Lord Gifford declared that the subject must be "natural theology," that science of God, his relation to the world, and human morality resulting from such knowledge, which is constructed by human reason in independence of special, supernatural revelation. Barth's answer to this stipulation is one of the most uncompromising in the history of Christianity —"I certainly see—with astonishment —that such a science as Lord Gifford had in mind does exist. . . . I am convinced that so far as it has existed and still exists, it owes its existence to a radical error." It is Barth's central insistence that any theologian of the Reformation, basing his faith, as he must, wholly upon God's revelation in Jesus Christ, is implicitly and explicitly opposed to all forms of natural theology. His Gifford Lectures are the attempt to clarify natural theology by exhibiting what he regards as its strongest and most vehement opponent —the theology of the Reformation. For this purpose Barth uses John Knox's Scottish Confession of 1560 as a systematic summary of Reformed theology.

But Barth's lectures have a second intent as well; not only is natural theology opposed, but the Church's compromising betrayal of its own foundations must be challenged. Judged by its ancient creeds, Protestantism must be driven back to Scripture as its sole authority.

For Barth, God can be known only when the distinction between Creator and creature is drawn. But since man in his self-righteousness universally makes himself or his works "god," such a distinction is acknowledged only when God *makes himself visible*, thereby drawing the bounds of creatureliness and smashing man's petty absolutes into the realm of the relative. Thus the *only* knowledge of God is faith, but it is unique knowledge, for it binds and commits one totally. Its objectivity comes not from human vindication, but only from its own universal validity in the life of the believer. Yet *the* revelation is not the elimination of mystery, for the one revealed is the Hidden God—God remains always above man's concepts and potentialities. In fact, for Barth, this is the paradox of revelation—the Hidden God of Majesty *is with us*—this is to call him "Father." Such a thing simply cannot be known by reason, for it is so only if one is personally addressed as "son." This relation rests not in necessity, but in divine decision; he who decides can be the only revealer of the decision.

The God-man revelation which is Jesus Christ reveals that God takes man seriously; although God does not need his creation, he wills it to be a reflection of his glory. All creation is indebted to God, for all exists by him (as Creator), through him (as Sustainer), and for him (as Redeemer). But Christ separates man from the rest of creation, for He reveals that *man has been called to present to the Creator the gratitude of the creation.* This is the meaning of man as the "image of God"—not that man possesses something, but that his destiny is to image God's glory through gratitude. It is on the basis of this broad cosmic context that Barth's position is so uncompromising. We know absolutely nothing about God, the world, or man outside of Jesus Christ; without His revelation of the creating, sustaining, and governing of the world, of God's glory and man's, everything is "confused myth and wild metaphysic."

There is likewise no anthropology except from the perspective of Christ; therein the validity of "original sin" is seen. In the light of man's intended vocation, man's existence in ingratitude and self-centeredness is seen as a "defacement of God's image in man." Because this is a matter not simply of acting against God but also of *being* against him, it can be undone by God alone. Here is where Barth takes fundamental exception to existentialist Christians such as Tillich. For Tillich, man's awareness of the human dilemma drives one *to* revelation. Barth's Christo-centricity operates even here: since man's dilemma is known only through Christ, "if we know that we cannot save ourselves, we know already that we are *saved* by God." This is the tension which is redemption—humiliation for the sake of exaltation.

Since history is the plane of relation between God and man, its meaning comes from Christ as its center. Through Him history assumes two parts. The first is the history of Israel—the history of God's faithfulness despite man's unfaithfulness. Israelites are chosen people, sought, judged, sustained by faith in God's promise of a deliverer. The second history is that of the promise fulfilled—the Church as the history of "God's becoming one with man." These histories repeat themselves in the sense that Adam's act is repeated throughout history, and the Church is sustained by the One who has come and will come again. The continuity of history is that of those who emerge while man again and again is unfaithful and is judged. Since the emerging ones are as guilty as all others, continuity is a miracle which rests in the fact that these saving few admit their guilt. The true Church through history is the few who live in the promise of God while knowing themselves unworthy. Although Christ appeared at one point in history, He is the savior of all believers in all times for they are saved through their faith in the promise of which He is the fulfillment.

In all this Barth is attempting to restore the orthodox belief of early and Reformation Christianity. But there is one important difference which distinguishes him from both "fundamentalists" and "liberals." Against the former he insists that the Bible is a *human* document requiring critical analysis for its proper understanding. Against the liberals, Barth insists that such Biblical criticism cannot prove or disprove the revelation itself. The revelation is not the Scripture but God's act in Christ. The former is simply the human account of the latter. The Holy Spirit witnesses to the revelation *through* the Scripture, and without such a witness revelation can never be known.

One of the most intriguing aspects of Barth's work is his attempt to untangle perennial theological knots by understanding them from his consistent Christo-centric perspective. Central is the problem of predestination. For Barth, Calvin's doctrine is totally unacceptable, for he distinguished between God's eternal decree and the existence of Christ, understanding the former in terms of an alien philosophical system. But when Christ alone is taken as presupposition, the problem is answered by seeing that God's eternal decree *is* Jesus Christ. It is Christ who is the only cursed man and the only elected man. In electing Christ, God takes all the incapacities of man upon himself; he who judges endures the judgment. Since it is through

Christ that God regards man, it is only in Christ that man can understand himself—so to understand is to be as Christ.

In consistency, this means for Barth that in Christ man is not simply restored; instead, he is made a new creature, higher than at Creation. This elevation comes from man's absolution in the Crucifixion and his affirmation as righteous in the Resurrection. In the face of man's rebellion, God in justice must be against man; yet in Christ he has decided for fellowship. The problem is that God alone can forgive, for Sin is against him; man alone can seek atonement, for he is responsible. It is in Christ that justice and mercy are brought together—in Christ, man is what he ought to be and is not; in Christ, God is what he is from eternity. In regarding man through Christ's perfect humanity, God's fellowship with man is proper; from the side of man, this "yea" spoken to sinful men appears as free mercy. Above all, Christ alone endured God's punishment, the realization of sin and death. This completeness of humiliation and self-sacrifice occurred not only in time; as God's very act it occurred also in eternity. Only because he is God can his infinite sacrifice and humiliation have infinite significance.

But this forgiveness can be consummated only in the Resurrection, the guarantee, as Barth says, that the Author of life is victorious over the Author of death. Since man's acquittal brings everlasting life, the fact that Christ has the power to forgive sin needs as thoroughgoing proof as the fact of His death. It is here that Barth's severance with liberalism is complete: "For if Jesus Christ has not risen . . . as man, and therefore visibly and corporally risen from the dead, then He has not revealed Himself as the Son of God, then we know nothing about His having been so, nor do we know anything of the infinite value of His sacrifice. In that case we would have no knowledge of the forgiveness of our sin or of our election or of God's gracious decision in our favour. In that case the whole Christian church is based on an illusion and the whole of what is called Christianity is one huge piece of moral sentimentalism. . . ." This is the core of Barth's wholesale rejection of natural theology in all forms—"our knowledge that this is no dream but the truth, and the fact that we have received that knowledge, rest entirely on the Easter message literally understood."

Redemption does not mean that the believer is visibly changed; the change is in Christ, and thus only by faith is it in man. The change is that all things, man's hopes, direction, future, are made to rest upon Christ. These are unknown, yet fully known, for they rest in the hands of One who cannot fail. This, for Barth, is faith, this is trust, this is perfect assurance, this is salvation. It is in this sense that the future is founded upon the past, and the future transforms the present.

What looms large in Barth's theology is the question of man's freedom, for "man's salvation is the work of God exclusively." This problem has to be balanced with Barth's view of salvation, which comes close to universalism—God is the one "who wills that all men be succoured and who acknowledges our sin only as forgiven sin. . . ." Now, faith can proceed only from the inspiration of the Holy Spirit. But, Barth affirms, it is only the man of faith who knows his incapacity to prepare for, persevere in, or perfect faith; only he can view the unfaith of the unbeliever as inevitable.

Yet, Barth affirms, everyone comes to faith who in his freedom does not evade the action of God in Jesus Christ appointed for him. To the unbeliever this freedom comes as a challenge to decide; from the perspective of the decision made, one can only confess that the decision itself was a Divine gift. This does not mean that man is passive or that reason has been sacrificed. For Barth, the Holy Spirit operates through the human spirit; faith occurs in "a perfectly human way." Thus the decision for faith is made in the same way as all other decisions, yet the fact that one does decide is the doing of the Holy Spirit.

In effect, what Barth is doing is insisting that such problems as predestination and freedom are made insoluble when systematized by logic; rather, they must be seen as soteriological inferences, as confessions of faith, not philosophical statements. Faith confesses election as a personal fact; reason insists on freedom as a universal fact. The believer can hold these in tension, for he has experienced as fact both responsibility for sin and Christ as the source of salvation. Barth's insights here have brought together aspects of liberalism and orthodoxy in such a way that St. Paul's theology and theological method have been reopened for fresh consideration.

Barth's understanding of man's proper service to God follows quite consistently. Once again, his understanding is in radical opposition to natural theology and to the Roman Catholic position. Although there are natural laws, there can be no distinction between the natural and divine ends of man. God's law demands unconditional obedience; no distinction of degree is possible. But in Christ we know that the one man who stands before the law is Christ; thus no man need justify himself before the law. Jesus Christ is both the law and its fulfillment. Salvation means simply this— that Christ's obedience, thankfulness, love, and service are imputed to man. As a result the believer is freed from what he cannot do, but yet made totally subject to a new law, the law of gratitude, and thus penitence and love to God and neighbor. Obedience now rests alone in holding to the fact of salvation in Christ; all things else, if not a reflection of this fact, are not righteousness but self-righteousness.

Evaluating Barth's position is as much an either/or as the theology he espouses. He does not address the philosopher and does not expect to be heeded by him. He is a Church theologian who claims nothing more. Yet the philosopher cannot escape him, for, as these Gifford Lectures indicate, part of his witness is to oppose philosophical theology unceasingly. This is done not by criticizing, arguing, or employing dialogue, but by proclaiming the teachings of the Reformation as the "exact opposite" of natural theology. Perhaps no other man has so exhibited to the philosophers the fundamental difference of kind between "rational knowledge of God" and the "religious life of faith." Perhaps, too—as many Protestant theologians firmly believe—it has been Barth more than any other man who has saved Protestant Christianity from slow death by innocuousness, extinction by amalgamation. Right or wrong, in stimulating in Protestants a passionate search for their fundamental *raison d'etre*, Barth is contributing significantly to the great theological renaissance of modern times.

LOGIC, THE THEORY OF INQUIRY

Author: John Dewey (1859-1952)
Type of work: Logic, epistemology
First published: 1938

PRINCIPAL IDEAS ADVANCED

Logic is inquiry given a theoretical formulation; logical theory is the comprehensive theory of how people solve problems through conducting inquiries.

The process of inquiry involves the following stages: (1) the indeterminate situation, a case of disturbed equilibrium between an organism and its environment; (2) the institution of a problem, the change of a situation from indeterminate to problematic as a result of the active interest of an inquirer; (3) the setting up of a hypothesis, an anticipation of the consequences of certain operations; (4) the deductive elaboration of the hypothesis, together with experimental test-

1033

ing; and (5) the termination of inquiry, the establishment of a settled outcome; the situation has become determinate.

Universal propositions which have existential import (which are about existing things) differ from those which do not have such import, but the difference is factual, not formal.

Since propositions are instruments used in the process of inquiry, it is proper to characterize them as effective or ineffective, rather than as true or false.

Logic, the Theory of Inquiry is John Dewey's third extensive statement of his views on logic. In 1903 he contributed five articles to the volume, *Studies in Logical Theory*. Thirteen years later, in 1916, he expanded these views in his book, *Essays in Experimental Logic*. *Logic, the Theory of Inquiry*, published in 1938, is the fullest and most recent statement of his position. (He wrote one other book on logic, *How We Think*, which appeared in 1910—a popular account rather than a technical, philosophical discussion.) These books, published over a period of thirty-five years, indicate that Dewey was concerned throughout his life with logical theory. He adopted a position quite early in his career, and retained it and elaborated on it as his own philosophical thinking developed and matured. The books also indicate the great importance Dewey attached to logical theory. It is no exaggeration to say that he regarded it as near the very center of his philosophical position. Inasmuch as Dewey is perhaps the most widely known and most influential philosopher America has produced, and since he regarded his logic as fundamental to his general philosophical orientation, it is clear that *Logic, the Theory of Inquiry*, his final word on the subject, is well worth study by anyone who wishes to understand the role Dewey has played in recent American philosophy.

Although the book is important, it is also forbidding. It is long, and it suffers from the defects found in almost all of Dewey's technical writing, namely, an odd technical vocabulary and a writing style that is tiring and hard to follow. The key points are not highlighted, but are almost buried in a text that is monotonously heavy. In spite of the many examples and illustrations Dewey gives, his writing remains abstract and colorless.

A great many questions are discussed in the book—too many, in fact, to be covered in a short review. But it is possible to give a brief résumé of the process of inquiry, as Dewey sees it, and to discuss a few of the more controversial elements in Dewey's theory.

The title of the book, *Logic, the Theory of Inquiry*, indicates the problem Dewey regarded as the chief one for logic. Logic is inquiry given a theoretical formulation; logical theory is the comprehensive theory of how people solve problems through conducting inquiries. Inquiry is *the* topic throughout the book, and it is Dewey's description of this process that gives the book its unique character as a study of logic.

Dewey, departing from the usual accounts of syllogism, immediate inference, and so on, discusses the role he feels they play in inquiry instead of treating them as kinds of formal patterns of deduction. It is appropriate, therefore, to begin by noting what

Dewey means by "inquiry." He defines it as the "controlled or directed transformation of an indeterminate situation into one that is . . . determinate." The original "indeterminate" situation is replaced, through inquiry, by one that is "determinate" or "unified."

Part of what Dewey meant by speaking of an "indeterminate situation" as becoming "unified" emerges out of the discussion which begins the book and precedes the account of inquiry proper. The first hundred pages of the book are devoted to an account of the emergence of inquiry out of a matrix of antecedent biological and cultural conditions. Dewey apparently believed that his naturalism required of him that he show a continuity between the prior biological and cultural activities which do not illustrate the peculiar characteristics of inquiry and the more specific activities which do. His point is that inquiry develops naturally out of behavior which is not inquiry. According to Dewey, the general pattern of life behavior out of which inquiry emerges is, of course, the pattern of adjustment between living organisms and their environment. Generally, organisms find themselves at times out of adjustment with the environment, and this forces them to take steps to restore the balance or harmony of a satisfactory adjustment. Inquiry is one specific technique—a most important technique—by means of which certain organisms (human beings) can sometimes restore a satisfactory adjustment between themselves and the environment. There is nothing mysterious about logical behavior to Dewey, then. It is a specific kind of human behavior that is properly subsumed under the general behavior of organisms as they seek to restore proper adjustment between themselves and the environment. An "indeterminate situation" is one in which the human organism is out of adjustment with the environment; when proper adjustment is restored, the situation is "unified" again.

There is another sense in which inquiry (logic) is not mysterious to Dewey. He spends a considerable amount of time arguing that the problem-solving in which all of us engage on the level of common sense and the problem-solving in which the technical expert engages are in their essentials identical. He proposes his theory of inquiry as an empirically derived and validated account of how people do, in fact, think. It is an attempt to explain how scientists, philosophers, machinists, housewives, and others proceed in trying to solve the problems they face in their lives. In all these cases, Dewey feels, people find themselves in indeterminate situations, and adopt as the intended outcome or consequence of action the desired resolution of these situations. Inquiry is thus a process of instituting means to reach desired ends, and logic is the general empirical theory of this process. The fundamental character of this means-consequence relation which logic seeks to describe and explain is qualitatively the same for common sense as it is for the most sophisticated scientific investigation.

The denial that there is any significant difference between common sense inquiry and the inquiries of the technical experts is related to Dewey's rejection of the position that logic is a formal science. He rejects the view that logic is the study of the formal conditions which justify valid inference. He believes that such formalistic logical theories are really derived from metaphysical and epistemological theories that are either out of date or mistaken. He calls such theories "spectator" theories which declare that the logician should spend his time investigating "the eternal nature of thought and its eternal validity in relation to an eternal reality." Dewey wanted nothing to do with "the eternal." In opposition to such views, Dewey thought that the emphasis should be on what he calls the "evolutionary method" of the "natural history of thought," and this, in turn, requires that common sense problem-solving be taken into account just as fully as scientific reasoning.

Dewey divides the process of inquiry proper into a series of steps or stages. These stages are (1) the indeterminate situation, (2) institution of a problem, (3) determination of a problem-solution: hypotheses, (4) reasoning, and (5) the construction of judgment. Each of these steps will now be described.

(1) *The Indeterminate Situation.* The process of inquiry is initiated in what Dewey calls the "indeterminate situation." He states that the indeterminate situation is "by its very nature" questionable, uncertain, unsettled, disturbed, troubled, confused, full of conflicting tendencies. These conditions, it should be noted, pervade the given materials of the particular situation which initiates inquiry. It is the situation itself which is marked by these characteristics; not merely the inquirer. The situation itself is a specific case of disturbed equilibrium between an organism and the environment; and this disturbed, indeterminate situation produces a need to restore equilibrium.

It is out of this situation that inquiry grows.

(2) *Institution of a Problem.* The second stage of inquiry is reached when the inquirer becomes aware of the indeterminateness of the situation in which he finds himself. He then begins to look for a way out of this uncomfortable situation, and when this happens the situation changes from an "indeterminate" to a "problematic" one. If Dewey is emphatic in saying that the indeterminateness of the initial situation is not merely in the mind of the inquirer, we may be just as emphatic in saying that a situation cannot become problematic unless the inquirer is himself mentally involved. When the doubt, confusion, and the rest do come to the attention of the inquirer— in a sense, when they are located in the mind of the inquirer—then the situation as a whole becomes problematic rather than indeterminate.

This movement from the indeterminate to the problematic involves two activities which really advance the inquiry. It involves both (a) seeing certain facts—the elements of the total situation which are or are not out of adjustment—and also (b) seeing just what the problem is. Problems always grow out of actual situations. Furthermore, to mistake the problem involved is to embark on a wrong-headed effort to resolve the disequilibrium. Thus the situation becomes problematic when the inquirer notes the facts and identifies the problem which he must solve to restore adjustment.

(3) *Determination of a Problem-Solution: Hypotheses.* In the third stage of inquiry the person involved must again take account of the facts of the situation and the problem with which he is faced, but now he must

1036

add to these a suggestion about how the problem can be solved. This fact indicates that, in contrast to the preceding steps, the third step is not a mere reading off of something concrete and actual; instead, it is an anticipation of future consequences—a possibility—which Dewey calls an "idea." The terms of the problem, the facts, are obtained by observation; the hypothesis or idea is an anticipation of what will happen when certain operations are performed on the materials of the problem. And this fact, that the hypothesis has future reference, that it is an anticipation, means that the hypothesis must be expressed in symbols. It is this that introduces the conceptual element into the procedure of inquiry.

(4) *Reasoning.* There are two related kinds of activity that are involved in the fourth step in the process of inquiry. The complex act of reasoning includes as one aspect what usually comes to mind when a logician mentions "reasoning"; namely, the deductive elaboration of the hypothesis. But it also includes the experimental testing of the deductive consequences of the hypothesis. Dewey's "reasoning," then, includes both the deductive elaboration of the hypothesis and its experimental testing. The two activities are said, by Dewey, to be "conjugate." That is to say, in inquiry the two go hand in hand; both are essential to the successful prosecution of an inquiry, and the one illuminates and sustains the other. This is characteristic of Dewey's position as a whole; he consistently relates conceptual elaboration to existential development, and he insists that failure to realize that these two activities go hand in hand is responsible for many of the inadequacies of other logical theories. (We

shall return again to this aspect of Dewey's view.)

(5) *The Construction of Judgment.* The outcome of inquiry is the resolution of the problem which initiated the inquiry. The indeterminate situation is transformed into a determinate one, the discordant elements are unified. Judgment, according to Dewey, is "the settled outcome of inquiry." It should be stressed here that Dewey is using the word "judgment" in a sense that differs from the usual one. Ordinarily, logicians mean by "judgment" the assertion of a proposition, but Dewey uses the word to refer to the settled outcome, the state of affairs that is established when an inquiry is successfully terminated. At the termination of the successful prosecution of the first four steps in inquiry a person is in a position to affirm a proposition which states the conclusion of the inquiry. Logicians often call this concluding proposition "final judgment," but Dewey prefers to call it a "warranted assertion" and reserve the word "judgment" for the settled situation which a warranted assertion describes.

Here again we see a correspondence between the conceptual elaboration and the existential development in inquiry. This is a persistent theme in Dewey's logical position, and it therefore merits a somewhat longer discussion.

A good way to begin the discussion of the parallelism between the conceptual and the existential is to restate Dewey's account of inquiry in other terms. Inquiry starts with discordance or lack of adjustment between the inquirer and his environment. It ends with the establishment of a settled relationship between the inquirer and the environment. Dewey's analysis

1037

consists of showing what takes place in the movement from the one situation to the other. The indeterminate situation is subjected to analysis and this gives rise to two parallel processes, one dealing with existential, material means (concrete, physical reality—"the facts"), which Dewey designates as "inference," and another dealing with conceptual, procedural means (possible future operations—conceptual meanings), which he calls "discourse" or "implication." The first products of analysis of the indeterminate situation are *data* (facts), on the one hand, and *meanings* (concepts), on the other. Data are material means which are used in inference and meanings are procedural means which are used in discourse or implication. These two initial products of analysis, data and meanings, are then elaborated by the parallel processes of experimental testing and deductive reasoning.

The relations between meanings or concepts permit the inquirer to formulate possible operations for settling the disturbed indeterminate situation. The relation of implication which joins meanings permits formulation in propositions, and these in turn can be elaborated and developed in conjunction with other propositions to reveal further implications of meanings. Such determination of implications between propositions discloses the possible future operations which may be engaged in to resolve the indeterminate situation.

Data, the existential or factual correlatives of meanings, are connected to one another by a relation called by Dewey "involvement." When data and their involvements are formulated in propositions they can be elaborated and developed in inference, a process

which parallels discourse but which holds between propositions about (factual) data, while discourse applies to propositions about (conceptual) meanings. In both cases, inference and discourse (implication), the fact that the inquirer is working with propositions and verbal symbols enables him to relate involvements and implications to one another without performing concrete physical operations. This is the factor which makes it possible for the inquirer to anticipate and control the course of inquiry. The use of verbal symbols in propositions enables the inquirer, as Dewey puts it, to behave toward the absent as though it were present. Finally, propositions which formulate possible operations are brought together with propositions about data and the result is experimentally tested. Some of the possibilities become actualities, thus providing a concrete resolution of the problem; that is to say, these actualities give rise to judgment.

Consistent with this doctrine that inquiry involves the parallel processes of inference and discourse is Dewey's theory of propositions, one of the debated elements of his theory. The usual doctrine concerning propositions begins with the traditional Aristotelian schedule of propositions, the "A," "E," "I," and "O" propositions that are the units of the standard discussion of immediate inference and the syllogism in introductory logic texts. The usual treatment of these four forms includes the point held by the older logicians, that universal propositions, the "A" and "E" forms (All S is P, and No S is P), had existential import; that is, the subject terms of universal propositions ("All" or "No" statements) were held to denote classes which did have members. The usual account then goes on to point out that, in the modern interpretation of propositions, universal propositions lack existential import while particular propositions have existential import. The universal affirmative proposition "All men are mortal" is interpreted, from the modern point of view, as saying, "If anything is a man, then it is mortal," but this does not necessarily imply that there are any men. The particular affirmative proposition ("Some men are mortal"), in contrast, is interpreted as, "There is at least one thing which both is a man and is mortal," and here the "there is . . ." does imply that there are men. In the case of a universal proposition which does have existential import an additional assertion to the effect that there are men is conjoined to it to yield, "If anything is a man, then it is mortal, and there are men." The point which is pertinent here is that a universal proposition which lacks existential import can be distinguished from one which has existential import by noting the *forms* of the two propositions. If a universal proposition has existential import, it is conjoined with another proposition which asserts this existential import.

Dewey does not accept this analysis. He distinguishes universal propositions which have existential import from those which do not, but the difference is not for him one of form. He makes the distinction by reference to the role played in inquiry. Those universal propositions which play a role in discourse or implication (the realm of conceptual meanings) he calls "universal" propositions, while those universal propositions which play a role in inference (the realm of existential data or facts) he calls "generic" proposi-

tions. Here, then, is another instance of how Dewey rejects the formal logicians' positions on behalf of his own nonformalist, instrumentalist position. He regarded the difference between the two kinds of propositions as not a formal difference; but in this case he was mistaken. Formal logicians can distinguish those universal propositions which lack existential import from those which have it, and they can do so on formal grounds.

It has been mentioned that Dewey distinguishes universal and generic propositions on instrumental grounds; that is, by noting what kind of means they are in the means-consequence relationship which governs inquiry. This concern with the means-consequence character of inquiry led Dewey to diverge in another way from usual logical doctrine. The usual doctrine is that propositions are either true or false. Dewey rejected this view. For Dewey, "truth-falsity is not a property of propositions." Instead of taking truth value as the fundamental property of propositions, Dewey takes their function as *means* in the process of inquiry to be their distinctive feature; propositions are *means* promoting the passage from a problematic situation to a determinate one. Furthermore, Dewey states that if they are fundamentally means, then they are to be characterized as *effective* or *ineffective* rather than as true or false.

This, of course, is a radical departure from the usual account of propositions, and the question naturally arises as to why Dewey made this departure. His case rests on his definition of propositions as means for conducting an inquiry. Many things function as means to ends; hammers, for example, function as means in the building of a house. Yet hammers are not said to be true or false, nor are other means of the same sort (tools). Not all means, then, are either true or false. From this Dewey moves to the conclusion that propositions, since they, too, are means, are also neither true nor false.

Surely Dewey reasoned incorrectly in this case. What his argument amounts to is a generalization from "Some means are not true or false" to "No means are true or false." This is an illegitimate inference. It may be that propositions are neither true nor false, but Dewey's argument has not shown this to be the case.

There are many other topics included in *Logic, the Theory of Inquiry*; Dewey's range of learning was enormous. However, the points mentioned above indicate the underlying thesis of the book together with the implications, as Dewey sees them, of this thesis for some of the questions that make up the substance of logical theory. Dewey was concerned to write out a logical theory which was oriented toward problem-solving, toward what is often called the logic of discovery. He kept his attention focused on this purpose, and his book is

very illuminating on a number of aspects of this problem. He tended to slight formal logic, and he failed to appreciate the contributions made by formal logic to the logic of exposition or justification. Nevertheless, Dewey's case is stated carefully and at length, and its implications are traced for many sub-areas within the larger domain of logic.

Dewey stands in the tradition of Bacon and Mill in logic, but surely he was more rigorous and relevant than either of them. His care and caution have made his book a notable advance over those of his predecessors in the tradition of empirical logic. He has avoided most of Bacon's and Mill's mistakes. Finally, Dewey's account has the merit of providing a bridge for better understanding between logicians and some of the other workers in the general province of knowledge. If logic is concerned with knowing, Dewey's account may help psychologists, biologists, and logicians to find some common ground for understanding their respective roles in determining the processes and conditions of knowing. This is a most valuable contribution for any scholar to make.

THE NATURE OF THOUGHT

Author: Brand Blanshard (1892-   )
Type of work: Philosophy of mind
First published: 1939

PRINCIPAL IDEAS ADVANCED

Thought aims at truth.

The activity of thinking and the object of thinking cannot be considered separately.

The test of truth, the nature of truth, and reality itself can all be understood by reference to coherence.

Reality is the coherent perfection of partially realized thoughts in finite minds.

Blanshard is a happy example of a philosopher who, early in his career, staked out a position sufficiently promising for him to devote his academic lifetime to its exploration and defense. The view that mind is an autonomous realm and that thought has no other goal than truth impressed itself on him before he knew that this lay in the great tradition of Plato and Hegel, and that it had been fully worked out by Bradley, Bosanquet, and Royce. *The Nature of Thought* is a protracted exposition of this thesis, composed over a period of fifteen years. Blanshard took time to study carefully all serious alternatives to his position, and the bulk of the work is the result of the painstaking care with which he has restated and assessed these alternatives.

In Hegelian fashion, Blanshard has tried to find some truth in every point of view. Making no great claims to originality, he has developed his thesis largely in terms of other men's statements. But he is no mere eclectic. From the opening sentence his thesis is clear and emphatic: "Thought is that activity of the mind which aims directly at truth." And the exposition, while ample and gracious, is straightforward and direct, reflecting the author's resolution to bring down to earth and make practical a mode of thinking which renowned philosophers have often been content to leave at Olympian heights.

There is a deliberate ambiguity in the book's title. Does the author mean to discuss the activity of thinking, or that which thinking has for its object? Both are called "thought." Blanshard deals with both, alternating between one and the other. In fact, his main contention is that they cannot be taken separately.

This brings him into sharp opposition to many contemporary philosophers. Students of logic, epistemology, ethics, and religion have in recent years declared that no light is shed on the objects of thought by considering its subjective conditions. They have seen a danger to free inquiry, and indeed to all meaningful human activity, in philosophical systems, whether idealistic or naturalistic, and have declared their independence not only of metaphysics, but also of historicism, which professes to explain everything in terms of historical development, and of psychologism, which makes a corresponding claim for the study of the human mind. Blanshard was certainly aware of these dangers. But he maintained that there is even greater danger in the fragmentization that characterizes the modern approach. In his view, to study logic or ethics apart from their grounds in thought and in reality can lead only to skepticism or irrationalism.

Blanshard states the problem by outlining the views of psychologist E. B. Titchener, who, in the interests of delimiting his science to include only intelligible matter, had insisted that it must exclude mind from its purview. Titchener had taught that it is possible to draw a line between man's sensitive life and the realm of meaning which attaches to it, and he had held that if psychology is to remain a distinct field of inquiry, it must not be drawn into discussions about ethics and logic. With this recommendation, however, Blanshard disagrees. Long connected with the University of Michigan, both as a student and as a professor, he echoes an idealist tradition which goes back to the days when John Dewey, then a disciple of Hegel, taught there. In a book called *Psychology* (1886), Dewey argued that psychology is a central science which, because it includes knowledge, includes every other science. Blanshard agrees with the early Dewey that knowledge implies a reference to mind and cannot be understood apart from psychological processes, and that as a result anyone who wants to know the nature of the world must study the nature of thought. In other words, a philosopher must not neglect psychology.

A difficulty is that, in recent times, psychology has sought to get free from philosophy and establish itself as an empirical science. Sometimes, as in the case of American behaviorism, it has only brought back a discredited philosophy—mechanistic materialism—in a new form; and Blanshard turns aside to devote a chapter to exposing this movement, which he regards as impossibly naïve. But other psychologists, by restricting themselves to description and analysis, have, in his opinion, let the fetish of method stand between them and an adequate account of our mental activities. Dewey's functionalism, according to Blanshard, was nearer the truth because it let no presuppositions obscure the teleological character of thinking. Blanshard was not attracted to Dewey's pragmatism, which, with its strong biological bias, makes thought subservient to organic impulses; but very often his own psychology echoes the language of the pragmatists (both William James and Dewey). The explanation is found in

his sympathy with their contention that the mind never works except when motivated by some purpose.

For pragmatism, an idea is an incipient act; but for Blanshard it is an incipient object. According to his view, the intellect does not merely serve the needs of the body: it has its own goal which it seeks to realize; namely, perfect union between mind and being. Common sense has grasped this fact and tried to express it by saying that the idea resembles its object. But the dualism which such an explanation creates between the two orders of being, mental and physical, is philosophically unsound—there being no intelligible way of explaining the sense in which the idea and its object are the same. Blanshard believes that the truth of common sense is preserved and the philosophical difficulty overcome by his theory. It agrees with common sense that ideas are not in fact identical with their objects; but it overcomes the qualitative dualism between them by maintaining that ideas are potentially what they represent. Their stand in relation to things is much like that in which acorns stand to oak trees: ideas are the same, and not the same, as things. They are halfway houses on the road to reality, to use an expression of Blanshard.

For Blanshard, as for the pragmatists, thinking is problem-solving. He speaks of the activity as analogous to building a bridge from the mainland to an island. The mainland is the body of understanding which a person already possesses, and the island is some factual knowledge that is as yet unassimilated by the mind. The aim of thought is to bring the new into intelligible relations with the old. We may want to know the cause of a thing, or the end which it serves, or its definition in terms of a familiar scheme of classification. Blanshard does not shirk the psychological questions here involved; for example, whether thoughts leave traces or dispositions which enable us to bring the past to bear upon the future; or, again, whether there is a subconscious activity of the mind involved in all creation and invention. But these questions are incidental to his main inquiry, which has to do with the mind's goal and fulfillment in truth.

Blanshard tries always to keep in view the two ways of viewing the movement of thought. When engaged in thinking, a person seems, on the one hand, to be seeking his own fulfillment as a rational being, exorcising the ignorance and doubt which limit his freedom. On the other hand, he seems to be trying to reach beyond himself and embrace something entirely transcendent to thought; namely, the nature of things as they are. In modern philosophy, according to Blanshard, critical realism and neo-realism have divided these two aspects between them. The former emphasizes the role played in knowledge by ideas, or contents of the mind, and sees thought mainly as an effort to bring these into consistent and orderly relations; but it loses sight of the transcendent end of knowledge. The latter emphasizes the direct acquaintance which thought has with objects, but it denies that specifically mental contents even exist. The one loses the world; the other loses its own soul. But Blanshard thinks that such half-views are unnecessary. The merit of his theory is that it saves both thought and its object, without permitting one to encroach on the other. The two are never in fact

identical, for reality is the perfection and fullness of being which is but imperfectly and partially realized in the finite mind. But the transcendence of the end over its immanent realization in thought is merely one of degree.

Blanshard's view leans hard on the coherence theory of truth. On the one hand, thought strives for coherence; on the other, reality possesses coherence: all that distinguishes them from each other is the difference in degree. Common sense, which thinks of truth as an agreement between the mind and the world it seeks to know, falls short of comprehending what knowledge actually involves. Suppose someone says, "That is a cardinal singing in the bush." It is naïve to think, with the man on the street, that the way to confirm the judgment is to inquire whether the fact agrees with our thoughts; for any new observation which we make will necessarily have the same problematic character as the one we are seeking to verify. What we finally affirm to be the truth is the state of affairs which renders the several aspects of experience coherent with each other and with our previous knowledge. Blanshard gives separate consideration to three related questions: What is the test of truth? What is the nature of truth? What is reality? But his answer in each case is the same, namely, "coherence." "Coherence is a pertinacious concept and, like the well-known camel, if one lets it get its nose under the edge of the tent, it will shortly walk off with the whole."

Blanshard admits that there is no proof that reality is coherent, much less that coherence exhausts the nature of being. His contention, however, is that only such a view of the world accounts for the accuracy, dependability, improvability, and scope which our thought possesses. Thought seeks understanding, and in the measure that we understand anything we see the necessity for it. Blanshard, therefore, devotes a major portion of his book to exploring the kinds of necessity in order to see which is adequate to account for knowledge.

Empirical philosophy has, in his opinion, totally failed to account for necessity. Mistakenly supposing that the contents of the mind are atomic sense impressions, each inherently independent of every other, it has tried to explain the order and connection that come to govern a man's thinking as having no other basis than habit, whether that of the individual (John Stuart Mill) or of the race (Herbert Spencer). Blanshard believes that this contention can be disproved at the psychological level because the laws of association by which the connections are allegedly explained do not describe the way learning actually takes place. But his chief line of argument is that the theory leads to skepticism and, if consistently applied, precludes our ever understanding anything, even how the mind works. Mill's account of syllogistic reasoning, for example, makes inference impossible to confide in because each step in the proof is held to be determined entirely by psychological laws.

Logical positivists have sought to save empiricism by locating intelligibility in language and in the conventions of formal logic. Thus, pushing empiricism to the limit, they deny that there is any necessary connection between being a man and being mortal; but they allow that there is a kind of necessity governing the use of the terms "man"

and "mortal," once we have agreed to relate them in a certain way. In their view, all inference is but an expanded tautology: it tells us nothing at all about matters of fact. Blanshard's criticism of formalism goes deep. Like the Hegelians, he objects to the principles of abstraction which underlie even traditional logic. There is a radical difference, according to Blanshard, between the concrete universal with which the mind actually advances toward knowledge of the world and the empty counters of the formal logician. "Man" is an example of the former: it is general but not abstract, a richly intensional term which the mind forms by moving from particular ideas to a more general one that embraces them. Contrast it with the abstract, purely extensional notion employed by the formal logician; for example, "the class of rational bipeds past, present, and future." Actual thought operates with terms like "man" and is concerned with following out relations which are actually given in experience. Thus, says Blanshard, when we affirm that being human implies being mortal, "we mean, foggily without doubt, and if you will, unjustifiably, but still beyond all question, that the *character* of being human has some special and intimate connection with liability to die." And he denies that the formal logician has shed any light on the necessity here uncovered when he points out that, by the rules of the syllogism or by the truth tables, the conjunction of the propositions "All men are mortal" and "Socrates is a man" implies the proposition "Socrates is mortal." On the contrary, we are plunged into deeper darkness. In their efforts to escape from the imperialism of metaphysics and psychologism and historicism, logicians have set up a dictatorship. In the language of A. J. Ayer, "Philosophy is a department of logic."

The scientific account of the world leads, in Blanshard's opinion, to a sounder view of things. In the first place, it takes for granted a course of nature in which every event is causally related, either directly or indirectly, to every other event; in the second place, it is committed to the belief that man's mind is capable of understanding these relations. If we hold fast to both of those principles, Blanshard says, we must come in the end to the view that events are constituted by their relations to all other aspects of reality. This is the theory of "internal relations" for which modern idealism has contended. A rival view, which has found favor with empirical philosophers, including such men as Ernst Mach and Bertrand Russell, is that no event really influences any other and that our knowledge of nature is limited to observing regular sequences between events. But Blanshard argues that when we state that water extinguishes fire, we affirm something more than the mere regularity with which the phenomenon occurs; namely, some connection between the natures of water and of fire. In his view, the meaning of water includes its relations to fire, as well as to other things such as soap and dirt. To understand anything, according to idealism, is to grasp the system of relations in which it is found. If the system is incomplete, we try to piece it out or if necessary modify it until the missing connections are found. Thus, we explain why water extinguishes fire by making use of hypotheses about temperature and oxidation. Scientific the-

ories such as these provide a larger area of coherence and present a higher level of truth than is available to our native experience; and, even though we do not claim, as common sense is prone to do, that our theories reproduce the actual structure of the world of things, still, the confidence which we repose in them would be without foundation if reality were itself without coherence.

Blanshard writes with a marked sense of mission. Like the common-sense philosophers of an earlier day, who battled skepticism and agnosticism, he is vexed that in an age of unprecedented intellectual achievement philosophers can find nothing better to do than to raise doubts as to whether knowledge is possible. He is sure that their misgivings are the result of mistaken theories and that a sound analysis not only permits but demands that we take a thoroughly rationalistic view of the world. At this point, his inquiry opens out onto the problems of metaphysics, which he does not venture to discuss. But he does admit his allegiance to that *perennial philosophy* which through the centuries has maintained "the doctrine that through different minds one intelligible world is in the course of construction or reconstruction . . . [and] that the secret of sound thinking is the surrender of individual will to an immanent and common reason." Concluding his work on the eve of World War II, he lamented the passing of a time when educated men recognized a common standard of judgment and obligation; but he refused to believe that the defeat of reason and truth was more than temporary, and ventured to think that his own "insistent and reiterated emphasis . . . on the membership of minds in one intelligible order [might] serve, however minutely, to confirm the belief in a common reason and the

hope and faith that in the end it will prevail."

AN ESSAY ON METAPHYSICS

Author: Robin George Collingwood (1889-1943)
Type of work: Philosophy of metaphysics
First published: 1940

PRINCIPAL IDEAS ADVANCED

Any intelligible statement finally rests upon certain absolute presuppositions. Ordinary presuppositions are either true or false; but absolute presuppositions are neither true nor false, for they are not factual.

Although it is a mistake to treat absolute presuppositions (such as the belief in the uniformity of nature) as if they were factual propositions to be confirmed by sense experience, it is also a mistake to suppose metaphysics impossible and to narrow rational investigation to empirical inquiry.

The metaphysician is a kind of historian whose task it is to discover absolute presuppositions in the thought of others.

In designating his philosophical books "essays," Collingwood, who preserved a keen sense for etymologies, meant to imply that they were not general "treatises," and he made no claim either to comprehensiveness or system. On the contrary, they were written, each one, to make a special point.

These remarks apply to the work in hand, both to its outline and to its texture. It is far from being a "metaphysical" book, in the usual sense of that word. Instead of propounding the author's metaphysics, it is a lively statement of the importance of metaphysics, sharpened by a polemic against certain anti-metaphysical tendencies, and it is enforced by three extended illustrations (which make up half of the volume).

Collingwood argued that any intelligible statement, if fully fathomed,

rests upon a series of presuppositions which terminate in one or more absolute presuppositions. And this is not a mere matter of fact that happens to be the case but a consequence of the nature of the understanding itself. Not merely philosophy, but everything that is included under science (taken in the sense of systematic thought about a determinate subject matter) involves logical or *a priori* elements.

Writing on board a freighter, Collingwood took as an example a cord which the crew had stretched above the deck. He recognized it as being a clothesline. But this supposition presupposes another thought; namely, that the line was put there on purpose. Had this assumption not been made, the thought which identified it as a clothesline would never have occurred. In other words, every thought which we can put into words is the answer to some question and can be understood only if the question is sensible. But a sensible question rests upon other thoughts which, if put into words, are likewise answers to questions—and so on, until we finally come to a thought which is not the answer to any question. It is an absolute presupposition.

R. G. Collingwood is almost as well known as a historian (Roman Britain) as he is as a philosopher. And the circumstance is relevant to understanding his views on metaphysics. (See *An Autobiography,* 1939.) As an excavator he formulated and was instrumental in giving currency to the methodological principle: never dig except to find the answer to a question. As a historian, he brought to new clarity the concept that the only subject matter of history is the thoughts of men who lived in the past. "Why did Caesar invade Britain? Did he achieve his purpose? If not, what determined him to conclude the campaign?" Armed with questions of this sort, the archaeologist becomes something more than an antiquarian and the historian something more than an editor of texts: they become scientists. They increase our store of relevant knowledge. And they do this by following Bacon's advice about interrogating nature.

Collingwood relates that it was this kind of intellectual discipline which overthrew in his mind the claims of the Oxford realists under whom he had studied philosophy. He abandoned their claim that knowledge is made up of simple truths which are independent of each other and immediately knowable; he maintained, to the contrary, that a fact is meaningful only as it fits into an inquiry. Moreover, he argued,

a particular inquiry is always part of a more comprehensive undertaking—civilization itself—which gives it backing and direction, for at any given moment, men of a living culture are engaged in solving the problems of human existence, starting from certain beliefs and commitments. But these are the considerations that are commonly called metaphysics, after the treatise by Aristotle in which they were first systematically dealt with.

In Aristotle, according to Collingwood, two quite different inquiries are confused. Aristotle perfected the logic of classification by genus and species. He saw that at the bottom of the table there must be *infimae species* which are fully differentiated and that, by the same logic, there must be at the top a *summum genus,* which because completely undifferentiated may be designated by the term Pure Being. In a different context, Aristotle dealt with the structure of the sciences. Much better than Plato, he understood the necessity of delimiting a particular subject matter and defining the presuppositions which it involved; and he saw that this task was a distinct one which required a new science to deal with it, which he called first philosophy, wisdom, or theology. So far, so good. But Aristotle made a mistake. Influenced too much by the ontological tradition from Parmenides to Plato, he allowed himself to suppose that the first principles of the sciences could be identified with the Pure Being of his logic of classification. And metaphysics, in the history of Western philosophy, has ever since had great difficulty in extricating itself from this confusion. In Collingwood's view, Kant's *Critique of Pure Reason* is a notable attempt to set it free. The Transcendental Aesthetic and the Analytic pursue the proper task of metaphysics —seeking for absolute presuppositions; and the Transcendental Dialectic exposes the fallacies of pseudo-metaphysics, which seeks to fit these absolute matters into a conditional scheme of things.

There is a significant agreement, at this point, between Collingwood and various anti-metaphysical groups in our own time. He insists that much of what is traditionally called metaphysics is bad science because it seeks to treat transcendental issues as matters of fact. Ordinary presuppositions are factual: they can be stated as propositions, and are either true or false. But absolute presuppositions are not factual: they do not answer any question and are neither true nor false. Properly speaking, they are not propositions at all.

But if Collingwood agrees with the realists and positivists in assailing the claims of ordinary metaphysics, his emphasis on the importance of absolute presuppositions represents a significant protest against this group. In his opinion, their radical empiricism is a species of anti-intellectualism. Such empiricism accounts for truths such as: "This is the back of my hand"; but it breaks down when called upon to account for complex truths which make up natural science, not to speak of ethics and politics. He sees it as part of a dangerous tendency in the contemporary world which he broadly designates as irrationalism and, in its philosophical expression, as anti-metaphysics.

The second part of *An Essay on Metaphysics* is given over to the discussion of two characteristic expressions of this anti-metaphysical tendency. The first is pseudo-psychology. Collingwood has no quarrel with psy-

chology so long as it sticks to its subject. It began as a distinct science when modern (sixteenth century) thought began to insist on a sharp distinction between mental (logical) and physiological (mechanical) explanations of human conduct. Emotion or feeling did not seem to fit in either of these realms; therefore, psychology arose to take account of this third realm. Properly it deals with problems of motivation which cannot be accounted for either by mechanical or by rational means. And there are such problems. But the problems of ethics, aesthetics, and religion are not among them. These are rational pursuits, each with its own logic and presuppositions. They are mental sciences which fall outside the province of psychology. But it is part of the irrational tendency of the past century (Collingwood can only reckon it as analogous to a disease, "a kind of epidemic withering of belief in the importance of truth") that we have suffered psychology to extend its principles of explanation to include these rational pursuits. Freud's *Totem and Taboo* (1913) is cited as an example of the errors and confusions which come when a great psychologist tries to apply to significant activity categories which are legitimately used to understand aberrant behavior. If the presumptions of psychology are not turned back, science itself is doomed. Citing at length three instances of careless thinking to be found in standard psychology books, Collingwood affects to think that psychology is a deliberate conspiracy to undermine our scientific habits.

The other characteristic expression of anti-metaphysics is positivism. Collingwood admits that it has greater respect than does psychology for the autonomy of man's rational activity; but in maintaining that science is made up entirely of empirical truths, it is a victim of the same irrationalist infection. John Stuart Mill set the pattern when he maintained that the principle of uniformity in nature is an inductive inference, whereas it is the absolute presupposition on which induction depends. Bradley, according to Collingwood, disclosed his own positivist affinities when he defined metaphysics as "the finding of bad reasons for what we believe on instinct." Mill saw rightly enough that the science of his day presupposed belief in the uniformity of nature: but he introduced radical incoherence when he treated it as a proposition which must be verified by experience.

The irrationalist propensities of positivism become most clear, however, in the dictum of the logical positivists that any proposition which cannot be verified by appeal to observed facts is nonsensical. That is to say, because they cannot be treated as factual statements, the absolute presuppositions of science, ethics, and politics, are subrational. Collingwood agrees with Ayer's strictures on pseudo-metaphysics; that is, a science which would treat absolute presuppositions as if they were facts; but he blames Ayer for what seems to him to be merely a petulant attack arising from the lunatic fear that in some way metaphysics is a threat to science. The threat which Collingwood sees is the habit of mind which narrows rational investigation to the limits of sense verification.

The remainder of the book is given to three examples which illustrate the thesis that metaphysics is the science of absolute presuppositions. The first is an illuminating account of the role

theology has played in Western intellectual history. One of the names which Aristotle gave to the science of first principles was "theology." And, according to Collingwood, the classic concern of Greek philosophy was to formulate the new convictions which had replaced the older Homeric beliefs. Thales is important because he gave expression to the new belief that the multiform spheres of nature are at bottom one; Heraclitus, because he saw that all change is according to law. These, according to Aristotle, are *divine* matters. And far from being hostile to art, ethics, and knowledge, they were the foundations upon which Greek achievement rested. They were also the measure of its limitations. The failure of the Greek polis and the later collapse of the Roman empire are traced by Collingwood to metaphysical causes; that is, to inadequacies in the fundamental axioms of the Hellenic mind. Men could not overcome the impression that the world falls into irreconcilable parts: necessity and contingency, or eternity and time, or virtue and fortune. And it was the sense of the contradictions in human existence which this world-view entailed that left them unnerved in the face of the progressively greater challenges to which their own achievements gave rise.

Then came Christianity. Of the host of religions that crowded the shores of the Mediterranean Sea during imperial times, it alone offered an improved metaphysics. Athanasius and Augustine are only the best known of a number of first-rank intellects who would have been drowned in a sea of trivialities if they had not been able to extract from the Gospel the basis for a new science. The trinitarian statements are properly understood as a highly fruitful solution to the metaphysical problem which had defeated the Greeks. In this connection, Collingwood chides Gibbon for obscuring an important truth in order to be clever. Gibbon said that the doctrine of the Logos was taught in the school of Alexandria in 300 B.C. and revealed to the Apostle John in A.D. 97. As Collingwood points out, Gibbon took this fact from Augustine, but he omitted the point which Augustine went on to make and which proved the key to Christianity's success; namely, that the Christians for the first time bridged the chasm between time and eternity, inasmuch as the Logos was made flesh. One must, Collingwood says, "regret the slipshod way in which Gibbon speaks of Plato as having 'marvelously anticipated one of the most surprising discoveries of the Christian revelation.'"

Collingwood maintains that Christian theology provided not merely a rallying point for good minds during the decline and fall of Rome, but that it also furnished the fundamental assumptions which enabled European science to make such advance over that of the Greeks. In part, Aristotle's presuppositions agree with those of modern man—that there is one God, and that there are many modes of God's activities—but in part they disagree, notably on the question as to the origin of motion, which Aristotle tried to explain but which modern science takes as a presupposition. In this connection, Collingwood analyzes the trinitarian confession. The "I believe" indicates from the very first that we are dealing not with propositions but with presuppositions. The doctrine of One God, in whom, however, are contained not merely the principle of Being but also those of Order and of Motion, places all these severally and together on the plane of absolute presuppositions. This doctrine, and not the metaphysics of Pythagoras, Plato, Aristotle, or Plotinus, provided the indispensable foundation upon which Galileo and Newton founded modern science.

We cannot deal at any length with Collingwood's further examples. They are "The Metaphysics of Kant," to which we have briefly alluded, and "Causation," a suggestive account of the perplexities involved in that essentially anthropomorphic concept. Collingwood reports that Western science has made varying assumptions about causation: Newton held that some events have causes and others not; Kant, that all events have causes; and modern physics, that no events have causes. And here we observe an important feature of the subject that has not hitherto been mentioned. Collingwood talks about absolute presuppositions; but he means no more than that they are taken as absolute by the person (or society) which makes use of them. They change unaccountably, as in the instance of causation. And they may change for the better or for the worse. But their change can never be a matter of indifference; rather, the whole well-being of a civilization is dependent upon them. For a civilization, Collingwood insists, is at bottom a way people live; and if the way turns out to be impracticable, the problem is not to save the old civilization, but to save the people by inducing them to live in a different way. The new way will be based upon different absolute presuppositions, and in time it will produce a new science and a new culture.

Now it is no task of the metaphysician to say what absolute presuppositions one should or should not hold. His business is merely to discover them. And he is most likely to find them, not in the writings of philosophers, but in those of constructive workers in the various fields of human interest; that is, in physics or law. Essentially, he is a historian. For it makes no difference whether he investigates the "so-called past" or the "so-called present." In either case, he has to do first-hand historical work, and the things he studies—namely, absolute presuppositions—are historical facts. It is thus that metaphysics takes its place among the sciences. For, as Collingwood has insisted, an absolute presupposition, taken in relation to the truths that are based upon it, is not a truth. But, viewed historically, it is. In order to preserve the distinction, Collingwood provides us with a special rubric to be applied to every metaphysical proposition: "In such and such a phase of scientific thought it is (or was) absolutely presupposed that. . . ." The statement as a whole is a proposition which may be true or false.

Taken in this way, metaphysics has the same importance as any other kind of history; namely, helping us understand the human enterprise. When it studies the so-called present, it has the special utility of disarming reactionary thinkers who, because of inattention to historical tensions, remain wedded to the errors of the past. We expect to find such reactionaries among pseudo-metaphysicians, with their commitment to eternal truths and deductive proofs. But there are just as many among anti-metaphysicians who, in their ignorance of the role played by absolute presuppositions, perpetuate outmoded assumptions under the guise of intuitions or inferences. Collingwood cites examples of new realists and analysts who continue to affirm the "law of causation." For instance, John Wisdom: "I do not know *how* we know that things are as they are because they were as they were. But *we* do know it." The "we," says Collingwood, can only be a group or society of persons whose reverence for the past has blinded them to the developments of twentieth century science. The group does not include contemporary natural scientists or those philosophers who understand what the natural scientists are doing. He quotes Russell: "The law of causality, I believe, like much that passes muster among philosophers, is a relic of a bygone age, surviving, like the monarchy, only because it is erroneously supposed to do no harm."

In Collingwood's opinion, the sciences (both natural and historical) are in flourishing condition, and prospects for their growth were never more promising—if the anti-intellectual threat does not overpower them. He sees two great danger spots: a political order in which reason is replaced by emotion and an academic atmosphere in which pseudo-sciences are nurtured alongside the true. Like the geese that saved the Capitol, Collingwood must warn men of the peril. "I am only a professorial goose, consecrated with a cap and gown and fed at a college table; but cackling is my job, and cackle I will."

1051

AN INQUIRY INTO MEANING AND TRUTH

Author: Bertrand Russell (1872-   )
Type of work: Epistemology
First published: 1940

PRINCIPAL IDEAS ADVANCED

Empirical knowledge has its basis in percepts (sense experiences); from basic propositions about percepts empirical knowledge is constructed.

Although basic propositions are not indubitably true, as propositions of the utmost particularity, referring to percepts, they are the most dependable propositions of empirical inquiry.

Empirical knowledge requires provision for general statements, for stating logical relationships, and for modes of inference.

Propositions are both objective and subjective; they are objective in that they indicate factually, and they are subjective in that they express the state of mind of the speaker (belief, denial, or doubt).

Sentences are true if what they indicate is the case; to know a sentence to be true one must perceive its verifier (the event the sentence indicates).

The phrase "theory of knowledge," Russell says, has two meanings. One kind of theory, the lesser, accepts whatever knowledge science presents, and seeks to account for it. Russell's concern is with the wider kind, which embraces all problems of establishing the nature and validity of all knowledge. Confining his attention in this work to empirical knowledge, he undertakes to discover two things, principally: (1) What is meant by "empirical evidence for the truth of a proposition"? (2) What can be inferred from the fact that there sometimes is such evidence?

Russell brings to the problem of a theory of empirical knowledge the full force of its counterpart, logical knowledge, to whose modern development he is a foremost contributor. He attacks the problems of his general task by translating their elements into formal logical symbols, so as to achieve a precision lacking in the language in which the problems are usually couched. Yet

the book does not consider problems of logic as such, except when they are relevant to epistemology.

To talk about epistemological matters, Russell sets up a modern linguistic apparatus. He conceives a hierarchy of languages, at whose base is the object-language or primary language. Terms in the object-language include subjects and predicates. While ordinary language may provide a beginning, we should transform every subject of the object-language into a unique proper *name,* making use of coördinates in the visual field and of measures of time for discriminating the object named. The name will apply to a complex; and sometimes we must give names to complex wholes without knowing what their constituents are. We learn the names of things ostensively, and only of those things we actually perceive while hearing or coining their names. The names are employed as subjects in propositions of the simplest sort, called *atomic* propositions. We may designate their predicates *relations*. Letting R stand for the relation "above," the proposition "A R B" consists of the relation R and the names A and B, and asserts that A is above B. This is a dyadic relation. Predicates may take any number of terms. The predicate of a single name is a monadic relation: "$f(A)$" states that a characteristic f is an attribute of A.

The secondary language consists of statements about the primary language (thus it must include the primary language within it). Therefore all words for logical conceptions, such as "is true," "is false," "or," "if," belong to the secondary language. All logical truths, since they depend for their truth on rules of syntax, are at least on this level, if not higher. An important group of propositions of the secondary language are those stating *propositional attitudes*, such as "A believes proposition *p*."

The distinctive feature of empirical rather than logical truth is, of course, its basis in percepts, the sense images by which perception is possible. Russell adapts A. J. Ayer's phrase "basic propositions" to designate those propositions arising as immediately as possible from percepts. A basic proposition "is a proposition which arises on occasion of a perception, which is the evidence for its truth, and it has a form such that no two propositions having this form can be mutually inconsistent if derived from different percepts." Examples in ordinary language are "I am hot," "That is red." Many basic propositions may arise describing a single percept, for we perceive a sensory whole combining the entire fields of vision, touch, and so on; and within this field we identify smaller wholes of sensory complexes—the individual objects of the world. Basic propositions need not be atomic propositions. An important group includes some propositions stating propositional attitudes— "I believe proposition *p*"—and thus basic propositions may occur in the secondary language as well as in the primary.

Unlike most prior writers, Russell does not affirm that basic propositions are indubitably true. He is quite willing to doubt them, particularly those involving the memory of percepts. But what distinguishes basic propositions from others is their immediacy, whereas other propositions rest to some degree on inference. The evidence for a basic proposition is the momentary percept which causes it, and nothing can ever make a percept more or less certain than it is at the moment of its occurrence. It is from basic propositions that Russell proceeds to erect the structure of empirical knowledge. Since basic propositions are based on the least questionable objects of experience, they are the most dependable propositions in empirical inquiry. Thus, empirical knowledge is founded on propositions of the utmost particularity. Russell criticizes other writers for failing to screen out all traces of inference in the propositions they have regarded as basic.

A pure empiricism, depending only upon percepts for validation, would be self-refuting. It must contain some general proposition, which cannot be a basic proposition, about the dependence of knowledge upon experience; and the consequence is that such a proposition could not itself be known. Empirical knowledge requires certain additional elements besides basic propositions. These include provisions for making general statements and for stating logical relationships. Empirical knowledge, in other words, needs some epistemological premises as well as factual premises. Modes of inference are also required. These modes include the usual logical operations of deduction. More important in empirical knowledge, however, are nonlogical patterns of inference; namely, reasoning by analogy and by induction. As an example: Russell throughout assumes that things perceived *cause* perceptions, and that perceptions *cause* propositions. His notion of cause is that it is a convenient device for collecting together propositions of certain percepts; it is something that we can arrive at inductively from appropriate combinations of percepts. Without some such organizing scheme for relating percepts, we would have nothing resembling empirical science. Yet neither causality nor induction is perceived, nor are they validated by logical syntax.

An innovation, no doubt startling to logicians, which Russell finds necessary to epistemology is to supply substantial meaning rather than merely formal meaning to logical terms. He finds these in psychological fact. "Or" rises from a hesitation, a conflict between two motor impulses when the organism is suspended between two courses of action. "Not" expresses a state of mind in which an impulse to action exists but is inhibited. "True" has its psychological ground in an expectation that is fulfilled; "false" in the surprise when an expectation is defeated. Such interpretations as these become possible when we accept into epistemology not only logic but psychology and physical science, as we must in order to account for empirical rather than purely logical knowledge.

Russell is now able to develop a theory of significance. Regarded epistemologically, a proposition has two sides, objective and subjective. The objective side is what it *indicates* factually. The subjective side is what it *expresses* about the state of mind of its originator; and this is called its *significance*. What it expresses may be belief, denial, or doubt. These distinctions, not needed in logic, solve many puzzles of epistemology. The points concerning significance are independent of truth or falsity of the proposition; truth and falsity come into the relation of the proposition to what it indicates. A proposition does not necessarily consist of words; it is psychological, of the stuff of belief, not language. But words may always be found to state the belief which, as a proposition, may underlie the many possible ways of saying it, in one or in various languages. Russell provides a sample language to show that the psychological conditions of significance can be translated into precise syntactical rules.

Logical sentence-patterns can start from particular propositions recording percepts and extend our thought over material that we have not experienced, and in this way we can expand our body of statement. If we know "Socrates is mortal" we can think "Something is mortal," or "Everything is mortal," and so on. Then further inquiry so as to have new percepts may test whether the new statements should be added to belief. Simple statements of immediate percepts may be expressed with constants—particular names—and predicates. But any statement covering a percept one has not actually had must contain a variable term in place of a constant, for one can neither give nor learn a name (in

Russell's sense) for an object one has not perceived. An epistemological language will need names, whereas a logical language does not deal with particulars and has no use for names. By the use of variables rather than names, it is possible to have propositions transcending one's experience. This is in fact what happens whenever one receives information from another person.

Thus far Russell has investigated meaning. In effect, he has constructed an epistemological language, so that one can know what kinds of sentences are possible as statements of percepts and their relationships. It remains to examine the relationship between meaning and truth, between language and the world.

Among the many possible theories of truth, Russell adheres firmly to a correspondence theory. Truth is defined by events, not percepts, although it becomes known by percepts. Truth is thus a broader concept than knowledge. The truth of a proposition is established by perception of its *verifier*. The sort of sentence which provides the model for truth is a spontaneous sentence that expresses what it indicates—that is, in which the subjective and the objective content coincide. Such a sentence is "I am hot!" Provided the sentence is stimulated by the immediate circumstances of the moment, there is no reason to doubt it. The verifier of a true sentence is what the sentence *indicates*; in other words, what makes that sentence true is that I was hot when I said it. Similarly, the verifier of a sentence about the future is the occurrence of what it indicates, and when that occurrence is perceived, the sentence is verified. A false sentence has no verifier, and it indicates nothing. Obviously, some verifiers may never be perceived, and there are some sentences whose truth or falsity we never know. Sentences are true if their verifiers occur, but when verifiers are not perceived the sentences cannot be said to be known. The presence of an observer, Russell affirms, is no requisite of verifiers occurring.

The verifier of a basic proposition is a single occurrence at a moment of time. As to sentences containing variables, there is (usually) not just one but a collection of verifiers for them. The actual verification of such sentences depends on what is said. "All men are mortal" says "For any x, if x is a man then x is mortal." This can never be verified by empirical knowledge because it would be impossible to examine all values of the variable—all men. "Some men live in Los Angeles" says "There is an x such that x is a man and x lives in Los Angeles." This can be verified by one of a very large number of verifiers, since any individual man living in Los Angeles can be the assigned value of the variable. In this fashion, propositions which are not basic, but which, rather, by the use of variables indicate occurrences beyond the speaker's experience, may be verified. We can give in advance a description of the occurrence which would make the proposition true, but we cannot name the occurrence. The relation between a sentence and its verifier is often much more remote than the explanation of simple cases would suggest.

Russell denies that either the verification or the verifier of a sentence constitutes its meaning. The verifier, as what the sentence indicates, relates to its truth; but we must know what the proposition means before we can know either its significance or its verifier; that is, before we can know either what it expresses or what it indicates. This knowledge is based ultimately on our ostensive learning of object-words.

Known error arises in the experience of surprise upon a disappointed expectation. Its simplest case requires a combination of expectation, perception, and memory, in which either the expectation or perception must be negative, the others being positive. This combination accounts for our perceptions which seem to be negative perceptions, such as in "There is no cheese in this cupboard." We examine every object in the cupboard having a size which might result in a percept of cheese, but in every such case the expectation is disappointed.

The relation of empirical knowledge to experience is explained by Russell as follows: I must depend completely upon my own experience for all beliefs whose verbal expression has no variables; these include only basic propositions of immediate experience and memory. Though not indubitable, they are highly trustworthy. All my knowledge of what transcends *my* experience, including everything I learn from others, includes variables. When someone tells me, "A is red," using a proper name for something I have not experienced, if I believe him, what I believe is not "A is red" since I am not immediately acquainted with A, but "There is an *x* such that *x* is red." (Future experience giving me a percept of A together with a percept of the name "A" may later entitle me to believe "A is red.") Such a view of the nature of empirical knowledge would commit us either to depleting the body of knowledge to an intolerably small set of beliefs, or else to relaxing our insistence that only the belief in true statements may be called knowledge. In order to admit the statements one believes on testimony, statements of things ever experienced anywhere by other human beings, and statements assumed in physical science, we should have to do the latter. In fact, upon examining the limitations of pure empiricism, Russell concludes there are no true empiricists.

Certain principles of logic make difficulties in our epistemological language when we attempt to apply non-syntactic criteria of truth. They are the principles of extensionality and atomicity. Loosely, the principle of extensionality allows us to insert any atomic proposition in the place of a given atomic proposition in a sentence in the secondary language. But this will obviously not do for sentences stating propositional attitudes. "A believes *p*" should not entitle us to say, by substitution, that A believes any or all propositions whatever. The principle of atomicity in effect requires us to reduce the complex parts of any proposition on a higher language level to their components on the atomic level, then be governed in assessing the truth of the whole by the relationships thus exhibited. Difficulties which these two principles raise in logic have been attacked by Wittgenstein and others by distinguishing between the assertion of a proposition and the mere consideration of a proposition. Russell affirms, however, that the appropriate distinction to be made is between indication and significance. The principle of extensionality will be found to apply to all occurrences of a proposition within a larger proposition when its indication is what is relevant, but not when only its significance is relevant, as is the case with sentences of propositional attitudes. Russell is less sure whether atomicity must be accepted or denied; upon considering the immediacy of perception and, in contrast, the elaborateness of inference involved in applying the principle of atomicity, he is inclined to believe that its application is irrelevant to the theoretical construction of empirical knowledge.

Another matter arising in logic is the challenge to the law of the excluded middle (which says that a proposition must be either true or false, not a third thing). It has been suggested that sentences as yet unverified should not be called either true or false. But Russell clings to a realism, and a correspondence theory of truth, declaring that a sentence is true if its verifier occurs, even though its perception may not be part of anyone's experience. This outlook is extremely helpful in framing hypotheses, he says, and we should not attempt to do without it.

A continually recurring question in any investigation involving logical and nonlogical knowledge is whether anything about the structure of the world can be inferred from the structure of language. Since words are sensible objects, Russell believes that such inference is possible. While we confine the investigation to names and their objects, we have no reason to attempt such inference. But on examining sentences, we find that those like "A is to the left of B" cannot be explained without raising the question of universals. There is no escape from admitting relations as part of the nonlinguistic constitution. A universal is the meaning of a relation-word. "Above" and "before," just as truly as proper names, mean something in perception. Thus, in a logical language there will be some distinctions of parts of speech

which correspond to objective distinctions. Again, when we ask whether the word "similar" in recurring instances means the same thing or only similar things, there is no logical escape from granting that it means the same thing, thus establishing the universal "similar." Russell concludes, although with admitted hesitation, that there are universals, and not merely general words. Knowledge must then be not of words alone but of the nonlinguistic world also. One who denies this fact must deny that he even knows when he is using a word; a complete agnosticism is not compatible with the maintenance of linguistic propositions. Hence, Russell believes that the study of syntax can assist us to considerable knowledge of the structure of the world.

With this work, given as the William James Lectures at Harvard University in 1940, Russell has performed at least three worthy services for modern epistemology. By asserting that more than one thing can be known from one experience, that there is more than a single kind of knowledge, and that the mind can attain negative knowledge through perception, he has assigned to the mind a fuller role in shaping its life than that accorded it by positivists and reductionistic philosophers. He has pointed out the necessity for a metaphysic, if only a very simple one, and in doing so has given strength to the counterclaim against logical positivism that logical positivism is itself a metaphysic. Most important, his penetrating criticism has shown the importance of the limitations upon empirical knowledge that its advocates, in their consciousness of the limitations of other kinds of knowledge, are prone to overlook.

1057

REVELATION AND REASON

Author: Heinrich Emil Brunner (1889-   )
Type of work: Theology, epistemology
First published: 1941

PRINCIPAL IDEAS ADVANCED

Divine revelation alone must be the ground, norm, and content of the Church's proclamation; for a believing Church, inquiry begins with revelation and works toward reason.

Revelation is Jesus Christ; and faith is not belief in doctrine, but knowledge through personal encounter.

Since God is Absolute Subject, there is no knowledge of God except by God's own action.

God known through reason is an abstraction; God known through revelation is a living person.

Reason is not a thing-in-itself, but a relation which is what it is because of the original revelation in Creation; man, the sinner, retains his rational nature, but what he has lost is the right attitude of reason.

Emil Brunner is one of the best-known spokesmen for the neo-orthodox movement in contemporary Protestant theology. Its leading representative is certainly Karl Barth, but Brunner has been more widely read in this country. The reason for this is threefold. First, Brunner's style is far more readable, and therefore his books have been translated into English sooner than Barth's primary works; second, Brunner has been the more systematic of the two; third, and most important, Brunner is not as extreme and uncompromising as Barth. Brunner's mediating attempt is more amenable to the Anglo-American temperament. While Barth takes the extreme Christianity-against-culture approach, thoroughly unsympathetic to all philosophical approaches to theism, and others such as Paul Tillich stand at the opposite pole, Brunner attempts to bridge these extremes, bringing the truths of revelation into meaningful

dialogue with the truths of reason.

Yet, in assuming such a mediating role, it is necessary for a theologian to make one end of the spectrum the foundation of his dialogue. In this Brunner clearly exhibits himself as belonging to the Barthian predilection. *Revelation and Reason* is one of his best and most representative works in this regard. Here he makes his point of departure quite clear. "It is no accident that there are plenty of books with the title *Reason and Revelation*, but that there is none with the title *Revelation and Reason*. The usual order, 'Reason and Revelation,' is derived from the medieval-Catholic doctrinal tradition. . . . The reversal of this order, suggested by the title of this book, is the necessary consequence of a theological outlook which understands even the man who has not been gripped by the Christian message— and his reason—from the standpoint

1058

of the Word of God. . . . We do not begin our inquiry with reason and then work up to revelation, but, as a believing Church, we begin our inquiry with revelation and then work outwards to reason." Brunner and Barth begin together, and are in fundamental agreement, but Brunner moves farther out beyond the confines of the Church.

This difference began early in Brunner's career and caused a split between the two men. The argument began over the problem of the *imago Dei*, the image of God. In Genesis 1:27 it is recorded that "God created man in His own image, in the image of God He created him." From the inception of Christian theology the problem which has emerged is this—what is this image in man, and what is its condition consequent to man's fall? While theologians such as St. Augustine, Luther, and Calvin speak vehemently of this image being "lost," "corrupted," or "thoroughly maimed," other theologians have regarded man's plight in a more optimistic light.

Saint Thomas Aquinas and consequently Roman Catholics in general translate the passage to read, "God created man in His image, in His likeness created He him." The distinction is thus made between "image" and "likeness." The image, characterized by reason, is not lost but was preserved after the fall in essential integrity. Man's reason, even outside the purgative affects of grace, can function correctly and permit man to know and fulfill the natural end of man, characterized by the natural virtues of justice, prudence, temperance, and fortitude. Further, natural (unaided) reason can know God's existence and some of his attributes. In other words,

reason is a powerful aid in bringing man to faith, and thus is the natural ally of the Church. It is the "likeness" of God in man which was lost in the fall. This likeness, those qualities which render man God-like, are characterized by the virtues of faith, hope, and love; the attainment of these is the theological end of man, for which divine grace, mediated through the sacraments of the Church, is indispensable.

During the Protestant Reformation this problem of the divine image became central. Man cannot "earn" salvation, Luther insisted; man can neither know nor follow God unless grace transforms the individual—"*all* man's righteousness is as filthy rags." Following St. Augustine, the Reformers insisted that it is the will, not reason, that is central in man; until the will is reoriented in love to God through grace, all acts, reasoning, and thoughts are sinful, for they have the self as center. The image in man is totally disoriented, and thus depraved; reason is not the agent of truth, but simply the act of rationalizing for the human *status quo*. Faith and faith alone justifies, and faith is God's doing and God's alone.

During the period of liberalism in Protestantism, the Reformation doctrine of man was largely lost; the chasm between reason and grace was glossed over, and revelation was judged before the bar of reason. With the theological renaissance in contemporary Protestantism, however, what was rediscovered (meriting for the movement the title "neo-orthodox" or "neo-Reformation") was this very matter of the Reformation doctrine of man. Taking their lead from Luther, and consequently St. Augustine and

St. Paul, theologians like Brunner and Barth insisted upon the impotence of the divine image in man. Barth, the father of this movement, was most uncompromising at this point; it is here, he insisted, that Roman Catholics and Protestants are forever divided. God is known only when the Eternal Subject acts toward men; this was done at one point in history. Since God is subject, all attempts of reason to know him are doomed to failure and perversion, for of necessity they make the Subject into an object.

With this Brunner agreed, but he saw clearly the difficulty involved in Barth's insistence. If the image is utterly lost, in what respect is man still man? Unless something of man's essential nature remains, two consequences are inevitable. First, the Christian theodicy collapses, for man can no longer be regarded responsible for his own actions and, consequently, for the continuation of the effects of the fall; second, if salvation is totally God's doing, in which man is the unconscious pawn, how can one say that it is man who is saved? Without freedom in some regard, salvation is simply God's answer to his own call. Brunner's fundamental difficulty is thus explained by this question: How can man be placed in true dialogue with the God of grace, responsible for his sin as well as capable of response, and still be regarded as impotent without divine grace?

Brunner's basic insistence is that, despite the present glorification of scientific method, divine revelation alone must be the ground, norm, and content of the Church's proclamation. The past error of the Church has been in mistaking Scripture or dogma for revelation. For Brunner, revelation *is* Jesus Christ, "God Himself in His self-manifestation within history." Revelation is event, and Scripture simply witnesses to it. Correlatively, faith is not belief in doctrine, but knowledge through personal encounter which creates obedient trust. Roman Catholicism and Protestantism have tended to forget this, the former absolutizing the Church, the latter absolutizing Scripture.

Science and Biblical criticism have destroyed the idea of Biblical infallibility and are making possible a correct understanding of revelation. What needs to be done now, Brunner holds, is to show that faith does not suppress any legitimate claim of reason; rather, "the true interest of reason is only rightly preserved and maintained in faith." Because revelation illumines the mind *through* man's acts of understanding and will, faith must be dialectical—God *and man* in dialogue. The theologian is thus characterized not by greater faith, but by "greater power of thought in the service of faith." Natural and revealed knowledge are poles apart, but without the former, the latter remains unexpressed and vaguely understood.

Brunner's fundamental insistence is that since God is "Absolute Subject," there is no true knowledge of God except that which is given by God's own action. This fact indicates human sin, for it implies man's separation from God; in the beginning there was an original revelation from which man turned. The aim of the second revelation, Jesus Christ, is not simply the communication of knowledge but human restoration, the creation of the community of love. This occurs when revelation effects the disclosure of the neighbor as a "Thou" because God replaces the "I" as center. It is for this reason that the history of revelation *is* the history of salvation.

Revelation is always unexpected, for man has no right to expect forgiveness. The most critical revelation is the sacrificial death of Jesus Christ, for on it alone divine forgiveness depends. But this revelation must not be separated from its reception—the subjective process is an integral part. Revelation is both fact and illumination. This total act of faith is *sui generis,* for it belongs totally in the "I-Thou" dimension, not that of "objective" knowledge. Faith is a subject-subject relation with Christ which *is itself* justifying; theology is reflection upon this faith.

Faith is supernatural in the sense that its origin is God. But, Brunner maintains, it is also natural, for it enables man to become that for which he was created. Man can love unselfishly only when he has first been loved; he can give himself unconditionally only because God so gave himself in Jesus Christ. Without this event, every human attempt makes God a means to an end, one relation among many.

Consequently, Brunner insists, the mode of "knowing" God affects completely the nature of the "God" known. The "God" known through reason is an object, an absolute, an abstraction. The God of Christian revelation, however, is a living person. In believing on faith, God is not first known as Creator, but in knowing God as Lord he is then known as Creator *ex nihilo.* Likewise, God is "wholly other," knowing wrath against human sin; still he reveals himself as willing to love the sinner. Such a paradox, resting in God's *decision,* cannot be known through reason—"this idea

of God bursts through and destroys all fundamental categories of thought." Further, in Christ God is revealed as Triune—God throughout history is he "who is to be revealed, who reveals, and who is being revealed: Father, Son, and Spirit." Herein the Incarnation is revealed as at the heart of God's eternal plan.

Revelation, however, is not only of God but of man. It is through Christ that man truly knows himself as sinner, as disobedient to the original revelation. If Christianity does not affirm this critical revelation, Brunner insists, it must affirm man as *essentially* sinful. But for Brunner, man's freedom is primary, and man is distinguished from other creatures by his ability to sin. It is this original revelation which makes man a responsible being.

Here we come to the heart of Brunner's understanding of reason. Reason is not a "thing-in-itself," but a relation, for it comes from perception. When the philosopher says that the core of reason is transcendental, he is pointing to what Christianity identifies as reason's essential relation to God. Every use of reason, Brunner insists, implies this relation which is the general revelation; for example, multiplication implies the presupposition of infinite number, verification implies the standard of "absolute Truth." But not only is reason what it is because of the general revelation, but therein is contained the cause of its unrest—it is "derived from God and has been made for God." Thus, for Brunner, reason is not ignored in faith, but fulfilled, restored to its created relation. Man is nothing in himself; the same is true of reason.

This original or general revelation is

revelation in Creation. It is further witnessed to in conscience. Man knows within himself what is commanded and forbidden, but not why or by whom. Barth mistakenly denies this revelation; Brunner affirms, because he sees it as competing with particular revelation. But for Brunner the former is the presupposition of the latter. Yet Brunner rejects "natural theology," for because of the fall only one "whose eyes have been opened by Jesus Christ" is in a position to recognize the general revelation which is given to all men. For the sinner, general revelation has no "saving significance," for in it God does not meet man personally. In both kinds of revelation the same Triune God is revealer; only the form differs. In this rests the significance of the Crucifixion: man is not simply ignorant but guilty in his ignorance, for he does not know because he *does not want to know*. Man retains the *imago Dei*, his rational nature, but what is lost is the right attitude of reason. Thus, for Brunner, general revelation is the basis for human responsibility, being the point of contact for the "call to repentance." This, Brunner insists, is the truth of Scripture which Barth refuses to admit because he does not clearly distinguish between "knowing" and "being."

In the Old Testament, God reveals *who* he is—herein rests the importance of God's name. In the New Testament, God reveals *what* he is—thus the importance of God's Word. Through revelation of his name God's presence is established as the "Thou," but, for Brunner, God is still not personally present—he is revealed as promise. The Old Testament prophecy of the "suffering servant" is the climax, for it is the supreme promise of the

divine act fulfilled in Jesus Christ. Christ could come only to people prepared by God's promise. In Christ, God's being and will are "finally and completely revealed." As a teacher Jesus is simply one among many. His uniqueness is that His message and person are identical, for revelation and atonement are one. Brunner's Christology is as "high" as any in contemporary theology—Jesus Christ "is God Himself. When He speaks, God Himself speaks; when He acts, God Himself acts; in His personal presence the personal presence of God has become real." All intellectual Trinitarian and Christological affirmations Brunner holds to be simply attempts to express this fact.

Scripture is necessary, but it belongs to the Old Testament revelation, for it is not itself the personal confrontation. Yet through it the confrontation occurs. And since reception is part of revelation, the apostolic response is an indispensable part of the divine act itself. The Scriptures are divinely inspired, but, for Brunner, this inspiration is far from "verbal" or literal. They are human testimonies under the guidance of the Spirit.

Man cannot be redeemed without the Scripture, yet the Scripture is not sufficient; each man must be addressed where he is. This is the task of the Church. Although its doctrine is not revelation, Christ is present only "through definite ideas." Thus, for Brunner, theology and preaching must remain in constant dialogue, both being confessional, and the temptation of a closed theological system must be totally dismissed.

Certainty of the Christian revelation is derived in only one way—one believes only when the Holy Spirit permits the Scriptural witness to dawn on one as Truth. In this manner the believer "knows" Jesus as the Christ in the identical manner as the first disciples. To so know is to be redeemed. But faith is always imperfect, for it is always a process of *"becoming* sure." The world contradicts the victory which the Resurrection promises. Consequently, in this life one lives by faith, not by "sight"—risk, doubt, uncertainty are always present. This wrestling with unfaith is man's continual temptation to sin, springing not from intellectual honesty but from the intellectual arrogance of making human reason the measure of all things. The Church's disastrous response was the attempt to provide "proof." The necessary weakness of all such attempts, Brunner contends, has greatly weakened contemporary Christianity. It is only to a man whose belief in the autonomy of reason has been shattered that it can be shown that revelation possesses its own logic and facts. God must not be given a place within reason, but the reverse. It is only when this reversal does not occur, Brunner claims, that revelation and reason are at odds.

Brunner attempts to bring this contention to play on some crucial relations between Christianity and other areas. First, in regard to other religions, Christianity must not assume itself to have a monopoly on revelation but other revelations are given only the preparatory and prophetic function which belongs to the Old Testament. In all religions there are distorted "relics" of the original revelation, but only in Christianity, Brunner insists, has the Word become flesh. Second, in regard to "naturalistic" philosophy of religion, he is uncompro-

mising—"A man is *either* a believing Christian *or* a religious man in the sense of Schleiermacher or Kant; but he cannot be both." Third, in regard to science, revelation provides no knowledge at all concerning the scientific structure of things. Biblical "science" is prescientific and must be rejected as extraneous. Science can understand miracles in a perfectly natural way, and this does not destroy revelation. Faith is not dependent on miracles, for a miracle is seen to be such only through the eyes of faith. A miracle declares nothing more than God's freedom from the limitations of the world. Jesus Christ is the only indispensable miracle. The scientist, Brunner claims, who is cognizant of the "miracle" of life and mind cannot be antagonistic to the Christian claim. The tension between Christianity and science arises only when either leaves its own sphere. And last, philosophy witnesses to revelation through its presuppositions. In the moral realm it points to the human condition with its bludgeoning "ought." The convincing power and content of the theistic arguments depend on their support by the Christian tradition, without which they are tentative and misleading.

What Brunner is attempting to do throughout is to restore the Augustinian understanding of faith and reason. For St. Augustine, they belong together. The correct relation is "faith seeking understanding." An autonomous philosophy is impossible. The reversal of St. Thomas Aquinas, understanding seeking faith, permitted the wedge which eventually ended in the contemporary autonomy of both spheres. While Barth has attempted to restore faith through the total rejection of autonomous philosophy, Brunner attempts the same restoration by bringing reason back to its former Augustinian relation. As Brunner says, the difference between the Christian theologian and the Christian philosopher is one of subject, not of method.

The problem of Christian philosophy is that of penetrating every sphere of life with the Christian spirit—"Christ conquers the reason and in so doing makes it free to serve."

THE NATURE AND DESTINY OF MAN

Author: Reinhold Niebuhr (1892-   )
Type of work: Theology
First published: 1941-1943

PRINCIPAL IDEAS ADVANCED

Man is both a child of nature and a spirit who stands outside nature.

Man has the capacity for self-transcendence; he can view himself as an object, thereby making himself a moral creature, subject to conscience.

Man's state of anxiety supplies him with the creative energy to transform the natural through the love of God.

The alternative to faith, made possible by man's freedom, is sin; and sin is an act of will whereby the self, rather than God, becomes the center of human concern.

God is agape, self-giving love, and such love is not possible in this life; but by commitment to such love man transcends himself and in the knowledge of God's forgiveness accepts judgment without despair.

Reinhold Niebuhr is perhaps more responsible for the contemporary renaissance of theology in America than any other single man. With the possible exceptions of Jonathan Edwards and Horace Bushnell, America has been rather unsuccessful in making unique contributions to Christian theology. Rather, the American contribution to religion, especially since the latter part of the nineteenth century, has been a unique social fervor, an ethical "activism," which is often absent in Continental Christianity.

This social passion grew during the last century into the movement known

as the "social gospel," fathered by Washington Gladden. Although it is dangerous to generalize concerning this diverse group, the social gospel became characterized by an accent on human capacity, the ethical side of religion, the "simple teachings of Jesus," and a rather wholesale de-emphasis of theology and dogma. Walter Rauschenbusch was the most moderate and profound representative of this movement. Niebuhr has called him not only the real founder of social Christianity but "its most brilliant and generally satisfying exponent to the present day."

As a young devotee of Rauschenbusch, Niebuhr entered a Detroit labor parish in 1915, prepared to establish social justice through the nurturing of human love. In the crucible of social conflict, Niebuhr discovered that the key problem was not one of personal ethics but of social structure and strategy. Detroit industrialists were no less moral in their personal relations than the average laborer, but in a system of competitive capitalism, operating by the impersonal laws of market, profit, supply, and demand, direct application of the "simple teachings of Jesus" to the social sphere was impossible. As a result of this practical conviction, Niebuhr wrote a volume in 1933 which shook the American theological scene as strongly as did Barth's *The Epistle to the Romans* on the Continent in 1918. While strongly tempered by liberal theology, Niebuhr's *Moral Man and Immoral Society* marked the beginning of social realism in contemporary American Christianity. Gone was the idealism of the liberal period; the Kingdom of God was not man's to build, not simply in this generation but in any generation. The Kingdom was the "impossible possibility" standing over against man eternally, the ideal perfect community of mutual love, judging all man's attempts to emulate it. The only possible possibilities were transient and imperfect forms of justice.

Accompanying these insights came Neibuhr's rejection of absolutism in ethics: there are no absolute goods and evils. The problem of ethics is the never-ending task of finding "proximate solutions for insoluble problems." Accompanying this position, classically formulated in Niebuhr's *An Interpretation of Christian Ethics,* was a growing shift in emphasis from the liberal stress on society as the molder of man, to the nature of man as the key to the nature and problems of society. The orthodox doctrine of original sin became increasingly more relevant for Niebuhr in understanding the problems of culture. Man is essentially self-centered, seeking self-aggrandizement and domination over others. While this tendency can be checked to a large degree on the personal level within the small confines of the interdependent family, in the larger dimensions of community, group, nation, and hemisphere, personal pride is compounded into impersonal, immoral, irresponsible pressure groups seeking their own untempered ends in hypocritical self-righteousness.

This understanding early led Niebuhr to sympathy with the Marxist analysis of social forces, but he saw that the Marxist realism about the present was naïvely undermined by an unfounded optimism about human capacity in the proletarian future. In 1944 these thoughts coalesced in a brilliant vindication of democracy, *The Children of Light and the Children of Darkness.* Here was combined Niebuhr's political movement to the "left" with his theological movement toward the "right." All previous apologies for democracy, he declared, were wrongly grounded on an optimistic doctrine of man, defending it as the only form of government which respected human capacity. Such a defense, Niebuhr insisted, can lead only to catastrophe; Locke must be tempered with Hobbes, as well as the reverse.

Man is capable of self-transcendence, but he is likewise motivated by an even stronger desire for domination. Socialism controls man, but in a manner which undercuts the creativity that emerges from self-transcendence; further, those tendencies which make control necessary undermine the integrity of those given the power to control. On the other hand, laissez faire democracy so liberates man that his selfish propensities, compounded by monopoly, by cartels, and by simple numbers, destroy the integrity of the less organized and less privileged, using them as tools for maintaining their competitive place in society. The plight of the worker several decades ago, exploited by the industrialist not out of vindictiveness but out of the necessity of competing in an uncontrolled business world, is Niebuhr's favorite case in point.

The only realistic answer for this dilemma Niebuhr sees in democracy. The only structure for social justice is that of competing pressure groups, deadlocked by their conflicting self-interests and thereby forced into self-transcendence for the mutual good. Since group power is never constant but changed by the circumstances of each new situation, democracy has two unique advantages. Its carefully designed system of internal checks and balances is alone in a position to prevent excessive governmental control, while its representative legislation can delegate power to the underprivileged and restrain the irresponsible. This system requires constant change and vigilance, for today's justice may be tomorrow's greatest injustice. To summarize with one of Niebuhr's most famous statements, "man's capacity for justice makes democracy possible; but man's inclination to injustice makes democracy necessary."

This is the basic understanding which runs throughout Niebuhr's prolific writings on economics, political theory, international relations, and the like. His writing career, however, was climaxed in 1939 with his two Gifford Lecture series, combined in a large volume entitled *The Nature and Destiny of Man: a Christian Interpretation*. It is indicative of the contemporary theological scene that a social ethicist, confessedly a minister and not a scholar, should have produced such a theological classic. Niebuhr's lifetime of practical thinking is here placed in a carefully created intellectual dialogue attempting to bring the various aspects of his thought into a systematic structure.

One appraisal of Niebuhr's general theological position may be helpful. Although he is often placed in the general school of "neo-orthodoxy" (see the article on Karl Barth's *The Knowledge of God and the Service of God*), this label is misleading. He has remained in essential agreement with Rauschenbusch on such theological matters as Christology, redemption, and eschatology, with one fundamental difference: his doctrine of man is far more "orthodox." But even here there are differences. It appears that the combination of a negative doctrine of man with an essentially "liberal" understanding of the remaining tenets of Christianity is the reason for much of the ambiguity in Niebuhr's thought. *The Nature and Destiny of Man* is Niebuhr's most conscientious attempt to reconcile these elements, but it remains an imperfect attempt. As a result, it is the first series of the lectures dealing with the nature of man, that is Niebuhr's best work; it is without doubt a unique and lasting contribution to American theology.

"Man has always been his own most vexing problem." Thus Niebuhr begins, analyzing rationalism, romanticism, Marxism, idealism, and naturalism as alternative attempts of Western thought to come to terms with the curious contradictions constituting the enigma which is man. For Niebuhr, anthropology is *the* problem from which all others follow, and theological anthropology alone is capable of dealing with the whole man. He systematically undermines every attempt to establish man as a simplex being, whether in terms of reason, animality, or the like.

For Niebuhr, every human contradiction points to two paradoxical facts about man. First, "man is a child of nature, subject to its vicissitudes, compelled by its necessities, driven by its impulses. . . ." Second, man is a "spirit who stands outside of nature, life, himself, his reason and the world." It is only the Christian view which succeeds in holding these two aspects together. Not to do this is to overestimate or underestimate man, both of which actions bring tragic practical consequences, whether they be the tyranny of totalitarianism or the exploitation by laissez-faire capitalism.

For the Christian, man is created in the "image of God," and in this rests his transcendence over nature. As Niebuhr understands this, the *imago* refers to man's capacity for self-transcendence, to make an object of himself, to stand continually outside himself in an indefinite regression. This is the root of "conscience," for it gives to man a capacity for objectivity about himself, viewing himself as an object, appraising the degree to which this "object" acts as he would want to be acted toward. This ability and this inborn "golden rule," similar to Kant's ethic of rational consistency, is the

source of morality for Niebuhr. Man is not only "spirit" but he is also "natural"; he is a finite creature. Finitude does not mean evil, but dependency, creatureliness. This polarity means that man is at the intersection of time and eternity, or finitude and infinity, or nature and spirit.

The law of man's nature is love, pointed to by man's self-transcendence but clearly revealed in the Christian revelation. God's intent was that man should have faith, trust, in the Creator, loving him for the gift of existence, and in gratitude loving his neighbor as he had been loved. Being at the intersection of nature (under the necessity of instinct, need, and drive) and spirit (under the freedom of infinite possibility), the inevitable condition of man is anxiety. If man trusts in God, he knows his anxious state to be God-intended, and anxiety therefore becomes the energy of creativity—infinite possibilities come as challenges, as leaven for humble achievement in service to God and man. The spirit transforms the natural by bringing it to fulfillment—this is to become a self. This was God's plan in creating the world.

Because of man's freedom, another option is open. This possibility Niebuhr finds classically portrayed in Genesis in terms of the Garden of Eden. This story, he insists, is not history but myth—myth, however, not in the sense of "falsehood," but in the Platonic sense or the sense in which it is used in literature. Myth is the vehicle for communicating truths which are beyond the capacity of concept to communicate. Adam, then, is not simply "first man," but *every* man. What Adam did, all men do, not because he did it but because man is what he is.

It is at this point that Niebuhr's difficult distinction arises—the fall of each man is "inevitable" but not "necessary." Reminiscent of Kierkegaard, from whom Niebuhr drew much of his analysis, the fall is a personal affair, something which cannot be universally understood, but something which I do, for which I know *myself* responsible, and which I understand *in myself*. The feeling of guilt attending all actions is the guarantee of responsibility despite inevitability.

This alternative is the way of sin, as opposed to the way of faith. Anxiety is its psychological condition, but it is not the cause—the cause is the will. If the self does not *accept* anxiety as God-given for creativity, he has no option but to try to eliminate it. This is sin, for it stems from disbelief, lack of trust —it is the substitution of the self and its own strength for God as center. This "elimination" of anxiety can be attempted in two ways, for anxiety, being the product of an intersection, can be denied by denying either dimension of the human polarity.

The first way, by far the most universal, is that of "pride." This is the denial of one's natural aspect, to reject one's limitations by deliberately mistaking one's self-transcendence for achievement. Man, with the capacity to envisage the whole, is tempted to imagine himself as the whole. This is not a matter of ignorance, but of willed self-deception. There are four basic types of pride: the pride of power (glorification in personal and group superiority, false or real), pride of knowledge (especially apparent in conflicting ideologies), pride of virtue (best exemplified by moral self-righteousness), and pride of spirit (religious fanaticism). These are all rooted in insecurity, tempting one to self-deception by deceiving others in a façade of word and deed. In effect, pride is the elevation of the relative to the Absolute.

The second way is that of sensuality. Anxiety is "eliminated" by denying one's freedom, one's capacity for self-transcendence, and one's responsibility, affirming animality as man's essential nature. This may be done either to assert the self or to escape the self. In reality sensuality is a result of pride, for one's own pleasure is made the only center. In whatever form it takes, sin is best understood as the attempt to hide contingency, to seek security at the expense of others. The continuity of sin rests in the fact that while anxiety tempts one to sin, the sin only compounds the insecurity in a vicious circle.

The fact that self-deception, rationalization, is involved in all sin is the living refutation, for Niebuhr, of the doctrine of total depravity; unless the will is successful in disguising its actions it cannot bring itself to do them. Thus there are no personal acts which are purely evil, and yet it must be affirmed that pride infects every human action, to a lesser or greater degree. But since the self, never deserving unconditional devotion, cannot ever fully convince itself, it craves allies to strengthen the deception. Herein lie the demonic proportions of group pride, formed by the attempt of individuals to escape insecurity in a blind, absolute devotion to race, religion, institution, nation, or party. Such idolatry is ruthless, for it possesses the instruments for power. There is no group which escapes "sinful pride and idolatrous pretensions." This means that all judgments and distinctions are relative, and always a matter of degree; they cannot be made previous to the occasion. A "Christian" group or nation is characterized not in its achievement but in its willingness to hear judgment. Since a nation has no collective capacity for self-transcendence, its hope rests in a creative minority, heard because of the tension of competitive forces.

Man, though "fallen," has a "vision of health," an awareness of the law of love as the "ought" of which he is incapable. This awareness is the "point of contact" for the Christian revelation. It is here that Niebuhr's liberal theology is apparent. Although Niebuhr is willing to use much of the traditional terminology concerning Jesus Christ, he makes it clear, as does Tillich, who greatly influenced him, that they have only symbolic meaning. Jesus is the fulfillment of prophetic religion, making vicarious suffering the final revelation of the meaning of history; for Niebuhr this means that God takes the sins of the world on himself in the sense that divine forgiveness is the reverse side of divine judgment. This forgiveness cannot be effective until man takes sin seriously, knowing that sin causes God to suffer—this is the message of the Crucifixion which brings man to contrition. Without such contrition divine forgiveness could not be appropriated. To the degree that man has faith in this fact as the truth of history, to that degree can anxiety become creative.

Niebuhr rejects the Chalcedonian and Nicene formulations of a two-nature Christology, declaring that although "it is possible for a character . . . to point symbolically beyond history and to become a source of disclosure of an eternal meaning, purpose and power which bears history," it is "not possible for any person to be historical and unconditioned at the same time." Through Jesus, love is established as the center of life, but only in principle, not in fact. In this life, love is suffering, not triumphant. The Kingdom of God is not in history nor ever will be—it is the hope which keeps man from the despair of the moment through his faith that the divine power cannot be overcome.

Through Jesus Christ it is known that God is *agape*, self-giving love, and that a life so lived can only end tragically, for it refuses "to participate in the claims and counterclaims of historical existence." Thus love as taught by Jesus is impossible, for to exist is to participate in the balance of competing wills which *is* the structure of this life. Such love transcends history; but to the degree that man is capable of self-transcendence, to that degree does this "impossibility" become "possible," not in the sense of being attainable but of being relevant—it judges every human attempt, revealing possibilities not realized or seen. Yet since this awareness of infinite possibility is that which tempts man to pride or sensuality, it is only in awareness of divine forgiveness that man can accept judgment without despair. This is the Christian answer for Niebuhr.

Such an understanding means that, for Niebuhr, there is no progress in history. This does not mean that there is no achievement, but since man's duality is never overcome, every greater possibility for good brings with it in direct proportion a greater possibility for evil. For example, atomic research brings the possibility of unlimited industrial energy, but also the possibility of total cosmic disaster. Mankind always walks the tightrope between antithetical possibilities, for each will walks the tightrope between the will-to-realization and the will-to-power.

What remains as an enigma in Niebuhr's position is the combination of a negative doctrine of man with a liberal Christology. In liberal theology, the optimism concerning the former is the respective "weakness" of the latter. But while Niebuhr's anthropology became more negative, his Christology and understanding of redemption did not change accordingly. It is for this reason that Niebuhr's ethic makes no fundamental distinction between the "redeemed" and "unredeemed" man. For him, social ethics and Christian ethics are identical, and what he calls "personal ethics" is totally unrelated to the former. Yet whatever other implications are involved here, it cannot be denied that, on the one hand, Niebuhr's doctrine of man has proved a powerful stimulus to the renaissance in American theology, and that, on the other, it has made ready contact with secular thinking in almost every area of group relations.

EXPERIENCE AND SUBSTANCE

Author: De Witt Henry Parker (1885-1949)
Type of work: Metaphysics, value theory
First published: 1941

Principal Ideas Advanced

Experience, as something concrete and given, is existentially ultimate; in the experience of the self we have an illuminating sample of reality.

What we regard as physical objects quite different from our sensations are actually constructions integrating sensory data and meanings.

The generic concepts of being derive their sense from the given characteristics of experience.

Hume's analysis of causation is inadequate for it fails to take into account the critical role of volition in influencing action.

Substances cannot be reduced to their characteristics; they are relatively independent, have casual efficacy, and endure through change.

Space is a manifold of actual and possible relations; time is a term for events and their coming into being and ceasing to be; the self is best understood as present in the focal self, and as having come out of the matrix self.

Experience and Substance is characterized by its author as belonging to the tradition initiated by Plato, Aristotle, and Plotinus, recast by Berkeley, Leibniz, and Fichte, and enriched in our own day by the insights of Bergson, James, and Whitehead. Its argument is along the lines of what is called speculative empiricism in which an empirical base is a point of departure for suggestions and inferences. The resultant point of view is labeled idealist, finitist, and monadistic. Quite naturally, there is a running polemic against materialism in its various forms, old and new. This polemic is of special interest since it brings out in a sharpened way Parker's own principles. When we get these clearly before us, we soon realize how logical the development of his thought is.

Essentially, Parker's thesis is that *experience*, as something concrete and given, is existentially ultimate; in the experience of the self we have an illuminating sample of reality. He denies that the verb "exists" has application in any meaningful way to anything other than ingredients of experience, such as sensa (the given elements of sensation), thoughts, desires, satisfactions, and frustrations, within the circuit of selves or monads. On this foundation the author builds the framework of what he calls an Omega System having eternal status. The analogy with the theses of Whitehead is evident, though Parker is opposed to the Platonic base in the latter's position, being himself more Aristotelian. Both, however, are theists and opposed to what is currently called naturalistic humanism.

Experience and Substance is a careful discussion of related topics, beginning with a definition of subject matter and taking up generic problems in succession.

The book is delightfully written. The style is vivid and concrete and technicalities are translated, as much as possible, into their empirical bases. Parker's training in aesthetics and his wide culture are drawn upon to illuminate his more abstract arguments. Realists and materialists will find in this book analyses which they cannot ignore. There is competent familiarity with modern logic and mathematics as well as with physics, biology, and psychology. Parker was a graduate of Harvard University in the days of its outstanding teachers in philosophy, and one observes something of the range and spirit of Josiah Royce. This is a mature book reflecting years of careful thought and decision.

There are few philosophical issues which are not explored in this volume. The examination of time, relations, and causality is, perhaps, particularly outstanding. As an unashamed metaphysician, Parker was concerned with the eternal and its relation to time and change. This framework is somewhat similar to that of Whitehead; both were opposed to positivism. Wrote Parker: "The traditional conception of the province of metaphysics was defined once and for all by Aristotle as the study of being as being." Ontology is a transcription of that dictum. It is worth noting that Parker differs from Whitehead and Russell in seeking to reform the category of substance.

Parker believed that metaphysics is maligned when it is associated with the transcendental or quasi-unknowable. It consists of necessary or foundational beliefs. It involves a catharsis of prejudices and analyzes what people often consider obvious, the nature of physical things and of other minds. As a matter of fact, Parker, like Berkeley, considered the things of common sense and science to be phenomenal constructions. He was well aware of the role played in modern thought by theory of knowledge, and he moved in the ambit of British empiricism and Kant. He mentions critical realism, but does not consider it critical enough.

In his account Parker regards sensations as being at once in the mind of the percipient and external to the mind as control, thus constituting a sort of boundary between monads. Contrary to Leibniz, Parker argues that monads are causally related. The result is somewhat akin to naïve, or presentational, realism. In fact, Parker makes much of the inseparability of so-called primary and secondary qualities as features of experienced *qualia*, in this resembling Berkeley and Whitehead. But the question is, of course, whether the properties we ascribe to things are mere transcripts of sensory qualia. Parker's view takes things to be constructions integrating sensory data and meanings.

For Parker, idea and object are capable of literal confrontation, both being experienced. Concepts apply to sensory data which demand interpretation. And some datum is always at the base of a concept. In fact, Parker's theory of universals is to the effect that they concern the generic features of the given. This position is in accordance with the traditions of British empiricism.

In Parker's empirical metaphysics the connection of all discourse with the *given* in experience is made explicit. However, the emphasis is upon those generic concepts which grasp the most fundamental stratum of being. These are called categories, and concern the basic characteristics of whatever exists, such as space, time, relations, and causality. In all this Parker was opposed to what we may call *a priori rationalism;* he wanted to check up on all assumptions. There are many insights in his speculative enlargement of empiricism. Perhaps realistic corpo-realism could profit from them. Cer-

tainly, one may find much that is admirable in Parker's suggestions about the generic characteristics of the cosmos. Concepts are responsible to the evidence of the senses and to the indications of life as lived.

Following Bradley, Parker speaks of centers of experience. These are his monads. In a way, *to be* is to experience. This approach fits in logically with Bradley's denial that anything but idea is thinkable and with Whitehead's rejection of *vacuous;* that is, nonsensuous, actualities.

The centricity of centers rests on activities such as symbolism, conception, and volition. In his treatment of these activities, Parker supplements Hume and Berkeley with Brentano. Here the Aristotelian tradition again enters. Much is made of symbols and meanings as additional to sensations. But Berkeley's framework is retained. Conception is an activity of the self which finds expression in belief and in description. Volition is the guidance of experience from within. In criticizing Hume's treatment of causation, Parker made much of volitional control: we can control our actions and affect other persons. He suggests that Hume was still influenced by Cartesian dualism in his rejection of volition as a true cause of movements.

Volition is the guidance of experience from within. Symbolizing, conceiving, and volition are integrated, although any one may be dominant for a time. A sensation is an event rather than an activity. Here Parker diverges from Brentano, on the one hand, and from G. E. Moore, on the other. At one time, at least, Moore described the consciousness as able to be directly aware of nonmental data. Parker regarded this as mythical, and interpreted sensations as mental events encompassed by activities. And he argues that Brentano overdid the emphasis on reference as a mark of the psychical. He refers to the serial dimension of sensory qualia as a mark against the polarities of conception and volition, such as acceptance and rejection.

To avoid the pitfall of a shut-in mind, the author appeals to the thesis that sensations are on the boundary between minds and nature. Here we *intuit* control and countercontrol. At the human level, one presses another's hand in greeting and the pressure is returned. Such communication is more basic than the argument from analogy. Language develops within this context of intercourse.

The strength of the Aristotelian tradition in Parker has already been mentioned. It now appears in his defense of the category of substance. His *empirical recasting* does not go as far as either Russell and Whitehead went, or the logical positivists. What he does is to modify the logic of Leibniz by developing relational statements; his monads have causal windows.

There are, he argues, four important features in the concept of substance. The first is to the effect that nothing can be reduced to its characteristics. The second concerns relative independence. The third bears on causal efficacy, while the fourth calls attention to conservation, or endurance, through change.

A polemical note of some interest enters. Parker argues that the materialist who identifies the mind with the brain must hold that experience is a predicate of the brain. It is evident that there are linguistic traps here. People do say that a man has a good brain much as they say that he has a good mind. But how does this functional goodness manifest itself? Parker argues, first, that materialism involves an enlargement of the notion of matter. "It is so enriched that it no longer means matter." But that is an appeal to definition. Parker treats the notion of emergence and levels with respect; his treatment of levels of causality is excellent.

As against pragmatism, Parker accepts a picturing notion of truth, a kind of correspondence theory. The pertinent question is whether meaningful statements have sensory data as their objects or refer to something beyond the data which is controlling them. It appears likely that Parker had the latter notion in mind for he was very much interested in other selves. His phenomenalism covers ontological panpsychism. It appears that he rejected C. I. Lewis's two types of knowledge—that which terminates on sensory data and that which is more open and nonterminating—as insufficient. To this extent, Parker was a realist. But he was not a physical realist. Material things are constructions, he argues; the Berkeleian view of perception was essentially held.

In considering the generic, or fundamental, categories, Parker had many valuable insights. Newtonian space is rejected, and space is thought of as a manifold of actual and possible relations and positions. Mathematical points should not be reified. Time is a term for events and their coming into being and their ceasng to be. Duration is a relational term pointing to parallel series of events. Even the matrix self has duration in time only in this sense. The author gives no analysis of the distinction between the ocurrent and the continuant, but there is something analogous in his distinction between the focal self and the matrix self. According to Parker, memory depends on traces, or echoes, of the past. This is the basis of his doctrine of historical truth as eternal. It leads him to a matrix self of the universe, which is eternal, and to creation. The resemblance to Whitehead's theism is evident.

The treatment of relations finds a middle ground between Russell and Bradley. Symbols must not be allowed to get in the way of thought. Ropes or brackets may be better symbols than words. Parker distinguishes between static and dynamic relations and between original and acquired properties. His stress on acquired properties represents his break with Leibniz and his recognition of time in an evolutionary sense.

As against Hume, Parker defends the objectivity of causality. Decisions and tendencies are at the foundation of causal sequences. Successful wagering rests on forces in nature itself. Thus Parker provides a metaphysical basis for induction which is in accord with the idea of initial probability. The treatment of levels of causality is quite in line with theories of emergence.

The summary of value theory in this book condenses what Parker worked out elsewhere in detail. Volition and satisfaction are the bases of value as an experience. In this way Parker links value and existence much as did Bosanquet. He is critical of Perry's formula to the effect that value is any object of any interest.

The concluding chapters are devoted to the consideration of the eternal. Passing by essences, or universals, as timeless, Parker develops the thesis that there is an ultimate level which is permanent and really highest; he calls this the Omega System. Roy Wood Sellars once called it the "floor of being." As a theist Parker exalts it. He argues that the whole must be more *complex* than any part.

Some interesting remarks are made on constants in nature such as the gravitational constant and Planck's *h*. These would be, in a sense, *a priori*, though in a non-Kantian sense. It may be recalled that Sir Arthur Eddington was seeking such factors in a rationalistic way. Science is often more ontologically inclined that positivists admit.

The topic now shifts to the meaning of the term, "existence." Parker regards it as involved with the given. To say that *this* sense-datum exists is tautological. Perhaps "existence" arises as a term in connection with the application of concepts. "There are lions" or "Lions exist" concerns the applicability of a concept to an observable world. The statement involves a terminal statement of the form *"This* is a lion."

In this book Parker argues for theism. The mystic may be right in his feeling that he is in communication with the Eternal. There is a touch here of Hocking's approach. What Parker argues for is the initial probability of the religious view of the world, and he supplements his argument with a pragmatic defense.

While sympathetic to the arguments of the Neosupernaturalists such as Tillich and Barth, Parker was not impressed by them; they are supports of a tradition.

In the last analysis, Parker turns to Plotinus and emanation. God created the universe because of his need for companionship. Parker is frank enough to say that the scientific view of the world is an alternative, but holds that it lacks the recognition of the ultimacy of experience.

There are other points which could be examined, for *Experience and Substance* is a mature book. It is a systematic development of a point of view. It

is delightfully written and reflects intimate acquaintance with the relevant literature. It was meant as a conscious challenge to naturalism and materialism. Such debates give vitality to philosophy.

INTRODUCTION TO SEMANTICS

Author: Rudolf Carnap (1891-   )
Type of work: Philosophy of semantics
First published: 1942

PRINCIPAL IDEAS ADVANCED

To study any language a metalanguage is needed—a language about language. Semantics is the study of linguistic expressions insofar as they serve to designate.

A semantical system is a system of rules, formulated in a metalanguage, for determining the truth-conditions of sentences in a language.

Sentences are logically true when they are true because of semantical rules.

Carnap is known as a logical empiricist with roots in the Vienna Circle of logical positivists, and as a prolific logician. Whereas other students of semantics have largely been interested in relating the use of language to the empirical world, Carnap is interested in pure semantics; that is, in discovering what languages are in and of themselves. *Introduction to Semantics* sets forth the chief principles of semantics upon which more specialized theory may be expected to depend.

In order to investigate a language, another language is needed in which the first may be discussed and described. The language investigated is called the *object language;* the other, the *metalanguage.* When the meta-

language is discussed, this is done in the metametalanguage, and so on. A metalanguage includes the object language, since that must be reproduced in the discussion of itself.

Carnap adopts the diversions of linguistic study suggested by C. W. Morris. If the investigation includes the user of a language, "we assign it to the field of **pragmatics. . . .** If we abstract from the user of the language and analyze only the expressions and their designata, we are in the field of **semantics.** And if, finally, we abstract from the designata also and analyze only the relations between the expressions, we are in (logical) **syntax.** The whole science . . . is called **semiotic."** *Descriptive semantics* is the study of historical languages; *pure semantics* is the construction and analysis of semantic systems. *Pure syntax* deals similarly with syntactical systems. Carnap's study is concerned with pure semantics and pure syntax; further, it is limited to declarative statements. His four chapters beyond the introductory one are addressed to the construction of semantical systems, the consideration of the semantics of logical truth, pure syntax, and finally the relation of semantics and syntax. After describing aims and principles within each section, Carnap usually gives precise definitions in the notation of formal logic and develops theorems from these. This material, impossible to reproduce in a brief review, comprises much of the wealth of the work. It may be remarked that while the work is an original contribution and not a textbook, it should be beneficial collateral reading for the beginning student of formal logic. The separation of semantical problems from logical ones enables one to deal precisely with questions concerning the foundations of logic.

The definition Carnap offers for "semantical system" stems from logical positivism. "By a **semantical system** (or interpreted system) we understand a system of rules, formulated in a metalanguage and referring to an object language, of such a kind that the rules determine a **truth-condition** for every sentence of the object language, i.e. a sufficient and necessary condition for its truth. In this way the sentences are *interpreted* by the rules, i.e. made understandable, because to understand a sentence, to know what is asserted by it, is the same as to know under what conditions it would be true. To formulate it in still another way: the rules determine the *meaning* or *sense* of the sentences." As a consequence of such a presupposition, the theory of truth and the theory of logical deduction depend on semantic considerations and belong to semantics.

To construct a semantical system, first a classification of its signs is given; then follow rules for the formation of its sentences, rules of designation, and finally rules of truth. Carnap offers several examples of semantical systems so constructed. The chief aim of each is the definition of what "true" means in the particular system; the rules are steps toward this result. The word "true" is used in the "semantical" sense described by the logician Tarski. That is, to assert that a sentence is true means the same thing as to assert the sentence itself. In pragmatics the two assertions may have different intents, emphasis, or effects, but in semantics such considerations are unnecessary. Rather, it is convenient to adopt the semantic conception of truth to enable ready passage from level to level, for example from metalanguage to object language. The semantic "definition" is not a definition of truth, but a criterion of the *adequacy* (accord with our intentions) of a predicate for the concept of truth within a given system. "True" thus becomes a predicate applicable by the rules of a system to sentences of the system. While practical considerations usually govern even the arbitrary language we devise, as well as the natural languages, the view of truth is divorced from that of verifiable belief. In pure semantics the conditions of the truth of sentences in a system need not be found outside the system but must be provided within it. The truth-tables often used in calculi to show the relations among sentences are semantical **rules stipulating** truth-conditions. From the radical concept of truth other usual radical concepts may be defined: "false," "implicate," "equivalent," and so on. Some concepts which are "absolute"—that is, not dependent on language—can then be introduced by showing to what kind of formations they correctly apply. In systems containing variables, rules of determination are required, to show which entities are determined by expressions with free variables and which attributes are determined by sentential functions.

Designation is a relation between an expression and another object; when the expression is a sentence and is true, it designates a proposition determined by the sentence. The terms of the sentence may be said to designate individuals, attributes, or relations. This conception of designation is made for convenience to extend the usual understanding of the word.

Carnap devotes a chapter to problems of logical truth. This branch of the inquiry he terms "L-semantics"; for example, logical truth is called "L-truth." The L-concepts are contrasted with the C-concepts, those pertaining to a calculus, and the F-concepts, those pertaining to empirical fact. The L-terms apply whenever the corresponding radical term applies for solely logical rather than factual reasons. For example, a sentence is L-true if it is true by reason of being a tautology —that is, true because of its logical structure as determined by semantical rules. The full meaning of the L-concepts is contained only in definitions of them. Carnap sets up a set of postulates and their derived theorems in order to lay grounds for the desired definitions. The need for this system is provisional, however, and

the system is replaced later by a method of developing the definitions in which postulates are not necessary. That the term for L-truth will apply when for logical reasons the radical term applies is at first seen as following from the semantical rules of the system in question. This understanding may be broadened, taking the metalanguage into account, by adding that a predicate for L-truth is adequate when it applies to a sentence in an object language and when the sentence in the metalanguage stating that it is true is itself L-true. To define a concept of L-truth with adequacy for general semantics rather than for a particular system remains still to be accomplished.

Concepts which do not depend upon reference to semantical systems are absolute concepts. The terms for them may be applied to the designata of expressions (rather than to the expressions, in which case the terms are L-terms). The designata of sentences are propositions. Carnap recognizes that the nature of propositions is controversial. There are two general usages: (1) a proposition is simply a declarative sentence; (2) a proposition is that which is expressed by a declarative sentence. Although in "Foundations of Logic and Mathematics" (1939), Carnap had used the first sense, in *Introduction to Semantics* he confines himself to the second. However, even upon eliminating the first sense there remains some controversy as to what propositions are and whether they are the "meanings" of sentences. Carnap makes a beginning of a general theory of propositions, and to do so he introduces the important ideas of L-state and L-range. An L-state with respect to a given semantical system is a possible state of affairs dealt with in that

1077

system with respect to all properties and relations dealt with in the system. Thus, an L-state is a proposition, something designated by a sentence (or a collection of propositions designated by one or a collection of sentences). The class of possible L-states admitted by a given sentence in the system is the L-range of that sentence. The basic premise mentioned earlier is seen again here. If we understand a sentence, we know what possible cases it admits; hence, semantical rules determine under what conditions the sentence is true, and factual knowledge is not required.

The concept of L-state may be broadened to include sentential classes as well as single sentences. Carnap develops methods for definite L-range in nonextensional systems and analogous concepts for systems with an extensional metalanguage.

Having expounded in detail the concepts of L-range and L-state, Carnap proceeds to develop from them, without the use of postulates, a general semantical system. First using as the primitive term the L-range of a sentence, he defines the universal L-range and the null L-range. Through these, respectively, he defines L-truth and L-falsity, as well as L-equivalence, L-disjunction, L-exclusion, and L-nonequivalence. Then, upon introducing the second primitive, the real L-state, he develops definitions of the radical concepts of truth, falsity, implication, equivalence, disjunction, and exclusion.

Not all sentences are tautologous; that is, L-true or the opposite. Those to which the radical term ("true" or "false") but not the L-term ("L-true" or "L-false") apply are *factual* sentences (traditionally, synthetic as op-posed to analytic). To determine their truth-value, factual knowledge is needed. To these we may apply F-terms, standing for F-concepts, generated from the pertinent radical concepts.

A final L-concept is that of L-content. When Carnap analyzes the concept *content* of a sentence as meaning "something like the strength or assertive power of a sentence," he notes that we commonly say that the content of one sentence is included within that of another. He expresses this in two postulates linking the content of such sentences with the relation of L-implication. It becomes evident that the relation of inclusion among L-contents is always inverse to that among L-ranges. That is, the L-content of a sentence is all that is dealt with by a system but excluded by that sentence. The assertive power of sentences resides in the power of a sentence to exclude cases, leaving a much narrower set of cases (its L-range) which may actually obtain.

Syntax, which Carnap finds in this volume to be founded on semantics, is the theory of syntactical systems or calculi. To construct a calculus, there are required a classification of the signs, rules of formation of sentences, and rules of deduction consisting, first, of a collection of primitive sentences and, second, of rules of inference. The calculus may optionally contain rules of refutation, and definitions. Carnap provides some sample calculi, together with descriptions in the metalanguage of their relations to one another and ways of passing back and forth among calculi. Definitions in *general syntax* of the terms "proof in a given calculus" and "derivation in a given calculus" give the explanations of the procedures of calculi of ordinary kinds. C-concepts and C-terms are elicited from the radical terms in a manner considerably analogous to that for the L-concepts and L-terms. In an appendix, Carnap comments on differences in the discussions of syntax in this book and in his earlier work, *The Logical Syntax of Language* (1934), differences arising out of the fact that in the later work he came to assign the foundation of syntax to semantics, whereas previously he had regarded it as complete in itself. The field of theoretical philosophy may even extend to pragmatics, he suggests.

A semantical system which contains all the sentences of a calculus is an *interpretation* of that calculus, and through its truth-conditions the sentences of the calculus may be interpreted. If, furthermore, all the C-concepts of the calculus are in agreement with the radical concepts of the semantic system, then that system is a *true* interpretation of the calculus; otherwise it is a *false* interpretation. Again, if the radical concepts apply correspondingly to the C-concepts by reason of logic alone, not fact, the semantical system is an *L-true* interpretation. Conversely, when a system is a true interpretation for a calculus, the calculus is said to be *in accordance with* the system; and when C-concepts coincide with the radical concepts (or the L-concepts) of the semantical system, the calculus is said to be an *exhaustive* calculus for (or an L-exhaustive calculus for) that system.

Two reservations must be held in mind in treating *Introduction to Semantics* as a contribution to philosophy. One is that it is a first volume of a series, providing the beginning points but not the complete developments of theories which have been projected for later volumes of the series. The second is that the author himself draws our attention to the fact that the book is a first attempt at setting forth the semantical principles required by logic and science; he often identifies for us problems for which satisfactory solutions are not yet completed. For example, the problems of defining L-truth and the other L-concepts for systems in general rather than particular systems, and of defining logical and descriptive signs distinctively, are yet unsolved. And in addition, some of the author's methods or assertions are under challenge; for instance, the question has been raised as to whether propositions are the designata of sentences, or whether sense or connotation are to be considered necessary concepts of semantics. *Introduction to Semantics* is, nevertheless, a central book in the field of semantics because the claims it makes are both so broad and so novel that their potential fruitfulness is not readily evident; and it deserves a long period of trial and consideration.

BEING AND NOTHINGNESS

Author: Jean-Paul Sartre (1905-   )
Type of work: Existential metaphysics
First published: 1943

Being is never exhausted by any of its phenomenal aspects; no particular perspective reveals the entire character of being.

Being-in-itself (en-soi) is fixed, complete, wholly given, absolutely contingent, with no reason for its being; it is roughly equivalent to the inert world of objects and things.

Being-for-itself (pour-soi) is incomplete, fluid, indeterminate; it corresponds to the being of human consciousness.

Being-in-itself is prior to being-for-itself; the latter is dependent upon the former for its origin; being-for-itself is derived from being-in-itself by an act of nihilation, for being-for-itself is a nothingness in the heart of being.

Freedom is the nature of man; in anxiety man becomes aware of his freedom, knows himself responsible for his own being by commitment, seeks the impossible reunion with being-in-itself, and in despair knows himself forever at odds with the "others" who by their glances can threaten a man, turning him into a mere object.

The subtitle of *Being and Nothingness, An Essay on Phenomenological Ontology,* states clearly the central intention of the author. Jean-Paul Sartre is at one with Parmenides and Plato in his contention that the chief problem of philosophy is the problem of being. Significant differences, however, emerge in a comparison of the ontological investigations of the ancient Greeks with those of the contemporary Frenchman. The adjective, "phenomenological," in the subtitle of Sartre's classic, indicates one of these significant differences.

Sartre's ontology is an ontology that follows in the wake of Immanuel Kant's critical philosophy, Edmund Husserl's phenomenological reduction, and Martin Heidegger's ontology of *Dasein. Being and Nothingness* has all of the Kantian reservations about any philosophy which seeks to proceed beyond the limits of possible experience, draws heavily from the phenomenological investigations of Husserl, and exhibits basically the same form of analysis and description as was used in

Heidegger's *Being and Time* (1927). Nonetheless, Kant, Husserl, and Heidegger intermittently throughout the work fall under some rather trenchant Sartrian criticism. Kant's chief mistake was his appeal to a "thing-in-itself" which somehow stands behind the phenomena. In Sartre's phenomenological ontology there is nothing concealed behind the phenomena or the appearances. The appearances embody full reality. They are indicative of themselves and refer to nothing but themselves. The Kantian dualism of phenomena and noumena, appearance and reality, is abolished, and being is made coextensive with phenomena. Husserl comes in for a similar criticism. His hypothesis of a transcendental ego is pronounced useless and disastrous. The fate of such a view, according to Sartre, is shipwreck on the "reef of solipsism." The faults of Heidegger are not as grievous as those of Kant and Husserl. As becomes apparent on every page of *Being and Nothingness,* Sartre's analysis is markedly informed by Heideggerian concepts. Yet Heidegger, argues the author, neglects the phenomenon of the lived body, has no explanation for the concrete relatedness of selves, and misinterprets the existential significance of death.

Being, in Sartre's analysis, evinces a *transphenomenal* character. Although there is no *noumena* and no *thing-in-itself* which lies concealed behind the phenomenal appearances of being, being is never exhausted in any of its particular phenomenal aspects. Being, in the totality of its aspects and manifestations, never becomes wholly translucent to consciousness. Everything which has being "overflows" whatever particular categories, designations, and descriptions human knowledge may attach to it. Being evinces relationships and qualities which escape any specific determination. Although being is reduced to the whole of its phenomenal manifestations, it is in no way exhausted by any *particular* perspective that man has of the phenomena. All phenomena overflow themselves, suggesting other phenomena yet to be disclosed. This primordial being, transphenomenal in character, expresses a fundamental rupture into "being-in-it-itself" (*en-soi*) and "being-for-itself" (*pour-soi*).

Being-in-itself designates being in the mode of fullness or plenitude. It is massive, fixed, complete in itself, totally and wholly given. It is devoid of potency and becoming, roughly equivalent to the inert world of objects and things. It has no inside and no outside. It expresses neither a relationship with itself nor a relationship to anything outside itself. It is further characterized by an absolute contingency. There is no reason for its being. It is superfluous (*de trop*). "Un-

created, without reason for being, without connection with any other being, being-in-itself is superfluous for all eternity."

Being-for-itself is fluid and vacuous rather than fixed and full. It is characterized by incompleteness, potency, and lack of determinate structure. As being-in-itself is roughly equivalent to the inert and solidified world of objectivized reality, so being-for-itself generally corresponds to the being of human consciousness. These two modes of being, however, are not granted an equal ontological status. Being-in-itself is both logically and ontologically prior to being-for-itself. The latter is dependent upon the former for its origin. Being-for-itself is inconceivable without being-in-itself and is derived from it through an original nihilation (*néantisation*). Being-for-itself thus constitutes a nihilation of being-in-itself. Being-for-itself makes its appearance as a nothingness which "lies coiled in the heart of being—like a worm." The being of the for-itself is a "borrowed" being which emerges from the in-itself by virtue of its power of negation. The source of the power of nothingness remains inexplicable and mysterious. The for-it-self simply finds itself *there*, separated and at a distance from the absolute fullness of the in-itself. The for-itself emerges as an irreducible and ultimate datum.

One of the fateful consequences of the primordial rupture of the for-it-self from the in-itself is the introduction of nothingness. Sartre makes it clear that it is through man or human consciousness that nothingness comes into the world. In his discussion on nothingness Sartre is intent upon rejecting the Hegelian dialectical approach and substituting for it a phenomenological account. For Hegel, being and nothingness are dialectical concepts which take their rise from the same ontological level of mediated reality. Sartre maintains in his phenomenological approach that nothingness is dependent upon being in a way that being is not dependent upon nothingness. Nothingness is not an abstract idea complementary to being, nor can it be conceived outside of being; it must be given at the heart of being. Nothingness demands a host, possessing the plenitude and full positivity of being, from which it borrows its power of nihilation. Thus, nothingness has only a borrowed or marginal being. Although Sartre never acknowledges his debt to Augustine on this point, his analysis seems to draw heavily from Augustinian sources. Augustine had already described evil as a tendency toward nothingness, the movement presupposing perfect being as a host in which evil exists as a privation of the good. It would indeed seem that in its basic outlines Sartre's analysis of nothingness is little more than a secularized Augustinianism. The introduction of nothingness raises the question of its relation to negative judgments.

As Heidegger had done before him, Sartre insists that nothingness is the origin and foundation of negative judgments, rather than vice versa. This foundation finds its clarification in the context of human expectations and projects. Sartre, as an example, tells of expecting to find a person (Pierre) in a café when in fact he is not present: my expectation of finding Pierre has caused the absence of Pierre to happen as a real event pertaining to the café. I discover his absence as an objective fact. I look for him and find that he is not there, thus disclosing a synthetic relation between Pierre and the setting in which I have expected him to be. There obtains a *real* relation between Pierre and the café, as distinct from the relation of *not-being* which characterizes the order of thought in simple negative judgments. To make the negative judgment that Pierre is not in the café has purely abstract meaning. It is without real or efficacious foundation.

We have observed that it is through man that nothingness comes into the world. The question then arises: what is it about the being of man that occasions nothingness? The answer is: freedom. The freedom which is here revealed should in no way be identified with a property or a quality which somehow attaches to man's original nature. Freedom *is* the "nature" of man. There is no difference between the being of man and his being-free. As becomes apparent later in *Being and Nothingness,* Sartre's ontology of man is a philosophy of radical and total freedom. This consciousness of freedom is disclosed in anxiety. "It is in anxiety that man gets the consciousness of his freedom, or if you prefer, anxiety is the mode of being of freedom as consciousness of being; it is in anxiety that freedom is, in its being, in question of itself." There is thus an internal connection among nothingness, freedom, and anxiety. These are interrelated structural determinants of the being of man.

Nothingness, freedom, and anxiety provide the conditions which make possible the movement of "bad faith" (*mauvaise foi*). Bad faith is a form of self-deception which in making use of freedom denies it. Bad faith is akin to lying, yet not identical with it.

In lying one hides the truth from others. In bad faith one hides the truth from oneself. In the former there is a duality of deceiver and deceived; in the latter there is a unity of a single consciousness. Bad faith does not come from the outside. Consciousness affects itself with it. In describing the pattern of bad faith Sartre develops the example of a woman who consents to go out with an amorous suitor. She is fully aware of his intentions and knows that sooner or later she will have to make a decision. An immediate decision is demanded when he caresses her hand. If she leaves her hand there she encourages his advances; if she withdraws it she may well preclude any future relationship with the suitor. She must decide, but she seeks means for postponing the decision. It is at this point that bad faith comes into play. She leaves her hand in his, but does not notice that she is doing so. She becomes all intellect, divorces her soul from her body, and transforms her body into an object or thing —into the mode of "being-in-itself." Her hand becomes "a thing," neither consenting nor resisting. She objectivizes her body, and ultimately herself, as in-itself, and thus stages a flight or an escape from herself as for-itself. She loses her subjectivity, her freedom, and her responsibility for decision. She exists in bad faith.

The pursuit of being leads to an awareness of nothingness, nothingness to an awareness of freedom, freedom to bad faith, and bad faith to the being of consciousness which provides the condition for its possibility. We are thus led to an interrogation of the immediate structures of the for-itself as consciousness. The immediate consciousness in which the self experiences presence is what Sartre calls the nonpositional consciousness. This consciousness characterizes the level of primitive awareness, and is prior to the positional consciousness which is the reflective consciousness of the intentional action. Nonpositional consciousness is pre-reflective; therefore, Sartre describes it as a pre-reflective cogito (*cogito pre-reflexif*). This pre-reflective cogito quite clearly precedes the Cartesian cogito, which is a movement of reflection, and becomes the foundation for it. Positional consciousness, on the other hand, is reflective in character, directed toward some intentional object. Sartre has taken over Husserl's doctrine of intentionality and has made it central to his description of the positional consciousness. Positional consciousness is always consciousness *of* something. It is directed outward into a *world*. But the positional consciousness can also be directed reflexively upon itself. Consciousness can become conscious of itself as being conscious. It is in this way that the ego or the self is posited or derived. Both the world and the ego or self are posited by the projecting activity of the for-itself in its nonpositional freedom, and they become correlative phenomena inextricably bound up at their very source. Without the world there is no ego, and without the ego there is no world. Both the world and the ego are hypostatized through reflection as unifying, ideal limits.

One of the central structural elements of the for-itself is facticity. The for-itself apprehends itself as a lack or decompression of being. It is not its own foundation. It is a "hole" in the heart of being, infected with nothingness, abandoned to a world without justification. It discovers itself thrown into a situation, buffeted by brute contingencies, for the most part superfluous and "in the way." Facticity indicates the utter contingency and irrevocable situationality of the being of the for-itself. Without facticity consciousness could choose its attachments to the world—it would be absolute and unfettered freedom. But the freedom which the for-itself experiences is always restricted by the situation in which it is abandoned. Nonetheless, the freedom of the for-itself is a *real* freedom and even in its facticity the for-itself perpetually relates itself to itself in freedom. I do not become a bourgeois or a Frenchman until I *choose* to become such. Freedom is always present, translating facticity into possibility. In the final analysis the for-itself is totally responsible for its being.

Value and possibility provide two additional structures of the for-itself. Value is an expression of an impossible striving toward a coincidence of being. The for-itself perpetually strives to surpass itself toward reunion with the in-itself, thus achieving totality by healing the fundamental rupture in being. But this totality is an impossible synthesis. As soon as the for-itself would become coincident with the in-itself it would lose itself as for-itself. A final totality remains forever unattainable because it would combine the incompatible characteristics of the in-itself (positivity and plenitude) and the for-itself (negativity and lack). The impossible striving for reunion gives rise to the unhappy or alienated consciousness. The for-itself is "sick in its being" because it is haunted by a totality which it seeks to attain but never can without losing itself as for-it-

self. "The being of human reality is suffering because it emerges in being as perpetually haunted by a totality which it is without being able to be it, since it would not be able to attain the in-itself without losing itself as for-itself. Human reality therefore is by nature an unhappy consciousness, without the possibility of surpassing its unhappy state." Now possibility, as an immediate structure of the for-itself, provides further clarification of the meaning of the for-itself as lack. The possible is what the for-itself lacks in its drive for completeness and totality. It indicates the *not yet* of human reality, the openness of its constant striving.

The structures of the for-itself are ontologically rooted in temporality, which provides their unifying ground. This temporality is understood in Sartre's phenomenological analysis as a synthesis of structured moments. The "elements" or directions of time (past, present, and future) do not constitute an infinite series of nows, or collected "givens," in which some are no longer and others are not yet. If time is understood as an infinite series of discrete nows, then the whole series is annihilated. The past nows are no longer real, the future nows are not yet real, and the present now is always slipping away, functioning only as a limit of an infinite division. In such a view time evaporates and is dissolved into an infinite "dust of instants" which are ontologically anemic. A phenomenological analysis of the time of the immediate consciousness avoids this dissolution of temporality by describing the elements of time as "structured moments of an original synthesis."

Following Heidegger, Sartre speaks of time as an *ecstatic* unity in which the past is *still* existentially real, the future *already* existentially real, and in which past and future coalesce in the present. However, Sartre differs from Heidegger in refusing to ascribe ontological priority to the future. No ecstasis of time has any priority over any of the others; none can exist without the other two. If, indeed, one is to accent any ecstasis, Sartre maintains that it would be phenomenologically closer to the facts to accent the present rather than the future. The past remains an integral part of my being. It is not something which I had or possessed at one time; it is something of which I am aware here and now. The past is always bound to my present. Man is always related to his past, but he is at the same time separated from it insofar as he engages in a constant movement from himself as past to himself as future. The past tends to become solidified and thus takes on the quality of an in-itself. It is defined as a for-itself which has become an in-itself. It takes on a character of completeness and fixity, but it still remains mine, and as long as it remains a part of my consciousness it can be recovered in an act of choice. The past provides the ontological foundation for facticity. In a very real sense the past and facticity indicate one and the same thing. The past makes possible my experience of abandonment and situationality. In contrast to the past which has become an in-itself, the present remains a full-embodied for-itself. The author defines the present as a "perpetual flight in the face of being." It exhibits a flight from the being that it was and a flight towards the being that it will be. Strictly speaking, the for-itself as present has its being outside of itself—behind it and before it.

It was its past and will be its future. The for-itself as present is not what it is (past) and is what it is not (future). The future is a mode of being which the for-itself must strive to be. As a mode of being it designates an existential quality which one *is*, rather than an abstract property which one *has*. The future is a lack which is constitutive of my subjectivity. As the past provides the foundation for facticity, so the future provides the foundation for possibility. The future constitutes the meaning of my present for-itself as a project of possibilities. The future is not a series of chronologically ordered nows which are yet to come. Rather, it is a region of my being, which circumscribes my expanding possibilities, and defines me as a for-itself who is always on the way.

The temporalized world of the for-itself is not an insulated world experienced in isolation. In the world of the for-itself the "others" (*autrui*) have already made their appearance. Hence, the being of the for-itself is always a being-for-others as well. The discussion of the problem of the interrelation of personal selves occupies a lengthy and important part of *Being and Nothingness*. The author begins with an examination and criticism of the views of Hegel, Husserl, and Heidegger, and then proceeds to a positive formulation of his own. The "other" is already disclosed in the movements of the prereflective, nonpositional consciousness. Shame affords an example of a prereflective, disclosure of the "other," as well as a disclosure of myself as standing before the other. Through shame I discover simultaneously the "other" and an aspect of my being. *I am ashamed of myself* before the "*other*." The "other" reveals myself to me. I need the "other" in order to realize fully all the structures of my being. It is thus that the structures of being-for-itself and being-for-others are inseparable.

In the phenomenon of "the look" (*le regard*) we find another example of the pre-reflective disclosure of the self and the other. It is through the look that the "other" irrupts into my world, decentralizes and dissolves it, and then by reference to his own projects reconstitutes it and the freedom which I experience. When I am "looked at" the stability of my world and the freedom which I experience as for-itself are threatened. The "other" is apprehended as one who is about to steal my world, suck me into the orbit of his concerns, and reduce me to the mode of being-in-itself—to an object or a thing. "Being-seen-by-the-other" involves becoming an object for the "other." When the movement of the look is completed I am no longer a free subject; I have fallen into the slavery of the "other." "Thus being-seen constitutes me as a being without defenses for a freedom which is not my freedom. It is in this sense that we can consider ourselves as slaves in so far as we appear to the other. But this slavery is not the result of a life in the abstract form of consciousness. I am a slave to the degree that my being is dependent at the center of a freedom which is not mine and which is the very condition of my being." It is in this way that the existence of the "other" determines my original fall—a fall which can be most generally described as a fall from myself as being-for-itself into the mode of being-in-itself. My only defense is the objectivization of the "other." Through *my* look I can seek to shatter the world of the "other" and divest him of his subjective freedom. Indeed I seek to remove the other from my world and put him out of play, but this can never succeed, because the existence of the other is a contingent and irreducible fact. I *encounter* the "other"; I do not *constitute* him. The "other" remains, threatening to counterattack my defenses with *his* look. Thus there results a constant cycle of mutual objectivization. I affirm my freedom by rendering the "other" into an object. Then the "other" affirms his freedom by rendering me into an object. Then I stage an existential counterattack, and the cycle repeats itself. According to the author there seems to be no end to this sort of thing. The upshot of all this is an irreconcilable conflict between the self and the "other," with a consequent breakdown of all communication. Alienation has the last word in Sartre's doctrine of inter-subjectivity. The reader who searches for a positive doctrine of community, searches in vain. All forms of "being-*with*" find their common denominator in an alienating "being-*for*."

In the relation of the for-itself with the "other" the body appears as a central phenomenon. The body is discussed in the context of three ontological dimensions: (1) the body as I exist it, (2) the body as utilized and known by the "other," and (3) the body as I exist it in reference to its being known by the "other." The body as I exist it is not the objectivized body constituted by nerves, glands, muscles, and organs. Such an objectivized body is present for the physician when he gives me a medical examination, but I do not apprehend my body in this way. I apprehend my body in its lived concreteness as that phenomenon which indicates my possibilities in the world. The body as *concretely lived* signifies a level of being which is fundamentally different from the body as *objectively known.* The body as concretely lived reveals an original relation to the world of immediate and practical concerns. I carry out my practical concerns through instruments or utensils.

Sartre, in the development of his concept of the world, draws heavily from Heidegger and defines the world of immediate experience as an instrumental world. Instruments refer to my body, insofar as the body apprehends and modifies the world through the use of instruments. My body and the world are thus coextensive. My body is spread out across the utensils which I use. My body is everywhere in the world. To have a body and to experience that there is a world are one and the same thing. However, not only do I exist my body, but my body is also utilized and known by the "other." This second ontological dimension indicates my body as a body-for-the-other. My body as known by the "other," and so also his body as known by me, is always a body-in-a-situation. The body of the "other" is apprehended within the movements of a situation as a synthetic totality of life and action. The isolated appendages and gestures of another's body have no significance outside the context of a situation. A clenched fist in itself means nothing. Only when the clenched fist is apprehended as an integral part of a synthetic totality of life movements is the lived body of the "other" disclosed. A corpse is no longer in a situation, and hence can be known only in its modality of death as an anatomical-physiological entity.

The third ontological dimension indicates the reappraisal of my body as a body which is known by and exists for the "other." Thus alienation enters my world. My body becomes a tool or an object for the "other." My body flows to the "other," who sucks it into the orbit of his projects and brings about the dissolution of my world. This alienation is made manifest through affective structures such as shyness. Blushing, for example, expresses the consciousness of my body not as I live it for myself, but as I live it for the "other." I cannot be embarrassed by my own body as I exist it. Only a body which exists for the "other" can become an occasion for embarrassment.

In the concrete relation of the for-itself with the "other," two sets of contradictory attitudes make their appearance. On the one hand, there are the attitudes of love and masochism, and on the other hand, the attitudes of hatred and sadism. In the love relationship the beloved is for the lover not simply a thing which he desires to possess. The analogy of ownership breaks down in an explanation of love. Love expresses a special kind of appropriation. The lover wants to assimilate the love of the beloved without destroying his or her freedom. But this relationship of love ultimately founders because it is impossible to maintain an absolute subjectivity or freedom without objectivizing another as the material for one's freedom. This accounts for the insecurity of love. The lover is perpetually in danger of being made to appear as an object. In masochism the annihilation of subjectivity is deliberately directed inward. The masochist puts himself forward as an in-itself for the "other." He sets up conditions so that he can be assimilated by the "other"; thus, he deliberately transforms himself into an object. Hatred and sadism constitute the reverse attitude. Here there is an attempt to objectivize the "other" rather than oneself. The sadist seeks to "incarnate" the "other" by using his body as a tool. The "other" becomes an instrument in his hands and thus is depriate the freedom of the "other." But simplest form, is an attempt to appropriate the freedom of the "other." But this attempt results in failure because the "other" can always turn back upon the sadist and make an object out of him. Thus, again, the reader is made aware of the futility of all attempts to establish harmonious relations with the "other." This inability to achieve genuine communication leads to a despair in which nothing remains for the for-itself but to become involved in the circularity of objectivization in which it passes from one to the other of the two fundamental attitudes.

The author concludes his phenomenological essay with a restatement and further elucidation of the nature and quality of human freedom, and a delineation of his program of existential psychoanalysis. Freedom is discussed in relation to the will, in relation to facticity, and finally in relation to responsibility. The will can never be the condition of freedom; it is simply a psychological manifestation of it. The will presupposes the foundation of an original freedom in order to be able to constitute itself as will. The will is derived or posited by reflective decision. It is a psychological manifestation which emerges within the complex of motives and ends already posited by the for-itself. Properly speaking, it is not the will that is free. Man

is free. The will is simply a manifestation of man's primordial freedom. Freedom in relation to facticity gives rise to the situation. The situation is that ambiguous phenomenon in which it is impossible clearly to distinguish the contribution of freedom and the determinants of brute circumstance. This accounts for the paradox of freedom. There is freedom only in a situation, and there is a situation only through freedom. Sartre delineates five structures of the situation in which freedom and facticity interpenetrate each other: (1) my place, (2) my past, (3) my environment, (4) my fellow man, and (5) my death. Insofar as freedom always interpenetrates facticity, man becomes wholly responsible for himself. I am responsible for everything except for the fact of my responsibility. I am free, but I am not free to obliterate fully my freedom. I am condemned to be free. This abandonment to freedom is an expression of my facticity. Yet I must assume responsibility for the fact that my facticity is incomprehensible and contingent. The result is that my facticity or my final abandonment consists simply in the fact that I am condemned to be wholly responsible for myself. Although freedom and facticity interpenetrate, it remains incontestable that freedom is given a privileged status in the Sartrian view of man.

The touchstone of existential psychoanalysis is a concentration on man's fundamental project (*projet fondamental*). This fundamental project is neither Heidegger's *Sein-zum-Tode*, nor is it Freud's libidinal cathexis. The method of existential psychoanalysis resembles that of the Freudians in that an effort is made to work back through secondary and superficial manifestations of personality to an ultimate and primary project, but the existentialist differs with Freud concerning the nature of this project. The Freudian localizes the project in a libidinal attachment which is determined by the past history of the self. The existential psychoanalyst broadens the framework of explanation to include the future projects of the self as well. The fundamental project is thus understood in the context of man's temporalized being, which includes the ecstatic unity of past, present, and future. The irreducible minimum of this fundamental project is the *desire to be*. Quite clearly, it is impossible to advance farther than being, but in having advanced thus far one has undercut the simple empirical determinants of behavior. The goal of this desire to be is to attain the impermeability, solidity, and infinite density of the in-itself. The ideal toward which consciousness strives is to be the foundation of its own being. It strives to become an "in-itself-for-itself," an ideal which can properly be defined as God. One can thus most simply express the fundamental project of man as the desire to be God. But the idea of God is contradictory, for in striving after this ideal the self can only lose itself as for-itself. Man's fundamental desire to give birth to God results in failure. He must thus reconcile himself to the fact that his is a useless passion.

ETHICS AND LANGUAGE

Author: Charles Leslie Stevenson (1908-   )
Type of work: Ethics
First published: 1944

PRINCIPAL IDEAS ADVANCED

Ethical disagreements usually involve both disagreement in belief and disagreement in attitude, but disagreement in attitude is the distinctive element in ethical disputes.

The judgment "This is good" usually functions both as the expression of an attitude and as an injunction; it is roughly equivalent to, "I approve of this; do so as well."

Ethical judgments are justified by the submission of reasons for acting; if the reasons do not appeal to the persons to whom they are addressed, and if there is no disagreement in belief, nothing can be done by the use of reasons.

No one explanation of the function of such a word as "good" is possible; emotive meanings are not so much defined as characterized, and they vary according to the context.

"This is good," according to a second pattern of analysis, means that the object has a particular set of qualities or relations in virtue of which the speaker approves of the object; the hearer tends to be encouraged to approve also. (Such a

1089

definition is normally persuasive; it alters descriptive meanings in order to re-direct attitudes.)

Ethics and Language propounds what has been called the emotive theory of ethics, a theory often associated particularly with the logical positivists. Stevenson, however, explores an area largely ignored by those writers. Anti-positivistic readers with a predisposition to disagree, on the basis that an emotive theory as previously propounded is oversimple, may be induced to set aside this judgment upon discovering Stevenson to observe human nature with acumen and to write with sensitivity and insight. One of Stevenson's avowed purposes is to remove from the term "emotive" any derogatory emotive meaning.

The work lies across several philosophical fields. While "the emotive theory" is a theory of ethics, emotive meaning is a feature of language, studied in semantics. The bases of emotive meaning, feelings, and attitudes, are objects of psychology. And as it combines these fields, the book is in large measure actually a rhetoric, following in a distinguished tradition founded by Aristotle. Stevenson himself calls the work "no more than a prolegomenon to further inquiry" in normative ethics.

Stevenson announces two chief objectives: to clarify the meaning of ethical terms, such as "good," "right," "just," and "ought," and to characterize the general methods by which ethical judgments are justified. He first examines the nature of cases of agreement and disagreement, the situations leading to ethical judgments. Disagreement, whose components are the more readily observed, is of two kinds, disagreement in belief and disagreement in attitude toward an object. "The former is concerned with how matters are truthfully to be described and explained; the latter is concerned with how they are to be favored or disfavored, and hence with how they are to be shaped by human efforts." What one believes to be the nature of an object will go far toward determining his attitude toward it. Furthermore, what one feels toward an object will also shape his belief of what its nature is. When an ethical controversy arises, almost always there is disagreement in both belief and attitude. Its resolution requires not only factual knowledge of the things involved but also recommendations of what is to be done, as well as consequent changes in the motivational attitudes of parties who will undertake pertinent action. Attitudes therefore earn constant attention in Stevenson's work. But since attitudes *alone* are not usually the sources of ethical disagreement, matters of establishing and testing beliefs, or organizing them practically, are vital in all normative discussion, and are likewise important in this exposition.

Efforts to approach ethical judgments as analogues of scientific judgments have been misleading, for, failing to take emotive meaning into account, they treat such judgments as expressive solely of belief. Rather than confine our attention to declarative statements of belief, we should be aware of the more emotion-laden imperative mode. An ethical judgment is closely related to an imperative: "You ought to defend your country" readily becomes "Defend your country." This clue gives Stevenson the working model for the first of two proposed patterns of analysis of ethical judgments. The judgment "This is good," he claims, roughly and partially means "I approve of this; do so as well." The first clause reports an attitude; the second is a command representing the speaker's effort to direct the hearer's attitudes according to his own. The formula should remind us explicitly that "good" is used "not only in expressing beliefs about attitudes, but in strengthening, altering, and guiding the attitudes themselves."

If ethical judgments have the significance of commands, how can they be justified? By the offering of a reason to obey. This may have the form of a description of the situation the speaker desires to alter, or of the new situation he desires to bring about, so that the hearer, upon realizing how obeying would satisfy a preponderance of his desires, will take the same attitude toward the object as the speaker. People who agree in belief generally agree in attitude, since most of us attain satisfaction in about the same things. It must be acknowledged at once that on some occasions two disputants could have precisely the same beliefs about an object, yet disagree radically in attitude, the one approving, the other not. As far as Stevenson's study is concerned, this situation is left as it is. "Those . . . who want to rule out the possibility of rival moral codes, each equally well supported by reasons, will find that the present account gives them less than they want."

Ethical judgments, however, do not have such a bald form in discourse as "I approve of this; do so as well." Neither do they function simply as the command of a superior to an inferior.

Rather, they have the power of suggestion through emotive meaning, the "power that the word acquires, on account of its history in emotional situations, to evoke or directly express attitudes, as distinct from describing or designating them. In simple forms it is typical of interjections; in more complicated forms it is a contributing factor to poetry; and it has familiar manifestations in the many terms of ordinary discourse that are laudatory or derogatory."

In order to account for emotive meaning and to relate it to descriptive meaning, we must have a general theory of signs. One requirement of a good view of meaning is that according to its definition meaning must not vary in a bewildering way as emotional associations would do, depending upon the individual user and occasion. This requirement is met by adopting and developing a view of meaning as causal, on the pattern of stimulus-response, understood as complex. Even a seemingly simple instance of cause and effect such as the stimulating effect of drinking coffee is actually complex, joining together many factors of greater or less immediate or ultimate bearing on the outcome, which itself may be measured in terms of greater and less. Some of the factors are in the coffee, and some in the drinker. We say that the relevant cluster of factors in the person stimulated comprise his disposition to be stimulated by coffee. We may equally well say the coffee has a disposition to stimulate its imbibers. A disposition is realized only when its response concretely occurs along with its conrete stimulus, but for convenience we talk of dispositions existing regardless of whether they are being realized at the moment.

1091

A disposition is actually a collection of causal factors, known or unknown, involving both stimulus and response, sometimes said to "belong to" the one, sometimes the other, as a dispositional property. Some dispositions are causes of other dispositions.

The meaning of a sign, Stevenson now can say, is a dispositional property of the sign, whose response, varying with the circumstances, consists of psychological processes in a hearer stimulated by his hearing of the sign. Correspondingly, for the speaker it is the word's disposition to be used for a certain effect, the stimulus of his choosing it. *Emotive* meaning is a meaning in which the response of the hearer is a range of emotions. For *descriptive* meaning, the processes of response relate to cognition rather than emotion. Although the basis of the disposition is the psychological make-up of the hearer, it is convenient to refer still to the emotive meaning as "of" the sign just as we do its descriptive meaning. Thus it may be an abiding property of the sign rather than an aspect of individuals upon particular occasions.

Stevenson emphasizes the importance of linguistic flexibility. One and the same word may be used in different circumstances to express favor, disfavor, or indifference, having no one "real" sense present on all occasions. Rather than being able to provide a single definition of "good" or other ethical terms, he must on this account provide patterns for forming definitions of them as used in particular contexts. It is important to remember that these terms have both descriptive and emotive meaning. The patterns should serve to show when emotive meaning is dependent upon or independent of the descriptive meaning of the same term, or quasi-dependent upon indefinite or confused meanings. Emotive meanings, in fact, may need to be *characterized* rather than defined. Because of these complications, the first of Stevenson's two patterns for ethical definition is fashioned expressly to restrict severely the descriptive meaning of ethical terms. It consists simply in the employment, according to particular contexts, of working models of restatement, in the fashion after which "This is good," above, was restated.

A benefit of the first pattern is that it helps make evident the distinctness of the peculiarly moral attitudes, those usually associated with the ethical terms. Conduct morally disapproved leads to responses of indignation, mortification, or shock, or if it is one's own conduct, to guilt or bad conscience. If the conduct is merely disliked, it leads to displeasure but not of these sorts. What one simply likes brings an ordinary sort of pleasure, whereas one "may feel a particularly heightened sense of security" when something he morally approves prospers. "These differences in response, given similar stimuli, help to distinguish the attitudes which are moral from those which are not."

The first pattern also makes evident the methods one uses to support ethical judgments to which it is applied. The reasons are psychologically, not logically, related to ethical judgments, although deductive and inductive logic apply to their descriptive meanings, which express beliefs rather than attitudes. Ethical judgments are supported by such means as showing the nature of what is judged, or of its consequences, or motives that attend it, or origins of the attitude to which it testifies, and so on. Personal decisions, rising from inner conflicts of attitudes, are decided in the same ways as disagreements among individuals. Since emotive factors as reasons are connected only empirically and not in any necessary way to ethical judgments, when an ethical dispute is rooted in disagreement of belief, "it may be settled by reasoning and inquiry to whatever extent the beliefs may be so settled. But if any ethical dispute is *not* rooted in disagreement in belief, then no *reasoned* solution of any sort is possible."

Yet even in such cases of radical disagreement in belief, ethical agreement is sometimes reached, and Stevenson's study of methodology shows certain nonrational ways in which this occurs. The most important are the "persuasive" methods, in a broadened sense of that word. They use the direct emotional impact of the proponent's presentation—"emotive meaning, rhetorical cadence, apt metaphor, stentorian, stimulating, or pleading tones of voice, dramatic gestures, care in establishing *rapport* with the hearer or audience, and so on." Rational and nonrational, and indeed irrational, elements may be woven tightly together; but when we separate them by analysis, among the nonrational we may find emotive means in the supporting reasons as well as the thesis, or merely suggested elements rather than explicit ones. An appeal leading to an *Einfühlung* may bring the hearer to his own reasons for accepting the judgment. Self-persuasion exists and has its place, for persuasion is as ubiquitous as choice. The term "persuasion" has so many legitimate references that, like "emotive," it should not bear an opprobrious emotive meaning.

The question of validity of ethical judgments has often been raised. There can be nothing applying to attitudes and feelings corresponding to deductive validity or soundness of induction in the field of beliefs. Rather, determining what method to use to justify an ethical judgment is itself an ethical problem, whose outcome in turn is determined by an ethical judgment. A moralist may choose either rational or "persuasive" methods; the reasons for his choice, involving both his attitudes and his beliefs, will be as complicated as in any other case of ethical choice. The question of norms for ethical judgments is and remains a normative question. Similarly, the question of what means are to be adopted toward what ends is a normative question. Any combination of approval and disapproval of means and ends may occur. Hence, it is unwarranted for moralists to assume that they can leave the choice of means to others as long as they indicate what ends are worthy. The artificial division between intrinsic and extrinsic goods should be abandoned.

Further, A and B may both agree on the worth of X, but as a means to different ends, or one as a means and the other as an end. And one of them may approve of X both as an end and as a means to another end. Still further, what is first approved as a means may later be approved as an end, or vice versa. As our knowledge of the world increases, these interrelationships of ourselves with our objects of approval, and of other persons with their and our objects of approval, become multiplied to a great number and variety. It is therefore better to substitute the notion of a "focal aim" for "intrinsic good," as a major goal toward which one or many together may strive, for either final or mediate purposes. The whole consideration shows that a study of means is of the utmost importance to normative ethics.

According to Stevenson's second pattern of analysis, "This is good" means "This has qualities or relations X, Y, Z, . . ." and the term "good" also has "a laudatory emotive meaning which permits it to express the speaker's approval, and tends to evoke the approval of the hearer." This pattern permits rich and varied descriptive meaning (interpretations of X, Y, Z . . .) whereas the first pattern stringently restricted it. The explicit report of the speaker's attitude ("I approve of this") has dropped out, now only to be suggested. Like the first pattern, this description is to be treated as a pattern, not itself a definition, for language and contexts are various and we cannot fill in permanent interpretations of X, Y, and Z. The apparently greater "content" of the second pattern allows it to do much more justice to linguistic richness. It is useful where contrary predications of the ethical terms accompany contrary assertions about what they mean.

The definitions of the second pattern are normally *persuasive definitions*. These are definitions of a familiar terms so as to alter the term's descriptive meaning, usually making the descriptive meaning more precise while retaining its previous emotive meaning. This is done, consciously or not, to redirect people's attitudes. For instance, we change the descriptive meaning of "temperance," a term with favorable emotive meaning for our opponent, from including only abstinence, which he admires, to including moderate imbiding, which he does not. When this procedure succeeds in redirecting his attitudes to some degree, the effect is not a rational but (in Stevenson's broad sense) a persuasive one. The definition not only clarifies but *participates in* moral issues. Hence great care is needed to keep separate the linguistic and moral aspects if one's purpose (unlike that of many moral philosophers, who are both analysts and moralists) is to achieve clarity and avoid confusion.

So far as norms are concerned, it is indifferent to the outcome of an ethical dispute whether the first or second pattern is used. With the second pattern, the definition itself is persuasive immediately. On the other hand, "instead of *defining* 'good' in terms of X, Y, and Z, as in the second pattern, one may use 'good' in a first-pattern sense and simply *predicate* it of X, Y, and Z. Either procedure will be persuasive . . ." and the choice of the linguistic mechanism to achieve the effect is only incidental.

To use an emotionally-laden word as a scientific term, we must first neutralize its emotive meaning. This may be done by carefully offsetting its emotive meaning with a compensating tone in its whole context, or by balancing particular laudatory terms and derogatory terms against one another, or by giving explicit admonition that emotive effects are to be resisted.

We have noticed that persuasive definitions change the descriptive meaning of a term while retaining the emotive meaning. The corollary process may also have persuasive effect; that is, creating a new emotive meaning without changing the descriptive meaning. Since changes in emotive meaning are not ordinarily said to be new definitions. Stevenson calls this latter process "persuasive quasi-definition." Most cases of persuasive definition exhibit this process to some extent also. Another class of definitions, including typically those of logic, are "detached." They are emotively neutral, persuasive only in the fact of their being the selection for others' attention of the authorities who give them. Related to these are "re-emphatic" definitions, which redirect attention forcibly by rhetorical means, such as a paradox or surprise. Some definitions indeed are both re-emphatic and persuasive. Definitions should not be rejected out-of-hand on account of strong persuasive favor, for the emphasis may suggest useful inquiry.

Showing that the understanding of definitions is often "central to the formulation and outcome of highly important issues," Stevenson introduces as a sample the question of freedom versus determinism. The controversy belongs to ethical methodology, involving as it does the relation of judgments and their reasons. Avoidability, not indeterminism, is what is required for responsibility for an action. "A's action was avoidable" means "If A had made a certain choice, which in fact he did not make, his action would not have occurred." (This does not say A's action was not determined. Avoidability has to do not with the causes of an actual choice, but with the effects of a different choice.) We do not assign blame for unavoidable action because ethical judgments are efforts to influence future actions, and blaming unavoidable actions would not accomplish this end. But an ethical judgment of blame for a past act may serve to alter attitudes; hence, to alter both choices and subsequent action. Far from presupposing indeterminism, this

view would seem to presuppose determinism, of the relation of attitudes, choices, and action. But while permitting full determinism, it *requires* only partial determinism, and may also permit partial indeterminism. The question of indeterminism, then, is actually quite irrelevant to ethics.

In assessing the prospects of normative ethics, we may expect any writer presenting his own moral views to follow the long-existing ideal of examining both sides of a normative question and bringing to it as much knowledge as possible. "Our conclusions about how reasons *can* be used, when wedded to the above ideal, become an indispensable guide for deciding how they *should* be used." Such a writer, if he wishes to embody general unifying principles in the face of the great multiplicity of people's actual attitudes, must attend to "focal aims." He will be aware that the value of a goal depends on the still radiating consequences of it, once attained. Before reaching basic principles, he must start with specific judgments and lesser aims, using the sciences in a detailed manner, making empirical inquiry pervade his whole ethics. As far as he provides his norms with rational support, his inquiry will be confined to relevant factual conclusions about human nature and its environment. This writer will probably use persuasion to hasten the effects of his reasons, or to stimulate further inquiry, or to insure full and healthy exercise of the emotions; but these aspects of language must not be allowed to stultify the descriptive. Rather, both aspects must be made to work smoothly together, neither overstepping its prerogatives. Normative writing and discussion "must draw from the *whole* of a man's knowledge, lending themselves very poorly to specialization, and they demand a full but controlled emotional vitality." With his last remarks, Stevenson makes it evident that he himself has been consciously using persuasive language in urging his views. To reject his doctrine, it should probably be necessary to reject his early tenet that ethical experience has its being in the feelings (and is characterized by feelings of a certain sort as against others),

and that therefore the ethical meanings of sentences are subsumed under their emotive meanings rather than those aspects which communicate belief. Stevenson has done a great service in showing the consequences of this tenet. Regardless of whether his contribution is an adequate prolegomenon to the art of morals, his study of emotive meaning is of great importance to rhetoric and semantics.

AN ANALYSIS OF KNOWLEDGE AND VALUATION

Author: Clarence Irving Lewis (1883-   )
Type of work: Epistemology, philosophy of value
First published: 1946

PRINCIPAL IDEAS ADVANCED

Empirical statements, describing matters of fact, are equivalent in meaning to hypothetical statements to the effect that if one were to act in certain ways, then one would come to have experiences of a certain anticipated sort.

An empirical statement is verified by finding out whether what is presented in experience as a result of action is what one would expect.

A priori statements (statements whose truth is independent of matters of fact) are true by virtue of the meanings of their terms and the logical relations between terms.

Value statements concerning objects are empirical statements to the effect that if one were to be concerned with the objects, one would be satisfied or pleased by them; value statements expressive of the value-quality of experience do not admit of error and therefore, unlike value statements concerning objects, cannot be known to be true.

C. I. Lewis undertook an examination of basic topics in ethics in preparation for the Carus Lectures, the Seventh Series, to be delivered in 1945. But during the course of his philosophical inquiries he came to realize that problems of value take semantical priority over problems of moral rightness

and duty, and that epistemological considerations, having to do with the knowledge of values, would have to come before further reflections on value. The problem for him became the problem of determining whether knowledge of values is possible. The conclusion he reached is that such knowledge is

1096

possible. The defense of his conclusion is *An Analysis of Knowledge and Valuation.*

The book begins with a pragmatic account of knowledge. "To know," he argues at the outset, "is to apprehend the future as qualified by values which action may realize." This theory of knowledge owes its basic character to Peirce and James. Statements describing matters of fact, whatever their grammatical form, are equivalent in meaning to hypothetical statements to the effect that *if* one were to act in certain ways, *then* one would come to have experiences of the sort anticipated. A statement is verified by acting and finding out whether what one receives in the way of experience is what one expected. "For example; this wall is hard: if I should bump my head against it, it would hurt." Knowledge, action, and evaluation are connected because knowledge is understandable only in terms of action; one seeks to know in order to inform action, and one seeks to act in a manner which will be satisfactory.

But this initial account of the nature of knowledge and of the relation of knowledge to action and evaluation is merely introductory in character. Lewis considers at some length problems of meaning and of analytic truth. His objective was to establish the point that *a priori* statements (statements whose truth is independent of matters of empirical fact) are dependent for their truth value on meanings alone. This involves the rejection of the synthetic *a priori* statement, for if a statement is synthetic and not analytic, it cannot be *a priori*. Empirical, synthetic statements, on the other hand, are true or false according to facts discoverable by sense experience; their truth values

have no necessary connection with meaning and form. Since Lewis takes as his thesis the proposition that values are empirically knowable, it is relevent to his defense to consider whether other philosophers have been right who have said that the basic value and duty claims of ethics are synthetic *a priori* propositions.

Book I, then, following the two chapters of the Introduction, is devoted to "Meaning and Analytic Truth." The following book considers the most important problems relating to empirical knowledge: the bases of empirical knowledge, the nature of empirical judgments and beliefs, the justification of empirical beliefs, probability, and probable knowledge. This is a careful elaboration of the fundamental pragmatic thesis which relates empirical knowledge to predictions of sense experience.

The concluding book, Book III, presents an analysis of value, making the familiar distinction between instrumental value and intrinsic value and building up to the unifying claim that questions of value are empirical questions.

Lewis's account of value depends upon his basic assertion that values finally involve satisfaction, if not actually, at least potentially. Roughly speaking, something is valuable if it is such that under certain circumstances it will lead to someone's satisfaction. For a full understanding of various types of value judgments, one has to make distinctions of the sort Lewis clarifies—distinctions between the intrinsically good, the immediately good, the instrumentally good, and so forth. But for an understanding of the kind of defense possible for one who claims that values are empirically knowable, it is enough to realize that if value judgments can be expressed by hypothetical propositions, and if they relate to matters falling within the range of possible experience, then they are empirical judgments. To say that something is valuable is to say that *if* it were to have its effect on someone acting in regard to it, *then* it would satisfy or please him. It is possible to say even in regard to objects which are neither known to exist nor accessible to observation that some of them are worth while in that *were* they to be discovered, they would, in some way, satisfy. Thus, he writes that "the term 'valuable' is to be applied to objects and other existents solely with the meaning 'capable of conducing to satisfaction in some possible experience.'" To verify a value judgment, then, one has only to determine whether the object in question *does,* under the circumstances *satisfy* the person or persons to whom reference is implicitly or explicitly made. The immediate content of experience can be worth while in the sense that the experience may be prized for its own sake.

Considering Lewis's argument in more detail, and turning back to the Introduction, we find that Lewis considers the following criteria of knowledge to be suggested by common usage of the term "knowledge": (1) knowledge involves belief in what is true; (2) knowledge involves meaning, a reference to some matter other than the experience of knowing; (3) knowledge involves a ground, or evidence; and (4) knowledge, in the strictest sense, is certain and not merely probable to some degree. However, if one were to define the term "knowledge" so as to include all these criteria, it would be difficult to find any instances of knowledge. A certain tolerance of the diversity of meanings and uses of the term "knowledge" is called for. Lewis decides to recognize three "types of apprehension": apprehension of "directly given data of sense," such as particular feelings, aches, conscious responses to light, and the like: apprehension of the empirically verifiable; and apprehension of what is involved in the meanings of terms. But of these three types of apprehension, only the latter two are called "knowledge" by Lewis; they are, then, empirical knowledge and the knowledge of meanings (or logical knowledge, analytic knowledge). The apprehension of feelings, since it involves no claims and thus gains no cognitive victories, is not called "knowledge" because the possibility of error is absent.

The discussion of meaning and analytic truth begins with an account of the four modes of meaning: *denotation,* the class of everything actual to which a term applies; *comprehension,* the class of everything possible to which the term could apply; *signification,* the property of anything in virtue of which the term applies; and *intension* (sometimes called "connotation" by other writers), the conjunction of all other terms applicable to anything to which the given term is correctly applicable. The most interesting and controversial claim made in connection with these distinctions is that the denotation of a propositional term, such as "Mary making pies now," is the actual world characterized by the state of affairs described. Every statement attributes a state of affairs to the actual world; true statements denote the actual world, but false statements denote nothing.

Since analytic statements are "certifiable from facts of intensional meaning," and thus can be known to be true by knowing nothing more than the definitions of the terms involved, they require nothing of the world in order to be true. Lewis calls the intension of an analytic statement considered as a whole its "holophrastic meaning"; and since all analytic statements have zero intension, the holophrastic meaning of an analytic statement is its zero intension. (For Lewis, the intension of a proposition is made up of whatever the proposition entails; since an analytic proposition entails nothing, it has zero intension.) The analytic meaning of an analytic statement is its meaning considered as a complex statement; that is, it is the meaning composed of the intensions of its terms. With this distinction, together with the distinction between implicitly analytic statements and explicitly analytic statements, Lewis is able to show that analytic statements are *a priori* since they can be known to be true by appeal to logic and to definitions. Since *a priori* truths are true independently of experience, they must be true by definition of terms; they must be analytic. The classes are equivalent; the *a priori* is the analytic; consequently there are no synthetic *a priori* statements.

Lewis does not accept the view that analytic truth merely expresses linguistic usage. The point is that once meanings are determined by use, the relationships of meanings are fixed and are not subject to linguistic stipulation. He maintains that language depends upon criteria for the applications of terms; the criteria are "sense meanings," understandable in advance of application in terms of "if . . . then . . ." propositions having to do with the experiential consequences of action. The source of analytic knowledge is to be found in the relations between sense meanings. "Such knowledge, like the meanings it concerns, is essentially independent of linguistic formulation. . . ."

Although all knowledge, whether of the analytic or of the synthetic, has reference to meanings which are "sense-representable," only empirical truth is such that one can acquire knowledge of it *only* through sense presentations. Analytic truths are known by the analysis of meanings; but synthetic, or empirical, truths are known only by the sense consequences of action. Lewis distinguishes three classes of empirical statements: *Formulations of the given* element in experience (such statements are expressive and involve no judgment); *terminating judgments* of the form, "Sensory cue S being given, if action A is undertaken, then experience E will occur"; and *non-terminating judgments* which present some state of affairs as being the case (such judgments have a significance which cannot be exhausted by any limited set of terminating judgments).

Lewis argues that perceptual knowledge involves two phases: the giving of some sense datum or complex of data, "qualia," and the interpretation of the given. Interpretation is a function of past experience, and makes empirical belief or knowledge possible. If one expects a particular kind of experience to follow a particular kind of action, the perceptual judgment is terminating; if one states an objective state of affairs, the judgment is non-terminating, for there is no end to the ways in which, by action, one could confirm to some degree the objective claim. Objective beliefs, then, are never more than probably true. (Along the way there is an interesting discussion of the if-then relation in terminating judgments; the relation, Lewis claims, is neither material implication nor formal implication.)

In order to handle the question "In what sense can what is presently uncertain be called knowledge?" Lewis considers the meaning of "probability." The discussion is careful and involved but its point is fairly clear. According to Lewis, probability theory which attempts to make relative frequencies the final criterion of validity is intrinsically circular. Not the frequencies themselves, but "valid estimates" of frequences, based on data, are the essential factors in probability judgments.

Passing on to a consideration of the justification of empirical judgments, Lewis argues that a body of empirical beliefs made up of beliefs which, considered singly, are of little weight, may nevertheless have considerable weight of probability as a result of the "congruence" of the beliefs. Congruence is described as a relationship somewhat stronger than consistency, and in Lewis's epistemology it takes precedence over coherency, the favorite of the idealists. *"A set of statements, or a set of supposed facts asserted, will be said to be congruent if and only if they are so related that the antecedent probability of any one of them will be increased if the remainder of the set can be assumed as given premises."* If present memory can be trusted to afford some reason for counting on what is presumably remembered—and it is reasonable to assume that memory provides some evidential weight—then memory, together with the congruency of particular items of evidence, provides all that we need to make empirical knowledge of probabilities possible. The

skeptic's reluctance to concede the reality of the objective world is a sign of a stultifying temperament with which Lewis has little sympathy.

Lewis's studies of meaning and empirical knowledge have prepared the way for the claims and arguments of Book III, "Valuation." "Evaluations are a form of empirical knowledge," he argues, and goes on to distinguish between "direct findings of value-quality in what is presented," the predictions of "a goodness or badness which will be disclosed in experience under certain circumstances and on particular occasions," and the evaluations of things, "appraisals of their potentialities for good or ill." The first—the direct findings of value-quality in experience—does not involve judgment. An expression of value found in experience is true or false, since lying is possible, but no judgment is involved since no predictions are made and one simply finds that the quality of experience is appealing or it is not. The second— the prediction that experience will have value if certain action is undertaken: "If I touch what is before me, I shall enjoy it"—involves terminating judgments, capable of verification and of being known to be true. The most frequent kind of evaluation is the third —ascribing value to objects—and, as with any ascription of properties to objects, this form of judgment involves nonterminating judgments and is, consequently, never completely confirmable. But in regard to this third kind of evaluation, it is possible to acquire knowledge of probabilities, and such judgments, whether we know for certain that they are true, are either true or false.

For Lewis, then, the goodness of any good object *"consists in the possibility* of [its] *leading to some realization of directly experienced goodness.*" The experience of goodness is simply the realization of some experience as being such that one likes it or, as is often said, "enjoys" it. Immediately realized values are described by Lewis as "subjective" when the prizing by the subject, the person, is a function more of his personality than it is of the quality of the experience. When the opposite is the case, the value is "objective," even though it is the value of an experience.

Immediate values are characterized as "intrinsic"; the values of objects are "extrinsic" or instrumental. When the object is such that in the presence of the object one realizes the value-quality of experience to which the object is conducive, the object is said to be "inherently" valuable. A beautiful object, for example, has inherent value because in contemplation of it a pleasant experience is realized; the experience itself is immediately, or intrinsically, valuable.

Developing his ideas of the aesthetic, Lewis argues that the object of aesthetic contemplation is what he calls "an aesthetic essence," contingent upon context and not merely subjective, a complexus of properties forming some kind of "configurational whole."

In commenting on the moral sense and contributory values, Lewis suggests that the life which serves as the norm in the activity of moral choice is the good life, a life in which individual experiences contribute, in virtue of their value-quality, to the worth of life as a whole. Choice is made on the basis of probabilities, and evidence as to the likelihood of achieving what one seeks through action is relative to past experience as remembered.

In the closing chapter, "Value in Objects," Lewis stresses a point which his analysis of empirical knowledge makes clear. A value property, like other empirical properties, need not be realized in order to be; something can be good in the sense that *were* it to affect someone, it *would* lead to satisfaction. He clears up various possible misconceptions: the fact that values are relative to circumstances and persons does not mean that they are subjective; the fact that a value is subjective does not entail that it is not genuine; the fact that something is of value to a person does not entail that it is objectively valuable (except as an object of his interest); and there are not simply one but several modes of value predication.

The closing remarks make the point that although determination of values is necessary to the application of ethical principles, it is not sufficient. Although valuation is always a matter of empirical knowledge, what is right and just cannot be decided by reference to empirical facts alone.

Lewis's presentation of important problems of meaning, knowledge, and value is both clear and convincing. Although he confines his attention to the empirical function of value terms, limiting his consideration of the expressive function to those occasions upon which one reports the value-quality of experience as immediately prized, his analysis stands as a credible addition to the literature of value theory. The fact that an analysis of this sort is possible and is able to withstand criticism across the years can serve to support the claim that value utterances are not always and exclusively the emotive expressions of attitudes.

SIGNS, LANGUAGE AND BEHAVIOR

Author: Charles W. Morris (1901-   )
Type of work: Semiotic
First published: 1946

PRINCIPAL IDEAS ADVANCED

The study of signs (semiotic) is facilitated by the invention of a more useful vocabulary for discussing signs and sign-functioning.

The behavioristic approach to semiotic is adapted because it is more precise, interpersonal, and unambiguous than the appeal to the "mental."

When something controls the behavior of an organism in the process of satisfying a need in a way in which the actual object needed would have controlled the organism, it is a sign.

A symbol is a sign produced by its interpreter which acts as a substitute for a synonymous sign.

Among the conditions which must be met if a language is to constituted by signs are the following: The signs must have common and constant signification, and they must be combinable.

Signs are used informatively, valuatively, incitively, and systematically.

Pragmatics is the study of the uses of signs, semantics is the study of the meanings of signs, and syntactics is the study of the modes of combining signs.

The publication of *The Meaning of Meaning* (1923), by C. K. Ogden and I. A. Richards, was only one indication of a rapidly increasing interest in the nature and role of signs in human and animal behavior. Studies appeared in such diverse areas as psychology, psychiatry, social science, linguistics, aesthetics, and logic. While there was unanimity in the conception of the problem involved, namely, the problem of what linguistic and nonlinguistic signs are and how they control and are controlled by human beings, there was no unity in the terminology in which such discussions were carried on. Words like "sign," "symbol," "meaning," "reference," "denotation," "connotation," and "expression" were used in almost as many ways as there were authors who used them. There was little evidence that the writers were examining essentially the same problem. The source material was distributed over so wide an area and the authors employed so diverse a terminology that coöperative effort was virtually impossible.

Morris attempted to remedy this situation by inventing a new vocabulary in which all of the basic terms used in discussing signs and sign-functioning are more or less precisely defined. His task, in some cases, involved taking over old words and giving them new and more precise meanings; but in the great majority of cases it required, as the reader will soon discover, devising new words to characterize heretofore unrecognized aspects of the sign-situation or aspects which had been recognized but had been named in such a variety of ways by different investigators that essential agreements in point of view had been more or less completely covered up. Morris is clearly aware of the fact that what he is presenting is simply a series of proposals; indeed, since his definitions are simply *stipulative* in character (let *"x"* mean such-and-such) rather than *legislative* (*"x" does* or *ought to* mean such-and-such), no one can reasonably object to what he has done. Whether such a term as "lansign-system," which he uses as substantially equivalent to "language," is or is not actually equivalent to it, is not his concern, and must be determined by the examination of actual languages; and whether his definition of "logic" in terms of analytic formative ascriptors would be accepted by logicians or authors of dictionaries in no way affects either the internal consistency of his scheme or its applicability to signs and sign-function as they exhibit themselves in our experience. He conceives his job to be simply one of examining the very complex situations in which signs occur, discriminating the various phases and aspects, hitherto either overlooked entirely or only confusedly recognized in these situations, and devising a terminology by which they can be accurately designated in such a way as to make coöperative study possible.

Of the possible approaches to the study of signs (semiotic) he chooses one—the behavioristic approach. This is based on his conviction that although the science of behavior (behavioristics) has not yet developed to the point where it can adequately explain either the more complex human actions or the signs which they employ, the only alternative, the "mentalistic" approach, is at a much greater disadvantage. The question is simply one of method, and reduces to the problem of whether such terms as "stimulus," "response-sequence," and "disposition to respond" are not, on the whole, much more precise, interpersonal, and unambiguous than such terms as "idea," "thought," and "mind." Morris makes it quite clear that he does not deny that such a term as "consciousness" is meaningful, nor that an individual can observe his feelings, or his thoughts, or his dreams in a way which is not possible to other individuals. He is therefore not taking sides on the metaphysical issue as to whether people have minds. He is simply recognizing that sign-functioning does occur in the case of animals, where mind in the usual sense of the word is undetectable, and that in studying this mode of sign operation we can learn much about the role of signs in human behavior.

Having adopted this approach to the study of signs, Morris begins by analyzing a case of animal behavior and a case of human behavior, both of which are instances of sign-behavior. A dog that goes to a certain place where food is seen or smelled is trained to go to this same place when a buzzer is sounded, even though the food is not seen or smelled. A person who is driving along a highway is stopped by another person who tells him that the road beyond is blocked by a landslide, and the driver turns off on a side-road and takes another route to his destination. In both cases something (the buzzer, the words of the informant) controls the behavior of an organism in the satisfaction of a need (hunger, desire to arrive at destination) in a way which is roughly similar to the way in which the object (actual food, actual landslide) would modify his behavior. Both are cases of goal-seeking behavior. Whatever exercises this type of control in such behavior is a *sign*, and the behavior which is thus exhibited is *sign-behavior*.

Important to this conception of sign-behavior is the notion that "sign" is defined not in terms of an actual response of the organism, but in terms of a "disposition to respond." This is described as a state of the organism which is such that under certain additional conditions the response *does* take place. The existence of this state in the organism is part of its goal-seeking behavior. But how shall we determine that an organism is *disposed* to act? Ideally, of course, by making the conditions available and showing that the organism *does* act. Another way is to define the response in terms of a wide *class* of responses (behavior-family) any one of which would constitute an instance of the disposition. Or we could introduce *partial* responses which are segments of the total response. Or we could define the response of the organism hypothetically, say, in terms of brain waves which have not yet been measured but may someday be recorded. Or we might, in the case of human beings, simply ask them whether the stimulus is a sign which produces the required disposition.

We are now ready to define the basis terms of semiotic. The organism for which something is a sign is called an *interpreter*. The disposition to respond in some way which is a member of a behavior-family is called an *interpretant*. That which would permit the termination of the responses to which the interpreter is disposed is called a *denotatum*, and the set of conditions satisfied by a denotatum terminating the responses is called a *significatum*. Thus in the case of the dog, the buzzer is the sign, the dog is the interpreter, the disposition to seek food in a specific way is the interpretant, the actual food in the proper place is the denotatum, and the condition of being an edible object of a certain kind in a certain place is the significatum. Other terms, such as *sign-vehicle, unisituational* and *plurisituational signs, vague signs, unambiguous* and *ambiguous signs,* and many others are defined by Morris. One distinction which he makes—that between *sign* and *symbol*—is important for his general thesis. A *symbol* is defined as "a sign produced by its interpreter which acts as a substitute for some other sign with which it is synonymous." Signs which are not so produced are called *signals*. It is clear from this that symbols are more autonomous and conventional than signals, for they may be created at will by interpreters, and they commonly vary considerably from interpreter to interpreter.

Morris now states the conditions under which signs constitute a language. He specifies five criteria. (1) A language consists of a plurality of signs. (2) Each sign has a signification common to a plurality of interpreters. (3) The signs constituting a language must be producible and have the same signification to the producers that they have to other interpreters. (4) The signs must have a relative constancy of signification in all situations in which they occur. (5) Signs in a language must be combinable in certain ways so as to form complex signs. Signs which possess these properties are to be called *lansigns* and a system of such signs a *lansign-system*. Whether any actual language possesses these characteristics and is therefore to be called a "lansign-system" is a matter to be decided by actual examination of the language in question.

After examining further the social role of signs, and the way in which the human use of signs may be differentiated from the animal use, Morris examines the very important problem of the modes of signifying. This problem takes its origin in current attempts to distinguish between cognitive and noncognitive signs, referential and expressive signs, referential and evocative signs, cognitive and instrumental signs, and many others. Illustrations of the problem are found in the need for distinguishing from one another such sentences as these: "What a fine fellow he is!" "Keep the wind ahead!" "There is a deer." Morris reduces the problem to its simplest terms by indicating three major factors which exhibit themselves in sign-behavior. These correspond, respectively, to the environment, the relevance of this environment to the needs of the organism, and the ways in which the organism must act upon the environment in order to satisfy its needs. The three parallel components of the sign-situation may be called the *designative,* the *appraisive,* and the *prescriptive* components. In the case of the blocked road situation the informant may designate the condition of the road, may appraise it as preventing further progress, and may prescribe that the man discontinue driving toward his destination. All sign-behavior contains components of these three kinds, but their relative importance varies from situation to situation. In sign-situations which are genetically early in the development of the organism, the components are not sharply distinguished; in symbol-situations, and especially in situations which employ language symbols, the differentiation becomes sharp. The word "deer" may be purely designative. But if we speak of a "fine deer" we are using language appraisively. And if we say that when hunting a deer we should approach it against the wind, we are using language prescriptively. What may be signified in a sign-situation is determined by the various dispositions to respond, and our ability to distinguish these forms of behavior-response is a measure of our ability to identify the modes of signifying.

The actual elements in the sign-situation which function in these different ways may be called the *designators* the *appraisors,* and the *prescriptors.* In addition to these there are the *indicators,* which are distinguished from the designators in that they direct responses to a certain spatial-temporal region. These all influence the behavior of the interpreter in different ways, and may be called *ascriptors.* They answer the questions of where what is signified is to be found, what characteristics it possesses, why it is relevant to the interpreter, and how he should respond to it. They may therefore be called "where," "what," "why," and "how," signs.

A special type of ascriptor, whose role in sign-behavior is difficult to explain, is the *formative ascriptor.* Signs of this type are best illustrated in language systems, and Morris exemplifies them by "or," "not," "some," "is," "plus," "five," variables, word order, suffixes, parts of speech, grammatical structure, punctuation devices, and the like. Whether these are properly to be called "signs" may be debated. Morris believes that since they do modify behavior-responses they should be so characterized, though this involves a more or less arbitrary decision as to how "sign" is to be defined. The most important aspect of formators is that they presuppose other signs and influence the significance of the specific sign combinations in which they appear. For example, given the signs "It will rain in Chicago" and "It will not rain in Chicago," we may use alternative formators in combining these signs, and thus produce different responses on the part of the interpreters: "Either it will rain in Chicago or it will not rain in Chicago," "It will rain in Chicago and it will not rain in Chicago," "If it rains in Chicago, it will not rain in Chicago." Or if we take certain arithmetical signs we may construct alternative complex signs by changing formators; for example, "2 plus (3 times 5)" may become "(2 plus 3) times 5." Or to return to the dog, we may train him to respond to two different signals in such a way as to permit us to characterize the signal as "S_1 or S_2 (at least one but not both)": in this situation the way in which S_1 and S_2 are combined by a formator produces a specific type of behavior response. Since formators are indicated usually by sign combinations, Morris contrasts them to *lexicators*, which are defined negatively as ascriptors which are not formators and which include indicators, designators, appraisors, and prescriptors.

Corresponding to the problem of the modes of signifying there is the parallel problem of sign use. This concerns the purpose for which an organism produces the signs which it uses and other organisms interpret. For example, a person may write a short story in order to earn money. There are so many purposes implied in the various usages of signs that no complete listing of them is possible. Some of the most common are: to gain prestige and power; to deceive or entertain; to excite or comfort; to record or to inform;

to satisfy a need or arouse a need in another person; to induce action; to enlist the aid of other people; to "express" oneself, and so on. Morris summarizes these in the four categories: the *informative*, the *valuative*, the *incitive*, and the *systemic*. These terms are self-explanatory: they indicate, respectively, attempts on the part of a user to provide information, to aid in preferential selection of objects, to incite certain responses, and to organize behavior into a determinate whole. Signs which succeed in their informative use may be said to be *convincing*, in their valuative use to be *effective*, in their incitive use to be *persuasive*, and in their systemic use to be *correct*. (Morris grants that the last term, "correct," is not particularly appropriate; in the systemic use of signs emphasis is placed on their interrelationships and on the corresponding integrative, or lack of integrative, character of the behavior responses.)

Having examined signs from the points of view of their modes of signifying and their use, Morris then proceeds to combine these two aspects of signs. This becomes the problem of *types of discourse*. An illustration is to be found in a classification of books; books may be characterized as scientific, mathematical, poetic, religious, fictional, technological, propagandistic, metaphysical, and the like. All such schemes are very crude indeed, containing overlapping classes and subdivisions almost without limit. Morris believes that his double approach to signs in terms of mode of signifying and utility provides a scheme which will eliminate some of the ambiguities in the layman's solution to the problem, and he presents a table containing examples of the sixteen major types of discourse which result when each mode (Designative, Appraisive, Prescriptive, Formative) of signifying is combined with each use (Informative, Valuative, Incitive, Systemic) of signs.

In explaining the sixteen types of discourse, Morris makes it quite clear that he is not proposing that any one of these—say, religious discourse—is to be *defined* in terms of his table. On the contrary, what he is doing is defining a type of discourse, the prescriptive-incitive type, and then showing that much literature which is commonly called "religious" would fall loosely in this area and would thus constitute an *illustration* of prescriptive-incitive discourse.

1. *Scientific discourse* (Designative-Informative) is essentially designative since it does not evaluate or prescribe modes of behavior, and it is primarily informative, since its main concern is with truth. 2. *Fictive discourse* (Designative-Valuative) tells tales, usually about unreal persons and places, with the design not to inform but to evaluate (heroes and villains). 3. *Legal discourse* (Designative-Incitive) prescribes what a person should do, not by saying that it is good or bad, but merely by specifying rewards and punishments; it thus tries to incite action (or inaction) by informing the person of what the consequences of his behavior will be. 4. *Cosmological discourse* (Designative-Systemic) is not a clear-cut type but can be illustrated by certain kinds of metaphysics which describe the universe as one or many, mental or material, purposive or mechanical, yet are not primarily informative since they are concerned more with that organization of sign-behavior which is provided by the emphasis on the systemic use of the signs.

5. *Mythical discourse* (Appraisive-Informative) is appraisive since it evaluates actions, but its main purpose is to inform the reader of the way in which these actions are approved or disapproved by some group. 6. *Poetic discourse* (Appraisive-Valuative) is appraisive-valuative because the poet uses words heavily charged with feeling to arouse feelings in the mind of the reader; thus, words which signify emotions are used to evoke emotions. 7. *Moral discourse* (Appraisive-Incitive) appraises actions as favorable or unfavorable from the standpoint of an individual or a group, and it tries to induce people to perform or avoid such actions. 8. *Critical discourse* (Appraisive-Systemic) consists of the measurement of appraisive judgments by their organization or lack of organization; it involves a grounded appraisal of appraisals, and may take the form of moral criticism, poetic criticism, religious criticism, or any other type.

9. *Technological discourse* (Prescriptive-Informative) may be popularly described as "how to" discourse; it provides information which is designed to make certain actions more effective in the production of certain desired ends. 10. *Political discourse* (Prescriptive-Valuative), exemplified by the Declaration of Independence, urges the adoption of a certain type of society which has a preferential status because of the rights, privileges, and happiness of its members. 11. *Religious discourse* (Prescriptive-Incitive), in its preoccupation with the "whole" man, both prescribes one type of personality as above all others and incites the individual to become this type of person. 12. *Propagandistic* (as Morris names it) *discourse* (Prescriptive-Systemic) consists of statements designed to produce ac-

1107

tion, but places emphasis on an integrated *program* of these statements, such as might characterize, for example, the policy of a newspaper, or the advertising techniques of a manufacturer, or the arguments of a speaker before Congress.

13. *Logico-mathematical discourse* (Formative-Informative) is illustrated by the syllogism, "If men are animals, and animals are mortal, then men are mortal." This is informative of a structural relation holding between propositions, but this relation is analytic in character, as shown by the formators —"if," "and," "then"; for example, to prove the validity of this argument one does not need to examine men, animals, and mortals to see whether the relation in question holds. 14. *Rhetorical discourse* (Formative-Valuative) is formative in mode of signifying but valuative in aim. If I say, "Children are children," I am using the formator "are" to create a sign-structure which is used for the purpose of expressing my approval of the actions of children when they behave in a manner contrary to that of adults. 15. *Grammatical discourse* (Formative-Incitive) incites the student, when he is given the conjugations of the verbs in a certain language, to use the language in accordance with these rules; thus it incites the individual to use formators properly. 16. *Metaphysical discourse* (Formative-Systemic) cannot be unequivocally placed in the category of forma-

tive-systemic discourse, since the term has so many meanings. But according to one commonly held conception, metaphysics consists of necessary truths having wide generality, and not being such as are refutable or irrefutable by the date of the special sciences. Judgments in this area will then be both formative, since their truth is determined merely by their structure, and systemic, since they are characterized by their extreme generality.

Morris concludes with a discussion of the social and individual import of signs, in which he examines such questions as whether the arts can be considered a language, how language may be at times "healthy" and at other times "pathic," how signs are related to personality disturbances, and how signs may be used for social control. He examines the scope and import of the semiotic which he has developed, showing how it can be divided into *pragmatics* (which deals with the origin, uses, and effects of signs within behavior), *semantics* (which deals with all modes of signification), and *syntactics* (which deals with combinations of signs in abstraction from signification or behavioral connections). He believes that an adequatic science of semiotic will do much to unify the sciences, to advance a scientific humanistics, and to increase the confidence of the individual in his own production and use of signs.

THE CONCEPT OF MIND

Author: Gilbert Ryle (1900-   )
Type of work: Philosophy of mind
First published: 1949

PRINCIPAL IDEAS ADVANCED

To suppose that the mind is a ghost mysteriously embodied in a machine is to commit the category mistake of confusing the logic of discourse about bodies and things with the logic of discourse about minds.

To talk of a person's mind is to talk of his ability to perform certain kinds of tasks; words such as "know" and "believe" are disposition words indicating that under certain circumstances certain kinds of performance would be forthcoming.

What are called mental processes are not processes; they are dispositions, or ways of acting, not themselves acts.

Pronouns, such as "I," do not function as proper names, but are index words; index words function in a variety of ways.

A man's knowledge of himself comes from observing his own behavior.

To imagine is not to look at pictures in the theater of the mind; it is to perform any one of a number of various kinds of acts (such as telling lies, or playing bears).

According to Gilbert Ryle, it is not the function of philosophy to furnish information about minds. Teachers, magistrates, historians, and plain people of all sorts already know the kinds of things that can be known about them, and knowing more is merely a matter of extending one's experience. The philosopher has access to no special facts. But if he rightly plies his trade, he can help "rectify the logical geography of the knowledge which we already possess."

As Ryle sees it, most people know how to make correct use of concepts which apply to mental situations but cannot state the "logical regulations governing their use." Consequently, they do not know how to correlate such concepts with one another or with concepts which refer to matters other than mental facts. The philosopher has the task of clearing up confusions and correcting mistakes which have their source in this kind of ineptness.

It is the more incumbent upon philosophers to do this because, in Ryle's opinion, most of the difficulties which have come to plague us when we talk about these matters—the mind-body problem, solipsism, our knowledge of "other minds," and so forth— have their origin in the errors of philosophers. In particular, modern European thinkers have great difficulty in throwing off the two-substance doctrine so forcibly stated by Descartes, according to which a man has immediate knowledge of his own mind by a kind of interior illumination, greatly superior to the kind of knowledge— never more than an inference—which he has of material things. According to this view, which Ryle calls "the official doctrine," minds dwell in bodies but

1109

share none of the characteristics of material things. He frequently stigmatizes it as "the dogma of the Ghost in the Machine."

In attacking this dogma, Ryle carries over into epistemology the battle which the logical positivists previously waged against metaphysics, and the lines of his attack, if not the weapons, are familiar. The first line of attack has to do with the logic of statements: whether the expressions are related to one another in a coherent fashion. The second has to do with the meaning of the statements: under which conditions they can be verified or confirmed. For the purpose of carrying through the former of these attacks, Ryle has set up a series of "categories," deliberately reviving the Aristotelian term, but relating the discovery of categories to linguistic analysis.

Ryle explains "the official doctrine" in terms of what he calls a "category mistake." To suppose that "the University" is an entity in the same sense that its component colleges, libraries, laboratories, and so forth are entities, would be to make a category mistake. Another would be to suppose that "team spirit" has the same kind of reality that batsmen, fielders, and umpires do. These extreme examples to one side, the danger is ever present, Ryle says, that people who know how to apply terms correctly in familiar situations will fall victims to the fallacy of mixing up terms of different orders when they try to think in abstract ways. In his opinion, most of our mistakes in thinking about "mind" are of this sort.

The categories which we use in describing the physical world are "thing," "stuff," "attribute," "state," "process," "change," "cause," and "effect." The error of philosophers, and of plain men when they try to theorize, consists in supposing that there are "things" called "minds" comparable to things called "bodies," except for having different attributes, and that there are mental "events," like physical ones, which have causes and effects. Ryle designates attempts to talk about minds in these terms as "para-mechanical." Mind is thought of as a ghost in the sense that it is regarded as immaterial; but it is believed to press levers, open windows, receive shocks, and exert reactions much as if it were material.

A special feature of "the official doctrine" which has impressed epistemologists is the teaching that mind knows itself in a peculiarly direct manner. Ryle supposes that this view reflects the strong influence upon seventeenth century European thought of the Protestant affirmation that men's minds are "illuminated" by divine truth—a mode of thought that was reinforced by a preoccupation with optical phenomena on the part of Galilean science. As a result, the para-mechanical hypothesis of the mind's working was supplemented by a para-optical hypothesis of its self-knowledge.

Ryle, on his part, does not admit that there is any such *thing* as mind. It is, he says, a solecism to speak of the mind as knowing this or choosing that. The correct thing to say is that a *person* knows or chooses. Some actions of men exhibit qualities of intellect and of character, and, says Ryle, the fact that a person knows or chooses can be classified as a "mental fact" about that person. But he regards it as "an unfortunate linguistic fashion" which leads men to say that there are "mental acts" or "mental processes" comparable to "physical acts" and "physical processes."

Ryle's book is an attempt to show how it is that, since there is no such thing as a mind, we sometimes talk as if there were. The fault derives from our failure to distinguish different types of statements, and from supposing that what is characteristic of words in one kind of sentence is also characteristic of words in other kinds of sentences.

Take, for example, words such as "know," "believe," "aspire," "clever," and "humorous." These are, in Ryle's terminology, *disposition-words*. Statements in which they occur do not assert matters of fact, but capacities, tendencies, propensities, and so forth. To say of a sleeping man that he knows French is not to affirm an additional fact about him comparable to saying that he has gray eyes and is wearing a blue suit. Dispositional statements correspond, rather, to the hypothetical propositions of modern logic: they are indicative sentences and may be true or false in the sense that they are verifiable under certain conditions. A man knows French *if*, when he is spoken to in French, he responds appropriately in French. But no one criterion of performance is sufficient. A mistake arises when it is supposed that every true or false statement is categorical and either asserts or denies that there exists some object or set of objects possessing a specified attribute.

Besides disposition-words there are *occurrence-words* which apply to the higher-grade activities of men which we call "mental." If, as suggested above, "knows" designates a disposition, "heeds" would seem to designate an occurrence, as, for example, when a person is said to heed what he is doing. A double-process misleadingly suggests itself in this instance, with the bodily activity (say, driving a car) going on more or less by itself and an intermittent mental process trying to parallel what is going on in the body. According to Ryle, however, there are not two processes, but one. Driving a car is an occurrence; paying heed is a state of readiness, or a disposition. To say that a person heeds what he is doing while driving is to make a semi-hypothetical, or a "mongrel categorical" statement. The heedful man drives differently, perhaps, in that he is alert to chuck-holes and pedestrians; but the heeding is not itself an act in addition to the act of driving, and it presupposes no agent other than the one who is driving the car.

Ryle suggests that the wide currency of "the official doctrine" is due in great part to the "bogy of mechanism." The successes of physical science since the days of Galileo have excited in many theorists the expectation that the world may ultimately be explicable in terms of the motions of bodies according to laws which have the necessity of mathematical demonstrations. Hence, in the interests of human freedom, moral and religious thinkers have countered this prospect by asserting the autonomy of mind. According to Ryle, however, the fear is baseless.

In the first place, "laws of nature" are not "fiats." Law-statements are "open" hypothetical sentences—that is, hypothetical sentences in which the conditional phrase contains a universal term such as "any" or "whenever." Such sentences do not, like categorical sentences, affirm the existence of anything. "Causal-connections," in other

1111

words, do not exist in the same sense as, say, the existence of bacteria and the disease they are alleged to cause. To assume that they do is "to fall back into the old habit of assuming that all sorts of sentences do the same sort of job, the job, namely, of ascribing a predicate to a mentioned object." Statements about physical laws do not "mention" anything. They are merely predictive of behavior.

In the second place, according to Ryle, the mechanistic account of nature is no threat to human freedom because many questions concerning human behavior cannot be answered in terms of physical law. Suppose that physicists eventually find the answer to all physical questions, the plain fact is that "not all questions are physical questions." The same process, says Ryle, is often viewed in terms of two or more principles of explanation, neither of which can be reduced to the other, although one commonly presupposes the other. For example, if a child asks a chess player why he moves a certain piece (say, a knight) to a certain spot, the answer he requires is a statement of the rules of the game; whereas, if an experienced player asks the question, the answer required will be in terms of "tactical canons." Another example is the rules of grammar, which apply equally to all books in the language irrespective of style or content. Just so, says Ryle, the laws of physics apply to everything—animate as well as inanimate; but they do not explain everything. Even for describing a game of billiards, mechanical principles, while necessary, are not sufficient. The purpose of the game, its rules, and its tactics are equally important. These "appraisal concepts" are not in conflict with the law-statements;

rather, they presuppose them, for there would be no place for planning if there were no predictability.

Ryle safeguards the meaning of purpose in human activity by distinguishing between questions about the *causes* of a man's acts and the *reasons* for it. Suppose the event to be explained is a man's passing the salt to his neighbor at the table. The question about causes demands to be answered in factual or categorical sentences such as, "He heard his neighbor ask for it," or "He saw his neighbor's eye wandering over the table." "Seeing" and "hearing" are events that may stand in the chain of causal explanations. The question about reasons does not admit of categorical answers. One might say, "He passed the salt from politeness," or, "He did it out of friendliness." These are reasons and not causes. They refer to motives or dispositional states, and are expressed in law-like or hypothetical propositions. That we constantly appeal to them in explaining human behavior testifies to the incompleteness of "causal" explanations. Moreover, according to Ryle, they express all that we actually intend when we speak of man's acts as being free or voluntary.

Ryle finds that there is good sense in saying, "I know that I am free." To infer, however, that the pronoun "I" must be the name of a distinct entity is to misunderstand the true function of pronouns. They do not function like proper names, but are "index" words which point now to one thing, now to another. Because of the complexity of our experience, the pronoun "I," (with "me," and "myself") is used in a variety of ways. Sometimes the speaker uses "I" to refer to his body, as when a man says, "I was cut in the collision." He may even use "I" to refer to his mechanical auxiliaries, such as his car, as in the sentence, "I collided with the police car." These cases offer no particular difficulty. But it is different when one says, "I am warming myself before the fire." Here, "myself" could be replaced by "my body," but not "I." Even more complex are such statements as, "I was ashamed of myself," and "I caught myself beginning to dream." Ryle's explanation is that the pronouns are "used in different senses in different sorts of contexts." Human behavior frequently involves what Ryle calls "higher order actions"; that is to say, actions in which the second agent is concerned with actions of a first agent, as in spying or applauding. And a person's higher order acts may be directed upon his own lower order acts, as in self-criticism. This, according to Ryle, is what we ordinarily mean by "self-consciousness." There is nothing here to support the view that one looks into his own mind and discovers its workings. What is known as "introspection" is in fact "retrospection." The attempt to glimpse ourselves in the act of thinking is hopeless.

The much-touted claims of introspective psychology, founded on the para-optical model of knowledge, are, therefore, rejected by Ryle. That we know our feelings immediately he does not deny. But he is careful to distinguish feelings, which are agitations, from moods and tendencies, which are dispositions. Of the latter we have no immediate knowledge. Only as they eventuate in actions can we form any estimate of them. A man's knowledge of himself, therefore, comes from observing his own *behavior* and is in principle no differ-

ent from his knowledge of other persons. Ryle recognizes many grades of self-knowledge: a man may know that he is whistling "Tipperary" and not know that he is doing so to keep up his courage. Or, he may be aware that he is trying to keep up his courage without realizing that what makes him afraid is a guilty conscience. But in no case does he have "privileged access" to his own mental states.

Ryle continues: "No metaphysical Iron Curtain exists compelling us to be forever absolute strangers to one another, though ordinary circumstances, together with some deliberate management, serve to maintain a reasonable aloofness. Similarly, no metaphysical looking-glass exists compelling us to be forever completely disclosed and explained to ourselves, though from the everyday conduct of our sociable and unsociable lives we learn to be reasonably conversant with ourselves."

Ryle's treatment of sensation and observation is refreshing in that he candidly admits that his analysis is not satisfactory to him. He attributes his difficulty to contamination by sophisticated language. In ordinary language the words "sensation" and "feel" signify perceptions, but in philosophical language they refer to presumed bases for perceptual inference. Words like "hurt" and "itch" are not the names of moods, nor are they the names of certain kinds of perceptions, nor are they terms by which achievements are reported. Ryle confesses: "I do not know what more is to be said about the logical grammar of such words, save that there is much more to be said."

His discussion of imagination is perhaps the most provocative part of the book. The ordinary myth-view of imagination is that in the private box or theater of our minds we view private pictures. But the logic of discourse involving the word "imagination" does not entail any such fanciful assumption. To imagine is to lie, to play bears, to write a story, or to invent a machine. There is no need to suppose some one internal, private operation to which the word "imagine" calls attention; in fact, the word does no such thing; it calls attention to publicly observable behavior.

In his discussion of "intellect" Ryle rejects, as by now one might expect, any analysis which describes intellect as an organ, an internal lecturer, a private thinker. As a result of producing various kinds of things—such as sums, books, theories—men are said to have been engaged in intellectual processes. Confusing the grammar of intellect with the grammar of production, and working out an erroneous analogy, we tend to regard intellect as a hidden faculty of mind. Ryle's analyses—here, as elsewhere in the book, careful and illuminating—discredit such a notion. He makes the interesting suggestion that such words as "judgment" and "deduction" are words belonging to "the classification of the products of pondering and are mis-rendered when taken as denoting acts of which pondering consists." Such words, he argues, are "referees' nouns, not biographers' nouns"—that is, they are properly used to describe the products which men have produced; they are misleadingly used to talk about some hidden performances within the mind.

Ryle, in concluding his book, discusses the relation between his approach to the "concept of mind" and that which engages psychologists. It is his stated opinion that, with the collapse of the two-world view, psychology has ceased to have an identifiable aim and is more like medicine, a "fortuitous federation of inquiries and techniques." The wrong sort of promise, he feels, is being made when we are told that psychology will disclose causes of human actions which are hidden from such observers as economists, historians, anthropologists, and novelists. "We know quite well what caused the farmer to return from the market with his pigs unsold. He found the prices were lower than he had expected." The explanation of our competent mental behavior does not require a psychologist; it is apparent to ordinary good sense. Where the psychologist can be of service is in explaining why our competencies often fail. "The question why the farmer will not sell his pigs at certain prices is not a psychological but an economic question; but the question why he will not sell his pigs at any price to a customer with a certain look in his eye might be a psychological question."

Ryle recognizes a certain debt to behaviorism. Often confused by its practioners with "a not very sophisticated mechanistic doctrine," it was originally a methodological program which insisted that the theories of psychologists "should be based upon repeatable and publicly checkable observations and experiments." This program, according to Ryle, has been of first importance in overthrowing the two-world myth. And it does not in any way entail mechanistic assumptions. For, says Ryle, the rise of the biological sciences and the fact that the Newtonian system is no longer the sole paradigm of natural science make it unnecessary for scientists to consider man as a machine. "He might, after all, be a sort of animal, namely, a higher mammal. There has yet to be ventured the hazardous leap to the hypothesis that perhaps he is a man."

ZEN BUDDHISM

Author: Daisetz T. Suzuki (1870-   )
Type of work: Metaphysics, ethics
First published: 1956 (Selections by Editor William Barrett from works published during the years 1949-1955)

PRINCIPAL IDEAS ADVANCED

Zen is a way of life, of seeing and knowing by looking into one's own nature.
The truth comes through active meditation, and enlightenment is sudden and intuitive.
Zen does not rely on the intellect, the scriptures, or the written word, but on a direct pointing at the soul of man, a seeing into one's own nature as making Buddhahood possible.
Zen masters make the moment of enlightenment (satori) possible by referring directly to some natural and commonplace matter; the immediate recognition of the unity of being follows.
The chief characteristics of satori are irrationality, intuitive insight, authoritativeness, affirmation, a sense of the Beyond, an impersonal tone, a feeling of exaltation, and momentariness.
The methods of Zen are paradox, going beyond the opposites, contradiction, affirmation, repetition, exclamation, silence, or direct action (such as a blow, or pointing).

Zen Buddhism shares with other philosophies and faiths which stress intuition and awareness the ironic condition of desiring to communicate what cannot be communicated. Like the theologies of the Middle Ages, it urges an understanding of true being by a kind of direct insight into one's own being, but it disdains any intellectual or formalistic methods of achieving that insight. The profession of conviction, then, is largely negative; the emphasis, insofar as discourse is concerned, is not on what can be said but on that concerning which we must be silent. A Zen master is not a lecturer; he is a director, or pointer, one who turns the attention of the disciple to some natural fact which, properly apprehended, reveals everything. Of those who have made the effort to explain Zen Buddhism, no one has been more successful than the Japanese philosopher and professor, Daisetz T. Suzuki, whose *Essays in Zen Buddhism* (1949, 1950, 1953), *The Zen Doctrine of No-Mind* (1949), and *Studies in Zen* (1955) provide the selections collected and edited by William Barrett under the title, *Zen*

Buddhism. As an introduction to Suzuki's work and to Zen Buddhism, this volume is admirably suited; it deals with the meaning of Zen Buddhism, its historical background, its techniques, its philosophy, and its relation to Japanese culture.

According to the legendary account of Zen, given by Suzuki, Zen originated in India, and the first to practice the Zen method was Sakyamuni himself, the Buddha. He is reputed to have held a bouquet of flowers before his disciples without saying a word. Only the venerable Mahakasyapa understood the "silent but eloquent teaching on the part of the Enlightened One." Consequently, Mahakasyapa inherited the spiritual treasure of Buddhism.

According to historical accounts however, Zen Buddhism originated in China in A.D. 520 with the arrival of Bodhi-Dharma from India (the twenty-eighth in the line of patriarchs of Zen, according to the orthodox followers). The message brought by Bodhi-Dharma became the four-phrase summation of the Zen principles:

"A special transmission outside the scriptures;

"No dependence upon words and letters;

"Direct pointing at the soul of man;

"Seeing into one's nature and the attainment of Buddhahood."

These are not the words of Bodhi-Dharma, but of later disciples who formulated his teachings. The method of "direct pointing," of referring to some natural thing or event as the focal point of meditation, preparatory to an instantaneous enlightenment, continues to be the most characteristic method of Zen Buddhism.

Dharma came to be known as the *pi-kuan* Brahman, the Wall-contemplating Brahman, because of his practice of contemplating a monastery wall —reputedly for nine years. One of the most familiar stories of his teaching has to do with the persistent seeker after truth, the monk Shen-kuang, described in legend as having stood in the snow until he was buried to his knees and as having cut off his arm in order to show the sincerity of his desire to learn. Finally, gaining audience with Dharma, he said, "My soul is not yet pacified. Pray, master, pacify it." Dharma replied, "Bring your soul here, and I will have it pacified." Suzuki finishes the story: "Kuang hesitated for a moment but finally said, 'I have sought it these many years and am still unable to get hold of it!'

"'There! it is pacified once for all.' This was Dharma's sentence."

The Chinese founder of Zen, Suzuki reports, was Hui-neng (638-713), who was so deeply touched by a recitation of the *Diamond Sutra* (*Vajracchedika-sutra*) that he made a month-long journey to beg the patriarch Hung-jen to allow him to study under him. Hung-jen recognized Hui-neng's spiritual quality and transferred the patriarchal robes to him. (The account may not be accurate, having been composed by the followers of Hui-neng.)

It was Hui-neng who taught that Zen is the "seeing into one's own Nature." According to Suzuki, "This is the most significant phrase ever coined in the development of Zen Buddhism." Allied with this idea was the "abrupt doctrine" of the Southern school of Hui-neng. According to the *Platform Sutra*, "When the abrupt doctrine is understood there is no need of disciplining oneself in things external.

Only let a man always have a right view within his own mind, no desires, no external objects will ever defile him. . . . The ignorant will grow wise if they abruptly get an understanding and open their hearts to the truth." In opposition to the view that enlightenment can be achieved by passive or quiet meditation, Hui-neng emphasized apprehending the nature of the self while the self is in the midst of action. Hui-neng began the Zen tradition of getting at the truth directly, intuitively, not intellectually. "When the monk Ming came to him and asked for instruction," Suzuki recounts, "[Hui-neng] said, 'Show me your original face before you were born.'" Suzuki comments: "Is not the statement quite to the point? No philosophic discourse, no elaborate reasoning, no mystic imagery, but a direct unequivocal dictum."

Suzuki's essay "The Sense of Zen," which is Chapter I of Barrett's collection, states at the outset that Zen is "the art of seeing into the nature of one's own being." He argues that Zen Buddhism contains the essence of Buddhism, although it differs from other forms of Buddhism in not stressing rules, scriptures, authorities, and the intellectual approach to the truth. Zen Buddhism assents to the Buddha's "Fourfold Noble Truth" which is built on the basic claim that life is suffering and that to escape suffering one must overcome desire and find truth. There is a struggle in the individual between the finite and the infinite, so that the nature of one's being, which provides a clue to the resolution of the conflict within the self, must be directly grasped. But books are of no help, nor is the intellect; the only way to Buddhahood is through a "direct

pointing to the soul of man," as one of the four statements claims. "For this reason, Suzuki writes, "Zen never explains but indicates. . . . It always deals with facts, concrete and tangible." Suffering is the result of ignorance, and ignorance "is wrought of nothing else but the intellect and sensuous infatuation. . . ."

Direct teaching or pointing is sometimes a silent reference, as with the Buddha's flower. But it may appear in the use of an apparently irrelevant, even ridiculous or apparently senseless remark. To appreciate the method of direct pointing, Suzuki cautions, one must regard the attempt to learn as no mere pastime; for Zen Buddhists, Zen is an ethical discipline, an attempt to elevate one's spiritual powers to their ideal limits. The brief answers of the masters to their students' questions were never intended to be intellectual riddles or symbolic utterances. To talk by the use of metaphorical imagery would not be to point directly. Perhaps one can say that although some of the statements attributed to the masters appear to be symbolic in import, there may very well be more direct meanings which are the significant meanings of the statements. Suzuki gives some illustrations of the Zen practice of uttering a few words and demonstrating with action: "What is Zen?" The master: "Boiling oil over a blazing fire." "What kind of man is he who does not keep company with any thing?" The master (Baso): "I will tell you when you have swallowed up in one draught all the waters in the West River."

There is perhaps no more difficult point to make than that such answers from the Zen masters are important not as charming and archaic riddles or ir-

1117

relevancies, but as "direct pointings" to the truth. The tendency of the Western mind is to go at these remarks intellectually, to "make" sense out of them. But Suzuki argues with convincing sincerity that for the Zen Buddhist such remarks are instruments of enlightenment that can be comprehended simply and naturally with the "opening of a third eye," the sudden enlightenment by which one sees into the nature of his own being. The name for the moment of enlightenment or awakening is *"satori,"* and the means to it is meditation of the proper sort. (As Mr. Barrett indicates, the term "Zen" comes from the Japanese term *zazen,* meaning "to sit or meditate," and is equivalent to the Chinese *ch'an* and the Indian *Dhyana.* The distinctive feature of Zen is that meditation and action are one. Suzuki says, "Zen has its own way of practicing meditation. Zen has nothing to do with mere quietism or losing oneself in a trance.")

To achieve *satori,* or enlightenment, involves "meditating on those utterances or actions that are directly poured out from the inner region undimmed by the intellect or the imagination. . . ." Again, examples from the masters are offered to suggest the direct method of Zen. Referring to his staff, Ye-ryo said, "When one knows what that staff is, one's life study of Zen comes to an end." Ye-sei said, "When you have a staff, I will give you one; when you have none, I will take it away from you."

Some suggestive remarks by Suzuki put the Zen method into a perspective accessible to Western minds. If we consider that the direct method is possible for the Zen masters because *any* point of meditation, properly caught in the fullness of its being, is infinitely illuminating, we can come to appreciate the pertinence of apparently irrelevant and abrupt remarks. If one's study of Zen ends with knowledge of the master's staff, it may be that it also ends, as Suzuki suggests, with knowledge of the flower in the crannied wall. Tennyson's image may have much the same significance as the Zen master's image. Referring to the Buddhist scriptures, Suzuki argues that "enlightenment and darkness are substantially one," that "the finite is the infinite, and *vice versa,*" and that "The mistake consists in our splitting into two what is really and absolutely one." All of this is reminiscent of the philosophy of the metaphysical mystics; there is a close resemblance to the views of such men as Nicholas of Cusa and Giordano Bruno. Suddenly to appreciate the unity of all being and to recognize that unity in an illuminating moment of knowing one's own nature to be the nature of all being, and therefore the nature of whatever it is to which the master's abrupt remark calls attention, is surely not an act of intellect. For intellect to "work it out" would be to spoil the whole effect, as if one were to try to embrace the quality of a rug as a whole by tracing out its separate threads and their relationships to other threads. *Satori,* if it occurs, has to be a moment of "grasping," of knowing "all at once," and it is not at all surprising that the masters of Zen have come to rely on the abrupt remark as a sudden direct pointing.

In the essay, "Satori, or Enlightenment," Suzuki defines *satori* as "an intuitive looking into the nature of things in contradistinction to the analytical or logical understanding of it." It involves a new view, a new way of looking at the universe. The emphasis of the Zen masters, as with the patriarch Hui-neng, is not on direction or on instruction, but on seeing into one's own nature in order to see the nature of all, to achieve Buddhahood and to escape the cycle of birth and death.

Here again Suzuki emphasizes the masters' methods of bringing the seekers of enlightenment abruptly to *satori*. "A monk asked Joshu . . . to be instructed in Zen. Said the master, 'Have you had your breakfast or not?' 'Yes, master, I have,' answered the monk. 'If so, have your dishes washed,' was an immediate response, which, it is said, at once opened the monk's mind to the truth of Zen." Such remarks are like the strokes and blows, or the twisting of noses, which the masters sometimes resorted to, as if suddenly to make the disciple aware of himself and of the obscuring tendencies of his old perspectives. By referring to commonplace matters in the context of a desire to know all, the masters somehow refer to all. By being apparently irrelevant, they show the relevance of everything.

The chief characteristics of *satori*, Suzuki writes, are *irrationality*, the nonlogical leap of the will; *intuitive insight*, or mystic knowledge; *authoritativeness*, the finality of personal perception; *affirmation*, the acceptance of all things; *a sense of the Beyond*, the loss of the sense of self together with the sense of all; *an impersonal tone*, the absence of any feeling of love or "supersensuality"; *a feeling of exaltation*, the contentment of being unrestricted and independent; and *momentariness*, an abruptness of experience,

a sudden realization of "a new angle of observation."

In "Practical Methods of Zen Instruction," Suzuki discusses methods for arriving at the realization of the absolute oneness of things. A proper appreciation of these methods, even in outline, depends upon unabridged explanations and examples, but the methods can be mentioned. Zen sometimes utilizes *paradox*, but by concrete images, not by abstract conceptions. Another method is to attempt to think the truth without using the ordinary logic of affirmation and denial; it is the method of *"going beyond the opposites."* The third method is the method of *contradiction*, the method of denying what has already been asserted or taken for granted. The method of *affirmation* is the method frequently referred to: stating almost blithely some commonplace matter of fact in answer to an abstruse and apparently unrelated question. *Repetition* serves to return the self to what it has already seen and not recognized. *Exclamation*, particularly when used as the only answer and when the sound is meaningless, is sometimes used; and even the method of *silence* has provoked *satori*. But of all the methods, the *direct method* of illuminating action—even though the action be commonplace or almost violent, such as a blow on the cheek of a questioner —is most characteristic of Zen, perhaps because it is the action of everything to which Zen directs attention.

The *koan* exercise is the Zen method of teaching the uninitiated by referring them to answers made by Zen masters. The student is either enlightened or encouraged to "search and contrive" in order to understand the state of mind of the master whose *koan* he is considering. Suzuki devotes an interesting chapter to a discussion of the *koan* exercise, and he offers several examples.

The basic principles of Zen, particularly as related to the teachings of Hui-neng, are examined anew in the essay, "The Zen Doctrine of No-Mind," in which the emphasis on the No-Mind, the Unconscious, brings out the essential concern with active, nondiscursive, intuitive insight. By avoiding the conscous effort, to understand intellectually and by participating in ordinary action, one prepares oneself for the moment of enlightenment.

Zen differs from pragmatism, Suzuki maintains, in that pragmatism emphasizes the practical usefulness of concepts, while Zen emphasizes purposelessness or "being detached from teleological consciousness. . . ." Suzuki describes Zen as life; it is entirely consistent with the nonintellectualism of Zen that Zen has implications for action in every sphere of human life. But Zen is concerned not so much with the quality or direction of action as with the perspective of the actor. The emphasis is on "knowing and seeing." Like existentialism, Zen recognizes the antinomy of the finite and the infinite and the possibilities which that relation of apparent opposition opens up; but unlike existentialism, Zen does not involve any conception of an absolute opposition and, consequently, does not entail any "unbearable responsibility," or nausea in the face of the necessity for action. Once the division of finite and infinite, individual and other, is seen to be the consequence of intellectual analysis, so that the idea of individuality is succeeded by the idea of oneness, there is no fear of plunging into the abyss.

In his discussion of Zen and Japanese culture Suzuki shows how Sumiye painting (ink sketching on fragile paper, with no corrections possible), swordsmanship, and the tea ceremony are expressions of Zen principles.

Suzuki's essays on Zen Buddhism are exotic material for the Western reader, but taken seriously—that is, as having some bearing on practice and perspective—they can contribute immeasurably to an appreciation of Oriental religion and philosophy. There is also the challenging possibility that these essays may lead to an understanding of the unifying intuitive mysticism which persistently runs through Western metaphysics despite its prevailing realistic and pragmatic directions. And the most hopeful possibility of all is that by a sincere effort to *learn by seeing* the Zen attitude, the Western mind may finally reach the enlightened freedom of finding that the opposition between realism and mysticism vanishes.

THE MYSTERY OF BEING

Author: Gabriel Marcel (1887-   )
Type of work: Existential ontology
First published: 1950

The peculiar task of philosophy is to describe what it means to be in a particular concrete situation.

Existential thinking, the thinking of an involved self, is threatened by the interest in abstractions and by bureaucratic societies which reduce individuals to averages.

Primary reflection is analytical; secondary reflection is recuperative, allowing the self to discover its being in action.

The immediate encounter with the mystery of being is in terms of a lived participation; being is an internal relation; the self, or the body, is not an object of knowledge, but the subject who knows himself as he acts.

To know others existentially is to encounter them, not as things, but in acknowledgment of them as persons.

Freedom is found when the self turns inward and becomes aware of its capability for commitment and treason.

Gabriel Marcel is one of the main figures associated with existential thought in France. His two-volume work, *The Mystery of Being*, is the final product of a series of Gifford Lectures which were given in 1949 and 1950 at the University of Aberdeen. Volume I is subtitled "Reflection and Mystery." The subtitle of Volume II is "Faith and Reality." Characteristic of *The Mystery of Being*, and one might say of Marcel's writings in general, is a philosophical approach which is oriented towards concrete descriptions and elucidations instead of systematic delineations. In this respect the existentialism of Marcel has greater affinities to the thought of Kierkegaard and Jaspers than to that of Heidegger and Sartre. Marcel will have nothing to do with the system builders. A philosophical system, even though it may have an existentialist cast, as in Heidegger and Sartre, entails for the author a falsification of lived experience as it is immediately apprehended.

On every page of Marcel's writings the reader is forced to acknowledge the author's concentrated efforts to remain with the concrete. Existential thinking is the thinking of the "involved self." This involved self is contrasted by the author with the "abstracted self." The abstracted self, in its movement of detachment, escapes to a privileged and intellectually rarefied sanctuary—an "Olympus of the Spirit"—from which it seeks to formulate a global and inclusive perspective of the whole of reality. Marcel's concrete philosophical elucidations express a continuing protest against any such Olympian view. "There is not, and there cannot be, any global abstraction, any final terrace to which we can climb by means of abstract thought, there to rest for ever; for our condition in this world does remain, in the last analysis, that of a wanderer, an itinerant being, who cannot come to absolute rest except by a fiction, a fiction which it is the duty of philosophic reflection to oppose with all its strength." Man as an "itinerant being" (or as a wayfarer, as the author has expressed it in the title of another of his works, *Homo Viator*, 1945) is always on the way, passing from one concrete situation to another. At no time can he shed his situationality and view himself and the rest of the world as completed. There is no *Denken überhaupt* which can tear itself loose from the concrete situation of the involved self and lay a claim for universal validity. This, for Marcel, as already for Kierkegaard, is the grievous fault in all varieties of idealism. Idealism fails to recognize the situational character of all human thinking. The philosophical reflection which the author prescribes is a reflection which retains its existential bond with the concrete situation. The peculiar task of philosophy is that of describing what it means to be in a situation. This task is a phenomenological one—phenomenological in the sense that it takes its point of departure from everyday, lived experience and seeks to follow through the implications which can be drawn from it.

Concrete existence is lost in the abstract movements of a detached reflection, but it is also threatened by the pervasive bureaucratization of modern life. In the chapter entitled, "A Broken World," Marcel develops a penetrating analysis of the dissolution of personality in the face of increased social regimentation. Man stands in danger of losing his humanity. Our modern bureaucratized world tends to identify the individual with the state's official record of his activities. Personality is reduced to an identity card. In such a situation man is defined in terms of replaceable functions rather than acknowledged as a unique and irreplaceable self. Creative activities are standardized and consequently depersonalized. Everything, including man himself, is reduced to a stultifying law of averages. In one passage the author speaks of an equality which is obtained by a process of "levelling *down*" to a point where all creativity vanishes. The language and theme are reminiscent of Kierkegaard's social critique in *The Present Age* (1846), in which he indicted the public for having effected a leveling process that virtually made the category of the individual extinct. This theme of depersonalization also links Marcel with the two German existentialists, Jaspers and Heidegger. Jaspers in his book, *Man in the Modern Age* (1931), has described how the masses have become our masters and reduced everything to an appalling mediocrity. Heidegger, in his notion of *das Man,* has expressed basically the same theme. In a later work, *Man Against Mass Society* (1952), Marcel gives special attention to this phenomenon, elucidating it in a descriptive analysis which is rich and penetrating.

The leading question in Marcel's philosophy of the concrete is the question, "Who am I?" Only through a pursuit of this question can man be liberated from the objectivizing tendencies in modern thought, and return to the immediacy of his lived experience. Reflection will illuminate this lived experience only as long as it remains a part of life. The author defines two levels of reflection—primary and secondary. Primary reflection is *analytical* and tends to dissolve the unity of experience as it is existentially disclosed to the involved self. Secondary reflection is *recuperative* and seeks to reconquer the unity that is lost through primary reflection. It is only with the aid of secondary reflection that man can penetrate to the depths of the self. The Cartesian *cogito* is derived by primary reflection, and therefore it is viewed as a mental object somehow united with the fact of existence. But this abstract reflection is already at a second remove from the reality of pure immediacy. If the "I exist" is to provide the Archimedean point, then it will need to be retrieved in its indissoluble unity as an immediate datum of secondary reflection. Existence, as Kant had already shown in his *Critique of Pure Reason* (1781), is not a property or a predicate which can be attached to a mental object. Existence indicates an irreducible status in a given sensory context. Secondary reflection uncovers my existence as it is sensibly experienced *in act*. This apprehension of my existence *in act* is what Marcel calls the "existential indubitable." In asking about myself, I am disclosed as the questioner in the very act of posing the question. It is here that we find ourselves up against existence in its naked "thereness."

The living body is for the author a central phenomenon in secondary or recuperative reflection. Secondary reflection discloses my existence as an *incarnated* existence—an existence which is tied to a body which I experience as peculiarly and uniquely my own. The "existential indubitable" is manifested in the experience of my body as it actually lives. Primary reflection tends to dissolve the link between me and my body; it transforms the "me" into a universal consciousness and my body into an objectivized entity which is in fact only one body among many others. The original unity of the experience of myself as body is thus dissolved. Primary reflection takes up the attitude of an objectivizing detachment. The body becomes an anatomical or physiological object, generalized as a datum for scientific investigation.

It becomes evident that the Cartesian dualism of mind and body springs from primary rather than secondary reflection. The body in Descartes' philosophy is a substantive entity which has been objectivized and viciously abstracted from the concrete experience of the living body as intimately mine. Secondary reflection apprehends my body as an irreducible determinant in my immediate experience. On the one hand, my body is disclosed as something which I *possess*, something that belongs to me. But as I penetrate deeper I find that the analogy of ownership does not succeed in fully expressing the incarnated quality of my existence. The analogy of ownership still tends to define the relation of myself to my body as an external one. It defines my body as a possession which is somehow accidental to my inner being. But this is not so. My body is constitutive of my inner being. Properly speaking, it is not something which I have; it designates who I am. "My body is *my* body just in so far as I do *not* consider it in this detached fashion, do not put a gap between myself and it. To put this point in another way, my body is mine in so far as for me my body is not an object but, rather, I *am* my body."

It is at this point that the author's distinction between being and having becomes relevant. The phenomenon of being can never be reduced to the phenomenon of having. In *having* the bond between the possessor and the possessed is an external relation; in the phenomenon of *being* the bond is internal rather than external and is expressed by Marcel in the language of participation. Man has or possesses external objects and qualities, but he participates in being. The implications of this phenomenological distinction for the immediate awareness of the living body are evident. On one level of experience my body is something which I have or possess. It is a material complex which is attached to myself, and defines me as a self with a body. But on a deeper level of experience I *am* my body, and I am my body in such a way that the simple materiality of my body as a possession is transcended. I *exist as body,* as an incarnated being for whom the experience of body and the experience of selfhood are inseparable phenomena. Speaking of my body is a way of speaking of myself. The body in such a view is existentialized. It is no longer an object possessed by a subject. It is apprehended as a determinant of subjectivity.

The immediate encounter with the mystery of being is thus in terms of a lived participation. The idea of participation, says the author, had taken on importance for him even in the days of his earliest philosophical gropings. Although the language of participation would seem to betray a Platonic influence, the author makes it clear that the idea of participation includes more than an intellectual assent. Indeed, the foundational mode of participation is feeling, inextricably bound up, as we have seen, with a bodily sense. The Platonic dualism of mind and body, with its perfervid intellectualism and depreciation of the senses, could not admit the existential quality of participation which Marcel seeks to establish. Marcel's favorite illustrations of feeling as a mode of participation are his illustrations of the link between the peasant and the soil, and the sailor and the sea. Here, he says, we can grasp what participation means. The peasant's attachment to the soil and the sailor's attachment to the sea transcend all relationships of simple utility. The peasant does not "have" the soil as a simple possession. The soil becomes a part of his being. He becomes existentially identified with the soil. A separation of himself from the soil would entail a loss of identity and a kind of incurable internal bleeding. This bond through participation, expressed in the link between the peasant and the soil, points to the fundamental relation of man to the mystery of being.

In Marcel's philosophy of participation, the notions of intersubjectivity, encounter, and community are decisive. In the second volume of *The Mystery of Being* the author seeks to replace the Cartesian metaphysics of "I think" with a metaphysics of intersubjectivity which is formulated in terms of "we are." Philosophical reflection, he argues, must emancipate its inquiry from the solipsism of an isolated epistemological subject or a transcendental ego. My existence is disclosed only in the context of a "living communication" with other selves. "The more I free myself from the prison of ego-centricism," concludes the author, "the more do I exist." Imbedded in all my existential reflections is a preliminary and precognitive awareness of a communal horizon of which I am inextricably a part. *"I concern myself with being only in so far as I have a more or less distinct consciousness of the underlying unity which ties me to other beings of whose reality I already have a preliminary notion."*

The basic phenomenon of communal intersubjectivity is further elucidated in the author's use of the notion of encounter. The intersubjectivity of human life becomes apparent only in the movements of personal encounter. Now the phenomenon of personal encounter expresses a relationship which is qualitatively diverse from that which obtains in a relationship between physical objects on the level of *thinghood*. Selfhood and thinghood constitute distinct modes of being, correspondingly requiring different modes of apprehension or knowledge. Another human self cannot be encountered as a thing. Every human self is a "thou," and must be encountered as a personal center of subjectivity. Only through encounter does one attain knowledge of another self. The French verb *"reconnaître"* is peculiarly suited to express the movement of encountering. The range of meaning in *reconnaître* is restricted if it is translated in its usual manner as "to recognize." The French usage denotes *acknowledgment* as well as *recognition*. In an *encounter* another self is known when he is acknowledged as a person. Knowledge is acknowledgment.

Allied with notions of the encounter and *reconnaître* are the notions of *disponibilité* and *indisponibilité*, which are elucidated at some length in a previous work by Marcel, *L'Être et Avoir* (*Being and Having*, 1949). The two notions have been rendered into English respectively as *availability* and *unavailability*. Marcel suggests, however, that it would be more natural if one spoke of handiness and unhandiness. The self-centered person is unhandy. He does not make himself and his resources available to other selves. He remains encumbered with himself, insensitive to openness and transparence. He is incapable of sympathizing with other people, and he lacks a requisite fellow feeling for understanding their situation. "He remains shut up in himself, in the petty circle of his private experience, which forms a kind of hard shell round him that he is incapable of breaking through. He is unhandy from his own point of view and unavailable from the point of view of others." The handy and available self is that self who can transcend his private, individual life and become open to a creative communion with other selves. He is ever ready to respond in love and sympathy. No longer enclosed upon himself, he acknowledges the inner freedom or subjectivity of the other, and thus reveals both himself and the other as something other than object. It is Marcel's accentuation of the theme of creative intersubjectivity which most clearly contrasts his existential reflections with those of his fellow countryman, Jean-Paul Sartre. In the existentialism of Sartre the final movement culminates in a disharmonious and alienating ego-centricism. In the existentialism of Marcel the last measure and note is one of harmony—creative communality.

The existential reflections in the author's two-volume work are geared to an elucidation of various facets of the presence of being. Being discloses itself as a mystery—hence, the appropriate title of his lectures, *The Mystery of Being*. In the concluding chapter of Volume I the author erects a signpost for the philosophical wayfarer to help him in his metaphysical journeyings. This signpost is the distinction between problem and mystery. A mystery is something in which I myself am involved. A problem is something from which I detach myself and seek to solve. One is involved in mystery, but one solves problems. Mystery has to do with the experience of presence. Problem has to do with the realm of objects which can be grasped through the determination of an objectivizing reason.

A problem is subject to an appropriate technique; it can be diagramed, quantified, and manipulated. A mystery by its very character transcends every determinable technique. Being is a mystery rather than a problem, and the moment that it is reduced to a problem its significance vanishes. By turning a mystery into a problem one degrades it. When the mystery of the being of the self is subject to a problematic approach, which by definition objectivizes its content, then the personal and subjective quality of selfhood is dissolved. When the mystery of evil is translated into a problem of evil, as is the case in most theodicies, then the issue is so falsified as to render impossible any existentially relevant illumination. In advancing his distinction between mystery and problem, however, Marcel is not delineating a distinction between the unknowable and the knowable. In fact, the unknowable belongs to the domain of the problematic. It points to the limiting horizon of that which can be conceived through objective techniques. The recognition of mystery involves a positive act or responsiveness on the part of self. It expresses a knowledge which is peculiar to its content— an immediate knowledge of participation as contrasted with an objectivizing knowledge of detachment. Knowledge is attainable both in the domain of mystery and in the domain of problem, but the knowledge in each case is irreducibly adapted to its intentional content.

In Volume II the author concludes his philosophical reflections by showing that his philosophy of being is at the same time a philosophy of freedom. Although the notion of freedom is not given as much attention in the existentialism of Marcel as in that of Kierkegaard, Jaspers, and Sartre, it plays a significant role in his elucidations of concrete experience. Freedom is disclosed in the domain of mystery rather than in the domain of problem. Freedom can never be found in a series of external acts. Freedom is found only when the self turns inward and becomes aware of its capacity for commitment and treason. Freedom is disclosed in the subjective movements of promise and betrayal. I am free to bind myself in a promise, and then I am free to betray the one who has taken me into his trust. Freedom is thus disclosed in both its creative and destructive implications. Both fidelity and treason are expressions of a free act. This freedom, which is experienced only *in concreto*, moves within the mystery of man's inner subjectivity. As a problem, freedom can be nothing more than a series of objectively observable psychological states. As a mystery, freedom constitutes the inner core of the self.

There is an inner connection between faith and freedom. In Volume II, which the author has subtitled "Faith and Reality," this inner connection is elaborated. Faith is itself a movement of freedom in the establishment of bonds of commitment—both with one's fellow man and with God. Faith is thus described as trust rather than as intellectual assent to propositional truth. Marcel distinguishes between *believing that* and *believing in*. Faith is not a matter of *believing that*. It is not oriented toward propositions which correspond to some objective reality. Faith is expressed through *believing in*. To believe in another person is to place confidence in him. In effect, this is to say to the other: "I am sure that you will not betray my hope, that you will respond to it, that you will fulfil it." Also, to have faith in God is to establish a relationship of trust in him. Man is free to enter into a covenant with God, invoking a bond of trust and commitment, but he is also free to betray him and revoke the covenant. Faith and freedom disclose the need for transcendence. Transcendence, for the author, is not simply a horizontal transcendence of going beyond in time —as it is for Heidegger and Sartre.

Transcendence has a vertical dimension as well—a going beyond to the eternal. The experience of transcendence is fulfilled only through participation in the life of a transcendent being. Marcel's philosophy of being, unlike that of Heidegger and Sartre, is not simply a philosophy of human finitude. It seeks to establish a path which reaches beyond the finite and temporal to the transcendent and eternal.

THE REBEL

Author: Albert Camus (1913-1960)
Type of work: Ethics
First published: 1951

PRINCIPAL IDEAS ADVANCED

When a person who is slave to the absurd conditions about him declares that there is a limit to what he will endure or approve, he becomes a man, he exists.

In creating value through rebellion, the rebel creates values for all men and makes himself part of the community of men.

Those who attempt to rebel by becoming nihilists or utopians fail to achieve authentic rebellion.

The genuine rebel combines the negative attitude of one who recognizes the relativity of values with the positive attitude of one who makes an absolute commitment which gives rise to spiritual values.

From Robespierre to Stalin, lovers of justice and equality have fallen time and again into contradiction and ended by outraging the humanity they were committed to save. *The Rebel* seeks to understand the failure of a century and a half of revolution and, by returning to its source in the spirit of revolt, to recover the ideal which has eluded the ideologues.

Camus' book is, in one aspect, a history of the whole anti-God, anti-authoritarian movement in literature, philosophy, and government. This is clearly indicated in the subtitle, *An Essay on Man in Revolt.* The historical study is divided into three parts. The first, entitled "Metaphysical Rebellion," examines a gallery of "immoralist" authors beginning with the Marquis de Sade and ending with André Breton. A longer section, called "Historical Rebellion," traces the fortunes of political nihilism both in its individualist and its collectivist forms. A third part, "Rebellion and Art,"

1127

briefly indicates the manner in which the same analysis may be carried over into the fine arts, particularly the history of the novel. Thus, the body of this considerable work is a series of essays in literary and historical criticism.

But the introductory and concluding essays are of a different sort. In them Camus conducts a phenomenological investigation into the data of Revolt, analogous to Max Scheler's study of Resentment and his own earlier analysis of the Absurd. These essays, which are the most original part of the book, provide the norm by which the failures of nihilism are judged, and point the direction of a more humane and creative endeavor.

The essay *The Myth of Sisyphus* (1942) was addressed to the problem of nihilism which engrossed the minds of intellectuals at the close of World War I. In it we are offered Camus' variant of existentialism, according to which the person who has been confronted with the meaninglessness of existence gives his own life a modicum of dignity and significance by holding the posture of revolt. An honest man, says Camus, acts according to his belief. If he affirms that the world is meaningless, he is bound to commit suicide, for to go on living is to cheat. According to Camus in this youthful work, the only honest reason for a man's putting up with the irrationality of things is to be able to feel superior to the forces that crush him—like Pascal's Thinking Reed. To the man of the Absurd, the world becomes as indifferent as he is to the world. He bears his burden without joy and without hope, like Sisyphus, who was condemned to roll his rock up the hill anew each day; but he preserves a titanic fury, refusing any of the pallia-

tives offered by religion or philosophy or by the distractions of pleasure or ambition.

When *The Rebel* was written, ten years later, the fashionable nihilism of the period between the wars was no longer relevant. The fall of France led to the taking of sides by many intellectuals, including Camus. The problem of suicide gave way to that of collaboration. People who had cultivated indifference suddenly found that they could not overlook the difference between Pierre Laval and Charles de Gaulle.

The new concern is plainly evident in Camus' novel *The Plague* (1947), where it is abundantly clear that those who are strong ought to bear the burdens of the weak. In this pest-hole of a world, no man can stir without the risk of bringing death to someone. But although we are all contaminated, we have the choice of joining forces with the plague or of putting up a fight against it. The immediate objective is to save as many as possible from death. But beyond this, and, in Camus' eyes even more important, is the task of saving men from loneliness. It is better to be in the plague with others than to be isolated on the outside.

In *The Rebel*, Camus tries to show that solidarity is logically implied even in the absurdist position; for to perceive that life is absurd there must be consciousness, and for there to be consciousness there must be life. But the moment human life becomes a value, it becomes a value for all men. In this way, absurdism may be extended to prohibit murder as well as suicide. But it offers no creative solution to an age of wholesale exportation, enslavement, and execution. We must turn, instead, to a different kind of revolt—that which on occasion is born in the heart of a slave who suddenly says, "No; there is a limit. So much will I consent to, but no more." At this moment a line is drawn between what it is to be a thing and what it is to be a man. Human nature is delineated, and a new value comes into being. To be sure, the universe ignores it, and the forces of history deny it. But it rises, none the less, to challenge these; and in doing so creates a new force, brotherhood. Out of rebellion Camus wrenches a positive principle of politics as Descartes had found certitude in the midst of doubt. "I rebel," says Camus, "therefore *we* exist."

Although the first stirrings of rebellion are full of promise, the path they mark out is straight and narrow, and few there be that follow it to the end. Like the moral virtues in Aristotle's *Ethics*, it is a mean between two extremes. The rebel, if he thinks out the implications of the impulse which moves within him, knows that he must never kill or oppress or deceive his fellow man. But in the actual world such a policy makes him accessory to the crimes of others. Therefore, he must on occasion perform acts of violence in the interest of suffering humanity. The difficulties of taking arms against oppression without becoming an oppressor are so great that it is small wonder most would-be rebels slip into one false position or another.

In *The Myth of Sisyphus,* Camus went to great lengths showing the inauthentic responses to the Absurd made by the existentialists Søren Kierkegaard, Franz Kafka, and Jean-Paul Sartre, who, according to Camus, rejected literal suicide, but substituted a kind of "philosophical suicide" by making believe that it is possible to escape Absurdity. Just so, in *The Rebel,* Camus' chief line of argument is to show that the great heroes in the literature of revolt and in the history of revolution, almost without exception, fall away from authentic rebellion. For some, the dominant impulse is to negate the forces that frustrate man's development: with them rebellion passes into hatred, and they can think of nothing but destruction. For others, the impulse is to enforce order and realize a standard good: love of their fellow man gives place to an abstract goal which they must achieve at any cost. The former are nihilists, the latter utopians.

Camus' discussion in "Rebellion in Art" provides a clear instance of the two kinds of false rebellion. All art, in his opinion, is essentially a revolt against reality. Art both needs the world and denies it. But contemporary art has allowed itself to be sidetracked. Formalism gravitates too exclusively toward negation, banishing reality and ending in delirium. Realism, however (he specifies the "tough" American variety), by reducing man to elemental and external reactions, is too eager to impose its own order on the world. Both arise, in a sense, out of the spirit of revolt, protesting the hypocrisy of bourgeois conventionality; both fail, as art, inasmuch as they lose touch with the springs of revolt. Proust is Camus' example of a genuine artist: rejecting those aspects of reality which are of no interest to man while lovingly affirming the happier parts, he recreates the universe by redistributing its elements after the heart's desire. This suggests that the creative way is not that of "all or nothing" but that of moderation and limit. The order and unity which make for genuine art do minimal violence to the matter they undertake to re-form. And the artist remains, above all, a friend of man.

Camus' classification of rebels into world-deniers and world-affirmers provides only a rough basis for division when he comes to consider the great figures in the history of revolt. The difficulty is that the contradictions into which their extremism leads renders them at last almost indistinguishable. Nevertheless there is merit in retaining the groupings. Under "Metaphysical Rebellion," Sade's advocacy of universal crime and Alfred de Vigny's Satanism exemplify rebellion which took the way of negation. With them we may place Rimbaud, who made a virtue of renouncing his genius, and the surrealist Breton, who talked of the beauty of shooting at random into a street crowd. On the other side are the partisans of affirmation—Max Stirner with his absolute egotism, and Nietzsche with his deification of fate. When we turn to "Historical Rebellion," there are the anarchists and nihilists such as Michael Bakunin and Dmitri Pisarev, for whom destruction was an end in itself. But they are more than balanced by the revolutionaries, whose ambition in overthrowing the present order was but a means toward fulfilling the destiny of a race or of mankind—Robespierre and St. Just, Mussolini and Hitler, Marx and Lenin.

The section on Metaphysical Revolt deals with those whose revolt was centered in the realm of imagination. Camus finds their archetype not in Prometheus but in Cain, because rebellion presupposes a doctrine of creation and a personal deity who is held to be responsible for the human condition. Their temper is rather that of blasphemy than of unbelief; and when they go so far as to deny that there is a God, their protest, lacking an object, turns into madness. Here Ivan Karamazov is more instructive than real-life rebels. Indignation causes him to reject God on the grounds that a world that entails suffering ought never to have been permitted. But he discovers that, having rejected God, there is no longer any limit—"everything is permitted." And Ivan acquiesces in the murder of his father—before going mad. Ivan rejects *grace* and has nothing to put in its place. This is the tragedy of nihilism.

Historical Revolt was directed less immediately against God than against the absolutism of divine right kings and the prerogatives of feudal lords and bishops. But it has its metaphysical dimension. In rejecting the old order, the revolutionaries too were rejecting grace, without, however, falling into nihilism; for instead of concluding that all things are permitted, they immediately divinized *justice*. They repudiated Christ, but retained the apparatus of an infallible institution within which alone salvation is possible. And in place of the madness of Ivan Karamazov, they find themselves swallowed up in Chigalov's despair. Their conclusion is a direct contradiction of their original premises: starting from unlimited freedom they arrive at unlimited despotism.

In Camus' opinion, just as the nineteenth century revolted against *grace*, the twentieth must revolt against *justice*. The kingdom of men which the revolutionaries sought to substitute for the kingdom of God has retreated into the distance and the goal has been brought not a step nearer. The fault is in the nature of revolution itself, which, as the word indicates, describes a full cycle. In rebellion, the slave rises against his master; in revolution, he aspires to take his master's place. Thus, the champions of justice have merely substituted a new domination for the old. And in many ways the new is less tolerable than that which it replaced. For the rule of God at least allowed man to preserve the human image; but when the sacred disappeared, man's dignity disappeared with it. Ivan Karamazov said that "everything is permitted"; Chigalov, the human-engineer, calculated that nine-tenths of the human race must be reduced to herd animals. This is what takes place when God is overthrown. It is a principle of all revolutions, says Camus, that human nature is infinitely malleable; in other words, that there is no special human nature. Under the kingdom of grace there was; and the rebel insists that there still is. This is the limit that he opposes to Caesarism. Rebellion rediscovers man, affirms that he is not a mere thing, insists that a distinctive nature sets him off from all other beings and, at the same time, unites him with every other man. From this point of view, the only alternative to grace is *rebellion*.

No doubt enough has been said about the defections into which rebels are prone to fall. Like many a preacher, Camus finds it easier to criticize the failures of others than to present a clear-cut statement of what authentic rebellion entails. We have, of course, his stories and dramas to fill out the picture. But so far as the present essay is concerned, the only vivid illustration of genuine revolt is found in his account of a group of Russian terrorists (the most exemplary were brought to trial in 1905) who combined nihilism

with definite religious principles. Camus calls them "fastidious nihilists." "In the universe of total negation, these young disciples try with bombs and revolvers and also with the courage with which they walk to the gallows, to escape from contradiction and to create the values they lack." They did not hesitate to destroy; but by their death they believed they were recreating a community founded on love and justice, thus resuming the mission the church had betrayed. They combined respect for human life in general with the resolution to sacrifice their own lives. Death was sought as payment for the crimes that the nihilists knew they must commit.

Transposed into a more moderate key, what Camus seems to be advocating is a life of tension in which contradictions may live and thrive. There must be a way between that of the Yogi and that of the Commissar, between absolute freedom and absolute justice. In this world, man has to be content with relative goods; but he does not have to give them anything less than his absolute commitment. This is humanism, though hardly of the Anglo-Saxon utilitarian variety. The values born of the spirit of rebellion are essentially spiritual. The rebel wills to serve justice without committing injustice in the process, to use plain language and avoid falsehood, to advance toward unity without denying the origins of community in the free spirit.

Politically, Albert Camus takes his stand with syndicalist and libertarian thought: as opposed to the revolutionists who would order society from the top down, he favors a society built out of local autonomous cells. Far from being romantic, he holds that a communal system is more realistic than the totalitarian, based as it is on concrete relations such as occupation and the village. Nor is it new. From the time of the Greeks, the struggle has been going on (especially around the Mediterranean) between city and empire, de-liberate freedom and rational tyranny, altruistic individualism and the manipulation of the masses. It is the endless opposition of moderation to excess in man's attempt to know and apply the measure of his stature, his refusal to be either beast or god.

NATURE, MIND, AND DEATH

Author: Curt John Ducasse (1881-   )
Type of work: Philosophy of philosophy, metaphysics, epistemology
First published: 1951

PRINCIPAL IDEAS ADVANCED

Philosophy can proceed scientifically from data statements in which terms crucial to philosophical problems are used to theorize concerning the meanings of such terms; the terms central to the philosophic enterprise are value-terms.

Causation is understandable in terms of a single change (the cause) prior to another event (the effect) in a specific environment.

Sensations are not objects of acts of sensing, but kinds of sensing, ways of responding sensibly.

Mind is a substance capable of receiving impressions, causing bodily action, and causing events in consciousness.

Although life after death cannot be proved, it is possible: what could survive is not personality, but individuality.

Nature, Mind, and Death is a comprehensive summary of the author's views concerning causality, nature, matter, mind, and the possibility of life after death. Its importance lies in the fact that its conclusions are presented not simply as metaphysical statements, but as illustrations of a general method which is applicable to all philosophical problems. The book consequently falls both in the area of metaphysics and in the area of epistemology, or theory of knowledge. It restates the author's view on philosophical method, which was earlier described in *Philosophy as a Sci-*ence (1941), and elaborates his views on causation, perception, and symbols, previously published in monographs and periodical articles.

The first section of this work is devoted to a discussion of the method of philosophy, with an illustration of its application to the problem of the nature of reality. Ducasse believes, contrary to the tenets of certain modern philosophers, that metaphysics is, or can be, a legitimate and profitable study. The reason for its being held in disrepute is that its problems, in general, have been so badly stated that

1132

it has been unable to avoid looseness of inference, ambiguity of terms, confusion of issues, and inadequate testing of its hypotheses. The tacit assumption has apparently been that one can attain satisfactory knowledge in this area by using the vague terms of ordinary language, and without bothering to introduce the technical apparatus of logic and the scientific method. The two maxims of a scientific philosophy are that the data with which it deals should be stated clearly and explicitly and that the problem whose solution is being sought should be defined as sharply and unambiguously as possible.

More explicitly, the philosophical method is substantially the same as the scientific method. It consists of data which are disclosed through observation and experimentation, formulations of these data in language appropriate to the problem, empirical generalization, analysis and confirmation of hypotheses, and practical application of the knowledge thus obtained. There are, in fact, two kinds of problems in science: problems "for" science, and problems "of" science. The former are the practical or technological problems; these have to do with means and ends, provided the ends are not the purely theoretical ends identified with mere knowledge. The latter are theoretical or epistemic problems, which characterize science as an explanation or understanding of nature. Problems of this kind are themselves of two sorts: those which concern, on the one hand, what is observable, what is primitive, and what must be taken as initial or empirically basis; and, on the other hand, the abstract theories which are derived from the primitive data and constitute their explanations and interpretations.

Ducasse believes that philosophy differs from science, not in method, but in the special character of its practical and theoretical problems and in the nature of its primitive data and its derived hypotheses. Practical philosophy always concerns itself with problems of *values*; it is therefore much interested in means and ends, as is science, but it goes beyond science in raising questions concerning the values of the means and the values of the ends, and whether acts *ought* or *ought not* to be performed in certain circumstances where value judgments are involved. Theoretically, philosophy centers its attention on procuring the knowledge which will permit us to make reliable judgments of value having the forms, "This syllogism is (or is not) valid," "This act is (or is not) moral," "This consideration is (or is not) important." These are the primitive, initial, and basic facts of philosophy. Theoretical philosophy then goes on to explain these data. Here its character is sharply distinguished from that of science, for its problems now become semantical; its task is to discover the meaning or meanings of terms. The data from which it starts are actual statements in which value-terms are used, and its problem is to formulate a linguistic hypothesis which will attempt to answer the question: "What does the value-term as employed in these statements mean?" The test of such a hypothesis lies in observing whether the proposed definition is actually substitutable in these assertions without altering any of their standard implications. If it is, then its validity is proportionate to the number of the original statements or to their representative character as samples of a large group; if it is not, it has to be rejected

1133

or revised. This procedure constitutes empirical confirmation, for the meanings are empirically discoverable. Furthermore, Ducasse's theory does not in any way reduce philosophy to a mere study of language, for statements *in* language can also be statements *of* extralinguistic facts; this is no more paradoxical than saying that a mathematical problem which is solvable by purely formal techniques may also be a problem about nature.

As an illustration of his philosophical method, Ducasse examines the problem of explaining what may be meant by an individual who utters a number of true judgments containing the word "real." That this *is* a value-predicate is not explicitly stated by Ducasse, though in the earlier book referred to above he makes this point quite clear: to be *real* is to be *interesting*, and "interesting" *is* a value-predicate. The problem of discovering the possible meanings of the word "real" is an *ontological problem*, and the solution may be termed an *ontological hypothesis*. Four hypotheses, each proposing a meaning for the word "real," are examined: (1) "real" as opposed to "apparent": a dog is not really ferocious though apparently so; (2) "real" as opposed to "nonexistent": black swans are real but green swans are not; (3) "real" in the sense of physical existence as opposed to mathematical or psychological existence: black swans are real but numbers are not, or ideas are not; (4) "real" in the sense of what is relevant to our purposes or interests as opposed to what is not: a table is really a cloud of minute particles at relatively vast distances from one another, not a hard and solid object. Solving the philosophical problem consists in substituting each of

these meanings of the word "real" in the statements initially uttered by the individual to see whether their implications would be altered. Any meaning which does not permit this substitution must be eliminated as a disconfirmed hypothesis; any meaning, if any, which permits the substitution is to that degree confirmed and constitutes a solution of the ontological problem.

In Part II of his book Ducasse turns to an application of his method to the clarification of some of the fundamental categories of philosophy. One of these is *causation*. The procedure to be used in examining this concept should not be that adopted by Russell when he collects a number of philosophical definitions of "cause" and tries to determine which is right; these are philosophical hypotheses, not data, and one cannot decide whether they are good or bad unless he has something on which to base his decision. The data must be a series of statements made by a certain individual (we should probably try to eliminate at the outset an individual who employs odd usages, or who is crude or careless in his speech, or who is a deliberate innovator) when he asserts, say, that the New England hurricane of 1938 caused the death of a number of persons and that its tidal wave caused a number of yachts to become lodged on the top of a bridge.

Ducasse finds that the meaning of "causation" which will best explain these statements, and similar ones, is a complex one, but one which can be rendered precise through careful formulation of its properties. Distinction must be made between "cause of" and "condition of," the first being synonymous with "sufficient to" and the second with "necessary to." We are permitted to speak of a cause *necessarily* producing its effect, but we must not confuse the necessity holding between natural events with the necessity holding between the premises and conclusion of a valid argument. Causes are never substances or forces, but always events or happenings. Causation is a relation in which only two changes occur, the earlier one being the cause, and the later one the effect; but it is a triadic rather than a dyadic relation, because there must also be present an environment in which the changes take place. Also, although causation is a relation between concrete, individual events, it may be generalized into a relation between *kinds* of events and may then be formulated as a causal law. Causal relations are empirically observable, but since the cause must be detected in every case as the *only* change in a certain neighborhood, and since to do so requires us to be sure that *no other* change is present, we can easily make mistakes and believe that we find causal relations when they are not really present.

The solution to the problem of whether the will is free is dependent upon the results of Ducasse's previous analysis of causation, which showed that while causal laws are *possible* in the case of repeated causal connections, the universality of causation does not of itself entail that there *are* such causal laws, or that every event which occurred was theoretically predictable. Since a cause is a cause only within a given state of affairs, it will produce its effect when it recurs only if this given state of affairs also recurs. Determinism, therefore, if it means universal predictability, cannot be proved to apply to our world. Freedom of the will exists in the sense that man can do, within limits, what he wills; this may

be called "freedom of efficacy." Freedom *to will,* as distinguished from freedom *to act as one wills,* is a special case of freedom of efficacy; in some cases man can will what he wants to, and in some cases he cannot. A volition is determined by the circumstances which a man believes himself to be facing at a certain time and by the consequences which he judges that volition to have. Without this determination moral acts would be irrational and erratic, and rewards and punishments would be senseless. Freedom of choice consists in awareness of alternative possible courses of action, the choice being determined by one's preference. There is no such thing as acting against one's will, for all such cases involve choosing among alternatives, all of which are repugnant, and what one does is merely to choose the *least* unpleasant. Furthermore, although one's choice in a given situation depends on his volitional nature, which is itself dependent on his heredity, upbringing, and social environment and seems therefore to be external to him, yet his volitional nature is still his own. This conclusion is established by the fact that his volitional nature is not fixed forever, but can be changed as a result of self-observation and self-appraisal. Finally, the predictability of a person's future acts is not in any way incompatible with the freedom which we believe him to possess.

Part III deals with nature, matter, mind, and the problem of perception. The naturalistic theory of mind argues that mind is not a special, psychical entity, which is the antithesis of everything that is material. On the contrary, it is simply the name for the way in which the biological organism behaves when it is adapting itself to its environment, or adapting its environment to itself, in a cognitive manner. Such a theory describes mind as a part of nature, if we mean by this term whatever is perceptually public and whatever is existentially implicit therein. The most extreme form of naturalism involves a radical behaviorism which denies the existence of mental events observable only by introspection.

This form of radical behaviorism Ducasse rejects, on the grounds that the meaning which it gives to the word "mind" is quite different from that given to it by the ordinary man. Thus, the behavioristic conception of mind is to be rejected because it clashes with the preëxisting, commonly accepted use of the term "mind." It does not represent a *fact* which naturalism has discovered, but only a deep-seated *resolution* to make the term applicable to something in the perceptually public world. Introspective knowledge, indicated by statements such as "I am conscious of such-and-such" must be interpreted by the behaviorist as a special kind of behavior response. But we do not ordinarily *mean* a behavior response when we are aware of our own consciousness, and there is no reason whatsoever why this awareness should always be *expressed* in this kind of statement.

The solution which Ducasse offers to the problem of perception seems to depart from, rather than to be in accord with, ordinary usage. But he permits the philosopher, in cases "where ordinary language hesitates," to "purge it of defects." He begins by making a linguistic distinction between two kinds of accusatives, illustrated by "I jumped an obstacle" and "I jumped a jump." He calls the former an "alien accusative" and the latter a "connate

accusative." Then he proceeds to subdivide each of these accusatives into special kinds: coördinate and subordinate. For example, a jump is coördinate with jumping, but a leap is subordinate to it; and an obstacle is coördinate with jumping, but a fence is subordinate to it. We then have four cases:

(1) coördinately alien accusative: jump an obstacle;

(2) subordinately alien accusative: jump a fence;

(3) coördinately connate accusative: jump a jump;

(4) subordinately connate accusative: jump a leap.

Now it is obvious that the accusatives in cases (1) and (2) may both exist independently of the processes, in that both obstacles and fences may exist without being jumped. But in cases (3) and (4) the accusatives cannot be independent, for a jump could not exist without the jumping, and a leap, since it is a special case of jumping, could not exist without the jumping. Now let us translate the problem into one of *perception,* and examine the distinction between "I see blue" and "I see lapis lazuli." Ducasse refers to G. E. Moore's argument that these are both cases of alien accusatives, that in both instances I am aware of a content, through *different* contents, of consciousness or experience. Ducasse disagrees with Moore. He insists that the lapis lazuli is an alien accusative because its nature is such that whenever I turn my eyes upon it in daylight it causes me to experience something called "blue." However, the blue is not an alien but a connate accusative. When I see blue I do not see a blue content; I see "bluely." Furthermore, when I see blue I am seeing a subordinate accusative, not a coördinate one; seeing

1136

blue is a special *kind* of seeing, not seeing a special *kind of content*. We are now ready for the final conclusion. Since in the case of connate accusatives the object cannot exist independently of the awareness, the blue which I see cannot exist independently of my awareness of it; to assert that it could exist independently would be as absurd as to say that leaping could exist without jumping.

The view of mind which Ducasse develops on the basis of these and similar considerations is that mind is a *substance*. This view is arrived at inductively from what introspection reveals, and it discloses that mind, like other substances, exhibits itself by its properties and capacities. The minimal properties which a mind would have to exhibit are three: the capacity for *impressions* of a certain kind, caused by physical stimulation of sense organs, by telepathy, by clairvoyance, or otherwise; the capacity for *causation of external effects* in the body or in the outside world *by means of impulses;* and the capacity for *causation of psychical events by other psychical events,* as in the case of causing an impulse by an impression.

If mind is this sort of thing it must have a certain kind of relation to the body, and the nature of this relation will determine the possibility of life after death. This is the topic of Part IV of the book.

What are the characteristics in terms of which I identify my body as my own, rather than that of someone else? Ducasse lists four. (1) It is the only physical object in which certain bodily changes can be caused or inhibited by my mind: *my* blushing can be caused only by *my* feeling of shame. (2) It is the only physical object in which

certain changes can cause changes in my mind: sticking a pin in *my* finger causes *me* to feel pain. (3) It is the only physical object in which mutilations of brain or sensory nerves causes alterations in my conscious mind: cutting *my* optical nerve causes *me* to lose my capacity for vision. (4) It is the only physical object in which structural connections among brain neurons can be brought about by my willing to acquire certain habits and skills: *my* brain pattern can be changed by *my* decision to learn a certain foreign language and *my* developing the skills which are required.

Ducasse thus concludes that there must be direct causal interactions between two different substances, mind and body. There is no more mystery about this causal interdependence than there is about physico-physical causation. Since minds and bodies are substances, and causal actions have been shown above to hold between certain kinds of events which are changes in substances, there is no reason for denying causal interaction between mind and body; the fact of interaction does not depend on the *kinds* of events interacting, but only on the *form* of the interrelation.

Life after death cannot, according to Ducasse, be either proved or disproved. The fact that some people believe in it and some do not can be explained by many factors: human credulity (the readiness to believe without having investigated); such human bias as the unfounded conviction that only the material can be real; the existence of certain phenomena—the so-called "Psi" phenomena, including clairvoyance, precognition, retrocognition and telepathy—which, supposing them to be genuine, have not yet been explained and *could*, therefore, constitute evidence for survival; the variations in the beliefs as to *what* survives death, in case anything survives; and the admitted existence of fraud and trickery on the part of certain people who had previously claimed to demonstrate immortality.

It is only the *possibility* of life after death that Ducasse proves. This he does by showing that the arguments against survival contain certain loopholes. To show, for example, that mind and body interact, and therefore that many psychical events are caused by physical events, does not establish the impossibility of psychical events which are not thus caused; hence, a disembodied mind *may* exist. And to show that mind cannot exist without body because mind is *defined* in terms of behavioral responses is to prove nothing, but only to attempt to make our language legislate over nature and thus prescribe what can and what cannot exist. On the positive side, Ducasse argues that certain forms of survival are perfectly consistent with what he has shown mind to be, with what he has shown the mind-body relation to

be, and with all empirical facts, whether normal or paranormal, now known. Furthermore, these forms, in addition to being possible, are *significant* enough to us now to be of interest.

The form of survival which Ducasse considers to be both possible and significant is the following: What survives is not man's *personality* (his habits, skills, and memories) but his *individuality* (his native aptitudes, instincts, and proclivities). This could be the distillation from a number of different personalities. For some time after death the personality could persist in a dream-like consciousness, and during this interval, through recollection of the acts and events of the preceding life, new dispositions and deep changes in attitude could be generated much as they are in life when experiencing a deep tragedy produces a change in values. Finally, our desire that the injustices of life should be redressed in the afterlife would be satisfied not only because a man's individuality shapes his personality but also because his personality shapes his individuality; therefore justice is immanent in the entire process.

SYSTEMATIC THEOLOGY
(Volume One)

Author: Paul Tillich (1886-   )
Type of work: Theology
First published: 1951

PRINCIPAL IDEAS ADVANCED

Man was created to be oriented by an ultimate concern; such a concern may be either for God or for some finite object.

Philosophy is the cognitive approach to reality in which reality is the object; theology is concerned with the meaning of being for men.

The sources of systematic theology are the Bible, tradition, and the history of religion and culture; these sources are perceived through the medium of experience.

Revelational answers are taken by the theologian from the source, through the medium, and under the norm (the New Being in Jesus as the Christ).

Revelation transcends the subject-object distinction; usually in a moment of "ontic shock," the abrupt confrontation with the power of being, one's finiteness is overcome by anticipation: this is salvation.

Religious symbols need not be true; it is enough that they be existentially effective, that they evoke awareness of the power of being.

There is little doubt that the two greatest Protestant theologians today are Paul Tillich and Karl Barth. These stand far above all others in originality and creativeness of thought; yet they stand near opposite ends of the theological spectrum. At one time or another they have both been classified as "neo-orthodox," presumably because both generally concur in their pessimistic doctrines on man. Yet their fundamental contrasts make such a designation meaningless. Theologically, Barth belongs solidly in the orthodox tradition of Luther and Calvin, and with Kant philosophically; Tillich, on the other hand, stands clearly in the liberal theological tradition of Schleiermacher and Otto, and philosophically in the train of such Idealists as Schelling and Hegel. The fittingness of the designation "neo" in both cases rests on the influence of Kierkegaard and the existentialists as well as the Biblical critics upon them.

Barth's greatness rests fundamentally on his ability to resurrect the orthodox dogma of Christendom in all its Reformation centrality in the aftermath of an epoch of liberalism that had largely undermined Biblical authority, the unique miracles of the Incarnation and Resurrection, the meta-physical significance of the Atonement, the necessity of special revelation, the legitimacy of original sin as a descriptive category, the indispensability of the "new birth," and the utter uniqueness of Christianity. Thus, Barth stated a radical rejection of all compromise with culture. In his opinion, Protestant theology since Schleiermacher has been what he called "Kultur-protestismus," or what H. Richard Niebuhr calls the "Christ of Culture" position; that is, instead of Christendom standing against culture, against the faith of secularism, it has become its product. Cultural concern has become cultural capitulation, for since the days of Kant Protestant theologians have seen their task as being one of defending the faith on culture's own terms; it was inevitable that culture should become Christianity's criterion of truth. Such is the irony of the impotent Christianity of the present.

Barth's solution is to have no dealings with culture; theology is strictly *Church* theology, or as he prefers to call it, Church dogmatics. He who would know the Truth must enter the community of the faithful, must participate in the action and liturgy that only believers understand. Here the

1139

Holy Spirit enters the human soul with the power to overwhelm and cure. If the faith be "proven," "defended," or "argued," the spirit relied upon is finite, and the word spoken is not the Word of God but the word of man.

It is here that the tremendous gulf between Barth and Tillich is most visible. Tillich is, above all, a theologian to, for, and of culture; in fact, the new enterprise called "theology of culture" is largely of his making. Tillich has been from the beginning an activist in politics, social work, art, and culture in general. It was his work with the Christian Socialists in Germany and his outspoken attitude toward the rising totalitarianism which drove Tillich from his homeland to permanent residency in the United States. Since then he has been actively writing in almost every area of the social sciences, defending Christianity in the categories of and from the problems of culture. In his well-known work entitled *The Religious Situation* (1929), Tillich early clarified his task—his concern is not with the religion of the churches but with the faith contained in and being witnessed to by every culture in every aspect of its work and product. Tillich's insistence is not upon any special revelation in Christianity, but upon the Christian faith, rightly reinterpreted, as the clue to the universal revelation of the eternal God-man relation, universally available and universally perceived.

Tillich's lifetime of thought and activity is presently being crystallized in a celebrated three-volume *Systematic Theology*. Volume One is by far the most important, for in it Tillich lays out his system as a whole, defines his basic categories, and develops his fundamental theological method. Charac-

teristic of Germans, but especially characteristic of Tillich, is the tendency to create new terminology with abandon. This makes his work particularly difficult to understand. For the reader not well versed in philosophical theology, it is suggested that he begin his reading of Tillich with *The Courage to Be* (1952), *The Religious Situation* (1929), or *The Dynamics of Faith* (1957). Although Volume One of *Systematic Theology* is by far his most important work, *The Dynamics of Faith* is the most lucid presentation of his basic approach which is available to the general reader; in its own right, it is a classic of clarity and simplicity, traits usually uncommon to Tillich.

Tillich's system is contained in his unique theological method, the "method of correlation." Theology must exist in the tension of revelational truths and the questions implied in man's concrete situation. This "situation" to which theology must respond is "the totality of man's creative self-interpretation in a special period." Underlying Tillich's thinking here is the Augustinian conception of community. For St. Augustine, man was created to be oriented by a supreme "love," or what Tillich calls an "ultimate concern." This concern is either for "God" or for some finite object, being, idea, or goal made "god." Communities are formed on the basis of their ultimate loyalty to some common object of love. For Tillich, every epoch, generation, people, and nation, is so characterized, drawing from this ultimate concern its vitality, values, and destiny.

Consequently, this ultimate concern permeates all of a culture's products, giving them their unique "style"; this is most true of art. The theologian must analyze these works, ascertaining

1140

through this style the "faith" of each cultural situation. Thereby the questions haunting a particular situation are seen expressed in the categories which that situation can understand; only by finding these can the theologian make revelation relevent and intelligible. As Tillich says, the only proper theology is "answering theology."

For Tillich, every attempt to understand human existence must begin with "an a priori of experience and valuation." That is, every such attempt is a circle, beginning and ending with a "mystical a priori," an immediate intuition of something ultimate in value and being that transcends the distinction between subject and object. This intuitive foundation is the common basis which Tillich sees between the realms of question and answer and which makes the correlating dialogue possible. This basis applies to the Christian theologian, but his circle is smaller, for he is committed to the Christian message as the criterion of all other circles.

The distinction between philosophy and theology appears here. Philosophy is *that cognitive approach to reality in which reality as such is the object,"* that is, the structure which makes reality a whole. *The* philosophical question concerns the "general structures" which make experience possible. The Kantian influence here is obvious. Theology, having as its object that which concerns man ultimately, raises the same question as philosophy, but in a manner of involvement, not detachment. While philosophy is interested in the *structure* of being, theology is concerned with the *meaning* of being *for us.* Although these two may be distinguished, the philosopher of

necessity operates from an ultimate concern, and the theologian must assume the structure of being. Yet they cannot contradict each other, for "no philosophy which is obedient to the universal *logos* can contradict the concrete *logos,* the Logos 'who became flesh.' "

The sources of systematic theology are threefold. The Bible is the basic source, interpreted not infallibly but as human response to historical events. The second source is tradition. The third is the history of religion and culture, for herein are the means of expression, their confirmation, and the formulations of the existential questions. These sources are perceived through the medium of "experience." In this regard, Tillich sees Christianity as divided between the Augustinian-Franciscan tradition and that of Aquinas and Duns Scotus. For the former there was an immediate awareness of being-itself, a mystic intuition underlying all human operations; the latter tradition, however, replaced such mystical immediacy with "analytical detachment," not experiencing the divine but inferring it from sense-data regarded as prior and more certain.

The Augustinian-Franciscan approach, on which Tillich insists, he sees classically formulated by Friedrich Schleiermacher, who defined religion as the "feeling of absolute dependence." This experience, having its religious roots in pietism and its philosophical roots in Spinoza and Schelling, Tillich sees as being "rather near" to his experience of "ultimate concern." The sources become revelatory only when in them one experiences the power of being as one's ultimate concern.

Over against the sources and medium Tillich places a "norm" by which these are formulated. This norm must be the basic existential question of an age. In the early Greek Church it was the question of finitude, death, and error; in the Reformation this question concerned a merciful God and the forgiveness of sins. In our age, Tillich insists, it is the question of "a reality in which the self-estrangement of our existence is overcome, a reality of reconciliation and reunion, of creativity, meaning and hope." Such a reality Tillich calls "the New Being." For the Christian, while the critical principle is that of ultimate concern, the norm is the New Being in Jesus as the Christ. The former judges all religion as to "form," the latter judges it as to "content."

Systematic theology is essentially a rational discipline, but rational in two special senses. For Tillich there are two types of reason—"ontological" and "technical." The former is reason as the capacity to participate in immediacy, for transcending the subject-object bifurcation—this is the experience which is revelation, whereby the whole man is grasped by an ultimate concern. Hereby the "content" of faith is received. "Technical" or formal reason is man's capacity for logical procedure; hereby the content of faith is systematized into theological concepts. This relation of form and content is always dialectical; thus theology is always changing, for since its method is that of "correlation," its formulations change with the situation. The revelational answers are taken by the theologian *from* the source, *through* the medium, *under* the norm. The content is revealed; the form is dependent on the structure of the questions.

For Tillich, such a method "escapes"

one of the basic religious quarrels. By considering only the *existential* validity of religious symbols, he "transcends" the inadequacies of supernaturalism, naturalism, and dualism or natural theology. As we shall see more clearly, Tillich rejects any supernatural realm and any theistic "object"; his concern is only with the existential nature of finite reality.

Having established his theological method and the ontological presuppositions implied by this method, Tillich develops his three-volume theology logically. The work is composed of five parts, each of which analyzes one portion of finite existence and provides an exposition on the basis of sources, medium, and norm. These parts are: "Reason and Revelation," "Being and God," "Existence and Christ," "Life and the Spirit," and "History and the Kingdom of God." Volume One consists of an Introduction and the first two parts.

In Part One, "Reason and Revelation," Tillich attempts to analyze reason in terms of the two types indicated. He insists that our age has made technical reason supreme, reducing reason to reasoning, concerned only with means to ends. The classical idea of ontological reason as the source of structures, values, and meanings, has been totally dismissed, and the "ends" are provided by non-rational forces. Religion has become the instrument of technical reason. In such a situation, the task of Christian theology, for Tillich, is to exhibit "the essence of ontological reason" as identical with "the content of revelation," thereby indicating the difference between ontological reason in its perfection and its predicament in the different stages of its actualization. It must show that such

1142

perfection rests in its unity with being-itself, and that its weakness is a result of the conditions of existence. Reason thereby raises the question of revelation.

Tillich defines ontological reason as "the structure of the mind which enables it to grasp and to shape reality." Such reason has its receptive side (constituted by a cognitive and aesthetic polarity) and its reactive side (constituted by an organizational and organic polarity). The affinity between the objective structure of reality and the structure of the mind points to something in both which transcends both; this Tillich calls "being-itself," that "power" which manifests itself inexhaustibly in everything. Each realm points to this in its own way, whether as Truth-Itself, Beauty-Itself, and the like.

This "depth of reason" which apprehends the depth in all things can be expressed only in terms of myth and symbol; but the fact that these contradict reason witnesses to reason as "fallen" in its existential condition. Herein reason raises the question of revelation. This Tillich sees exhibited in Kant's near-perfect description of finite reason. Finite reason cannot grasp being-itself, for the mind's categories are finite. But Kant's doctrine of the categorical imperative points to the depth of practical reason, just as his doctrine of the teleological principle in art and nature points to the depth of "ontological reason." Thus, since the component elements (polarities) of reason operate in relative isolation and conflict, they raise the question of revelation, "the reintegration of reason."

Further, knowing is a form of union between knower and known. Yet finite knowledge is characterized by detachment, separation, the chasm between subject and object. Likewise, knowledge is desired in order to heal, to reunite; yet in finite knowing the alienation remains even more strongly. Thus, what is asked for is a type of "knowing" which transcends such conditions. And last, knowledge which is certain is not ultimately significant, while that which is ultimately significant cannot be given certainty. This dilemma likewise gives rise to the desperate search for revelation in which ultimate significance and certainty are present.

Revelation is the answer for this existential dilemma of reason, for it transcends the subject-object distinction in immediacy. It is the ecstatic, mystic, intuitive experience of the "ground of being" as that which is our ultimate concern. It is usually derived through an "ontic shock," through being driven to the boundary of human capacity where one is still sustained in a "nevertheless" by the power of being beyond him. This is revelation, and it is "salvation," for one's finiteness is "overcome in anticipation."

Reason is grasped from beyond itself, yet the beyond is the mystery in reason's own depth. In it the person is grasped as a whole, and the polarities of reason are sustained in a unitary function. This is revelation, for the mind is made one with itself. The "objective" event or "source" with which such experience is correlated is a "miracle," but not miracle in the sense of supernatural interference. For Tillich, "miracle" is a special constellation of elements whereby they become a "medium" of the ground of being, becoming "transparent" by pointing beyond themselves to the power of being which sustains them. They are miracles only for those who receive them as such, who enter into a subject-subject relation of immediacy.

Because, for Tillich, revelation is the correlation between mind and the ground of being, and since all things exist through their participation in this ground, all things may become media of this power; that is, all things may be seen as transparent, as revelational. This is the meaning of sacraments: that bread, stone, a book or person, may become the instrument of the revelational correlation. And yet a distinction may be made between original and dependent revelation. Men may come into a revelational relation with a constellation seen as miracle by other men in the past; the same power is experienced, but the medium ("source") is derived. In this sense Jesus is revelatory; unlike orthodox Christians, Tillich understands Jesus himself as not the revelation, but as the *medium* of revelation for any who accept him *as the Christ*. In this fashion Tillich attempts to escape (his word is "transcend") the problem of Biblical historicity. As he says in other works, if it could be shown with probability that the historical man Jesus never lived, it would not change Christianity. The basis of Christian revelation is not Jesus Christ, but Jesus *as* the Christ. For all those moved by the power of being *through* the Biblical "portrait" of Jesus as the Christ, this "revelation" is valid; that is, the power of being is existentially efficacious. So with all "knowledge" of the divine—all designations are "symbolic" in the sense that their "truth" is their capacity to evoke awareness of the power of being. Since they provide no "knowledge" of the divine, their "truth" comes into being and dies. Symbols are born of the collective unconscious of believers and are valid only as long as they retain this connotative capacity.

For Tillich, the uniqueness of the Christian revelation rests in the insistence on Jesus as the *final* revelation, "final" meaning the criterion of all other revelational correlations. The criteria of finality are these: awareness of uninterrupted unity with the ground of being and constant negation of self to this ground. This is to be completely transparent, therefore the most complete medium, for it witnesses to what all things are ontologically. The Christ is Christ only because he was constantly conscious of God and was denied equality with God, who sacrificed through the Cross "the Jesus who is Jesus to Jesus who is the Christ." This means that an object or being is "redeemed," restored to its essential being, when it rejects all claims for the finite to be absolute and points beyond itself to its true source of power.

As his other volumes make clearer, to stand in such transparency is to know oneself as a "new being," for one knows that despite the fact that he is unacceptable, he is nevertheless sustained in being—he is "accepted." This, for Tillich, is the meaning of the Protestant norm of justification by faith, reinterpreted as norm for our contemporary situation. Being so redeemed, one can apprehend all things with the "vision of the New Being," that is, can enter into "I-Thou" relations with all of reality, perceiving in all things the power of being which permeates all things. This is the vision of universal salvation of which such revelation makes promise.

In regard to culture, the final criterion judges all cultures, determining the degree to which the products of each are transparent to their ground. The ideal is a "theonomous" culture, as opposed to the "autonomous" culture of the twentieth century in which its bankrupt products witness only to the hollowness of "self-sufficient finitude." Such judgment drives a culture to the "abyss" whereby in disillusionment it may apprehend the power of being operative even when denied. This is the positive function of theology of culture, the fullest completion of Tillich's method of correlation.

This "ground of being" towards which the symbol "God" points cannot be known, only experienced. The only literal statement possible is that "God is being-itself"; all other declarations are symbolic. For example, God is both "cause" and "substance," yet transcends both. Perhaps Tillich's most indicative statement is that God can be thought of only through a double negative—God is the negation of the negation of being. Here we see the fuller significance of Tillich's rejection of supernaturalism. God is neither an object nor a subject—"He" transcends both. It is not even true to say that God exists. All affirmations of God are only affirmations about finite existence. To say, for example, that "God is good" means that God is the ground of finite good. God as "living" means he is the ground of life.

This is why Tillich's section on God begins with the questions of finite Being from which the affirmation of God arises. It is from the awareness of anxiety that man's affirmation of God begins. God is the name for the ultimate concern which answers this question of existence. The tension in *man's* ultimate concern is the basis for the different types of ideas of God in history.

It is here that the radicalness of Tillich's conception of both metaphysics and theology can be seen. When living and nonliving, personal and nonpersonal, free and determined, static and dynamic, unity and diversity, potentiality and actuality, and the like, are all finite polarities which the divine transcend, truth in both the philosophical and theological senses is radically reinterpreted. Theologically, dogma provides not knowledge of the divine being, but symbols of *finite* experience in relation to an undifferentiated ground. Metaphysically, ontology is not knowledge of the structures of Being Itself, but knowledge of the *structures* of finite existence. It is for this reason that the label "religious naturalist" is not completely inappropriate for Tillich.

In effect, what Tillich has done is to affirm the ontological argument, not as argument but as finite experience. No longer is Christian revelation understood as divine activity in history, but the Christian doctrine of God is reinterpreted in terms of symbols having the power to effect the experience of absolute dependence and exhibit it in human and cultural action. Nowhere has the "liberal" tradition of Schleiermacher, Otto, and Bergson been so consistently developed as an explication of Christianity.

1145

THE COURAGE TO BE

Author: Paul Tillich (1886-   )
Type of work: Ontology, ethics
First published: 1952

PRINCIPAL IDEAS ADVANCED

Considered from the ethical point of view, courage in a man is a sign of his caring for something enough to decide and to act despite opposition; considered in terms of its effect on his being (ontologically), courage is the self-affirmation of one's being.

These points of view are united in the conception of courage as the self-affirmation of one's being in the presence of the threat of nonbeing; anxiety is the felt awareness of the threat of nonbeing, and courage is the resolute opposition to the threat in such a manner that being is affirmed.

Three types of anxiety—ontic, moral, and spiritual (the anxiety of fate and death, of guilt and condemnation, of emptiness and meaninglessness)—are present in all cultural ages, but spiritual anxiety is predominant in the modern period.

Existential anxiety cannot be removed; it can be faced only by those who have the courage to be.

The courage to be involves the courage to participate, to be oneself, and to unite the two by absolute faith in the God above God, "being-itself."

The material in Tillich's book, *The Courage to Be,* was first presented in the form of a series of lectures given at Yale University in 1950-51, under the sponsorship of the Terry Foundation. The central task which the author has assumed in these lectures is that of a dialectical analysis and phenomenological description of courage as a structural category of the human condition.

Courage, as understood by the author, is both an ethical reality and an ontological concept. As an ethical reality courage indicates concrete action and decision which expresses a valuational content. As an ontological concept—that is, as illuminating a feature of being—courage indicates the universal and essential self-affirmation of one's being. Tillich argues that these two meanings of courage must be

united if a proper interpretation of the phenomenon is to be achieved. In the final analysis the ethical can be understood only through the ontological. Courage as an ethical reality is ultimately rooted in the structure of being itself.

These two meanings of courage have been given philosophic consideration throughout the whole history of Western thought. The author provides a brief historical sketch of the attempt to deal with the phenomenon of courage by tracing its development from Plato through Nietzsche. There is first the tradition which begins with Plato and leads to Thomas Aquinas. In the thought of Plato and Aristotle the heroic-aristocratic element in courage was given priority. Plato aligned courage with the spirited part of the soul, which lies between reason and desire, and then aligned both courage and spirit with the guardian class (*phýlakes*), which lies between the rulers and the producers. The class of guardians, as the armed aristocracy, thus gave the Platonic definition of courage an indelible heroic-aristocratic stamp. Aristotle preserved the aristocratic element by defining the courageous man as one who acts for the sake of what is noble. However, there was another current of thought developing during this period. This was the understanding of courage as rational-democratic rather than heroic-aristocratic. The life and death of Socrates, and later the Christian tradition, gave expression to this view. The position of Thomas Aquinas is unique in that it marks the synthesis of a heroic-aristocratic ethic and society with a rational-democratic mode of thought. With Stoicism a new emphasis emerges. Taking as the ideal sage the Athenian Socrates, Stoics became the spokesmen for an emphatic rational-democratic definition of courage. Wisdom replaces heroic fortitude and the democratic-universal replaces the aristocratic ideal. The "courage to be" for the Stoics was a rational courage, indicating an affirmation of one's reasonable nature, or Logos, which countered the negativities of the nonessential or accidental. But this courage to be, formulated independently of the Christian doctrine of forgiveness and salvation, was ultimately cast in terms of a cosmic resignation. The historical significance of the ethical thought of Spinoza, according to the author, is that it rendered explicit an ontology of courage. This ontology of courage was one which made the Stoic doctrine of self-affirmation central, but which replaced the Stoic idea of resignation with a positive ethical humanism. Nietzsche stands at the end of the era, and in a sense is its culmination. Nietzsche transforms Spinoza's "substance" into "life." Spinoza's doctrine of self-affirmation is restated in dynamic terms. Will becomes the central category. Life is understood as "will-to-power." Courage is thus defined as the power of life to affirm itself in spite of its negativities and ambiguities—in spite of the abyss of nonbeing. Nietzsche expressed it thus: "he who with eagle's talons *graspeth* the abyss: he hath courage."

Tillich, in formulating his ontology of courage, keeps the tradition from Plato to Nietzsche in mind. His definition of courage, as the universal self-affirmation of one's being in the presence of the threat of nonbeing, receives its final clarification only in light of the historical background which he has sketched. In the author's definition of courage the phenomenon of anxiety is disclosed as an unavoidable consideration. Courage and anxiety are interdependent concepts. Anxiety is the existential awareness of the threat of nonbeing. Courage is the resolute facing of this anxiety in such a way that nonbeing is ultimately embraced or taken up into being. Thus, the author is driven to formulate an ontology of anxiety. There is first a recognition of the interdependence of fear and anxiety. Fear and anxiety are distinct, but not separate. Fear has a determinable object—a pain, a rejection by someone who is loved, a misfortune, the anticipation of death. Anxiety, on the other hand, has no object, or paradoxically stated, its object is the negation of every object. Anxiety is the awareness that nonbeing is irremovably a part of one's being, which constitutes the definition of human finitude. Anxiety and fear are thus distinct. Yet they are mutually immanent within each other. Fear, when it is deepened, reveals anxiety; and anxiety strives toward fear. The fear of dying ultimately ceases to be a fear of an object—a sickness or an accident—and becomes anxiety over the nonbeing envisioned "after death." And conversely, anxiety strives to become fear, because the finite self cannot endure the threatening disclosure of nonbeing for more than a moment. The mind seeks to transform anxiety into fear, so that it can have a particular object to deal with and overcome. But the basic anxiety of nonbeing cannot, as such, be eliminated. It is a determinant of human existence itself.

The author distinguishes three types of anxiety: (1) *ontic anxiety* or the anxiety of fate and death; (2) *moral anxiety* or the anxiety of guilt and condemnation; and (3) *spiritual anxiety* or the anxiety of emptiness and meaninglessness.

Fate threatens man's ontic self-affirmation relatively; death threatens it absolutely. The anxiety of fate arises from an awareness of an ineradicable contingency which penetrates to the very depth of one's being. Existence exhibits no ultimate necessity. It manifests an irreducible element of irrationality. Behind fate stands death as the absolute threat to ontic self-affirmation. Death discloses the total ontic annihilation which is imminent in every moment of our existence. For the most part man attempts to transform this anxiety into fear, which has a definite object. He partly succeeds but then realizes that the threat can never be embodied in a particular object. It arises from the human situation as

such. The question then is posed: "Is there a courage to be, a courage to affirm oneself in spite of the threat against man's ontic self-affirmation?"

Nonbeing threatens on another level. It threatens by producing moral anxiety—the anxiety of guilt, which threatens relatively, and the anxiety of condemnation, which threatens absolutely. The self seeks to affirm itself morally by actualizing its potentialities. But in every moral action nonbeing expresses itself in the inability of man to actualize fully all of his potential. He remains estranged from his essential being. All of his actions are pervaded with a moral ambiguity. The awareness of this ambiguity is guilt. This guilt can drive man toward a feeling of complete self-rejection, in which he experiences the absolute threat of condemnation. The question then arises whether man can find a courage to affirm himself in spite of the threat against his moral self-affirmation.

Lastly, there is the anxiety of emptiness and meaninglessness, which reveals the threat to man's spiritual self-affirmation. Emptiness threatens this self-affirmation relatively, meaninglessness threatens it absolutely. Emptiness arises out of a situation in which the self fails to find satisfaction through a participation in the contents of its cultural life. The beliefs, attitudes, and activities of man's tradition lose their meaning and are transformed into matters of indifference. Everything is tried but nothing satisfies. Creativity vanishes and the self is threatened with boredom and tedium. The anxiety of emptiness culminates in the anxiety of meaninglessness. Man finds that he can no longer hold fast to the affirmations of his tradition nor to those of his personal convictions. Truth itself is called into question. Spiritual life is threatened with total doubt. Again, the question arises: Is there a courage to be which affirms itself in spite of nonbeing—in this case, nonbeing expressed in the threat of doubt which undermines one's spiritual affirmation through the anxiety of emptiness and meaninglessness?

These three types of anxiety find a periodic exemplification in the history of Western civilization. Although the three types are interdependently present in all cultural ages, we find that ontic anxiety was predominant at the end of ancient civilization, moral anxiety at the end of the Middle Ages, and spiritual anxiety at the end of the modern period. The anxiety of fate and death was the central threat in the Stoic doctrine of courage; it received expression in the transition from Hellenic to Hellenistic civilization, which saw the crumbling of the independent city states and the rise of universal empires, introducing a political power beyond control and calculation; and it is present on every page of Greek tragical literature. In the Middle Ages the anxiety of guilt and condemnation was dominant, expressed in the theological symbol of the "wrath of God" and in the imagery of hell and purgatory. Ascetic practices, pilgrimages, devotion to relics, institution of indulgences, heightened interest in the mass and penance—all witness to the moral threat of nonbeing as it manifests itself in guilt and condemnation. Modern civilization, born of the victory of humanism and the Enlightenment, found its chief threat in the threat to man's spiritual self-affirmation. Here the anxiety of emptiness and meaninglessness becomes dominant. Demo-

cratic liberalism calls into question the security and supports of an absolute state; the rise of technology tends to transform selves into tools and thus displace man's spiritual center; skepticism replaces philosophical certitude. All cultural contents which previously gave man security no longer afford satisfaction and meaning. Modern man is threatened with the attack of emptiness and meaninglessness.

The author concludes his ontology of anxiety by distinguishing existential anxiety, in the three types discussed, from pathological or neurotic anxiety. Existential anxiety has an ontological character and is thus understood as a universal determinant of the human condition. Existential anxiety cannot be removed; it can only be courageously faced. Pathological anxiety, on the other hand, as the result of unresolved conflicts in the socio-psychological structure of personality, is the expression of universal anxiety under special conditions. It is the consequence of man's inability to face courageously his existential anxiety and thus take the nonbeing which threatens into himself. The neurotic self still affirms itself, but it does so on a limited scale. Such affirmation is the affirmation of a reduced self which seeks to avoid the nonbeing that is constitutive of his universal finite condition. But in thus seeking to avoid nonbeing the neurotic self retreats from the full affirmation of his being. Hence, the author's definition of neurosis as *the way of avoiding nonbeing by avoiding being.* The neurotic personality always affirms something less than what he essentially is. His potentialities are sacrificed in order to make possible a narrow and intensified affirmation of what remains of his reduced self. The neurotic is unable to take creatively into himself the universal existential anxieties. In relation to the anxiety of fate and death this produces an unrealistic security, comparable to the security of a prison. Since the neurotic cannot distinguish what is to be realistically feared from those situations in which he is realistically safe, he withdraws into a castle of false security so as to insulate himself from all threats of existence. In relation to the anxiety of guilt and condemnation, pathological anxiety expresses an unrealistic perfection. The neurotic sets up moralistic self-defenses against all actions which would widen the horizons of his reduced and limited actualized state, which he considers to be absolutely perfect. In relation to the anxiety of emptiness and meaninglessness, which expresses itself in a radical existential doubt, pathological anxiety drives the self to an unrealistic certitude. Unable to face the doubt regarding the contents of his cultural tradition and his personal beliefs, the neurotic constructs a citadel of certainty, from which he fends off all threat of doubt on the basis of an absolutized authority. This absolutized authority may be either a personal revelation, a social or religious institution, or a fanatical leader of a movement. In any case, he refuses to accept doubt and rejects all questions from the outside. He is unable courageously to accept the reality of meaninglessness as a universal phenomenon in existential reality.

The courage to be is the movement of self-affirmation in spite of the threat of anxiety as the existential awareness of nonbeing. This courage is conceptually clarified by the author through the use of the polar ontological princi-

ples of participation and individualization. The basic polar structure of being is the polarity of self and world. The first polar elements which emerge out of this foundational polar structure are the elements of participation and individualization. The relevance of these elements to Tillich's doctrine of courage is evident. Courage expresses itself as "the courage to be as a part," exemplifying the polar element of participation, and as "the courage to be as oneself," exemplifying the polar element of individualization. Finally, these two polar exemplifications of courage are transcended and united in "absolute faith." Absolute faith, grounded in transcendence, provides the final definition of the courage to be.

First the author examines the manifestation of courage as the courage to be *as a part*. This is one side of man's self-affirmation. He affirms himself as a participant in the power of a group, a historical movement, or being as such. This side of courage counters the threat of losing participation in his world. The social forms which embody this manifestation of courage are varied. The author briefly discusses four of these forms: *collectivism, semicollectivism, neocollectivism,* and *democratic conformism.*

All of these forms attempt to deal with the three types of anxiety—ontic, moral, and spiritual—by channeling their individual expressions into an anxiety about the group. Thus, it becomes possible to cope with these existential anxieties with a courage that affirms itself through collective or conformal participation. The individual anxiety concerning fate and death is transcended through a collective identification. There is a part of oneself, belonging to the group, which cannot be hurt or destroyed. It is as eternal as the group is eternal—an essential manifestation of the universal collective. So, also, a self-affirmation is made possible in spite of the threat of guilt and condemnation. Individual guilt is translated into a deviation or transgression of the norms of the collective, and the courage to be as a part accepts guilt and its consequences as public guilt. The anxiety of emptiness and meaninglessness is dealt with in the same way. The group becomes the bearer of universal meaning, and the individual derives his personal meaning through a participation in the group. The ever present danger in the radical affirmation of the courage to be as a part is the absorption of the self into the collective, with the consequent loss of the unique, unrepeatable, and irreplaceable individual.

The courage to be *as oneself* expresses the other side of man's self-affirmation. This movement is made possible through the ontological polar element of individualization. The courage to be as oneself has found a concrete embodiment in *romanticism, naturalism,* and *existentialism.*

Romanticism elevated the individual beyond all cultural content, and conferred upon him a radical autonomy. In some of its extreme expressions, as in Friedrich von Schlegel, the courage to be as oneself led to a complete rejection of participation.

Naturalism, whether of the "philosophy of life" variety or of the American pragmatic variety, follows basically the same path. Nietzsche, in his definition of nature as the will-to-power, granted priority to the individual will and made it the decisive element in the drive toward creativity.

In Nietzsche individual self-affirmation reaches a climactic point. American pragmatism, in spite of its roots in democratic conformism, shares much of the individualistic attitude characteristic of European naturalism. It finds its highest ethical principle in growth, sees the educational process as one which maximizes the individual talents of the child, and seeks its governing philosophical principle in personal creative self-affirmation.

It is in *existentialism* that the courage to be as oneself is most powerfully presented. Tillich distinguishes two basic expressions of existentialism—as an attitude and as a philosophical and artistic content. Existentialism as an attitude designates an attitude of concrete involvement as contrasted with an attitude of theoretical detachment. Existentialism as a content is at the same time a point of view, a protest, and an expression. But in all of its varieties existentialism is the chief protagonist for the reality of the individual and the importance of personal decision. It is concerned to salvage the individual from the objectivization of abstract thought, society, and technology alike. The existentialist struggles for the preservation of the self-affirmative person. He fights against dehumanization in all of its forms. The task of every individual, according to the existentialist, is to be himself. Heidegger has profoundly expressed this existentialist courage to be as oneself in his concept of resolution (*Entschlossenheit*). The resolute individual derives his directives for action from no external source. Nobody can provide for one's security against the threat of ontic annihilation, moral disintegration, or spiritual loss of meaning. He himself must decide how to face his imminent

1151

death, how to face his moral ambiguity, and how to face the threat of meaninglessness which strikes at the root of his existence.

We have seen that the danger in the courage to be as a part is a loss of the self in the collective. The opposite danger becomes apparent in the various forms of the courage to be as oneself—namely, a loss of the world as a polar structure of selfhood. The question then arises whether there can be a courage which unites both sides of man's self-affirmation by transcending them.

Courage understood as absolute faith exemplifies this union through transcendence. A courage which can take the three types of anxiety creatively into itself must be grounded in a power of being that transcends both the power of oneself and the power of one's world. The self-world correlation is still on this side of the threat of nonbeing; hence, neither self-affirmation as oneself nor self-affirmation as a part can cope successfully with nonbeing. The courage to be, in its final movement, must be rooted in the power of being-itself, which transcends the self-world correlation. Insofar as religion is the state of being grasped by the power of being-itself, it can be said that courage always has either an explicit or implicit religious character. The courage to be finds its ultimate source in the power of being-itself, and becomes manifest as absolute faith. As long as participation remains dominant the relation to being-itself is mystical in character; as long as individualization remains dominant the relationship is one of personal encounter; when both sides are accepted and transcended the relation becomes one of absolute faith. The

two sides are apprehended as contrasts, but not as contradictions which exclude each other.

This absolute faith is able to take the threefold structure of anxiety into itself. It conquers the anxiety of fate and death in its encounter with providence. Providence gives man the courage of confidence to say "in spite of" to fate and death. Providence must not be construed in terms of God's activity, but as a religious symbol for the courage of confidence which conquers fate and death. Guilt and condemnation are conquered through the experience of divine forgiveness which expresses itself in the courage to accept acceptance. The courage to be in relation to guilt is "the courage to accept oneself as accepted in spite of being unacceptable." In relation to the anxiety of emptiness and meaninglessness the courage to be, based on absolute faith, is able to say "yes" to the undermining doubt and to affirm itself in spite of the threat. Any decisive answer to the question of meaninglessness must first accept the state of meaninglessness; this acceptance constitutes a movement of faith. "The act of accepting meaninglessness is in itself a meaningful fact. It is an act of faith." Through his participation in the power of being-itself man is able to conquer emptiness and meaninglessness by taking them into himself and affirming himself "in spite of."

The content of absolute faith is the "God above God." Tillich rejects the God of theological theism, who remains bound to the subject-object structure of reality. A God who is understood as an object becomes an invincible tyrant who divests man of his subjectivity and freedom. This is the God whom Nietzsche pronounced dead, and against whom the existentialists

1152

have justifiably revolted. Theism must be transcended if absolute faith is to become a reality. The "God above God" is the power of being-itself, which, as the source of absolute faith, is not bound to the subject-object structure of reality. Being-itself transcends both self and world and unites the polarities of individualization and participation. The courage to be, which is ultimately grounded in the encounter with the "God above God," thus unites and transcends the courage to be as oneself and the courage to be as a part. This courage avoids both the loss of oneself by participation and the loss of one's world by individualization.

PHILOSOPHY AND PSYCHO-ANALYSIS

Author: John Wisdom (1904-   )
Type of work: Philosophy of philosophy
First published: 1953

PRINCIPAL IDEAS ADVANCED

Philosophical questions are verbal in the sense that they turn upon unconventional uses of language; but they are not merely verbal, for, in virtue of their oddity, in the process of justifying their use, one's attention is called to matters obscured by conventional language.

Metaphysical paradoxes and platitudes function as penetrating suggestions as to how language might be used to reveal what is hidden by the actual use of language.

In philosophical analysis penumbral facts (matters to which certain conventional sentences call attention) are compared to non-penumbral facts (matters to which the penumbral are presumably reducible) in order to determine whether the switch from one kind of statement to another is advisable and illuminating.

The goal of philosophy is the clarification of the structure of facts.

Philosophers do not uncover new facts, but they show us old facts in a new way.

The title of this book is somewhat misleading. Only two of the fifteen essays are concerned with psychoanalysis. Even these two do not face squarely the question as to the sense, if any, in which the perplexities which the ordinary man experiences when he wonders about the universe and is led to the philosopher for help are like the perplexities which the psy- chotic and the neurotic experience when they develop conflicts and are directed to the psychoanalyst for treatment. The author does show that there are certain similarities between the approach of the metaphysician and the approach of the psychoanalyst, but he also shows that there are similarities between the approach of the metaphysician and that of the lawyer, or the mathematician, the logician, the scientist, the art critic, or even that of the novelist. Thus his design is really to clarify the term "metaphysics." He suggests in one place that his task is one of "meta-metaphysics," that is, one of determining the status of metaphysical problems and metaphysical judgments. The essays are united only in their common concern with this problem. They extend in time of publication from 1932 to 1953 and are arranged, roughly, in chronological order. Several are critical book reviews. Only one, the last, is not indicated as having been previously published.

The importance of the book lies in the fact that it clarifies the position of the author in relation to the current attempts to define philosophy as some form of linguistic analysis. Though Wisdom was strongly influenced by the late Ludwig Wittgenstein, he does not believe, as Wittgenstein and many of the logical positivists did, that metaphysics is nonsense of some sort which becomes evident when its statements are properly analyzed; nor does he believe that metaphysical statements are *merely* linguistic and that all difficulties can be eliminated by substituting clear words for vague ones and precise grammatical constructions for ambiguous ones; nor does he follow the Oxford School in stressing either the *language* of man in the street or his *beliefs* on certain philosophical matters as the final court of appeal for settling all philosophical disputes. He examines these views, as well as others which associate philosophical problems with their mode of expression and endeavors to state his own view in contrast to them.

Let us begin by taking some typical philosophical problems: "Can we really know what is going on in someone else's mind?" "Can we really know the causes of our sensations?" "What is a chair?" These are the kinds of questions philosophers ask, and we must attempt to determine what they are seeking when they ask them, and what they mean when they reply, "We can never really know what is going on in someone else's mind," "A chair is nothing but our sensations," or, "A chair is something over and above our sensations."

In a sense, Wisdom says, philosophy gives rise to verbal disputes. To state that we cannot know what is going on in someone else's mind is to utter something which is obviously untrue unless we adopt an unusual meaning for the word "know." Thus we might say that one who makes a statement of this kind is uttering nonsense. Or suppose a philosopher asks whether two plus three can ever equal six? Again the question becomes nonsense unless we adopt unconventional meanings for some of the words which it contains. But the fact that both statements are nonsensical does not mean that they are nonsensical in the same way. And in order to determine how they differ in their portrayal of nonsense we should have to make a study which would be at least partially verbal. Thus, philosophical clarification is achieved through an examination of language. Similarly, if a philosopher says that a chair is something over and above our sensations he is not proposing a new definition of "chair," nor a new use for chairs, but he is suggesting the need for a clarification of the meaning of a word. Hence, philosophical questions and answers seem to be verbal.

1154

But although the philosopher's statements are formulated *in* words, his intention is not to raise verbal issues; he is not taking over the role of the translator. A translator substitutes a sentence S for a sentence S', for the purpose of telling us the meaning of S'. The philosopher does not wish merely to substitute one statement of a fact for another; he wishes to transmit insight—insight into the structure of the fact which is asserted by S'. He equates S with S' because he believes that S better indicates the structure of a certain fact than does S'. This is not a verbal matter.

The nature of philosophical statements can be further clarified by distinguishing their *content* from their *point*. Suppose we have a philosophical statement containing the word "monarchy." Now anybody who knows that "monarchy" means the same as "set of persons ruled by the same king," and who also knows the meaning of *either* of these expressions, will find that the philosophical statement becomes clarified if one is substituted for the other. But this involves merely clarification in *content* and is the concern of the decoder rather than of the philosopher. The philosopher achieves his clarification (the *point* of his utterance) only if his hearer already uses and understands the meaning of *both* "monarchy" and "set of persons ruled by the same king." Philosophical statements thus appear to be very curious; they provide information only if the hearer already knows what is to be told him. Philosophy is trying to show the "structure" of a monarchy by bringing together the sphere in which "monarchy" is used, and the sphere in which "set of persons ruled by the same king" is used. These are differ-

ent categories, and the philosophical problem is that of showing by means of the structure of the statement how these are related. Wisdom suggests a certain mnemonic device: "It's not the stuff, it's the style that stupifies." It is not *what* the philosopher talks about that makes him unique, but the *form* in which he expresses himself. Wisdom apologizes for a suspicion of smartness when he says, "Philosophers should be continually trying to say what cannot be said."

What is really involved in this disclosure of "structure" can be understood only by an examination of what Wisdom means by *analysis* as the method of all philosophy. But since his use of this word is somewhat technical, the way may be prepared by an examination of the conception of the world which, according to Wisdom, is held by all metaphysicians. They believe, in his words, "that the actual world is made up solely of positive, specific, determinate, concrete, contingent, individual, sensory facts." But they also believe in an apparent "penumbra of fictional, negative, general, indeterminate, abstract, necessary, super-individual, physical facts." This penumbra is only apparent because we have not penetrated deeply enough. Now philosophers feel that there are not two ways of knowing—one for the nonpenumbral facts and another for the penumbral. Yet they also feel that since the nonpenumbral and the penumbral are not identical, there *must* be two ways of knowing. This produces philosophical perplexity.

Let us take some examples. "The height of the average man is simply the sum of the heights of the individual men divided by their number." "A chair is simply a collection of sense-data." "A person's mind is nothing more than his behavior." "The State is something over and above the individuals who make it up." "The statement 'Not three people are interested in mathematical logic' may be expressed in the form: 'If x is interested in mathematical logic, and also y is interested, and also z is interested, then x is identical with y, or y is identical with z, or x is identical with z.'" "'All men are mortal' can be reduced to 'John is mortal, and George is mortal, and James is mortal, and so on.'" "*Time* means (G. E. Moore) that lunch is over, supper to come, that Smith's anger is past, and so on." "Analytic propositions are merely verbal propositions."

In all of these examples what is given first may be designated as the penumbral fact, and what is given second as the nonpenumbral fact. Then average men, physical objects, minds, States, numerical statements, general statements, time, and analytic propositions are all penumbral. And actual men, sense-data, behavior, individual citizens, identity of x's and y's, John and George being mortal, supper following lunch, and verbal propositions are non-penumbral. Call the former "X facts," and the latter "Y facts." Then the question becomes simply this: Are X facts ultimate or are they reducible to Y facts? If they are reducible, are they *completely* reducible, that is, are X facts *equivalent to* Y facts? If they are not completely reducible, are X facts something *over and above* Y facts?

Wisdom believes that it is misleading to formulate the problem in terms of *facts*, for it suggests that the issue can be decided simply by examining the world, either the logical world or the natural world. This is not the case. The question should therefore be expressed in terms of propositions or sentences: Do X sentences stand for the same proposition as any combination of Y sentences? Are X sentences used in the same way as some combination of Y sentences? When we have an X sentence can we find a Y sentence which serves the same purpose?

This approach suggests that we examine the sentences to see under what circumstances we would be inclined to answer the question, "Yes," and under what circumstances, "No." There is no right or wrong answer to these questions. But dispute can be resolved by explaining what induces each disputant to claim what he does. Thus, statements which are metaphysical paradoxes, and statements which are metaphysical platitudes are revealed to be not simply false statements and true statements, but penetrating suggestions as to how language *might be used* to reveal what is completely hidden by its *actual use*. "Thus it appears how it is that, to give metaphysicians what they want, we have to do little more than remove the spectacles through which they look at their own work. Then they see how those hidden identities and diversities which lead to the 'insoluble' reduction questions about forms, categories and predicates, have already been revealed, though in a hidden way."

We are now ready to turn to an examination of what Wisdom means by *analysis*. A distinction must first be made between *material* analysis and *philosophical* analysis. To give a material analysis is simply to give a definition: "*Wealth* is defined as *what is useful, transferable, and limited in supply*." A definition of *wealth* as *riches* would not be materially analytic, for it does nothing to render explicit the connotation of the word defined. But a philosophical analysis is given by a rule for translating sentences about any abstraction ("the State") into sentences about what it is an abstraction from ("the individual citizens"). A second distinction must be made between *formal* analysis and *philosophical* analysis. A formal analysis is the replacement of a sentence by another which more clearly indicates the form of the fact asserted: " 'Two horses passed him' means 'A horse passed him and then another.' " This would not be a material analysis for *two* is not an adjective, and it is not a philosophical analysis for it merely exhibits clearly the structure of something whose structure was not clear. The distinction between the three types of analysis can be illustrated by the statement, "Two men are good." A *formal* analysis would be, "A man is good and another man is good"; a *philosophical* analysis would be, "A *mannish* pattern of states contains a high proportion of good ones and another *mannish* pattern does so also"; and a *material* analysis would be, "A *mannish* pattern of states contains a high proportion of states likely to cause approval and another does so also."

Analysis (philosophical analysis) cannot be understood without explaining *ostentation*. Philosophers have always employed ostentation, though because of their preoccupation *with* philosophy they have had little time to *talk about* ostentation. Ostentation is a kind of substitution; we use ostentation on a sentence S′ when we substitute for S′ another sentence S which more clearly reveals the ultimate structure of the fact they assert. Let us take the sentence, "England invaded France." This has a dyadic structure exhibited by "EIF" where "E" is a term, "I" is a relation, and "F" is another term. But the sentence "EIF" does not exhibit the *ultimate* structure of its fact. In order to show this we should have to formulate sentences about Tom, Dick, and Harry, and about Henri, François, and Jean, and about the former being sent threateningly into land owned by the latter, and so on. We can say that "EIF" *directly* locates a fact of which England is an element; but it *indirectly* locates a fact of which Tom, Dick, and the rest, are elements. The analysis of the sentence "EIF" into sentences about Englishmen and Frenchmen is a philosophical analysis because the predicates which are applicable to England are definable in terms of the predicates which are applicable to Englishmen. They are, of course, different *kinds* of predicates because they are exhibited in different *kinds* of structure. The sentences about Englishmen and Frenchmen become an ostentation of the sentence about England and France; S is an ostentation of S′. When this is the case the facts displayed, though not two, are not identical. Thus the distinction between the penumbral and the nonpenumbral facts has been recognized, and the question as to whether the former can be "reduced" to the latter (whether the former are "logical constructions out of" the latter) can be intelligently discussed, pro and con. What is introduced by ostentation is not merely a clearer understanding of the structure of a fact, but an increased clearness in the apprehension of the *ultimate* structure of the fact. We should not say that S is merely a translation of S′ but that S displays directly what S′ displays indirectly, or that S′ displays a fact which is secondary to the fact which S displays. The sentence about Tom, Dick, and the others displays directly what the sentence about England and France displays indirectly, or the fact displayed by the sentence about England and France is secondary to the fact displayed by the sentence about Tom, Dick, and the others. Wisdom concludes the discussion of this topic by stating that the philosopher makes a prayer: *"Please give me clearer apprehension of the Arrangement of the Elements of the Fact finally located by the sentence* 'aRb.' " (In this statement Wisdom uses capital letters to indicate that what the philosopher is seeking is the *ultimate* arrangement of the *ultimate* elements of the *ultimate* fact, not merely the structure which is obviously exhibited by "aRb.")

The question of whether the penumbral can be reduced to the nonpenumbral has divided philosophers into two schools. On the one hand are the naturalists, empiricists, and positivists. They accept the Verification Principle. On the other hand are the realists and the transcendentalists, who accept the Idiosyncrasy Platitude. The former maintain such statements as "A cherry is nothing but sensations and possibilities of more," "A mind is nothing but a pattern of behavior," "There are no such things as numbers, only numerals." The latter argue that every statement has its own sort of meaning, and "everything is what it is and not another thing." Examples can be found in "Ethical propositions involve value predicates and are ultimate," "Mathematical propositions are necessary synthetic propositions—an

ultimate sort of proposition," "Statements about nations are not to be reduced to statements about individuals, they are about a certain sort of concrete universal."

Wisdom's contention with regard to both of these principles is that we should examine what we mean when we say that either of them is true. To say this is to suppose that the principles in question can be confirmed or disconfirmed. But this is not the case; neither principle is a scientific theory. The issue should, therefore, be formulated in terms of the question whether we should accept the Verification Principle, or the Idiosyncrasy Platitude. But now what has the issue become? Can we say that the Verification Principle is a metaphysical theory? Yes, says Wisdom, in a certain sense. It is not so much a metaphysical theory as a recipe for framing metaphysical theories; it is a mnemonic device which tells those who accept it how to proceed in settling certain metaphysical issues. It draws their attention to "the deplorably old-fashioned clothes in which it presents itself," since it appears in the disguise either of a scientific discovery which removes a popular illusion or of a logical proposition from which deductions can be made. Furthermore, the principle serves to draw the attention of those who reject it to the fact that underneath its disguise it has obvious merits. The principle, therefore, has the characteristics of all metaphysical statements in that it covers up what it really intends to say. The same is true of the Idiosyncrasy Platitude. Whether either of these is called "metaphysical" is of no great importance; the point is that in examining the reasons for or against accepting

1158

one of these principles we are led into the activity which is designed to eliminate metaphysical perplexities, and to arrive at that clarification of structure which is the goal of philosophy.

Finally, Wisdom attempts to show in what sense philosophical difficulties are like psychopathic difficulties. Wittgenstein said that he held no opinions in philosophy but tried to remove "a feeling of puzzlement, to cure a sort of mental cramp" which is associated with philosophical problems. Wisdom gives an example in which an individual wrestles with the problem of whether he can or cannot know what other creatures are thinking about. He points out that such an individual, first skeptical about the minds of other people, is led inevitably into skepticism about his senses, and finally into a skepticism about everything. But this is obviously an absurd position, and he develops a stress which is quite analogous to that of the businessman who is trying to meet his financial obligations and becomes neurotic as a result. In what respects are these stresses alike, and in what respect is the cure which the philosopher might administer to the puzzled thinker like the cure which the psychoanalyst might administer to the neurotic businessman?

Philosophy has never been a purely psychogenic disorder and it is not ordinarily considered to be a therapy. But when philosophers proceed by trying to show us "not new things but old things anew," they are adopting procedures much like those of the psychoanalyst. Philosophical discussion aims to bring out latent opposing forces, and not to teach what is behind closed doors or whether 235 times 6 equals 1410. Philosophy often shows that behind the latent linguistic sources of confusion there are much more deeply hidden nonlinguistic forces, and that a purely linguistic treatment of philosophy cannot therefore be adequate. Philosophy also shows that the nonlinguistic sources are the same as those that trouble us elsewhere in our lives; hence, that the philosophical riddles are the true "riddles of the Sphinx."

Philosophy is concerned with what is paradoxical and unconventional. Such matters are not to be settled by experiment and observation. Many philosophers have said that questions which cannot be settled by experiment and observation are questions merely of words. In saying this they are speaking wildly. But so are those "scientists, philosophers, or poets who say one cannot stir a flower without troubling of a star. What they say is mad but there's method in it."

PHILOSOPHICAL INVESTIGATIONS

Author: Ludwig Wittgenstein (1889-1951)
Type of work: Philosophy of philosophy, philosophy of language
First published: 1953

Language is best conceived as an activity involving the uses of words as tools.

Words are used in a multiplicity of ways and are to be understood by engaging in the language "games" in which they are employed; words are not labels for things.

For a large number of cases in which the word "meaning" is used, the meaning of a word is its use in the language.

Discourse about sensations is understandable because there is a grammar of the word "sensations," and of such words as "pain" and "remember," which can be grasped by anyone acquainted with the relevant language games; no reference to what one has in mind or feels privately makes sense unless it makes sense in this way.

Expecting, intending, remembering—these are ways of life made possible by the use of language; and language is itself a way of life.

Philosophical Investigations, published posthumously, contains in Part I a body of work completed by Wittgenstein by 1945. This material includes a preface in which he comments on the book, characterizing it as an "album" of "sketches of landscapes," in virtue of its being a collection of philosophical remarks by the use of which Wittgenstein attacked the problems with which he concerned himself. Parts II and III, written between 1947 and 1949, were added by the editors, G. E. M. Anscombe (who translated the work from the German), and R. Rhees. The German and English versions appear side by side.

Although the work has been in translation only a few years, discussion of its contents preceded the publication of the work because of the appearance of the "Blue Book" and the "Brown Book," collections of typescripts and notes based on Wittgenstein's lectures at Cambridge. In part, the author's interest in the publication of the work during his lifetime came from a reluctance to rest his reputation on second-hand reports of his philosophical remarks.

An aura of mystery, then, surrounded *Philosophical Investigations* when it finally appeared—and something of the aura yet remains as arguments having to do with the interpretation of the sense and direction of Wittgenstein's remarks tend to condition the understanding of the book. Nevertheless, there is little argument about the central theme; in spite of Wittgenstein's erratic and peripatetic method, the purpose of his remarks manages to become clear.

The point of the book appears to be that language is best conceived as an activity involving the uses of words as tools. There is a multiplicity of uses to which words can be put. To understand the meaning of an utterance is to understand the use to which it is put. Consequently, it is misleading and confusing to think of language as being made up of words which stand for objects. Understanding the uses of words is like understanding the rules of games, and just as confusion results when a player in a game makes up new rules as he goes along, or misapplies the rules, or conceives of the game in some static fashion—so it causes confusion and perplexity when a user of language creates new rules, violates old ones, or misconceives language. To be clear about language, one must look to its uses.

But if all that Wittgenstein meant to do with his remarks were to say this, he could have done the job with a great deal less effort and at considerably less length. The *Investigations* is not so much a report of the results of Wittgenstein's philosophical investigations, as it is itself an investigation *in progress* —and what it deals with and exhibits are philosophical investigations. In other words, Wittgenstein's remarks are used to show that certain philosophical problems arise because language is misconceived; and because of the author's adroit uses of language we are led to conceive of language as instrumental. In a sense, then, the book *is* what it is *about*; its process, as a proof, is its evidence.

What is it to investigate *philosophically?* Wittgenstein's answer is: It is *not* to seek theses or theories, and it is *not* to find static meanings (objects) for which words are permanent labels; it is, rather, to understand by attending to the uses of language relevant to the problem at hand in order to discover how philosophical problems arise "when language *goes on holiday*"—that is, when a user of languages takes off in new, unpredictable directions as a result of failing to abide by the rules of a particular "language-game." One might support Wittgenstein at this point by saying that what poets do intentionally, in order to be poets, philosophers do in ignorance— and hence are philosophers.

In the Preface to the book, Wittgenstein declares that he had hoped to bring the remarks of the book into some coherent whole, but such an attempt—he came to realize—could never succeed. He suggests that philosophical investigation involves coming at a problem from a number of different directions.

On the point concerning coherence one may justly dissent. Though it is true that escape from a static conception of language is made possible by a series of relevant demonstrations of the uses of language, there is no reason why the points of the book could not have been clearly made seriatim—even if, to do so, eccentric uses of language would have been necessary. A number of problems could then have been dealt with in the Wittgenstein fashion, a fashion which would have illuminated the eccentric uses of language. In fact, this is what *almost* happens in the *Investigations*: now and then we catch the author presenting a thesis, and it is clear that the problems he considers —suggested by his own odd uses of language in the expression of his theses —are intended to illustrate and support his points. Yet Wittgenstein had a streak of philosophical coyness—sometimes disguising itself as a kind of insight—which led him, presumably for theoretical reasons, but more likely for effect, sometimes to withhold the moral of the tale, the destination of his philosophical wanderings.

There are two principal metaphors by the use of which Wittgenstein has sought to make his meaning clear: the metaphor of language as a game and the metaphor of language as a tool. Or, to be more accurate, the metaphors of languages as games or as tools. After describing a primitive language which could be described as involving a process of calling for objects by the use of words, Wittgenstein writes: "We can

. . . think of the whole process of using words . . . as one of those games by means of which children learn their native language. I will call these games 'language-games' and will sometimes speak of a primitive language as a language-game. . . . I shall also call the whole, consisting of language and the actions into which it is woven, the 'language-game.'" (7) (In Part I, which comprises the largest section of the work, the remarks are numbered. For convenience in referring to the work—since there are no chapters, section headings, or other devices for locating oneself—these numbers are mentioned here.)

Then, in 11, Wittgenstein writes: "Think of the tools in a toolbox: there is a hammer, pliers, a saw, a screwdriver, a rule, a glue-pot, glue, nails and screws.—The functions of words are as diverse as the function of these objects."

But what is the point of using the expression, "language-game"? Wittgenstein answers: "Here the term 'language-*game*' is meant to bring into prominence the fact that the *speaking* of language is part of an activity, or of a form of life." (23) He then presents a list of some of the functions of language—for example, giving orders, describing, reporting events, making up stories, translating—and comments: "It is interesting to compare the multiplicity of the tools in language and of the ways they are used, the multiplicity of kinds of word and sentence, with what logicians have said about the structure of language. (Including the author of the *Tractatus Logico-Philosophicus*.)" (23) Here the reference is to his own earlier work (1921) in which he defended a logical atomism —a philosophy which would elucidate problems by devising an ideal language in which for each simple object or property there would be a fixed, unambiguous symbol—ironically, the very conception of language which the *Investigations* examines and rejects.

The simile that using an utterance is like making a move in a game suggests the problem, "What is a game?" If language involves simply the use of names as labels, then there is a definite answer to that question. But if the word "game" is used in various ways, it may very well be that there is no "object," no essential nature, to which the word "game" calls attention. Indeed, this conclusion is what Wittgenstein argues. In response to the supposition that there must be something common to the proceedings called "games," he urges everyone to *"look and see* whether there is anything common to all," and he ends a survey of games by remarking: "And the result of this examination is: we see a complicated network of similarities overlapping and criss-crossing: sometimes overall similarities, sometimes similarities of detail." (66) He introduces the expression "family resemblances" to characterize the similarities.

The point is that just as games form a "family," so do the various uses of an expression. To look for common meanings, then, is as fruitless as to look for the essential nature of games. The only way of making sense out of a problem having to do with the essence of language (or the meaning of a word) is by examining language as it is actually used in a multiplicity of ways.

The theme of the *Investigations* is introduced shortly before the philosophical investigation into the essence of games: "For a *large* class of cases—

though not for all—in which we employ the word 'meaning' it can be defined thus: the meaning of a word is its use in the language." (43)

To understand this critical sentence is to understand the *Investigations*. At first the claim that, as the word "meaning" is often used, the meaning of a word is its use in the language might appear to be a variant of the familiar pragmatic claim that verbal disputes are resolved by decisions as to the practical use of language. William James considered the question "Does the man go round the squirrel?" in an imagined situation in which, as the man walks round a tree, the squirrel moves about the tree trunk, keeping the tree between himself and the man. Some persons would be inclined to say that the man *does* go round the squirrel, since the man's path enclosed the squirrel's path; but others would say that the man does *not* go round the squirrel since the squirrel keeps the same part of its body turned toward the man. James would settle the issue by deciding how to use the word "round." He did not *answer* the question, but he settled the problem; he settled it by resolving the issue as a problem. In an analogous fashion, it might seem, Wittgenstein proposed resolving problems, not by answering them, but by showing that they involve confusions concerning the use of language.

But to interpret "the meaning is the use" in this manner is to fail to understand the function of the sentence in Wittgenstein's remarks. For Wittgenstein is not suggesting that meanings be determined by reference to use, or that meanings be explicated by reference to human attitudes in the use of language. What he suggests is what he says (but he says it oddly): the meaning of a word is its use in the language. For anyone who takes the word "meaning" as if the meaning of a term were an object, or a class of objects, or a property of a class of objects—in other words, something to which a word, as a label, refers—it is nonsense to say "the meaning of a word is its use." If the word "man" means rational animal, for example, what would be the sense of saying, "The meaning of the word 'man,' namely, rational animal, is its use in the language"? That is indeed philosophic garble. But if, now, we take the word "meaning" as it is used in discourse about the *meaning* of conduct, the *meaning* of an act, the *meaning* of a form of life—then it makes sense (even though it is *new* sense, since we do not usually talk about the meaning of a word in this sense of the word "meaning") to talk about the meaning of a word as being the use of the word in the language: it makes sense if by the "use" of something we mean what we would mean—more or less—in talking about the "purpose" of something. To understand a word, then, is much like understanding an act which makes no sense until one notices what the act does and, consequently, realizes what the act is *for,* what the purpose of it is, what *meaning* it has.

There is no more difficult demand upon philosophers accustomed to the sign-referent way of analyzing language than this demand that philosophers stop thinking of words as names for objects (a conception that has some use only in reference to a primitive language quite different from ours) and start thinking of words as tools that can be used in various ways and can be understood as bringing about certain changes in behavior or in ways of looking at things. Figurative description of language as a game is meant to stress "the fact that the *speaking* of language is part of an activity, or of a form of life": one does something with the use of a word that is much like what one does in making a move in a game; and just as it would be senseless to ask what the move *stands for* or *represents* (as if somehow it were a symbol for the victory toward which the player moves), so it is senseless to ask what the word, as used, *stands for* or *represents*. To be sure, conventional answers can be given to questions of the latter sort, but conventional answers are not illuminating; one comes to understand what language is and what language means in noticing (seeing) what is done with it (just as one can come to understand a machine by watching its operation).

This interpretation of Wittgenstein's remark that "the meaning of a word is its use in the language" gains strength with the realization that a considerable number of the remarks are directed against the idea that the meaning of a word is whatever the speaker has in mind or feels privately. Here again the problem "What is the essential nature of games?" is illuminating. By a survey of the various activities to which attention is called by various uses of the word "game," one comes to understand the word "game" and games; and the problem dissolves because one is satisfied with the survey of the family of games, and there is nothing more to wonder about. Similarly, to understand the meaning of the word "pain" is to have acquired the technique of using the word; there is nothing hidden or private to wonder about.

But this conclusion—that discourse about sensations is meaningful because the word "sensation" has a use in our language, and that the word "sensation" cannot be part of a private language significant only to the speaker— is intolerable to philosophers who like to say that "Sensations are private," "Another person can't have my pains," or "I can only *believe* that someone else is in pain, but I *know* it if I am." (These are Wittgenstein's examples— which he discusses in a series of related remarks.) Wittgenstein realized that much of what he had to say is intolerable to some philosophers, but he writes that philosophers have the habit of throwing language out of gear; and sometimes the philosophical use of language is so extreme, so abnormal, that what is called for is *treatment* by one who understands that philosophical problems arise and philosophical theories are advanced when philosophers develop the disease of taking expressions that fit into the language in one way and then using the expressions in some other, problem-provoking, paradox-generating way. Hence, "The [enlightened] philosopher's treatment of a question is like the treatment of an illness." (255)

Thus, if someone comes forth with the philosophical "discovery" that "Sensations are private," what he needs is treatment: a philosopher who talks about private sensations has made the error of confusing a discovery about the "grammar" (the systematic use) of the *word* "sensation" with a nonlinguistic fact. "The truth is: it makes sense to say about other people that they doubt whether I am in pain; but not to say it about myself." (246) But it does not follow from the grammatical point— that it would be senseless to *say* that I doubt whether I am in pain—that therefore I *know* that I am in pain: the expression "I know I am in pain" has no use in our language—except, perhaps, to emphasize (do somewhat better) the job that is done with the expression "I am in pain." To confuse the use of the word "know" in such an expression as "I know he is in pain" (for he is writhing, clenching his teeth, and the like) with its use in the expression "I know I am in pain" is to breed perplexity which only an investigation into the multiplicity of uses of the word "know" can resolve.

In his discussions of understanding, memory, and sensations, Wittgenstein characteristically sketches the range of uses of the terms "sensation," "understand," and "remember." He resists the tendency to settle upon one use, one way of looking at things, one definition as somehow settling anything. For even if one considers what one takes to be a "single" use of a term, it soon develops that there are borderline cases, areas in which one use imperceptibly merges into another, so that any decision as to the use of language by way of definition settles nothing (the complex network remains) and may lead to further paradox. Philosophical difficulties in this area (as well as in others) arise when one kind of grammar is mistaken for another, when an expression appropriate in one context is used in another: "Perhaps the word 'describe' tricks us here. I say 'I describe my state of mind' and 'I describe my room.' You need to call to mind the differences between the language-games." (290)

Expecting, intending, remembering —these are ways of life made possible by the use of language; and language is itself a way of life. What we find when we try to find the criteria of these states are the uses of various ex-pressions—or by noticing the uses of various expressions we come to learn what kind of behavior prompts our use of these terms. No reference to *inner* thoughts, sensations, intentions, or memories is necessary.

For Wittgenstein *"Essence* is expressed by grammar." (371) To understand the nature of something is to acquire the technique of using the language which prompted the question and the investigation concerning it. There are, however, no simple answers; in a sense, there are no answers at all. One gets acquainted with the multiplicity of uses and one surveys the scene accordingly: there is nothing left to wonder about.

Wittgenstein does not deny the existence of feelings, of pains, memories, and expectations. In response to the charge that "you again and again reach the conclusion that the sensation itself is a *nothing*," he responds, "Not at all. It is not a *something*, but not a *nothing* either! The conclusion was only that a nothing would serve just as well as a something about which nothing can be said. We have only rejected the grammar which tries to force itself on us here." (304) Again, in response to the query "Are you not really a behaviorist in disguise? Aren't you at bottom really saying that everything except human behavior is a fiction?" he replies, "If I do speak of a fiction, then it is of a *grammatical* fiction." (307) The effort throughout is to argue against the tendency philosophers sometimes have of studying "inner processes" in order to acquire knowledge about sensations, memory, and so forth; the proper procedure, according to Wittgenstein, is to attend to the use of the relevant terms. If we do observe the uses of such terms as "sensation," "pain," "think," "remember," and so forth, we come to see that the technique of using these terms in no way depends upon introspecting private processes. An analogous mistake is made when it is assumed that to mean something is to think something. We can say that we meant a person to do one thing, and he did another—and we can say this even though we did not think of the possibility in question: " 'When I teach someone the formation of the series . . . I surely mean him to write . . . at the hundreth place.'—Quite right; you mean it. And evidently without necessarily even thinking of it. This shows you how different the grammar of the verb 'to mean' is from that of 'to think.' And nothing is more wrong-headed than calling meaning a mental activity!" (693)

In Part II of the *Investigations* the theme of the latter section of Part I is made perfectly clear: meaning, intending, understanding, feeling, and seeing (whether it is visual apprehension or the understanding of something; and these are related) are techniques, forms of life, modes of action about which we could be clear were we not confused by misleading parallelisms of grammar. To understand, to see clearly, is to master techniques to which our attention is called when language is used; and the use of language is itself a technique.

Philosophical Investigations is Wittgenstein's mature discourse on method. It corrects the basic error of the *Tractatus Logico-Philosophicus*—the error of supposing that there are atomic facts involving unanalyzable simples, an error which arose from the mistaken conception of language as a naming of objects. This book not only makes the correction by conceiving of language as a tool and of the use of language as a form of life involving techniques, but it also exhibits the multifarious character of philosophical investigations by showing them as criss-crossing sightseeing excursions made possible by tracing out families of similarities to which the multiplicty of language uses calls attention.

If there is a weakness in this revolutionary work, it is the weakness of glossing over the multiplicity of *limited* philosophical concerns. Not all philosophers can be satisfied with the restless philosophical excursions which so delighted Wittgenstein and at which he was so adept; many philosophers are more content to stay at home with their limiting and precising definitions, their fanciful speculations, their penchants for single uses of single terms. Nevertheless, Wittgenstein's work can serve as a foundation for argument against philosophic dogmatism; it makes possible an *enlightened* staying-at-home. From it a philosopher can learn that there is more between heaven and earth than can be seen by the use of his vocabulary; and there is then some hope that, though he spends his days looking at the world from his single window, he will not confuse the complexity of the world with the simplicity of some grammatical fiction.

AUTHOR INDEX

I

AUTHOR INDEX